W9-CEW-987

CHILDREN

2024 Release

JOHN W. SANTROCK
University of Texas at Dallas

JENNIFER E. LANSFORD
Duke University

KIRBY DEATER-DECKARD
University of Massachusetts Amherst

CHILDREN, 2024 RELEASE

Published by McGraw Hill LLC, 1325 Avenue of the Americas, New York, NY 10121. Copyright ©2024 by McGraw Hill LLC. All rights reserved. Printed in the United States of America. Previous editions ©2022, 2019, and 2016. No part of this publication may be reproduced or distributed in any form or by any means, or stored in a database or retrieval system, without the prior written consent of McGraw Hill LLC, including, but not limited to, in any network or other electronic storage or transmission, or broadcast for distance learning.

Some ancillaries, including electronic and print components, may not be available to customers outside the United States.

This book is printed on acid-free paper.

1 2 3 4 5 6 7 8 9 LWI 29 28 27 26 25 24

ISBN 978-1-266-25304-1 (bound)
MHID 1-266-25304-1 (bound)
ISBN 978-1-264-92537-7 (loose-leaf)
MHID 1-264-92537-9 (loose-leaf)

Executive Portfolio Manager: *Ryan Treat*
Senior Product Development Manager: *Dawn Groundwater*
Marketing Manager: *Isfa Syed*
Content Project Managers: *Mary E. Powers (Core), Jodi Banowetz (Assessment)*
Manufacturing Project Manager: *Sandy Ludovissy*
Designer: *Beth Blech*
Content Licensing Specialist: *Carrie Burger*
Cover Image: *RichVintage/Getty Images*
Compositor: *Aptara®, Inc.*

All credits appearing on page or at the end of the book are considered to be an extension of the copyright page.

Library of Congress Cataloging-in-Publication Data

Names: Santrock, John W., author. | Lansford, Jennifer E., author. |
    Deater-Deckard, Kirby D., author.
Title: Children / John W. Santrock, Jennifer E. Lansford, Kirby
    Deater-Deckard.
Description: 2024 Release. | New York, NY : McGraw Hill LLC, 2025. |
    Includes bibliographical references and index.
Identifiers: LCCN 2023035226 (print) | LCCN 2023035227 (ebook) | ISBN
    9781266253041 (hardcover) | ISBN 9781264925377 (spiral bound) | ISBN
    9781264925049 (ebook) | ISBN 9781264931415 (ebook other)
Subjects: LCSH: Child development. | Adolescence.
Classification: LCC HQ767.9 .S268 2025 (print) | LCC HQ767.9 (ebook) |
    DDC 305.231—dc23/eng/20230808
LC record available at https://lccn.loc.gov/2023035226
LC ebook record available at https://lccn.loc.gov/2023035227

Dedication

With special appreciation to my grandchildren: Jordan, Alex, and Luke.

—John W. Santrock

I gratefully acknowledge my parents, David and Maxine Kuehn, my husband, Chris Lansford, and our children, Katherine and Nick, who have guided my development and given me insights into theirs.

—Jennifer E. Lansford

I am dedicating this release to all of the wonderful "kids" in my family who continue to teach me about human development—my children Anna and Lee, and many nieces and nephews.

—Kirby Deater-Deckard

brief contents

Mc Graw Hill connect   McGraw Hill Education Psychology APA Documentation Style Guide

contents

SECTION 1   THE NATURE OF CHILDREN'S DEVELOPMENT   1

Ariel Skelley/Blend Images

SECTION 2   BEGINNINGS   43

MedicalRF/Getty Images

SECTION 3 **INFANCY 118**

Jamie Grill/Brand X Pictures/Getty Images

FatCamera/E+/Getty Images

SECTION 6 ADOLESCENCE 418

Carlos Barquero/Alamy Stock Photo

CHAPTER 16
Socioemotional Development in Adolescence   477

Mc Graw Hill **connect** McGraw Hill Education Psychology APA Documentation Style Guide

guide to diversity, equity, and inclusion

Special attention is given to diversity, equity, and inclusion (DEI) in order to understand their influence on many aspects of our physical, cognitive, and social development. Preferred pronouns and terminology used to refer to different racial and ethnic groups have been updated, and a new discussion has been added to explain why certain terms are used throughout the text. Studies conducted by researchers representing diverse and global populations and topics are included throughout to ensure a balanced view of child development.

Additionally, all of the *Connecting with Careers* profiles have been updated, and many new profiles introduce the reader to a diverse group of active professionals.

Following is a chapter-by-chapter list of examples of current content and revisions involving DEI issues and research.

Chapter 1: Introduction

- New *Connecting with Diversity* box highlighting ongoing discussions regarding preferred terminology for describing ethnic and racial groups and how this terminology will be addressed throughout the chapters
- Section on sociocultural contexts and diversity sets the stage for the rest of the book in situating development within cultural contexts that encompass race, ethnicity, and socioeconomic status
- Updated content on discrimination and prejudice experienced by ethnic minority children and youth (Clauss-Ehlers, Roysircar, & Hunter, 2021)
- New research indicating that pride in one's ethnic identity group and exploration of ethnic identity have positive outcomes (Sladek, Umaña-Taylor, & others, 2020; Umaña-Taylor & Hill, 2020)
- New research on socioeconomic differences in access to opportunities and effects of socioeconomic status on development during childhood and adolescence (Mayo & Wadsworth, 2020; Peverill & others, 2021)
- Recent conceptualizations of gender identity and development
- Content on the role of gender in child development around the world
- Updated demographic data related to poverty (OECD, 2021; Semega & others, 2020) and how the COVID-19 pandemic exacerbated socioeconomic disparities (Perry & others, 2021)
- Inclusion of recommendations related to dual-language learning (Diaz-Rico, 2020)
- Strategies for minimizing bias related to gender, race/ethnicity, and culture in the study of child development

Chapter 2: Biological Beginnings

- Revised key terms and definitions throughout the chapter to align with the latest theory and evidence on biological factors in child development and functioning, including correcting all terminology with regard to genetic-associated sex (binary genetic male and female)
- Inclusion of the latest science on stem-cell engineering approaches to curing sickle-cell disease that disproportionally affects Black and African individuals (Kanter & others, 2022)

Chapter 3: Prenatal Development

- Discussion of factors that affect fetal growth around the world (Papageorghiou & others, 2018)
- Content on cultural beliefs about pregnancy
- Inclusion of a global review of 55 studies linking smoking during pregnancy to low birth weight (Di & others, 2022)

Chapter 4: Birth

- Description of cultural differences in typical childbirth settings and attendants
- Coverage of the differences across countries in rates of cesarean delivery
- Discussion about cross-cultural variations in the incidence and causes of low birth weight
- Inclusion of a recent study showing the benefits of increasing partner support to decrease postpartum depression in sexual minority women (Marsland, Treyvaud, & Pepping, 2022)

Chapter 5: Physical Development in Infancy

- Updated data on rates of breast feeding and formula feeding practices with infants in the United States from the Centers for Disease Control and Prevention (2022), along with revised recommendations for breast feeding in all countries and economic and sociocultural contexts, based on ongoing policy development of the World Health Organization (2021)
- Inclusion of results from the largest comprehensive longitudinal study to date of nutritional effects on subsequent child development across eight low- and middle-income countries, showing beneficial effects of combined good nutrition, nurturing caregiving, and adequate socioeconomic resources (McCormick & others, 2019)

- Substantial revision showing the latest data and policy recommendations regarding infant malnutrition in low- and middle-income countries and low-income communities within high-income countries (FAO, IFAD, UNICEF, WFP, & WHO, 2022; Nisbett & others, 2022; World Health Organization, 2023), including latest results from the positive effects of infant and maternal nutrition programs for low-income families in the United States (Testa & Jackson, 2021)

Chapter 6: Cognitive Development in Infancy

- Major updates to *Connecting with Diversity* box, addressing countering the "deficit" thinking in prior research on socioeconomic status and infants' development (Florit & others, 2021; Masek & others, 2021)

Chapter 7: Socioemotional Development in Infancy

- Updated evidence regarding individual differences in maternal and paternal caregiving behaviors and infant attachment security (Fourment, Espinoza, Ribeiro, & Mesman, 2022; Luby, 2020; Thompson, 2021), including results showing that sensitivity in parenting was related to secure attachment in infants in Colombia, Mexico, Peru, and the United States (Posada & others, 2016)
- Latest evidence from social neuroscience perspectives of the role of nervous and endocrine systems in attachment in infancy (Hannan & others, 2023; Storey, Alloway, & Walsh, 2020), including results from a recent study of first-time fathers in Japan showing changes in their brain functioning and hormone levels during their partner's pregnancy and after the birth (Diaz-Rojas & others, 2023)
- Revision of description of family systems theories and definitions (Perez-Brena & others, 2022) and expansion of inclusive terminology and language with regard to parent and caregiver sex and gender throughout this and all chapters
- Updated information about the Nordic countries' policies of shared caregiving and workplace leave for mothers and fathers (Greve & Hussain, 2021; OECD, 2022; Thébaud & Pedulla, 2022)
- Substantially revised consideration of out-of-home infant child care and the challenges of improving high quality of care and equitable access for low-income and marginalized families, including the positive effects of such high-quality infant care (Hatfield & others, 2021; Haynie & others, 2023; Pilarz, Sandstrom, & Henly, 2022)

Chapter 8: Physical Development in Early Childhood

- New information from a large international team about a set of benchmarks for children's overall physical activity, as well as in specific domains such as active play and organized sports and in specific settings such as at home and in school (Aubert & others, 2022)

- New nutritional guidelines from within the U.S. (Dallacker, Hertwig, & Mata, 2018) and globally (World Health Organization, 2020)
- Updated international statistics on the prevalence of overweight and obesity during childhood (World Health Organization, 2021)
- Discussion of the findings on how structural racism and barriers to health care have contributed to health disparities in the United States (Goyal & others, 2020)
- Discussion of a longitudinal study showing that children who lived in high-poverty neighborhoods were more likely to be exposed to lead, which in turn led to lower vocabulary skills (Wodtke, Ramaj, & Schachner, 2022)
- Coverage of the state of children's illness and health globally

Chapter 9: Cognitive Development in Early Childhood

- Updated information about Head Start and Early Head Start child care preschool programs for low-income children in the United States, including evidence of its impact on subsequent child development outcomes (Administration for Children and Families, 2023; Slater & others, 2021)
- Revised coverage of three controversies in early childhood education regarding curriculum, universal access, and priorities for school readiness (Cascio, 2023; Morrison & others, 2022) and how these controversies intersect with socioeconomic and family policy
- Newly updated *Connecting with Careers* box introducing Rakaya Humphries, Head Start/Early Head Start program director in Tennessee, whose vocation and work support the healthy development and learning of hundreds of low-income children

Chapter 10: Socioemotional Development in Early Childhood

- Inclusion of research on discipline strategies used in different cultural contexts (Fung, Li, & Lam, 2017)
- New conceptualizations and research on gender identity (Best & Puzio, 2019; Erickson-Schroth & Davis, 2021; Halim & others, 2017; Li, Kung, & Hines, 2017; Spencer & others, 2021)
- Discussion of gender stereotypes in different cultural contexts (Koenig, 2018)
- Updated demographics of families with half siblings and stepsiblings (Knop, 2020)
- Contemporary research on child development in different family structures, including families with divorced or remarried parents and LGBTQ parents (Raley & Sweeney, 2020; Roper, Fife, & Seedall, 2020; Walker & Taylor, 2021)
- Inclusion of an analysis of 72 reviews of the literature concluding that parents' sexual orientation is not related to their children's sexual orientation (Schumm & Crawford, 2019)
- Section on cultural, ethnic, and socioeconomic variations in parenting

- New research showing that parental monitoring varies across cultures in ways that are related to cultural expectations regarding adolescent autonomy and how much control parents should have over adolescents' decisions and activities (Soenens & Vansteenkiste, 2020)
- Coverage of parenting in immigrant and ethnic minority families

Chapter 11: Physical Development in Middle and Late Childhood

- Inclusion of evidence of a large longitudinal study in Spain showing the benefits of organized sports participation on a wide range of developmental outcomes in middle and late childhood (Menescardi & others, 2023)
- Addition of evidence from the largest meta-analysis to date spanning many countries and cultural contexts, showing the important role of increasing nutritious food options in schools for supporting children's weight management (Pineda, Bascunan, & Sassi, 2021)
- Updated background, evidence, and policies regarding all major categories of developmental and learning disabilities in childhood (Astle & others, 2022; Condition of Education, 2022; Hallahan & others, 2023)
- Revised sections about attention deficit hyperactivity disorder (ADHD) and autism spectrum disorders (ASD) regarding prevalence, causes, and interventions to support development (Hallahan, Kauffman, & Pullen, 2023; Hudry & others, 2022; Ivanov & others, 2022)
- Inclusion of recent sources and information regarding the policies and practices in schools for assessment, evaluation, and implementation of inclusive education plans to support learning and development of all children with a wide range of disabilities (Etscheidt & others, 2023; Kauffman & others, 2022)

Chapter 12: Cognitive Development in Middle and Late Childhood

- Addition of findings from a recent study of bilingual school-age children showing a link between working memory improvements with better math problem solving (Swanson, Arizmendi, & Li, 2021)
- Revised emphasis on the importance of family relationships, stories, and narratives for transmitting and supporting memory development that is consistent with the child's cultural context (Wang, 2021)
- Revised information about metalinguistic strategies for learning that develop across childhood, including emphasis on pragmatics involving culturally defined appropriate language use (Gleason & Ratner, 2023; Nadasdi, 2021)
- Updated *Connecting with Diversity* box emphasizing methods for supporting bilingual children's English language learning (Herrell & Jordan, 2020; Tao & others, 2021)
- Expanded revision on background and evidence regarding culturally distinct definitions of intelligence and efforts to

reduce or eliminate bias in intelligence assessments (Ang, Ng, & Rockstuhl, 2020; Gonthier, 2022)

- Updated definitions of and educational approaches for "gifted" students, including efforts to address underrepresentation of minoritized children in gifted programs in the United States (Bucaille & others, 2022; Sternberg, Ambrose, & Karami, 2022; Wright, Ford, & Moore, 2022)
- Addition of theory and evidence regarding the negative effects of exposure to racial and ethnic discrimination on children's achievement and learning, and approaches that families and communities can take to tackle this in a new *Connecting with Research* box (Lash, Akpovo, & Cushner, 2022; Whaley, 2020)
- Updated results from international assessments of over 70 countries to understand cultural differences in educational practices that promote or impede children's and adolescents' academic achievement (Gomendio, 2023)

Chapter 13: Socioemotional Development in Middle and Late Childhood

- Inclusion of the largest study to date, a meta-analysis of 15 studies and almost 23,000 children, regarding COVID-19 pandemic impacts on school-age children's emotional problems in numerous countries around the world (Kumar Panda & others, 2021)
- Revised background on moral development and prosocial behavior in childhood, including evidence of consistency of prosocial behavioral development in many cultures (Callaghan & Corbit, 2018; Misch & Dunham, 2021)
- Substantially revised description of theory and research on gender group and individual differences and similarities in childhood, including examination of the brain and nervous system, cognition, emotions, and behavior (Brandes & others, 2021; Eliot & others, 2021; Grabowska, 2020)
- Updated examination of the impact of educational environments (including same-sex education settings) and exposure to gender bias and discrimination on gender differences in academic and socioemotional functioning in childhood (Denessen & others, 2020; Herr, Grant, & Price, 2020)
- Updated data on the prevalence of children and youth who identify as transgender, and evidence regarding the particular challenges transgender youth face in regard to bullying and discrimination (Potter & others, 2021; Sherman & others, 2020)
- Substantially revised description of peer bullying and its effects, including description of cross-cultural similarities in these patterns, across middle and late childhood
- Major update to examination of race, ethnic, and socioeconomic status bias and discrimination in educational systems and schools, their influences on children's learning and socioemotional well-being, and interventions that seek to reduce and eliminate such experiences (Banks, 2020; Cushner, McClelland, & Safford, 2022; Jarvis & Okonofua, 2020; Le Menestrel & Duncan, 2019)

Chapter 14: Physical Development in Adolescence

- Inclusion of a research review of 30 studies in different countries around the world concluding that the age at which breast development began in girls had declined by almost three months per decade since the 1970s (Eckert-Lind & others, 2021)

- Coverage of the development of sexual identity

- Addition of a new study on how gender differences in body perceptions are often exacerbated by heavy social media use (Harriger, Thompson, & Tiggemann, 2023)

- Discussion of ethnic and racial differences and similarities in adolescents' sexual experiences

- Updated data on adolescent pregnancy and birth rates in the United States and globally (UNICEF, 2022; World Bank, 2023)

- Coverage of cross-cultural differences in adolescent pregnancy

- New *Connecting with Careers* profile on Terrance Weeden, a pediatrician whose clinical and research interests include LGBTQ+ health care and eradicating disparities in health care among youth in underserved communities

- New information from the World Health Organization (2022) that in many countries, there is a large unmet need for contraceptives, including condoms to help prevent transmission of HIV and other sexually transmitted infections

- New information on the need for comprehensive sexuality education programs that include information on how to communicate with a partner about consent, sexual history, pregnancy, and sexually transmitted infections, as well as addressing the needs of LGBTQ adolescents (Grasso & Trumbull, 2023)

- New *Connecting with Careers* profile on Bonnie Halpern-Felsher, university professor in pediatrics and director of community efforts to improve adolescents' health, who also coordinates the STEP-UP program (Short-Term Research Experience for Underrepresented Persons) in which she has personally mentored and supervised 22 to 25 middle and high school students every year since 2007

- New research on family risk factors for eating pathology as well as eating disorders in boys and sexual minority youth (Breton, Juster, & Booji, 2023; Cao & others, 2023; Potterton & others, 2020)

Chapter 15: Cognitive Development in Adolescence

- Current prevalence of religious affiliations around the world (Jensen, 2021; Pew-Templeton Global Religious Future Project, 2022)

- Contemporary research on how individuals perceive and navigate the intersectionality of their identities, including their religious identity (Azmitia & others, 2023; Martin, Butler-Barnes, & Hope, 2023; Shen & others, 2023)

- Updated research on poverty and barriers to learning (Lampert & others, 2020)

- Cross-cultural comparisons of secondary schools

- Updated demographics related to school dropout (National Center for Education Statistics, 2023)

Chapter 16: Socioemotional Development in Adolescence

- Section on cultural and racial/ethnic identity

- New research on the major factors in identity narratives (McLean & others, 2020)

- Inclusion of a longitudinal study of more than 5,000 young people finding that greater identity synthesis (as opposed to confusion) was related to greater life satisfaction (Hatano & others, 2022)

- New *Connecting with Careers* profile on Anna Boyer-Chadwick, academic advisor, whose university's counseling program has won national awards as a model for Latinos' academic success

- Coverage of a recent study of immigrant and nonimmigrant adolescents in Greece finding that national identity and friendship networks developed in tandem, with identity influencing friendship choices, and friends influencing identity development (Umaña-Taylor & others, 2020)

- Description of an influential life-span model of ethnic-racial identity describing five dimensions of ethnic-racial identity (Williams & others, 2020)

- New *Connecting with Careers* profile on Adriana Umaña-Taylor, a professor who studies ethnic-racial identity

- New research on adolescents' bicultural or multicultural identities (Ferguson, Iturbide, & Raffaelli, 2020)

- Discussion of flexibility and specific situations in understanding gender identity (Martin, Cook, & Andrews, 2017)

- Updated demographics regarding transgender youth (Herman, Flores, & O'Neill, 2022)

- New *Connecting with Careers* profile on Stephanie Budge, a psychotherapist and professor who specializes in transgender research

- Inclusion of a five-year longitudinal study of transgender children (Olson & others, 2022)

- Coverage of a review of research on parental autonomy support among Black, White, Latino, and Asian American families concluding that understanding this aspect of parenting needs to be grounded in cultural concepts related to independence and expectations of parents (Benito-Gomez & others, 2020)

- Inclusion of recent research on the importance and functions of friendship in different cultures (Chen, Lee, & Chen, 2018)

- Section on sociocultural contexts of dating

- Inclusion of recent research recognizing fluidity in sexual orientation and gender identity and expression (Diamond, 2021)

- Coverage of a qualitative study of Latino adolescents' perceptions of their parents' roles in their daughters' and sons' romantic relationships (Killoren & others, 2023)
- Current global statistics showing that in 51 percent of countries, boys have more access to primary school education than do girls, and in 76 percent of countries, boys have more access to upper secondary school education than do girls (UNICEF, 2022)
- Coverage of recent research demonstrating that how immigrant youth fare depends on opportunities available in the country of destination, discrimination they might experience, their families' socioeconomic status, and a range of other factors (Motti-Stefanidi, 2023)
- Inclusion of a study of over 470,000 youth in Canada finding that both first- and second-generation immigrant youth had lower rates of conduct disorders, ADHD, and mood disorders than nonimmigrant youth (Gadermann & others, 2022)
- Inclusion of a recent study of over 5,000 individuals in 11 countries showing that improvements in aspects of psychosocial maturity involved in decision making in emotionally charged situations continued beyond age 18 (Icenogle & others, 2019)
- Current statistics on the national prevalence of mental health problems among adolescents in the United States (Centers for Disease Control and Prevention, 2022) and globally (World Health Organization, 2021)
- Inclusion of research on gender differences in depression (de la Torrs & others, 2021; Porter & others, 2021)
- Extensive discussion on why culture is an important context for adolescent development

about the authors

John W. Santrock

John Santrock (back row middle) with recipients of the Santrock Travel Scholarship Award in developmental psychology. Created by Dr. Santrock, this annual award gives undergraduate students the opportunity to attend professional meetings. Some of the students shown here attended the meeting of the Society for Research in Child Development.

Courtesy of Jessica Serna

John Santrock received his Ph.D. from the University of Minnesota. He taught at the University of Charleston and the University of Georgia before joining the Program in Psychology at the University of Texas at Dallas, where he has taught a number of undergraduate courses and has received the University's Effective Teaching Award. In 2010, he created the UT–Dallas Santrock undergraduate travel scholarship, an annual award that is given to outstanding undergraduate students majoring in developmental psychology to enable them to attend research conventions. In 2019, he created an endowment that will provide the travel awards for students at UT–Dallas for decades to come. Additionally, Dr. Santrock and his wife, Mary Jo, created a permanent endowment that will provide academic scholarships for six to ten undergraduate psychology students per year, with preference given to those majoring in developmental psychology.

Dr. Santrock has been a member of the editorial boards of *Child Development* and *Developmental Psychology*. His research on father custody is widely cited and used in expert witness testimony to promote flexibility and alternative considerations in custody disputes. He also has authored these exceptional McGraw Hill texts: *Life-Span Development* (19th edition), *Essentials of Life-Span Development* (8th edition), *Adolescence* (18th edition), *A Topical Approach to Life-Span Development* (11th edition), and *Educational Psychology* (7th edition).

For many years, Dr. Santrock was involved in tennis as a player, teaching professional, and coach of professional tennis players. As an undergraduate, he was a member of the University of Miami (FL) tennis team that still holds the record for most consecutive wins (137) in any NCAA Division I sport. He has been married for four decades to his wife, Mary Jo, who created and directed the first middle school program for children with learning disabilities and behavioral disorders in the Clarke County Schools in Athens, Georgia. More recently, she has worked as a Realtor. He has two daughters—Tracy and Jennifer—both of whom are Realtors after long careers in technology marketing and medical sales, respectively. Jennifer was inducted into the SMU sports hall of fame, only the fifth female to receive this award. He has one granddaughter, Jordan, who works for Ernst & Young, and two grandsons: Alex, age 18, and Luke, age 17. In the last two decades, Dr. Santrock has spent time painting divisionist and expressionist art.

Jennifer E. Lansford

Courtesy of Erika Hanzely-Layko

Jennifer E. Lansford is the S. Malcolm Gillis Distinguished Research Professor of Public Policy and Director of the Center for Child and Family Policy at Duke University. She earned her Ph.D. in Developmental Psychology from the University of Michigan in 2000. Dr. Lansford has authored more than 300 publications that focus on the development of aggression and other behavior problems during childhood and adolescence, with particular attention to how parent, peer, and cultural factors contribute to or protect against these problems. Dr. Lansford leads the Parenting Across Cultures Project, a longitudinal study of mothers, fathers, and children from nine countries (China, Colombia, Italy, Jordan, Kenya, Philippines, Sweden, Thailand, and the United States). In addition, Dr. Lansford has consulted for UNICEF on the evaluation of parenting programs in several low- and middle-income countries and on the development of a set of international standards for parenting programs. She is editor-in-chief of the *International Journal of Behavioral Development* and has served in a number of national and international leadership roles, including chairing the U.S. National Institutes of Health Psychosocial Development, Risk and Prevention Study Section; chairing the U.S. National Committee for Psychological Science of the National Academies of Sciences, Engineering, and Medicine; serving on the Secretariat of the International Consortium for Developmental Science Societies; and serving as president-elect of the Society for Research in Child Development. Dr. Lansford's husband, Chris, is a surgeon who specializes in head and neck cancer. They have two children: Katherine, age 20, and Nick, age 17.

Kirby Deater-Deckard

Courtesy of Michael McDermott

Kirby Deater-Deckard is a professor in the Department of Psychological and Brain Sciences at the University of Massachusetts Amherst, where he serves as a graduate program leader in developmental science, and he is also a faculty member in neuroscience and behavior. He is a Fellow of the Association for Psychological Science and leader of collaborative research group in Springfield, Massachusetts. He earned his Ph.D. in Developmental Psychology from the University of Virginia in 1994. Dr. Deater-Deckard has authored more than 200 publications that focus on the biological and environmental influences in the development of individual differences in social-emotional and cognitive outcomes in childhood and adolescence. The emphasis of his recent work is on parenting and intergenerational transmission of self-regulation (e.g., executive function, emotion regulation) that uses behavioral, cognitive neuroscience, and physiological research methods. He is principal or co-investigator on several ongoing studies funded by the National Institutes of Health and the National Science Foundation. Dr. Deater-Deckard serves as a consulting investigator on several longitudinal research project teams around the globe and is a scientific review panelist for multiple national and international funding agencies and organizations. He is former co-editor of the book series *Frontiers in Developmental Science* (Taylor & Francis) and serves on editorial boards for journals in developmental and family sciences. Dr. Deater-Deckard's wife, Keirsten, is a community volunteer, and they have two children, Anna, age 26, and Lee, age 19.

expert consultants

Children's development is an enormous and complex field. No one author or co-authors can possibly keep up with all of the rapidly changing content across ages and domains. To solve this problem, the authors have sought the input of leading experts about content in a number of areas of children's development. These experts have provided detailed evaluations and recommendations in their area(s) of expertise.

The following individuals were among those who served as expert consultants for one or more of the previous editions of this text:

Karen Adolph, *New York University*
John Bates, *Indiana University*
Diana Baumrind, *University of California-Berkeley*
Martha Ann Bell, *Virginia Tech University*
Maureen Black, *University of Maryland*
Urie Bronfenbrenner, *Cornell University*
Rosalind Charlesworth, *Weber State University*
Florence Denmark, *Pace University*
Janet DiPietro, *Johns Hopkins University*
Tiffany Field, *University of Miami*
Elizabeth Gershoff, *University of Texas*
James Graham, *The College of New Jersey*
Sandra Graham, *University of California-Los Angeles*
Joan Grusec, *University of Toronto*
Algea Harrison-Hale, *Oakland University*
Marilou Hyson, *University of Pennsylvania*

Campbell Leaper, *University of California-Santa Cruz*
Esther Leerkes, *University of North Carolina-Greensboro*
Virginia Marchman, *Stanford University*
James Marcia, *Simon Fraser University*
Megan McClelland, *Oregon State University*
David Moore, *Pitzer College and Claremont Graduate University*
Nel Noddings, *Stanford University*
Barbara Pan, *Harvard University*
Karl Rosengren, *University of Rochester*
David Sadker, *The American University-Washington, DC*
Peter Scales, *Search Institute*
Susan Spieker, *University of Washington*
Ross Thompson, *University of California-Davis*
Allan Wigfield, *University of Maryland-College Park*
Philip David Zelazo, *University of Minnesota*

Following are the expert consultants for this revision who, like previous consultants, represent a *Who's Who* in the field of child and adolescent development.

Courtesy of
Jim Hoste

Mary Gauvain Mary Gauvain is a developmental psychologist with expertise in cognitive development in early and middle childhood. She obtained her Ph.D. from the University of Utah and currently is Distinguished Professor of Psychology at the University of California-Riverside. Dr. Gauvain's research concentrates on social and cultural contributions to the development of thinking, principally in the areas of spatial cognition, problem solving, and planning skills. In recent years, she has studied children's learning within and outside of school, children's concept development regarding water and food contamination in sub-Saharan Africa, and child development during cultural change. Dr. Gauvain is a Fellow of the American Association for the Advancement of Science, the American Educational Research Association, the American Psychological Association, and the Association for Psychological Science. She has held leadership roles in the Society for Research in Child Development and Division 7 (Developmental Psychology) of the American Psychological Association. She is the author of *The Social Context of Cognitive Development* (2001) and recently served as the principal investigator on an interdisciplinary NSF-IGERT award, *Water SENSE: Social, Engineering, and Natural Sciences Engagement.* Dr. Gauvain's work has been published in leading research journals such as *Child Development, Developmental Psychology, Cognitive Development,* and *Current Directions in Psychological Science.* She has served as associate editor for the journals *Child Development* and *The Merrill-Palmer Quarterly* and has been on the editorial boards of several other major developmental journals.

Courtesy of
Jennifer Hogan

Melinda Gonzales-Backen Melinda Gonzales-Backen is an expert in the formation of ethnic-racial identity and other cultural processes among Latino adolescents and families. She obtained her Ph.D. in Family and Human Development from Arizona State University. She is currently an Associate Professor in the Department of Human Development and Family Science at Florida State University. Her research focuses on the psychosocial well-being of Latino youth and families. Specifically, Dr. Gonzales-Backen is interested in how cultural stressors (e.g., discrimination, acculturative stress, etc.), cultural strengths (e.g., ethnic identity, familial ethnic socialization, etc.), adolescent development, and family processes intersect to predict adolescent adjustment. Dr. Gonzales-Backen is currently an associate editor of *Developmental Psychology* and a member of the editorial boards of the *Journal of Youth and Adolescence* and *Cultural Minority and Ethnic Diversity Psychology.* Her work has been published in top journals such as *Child Development, Developmental Psychology,* and *Family Process.*

Courtesy of Lionel
Howard

Lionel C. Howard Lionel C. Howard is an Associate Professor in the Graduate School of Education and Human Development at The George Washington University. Dr. Howard received his Ed.D. in Human Development and Psychology from Harvard University, Graduate School of Education, and completed a National Institute of Child Health and Development postdoctoral fellowship at the University of North Carolina at Chapel Hill. He also has an M.A. in Measurement, Statistics, and Evaluation from the University of Maryland, College Park, and a B.A. in Applied Mathematics and Statistics from William Paterson University of New Jersey. Dr. Howard is a developmental psychologist whose research interests include gender and racial identity development and socialization, motivation and academic achievement, and research methodology. He has worked on several local and national research projects focused on Black child development and improving the educational trajectory and schooling experiences of minoritized students. Dr. Howard has published in the *Journal of Applied Developmental Psychology, Journal of Black Psychology, Journal of Orthopsychiatry, Journal of Boyhood, International Journal of Inclusive Education, Journal of Homosexuality, International Journal of Qualitative Studies in Education,* and *Harvard Educational Review.* He is co-editor of *Facing Racism in Education* (3rd ed.), published by Harvard University Press, and is completing a manuscript on researcher vulnerability in social science research and a manuscript on Black boys' socioemotional learning and development during the formative years.

Courtesy of Seth Odell/UCLA Newsroom

Scott Johnson Scott Johnson is one of the world's leading experts on perceptual and cognitive development in infancy. He is currently a Professor of Psychology and Professor of Psychiatry and Biobehavioral Sciences at UCLA. Dr. Johnson obtained his Ph.D. from Arizona State University and then did postdoctoral work in the Center for Visual Science at the University of Rochester. His research interests center on mechanisms of perceptual, cognitive, motor, social, and cortical development, and relations among different developmental processes. Current research topics include object perception, face perception, intermodal perception, visual attention, early language development, and learning mechanisms in typical and at-risk populations. In studying infants, Dr. Johnson uses a combination of methods, including preferential looking, eye movements, electroencephalography, and modeling. He has served on numerous grant review panels in the United States and Europe as well as the editorial boards of *Infancy, Infant Behavior and Development, Child Development, Cognition, Developmental Psychology, Early Development and Parenting, The British Journal of Developmental Psychology,* and *Frontiers in Neuroscience.*

Courtesy of Robert Lickliter

David S. Moore David S. Moore is a professor of psychology at Pitzer College. He received his Ph.D. in developmental and biological psychology from Harvard University. As a developmental cognitive neuroscientist with expertise in infant cognition, he has explored the contributions of genetic, environmental, and epigenetic factors to human development. His book *The Dependent Gene* has been widely adopted for use in undergraduate education and was nominated for the Cognitive Development Society's Best Authored Volume award. His book *The Developing Genome* won both the William James Book Award and the Eleanor Maccoby Book Award from the American Psychological Association, recognizing a book expected to have a profound effect on developmental psychology. Dr. Moore has served on the consulting editorial board for *Child Development Perspectives* and has been the editor of special issues of *New Ideas in Psychology, Developmental Psychobiology,* and *Infant Behavior and Development.* From 2016 to 2018, Dr. Moore served as the director of the U.S. National Science Foundation's Developmental Sciences Program in Washington, D.C. He was elected a Fellow of the American Psychological Association in 2021.

Courtesy of Alejandra Livas

Gabriela Livas Stein Gabriela Livas Stein is a leading expert on Latinx youth and their families. She is a licensed psychologist and chair of The University of Texas at Austin's Department of Human Development and Family Sciences. Dr. Stein received her doctoral degree in clinical psychology with a specialization in child and family psychology from the University of North Carolina–Chapel Hill. Broadly, her research uses developmental psychopathology and cultural-ecological frameworks to investigate the impact of culturally relevant factors on the development of psychopathology in minoritized youth and their families. She has served as the Vice President of Programming for the Society of Research on Adolescence, as a co-chair of the Ethnic Racial Issues Committee of the Society for Research in Child Development, and a past chair of the Latinx Caucus of the Society for Research in Child Development. She has also served as an associate editor for the *Journal of Research on Adolescence* and has been a consulting editor for *Child Development* and *Developmental Psychology.* Dr. Stein's work has been published in leading research journals such as *Developmental Psychology, Journal of Research on Adolescence,* and *Journal of Youth and Adolescence.*

Connecting *Research* and *Results*

Children connects current research and real-world applications. Through an integrated, personalized digital learning program, students gain the insight they need to study smarter and improve performance.

McGraw Hill Connect is a digital assignment and assessment platform that strengthens the link between faculty, students, and coursework, helping everyone accomplish more in less time. *Connect Psychology* includes assignable and assessable videos, quizzes, exercises, and interactivities, all associated with learning objectives. Interactive assignments and videos allow students to experience and apply their understanding of psychology to the world with fun and stimulating activities.

Apply Concepts and Theory in an Experiential Learning Environment

An engaging and innovative learning game, **Quest: Journey Through the Lifespan**® provides students with opportunities to apply content from their human development curriculum to real-life scenarios. Students play unique characters who range in age and make decisions that apply key concepts and theories for each age as they negotiate events in an array of authentic environments. Additionally, as students analyze real-world behaviors and contexts, they are exposed to different cultures and intersecting biological, cognitive, and socioemotional processes. Each quest has layered replayability, allowing students to make new choices each time they play—or offering different students in the same class different experiences. Fresh possibilities and outcomes shine light on the complexity of and variations in real human development. This experiential learning game includes follow-up questions, assignable in Connect and auto-graded, to reach a higher level of critical thinking.

Evergreen

Content and technology are ever-changing, and it is important that you keep your course up to date with the latest information and assessments. That's why we want to deliver the most current and relevant content for your course, hassle-free.

Children is moving to an Evergreen delivery model, which means it has content, tools, and technology that are current and relevant, with updates delivered directly to your existing McGraw Hill Connect® course. Engage students and freshen up assignments with up-to-date coverage of select topics and assessments, all without having to switch editions or build a new course.

Diversity, Equity, and Inclusion

Substantial discussion is devoted to addressing issues of diversity, equity, and inclusion. When relevant, each chapter includes citations of studies and topical coverage that represent diverse U.S. and global populations. A comprehensive list of diversity, equity, and inclusion coverage can be found on pages xii–xvi.

In addition, all of the ***Connecting with Careers*** features have been updated, and two-thirds are new profiles that introduce the reader to a diverse group of active professionals. For example, pediatrician Terrance Weeden is a vocal advocate for LGBTQ youth; Anna Boyer-Chadwick is an academic advisor whose university's advising and retention program is a nationally recognized model for Latino student success; and midwife Jennifer Nguyen works with diverse communities to reduce inequities in health care in rural and remote areas of Canada.

McGraw Hill Immersive Brain Program

The McGraw Hill Immersive Brain Program provides opportunities for students to learn about the brain and its connection to behavior through interaction. Embedded within the ebook, SmartBook, and ReadAnywhere App are three-dimensional, dynamic figures of the brain. Students have the opportunity to navigate within these dynamic figures to explore key structures and functions to support their understanding of key concepts. Sample figures include:

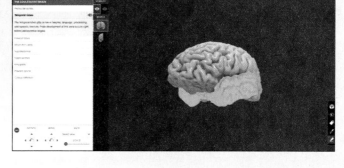

- Lobes of the Brain
- The Neuron
- The Adolescent Brain
- Alzheimer's Disease and the Brain
- Infant Attachment and the Brain

Additionally, Brain Lab Activities are assignable as Application-Based Activities through Connect. These activities, which incorporate the dynamic brain figures, allow students to practice with and apply their understanding of the brain's structures and functions. Sample Brain Lab Activities include Reaction Time, Classical Conditioning, Stereotypes and Prejudice, Fight or Flight, Memory Creation and Retention, and Morality.

Real People, Real World, Real Life

At the higher end of Bloom's taxonomy (analyze, evaluate, create), the **McGraw Hill Milestones** video series is an observational tool that allows students to experience life as it unfolds, from infancy to late adulthood. This ground-breaking, longitudinal video series tracks the development of real children as they progress through the early stages of physical, social, and emotional development in their first few weeks, months, and years of life. Assignable and assessable within Connect Psychology, Milestones also includes interviews with adolescents and adults to reflect development throughout the entire life span. Milestones is available in a WCAG-compliant format. Ask your McGraw Hill representative about this upgrade!

Develop Effective Responses

McGraw Hill's **Writing Assignment** tool delivers a learning experience that improves students' written communication skills and conceptual understanding with every assignment. Assign, monitor, and provide feedback on writing more efficiently and grade assignments within McGraw Hill Connect.

McGraw Hill GO

McGraw Hill GO is an easy-to-use, quick-to-set-up eBook+ that lives within the learning management system (LMS). GO equips instructors and students with essential course materials: trusted, assignable content and auto-graded chapter questions that sync directly into the LMS. GO makes it easier to keep up with progress and direct attention where it matters.

Prepare Students for Higher-Level Thinking

Also at the higher end of Bloom's taxonomy, **Power of Process** for Psychology helps students improve critical thinking skills and allows instructors to assess these skills efficiently and effectively in an online environment. Available through Connect, pre-loaded journal articles are available for instructors to assign. Using a scaffolded framework such as understanding, synthesizing, and analyzing, Power of Process moves students toward higher-level thinking and analysis. ⟶

Inform and Engage on Psychological Concepts

At the lower end of Bloom's taxonomy, students are introduced to **Concept Clips**—the dynamic, colorful graphics and stimulating animations that break down some of psychology's most difficult concepts in a step-by-step manner, engaging students and aiding in retention. They are assignable and assessable in Connect or can be used as a jumping-off point in class. For example, there are Concept Clips on topics such as object permanence and conservation, as well as theories and theorists like Bandura's social cognitive theory, Vygotsky's sociocultural theory, Buss's evolutionary theory, and Kuhl's language development theory. New to this release, Concept Clips feature a more modern visual style, updated scripts and assessment items, and enhanced accessibility.

Connect Media Sources to Content

Also at the lower end of Bloom's and located in Connect, **NewsFlash** is a multimedia assignment tool that ties current news stories, TedTalks, blogs, and podcasts to key psychological principles and learning objectives. Students interact with relevant news stories and are assessed on their ability to connect the content to the research findings and course material. NewsFlash is updated annually and uses expert sources to cover a wide range of topics, such as emotion, personality, stress, drugs, COVID-19, abilities and disabilities, social justice, stigma, bias, inclusion, gender, LGBTQA+, and many more.

SMARTBOOK™ Better Data, Smarter Revision, Improved Results

McGraw Hill's **SmartBook** helps students distinguish the concepts they know from the concepts they don't, while pinpointing the concepts they are about to forget. SmartBook's real-time reports help both students and instructors identify the concepts that require more attention, making study sessions and class time more efficient.

SmartBook is optimized for mobile and tablet use and is accessible for students with disabilities. Content-wise, measurable and observable learning objectives help improve student outcomes. SmartBook personalizes learning to individual student needs, continually adapting to pinpoint knowledge gaps and focus learning on topics that need the most attention. Study time is more productive and, as a result, students are better prepared for class and coursework. For instructors, SmartBook tracks student progress and provides insights that can help guide teaching strategies.

Online Instructor Resources

The resources listed here accompany *Children*. Contact your McGraw Hill representative for details concerning the availability of these and other valuable materials that can help you design and enhance your course.

Instructor's Manual   Broken down by chapter, this resource provides chapter outlines, suggested lecture topics, classroom activities and demonstrations, suggested student research projects, essay questions, and critical thinking questions.

Test Bank and Test Builder   This comprehensive Test Bank includes more than 1,500 multiple-choice, short answer, and essay questions. Organized by chapter, the questions are designed to test factual, applied, and conceptual knowledge. Available within Connect, Test Builder is a cloud-based tool that enables instructors to format tests that can be printed and administered within a learning management system. Test Builder offers a modern, streamlined interface for easy content configuration that matches course needs, without requiring a download. Test Builder enables instructors to:

- Access all test bank content from a particular title
- Easily pinpoint the most relevant content through robust filtering options
- Manipulate the order of questions or scramble questions and/or answers
- Pin questions to a specific location within a test
- Determine your preferred treatment of algorithmic questions
- Choose the layout and spacing
- Add instructions and configure default settings

PowerPoint Slides   The PowerPoint presentations are WCAG compliant, highlight the key points of the chapter, and include supporting visuals. All of the slides can be modified to meet individual needs.

Remote Proctoring   New remote proctoring and browser-locking capabilities are seamlessly integrated within Connect to offer more control over the integrity of online assessments. Instructors can enable security options that restrict browser activity, monitor student behavior, and verify the 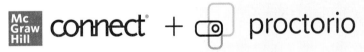 identity of each student. Instant and detailed reporting gives instructors an at-a-glance view of potential concerns, thereby avoiding personal bias and supporting evidence-based claims.

Polling   Every learner has unique needs. Uncover where and when you're needed with the new Polling tool in McGraw Hill Connect. Polling allows you to discover where students are in real time. Engage students and help them create connections with your course content while gaining valuable insight during lectures. Leverage polling data to deliver personalized instruction when and where it is needed most.

preface

Making Connections . . . From Our Classrooms to *Children* to You

The material in *Children* has been shaped by thousands of students taking countless undergraduate developmental courses across four decades. These students have consistently said that when instructors highlight the connections among the different aspects of children's development, they can more readily understand the concepts, theories, and research presented in the course. As a result, *Children* has focused on providing a systematic, integrative approach that helps students make these connections in their learning and practice. This release continues that philosophy, with the main goals of the text as follows:

1. **Connecting with today's students** to help students learn about children's development more effectively;

2. **Connecting with research on children's development** to provide students with the best and most recent theory and research in the world today about each of the periods of children's development;

3. **Connecting development processes** to guide students in making developmental connections across different points in children's development;

4. **Connecting development to real life** to help students understand ways to apply content about child development to the real world and improve children's lives, and to motivate students to think deeply about their own personal journey through life and better understand who they were as children and how their experiences and development have influenced who they are today.

Connecting with Today's Students

Today's students are as different in some ways from the learners of the last generation as today's discipline of child development is different from the field 30 years ago. Students now learn in multiple modalities; rather than sitting down and reading traditional printed chapters in linear fashion from beginning to end, their work preferences tend to be more visual and more interactive, and their reading and study often occur in short bursts. For many students, a traditionally formatted printed textbook is no longer enough when they have instant, 24/7 access to news and information from around the globe. Two features that specifically support today's students are the adaptive ebook (SmartBook, see page xxii) and the learning goals system.

The Learning Goals System

Students often report that development courses are challenging because so much material is covered. To help today's students focus on the key ideas, the Learning Goals System for *Children* provides extensive learning connections throughout the chapters. The learning system connects the chapter-opening outline, learning goals for the chapter, mini-chapter maps that open each main section of the chapter, *Review, Connect, Reflect* questions at the end of each main section, and the chapter summary at the end of each chapter.

The learning system keeps the key ideas in front of the student from the beginning to the end of the chapter. The main headings of each chapter correspond to the learning

1 Why Is Caring for Children Important?	**LG1** Explain why it is important to study children's development, and identify five areas in which children's lives need to be improved.
The Importance of Studying Children's Development	Improving the Lives of Children

goals, which are presented in the chapter-opening spread. Mini-chapter maps that link up with the learning goals are presented at the beginning of each major section in the chapter.

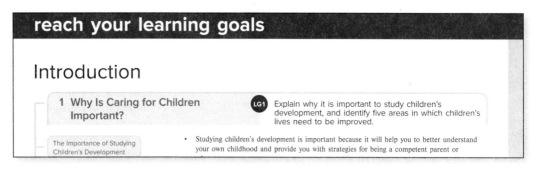

reach your learning goals

Introduction

1 Why Is Caring for Children Important?

LG1 Explain why it is important to study children's development, and identify five areas in which children's lives need to be improved.

The Importance of Studying Children's Development

- Studying children's development is important because it will help you to better understand your own childhood and provide you with strategies for being a competent parent or

Then, at the end of each main section of a chapter, the learning goal is repeated in *Review, Connect, Reflect,* which prompts students to review the key topics in the section, to connect these topics to existing knowledge, and to relate what they have learned to their own personal journey through life. *Reach Your Learning Goals,* at the end of each chapter, guides students through the bulleted chapter review, connecting with the chapter outline/learning goals at the beginning of the chapter and the *Review, Connect, Reflect* material at the end of major chapter sections.

Connecting with Research on Children's Development

It is critical to include the most up-to-date research available. As with previous editions, we continue to look closely at specific areas of research, involve experts in related fields, and update research throughout. *Connecting with Research* describes a study or program to illustrate how research in child development is conducted and how it influences our understanding of the discipline. Key Points are included that summarize the take-away points of the discussion. Topics range from "How Can We Study Newborns' Perception?" to "Evaluating a Service-Learning Program Designed to Increase Civic Engagement" to "Do Parental Expectations Influence Black Boys' Math Scores?"

The tradition of obtaining detailed, extensive input from a number of leading experts in different areas of child development also continues. Biographies and photographs of the leading experts in the field of child development appear on pages xviii and xix. Finally, the research discussions have been updated for each developmental period and topic in order to keep *Children* as contemporary and up-to-date as possible. To that end, there are more than 1,300 citations from 2021 to 2023. Highlighted research focuses on relevant classic and current findings by a diverse group of researchers.

connecting with research

Caregivers' Emotional Expressiveness, Children's Emotion Regulation, and Behavior Problems in Head Start Children

Key Points:

- Children whose caregivers expressed more negative emotions and children with poorer emotion regulation had more internalizing behavior problems.
- Children whose caregivers expressed more positive emotions had fewer externalizing behavior problems.

A foundational study by Dana McCoy and Cybele Raver (2011) explored links between caregivers' reports of their positive and negative emotional expressiveness, observations of young children's emotion regulation, and teachers' reports of the children's internalizing and externalizing behavior problems. The study focused on 97 children,

What did Dana McCoy and Cybele Raver discover about the importance of caregivers' emotions and children's emotion regulation in children's development?
Tatyana Dzemileva/Shutterstock

Connecting Developmental Processes

Too often we forget or fail to notice the many connections from one point in child development to another. Thus, several features have been designed to help students connect topics across the stages of child development.

Developmental Connections, which appear multiple times in each chapter, point readers to places where the topic is discussed in a previous, current, or subsequent chapter. This feature highlights links across topics of development *and* connections among biological, cognitive, and socioemotional processes. The key developmental processes are typically

developmental connection
Gender
Gender stereotyping continues to be extensive. Recent research indicates that girls and older children use a higher percentage of gender stereotypes than younger children and boys. Connect to "Socioemotional Development in Middle and Late Childhood."

discussed in isolation from each other, so students often fail to see the connections among them. Included in **Developmental Connections** is a brief description of the backward or forward connection.

---topical **connections**   *looking **back*** ---

You have learned about the evolutionary perspective, genetic foundations of development, the reproductive challenges and choices parents today may face, and the interaction of nature and nurture. Now we will explore the remarkable course of prenatal development, including the phenomenal growth of the brain. Potential hazards to the offspring's and the mother's health also are covered.

Furthermore, a Connect question is included in the self-reviews at the end of each section—**Review, Connect, Reflect**—so students can practice making connections among topics.

Topical Connections: Looking Back and *Looking Forward* begin and conclude each chapter by placing the chapter's coverage in the larger context of development. The Looking Back section reminds the reader of what happened developmentally in previous periods of development.

Connecting Development to Real Life

In addition to helping students make research and developmental connections, *Children* shows the important real-life connections to the concepts discussed. Real-life connections are explicitly made in the chapter-opening vignette as well as in *Caring Connections, Connecting with Diversity,* the *Milestones* video program, *Connecting with Careers, How Would You . . . ?* questions that pertain to five career areas, and *Reflect: Your Own Personal Journey of Life.*

Each chapter begins with a story designed to spark students' interest and motivate them to read the chapter. *Caring Connections* provides applied information about parenting, education, or health and well-being related to topics ranging from "From Waterbirth to Music Therapy" to "Parenting Strategies for Helping Overweight Children Lose Weight" to "Guiding Children's Creativity."

Children puts a strong emphasis on diversity. A new discussion is included regarding debates on current terminology used for various demographic groups, and related terms are updated and consistent throughout the text.

Diversity is discussed in every chapter. *Connecting with Diversity* interludes also appear in every chapter, focusing on a diversity topic related to the material at that point in the chapter. Topics range from "The Increased Diversity of Adopted Children and Adoptive Parents" to "How Does Family Environment Affect Young Children's Language?" to "English Language Learners" to "Cross-Cultural Comparisons of Secondary Schools."

The *Milestones* video program shows students what developmental concepts look like by letting them watch actual humans develop. Students are able to track several individuals starting from infancy and watch them achieve major developmental milestones, both physically and cognitively. (See page xxi for further details.)

caring connections

Improving the Nutrition of Infants and Young Children Living in Low-Income Families

Incomplete or insufficient nutrition is a special concern in the lives of infants in low-income families. To address this problem in the United States, the WIC (Women, Infants, and Children) program provides federal grants to states for healthy supplemental foods, health-care referrals, and nutrition education for women from low-income families beginning in pregnancy, and to infants and young children up to 5 years of age who are at nutritional risk (S.W. Ng & others, 2018). WIC serves approximately 7 million participants in the United States.

Positive influences on infants' and young children's nutrition and health have been found for participants in WIC (Paolicelli & others, 2021). One study revealed that a WIC program that introduced peer counseling services for pregnant women increased breast feeding substantially (McCoy & others, 2018). Another study found that entry in the first trimester of pregnancy to the WIC program in Rhode Island reduced maternal cigarette smoking (Brodsky, Viner-Brown, & Handler, 2009). And a multiple-year literacy intervention with Spanish-speaking families in the WIC program in Los Angeles increased literacy resources and activities at home, which in turn led to a higher level of school readiness in children (Whaley & others, 2011). And a longitudinal

Participants in the WIC program. *What are some of the benefits of participating in the WIC program?*
USDA Food and Nutrition Service, Supplemental Nutrition Assistance Program

analysis of nine years of infant health and mortality data in the United States indicated that WIC participation during pregnancy reduced racial and ethnic group disparities in infant mortality, low birth weight, preterm birth, and other outcomes (Testa & Jackson, 2021).

connecting with diversity

Cultural Beliefs About Pregnancy

All cultures have beliefs and practices that surround life's major events, and one such event is pregnancy. When a woman who has immigrated to the United States becomes pregnant, the beliefs and practices of her native culture may be as important as, or more important than, those of the mainstream U.S. culture that now surrounds her. The conflict between cultural traditions and Western medicine may pose a risk for the pregnancy and a challenge for the health-care professional who wishes to give proper care while respecting the woman's values.

The American Public Health Association (2006) identified a number of cultural beliefs and practices that are observed among various immigrant groups, and these findings have been replicated in a variety of research studies (e.g., Goswami & Thakur, 2019; Withers, Kharazmi, & Lim, 2018). These beliefs and practices include the following:

- *Food cravings.* Latin American, Asian, and some African cultures believe that it is important for a pregnant woman's food cravings to be satisfied because they are thought to be the cravings of the baby. If cravings are left unsatisfied, the baby might take on certain unpleasant personality and/or physical traits, perhaps characteristic of the food (Kavle & Landry, 2018; Taylor, Ko, & Pan, 1999). As

In India, a midwife checks on the size, position, and heartbeat of a fetus. Midwives deliver babies in many cultures around the world. *What are some cultural variations in prenatal care?*
Viviane Moos/Corbis/Getty Images

All of the *Connecting with Careers* features have been updated, and two-thirds are new profiles that introduce the reader to a diverse group of active professionals. For example, pediatrician Terrance Weeden is a vocal advocate for LGBTQ youth; Anna Boyer-Chadwick is an academic advisor whose university's advising and retention program is a nationally recognized model for Latino student success; and midwife Jennifer Nguyen works with diverse communities to reduce inequities in health care in rural and remote areas of Canada. The careers highlighted extend from the Careers Appendix, which provides a comprehensive overview of careers to show students where knowledge of child development could lead them.

connecting with careers

Salvador Tamayo, Teacher of English Language Learners

Salvador Tamayo is a middle school broadcasting communications teacher in West Chicago, Illinois. He received a National Educator Award from the Milken Family Foundation for his work in educating English language learners (ELLs). Tamayo is especially adept at integrating technology into his ELL classes. He and his students created several award-winning Web sites about the West Chicago City Museum, the local Latino community, and the history of West Chicago. His students also developed an "I Want to Be an American Citizen" Web site to assist family and community members in preparing for the U.S. citizenship test. Tamayo mentors a student club in which participants learn to produce, write, and anchor school broadcasts, such as an informational podcast on Latinos In Action, a group that aims to empower Latino youth to lead and strengthen their communities through college and career readiness.

Salvador Tamayo works with broadcasting communications students in West Chicago.
Sal Tamayo

How Would You . . . ? questions in the margins of each chapter highlight issues involving five main career areas of children's development: psychology, human development and family studies, education, health professions (such as nursing and pediatrics), and social work. The *How Would You . . . ?* questions ensure that this book orients students to concepts that are important to their understanding of children's development. Instructors specializing in these fields have contributed *How Would You . . . ?* questions for each chapter. Strategically placed in the margin next to the relevant chapter content, these questions highlight essential ideas for students to take away from chapter content.

How Would You...?
If you were an **educator,** how would you work with low-socioeconomic-status families to increase parental involvement in their children's educational activities?

Finally, part of applying knowledge of children's development to the real world is understanding how it affects oneself. Accordingly, one of the goals of *Children* is to motivate students to think deeply about their own journey of life. To encourage students to make personal connections to the topics in each section, we include a *Reflect: Your Own Personal Journey of Life* prompt in the end-of-section review. This question asks students to reflect on some aspect of the discussion in the section they have just read and connect it to their own life. For example, in relation to a discussion of the early-later experience issue in development, students are asked,

- Can you identify an early experience that you believe contributed in important ways to your development? Can you identify a recent or current (later) experience that you think had (is having) a strong influence on your development?

Content Revisions

A significant reason *Children* has been successfully used by instructors for many years is the painstaking effort and review that go into making sure it provides the latest research on all topic areas discussed in the classroom. This release is no exception, with more than 1,300 citations from 2021 to 2023. The highlighted research reflects relevant classic and current findings by a diverse group of researchers. Additionally, new discussion is included regarding debates on current terminology used for various demographic groups, and related terms are updated and consistent throughout the text.

In order to provide students with more current examples of related and attainable career opportunities, all of the *Connecting with Careers* boxes have been updated, and many new profiles introduce the reader to additional careers and a very diverse group of active professionals.

Following is a sample of the many chapter-by-chapter changes that were made in this release of *Children*.

Chapter 1: Introduction

- New *Connecting with Diversity* box highlighting ongoing discussions regarding preferred terminology for describing ethnic and racial groups and how this terminology will be addressed throughout
- Updated content on discrimination and prejudice experienced by ethnic minority children and youth (Clauss-Ehlers, Roysircar, & Hunter, 2021)
- New research indicating that pride in one's ethnic identity group and exploration of ethnic identity have positive outcomes (Sladek, Umaña-Taylor, & others, 2020; Umaña-Taylor & Hill, 2020)
- New research on socioeconomic differences in access to opportunities and effects of socioeconomic status on development during childhood and adolescence (Mayo & Wadsworth, 2020; Peverill & others, 2021)
- Recent conceptualizations of gender identity and development
- Updated demographic data related to poverty (OECD, 2021; Semega & others, 2020) and how the COVID-19 pandemic exacerbated socioeconomic disparities (Perry & others, 2021)
- Research on generational differences in the role of technology in development
- Inclusion of recommendations related to dual-language learning (Diaz-Rico, 2020)
- New studies on epigenetics that demonstrate bidirectional influences of genes and the environment on development (Champagne, 2021; Franzago & others, 2020)

Chapter 2: Biological Beginnings

- Updated theory and coverage on the latest research on evolution, natural selection, and adaptation and their roles in advancing our understanding of child development (De Baca & Ellis, 2021; Johansson & others, 2021; Maharian & others, 2021) and critiques of these theoretical perspectives (Davis, 2021)
- Revised key terms and definitions throughout chapter to align with the latest theory and evidence on biological factors in child development and functioning, including correcting all terminology with regard to genetic-associated sex (binary genetic male and female)
- Latest evidence of genetic markers for a wide variety of diseases and disorders of development, e.g., physical illnesses, depression, autism spectrum disorder (Hikino & others, 2022; Wainberg & others, 2022)
- Comprehensively revised description of the latest approaches to identifying genes and genetic effects in child development, including linkage analysis, genomewide association studies, and next-generation sequencing analysis (Akiyama, 2021; Blanton, 2021; Byrska-Bishop & others, 2022)
- Latest available data regarding the number and distribution of protein-coding genes in humans (Nurk & others, 2022)
- Updated theory and evidence regarding epigenetic changes (e.g., DNA methylation) and how they influence gene expression or function (Christiansen & others, 2021; Yang & Chen, 2023)
- Revised information reflecting the latest knowledge about X-linked inheritance, gene imprinting, and polygenic inheritance (Bourn, 2022; J. Chen & others, 2023)
- Major updating of the science regarding a wide range of genetically caused abnormalities, such as Down syndrome, Klinefelter syndrome, and Turner syndrome (Bolling & others, 2023; Tanner & others, 2022)
- Inclusion of the latest science on stem-cell engineering approaches to curing sickle-cell disease (Kanter & others, 2022)
- New *Connecting with Careers* profile on Jennifer Leonhard, a genetic counselor who works with families to understand and make decisions based on the results of genetic testing
- Comprehensive update of most recent information available on the variety of prenatal tests and screening tools being used, e.g., sonography, MRI (Davidson & others, 2022; Navaratnam & others, 2022; Santirocco & others, 2021)
- Latest prevalence rates of infertility, and information regarding methods and interventions available for individuals and couples facing infertility challenges (Agerwal & others, 2021; Graham & others, 2023)
- Thorough revision of data, policy, and practices regarding adoption and adoptive families, including recognition that the recent U.S. Supreme Court decision overturning *Roe v. Wade* may have a dramatic impact on fostering and adoption in the United States (Jones & others, 2021; Koh & others, 2022; U.S. Department of Health and Human Services, 2022)
- Updating of the latest theory and findings regarding heritability, gene-environment interactions, and gene-environment correlations in child development (Davidson & others, 2021; Harden, 2021)

Chapter 3: Prenatal Development

- Discussion of factors that affect fetal growth around the world (Papageorghiou & others, 2018)
- New research on how maternal exposure to indoor air pollution and secondhand tobacco smoke is related to neural tube defects (Chen & others, 2023)
- Discussion of a recent meta-analysis finding that for women with depression, doing yoga during pregnancy reduced depression scores (Lin & others, 2022)
- New *Connecting with Careers* profile on Barbara Greedan, perinatal nurse navigator
- Updated studies on the CenteringPregnancy program (Liu & others, 2021)
- New research on nurse home visiting programs (Goodman & others, 2022)
- Recent data on the effects of maternal caffeine intake during pregnancy (Christensen, Freedman, & Foxe, 2021; Gleason & others, 2021)
- Inclusion of a global review of 55 studies linking smoking during pregnancy to low birth weight (Di & others, 2022)
- New research showing that e-cigarette use during pregnancy is associated with the same risks for premature birth and low birth weight as is smoking combustible cigarettes (Regan & Pereira, 2021)
- Information on withdrawal experienced after birth for infants exposed to cocaine in utero (Mark, 2022)
- New research on effects of prenatal methamphetamine exposure on development (Kalaitzo-poulos & others, 2018; Kunkler & others, 2022; Warton & others, 2018)
- Inclusion of recent studies demonstrating the detrimental effects of prenatal marijuana exposure on outcomes not only in infancy (Corsi & others, 2019) but also into adolescence (Schreiber & Pick, 2019)
- Research linking more negative birth outcomes to fathers' radiation exposure (Andreassi & others, 2021)
- Recent studies on whether exposure to COVID-19 affects fetal development (Rasmussen & Jamieson, 2020; Yang & others, 2022)
- Discussion of the factors to consider in using antidepressants during pregnancy (Biffi & others, 2020; Galbally & others, 2020)
- Paternal factors that can increase the risk of autism spectrum disorders (Kavanaugh & others, 2022)
- Inclusion of the risks of intimate partner violence during pregnancy for the mother and fetus (Drexler & others, 2022)

Chapter 4: Birth

- New *Connecting with Careers* profile on Jennifer Nguyen, an assistant professor with the University of British Columbia midwifery education program who practices in Campbell River, British Columbia, Canada

- New discussion reviewing birth outcomes for doula-assisted mothers (Knocke & others, 2022)
- New section on benefits of yoga during pregnancy on birth outcomes (Kwon & others, 2020; Pais & others, 2021)
- Inclusion of a review of research concluding that preterm and low birth weight infants are at greater risk than full-term and normal birth weight infants of a range of developmental difficulties (Morgan & others, 2022)
- New meta-analysis finding that kangaroo care provided pain relief to preterm infants during painful procedures (Wang & others, 2022)
- Discussion of a randomized controlled trial concluding that kangaroo care starting immediately after birth decreases the risk of mortality in low birth weight infants (WHO Immediate KMC Study Group, 2021)
- New research on the benefits of infant massage for infants and parents (Fan & others, 2022; Rana & others, 2022)
- Discussion of the barriers to seeking help for postpartum depression (Bina, 2020)
- Inclusion of a recent study showing the benefits of increasing partner support to decrease postpartum depression in sexual minority women (Marsland, Treyvaud, & Pepping, 2022)

Chapter 5: Physical Development in Infancy

- Revised coverage of the major tools and strategies being used to study infant brain development, e.g., EEG, fNIRS (Anderson, Perone, & Gartstein, 2022; Fiske & others, 2022)
- Latest cutting-edge research findings regarding infant brain development and its connections to growth and healthy development (Conte & Richards, 2022; Elansary & others, 2022; McMurray & others, 2022; Meza-Cervera & others, 2022)
- Newest evidence regarding neuron functioning and development in infancy including proliferation and pruning of synapses and myelination (Norbom & others, 2021; Schneider, Greenstreet, & Deoni, 2022a and 2022b)
- Update of latest theory and empirical evidence regarding neuroconstructivist viewpoints regarding brain development, plasticity, and learning in infancy (Esteves & others, 2021; Tooley, Bassett, & Mackey, 2021)
- Revised information regarding sleep and its role in infant development (Honaker & others, 2021; Kalogeropoulos & others, 2022; Mason & others, 2021; Tsunematsu, 2023), along with the latest information regarding shared sleeping practices (Barry & McKenna, 2022; Moon & others, 2022)
- Comprehensive revision of data and recommendations regarding preventing sudden infant death syndrome (SIDS) (Byard, 2021; Jani & others, 2022; National Institute of Child Health and Human Development, 2022)
- Updated data on rates of breast feeding and formula feeding practices with infants in the United States from the Centers

for Disease Control and Prevention (2022), along with revised recommendations for breast feeding in all countries and economic and sociocultural contexts, based on ongoing policy development of the World Health Organization (2021)

- Updated information regarding positive benefits of breast feeding for infant and maternal health and functioning (Landa-Rivera & others, 2022; Tschiderer & others, 2022)
- Inclusion of results from the largest comprehensive longitudinal study to date of nutritional effects on subsequent child development across eight low- and middle-income countries, showing beneficial effects of combined good nutrition, nurturing caregiving, and adequate socioeconomic resources (McCormick & others, 2019)
- Substantial revision showing the latest data and policy recommendations regarding infant malnutrition in low- and middle-income countries and low-income communities within high-income countries (FAO, IFAD, UNICEF, WFP, & WHO, 2022; Nisbett & others, 2022; World Health Organization, 2023), including the latest results from the positive effects of infant and maternal nutrition programs for low-income families in the United States (Testa & Jackson, 2021)
- Latest information about reflexes and gross and fine motor development in infancy, including early crawling and walking (Bednarski, Musholt, & Wiesmann, 2022; de Barbaro & Fausey, 2022; Kornafel, Paremski, & Prosser, 2022)
- Updated theory and research on infant development of sensation and perception, including hearing, vision, touch, and pain perception, as well as perceptual-motor coupling (Adolph, Kaplan, & Kretch, 2021; Esteban-Ibañez & others, 2022; Yuan & others, 2022)

Chapter 6: Cognitive Development in Infancy

- Updated description of object permanence and its development in infancy, including the latest theory and empirical evidence (Lin, Stavans, & Baillargeon, 2021)
- Revised critical analysis of Piaget's theory and view on sensorimotor stage of development (Adolph & Hoch, 2021; Hayne & Herbert, 2021; Yates, Ellis, & Turk-Browne, 2021)
- Substantial updating and revision of information about the debate regarding "innate" core knowledge of newborns
- Latest theory and research regarding newborn and infant memory and attention, as well as joint attention with others, and their roles in cognitive functioning and development (Bell & Broomell, 2022; Masek & others, 2021; Richards & Conte, 2021; Riggins & Bauer, 2022)
- Comprehensive update of information regarding early language and communication including rule systems, e.g., morphology, syntax, semantics (Bruhn de Garavito, 2021a, b, c; Levine, Hirsh-Pasek, & Golinkoff, 2021)
- Revised foundational research on early infant communication and language development including speech recognition, babbling, gestures, and early word learning (Kuhl, 2022; Meyer & Hunnius, 2021)

- Major updates to *Connecting with Diversity* box, addressing countering the "deficit" thinking in prior research on socio-economic status and infants' development (Florit & others, 2021; Masek & others, 2021)

Chapter 7: Socioemotional Development in Infancy

- Latest theory and evidence regarding the role and influence of fathers in young infants' development (Carone & Lingiardi, 2022; Kuo & others, 2019; Matte-Gagné, Turgeon, Bernier, & Cyr, 2023; Schoppe-Sullivan & others, 2021)
- Updated information on infants' emotions and their links with cognition and behavior (Davis, Parsafar, & Brady, 2023; Rattaz & others, 2022)
- Recent evidence and ideas regarding early emergence in infancy of dyadic synchrony or coordination of emotions and behavioral states between infant and caregiver (Henderson, Burrows, & Usher, 2020; Ogren & Johnson, 2021)
- Revised sections regarding early emerging emotion regulation in infancy and the role of social environment and context (Dollar & Calkins, 2021; Geyer & Ogbonnaya, 2021; Godleski & others, 2020)
- Significant updates to definitions of key terms, examples, and hypotheses regarding causes and effects of individual differences in infant temperament (Fox & others, 2021; Kagan, 2019; Pozzi & others, 2021; Rothbart, Posner, & Sheese, 2021)
- Addition of evidence from one of the longest running longitudinal studies conducted, showing effect of fearful inhibition in infancy predicting social difficulties and symptoms of depression and anxiety 25 years later (Tang & others, 2020)
- Updated description of "goodness of fit" concept in temperament research, integrated with consideration of the latest theories about differential susceptibility and biological sensitivity (Belsky, Zhang, & Sayler, 2022; Dagan & Sagi-Schwartz, 2021)
- Revised background theory and research regarding the important role of face-to-face play, gaze following, and scaffolding in social interaction in infancy for healthy early socioemotional development (Abels, Osokina, & Kilale, 2023; Gao & others, 2023; Stout & others, 2021; Terrace, Bigelow, & Beebe, 2022; Thompson, 2022)
- Updated evidence regarding individual differences in maternal and paternal caregiving behaviors and infant attachment security (Fourment, Espinoza, Ribeiro, & Mesman, 2022; Luby, 2020; Thompson, 2021), including results showing that sensitivity in parenting was related to secure attachment in infants in Colombia, Mexico, Peru, and the United States (Posada & others, 2016)
- Inclusion of results from a long-term longitudinal study showing that insecure attachment in infancy was linked to difficulties with emotion expression and regulation in close relationships 25 to 30 years later (Girme & others, 2021)

- Latest evidence from social neuroscience perspectives of the role of nervous and endocrine systems in attachment in infancy (Hannan & others, 2023; Storey, Alloway, & Walsh, 2020), including results from a recent study of first-time fathers in Japan showing changes in their brain functioning and hormone levels during their partner's pregnancy and after the birth (Diaz-Rojas & others, 2023)
- Revision of the descriptions of family systems theories and definitions (Perez-Brena & others, 2022) and expansion of inclusive terminology and language with regard to parent and caregiver sex and gender throughout this and all chapters
- Addition of information about the potential impact of the COVID-19 pandemic on differential effects on men and women on staying at work versus staying at home with the infant and the potential effects of these rapid changes on infant development (Volling & Palkovitz, 2021; Zamarro & Prados, 2021)
- Updated information about the Nordic countries' policies of shared caregiving and workplace leave for mothers and fathers (Greve & Hussain, 2021; OECD, 2022; Thébaud & Pedulla, 2022)
- Substantially revised consideration of out-of-home infant child care and the challenges of improving high quality of care and equitable access for low-income and marginalized families, including the positive effects of such high-quality infant care (Hatfield & others, 2021; Haynie & others, 2023; Pilarz, Sandstrom, & Henly, 2022)

Chapter 8: Physical Development in Early Childhood

- Inclusion of a new study finding that children with growth hormone deficiencies were at high risk of psychiatric problems such as social anxiety disorders and were often victimized by peers (Çoban & others, 2022)
- Recent research on brain development in young children (Gualtieri & Finn, 2022; Schneider, Greenstreet, & Deoni, 2022)
- Discussion of a recent study showing that children who were randomly assigned to an intervention group that focused on improving both motor and cognitive skills improved not only in motor skills and academic skills but also in perceived competence, self-worth, and social acceptance compared to a control group (Nobre, Nobre, & Valentini, 2023)
- Inclusion of recent research demonstrating that incorporating movement into academic subjects can increase children's enjoyment of these subjects (Liang & others, 2023)
- New information from a large international team about a set of benchmarks for children's overall physical activity, as well as in specific domains such as active play and organized sports and in specific settings such as at home and in school (Aubert & others, 2022)
- Addition of a recent study that used drawing to help prepare children to return to school following the COVID-19 pandemic (Alabdulkarim & others, 2021)

- Inclusion of a study linking better parent-child relationships with better sleep (Dubois-Comtois & others, 2020)
- New research showing that having nightmares at 24 months and restless sleep at 48 months were linked to ADHD at 11 years of age (Carpena & others, 2020)
- New nutritional guidelines from within the U.S. (Dallacker, Hertwig, & Mata, 2018) and globally (World Health Organization, 2020)
- New research on the long-term effects of childhood obesity (Weihrauch-Blüher, Schwarz, & Klusmann, 2019)
- Updated international statistics on the prevalence of overweight and obesity during childhood (World Health Organization, 2021)
- Inclusion of a new study demonstrating that positive parenting that emphasized praise for healthy eating behavior improved young children's eating behavior and helped overweight children lose weight better than negative comments by parents did (Rotman & others, 2020)
- Discussion of a meta-analysis finding that interventions that communicated with parents information about nutrition and social behavior change were effective in improving children's growth (Mahumud & others, 2022)
- New *Connecting with Careers* profile on Alyssa Cantal, a pediatric occupational therapist
- New research showing that preschool children are more physically active if they spend time outdoors and live in a safe neighborhood where families feel that they can trust their neighbors (Parent & others, 2021)
- Updated data on child deaths from firearms (Centers for Disease Control and Prevention, 2021; McGough & others, 2022)
- Inclusion of safety precautions that can help protect children from injury and death (Burr & others, 2023)
- New research on early physical and cognitive development being negatively affected by inadequate nutrition and food insecurity that often accompany poverty (Alam & others, 2020)
- Discussion of the findings on how structural racism and barriers to health care have contributed to health disparities in the United States (Goyal & others, 2020)
- Inclusion of a recent study finding that children with a smoker in the home were 30 percent more likely to be diagnosed with asthma than children with no smokers in the home (Xie & others, 2021)
- Discussion of a longitudinal study showing that children who lived in high-poverty neighborhoods were more likely to be exposed to lead, which in turn led to lower vocabulary skills (Wodtke, Ramaj, & Schachner, 2022)

Chapter 9: Cognitive Development in Early Childhood

- Updated framing of Piaget's and Vygotsky's theories as historical and scholarly precedents and foundations, in the context of contemporary neo-Piagetian and neo-Vygotskian perspectives and their applications

- Revised sources for the latest thinking regarding Piaget's pre-operational stage and substages of cognitive development (Goldman & others, 2022; Kurkul & others, 2022; Panesi & Morra, 2022)

- Inclusion of contemporary accounts of key elements of Vygotsky's theory, e.g., zone of proximal development, scaffolding, private speech (Alcalá, Montejano, & Fernandez, 2021; Groot & others, 2020; Mulvihill & others, 2023)

- Expanded recommendations for applying Vygotsky's theory in practical ways in young children's education, e.g., guided reading, play-based math learning, "flipped" classrooms (Dunphy, 2020; Hew & others, 2021; Nicholas, Veresov, & Clark, 2021)

- Updated description in *Caring Connections* box of the *Tools of the Mind* curriculum and evaluations of its effectiveness for supporting young children's self-regulated learning

- Coverage of the latest work regarding growth in attention skills in early childhood and its links with a variety of learning and other cognitive processes (Dotan, Eliahou, & Cohen, 2021; Gonzalez & others, 2021; Savina, 2021)

- Revised theory and evidence regarding early childhood memory skills and development (Alghamdi, Murphy, & Crewther, 2021; Brown, 2022; Kangaslampi, 2023)

- Addition of recent research on the remarkable developmental progression of executive function skills across early childhood and their links with other cognitive and academic skills (Bell & Garcia Meza, 2020; Nakamichi & others, 2022; Zelazo & Carlson, 2022)

- Updated theory and empirical evidence on growth and changes in theory of mind across early childhood, and its connections with a variety of other cognitive and socioemotional capacities (Fujita, Devine, & Hughes, 2022; Rakoczy, 2022; Visu-Petra, Prodan, & Talwar, 2022; Yates, Ellis, & Turk-Browne, 2021)

- Expanded coverage of research on theory of mind and autism spectrum disorder (Martínez-González & others, 2022; Rice & others, 2022)

- Revised information on early emerging language and literacy skills and their connections to subsequent academic and cognitive competencies (McBride, Pan, & Mohseni, 2021; Pakarinen & others, 2021)

- Inclusion of contemporary background and data regarding early childhood education (e.g., preschool) programming and its connections with a variety of family, community, and cultural factors (Friedman-Krauss & others, 2022; Lillard, 2021; Morrison & others, 2022), including updating of sources regarding Montessori and child-centered kindergarten pedagogies

- Substantial updates to information about Head Start and Early Head Start child care preschool programs for low-income children in the United States, including evidence of its impact on subsequent child development outcomes (Administration for Children and Families, 2023; Slater & others, 2021)

- Revised coverage of three controversies in early childhood education regarding curriculum, universal access, and priorities for school readiness (Cascio, 2023; Morrison & others, 2022) and how these controversies intersect with socioeconomic and family policy

- New *Connecting with Careers* profile on Rakaya Humphries, a Head Start/Early Head Start program director in Tennessee whose vocation and work support the healthy development and learning of hundreds of low-income children

Chapter 10: Socioemotional Development in Early Childhood

- Inclusion of research on discipline strategies used in different cultural contexts (Fung, Li, & Lam, 2017)

- New research demonstrating that children who are better at understanding and regulating emotions are then able to form better relationships with peers and teachers, perform better academically, and show fewer behavior problems (Denham, 2023)

- Elaboration on how moral behavior is influenced by situational determinants (Misch & Dunham, 2021)

- New conceptualizations and research on gender identity (Best & Puzio, 2019; Erickson-Schroth & Davis, 2021; Halim & others, 2017; Li, Kung, & Hines, 2017; Spencer & others, 2021)

- Inclusion of a recent study on gendered parenting roles (Deichmann & Ahnert, 2021)

- Discussion of gender stereotypes in different cultural contexts (Koenig, 2018)

- Updated research on parents' use of corporal punishment, which is now outlawed in over 65 nations (End Violence Against Children, 2023)

- Current recommendations from several professional organizations that parents not use corporal punishment because of its detrimental effects on child development (American Psychological Association, 2019; Sege & others, 2018)

- Inclusion of recent findings from an intervention to improve coparenting and, in turn, children's emotional and behavioral adjustment (Tomfohr-Madsen & others, 2020)

- New *Connecting with Careers* profile on Allison Tomlinson, a marriage and family therapist

- New *Connecting with Careers* profile on Stacie Padilla, a child welfare case manager

- Discussion of longitudinal studies demonstrating the long-term negative effects into adulthood of being physically abused as a child (Angelakis, Gillespie, & Panagioti, 2019; Lansford & others, 2021)

- Updated demographics of families with half siblings and stepsiblings (Knop, 2020)

- Inclusion of research on birth order and being an only child (Stronge & others, 2019; Volling & others, 2023)

- Discussion of the historical changes in parental employment (Bastian, 2020; Bureau of Labor Statistics, 2021)
- Contemporary research on child development in different family structures, including families with divorced or remarried parents and LGBTQ parents (Raley & Sweeney, 2020; Roper, Fife, & Seedall, 2020; Walker & Taylor, 2021)
- New research on effects of interparental conflict on child development and interventions to reduce interparental conflict and enhance parenting (Cummings & others, 2021; DeGarmo & Jones, 2023; Hoegler, Mills, Feda, & Cummings, 2023)
- Inclusion of an analysis of 72 reviews of the literature concluding that parents' sexual orientation is not related to their children's sexual orientation (Schumm & Crawford, 2019)
- New research showing that parental monitoring varies across cultures in ways that are related to cultural expectations regarding adolescent autonomy and how much control parents should have over adolescents' decisions and activities (Soenens & Vansteenkiste, 2020)
- New research on young children's peer relationships (Lenz & others, 2021) and how peer relationships are related to family relationships (Kaufman & others, 2020)
- Description of how, with the advent of digital games on mobile devices, game playing has become widely available and used by older children, adolescents, and adults (Pew Research Center, 2018)
- Updated recommendations regarding the importance of play for children's healthy development (Hassinger-Das, Hirsh-Pasek, & Golinkoff, 2017; Yogman & others, 2018)
- Updated guidelines regarding children's screen time and the large proportion of children who exceed recommended limits on screen time (McArthur & others, 2022)
- Inclusion of a recent meta-analysis showing that more screen time was related to children's poorer language skills, but the quality of screen use mattered too (Madigan & others, 2020)
- New research on the physical, cognitive, and behavioral effects of excessive screen time (LeBourgeois & others, 2017; Simonato & others, 2018)
- Discussion of research reviews that concluded children and adolescents who experience a heavy media diet of violence are more likely to perceive the world as a dangerous place and to view aggression as more acceptable than their counterparts who see media violence less frequently (Greitemeyer, 2022; Groves, Prot, & Anderson, 2020)
- Inclusion of a recent research finding that playing prosocial video games is related to more subsequent prosocial thoughts and behaviors (Li & Zhang, 2023)

Chapter 11: Physical Development in Middle and Late Childhood

- Updated statistics on physical growth trajectories and percentiles across middle and late childhood (National Center for Health Statistics, 2022)

- Recent empirical evidence for the wide range of changes in brain structure and function in middle and late childhood, e.g., neural pruning, myelination, cortical thickness (Bell, 2022; Frangou & others, 2022; Kraus & Horowitz-Kraus, 2022)
- Revised background information about motor development in middle childhood (Hockenberry, Wilson, & Rodgers, 2021; Wuest & Walton-Fisette, 2024)
- Updated background evidence and recommendations for healthy balanced diet and nutrition in middle and late childhood (Sorte & others, 2020; USDA, 2023)
- Addition of recent evidence and policy recommendations for reducing "screen time" and increasing moderate and vigorous physical activity, and regarding links with physical and cognitive benefits (Ramírez-Coronel & others, 2023; Sardinha & others, 2022; Sun & others, 2021)
- Inclusion of evidence of large longitudinal study in Spain showing the benefits of organized sports participation on a wide range of developmental outcomes in middle and late childhood (Menescardi & others, 2023)
- Updated resources for recommended practices of parents and coaches for involving and supporting children's participation in sports (Families in Sport Lab at Utah State University, 2023; Women's Sports Foundation, 2023)
- Updated theory, evidence, and recommendations regarding causes and consequences of childhood obesity (Centers for Disease Control and Prevention, 2022; Flynn & others, 2023; Hemmingsson & others, 2023)
- Addition of evidence from the largest meta-analysis to date spanning many countries and cultural contexts, showing the important role of increasing nutritious food options in schools for supporting children's weight management (Pineda, Bascunan, & Sassi, 2021)
- Substantially revised data, evidence, and interventions for addressing injuries and diseases in childhood, e.g., accident prevention, cancer, diabetes, asthma (Cosottile & Damashek, 2022; Di Cicco & others, 2023; Harnois-Leblanc & others, 2023; National Cancer Institute, 2023)
- Updated background, evidence, and policies regarding all major categories of developmental and learning disabilities in childhood (Astle & others, 2022; Condition of Education, 2022; Hallahan & others, 2023)
- Revised sections about attention deficit hyperactivity disorder (ADHD) and autism spectrum disorders (ASD) regarding prevalence, causes, and interventions to support development (Hallahan, Kauffman, & Pullen, 2023; Hudry & others, 2022; Ivanov & others, 2022)
- Inclusion of recent sources and information regarding the policies and practices in schools for assessment, evaluation, and implementation of inclusive education plans to support learning and development of all children with a wide range of disabilities (Etscheidt & others, 2023; Kauffman & others, 2022)

Chapter 12: Cognitive Development in Middle and Late Childhood

- Additional recent sources to emphasize the importance of culture and education on childhood cognitive development in response to some of the ideas in Piaget's theory (Kirmayer & others, 2021; Riccio & Castro, 2021)
- Updated definition of short-term memory to distinguish it more clearly from working memory
- Inclusion of the most recent theory and evidence regarding growth in and effects of memory capacities across middle and early childhood (Baddeley, 2021; Bjorklund, 2022; Nelwan & others, 2022)
- Addition of findings from a recent study of bilingual school-age children showing a link between working memory improvements with better math problem solving (Swanson, Arizmendi, & Li, 2021)
- Revised emphasis on the importance of family relationships, stories, and narratives for transmitting and supporting memory development that is consistent with the child's cultural context (Wang, 2021)
- Updated evidence regarding activities and practices that support growth in executive function skills in middle childhood, e.g., aerobic activity, child-centered instructional methods (Doebel & Lillard, 2023; Zhang & others, 2023)
- Addition of recent theory and evidence on mindfulness practices for improving cognitive functions in school-age children (Amundsen & others, 2020; Roeser & others, 2022)
- Inclusion of latest theory and empirical evidence about the development and importance of meta-cognition across middle and late childhood (Dos Santos Kawata & others, 2021; Forsberg, Blume, & Cowan, 2021)
- Revised information about metalinguistic strategies for learning that develop across childhood, including emphasis on pragmatics involving culturally defined appropriate language use (Gleason & Ratner, 2023; Nadasdi, 2021)
- Updated *Connecting with Diversity* box emphasizing methods for supporting bilingual children's English language learning (Herrell & Jordan, 2020; Tao & others, 2021)
- Substantial revision of sources regarding theories and measurement of intelligence in middle and late childhood (Bjorklund, 2022; Coyle, 2021; Sternberg, 2021a; Wright, 2020), and on genetic and environmental influences on intelligence (Mahmassani & others, 2022; von Stumm & Plomin, 2021)
- Expanded discussion on the background and evidence regarding culturally distinct definitions of intelligence and efforts to reduce or eliminate bias in intelligence assessments (Ang, Ng, & Rockstuhl, 2020; Gonthier, 2022)
- Updated definitions and discussion of educational approaches for "gifted" students, including efforts to address underrepresentation of minoritized children in gifted programs in the United States (Bucaille & others, 2022; Sternberg, Ambrose, & Karami, 2022; Wright, Ford, & Moore, 2022)

- New *Connecting with Careers* profile on Geoffrey Moon, gifted education specialist
- Revised background on the importance of children's motivation, mindset, and self-efficacy to growth in learning and cognitive skills (Dweck, 2019; Reeve & Cheon, 2021; Schunk, 2020; Shin & Bolkan, 2021)
- Expanded and updated description of the roles of parents and teachers in supporting cognitive development and academic achievement in middle and late childhood (Grolnick & Pomerantz, 2022; Skinner & others, 2022; Urhahne & Wijnia, 2021)
- Addition of theory and evidence regarding the negative effects of exposure to racial and ethnic discrimination on children's achievement and learning, and approaches that families and communities can take to tackle this in a new *Connecting with Research* box (Lash, Akpovo, & Cushner, 2022; Whaley, 2020)
- Up-to-date results from international assessments of over 70 countries to understand cultural differences in educational practices that promote or impede children's and adolescents' academic achievement (Gomendio, 2023)

Chapter 13: Socioemotional Development in Middle and Late Childhood

- New opening story about a Girl Scout who showed the importance and impact of honesty and integrity, as shared by broadcaster and journalist Steve Hartman and his family
- Updated background and evidence regarding developmental changes across middle and late childhood in perspective-taking skills (Amemiya & others, 2021; Lagattuta & Kramer, 2021)
- Revised sections on self-esteem, self-concept, and self-regulation across childhood (Arens & Niepel, 2023; Clark & others, 2023; Lichtenfeld & others, 2023)
- Inclusion of the latest theory and evidence regarding developmental changes in attachment security and relationships in middle and late childhood (Dagan & Sagi-Schwartz, 2021; Gastelle & Kerns, 2022)
- New *Connecting with Careers* profile on child psychiatrist Dr. Melissa Jackson, who helps children facing many types of challenges and trauma
- Inclusion of the largest study to date, a meta-analysis of 15 studies and almost 23,000 children, regarding COVID-19 pandemic impacts on school-age children's emotional problems in numerous countries around the world (Kumar Panda & others, 2021)
- Revised background on moral development and prosocial behavior in childhood, including evidence of consistency of prosocial behavioral development in many cultures (Callaghan & Corbit, 2018; Misch & Dunham, 2021)
- Updated terminology (e.g., added term "sex assigned at birth" to replace "natal sex") along with the latest research on gender identity development and stereotyping across middle and late childhood (Foster-Hanson & Rhodes, 2023)

- Substantially revised description of theory, definitions, and research on gender group and individual differences and similarities in childhood, including examination of the brain and nervous system, cognition, emotions, and behavior (Brandes & others, 2021; Eliot & others, 2021; Grabowska, 2020)
- Updated examination of the impact of educational environments (including same-sex education settings) and exposure to gender bias and discrimination on gender differences in academic and socioemotional functioning in childhood (Denessen & others, 2020; Herr, Grant, & Price, 2020)
- Up-to-date data on the prevalence of children and youth who identify as transgender, and evidence regarding the particular challenges transgender youth face in regard to bullying and discrimination (Potter & others, 2021; Sherman & others, 2020)
- Revised description of diversity of family structures (e.g., single parent, stepparent) and the potential links between family structure and form and child development (Bean & others, 2021; Ganong & others, 2022; Michas, 2023)
- Comprehensive updating of sources and studies describing the peer group relationships and structures that influence child development in middle and late childhood, e.g., peer neglect and rejection, as well as updates to information about close friendships (Normand & others, 2022; Sørlie & others, 2021)
- Substantially revised description of peer bullying and its effects, including description of cross-cultural similarities in these patterns across middle and late childhood
- New *Connecting with Careers* profile on Yolanda Curry, a high school counselor
- Updated background on educational methods in middle and late childhood, e.g., constructivist and direct instruction approaches (Kauchak & Eggen, 2021; Sadker, Zittleman, & Koch, 2022), and the latest data on national differences in achievement based on the PISA (Programme for International Student Assessment) and TIMMS (Trends in International Mathematics and Science Study) assessments
- Major update to the examination of race, ethnic, and socioeconomic status bias and discrimination in educational systems and schools, their influences on children's learning and socioemotional well-being, and interventions that seek to reduce and eliminate such experiences (Banks, 2020; Cushner, McClelland, & Safford, 2022; Jarvis & Okonofua, 2020; Le Menestrel & Duncan, 2019)

Chapter 14: Physical Development in Adolescence

- New chapter opener that introduces two adolescents who are contributing in positive ways to their communities and competently making the transition through adolescence
- Inclusion of a research review of 30 studies in different countries around the world concluding that the age at which breast development began in girls had declined by almost three months per decade since the 1970s (Eckert-Lind & others, 2021)

- Updated research on factors leading to earlier pubertal onset (Argente & others, 2023; Colich & McLaughlin, 2022; Wang & others, 2023)
- Addition of a new study on how gender differences in body perceptions are often exacerbated by heavy social media use (Harriger, Thompson, & Tiggemann, 2023)
- Contemporary research on early maturation effects for boys, which is mixed with regard to negative and positive outcomes (Klopack & others, 2020)
- Longitudinal research finding that early-maturing girls are more likely to become pregnant and bear children as teenagers and are less likely to graduate from high school, which predicts depressive symptoms and antisocial behavior into adulthood (Mendle, Ryan, & McKone, 2019)
- Inclusion of a new study illustrating a range of responses to unwanted sexual texts (Lunde & Joleby, 2023)
- New *Connecting with Careers* profile on Terrance Weeden, a pediatrician whose clinical and research interests include LGBTQ+ health care and eradicating disparities in health care among youth in underserved communities
- Updated statistics on risky sexual behavior (Centers for Disease Control and Prevention, 2023)
- Discussion of the changes in risky sexual behavior over the last decade (Centers for Disease Control and Prevention, 2023)
- Recent research on how having siblings who use alcohol or cannabis or are sexually active is a risk factor for adolescents' own risky sexual behavior (Thomas & others, 2022)
- Inclusion of a large study of 88,815 high school students in Minnesota finding that students with poorer self-regulation were more likely to have initiated sexual activity and to engage in risky sexual behavior (Song & Qian, 2020)
- Discussion of findings that approximately half of all new sexually transmitted infections occur in young people ages 15 to 24 (Centers for Disease Control and Prevention, 2023)
- Updated information on the vaccine to protect against the human papillomavirus
- New information from the World Health Organization (2022) that in many countries, there is a large unmet need for contraceptives, including condoms to help prevent transmission of HIV and other sexually transmitted infections
- Updated data on adolescent pregnancy and birth rates in the United States and globally (UNICEF, 2022; World Bank, 2023)
- Inclusion of a meta-analysis of 35 studies finding that offspring born to mothers younger than age 21 had more cognitive, externalizing, and internalizing problems across the life span than did offspring born to mothers who were 21 or older (Cresswell & others, 2022)
- Addition of a meta-analysis finding that offspring of adolescent fathers were at greater risk of being born prematurely, having low birth weight, and having psychological disorders later in development (Bamishigbin, Schetter, & Stanton, 2019)

- Discussion of a meta-analysis of 15 surveys in the United States demonstrating that 88 percent of respondents in nationally representative samples supported sexuality education in schools (Szucs & others, 2022)

- New information on the need for comprehensive sexuality education programs that include information on how to communicate with a partner about consent, sexual history, pregnancy, and sexually transmitted infections, as well as addressing the needs of LGBTQ adolescents (Grasso & Trumbull, 2023)

- Contemporary research on adolescents' physical activity (Chong & others, 2020; Underwood & others, 2020)

- Inclusion of a study showing that engaging in more physical exercise during quarantine periods helped to reduce the link between experiences during the COVID-19 pandemic and adolescents' depressive symptoms (Ren & others, 2021)

- Discussion of a study revealing that adolescents' participation in physical activities was predicted by more parental support for those activities, and girls' participation in physical activities was also linked to their friends' support of those activities (Lawler & others, 2022)

- New research showing that adolescents who engage in low physical activity and high screen-based activity are more likely to be overweight or obese compared to peers who are physically active (Zhu & others, 2019)

- Historical changes in the amount of sleep adolescents report getting (Gariepy & others, 2020; Kann & others, 2018)

- New research using statewide administrative data finding that later school start times reduce absences and suspensions and improve adolescents' math and reading test scores (Bastian & Fuller, 2023)

- New data showing that the United States is the only large or wealthy country in which guns are a leading cause of death in adolescents (McGough & others, 2022)

- Inclusion of reports showing an exponential growth in mental health problems and suicidal ideation in adolescents following the COVID-19 pandemic (Centers for Disease Control and Prevention, 2023)

- Updated statistics on the prevalence of current substance use by adolescents in the United States based on national surveys (National Institute on Drug Abuse, 2022)

- New *Connecting with Careers* profile on Bonnie Halpern-Felsher, university professor in pediatrics and director of community efforts to improve adolescents' health, who also coordinates the STEP-UP program (Short-Term Research Experience for Underrepresented Persons) in which she has personally mentored and supervised 22 to 25 middle and high school students every year since 2007

- New research on vaping (National Institute on Drug Abuse, 2022)

- Inclusion of studies on family (Afifi & others, 2022) and peer (Henneberger, Gest, & Zadzora, 2019; Marmet & others, 2021) influences on adolescents' substance use

- Coverage of a meta-analysis of longitudinal studies showing reciprocal links with low self-esteem predicting more eating pathology and more eating pathology predicting worse self-esteem over time (Krauss, Dapp, & Orth, 2023)

- New research on family risk factors for eating pathology as well as eating disorders in boys and sexual minority youth (Breton, Juster, & Booji, 2023; Cao & others, 2023; Potterton & others, 2020)

- Contemporary research suggesting that extensive use of social media contributes to more body dissatisfaction for girls and boys (Vandenbosch, Fardouly, & Tiggemann, 2022)

Chapter 15: Cognitive Development in Adolescence

- New research indicating that working memory is a foundational cognitive activity, with the frontoparietal brain network playing a key role in its development (Rosenberg & others, 2020)

- Inclusion of a recent study showing that adolescents with poorer working memory were more at risk for internalizing problems, such as anxiety and depression (Blok & others, 2023)

- Description of how college professors can embed metacognitive strategies, such as helping students monitor their own learning to be more accurate about gaps in knowledge, into their teaching practices to improve students' learning (Voorhees & others, 2022)

- Coverage of a meta-analysis of 10 service-learning programs in the United States, identifying eight important standards to be considered in the implementation of such programs (Filges & others, 2022)

- New research on service learning and predictors and outcomes of adolescents' volunteerism (Ramey & others, 2022)

- Inclusion of a recent study of the development of forgiveness finding that older children are more likely than younger children to pay attention to intentions and to forgive accidental than purposeful transgressions (Amir & others, 2021)

- New research on how parents socialize their children's gratitude (Hussong, Coffman, & Halberstadt, 2021)

- New *Connecting with Careers* profile on Gabriel Dy-Liacco, a professor and pastoral counselor

- Current prevalence of religious affiliations around the world (Jensen, 2021; Pew-Templeton Global Religious Future Project, 2022)

- Contemporary research on how individuals perceive and navigate the intersectionality of their identities, including their religious identity (Azmitia & others, 2023; Martin, Butler-Barnes, & Hope, 2023; Shen & others, 2023)

- Inclusion of a longitudinal study of a nationally representative sample of Americans finding that attending religious services regularly during adolescence predicted a lower likelihood of having engaged in sex in early adulthood (Vasilenko, 2022)

- New *Connecting with Careers* profile on Willie Howard, a high school activities director

- Updated research on poverty and barriers to learning (Lampert & others, 2020)
- Updated demographics related to school dropout (National Center for Education Statistics, 2023)

Chapter 16: Socioemotional Development in Adolescence

- New chapter opener that introduces three teenage girls' efforts to tackle environmental issues
- New research on the major factors in identity narratives (McLean & others, 2020)
- Inclusion of a longitudinal study of more than 5,000 young people finding that greater identity synthesis (as opposed to confusion) was related to greater life satisfaction (Hatano & others, 2022)
- New *Connecting with Careers* profile on Anna Boyer-Chadwick, academic advisor, whose university's counseling program has won national awards as a model for Latinos' academic success
- Coverage of a recent study of immigrant and nonimmigrant adolescents in Greece finding that national identity and friendship networks developed in tandem, with identity influencing friendship choices, and friends influencing identity development (Umaña-Taylor & others, 2020)
- Description of an influential life-span model of ethnic-racial identity describing five dimensions of ethnic-racial identity (Williams & others, 2020)
- New *Connecting with Careers* profile on Adriana Umaña-Taylor, a professor who studies ethnic-racial identity
- New research on adolescents' bicultural or multicultural identities (Ferguson, Iturbide, & Raffaelli, 2020)
- Discussion of flexibility and specific situations in understanding gender identity (Martin, Cook, & Andrews, 2017)
- Updated demographics regarding transgender youth (Herman, Flores, & O'Neill, 2022)
- New *Connecting with Careers* profile on Stephanie Budge, a psychotherapist and professor who specializes in transgender research
- Inclusion of a five-year longitudinal study of transgender children (Olson & others, 2022)
- Updated conceptualizations of families as being best understood as systems in which relationships between coparents, siblings, and extended family members affect parent-adolescent relationships (Updegraff & Perez-Brena, 2023)
- New studies of the role of monitoring in parent-adolescent relationships and adolescents' adjustment (Jaggers & others, 2021; Khetarpai & others, 2022; Pizarro, Surkan, & Bustamante, 2021; Spirito & others, 2021)
- Coverage of a review of research on parental autonomy support among Black, White, Latino, and Asian American families concluding that understanding this aspect of parenting needs to be grounded in cultural concepts related to independence and expectations of parents (Benito-Gomez & others, 2020)

- Inclusion of a systematic review of 19 studies concluding that secure attachment to parents during adolescence is related to better peer relationships in terms of communication, support, intimacy, trust, and quality (Delgado & others, 2022)
- New studies of adolescents' and young adults' communication and conflict with their parents (Martin & others, 2019; Mokhtarnia & others, 2023; Skinner & others, 2021; Sumner & Ramirez, 2019)
- Inclusion of recent research on the importance and functions of friendship in different cultures (Chen, Lee, & Chen, 2018)
- New information on the relationship among pubertal timing, adolescents' associations with older peers, and engagement in substance use and other problem behaviors (Bucci & Staff, 2020)
- New section on peer relationships, social distancing, online engagement, and psychological well-being in the context of the COVID-19 pandemic (Loades & others, 2020; Magis-Weinberg & others, 2021; Magson & others, 2021)
- Inclusion of recent research recognizing fluidity in sexual orientation and gender identity and expression (Diamond, 2021)
- Coverage of a qualitative study of Latino adolescents' perceptions of their parents' roles in their daughters' and sons' romantic relationships (Killoren & others, 2023)
- Inclusion of a review of studies concluding that whether romantic partners enhance or diminish adolescents' adjustment depends on the quality of the romantic relationship and the adjustment of the romantic partner (Austin & others, 2022)
- New demographics regarding the use of dating apps (Pew Research Center, 2020)
- Current global statistics showing that in 51 percent of countries, boys have more access to primary school education than do girls, and in 76 percent of countries, boys have more access to upper secondary school education than do girls (UNICEF, 2022)
- Coverage of recent research demonstrating that how immigrant youth fare depends on opportunities available in the country of destination, discrimination they might experience, their families' socioeconomic status, and a range of other factors (Motti-Stefanidi, 2023)
- Inclusion of a study of over 470,000 youth in Canada finding that both first- and second-generation immigrant youth had lower rates of conduct disorders, ADHD, and mood disorders than nonimmigrant youth (Gadermann & others, 2022)
- Discussion of a study of college students showing that media multitasking led to attention biases in taking in negative information, which in turn predicted more depression and anxiety (Li & Fan, 2022)
- New data on the possible associations of social media use and screen time with adolescents' physical and mental health (Calandri, Cattelino, & Graziano, 2023; Hamilton, Nesi, & Choukas-Bradley, 2022; Twenge, 2020)

- New section on ways that parents engage with adolescents regarding their online lives (Beyens, Keijsers, & Coyne, 2022)
- Inclusion of a recent study of over 5,000 individuals in 11 countries showing that improvements in aspects of psychosocial maturity involved in decision making in emotionally charged situations continued beyond age 18 (Icenogle & others, 2019)
- Description of recent research showing that a developmental pathway from behavior problems in childhood to delinquency in adolescence can be disrupted by parental monitoring, which reduces adolescents' opportunities to spend time with antisocial peers (Jaggers & others, 2021)
- Inclusion of a meta-analysis of 18 longitudinal studies finding that both older and younger siblings who engaged in deviant behaviors increase their siblings' risk for future delinquency (Maneiro & others, 2022)
- New research on deviant peer contagion demonstrating how peers can reinforce one another's antisocial behaviors by laughing or going along with plans to engage in delinquency (Kornienko, Ha, & Dishion, 2020)
- Current statistics on the national prevalence of mental health problems among adolescents in the United States

(Centers for Disease Control and Prevention, 2022) and globally (World Health Organization, 2021)
- Inclusion of research on gender differences in depression (de la Torrs & others, 2021; Porter & others, 2021)
- New research demonstrating that one of the reasons that parental depression is a risk factor for the development of adolescents' own depression is that parents who are depressed parent less consistently and adaptively than parents who are not depressed (Pine & Garber, 2023)
- Description of studies of associations between friendships, bullying, victimization, and depression (Sutter & others, 2023; van der Mey-Baijens & others, 2023)
- Contemporary data on the prevalence of suicide attempts in different sociodemographic groups (Centers for Disease Control and Prevention, 2022)
- Inclusion of an explanation of reasons that adolescents sometimes exhibit a range of problem behaviors
- New research on long-term effects of the Fast Track intervention on adult outcomes and outcomes into the next generation (Godwin & Conduct Problems Prevention Research Group, 2020; Rothenberg & others, 2023)

acknowledgments

We very much appreciate the support and guidance provided by many people at McGraw Hill. Ryan Treat, Executive Portfolio Manager for Psychology, has provided excellent guidance, vision, and direction for this book. Vicki Malinee provided considerable expertise in coordinating many aspects of the editorial process. Kevin Campbell did an outstanding job as the book's copy editor. Mary Powers did a terrific job in coordinating the book's production. Dawn Groundwater, Senior Product Development Manager, did excellent work on various aspects of the book's development, technology, and learning systems. And Steve Rouben provided excellent choices of new photographs. We also wish to thank Sophie Sharp and Anna Deater-Deckard, who assisted with library literature research.

QUEST: JOURNEY THROUGH THE LIFESPAN BOARD OF ADVISORS AND SUBJECT MATTER EXPERTS

Admiration and appreciation go to the following experts who have devoted a significant portion of their time and expertise to creating the first of its kind learning game for Developmental Psychology: Cheri Kittrell, *State College of Florida;* Brandy Young, *Cypress College;* Becky Howell, *Forsyth Technical College;* Gabby Principe, *College of Charleston;* Karen Schrier Shaenfield, *Marist College;* Steven Prunier, *Ivy Tech;* Amy Kolak, *College of Charleston;* Kathleen Hughes Stellmach, *Pasco-Hernando State College;* Lisa Fozio-Thielk, *Waubonsee Community College;* Tricia Wessel-Blaski, *University of Wisconsin-Milwaukee, Washington County;* Margot Underwood, *Joliet Junior College;* Claire Rubman, *Suffolk County Community College;* Alissa Knowles, *University of California-Irvine;* Cortney Simmons, *University of California-Irvine;* Kelli Dunlap, *Level Access-WCAG Accessibility Partners.*

EXPERT CONSULTANTS

As each revision is developed, we consult with leading experts in their respective areas of child and adolescent development. Their invaluable feedback ensures that the latest research, understandings, and perspectives are presented. Their willingness to devote their time and expertise to this endeavor is greatly appreciated. Coverage of the Expert Consultants who contributed to this release can be found on pages xviii and xix.

REVIEWERS

A special debt of gratitude goes to the reviewers who have provided detailed feedback on *Children* over the years.

John A. Addleman, *Messiah College;* Linda Anderson, *Northwestern Michigan College;* Christine Anthis, *Southern Connecticut State University;* Harry H. Avis, *Sierra College;* Diana Baumrind, *University of California-Berkeley;* Lori A. Beasley, *University of Central Oklahoma;* Patricia J. Bence, *Tompkins Cortland Community College;* Michael Bergmire, *Jefferson College;* Belinda Blevins-Knabe, *University of Arkansas-Little Rock;* Albert Bramante, *Union County College;* Ruth Brinkman, *St. Louis Community College, Florissant Valley;* Eileen Donahue Brittain, *City College of Harry S Truman;* Urie Bronfenbrenner, *Cornell University;* Phyllis Bronstein, *University of Vermont;* Dan W. Brunworth, *Kishwaukee College;* Carole Burke-Braxton, *Austin Community College;* Jo Ann Burnside, *Richard J. Daley College;* Victoria Candelora, *Brevard Community College;* Alison S. Carson, *Hofstra University;* Kelly Champion, *Northern Illinois University;* Rosalind Charlesworth, *Weber State University;* Martha Cipullo, *Bunker Hill Community College;* Nancy Coghill, *University of Southwest Louisiana;* Malinda Jo Colwell, *Texas Tech University;* Jennifer Cousins, *University of Houston;* Dixie R. Crase, *Memphis State University;* Kathleen Crowley-Long, *The College of Saint Rose;* Florence Denmark, *Pace University;* Sheridan DeWolf, *Grossmont Community College;* Swen H. Digranes, *Northeastern State University;* Ruth Doyle, *Casper College;* Laura Duvall, *Heartland Community College;* Celina V. Echols, *Southeastern Louisiana State University;* Beverly Edmondson, *Buena Vista University;* Timothy P. Eicher, *Dixie Community College;* Sarah Erikson, *University of New Mexico;* Jennifer Fager, *Western Michigan University;* Karen Falcone, *San Joaquin Delta College;* JoAnn Farver, *Oklahoma State University;* Greta Fein, *University of Maryland;* Tiffany Field, *University of Miami (FL);* Johanna Filp, *Sonoma State University;* Kate Fogarty, *University of Florida-Gainesville;* Cheryl Fortner-Wood, *Winthrop College;* Dale Fryxell, *Chaminade University;* Janet Fuller, *Mansfield University;* Thomas Gerry, *Columbia Greene Community College;* Sam Givhan, *Minnesota State University;* Art Gonchar, *University of La Verne;* Sandra Graham, *University of California-Los Angeles;* Susan Hale, *Holyoke Community College;* Barbara Springer Hammons, *Palomar College;* Cory Anne Hansen, *Arizona State University;* Barbara H. Harkness, *San Bernardino Valley College;* Algea Harrison, *Oakland University;* Archana Hegde, *East Carolina University;* Susan Heidrich, *University of Wisconsin;* Ashleigh Hillier, *Ohio University;* Alice S. Hoenig, *Syracuse University;* Sally Hoppstetter, *Palo Alto College;* Robert J. Ivy, *George Mason University;* Diane Carlson Jones, *Texas A&M University;* Ellen Junn, *Indiana University;* Marcia Karwas, *California State University-Monterey;* Melvyn B. King, *State College of New York at Cortland;* Kathleen Kleissler, *Kutztown University;* Dene G. Klinzing, *University of Delaware;* Claire B. Kopp, *University of California-Los Angeles;* Cally Beth Kostakis, *Rockland Community College;* Tara L. Kuther, *Western Connecticut State University;* Linda Lavine, *State University of New York-Cortland;* Sara Lawrence, *California State University-Northridge;* Hsin-Hui Lin, *University of Houston-Victoria;* Gloria Lopez, *Sacramento City College;* James E. Marcia, *Simon Fraser University;* Deborah N. Margolis, *Boston College;* Julie Ann McIntyre, *Russell Sage College;* Mary Ann McLaughlin, *Clarion University;* Chloe Merrill, *Weber State College;* Karla Miley, *Black Hawk College;* Jody Miller, *Los Angeles Pierce College;* Carrie L. Mori, *Boise State University;* Joyce Munsch, *California State University-Northridge;* Barbara J. Myers, *Virginia Commonwealth University;* Jeffrey Nagelbush, *Ferris State University;* Sonia Nieves, *Broward*

Community College; **Caroline Olko,** *Nassau Community College;* **Sandy Osborne,** *Montana State University;* **William H. Overman,** *University of North Carolina-Wilmington;* **Michelle Paludi,** *Michelle Paludi & Affiliates;* **Susan Peet,** *Bowling Green State University;* **Pete Peterson,** *Johnson County Community College;* **Joe Price,** *San Diego State University;* **Charles L. Reid,** *Essex County College;* **Barbara Reynolds,** *College of the Sequoias;* **Cynthia Rickert,** *Dominican College;* **Richard Riggle,** *Coe College;* **Naitcka Robinson,** *J. Sargeant Community College;* **Lynne Rompelman,** *Concordia University-Wisconsin;* **James A. Rysberg,** *California State University-Chico;* **Marcia Rysztak,** *Lansing Community College;* **David Sadker,** *The American University, Washington, DC;* **Peter C. Scales,** *Search Institute;* **Pamela Schuetze-Pizarro,** *Buffalo State College;* **Pamela A. Schulze,** *University of Akron;* **Diane Scott-Jones,** *University of Illinois;* **Sawa Senzaki,** *University of Wisconsin-Green Bay;* **Clyde Shepherd,** *Keene State College;* **Carol S. Soule,** *Appalachian State University;* **Dorothy D. Sweeney,** *Bristol Community College;* **Anita Thomas,** *Northeastern Illinois University;* **Ross A. Thompson,** *University of Nebraska-Lincoln;* **Kourtney Vaillancourt,** *New Mexico State University;* **Naomi Wagner,** *San Jose State University;* **Richard L. Wagner,** *Mount Senario College;* **Patricia J. Wall,** *Northern Arizona University;* **Dorothy A. Wedge,** *Fairmont State College;* **Carla Graham Wells,** *Odessa College;* **Teion Wells,** *Florida State University;* **Becky G. West,** *Coahoma Community College;* **Alida Westman,** *Eastern Michigan University;* **Allan Wigfield,** *University of Maryland, College Park;* **Angela Williamson,** *Tarrant County College;* **Marilyn E. Willis,** *Indiana University of Pennsylvania;* **Mary E. Wilson,** *Northern Essex Community College;* **Susan D. Witt,** *University of Akron;* **Bonnie Wright,** *Gardner Webb University;* **Sarah Young,** *Longwood College;* **William H. Zachry,** *University of Tennessee-Martin*

Kids deserve the right to think that they can change the world.

—LOIS LOWRY
Author of Children's Literature

The Nature of Children's Development

Examining the shape of childhood allows us to understand it better. Every childhood is distinct, the first chapter of a new biography in the world. This release is about children's development, its universal features, its individual variations, its nature during the twenty-first century. *Children* is about the rhythm and meaning of children's lives, about turning mystery into understanding, and about weaving together a portrait of who each of us was, is, and will be. In Section 1 you will read "Introduction."

chapter 1

INTRODUCTION

chapter **outline**

① Why Is Caring for Children Important?

Learning Goal 1 Explain why it is important to study children's development, and identify five areas in which children's lives need to be improved.

The Importance of Studying Children's Development
Improving the Lives of Children

② What Characterizes Development?

Learning Goal 2 Discuss processes, periods, cohort effects, and issues in development.

Biological, Cognitive, and Socioemotional Processes
Periods of Development
Cohort Effects
Issues in Development

③ How Is Child Development a Science?

Learning Goal 3 Summarize why research is important in child development, the main theories of child development, and research methods, designs, and challenges.

The Importance of Research
Theories of Child Development
Research Methods for Collecting Data
Research Designs
Research Challenges

Hero Images/Corbis

Ted Kaczynski sprinted through high school, not bothering with his junior year and making only passing efforts at social contact. Off to Harvard at age 16, Kaczynski was a loner during his college years. One of his roommates at Harvard said that he avoided people by quickly shuffling by them and slamming the door behind him. After obtaining his Ph.D. in mathematics at the University of Michigan, Kaczynski became a professor at the University of California at Berkeley. His colleagues there remember him as hiding from social interaction—no friends, no allies, no networking.

After several years at Berkeley, Kaczynski resigned and moved to a rural area of Montana, where he lived as a hermit in a crude shack for 25 years. Town residents described him as a bearded eccentric. Kaczynski traced his own difficulties to growing up as a genius in a kid's body and sticking out like a sore thumb in his surroundings as a child. In 1996, he was arrested and charged as the notorious Unabomber. Over the course of 17 years, Kaczynski had sent 16 mail bombs that left 23 people wounded or maimed and 3 people dead. In 1998, he pleaded guilty to the offenses and was sentenced to life in prison.

A decade before Kaczynski mailed his first bomb, Alice Walker spent her days battling racism in Mississippi. She had recently won her first writing fellowship, but rather than use the money to follow her dream of moving to Senegal, Africa, she put herself into the heart and heat of the civil rights movement. Walker had grown up knowing the brutal effects of poverty and racism. Born in 1944, she was the eighth child of Georgia sharecroppers who earned $300 a year. When Walker was 8, her brother accidentally shot her in the left eye with a BB gun. Because her parents had no car, it took them a week to get her to a hospital. By the time she received medical care, she was blind in that eye, and it had developed a disfiguring layer of scar tissue. Despite these challenges, Walker overcame pain and anger and went on to win a Pulitzer Prize for her book *The Color Purple*. She became not only a novelist but also an essayist, a poet, a short-story writer, and a social activist.

What leads one individual, so full of promise, to commit brutal acts of violence and another to turn poverty and trauma into a rich literary harvest? If you have ever wondered why people turn out the way they do, you have asked yourself the central question we will explore.

Ted Kaczynski, the convicted Unabomber, traced his difficulties to growing up as a genius in a kid's body and not fitting in when he was a child.
Seanna O'Sullivan

Ted Kaczynski, about age 14.
WBBM-TV/AFP/Getty Images

What might be some reasons Alice Walker was able to overcome trauma in her childhood and develop in impressive ways?
Monica Morgan/WireImage/Getty Images

Alice Walker, about age 8.
Courtesy of Alice Walker

preview

Why study children? Perhaps you are, or will be, a parent or teacher, and responsibility for children is, or will be, a part of your everyday life. The more you learn about children, the better you can guide them. Perhaps you hope to gain an understanding of your own history—as an infant, as a child, and as an adolescent. Perhaps you accidentally came across the course description and found it intriguing. Whatever your reasons, you will discover that the study of child development is provocative, intriguing, and informative. In this chapter, we explore why caring for children is so important, describe historical changes in the study of children's development, examine the nature of development, and outline how science helps us to understand it.

1 Why Is Caring for Children Important?

 LG1 Explain why it is important to study children's development, and identify five areas in which children's lives need to be improved.

The Importance of Studying Children's Development   Improving the Lives of Children

Caring for children is an important theme of this text. To think about why caring for children is such an important theme, we will explore why it is beneficial to study children's development and identify some areas in which children's lives need to be improved.

Just what do we mean when we speak of an individual's development? **Development** is the pattern of change that begins at conception and continues throughout the life span. Most development involves growth, although it also includes decline.

THE IMPORTANCE OF STUDYING CHILDREN'S DEVELOPMENT

How might you benefit from examining children's development? Perhaps you are, or will be, a parent or teacher and you want to learn about children so that you can become a better parent or an educator. Perhaps you hope to gain some insight about how your childhood experiences have shaped the person you are today. Or perhaps you think that the study of children's development might raise some provocative issues. Whatever your reasons for reading this book, you will discover that the study of children's development is fascinating and filled with information about who we are and how we came to be this way.

As we indicated earlier, most human development involves growth, but it also includes decline. For example, think about how your ability to speak and write your native language has grown since you were a young child. But your ability to achieve a high level of competence in learning to speak a new language has probably declined with age. In this book, we examine children's development from conception through adolescence. You will see yourself as an infant, as a child, and as an adolescent—and begin to think about how those years influenced you.

IMPROVING THE LIVES OF CHILDREN

If you were to read the headlines in any newsfeed or magazine today, you might see information like this: "Political Views May Be Written in the Genes," "Mother Accused of Tossing Children into Bay," "Gender Gap Widens," and "FDA Warns About ADHD Drug." Researchers are examining these and many other topics of contemporary concern. The roles that health and well-being, parenting, education, and sociocultural contexts play in children's development, as well as how social policy is related to these issues, are a special focus of this release.

Health and Well-Being   Does a pregnant woman endanger her fetus if she drinks a few beers a week? How does a poor diet affect a child's behaviors and learning skills? Are children less physically active today than in the past? What roles do parents and peers play in whether adolescents abuse drugs? Throughout this release we discuss many questions like these

development The pattern of movement or change that begins at conception and continues through the human life span.

Gustavo Medrano, Clinical Psychologist

Gustavo Medrano specializes in helping children, adolescents, and adults improve their lives when they are struggling with depression, anxiety, emotion regulation, chronic health conditions, and life transitions. He works individually with clients and also provides therapy for couples and families. As a native Spanish speaker, he provides bicultural and bilingual therapy for clients.

Dr. Medrano is a faculty member in the Department of Psychiatry at the University of Illinois–Chicago. He obtained his undergraduate degree in psychology at Northwestern and then became a high school teacher through Teach for America, a program where participants spend at least two years teaching in a high-poverty area. He received his master's and doctoral degrees in clinical psychology at the University of Wisconsin–Milwaukee. As a faculty member, in addition to doing clinical therapy with clients, he has conducted research focusing on how family experiences, especially parenting, influence children's and adolescents' ability to cope with chronic pain and other challenges.

Gustavo Medrano is a clinical psychologist who provides therapy for children, adolescents, and adults. His bilingual background and skills help him to work effectively with Latino clients.
Avis Mandel Pictures

regarding physical and psychological health and well-being. Investigating these questions, and exploring possible answers, is an important goal for just about everyone.

Health professionals today recognize the influence of lifestyles and psychological states on health and well-being (Schell & Rousham, 2022). In every chapter of this release, issues of health and well-being are integrated into our discussion.

Clinical psychologists are among the health professionals who help people improve their well-being. In this chapter's *Connecting with Careers* profile, you can read about clinical psychologist Gustavo Medrano, who helps adolescents with problems. The Careers Appendix for this text describes the education and training required to become a clinical psychologist and to pursue other careers in child development.

Parenting   Are young children harmed if both parents work outside the home? Does parental divorce damage children's mental health? Do the gender and sexual orientation of parents affect their children's development? The answers to potentially controversial questions like these reflect pressures on the contemporary family (Recksiedler, Bernhardt, & Heintz-Martin, 2023). We'll examine these questions and others in order to understand factors that influence parents' lives and support or detract from their effectiveness in raising their children. Another major emphasis in this release involves the ways in which parents and other adults make a positive difference in children's lives.

You might become a parent someday or might already be one. You should take seriously the importance of rearing your children, because they are the future of our society. Effective parenting takes considerable time and effort. If you plan to become a parent, commit yourself to providing your children with a warm, supportive, safe, and stimulating environment that will make them feel secure and allow them to reach their full potential as human beings.

Understanding the nature of children's development can help you become a better parent (Jeong & others, 2021). Many parents learn parenting practices from their parents. Unfortunately, when parenting practices and child-care strategies are passed from one generation to the next, both desirable and undesirable ones are usually perpetuated. This release and your instructor's lectures in this course can help you become more knowledgeable about children's development and decide which practices in your own upbringing you should continue with your children and which you should abandon.

Good parenting requires a lifetime commitment to providing your child with a supportive and safe environment.
kate_sept2004/Getty Images

What are some questions that need to be answered when thinking about improving schools?

lofoto/iStockphoto/Getty Images

How Would You...?

If you were a **psychologist,** how would you explain the importance of examining sociocultural factors in developmental research?

Education   There is widespread agreement that society needs to continuously improve education for all children (Schiariti, Simeonsson, & Hall, 2021). A number of questions are involved in improving schools. For example, how successful are schools in teaching children to read, write, and calculate? Should there be more accountability in schools, with effectiveness of student learning and teaching assessed by formal tests? Should teachers have higher expectations for students? Should schooling involve less memorization and more attention to the development of children's ability to process information efficiently? In this release, we examine such questions about the state of education (primarily in the United States) and consider recent research on solutions to educational challenges.

Sociocultural Contexts and Diversity   Health and well-being, parenting, and education—like development itself—are all shaped by their sociocultural context (McEwen, 2021). The term **context** refers to the settings in which development occurs. These settings are influenced by historical, economic, social, and cultural factors (Khaleque, 2021). Four contexts to which we pay special attention in this text are culture, ethnicity, socioeconomic status, and gender.

Culture encompasses the behavior patterns, beliefs, and all other products of a specific group of people that are passed on from generation to generation. Culture results from the interaction of people over many years (Kulich & others, 2021). A cultural group can be as large as the United States or as small as a single rural Appalachian town. Whatever its size, the group's culture influences the behavior of its members. **Cross-cultural studies** compare aspects of two or more cultures. The comparison measures the degree to which development is similar, or universal, across cultures, or is instead culture-specific (Khaleque, 2021; Keith, 2019).

Ethnicity (the word *ethnic* comes from the Greek word for "nation") is rooted in cultural heritage, nationality, race, religion, and language. Black Americans, Latino Americans, Asian Americans, Native Americans, European Americans, and Arab Americans are a few examples of ethnic groups. Diversity also exists within each ethnic group (Gollnick & Chinn, 2021). Additionally, there is continual discussion about the terms used to identify various cultural, racial, and ethnic groups. See the *Connecting with Diversity* feature about the use of terminology in this release.

Relatively high rates of minority immigration have contributed to the growth in the proportion of ethnic minority groups in the U.S. population (Frey, 2019). The growing proportion of ethnic minorities in the U.S. population is expected to continue throughout the rest of the twenty-first century. Asian Americans are expected to be the fastest-growing ethnic group of adolescents, with a growth rate of almost 600 percent between 2000 and 2100. Latino adolescents are projected to increase almost 400 percent by 2100. By 2100, Latino adolescents are expected to outnumber non–Latino White adolescents. In contrast, the percentage of Black American children is anticipated to increase only slightly over the rest of this century.

Within-group variation and differences in people contradict stereotypes about ethnic groups. A special concern is the discrimination and prejudice experienced by ethnic minority children and youth (Clauss-Ehlers, Roysircar, & Hunter, 2021). Recent research by Adriana Umaña-Taylor and her colleagues indicates that pride in one's ethnic identity group and

context The settings, influenced by historical, economic, social, and cultural factors, in which development occurs.

culture The behavior patterns, beliefs, and all other products of a group that are passed on from generation to generation.

cross-cultural studies Comparisons of one culture with one or more other cultures. These comparisons provide information about the degree to which children's development is similar, or universal, across cultures, and the degree to which it is culture-specific.

ethnicity A characteristic based on cultural heritage, nationality, race, religion, and language.

(a)   **(b)**

(*a*) These two Korean-born children on the day they became U.S. citizens represent the dramatic increase in the percentage of ethnic minority children in the United States. (*b*) Inderjeet Poolust, 5, from India celebrates being one of 27 schoolchildren who recently became U.S. citizens at an induction ceremony in Queens, New York.

(*a*) Zuma Press Inc./Alamy Stock Photo; (*b*) Debbie Egan-Chin/NY Daily News Archive/Getty Images

Terminology for Describing Ethnic and Racial Groups

Over historical time, the preferred terms for referring to ethnic and racial groups have changed. Research studies, professional organizations, the media, and individuals themselves have modified the way they refer to ethnic and racial groups. For example, in 2020, members of the Latino Caucus of the Society for Research on Child Development, a leading professional organization, voted to change the name to the Latinx Caucus, in part because Latinx was considered more inclusive of LGBTQ, gender diverse, and nonbinary members. In 2021, around the same time, the League of United Latin American Citizens, a civil rights organization, dropped the term Latinx from their official communication. The organization's president, Domingo García, explained that the term was "very unliked" by most Latinos and was perceived as being used primarily in academic circles. Results of a

Pew Research Center poll reflect this position. The poll found that only 23 percent of adults who identify themselves as Latino or Hispanic had even heard of the term Latinx and of those who had heard the term, only 3 percent used it themselves (Noe-Bustamante, Mora, & Lopez, 2020).

Preferred terminology for identifying Black Americans has changed over time, too. The 2020 U.S. Census Bureau question includes the option "Black or African American." The shift in terminology from African American to Black American is intended to be more inclusive because many people, such as immigrants from the Caribbean, identify themselves as Black but not as African American. In this release, we generally use the terms Latino or Latina, non–Latino White, and Black American to refer to these groups, which corresponds with current terminology for these demographic groups. However, we recognize that these and other terms will not represent every individual's or group's point of view.

exploration of ethnic identity development have positive outcomes (Sladek, Umaña-Taylor, & others, 2020; Umaña-Taylor & Hill, 2020).

Socioeconomic status (SES) refers to a person's position within society based on occupational, educational, and economic characteristics. Socioeconomic status reflects certain inequalities. Generally, members of a society have (1) occupations that vary in prestige, with some individuals having more access than others to higher-status occupations; (2) different levels of educational attainment, with some individuals having more access than others to advanced education; (3) different economic resources; and (4) different levels of power to influence a community's institutions. Differences in the ability to control resources and to participate in society's rewards produce unequal opportunities (Mayo & Wadsworth, 2020). For example, a recent research review of 3- to 19-year-old U.S. children and adolescents concluded that growing up in low-SES settings is associated with higher levels of psychopathology (Peverill & others, 2021).

Gender   Gender is another key dimension of children's development. **Gender** refers to the characteristics of people as girls/women and boys/men. In addition, gender development and identity encompass more genders than this, such as transgender and nonbinary gender (Hammack & others, 2022). Few aspects of our development are more central to our identity and social relationships than gender (Erickson-Schroth & Davis, 2021). How you view yourself, your relationships with other people, your life, and your goals are shaped to a great extent by your gender and how your culture defines gender roles (Gutierrez & others, 2020).

Each of these dimensions of the sociocultural context—culture, ethnicity, SES, and gender—helps to mold how an individual develops through life, as discussions in later chapters demonstrate. We explore, for example, questions such as the following:

- Do infants around the world form attachments with their parents in the same way, or do these attachments differ from one culture to another?
- Does poverty influence the likelihood that young children will be provided with fewer educational opportunities than children growing up in more affluent families?
- Is there a parenting style that is universally effective, or does the effectiveness of different types of parenting depend on the ethnic group or culture?
- If adolescents from minority groups identify with their ethnic culture, is that likely to help or hinder their socioemotional development?

> **developmental connection**
>
> **Socioeconomic Status**
>
> Growing up in poverty is linked to negative outcomes for children's language skill. Connect to "Cognitive Development in Infancy."

socioeconomic status (SES) An individual's position within society based on occupational, educational, and economic characteristics.

gender The characteristics of people as girls/women and boys/men.

Gender, Families, and Children's Development

Around the world, the experiences of male and female children and adolescents continue to be quite different (Ozdenerol, 2021). Except in a few areas, such as Japan, the Philippines, and Western countries, males have far greater access to educational opportunities than females. In many countries, adolescent girls have less freedom to pursue a variety of careers and engage in various leisure acts than boys. Gender differences in sexual expression are widespread, especially in India, Southeast Asia, Latin America, and Arab countries—where there are far more restrictions on the sexual activity of adolescent girls than on boys. In certain areas around the world, these gender differences do appear to be narrowing over time. In some countries, educational and career opportunities for women are expanding, and in some parts of the world control over adolescent girls' romantic and sexual relationships is weakening. However, in many countries girls and women still experience considerable discrimination, and much work is needed to bridge the gap between the rights of girls and boys (Haack, 2022). Many girls continue to be denied access to education, and women continue to be denied access to jobs. For example, after the Taliban took control of Afghanistan in 2021, girls were no longer allowed access to a secondary education, and women were banned from working in most sectors (Popalzai & Kottasová, 2022). These inequalities sometimes lead to protests, such as the uprising in Iran following the death of Mahsa Amini in 2022, who died while in custody after being arrested by the country's morality police for a clothing violation. Oftentimes, however, these protests have been met with strict resistance by authoritarian regimes.

Doly Akter is from Dhaka, Bangladesh, a city with a metropolitan area of nearly 22 million people that is challenged with providing access to basic necessities to its poorest residents. Just over half of the girls in Bangladesh get married before they are 18 (UNICEF, 2020). As a teenager, Doly began her work striving for gender equity and safety for girls and women. She organized a club supported by UNICEF in which girls go door-to-door to monitor the hygiene habits of households in their neighborhood. This has led to improved hygiene and health in the families. Also, her group has managed to stop child marriages by meeting with parents and convincing them that it is not in their daughter's best interests. When talking with parents, they emphasize the importance of staying in school and how this will improve their daughter's future. Doly has continued her social justice work for girls and women in Dhaka, most recently focusing on protecting them from sexual harassment and assault at work (The Guardian, 2019).
Naser Siddique/UNICEF Bangladesh

Ann Masten with a homeless family who is participating in her research on resilience. She and her colleagues have found that good parenting skills and good cognitive skills (especially attention and self-control) improve the likelihood that children in challenging circumstances will do better when they enter elementary school.
©Dawn Villella Photography

We discuss sociocultural contexts and diversity in each chapter. In addition, a *Connecting with Diversity* interlude appears in every chapter. See the first *Connecting with Diversity* interlude, which focuses on gender, families, and children's development around the world.

Resilience, Social Policy, and Children's Development

Some children develop confidence in their abilities despite negative stereotypes about their gender or their ethnic group. And some children triumph over poverty or other adversities. They show resilience. Think back to the chapter-opening story about Alice Walker. In spite of racism, poverty, her low socioeconomic status, and a disfiguring eye injury, she went on to become a successful author and champion for equality.

Are there certain characteristics that cause children like Alice Walker to be resilient? Are there other characteristics that influence children to behave like Ted Kaczynski, who despite his intelligence and education became a killer? After analyzing research on this topic, Ann Masten (2017; Masten & others, 2021) concludes that a number of individual factors, such as good intellectual functioning, influence resiliency. In addition, as Figure 1 shows, resources within and outside of resilient children's families tend to show certain features. For example, resilient children are likely to have a close relationship to a caring parent figure and bonds with caring adults outside the family.

Should governments take action to improve the contexts of children's development and aid their resilience? **Social policy** is a government's course of action designed to promote the welfare of its citizens. The shape and scope of social policy related to children are tied to the political and economic system. The values held by citizens and elected officials, the nation's economic strengths and weaknesses, and partisan politics all influence the policy agenda.

When concern about broad social issues is widespread, comprehensive social policies often result. Child labor laws were established in the early twentieth century not only to protect children but also to provide jobs for adults; federal child-care funding during World War II was justified by the need for women laborers in factories; and Head Start and other War on Poverty programs in the 1960s were implemented to decrease intergenerational poverty (Stern & Axinn, 2017).

Out of concern that policy makers are doing too little to protect the well-being of children as well as other vulnerable age groups, researchers increasingly are undertaking studies that they hope will lead to wise and effective decision making about social policy around the world (Vescio & Kosakowska-Berezecka, 2021). In 2019, 14.4 percent of U.S. children under 18 years of age were living in families with incomes below the poverty line, a decrease from 2018 (16.2 percent) as well as a decrease from a peak of 23 percent in 1993 (Semega & others, 2020). In 2019, Black American (26.4 percent, down from 30.1 percent in 2018) and Latino (20.9 percent, down from 23.7 percent in 2018) families with children had especially high rates of poverty (Semega & others, 2020). In 2019, 7.3 percent of Asian American children (down from 11.3 percent in 2018) and 8.3 percent of non–Latino White U.S. children (down from 8.9 percent) were living below the poverty line. The COVID-19 pandemic further exacerbated economic disparities between ethnic groups (Perry, Aronson, & Pescosolido, 2021).

As indicated in Figure 2, one classic study found that a higher percentage of U.S. children in poor families than in middle-income families were exposed to family turmoil, separation from a parent, violence, crowding, excessive noise, and poor housing (Evans & English, 2002). Another more recent study also revealed that the years children spend living in poverty, when household chaos and family conflict are also present, are linked with hormonal and other physiological measures (Schmidt & others, 2021). The U.S. figure of more than 20 percent of children living in relative poverty is much higher than those of other industrialized nations (OECD, 2021). The average is 13 percent among the 36 members of the Organization for Economic Cooperation and Development, ranging from 3 percent in Finland to 33 percent in China (OECD, 2021).

In the United States, the national government, state governments, and city governments all play a role in influencing the well-being of children (Doob, 2021; Duncan, 2021). When families fail or seriously endanger a child's well-being, governments often step in to help. Nonprofit organizations like the Children's Defense Fund also play a key role in ensuring that all children receive the care and resources they need to thrive. At the national and state levels, policy makers have debated for decades whether helping low-income parents ends up helping their children as well. Researchers are providing some answers by examining the effects of specific policies (Duncan, Magnuson, & Votruba-Drzal, 2017; Gottlieb & DeLoache, 2017).

For example, the Minnesota Family Investment Program (MFIP) was designed in the 1990s primarily to influence the behavior of adults—specifically, to move adults off the welfare rolls and into paid employment. A key element of the program was its guarantee that adults participating in the program would receive more income if they worked than if they did not. When the adults' income rose, how did that affect their children? An early study

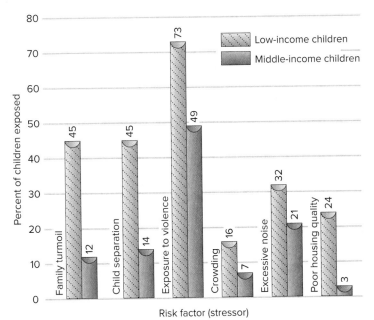

Source	Characteristic
Individual	Good intellectual functioning Appealing, sociable, easygoing disposition Self-confidence, high self-esteem Talents Faith
Family	Close relationship to caring parent figure Authoritative parenting: warmth, structure, high expectations Socioeconomic advantages Connections to extended supportive family networks
Extrafamilial Context	Bonds to caring adults outside the family Connections to positive organizations Attending effective schools

FIGURE 1

CHARACTERISTICS OF RESILIENT CHILDREN AND THEIR CONTEXTS

social policy A government's course of action designed to promote the welfare of its citizens.

FIGURE 2

EXPOSURE TO SIX STRESSORS AMONG LOW- AND MIDDLE-INCOME CHILDREN. One study analyzed the exposure to six stressors among low-income children and middle-income children (Evans & English, 2002). Low-income children were much more likely to face each of these stressors. *Source:* Evans, G.W., & English, K. (2002). The environment of poverty. *Child Development,* 73, 1238–1248.

This mother and her daughter are participating in the Ascend program. *What characterizes the Ascend program?*

Tetra Images, LLC/Alamy Stock Photo

of the effects of MFIP found that increases in the incomes of working poor parents were linked with benefits for their children (Gennetian & Miller, 2002). The children's achievement in school improved, and their behavior problems decreased.

The MFIP is one of many such interventions and studies. These interventions have shown that raising the incomes of families living in poverty sometimes does not affect children's development, but often it does. Benefits include reduced exposure to developmental risks such as abuse and maternal depression, along with improvements in supportive factors such as safety, cognitive stimulation, and sensitive parenting (Cooper & Stewart, 2017; Webb & others, 2020).

There is ongoing interest in developing two-generation educational interventions to improve the academic success of children living in poverty. For example, a recent large-scale effort to help children escape from poverty is the Ascend two-generation educational intervention being conducted by the Aspen Institute (2022). The intervention emphasizes education (increasing post-secondary education for mothers and improving the quality of their children's early childhood education), economic support (housing, transportation, financial education, health insurance, and food assistance), and social capital (peer support including friends and neighbors; participation in community and faith-based organizations; school and work contacts).

Developmental psychologists and other researchers have examined the effects of many government policies. They are seeking ways to help families living in poverty improve their well-being, and they have offered many suggestions for improving government policies (Crosby, 2021; Duncan, 2021).

Review Connect Reflect

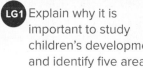 **LG1** Explain why it is important to study children's development, and identify five areas in which children's lives need to be improved.

Review

- Why is it important to study children's development?
- What are five aspects of children's development that need to be improved?

Connect

- How is the concept of resilience related to the story about Ted Kaczynski and Alice Walker?

Reflect *Your Own Personal Journey of Life*

- Imagine what your development as a child would have been like if you had grown up in a culture that offered more or fewer choices. How might your development have been different if your family had been significantly richer or poorer than it was?

2 What Characterizes Development? **LG2** Discuss processes, periods, cohort effects, and issues in development.

| Biological, Cognitive, and Socioemotional Processes | Periods of Development | Cohort Effects | Issues in Development |

Each of us develops in certain ways like all other individuals, like some other individuals, and like no other individuals. Most of the time, our attention is directed to a person's uniqueness, but psychologists who study development are drawn to our shared characteristics as well as what makes us unique. As humans, we all have traveled some common paths. Each of us walked at about the age of 1, engaged in fantasy play as a young child, and became more independent as a youth. What shapes this common path of human development, and what are its milestones? Two concepts help provide a framework for describing and understanding an individual's development: developmental processes (*biological, cognitive, and socioemotional*), and *periods of development.*

BIOLOGICAL, COGNITIVE, AND SOCIOEMOTIONAL PROCESSES

The pattern of human development is created by the interplay of different kinds of processes—biological, cognitive, and socioemotional. **Biological processes** produce changes in an individual's body. Genes inherited from parents, the development of the brain, height and weight gains, motor skills, and the hormonal changes of puberty all reflect the role of biological processes in development.

Cognitive processes lead to changes in an individual's thoughts, intelligence, and language. The tasks of watching a mobile swinging above a crib, putting together a two-word sentence, memorizing a poem, solving a math problem, and imagining what it would be like to be a movie star all involve cognitive processes.

Socioemotional processes produce changes in an individual's relationships with other people, changes in emotions, and changes in personality. An infant's smile in response to a mother's touch, a toddler's attack on a playmate, a third-grader's development of assertiveness, and an adolescent's joy at a party all reflect socioemotional development.

Biological, cognitive, and socioemotional processes are deeply intertwined (Boyce & others, 2021). Consider a baby smiling in response to a parent's touch. This response depends on biological processes (the physical nature of touch and responsiveness to it), cognitive processes (the ability to understand intentional acts), and socioemotional processes (smiling often reflects positive emotions, and helps connect us in positive ways with other human beings). The connection across biological, cognitive, and socioemotional processes is most obvious in two rapidly emerging fields:

- *Developmental cognitive neuroscience,* which explores links between development, cognitive processes, and the brain (Bell & Broomell, 2021)
- *Developmental social neuroscience,* which examines connections between socioemotional processes, development, and the brain (Kirmayer & others, 2020)

Biological, cognitive, and socioemotional processes interact and can influence each other. For example, biological processes can influence cognitive processes and vice versa. Thus, although usually we will explore the different processes of development (biological, cognitive, and socioemotional) separately, keep in mind that our discussion is about the development of an integrated human child with a mind and body that are interdependent (see Figure 3). In many places throughout this release we will call attention to these connections.

PERIODS OF DEVELOPMENT

For the purposes of organization and understanding, a child's growth is commonly described in terms of developmental periods, which are given approximate age ranges. The most widely used classification of developmental periods includes the prenatal period, infancy, early childhood, middle and late childhood, and adolescence.

The **prenatal period** is the time from conception to birth, roughly a nine-month period. During this stage of incredibly rapid development, a single cell grows into a fetus and then a baby with a brain and a wide range of capabilities.

Infancy is the developmental period that extends from birth to about 18 to 24 months of age. Infancy is a time of extreme dependence on adults. Many psychological activities are just beginning—the ability to speak, to coordinate sensations and physical actions, to think with symbols, and to imitate and learn from others.

Early childhood is the developmental period that extends from the end of infancy to about 5 or 6 years of age; sometimes this period is called the preschool years. During this time, young children learn to become more self-sufficient; they develop school readiness skills (following instructions, identifying letters), and they spend many hours in play and with peers. First grade typically marks the end of this period.

Middle and late childhood is the developmental period from about 6 to 11 years of age; sometimes this period is referred to as the elementary school years. Children master the fundamental skills of reading, writing, and arithmetic, and they are formally exposed to the larger world and its cultures. Achievement becomes a more central theme of the child's world, and self-control increases.

Adolescence is the developmental period of transition from childhood to early adulthood, beginning at approximately 10 to 12 years of age and ending at 18 to 22 years of age. Adolescence begins with rapid physical changes—dramatic gains in height and weight; changes in

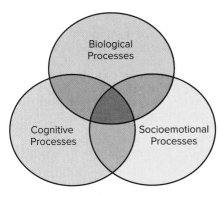

FIGURE 3

CHANGES IN DEVELOPMENT ARE THE RESULT OF BIOLOGICAL, COGNITIVE, AND SOCIOEMOTIONAL PROCESSES. The processes interact as individuals develop.

biological processes Changes in an individual's body.

cognitive processes Changes in an individual's thought, intelligence, and language.

socioemotional processes Changes in an individual's relationships with other people, changes in emotions, and changes in personality.

prenatal period The time from conception to birth.

infancy The developmental period that extends from birth to 18 to 24 months of age.

early childhood The developmental period that extends from the end of infancy to about 5 to 6 years of age; sometimes called the preschool years.

middle and late childhood The developmental period that extends from about 6 to 11 years of age; sometimes called the elementary school years.

adolescence The developmental period of transition from childhood to early adulthood, entered at approximately 10 to 12 years of age and ending at 18 to 22 years of age.

FIGURE **4**

PROCESSES AND PERIODS OF DEVELOPMENT. Development moves through the prenatal, infancy, early childhood, middle and late childhood, and adolescence periods. These periods of development are the result of biological, cognitive, and socioemotional processes.

(left to right): Steve Allen/Brand X Pictures/Getty Images; Dr. John Santrock; Laurence Mouton/PhotoAlto/Getty Images; Ken Karp/McGraw Hill; SW Productions/Brand X Pictures/Getty Images

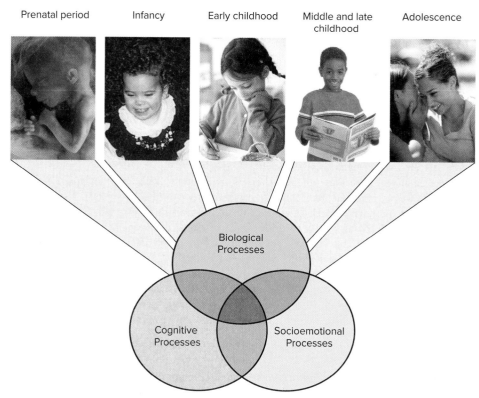

Prenatal period   Infancy   Early childhood   Middle and late childhood   Adolescence

Biological Processes

Cognitive Processes

Socioemotional Processes

Processes of Development

body shape; and the development of secondary sexual characteristics such as enlargement of the breasts and widening of the hips in females and the development of facial hair in males. The pursuit of independence and an identity are prominent features of this period of development, although this varies widely between cultures. More and more time is spent outside the family. Thought becomes more abstract, idealistic, and logical.

Today, developmental scientists do not suggest that change ends with adolescence (Bornstein, 2018; Somerville & others, 2018). Instead, they describe development as a lifelong process. However, the purpose of this text is to describe the changes in development that take place from conception through adolescence. All of these periods of development are produced by the interplay of biological, cognitive, and socioemotional processes (see Figure 4).

COHORT EFFECTS

In addition to considering developmental periods that emerge and change with age, we also must consider the points in time and history when groups of people were born and grew up. A *cohort* is a group of people who are born at a similar point in history and share similar experiences such as growing up in the same city at around the same time. These shared experiences can produce differences in development between cohorts (Vaz & others, 2021). For example, children and their parents who grew up during the Great Depression and World War II are likely to differ from their counterparts during the economically booming 1990s in their educational opportunities and economic status, how they were raised, their attitudes and experiences related to gender, and their exposure to technology. In research on development, **cohort effects** are due to a person's time of birth, era, or generation but not to actual age.

In recent decades, generations have been given labels by the popular culture. The most recent group to have "grown up" are called **Millennials,** the generation born roughly between 1980 and 1999, that is the first to come of age and enter emerging adulthood in the new millennium. Thus, many of today's parents are Millennials. Two characteristics of Millennials stand out: (1) their ethnic diversity and (2) their connection to technology (Dimock, 2019). As their ethnic diversity has increased in comparison with prior generations, many Millennials are more tolerant and open-minded than their counterparts in older cohorts (Frey, 2018).

cohort effects Effects due to a person's time of birth, era, or generation but not to actual age.

Millennials The generation born after 1980, which is the first generation to come of age and enter emerging adulthood in the new millennium; members of this generation are characterized by their ethnic diversity and their connection to technology.

Another major cohort change involving Millennials is the dramatic increase in their use of media and technology.

Anyone born in 1997 or later is part of a new generation. The name of this new generation has not yet been selected, but two potential names are Generation Z and Post-millennial. The oldest members of this new generation turned 23 in 2020, while the oldest Millennials turned 39 in 2020. What characterizes this new Z/Post-millennial generation? They are even more technologically sophisticated and ethnically diverse than Millennials. These young people have technological devices that are always available and always on, they are immersed in social media, and they tend to communicate with others online and through mobile devices far more than in person. Also, Generation Z/Post-millennials are the best-educated generation ever: They are more likely to go to college and to have a college-educated parent than Millennials are (Fry & Parker, 2018).

Sanda Stanca/123RF

ISSUES IN DEVELOPMENT

Many questions about children's development remain unanswered. For example, what exactly drives the biological, cognitive, and socioemotional processes of development, and how do experiences during infancy influence middle childhood or adolescence? Despite all of the knowledge that researchers have acquired, debate continues about the relative importance of factors that influence the developmental processes and about how the periods of development are related. The most important issues in the study of children's development include nature and nurture, continuity and discontinuity, and early and later experience.

nature-nurture issue The issue regarding whether development is primarily influenced by nature or nurture. Both "nature" (biological inheritance) and "nurture" (environmental experiences) are important to development.

Nature and Nurture   The **nature-nurture issue** involves an old debate about whether development is primarily influenced by nature or by nurture. Nature refers to an organism's biological inheritance, nurture to its environmental experiences. Almost no one today argues that development can be explained by nature alone or by nurture alone. However, it is important to understand the history of the old nature-nurture positions. Some ("nature" proponents) claim that the more important influence on development is biological inheritance, and others ("nurture" proponents) claim that environmental experiences are the more important influence.

According to the nature proponents, just as a sunflower grows in an orderly way—unless it is defeated by an unfriendly environment—so does a person. The range of environments can be vast, but evolutionary and genetic foundations produce commonalities in growth and development (Mason, Duncan, & Losos, 2021). We walk before we talk, speak one word before two words, grow rapidly in infancy and less so in early childhood, and experience a rush of sexual hormones in puberty. Proponents of the developmental influence of nature acknowledge that extreme environments—those that are psychologically barren or hostile—can depress development. However, they believe that basic growth tendencies are genetically programmed into humans (Hoefnagels, 2021).

By contrast, others have emphasized the influence of nurture, or environmental experiences, on development (Bembenutty, 2021; Kuo, 2021). Experiences run the gamut from the individual's biological environment (nutrition, medical care, drugs, and physical accidents) to the social environment (family, peers, schools, community, media, and culture). For example, a child's diet can affect how tall the child grows and even how effectively the child can think and solve problems. Despite genes, a child born and raised in an impoverished village in a low-income country and a child in the suburbs of a wealthy city are likely to have different skills, different ways of thinking about the world, and different ways of relating to people. Today, there are few proponents of only nature or only nurture as being important; we now understand that nature and nurture work together in explaining development.

There has been a dramatic increase in the number of studies that reflect the epigenetic view, which states that development reflects an ongoing, bidirectional interchange between genes and the environment. These studies involve specific DNA sequences (Franzago & others, 2020). The epigenetic mechanisms involve the actual molecular modification of the DNA strand as a result of environmental inputs in ways that alter gene functioning (Champagne, 2021).

Continuity and Discontinuity   Think about your own development for a moment. Did you become the person you are gradually, like the seedling that slowly, cumulatively grows into a giant oak? Or did you experience sudden, distinct changes, like the caterpillar that changes into a butterfly (see Figure 5)? For the most part, developmentalists who

Continuity

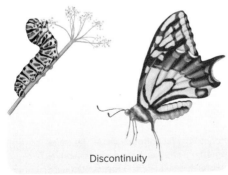

Discontinuity

FIGURE 5
CONTINUITY AND DISCONTINUITY IN DEVELOPMENT. *Is our development like that of a seedling gradually growing into a giant oak? Or is it more like that of a caterpillar suddenly becoming a butterfly?*

How Would You...?

If you were an **educator,** how would you apply your understanding of the developmental influences of nature and nurture to create appropriate classroom strategies for students who display learning or behavioral problems?

emphasize nurture usually describe development as a gradual, continuous process, like the seedling's growth into an oak. Those who emphasize nature often describe development as a series of distinct stages, like the change from caterpillar to butterfly. The **continuity-discontinuity issue** focuses on the extent to which development involves gradual, cumulative change (continuity) or distinct stages (discontinuity).

Consider continuity first. As the oak grows from seedling to giant oak, it becomes more oak—its development is continuous. Similarly, a child's first word, though seemingly an abrupt, discontinuous event, is actually the result of weeks and months of growth and practice. Puberty, another seemingly abrupt, discontinuous occurrence, is actually a gradual process occurring over several years.

Viewed in terms of discontinuity, each person is described as passing through a sequence of distinct stages. As the caterpillar changes to a butterfly, it is not more caterpillar but an altogether different kind of organism—its development is discontinuous. Similarly, at some point a child moves from not being able to think abstractly about the world to being able to do so. This change is a "qualitative," discontinuous change in development, not a "quantitative," continuous change.

Early and Later Experience

The **early-later experience issue** focuses on the degree to which early experiences (especially in infancy) or later experiences are the key determinants of the child's development. That is, if infants experience harmful circumstances, can those experiences be overcome by later, positive ones? Or are the early experiences so critical—possibly because they are the infant's first, essential experiences—that their influence cannot be overridden by a later, better environment? To those who emphasize early experiences, life is an unbroken trail on which a psychological quality can be traced back to its origin. In contrast, to those who emphasize the impact of recent experiences, development is like a river, continually ebbing and flowing.

The early-later experience issue has a long history and continues to be hotly debated among developmentalists (Dagan & Sagi-Schwartz, 2021). Some argue that unless infants experience warm, nurturant caregiving in the first year or so of life, their development will be less optimal (Waters, Waters, & Waters, 2021). The later-experience advocates see children as malleable throughout development, with sensitive caregiving and positive close relationships playing important roles later in child development, adolescence, and adulthood, just as they do in infancy (Mikulincer & Shaver, 2021).

A number of experts on life-span development stress that too little attention has been given to the impact of later experiences on development. They accept that early experiences are important contributors to development but hold them to be no more important than later experiences (McCrae & others, 2021). Jerome Kagan (2013) points out that even children who show the qualities of an inhibited temperament, which is linked to heredity, have the capacity to change their behavior. In one classic study, almost one-third of a group of children who had an inhibited temperament at 2 years of age were not unusually shy or fearful when they were 4 years of age (Kagan & Snidman, 1991).

Evaluating the Developmental Issues

Most developmentalists recognize that it is unwise to take an extreme position on the issues of nature and nurture, continuity and discontinuity, and early and later experiences. Development is not all nature or all nurture; not all continuity or all discontinuity; and not all early or later experiences. Nature and nurture, continuity and discontinuity, and early and later experiences all play a part in development throughout the human life span. Along with this consensus, however, there is still spirited debate about how strongly development is influenced by each of these factors. Are there gender differences in certain skills because of inherited characteristics or because of society's expectations and because of how girls and boys are raised? Can enriched experiences during adolescence remove negative effects on development resulting from poverty, neglect, and poor schooling during childhood? The answers to these and many other related questions also have a bearing on social policy decisions about children and adolescents—and consequently on each of our lives.

What is the "early-later experience issue," and why is it important when thinking about child and adolescent development?

Jamie Grill/JGI/Blend Images/Getty Images

developmental **connection**

Biological Processes

Can specific genes be linked to specific environmental experiences in influencing the child's development? Connect to "Biological Beginnings."

continuity-discontinuity issue The issue regarding whether development involves gradual, cumulative change (continuity) or distinct stages (discontinuity).

early-later experience issue The issue of the degree to which early experiences (especially infancy) or later experiences are the key determinants of the child's development.

Review Connect Reflect

LG2 Discuss processes, periods, cohort effects, and issues in development.

Review

- What are biological, cognitive, and socioemotional processes?
- What are the main periods of development?
- What are cohort effects?
- What are three important issues in development?

Connect

- Based on what you read earlier in the chapter, what do you think Ted Kaczynski would say about the early-later experience issue?

Reflect *Your Own Personal Journey of Life*

- Can you identify an early experience that you believe contributed in important ways to your development? Can you identify a recent or current (later) experience that you think had (is having) a strong influence on your development?

3 How Is Child Development a Science?

 LG3 Summarize why research is important in child development, the main theories of child development, and research methods, designs, and challenges.

| The Importance of Research | Theories of Child Development | Research Methods for Collecting Data | Research Designs | Research Challenges |

This section introduces the theories and methods that are the foundation of the science of child development. We consider why research is important in understanding children's development and examine the main theories of children's development, as well as the main methods and research designs that researchers use. At the end of the section, we explore some of the ethical challenges researchers face and the biases they must guard against to protect the integrity of their results and respect the rights of the participants in their studies.

THE IMPORTANCE OF RESEARCH

Some individuals have difficulty thinking of child development as a science like physics, chemistry, and biology. Can a scientific discipline that studies how parents nurture children, how peers interact, what are the developmental changes in children's thinking, and whether unlimited screen time hour after hour is linked with being overweight be equated with disciplines that study the molecular structure of a compound and how gravity works? Is child development really a science? The answer is yes. Science is defined not by *what* it investigates, but by *how* it investigates. Whether you're studying photosynthesis, butterflies, Saturn's moons, or children's development, it is the way you study that makes the approach scientific or not.

Scientific research is objective, systematic, and testable. It reduces the likelihood that information will be based on personal beliefs, opinions, and feelings, and it places emphasis on being able to replicate studies and find the same results (Gundersen, 2021). Scientific research is based on the **scientific method**, an approach that can be used to discover accurate information. It includes four steps: conceptualize the problem, collect data, analyze the data to reach conclusions, and revise research conclusions and theory.

The first step, *conceptualizing a problem,* involves identifying the problem. At a general level, this may not seem like a difficult task. However, researchers must go beyond a general description of the problem by isolating, analyzing, narrowing, and focusing more specifically

scientific method An approach that can be used to obtain accurate information. It includes these steps: (1) conceptualize the problem, (2) collect data, (3) draw conclusions, and (4) revise research conclusions and theory.

A high school senior mentors a younger student as part of the Book Buddy mentoring program. *If a researcher wanted to study the effects of the mentoring program on children's academic achievement by following the scientific method, what steps would the researcher take in setting up the study?*

SDI Productions/E+/Getty Images

on what they want to study. For example, a team of researchers decides to study ways to improve the achievement of children from impoverished backgrounds. Perhaps they choose to examine whether mentoring that involves sustained support, guidance, and concrete assistance can improve the children's academic performance. At this point, even more narrowing and focusing takes place. For instance, what specific strategies should the mentors use? How often will they see the children? How long will the mentoring program last? What aspects of the children's achievement will be assessed?

As part of the first step in formulating a problem to study, researchers often *draw on theories and develop a hypothesis*. A **theory** is an interrelated, coherent set of ideas that helps to explain and to make predictions. For example, a theory on mentoring might attempt to explain and predict why sustained support, guidance, and concrete experience make a difference in the lives of children from impoverished backgrounds. The theory might focus on children's opportunities to model the behavior and strategies of mentors, or it might focus on the effects of individual attention, which might be missing in the children's lives. A **hypothesis** is a specific testable assumption or prediction. A hypothesis is often written as an if-then statement. In our example, a sample hypothesis might be: If children from impoverished backgrounds are given individual attention by mentors, the children will spend more time studying and earn higher grades. Testing a hypothesis can inform researchers whether or not a theory may be accurate.

The second step in the scientific method is to *collect information (data)*. In the study of mentoring, the researchers might decide to conduct the mentoring program for six months. Their data might consist of classroom observations, teachers' ratings, and achievement tests given to the mentored children before the mentoring began and at the end of six months of mentoring.

Once data have been collected, child development researchers use statistical procedures to understand the meaning of the data. Then they try to *draw conclusions*. In this third step, statistics help to determine whether or not the researchers' observations are due to chance.

After data have been collected and analyzed, researchers compare their findings with those of other researchers on the same topic. The final step in the scientific method is *revising research conclusions and theory.*

How Would You...?
If you were a **health-care professional,** how would you apply the scientific method to examine developmental concerns such as adolescent pregnancy?

THEORIES OF CHILD DEVELOPMENT

Having a wide range of theories to choose from makes understanding children's development a challenging undertaking. Just when you think one theory has the most helpful explanation of children's development, another theory crops up and makes you rethink your earlier conclusion. To keep from getting frustrated, remember that child development is a complex, multifaceted topic. No single theory has been able to account for all aspects of child development. Each theory contributes an important piece to the child development puzzle. Although the theories sometimes disagree, much of their information is complementary rather than contradictory. Together they let us see the total landscape of development in all its richness.

We briefly explore five major theoretical perspectives on development: psychoanalytic, cognitive, behavioral and social cognitive, ethological, and ecological. As you will see, these theoretical approaches examine in varying degrees the three major processes involved in children's development: biological, cognitive, and socioemotional.

theory An interrelated, coherent set of ideas that helps to explain and make predictions.

hypothesis A specific assumption or prediction that can be tested to determine its accuracy.

psychoanalytic theories Describe development as primarily unconscious and heavily colored by emotion. Behavior is merely a surface characteristic, and the symbolic workings of the mind have to be analyzed to understand behavior. Early experiences with parents are emphasized.

Psychoanalytic Theories **Psychoanalytic theories** describe development as primarily unconscious (beyond awareness) and heavily colored by emotion. Psychoanalytic theorists emphasize that behavior is merely a surface characteristic and that a true understanding of development requires analyzing the symbolic meanings of behavior and the deep inner workings of the mind. Psychoanalytic theorists also stress that early experiences with parents extensively shape development. These characteristics are highlighted in the psychoanalytic theory of Sigmund Freud (1856–1939).

Freud's Theory   Freud (1917) proposed that personality has three structures: the id, the ego, and the superego. The *id* is the Freudian structure of personality that consists of instincts, which are an individual's reservoir of psychic energy. In Freud's view, the id is totally unconscious; it has no contact with reality. As children experience the demands and constraints of reality, a new structure of personality emerges—the *ego*. It deals with the demands of reality and is called the "executive branch" of personality because it uses reasoning to make decisions. The id and the ego have no morality—they do not take into account whether something is right or wrong. The *superego* is the Freudian structure of personality that is the moral branch of personality, the part that considers whether something is right or wrong. Think of the superego as what we often refer to as our "conscience."

As Freud listened to, probed, and analyzed his patients, he became convinced that their problems were the result of experiences early in life. He thought that as children grow up, their focus of pleasure and sexual impulses shifts from the mouth to the anus and eventually to the genitals. As a result, we go through five stages of psychosexual development: oral, anal, phallic, latency, and genital (see Figure 6). Our adult personality, Freud claimed, is determined by the way we resolve conflicts between sources of pleasure and the demands of reality at each stage.

Freud's theory has been significantly revised by a number of psychoanalytic theorists. Many contemporary psychoanalytic theorists maintain that Freud overemphasized sexual instincts; they place more emphasis on cultural experiences as determinants of an individual's development. Unconscious thought remains a central theme, but most contemporary psychoanalysts stress that conscious thought plays a greater role than Freud envisioned. Next, we outline the ideas of an important revisionist of Freud's theory—Erik Erikson.

Erikson's Psychosocial Theory   Erik Erikson (1902–1994) recognized Freud's contributions but argued that Freud misjudged some important dimensions of human development. For one thing, Erikson (1950, 1968) said we develop in psychosocial stages rather than in psychosexual stages, as Freud maintained. According to Freud, the primary motivation for human behavior is sexual; according to Erikson, it is social and reflects a desire to affiliate with other people. According to Freud, our basic personality is shaped in the first five years of life; according to Erikson, developmental change occurs throughout the life span. Thus, in terms of the early versus later experience issue described earlier in this chapter, Freud argued that early experience is far more important than later experiences, whereas Erikson emphasized the importance of both early and later experiences.

Sigmund Freud, the pioneering architect of psychoanalytic theory. *What are some characteristics of Freud's theory?*
Chronicle/Alamy Stock Photo

Erik Erikson with his wife, Joan, an artist. Erikson generated one of the most important developmental theories of the twentieth century. *Which stage of Erikson's theory are you in? Does Erikson's description of this stage characterize you?*
Jon Erickson/Science Source

FIGURE 6
FREUDIAN STAGES.

Oral Stage	Anal Stage	Phallic Stage	Latency Stage	Genital Stage
Infant's pleasure centers on the mouth.	Child's pleasure focuses on the anus.	Child's pleasure focuses on the genitals.	Child represses sexual interest and develops social and intellectual skills.	A time of sexual reawakening; source of sexual pleasure becomes someone outside the family.
Birth to 1½ Years	**1½ to 3 Years**	**3 to 6 Years**	**6 Years to Puberty**	**Puberty Onward**

Erikson's Stages	Developmental Period
Integrity versus despair	Late adulthood (60s onward)
Generativity versus stagnation	Middle adulthood (40s, 50s)
Intimacy versus isolation	Early adulthood (20s, 30s)
Identity versus identity confusion	Adolescence (10 to 20 years)
Industry versus inferiority	Middle and late childhood (elementary school years, 6 years to puberty)
Initiative versus guilt	Early childhood (preschool years, 3 to 5 years)
Autonomy versus shame and doubt	Infancy (1 to 3 years)
Trust versus mistrust	Infancy (first year)

FIGURE 7
ERIKSON'S EIGHT LIFE-SPAN STAGES

How Would You...?
If you were a **human development and family studies professional,** how would you apply psychoanalytic theory to advise the family of a child who has no reported history of abuse yet shows violent behavior?

Erikson's theory Includes eight stages of human development. Each stage consists of a unique developmental task that confronts individuals with a crisis that must be resolved.

In **Erikson's theory,** eight stages of development unfold as we go through life (see Figure 7). At each stage, a unique developmental task confronts individuals with a crisis that must be resolved. According to Erikson, this crisis is not a catastrophe but a turning point marked by both increased vulnerability and enhanced potential. The more successfully an individual resolves the crisis, the healthier his or her development will be.

Trust versus mistrust is Erikson's first psychosocial stage, which is experienced in the first year of life. Trust during infancy sets the stage for a lifelong expectation that the world will be a good and pleasant place to live.

After gaining trust in their caregivers, infants begin to discover that their behavior is their own. They start to assert their sense of independence, or autonomy. If infants are restrained too much or punished too harshly, they are likely to develop a sense of shame and doubt. This is Erikson's second stage of development, *autonomy versus shame and doubt,* which occurs in late infancy and toddlerhood (1 to 3 years of age).

Initiative versus guilt, Erikson's third stage of development, occurs during the preschool years. As preschool children encounter a widening social world, they face new challenges that require active, purposeful behavior. Children are asked to assume responsibility for their bodies, their behavior, their toys, and their pets—and they take initiative. Feelings of guilt may arise, though, if the child is irresponsible and is made to feel too anxious.

Industry versus inferiority is Erikson's fourth developmental stage, occurring approximately in the elementary school years. Children's initiative brings them in contact with a wealth of new experiences. As they move into middle and late childhood, they direct their energy toward mastering knowledge and intellectual skills. At no other time is the child more enthusiastic about learning than at the end of early childhood's period of expansive imagination. The danger is that the child can develop a sense of inferiority—feeling incompetent and unproductive.

During the adolescent years, individuals are faced with finding out who they are, what they are all about, and where they are going in life. This is Erikson's fifth developmental stage, *identity versus identity confusion.* Adolescents are confronted with many new roles and adult statuses—vocational and romantic, for example. If they explore roles in a healthy manner and arrive at a positive path to follow in life, then they achieve a positive identity. If parents push an identity on adolescents, and if adolescents do not adequately explore many roles and define a positive future path, then identity confusion reigns.

Intimacy versus isolation is Erikson's sixth developmental stage, which individuals experience during early adulthood. At this time, individuals face the developmental task of forming intimate relationships. Erikson describes intimacy as finding oneself yet losing oneself in another. If the young adult forms healthy friendships and an intimate relationship with another, intimacy will be achieved; if not, isolation will result.

Generativity versus stagnation, Erikson's seventh developmental stage, occurs during middle adulthood. By generativity Erikson means primarily a concern for helping the younger generation to develop and lead useful lives. The feeling of having done nothing to help the next generation is stagnation.

Integrity versus despair is Erikson's eighth and final stage of development, which individuals experience in late adulthood. During this stage, a person reflects on the past. Through many different routes, the person may have developed a positive outlook in most or all of the previous stages of development. If so, the person's life review will reveal a life well spent, and the person will feel a sense of satisfaction—integrity will be achieved. If the person has resolved many of the earlier stages negatively, the retrospective glances likely will yield doubt or gloom—the despair Erikson described.

Each of Erikson's stages has a "positive" pole, such as trust, and a "negative" pole, such as mistrust. In the healthy solution to the crisis of each stage, the positive pole dominates, but Erikson maintained that some exposure or commitment to the negative side is sometimes inevitable. For example, learning to trust is an important outcome of Erikson's first stage, but you cannot trust all people under all circumstances and survive. We discuss Erikson's theory again in the chapters on socioemotional development. In the *Caring Connections* interlude, you can read about some effective strategies for improving the lives of children based on Erikson's view.

Evaluating the Psychoanalytic Theories The contributions of psychoanalytic theories include these ideas: (1) early experiences play an important part in development; (2) family relationships are a central aspect of development; (3) personality can be better

caring connections

Strategies for Parenting, Educating, and Interacting with Children Based on Erikson's Theory

Parents, child-care specialists, teachers, counselors, youth workers, and other adults can adopt positive strategies for interacting with children based on Erikson's theory. These strategies are described below.

1. ***Nurture infants and develop their trust, then encourage and monitor toddlers' autonomy.*** Because infants depend on others to meet their needs, it is critical for caregivers to consistently provide positive, attentive care for infants. Infants who experience consistently positive care feel safe and secure, sensing that people are reliable and loving, which leads them to develop trust in the world. Caregivers who neglect or abuse infants are likely to have infants who develop a sense of mistrust in their world. Having developed a sense of trust in their world, as infants move into the toddler years, it is important that they are given the freedom to explore it. Toddlers whose caregivers are too restrictive or harsh are likely to develop shame and doubt, sensing that they can't adequately do things on their own. As toddlers gain more independence, caregivers need to monitor their exploration and curiosity because there are many things that can harm them, such as running into the street or touching a hot stove.

2. ***Encourage initiative in young children.*** Children should be given a great deal of freedom to explore their world. They should be allowed to choose some of the activities they engage in. If their requests for doing certain activities are reasonable, the requests should be honored. Children need to be provided with exciting materials that will stimulate their imagination. Young children at this stage love to play. It not only benefits their socioemotional development but also is an important medium for their cognitive growth. Criticism should be kept to a minimum so that children will not develop high levels of guilt and anxiety. Young children are going to make lots of mistakes and have lots of spills. They need good models far more than harsh critics. Structure their activities and environment for success rather than failure by giving them

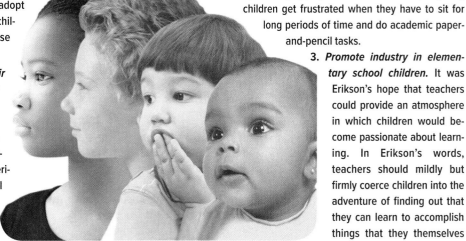

What are some applications of Erikson's theory for effective parenting?
(*Left to Right*): Valerie Berry/iStock/Getty Images; Tomas Rodriguez/Corbis/Getty Images; Fuse/Corbis/Getty Images; Image Source/Getty Images

developmentally appropriate tasks. For example, young children get frustrated when they have to sit for long periods of time and do academic paper-and-pencil tasks.

3. ***Promote industry in elementary school children.*** It was Erikson's hope that teachers could provide an atmosphere in which children would become passionate about learning. In Erikson's words, teachers should mildly but firmly coerce children into the adventure of finding out that they can learn to accomplish things that they themselves would never have thought they could do. In elementary school, children thirst to know. Most arrive at elementary school steeped in curiosity and motivated to master tasks. In Erikson's view, it is important for teachers to nourish this motivation for mastery and curiosity. Teachers need to challenge students but not overwhelm them; be firm in requiring students to be productive without being overly critical; and especially be tolerant of honest mistakes and make sure that every student has opportunities for many successes.

4. ***Stimulate identity exploration in adolescence.*** It is important to recognize that the adolescent's identity is multidimensional. Aspects include vocational goals; intellectual achievement; and interests in hobbies, sports, music, and other areas. Adolescents can be asked to write essays about such dimensions, exploring who they are and what they want to do with their lives. They should be encouraged to think independently and to freely express their views, which stimulates their self-exploration. Adolescents can also be encouraged to listen to debates on political and ideological issues, which stimulates them to examine different perspectives. Another good strategy is to encourage adolescents to talk with a school counselor about career options as well as other aspects of their identity. Teachers can have people from different careers come into the classroom and talk about their work with students regardless of grade level.

understood if it is examined developmentally; (4) activities of the mind are not entirely conscious—unconscious aspects need to be considered; and (5) in Erikson's theory, changes take place in adulthood as well as in childhood.

Psychoanalytic theories have been criticized for several reasons. First, the main concepts of psychoanalytic theories are difficult to test scientifically. Second, many of the data used to support psychoanalytic theories come from individuals' reconstruction of the past, often the distant past, and are of unknown accuracy. Third, the sexual underpinnings of development are given too much importance (especially in Freud's theory), and the unconscious mind is given too much credit for influencing development. In addition, psychoanalytic theories (especially Freud's theory) present an overly negative image of humans and are culture- and gender-biased, treating Western culture and males as the measure for evaluating everyone.

Cognitive Theories   Whereas psychoanalytic theories stress the importance of the unconscious, cognitive theories emphasize conscious thoughts. Three important cognitive theories are Piaget's cognitive developmental theory, Vygotsky's sociocultural cognitive theory, and information-processing theory.

Piaget's Cognitive Developmental Theory   **Piaget's theory** states that children actively construct their understanding of the world and go through four stages of cognitive development. Two processes move us through the four stages of development in Piaget's theory: organization and adaptation. To make sense of our world, we *organize* our experiences. For example, we separate important ideas from less important ideas, and we connect one idea to another. In addition to organizing our observations and experiences, we *adapt,* adjusting to new environmental demands (Miller, 2016).

Piaget (1896–1980) also proposed that we go through four stages in understanding the world (see Figure 8). Each stage is age-related and consists of a distinct way of thinking, a different way of understanding the world. Thus, according to Piaget (1954), the child's cognition is *qualitatively* different in one stage compared with another.

---

developmental **connection**

Cognitive Theory

The entire field of children's cognitive development began with Piaget, but a number of criticisms of his theory have been made. Connect to "Cognitive Development in Middle and Late Childhood."

Piaget's theory States that children actively construct their understanding of the world and go through four stages of cognitive development.

Sensorimotor Stage

The infant constructs an understanding of the world by coordinating sensory experiences with physical actions. An infant progresses from reflexive, instinctual action at birth to the beginning of symbolic thought toward the end of the stage.

Birth to 2 Years of Age

Preoperational Stage

The child begins to represent the world with words and images. These words and images reflect increased symbolic thinking and go beyond the connection of sensory information and physical action.

2 to 7 Years of Age

Concrete Operational Stage

The child can now reason logically about concrete events and classify objects into different sets.

7 to 11 Years of Age

Formal Operational Stage

The adolescent reasons in more abstract, idealistic, and logical ways.

11 Years of Age Through Adulthood

FIGURE **8**
PIAGET'S FOUR STAGES OF COGNITIVE DEVELOPMENT.
(left to right): Stockbyte/Getty Images; Jacobs Stock Photography/BananaStock/Getty Images; Fuse/image100/Corbis; Hero Images Inc./Alamy Stock Photo

The *sensorimotor stage,* which lasts from birth to about 2 years of age, is the first Piagetian stage. In this stage, infants construct an understanding of the world by coordinating sensory experiences (such as seeing and hearing) with physical, motoric actions—hence the term *sensorimotor.*

The *preoperational stage,* which lasts from approximately 2 to 7 years of age, is Piaget's second stage. In this stage, children begin to go beyond simply connecting sensory information with physical action by representing the world with words, images, and drawings. However, according to Piaget, preschool children still lack the ability to perform what he calls operations, which are internalized mental actions that allow children to do mentally what they previously could only do physically. For example, if you imagine putting two sticks together to see whether they would be as long as another stick, without actually moving the sticks, you are performing a concrete operation.

The *concrete operational stage,* which lasts from approximately 7 to 11 years of age, is the third Piagetian stage. In this stage, children can perform operations that involve objects, and they can reason logically as long as reasoning can be applied to specific or concrete examples. For example, concrete operational thinkers understand that two rows of four nickels have the same number of nickels regardless of how far apart the nickels in the row are spaced. However, concrete operational thinkers cannot imagine the steps necessary to complete an algebraic equation, which is too abstract for thinking at this stage of development.

The *formal operational stage,* which appears between the ages of 11 and 15 and continues through adulthood, is Piaget's fourth and final stage. In this stage, individuals move beyond concrete experiences and think in abstract and more logical terms. As part of thinking more abstractly, adolescents develop images of ideal circumstances. They might think about what an ideal parent is like and compare their parents to this ideal standard. They begin to entertain possibilities for the future and are fascinated with what they can be. In solving problems, they become more systematic, developing hypotheses about why something is happening the way it is and then testing these hypotheses.

In sum, this brief introduction to Piaget's theory that children's cognitive development goes through four stages is provided here, along with other theories, to give you a broad understanding. Later in the text, when we study cognitive development in infancy, early childhood, middle and late childhood, and adolescence, we will examine Piaget's theory in more depth.

Vygotsky's Sociocultural Cognitive Theory   Like Piaget, the Russian developmentalist Lev Vygotsky (1896–1934) said that children actively construct their knowledge. Unlike Piaget, Vygotsky (1962) did not propose that cognitive development occurs in stages, and he gave social interaction and culture far more important roles in cognitive development than Piaget did. **Vygotsky's theory** is a sociocultural cognitive theory that emphasizes how culture and social interaction guide cognitive development.

Vygotsky portrayed the child's development as inseparable from social and cultural activities (Veraksa & Sheridan, 2018). He argued that development of memory, attention, and reasoning involves learning to use the inventions of society, such as language, mathematical systems, and memory strategies. Thus in one culture, children might learn to count with the help of a computer; in another, they might learn by using beads. According to Vygotsky, children's social interaction with more-skilled adults and peers is indispensable to their cognitive development. Through this interaction, they learn to use the tools that will help them adapt and be successful in their culture. For example, if you regularly help a child learn how to read, you not only advance a child's reading skills but also communicate to the child that reading is an important activity in his or her culture.

Vygotsky's theory has stimulated considerable interest in the view that knowledge is situated and collaborative (Holzman, 2016). In this view, knowledge is not generated from within the individual but rather is constructed through interaction with other people and objects in the culture, such as books. This suggests that knowledge grows through interaction with others in cooperative activities.

Vygotsky's theory, like Piaget's, remained virtually unknown to American psychologists until the 1960s, but eventually both became influential among educators as well as psychologists. We will examine ideas about learning and teaching that are based on Vygotsky's theory when we study cognitive development in early childhood.

Jean Piaget, the famous Swiss developmental psychologist, changed the way we think about the development of children's minds. *What are some key ideas in Piaget's theory?*

Vygotsky's theory A sociocultural cognitive theory that emphasizes how culture and social interaction guide cognitive development.

There is considerable interest today in Lev Vygotsky's sociocultural cognitive theory of child development. *What were Vygotsky's basic ideas about children's development?*

A. R. Lauria/Dr. Michael Cole, Laboratory of Human Cognition, University of California, San Diego

information-processing theory Emphasizes that individuals manipulate information, monitor it, and strategize about it. Central to this theory are the processes of memory and thinking.

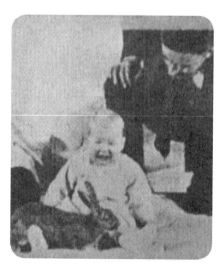

In 1920, John Watson and Rosalie Rayner conditioned 11-month-old Albert to fear a white rat by pairing the rat with a loud noise. When little Albert was subsequently presented with other stimuli similar to the white rat, such as the rabbit shown here with little Albert, he was afraid of them, too. This illustrates the principle of stimulus generalization in classical conditioning.

Courtesy of Dr. Benjamin Harris

The Information-Processing Theory   Early computers may be the best candidates for the title of "creators" of information-processing theory. Although many factors stimulated the growth of this theory, none was more important than the computer. Psychologists began to wonder whether the logical operations carried out by computers might tell us something about how the human mind works. They drew analogies between a computer's hardware and the brain and between computer software and cognition.

This line of thinking helped to generate **information-processing theory,** which emphasizes that individuals manipulate information, monitor it, and strategize about it. Unlike Piaget's theory, but like Vygotsky's theory, information-processing theory does not describe development as stage-like. Instead, according to this theory, individuals develop a gradually increasing capacity for processing information, which allows them to acquire increasingly complex knowledge and skills (Gordon & others, 2020).

Robert Siegler (2016a, b, 2017), a leading expert on children's information processing, states that thinking is information processing. In other words, when individuals perceive, encode, represent, store, and retrieve information, they are thinking. Siegler emphasizes that an important aspect of development is learning good strategies for processing information (Fazio, DeWolf, & Siegler, 2016; Siegler & Braithwaite, 2017). For example, becoming a better reader might involve learning to monitor the key themes of the material being read.

Siegler (2016a, b, 2017) also argues that the best way to understand how children learn is to observe them while they are learning. He emphasizes the importance of using the *microgenetic method* to obtain detailed information about processing mechanisms as they are occurring moment to moment. Siegler concludes that most research methods indirectly assess cognitive change, being more like snapshots than movies. The microgenetic method seeks to discover not just what children know but the cognitive processes involved in how they acquired the knowledge. A typical microgenetic study will be conducted across a number of trials assessed at various times over weeks or months (Miller, 2016). A number of microgenetic studies have focused on a specific aspect of academic learning, such as how children learn whole number arithmetic, fractions, and other areas of math (Siegler, 2022). Microgenetic studies also have been used to discover how children learn a particular issue in science or a key aspect of learning to read.

Evaluating the Cognitive Theories   The primary contributions of cognitive theories are that (1) they present a positive view of development, emphasizing conscious thinking; (2) they emphasize the individual's active construction of understanding (especially Piaget's and Vygotsky's theories); (3) Piaget's and Vygotsky's theories underscore the importance of examining developmental changes in children's thinking; and (4) information-processing theory offers detailed descriptions of cognitive processes.

There are several criticisms of cognitive theories. First, Piaget's stages are not as uniform as he theorized. Piaget also underestimated the cognitive skills of infants and overestimated the cognitive skills of adolescents. Second, the cognitive theories do not give adequate attention to individual variations in cognitive development. Third, information-processing theory does not provide an adequate description of developmental changes in cognition. In addition, some theorists argue that the cognitive theories do not give enough credit to unconscious thought.

Behavioral and Social Cognitive Theories   In the early twentieth century, as Freud was interpreting patients' unconscious minds through their early childhood experiences, Ivan Pavlov and John B. Watson were conducting detailed observations of behavior in controlled laboratory settings. Their work provided the foundations of *behaviorism,* which holds that we can study scientifically only what can be directly observed and measured. Out of the behavioral tradition grew the belief that development is defined as observable behavior that can be learned through experience with the environment (Schunk, 2020). In terms of the continuity-discontinuity issue discussed earlier in this chapter, the behavioral and social cognitive theories emphasize continuity in development and argue that development does not occur in stage-like fashion. The three versions of the behavioral and social cognitive theories that we explore are Pavlov's classical conditioning, Skinner's operant conditioning, and Bandura's social cognitive theory.

Pavlov's Classical Conditioning   In the early 1900s, the Russian physiologist Ivan Pavlov (1927) knew that dogs salivate when they taste food. He became curious when he observed that dogs salivate to various sights and sounds before eating their food. For example, when an individual paired the ringing of a bell with the food, the bell ringing subsequently elicited salivation from the dogs when it was presented by itself. With this experiment, Pavlov discovered the principle of *classical conditioning*, in which a neutral stimulus (in our example, ringing a bell) produces a response originally produced by another stimulus (in our example, food).

In the early twentieth century, John Watson demonstrated that classical conditioning occurs in humans. He showed an infant named Albert a white rat to see if he was afraid of it. He was not. As Albert played with the rat, a loud noise was made behind his head. As you might imagine, the noise caused little Albert to cry. After several pairings of the loud noise and the white rat, Albert began to cry at the sight of the rat even when the noise did not occur (Watson & Rayner, 1920). Albert had been classically conditioned to fear the rat. Similarly, many of our fears may result from classical conditioning: Fear of the dentist may be learned from a painful experience, fear of driving from being in an automobile accident, fear of heights from falling off a high chair when we were infants, and fear of dogs from being bitten.

Skinner's Operant Conditioning   Classical conditioning may explain how we develop many involuntary responses such as fears, but B. F. Skinner argued that a second type of conditioning accounts for the development of other types of behavior. According to Skinner (1938), through *operant conditioning* the consequences of a behavior produce changes in the future probability of the behavior's occurrence. A behavior followed by a rewarding stimulus is more likely to recur, whereas a behavior followed by a punishing stimulus is less likely to recur. For example, when a person smiles at a child after the child has done something, the child is more likely to repeat the action than if the person gives the child a nasty look.

According to Skinner, such rewards and punishments shape development: For example, shy people learned to be shy as a result of experiences they had while growing up. It follows that modifications in an environment can help a shy person become more socially oriented. Also, for Skinner the key aspect of development is behavior, not thoughts and feelings. He emphasized that development consists of the pattern of behavioral changes that are brought about by rewards and punishments.

Bandura's Social Cognitive Theory   Some psychologists agree with the behaviorists' notion that development is learned and is influenced strongly by the environment. However, unlike Skinner, they argue that our thoughts (that is, cognition) are also important in understanding development. **Social cognitive theory** states that behavior, environment, and cognition are the key factors in development.

Canadian American psychologist Albert Bandura (1925–2021) was the leading architect of social cognitive theory. Bandura (2015, 2018) emphasized that cognitive processes have important links with the environment and behavior. His early research focused heavily on *observational learning* (also called *imitation,* or *modeling*), which is learning that occurs through observing what others do. For example, a young child might observe a parent yelling in anger and treating other people with hostility; with peers, the young child later acts very aggressively, showing behavior similar to the parent's. Another child might adopt the dominant and sarcastic style of a teacher, saying to a younger brother, "You are so slow. How can you do this work so slowly?" Social cognitive theorists stress that people acquire a wide range of behaviors, thoughts, and feelings through observing others' behavior and that these observations powerfully influence children's development.

According to Bandura, what is cognitive about observational learning? He proposed that people cognitively represent the behavior of others and then sometimes adopt this behavior themselves. Bandura's (2018) most recent model of learning and development included three elements: behavior, the person/cognition, and the environment. A person's sense of being in control of success is an example of a person factor; strategies are an example of a cognitive

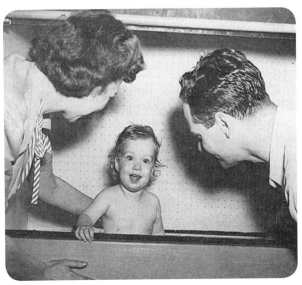

B. F. Skinner was a tinkerer who liked to make new gadgets. The younger of his two daughters, Deborah, spent much of her infancy in Skinner's enclosed Air-Crib, which he invented because he wanted to ensure her comfort while minimizing the need for heavy blankets and pajamas. The Air-Crib was temperature-controlled. Debbie, shown here as a child with her parents, is currently a successful artist, is married, and lives in London. *What do you think about Skinner's Air-Crib?*
AP Images

social cognitive theory The view of psychologists who emphasize behavior, environment, and cognition as the key factors in development.

Albert Bandura was one of the leading architects of social cognitive theory. *What is the nature of his theory?*
Courtesy of Dr. Albert Bandura

developmental **connection**

Achievement

Bandura emphasized that self-efficacy is a key person/cognitive factor in children's achievement. Connect to "Cognitive Development in Middle and Late Childhood."

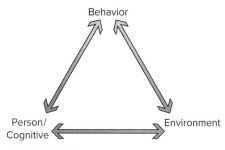

Behavior

Person/
Cognitive   Environment

FIGURE 9

BANDURA'S SOCIAL COGNITIVE MODEL.
The arrows illustrate how relations between behavior, person/cognition, and environment are reciprocal rather than unidirectional.

ethology Stresses that behavior is strongly influenced by biology, is tied to evolution, and is characterized by critical or sensitive periods.

Konrad Lorenz, a pioneering student of animal behavior, is followed through the water by three imprinted greylag geese. Describe Lorenz's experiment with the geese. *Do you think his experiment would have the same results with human babies? Explain.*
Nina Leen/The LIFE Picture Collection/Shutterstock

factor. As shown in Figure 9, behavior, person/cognitive, and environmental factors operate interactively. Behavior can influence person factors and vice versa. Cognitive activities can influence the environment, the environment can change the person's cognition, and so on.

Evaluating the Behavioral and Social Cognitive Theories Contributions of the behavioral and social cognitive theories include (1) their emphasis on the importance of scientific research; (2) their focus on environmental causes of behavior; (3) the identification and explanation of observational learning (by Bandura); and (4) the inclusion of person/cognitive factors (in social cognitive theory).

Criticisms of the behavioral and social cognitive theories include the objections that they give (1) too little emphasis to cognition (in Pavlov's and Skinner's theories); (2) too much emphasis to environmental determinants; (3) inadequate attention to developmental changes; and (4) inadequate recognition to human spontaneity and creativity.

Behavioral and social cognitive theories emphasize the importance of environmental experiences in human development. Next we turn our attention to a theory that underscores the importance of the biological foundations of development—ethological theory.

Ethological Theory Developmental psychologists began to pay attention to the biological bases of development thanks to the work of zoologists who pioneered the field of ethology. **Ethology** stresses that behavior is strongly influenced by biology, is tied to evolution, and is characterized by critical or sensitive periods. These are specific time frames during which, according to ethologists, the presence or absence of certain experiences has a long-lasting influence on individuals.

Austrian zoologist Konrad Lorenz (1903–1989) helped bring ethology to prominence. In his best-known experiment, Lorenz (1965) studied the behavior of greylag geese, which will follow their mother as soon as they hatch. In a remarkable set of experiments, Lorenz separated the eggs laid by one goose into two groups. One group he returned to the goose to be hatched by her. The other group was hatched in an incubator. The goslings in the first group performed as predicted. They followed their mother as soon as they hatched. However, those in the second group, which saw Lorenz when they first hatched, followed him everywhere, as though he were their mother. Lorenz marked the goslings and then placed both groups under a box. Mother goose and "mother" Lorenz stood nearby as the box was lifted. Each group of goslings went directly to its "mother." Lorenz called this process *imprinting,* the rapid, innate learning within a limited critical period of time that involves attachment to the first moving object seen.

Ethological research and theory at first had little to say about the nature of social relationships across the human life span, and the theory stimulated few studies with humans.

Ethologists' view that normal development requires that certain behaviors emerge during a critical period, a fixed time period very early in development, seemed to be overstated.

However, John Bowlby (1989) illustrated an important application of ethological theory to human development. Bowlby argued that attachment to a caregiver over the first year of life has important consequences throughout the life span. Bowlby stated that if this attachment is positive and secure, the individual will likely develop positively in childhood and adulthood. If the attachment is negative and insecure, life-span development will likely not be optimal. Thus, the first year of life is a sensitive period for the development of social relationships. In the chapter "Socioemotional Development in Infancy," we explore the concept of infant attachment in much greater detail.

Contributions of ethological theory include (1) an increased focus on the biological and evolutionary basis of development; (2) use of careful observations in naturalistic settings; and (3) an emphasis on sensitive periods of development.

Criticisms of ethological theory include the following: (1) the concepts of critical and sensitive periods are perhaps too rigid; (2) the emphasis on biological foundations is too strong; (3) cognition receives inadequate attention; and (4) the theory is better at generating research with animals than with humans.

Another theory that emphasizes the biological aspects of human development—evolutionary psychology—is presented in the chapter "Biological Beginnings," along with views on the role of heredity in development.

Ecological Theory

Ethological theory stresses biological factors, whereas ecological theory emphasizes environmental factors. One ecological theory that has important implications for understanding children's development was created by Urie Bronfenbrenner (1917–2005).

Bronfenbrenner's ecological theory (Bronfenbrenner & Morris, 2006; Tudge & others, 2021) holds that development reflects the influence of several environmental systems. The theory identifies five environmental systems (see Figure 10):

- *Microsystem*—the setting in which the individual lives. These contexts include the person's family, peers, school, neighborhood, and work. It is in the microsystem that the most direct interactions with social agents take place— with parents, peers, and teachers, for example.

- *Mesosystem*—relations between microsystems or connections between contexts. Examples are the relation of family experiences to school experiences, school experiences to church experiences, and family experiences to peer experiences. For example, children whose parents have rejected them may have difficulty developing positive relations with teachers.

- *Exosystem*—links between a social setting in which the individual does not have an active role and the individual's immediate context. For example, a husband's or child's experience at home may be influenced by a mother's experiences at work. The mother might receive a promotion that requires more travel, which might increase conflict with the husband and change patterns of interaction with the child.

developmental **connection**

Attachment

Human babies go through a series of phases in developing an attachment to a caregiver. Connect to "Socioemotional Development in Infancy."

Bronfenbrenner's ecological theory An environmental systems theory that focuses on five environmental systems: microsystem, mesosystem, exosystem, macrosystem, and chronosystem.

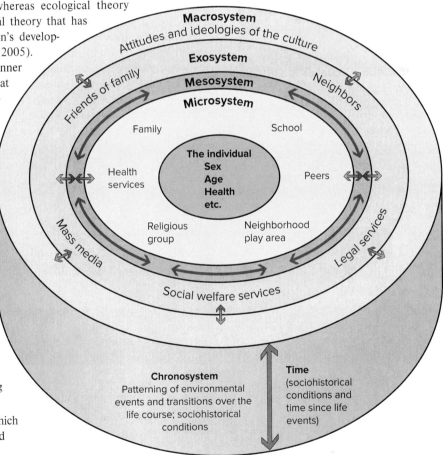

FIGURE **10**

BRONFENBRENNER'S ECOLOGICAL THEORY OF DEVELOPMENT. Bronfenbrenner's ecological theory consists of five environmental systems: microsystem, mesosytem, exosystem, macrosystem, and chronosystem.
Source: Simmons, J. "Bronfenbrenner's Ecological Theory of Development," in *Child Development in a Social Context*, Kopp, C. B., & Krakow, J. B., eds. New York: Addison-Wesley Longman, Inc., 1982, 648.

How Would You...?

If you were an **educator,** how might you explain a student's chronic failure to complete homework from the mesosystem level? From the exosystem level?

• *Macrosystem*—the culture in which individuals live. Remember from earlier in this chapter that *culture* refers to the behavior patterns, beliefs, and all other products of a group of people that are passed on from generation to generation. Remember also that cross-cultural studies—comparisons of one culture with one or more other cultures—provide information about the generality of development (Khaleque, 2021).

• *Chronosystem*—the patterning of environmental events and transitions over the life course, as well as historical circumstances. For example, divorce is one transition. Researchers have found that the negative effects of divorce on children often peak in the first year after the divorce (Mahrer & others, 2018). By two years after the divorce, family interaction is less chaotic and more stable. As an example of historical circumstances, consider how the opportunities for women to pursue a career have increased during the last 40 years.

Bronfenbrenner (Bronfenbrenner & Morris, 2006) added biological influences to his theory and described it as a *bioecological* theory. Nonetheless, ecological, environmental contexts still predominate in Bronfenbrenner's theory (Tudge & others, 2021).

Contributions of the theory include a systematic examination of macro and micro dimensions of environmental systems, and attention to connections between environmental systems. A further contribution of Bronfenbrenner's theory is its emphasis on a range of social contexts beyond the family, such as neighborhood, religious community, school, and workplace, as influences in children's development (Wei & others, 2021). Criticisms include giving inadequate attention to biological factors and placing too little emphasis on cognitive factors.

An Eclectic Theoretical Orientation   The theories that we have discussed were developed at different points in the twentieth century, as Figure 11 shows. No single theory described in this chapter can explain entirely the rich complexity of children's development, but each has contributed to our understanding of development. Psychoanalytic theory best explains the unconscious mind. Erikson's theory best describes the changes that occur in adult development. Piaget's, Vygotsky's, and the information-processing views provide the most complete description of cognitive development. The behavioral and social cognitive and ecological theories have been the most useful for examining the environmental determinants of development. The ethological theories have highlighted biology's role and the importance of sensitive periods in development.

Urie Bronfenbrenner developed ecological theory, a perspective that is receiving increased attention. *What is the nature of ecological theory?*

Courtesy of Cornell University Photography

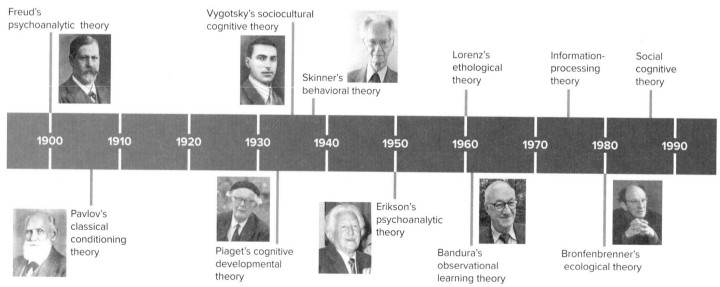

FIGURE **11**

TIME LINE FOR MAJOR DEVELOPMENTAL THEORIES.

Source: Kopp, C. B., & Krakow, J. B., "Time Line for Major Developmental Theories," in *Child Development in a Social Context*, Kopp, C. B., & Krakow, J. B., eds., New York: Addison-Wesley Longman, Inc., 1982.

(Freud) Chronicle/Alamy Stock Photo (Pavlov): Bettmann/Getty Images; (Piaget): Yves DeBraine/Black Star/Stock Photo; (Vygotsky): A.R. Lauria/Dr. Michael Cole, Library of Human Cognition, UCSD; (Skinner): Harvard University Photo Services; (Erikson): Bettmann/Getty Images; (Bandura): Courtesy of Dr. Albert Bandura; (Bronfenbrenner): Courtesy of Cornell University Photography

THEORY	ISSUES		
	Nature and nurture	**Early-and-later experience**	**Continuity and discontinuity**
Psychoanalytic	Freud's biological determinism interacting with early family experiences; Erikson's more balanced biological/cultural interaction perspective	Early experiences in the family are very important influences	Emphasis on discontinuity between stages
Cognitive	Piaget's emphasis on interaction and adaptation; environment provides the setting for cognitive structures to develop. Vygotsky's theory involves interaction of nature and nurture with strong emphasis on culture. The information-processing approach has not addressed this issue extensively; mainly emphasizes biological/environment interaction.	Childhood experiences are important influences	Discontinuity between stages in Piaget's theory; no stages in Vygotsky's theory or the information-processing approach
Behavioral and Social Cognitive	Environment viewed as the main influence on development	Experiences are important at all points in development	Continuity with no stages
Ethological	Strong biological view	Early experience is very important and can contribute to change early in development; after the early critical or sensitive period has passed, stability is likely to occur	Discontinuity because of early critical or sensitive period; no stages
Ecological	Strong environmental view	Experiences involving the five environmental systems are important at all points in development	No stages but little attention to the issue

FIGURE 12
A COMPARISON OF THEORIES AND ISSUES IN CHILD DEVELOPMENT

In short, although theories are helpful guides, relying on a single theory to explain development is probably a mistake. This release instead takes an **eclectic theoretical orientation,** which does not follow any one theoretical approach but rather selects from each theory whatever is considered its best features. With this orientation, you can view the study of development as it actually exists—with different theorists making different assumptions, stressing different research questions, and using different strategies to discover information. Figure 12 compares the main theoretical perspectives in terms of how they view important issues in children's development.

eclectic theoretical orientation An orientation that does not follow any one theoretical approach but rather selects from each theory whatever is considered the best in it.

RESEARCH METHODS FOR COLLECTING DATA

If they follow an eclectic orientation, how do scholars and researchers determine that one feature of a theory is somehow better than another? The scientific method discussed earlier in this chapter provides the guide. Recall that the steps in the scientific method involve conceptualizing the problem, collecting data, drawing conclusions, and revising research conclusions and theories. Through scientific research, the features of theories can be tested and refined.

Whether we are interested in studying attachment in infants, the cognitive skills of children, or the peer relations of adolescents, we can choose from several ways of collecting data. Here we outline the methods most often used, including their advantages and disadvantages, beginning with observation.

Observation   Scientific observation requires an important set of skills (Gravetter & Forzano, 2019). Unless we are trained observers and practice our skills regularly, we might not know what to look for, we might not remember what we saw, we might not realize that what we are looking for is changing from one moment to the next, and we might not communicate our observations effectively.

For observations to be effective, they have to be systematic. We need to have some idea of what we are looking for. We have to know whom we are observing, when and where we will observe, how the observations will be made, and how they will be recorded.

What are some important strategies in conducting observational research with children?
Marmaduke St. John/Alamy Stock Photo

laboratory A controlled setting in which many of the complex factors of the "real world" are absent.

naturalistic observation Observing behavior in real-world settings.

standardized test A test with uniform procedures for administration and scoring. Many standardized tests allow a person's performance to be compared with the performance of other individuals.

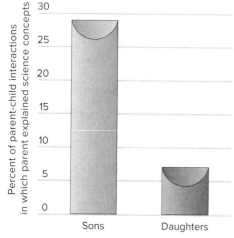

FIGURE **13**

PARENTS' EXPLANATIONS OF SCIENCE TO SONS AND DAUGHTERS AT A SCIENCE MUSEUM. In a naturalistic observation study at a children's science museum, parents were more than three times more likely to explain science to their sons than to their daughters (Crowley & others, 2001). The gender difference occurred regardless of whether the father, the mother, or both parents were with the child, although the gender difference was greatest for fathers' science explanations to sons and daughters.

Where should we make our observations? We have two choices: the laboratory and the everyday world. When we observe scientifically, we often need to control certain factors that determine behavior but are not the focus of our inquiry (Leary, 2017; Stangor, 2015). For this reason, some research in children's development is conducted in a **laboratory,** a controlled setting with many of the complex factors of the "real world" removed. For example, suppose you want to observe how children react when they see other people act aggressively. If you observe children in their homes or schools, you have no control over how much aggression the children observe, what kind of aggression they see, which people they see acting aggressively, or how other people treat the children. In contrast, if you observe the children in a laboratory, you can control these and other factors and therefore have more confidence about how to interpret your observations.

Laboratory research does have some drawbacks, however. First, it is almost impossible to conduct research without the participants' knowing they are being studied. Second, the laboratory setting is unnatural and therefore can cause the participants to behave unnaturally. Third, people who are willing to come to a university laboratory may not fairly represent groups from diverse cultural and socioeconomic backgrounds. Fourth, people who are unfamiliar with university settings and with the idea of "helping science" may be intimidated by the laboratory setting. In addition, some aspects of children's development are difficult, if not impossible, to examine in the laboratory. Last, laboratory studies of certain types of stress may even be unethical.

Naturalistic observation provides insights that we sometimes cannot achieve in the laboratory (Graziano & Raulin, 2020). **Naturalistic observation** means observing behavior in real-world settings, making no effort to manipulate or control the situation. Researchers conduct naturalistic observations at sporting events, child-care centers, work settings, malls, and other places people live in and frequent.

Naturalistic observation was used in one classic study that focused on conversations in a children's science museum (Crowley & others, 2001). Parents were more than three times more likely to engage boys than girls in explanatory talk while visiting exhibits at the science museum, suggesting a gender bias that encourages boys more than girls to be interested in science (see Figure 13). In another museum study, in a sample of Mexican American families, parents who had completed high school used more explanations with their children when visiting a science museum than those who had not completed high school (Tenenbaum & others, 2002).

Survey and Interview Sometimes the best and quickest way to get information about people is to ask them for it. One technique is to *interview* them directly. A related method is the *survey* (sometimes referred to as a questionnaire), which is especially useful when information from many people is needed (Neuman, 2020). A standard set of questions is used to obtain people's self-reported attitudes or beliefs about a specific topic. In a good survey, the questions are clear and unbiased, allowing respondents to answer unambiguously.

Surveys and interviews can be used to study a wide variety of topics, ranging from religious beliefs to sexual habits to attitudes about gun control to beliefs about how to improve schools. Surveys and interviews today are conducted in person, over the phone, and over the Internet.

One problem with surveys and interviews is the tendency of participants to answer questions in a way that they think is socially acceptable or desirable rather than telling what they truly think or feel (Yan, 2021). For example, on a survey or in an interview some individuals might say that they do not take drugs even though they do.

Standardized Test A **standardized test** has uniform procedures for administration and scoring. Many standardized tests allow a person's performance to be compared with that of other individuals to provide information about individual differences among people (Cohen, 2022). One example is the Stanford-Binet intelligence test, which is described in the chapter entitled "Cognitive Development in Middle and Late Childhood." Your score on the Stanford-Binet test tells you how your performance compares with that of thousands of other people who have taken the test.

Standardized tests have three key weaknesses. First, they do not always predict behavior in nontest situations. Second, standardized tests are based on the belief that a person's behavior is consistent and stable, yet personality and intelligence—two primary targets of standardized testing—can vary with the situation. For example, individuals may perform poorly on a standardized intelligence test in an office setting but score much higher at home where they are less anxious. A third weakness of standardized tests is that many psychological tests developed in Western cultures might not be appropriate in other cultures. The experiences of people in differing cultures may lead them to interpret and respond to questions differently (Sireci & Randall, 2021).

Case Study   A **case study** is an in-depth look at a single individual. Case studies are performed mainly by mental health professionals, when—for either practical or ethical reasons—the unique aspects of an individual's life cannot be duplicated and tested in other individuals. A case study provides information about one person's fears, hopes, fantasies, traumatic experiences, upbringing, family relationships, health, or anything else that helps the psychologist understand the person's mind and behavior. In later chapters, we discuss vivid case studies, such as studies of Michael Rehbein, who had much of the left side of his brain removed at 7 years of age to end severe epileptic seizures.

Case studies provide dramatic, in-depth portrayals of people's lives, but we must be cautious about generalizing from this information (McWhorter & Ellinger, 2018). The subject of a case study is unique, with a genetic makeup and personal history that no one else shares. In addition, case studies involve judgments of unknown reliability. Psychologists who conduct case studies rarely check to see whether other psychologists agree with their observations.

Mahatma Gandhi was the spiritual leader of India in the middle of the twentieth century. Erik Erikson conducted an extensive case study of Gandhi's life to determine what contributed to his identity development. *What are some limitations of the case study approach?*
Bettmann/Getty Images

Physiological Measures   Researchers are increasingly using physiological measures when they study children's development (Turk & others, 2022). For example, hormone levels are increasingly measured and used in developmental research. Cortisol is a hormone produced by the adrenal gland that is linked to the body's stress level and has been used in studies of temperament, emotional reactivity, and peer relations (Jacoby & others, 2016). Also, as puberty unfolds, the blood levels of certain hormones increase. To determine the nature of these hormonal changes, researchers analyze blood samples from adolescent volunteers (Carmina, Stanczyk, & Lobo, 2019).

Another physiological measure that is increasingly being used is neuroimaging, especially *functional magnetic resonance imaging* (fMRI), in which electromagnetic waves are used to construct images of a person's brain tissue and biochemical activity (Crone, 2017; White & Poldrack, 2018). Figure 14 compares the brain images of two adolescents—one a non-drinker and the other a heavy alcohol drinker—while they are engaged in a memory task.

case study An in-depth look at a single individual.

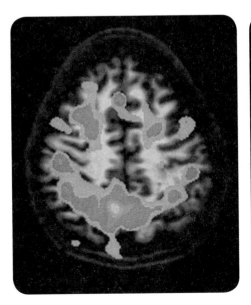 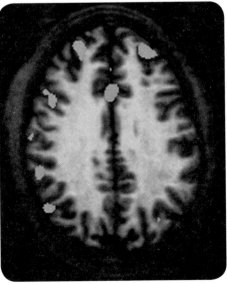

FIGURE **14**

BRAIN IMAGING OF 15-YEAR-OLD ADOLESCENTS. The two brain images indicate how alcohol can influence the functioning of an adolescent's brain. Notice the pink and red coloring (which indicates effective brain functioning involving memory) in the brain of the 15-year-old non-drinker (*left*) while engaging in a memory task and the lack of those colors in the brain of the 15-year-old under the influence of alcohol (*right*).

(*both*): Dr. Susan F. Tapert, University of California, San Diego

Electroencephaly (EEG) is a physiological measure that has been used for many decades to monitor overall electrical charges in the brain (Najjar & Brooker, 2017). Recent electroencephalograph research includes studies of infants' attention and memory (Bell & others, 2018). The latest brain imaging technique to emerge in developmental studies is functional near-infrared spectroscopy (fNIRS) imaging, in which light is used to measure changes in oxygenation of blood that correspond with brain activity (Larrivee, 2019).

Heart rate has been used as an indicator of infants' and children's development of perception, attention, and memory (Kim, Yang, & Lee, 2015). Further, heart rate and its variability have been used as an index of different aspects of emotional development, such as inhibition, stress, and anxiety (Amole & others, 2017; Blood & others, 2015).

Eye movement is increasingly being assessed to learn more about perceptual development and other developmental topics (Slone & others, 2018). Sophisticated eye-tracking equipment is especially being used to discover more detailed information about infants' perception, attention, memory, and language in typically and atypically developing children (Berdasco-Muñoz, Nazzi, & Yeung, 2019; Ishikawa & Itakura, 2019; Stone & Bosworth, 2019).

Yet another dramatic change in physiological measures is the advancement in methods to assess the actual units of hereditary information–genes–in studies of biological influences on development (Tam & others, 2019). For example, recent advances in assessing genes have revealed several specific genes that are linked to childhood obesity (Zandoná & others, 2017). We will have much more to say about these and other physiological measures in other chapters.

RESEARCH DESIGNS

Suppose you want to find out whether the children of permissive parents are more likely than other children to be rude and unruly. The data-collection method that researchers choose often depends on the goal of their research. The goal may be to describe a phenomenon, to describe relationships between phenomena, or to determine the causes or effects of a phenomenon.

Perhaps you decide that you need to observe both permissive and strict parents with their children and compare them. How would you do that? In addition to choosing a method for collecting data, you would need a research design (Neuman, 2020). There are three main types of research designs: descriptive, correlational, and experimental.

Descriptive Research   All of the data-collection methods that we have discussed can be used in **descriptive research,** which aims to observe and record behavior. For example, a researcher might observe whether people are altruistic or aggressive toward each other. By itself, descriptive research cannot prove what causes some phenomenon, but it can reveal important information about people's behavior.

Correlational Research   Correlational research goes beyond describing phenomena to provide information that will help us to predict how people will behave (Gravetter & others, 2021). In **correlational research,** the goal is to describe the strength of the relationship between two or more events or characteristics. The more strongly the two events are correlated (or related or associated), the more effectively we can predict one event from the other (Leedy & Ormrod, 2019).

For example, to study whether children of permissive parents have less self-control than other children, you would need to carefully record observations of parents' permissiveness and their children's self-control. The data could then be analyzed statistically to yield a numerical measure, called a **correlation coefficient,** a number based on a statistical analysis that is used to describe the degree of association between two variables. The correlation coefficient ranges from −1.00 to +1.00. A negative number means an inverse relation. For example, researchers often find a negative correlation between permissive parenting and children's self-control. By contrast, they often find a positive correlation between parental monitoring of children and children's self-control.

The higher the correlation coefficient (whether positive or negative), the stronger the association between the two variables. A correlation of 0.00 means that there is no association between the variables. A correlation of −0.40 is stronger than a correlation of +0.20 because we disregard whether the correlation is positive or negative in determining the strength of the correlation.

descriptive research A research design that has the purpose of observing and recording behavior.

correlational research A research design whose goal is to describe the strength of the relationship between two or more events or characteristics.

correlation coefficient A number based on statistical analysis that is used to describe the degree of association between two variables.

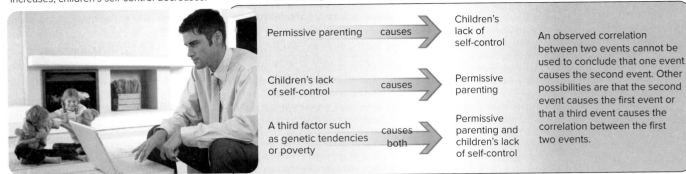

Observed Correlation: As permissive parenting increases, children's self-control decreases.

Possible explanations for this observed correlation

Permissive parenting → causes → Children's lack of self-control

Children's lack of self-control → causes → Permissive parenting

A third factor such as genetic tendencies or poverty → causes both → Permissive parenting and children's lack of self-control

An observed correlation between two events cannot be used to conclude that one event causes the second event. Other possibilities are that the second event causes the first event or that a third event causes the correlation between the first two events.

FIGURE **15**

POSSIBLE EXPLANATIONS OF CORRELATIONAL DATA

Jupiterimages/Pixland/Getty Images

A caution is in order, however. Correlation does not equal causation (Graziano & Raulin, 2020). The correlational finding just mentioned does not mean that permissive parenting necessarily causes low self-control in children. It could mean that, but it also could mean that a child's lack of self-control caused the parents to give up on trying to control the child. It also could mean that other factors, such as heredity or poverty, caused the correlation between permissive parenting and low self-control in children. Figure 15 illustrates these possible interpretations of correlational data.

Throughout this release, you will read about numerous correlational research studies. Keep in mind how easy it is to assume causality when two events or characteristics merely are correlated.

Experimental Research   To study causality, researchers turn to experimental research. An **experiment** is a carefully regulated procedure in which one or more factors believed to cause the behavior being studied are manipulated, while all other factors are held constant. If the behavior under study changes when a factor is manipulated, we say that the manipulated factor has caused the behavior to change (Christensen, Johnson, & Turner, 2020). In other words, the experiment has demonstrated cause and effect. The cause is the factor that was manipulated. The effect is the behavior that changed because of the manipulation. Descriptive and correlational research cannot establish cause and effect because they do not involve manipulating factors in a controlled way.

Independent and Dependent Variables   Experiments include two types of changeable factors, or variables: independent and dependent. An *independent variable* is a manipulated, influential, experimental factor. It is a potential cause. The label *independent* is used because this variable can be manipulated independently of other factors to determine its effect. One experiment may include several independent variables. A *dependent variable* is a factor that can change in an experiment, in response to changes in the independent variable. As researchers manipulate the independent variable, they measure the dependent variable for any resulting effect.

For example, in the experiment described in Figure 16, the amount of exercise performed by the pregnant women is the independent variable, the factor being manipulated in the experiment. When the infants are born, you would observe and measure their breathing and sleeping patterns. These patterns are the dependent variable, the factor that changes as the result of your manipulation of the mothers' exercise.

Experimental and Control Groups   Experiments can involve one or more experimental groups and one or more control groups. An *experimental group* is a group whose experience is manipulated. A *control group* is a comparison group that is as much like the experimental group as possible and that

experiment A carefully regulated procedure in which one or more of the factors believed to influence the behavior being studied are manipulated, while all other factors are held constant.

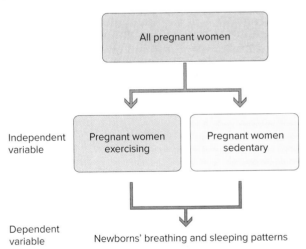

Independent variable

Dependent variable

FIGURE **16**

PRINCIPLES OF EXPERIMENTAL RESEARCH. Imagine that you conduct an experimental study of the effects of aerobic exercise by pregnant women on their newborns' breathing and sleeping patterns. You would randomly assign pregnant women to experimental and control groups. The experimental-group women would engage in aerobic exercise over a specified number of sessions and weeks. The control group would not. Then, when the infants are born, you would assess their breathing and sleeping patterns. If the breathing and sleeping patterns of newborns whose mothers were in the experimental group are different from those of the control group, you would conclude that aerobic exercise caused these effects.

is treated in every way like the experimental group except for the manipulated factor (independent variable). The manipulated condition can then be compared to the control condition.

Random assignment is an important principle for deciding whether each participant will be placed in the experimental group or in the control group. Random assignment means that researchers assign participants to experimental and control groups by chance. It reduces the likelihood that the experiment's results will be due to any preexisting differences between groups (Gravetter & Forzano, 2019). In the example of the effects of aerobic exercise by pregnant women on the breathing and sleeping patterns of their newborns (see Figure 16 again), you would randomly assign half of the pregnant women to engage in aerobic exercise over a period of weeks (the experimental group) and the other half not to exercise over the same number of weeks (the control group).

Time Span of Research   Researchers in child development have a special concern with studies that focus on the relation of age to some other variable. To do this, they can study different individuals of various ages and compare them, or they can study the same individuals as they age over time.

Cross-Sectional Approach   The **cross-sectional approach** is a research strategy in which individuals of different ages are compared at one time. A typical cross-sectional study might include a group of 5-year-olds, 8-year-olds, and 11-year-olds. The groups can be compared with respect to a variety of dependent variables: intelligence, memory, peer relations, attachment to parents, hormonal changes, and so on. All of these comparisons can be accomplished in a short time. In some studies, data are collected in a single day. Even in large-scale cross-sectional studies with hundreds of participants, data collection does not usually take longer than several months to complete.

The main advantage of the cross-sectional study is that researchers don't have to wait for children to grow older. Despite its efficiency, the cross-sectional approach has its drawbacks. It gives no information about how individual children change or about the stability of their characteristics. It can obscure the increases and decreases of development—the hills and valleys of growth and development.

Longitudinal Approach   The **longitudinal approach** is a research strategy in which the same individuals are studied over time, usually several years or more. For example, if a study of self-esteem were conducted longitudinally, the same children might be assessed three times— at 5, 8, and 11 years of age. Some longitudinal studies take place over time frames as short as one year or less.

Longitudinal studies provide a wealth of information about important issues such as stability and change in development and the influence of early experience on later development, but they are not without problems (Kramer & Rodgers, 2020). They are expensive and time-consuming. Also, the longer the study lasts, the more participants drop out. For example, children's families may move, get sick, lose interest, and so forth. Those who remain in the study may be dissimilar to those who drop out, biasing the results. For example, individuals who remain in a longitudinal study over a number of years may be more compulsive and conformity-oriented or they might have more stable lives than those who drop out.

Earlier in the chapter we described *cohort effects,* which are effects due to a person's time of birth, era, or generation, but not to actual age. Cohort effects are important in research on children, adolescents, and their parents because they can powerfully affect the dependent measures in a study meant to be concerned with age (Halfon & Forrest, 2018). Cross-sectional studies can show how different cohorts develop, but they can confuse age and cohort influences. Longitudinal studies are effective in studying age changes but only within one cohort.

So far we have discussed many aspects of scientific research in child development. In the *Connecting with Research* interlude, you can read about the research journals in which the findings of research studies are published.

RESEARCH CHALLENGES

The scientific foundation of research in child development helps to minimize the effect of research bias and maximize the objectivity of the results. Still, subtle challenges remain for each researcher to resolve. One is to ensure that research is conducted in an ethical way; another is to recognize, and try to overcome, deeply buried personal biases related to gender and ethnicity.

cross-sectional approach A research strategy in which individuals of different ages are compared at one time.

longitudinal approach A research strategy in which the same individuals are studied over a period of time, usually several years or more.

Why Are Research Journals Important in the Field of Child Development?

Key Points:

- Scientific journals publish scholarly and academic articles.
- Research articles contain technical language and terms.
- Peer review determines whether an article is accepted for publication.

Regardless of whether you pursue a career in child development, psychology, or some related scientific field, you can benefit by learning about the journal process. As a student you might be required to look up original research in journals. As a parent, teacher, or nurse you might want to consult journals to obtain information that will help you understand and work more effectively with people. And as an inquiring person, you might look up information in journals after you have heard or read something that piqued your curiosity.

A journal publishes scholarly and academic information, usually in a specific domain—like physics, math, sociology, or our current interest, child development. Scholars in these fields publish most of their research in journals, which are the source of core information in virtually every academic discipline.

An increasing number of journals publish information about child development. Among the leading journals in child development are *Developmental Psychology*, *Child Development*, *Developmental Psychopathology*, *Pediatrics*, *Pediatric Nursing*, *Infant Behavior and Development*, *Journal of Research on Adolescence*, *Human Development*, and many others. Also, a number of journals that do not focus solely on development publish articles on various aspects of human development. These journals include *Journal of Educational Psychology*, *Sex Roles*, *Journal of Cross-Cultural Research*, *Journal of Marriage and Family*, *Exceptional Children*, and *Journal of Consulting and Clinical Psychology*.

Every journal has a board of experts who evaluate articles submitted for publication. Each submitted paper is accepted or rejected on the basis of factors such as its contribution to the field, methodological excellence, and clarity of writing. Some of the most prestigious journals reject as many as 80 to 90 percent of the articles submitted.

Journal articles are usually written for other professionals in the specialized field of the journal's focus—therefore, they often contain technical language and terms specific to the discipline that are difficult for nonprofessionals to understand. Their organization often takes this course: abstract, introduction, method, results, discussion, and references.

The *abstract* is a brief summary that appears at the beginning of the article. The abstract lets readers quickly determine whether the article is relevant to their interests. The *introduction* introduces the problem or issue that is being studied. It includes a concise review of research relevant to the topic, theoretical ties, and one or more hypotheses to be tested. The *method* section consists of a clear description of the subjects evaluated in the study, the measures used, and the procedures that were followed. The method section should be sufficiently clear and detailed so that by reading it another researcher could repeat or replicate the study. The *results* section reports the analysis of the data collected. In most cases, the results section includes statistical analyses that are difficult for nonprofessionals to understand. The *discussion* section describes the author's conclusions, inferences, and interpretation of what was found. Statements are usually made about whether the hypotheses presented in the introduction were supported, limitations of the study, and suggestions for future research. The last part of the journal article, called *references*, includes bibliographic information for each source cited in the article. The references section is often a good resource for finding other articles relevant to a topic that interests you.

Where do you find journals such as those we have described? Your college or university library likely has some of them, and some public libraries also carry journals. Most journals are now fully online, and the articles can be accessed through libraries. Online resources such as PsycINFO and PubMed, which can facilitate the search for journal articles, are available to students on many campuses.

Conducting Ethical Research The explosion in technology has forced society to grapple with looming ethical questions that were unimaginable only a few decades ago. The same line of research that enables previously infertile couples to have children might someday let prospective parents "call up and order" the characteristics they prefer in their children. As another example of an ethical dilemma, should embryos left over from procedures for increasing fertility be saved or discarded? Should people with inherited fatal diseases (such as Huntington disease) be discouraged from having children?

Researchers also face ethical questions both new and old. They have a responsibility to anticipate the personal problems their research might cause and to at least inform the participants of the possible fallout. Safeguarding the rights of research participants is a challenge because the potential harm is not always obvious (Graziano & Raulin, 2020).

Ethics in research may affect you personally if you ever serve as a participant in a study. In that event, you need to know your rights as a participant and the responsibilities of researchers to ensure that these rights are safeguarded. If you ever become a researcher in child development yourself, you will need an even deeper understanding of ethics. Even if you only carry out experimental projects in psychology courses, you must consider the rights of the participants in those projects.

Today, proposed research at colleges and universities must pass the scrutiny of a research ethics committee before the research can be initiated. In addition, the American Psychological Association (APA) has developed ethics guidelines for its members, and these guidelines are used as a foundation for other national and international associations of researchers. The APA's code of ethics instructs psychologists to protect their participants from mental and physical harm. The participants' best interests need to be kept foremost in the researcher's mind. The APA's guidelines address four important issues: informed consent, confidentiality, debriefing, and deception.

- *Informed consent.* All participants must know what their participation will involve and what risks might develop. For example, participants in a study on dating should be told beforehand that a questionnaire might stimulate thoughts about issues in their relationship that they have not considered. Participants also should be informed that in some instances a discussion of the issues might improve their relationship, but in others it might worsen the relationship and even end it. Even after informed consent is given, participants have the right to withdraw from the study at any time and for any reason.

- *Confidentiality.* Researchers are responsible for keeping all of the data they gather on individuals completely confidential and, when possible, completely anonymous.

- *Debriefing.* After the study has been completed, participants should be informed of its purpose and the methods that were used. In most cases, the experimenter also can inform participants in a general manner beforehand about the purpose of the research without leading participants to behave in a way they think that the experimenter is expecting. When preliminary information about the study is likely to affect the results, participants can at least be debriefed after the study has been completed.

- *Deception.* This is an ethical issue that researchers debate extensively. In some circumstances, telling the participants beforehand what the research study is about substantially alters the participants' behavior and invalidates the researcher's data. In all cases, however, the psychologist must ensure that the deception will not harm the participants and that the participants will be told the complete nature of the study (debriefed) as soon as possible after the study is completed.

Minimizing Bias   Studies of children's development are most useful when they are conducted without bias or prejudice toward any specific group of people. Of special concern is bias based on gender and bias based on culture or ethnicity.

Gender Bias   For most of its existence, our society has had a strong gender bias, a preconceived notion about the abilities of males and females that prevented individuals from pursuing their own interests and achieving their potential (Garg & others, 2018). Gender bias also has had a less obvious effect within the field of child development. For example, it is not unusual for conclusions to be drawn about females' attitudes and behaviors from research conducted with males as the only participants (Helgeson, 2021).

Furthermore, when researchers find gender differences, their reports sometimes magnify those differences (Hyde & others, 2019). For example, a researcher might report that 74 percent of the boys in a study had high achievement expectations versus only 67 percent of the girls and go on to talk about the differences in some detail. In reality, this might be a rather small difference. It also might disappear if the study were repeated, or the study might have methodological problems that don't allow such strong interpretations.

See the *Connecting with Careers* feature to read about Pamela Trotman Reid, a leading researcher who has studied gender and ethnic bias in development, and who later became a university provost and then president.

Cultural and Ethnic Bias   For years, there has been a growing realization that research on children's development needs to include more children from diverse ethnic groups (Causadias & Umaña-Taylor, 2018; Giuntella, 2017). Historically, children from ethnic minority groups (Black American, Latino American, Asian American, and Native American) were excluded

developmental **connection**

Gender

Gender stereotyping continues to be extensive. Recent research indicates that girls and older children use a higher percentage of gender stereotypes than younger children and boys. Connect to "Socioemotional Development in Middle and Late Childhood."

Pamela Trotman Reid, Educational and Developmental Psychologist

When she was a child, Pam Reid liked to play with chemistry sets. Reid majored in chemistry during college and wanted to become a doctor. However, when some of her friends signed up for a psychology class as an elective, she also decided to take the course. She was intrigued by learning about how people think, behave, and develop—so much so that she changed her major to psychology. Reid went on to obtain her Ph.D. in psychology (American Psychological Association, 2003, p. 16).

For many years, Reid was a professor of education and psychology at the University of Michigan, where she also was a research scientist at the Institute for Research on Women and Gender, focusing on how children and adolescents develop social skills, with a special interest in the development of Black American girls (Reid & Zalk, 2001). She has been involved in numerous community activities, including the creation of a math and technology enrichment program for middle-school girls. In 2004, Reid became provost and executive vice-president at Roosevelt University in Chicago, and subsequently she served as president of the University of Saint Joseph in Hartford,

Pamela Trotman Reid (*center*) with students at the University of Saint Joseph, where she was the president of the university.
Courtesy of Dr. Pam Reid

Connecticut, from 2008 until she retired in 2015. Reid and her husband Irvin Reid (also a psychologist and university president) have established a $1 million endowment fund at Howard University, their alma mater, to support the students and faculty in the Department of Psychology for years to come.

from most research in the United States and simply thought of as variations from the norm or average. If minority children were included in samples and their scores didn't fit the norm, the information was viewed as confounds or "noise" in data and discounted (Gollnick & Chinn, 2021). Given the fact that children from diverse ethnic groups were excluded from research on child development for so long, we can reasonably conclude that children's real lives are perhaps more varied than research data have indicated in the past.

Researchers also have tended to overgeneralize about ethnic groups. **Ethnic gloss** is the use of an ethnic label such as Black American in a superficial way that portrays an ethnic group as being more homogeneous than it really is (Trimble, 2021). For example, a researcher

ethnic gloss The use of an ethnic label such as Black American or Latino in a superficial way that portrays an ethnic group as being more homogeneous than it really is.

Look at these two photographs, one (*left*) of all non–Latino White boys, the other (*right*) of boys and girls from diverse ethnic backgrounds. Consider a topic in child development such as independence seeking, cultural values, parenting education, or health care. *If you were conducting research on this topic, might the results of the study be different depending on whether the participants in your study were the children in the photo on the left or the photo on the right?*
(*left*): Nick David/Getty Images; (*right*): Rolf Bruderer/Getty Images

might describe a research sample like this: "The participants were 60 Latinos." A more complete description of the group might look like this: "The 60 Latino participants were Mexican Americans from middle-income neighborhoods in the southwestern area of Los Angeles. Thirty-six were from homes in which Spanish is the dominant language spoken, 24 from homes in which English is the main language spoken. Thirty were born in the United States, 30 in Mexico. Twenty-eight described themselves as Mexican American, 14 as Mexican, 9 as American, 6 as Chicano, and 3 as Latino." Ethnic gloss can cause researchers to obtain samples of ethnic groups that are not representative of the group's diversity, which can lead to overgeneralization and stereotyping.

Research on the racial and ethnic diversity of children and their families has not been given adequate attention, especially in light of their significant rate of growth within the overall population. Until recently, ethnic minority families were combined in the category "minority," which masks important differences among ethnic groups as well as diversity within an ethnic group. At present and in the foreseeable future, the growth of minority families in the United States will be mainly due to the immigration of Latino and Asian families (U.S. Census Bureau, 2021). Researchers must consider the acculturation level as well as the generational status of parents and children and examine how these factors influence family relationships and child outcomes (Parke, Roisman, & Rose, 2020). More attention needs to be given to biculturalism because many immigrant children and adolescents identify with two or more racial or ethnic groups (Clauss-Ehlers, Roysircar, & Hunter, 2021). In addition, more focus on dual-language learning is needed, given how many children in the United States and the world speak more than one language, especially once they begin formal schooling (Diaz-Rico, 2020).

Review Connect Reflect

(LG3) Summarize why research is important in child development, the main theories of child development, and research methods, designs, and challenges.

Review

- Why is research on child development important?
- What are the main theories of child development?
- What are the main research methods for collecting data about children's development?
- What types of research designs do child development researchers use?
- What are some research challenges in studying children's development?

Connect

- Which of the research methods for collecting data would be appropriate or inappropriate for studying Erikson's stage of trust versus mistrust? Why?

- When you review the timeline in Figure 11, it is quite noticeable that those credited as authoring early developmental theories are all non–Latino White men. How do you think this may have affected their ideas about development and the research their theories instigated?

Reflect Your Own Personal Journey of Life

- Imagine that you are conducting a research study on the sexual attitudes and behaviors of adolescents. What ethical safeguards should you use in conducting the study?

topical connections *looking forward*

You will continue to learn more about theory and research as we further explore the biological underpinnings of children's development. You will read about the evolutionary perspective and the genetic foundations of development. Challenges and choices people encounter when deciding to reproduce are covered, including the new reproductive choices made possible by advancing technology. Many aspects of adopting children also are examined. These topics set the stage for an introduction to the complex interaction of heredity and environment in children's development.

Introduction

1 Why Is Caring for Children Important?

 Explain why it is important to study children's development, and identify five areas in which children's lives need to be improved.

The Importance of Studying Children's Development

Improving the Lives of Children

- Studying children's development is important because it will help you to better understand your own childhood and provide you with strategies for being a competent parent or educator.

- Health and well-being are important areas in which children's lives can be improved. Today, many children in the United States and around the world need improved health care. We now recognize the importance of lifestyles and psychological states in promoting health and well-being.

- Parenting is an important influence on children's development. One-parent families, working parents, and child care are among the family issues that influence children's well-being.

- Education can also contribute to children's health and well-being. There is widespread concern that the education of children needs to be more effective, and there are many views in contemporary education about ways to improve schools.

- Sociocultural contexts are important influences on children's development. Culture, ethnicity, socioeconomic status, and gender are four key aspects of sociocultural contexts.

- Social policy is a national government's course of action designed to influence the welfare of its citizens. Researchers increasingly are conducting studies that are related to social policy.

2 What Characterizes Development?

 Discuss processes, periods, cohort effects, and issues in development.

Biological, Cognitive, and Socioemotional Processes

Periods of Development

Cohort Effects

Issues in Development

- Three key processes of development are biological, cognitive, and socioemotional. Biological processes (such as genetic inheritance) involve changes in an individual's physical nature. Cognitive processes (such as thinking) consist of changes in an individual's thought, intelligence, and language. Socioemotional processes (such as smiling) include changes in an individual's relationships with others, in emotions, and in personality.

- Childhood's five main developmental periods are (1) prenatal—conception to birth, (2) infancy—birth to 18 to 24 months, (3) early childhood—end of infancy to about 5 to 6 years of age, (4) middle and late childhood—about 6 to 11 years of age, and (5) adolescence—begins at about 10 to 12 and ends at about 18 to 22 years of age.

- Cohort effects are due to a person's time of birth, era, or generation but not to actual age. Two characteristics of the generation labeled Millennials are (1) their ethnic diversity and (2) their connection to technology.

- The nature-nurture issue focuses on the extent to which development is mainly influenced by nature (biological inheritance) or nurture (environmental experience).

- Some developmentalists describe development as continuous (gradual, cumulative change), whereas others describe it as discontinuous (a sequence of abrupt stages).

- The early-later experience issue focuses on whether early experiences (especially in infancy) are more important in development than later experiences.

- Most developmentalists recognize that extreme positions on the nature-nurture, continuity-discontinuity, and early-later experience issues are not supported by research. Despite this consensus, they continue to debate the degree to which each factor influences children's development.

3 How Is Child Development a Science?

LG3 Summarize why research is important in child development, the main theories of child development, and research methods, designs, and challenges.

The Importance of Research

- When we base information on personal experience, we aren't always objective. Research provides a vehicle for evaluating the accuracy of information. Scientific research is objective, systematic, and testable. Scientific research is based on the scientific method, which includes these steps: conceptualize the problem, collect data, draw conclusions, and revise research conclusions and theory.

Theories of Child Development

- Psychoanalytic theories describe development as primarily unconscious and as heavily colored by emotion. The two main psychoanalytic theories in developmental psychology are Freud's and Erikson's. Freud proposed that individuals go through five psychosexual stages—oral, anal, phallic, latency, and genital. Erikson's theory emphasizes eight psychosocial stages of development.

- The three main cognitive theories are Piaget's cognitive developmental theory, Vygotsky's sociocultural cognitive theory, and information-processing theory. Cognitive theories emphasize conscious thoughts. In Piaget's theory, children go through four cognitive stages: sensorimotor, preoperational, concrete operational, and formal operational. Vygotsky's sociocultural cognitive theory emphasizes how culture and social interaction guide cognitive development. The information-processing theory emphasizes that individuals manipulate information, monitor it, and strategize about it.

- Three versions of the behavioral and social cognitive approach are Pavlov's classical conditioning, Skinner's operant conditioning, and Bandura's social cognitive theory.

- Ethology stresses that behavior is strongly influenced by biology, is tied to evolution, and is characterized by critical or sensitive periods.

- Ecological theory is Bronfenbrenner's environmental systems view of development. It consists of five environmental systems: microsystem, mesosystem, exosystem, macrosystem, and chronosystem. An eclectic theoretical orientation does not follow any one theoretical approach but rather selects from each theory whatever is considered the best aspects of it.

Research Methods for Collecting Data

- Research methods for collecting data about child development include observation (in a laboratory or a naturalistic setting), survey (questionnaire) or interview, standardized test, case study, and physiological measures.

Research Designs

- Descriptive research aims to observe and record behavior. In correlational research, the goal is to describe the strength of the relationship between two or more events or characteristics.

- Experimental research involves conducting an experiment, which can determine cause and effect. An independent variable is the manipulated, influential, experimental factor. A dependent variable is a factor that can change in an experiment in response to changes in the independent variable.

- Experiments can involve one or more experimental groups and control groups. In random assignment, researchers assign participants to experimental and control groups by chance. When researchers decide about the time span of their research, they can conduct cross-sectional or longitudinal studies.

Research Challenges

- Researchers' ethical responsibilities include seeking participants' informed consent, ensuring their confidentiality, debriefing them about the purpose and potential personal consequences of participating, and avoiding unnecessary deception of participants.

- Researchers need to guard against gender, cultural, and ethnic bias in research. Every effort should be made to make research equitable for all participants. Individuals from varied ethnic backgrounds need to be included as participants in child development research, and overgeneralization about diverse members within a group must be avoided.

key terms

adolescence	cross-sectional approach	gender	psychoanalytic theories
biological processes	culture	hypothesis	scientific method
Bronfenbrenner's ecological theory	descriptive research	infancy	social cognitive theory
case study	development	information-processing theory	social policy
cognitive processes	early childhood	laboratory	socioeconomic status (SES)
cohort effects	early-later experience issue	longitudinal approach	socioemotional processes
context	eclectic theoretical orientation	middle and late childhood	standardized test
continuity-discontinuity issue	Erikson's theory	Millennials	theory
correlation coefficient	ethnic gloss	naturalistic observation	Vygotsky's theory
correlational research	ethnicity	nature-nurture issue	
cross-cultural studies	ethology	Piaget's theory	
	experiment	prenatal period	

key people

Albert Bandura	Erik Erikson	Ivan Pavlov	Lev Vygotsky
John Bowlby	Sigmund Freud	Jean Piaget	
Urie Bronfenbrenner	Konrad Lorenz	Robert Siegler	
Marian Wright Edelman	Ann Masten	B. F. Skinner	

Improving the Lives of Children

STRATEGIES

Lessons for Life

Marian Wright Edelman, founder and former president of the Children's Defense Fund, has been one of the foremost advocates of children's rights and has been instrumental in calling attention to the needs of children. Here are some of the main strategies she advocates for improving not only children's lives but our own as well (Edelman, 1992, pp. xxi, 42, 60):

- *"Don't feel as if you are entitled to anything that you don't sweat and struggle for."* Take the initiative to create opportunities. Don't wait around for people to give you favors. A door never has to stay closed. Push on it until it opens.

- *"Don't be afraid of taking risks or of being criticized."* We all make mistakes. It is only through making mistakes that we learn how to do things right. "It doesn't matter how many times you fall down. What matters is how many times we get up." We need "more courageous shepherds and fewer sheep."

- *"Don't ever stop learning and improving your mind or you're going to get left behind."* College is a great investment, but don't think you can park your mind there and everything you need to know will somehow be magically poured into it. Be an active learner. Be curious and ask questions. Explore new horizons.

- *"Stand up for children."* According to Edelman, this is the most important mission in the world. Parenting and nurturing the next generation of children are our society's most important functions, and we need to take these responsibilities more seriously than we have in the past.

RESOURCES

Children's Defense Fund
www.childrensdefense.org

The Children's Defense Fund provides a strong and effective voice for children and adolescents who cannot vote, lobby, or speak for themselves. The Children's Defense Fund is especially interested in the needs of poor, minority, and handicapped children and adolescents. The fund provides information, technical assistance, and support to a network of state and local child and youth advocates. The Children's Defense Fund publishes a number of excellent books and pamphlets related to children's needs.

Social Policy for Children and Families: A Risk and Resilience Perspective (4th ed., 2021)
William J. Hall, Pal Lanier, Jeffrey M. Jenson, and Mark W. Fraser, Editors
Los Angeles: SAGE

Provides up-to-date coverage of social policy in children's lives to improve their well-being and development.

The SAGE Encyclopedia of Lifespan Human Development (2018)
Marc Bornstein, Editor
Thousand Oaks, CA: SAGE

Leading experts provide up-to-date discussions of many topics in child development.

appendix

Careers in Children's Development

Each of us wants to find a rewarding career and enjoy the work we do. The field of child development offers an amazing breadth of career options that can provide extremely satisfying work.

If you decide to pursue a career in child development, what career options are available to you? There are many. Professors in colleges and universities teach courses in areas of child development, education, family development, nursing, and medicine. Teachers impart knowledge, understanding, and skills to children and adolescents. Counselors, clinical psychologists, nurses, and physicians help parents and children of different ages to cope more effectively with their lives and maintain their well-being. Various professionals work with families to improve the quality of family functioning.

Although an advanced degree is not absolutely necessary in some areas of child development, you usually can expand your opportunities (and income) considerably by obtaining a graduate degree. Many careers in child development pay reasonably well. For example, psychologists earn well above the median salary in the United States. Also, by working in the field of child development you can guide people in improving their lives, understand yourself and others better, possibly advance the state of knowledge in the field, and have an enjoyable time while you are doing these things.

If you are considering a career in child development, would you prefer to work with infants? Children? Adolescents? Parents? Caregivers? As you go through this term, try to spend some time with children of different ages. Observe their behavior. Talk with them about their lives. Think about whether you would like to work with children of this age in your life's work.

Another important aspect of exploring careers is talking with people who work in various jobs. For example, if you have some interest in becoming a school counselor, call a school, ask to speak with a counselor, and set up an appointment to discuss the counselor's career and work.

Something else that should benefit you is working in one or more jobs related to your career interests while you are in college. Many colleges and universities have internships or work experiences for students who major in fields such as child development. In some instances, these jobs earn course credit or pay; in others, they are strictly on a volunteer basis. Take advantage of these opportunities. They can provide you with valuable experiences to help you decide if this is the right career for you—and they can help you get into graduate school, if you decide you want to go.

In the upcoming sections, we profile careers in four areas: education and research; clinical and counseling; medical, nursing, and physical development; and families and relationships. These are not the only career options in child development, but they should provide you with an idea of the range of opportunities available and information about some of the main career avenues you might pursue. In profiling these careers, we address the amount of education required, the nature of the training, and a description of the work.

Education and Research

Numerous career opportunities in child development involve education or research. These range from college professor to child-care director to school psychologist.

College/University Professor

Courses in child development are taught in many programs and schools within colleges and universities, including psychology, education, nursing, child and family studies, social work, and medicine. The work that college professors do includes teaching courses at either the undergraduate or graduate level (or both), conducting research in a specific area, advising students and/or directing their research, and serving on college or university committees. Some college instructors do not conduct research as part of their jobs but instead focus mainly on teaching. Research is most likely to be part of the job description at universities with master's and Ph.D. programs. A Ph.D. or master's degree almost always is required to teach in some area of child development in a college or university. Obtaining a doctoral degree usually takes four to six years of graduate work, and it is becoming common to do additional "post-doctoral" training to further build and refine skills. A master's degree requires approximately two years of graduate work. The training involves taking graduate courses, learning to conduct research, and attending and presenting papers at professional meetings. Many graduate students work as teaching or research assistants for professors in an apprenticeship relationship that helps them to become competent teachers and researchers.

If you are interested in becoming a college or university professor, you might want to make an appointment with your instructor in this class on child development to learn more about the instructor's profession and work.

Researcher

Some individuals in the field of child development work in research positions. In most instances, they have either a master's degree or Ph.D. in some area of child development. The researchers might work at a university, in some cases in a university professor's research program, in a government agency such as the National Institute of Mental Health, or in private industry. Individuals who have full-time research positions in child development generate innovative research ideas, plan studies, and carry out the research by collecting data, analyzing the data, and then interpreting it. Then they will usually attempt to publish the research in a scientific journal. A researcher often works in a collaborative manner with other researchers on a project and may present the research at scientific meetings. One researcher might spend much of the time in a laboratory; another researcher might work primarily in the field, such as in schools, hospitals, and so on.

Elementary School Teacher

The work of an elementary or secondary school teacher involves teaching in one or more subject areas, preparing the curriculum, giving tests, assigning grades, monitoring students' progress, conducting parent-teacher conferences, and attending in-service workshops. Becoming an elementary or secondary school teacher requires a minimum of an undergraduate degree. The training involves taking a wide range of courses with a major or concentration in education, as well as completing a supervised practice-teaching internship.

Exceptional Children (Special Education) Teacher

A teacher of exceptional children spends concentrated time with individual children who have a disability or are gifted. Among the children a teacher of exceptional children might work with are children with learning disabilities, ADHD (attention deficit hyperactivity disorder), intellectual disabilities, or a physical disability such as cerebral palsy. Some of this work will usually be done outside of the student's regular classroom, and some of it will be carried out when the student is in the regular classroom. A teacher of exceptional children works closely with the student's regular classroom teacher and parents to create the best educational program for the student. Becoming a teacher of exceptional children requires a minimum of an undergraduate degree. The training consists of taking a wide range of courses in education and a concentration of courses in educating children with disabilities or children who are gifted. Teachers of exceptional children often continue their education after obtaining their undergraduate degree and attain a master's degree.

Early Childhood Educator

Early childhood educators work on college faculties and have a minimum of a master's degree in their field. In graduate school, they take courses in early childhood education and receive supervisory training in child-care or early childhood programs. Early childhood educators usually teach in community colleges that award an associate's degree in early childhood education.

Preschool/Kindergarten Teacher

Preschool teachers teach mainly 4-year-old children, and kindergarten teachers primarily teach 5-year-old children. They usually have an undergraduate degree in education, specializing in early childhood education. State certification to become a preschool or kindergarten teacher usually is required.

Family and Consumer Science Educator

Family and consumer science educators may specialize in early childhood education or instruct middle and high school students about such matters as nutrition, interpersonal relationships, sexuality, parenting, and human development. Hundreds of colleges and universities throughout the United States offer two- and four-year degree programs in family and consumer science. These programs usually include an internship requirement. Additional education courses may be needed to obtain a teaching certificate. Some family and consumer educators go on to graduate school for further training, which provides a background for possible jobs in college teaching or research.

Educational Psychologist

An educational psychologist most often teaches in a college or university and conducts research in areas of educational psychology such as learning, motivation, classroom management, and assessment. Most educational psychologists have a doctorate in education, which takes four to six years of graduate work. They help to train students who will take various positions in education, including educational psychologist, school psychologist, and teacher.

School Psychologist

School psychologists focus on improving the psychological and intellectual well-being of elementary and secondary school students. They may work in a centralized office in a school district or in one or more schools. They give psychological tests, interview students and their parents, consult with teachers, and may provide counseling to students and their families.

School psychologists usually have a master's or doctoral degree in school psychology. In graduate school, they take courses in counseling, assessment, learning, and other areas of education and psychology.

Clinical and Counseling

There are a wide variety of clinical and counseling jobs that are linked with child development. These range from child clinical psychologist to adolescent drug counselor.

Clinical Psychologist

Clinical psychologists seek to help people with psychological problems. They work in a variety of settings, including colleges and universities, clinics, medical schools, and private practice. Some clinical psychologists only conduct psychotherapy; others do psychological assessment and psychotherapy; and some also do research. Clinical psychologists may specialize in a particular age group, such as children (child clinical psychologist).

Clinical psychologists have either a Ph.D. (which involves clinical and research training) or a Psy.D. degree (which involves only clinical training). This graduate training usually takes five to seven years and includes courses in clinical psychology and a one-year supervised internship in an accredited setting toward the end of the training. In most cases, they must pass a test to become licensed in a state and to call themselves clinical psychologists.

Psychiatrist

Like clinical psychologists, psychiatrists might specialize in working with children (child psychiatry) or adolescents (adolescent psychiatry). Psychiatrists might work in medical schools in teaching and research roles, in a medical clinic, or in private practice. In addition to administering drugs to help improve the lives of people with psychological problems, psychiatrists also may conduct psychotherapy. Psychiatrists obtain a medical degree and then do a residency in psychiatry. Medical school takes approximately four years, and the psychiatry residency takes another three to four years. Unlike psychologists (who do not go to medical school), in most states psychiatrists can administer drugs to clients.

Counseling Psychologist

Counseling psychologists work in the same settings as clinical psychologists and may do psychotherapy, teach, or conduct research. In many instances, however, counseling psychologists do not work with individuals who have a severe mental disorder. A counseling psychologist might specialize in working with children, adolescents, and/or families.

Counseling psychologists go through much of the same training as clinical psychologists, but in a graduate program in counseling rather than clinical psychology. Counseling psychologists have either a master's degree or a doctoral degree. They

also must go through a licensing procedure. One type of master's degree in counseling leads to the designation of licensed professional counselor.

School Counselor

School counselors help to identify students' abilities and interests, guide students in developing academic plans, and explore career options with students. They may help students cope with adjustment problems. They may work with students individually, in small groups, or even in a classroom. They often consult with parents, teachers, and school administrators when trying to help students with their problems.

High school counselors advise students on choosing a major, fulfilling admissions requirements for college, taking entrance exams, applying for financial aid, and enrolling in appropriate vocational and technical training. Elementary school counselors are mainly involved in counseling students about social and personal problems. They may observe children in the classroom and at play as part of their work. School counselors usually have a master's degree in counseling.

Career Counselor

Career counselors help individuals to identify their best career options and guide them in applying for jobs. They may work in private industry or at a college or university. They usually interview individuals and give them vocational or psychological tests to target careers that fit their interests and abilities. Sometimes they help individuals to create résumés or conduct mock interviews to help them feel comfortable in a job interview. They may create and promote job fairs or other recruiting events to help individuals obtain jobs.

Social Worker

Social workers often are involved in helping people with social or economic problems. They may investigate, evaluate, and attempt to rectify reported cases of abuse, neglect, endangerment, or domestic disputes. They can intervene in families if necessary and provide counseling and referral services to individuals and families.

Social workers have a minimum of an undergraduate degree from a school of social work that includes course work in various areas of sociology and psychology. Some social workers also have a master's or doctoral degree. They often work for publicly funded agencies at the city, state, or national level, although increasingly they work in the private sector in areas such as drug rehabilitation and family counseling.

In some cases, social workers specialize in a certain area, as is true of a medical social worker who has a master's degree in social work (MSW). This involves graduate course work and supervised clinical experiences in medical settings. A medical social worker might coordinate a variety of support services provided to people with a severe or long-term disability. Family-care social workers often work with families who need support services.

Drug Counselor

Drug counselors provide counseling to individuals with drug abuse problems. They may work on an individual basis with a substance abuser or conduct group therapy sessions. They may work in private practice, with a state or federal government agency, with a company, or in a hospital setting. Some drug counselors specialize in working with adolescents or families. Most states provide a certification procedure for obtaining a license to practice drug counseling.

At a minimum, drug counselors go through an associate's or certificate program. Many have an undergraduate degree in substance-abuse counseling, and some have master's and doctoral degrees.

Medical, Nursing, and Physical Development

Careers in child development include a wide range of occupations in the medical and nursing areas, as well as jobs that pertain to improving some aspect of the child's physical development.

Obstetrician/Gynecologist

An obstetrician/gynecologist provides prenatal and postnatal health care and performs deliveries in maternity cases. The individual also treats diseases and injuries of the female reproductive system. Obstetricians may work in private practice, in a medical clinic, in a hospital, or in a medical school. Becoming an obstetrician/gynecologist requires a medical degree plus three to five years of residency in obstetrics/gynecology.

Pediatrician

A pediatrician monitors infants' and children's health, works to prevent disease or injury, helps children attain optimal health, and treats children with health problems. Pediatricians may work in private practice, in a medical clinic, in a hospital, or in a medical school. As medical doctors, they can administer drugs to children and may counsel parents and children on ways to improve the children's health. Many pediatricians on the faculty of medical schools also teach and conduct research on children's health and diseases. Pediatricians have attained a medical degree and completed a three- to five-year residency in pediatrics.

Neonatal Nurse

A neonatal nurse is involved in the delivery and care of the newborn infant. The neonatal nurse may work to improve the health and well-being of full-term infants or be involved in the delivery of care to premature and critically ill neonates.

A minimum of an undergraduate degree in nursing with a specialization in the newborn is required. This training involves course work in nursing and the biological sciences, as well as supervisory clinical experiences.

Nurse-Midwife

A nurse-midwife formulates and provides comprehensive care to selected maternity patients, cares for the expectant mother as she prepares to give birth and guides her through the birth process, and cares for the postpartum patient. The nurse-midwife also may provide care to the newborn, counsel parents on the infant's development and parenting, and provide guidance about health practices. Becoming a nurse-midwife generally requires an undergraduate degree from a school of nursing. A nurse-midwife most often works in a hospital setting.

Pediatric Nurse

Pediatric nurses have a degree in nursing that takes from two to five years to complete. Some also may obtain a master's or doctoral degree in pediatric nursing. Pediatric nurses take courses in biological sciences, nursing care, and pediatrics, usually in a school of nursing. They also undergo supervised clinical experiences in medical settings. They monitor infants' and children's health, work to prevent disease or injury, and help children attain optimal health. They may work in hospitals or schools of nursing, or with pediatricians in private practice or at a medical clinic.

Audiologist

An audiologist has a minimum of an undergraduate degree in hearing science. This includes courses and supervisory training. Audiologists assess and identify the presence and severity of hearing loss, as well as problems in balance. Some audiologists also go on to obtain a master's and/or doctoral degree. They may work in a medical clinic, with a physician in private practice, in a hospital, or in a medical school.

Speech Therapist

Speech therapists are health-care professionals who are trained to identify, assess, and treat speech and language problems. They may work with physicians, psychologists, social workers, and other health-care professionals as a team to help individuals with physical or psychological problems that include speech and language disorders. Speech pathologists have a minimum of an undergraduate degree in speech and hearing science or communication disorders. They may work in private practice, in hospitals and medical schools, and in government agencies with individuals of any age. Some specialize in working with children or with a particular type of speech disorder.

Genetic Counselor

Genetic counselors work as members of a health-care team, providing information and support to families who have members with birth defects or genetic disorders and to families who may be at risk for a variety of inherited conditions. They identify families at risk and provide supportive counseling. They serve as educators and resource people for other health-care professionals and the public. Almost half of these individuals work in university medical centers, and another one-fourth work in private hospital settings.

Most genetic counselors enter the field after majoring in undergraduate disciplines such as biology, genetics, psychology, nursing, public health, and social work. They have specialized graduate degrees and experience in medical genetics and counseling.

Families and Relationships

A number of careers involve working with families and relationship problems. These range from being a child welfare worker to a marriage and family therapist.

Child Welfare Worker

A child welfare worker is employed by the child protective services unit of each state. The child welfare worker protects the child's rights, evaluates any maltreatment the child might experience or grief a child feels if a parent dies, and may have the child removed from the home if necessary. A child social worker has a minimum of an undergraduate degree in social work.

Child Life Specialist

Child life specialists work with children and their families when the child needs to be hospitalized. They monitor the child patient's activities, seek to reduce the child's stress, help the child cope effectively, and assist the child in enjoying the hospital experience as much as possible. Child life specialists may provide parent education and develop individualized treatment plans based on an assessment of the child's development, temperament, medical plan, and available social supports.

Child life specialists have an undergraduate degree. As undergraduates, they take courses in child development and education and usually take additional courses in a child life program.

Marriage and Family Therapist

Marriage and family therapists work on the principle that many individuals who have psychological problems benefit when psychotherapy is provided in the context of a marital or family relationship. Marriage and family therapists may provide marital therapy, couples therapy to individuals in a relationship who are not married, and family therapy to two or more members of a family.

Marriage and family therapists have a master's or doctoral degree. They go through a training program in graduate school similar to that of a clinical psychologist but with a focus on marital and family relationships. To practice marital and family therapy in most states, it is necessary to go through a licensing procedure.

These are only a handful of careers that require knowledge of developmental psychology. *What other careers can you think of that require knowledge of children's development?*

section two

There are one hundred and ninety-three living species of monkeys and apes. One hundred and ninety-two of them are covered with hair. The exception is the naked ape, self-named Homo sapiens.

—**Desmond Morris**
British Zoologist, 20th Century

Beginnings

The rhythm and meaning of life involve beginnings. Questions are raised about how, from so simple a beginning, endless forms develop, grow, and mature. What was this organism, what is this organism, and what will this organism be? In this section, you will read "Biological Beginnings," "Prenatal Development," and "Birth."

chapter 2

BIOLOGICAL BEGINNINGS

chapter outline

① What Is the Evolutionary Perspective?

Learning Goal 1 Discuss the evolutionary perspective on development.

Natural Selection and Adaptive Behavior
Evolutionary Psychology

② What Are the Genetic Foundations of Development?

Learning Goal 2 Describe what genes are and how they influence human development.

The Collaborative Gene
Genes and Chromosomes
Genetic Principles
Chromosomal and Gene-Linked Abnormalities

③ What Are Some Reproductive Challenges and Choices?

Learning Goal 3 Identify some important reproductive challenges and choices.

Prenatal Diagnostic Tests
Infertility and Reproductive Technology
Adoption

④ How Do Heredity and Environment Interact?

Learning Goal 4 Explain some of the ways that heredity and environment interact to produce individual differences in development.

Behavior Genetics
Heredity-Environment Correlations
The Epigenetic View and Gene × Environment (G × E) Interaction
Conclusions About Heredity-Environment Interaction

Image Source/Getty Images

Jim Springer and Jim Lewis are identical twins. They were separated at 4 weeks of age and did not see each other again until they were 39 years old. Both worked as part-time deputy sheriffs, vacationed in Florida, drove Chevrolets, had dogs named Toy, and married and divorced women named Betty. One twin named his son James Allan, and the other named his son James Alan. Both liked math but not spelling, enjoyed carpentry and mechanical drawing, chewed their fingernails down to the nubs, had almost identical drinking and smoking habits, had hemorrhoids, put on 10 pounds at about the same point in development, first suffered headaches at the age of 18, and had similar sleep patterns.

Jim and Jim do have some differences. One wears his hair over his forehead, the other slicks it back and has sideburns. One expresses himself best orally; the other is more proficient in writing. But, for the most part, their profiles are remarkably similar.

Jim and Jim were part of the Minnesota Study of Twins Reared Apart, directed by Thomas Bouchard and his colleagues (Bouchard, 1995, 2008; Johnson & others, 2007). The study brings identical twins (identical genetically because they come from the same fertilized egg) and fraternal twins (who come from different fertilized eggs) from all over the world to Minneapolis to investigate their lives. There the twins complete personality

The Jim and Jim twins.
Ira Berger/Alamy Stock Photo

and intelligence tests, and they provide detailed medical histories, including information about diet and smoking, exercise habits, chest X-rays, heart stress tests, and electroencephalograms (EEGs). The twins are asked more than 15,000 questions about their family and childhood, personal interests, vocational orientation, values, and aesthetic judgments.

Another pair of identical twins in the Minnesota study, Daphne and Barbara, are called the "giggle sisters" because, after being reunited, they were always making each other laugh. A thorough search of their adoptive families' histories revealed no gigglers. The giggle sisters ignored stress, avoided conflict and controversy whenever possible, and showed no interest in politics.

topical connections   looking *back*

We have reviewed the historical background of child development, its growing importance as a field of study, and the way its researchers conduct their work. You studied the key processes and periods in child development and identified ways in which the science of child development can improve the lives of children. The forthcoming discussion of genetics and the previous coverage of theories (psychoanalytic, cognitive, behavioral and social cognitive, ethological, and ecological) in the "Introduction" chapter provide the background knowledge to help you examine one of development's major issues—how development is influenced jointly by heredity (nature) and environment (nurture).

Two other identical twin sisters were separated at 6 weeks and reunited in their fifties. Both described hauntingly similar nightmares in which they had doorknobs and fishhooks in their mouths as they suffocated to death. The nightmares began during early adolescence and had stopped within the past 10 to 12 years. Both women were bed wetters until about 12 or 13 years of age, and their educational and marital histories are remarkably similar.

When genetically identical twins who were separated as infants show such striking similarities in their tastes and habits and choices, can we conclude that their genes must have caused the development of those tastes and habits and choices? Other possible causes need to be considered. The twins shared not only the same genes but also some experiences. Some of the separated twins lived together for several months prior to their adoption; some of the twins had been reunited prior to testing (in some cases, many years earlier); adoption agencies often place twins in similar homes; and even strangers who spend several hours together and start comparing their lives are likely to come up with some coincidental similarities (Segal, Montoya, & Becker, 2018). The Minnesota study of identical twins points to both the importance of the genetic basis of human development and the need for further research on genetic and environmental factors.

preview

The examples of Jim and Jim, the giggle sisters, and the identical twins who had the same nightmares stimulate us to think about our genetic heritage and the biological foundations of our existence. Organisms are not like billiard balls, moved by simple, external forces to predictable positions on life's pool table. Environmental experiences and biological foundations work together to make us who we are. Our exploration of life's biological beginnings focuses on evolution, genetic foundations, challenges and choices regarding reproduction, and the interaction of heredity and environment.

1 What Is the Evolutionary Perspective?

 LG1 Discuss the evolutionary perspective on development.

Natural Selection and Adaptive Behavior

Evolutionary Psychology

As our earliest ancestors left the forest to feed in the savannahs and then to form hunting societies on the open plains, their minds and behaviors changed as humans gradually became the dominant species on Earth. How did this evolution come about?

NATURAL SELECTION AND ADAPTIVE BEHAVIOR

Natural selection is the evolutionary process by which those individuals of a species that are best adapted are the ones that survive and reproduce. To understand what this means, let's return to the middle of the nineteenth century, when the British naturalist Charles Darwin was traveling around the world, observing many different species of animals in their natural surroundings. Darwin, who published his observations and thoughts in *On the Origin of Species* (1859), noted that most organisms reproduce at rates that would cause enormous increases in the population of most species, and yet populations remain nearly constant. He reasoned that an intense, constant struggle for food, water, and resources must occur among the many young born in each generation, because many of the young do not survive. Those that do survive, and reproduce, pass on their characteristics to the next generation. Darwin observed that these survivors are better *adapted* to their world than are the nonsurvivors (Johansson & others, 2021; Johnson, 2017). The best-adapted individuals survive to leave the most offspring. Over the course of many generations, organisms with the characteristics needed for survival make up an increasing percentage of the population. Over many, many generations, this could produce a gradual modification of the whole population. If environmental conditions change, however, other characteristics might become favored by natural selection, moving the species in a different direction (Al-Shawaf, Zreik, & Buss, 2021).

All organisms must adapt to particular places, climates, food sources, and ways of life (Simon, 2017; Maharian & others, 2021). An eagle's claws are a physical adaptation that facilitates predation. *Adaptive behavior* is behavior that promotes an organism's survival in the natural habitat. For example, attachment between a caregiver and a baby ensures the infant's closeness to a caregiver for feeding and protection from danger, thus increasing the infant's chances of survival. Or consider pregnancy sickness, which is a tendency for women to become nauseated during pregnancy and avoid certain foods (Placek, Madhivanan, & Hagen, 2017). Women with pregnancy sickness tend to avoid foods that are more likely to be higher in toxins that could harm the fetus. Thus, pregnancy sickness may be an evolution-based adaptation that enhances the offspring's survival.

How does the attachment of this Vietnamese baby to its mother reflect the evolutionary process of adaptive behavior?
Matt Hahnewald Photography/Alamy Stock Photo

EVOLUTIONARY PSYCHOLOGY

Although Darwin introduced the theory of evolution by natural selection in 1859, his ideas have only recently become a popular framework for explaining behavior (Colmenares & Hernandez-Lloreda, 2017; Whiten, 2017). Psychology's newest approach, **evolutionary psychology,** emphasizes the importance of adaptation, reproduction, and "survival of the fittest" in shaping behavior. "Fit" in this sense refers to the ability to bear offspring that survive long enough to bear offspring of their own. In this view, natural selection favors behaviors that increase reproductive success: the ability to pass your genes to the next generation (Workman & Reader, 2021).

David Buss (2020) has been especially influential in stimulating new interest in how evolution can explain human behavior. He argues that just as evolution shapes our physical features, such as body shape and height, it also pervasively influences our decision making, our degree of aggression, our fears, and our mating patterns. For example, assume that our ancestors were hunters and gatherers on the plains and that men did most of the hunting and women stayed close to home, gathering seeds and plants for food. If you have to travel some distance from your home in an effort to find and slay a fleeing animal, you need not only certain physical traits but also the ability to use certain types of spatial thinking. Men born with these traits would be more likely than men without them to survive, to bring home lots of food, and to be considered attractive mates—and thus to reproduce and pass on these characteristics to their children. In other words, if such assumptions were correct, these traits would provide a reproductive advantage for males and, over many generations, men with good spatial thinking skills might become more numerous in the population. Critics point out that this scenario might or might not have actually happened.

Anthropological research in current hunter-gatherer societies, such as the Hadza in Tanzania, suggests that mothers' and grandmothers' foraging supplies the large majority of families' caloric intake, as male hunters are successful on only 3.4 percent of hunting excursions (Hawkes, 2020). First-time mothers' foraging skills are correlated with infants' growth, but after the birth of a second infant and as mothers' caregiving responsibilities increase, the correlation between mothers' foraging skills and infant growth disappears and a correlation between grandmothers' foraging skills and infant growth emerges as grandmothers more actively participate in foraging to support the family (Hawkes, 2020). These findings have several implications for understanding aspects of human evolution such as the fact that humans are the only primate species in which women live long past reproductive age and why social orientation and cooperation are so central to our species (Hrdy & Burkart, 2020).

Evolutionary Developmental Psychology Recently, researchers have shown increasing interest in using the concepts of evolutionary psychology to understand human

evolutionary psychology Branch of psychology that emphasizes the importance of adaptation, reproduction, and "survival of the fittest" in shaping behavior.

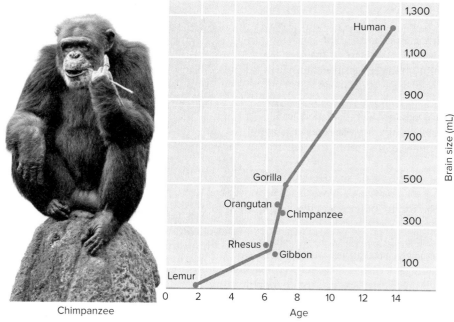

Chimpanzee

FIGURE 1

THE BRAIN SIZES OF VARIOUS PRIMATES AND HUMANS IN RELATION TO THE LENGTH OF THE CHILDHOOD PERIOD. Compared with other primates, humans have both a larger brain and a longer childhood period. *What conclusions can you draw from the relation indicated by this graph?* *Source:* Bonner, J., "Brain Sizes of Various Primates and Humans," in *The Evolution of Culture in Animals*, Princeton, NJ: Princeton University Press, 1983.

Photo: Tier Und Naturfotografie J und C Sohns/Getty Images

Children in all cultures are interested in the tools that adults in their cultures use. For example, this child near the Angkor Temples in Cambodia is using a machete. *Might the child's behavior be biologically based or due to both biological and environmental influences?*

Sirapanitkul/123RF

development (De Baca & Ellis, 2021; Lickliter, 2017). Following are some ideas proposed by evolutionary developmental psychologists (Bjorklund, 2020).

An extended childhood period might have evolved because humans require time to develop a large brain and learn the complexity of human societies (see Figure 1). Humans take longer to become reproductively mature than any other mammal. During this extended childhood period, they develop a large brain and the experiences needed to become competent adults in a complex society.

Many evolved psychological mechanisms are domain-specific. That is, the mechanisms apply only to a specific aspect of a person's makeup. According to evolutionary psychology, information processing is one example. In this view, the mind is not a general-purpose device that can be applied equally to a vast array of problems. Instead, as our ancestors dealt with certain recurring problems such as hunting and finding shelter, specialized modules might have evolved that processed information related to those problems. For example, such specialized modules might include a module for physical knowledge about tracking animals, a module for mathematical knowledge for trading, and a module for language.

Evolved mechanisms are not always adaptive in contemporary society. Some behaviors that were adaptive for our prehistoric ancestors may not serve us well today. For example, the food-scarce environment of our ancestors likely led to humans' propensity to gorge when food is available and to crave high-caloric foods, a trait that might lead to an epidemic of obesity when food is plentiful.

Evaluating Evolutionary Psychology

Although evolutionary psychology is getting increased attention, it is just one theoretical approach among many (Hyde, 2014). Like the theories described earlier, it has limitations, weaknesses, and critics (Davis, 2021). Albert Bandura (1998), whose social cognitive theory was described earlier, acknowledges the important influence of evolution on human adaptation. However, he rejects what he calls "one-sided evolutionism," which sees social behavior as the product of evolved biology. An alternative is a *bidirectional view* in which environmental and biological conditions influence each other. In this view evolutionary pressures created changes in biological structures that allowed the use of tools, which enabled our ancestors to manipulate their environment, constructing new environmental conditions. In turn, environmental innovations produced new selection pressures that led to the evolution of specialized biological systems for consciousness, thought, and language.

In other words, evolution gave us bodily structures and biological potentialities; it does not dictate behavior. People have used their biological capacities to produce diverse cultures—aggressive and peaceful, egalitarian and autocratic. As American scientist Stephen Jay Gould (1981) concluded, in most domains of human functioning, biology allows a broad range of cultural possibilities.

The "big picture" idea of natural selection leading to the development of human traits and behaviors is difficult to refute or test because evolution occurs on a time scale that does not lend itself to empirical study. Thus, studying specific genes in humans and other species—and their links to traits and behaviors—may be the best approach for testing ideas that emerge from the evolutionary psychology perspective.

2 What Are the Genetic Foundations of Development?

LG2 Describe what genes are and how they influence human development.

| The Collaborative Gene | Genes and Chromosomes | Genetic Principles | Chromosomal and Gene-Linked Abnormalities |

Genetic influences on behavior evolved over time and across many species. Our many traits and characteristics that are genetically influenced have a long evolutionary history that is retained in our DNA. In other words, our DNA is not just inherited from our parents; it includes what we inherited as a species from other species that were our ancestors.

How are characteristics that suit a species for survival transmitted from one generation to the next? Darwin could not answer this question because genes and the principles of genetics had not yet been discovered. Each of us carries a human "genetic code" that we inherited from our parents. Because a fertilized egg carries this human code, a fertilized human egg cannot grow into an egret, eagle, or elephant.

THE COLLABORATIVE GENE

Each of us began life as a single cell weighing about one twenty-millionth of an ounce! This tiny piece of matter housed our entire genetic code—information that helped us grow from that single cell to a person made of trillions of cells, each containing a replica of the original code. That code is carried by DNA, which includes our genes. What are genes and what do they do? For the answer, we need to look into our cells.

The nucleus of each human cell contains **chromosomes,** which are threadlike structures made up of deoxyribonucleic acid, or DNA. **DNA** is a complex molecule that has a double helix shape, like a spiral staircase, and contains genetic information. **Genes,** the units of hereditary information, are short segments of DNA, as you can see in Figure 2. They help cells to reproduce themselves and to assemble proteins. Proteins, in turn, are the building blocks of cells as well as the regulators that direct the body's processes (Kieler, Hofmann, & Schabbauer, 2021).

Each gene has its own location, its own designated place on a particular chromosome. Today, there is a great deal of enthusiasm about efforts to discover the specific locations of genes that are linked to certain functions and developmental outcomes (Rood & Regev, 2021). An important step in this direction was accomplished when the Human Genome Project completed a preliminary map of the human *genome*—the complete set of developmental information for creating proteins that initiate the making of a human organism (Johnson, 2017).

chromosomes Threadlike structures that come in 23 pairs, with one member of each pair coming from each parent. Chromosomes contain the genetic substance DNA.

DNA A complex molecule with a double helix shape; contains genetic information.

genes Units of hereditary information composed of DNA. Genes help cells to reproduce themselves and manufacture the proteins that maintain life.

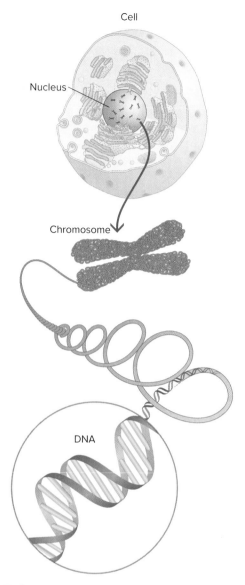

Cell

Nucleus

Chromosome

DNA

FIGURE 2

CELLS, CHROMOSOMES, DNA, AND GENES.
(*Top*) The body contains trillions of cells. Each cell contains a central structure, the nucleus. (*Middle*) Chromosomes are threadlike structures located in the nucleus of the cell. Chromosomes are composed of DNA. (*Bottom*) DNA has the structure of a spiral staircase. A gene is a segment of DNA.

How Would You...?
If you were a **psychologist,** how would you explain to an enthusiast of the Human Genome Project that genes don't provide an exact blueprint for how children's development will unfold?

Among the major approaches to gene identification and discovery that are being used today are the genome-wide association method, linkage analysis, next-generation sequencing, and the 1,000 Genomes Project:

- Completion of the Human Genome Project has led to use of the *genome-wide association method* to identify genetic variations linked to a particular disease, such as obesity, cancer, or cardiovascular disease (Akiyama, 2021). To conduct a genome-wide association study, researchers obtain DNA from individuals who have the disease and those who don't have it. Then, each participant's complete set of DNA, or genome, is purified from the blood or other cells and scanned on machines to determine markers of genetic variation. If the genetic variations occur more frequently in people who have the disease, the variations point to the region in the human genome where the disorder-causing problem exists. Genome-wide association studies have been conducted for cancer (Hikino & others, 2022); obesity (Loos & Yeo, 2022); cardiovascular disease (Tcheandjieu & others, 2022); depression (Wainberg & others, 2022); and many other disorders.

- *Linkage analysis*, in which the goal is to discover the location of a gene (or genes) in relation to a marker gene (whose position is already known), is often used in the search for a disease-related gene (Blanton, 2021). Genes transmitted to offspring tend to be in close proximity to each other, so the gene(s) involved in the disease is usually located near the marker gene. Gene linkage studies are now being conducted on a wide variety of disorders, including attention deficit hyperactivity disorder (Corominas & others, 2020), autism spectrum disorders (Choi & An, 2021), and depression (Wong & others, 2017).

- *Next-generation sequencing* is a term used to describe the vast increase in genetic data generated at a much reduced cost and in a much shorter period of time. Next-generation sequencing has considerably increased knowledge about genetic influences on development in recent years (Remec & others, 2021). Using recently developed next-generation sequencing, an entire human genome can be sequenced in one day. Prior to recent improvements, deciphering the human genome took more than 10 years! The new technology sequences millions of small DNA fragments (Foox & others, 2021).

- The human genome varies between individuals in small but very important ways. Understanding these variations will require examination of the whole genomes of many individuals. A current project that began in 2008, the Thousand Genomes Project, is the most detailed study of human genetic variation to date. This project is determining the genomic sequences of more than 1,000 individuals from different ethnic groups around the world (Byrska-Bishop & others, 2022). Compiling complete descriptions of the genetic variations of many people will make it possible for researchers to conduct studies of genetic variations in disease in a more detailed manner.

As scientists learn more about the human genome, the estimated number of human genes continues to change. Currently it is estimated that humans have 20,000 protein-coding genes (Nurk & others, 2022). Previously, scientists had thought that humans had 100,000 or more genes. They had also believed that each gene programmed just one protein. In fact, humans appear to have far more proteins than they have genes, so there cannot be a one-to-one correspondence between genes and proteins (Zaslavsky & others, 2021).

A gene is not translated, in automaton-like fashion, into one and only one protein. Genes do not act independently, but rather in combination with other genes and the environment.

Rather than being a group of independent genes, the human genome consists of many genes that collaborate with each other and with nongenetic factors inside and outside the body (Moore, 2018). The collaboration operates at many points. For example, the cellular machinery mixes, matches, and links small pieces of DNA to reproduce the genes, and that machinery is influenced by what is going on around it.

Whether a gene is turned "on"—that is, working to assemble proteins—is also a matter of collaboration. The activity of genes (genetic expression) is affected by their environment

(Moore, 2018). For example, hormones that circulate in the blood make their way into the cell where they can turn genes "on" and "off." And the flow of hormones can be affected by environmental conditions, such as light, day length, nutrition, and behavior. Numerous studies have shown that external events outside the original cell and the person, as well as events inside the cell, can excite or inhibit gene expression (Lickliter & Witherington, 2017).

Factors such as stress, exercise, nutrition, respiration, radiation, temperature, and sleep can influence gene expression (Zhang & others, 2017). For example, an increase in the concentration of stress hormones such as cortisol produces an increase in DNA damage and slows the rate of repair if damage occurs (Hare & others, 2018). Exposure to radiation also changes the rate of DNA synthesis in cells (Kim & others, 2017).

Scientists also have found that certain genes can be turned off or on as a result of exercise and diet through the process of *methylation*, in which a methyl group of atoms attaches to the outside of a gene (Ying & Chen, 2023). This process alters the gene's expression. Researchers also have found that tobacco use may affect gene behavior through the process of methylation (Christiansen & others, 2021; Godfrey & others, 2017).

GENES AND CHROMOSOMES

Genes are not only collaborative, but they are enduring. How do the genes manage to get passed from generation to generation and end up in all of the trillion cells in the body? Three processes explain the heart of the story: mitosis, meiosis, and fertilization.

Mitosis, Meiosis, and Fertilization   All of the cells in your body, except the sperm and egg, have 46 chromosomes arranged in 23 pairs. These cells reproduce through a process called mitosis. During **mitosis,** the cell's nucleus—including the chromosomes—duplicates itself and the cell divides. Two new cells are formed, each containing the same DNA as the original cell, arranged in the same 23 pairs of chromosomes.

However, a different type of cell division—**meiosis**—forms eggs and sperm (which also are called *gametes*). During meiosis, a cell of the testes (in men) or ovaries (in women) duplicates its chromosomes but then divides *twice*, thus forming four cells, each of which has only half of the genetic material of the parent cell. By the end of meiosis, each egg or sperm has 23 *unpaired* chromosomes.

During **fertilization,** an egg and a sperm fuse to create a single cell, called a **zygote** (see Figure 3). In the zygote, the 23 unpaired chromosomes from the egg and the 23 unpaired chromosomes from the sperm combine to form one set of 23 paired chromosomes—one chromosome of each pair having come from the mother's egg and the other from the father's sperm. In this manner, each parent contributes half of the offspring's genetic material.

Figure 4 shows 23 paired chromosomes of a male and a female. The members of each pair of chromosomes are both similar and different: Each chromosome in the pair contains varying forms of the same genes, at the same location on the chromosome. A gene that influences hair color, for example, is located on both members of one pair of chromosomes, in the same

mitosis Cellular reproduction in which the cell's nucleus duplicates itself with two new cells being formed, each containing the same DNA as the parent cell, arranged in the same 23 pairs of chromosomes.

meiosis A specialized form of cell division that occurs to form eggs and sperm (also known as *gametes*).

fertilization A stage in reproduction when an egg and a sperm fuse to create a single cell, called a zygote.

zygote A single cell formed through fertilization.

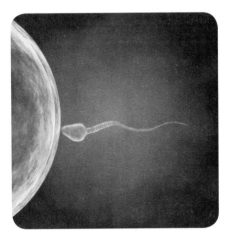

FIGURE **3**

A SINGLE SPERM PENETRATING AN EGG AT THE POINT OF FERTILIZATION

3Dalia/Shutterstock

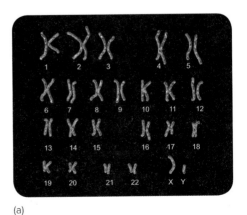

(a)

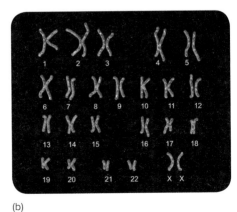

(b)

FIGURE **4**

THE GENETIC DIFFERENCE BETWEEN MALES AND FEMALES. Set (*a*) shows the chromosome structure of a male, and set (*b*) shows the chromosome structure of a female. The last pair of 23 pairs of chromosomes is in the bottom right box of each set. Notice that the Y chromosome of the male is smaller than the X chromosome of the female. To obtain this kind of chromosomal picture, a cell is removed from a person's body, usually from the inside of the mouth. The chromosomes are stained by chemical treatment, magnified extensively, and then photographed.

Kateryna Kon/Shutterstock

location on each. However, one of those chromosomes might carry a gene associated with blond hair; the other chromosome in the pair might carry the gene associated with brown hair.

Do you notice any obvious differences between the chromosomes of the male and the chromosomes of the female in Figure 4? The difference lies in the 23rd pair. Ordinarily, in females this pair consists of two chromosomes called *X chromosomes;* in males the 23rd pair consists of an X and a *Y chromosome.* The presence of a Y chromosome makes an individual genetically male, and the presence of two X chromosomes makes an individual genetically female.

Sources of Variability Combining the genes of two parents in offspring increases genetic variability in the population, which is valuable for a species because it provides more characteristics for natural selection to operate on (Simon, 2017). In fact, the human genetic process creates several important sources of variability.

First, the chromosomes in the zygote are not exact copies of those in the mother's ovaries or the father's testes. During the formation of the sperm and egg in meiosis, the members of each pair of chromosomes are separated, but which chromosome in the pair goes to the gamete is a matter of chance. In addition, before the pairs separate, pieces of the two chromosomes in each pair are exchanged, creating a new combination of genes on each chromosome (Mader & Windelspecht, 2017). Thus, when chromosomes from the mother's egg and the father's sperm are brought together in the zygote, the result is a truly unique combination of genes.

If each zygote is unique, how do identical twins like those discussed in the opening of the chapter exist? *Identical twins* (also called monozygotic twins) develop from a single zygote that splits into two genetically identical replicas, each of which becomes a person. *Fraternal twins* (called dizygotic twins) develop when two eggs are each fertilized by a different sperm, creating two zygotes that are genetically no more similar than ordinary siblings.

Another source of variability comes from within the DNA itself (Akingbuwa & others, 2021). Chance, a mistake by cellular machinery, or damage from an environmental agent such as radiation may produce a *mutated gene,* which is a permanently altered segment of DNA (Cowan & Bunn, 2016).

Even when their genes are identical, however, people vary. The difference between genotypes and phenotypes helps us to understand this source of variability (Klug & others, 2017). All of a person's genetic material makes up their **genotype.** However, not all of the genetic material is apparent in our observed and measurable characteristics. A **phenotype** consists of observable characteristics. Phenotypes include physical characteristics (such as height, weight, and hair color) and psychological characteristics (such as personality and intelligence).

How does the process from genotype to phenotype work? It's very complex, but at a very basic level in a cell, DNA information is transcribed to RNA (ribonucleic acid), which in turn is translated into amino acids that will become proteins (Starr, Evers, & Starr, 2018). Once proteins have been assembled, they become capable of producing phenotype traits and characteristics. Also, environments interact with genotypes to produce phenotypes.

Thus, for each genotype, a range of phenotypes can be expressed, providing another source of variability (Freeman & others, 2017). An individual can inherit the genetic potential to grow very large, for example, but environmental influences involving good nutrition, among other things, will be essential to determining that person's height. This is referred to as heredity-environment interaction (or gene-environment interaction).

GENETIC PRINCIPLES

What determines how a genotype is expressed to create a particular phenotype? Much is unknown about the answer to this question (Moore, 2018). However, a number of genetic principles have been discovered, among them those of dominant-recessive genes, sex-linked genes, genetic imprinting, and polygenically determined characteristics.

genotype A person's genetic heritage; the actual genetic material.

phenotype The way an individual's genotype is expressed in observed and measurable characteristics.

Dominant-Recessive Genes Principle In some cases, one gene of a pair always exerts its effects; it is *dominant,* overriding the potential influence of the other gene, called the *recessive* gene. This is the *dominant-recessive genes principle.* A recessive gene exerts its influence only if the two genes of a pair are both recessive. If you inherit a recessive gene for a trait from each of your parents, you will show the trait. If you inherit a recessive gene from only one parent, you may never know you carry the gene. For example, brown hair, farsightedness, and dimples are genetically dominant phenotypes, and blond hair, nearsightedness, and freckles are recessive.

Can two brown-haired parents have a blond-haired child? Yes, they can. Suppose that each parent has a dominant gene for brown hair and a recessive gene for blond hair. Because dominant genes override recessive genes, the parents have brown hair, but both are carriers of genes that contribute to blondness and pass on their recessive genes for producing blond hair. With no dominant gene to override them, the recessive genes can make the child's hair blond.

Sex-Linked Genes Most mutated genes are recessive. When a mutated gene is carried on the X chromosome, the result is called *X-linked inheritance*. The implications for males may be very different from those for females (Bourn, 2022). Remember that males have only one X chromosome. Thus, if there is an absent or altered, disease-relevant gene on the X chromosome, males have no "backup" copy to counter the harmful gene and therefore may develop an X-linked disease. However, females have a second X chromosome, which is likely to be unchanged. As a result, they are not likely to have the X-linked disease. Thus, most individuals who have X-linked diseases are males. Females who have one copy of the gene for the disease on the X chromosome are known as "carriers," and they usually do not show any signs of the X-linked disease (Lykken & others, 2018).

Genetic Imprinting *Genetic imprinting* occurs when genes have differing effects depending on whether they are inherited from the mother or the father (Eggermann & others, 2021). A chemical process "silences" one member of the gene pair. For example, as a result of imprinting, only the maternally derived copy of a gene might be active, while the paternally derived copy of the same gene is silenced—or vice versa (John, 2017). Only a small percentage of human genes appears to undergo imprinting, but it is a normal and important aspect of development. When imprinting goes awry, development is disturbed, as in the case of Beckwith-Wiedemann syndrome, a growth disorder, and Wilms tumor, a type of cancer (Bachmann & others, 2017).

Polygenic Inheritance Genetic transmission is usually more complex than the simple examples we have examined thus far (Moore, 2018). Few characteristics reflect the influence of only a single gene or pair of genes. Most are determined by the interaction of many different genes; they are said to be *polygenically determined* (Oreland & others, 2017; Zabaneh & others, 2017). Even simple characteristics such as height, for example, reflect the interaction of many genes, as well as the influence of the environment.

The term *gene-gene interaction* is used to describe studies that focus on the interdependence of two or more genes in influencing characteristics, behavior, diseases, and development (Hébert, Causeur, & Emily, 2022). For example, studies have documented gene-gene interaction in immune system functioning (Törmänen & others, 2017); asthma (Dębińska & others, 2019); obesity (Bordoni & others, 2017); type 2 diabetes (Saxena, Srivastava, & Banerjee, 2017); cancer (J. Chen & others, 2023); and cardiovascular disease (Luizon, Pereira, & Sandrim, 2018).

CHROMOSOMAL AND GENE-LINKED ABNORMALITIES

Sometimes abnormalities characterize the genetic process. Some of these abnormalities involve whole chromosomes that do not separate properly during meiosis. Other abnormalities are produced by harmful genes.

Chromosomal Abnormalities Occasionally when a gamete is formed, the sperm and ovum do not have their set of 23 chromosomes. The most notable examples involve Down syndrome and abnormalities of the sex chromosomes (see Figure 5).

Down Syndrome **Down syndrome** is a chromosomally transmitted form of intellectual disability caused by the presence of an extra copy of chromosome 21 (Daunhauer, 2018). It is not known why the extra chromosome is present, but the health of the male sperm or the female ovum may be involved. An individual with Down syndrome has a round face, a flattened skull, an extra fold of skin over the eyelids, a protruding tongue, short limbs, and motor and intellectual disabilities.

Down syndrome A chromosomally transmitted form of intellectual disability that is caused by the presence of an extra copy of chromosome 21.

Name	Description	Treatment	Incidence
Down syndrome	An extra chromosome causes mild to severe intellectual disabilities and physical abnormalities.	Surgery, early intervention, infant stimulation, and special learning programs	1 in 1,900 births at age 20 1 in 300 births at age 35 1 in 30 births at age 45
Klinefelter syndrome (XXY)	An extra X chromosome causes physical abnormalities.	Hormone therapy can be effective	1 in 500 to 1,000 male births
Fragile X syndrome	An abnormality in the X chromosome can cause intellectual disabilities, learning disabilities, or short attention span.	Special education, speech and language therapy	More common in males than in females
Turner syndrome (XO)	A missing X chromosome in females can cause intellectual disabilities and sexual underdevelopment.	Hormone therapy in childhood and puberty	1 in 2,500 female births
XYY syndrome	An extra Y chromosome can cause above-average height.	No special treatment required	1 in 1,000 male births

FIGURE 5

SOME CHROMOSOMAL ABNORMALITIES. The treatments are not cures but may improve the individual's adaptive behavior and quality of life.

These athletes who have Down syndrome are participating in the Trisome Games. *What causes Down syndrome?*

lorenzo codacci/Alamy Stock Photo

Klinefelter syndrome A chromosomal disorder in which males have an extra X chromosome, making them XXY instead of XY.

fragile X syndrome A genetic disorder involving an abnormality in the X chromosome, which becomes constricted and often breaks.

Turner syndrome A chromosomal disorder in females in which either an X chromosome is missing, making the person XO instead of XX, or the second X chromosome is partially deleted.

Down syndrome appears approximately once in every 700 live births. Women between the ages of 16 and 34 are less likely to give birth to a child with Down syndrome than are younger or older women.

Sex-Linked Chromosomal Abnormalities Recall that a newborn normally has either an X and a Y chromosome, or two X chromosomes. Human embryos must possess at least one X chromosome to be viable. The most common sex-linked chromosomal abnormalities involve the presence of an extra chromosome (either an X or Y) or the absence of one X chromosome in females.

Klinefelter syndrome is a chromosomal disorder in which males have an extra X chromosome, making them XXY instead of XY. Males with this disorder have undeveloped testes, and they usually have enlarged breasts and become tall (Kanakis & Nieschlag, 2018). Males with Klinefelter syndrome often have impairment in language, academic, attentional, and motor abilities (Van Rijn, de Sonneville, & Swaab, 2018). Klinefelter syndrome occurs approximately once in every 650 live male births. The majority of individuals are not identified until adulthood, and many are never identified because there is so much variation in the phenotypes (Tanner & others, 2022).

Fragile X syndrome is a genetic disorder that results from an abnormality in the X chromosome, which becomes constricted and often breaks (Rivera, 2018). Children with fragile X syndrome typically have prominent ears, a long face, a high-arched palate, and soft skin. An intellectual difficulty frequently is an outcome, which may take the form of an intellectual disability, autism spectrum disorder, a learning disability, or a short attention span (Thurman & others, 2017). Males with fragile X syndrome are characterized by cognitive deficits in inhibition, memory, and planning (Hooper & others, 2018). This disorder occurs more frequently in males than in females, possibly because the second X chromosome in females negates the effects of the abnormal X chromosome (Hooper & others, 2018).

Turner syndrome is a chromosomal disorder in females in which either an X chromosome is missing, making the person XO instead of XX, or part of one X chromosome is deleted

(Bollig & others, 2023). Females with Turner syndrome are short in stature and have a webbed neck (Apperley & others, 2018). They might be infertile and have difficulty in mathematics, but their verbal ability often is quite good.

The **XYY syndrome** is a chromosomal disorder in which the male has an extra Y chromosome (Green, Flash, & Reiss, 2019). Early interest in this syndrome focused on the belief that the extra Y chromosome found in some males contributed to aggression and violence. However, researchers subsequently found that XYY males are no more likely to commit crimes than are normal XY males (Navon & Thomas, 2021).

Gene-Linked Abnormalities

Abnormalities can be produced not only by an abnormal number of chromosomes but also by harmful genes. More than 7,000 such genetic disorders have been identified, although most of them are rare.

Phenylketonuria (PKU) is a genetic disorder in which the individual cannot properly metabolize phenylalanine, an amino acid. This condition results from a recessive gene and occurs about once in every 10,000 to 20,000 live births. Today, phenylketonuria is easily detected, and it is treated by a diet that prevents an excess accumulation of phenylalanine (Ahring & others, 2018). If phenylketonuria is left untreated, however, excess phenylalanine builds up in the child, producing intellectual disabilities and hyperactivity. Phenylketonuria accounts for approximately 1 percent of individuals who are institutionalized for intellectual disabilities, and it occurs primarily in non–Latino Whites.

The story of phenylketonuria has important implications for the nature-nurture issue. Although phenylketonuria is often described as a genetic disorder (nature), how or whether a gene's influence in phenylketonuria is played out depends on environmental influences because the disorder can be treated by an environmental manipulation (nurture). That is, the presence of a genetic defect *does not* inevitably lead to the development of the disorder *if* the individual develops in the right environment (one free of phenylalanine). This is one example of the important principle of heredity-environment interaction. Under one environmental condition (phenylalanine in the diet), intellectual disability results, but when other nutrients replace phenylalanine, intelligence develops in the normal range. The same genotype has different outcomes depending on the environment (in this case, the nutritional environment).

Sickle-cell anemia, which occurs most often in African and Black Americans, is a genetic disorder that impairs the functioning of the body's red blood cells. More than 300,000 infants worldwide are born with sickle-cell anemia each year (Azar & Wong, 2017). Red blood cells carry oxygen to the body's other cells and are usually disk-shaped. In sickle-cell anemia, a recessive gene causes the red blood cell to become a hook-shaped "sickle" that cannot carry oxygen properly and dies quickly. As a result, the body's cells do not receive adequate oxygen, causing anemia and early death (Pecker & Little, 2018). About 1 in 400 Black American babies is affected by sickle-cell anemia. One in 10 Black Americans is a carrier, as is 1 in 20 Latino Americans. The drug hydroxyurea has been used successfully to treat sickle cell anemia in children, adolescents, and adults (Phillips & others, 2018). Genetically engineered stem cell transplantation is showing potential promise as an effective treatment (Kanter & others, 2022).

Other diseases that result from genetic abnormalities include cystic fibrosis, some forms of diabetes, hemophilia, spina bifida, Tay-Sachs disease, cardiovascular disease, and Alzheimer disease (Taylor & Galichet, 2021). Figure 6 provides further information about these diseases. Someday scientists may identify why these and other genetic abnormalities occur and discover how to cure them.

Dealing with Genetic Abnormalities

Every individual carries DNA variations that might predispose the person to serious physical diseases or mental disorders. But not all individuals who carry a genetic risk develop the disorder. Other genes or developmental events sometimes compensate for genetic abnormalities (Moore, 2018). For example, recall the earlier example of phenylketonuria: Even though individuals might carry the genetic disorder associated with phenylketonuria, the phenotype does not develop when phenylalanine is replaced by other nutrients in their diet.

Thus, genes are not destiny, but genes that are missing, nonfunctional, or mutated can be associated with disorders (Russell, Hertz, & McMillan, 2017). Identifying such genetic variations could enable doctors to predict an individual's risks, recommend healthy practices, and prescribe the safest and most effective drugs (Chen & others, 2018). A decade or so from now,

XYY syndrome A chromosomal disorder in which males have an extra Y chromosome.

phenylketonuria (PKU) A genetic disorder in which the individual cannot properly metabolize phenylalanine, an amino acid. PKU is now easily detected—but if left untreated, results in intellectual disability and hyperactivity.

sickle-cell anemia A genetic disorder that affects the red blood cells and occurs most often in people of sub-Saharan African descent.

developmental **connection**

Conditions, Diseases, and Disorders

Intellectual disabilities can be classified in several ways. Connect to "Cognitive Development in Middle and Late Childhood."

Name	Description	Treatment	Incidence
Cystic fibrosis	Glandular dysfunction that interferes with mucus production; breathing and digestion are hampered, resulting in a shortened life span.	Physical and oxygen therapy, synthetic enzymes, and antibiotics; most individuals live to middle age.	1 in 2,000 births
Diabetes	Body does not produce enough insulin, which causes abnormal metabolism of sugar.	Early onset can be fatal unless treated with insulin.	1 in 2,500 births
Hemophilia	Delayed blood clotting causes internal and external bleeding.	Blood transfusions/injections can reduce or prevent damage due to internal bleeding.	1 in 5,000 male births
Huntington's disease	Central nervous system deteriorates, producing problems in muscle coordination and mental deterioration.	Does not usually appear until age 35 or older; death likely 10 to 20 years after symptoms appear.	1 in 20,000 births
Phenylketonuria (PKU)	Metabolic disorder that, left untreated, causes intellectual disability.	Special diet can result in average intelligence and normal life span.	1 in 10,000 to 1 in 20,000 births
Sickle-cell anemia	Blood disorder that limits the body's oxygen supply; it can cause joint swelling, as well as heart and kidney failure.	Penicillin, medication for pain, antibiotics, and blood transfusions.	1 in 400 African and Black American children (lower among some but higher among other groups)
Spina bifida	Neural tube disorder that causes brain and spine abnormalities.	Corrective surgery at birth, orthopedic devices, and physical/medical therapy.	1 in 500 births
Tay-Sachs disease	Deceleration of mental and physical development caused by an accumulation of lipids in the nervous system.	Medication and special diet are used, but death is likely by 5 years of age.	1 in 30 American Jews is a carrier.

FIGURE 6
SOME GENE-LINKED ABNORMALITIES

parents of a newborn baby may be able to leave the hospital with a full genome analysis of their offspring that reveals disease risks.

However, this knowledge might bring important costs as well as benefits. Who would have access to a person's genetic profile? An individual's ability to land and hold jobs or obtain insurance might be threatened if it is known that a person is considered at risk for some disease. For example, should an airline pilot or a neurosurgeon who is predisposed to develop a disorder that makes one's hands shake be required to leave that job early?

Genetic counselors, including some physicians or biologists who are well versed in the field of medical genetics, understand the kinds of problems just described, the odds of encountering them, and helpful strategies for offsetting some of their effects (Borle & others, 2018; Lohn & others, 2022). Many individuals who receive genetic counseling find it difficult to quantify risk and tend to overestimate risk (Johansson & others, 2018). To read about the career and work of a genetic counselor, see the *Connecting with Careers* profile.

Review *Connect* Reflect

 LG2 Describe what genes are and how they influence human development.

Review
- What are genes?
- How are genes passed on from one generation to another?
- What basic principles describe how genes interact?
- What are some chromosomal and gene-linked abnormalities?

Connect
- Explain how environment interacts with genes in gene-linked abnormalities.

Reflect *Your Own Personal Journey of Life*
- Would you want to be able to access a full genome analysis of yourself or your offspring? Why or why not?

Jennifer Leonhard, Genetic Counselor

Jennifer Leonhard is a genetic counselor at Sanford Bemidji Health Clinic in Bemidji, Minnesota. She obtained an undergraduate degree from Western Illinois University and a master's degree in genetic counseling from the University of Arkansas for Medical Sciences.

Genetic counselors like Leonhard work as members of a health-care team, providing information and support to families with birth defects or genetic disorders. They identify families at risk by analyzing inheritance patterns and then explore options with the family. Some genetic counselors, like Leonhard, specialize in prenatal and pediatric genetics, while others focus on cancer genetics or psychiatric genetic disorders.

Genetic counselors have specialized graduate degrees in medical genetics and counseling. They enter graduate school from undergraduate programs in a variety of disciplines, including biology, genetics, psychology, public health, and social work. There are approximately 30 graduate genetic counseling programs in the United States. If you are interested in this profession, you can obtain further information from the National Society of Genetic Counselors at www.nsgc.org.

Jennifer Leonhard, shown here talking with a young couple about genetic influences on development, is a genetic counselor in Bemidji, Minnesota.

Courtesy of Jennifer Leonhard

3 What Are Some Reproductive Challenges and Choices?

 LG3 Identify some important reproductive challenges and choices.

| Prenatal Diagnostic Tests | Infertility and Reproductive Technology | Adoption |

The facts and principles we have discussed regarding meiosis, genetics, and genetic abnormalities are a small part of the recent explosion of knowledge about human biology. This knowledge not only helps us understand human development but also opens up many new choices to prospective parents, choices that can also raise ethical questions.

PRENATAL DIAGNOSTIC TESTS

One choice open to prospective mothers is the extent to which they should undergo prenatal testing. A number of tests can indicate whether a fetus is developing normally; these include ultrasound sonography, fetal MRI, chorionic villus sampling, amniocentesis, and maternal blood screening. There has been a dramatic increase in research on the use of less invasive techniques, such as fetal MRI, which poses lower risks to the fetus than more invasive techniques such as chorionic villus sampling and amniocentesis.

Ultrasound Sonography An ultrasound test is often conducted seven weeks into a pregnancy and at various times later in pregnancy. *Ultrasound sonography* is a prenatal medical procedure in which high-frequency sound waves are directed into the pregnant woman's abdomen (Santirocco & others, 2021). The echo from the sounds is transformed into a visual representation of the fetus's inner structures. This technique can detect many structural abnormalities in the fetus,

A 6-month-old infant poses with the ultrasound sonography record taken four months into the baby's prenatal development. *What is ultrasound sonography?*

Jacques Pavlovsky/Sygma/Corbis/Getty Images

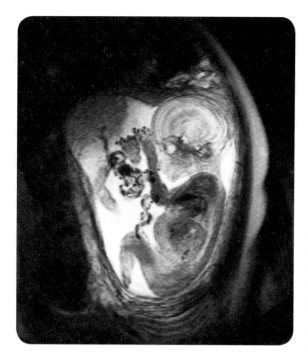

FIGURE 7

A FETAL MRI, WHICH IS INCREASINGLY BEING USED IN PRENATAL DIAGNOSIS OF FETAL MALFORMATIONS

Du Cane Medical Imaging Ltd./Science Source

---

developmental **connection**

Biological Processes

Discover what the development of the fetus is like at the times when chorionic villus sampling and amniocentesis can be used. Connect to "Prenatal Development."

How Would You...?

If you were a **health-care professional,** how would you discuss the benefits and risks of prenatal diagnostic testing with someone who has recently become pregnant?

---

including microcephaly, a form of intellectual disability involving an abnormally small brain; it can also determine the number of fetuses (if a woman is carrying twins or triplets) and give clues to the baby's sex (Sanapo & others, 2021). A research review concluded that many aspects of the developing prenatal brain can be detected by ultrasound in the first trimester and that about 50 percent of spina bifida cases can be identified at this time, most of these being severe cases (Engels & others, 2016). Ultrasound involves virtually no risk to the woman or fetus.

Fetal MRI   The development of brain-imaging techniques has led to increasing use of *fetal MRI* to diagnose fetal malformations (Manganaro & others, 2018) (see Figure 7). MRI stands for magnetic resonance imaging, which uses a powerful magnet and radio images to generate detailed images of the body's organs and structure. Currently, ultrasound is still the first choice in fetal screening, but fetal MRI can provide more detailed images than ultrasound. In many instances, ultrasound will indicate a possible abnormality, and then fetal MRI will be used to obtain a clearer, more detailed image (Manganaro & others, 2018). Among the fetal malformations that fetal MRI may be able to detect better than ultrasound sonography are certain abnormalities of the central nervous system, chest, gastrointestinal tract, genital/urinary organs, and placenta (Davidson & others, 2022). A research review concluded that fetal MRI often does not provide good results in the first trimester of pregnancy because of small fetal structures and movement artifacts (Wataganara & others, 2016). Also, in this review, it was argued that fetal MRI can be especially beneficial in assessing central nervous system abnormalities in the third trimester of pregnancy.

Chorionic Villus Sampling   At some point between 10 and 14 weeks of pregnancy, chorionic villus sampling may be used to detect genetic defects and chromosomal abnormalities such as the ones discussed in the previous section. Diagnosis takes approximately 10 days. *Chorionic villus sampling (CVS)* is a prenatal medical procedure in which a small sample of the placenta (the vascular organ that links the fetus to the mother's uterus) is removed (Navaratnam & others, 2022). There is a small risk of limb deformity, bleeding, infection, early labor, or even miscarriage when CVS is used.

Amniocentesis   Between the 14th and 20th weeks of pregnancy, amniocentesis may be performed. *Amniocentesis* is a prenatal medical procedure in which a sample of amniotic fluid is withdrawn by syringe and tested for chromosomal or metabolic disorders (Wertheimer & others, 2021). The amniotic fluid is found within the amnion, a thin sac in which the embryo is suspended. Ultrasound sonography is often used during amniocentesis so that the syringe can be placed precisely. The later amniocentesis is performed, the better its diagnostic potential. The earlier it is performed, the more useful it is in deciding how to handle a pregnancy. It may take two weeks for enough cells to grow so that amniocentesis test results can be obtained. Amniocentesis brings a small risk of miscarriage—about 1 woman in every 200 to 300 miscarries after amniocentesis.

Maternal Blood Screening   During the 16th to 18th weeks of pregnancy, maternal blood screening may be performed. *Maternal blood screening* identifies pregnancies that have an elevated risk for birth defects such as spina bifida (a defect in the spinal cord) and Down syndrome, as well as congenital heart disease risk for children (Findley & Northrup, 2021). The current blood test is called the *triple screen* because it measures three substances in the mother's blood. After an abnormal triple screen result, the next step is usually an ultrasound examination. If an ultrasound does not explain the abnormal triple screen results, amniocentesis is typically used.

Fetal Sex Determination   Chorionic villus sampling has often been used to determine the genetic sex of the fetus at some point between 11 and 13 weeks of gestation. Also, ultrasound accurately identifies the sex of the fetus between 11 and 13 weeks of gestation (Manzanares & others, 2016). Recently, however, some noninvasive techniques have been able to determine the sex of the fetus at an earlier point by assessing cell-free DNA in maternal plasma (Byrou & others, 2018). A meta-analysis concluded that the baby's sex can be determined as early as seven weeks into pregnancy (Devaney & others, 2011). Being able to detect an offspring's sex and to identify various diseases and defects so early raises ethical concerns about couples' motivation to terminate a pregnancy (Zaami & others, 2021).

INFERTILITY AND REPRODUCTIVE TECHNOLOGY

Recent advances in biological knowledge have also opened up many choices for infertile individuals (Graham & others, 2023). Approximately 10 to 15 percent of couples in the United States experience infertility, which is defined as the inability to conceive a child after 12 months of regular intercourse without contraception. The cause of infertility can rest with the woman or the man (Barbieri, 2019). The woman may not be ovulating (releasing eggs to be fertilized), she may be producing abnormal ova, her fallopian tubes through which fertilized ova normally reach the womb may be blocked, or she may have a disease that prevents implantation of the embryo into the uterus. The man may produce too few sperm, his sperm may lack motility (the ability to move adequately), or he may have a blocked passageway (Agarwal & others, 2021).

Globally, infertility is estimated to affect 8 to 12 percent of couples, with a male factor being the primary or a contributing cause in 50 percent of infertility cases (Agarwal & others, 2021). In the United States, more than 2 million couples seek help for infertility every year. In some cases of infertility, surgery may correct the cause; in others, hormone-based drugs may improve the probability of having a child. Of the 2 million couples who seek help for infertility each year, about 40,000 try high-tech assisted reproduction. By far the most common technique used is *in vitro fertilization (IVF),* in which eggs and sperm are combined in a laboratory dish (Sunderam & others, 2017). If any eggs are successfully fertilized, one or more of the resulting embryos are transferred into the woman's uterus. A foundational national U.S. study in 2004 by the Centers for Disease Control and Prevention found that the success rate of IVF depends on the mother's age (see Figure 8). Approximately 1.7 percent of births in the United States today result from IVF (Kawwass & Badell, 2018).

The creation of families by means of the new reproductive technologies raises important questions about the physical and psychological consequences for children (Graham & others, 2023; Sunderam & others, 2017). One result of fertility treatments is an increase in multiple births (Chambers & others, 2020). Twenty-five to 30 percent of pregnancies achieved by fertility treatments—including in vitro fertilization—now result in multiple births. Fertility drugs are more likely to produce multiple births than in vitro fertilization (March of Dimes, 2017). Any multiple birth increases the likelihood that the babies will have life-threatening and costly problems, such as extremely low birth weight (March of Dimes, 2017). Twins born through IVF, compared with twins born through natural conception, are at slightly higher risk of low birth weight, prematurity, and adverse neonatal outcomes (Wang & others, 2018); therefore, additional prenatal care and attention following birth may be needed for twins born through assisted reproductive technology.

Not nearly as many studies have examined the psychological outcomes of IVF as the physical outcomes. To read about a study that addresses these consequences, see the *Connecting with Research* interlude that follows.

ADOPTION

Although surgery and fertility drugs can sometimes resolve infertility problems, another choice is to adopt a child (Jones & others, 2021). Adoption is the social and legal process by which a parent-child relationship is established between persons unrelated at birth. As we see next in the *Connecting with Diversity* interlude, an increase in diversity has characterized the adoption of children in the United States in recent years.

How do adopted children fare after they are adopted? Children who are adopted very early in their lives are more likely to have positive outcomes than children adopted later in life, most likely because early adoption minimizes the amount of time children spend prior to adoption in adverse, traumatic situations that are often characterized by deprivation and other environmental risks (McCall & others, 2019). In a review of studies of children living in orphanages in the Russian Federation compared with children

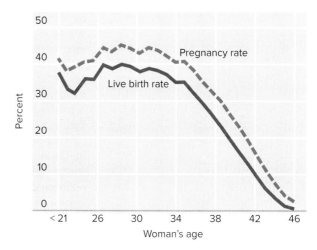

FIGURE 8

SUCCESS RATES OF IN VITRO FERTILIZATION VARY ACCORDING TO THE WOMAN'S AGE

Are There Developmental Outcomes in Childhood and Adolescence of In Vitro Fertilization?

Key Points:

- Rates of psychiatric disorders were compared in children conceived through assisted reproductive technologies (ART) and a control group.
- No significant differences were found between the two groups.

A longitudinal study sampled singleton children and twins who were conceived through assisted reproductive technologies (ART) and born in Denmark in 1995 (Klausen & others, 2017). The sample included 858 children born through ART, each of whom was matched demographically to four spontaneously conceived children, resulting in a sample of 3,436 spontaneously conceived children.

The children were assessed at ages 3, 7, 14, and 18 years to measure their behavior problems (such as aggression and delinquency) and mental health problems (such as anxiety and depression). In a cumulative analysis of mental health disorders identified through age 18, no significant differences were found between children born through ART and children conceived spontaneously (see Figure 9). More recent comprehensive reviews of the entire literature on long-term effects of ARTs suggest that they are safe with small, if any, effects on health and development (Graham & others, 2023).

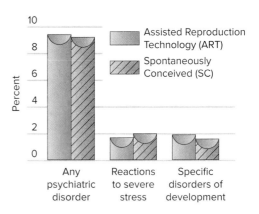

FIGURE **9**

CUMULATIVE PREVALENCE OF PSYCHIATRIC DISORDERS AT AGE 18. No significant differences in any diagnostic categories were found between children who were born through assisted reproductive technologies and those who were spontaneously conceived (Klausen & others, 2017).

What additional types of studies do you think researchers might conduct to study possible developmental effects of new reproductive technologies? How long do you think the children in such studies should be followed?

adopted in the Russian Federation or the United States, children who were adopted before the age of 18 months generally showed typical healthy development (McCall & others, 2019). However, children adopted after the age of 18 months had higher levels of behavior problems and poorer cognitive function years after the adoption. An intervention that focused on improving caregiver-child interactions in orphanages was found to improve orphans' physical, cognitive, and socioemotional outcomes (McCall & others, 2019). In a research review of internationally adopted adolescents, although a majority were well adjusted, adoptees had a higher level of mental health problems than their non-adopted counterparts (Askeland & others, 2017). Yet despite risks associated with early deprivation prior to adoption, the majority of adopted children and adolescents (including those adopted at older ages, transracially, and across national borders) adjust well, and their parents report considerable satisfaction with their decision to adopt (Compton, 2016; Finet & others, 2020).

An ongoing issue in adopting children is whether there should be any contact with the child's biological parents (Grant-Marsney, Grotevant, & Sayer, 2015). Open adoption involves sharing identifying information and having contact with the biological parents, while closed adoption does not include such sharing and contact. Most adoption agencies today offer birth parents and adoptive parents the opportunity to have either an open or a closed adoption. A longitudinal study found that when their adopted children reached adulthood, adoptive parents described open adoption positively and saw it as serving the child's best interests (Siegel, 2013). Another longitudinal study found that birth mothers, adoptive parents, and birth children who had contact were more satisfied with their arrangements than those who did not have contact (Grotevant & others, 2013). Also, in this study, contact was linked to more optimal adjustment for adolescents and emerging adults (Grotevant & others, 2013).

The Increased Diversity of Adopted Children and Adoptive Parents

A number of changes have characterized adopted children and adoptive parents in the last three to four decades (Koh & others, 2022; Zill, 2017). In the first half of the twentieth century, most children adopted in the United States were healthy, non–Latino White infants who were adopted at birth or soon after; however, in recent decades as contraception use increased, abortion became legal, and unmarried mothers became increasingly likely to raise their children as single mothers or with the help of their own parents, fewer non–Latino White infants became available for adoption. Increasingly, U.S. couples adopted a much wider diversity of children—from other countries, from other ethnic groups, children with physical and/or mental problems, and children who had been neglected or abused. For example, between 1999 and 2011, the number of kindergarten adoptees being raised by a mother of a different ethnicity rose by 50 percent (Zill, 2017).

It is still unclear what the implications of the overturning of *Roe v. Wade* will be for adoption in the United States. It is too soon to know if recent changes in abortion legislation will affect adoption trends. The rates of adoption in the United States decreased dramatically during the COVID-19 pandemic, but it is not yet known whether or not rates will return to pre-pandemic levels (Koh & others, 2022).

Changes also have characterized adoptive parents in the last three to four decades (Zill, 2017). In the first half of the twentieth century, most adoptive parents were straight couples from non–Latino White middle or upper socioeconomic status backgrounds who were married and did not have any type of disability. Although adoptive parents are still, on average, more likely to be non–Latino White and from higher socioeconomic backgrounds than the general population, increased diversity has characterized adoptive parents in recent decades. Many adoption agencies today have no income requirements for adoptive parents and now allow adults from a wide range of backgrounds and identities to adopt children, including single adults, gay and lesbian adults, trans and nonbinary adults, and older adults (Farr, 2017; Goldberg & others, 2020).

Further, many adoptions involve other family members (aunts/uncles/grandparents); the most recent national data indicate that 37 percent of U.S. domestic adoptions are made by relatives (Jones & Placek, 2017). And slightly more than 50 percent of U.S. adoptions occur through the foster care system; more than 100,000 children in the U.S. foster care system are waiting for someone to adopt them (U.S. Department of Health & Human Services, 2022).

Three major pathways to adoption are (1) domestic adoption from the public welfare system; (2) domestic infant adoption through private agencies and intermediaries; and (3) international adoption. In the next decade, the mix of U.S. adoptions is likely to include fewer domestic infant and international adoptions and more adoptions via the child welfare system (Koh & others, 2022; Zill, 2017).

Keep in mind that changes in adoption practice over the last several decades make it difficult to generalize about the average adopted child or average adoptive parent. For example, one longitudinal study of openness in adoption found at least four distinct patterns over time (no birth parent contact, limited contact, initiated but stopped contact, and extended contact) (Grotevant & others, 2019). To read more about adoption, see the *Caring Connections* interlude that describes effective parenting strategies with adopted children.

Review Connect Reflect

 LG3 Identify some important reproductive challenges and choices.

Review

- What are some common prenatal diagnostic tests?
- What are some techniques that help infertile people to have children?
- How does adoption affect children's development?

Connect

- Earlier you learned about different methods for collecting data. How would you characterize the methods used in prenatal diagnostic testing?

Reflect *Your Own Personal Journey of Life*

- If you were an adult who could not have biological children, would you want to adopt a child? Why or why not?

Parenting Adopted Children

Many of the keys to effectively parenting adopted children are no different from those for effectively parenting biological children: Be supportive and caring, be involved and monitor the child's behavior and whereabouts, be a good communicator, and help the child learn to develop self-control. Research by Ellen Pinderhughes, a professor and clinical psychologist who specializes in research on adoption in diverse families, along with scholarly work by others, indicates that parents of adopted children face some unique circumstances (see also Lee & others, 2018). They need to recognize the differences involved in adoptive family life, communicate about these differences, show respect for the birth family, and support the child's search for self and identity.

Following are some of the challenges parents face when their adopted children are at different points in development and some recommendations for how to face these challenges (Brodzinsky & Pinderhughes, 2002, pp. 288–292; see also Pinderhughes & Brodzinsky, 2019):

- *Infancy.* Researchers have found few differences in the attachment that adopted and nonadopted infants form with their parents. However, attachment can become problematic if parents have unresolved fertility issues or the child does not meet the parents' expectations. Counselors can help prospective adoptive parents develop realistic expectations.
- *Early childhood.* Because many children begin to ask where they came from when they are about 4 to 6 years old, this is a natural time to begin to talk in simple ways to children about their adoption status. Some parents (although not as many as in the past) decide not to tell their children about the adoption. This secrecy may create psychological risks for the child if he or she later finds out about the adoption. Adoptions today are more likely to be open than closed; in an open adoption the adoptive parents and adoptive children have information about the birth parents and the potential to have contact with the birth parents. Gay men and lesbian women who adopt have been found to maintain more contact with birth parents than do heterosexual couples who adopt (Brodzinsky & Goldberg, 2016).
- *Middle and late childhood.* During the elementary school years, children begin to show more interest in their origins and may ask

What are some strategies for parenting adopted children at different points in their development?
Photodisc/Getty Images

questions related to where they came from, what their birth parents looked like, and why their birth parents chose not to raise them.

As they grow older, children may develop mixed feelings about being adopted and question their adoptive parents' explanations. It is important for adoptive parents to recognize that this ambivalence is normal. Also, problems may arise from the desire of adoptive parents to make life too perfect for the adopted child and to present a perfect image of themselves to the child. The result too often is that adopted children feel that they cannot release any angry feelings or openly discuss problems.

- *Adolescence.* Adolescents are likely to develop more abstract and logical thinking, to focus their attention on their bodies, and to search for an identity. These characteristics provide the foundation for adopted adolescents to reflect on their adoption status in more complex ways, such as focusing on looking different from their adoptive parents. As they explore their identity, adopted adolescents may have difficulty incorporating their adoptive status into their identity in positive ways. It is important for adoptive parents to understand the complexity of the adopted adolescent's identity exploration and be patient with the adolescent's lengthy identity search.

---

4 How Do Heredity and Environment Interact?

 LG4 Explain some of the ways that heredity and environment interact to produce individual differences in development.

| Behavior Genetics | Heredity-Environment Correlations | The Epigenetic View and Gene x Environment (G x E) Interaction | Conclusions about Heredity-Environment Interaction |

In each section of this chapter so far, we have examined how heredity and environment interact in ways that affect individual differences in development. We have seen how the environment exerts selective pressures on the characteristics of species over generations, examined how genes are passed from parents to children, and discussed how reproductive technologies and adoption influence the course of children's lives. But in all of these situations, heredity and environment interact to produce development. After all, Jim and Jim (and each of the other pairs of identical twins discussed in the opening of the chapter) have the same genotype, but they are not the same person; each is unique. What made them different? Whether we are studying how genes produce proteins, their influence on how tall a person is, or how PKU might affect an individual, we end up needing to consider heredity-environment interactions.

Is it possible to untangle the influence of heredity from that of environment and discover the role of each in producing individual differences in development? When heredity and environment interact, how does heredity influence the environment, and vice versa?

developmental **connection**

Nature and Nurture

The nature and nurture interaction is one of the main issues in the study of children's development. Connect to "Introduction."

BEHAVIOR GENETICS

Behavior genetics is the field that seeks to discover the influence of heredity and environment on individual differences in human traits and development (Harden, 2021). Note that behavior genetics does not determine the extent to which genetics or the environment affects an individual's traits. Instead, behavior geneticists try to figure out what is responsible for the differences among people—that is, to what extent do people differ because of differences in genes, environment, or a combination of these (Krueger & Johnson, 2021)? To study the influence of heredity on behavior, behavior geneticists often use either twins or adoption situations.

In the most common **twin study,** the behavioral similarity of identical twins (who are genetically identical) is compared with the behavioral similarity of fraternal twins. Recall that although fraternal twins share the same womb, they are no more genetically alike than non-twin siblings. Thus, by comparing groups of identical and fraternal twins, behavior geneticists capitalize on the basic knowledge that identical twins are more similar genetically than are fraternal twins (Li & others, 2018). For example, identical twins are more similar to one another on measures of conduct problems than are fraternal twins, suggesting the importance of heredity in conduct problems (Saunders & others, 2019).

Certain issues complicate the interpretation of twin studies. For example, perhaps the environments of identical twins are more similar than the environments of fraternal twins. Adults might stress the similarities of identical twins more than those of fraternal twins, and identical twins might perceive themselves as a "set" and play together more than fraternal twins do. If so, the influence of the environment on the observed similarities between identical and fraternal twins might be very significant.

In an **adoption study,** investigators seek to discover whether the behavior and psychological characteristics of adopted children are more like those of their adoptive parents, who have provided a home environment, or more like those of their biological parents, who have contributed their DNA (Kendler & others, 2018). Another form of the adoption study compares adopted and biological siblings.

Twin studies compare identical twins with fraternal twins. Identical twins develop from a single fertilized egg that splits into two genetically identical organisms. Fraternal twins develop from separate eggs, making them genetically no more similar than nontwin siblings. *What is the nature of the twin study method?*
Digital Vision/Getty Images

HEREDITY-ENVIRONMENT CORRELATIONS

The difficulties that researchers encounter when they interpret the results of twin studies and adoption studies reflect the complexities of heredity-environment interaction. Some of these interactions are *heredity-environment correlations,* which means that individuals' genes may be systematically related to the types of environments to which they are exposed (Klahr & Burt, 2014). In a sense, individuals "inherit," seek out, or "construct" environments that may be related or linked to genetic "propensities." Behavior geneticist Sandra Scarr (1993) described three ways that heredity and environment can be correlated (see Figure 10):

- **Passive genotype-environment correlations** occur because biological parents, who are genetically related to the child, provide a rearing environment for the child. For example, the parents might have a genetic predisposition to read skillfully. Because they read

behavior genetics The field that seeks to discover the influence of heredity and environment on individual differences in human traits and development.

twin study A study in which the behavioral similarity of identical twins is compared with the behavioral similarity of fraternal twins.

adoption study A study in which investigators seek to discover whether, in behavior and psychological characteristics, adopted children are more like their adoptive parents, who provided a home environment, or more like their biological parents, who contributed their heredity. Another form of the adoption study compares adopted and biological siblings.

passive genotype-environment correlations Correlations that exist when the biological parents, who are genetically related to the child, provide a rearing environment for the child.

Heredity-Environment Correlation	Description	Examples
Passive	Children inherit genetic tendencies from their parents, and parents also provide an environment that matches their own genetic tendencies.	Musically inclined parents usually have musically inclined children and they are likely to provide an environment rich in music for their children.
Evocative	The child's genetic tendencies elicit stimulation from the environment that supports a particular trait. Thus genes evoke environmental support.	A happy, outgoing child elicits smiles and friendly responses from others.
Active (niche-picking)	Children actively seek out "niches" in their environment that reflect their own interests and talents and are thus in accord with their genotype.	Libraries, sports fields, and a store with musical instruments are examples of environmental niches children might seek out if they have intellectual interests in books, talent in sports, or musical talents, respectively.

FIGURE 10

EXPLORING HEREDITY-ENVIRONMENT CORRELATIONS

well and enjoy reading, they provide their children with books to read. The likely outcome is that their children, because of both their own inherited predispositions and their book-filled environment, will become skilled readers.

- **Evocative genotype-environment correlations** occur because a child's genetically influenced characteristics elicit certain types of environments. For example, active, smiling children receive more social stimulation than passive, quiet children do. Cooperative, attentive children evoke more pleasant and instructional responses from the adults around them than uncooperative, distractible children do.

- **Active (niche-picking) genotype-environment correlations** occur when children seek out environments that they find compatible and stimulating. *Niche-picking* refers to finding a setting that is suited to one's genetically influenced interests or abilities. Children select from their surrounding environment some aspect that they respond to, learn about, or ignore. Their active selections of environments are related to their particular genotype. For example, outgoing children tend to seek out social contexts in which to interact with people, whereas shy children don't. Children who are musically inclined are likely to select musical environments in which they can successfully perform their skills. How these "tendencies" come about will be discussed later in this chapter under the topic of the epigenetic view.

Scarr argued that the relative importance of the three genotype-environment correlations changes as children develop from infancy through adolescence. In infancy, much of the environment that children experience is provided by adults. Thus, passive genotype-environment correlations are more common in the lives of infants and young children than they are in the lives of older children and adolescents who can extend their experiences beyond the family's influence and create or select their environments to a greater degree.

THE EPIGENETIC VIEW AND GENE × ENVIRONMENT (G × E) INTERACTION

Critics argue that the concept of heredity-environment correlation gives heredity too much of a one-sided influence in determining development because it does not consider the role of prior environmental influences in shaping the correlation itself (Breton & others, 2021). Consistent with this view, earlier in the chapter we discussed how genes are collaborative, not determining an individual's traits in an independent manner but rather in an interactive manner with the environment.

The Epigenetic View In line with the concept of a collaborative gene, Gilbert Gottlieb (2007) emphasized the **epigenetic view,** which states that development reflects an ongoing, bidirectional interchange between heredity and the environment. Figure 11 compares the heredity-environment correlation and epigenetic views of development.

How Would You...?

If you were a **health-care professional,** how would you explain heredity-environment interaction to new parents who are upset about discovering that their child has a treatable genetic defect?

evocative genotype-environment correlations Correlations that exist when the child's genetically influenced characteristics elicit certain types of physical and social environments.

active (niche-picking) genotype-environment correlations Correlations that exist when children seek out environments they find compatible and stimulating. *Niche-picking* refers to finding a setting that is suited to one's genetically influenced interests or abilities.

epigenetic view Emphasizes that development reflects an ongoing, bidirectional interchange between heredity and environment.

Let's look at an example that reflects the epigenetic view. A baby inherits genes from both parents at conception. During prenatal development, toxins, nutrition, and stress can influence some genes to stop functioning while others become more active or less active (Pluess & others, 2011). During infancy, environmental experiences such as toxins, nutrition, stress, learning, and encouragement continue to modify the genetic activity and the activity of the nervous system that directly underlie behavior (Gottlieb, 2007). Heredity and environment operate together—or collaborate—to produce a person's well-being, intelligence, temperament, height, weight, skill in pitching a baseball, ability to read, and so on (Moore, 2018; O'Donnell & Meaney, 2020).

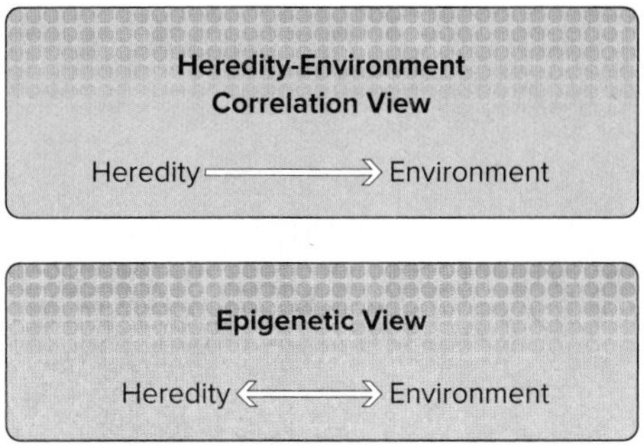

Gene × Environment (G × E) Interaction   An increasing number of studies are exploring how the interaction between heredity and environment influences development, including interactions that involve specific DNA sequences (Zhou & others, 2018). The epigenetic mechanisms involve the actual molecular modification of the DNA strand as a result of environmental inputs in ways that alter gene functioning (O'Donnell & Meaney, 2020).

An influential early study that generated a large body of follow-up tests found that individuals who have a short version of a gene labeled 5-HTTLPR (a gene involving the neurotransmitter serotonin) have an elevated risk of developing depression only if they *also* lead stressful lives (Caspi & others, 2003). Thus, the specific gene did not directly cause the development of depression; rather, the gene interacted with a stressful environment in a way that allowed the researchers to predict whether individuals would develop depression. More recent studies also have found support for the interaction between the 5-HTTLPR gene and stress levels in predicting depression in adolescents and older adults (Saul & others, 2019), yet they have also emphasized the importance of taking a polygenic approach across the whole genome rather than focusing on only single genes (Davidson & others, 2021).

Other research involving interaction between genes and environmental experiences has focused on attachment, parenting, and supportive or adverse child-rearing environments (Lovallo & others, 2017). For example, some genes are a risk factor for psychological disorders only if an individual also has experienced early adversity, such as physical or sexual abuse during childhood (Bulbena-Cabre, Nia, & Perez-Rodriguez, 2018).

The type of research just described is referred to as studies of **gene × environment (G × E) interaction**—the interaction between a specific measured variation in DNA and a specific measured aspect of the environment (Truzzi & others, 2017). Although there is considerable enthusiasm about the concept of gene × environment interaction (G × E), multiple research reviews have concluded that the area is plagued by difficulties in replicating results (Border & others, 2019; Manuck & McCaffery, 2014). The science of G × E interaction is very young, and during the next several decades it will likely produce more precise findings.

CONCLUSIONS ABOUT HEREDITY-ENVIRONMENT INTERACTION

If a strong, fast, athletic teenager wins a championship tennis match in high school, is their success due to heredity or to environment? Of course, the answer is both.

The relative contributions of heredity and environment are not additive. That is, we can't say that such-and-such a percentage of nature and such-and-such a percentage of experience make us who we are. Nor is it accurate to say that full genetic expression happens once, around conception or birth, after which we carry our genetic legacy into the world to see how far it takes us. Genes produce proteins throughout the life span, in many different environments. Or they don't produce these proteins, depending in part on how harsh or nourishing those environments are.

The emerging view is that complex behaviors are influenced by genes in a way that gives people a propensity for a particular developmental trajectory (Wertz & others, 2018). However, the actual development requires more: an environment. And that environment is complex, just like the mixture of genes we inherit (Gartstein & Skinner, 2018). Environmental influences range from the things we lump together under "nurture" (such as parenting, family dynamics, schooling, and neighborhood quality) to biological encounters (such as viruses, birth complications, and even biological events in cells).

Heredity-Environment Correlation View

Heredity ⟶ Environment

Epigenetic View

Heredity ⟵⟶ Environment

FIGURE 11

COMPARISON OF THE HEREDITY-ENVIRONMENT CORRELATION AND EPIGENETIC VIEWS

How Would You...?
If you were a **human development and family studies professional,** how would you apply the epigenetic view to explain why one identical twin can develop alcoholism while the other twin does not?

gene × environment (G × E) interaction The interaction of a specific measured variation in the DNA and a specific measured aspect of the environment.

Tennis stars Venus and Serena Williams. *What might be some of the environmental experiences they had while they were growing up that contributed to their tennis stardom?*

Greg Wood/AFP/Getty Images

In developmental psychologist David Moore's (2018) view, the biological systems that generate behaviors are extremely complex, and too often these systems have been described in overly simplified ways that can be misleading. Thus, although genetic factors clearly contribute to behavior and psychological processes, they don't determine these phenotypes independently from the contexts in which they develop. From Moore's (2018) perspective, it is misleading to talk about "genes for" eye color, intelligence, personality, or other characteristics. Moore commented that in retrospect we should not have expected to be able to make the giant leap from DNA's molecules to a complete understanding of human behavior any more than we should anticipate being able to make the leap from understanding how sound waves move in a concert hall to a full-blown appreciation of a symphony's wondrous experience.

Consider for a moment the cluster of genes associated with diabetes. The child who carries this genetic mixture might experience a world of loving parents, nutritious meals, and regular medical intervention. Or the child's world might include parental neglect, a diet high in sugar, and little help from competent physicians. In which of these environments are the child's genes likely to result in diabetes?

If heredity and environment interact to determine the course of development, is that all there is to answering the question of what causes development? Are children completely at the mercy of their genes and environment as they develop? Children's genetic heritage and environmental experiences are pervasive influences on their development (Franke & Buitelaar, 2018). But children's development is not only the outcome of their heredity and the environment they experience. Children also can author a unique developmental path by changing their environment. As one psychologist concluded:

> In reality, we are both the creatures and creators of our worlds. We are . . . the products of our genes and environments. Nevertheless . . . the stream of causation that shapes the future runs through our present choices. . . . Mind matters. . . . Our hopes, goals, and expectations influence our future. (Myers, 2010, p. 168)

Review *Connect* Reflect

LG4 Explain some of the ways that heredity and environment interact to produce individual differences in development.

Review

- What is behavior genetics?
- What are three types of heredity-environment correlations?
- What is the epigenetic view of development? What characterizes gene x environment (G x E) interaction?
- What conclusions can be reached about heredity-environment interaction?

Connect

- Of passive, evocative, and active genotype-environment correlations, which is the best explanation for the

similarities discovered between the twins (Jim and Jim, for example) discussed in the story that opened the chapter?

Reflect *Your Own Personal Journey of Life*

- Someone has analyzed your genetic background and environmental experiences and reached the conclusion that environment definitely has had little influence on your personality. What would you say about this analysis?

topical connections *looking forward*

In the remaining chapters, you will continue to read about biological influences on development, especially in the chapters on prenatal development, birth, and physical development in infancy, early childhood, middle and late childhood, and adolescence, and also in the chapters on cognitive and socioemotional development. Next you will learn about the amazing developmental journey from conception to birth, including how expectant mothers can best promote their offspring's health and well-being during pregnancy.

Biological Beginnings

1 What Is the Evolutionary Perspective?

 Discuss the evolutionary perspective on development.

Natural Selection and Adaptive Behavior

Evolutionary Psychology

- Natural selection is the process by which those individuals of a species that are best adapted survive and reproduce. Darwin proposed that natural selection fuels evolution. In evolutionary theory, adaptive behavior is behavior that promotes the organism's survival in a natural habitat.

- Evolutionary psychology holds that adaptation, reproduction, and "survival of the fittest" are important in shaping behavior. Ideas proposed by evolutionary developmental psychology include the view that we humans need an extended juvenile period to develop a large brain and learn the complexity of human social communities.

- Many evolved psychological mechanisms are domain-specific. Like other theoretical approaches to development, evolutionary psychology has limitations. Bandura rejects "one-sided evolutionism" and argues for a bidirectional link between biology and environment. Biology allows for a broad range of cultural possibilities.

2 What Are the Genetic Foundations of Development?

 Describe what genes are and how they influence human development.

The Collaborative Gene

Genes and Chromosomes

Genetic Principles

Chromosomal and Gene-Linked Abnormalities

- Short segments of DNA constitute genes, the units of hereditary information that help cells to reproduce and manufacture proteins. Except in the sperm and egg, the nucleus of each human cell contains 46 chromosomes (arranged in 23 pairs), which are composed of DNA. Genes act collaboratively, not independently.

- Genes are passed on to new cells when chromosomes are duplicated during the processes of mitosis and meiosis, which are two ways in which new cells are formed. When an egg and a sperm unite in the fertilization process, the resulting zygote contains the genes from the chromosomes in the father's sperm and the mother's egg. Despite this transmission of genes from generation to generation, variability is created in several ways, including through the exchange of chromosomal segments during meiosis, through mutations, and through environmental influences.

- Genetic principles that describe how genes interact include those involving dominant-recessive genes, sex-linked genes, genetic imprinting, and polygenic inheritance.

- Chromosomal abnormalities produce Down syndrome, which is caused by the presence of an extra copy of chromosome 21. Other sex-linked conditions include Klinefelter syndrome, fragile X syndrome, Turner syndrome, and XYY syndrome. Gene-linked abnormalities involve harmful or absent genes. Gene-linked disorders include phenylketonuria (PKU) and sickle-cell anemia. Genetic counseling offers people information about their risk of having a child with inherited abnormalities.

3 What Are Some Reproductive Challenges and Choices?

LG3 Identify some important reproductive challenges and choices.

Prenatal Diagnostic Tests

- Amniocentesis, ultrasound sonography, fetal MRI, chorionic villus sampling, and maternal blood screening are used to determine whether a fetus is developing normally. Noninvasive prenatal diagnosis is increasingly being explored. Sex determination of the fetus is occurring much earlier than in the past.

Infertility and Reproductive Technology	• Approximately 10 to 15 percent of U.S. couples have infertility problems, some of which can be addressed through surgery or fertility drugs. An additional option is in vitro fertilization.
Adoption	• Although adopted children and adolescents have more problems than their nonadopted counterparts, the vast majority of adopted children adapt effectively. When adoption occurs very early in development, the outcomes for the child are improved. Because of the dramatic changes that have occurred in adoption in recent decades, it is difficult to generalize about the average adopted child or average adoptive family.

4 How Do Heredity and Environment Interact?

 LG4 Explain some of the ways that heredity and environment interact to produce individual differences in development.

Behavior Genetics

• Behavior genetics seeks to discover the influence of heredity and environment on individual differences in the traits and development of humans. Methods used by behavior geneticists include twin studies and adoption studies.

Heredity-Environment Correlations

• In Scarr's view of heredity-environment correlations, heredity directs the types of environments that children experience. She described three genotype-environment correlations: passive, evocative, and active (niche-picking). Scarr maintained that the relative importance of these three genotype-environment correlations changes as children develop.

The Epigenetic View and Gene × Environment (G × E) Interaction

• The epigenetic view emphasizes that development reflects an ongoing, bidirectional interchange between heredity and environment. Gene × environment interaction involves the interaction of a specific measured variation in the DNA and a specific measured aspect of the environment. An increasing number of G × E studies are being conducted.

Conclusions About Heredity-Environment Interaction

• Behaviors are influenced by genes and environments in a way that gives people a propensity for a particular developmental trajectory. The actual development also requires both genes and an environment, and that environment is complex. The interaction of heredity and environment is extensive. Much remains to be discovered about the specific ways that heredity and environment interact to influence development.

key terms

active (niche-picking) genotype-environment correlations
adoption study
behavior genetics
chromosomes
DNA
Down syndrome
epigenetic view

evocative genotype-environment correlations
evolutionary psychology
fertilization
fragile X syndrome
gene × environment (G × E) interaction
genes

genotype
Klinefelter syndrome
meiosis
mitosis
passive genotype-environment correlations
phenotype
phenylketonuria (PKU)

sickle-cell anemia
Turner syndrome
twin study
XYY syndrome
zygote

key people

Albert Bandura
Thomas Bouchard

David Buss
Charles Darwin

Gilbert Gottlieb
David Moore

Ellen Pinderhughes
Sandra Scarr

Improving the **Lives of Children**

STRATEGIES

Preparing for Pregnancy

Even before a woman becomes pregnant, she can adopt some strategies that may make a difference in how healthy the pregnancy is and in her child's developmental outcomes:

- Become knowledgeable about prepregnancy planning and health-care providers. The kinds of health-care providers who are qualified to provide care for pregnant women include an obstetrician/gynecologist, a family practitioner, a nurse practitioner, and a certified nurse-midwife.

- Meet with a health professional before conception. A good strategy is for potential parents to meet with a health professional prior to conception to assess their health and review personal and family histories. During this meeting, the health professional will discuss nutrition and other aspects of health that might affect the baby.

- Find a health-care provider who is competent. The health-care provider should (1) take time to do a thorough family history; (2) not be patronizing; (3) be knowledgeable and stay current on prenatal testing; (4) be honest about risks, benefits, and side effects of any tests or treatments; and (5) inspire trust.

RESOURCES

***The Developing Genome: An Introduction to Behavioral Epigenetics* (2017)**
David S. Moore
New York: Oxford University Press

A superb overview of recent thinking and research on epigenetics, including many studies focused on gene × environment interaction.

American Society for Reproductive Medicine
www.asrm.org/

The American Society for Reproductive Medicine provides information about infertility and possible solutions to it.

***The Family Tree Guide to DNA Testing and Genetic Genealogy* (2nd ed., 2019)**
Blaine T. Bettinger
Blue Ash, OH: Family Tree Books

In this book, you will learn about the kinds of DNA tests available and how to interpret them to understand your family tree.

National Down Syndrome Society
www.ndss.org

The National Down Syndrome Society (NDSS) provides resources and advocacy for individuals with Down syndrome and their families.

National Organization for Rare Disorders (NORD)
www.rarediseases.org

NORD supports awareness and education about rare birth defects and genetic disorders.

The Twins Trust
www.twinstrust.org

For information about twins and multiple births, explore The Twins Trust.

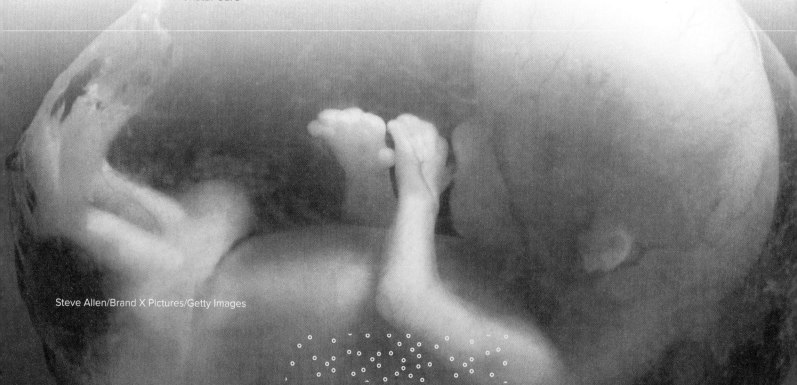

chapter 3

PRENATAL DEVELOPMENT

chapter **outline**

Steve Allen/Brand X Pictures/Getty Images

Diana and Roger married when he was 38 and she was 34. Both worked full-time and were excited when Diana became pregnant. Two months later, Diana began to have some unusual pains and bleeding. Just two months into her pregnancy she had lost the baby. Although most early miscarriages are the result of embryonic defects, Diana thought deeply about why she had been unable to carry the baby to full term and felt guilty that she might have done something "wrong."

Alex, also known as "Mr. Littles."
Dr. John Santrock

Six months later, Diana became pregnant again. Because she was still worried about her prior loss, she made sure to follow every government recommendation such as getting enough folic acid, avoiding certain types of dairy products that might harbor bacteria, and letting someone else change their cat's litterbox to avoid toxoplasmosis. She and Roger read about pregnancy, prenatal development, and birth, and signed up for birth preparation classes. Each Friday night for eight weeks they practiced simulated contractions. They talked about what kind of parents they wanted to be and discussed what changes in their lives the baby would make. When they found out that their baby was going to be a boy, they gave him a nickname: "Mr. Littles."

This time, Diana's pregnancy went well, and Alex, also known as Mr. Littles, was born. During the birth, however, Diana's heart rate dropped precipitously and she was given a stimulant to raise it. Apparently the stimulant also increased Alex's heart rate and breathing to a dangerous point, and he had to be placed in a neonatal intensive care unit (NICU).

Several times a day, Diana and Roger visited Alex in the NICU. A number of babies in the NICU who had a very low birth weight had been in intensive care for weeks, and some of these babies were not doing well. Fortunately, Alex was in better health. After several days in the NICU, his parents were permitted to take home a very healthy Alex.

-topical connections   *looking **back***

You have learned about the evolutionary perspective, genetic foundations of development, the reproductive challenges and choices parents today may face, and the interaction of nature and nurture. Now we will explore the remarkable course of prenatal development, including the phenomenal growth of the brain. Potential hazards to the offspring's and the mother's health also are covered.

preview

This chapter describes the truly amazing changes that take place from conception to birth. Imagine . . . at one time you were suspended in a sea of fluid in your mother's womb. In this chapter, you will explore the course of prenatal development, expectant parents' experiences, and some potential hazards to prenatal development.

1 What Is the Course of Prenatal Development?

 LG1 Discuss the three periods of prenatal development.

The Germinal Period   The Embryonic Period   The Fetal Period   The Brain

Imagine how Alex ("Mr. Littles") came to be. Out of thousands of eggs and millions of sperm, one egg and one sperm united to produce him. Had the union of sperm and egg come a day or even an hour earlier or later, he would have been very different in his psychological and physical characteristics. Conception occurs when a single sperm cell from the male unites with an ovum (egg) in the female's fallopian tube in a process called fertilization. Over the next few months, the genetic code directs a series of changes in the fertilized egg, but many events and hazards will influence how that egg develops and becomes tiny Alex.

Typical prenatal development begins with fertilization and ends with birth, lasting 266 days (38 weeks) from conception. It can be divided into three periods: germinal, embryonic, and fetal.

THE GERMINAL PERIOD

germinal period The period of prenatal development that takes place in the first two weeks after conception. It includes the creation of the zygote, continued cell division, and the attachment of the zygote to the uterine wall.

The **germinal period** is the period of prenatal development that takes place in the first two weeks after conception. It includes the creation of the fertilized egg, called a *zygote,* cell division, and the attachment of the zygote to the uterine wall.

Rapid cell division by the zygote continues throughout the germinal period. (Recall that this cell division occurs through a process called *mitosis.*) By approximately one week after conception, the differentiation of these cells—their specialization for different tasks—has already begun. At this stage, the group of cells, now called the **blastocyst,** consists of an inner mass of cells that will eventually develop into the embryo and the **trophoblast,** an outer layer of cells that later provides nutrition and support for the embryo. *Implantation,* the attachment of the zygote to the uterine wall, takes place about 10 to 14 days after conception. Figure 1 illustrates some of the most significant developments during the germinal period.

blastocyst The inner mass of cells that develops during the germinal period. These cells later develop into the embryo.

trophoblast The outer layer of cells that develops in the germinal period. These cells later provide nutrition and support for the embryo.

THE EMBRYONIC PERIOD

embryonic period The period of prenatal development that occurs two to eight weeks after conception. During the embryonic period, the rate of cell differentiation intensifies, support systems for the cells form, and organs appear.

The **embryonic period** is the period of prenatal development that occurs from two to eight weeks after conception. During the embryonic period, the rate of cell differentiation intensifies, support systems for cells form, and organs appear.

This period begins as the blastocyst attaches to the uterine wall. The mass of cells is now called an *embryo,* and three layers of cells form. The embryo's **endoderm** is the inner layer of cells, which will develop into the digestive and respiratory systems. The **mesoderm** is the middle layer, which will become the circulatory system, bones, muscles, excretory system, and reproductive system. The **ectoderm** is the outermost layer, which will become the nervous system and brain, sensory receptors (ears, nose, and eyes, for example), and skin parts (hair and nails, for example). Every body part eventually develops from these three layers. The endoderm primarily produces internal body parts, the mesoderm primarily produces parts that surround the internal areas, and the ectoderm primarily produces surface parts.

endoderm The inner layer of cells, which develops into digestive and respiratory systems.

mesoderm The middle layer of cells, which becomes the circulatory system, bones, muscles, excretory system, and reproductive system.

ectoderm The outermost layer of cells, which becomes the nervous system and brain, sensory receptors (ears, nose, and eyes, for example), and skin parts (hair and nails, for example).

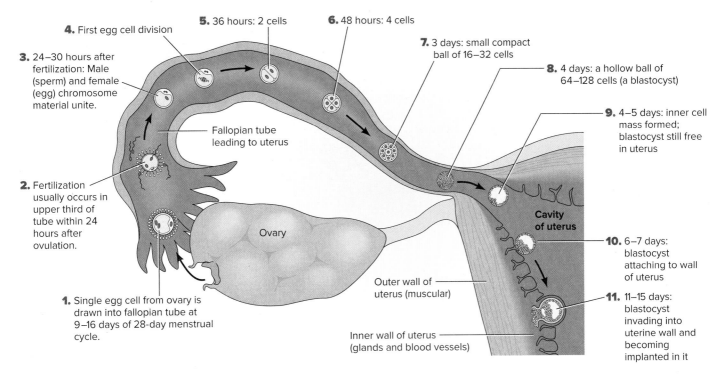

4. First egg cell division

5. 36 hours: 2 cells

6. 48 hours: 4 cells

7. 3 days: small compact ball of 16–32 cells

3. 24–30 hours after fertilization: Male (sperm) and female (egg) chromosome material unite.

8. 4 days: a hollow ball of 64–128 cells (a blastocyst)

9. 4–5 days: inner cell mass formed; blastocyst still free in uterus

Fallopian tube leading to uterus

2. Fertilization usually occurs in upper third of tube within 24 hours after ovulation.

Ovary

Cavity of uterus

10. 6–7 days: blastocyst attaching to wall of uterus

1. Single egg cell from ovary is drawn into fallopian tube at 9–16 days of 28-day menstrual cycle.

Outer wall of uterus (muscular)

Inner wall of uterus (glands and blood vessels)

11. 11–15 days: blastocyst invading into uterine wall and becoming implanted in it

FIGURE **1**

SIGNIFICANT DEVELOPMENTS IN THE GERMINAL PERIOD. Just one week after conception, cells of the blastocyst have already begun specializing. The germinal period ends when the blastocyst attaches to the uterine wall. *Which of the steps shown in the drawing occur in the laboratory when IVF (described in the "Biological Beginnings" chapter) is used?*

As the embryo's three layers form, life-support systems for the embryo develop rapidly. These life-support systems include the amnion, the umbilical cord (both of which develop from the fertilized egg, not the mother's body), and the placenta. The **amnion** is like a bag or an envelope and contains a clear fluid in which the developing embryo floats. The amniotic fluid provides an environment that is temperature and humidity controlled, as well as shockproof. The **umbilical cord** contains two arteries and one vein that connect the baby to the placenta. The **placenta** consists of a disk-shaped group of tissues in which small blood vessels from the mother and the offspring intertwine but do not join.

Figure 2 illustrates the placenta, the umbilical cord, and the blood flow in the expectant mother and developing organism. Very small molecules—oxygen, water, salt, and food from the mother's blood, as well as carbon dioxide and digestive wastes from the offspring's blood—pass back and forth between the mother and embryo or fetus (Whittington & others, 2022). Virtually any drug or chemical substance the pregnant woman ingests can cross the placenta to some degree, unless it is metabolized or altered during passage, or is too large (Hove & others, 2022). A comprehensive review of the research revealed that cigarette smoke weakened and increased the oxidative stress of fetal membranes from which the placenta develops (Lu & others, 2018). Large molecules that cannot pass through the placental wall include red blood cells and harmful substances such as most bacteria, maternal wastes, and hormones. The complex mechanisms that control the movement of substances across the placental barrier are still not entirely understood (Saunders & others, 2018; Zhu & others, 2018).

By the time most women find out that they are pregnant, the major organs have begun to form. **Organogenesis** is the name given to the process of organ formation during the first two months of prenatal development. While the organs are being formed, they are especially vulnerable to environmental influences (Sebastiani & others, 2018). In the third week after conception, the neural tube that eventually becomes the spinal cord forms. At about 21 days, eyes begin to appear, and at 24 days the cells for the heart begin to differentiate. During the fourth week, the urogenital system becomes apparent, and arm and leg buds emerge. Four

amnion The fetal life-support system, which consists of a thin bag or envelope that contains a clear fluid in which the developing embryo floats.

umbilical cord Contains two arteries and one vein, and connects the baby to the placenta.

placenta A disk-shaped group of tissues in which small blood vessels from the mother and the offspring intertwine but don't join.

organogenesis Process of organ formation that takes place during the first two months of prenatal development.

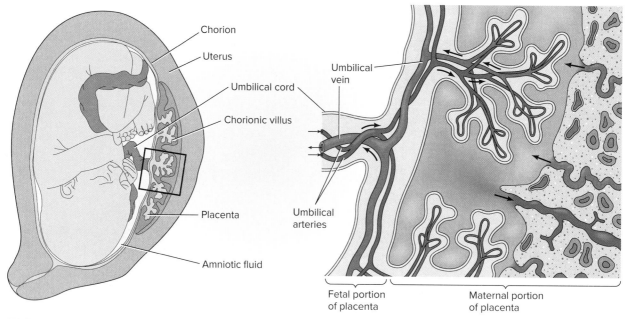

FIGURE 2

THE PLACENTA AND THE UMBILICAL CORD. The area bound by the square in the left illustration is enlarged on the right to show a segment of the placenta. Arrows indicate uterine veins to the maternal circulation. The exchange of materials takes place across the layer separating the maternal and fetal blood supplies, so the bloods never come into contact. *What is known about how the placenta works and its importance?*

chambers of the heart take shape, and blood vessels appear. From the fifth to eighth week, arms and legs differentiate further; at this time, the face starts to form but still is not very recognizable. The intestinal tract develops and the facial structures fuse. At eight weeks, the developing organism weighs about 1/30 ounce and is just over 1 inch long.

THE FETAL PERIOD

The **fetal period**, lasting about seven months, is the prenatal period between two months after conception and birth in typical pregnancies. Growth and development continue their dramatic course during this time.

Three months after conception (13 weeks), the fetus is about 3 inches long and weighs about four-fifths of an ounce. Its arms, legs, and head move randomly (or spontaneously), and its mouth opens and closes. The face, forehead, eyelids, nose, and chin are distinguishable, as are the upper arms, lower arms, hands, and lower limbs. In most cases, the genitals can be identified as male or female. By the end of the fourth month of pregnancy (17 weeks), the fetus has grown to about 5.5 inches in length and weighs about 5 ounces. At this time, a growth spurt occurs in the body's lower parts. For the first time, the mother can feel the fetus move.

By the end of the fifth month (22 weeks), the fetus is about 11 inches long and weighs close to a pound. Structures of the skin have formed—toenails and fingernails, for example. The fetus is more active, showing a preference for a particular position in the womb. By the end of the sixth month (26 weeks), the fetus is about 14 inches long and has gained another half pound to a pound. The eyes and eyelids are completely formed, and a fine layer of hair covers the head. A grasping reflex is present and irregular breathing movements occur.

As early as six months of pregnancy (about 24 to 25 weeks after conception), the fetus for the first time has a chance of surviving outside the womb—that is, it is *viable*. Infants born between 24 and 37 weeks of pregnancy usually need help breathing because their lungs are not yet fully mature. By the end of the seventh month, the fetus is about 16 inches long and weighs about 3 pounds.

During the last two months of prenatal development, fatty tissues develop, and the functioning of various organ systems—heart and kidneys, for example—steps up. During the eighth and ninth

How Would You...?
If you were a **human development and family studies professional,** how would you characterize the greatest risks at each period of prenatal development?

fetal period The prenatal period of development that begins two months after conception and lasts for seven months on average.

months, the fetus grows longer and gains substantial weight—about another 4 pounds. At birth, the average American baby weighs 8 pounds and is about 20 inches long. When mothers have access to adequate nutrition and prenatal care, less than 3.5 percent of fetal growth is due to differences between populations around the globe (Papageorghiou & others, 2018). Instead, most differences in the rate of fetal growth are a result of environmental, nutritional, and socioeconomic factors.

Figure 3 gives an overview of the main events during prenatal development. Notice that instead of describing development in terms of germinal, embryonic, and fetal periods, Figure 3 divides prenatal development into equal periods of three months, called *trimesters*. Remember that the three trimesters are not the same as the three prenatal periods we have discussed. The germinal and embryonic periods occur in the first trimester. The fetal period begins toward the end of the first trimester and continues through the second and third trimesters. Viability (the potential to survive outside the womb) occurs at the very end of the second trimester.

First trimester (first 3 months): Germinal and embryonic periods, and beginning of fetal period

Conception to 4 weeks
- Is less than 1/10 inch long
- Beginning development of spinal cord, nervous system, gastrointestinal system, heart, and lungs
- Amniotic sac envelops the preliminary tissues of entire body
- Is called a "zygote"

8 weeks
- Is just over 1 inch long
- Face is forming with rudimentary eyes, ears, mouth, and tooth buds
- Arms and legs are moving
- Brain is forming
- Fetal heartbeat is detectable with ultrasound
- Is called an "embryo"

12 weeks
- Is about 3 inches long and weighs about 1 ounce
- Can move arms, legs, fingers, and toes
- Fingerprints are present
- Can smile, frown, suck, and swallow
- Sex is distinguishable
- Can urinate
- Is called a "fetus"

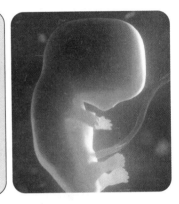

Second trimester (middle 3 months): Fetal period

16 weeks
- Is about 6 inches long and weighs about 4 to 7 ounces
- Heartbeat is strong
- Skin is thin, transparent
- Downy hair (lanugo) covers body
- Fingernails and toenails are forming
- Has coordinated movements; is able to roll over in amniotic fluid

20 weeks
- Is about 12 inches long and weighs close to 1 pound
- Heartbeat is audible with ordinary stethoscope
- Sucks thumb
- Hiccups
- Hair, eyelashes, eyebrows are present

24 weeks
- Is about 14 inches long and weighs 1 to 1½ pounds
- Skin is wrinkled and covered with protective coating (vernix caseosa)
- Eyes are open
- Waste matter is collected in bowel
- Has strong grip

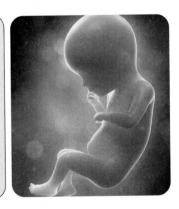

Third trimester (last 3 months): Fetal period

28 weeks
- Is about 16 inches long and weighs about 3 pounds
- Is adding body fat
- Is very active
- Rudimentary breathing movements are present

32 weeks
- Is 16½ to 18 inches long and weighs 4 to 5 pounds
- Has periods of sleep and wakefulness
- Responds to sounds
- May assume the birth position
- Bones of head are soft and flexible
- Iron is being stored in liver

36 to 38 weeks
- Is 19 to 20 inches long and weighs 6 to 7½ pounds
- Skin is less wrinkled
- Vernix caseosa is thick
- Lanugo is mostly gone
- Is less active
- Is gaining immunities from mother

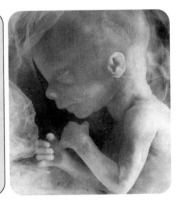

FIGURE **3**

THE THREE TRIMESTERS OF PRENATAL DEVELOPMENT. Both the germinal and embryonic periods occur during the first trimester. The end of the first trimester as well as the entire second and third trimesters are part of the fetal period.

(top) Konstantin Ermolaev/unlim3d/123RF; *(middle)* SCIEPRO/Science Photo Library/Getty Images; *(bottom)* Steve Allen/Brand X Pictures/Getty Images

neurons The term for nerve cells, which handle information processing at the cellular level.

neurogenesis The formation of new neurons.

THE BRAIN

One of the most remarkable aspects of the prenatal period is the development of the brain (Andescavage & others, 2017; Arck & others, 2018). By the time babies are born, they have approximately 100 billion **neurons**, or nerve cells, which handle information processing at the cellular level in the brain. During prenatal development, neurons gradually move to the right locations and start to become connected. The basic architecture of the human brain is assembled during the first two trimesters of prenatal development. In typical development, the third trimester of prenatal development and the first two years of postnatal life are characterized by increasing connectivity and functioning of neurons (Kostović & others, 2021).

Four important phases of the brain's development during the prenatal development involve (1) the neural tube, (2) neurogenesis, (3) neural migration, and (4) neural connectivity.

Neural Tube   As the human embryo develops inside its mother's womb, the nervous system begins forming as a long, hollow tube located on the embryo's back. This pear-shaped *neural tube,* which forms about 18 to 24 days after conception, develops out of the ectoderm. The tube closes at the top and bottom about 27 days after conception (Keunen, Counsell, & Benders, 2017). Figure 4 shows that the nervous system still has a tubular appearance six weeks after conception.

Two birth defects related to a failure of the neural tube to close are anencephaly and spina bifida. When *anencephaly* occurs (that is, when the head end of the neural tube fails to close), the highest regions of the brain fail to develop and the fetus dies in the womb, during childbirth, or shortly after birth (Özel & others, 2019). *Spina bifida,* an incomplete development of the spinal cord, results in varying degrees of paralysis of the lower limbs (Ho & others, 2021). Individuals with spina bifida usually need assistive devices such as crutches, braces, or wheelchairs. A strategy that can help to prevent neural tube defects is for pregnant women to take adequate amounts of the B vitamin folic acid, a topic covered later in this chapter (Best & others, 2021). A large-scale study in Brazil found that when flour was fortified with folic acid it produced a significant reduction in neural tube defects (Santos & others, 2016). Turning to other risk factors, maternal diabetes and obesity also place the fetus at risk for developing neural tube defects (Vena & others, 2022). Maternal exposure to indoor air pollution and secondhand tobacco smoke has been linked to neural tube defects (Chen & others, 2023). Further, a comprehensive research review and meta-analysis of many studies revealed that a high level of maternal stress during pregnancy was associated with neural tube defects in offspring (Jia & others, 2019).

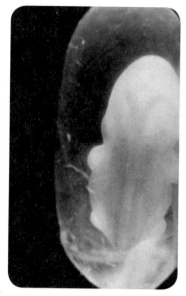

FIGURE 4

EARLY FORMATION OF THE NERVOUS SYSTEM. The photograph shows the primitive, tubular appearance of the nervous system at six weeks in the human embryo.
Claude Edelmann/Science Source

Yelyi Nordone of New York City, shown here as a 12-year-old casting her fishing line out into the pond during Camp Spifida in rural Pennsylvania. Camp Spifida is a week-long residential camp for children with spina bifida.
Bill Hughes/Bloomsburg Press Enterprise/AP Images

Neurogenesis   In a normal pregnancy, once the neural tube has closed, massive growth of new immature neurons begins to take place at about the fifth prenatal week and continues throughout the remainder of the prenatal period. The generation of new neurons is called **neurogenesis,** a process that continues through the remainder of the prenatal period although it is largely complete by the end of the fifth month after conception (Licari & others, 2019). At the peak of neurogenesis, it is estimated that as many as 200,000 neurons are being generated every minute.

Neural Migration   At approximately 6 to 24 weeks after conception, *neuronal migration* occurs (Licari & others, 2019). This involves cells moving outward from their point of origin to their appropriate locations and creating the different levels, structures, and regions of the brain. Once a cell has migrated to its target destination, it must mature and develop a more complex structure.

Neural Connectivity   At about 23 prenatal weeks, connections between neurons begin to occur, a process that continues postnatally (Hadders-Algra, 2018). We will have much more to consider about the structure of neurons, their connectivity, and the development of the infant brain in "Physical Development in Infancy."

Review *Connect* Reflect

 LG1 Discuss the three periods of prenatal development.

Review

- How can the germinal period be characterized?
- What takes place during the embryonic period?
- How can the fetal period be described?
- How does the brain develop in the prenatal period?

Connect

- You have learned about the issue of continuity and discontinuity. Does thinking about prenatal development in terms of germinal, embryonic, and fetal periods reflect continuity or discontinuity? Explain.

Reflect *Your Own Personal Journey of Life*

- What is the most important thing you learned in the section on exploring prenatal development that you did not previously know?

2 What Are Some Important Strategies That Enhance the Expectant Mother's Health and Prenatal Care?

LG2 Summarize how nutrition, exercise, and prenatal care are important aspects of the expectant mother's pregnancy.

The Expectant Mother's Nutrition and Weight Gain

Exercise

Prenatal Care

What can an expectant mother do to stay healthy and to improve her baby's chances of being born healthy? Some of the most important strategies she can adopt involve nutrition, exercise, and prenatal care.

THE EXPECTANT MOTHER'S NUTRITION AND WEIGHT GAIN

The mother's nutrition can have a strong influence on the development of the fetus. Here we discuss the mother's nutritional needs and optimal nutrition during pregnancy.

The best assurance of an adequate caloric intake during pregnancy is a satisfactory weight gain over time (Baugh & others, 2017). The optimal weight gain depends on the expectant mother's height, bone structure, and prepregnant nutritional state. For women of average weight and stature, a maternal weight gain of 25 to 35 pounds is associated with the best reproductive outcomes.

An increasing number of pregnant women gain more than this recommended amount. Maternal obesity adversely affects pregnancy outcomes through increased rates of hypertension, diabetes, respiratory complications, and infections in the mother (Baugh & others, 2017; McIntyre & others, 2020). Also, pregnancies in obese women are characterized by higher rates of neural tube defects, preterm deliveries, and late-term fetal deaths (Creanga & others, 2022). Studies also have found that maternal overweight and obesity during pregnancy were associated with an increased risk of preterm birth, especially extremely preterm delivery (Onishi, 2020). Further, research indicates that maternal obesity during pregnancy is linked to cardiovascular disease and type 2 diabetes in the adolescent and adult offspring of these mothers (Kominiarek & Chauhan, 2016; Lahti-Pulkkinen & others, 2019).

Management of obesity including weight loss and increased exercise prior to pregnancy is likely to benefit the mother and the baby (Hart & others, 2022). For example, one study found that higher maternal pre-pregnancy body mass was linked to a higher incidence of adiposity (body fat) and inflammation in newborns (McCloskey & others, 2017). For pregnant women who are obese, limiting gestational weight gain to 11 to 20 pounds is likely to improve outcomes for the mother and the child (McIntyre & others, 2020). We further discuss obesity as a potential hazard to prenatal development later in the chapter.

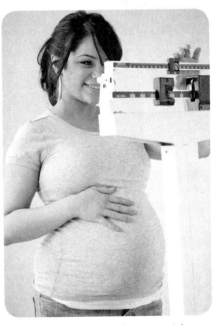

How much do you know about prenatal development and maintaining a healthy pregnancy? How much weight gain on average should occur during pregnancy?
JGI/Jamie Grill/Getty Images

The pattern of weight gain is also important. The ideal pattern of weight gain during pregnancy is 2 to 4.4 pounds during the first trimester, followed by an average gain of 1 pound per week during the last two trimesters. In the second trimester, most of the weight gain is due to increased blood volume; the enlargement of breasts, uterus, and associated tissue and fluid; and storage of maternal fat. In the third trimester, weight gain mainly involves the fetus, placenta, and amniotic fluid. A 25-pound weight gain during pregnancy is generally distributed in this way: 11 pounds: fetus, placenta, and amniotic fluid; 5 pounds: maternal fat stores; 4 pounds: increased blood volume; 3 pounds: tissue fluid; and 2 pounds: uterus and breasts.

During the second and third trimesters, inadequate gains of less than 2.2 pounds per month or excessive gains of more than 6.6 pounds per month should be evaluated and the need for nutritional counseling considered. Inadequate maternal weight gain has been associated with low birth weight of offspring. Sudden sharp increases in weight of 3 to 5 pounds in a week may result from fluid retention and may require evaluation.

The recommended daily allowance (RDA) for all nutrients increases during pregnancy. The expectant mother should eat three meals a day, with nutritious snacks of fruits, cheese, milk, or other foods between meals if desired. More frequent, smaller meals also are recommended. Water is an essential nutrient. Four to six 8-ounce glasses of water and a total of 8 to 10 cups (64 to 80 ounces) of total fluid should be consumed daily. The need for protein, iron, vitamin D, folacin, calcium, phosphorus, and magnesium increases by 50 percent or more. Recommended increases for other nutrients range from 15 to 40 percent (see Figure 5). Researchers have found that women who take a multivitamin prior to pregnancy may be at reduced risk for delivering a preterm infant and a number of other adverse birth outcomes (Miranda & others, 2019).

What are some guidelines for expectant mothers' eating patterns?

JGI/Tom Grill/Blend Images LLC

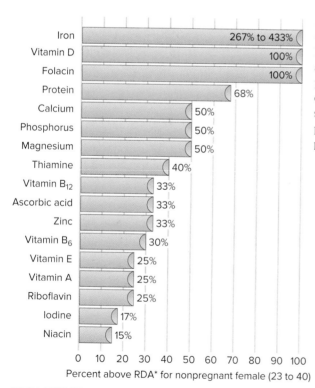

Iron 267% to 433%
Vitamin D 100%
Folacin 100%
Protein 68%
Calcium 50%
Phosphorus 50%
Magnesium 50%
Thiamine 40%
Vitamin B$_{12}$ 33%
Ascorbic acid 33%
Zinc 33%
Vitamin B$_6$ 30%
Vitamin E 25%
Vitamin A 25%
Riboflavin 25%
Iodine 17%
Niacin 15%

Percent above RDA* for nonpregnant female (23 to 40)

FIGURE **5**

RECOMMENDED NUTRIENT INCREASES FOR EXPECTANT MOTHERS

*Recommended Dietary Allowance

EXERCISE

How much and what type of exercise is best during pregnancy depend to some degree on the course of the pregnancy, the expectant mother's fitness, and her customary activity level. These factors are influenced by individual beliefs and practices, as well as cultural factors and adequate access to resources that permit activity and exercise. Normal participation in physical activity and exercise can continue throughout an uncomplicated pregnancy. In general, a skilled sportswoman or a physically active worker is not discouraged from participating in activities they participated in prior to pregnancy. However, pregnancy is not the appropriate time to begin strenuous activity.

How might a woman's exercise in pregnancy benefit her and her offspring?

JGI/Jamie Grill/Getty Images

Because of the increased emphasis on physical fitness in our society, more women routinely jog as part of a physical fitness program prior to pregnancy. There are few concerns about continuing to jog during the early part of pregnancy, but in the latter part of pregnancy there is some concern about the jarring effect of jogging on the breasts and abdomen. As pregnancy progresses, low-impact activities such as walking, swimming, water aerobics, and bicycling are safer and provide fitness as well as greater comfort, eliminating the bouncing associated with jogging (Bowersock & Lin, 2020). An increasing number of studies are finding that exercise either benefits the mother's health and has positive infant outcomes or that there are no differences in outcomes (for meta-analysis studies, see Craemer & others, 2019, and Du & others, 2019). Exercise during pregnancy helps prevent constipation, conditions the body, reduces the likelihood of excessive weight gain, lowers the risk of developing hypertension, and is associated with a more positive mental state, including a reduced level of depression (Nakamura & others, 2019). The following positive outcomes of exercise for pregnant women have been revealed by many studies and research reviews:

- A research review indicated that engaging in frequent exercise with a combination of aerobic and resistance activity during pregnancy has positive benefits for maternal cardiorespiratory fitness and weight management (Wang & others, 2019).
- A meta-analysis concluded that aerobic exercise for 35 to 90 minutes 3 to 4 times a week during pregnancy was not associated with an increased rate of preterm birth and was linked to a higher incidence of vaginal birth, as well as a lower occurrence of caesarean delivery (Di Mascio & others, 2016).
- Although results are mixed across studies, some show that women who exercise regularly during pregnancy are less likely to have high blood pressure (Du & others, 2019).
- A meta-analysis of 13 studies found that for women with depression, doing yoga during pregnancy reduced depression scores (Lin & others, 2022).
- Two weekly 70-minute yoga sessions reduced pregnant women's stress and enhanced their immune system functioning (Chen & others, 2017).
- Moderate exercise throughout pregnancy does not increase the risk of preterm delivery or other outcomes that threaten the life of the newborn (Davenport & others, 2019).
- Regular exercise by pregnant women was linked to more advanced development of the neonatal brain (Laborte-Lemoyne, Currier, & Ellenberg, 2017).

To read about some guidelines for exercise during pregnancy, see the *Caring Connections* interlude.

PRENATAL CARE

Although prenatal care varies enormously, it usually involves a defined schedule of visits for medical care, which typically includes screening for manageable conditions and treatable diseases that can affect the baby or the mother (Ickovics & others, 2019; Jarris & others, 2017). In addition to medical care, prenatal programs often include comprehensive educational, social, and nutritional services in most countries around the globe (Moller & others, 2017).

The education provided in prenatal care varies during the course of pregnancy. Those in the early stages of pregnancy as well as couples who are anticipating a pregnancy may participate in early prenatal classes. In addition to providing information on dangers to the fetus, early prenatal classes often discuss the development of the embryo and the fetus; sexuality during pregnancy; choices about the birth setting and care providers; nutrition, rest, and exercise; common discomforts of pregnancy and relief measures; psychological changes in the expectant mother and her partner; and factors that increase the risk of preterm labor and possible symptoms of preterm labor. Early classes also may include information about the advantages and disadvantages of breast feeding and bottle feeding. (Fifty to eighty percent of expectant mothers decide how they will feed their infant prior to the sixth month of pregnancy.) During the second or third trimester of pregnancy, prenatal classes focus on preparing for the birth, infant care and feeding, choices about birth, and postpartum self-care.

Partners or friends take classes with prospective mothers in many prenatal care programs. *What characterizes the content of prenatal care programs?*
MBI/Alamy Stock Photo

Exercise Guidelines for Expectant Mothers

Exercise is just as important during pregnancy as it is before or after pregnancy. The following guidelines for exercise are recommended for expectant mothers by the American College of Obstetricians and Gynecologists (2019), and affirmed by the World Health Organization (2018) for all women around the globe as part of prenatal care and counseling:

- *Adapting to changes in the woman's body.* Some of the changes in the woman's body during pregnancy require adaptations in exercise. Joints and ligaments become more mobile during pregnancy. Avoiding jerky, bouncy, or high-impact motions can reduce the risk of injuring joints and ligaments. During pregnancy women carry extra weight, and the pregnant woman's center of gravity shifts, placing stress on joints and muscles, especially in the pelvis and lower back. Thus, maintaining balance while exercising during pregnancy is sometimes difficult and requires attention. The extra weight pregnant women carry makes their bodies work harder, so it is important not to exercise too strenuously.
- *Getting started.* Before starting an exercise program, pregnant women should talk with their doctor to ensure that they don't have an obstetric or health condition that might limit their activity. Women with the following conditions will be advised by their doctor not to exercise during pregnancy: risk factors for preterm labor, vaginal bleeding, and premature rupture of membranes.
- *Choosing safe exercises.* Most types of exercise are safe during pregnancy, but some types involve positions and movements that may be uncomfortable, tiring, or harmful. For example, after the first trimester of pregnancy, women should not do exercises that require them to lie flat on their backs. Some sports are safe during pregnancy, even for beginners. Walking is a good exercise for anyone, and swimming is excellent because it works so many muscles, cycling provides a good aerobic workout (because balance is affected by pregnancy, a stationary bicycle is recommended in later pregnancy); aerobic exercise is effective in keeping the heart

What are some recommended guidelines for exercise during pregnancy?
Stockbyte/Getty Images

and lungs strong; and strength training can tone muscles and help prevent some common aches and pains during pregnancy. Women who were runners or played racquet sports before becoming pregnant should talk with their doctor about taking certain precautions if they plan to continue these activities during pregnancy. The following activities should be avoided during pregnancy: downhill snow skiing, contact sports, and scuba diving.

- *Establishing a routine.* Exercise is most practical during the first 24 weeks of pregnancy; during the last three months many exercises that were easy earlier in pregnancy are often difficult. It is important to begin each exercise session with a 5- to 10-minute warm-up and end each session with a 5- to 10-minute cool-down. During the warm-up and cool-down periods, stretching exercises should be done. Pregnant women should not exercise to the point of exhaustion. If pregnant women experience any of the following problems, they should stop exercising and call their doctor: vaginal bleeding, dizziness or feeling faint, increased shortness of breath, chest pain, headache, muscle weakness, calf pain or swelling, uterine contractions, decreased fetal movement, or fluid leaking from the vagina.

How Would You...?
If you were a **human development and family studies professional,** how would you justify the need for prenatal education classes for individuals and couples expecting a child?

Does prenatal care matter? Information about pregnancy, labor, delivery, and caring for the newborn can be especially valuable for first-time mothers (Hetherington & others, 2018). Prenatal care is also very important for women in poverty because it links them with other social services (Hughson & others, 2018; Mazul, Salm Ward, & Ngui, 2017). The legacy of prenatal care continues after the birth because women who experience this type of care are more likely to get preventive care for their infants.

Research contrasting the experiences of mothers who had prenatal care and those who did not supports the importance of prenatal care (Roman & others, 2022). One large study found that Canadian women who had no prenatal care were far more likely than their counterparts who received prenatal care to have infants who had low birth weight, increased mortality, and a number of other physical problems (Heaman & others, 2019). Another large study conducted in western China also found that inadequate prenatal care was associated with very low birth weight (Zhou & others, 2019). In many other studies, low birth weight and preterm deliveries were common among U.S. mothers who received no prenatal care, and the absence

Barbara Greedan, Perinatal Nurse Navigator

Pregnancy can be a stressful time for anyone and especially for first-time mothers and those who may be susceptible to high-risk pregnancies. A perinatal nurse navigator is a specialist within hospitals or women's clinics who can help guide a patient from conception through postpartum care.

Barbara Greedan is a perinatal nurse navigator with Chippenham & Johnston-Willis Hospitals in Virginia. Greedan started her career in the military, obtaining a degree in aerospace propulsion. After leaving the military, she used the GI Bill to transition to nursing, working in various clinical settings as she completed her BSN and a master's degree in informatics (Chippenham & Johnston-Willis Hospitals, 2022).

Once Greedan began working in labor and delivery, she knew she had found her calling, and she decided to focus on helping patients through their pregnancy experience. As a perinatal navigator, she works as a member of a team with the patient and her doctor to determine each client's specific needs, which may include connecting with other specialists—such as a pediatric cardiologist or neurologist—to protect the health of the mother and baby.

Greedan connects with her patients as least once a month to answer questions and discuss concerns, assess health issues, provide hospital tours, and suggest additional community resources to help support the patient's personal situation. "I bridge the gap for my moms to help them understand that they are cared for emotionally and physically throughout their pregnancy."

Barbara Greedan is a perinatal nurse navigator who helps patients in all aspects of their pregnancies.

Courtesy of Barbara Greedan

of prenatal care can increase the risk for preterm birth up to threefold in most ethnic groups (Mydam & others, 2019).

Inadequate prenatal care may help explain a disturbing fact: Rates of infant mortality and low birth weight indicate that many other nations have healthier babies than the United States (Blencowe & others, 2019). In many countries that have a lower percentage of low birth weight infants than the United States, mothers receive either free or very low cost prenatal and postnatal care, and can receive paid maternity leave from work that ranges from 9 to 40 weeks. In Norway and the Netherlands, for instance, prenatal care is coordinated among a general practitioner, an obstetrician, and a midwife. To read about the work and career of a perinatal nurse navigator, see the *Connecting with Careers* profile.

Why do some U.S. women receive inadequate prenatal care? The reasons may be linked to lack of access, the health-care system, provider practices, and their own individual and social characteristics (Kauer, Callaghan, & Regan, 2023). Women who do not want to be pregnant, who have negative attitudes about being pregnant, or who unintentionally become pregnant are more likely to delay prenatal care or to miss appointments. As we noted earlier, adolescent girls are less likely than adult women to obtain prenatal care.

Usage of prenatal care in the United States has been improving. A classic study examining births throughout the United States showed that from 1990 to 2004, the use of timely prenatal care increased among women from a variety of ethnic backgrounds, although non–Latina White women were still more likely to obtain prenatal care than Black American and Latina women (Martin & others, 2005) (see Figure 6). Since 2004, access to prenatal care has continued to increase, though these ethnic group disparities persist due in part to inequities in health-care access (Baer & others, 2019). The United States needs more comprehensive medical and

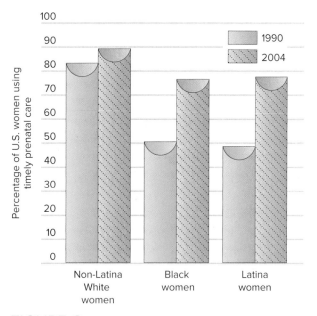

FIGURE 6

PERCENTAGE OF U.S. WOMEN USING TIMELY PRENATAL CARE: 1990 TO 2004. A classic study examining birth data in the United States found that from 1990 to 2004 the use of timely prenatal care increased by 7 percent (to 89.1) for non–Latina White women, by 25 percent (to 76.5) for Black women, and by 28 percent (to 77.4) for Latina women in the United States.

educational services to improve the quality of prenatal care and to reduce the number of low birth weight and preterm infants.

An innovative program that is rapidly expanding in the United States and other countries is CenteringPregnancy (Liu & others, 2021). This relationship-centered program provides complete prenatal care in a group setting. CenteringPregnancy replaces traditional 15-minute physician visits with 90-minute peer group support sessions and self-examination led by a physician or certified nurse-midwife. Groups of up to 10 women (and often their partners) meet regularly beginning at 12 to 16 weeks of pregnancy. The sessions emphasize empowering women to play an active role in experiencing a positive pregnancy. In one study, Centering Pregnancy was successful in getting participants to increase their prenatal visits, to breast feed, and to have healthier newborns (Grant & others, 2018). A meta-analysis of seven randomized controlled trials showed no differences in infants' birth weight or preterm births for mothers who participated in CenteringPregnancy compared to obstetric-led prenatal care, but mothers who participated in CenteringPregnancy did have lower rates of postpartum depression six months after delivery (Liu & others, 2021).

Some prenatal programs for parents focus on home visitation (Beatson & others, 2021). A research review concluded that prenatal home visits were linked to improved use of prenatal care, although there was less evidence that they improve newborns' birth weight (Issel & others, 2011). However, a subsequent study found that home visiting services reduced the risk of low birth weight (Shah & Austin, 2014). A large meta-analysis of experiments with random assignment to home visiting conditions showed some benefit for higher birth weights but no protection against premature birth (Liu & others, 2019).

A classic series of research evaluations indicates that one of the most successful home visitation programs is the Nurse-Family Partnership created by David Olds and his colleagues (2019). The Nurse-Family Partnership involves home visits by trained nurses beginning in the second or third trimester of prenatal development. The extensive program consists of approximately 50 home visits from the prenatal period through 2 years of age. The home visits focus on the mother's health, access to health care, parenting, and improvement of the mother's life by providing her with guidance in education, work, and

The popular CenteringPregnancy program alters routine prenatal care by bringing women out of exam rooms and into relationship-oriented groups.

Stephen Maturen

Cultural Beliefs About Pregnancy

All cultures have beliefs and practices that surround life's major events, and one such event is pregnancy. When a woman who has immigrated to the United States becomes pregnant, the beliefs and practices of her native culture may be as important as, or more important than, those of the mainstream U.S. culture that now surrounds her. The conflict between cultural traditions and Western medicine may pose a risk for the pregnancy and a challenge for the health-care professional who wishes to give proper care while respecting the woman's values.

The American Public Health Association (2006) identified a number of cultural beliefs and practices that are observed among various immigrant groups, and these findings have been replicated in a variety of research studies (e.g., Goswami & Thakur, 2019; Withers, Kharazmi, & Lim, 2018). These beliefs and practices include the following:

- *Food cravings.* Latin American, Asian, and some African cultures believe that it is important for a pregnant woman's food cravings to be satisfied because they are thought to be the cravings of the baby. If cravings are left unsatisfied, the baby might take on certain unpleasant personality and/or physical traits, perhaps characteristic of the food (Kavle & Landry, 2018; Taylor, Ko, & Pan, 1999). As an example, in African cultures women often eat soil, chalk, or clay during pregnancy; this is believed to satisfy the baby's hunger as well as affirming soil as a symbol of female fertility (American Public Health Association, 2006).

- *"Hot-cold" theory of illness.* Many cultures in Latin America, Asia, and Africa characterize foods, medications, and illnesses as "hot" or "cold"; this has nothing to do with temperature or spiciness, but with traditional definitions and categories. Most of these cultures view pregnancy as a "hot" condition, although the Chinese view it as "cold" (Taylor, Ko, & Pan, 1999; Withers, Kharazmi, & Lim, 2018). As a result, a woman may resist taking a prescribed medication because of concern that it could create too much "heat" and cause a miscarriage. In Indian culture, iron-rich foods are also considered unacceptably "hot" for pregnant women (DeSantis, 1998);

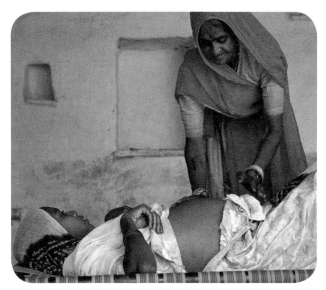

In India, a midwife checks on the size, position, and heartbeat of a fetus. Midwives deliver babies in many cultures around the world. *What are some cultural variations in prenatal care?*
Viviane Moos/Corbis/Getty Images

the resulting avoidance of iron has contributed to high rates of anemia during pregnancy (Nivedita & Shanthini, 2016).

- *Extended family.* In many immigrant cultures, the extended family is a vital support system, and health-care decisions are made that prioritize the needs of the family over those of the individual (Pangas & others, 2019). Western health-care providers need to be sensitive to this dynamic, which runs counter to today's practices of protecting patient confidentiality and autonomy.

- *Stoicism.* In many Asian cultures, stoicism is valued, as suffering is seen as part of life (Tung & Li, 2015; Uba, 1992). Physicians are also viewed with great respect. As a result, a pregnant Asian woman may behave submissively and avoid voicing complaints to her health-care provider, but may privately refrain from following the provider's advice (Assanand & others, 1990).

relationships. The evaluation studies revealed that the Nurse-Family Partnership has numerous positive outcomes including fewer pregnancies, better work circumstances, and stability in relationship partners for the mother and improved academic success and social development for the child. Most recently, evidence for programs such as Family Connects suggests that many of these benefits can be generated with fewer visits (Goodman & others, 2022).

Cultures around the world have differing views of pregnancy. In the *Connecting with Diversity* interlude, we explore some of these beliefs. Some cultures treat pregnancy simply as a natural occurrence; others see it as a medical condition (McCauley & others, 2019). How expectant mothers behave during pregnancy may depend in part on the prevalence of traditional home-care remedies and folk beliefs, the importance of indigenous healers, and the influence of health-care professionals in their culture. In various cultures women may consult herbalists and/or faith healers during pregnancy (Robbins & others, 2021). Health-care workers should assess whether a woman's beliefs or practices pose a threat to her or the fetus. If a health risk is posed, health-care professionals should consider a culturally sensitive way to handle the problem (Nagle & others, 2019).

Review *Connect* Reflect

Summarize how nutrition, exercise, and prenatal care are important aspects of the expectant mother's pregnancy.

Review

- What are some recommendations for the expectant mother's nutrition and weight gain?
- What role does exercise play in the mother's health during pregnancy?
- What are some important aspects of prenatal care?

Connect

- How would nutrition and exercise be incorporated into an ideal prenatal care program?

Reflect *Your Own Personal Journey of Life*

- What are some beliefs about pregnancy and prenatal development in your culture?

---

3 What Are Some Potential Hazards to Prenatal Development?

 Describe potential hazards during prenatal development.

Some General Principles	Prescription and Nonprescription Drugs	Psychoactive Drugs	Incompatible Blood Types	Environmental Hazards	Maternal Diseases	Other Parental Factors

For Alex, the baby discussed at the opening of this chapter, the course of prenatal development went smoothly. His mother's womb protected him as he developed. Despite this protection, however, the environment can affect the embryo or fetus in many well-documented ways.

SOME GENERAL PRINCIPLES

A **teratogen** is any agent that can potentially cause a physical birth defect. (The word comes from the Greek word *tera,* meaning "monster.") The field of study that investigates the causes of birth defects is called *teratology* (Holmes, 2020). Some exposures to teratogens do not cause physical birth defects but can alter the developing brain and influence cognitive and behavioral functioning, in which case the field of study is called *behavioral teratology*.

Teratogens include drugs, incompatible blood types, environmental pollutants, infectious diseases, nutritional deficiencies, maternal stress, advanced maternal and paternal age, and environmental pollutants. In fact, thousands of babies are born each year with physical deformities or intellectual disabilities as a result of events that occurred in the mother's life as early as one or two months before conception. As we further discuss teratogens, you will see that factors related to the father also can influence prenatal development.

So many teratogens exist that practically every fetus is exposed to at least some of them. For this reason, it is difficult to determine which teratogen causes which problem. In addition, it may take a long time for the effects of a teratogen to show up. Only about half of all potential effects appear at birth.

The time of exposure, dose, and genetic susceptibility to a particular teratogen influence both the type of defect and the severity of the damage to an embryo or fetus:

- *Time of Exposure.* Teratogens do more damage when they occur at some points in development than at others. Damage during the germinal period may even prevent implantation. In general, the embryonic period is more vulnerable than the fetal period (Buckley, Hamra, & Braun, 2019).
- *Dose.* The dose effect is rather obvious—the greater the dose of an agent, such as a drug, the greater the effect.

teratogen Any agent that can potentially cause a physical birth defect. The field of study that investigates the causes of birth defects is called *teratology*.

- *Genetic Susceptibility.* The type or severity of abnormalities caused by a teratogen is linked to the genotype of the pregnant woman and the genotype of the embryo or fetus (Minatoya, Hanaoka, & Kishi, 2020). For example, how a mother metabolizes a particular drug can influence the degree to which the drug effects are transmitted to the embryo or fetus. Differences in placental membranes and placental transport also affect exposure. The extent to which an embryo or a fetus is vulnerable to a teratogen may also depend on its genotype (Middleton & others, 2017). Also, for unknown reasons, male fetuses are far more likely to be affected by teratogens than are female fetuses (Traccis, Frau, & Melis, 2020).

Figure 7 summarizes additional information about the effects of time of exposure to a teratogen. The probability of a structural defect is greatest early in the embryonic period, when organs are being formed (Chudley, 2017). Each body structure has its own critical period of formation. Recall that a *critical period* is a fixed time period very early in development during which certain experiences or events can have a long-lasting effect on development. The critical period for the nervous system (week 3) is earlier than that for arms and legs (weeks 4 and 5).

After organogenesis is complete, teratogens can no longer cause anatomical defects. Instead, exposure during the fetal period is more likely to stunt growth or to create problems in the way organs function. This is especially true for the developing fetal brain, which continues to develop connections throughout pregnancy. To examine some key teratogens and their effects, let's begin with drugs.

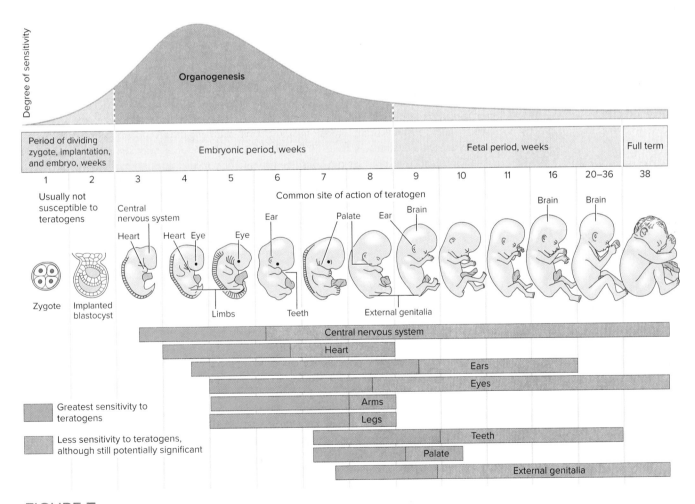

FIGURE 7

TERATOGENS AND THE TIMING OF THEIR EFFECTS ON PRENATAL DEVELOPMENT. The danger of structural defects caused by teratogens is greatest early in embryonic development. The period of organogenesis (red color) lasts for about six weeks. Later effects of teratogens (blue color) mainly occur in the fetal period and instead of causing structural defects are more likely to stunt growth or cause problems with organ function.

PRESCRIPTION AND NONPRESCRIPTION DRUGS

Many U.S. women are given prescriptions for drugs while they are pregnant—especially antibiotics, pain and fever reducers, and asthma medications. Prescription as well as nonprescription drugs, however, may have effects on the embryo or fetus that the women never imagined.

The damage that drugs can do was tragically highlighted in 1961, when many pregnant women took a popular sedative, thalidomide, to alleviate their morning sickness. In adults, the effects of thalidomide are typically not damaging; in embryos, however, they are devastating. Not all infants were affected in the same way. If the mother took thalidomide on day 26 (probably before she knew she was pregnant), an arm might not grow. If she took the drug two days later, the arm might not grow past the elbow. The thalidomide tragedy shocked the medical community and parents and taught a valuable lesson: Taking the wrong drug at the wrong time is enough to physically handicap the offspring for life.

Prescription drugs that can function as teratogens include antibiotics, such as streptomycin and tetracycline; some antidepressants; certain hormones such as progestin and synthetic estrogen; and isotretinoin (Accutane, often prescribed for acne) (Blotière & others, 2021). In a comprehensive review of teratogens that should never be taken during the first trimester of pregnancy, isotreninoin was on the prohibited list (Eltonsy & others, 2016). Nonprescription drugs that can be harmful include diet pills and high doses of aspirin.

PSYCHOACTIVE DRUGS

Psychoactive drugs are drugs that act on the nervous system to alter states of consciousness, modify perceptions, and change moods. Examples include caffeine, alcohol, and nicotine, as well as illicit drugs such as cocaine, methamphetamine, and heroin.

Caffeine   People often consume caffeine when they drink coffee, tea, an energy drink, or cola, or when they eat chocolate. Somewhat mixed results have been found for the extent to which maternal caffeine intake influences fetal development, but there is evidence that more maternal caffeine intake during pregnancy predicts lower birth weight (Gleason & others, 2021) and structural brain alterations and poorer neurocognitive outcomes during childhood (Christensen, Freedman, & Foxe, 2021). The U.S. Food and Drug Administration recommends that pregnant women either not consume caffeine or consume it only sparingly.

Alcohol   Heavy drinking by pregnant women can have devastating consequences for their offspring (Zhang, Hashimoto, & Guizzetti, 2018). **Fetal alcohol spectrum disorders (FASD)** are a cluster of abnormalities and problems that appear in the offspring of mothers who drink alcohol heavily during pregnancy (Broccia & others, 2023). The abnormalities include facial deformities and defects of the limbs, face, and heart (Blanck-Lubarsch & others, 2020). Some children with FASD have these bodily malformations, but others don't. Most children with FASD are characterized by neurocognitive difficulties and learning problems, and many are below average in intelligence or have an intellectual disability (Khoury & Milligan, 2019). A comprehensive review of studies revealed that children with FASD have deficiencies in the brain pathways involved in many aspects of perception, cognition, and behavior (Nguyen & others, 2017). Also, in a very large study in Alberta, Canada, the life expectancy of individuals with FASD was only 34 years of age, about 42 percent of the average life expectancy in the general population (Thanh & Jonsson, 2016). In this study, the most common causes of death among individuals with FASD were suicide (15 percent), accidents (14 percent), and poisoning by illegal drugs or alcohol (7 percent).

A thorough research review concluded that FASD is linked to a lower level of many neurocognitive and behavioral outcomes in children (Mattson, Bernes, & Doyle, 2019). For example, in one such study, FASD was associated with both externalized and internalized behavior problems in childhood (Tsang & others, 2016).

Although women who drink heavily during pregnancy are at a higher risk of having a child with FASD, not all pregnant heavy drinkers have children with FASD. What are some guidelines for alcohol use during pregnancy? Even drinking just one or two servings of beer or wine or one serving of hard liquor a few days a week may have negative effects on the fetus, although it is generally agreed that this level of alcohol use will not cause fetal alcohol spectrum disorders (Noor & Milligan, 2018). The U.S. Surgeon General recommends that no alcohol

Fetal alcohol spectrum disorders (FASD) are characterized by a number of physical abnormalities and learning problems. Notice the wide-set eyes, flat cheekbones, and thin upper lip in this child with FASD.

Streissguth, A. P., S. Landesman-Dwyer, J. C. Martin, and D. W. Smith. "Teratogenic Effects of Alcohol in Humans and Laboratory Animals." *Science* 209 (1980): 353–361.

fetal alcohol spectrum disorders (FASD) A cluster of abnormalities and problems that appears in the offspring of mothers who drink alcohol heavily during pregnancy.

be consumed during pregnancy, as does the World Health Organization and other public health bodies around the globe. Despite such recommendations, a large-scale U.S. study found that 11.5 percent of adolescent and 8.7 percent of adult pregnant women reported using alcohol in the previous month (Oh & others, 2017).

In addition, research suggests that it may not be wise to consume alcohol at the time of conception. Doing so can lead to increased risk for problems during fertilization and implantation that cause miscarriage (Kalisch-Smith & Moritz, 2017).

Nicotine Cigarette smoking by pregnant women also can adversely influence prenatal development, birth, and postnatal development. Preterm births and low birth weights, fetal and neonatal deaths, and respiratory problems and sudden infant death syndrome (SIDS, also known as crib death) are more common among the offspring of mothers who smoked during pregnancy (Dessì & others, 2018; Zhang & others, 2017). In a global review of 55 studies published from 1986 to 2020, smoking during pregnancy was linked to low birth weight, with worse outcomes linked to smoking more cigarettes per day and for longer periods over the course of pregnancy (Di & others, 2022). Other research has also linked heavy smoking during pregnancy to nicotine withdrawal symptoms in newborns (Bertini & others, 2019).

Maternal smoking during pregnancy has been identified as a risk factor for the development of attention deficit hyperactivity disorder in offspring (Abreu-Villaça & others, 2018; Weissenberger & others, 2017). And in a series of studies, maternal cigarette smoking during pregnancy was linked to higher rates of cigarette smoking among offspring at 16 years of age and through early adulthood (De Genna & others, 2016, 2018). Further, another study revealed that daughters whose mothers smoked during their pregnancy were more likely to subsequently smoke during their own pregnancy (Ncube & Mueller, 2017). A thorough meta-analysis indicated that maternal smoking during pregnancy was linked to a modest increase in risk for childhood non-Hodgkins lymphoma (Antonopoulos & others, 2011). Also, a series of studies, including one study of over 10,000 youths in Sweden, Germany, and the Netherlands, found that maternal smoking during pregnancy was associated with increased risk of asthma and wheezing in adolescence (Hollams & others, 2014; Thacher & others, 2018). Despite the plethora of negative outcomes for maternal smoking during pregnancy, in one study 23 percent of adolescent and 15 percent of adult pregnant women reported using tobacco in the previous month (Oh & others, 2017).

Smoking by pregnant women is not the only source of prenatal risk posed by tobacco use. Maternal exposure to environmental tobacco smoke, or secondhand smoke, has been linked to an increased risk of low birth weight and smaller head size in offspring (Soesanti & others, 2019), higher rates of stillbirth (Reece & others, 2019), and to diminished ovarian functioning in female offspring (Budani & Tiboni, 2017). And in another line of research, environmental tobacco smoke has been linked to many alterations in gene functioning in offspring (Dessì & others, 2018; Votavova & others, 2012). And still other research indicates that simultaneous exposure to environmental tobacco smoke and alcohol during pregnancy can increase the offspring's risk of having ADHD (Han & others, 2015).

A final point about nicotine use during pregnancy involves the recent dramatic increase in the use of e-cigarettes (Centers for Disease Control, 2020b; Rostron & others, 2020). Researchers already have found widespread misconceptions about e-cigarettes among pregnant women (Breland, McCubbin, & Ashford, 2019). For instance, one study found that the most common reasons pregnant women gave for using e-cigarettes were the perceptions that they are less harmful than regular cigarettes (74 percent) and that they promote smoking cessation (72 percent) (Mark & others, 2015). However, e-cigarette use during pregnancy is associated with the same risks for premature birth and low birth weight as is smoking combustible cigarettes (Regan & Pereira, 2021).

Intervention programs designed to help pregnant women stop smoking can reduce some of smoking's negative effects, especially by raising birth weights. A comprehensive meta-analysis of 16 intervention experiments involving over 6,000 women in multiple countries revealed that women who quit smoking during pregnancy had offspring with higher birth weights than their counterparts who continued smoking (Veisani & others, 2019). To read further about the negative outcomes of smoking during pregnancy, see the *Connecting with Research* interlude.

Cocaine Does cocaine use during pregnancy harm the developing embryo and fetus? Cocaine quickly crosses the placenta to reach the fetus. The most consistent finding is that

How Would You...?
If you were a **social worker**, how would you counsel a woman who continues to drink alcohol in the early weeks of pregnancy because she believes alcohol can't harm the baby until it has developed further?

What are some links between expectant mothers' drinking and cigarette smoking and outcomes for their offspring?
Monkey Business Images/Getty Images

Is Expectant Mothers' Cigarette Smoking Related to Cigarette Smoking by Their Adolescent Offspring?

Key Points:

- Nicotine and other substances are passed through the placenta from mother to fetus during pregnancy.
- Adolescents whose mothers smoked while they were pregnant were more than twice as likely to smoke as adolescents whose mothers did not smoke while they were pregnant.

Nicotine and other substances in cigarette smoke cross the placental barrier and pass from the expectant mother to the fetus, stimulating the fetal brain as early as the first trimester of pregnancy (Menon & others, 2011). Researchers are exploring the possibility that this prenatal exposure of the brain to cigarette smoke may predispose individuals to be more vulnerable to addiction in adolescence.

One of the first studies on this topic explored whether expectant mothers' cigarette smoking and marijuana use were linked to an increased risk for substance use in adolescence by their offspring (Porath & Fried, 2005). One hundred fifty-two 16- to 21-year-olds were asked to complete a drug history questionnaire that included their past and current cigarette smoking. A urine sample was also obtained from the participants and analyzed for the presence of drugs. The adolescent participants' mothers had been asked about the extent of their cigarette smoking during their pregnancy as part of the Ottawa Prenatal Prospective Study.

The results indicated that adolescent offspring of mothers who reported having smoked cigarettes during pregnancy were more than twice as likely to have initiated smoking during adolescence compared with their counterparts whose mothers reported not smoking during their pregnancy. These findings indicate that cigarette smoking by expectant mothers is a risk factor for later cigarette smoking by their adolescent offspring. Such results add to the strength of the evidence that supports drug use prevention and cessation among expectant mothers.

How do you think health-care professionals might use this type of evidence to counsel expectant mothers about cigarette smoking during pregnancy? Should the government include this evidence as part of its antismoking campaign?

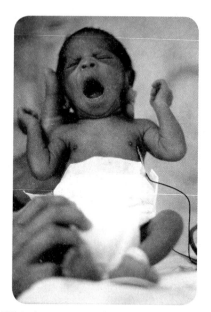

This baby was exposed to cocaine prenatally. *What are some of the possible effects on development of being exposed to cocaine prenatally?*
Chuck Nacke/Alamy Stock Photo

cocaine exposure during prenatal development is associated with reduced birth weight, length, and head circumference (dos Santos & others, 2018). Also, although the results vary, prenatal cocaine exposure has been linked to lower arousal, less effective self-regulation, higher excitability, and poorer reflexes in neonates; impaired motor development; slower growth rate throughout childhood; higher blood pressure; impaired language development and information processing; attention deficits and impulsivity; learning disabilities; increased likelihood of needing special education supports in school; and increased rates of aggression and other behavioral problems (Ackerman, Riggins, & Black, 2010; Buckingham-Howes & others, 2013; Viteri & others, 2015). In addition, after birth, infants who were exposed to cocaine regularly in utero experience withdrawal (Mark, 2022).

Some researchers argue that these findings should be interpreted cautiously. Why? Because other factors in the lives of pregnant women who use cocaine (such as poverty, malnutrition, and other substance abuse) often cannot be ruled out as possible contributors to the problems found in their children (Lowell & Mayes, 2019). For example, cocaine users are more likely than nonusers to smoke cigarettes, use marijuana, drink alcohol, and take amphetamines.

Despite these cautions, the weight of research evidence indicates that children born to mothers who use cocaine are likely to have neurological and cognitive deficits. Cocaine should never be used by pregnant women.

Methamphetamine Methamphetamine, like cocaine, speeds up an individual's nervous system. Babies born to mothers who use methamphetamine, or "meth," during pregnancy are at risk for a number of problems, including high infant mortality, low birth weight, and developmental and behavioral problems (Kwiatkowski & others, 2018). A meta-analysis of studies revealed that prenatal meth exposure was associated with smaller head circumference, lower birth weight, and premature birth (Kalaitzopoulos & others, 2018). And another study of newborns found that prenatal exposure to meth was linked to smaller brain structures in a number of areas, especially in the thalamus and caudate areas in the center of the brain (Warton & others, 2018). A meta-analysis of longer-term outcomes of prenatal methamphetamine exposure revealed detriments to language development, memory, and intellectual functioning that persisted across the life span (Kunkler & others, 2022).

Marijuana At the time of publication of this release, recreational marijuana use is legal or decriminalized in 31 states, even though it remains illegal in federal law. An increasing number of studies find that marijuana use by pregnant women also has negative outcomes for their offspring (Krishnamoorthy & Kaminer, 2020). For example, researchers have found that prenatal marijuana exposure was related to poorer functioning after birth, lower birth weight, premature birth, and a higher likelihood of neonatal intensive care admission (Corsi & others, 2019). Beyond infancy, a number of studies have linked prenatal marijuana exposure to a wide range of child and adolescent outcomes, including lower intelligence, depressive symptoms, and marijuana use in adolescence (Schreiber & Pick, 2019). In sum, pregnant women should not use marijuana.

Despite the widespread evidence of negative outcomes, a series of surveys over the past two decades found that marijuana use by pregnant women increased from 2.4 percent in 2002 to 3.85 percent in 2014 and 7.0 percent in 2017 (Brown & others, 2016; Volkow & others, 2019). There is considerable concern that marijuana use by pregnant women may increase further given the increasing number of states that are legalizing or decriminalizing marijuana (Kees & others, 2020).

Heroin It is well documented that infants whose mothers are addicted to heroin show several behavioral difficulties at birth (Larson & others, 2019). These difficulties include withdrawal symptoms such as tremors, irritability, abnormal crying, disturbed sleep, and impaired motor control. Many infants still show behavioral problems at their first birthday, and attention deficits may appear later in development. The most common treatment for heroin addiction, methadone, is associated with very severe withdrawal symptoms in newborns as well as birth complications; these effects may be less severe for other heroin replacement drug therapies (Wouldes & Woodward, 2020).

INCOMPATIBLE BLOOD TYPES

Incompatibility between the mother's and father's blood types poses another risk to prenatal development. Blood types are created by differences in the surface structure of red blood cells. One type of difference in the surface of red blood cells creates the familiar blood groups—A, B, O, and AB. A second difference creates what is called Rh-positive and Rh-negative blood. If a surface marker, called the Rh factor, is present in an individual's red blood cells, the person is said to be Rh-positive; if the Rh marker is not present, the person is said to be Rh-negative. If a pregnant woman is Rh-negative and her partner is Rh-positive, the fetus may be Rh-positive. If the fetus' blood is Rh-positive and the mother's is Rh-negative, the mother's immune system may produce antibodies that will attack the fetus. Such an assault can result in any number of problems, including miscarriage or stillbirth, anemia, jaundice, heart defects, brain damage, or death soon after birth (Myle & Al-Khattabi, 2021).

Generally, the first Rh-positive baby of an Rh-negative mother is not at risk, but with each subsequent pregnancy the risk increases. A vaccine (RhoGAM) may be given to the mother within three days of the first child's birth to prevent her body from making antibodies that will attack any future Rh-positive fetuses in subsequent pregnancies. Also, babies affected by Rh incompatibility can be given blood transfusions before or immediately after birth (Tyndall, Cuzzilla, & Kane, 2020).

ENVIRONMENTAL HAZARDS

Many aspects of our modern industrial world can endanger the embryo or fetus. Some specific hazards to the embryo or fetus that are worth a closer look include radiation, toxic wastes, and other chemical pollutants in neighborhoods and in workplace environments (Gómez-Roig & others, 2021).

Radiation can cause a gene mutation (an abrupt, permanent change in DNA). Offspring of fathers exposed to high levels of radiation in their occupations have worse birth outcomes (e.g., low birth weight) than offspring of fathers without radiation exposure (Andreassi & others, 2021). Radiation also can affect the developing embryo or fetus, especially during the first several weeks after conception when women do not yet know they are pregnant. Possible effects include microencephaly (an abnormally small brain), intellectual disabilities, and leukemia.

An explosion at the Chernobyl nuclear power plant in Ukraine produced radioactive contamination that spread to surrounding areas. Thousands of infants were born with health problems and deformities as a result of the nuclear contamination, including this boy whose arm did not form and whose legs were malformed. *Other than radioactive contamination, what are some types of environmental hazards to prenatal development?*

Sergey Guneev/RIA Novosti

Women and their physicians should weigh the risk of an X-ray when an actual or potential pregnancy is involved (Reitan & Sanderud, 2021). However, a routine diagnostic X-ray of a body area other than the abdomen, with the woman's abdomen protected by a lead apron, is generally considered safe (Chansakul & Young, 2017).

Environmental pollutants and toxic wastes are also sources of danger to unborn children. Among the dangerous pollutants are carbon monoxide, mercury, and lead, as well as certain fertilizers and pesticides (Yang & others, 2020). Exposure to lead can come from lead-based paint that flakes off the walls of a home or from corroded lead plumbing. Early exposure to lead can affect children's mental and behavioral development (Lin & others, 2020). For example, research has revealed that a moderately high maternal lead level in the first trimester of pregnancy is linked to lower scores on measures of mental development in infancy (Hu & others, 2007).

MATERNAL DISEASES

Maternal diseases and infections can produce defects in offspring by crossing the placental barrier, or they can cause damage during birth (Megli & Coyne, 2022). Rubella (German measles) is one disease that can cause prenatal defects. The greatest damage occurs if a mother contracts rubella in the third or fourth week of pregnancy, although infection during the second month is also damaging (Boucoiran & Castillo, 2018). One illustrative study found that cardiac defects, pulmonary problems, and microcephaly (a condition in which the baby's head is significantly smaller and less developed than normal) were among the most common fetal and neonatal outcomes when pregnant women have rubella (Yazigi & others, 2017). A vaccine that prevents German measles is now routinely administered to children, and women who plan to have children should have a blood test before they become pregnant to determine whether they are immune to the disease (Bukasa & others, 2018).

Syphilis (a sexually transmitted infection) is more damaging later in prenatal development—four months or more after conception. Rather than affecting organogenesis, as rubella does, syphilis damages organs after they have formed. Damage includes eye lesions, which can cause blindness, and skin lesions (Qin & others, 2014). When syphilis is present at birth, problems can develop in the central nervous system and gastrointestinal tract (Braccio, Sharland, & Ladhani, 2016). Penicillin is the only known treatment for syphilis during pregnancy (Moline & Smith, 2016), though alternative treatments are being developed and tested (Roberts & others, 2019).

Another infection that has received widespread attention recently is genital herpes. Newborns contract this virus when they are delivered through the birth canal of a mother with genital herpes (Johnston, 2022). About one-third of babies delivered through an infected birth canal die; another one-fourth become brain damaged. If an active case of genital herpes is detected in a pregnant woman close to her delivery date, a cesarean section can be performed (delivery of the infant through an incision in the mother's abdomen) to keep the virus from infecting the newborn (Sénat & others, 2018).

AIDS is a sexually transmitted infection that is caused by the human immunodeficiency virus (HIV), which destroys the body's immune system. A mother can infect her offspring with HIV/AIDS in three ways: (1) during gestation across the placenta, (2) during delivery through contact with maternal blood or fluids, and (3) postpartum (after birth) through breast feeding. The transmission of AIDS through breast feeding is especially a problem in many low-income countries (UNICEF, 2021). Babies born to HIV-infected mothers can be (1) infected and symptomatic (show HIV symptoms), (2) infected but asymptomatic (not show HIV symptoms), or (3) not infected at all. An infant who is infected and asymptomatic may still develop HIV symptoms until 15 months of age.

In the early 1990s, before preventive treatments were available, 1,000 to 2,000 infants were born with HIV infection each year in the United States. Since then, transmission of HIV from mothers to fetuses has been reduced dramatically (Blanche, 2020). Only about one-third as many cases of newborns with HIV appear today as in the early 1990s. This decline is due to the increase in counseling and voluntary testing of pregnant women for HIV and to the administration of zidovudine (AZT) to infected women during pregnancy and to the infant after birth. In many poor countries, however, treatment with AZT is limited, and HIV infection of infants remains a major problem.

developmental **connection**

Conditions, Diseases, and Disorders
The highest incidence of HIV/AIDS is in sub-Saharan Africa; many are unaware that they are infected with the virus. Connect to "Physical Development in Infancy," "Physical Development in Early Childhood," and "Physical Development in Adolescence."

The more widespread disease of diabetes, characterized by high levels of sugar in the blood, also affects offspring (Wahabi & others, 2020). The largest study to date (over 41,000 infants born in the United States) indicated that newborns with physical defects are more likely to have diabetic mothers than newborns without such defects (Tinker & others, 2019). Moreover, women who have gestational diabetes (a condition in which women without previously diagnosed diabetes develop high blood glucose levels during pregnancy) may deliver very large infants (weighing 10 pounds or more), and the infants themselves are at risk for diabetes (Alberico & others, 2014) and cardiovascular disease (Amrithraj & others, 2017). More recently, concerns have been raised about whether fetuses are affected by COVID-19 (Rasmussen & Jamieson, 2020). A review of early evidence suggested that although newborns can be infected with COVID-19, the infections did not appear to have occurred in utero (Yang & others, 2022). Additional research will be needed to determine the long-term effects of prenatal exposure to COVID-19.

Because the fetus depends entirely on its mother for nutrition, it is important for the pregnant woman to have good nutritional habits. In Kenya, this government clinic provides pregnant women with information about how their diet can influence the health of their fetus and offspring. *What might the information about diet be like?*

Delphine Bousquet/AFP/Getty Images

OTHER PARENTAL FACTORS

So far we have discussed drugs, environmental hazards, maternal diseases, and incompatible blood types that can harm the embryo or fetus. Here we explore other characteristics of the mother and father that can affect prenatal and child development, including nutrition, age, and emotional states and stress.

Maternal Diet and Nutrition   A developing embryo or fetus depends completely on its mother for nutrition, which comes from the mother's blood. The nutritional status of the embryo or fetus is determined by the mother's total caloric intake and by her intake of proteins, vitamins, and minerals. Children born to malnourished mothers are more likely than other children to have malformations and other developmental problems.

Being overweight before and during pregnancy can also put the embryo or fetus at risk, and an increasing number of pregnant women in many middle- and high-income countries are overweight (Harrison & others, 2021). Maternal obesity adversely affects pregnancy outcomes through elevated rates of hypertension, diabetes, respiratory complications, and infections in the mother (Cheng & others, 2017). Another area of research indicates that pregestational diabetes increases the risk of fetal heart disease (Pauliks, 2015; Zablah & others, 2017). Recent research studies have found that maternal obesity is linked to an increase in stillbirth (Browne & others, 2019) and increased likelihood that the newborn will be placed in a neonatal intensive care unit (Melchor & others, 2019). Further, two research reviews concluded that maternal obesity during pregnancy is associated with an increased likelihood of offspring being obese in childhood and adulthood (Pinto Pereira & others, 2016; Santangeli, Sattar, & Huda, 2015). Management of obesity that includes weight loss and increased exercise prior to pregnancy is likely to benefit the mother and the baby (Hanson & others, 2017; Mitanchez & Chavatte-Palmer, 2018).

One aspect of maternal nutrition that is important for normal prenatal development is folic acid, a B-complex vitamin. As we indicated earlier in the chapter, a lack of folic acid during prenatal development is linked with neural tube defects such as spina bifida in offspring (Best & others, 2021). A classic study of more than 34,000 pregnant women revealed that taking folic acid either alone or as part of a multivitamin for at least one year prior to conceiving was linked with a 70 percent lower risk of delivering between 20 to 28 weeks and a 50 percent lower risk of delivering between 28 and 32 weeks (Bukowski & others, 2008). The U.S. Department of Health and Human Service's Womenshealth.gov Web site (U.S. Department of Health and Human Services, 2023) recommends that pregnant women consume a minimum of 400 micrograms of folic acid per day (about twice the amount the average woman gets in one day). Orange juice and spinach are examples of foods rich in folic acid.

Fish is often recommended as part of a healthy diet and in general fish consumption during pregnancy has positive benefits for children's development (Bramante, Spiller, & Landa, 2018). However, pollution has made some kinds of fish a risky choice for pregnant women.

developmental **connection**

Conditions, Diseases, and Disorders

What are some key factors that influence whether individuals will become overweight or obese? Connect to "Physical Development in Early Childhood," "Physical Development in Middle and Late Childhood," and "Physical Development in Adolescence."

George Peters/Getty Images

Some fish contain high levels of mercury, which is released into the air both naturally and by industrial processes (Kosik-Bogacka & others, 2018). Mercury that falls into the water can accumulate in large fish, such as shark, swordfish, king mackerel, and some species of large tuna (American Pregnancy Association, 2023). Researchers have found that prenatal mercury exposure is linked to adverse outcomes, including miscarriage, preterm birth, and lower intelligence, but these effects are reduced by public health knowledge about risk of mercury exposure during pregnancy (Murakami, Suzuki, & Yamaguchi, 2017).

The American Pregnancy Association and the U.S. Food and Drug Administration recommend avoiding fish with a high mercury content, such as tilefish from the Gulf of Mexico, swordfish, shark, and king mackerel. However, these associations recommend that pregnant women increase their consumption of fish that have a low mercury content, such as salmon, shrimp, tilapia, and cod.

Maternal Age   When possible harmful effects on the fetus and infant are considered, two maternal ages are of special interest: adolescents and women 35 years of age and older (Frick, 2021; Macedo & others, 2020). Many studies conducted in numerous countries have revealed that the rate of stillbirth was elevated for adolescent girls and for women 35 years and older (Permana & others, 2019; Wie & others, 2019).

The mortality rate of infants born to adolescent mothers is double that of infants born to mothers in their twenties. Although this high rate probably reflects the immaturity of the mother's reproductive system, other factors such as poor nutrition, lack of prenatal care, and low socioeconomic status may also play a role (Mayo & others, 2019). Adequate prenatal care decreases the probability that a child born to an adolescent girl will have physical problems. However, adolescents are the least likely age group to obtain prenatal health care from clinics and health services.

Maternal age is also linked to the risk that a child will have Down syndrome (Jaruratanasirikul & others, 2017). An individual with *Down syndrome* has distinctive facial characteristics, short limbs, and impaired development of motor and mental abilities. Advanced maternal age confers a much greater risk of having a baby with Down syndrome (Tamminga & others, 2018). When the mother reaches 40 years of age, the probability is slightly more than 1 in 100 that a baby born to her will have Down syndrome, and by age 50 it is almost 1 in 10.

When mothers are 35 years and older, risks also increase for low birth weight, for preterm delivery, and for fetal death (Arya, Mulla, & Plavsic, 2018). Also, a Norwegian study found that maternal age of 30 years or older was linked to the same level of increased risk for fetal deaths as 25- to 29-year-old pregnant women who were overweight/obese or were smokers (Waldenstrom & others, 2014). Still other studies have shown that very advanced maternal age (40 years and older) is linked to adverse perinatal outcomes, including spontaneous abortion, preterm birth, stillbirth, and fetal growth restriction (Traisrisilp & Tongsong, 2015; Waldenstrom & others, 2015).

We still have much to learn about the role of the mother's age in pregnancy and childbirth. As women age but remain active, exercise regularly, and are careful about their nutrition, their reproductive systems may remain healthier at older ages than was thought possible in the past. In addition, women in many countries and cultures are delaying childbirth, leading to older maternal ages around the globe.

Emotional States and Stress   When a pregnant woman experiences intense fears, anxieties, and other emotions or negative mood states, physiological changes occur that may affect her fetus.

High maternal anxiety and stress during pregnancy can have long-term consequences for the offspring (Bowers & Yehuda, 2020). One study found that high levels of depression, anxiety, and stress during pregnancy were linked to internalizing problems in adolescence (Betts & others, 2014). A highly influential research review established that pregnant women with high levels of stress are at increased risk for having a child with emotional or cognitive problems, attention deficit hyperactivity disorder (ADHD), and language delay (Talge & others, 2007). A more recent research review concluded that regardless of the form of maternal prenatal stress or anxiety and the prenatal trimester in which the stress or anxiety occurred, during their first two years of life the offspring displayed lower levels of self-regulation (Korja & others, 2017). Maternal emotions and stress also can influence the fetus indirectly by increasing the likelihood that the mother will engage in unhealthy behaviors such as taking drugs and receiving inadequate prenatal care.

Might maternal depression also have an adverse effect on birth outcomes? Research indicates that maternal depression during pregnancy is linked to preterm birth as well as low birth

What are some of the risks for infants born to adolescent mothers?

Courtney Hale/Getty Images

How Would You...?

If you were a **health-care professional,** how would you advise an individual or a couple in their late thirties or early forties who are considering having a baby?

weight in full-term offspring (Venkatesh & others, 2019). Some of the effects can be delayed for decades. For example, one study revealed that maternal depression during pregnancy was related to increased risk for depression in their offspring 18 years later (Pearson & others, 2013). There also is a concern about taking antidepressant medications during pregnancy. A review of 22 meta-analyses concluded that using antidepressants during pregnancy might increase the risk of preterm birth, newborns' respiratory distress, and cardiovascular malformations (Biffi & others, 2020). However, some of these effects depended on the specific type of antidepressant and the point during pregnancy that the antidepressant was taken. Maternal mental health is also important to prenatal development, so decisions about antidepressant use should be made in careful consultation with physicians (Galbally & others, 2020).

Positive emotional states in mothers also appear to make a difference to the fetus. A growing body of evidence shows that positive mood and overall good emotional health during pregnancy benefit the fetus, the newborn baby, and the developing child for years to come (Phua, Kee, & Meaney, 2019).

Paternal Factors   So far, we have discussed how characteristics of the mother—such as drug use, disease, diet and nutrition, age, and emotional states—can influence prenatal development and the development of the child. This is also true for some paternal risk factors (Pedersen & others, 2014). Men's exposure to lead, radiation, certain pesticides, and petrochemicals may cause abnormalities in sperm that lead to miscarriage or to diseases such as childhood cancer (Andreassi & others, 2021).

The father's smoking during the mother's pregnancy also can cause problems for the offspring (Agricola & others, 2016). In one of the first studies conducted on this subject, the newborns of fathers who smoked around their wives during the pregnancy were 4 ounces lighter at birth for each pack of cigarettes smoked per day than were the newborns whose fathers had not smoked while their wives were pregnant (Rubin & others, 1986). In a similarly groundbreaking study in China, the longer the fathers smoked, the higher the risk that their children would develop cancer (Ji & others, 1997). A subsequent study showed that paternal smoking around the time of the child's conception was linked to an increased risk of the child developing leukemia (Milne & others, 2012). In another series of studies conducted in multiple countries (for example, the United States and China), heavy paternal smoking was associated with increased risk of early pregnancy loss (L. Wang & others, 2018). All of these negative effects may be related to maternal exposure to secondhand smoke. Also, research reviews have concluded that there is an increased risk of spontaneous abortion, autism, and schizophrenic disorders when the father is 40 years of age or older at the time of conception (Brandt & others, 2019). For example, children born to older fathers are at greater risk of autism spectrum disorders (Kavanaugh & others, 2022).

There are also risks to offspring in some circumstances when both the mother and father are older. In one illustrative study, taking into account the mother's and the father's age increased the accuracy of predictions of whether a pregnancy would end in miscarriage (du Fossé & others, 2022). Research examining the combined roles of advanced maternal and paternal age has shown somewhat mixed results, but overall, birth and newborn infant risks increase when both parents are older.

In terms of the benefits of fathers on a healthy pregnancy, the father may contribute to positive outcomes for the fetus by providing support to the mother and having a positive attitude toward the pregnancy. Earlier you read about how maternal stress and depression have negative developmental outcomes for offspring. Fathers can play an important role in helping to reduce stress and depression in the mothers by contributing to a positive marital relationship, not engaging in spousal abuse, sharing more in household tasks, and participating in childbirth classes. The risk of intimate partner violence increases during pregnancy and poses significant risks for the mother and fetus (Drexler & others, 2022). In contrast, another study of a large cohort of low-income Black American and Latino fathers found that fathers' involvement and

How Would You...?

If you were a **health-care professional,** how would you advise an expectant mother who is experiencing extreme psychological stress?

In a classic study conducted in China, the longer fathers smoked the greater the risk that their children would develop cancer (Ji & others, 1997). *What are some other paternal factors that can influence the development of the fetus and the child?*

David Butow/Corbis/Getty Images

support of the mother predicted healthier pregnancies and reduced rates of low birth weight (Surkan & others, 2019).

Much of our discussion in this chapter has focused on what can go wrong with prenatal development. Prospective parents should take steps to avoid the hazards to fetal development that we have described. But it is important to keep in mind that most of the time, prenatal development does not go awry and development occurs along the positive path that we described at the beginning of the chapter.

Review *Connect* Reflect

 LG3 Describe potential hazards during prenatal development.

Review

- What is teratology? What are some general principles regarding teratogens?
- Which prescription and nonprescription drugs can influence prenatal development?
- How do different psychoactive drugs affect prenatal development?
- How do incompatible blood types influence prenatal development?
- What are some environmental hazards that can influence prenatal development?
- Which maternal diseases can affect prenatal development?
- What other parental factors can affect prenatal development?

Connect

- Earlier you read about chromosomal and gene-linked abnormalities that can affect prenatal development. How are the symptoms of the related conditions or risks similar to or different from those caused by teratogens or other hazards?

Reflect *Your Own Personal Journey of Life*

- Imagine that you have just found out you are pregnant. What health-enhancing strategies will you follow during the prenatal period? Now imagine you are the partner of a woman who has just learned that she is pregnant. What can you do to increase the likelihood that the prenatal period will go smoothly?

topical connections *looking forward*

Next you will learn about the birth process and the transition from fetus to newborn, see how the newborn's health and responsiveness are assessed, read about low birth weight and preterm babies and find out about special ways to nurture these fragile newborns, and examine what happens during the postpartum period.

reach your **learning goals**

Prenatal Development

1 What Is the Course of Prenatal Development?

LG1 Discuss the three periods of prenatal development.

The Germinal Period

- The germinal period lasts from conception until about two weeks later. It includes the creation of a fertilized egg, which is called a zygote, and cell division. The period ends when the zygote attaches to the uterine wall in a process called implantation.

- The Embryonic Period

- The Fetal Period

- The Brain

- The embryonic period lasts from about two to eight weeks after conception. The embryo differentiates into three layers of cells (endoderm, mesoderm, and ectoderm), life-support systems develop, and organ systems form (organogenesis).

- The fetal period lasts from about two months after conception until nine months, or when the infant is born. Growth and development continue their dramatic course, and organ systems mature to the point at which life can be sustained outside the womb.

- The growth of the brain during prenatal development is nothing short of remarkable. By the time babies are born, they have approximately 100 billion neurons, or nerve cells. Neurogenesis is the term that means the formation of new neurons.

- Development of the nervous system begins with the formation of a neural tube at 18 to 24 days after conception. Proliferation and neuronal migration are two processes that characterize brain development in the prenatal period. The basic architecture of the brain is formed in the first two trimesters of prenatal development.

2 What Are Some Important Strategies That Enhance the Expectant Mother's Health and Prenatal Care?

 Summarize how nutrition, exercise, and prenatal care are important aspects of the expectant mother's pregnancy.

The Expectant Mother's Nutrition and Weight Gain

Exercise

Prenatal Care

- The best assurance of adequate caloric intake during pregnancy is a satisfactory weight gain over time. Maternal weight gain that averages 25 to 35 pounds is often linked with the best reproductive outcomes. The RDA for all nutrients increases during pregnancy, and the need for such nutrients as vitamin D, folacin, and iron increases by more than 50 percent.

- If the expectant mother's health allows, exercise can benefit her well-being during pregnancy and may reduce the risk of a preterm birth. How much and what type of exercise are appropriate depends to some extent on the course of pregnancy, the expectant mother's fitness, and her customary activity level.

- Prenatal care varies extensively but usually involves medical care services with a defined schedule of visits and often includes educational, social, and nutritional services. Much needs to be done to improve prenatal care in the United States, especially for low-income families.

3 What Are Some Potential Hazards to Prenatal Development?

 Describe potential hazards during prenatal development.

Some General Principles

Prescription and Nonprescription Drugs

Psychoactive Drugs

- Teratology is the field that investigates the causes of birth defects. Any agent that can potentially cause birth defects is called a teratogen. The time of exposure, dose, and genetic susceptibility influence the severity of the damage to an unborn child and the type of defect that occurs.

- Prescription drugs that can harm a developing fetus include antibiotics, some antidepressants, and certain hormones. Nonprescription drugs that can be harmful include diet pills and aspirin.

- Legal psychoactive drugs that are potentially harmful to prenatal development include alcohol, nicotine, and caffeine. Fetal alcohol spectrum disorders (FASD) consist of a cluster of abnormalities that appear in offspring of mothers who drink heavily during pregnancy. Even when pregnant women drink moderately, negative effects on their offspring have been found. Cigarette smoking by pregnant women can have serious adverse effects on prenatal and child development (such as low birth weight and SIDS). Exposure to secondhand smoke is also detrimental to fetal development.

- Other psychoactive drugs that are harmful to offspring include methamphetamine, which can produce high infant mortality, low birth weight, and developmental problems; marijuana, which can result in a child's impaired information processing; cocaine, which is associated with reduced birth weight, length, and head circumference; and heroin, which produces behavioral problems at birth and may result in attention deficits later in development.

Incompatible Blood Types

Environmental Hazards

Maternal Diseases

Other Parental Factors

- Incompatibility of the mother's and the father's blood types can also be harmful to the fetus. A woman is at risk when she has a negative Rh factor and her partner has a positive Rh factor. If the fetus is Rh-positive and the mother is Rh-negative, the mother's immune system may attack the fetus, resulting in problems such as miscarriage or brain damage.

- Environmental hazards include radiation, environmental pollutants, and toxic wastes.

- Syphilis, rubella (German measles), genital herpes, and AIDS are infectious diseases that can harm the fetus.

- Other parental factors that affect prenatal development include maternal diet and nutrition, age, emotional states and stress, and paternal factors. A developing fetus depends entirely on its mother for nutrition. One nutrient that is especially important very early in development is folic acid. A potential hazard to prenatal development occurs when the mother consumes fish with a high mercury content. Maternal age can negatively affect the offspring's development if the mother is an adolescent or over 35. High stress in the mother is linked with less than optimal prenatal and birth outcomes. Paternal factors that can adversely affect prenatal development include exposure to lead, radiation, certain pesticides, and petrochemicals, as well as smoking.

key **terms**

amnion
blastocyst
ectoderm
embryonic period
endoderm

fetal alcohol spectrum disorders
   (FASD)
fetal period
germinal period
mesoderm

neurogenesis
neurons
organogenesis
placenta
teratogen

trophoblast
umbilical cord

key **people**

David Olds

improving the **lives of children**

STRATEGIES

Maximizing Positive Prenatal Outcomes

What are some strategies during pregnancy that are likely to maximize positive outcomes for prenatal development?

- *Eat nutritious foods and monitor weight gain.* The recommended daily allowances for all nutrients increase during pregnancy. A pregnant woman should eat three balanced meals a day and nutritious snacks between meals if desired. Weight gains that average 25 to 35 pounds are associated with the best reproductive outcomes.

- *Engage in safe exercise.* How much and what type of exercise is best during pregnancy depends to some degree on the course of the pregnancy, the expectant mother's fitness, and her customary activity level. Normal participation in exercise can continue throughout an uncomplicated pregnancy. It is important to remember not to overdo exercise. Exercising for shorter intervals and decreasing the intensity of exercise as pregnancy proceeds are good strategies. Pregnant women should always consult a physician before starting an exercise program.

- *Don't drink alcohol or take other potentially harmful drugs.* An important strategy for pregnancy is to totally abstain from alcohol and other drugs such as nicotine and cocaine. In this chapter, we considered the harmful effects that these drugs can have on the developing fetus. Fathers also need to be aware of potentially harmful effects of their behavior on prenatal development.

- *Have a support system of family and friends.* The pregnant woman benefits from a support system of family members and friends. A positive relationship with a spouse helps keep stress levels down, as does a close relationship with one or more friends.

- *Reduce stress and stay calm.* Try to maintain an even, calm emotional state during pregnancy. High stress levels can harm the fetus. Pregnant women who are feeling a lot of anxiety can reduce their anxiety level through a relaxation or stress management program.

- *Stay away from environmental hazards.* We saw in this chapter that some environmental hazards, such as pollutants and toxic wastes, can harm prenatal development. Be aware of these hazards and avoid them.

- *Get excellent prenatal care.* The quality of prenatal care varies extensively. The education the mother receives about pregnancy, labor and delivery, and care of the newborn can be valuable, especially for first-time mothers.
- *Read a good book for expectant mothers.* An excellent one is *What to Expect When You're Expecting,* which is described under Resources.

RESOURCES

March of Dimes
www.marchofdimes.com

The March of Dimes organization strives to promote healthy pregnancy. Their Web site includes extensive information about many aspects of pregnancy and prenatal development.

National Center for Education in Maternal and Child Health (NCEMCH)
www.ncemch.org

NCEMCH answers questions about pregnancy and childbirth, high-risk infants, and maternal and child health programs. It also publishes free maternal and child health publications.

Pregnancy.org
www.pregnancy.org

This extensive Web site provides up-to-date information about pregnancy and prenatal development.

What to Expect When You're Expecting (5th ed., 2016)
Heidi Murkoff
New York: Workman

This highly popular book on pregnancy and prenatal development provides detailed month-by-month descriptions of pregnancy and prenatal growth.

Prenatal Care Tips

Pregnant women can call this toll-free number provided by the federal government for prenatal care advice and referral to local health-care providers: 1-800-311-BABY (2229); for Spanish speakers, 1-800-504-7081.

chapter 4

BIRTH

chapter **outline**

① **What Happens During the Birth Process?**

Learning Goal 1 Discuss the stages, decisions involved, and transitions in birth.

Stages of the Birth Process
Childbirth Setting and Attendants
Methods of Childbirth
The Transition from Fetus to Newborn

② **What Are Some Measures of Neonatal Health and Responsiveness?**

Learning Goal 2 Describe three measures of neonatal health and responsiveness.

③ **How Do Low Birth Weight and Preterm Infants Develop?**

Learning Goal 3 Characterize the development of low birth weight and preterm infants.

Preterm and Small for Gestational Age Infants
Consequences of Preterm Birth and Low Birth Weight
Nurturing Preterm Infants

④ **What Happens During the Postpartum Period?**

Learning Goal 4 Explain the physical and psychological aspects of the postpartum period.

Physical Adjustments
Emotional and Psychological Adjustments
Bonding

ERproductions Ltd/Blend Images/Getty Images

Tanner Roberts was born in a suite at St. Joseph's Medical Center in Burbank, California (Warrick, 1992). Let's examine what took place in the hours leading up to his birth. It is day 266 of his mother Cindy's pregnancy. She is in the frozen-food aisle of a convenience store and feels a sharp pain, starting in the small of her back and reaching around her middle, which causes her to gasp. For weeks, painless Braxton Hicks spasms (named for the gynecologist who discovered them) have been flexing her uterine muscles. But these practice contractions were not nearly as intense and painful as the one she just experienced. After six hours of irregular spasms, her uterus settles into a more predictable rhythm.

At 3 a.m., Cindy and her husband Tom are wide awake. They time Cindy's contractions with a stopwatch. The contractions are now only six minutes apart. It's time to call the hospital. A short time later, Tom and Cindy arrive at the hospital's labor-delivery suite. A nurse puts a webbed belt and fetal monitor around Cindy's middle to measure her labor. The monitor picks up the fetal heart rate. With each contraction of the uterine wall, Tanner's heartbeat jumps from its resting state of about 140 beats to 160 to 170 beats per minute. When the cervix is dilated to more than 4 centimeters, or almost half open, Cindy receives her first medication. As Demerol begins to drip into her veins, the pain of her contractions is less intense. Tanner's heart rate dips to 130 and then 120.

Contractions are now coming every three to four minutes, each one lasting about 25 seconds. The Demerol does not completely obliterate Cindy's pain. She hugs her husband as the nurse urges her to "Relax those muscles. Breathe deep. Relax. You're almost there."

Each contraction briefly cuts off Tanner's source of oxygen, his mother's blood. However, in the minutes of rest between contractions, Cindy's deep breathing helps rush fresh blood to the baby's heart and brain.

At 8 a.m., Cindy's cervix is almost completely dilated and the obstetrician arrives. Using a tool made for the purpose, he reaches into the birth canal and tears the membranes of the amniotic sac, and about half a liter of clear fluid flows out. Contractions are now coming every two minutes, and each one is lasting a full minute.

By 9 a.m., the labor suite has been transformed into a delivery room. Tanner's body is compressed by his mother's contractions and pushes. As he nears his entrance into the world, the compressions help press the fluid from his lungs in preparation for his first breath. Squeezed tightly in the birth canal, the top of Tanner's head emerges. His face is puffy and scrunched. Although he is fiercely squinting because of the sudden light, Tanner's eyes are open. Tiny bubbles of clear mucus are on his lips. Before any more of his body emerges, the nurse cradles Tanner's head and suctions his nose and mouth. Tanner takes his first breath, a large gasp followed by whimpering, and then a loud cry. Tanner's body is wet but only slightly bloody as the doctor lifts him onto his mother's abdomen.

topical connections *looking **back***

You have read about prenatal development and the strategies expectant mothers can use to enhance their health and their offspring's health. You also learned about some potential hazards that can occur during prenatal development. And you read about the remarkable prenatal development of the brain, which contains approximately 100 billion neurons when birth takes place. This chapter takes you through the birth process and its immediate aftermath—the postpartum period.

The umbilical cord, still connecting Tanner with his mother, slows and stops pulsating. The obstetrician cuts it, severing Tanner's connection to his mother's womb. Now Tanner's blood flows not to his mother's body for nourishment—but to his own lungs, intestines, and other organs.

Warrick, P. "The Fantastic Voyage of Tanner Roberts," *Los Angeles Times,* 1992, E1, E12, and E13. Copyright ©1992 Los Angeles Times. All rights reserved. Used with permission.

preview

As the story of Tanner Roberts's birth reveals, many changes take place during the birth of a baby. In this chapter, we explore what happens during the birth process, describe measures of neonatal health and responsiveness, discuss the development of preterm and low birth weight infants, and identify characteristics of the postpartum period.

1 What Happens During the Birth Process?

LG1 Discuss the stages, decisions involved, and transitions in birth.

| Stages of the Birth Process | Childbirth Setting and Attendants | Methods of Childbirth | The Transition from Fetus to Newborn |

Nature writes the basic script for how birth occurs, but parents make important choices about conditions surrounding birth. What is the sequence of physical steps when a child is born?

STAGES OF THE BIRTH PROCESS

The birth process occurs in three stages. The first stage is the longest of the three. Uterine contractions are 15 to 20 minutes apart at the beginning and last up to a minute apiece. These contractions cause the woman's cervix to stretch and open. As the first stage progresses, the contractions come closer together, appearing every two to five minutes. Their intensity increases. By the end of the first birth stage, contractions dilate the cervix to an opening of about 4 inches so that the baby can move from the uterus to the birth canal. For a woman having her first child, the first stage lasts an average of 12 to 14 hours; for subsequent children, this stage may be shorter.

The second birth stage begins when the baby's head starts to move through the cervix and the birth canal. It terminates when the baby completely emerges from the mother's body. With each contraction, the mother bears down hard to push the baby out of her body. By the time the baby's head is out of the mother's body, the contractions come almost every minute and last for about a minute. This stage typically lasts approximately 45 minutes to an hour.

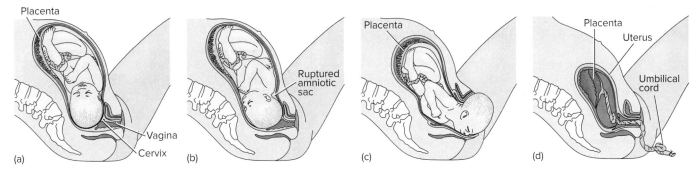

FIGURE 1

THE STAGES OF BIRTH. (*a*) First stage: cervix is dilating; (*b*) late first stage (transition stage): cervix is fully dilated and the amniotic sac has ruptured, releasing amniotic fluid; (*c*) second stage: birth of the infant; and (*d*) third stage: delivery of the placenta (afterbirth).

Afterbirth is the third stage, at which time the placenta, umbilical cord, and other membranes are detached and expelled. This final stage is the shortest of the three birth stages, lasting only minutes (see Figure 1).

CHILDBIRTH SETTING AND ATTENDANTS

In the United States, over 98 percent of births take place in hospitals (National Academies of Science, Engineering, & Medicine, 2020). Of the 1.5 percent of births occurring outside of a hospital, 63 percent took place in homes and almost 31 percent in free-standing birthing centers. The percentage of U.S. births at home is the highest since reporting of this context began in 1989. An increase in home births has occurred mainly among non-Latina White women, especially those who are older and married. For these non-Latina White women, two-thirds of their home births are attended by a midwife.

Some women with good medical histories and low risk for problems may choose a delivery at home or in a free-standing birth center, which is usually staffed by nurse-midwives. Births at home are far more common in many other countries—for example, in Holland 35 percent of the babies are born at home. Some critics worry that the U.S. tendency to view birth through a medical lens may lead to unnecessary medical procedures (Mueller, Webb, & Morgan, 2020).

The people who assist a mother during birth vary across cultures. In U.S. hospitals, it has become the norm for fathers or birth coaches to remain with the mother throughout labor and delivery. In the East African Nigoni culture, men are completely excluded from the childbirth process. When a woman is ready to give birth, female relatives move into the woman's hut and the husband leaves, taking his belongings (clothes, tools, weapons, and so on) with him. He is not permitted to return until after the baby is born. In some cultures, childbirth is an open, community affair. For example, in the Pukapukan culture in the Pacific Islands, women give birth in a shelter that is open for villagers to observe.

Midwives A *midwife* is a trained health practitioner who helps women during their labor, delivery, and afterbirth of their baby (World Health Organization, 2023). Midwives also may give women information about reproductive health and annual gynecological examinations (Hall & others, 2023). They may refer women to general practitioners or obstetricians if a pregnant woman needs medical care beyond a midwife's expertise and skill.

Midwifery is practiced in most countries throughout the world (World Health Organization, 2023). In Holland, more than 40 percent of babies are delivered by midwives rather than by doctors. However, in the United States, only 8 percent of all hospital births are attended by a midwife (Martin & others, 2017; Weisband & others, 2018). Nonetheless, the 8 percent figure represents a substantial increase from less than 1 percent in 1975.

Compared with physicians, certified nurse-midwives generally spend more time with patients during prenatal visits, place more emphasis on patient counseling and education, provide more emotional support, and are more likely to stay with the patient during the entire labor and delivery process, which may explain the higher rate of positive outcomes for babies delivered by certified nurse-midwives than for those delivered by doctors (Raipuria & others, 2018). See the *Connecting with Careers* profile to learn more about the many functions a midwife performs.

afterbirth The third stage of birth, when the placenta, umbilical cord, and other membranes are detached and expelled from the uterus.

Jennifer Nguyen, Midwife

Growing up in Nova Scotia, Canada, Jennifer Nguyen had never heard of midwives except for the stereotypes portrayed in media. When pursuing her master's degree, she conducted her thesis research with Aboriginal women and encountered inequities in health care in rural and remote communities. Learning more about midwifery, she decided a career in the field would allow her to contribute to improving access to quality health care.

Midwives are primary health care providers who center their work around the midwifery model of care, which incorporates informed choice, continuity of care, and choice of birthplace. Midwives provide complete care to clients and their families during pregnancy, labor, birth, and at least six weeks postpartum, including regular visits, diagnostic tests, routine bloodwork, and emotional support (Canadian Association of Midwives, 2022). In Canada, where Nguyen practices, midwifery programs are a 3- to 4-year direct entry baccalaureate level program, and the profession is regulated by each province/territory. In the United States, many certified nurse-midwives (CNM) and certified midwives (CM) have master's degrees. As of 2010, new applicants are required to have graduate degrees (American College of Nurse-Midwives, 2015). In 2019, CNMs and CMs attended almost 370,000 births in the United States (Centers for Disease Control and Prevention, 2020).

Nguyen graduated from the midwifery education program at McMaster University in Hamilton, Ontario, and holds a master's degree in

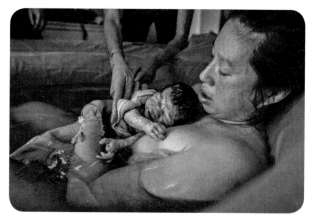

Jenn Nguyen, midwife, assists in the birth of her own baby.
Courtesy of Jennifer Nguyen. Photography by Ashley Marston Photography.

community health science. She is an assistant professor with the University of British Columbia midwifery education program and practices in Campbell River, British Columbia. As a fluent speaker of Mandarin and Vietnamese, she serves a variety of clients. Working in both rural and urban centers, she witnesses the health disparities in rural and remote communities, which has ignited her passion for ensuring equal access to quality perinatal care. Her philosophy of midwifery care is rooted in anti-oppression and trauma-informed practice, and her goal is for all her clients to feel supported and empowered to make the choices that are right for them and their families.

Doulas In many countries, a doula attends a childbearing woman. *Doula* is a Greek word that means "a woman who helps," although men can also be doulas. A **doula** is a caregiver who provides continuous physical, emotional, and educational support for the mother before, during, and after childbirth. Doulas remain with the mother throughout labor, assessing and responding to her needs. Researchers have found positive effects when a doula is present at the birth of a child (Howard & Low, 2020). A review of evidence concluded that doula-assisted mothers were less likely to have a low birth weight baby, less likely to experience birth complications involving themselves or their baby, and less likely to require cesarean delivery (Knocke & others, 2022). Thus, increasing doula-supported births could substantially lower the cost of a birth by reducing cesarean rates and birth complications.

In the United States, most doulas work as independent providers hired by the expectant mother. Doulas typically function as part of a "birthing team," serving as an adjunct to the midwife or the hospital's obstetric staff (Howard & Low, 2020). Managed care organizations are increasingly offering doula support as a part of regular obstetric care.

METHODS OF CHILDBIRTH

U.S. hospitals often allow the mother and her obstetrician to choose from a range of options available for delivering a baby. Key choices involve the use of medication, whether to use any of a number of nonmedicated techniques to reduce pain, and when to resort to a cesarean delivery.

Medication Three basic kinds of drugs are used for labor: analgesics, anesthesia, and oxytocics. **Analgesics** are used to relieve pain. Analgesics include tranquilizers, barbiturates, and narcotics (such as Demerol).

doula A caregiver who provides continuous physical, emotional, and educational support to the mother before, during, and after childbirth.

analgesics Drugs used to alleviate pain, such as tranquilizers, barbiturates, and narcotics.

Anesthesia is used in late first-stage labor and during expulsion of the baby to block sensation in an area of the body or to block consciousness. There is a trend toward not using general anesthesia, which blocks consciousness, in normal births because general anesthesia can be transmitted through the placenta to the fetus (Kannan, 2020). An *epidural block* is regional anesthesia that numbs the woman's body from the waist down. Even this drug, thought to be relatively safe, has come under recent criticism because it is associated with fever, extended labor, and increased risk for cesarean delivery (Wang, 2020). Researchers are continuing to explore safer drug mixtures for use at lower doses to improve the effectiveness and safety of epidural anesthesia (Wang, 2020).

Oxytocin is a hormone that promotes uterine contractions; a synthetic form called Pitocin™ is widely used to decrease the first stage of labor. The relative benefits and risks of administering synthetic forms of oxytocin during childbirth continue to be debated (Blanc-Petitjean & others, 2020).

Predicting how a drug will affect an individual woman and her fetus is difficult. A particular drug might have only a minimal effect on one fetus yet have a much stronger effect on another. The drug's dosage also is a factor (Sood & Sood, 2020). Stronger doses of tranquilizers and narcotics given to decrease the mother's pain potentially have a more negative effect on the fetus than mild doses. It is important for the mother to assess her level of pain and have a voice in deciding whether she should receive medication.

Natural and Prepared Childbirth

For a brief time not long ago, the idea of avoiding all medication during childbirth gained favor in the United States. Instead, many women chose to reduce the pain of childbirth through techniques known as natural childbirth, and a method called prepared childbirth became popular. Today, at least some medication is used in the typical childbirth, but elements of natural childbirth and prepared childbirth remain popular (Sood & Sood, 2020).

Natural childbirth is a method that aims to reduce the mother's pain by decreasing her fear through education about childbirth and by teaching her to use breathing methods and relaxation techniques during delivery (Mueller, Webb, & Morgan, 2020). This approach was developed in 1914 by English obstetrician Grantly Dick-Read. Dick-Read believed that the doctor's relationship with the mother plays an important role in reducing her perception of pain and that the doctor should be present, providing reassurance, during her active labor prior to delivery. One type of natural childbirth that is used today is the *Bradley Method,* which involves husbands as coaches, relaxation for easier birth, and prenatal nutrition and exercise.

French obstetrician Ferdinand Lamaze developed a method similar to natural childbirth that is known as **prepared childbirth,** or the Lamaze method. It includes a special breathing technique to control pushing in the final stages of labor, as well as more detailed education about anatomy and physiology than Dick-Read's approach provides. The Lamaze method has become very popular in the United States (Qumer & Ghosh, 2019). The pregnant woman's partner usually serves as a coach who attends childbirth classes with her and encourages her to use specific breathing and relaxation techniques during delivery.

Many other prepared childbirth techniques have been developed (Bindler & others, 2017; Smith, 2017). They usually include elements of Dick-Read's natural childbirth or Lamaze's method, plus one or more other components. For instance, the Bradley method emphasizes the father's role as a labor coach. Virtually all of the prepared childbirth methods emphasize education, relaxation and breathing exercises, and support.

In sum, proponents of current natural and prepared childbirth methods believe that when information and support are provided, women know how to give birth. To read about the increased variety of techniques being used to reduce stress and control pain during labor, see the *Caring Connections* interlude.

anesthesia Drugs used in late first-stage labor and during expulsion of the baby to block sensation in an area of the body or to block consciousness.

oxytocin A hormone that is sometimes administered during labor to stimulate contractions.

natural childbirth Method developed in 1914 by English obstetrician Grantly Dick-Read that attempts to reduce the mother's pain by decreasing her fear through education about childbirth and breathing methods and relaxation techniques during delivery.

prepared childbirth Developed by French obstetrician Ferdinand Lamaze, this childbirth method is similar to natural childbirth but teaches a special breathing technique to control pushing in the final stages of labor and also provides a more detailed anatomy and physiology course.

Expectant parents take a Lamaze class. *What characterizes the Lamaze method?*
Shutterstock

From Waterbirth to Music Therapy

The effort to reduce stress and control pain during labor has recently led to increased use of some older and some newer nonmedicated techniques (Sood & Sood, 2020). These include waterbirth, massage, yoga, acupuncture, hypnosis, and music therapy.

Waterbirth

Waterbirth involves giving birth in a tub of warm water. Some women go through labor in the water and get out for delivery, while others remain in the water during the delivery. The rationale for waterbirth is that the baby has been in a fluid-filled amniotic sac for many months and that delivery in a similar environment is likely to be less stressful for the baby and the mother (Charles, 2018; Taylor & others, 2016). Mothers get into the warm water when contractions become closer together and more intense. Getting into the water too soon can cause labor to slow or stop. An increasing number of studies are either showing no differences in neonatal and maternal outcomes for waterbirth and non-waterbirth deliveries or positive outcomes for waterbirth (Darsareh, Nourbakhsh, & Dabiri, 2018; Davies & others, 2015; Taylor & others, 2016). For example, a large-scale study of more than 16,000 waterbirth and non-waterbirth deliveries found fewer negative outcomes for the waterbirth newborns (Bovbjerg, Cheyney, & Everson, 2016). Further, a research review concluded that waterbirth is associated with high levels of maternal satisfaction and reduced use of drugs for pain relief during childbirth (Nutter & others, 2014). Waterbirth has been practiced more often in European countries such as Switzerland and Sweden than in the United States in recent decades, but it is increasingly being included in U.S. birth plans.

Massage

Massage is increasingly used to assist mothers prior to and during delivery (Sood & Sood, 2020). Researchers have found that massage can reduce pain and anxiety during labor (Erdogan, Yanikkerem, & Goker, 2017; Jones & others, 2012). One study revealed that massage therapy reduced pain in pregnant women and alleviated prenatal depression in both parents and improved their relationship (Field, Diego, & Hernandez-Reif, 2008). One variation in traditional massage that is being used to relieve labor pain is Hoku point ice massage (Dehcheshmeh & Rafiel, 2015).

Yoga

A research review concluded that practicing yoga during pregnancy may decrease women's stress levels, anxiety, depression, and pain response as well as improving emotional well-being (Kwon & others, 2020). In addition, an experiment that randomly assigned women to a

Shafia Monroe (*second from left*) is a renowned midwife who advocates for providing culturally competent maternity care. Her mission is to reduce infant mortality through various homebirth services and prenatal education.
Courtesy of Shafia Monroe Consulting

yoga condition or a control group found that women in the yoga condition were less likely to experience birth complications and preterm delivery, and the newborns had better health assessments at birth (Pais & others, 2021).

Acupuncture

Acupuncture, the insertion of very fine needles into specific locations in the body, is used as a standard procedure to reduce the pain of childbirth in China, although only recently has it been used in the United States for this purpose (Jo & Lee, 2017). Recent research indicates that acupuncture can have positive effects on labor and delivery (Atkins, Fogarty, & Feigel, 2021). For example, in one study, acupuncture was successful in reducing labor pain 30 minutes after the intervention (Allameh, Tehrani, & Ghasemi, 2015).

Hypnosis

Hypnosis, the induction of a psychological state of altered attention and awareness in which the individual is unusually responsive to suggestions, is increasingly being used during childbirth (Madden & others, 2016; McAllister & others, 2017). Some studies have indicated positive effects of hypnosis for reducing pain during childbirth (Eason & Parris, 2018).

Music Therapy

Music therapy during childbirth, in which music is played to reduce stress and manage pain, is increasingly used (McCaffrey & others, 2020). There is preliminary evidence that it may be effective for reducing labor pain and stress (Wan & Wen, 2018).

---

cesarean delivery Delivery in which the baby is removed from the mother's uterus through an incision made in her abdomen. This also is sometimes referred to as a cesarean section.

Cesarean Delivery   In a **cesarean delivery,** the baby is removed from the mother's uterus through an incision made in her abdomen. Cesarean deliveries also are performed if the baby is lying crosswise in the uterus, if the baby's head is too large to pass through the mother's pelvis, if the baby develops complications, or if the mother is bleeding vaginally.

Because of increased rates of respiratory complications, elective cesarean delivery is not recommended prior to 39 weeks of gestation (American College of Obstetricians and Gynecologists, 2019). The benefits and risks of cesarean deliveries continue to be debated (Cohen & Friedman, 2020). Some critics believe that too many babies are delivered by cesarean section in the United States and other countries such as India and China (Mahadik, 2019). The World Health Organization states that a country's cesarean rate should be 10 percent or less. The U.S. cesarean birth rate in 2015 was 32 percent, the lowest rate since 2007 (J.A. Martin & others, 2017). The highest cesarean rates are in the Dominican Republic and Brazil (56 percent); among the countries with the lowest rates are New Zealand and the Czech Republic (26 percent)—and the country with the very lowest rate (less than 1 percent) is South Sudan (Boerma & others, 2018).

What are some of the specific reasons that physicians perform cesarean deliveries? One of the most common reasons is failure to progress through labor (hindered by epidurals, for example) and fetal distress. Another reason for cesarean delivery involves the baby's positioning in the uterus. Normally the baby's head comes through the vagina first. But if the baby is in a **breech position,** the baby's buttocks would be the first part to emerge from the vagina. In 1 of every 25 deliveries, the baby's head is still in the uterus when the rest of the body is out. Breech births can cause respiratory problems.

breech position Position of the baby within the uterus that causes the buttocks to be the first part to emerge from the vagina.

THE TRANSITION FROM FETUS TO NEWBORN

Much of our discussion of birth so far has focused on the mother. Being born also involves considerable stress for the baby. During each contraction, when the placenta and umbilical cord are compressed as the uterine muscles draw together, the supply of oxygen to the fetus decreases. If the delivery takes too long, the baby can develop *anoxia,* a condition in which the fetus or newborn receives an insufficient supply of oxygen. Anoxia can cause brain damage (Siegel, 2020).

The baby has considerable capacity to withstand the stress of birth. Large quantities of adrenaline and noradrenaline, hormones that protect the fetus in the event of oxygen deficiency, are secreted in stressful circumstances. These hormones increase the heart's pumping activity, speed up heart rate, channel blood flow to the brain, and raise the blood-sugar level. Never again in life will such large amounts of these hormones be secreted. This circumstance underscores how stressful it is to be born and also how well prepared and adapted the fetus is for birth.

At the time of birth, the baby is covered with a protective skin grease called *vernix caseosa.* This substance, which consists of fatty secretions and dead cells, is thought to help protect the baby's skin against heat loss before and during birth.

Immediately after birth, the umbilical cord is cut and the baby is on its own. Before birth, oxygen came from the mother via the umbilical cord, but now the baby is self-sufficient and can breathe on its own. Now 25 million little air sacs in the lungs must be filled with air. These first breaths may be the hardest ones an individual takes.

What characterizes the transition from fetus to newborn?

ERproductions Ltd/Blend Images LLC

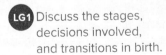

Review Connect Reflect

LG1 Discuss the stages, decisions involved, and transitions in birth.

Review

- What are the three stages involved in the birth process?
- What characterizes the childbirth setting and attendants?
- What are the main methods of childbirth?
- What is the fetus/newborn transition like?

Connect

- How might prenatal care be linked to the difficulty of the birth process?

Reflect *Your Own Personal Journey of Life*

- If you were having a baby, which birth strategy would you prefer? Why? If you could choose to be involved with childbirth, would you want to help your partner through the birth of the baby?

2 What Are Some Measures of Neonatal Health and Responsiveness?

 LG2 Describe three measures of neonatal health and responsiveness.

Almost immediately after birth, after the baby and mother have been introduced, a newborn is taken to be weighed, cleaned up, and tested for signs of problems that might require urgent attention. The **Apgar Scale** is widely used to assess the newborn's chances of survival and determine whether medical attention is needed. The Apgar Scale is used one and five minutes after birth and evaluates infants' heart rate, respiratory effort, muscle tone, body color, and reflex irritability. An obstetrician or a nurse does the evaluation and gives the newborn a score, or reading, of 0, 1, or 2 on each of these five health signs (see Figure 2). A total score of 7 to 10 indicates that the newborn's condition is good; lower scores may indicate an emergency that requires medical attention.

The Apgar Scale is especially good at assessing the newborn's ability to respond to the stress of delivery and the demands of a new environment (Ladewig, London, & Davidson, 2017; Michalczyk, Torbé, & Torbé, 2018). It also identifies high-risk infants who need resuscitation. One study revealed that in comparison with children who have high Apgar scores (9 to 10), the risk of developing attention deficit hyperactivity disorder (ADHD) in childhood was significantly higher for those with Apgar scores of 6 or less (Sucksdorff & others, 2018). Other studies have found that low Apgar scores are associated with long-term needs for additional support in education and educational attainment (Tweed & others, 2016), risk of developmental vulnerability at 5 years of age (Razaz & others, 2016), and risk for developing ADHD (Hanc & others, 2018).

For a more thorough assessment of the newborn, however, the Brazelton Neonatal Behavioral Assessment Scale or the Neonatal Intensive Care Unit Network Neurobehavioral Scale may be used. The **Brazelton Neonatal Behavioral Assessment Scale (NBAS)** is typically performed within 24 to 36 hours after birth. It is also used as a sensitive index of neurological competence, behavior, and emotion up to one month after birth for typical infants and in many studies as a measure of infant development. The NBAS assesses the newborn's neurological development, reflexes, and reactions to people and objects. Sixteen reflexes, such as sneezing, blinking, and rooting, are assessed, along with reactions to circumstances, such as the infant's reaction to a rattle.

Apgar Scale A widely used method to assess the newborn's chances of survival and determine whether medical attention is needed.

Brazelton Neonatal Behavioral Assessment Scale (NBAS) A test performed within 24 to 36 hours after birth to assess newborns' neurological development, reflexes, and reactions to people.

developmental **connection**

Physical Development

What are some individual differences in the reflex of sucking in young infants? Connect to "Physical Development in Infancy."

Score	0	1	2
Heart rate	Absent	Slow—less than 100 beats per minute	Fast—100–140 beats per minute
Respiratory effort	No breathing for more than one minute	Irregular and slow	Good breathing with normal crying
Muscle tone	Limp and flaccid	Weak, inactive, but some flexion of extremities	Strong, active motion
Body color	Blue and pale	Body pink, but extremities blue	Entire body pink
Reflex irritability	No response	Grimace	Coughing, sneezing, and crying

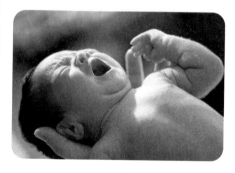

FIGURE 2

THE APGAR SCALE. A newborn's score on the Apgar Scale indicates whether the baby has urgent medical problems. *What are some subsequent outcomes associated with lower Apgar scores of babies?*
Art: *Source:* Apgar, V. "A Proposal for a New Method of Evaluation of the Newborn Infant," from *Anesthesia and Analgesia, 32,* 250–259. New York: Lippincott, Williams & Wilkins, 1953.
Photo: Francisco Cruz/Purestock/SuperStock

A very low NBAS score can indicate brain damage, or stress to the brain that may heal in time. If an infant merely seems sluggish, parents are encouraged to give the infant attention and become more sensitive to the infant's needs. Parents are shown how the newborn can respond to people and how to stimulate such responses. These communications with parents can improve their interaction skills with both high-risk infants and healthy, responsive infants (Candilis-Huisman, 2019).

An "offspring" of the NBAS, the **Neonatal Intensive Care Unit Network Neurobehavioral Scale (NNNS),** provides a more comprehensive analysis of the newborn's behavior, neurological and stress responses, and regulatory capacities. Whereas the NBAS was developed to assess typical, healthy, full-term infants, the NNNS was developed by T. Berry Brazelton, along with Barry Lester and Edward Tronick, to assess "at-risk" infants. It is especially useful for evaluating preterm infants (Hofheimer & others, 2022).

Neonatal Intensive Care Unit Network Neurobehavioral Scale (NNNS) An "offspring" of the NBAS, the NNNS provides a more comprehensive analysis of the newborn's behavior, neurological and stress responses, and regulatory capacities.

Review Connect Reflect

 Describe three measures of neonatal health and responsiveness.

Review
- How can the Apgar Scale, the Brazelton Neonatal Behavioral Assessment Scale, and the Neonatal Intensive Care Unit Network Neurobehavioral Scale be characterized?

Connect
- What tests are used to assess individual differences in older infants? (See the chapter on "Cognitive Development.")

Reflect *Your Own Personal Journey of Life*
- Imagine you are the parent of a newborn. Why might you want your offspring assessed by the NBAS or the NNNS in addition to the Apgar Scale?

---

3 How Do Low Birth Weight and Preterm Infants Develop?

 Characterize the development of low birth weight and preterm infants.

| Preterm and Small for Gestational Age Infants | Consequences of Preterm Birth and Low Birth Weight | Nurturing Preterm Infants |

Various conditions that pose threats for newborns have been given different labels. We next examine these conditions and discuss interventions for improving outcomes of preterm infants.

PRETERM AND SMALL FOR GESTATIONAL AGE INFANTS

Three related conditions pose threats to many newborns: having a low birth weight, being preterm, and being small for gestational age. **Low birth weight infants** weigh less than 5½ pounds at birth. *Very low birth weight* newborns weigh less than 3½ pounds, and *extremely low birth weight* newborns weigh less than 2 pounds. **Preterm infants** are those born three weeks or more before the pregnancy has reached its full term—in other words, before the completion of 37 weeks of gestation (the time between fertilization and birth). **Small for gestational age infants** are those whose birth weight is below normal when the length of the pregnancy is considered. They weigh less than 90 percent of what all babies of the same gestational age weigh. Small for gestational age infants may be preterm or full term. Small for gestational age infants have more birth complications and medical and developmental problems and are at greater risk of dying soon after birth (Boghossian & others, 2018).

<aside>
developmental **connection**
Nutrition
One study revealed that taking folic acid either alone or as part of a multivitamin for one year prior to conceiving was linked to a substantial reduction in preterm birth (Bukowski & others, 2008). Connect to "Prenatal Development."
</aside>

low birth weight infants Babies that weigh less than 5½ pounds at birth.

preterm infants Babies born three weeks or more before the pregnancy has reached its full term.

small for gestational age infants Babies whose birth weight is below normal when the length of pregnancy is considered.

Cross-Cultural Variations in the Incidence and Causes of Low Birth Weight

In some countries, such as Pakistan and Uganda, where poverty is common and the health and nutrition of mothers are poor, the percentage of low birth weight babies reaches as high as 35 percent (see Figure 3). In the United States, there has been an increase in low birth weight infants in the last two decades. The U.S. low birth weight rate of 8.1 percent in 2016 is considerably higher than that of many other high-income countries (Mahumud, Sultana, & Sarker, 2017; Organization for Economic Cooperation and Development, 2018). For example, only 4 percent of the infants born in Finland, Estonia, and Latvia are low birth weight, and only 5 percent of those born in New Zealand, the Netherlands, and Israel are low birth weight.

In both high- and low-income countries, adolescents who give birth when their bodies have not fully matured are at risk for having low birth weight babies. In the United States, the increase in the number of low birth weight infants has been attributed to drug use, poor nutrition, multiple births, reproductive technologies, and improved technology and prenatal care that result in more high-risk babies surviving (Khatun & others, 2017). Nonetheless, poverty continues to be a major factor in preterm birth in the United States. Women living in poverty are more likely to be obese, to have diabetes and hypertension, to use cigarettes and illicit drugs, and to be depressed or anxious, and they are less likely to receive regular prenatal care (Congdon & others, 2016).

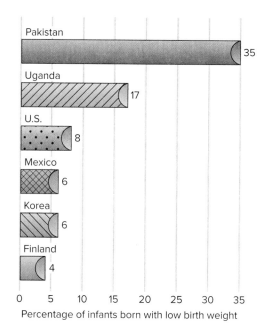

Percentage of infants born with low birth weight

FIGURE 3
PERCENTAGE OF INFANTS BORN WITH LOW BIRTH WEIGHT IN SELECTED COUNTRIES

As mentioned, women living in poverty are less likely to receive regular prenatal care. What did you learn earlier in the chapter about the benefits of regular prenatal care? Aside from women living in poverty, which other demographic group is not likely to receive adequate prenatal care?

How Would You...?
If you were a **social worker**, how would you advise individuals and couples living in poverty who are considering having a child about ways to reduce the risk of having a low birth weight child?

In 2021, 10.5 percent of U.S. infants were born preterm—a significant increase since the 1980s (Centers for Disease Control and Prevention, 2023). The increase in preterm birth is likely due to such factors as the increasing number of births to women 35 years of age or older, increasing rates of multiple births, increased management of maternal and fetal conditions (for example, inducing labor preterm if medical technology indicates that it will increase the likelihood of survival), increased maternal substance abuse (tobacco, alcohol), and increased stress. Ethnic variations characterize preterm birth (DeSisto & others, 2018). In 2021, the likelihood of being born preterm in the United States was 9.5 percent for non-Latino White infants, down from 11.4 percent in 2011. The preterm birth rate was 14.8 percent for Black infants (down from 16.7 percent in 2011) and 10.2 for Latino infants, down from 11.6 percent in 2011 (Centers for Disease Control and Prevention, 2023; J.A. Martin & others, 2017). In 2020, the world was confronted with a new concern—maternal novel coronavirus infection. Emerging evidence suggests this viral infection increases risk for premature birth, and there is a high risk of mother-newborn transmission after delivery (Segars & others, 2020).

See the *Connecting with Diversity* interlude to learn how the incidence and causes of low birth weight vary across countries.

CONSEQUENCES OF PRETERM BIRTH AND LOW BIRTH WEIGHT

Although most preterm and low birth weight infants are healthy, as a group they have more health and developmental problems than normal birth weight infants (Cheong & others, 2020). For preterm birth, the terms *extremely preterm* and *very preterm* are increasingly used

(Bell & others, 2022). *Extremely preterm infants* are those born at less than 28 weeks gestation, and *very preterm infants* are those born between 28 and 33 weeks of gestational age. Figure 4 shows the results of a foundational Norwegian study indicating that the earlier preterm infants are born, the more likely they are to eventually drop out of school (Swamy, Ostbye, & Skjaerven, 2008).

The number and severity of these problems increase when infants are born very early and as their birth weight decreases (Dilworth-Bart & others, 2018; FitzGerald & others, 2018). Survival rates for infants who are born very early and very small have risen, but with this improved survival rate have come increased rates of severe brain damage as well as less severe developmental problems (Bell & others, 2022). A review of research concluded that preterm and low birth weight infants are at greater risk than full-term and normal birth weight infants for motor problems, low IQ, poorer academic performance, attention deficit hyperactivity disorder, autism spectrum disorders, and difficulties with social interactions (Morgan & others, 2022). Approximately 50 percent of all low birth weight children are enrolled in special education programs.

An eight-year longitudinal study of genetically identical twin pairs examined the possible influence of genetic and prenatal environmental factors on whether an infant would be born preterm (Deater-Deckard, 2016). In this study, especially in very preterm infants, the identical twin who was smaller at birth (an index of prenatal environmental experience) than the genetically identical co-twin was far more likely to have poorer self-regulation of cognition, behavior, and emotion at 8 years of age. This study documents how the prenatal environment can be a powerful influence on development, even when genetic influences are controlled (indexed by the twins' identical genetic makeup). Further, the most likely explanation of the outcomes in this study involves epigenetic factors.

NURTURING PRETERM INFANTS

An important strategy when considering how to treat low birth weight and preterm births is to reduce the risk of low birth weight before it occurs. Some effects of being born low in birth weight can be reduced or even reversed. Intensive enrichment programs that provide medical and educational services for both the parents and children can improve short-term outcomes for low birth weight children (Petty & others, 2020).

At present, federal laws mandate that services for school-aged children must be expanded to include family-based care for infants born with severe disabilities. The availability of services for moderately low birth weight children who do not have severe physical problems varies, but most states do not provide these services.

Two increasingly used interventions in the neonatal intensive care unit (NICU) are kangaroo care and massage therapy. **Kangaroo care** involves skin-to-skin contact, in which the baby, wearing only a diaper, is held upright against the parent's bare chest, much as a baby kangaroo is carried by its mother (Stadd & others, 2020). Kangaroo care is typically practiced for two to three hours per day, skin-to-skin over an extended time in early infancy.

Why use kangaroo care with preterm infants? Preterm infants often have difficulty coordinating their breathing and heart rate, and the close physical contact with the parent provided by kangaroo care can help to stabilize the preterm infant's heartbeat, temperature, and breathing (Özdel & Sari, 2020). Preterm and low birth weight infants who experience kangaroo care also gain more weight than their counterparts who are not given this care (Charpak, Montealegre-Pomar, & Bohorquez, 2021). This intervention also may have long-term positive effects on cognitive functioning into early adulthood (Ropars & others, 2018). A meta-analysis found that kangaroo care provided pain relief to preterm infants during painful procedures (Wang & others, 2022). One study revealed that kangaroo care led to better physical development in low birth weight infants (Bera & others, 2014). Further, another study found that kangaroo care significantly reduced the amount of crying and improved the stability of heart rates in preterm infants (Choudhary & others, 2016). Also, a

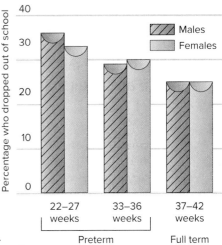

FIGURE 4

PERCENTAGE OF PRETERM AND FULL-TERM BIRTH INFANTS WHO DROPPED OUT OF SCHOOL

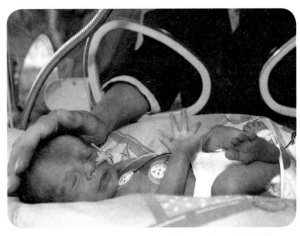

A "kilogram kid," weighing less than 2.3 pounds at birth. *What are some long-term outcomes for weighing so little at birth?*
Diether Endlicher/AP Images

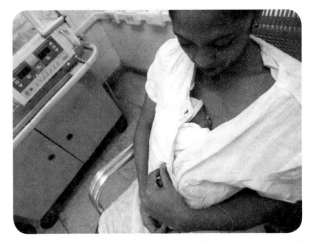

A new mother practicing kangaroo care. *What is kangaroo care?*
Claudia Daut/Reuters/Alamy Stock Photo

kangaroo care A way of holding a preterm infant so that there is skin-to-skin contact.

How Does Massage Therapy Benefit the Health and Well-Being of Babies?

Key Points:

- Researchers explored how human touch might improve outcomes for at-risk infants.
- One study found that massage therapy reduced the stress of preterm infants.
- Research indicates that massage therapy increases weight gain of preterm infants and reduces their hospital stay.

Throughout history and in many cultures, caregivers have massaged infants. In Africa and Asia, infants are routinely massaged by parents or other family members for several months after birth. In the United States, interest in using touch and massage to improve the growth, health, and well-being of infants has been stimulated by the foundational research and series of studies by Tiffany Field (for a complete review of studies, see Field, 2021). Field is the director of the Touch Research Institute at the University of Miami School of Medicine.

In a typical study, preterm infants in a neonatal intensive care unit (NICU) were randomly assigned to a massage therapy group or a control group. For five consecutive days, the preterm infants in the massage group were given three 15-minute moderate-pressure massages (Hernandez-Reif, Diego, & Field, 2007). Behavioral observations of the following stress behaviors were made on the first and last days of the study: crying, grimacing, yawning, sneezing, jerky arm and leg movements, startles, and finger flaring. The various stress behaviors were summarized in a composite stress behavior index. As indicated in Figure 5, massage had a stress-reducing effect on the preterm infants, which is especially important because they encounter numerous stressors while they are hospitalized.

Field (2021) has demonstrated the benefits of massage therapy for infants who face a variety of problems. For example, preterm infants exposed to opioids (such as heroin) in utero who received massage therapy had improvements in biomarkers of stress, such as a reduced heart rate and lowered blood pressure, following massage (Rana & others, 2022). In other research, massage therapy improved the scores of HIV-exposed infants on both physical and mental scales, while also improving their hearing and speech development (Perez & others, 2015). In addition to improving outcomes for infants, infant massage has benefits for parents, too. For example, maternal postpartum depression appears to be reduced by performing infant massage (Fan & others, 2023).

In the most comprehensive and up-to-date research review of massage therapy with preterm infants, Field (2021) concluded that the most consistent findings involve two positive results: (1) increased weight gain and (2) discharge from the hospital several days earlier. One study revealed that the mechanisms responsible for increased weight gain as a result of massage therapy were stimulation of the

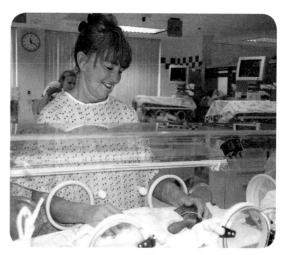

Tiffany Field massages a newborn infant. *What types of infants benefit from massage therapy?*
Courtesy of Dr. Tiffany Field

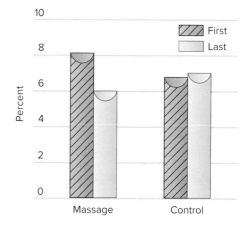

FIGURE 5

PRETERM INFANTS SHOW REDUCED STRESS BEHAVIORS AND ACTIVITY AFTER FIVE DAYS OF MASSAGE THERAPY (HERNANDEZ-REIF, DIEGO, & FIELD, 2007)

vagus nerve (one of 12 cranial nerves leading to the brain), which in turn promoted the release of insulin (a food absorption hormone) (Field, Diego, & Hernandez-Reif, 2010). Another study found that both massage therapy (moderate-pressure stroking) and exercise (flexion and extension of the limbs) led to weight gain in preterm infants (Diego, Field, & Hernandez-Reif, 2014). In this study, massage was linked to increased vagus nerve activity while exercise was associated with increased calorie consumption.

In light of Field's findings, do you think expectant parents should routinely be taught how to massage their infants, even when prenatal development and birth have gone smoothly? Why or why not?

How Would You...?

If you were a **health-care professional,** how would you advise hospital administrators about implementing kangaroo care or massage therapy in the neonatal intensive care unit?

developmental **connection**

Attachment

A classic study of infant monkeys with cloth and wire surrogate mothers demonstrated the important role that touch plays in infant attachment. Connect to "Socioemotional Development in Infancy."

study in the United Kingdom found that the use of kangaroo care in neonatal units resulted in substantial cost savings mainly because of reduced rates of diseases such as gastroenteritis and colitis (Lowson & others, 2015). Perhaps most important, a randomized controlled trial in five countries concluded that kangaroo care starting immediately after birth decreased the risk of mortality in low birth weight infants (WHO Immediate KMC Study Group, 2021). And in a longitudinal study, the nurturing positive effects of kangaroo care with preterm and low birth weight infants that were initially found for intelligence and home environment at 1 year of age were still positive 20 years later in emerging adults' reduced school absenteeism, reduced hyperactivity, lower aggressiveness, and higher levels of social skills (Charpak & others, 2017).

A U.S. survey found that mothers had a much more positive view of kangaroo care than did neonatal intensive care nurses and that the mothers were more likely to think it should be provided daily (Hendricks-Munoz & others, 2013). There is concern that kangaroo care is not used more often in neonatal intensive care units (Smith & others, 2017). Increasingly, kangaroo care is recommended as standard practice for all newborns (Stadd & others, 2020).

Many preterm infants experience less touch than full-term infants because they are isolated in temperature-controlled incubators. One illustrative study found that kangaroo care and massage therapy were equally effective in improving body weight and reducing length of hospital stay for low birth weight infants (Rangey & Sheth, 2014). The research of Tiffany Field has led to a surge of interest in the role that massage might play in improving developmental outcomes for preterm infants. To read about Field's research, see the *Connecting with Research* interlude.

Review Connect Reflect

LG3 Characterize the development of low birth weight and preterm infants.

Review

- What is a low birth weight infant? How can preterm and small for gestational age infants be distinguished?
- What are the long-term outcomes for low birth weight infants?
- What is known about the roles of kangaroo care and massage therapy with preterm infants?

Connect

- What are some different types of learning disabilities?

Reflect *Your Own Personal Journey of Life*

- Imagine that you are the parent of a newborn. Would you rather have your newborn experience kangaroo care or massage therapy?

4 What Happens During the Postpartum Period?

LG4 Explain the physical and psychological aspects of the postpartum period.

Physical Adjustments   Emotional and Psychological Adjustments   Bonding

The weeks after childbirth present challenges for many new parents and their offspring. This is the **postpartum period,** the period after childbirth or delivery that lasts for about six weeks or until the mother's body has completed its adjustment and has returned to a nearly prepregnant state. It is a time when the woman adjusts, both physically and psychologically, to the process of childbearing.

The postpartum period involves a great deal of adjustment and adaptation. The baby has to be cared for. The mother has to recover from childbirth, to learn how to take care of the baby, and to learn to feel good about herself as a mother. The father or partner needs to learn how to take care of the recovering mother, to learn how to take care of the baby, and to learn

postpartum period The period after childbirth when the mother adjusts, both physically and psychologically, to the process of childbearing. This period lasts for about six weeks, or until her body has completed its adjustment and has returned to a near-prepregnant state.

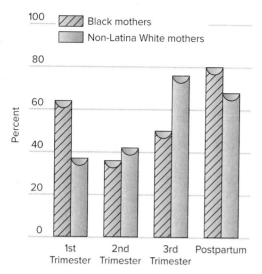

FIGURE 6

POOR SLEEP QUALITY IN PREGNANT AND POSTPARTUM BLACK AND NON-LATINA WHITE WOMEN

Postpartum blues
Symptoms appear 2 to 3 days after delivery and usually subside within 1 to 2 weeks.

70%

10%

20%

Postpartum depression
Symptoms linger for weeks or months and interfere with daily functioning.

No symptoms

FIGURE 7

POSTPARTUM BLUES AND POSTPARTUM DEPRESSION AMONG U.S. WOMEN. Some health professionals refer to the postpartum period as the "fourth trimester." Though the time span of the postpartum period does not necessarily cover three months, the term "fourth trimester" suggests continuity and the importance of the first several months after birth for the mother.
Source: American College of Obstetricians and Gynecologists, Postpartum

involution The process by which the uterus returns to its prepregnant size.

postpartum depression Involves a major depressive episode characterized by strong feelings of sadness, anxiety, or despair in new mothers, making it difficult for them to carry out daily tasks.

how to feel good about being a coparent. Many health professionals believe that the best way to meet these challenges is with a family-centered approach that uses the family's resources to support an early and smooth adjustment to the newborn by all family members. The adjustments needed are physical, emotional, and psychological.

PHYSICAL ADJUSTMENTS

A woman's body makes numerous physical adjustments in the first days and weeks after childbirth (Sardi & others, 2020). She may have a great deal of energy or feel exhausted and let down. Most new mothers feel tired and need rest. Though these changes are normal, the fatigue can undermine the new mother's sense of well-being and confidence in her ability to cope with a new baby and a new family life (Dennis & Vigod, 2020).

A concern is the loss of sleep that the primary caregiver experiences in the postpartum period (McBean, Kinsey, & Montgomery-Downs, 2016). One illustrative analysis indicated that the primary caregiver loses as much as 700 hours of sleep in the first year following the baby's birth (Maas, 2008). In many Western industrialized countries including the United States, a substantial percentage of women report loss of sleep during pregnancy and in the postpartum period (Parsons & others, 2023) (see Figure 6). The loss of sleep can contribute to stress, relationship conflict, and impaired decision making (Thomas & Spieker, 2016). Postpartum depression may be linked to poor sleep quality (such as disrupted, fragmented sleep) rather than to lower amounts of sleep (Park, Meltzer-Brody, & Stickgold, 2013).

After delivery, a mother's body undergoes sudden and dramatic changes in hormone production. When the placenta is delivered, estrogen and progesterone levels drop steeply and remain low until the ovaries start producing hormones again. **Involution** is the process by which the uterus returns to its prepregnant size five or six weeks after birth. Immediately following birth, the uterus weighs 2 to 3 pounds. By the end of five or six weeks, the uterus weighs 2 to 3½ ounces. Nursing the baby helps contract the uterus at a rapid rate.

If a woman has regularly engaged in conditioning exercises during pregnancy, exercise will help her recover her former body contour and strength. With a caregiver's approval, the new mother can begin some exercises as soon as one hour after delivery. One classic study found that women who maintained or increased their exercise from prepregnancy to postpartum had better well-being than women who engaged in no exercise or decreased their exercise from prepregnancy to postpartum (Blum, Beaudoin, & Caton-Lemos, 2005). A subsequent comprehensive review of the research literature shows clear evidence for the benefit of exercise in improving emotional and physical well-being (Kołomańska-Bogucka & Mazur-Bialy, 2019).

Relaxation techniques are also helpful during the postpartum period. Five minutes of slow breathing on a stressful day during the postpartum period can relax and refresh the new mother, and this will indirectly benefit the new baby.

EMOTIONAL AND PSYCHOLOGICAL ADJUSTMENTS

Emotional fluctuations are common for mothers in the postpartum period. For some women, emotional fluctuations decrease within several weeks after the delivery, but other women experience more long-lasting emotional swings (Li & others, 2020).

As shown in Figure 7, about 70 percent of new mothers in the United States have what are called "baby blues." About two to three days after birth, they begin to feel depressed, anxious, and upset. These feelings may come and go for several weeks after the birth, often peaking about three to five days after birth.

Postpartum depression involves a major depressive episode that typically occurs about four weeks after delivery. In other words, women with postpartum depression have such strong feelings of sadness, anxiety, or despair that for at least a two-week period they have trouble coping with their daily tasks. Without treatment, postpartum depression may become worse and last for many months (Wilcox & others, 2020). And many women with postpartum depression don't seek help. Barriers to seeking help for postpartum depression may be individual, such as perceived stigma, or societal, such as lack of access to services (Bina, 2020). A comprehensive review of studies conducted in many countries shows that many such women do not seek out assistance (Bina, 2020). Estimates indicate that 10 to 15 percent of new mothers experience postpartum depression.

A comprehensive research review concluded that the following are risk factors for developing postpartum depression: a history of depression, depression and anxiety during pregnancy, neuroticism, low self-esteem, postpartum blues, a poor marital relationship, and a low level of social support (O'Hara & McCabe, 2013). Also, in this research review, a number of perinatal-related stressors such as perinatal complications, infant health and temperament, and type of delivery (emergency cesarean section, for example) were found to be potential risk factors for postpartum depression. A subset of women are likely to develop postpartum depression in the context of hormonal changes associated with late pregnancy and childbirth (O'Hara & McCabe, 2013). Further, a subsequent study found that depression during pregnancy, a history of physical abuse, migrant status, and postpartum physical complications were major risk factors for postpartum depression (Gaillard & others, 2014). And a more recent study revealed that women who had a history of depression were 20 times more likely to develop postpartum depression than women who had no history of depression (Silverman & others, 2017).

Several antidepressant drugs have been proposed as possibly effective in treating postpartum depression, although it is not yet clear whether these are safe to take while breast feeding (Kaufman & others, 2022). Psychotherapy, especially cognitive-behavioral therapy, also is effective in treating postpartum depression for many women, and recent evidence suggests such therapy can be effectively delivered online (Roman & others, 2020). The effectiveness of psychotherapy may depend in part on cultural and socioeconomic factors (Ponting & others, 2020). In addition, engaging in regular exercise may help reduce postpartum depression (Kołomańska-Bogucka & Mazur-Bialy, 2019).

A mother's postpartum depression can affect the way she interacts with her infant (Brummelte & Galea, 2016). A foundational research review concluded that the interaction difficulties of depressed mothers and their infants occur across cultures and socioeconomic status groups, and encompass less sensitivity of the mothers and less responsiveness on the part of infants (Field, 2010). In one study, postpartum depression was associated with an increase in 4-month-old infants' unintentional injuries (Yamaoka, Fujiwara, & Tamiya, 2016). Further, a recent study revealed that mothers' postpartum depression, but not generalized anxiety, were linked to their children's emotional negativity and behavior problems at 2 years of age (Prenoveau & others, 2017). Several caregiving activities also are compromised, including feeding, sleep routines, and safety practices.

How is postpartum depression linked to children's development? Research indicates that children's physical health and cognitive development are affected (Netsi & others, 2018). Studies link postpartum depression to a lower level of cardiovascular functioning in children and higher rates of gastrointestinal and respiratory infections (Ban & others, 2010; Gump & others, 2009; Ullah & others, 2019). In terms of cognitive development, children whose mothers have postpartum depression are more likely to have a lower level of intelligence and poorer language development (Y. Liu & others, 2017), although for some children these effects dissipate over the course of childhood.

To read about an individual who has specialized in helping women adjust during the postpartum period, see the *Connecting with Careers* profile.

Fathers also undergo considerable adjustment in the postpartum period, even when they work away from home all day (Walsh, Davis, & Garfield, 2020). When the mother develops postpartum depression, many fathers also experience depressed feelings (Johansson, Benderix, & Svensson, 2020). Many fathers feel that the baby comes first and gets all of the mother's attention; some feel that they have been replaced by the baby. One typical study found 5 percent of fathers had depressive symptoms in the first two weeks following delivery (Anding & others, 2016).

The father's support and caring can play a role in whether the mother develops postpartum depression (Darwom & others, 2017; Mahalik, Di Bianca, & Sepulveda, 2020). A meta-analysis of 10 studies revealed that a higher level of support by fathers was related to a lower incidence of postpartum depression in Latina women (Edwards & others, 2021). Another study found that depressive symptoms in both the mother and father were associated with impaired bonding with their infant during the postpartum period (Kerstis & others, 2016). And in a study of women in the United States and Australia who identified as lesbian, bisexual, or as another orientation, such as pansexual or queer, increasing partner support was recommended as a way to decrease postpartum depression (Marsland, Treyvaud, & Pepping, 2022).

How Would You...?
If you were a **human development and family studies professional,** how would you talk with mothers and fathers about vulnerabilities involving mental health and relationships in the postpartum period?

The postpartum period is a time of considerable adjustment and adaptation for both the mother and the father. Fathers can provide an important support system for mothers and loving care for young infants. *What kinds of tasks might the father of a newborn do to care for his infant?*
Cavan Images/Alamy Stock Photo

developmental connection
Theories
Lorenz demonstrated the importance of bonding in greylag geese, but the first few days of life are unlikely to be a critical period for bonding in human infants. Connect to "Introduction."

Diane Sanford, Clinical Psychologist and Postpartum Expert

Diane Sanford, Ph.D., is a licensed psychologist, author, and educator who specializes in women's reproductive mental health. Sanford has written a number of print and online resources, including *Stress Less, Live Better: For Pregnancy, Postpartum, and Early Motherhood* (with Megan Demsky), which describes five skill sets to improve mental health and well-being for all pregnant and postpartum moms. Postpartum depression can be experienced both by those who have recently delivered a baby and by women who have miscarried or had a stillbirth. It is estimated that 900,000 U.S. women experience postpartum depression each year, making this a significant mental health concern.

In 2022, Dr. Sanford and her daughter Rachel Sanford, MSW, LCSW, started Sanford Counseling and Consulting. Rachel, who also focused on prenatal health issues in her academic studies, is health promotions manager for the American Lung Association and graduated in 2018 with a concentration in mental health from the Brown School of Social Work at Washington University in St. Louis, Missouri.

Diane Sanford (*sitting*) is a leading expert on postpartum depression. Her daughter, Rachel Sanford, is also a practicing counselor.
Courtesy of Diane and Rachel Sanford

Some fathers develop postpartum depression, and it can be detrimental to the child's development (Walsh, Davis, & Garfield, 2020). One example is seen in a study that revealed that paternal postpartum depression (independent of maternal postpartum depression) was linked to psychological disorders in their children seven years later (Ramchandani & others, 2008).

To help the father adjust, parents should set aside some special time to spend together. The father's postpartum reaction also likely will be improved if he has taken childbirth classes with the mother and is an active participant in caring for the baby.

BONDING

A special component of the parent-infant relationship is **bonding,** the formation of a connection, especially a physical bond involving touch, between parents and the newborn in the period shortly after birth. Sometimes hospitals seem determined to deter bonding. Drugs given to the mother to make her delivery less painful can make the mother drowsy, interfering with her ability to respond to and stimulate the newborn. Mothers and newborns are often separated shortly after delivery, and preterm infants are isolated from their mothers even more than are full-term infants.

Do these practices do any harm? Some physicians believe that during the period shortly after birth, direct skin-to-skin contact between the parents and newborn is necessary to form an emotional attachment as a foundation for optimal development in years to come. Is there evidence that close contact between mothers in the first several days after birth is critical for optimal development later in life? Although some older research supports this bonding hypothesis (Kennell, 2006), a body of research, including several classic studies, challenges the significance of the first few days of life as a critical period (Bakeman & Brown, 1980; Rode & others, 1981). Indeed, the extreme form of the bonding hypothesis—the idea that the newborn must have close contact with the mother in the first few days of life to develop optimally—simply is not true.

Nonetheless, the weakness of the bonding hypothesis should not be used as an excuse to keep motivated mothers from interacting with their newborns. Such contact brings pleasure to many mothers. In some mother-infant pairs—including preterm infants, adolescent mothers,

A mother bonds with her infant moments after it is born. *How critical is bonding for the development of social competence later in childhood?*
FatCamera/E+/Getty Images

bonding A close connection, especially a physical bond, between parents and their newborn in the period shortly after birth.

and mothers from disadvantaged circumstances—early close contact may establish a climate for improved interaction after the mother and infant leave the hospital.

Most hospitals offer a rooming-in arrangement, in which the baby remains in the mother's room most of the time during their hospital stay. However, if parents choose not to use this rooming-in arrangement, the weight of the research suggests that this decision will not harm the infant (Theo & Drake, 2017).

Review Connect Reflect

 LG4 Explain the physical and psychological aspects of the postpartum period.

Review
- What does the postpartum period involve? What physical adjustments does the woman's body make during this period?
- What emotional and psychological adjustments characterize the postpartum period?
- Is bonding critical for optimal development?

Connect
- How can exercise help pregnant women before delivery and women with postpartum depression?

Reflect *Your Own Personal Journey of Life*
- If you plan to have children, what can you do to adjust effectively in the postpartum period? If you were the partner of a new mother, what could you do to help during the postpartum period?

topical connections   *looking forward*

You will explore the physical, cognitive, and socioemotional development of infants, including key theoretical, research, and applied aspects of the first 18 to 24 months of life. You will learn about the remarkable and complex physical development of infants' motor skills, such as learning to sit and walk; read about the early development of infants' cognitive skills, such as the ability to form concepts; and examine infants' surprisingly sophisticated socioemotional development, as reflected in their motivation to share and perceive others' actions as intentionally motivated.

Next, you will follow the dramatic physical development of the infant through the first months of life, tracing how motor skills are acquired and how perception and the senses develop during a period of remarkable physical growth and change.

reach your **learning goals**

Birth

1 What Happens During the Birth Process?

 LG1 Discuss the stages, decisions involved, and transitions in birth.

Stages of the Birth Process

- The first stage of birth is the longest and lasts about 12 to 14 hours for a woman having her first child. During it, the cervical opening dilates to about 4 inches in diameter. The second stage begins when the baby's head starts to move through the cervix and ends with the baby's complete emergence. The third stage is delivery of the afterbirth.

Childbirth Setting and Attendants	• In the United States, the vast majority of births occur in hospitals and are attended by physicians. Many hospitals now have birthing centers. Some women who have good medical histories and who are at low risk for problem deliveries have babies at home. In many countries, such as Holland, much higher percentages of babies are born at home. Some births are attended by a midwife, and in many countries a doula attends.
Methods of Childbirth	• Among the methods of delivery are medicated, natural and prepared, and cesarean. The three basic kinds of drugs used in delivering a baby are analgesics, anesthesia, and oxytocics. Predicting how a particular drug will affect an individual pregnant woman and her fetus is difficult. Today the trend is toward using some medication during childbirth but keeping it to a minimum, if possible. Some believe that the U.S. cesarean rate is too high. The Lamaze method of prepared childbirth is widely used in the United States.
The Transition from Fetus to Newborn	• In some cases, if the delivery takes too long, anoxia can occur. Anoxia involves an insufficient supply of oxygen during the fetus/newborn transition. Being born involves considerable stress, but the baby is well prepared and adapted to handle the stress. Large quantities of stress-related hormones (adrenaline and noradrenaline) are secreted during the fetus/newborn transition.

2 What Are Some Measures of Neonatal Health and Responsiveness?

 LG2 Describe three measures of neonatal health and responsiveness.

- For many years, the Apgar Scale has been used to assess the newborn's health. It is used one and five minutes after birth and assesses heart rate, respiratory effort, muscle tone, body color, and reflex irritability.

- The Brazelton Neonatal Behavioral Assessment Scale (NBAS) is performed within 24 to 36 hours after birth to evaluate the newborn's neurological development, reflexes, and reactions to people.

- Recently, the Neonatal Intensive Care Unit Network Neurobehavioral Scale (NNNS) was constructed; it provides a more comprehensive analysis of the newborn's behavior, neurological and stress responses, and regulatory capacities.

3 How Do Low Birth Weight and Preterm Infants Develop?

 LG3 Characterize the development of low birth weight and preterm infants.

Preterm and Small for Gestational Age Infants	• Low birth weight infants weigh less than 5½ pounds at birth. Low birth weight babies may be preterm (born three weeks or more before the pregnancy has reached full term) or small for gestational age (which refers to infants whose birth weight is below normal when the length of pregnancy is considered). Small for gestational age infants may be preterm or full term.
Consequences of Preterm Birth and Low Birth Weight	• Although most low birth weight babies are normal and healthy, as a group they have more health and developmental problems than full-term babies do. The number and severity of the problems increase when infants are born very early and at very low birth weight.
Nurturing Preterm Infants	• Kangaroo care, a way of holding a preterm infant so that there is skin-to-skin contact, has positive effects on preterm infants. Massage therapy is increasingly being used with preterm infants and has positive outcomes.

4 What Happens During the Postpartum Period?

 LG4 Explain the physical and psychological aspects of the postpartum period.

Physical Adjustments	• The postpartum period is the period after childbirth or delivery. It is a time when the woman adjusts, both physically and psychologically, to the process of childbearing. It lasts for about six weeks, or until the body has completed its adjustment. Physical adjustments include fatigue, involution, hormonal changes that include a dramatic drop in estrogen and progesterone, and exercises to recover former body contour and strength.
Emotional and Psychological Adjustments	• Emotional fluctuations are common among mothers during the postpartum period. These fluctuations may be due to hormonal changes, fatigue, inexperience or lack of confidence in caring for a newborn, or the extensive demands involved in caring for a newborn. For some,

these emotional fluctuations are minimal and disappear within a few weeks, but for others they can be more long-lasting. Postpartum depression involves such strong feelings of sadness, anxiety, or despair that new mothers have difficulty carrying out daily tasks. Postpartum depression affects approximately 10 to 15 percent of new mothers.

- The father also goes through a postpartum adjustment. He may feel that the baby now receives all of his partner's or wife's attention. Being an active participant in caring for the baby helps ease the father's postpartum reaction. Parents need to set aside special time to spend together.

- Bonding refers to the formation of a connection between parents and the newborn shortly after birth. Bonding has not been found to be critical in the development of a competent infant or child, although it may stimulate positive interaction in some mother-infant pairs.

Bonding

key **terms**

afterbirth
analgesics
anesthesia
Apgar Scale
bonding
Brazelton Neonatal Behavioral
   Assessment Scale (NBAS)

breech position
cesarean delivery
doula
involution
kangaroo care
low birth weight infants
natural childbirth

Neonatal Intensive Care Unit
   Network Neurobehavioral
   Scale (NNNS)
oxytocin
postpartum depression
postpartum period
prepared childbirth

preterm infants
small for gestational age
   infants

key **people**

T. Berry Brazelton
Grantly Dick-Read

Tiffany Field
Ferdinand Lamaze

Barry Lester

Edward Tronick

improving the **lives of children**

STRATEGIES

Preparing for Childbirth

Here are some birth strategies that may benefit the baby and the mother:

- *Take a childbirth class.* These classes provide information about the childbirth experience.

- *Become knowledgeable about different childbirth techniques.* We considered a number of different childbirth techniques in this chapter, including Lamaze and use of doulas. Obtain more detailed information about such techniques by reading an informative book, such as *The Expectant Father: The Ultimate Guide for Dads-to-Be* (5th ed.), by Armin Brott and Jennifer Ash Rudick (New York: Abbeville Press, 2021).

- *Use positive intervention with at-risk infants.* Massage can improve the developmental outcomes of at-risk infants. Intensive enrichment programs that include medical, educational, psychological, occupational, and physical domains can benefit low birth weight infants. Intervention with low birth weight infants should involve an individualized plan.

- *Involve the family in the birth process.* If they are motivated to participate, the husband, partner, and siblings can benefit from being involved in the birth process. A mother, sister, or friend can also provide support.

- *Know about the adaptation required in the postpartum period.* The postpartum period involves considerable adaptation and adjustment by mothers and fathers. The mother's adjustment is both physical and emotional. Exercise and relaxation techniques can benefit mothers during the postpartum period. So can an understanding, supportive partner.

RESOURCES

Lamaze International
www.lamaze.org

Lamaze provides information about the Lamaze method and taking or teaching Lamaze classes.

Birth: Issues in Perinatal Care

This multidisciplinary journal on perinatal care is written for health professionals and contains articles on research and clinical practice, review articles, and commentary.

International Cesarean Awareness Network
www.ican-online.org

This organization provides extensive information and advice about cesarean birth.

Postpartum Support International (PSI)
www.postpartum.net

PSI provides information about postpartum depression.

section three

Babies are such a nice way to start people.

—DON HEROLD
American Writer, 20th Century

Infancy

As newborns, we were not empty-headed organisms. We had some basic competencies. We slept a lot, and occasionally we smiled, although the meaning of our first smiles was not entirely clear. We ate and we grew. We crawled and then we walked, a journey of a thousand miles beginning with a single step. Sometimes we conformed; sometimes others conformed to us. Our development was a continuous creation of more complex forms. Our helplessness demanded loving caregiving. We juggled the necessity of controlling our will with becoming who we willfully were becoming. Section 3 contains three chapters: "Physical Development in Infancy," "Cognitive Development in Infancy," and "Socioemotional Development in Infancy."

chapter 5

PHYSICAL DEVELOPMENT IN INFANCY

chapter **outline**

Image Source/Getty Images

Efia is a newborn baby in Ghana. During her first days after birth, she has been kept apart from her mother and bottle fed. Manufacturers of infant formula provide the hospital where she was born with free or subsidized milk powder. Her mother has been persuaded to bottle-feed rather than breast-feed her. When her mother bottle-feeds Efia, she dilutes the milk formula with unclean water. Efia's feeding bottles cannot be thoroughly sterilized. Efia becomes very sick. She dies before her first birthday.

Ajani was born in a Nigerian hospital with a "baby-friendly" program. In this program, babies are not separated from their mothers when they are born, and the mothers are encouraged to breast-feed them. The mothers are told of the risks that bottle feeding can bring because of unsafe water and unsterilized bottles. They also are informed about the advantages of breast milk, which include its nutritious and hygienic qualities, its ability to immunize babies against common illnesses, and its role in reducing the mother's risk of breast and ovarian cancers. Ajani's mother is breast feeding him. At 1 year of age, Ajani is very healthy.

For many years, maternity units in hospitals favored bottle feeding and did not give mothers adequate information about the benefits of breast feeding. In recent years, the World Health Organization and UNICEF have tried to reverse the trend toward bottle feeding of infants in many countries by instituting programs. They also persuaded the International Association of Infant Formula Manufacturers to stop marketing their baby formulas to hospitals in countries where the government supports their initiatives. For the hospitals themselves, costs actually were reduced as infant formula, feeding bottles, and separate nurseries became unnecessary. For example, Jose Fabella Memorial Hospital in the Philippines reported saving 8 percent of its annual budget. Still, there are many places in the world where these initiatives have not been implemented (World Health Organization, 2021).

The advantages of breast feeding, especially in low- and middle-income countries, are substantial (UNICEF, 2017). However, these advantages must be balanced against the risk of passing HIV to the baby through breast milk if the mother has the virus; many mothers don't know their HIV status (Fox & others, 2018).

(Top) A mother breast feeding her baby in Nairobi, Kenya. *(Bottom)* A Rwandan mother bottle feeding her baby. *What are some concerns about breast feeding versus bottle feeding?*

(Top) Wendy Stone/Corbis Documentary/Getty Images; *(bottom)* Horizon International Images/Alamy Stock Photo

¬topical connections *looking **back***

You have read about the transformation from fetus to newborn, and the baby's remarkable capacity to withstand the stress of the birth process. You learned how preterm and low birth weight babies can be nurtured in their first days and weeks after birth, and how new mothers adjust—physically and psychologically—during the postpartum period. In this chapter, you will read about many aspects of the infant's physical development, including breathtaking advances in the development of the brain, motor skills, and perception.

preview

It is very important for infants to get a healthy start. When they do, their first two years of life are likely to be a time of amazing development. In this chapter, we focus on the biological domain and the infant's physical development, exploring physical growth, motor development, and sensory and perceptual development.

1 How Do Infants Grow and Develop Physically?

LG1 Discuss physical growth and development in infancy.

| Patterns of Growth | Height and Weight | The Brain | Sleep | Nutrition | Health |

PATTERNS OF GROWTH

An extraordinary proportion of the total body is occupied by the head during prenatal development and early infancy (see Figure 1). The **cephalocaudal pattern** is the sequence in which the earliest growth always occurs at the top—the head—with physical growth and differentiation of features gradually working their way down from top to bottom (for example, shoulders, middle trunk, and so on). This same pattern occurs in the head area because the top parts of the head—the eyes and brain—grow faster than the lower parts, such as the jaw.

Sensory and motor development generally proceed according to the cephalocaudal principle (London & others, 2017). For example, infants see objects before they can control their torso, and they can use their hands long before they can crawl or walk. However, development does not follow a rigid blueprint. For example, infants reach for toys with their feet prior to reaching with their hands (Ali & others, 2021). On average, infants first touch toys with their feet when they are 12 weeks old and with their hands when they are 16 weeks old.

Growth also follows the **proximodistal pattern,** the sequence in which growth starts at the center of the body and moves toward the extremities. For example, infants control the muscles of their trunk and arms before they control their hands and fingers, and they use their whole hands before they can control several fingers.

cephalocaudal pattern The sequence in which the earliest growth always occurs at the top—the head—with physical growth and feature differentiation gradually working from top to bottom.

proximodistal pattern The sequence in which growth starts at the center of the body and moves toward the extremities.

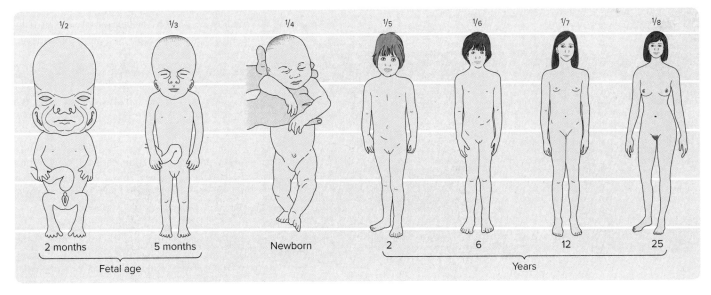

FIGURE 1

CHANGES IN PROPORTIONS OF THE HUMAN BODY DURING GROWTH. As individuals develop from infancy through adulthood, one of the most noticeable physical changes is that the head becomes smaller in relation to the rest of the body. The fractions listed refer to head size as a proportion of total body length at different ages.

HEIGHT AND WEIGHT

The average North American newborn is 20 inches long and weighs 7½ pounds. Ninety-five percent of full-term newborns are 18 to 22 inches long and weigh between 5½ and 10 pounds.

In the first several days after birth, most newborns lose 5 to 7 percent of their body weight before they adjust to feeding by sucking, swallowing, and digesting. Then they grow rapidly, gaining an average of 5 to 6 ounces per week during the first month. They have doubled their birth weight by the age of 4 months and have nearly tripled it by their first birthday. Infants grow about 1 inch per month during the first year, reaching approximately 1½ times their birth length by their first birthday.

Growth slows considerably in the second year of life (Hockenberry, Rogers, & Wilson, 2021). By 2 years of age, infants weigh approximately 26 to 32 pounds, having gained a quarter to half a pound per month during the second year; now they have reached about one-fifth of their adult weight. At 2 years of age, the average infant is 32 to 35 inches in height, which is nearly half of their adult height.

An important point about growth is that it often is not smooth and continuous but rather is *episodic,* occurring in spurts (Adolph & Berger, 2015). In infancy, growth spurts may occur in a single day and alternate with long time frames characterized by little or no growth for days and weeks (Lampl & Schoen, 2017). In two foundational studies, in a single day, infants grew 0.7 inch in length (Lampl, 1993), and their head circumference increased 0.3 inch (Caino & others, 2010).

THE BRAIN

How Would You...?
If you were a **health-care professional,** how would you talk with parents about shaken baby syndrome?

We described the amazing growth of the brain from conception to birth in "Prenatal Development." By the time it is born, the infant that began as a single cell is estimated to have a brain that contains approximately 100 billion nerve cells, or neurons. Extensive brain development continues after birth, through infancy and later (Sullivan & Wilson, 2018; Wass, 2021).

Because the brain is still developing so rapidly in infancy, the infant's head should be protected from falls or other injuries and the baby should never be shaken. *Shaken baby syndrome,* which includes brain swelling and hemorrhaging, affects hundreds of babies in the United States each year (Conrad & others, 2021). The biggest trigger for shaking a baby is frustration with the infant's crying, but shaking a baby is dangerous; approximately 25 percent of victims of shaken baby syndrome die (National Center on Shaken Baby Syndrome, 2023).

Researchers have been successful in using the electroencephalogram (EEG), a measure of the brain's electrical activity, to learn about the brain's development in infancy (Anderson, Perone, & Gartstein, 2022) (see Figure 2). For example, one study found that higher-quality mother-infant interaction early in infancy predicted higher-quality frontal lobe functioning that was assessed with EEG later in infancy (Bernier, Calkins, & Bell, 2016).

Patricia Kuhl and her colleagues at the Institute for Learning and Brain Sciences at the University of Washington have been using magnetoencephalography, or MEG, brain-imaging machines to assess infants' brain activity. MEG maps brain activity by recording magnetic fields produced by electrical currents and is being used with infants to assess perceptual and cognitive activities such as vision, hearing, and language.

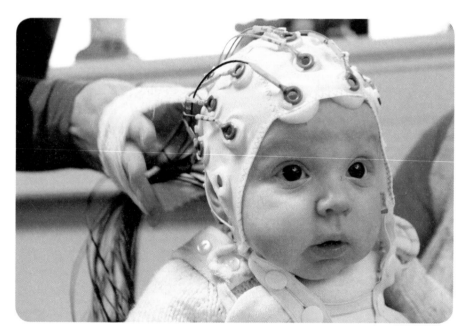

FIGURE 2

MEASURING THE ACTIVITY OF AN INFANT'S BRAIN. By attaching up to 128 electrodes to a baby's scalp to measure the brain's activity, Nelson & others (2006) have found that even newborns produce distinctive brain waves that reveal they can distinguish their mother's voice from another woman's, even while they are asleep. *Why is it so difficult to measure infants' brain activity?*

Owen Humphreys/PA Images/Getty Images

Researchers also are increasingly using functional near-infrared spectroscopy (fNIRS), which uses very low levels of near-infrared light to monitor changes in blood oxygen, to study infants' brain activity (Fiske & others, 2022) (see Figure 3). Unlike fMRI, which uses magnetic fields or electrical activity, fNIRS is portable and allows the infants to be assessed as they explore the world around them.

The following are just a few examples of research that is uncovering new information about the brain's development in infancy:

- Martha Ann Bell and her colleagues (Meza-Cervera & others, 2022) are studying brain-behavior links, emotion regulation, and the integration of cognition and emotion.
- Charles Nelson and his colleagues (Elansary & others, 2022) are exploring various aspects of memory development, face recognition and facial emotion, and the role of experience in influencing the course of brain development.
- Mark Johnson and his colleagues (Johnson, Jones, & Gliga, 2015; Saez de Urabain & others, 2017) are examining neuroconstructivist links between the brain, cognitive and perceptual processes, and environmental influences; their research focuses on the development of the prefrontal cortex and its function, early identification of autism, face processing, and early social experiences.
- Patricia Kuhl and her colleagues (Weiss & others, 2022) are studying early language and brain development in infancy and the neural and learning mechanisms associated with language and cognitive processing.
- John Richards and his colleagues (Conte & Richards, 2022; Xie, Mallin, & Richards, 2019) are examining sustained attention, perception of TV programs, and eye movements.
- Richard Aslin and his colleagues (McMurray & others, 2022) are examining how patterns of neural responses using EEG are related to infants' responses to different words to better understand the brain foundations of infant language development.

FIGURE **3**

FUNCTIONAL NEAR-INFRARED SPECTROSCOPY (FNIRS). This brain-imaging technique is increasingly being used to examine the brain activity of infants. fNIRS is noninvasive and can assess infants as they move and explore their environment.

Oli Scarff/Getty Images

The Brain's Development

At birth, the newborn's brain is about 25 percent of its adult weight. By the second birthday, the brain has attained about 75 percent of its adult weight. However, the brain's areas do not mature uniformly.

Mapping the Brain   Scientists analyze and categorize areas of the brain in numerous ways. We are most concerned with the portion farthest from the spinal cord, known as the **forebrain,** which includes the cerebral cortex and several structures beneath it. The **cerebral cortex** covers the forebrain like a wrinkled cap. It has two halves or hemispheres (see Figure 4). Based on ridges and valleys in the cortex, scientists distinguish four main areas, called lobes, in each hemisphere. Although the lobes usually work together, each has a somewhat different primary function (see Figure 5):

FIGURE **4**

THE HUMAN BRAIN'S HEMISPHERES. The two hemispheres of the human brain are clearly seen in this photograph. It is a myth that the left hemisphere is the exclusive location of language and logical thinking or that the right hemisphere is the exclusive location of emotion and creative thinking.

IgorZD/Shutterstock

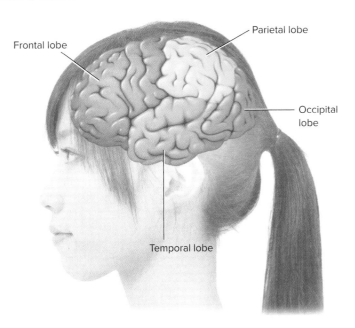

FIGURE **5**

THE BRAIN'S FOUR LOBES. Shown here are the locations of the brain's four lobes: frontal, occipital, temporal, and parietal.

Takayuki/Shutterstock

- *Frontal lobes* are involved in voluntary movement, thinking, personality, emotion, memory, sustained attention, and intentionality or purpose.
- *Occipital lobes* function in vision.

forebrain The region of the brain that is farthest from the spinal cord and includes the cerebral cortex and several structures beneath it.

cerebral cortex Tissue that covers the forebrain like a wrinkled cap and includes two halves, or hemispheres.

lateralization Specialization of function in one hemisphere of the cerebral cortex or the other.

developmental **connection**

Brain Development

How does the brain change from conception to birth? Connect to "Prenatal Development."

- *Temporal lobes* have an active role in hearing, language processing, and memory.
- *Parietal lobes* play important roles in registering spatial location, maintaining attention, and administering motor control.

To some extent, the type of information handled by neurons depends on whether they are in the left or right hemisphere of the cortex—a pattern that has evolved over many millennia (Güntürkün, Ströckens, & Ocklenburg, 2020; Yang, Marslen-Wilson, & Bozic, 2017). Speech and grammar, for example, depend on activity in the left hemisphere in most people; humor and the use of metaphors depend on activity in the right hemisphere (Holler-Wallscheid & others, 2017; Perchtold-Stefan & others, 2020). This specialization of function in one hemisphere of the cerebral cortex or the other is called **lateralization.** However, most neuroscientists agree that complex functions such as reading or performing music involve both hemispheres. Labeling people as "left-brained" because they are logical thinkers and "right-brained" because they are creative thinkers does not correspond to the way the brain's hemispheres work (Rao & Vaid, 2017; Shin, Lee, & Bong, 2022). Complex thinking is the outcome of communication between both hemispheres of the brain (Nora & others, 2017; Vohryzek & others, 2022).

At birth, regions of the brain already have started to specialize, and infants are neurologically primed for certain types of stimuli; for example, anterior temporal areas of the newborn's cortex are more activated in response to speech than to nonspeech sounds (May & others, 2018). How do the areas of the brain in the newborn and the infant differ from those in an adult, and why do the differences matter? Important differences have been documented at both cellular and structural levels.

Changes in Neurons   Within the brain, the type of nerve cells called neurons send electrical and chemical signals, communicating with each other. As we discussed in "Prenatal Development," a *neuron* is a nerve cell that handles information processing (see Figure 6). Extending from the neuron's cell body are two types of fibers known as axons and dendrites. Generally, the axon carries signals away from the cell body and dendrites carry signals toward it. A *myelin sheath,* which is a layer of fat cells, encases many axons (see Figure 6). The myelin sheath insulates axons and helps electrical signals travel faster down the axon (Wang & others, 2021). Myelination also is involved in providing energy to neurons and in facilitating communication between them (Moss & others, 2021). At the end of the axon are terminal buttons that release chemicals called *neurotransmitters* into synapses, which are tiny gaps between neurons' fibers. Chemical interactions in synapses connect axons and dendrites, allowing information to pass from neuron to neuron (De Deurwaerdere & Di Giovanni, 2021).

Think of the synapse as a river that blocks a road. A delivery truck arrives at one bank of the river, crosses by ferry, and continues its journey to its destination. Similarly, a message in the brain is "ferried" across the synapse by a neurotransmitter, which pours out information contained in chemicals when it reaches the other side of the river.

How complex are these neural connections? In one analysis, it was estimated that each of the billions of neurons is connected to as many as 1,000 other neurons, producing neural networks with trillions of connections (de Haan, 2015).

Neurons change in two very significant ways during the first years of life. First, *myelination,* the process of encasing axons with fat cells, begins prenatally and continues after birth, even into adolescence and emerging adulthood (Juraska & Willing, 2017; Schneider, Greenstreet, & Deoni, 2022a). Second, connectivity among neurons increases, creating new neural pathways. New dendrites grow, connections among dendrites increase, and synaptic connections between axons and dendrites proliferate. Whereas myelination speeds up neural transmissions, the expansion of dendritic connections facilitates the spreading of neural pathways in infant development.

Researchers have discovered an intriguing aspect of synaptic connections: Nearly twice as many of these connections are made as will ever be used (Huttenlocher & Dabholkar, 1997). The connections that are used grow stronger and survive, while the unused ones are replaced

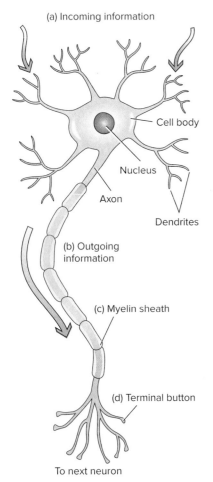

(a) Incoming information

Cell body

Nucleus

Axon

Dendrites

(b) Outgoing information

(c) Myelin sheath

(d) Terminal button

To next neuron

FIGURE **6**

THE NEURON. (*a*) The dendrites of the cell body receive information from other neurons, muscles, or glands through the axon. (*b*) Axons transmit information away from the cell body. (*c*) A myelin sheath covers most axons and speeds information transmission. (*d*) As the axon ends, it branches out into terminal buttons.

by other pathways or disappear (Lieberman & others, 2019; Sakai, 2020). In the language of neuroscience, these connections are "pruned." For example, the more a baby engages in physical activity or uses language, the more those pathways will be strengthened.

Changes in Regions of the Brain Figure 7 vividly illustrates the dramatic growth and later pruning of synapses in the visual, auditory, and prefrontal cortex (Huttenlocher & Dabholkar, 1997). Notice that "blooming and pruning" vary considerably by brain region. In the prefrontal cortex, the area of the brain where higher-level thinking and self-regulation occur, the peak of overproduction occurs at just over 3 years of age; it is not until middle to late adolescence that the adult density of synapses is achieved. Both heredity and environment are thought to influence the timing and course of synaptic overproduction and subsequent retraction.

Meanwhile, the pace of myelination also varies in different areas of the brain and at different points in childhood and adolescence (Croteau-Chonka & others, 2016; Norbom & others, 2021). Myelination for visual pathways occurs rapidly after birth and is completed in the first six months. Auditory myelination is not completed until 4 or 5 years of age. More advanced myelination is related to more advanced verbal and nonverbal cognitive abilities and has been described as a mechanism through which breast feeding promotes cognitive development, as breast feeding results in better myelination than does formula feeding due to differences in their levels of key nutrients (Deoni & others, 2018; Schneider & others, 2022b).

In general, some areas of the brain, such as the primary motor areas, develop earlier than others, such as the primary sensory areas. The frontal lobes are immature in the newborn. However, as neurons in the frontal lobes become myelinated and interconnected during the first year of life, infants develop an ability to regulate their physiological states, such as sleep, and gain more control over their reflexes. Cognitive skills that require deliberate thinking do not emerge until later in the first year (Whedon, Perry, & Bell, 2020). Indeed, the prefrontal region of the frontal lobe has the most prolonged development of any brain region, with changes detectable at least into adolescence and emerging adulthood (Juraska & Willing, 2017).

developmental **connection**

Brain Development

Changes in the prefrontal cortex in adolescents have important implications for their development. Connect to "Physical Development in Adolescence."

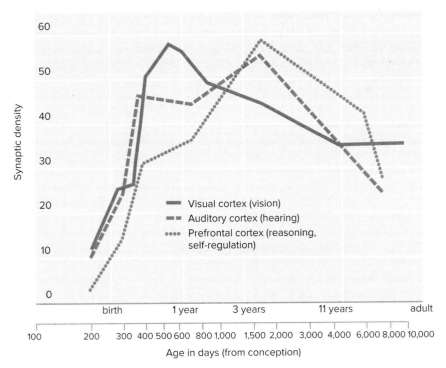

FIGURE **7**

SYNAPTIC DENSITY IN THE HUMAN BRAIN FROM INFANCY TO ADULTHOOD. The graph shows the dramatic increase and then pruning in synaptic density for three regions of the brain: visual cortex, auditory cortex, and prefrontal cortex. Synaptic density is believed to be an important indication of the extent of connectivity between neurons.

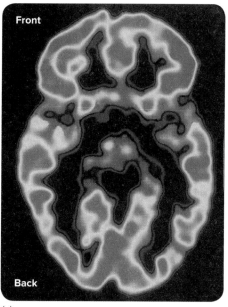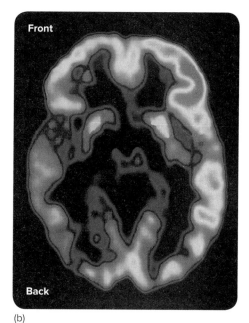

(a)   (b)

FIGURE 8

EARLY DEPRIVATION AND BRAIN ACTIVITY. These two photographs are PET (positron emission tomography) scans—which use radioactive tracers to image and analyze blood flow and metabolic activity in the body's organs. These scans show the brains of (*a*) a typically developing child and (*b*) an orphan who was institutionalized in Romania who experienced substantial deprivation since birth. In PET scans, the highest to lowest brain activity is reflected in the colors of red, yellow, green, blue, and black, respectively. As can be seen, red and yellow show up to a much greater degree in the PET scan of the typically developing child than in that of the deprived Romanian orphan.

(*both*): Courtesy of Dr. Harry T. Chugani, Children's Hospital of Michigan

(a)

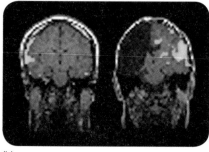

(b)

FIGURE 9

PLASTICITY IN THE BRAIN'S

HEMISPHERES. (*a*) Michael Rehbein at 14 years of age. (*b*) Michael's right hemisphere has reorganized to take over the language functions normally carried out by corresponding areas in the left hemisphere of an intact brain (shown at left). However, the right hemisphere is not as efficient as the left, and more areas of the brain are recruited to process speech.

Courtesy of The Rehbein Family

Early Experience and the Brain   Children who grow up in a deprived environment may have depressed brain activity (McLaughlin, Sheridan, & Nelson, 2017; Wade & others, 2020). As shown in Figure 8, a child who grew up in the unresponsive and unstimulating environment of a Romanian orphanage showed considerably depressed brain activity compared with a child who grew up in a nondeprived environment.

Are the effects of deprived environments reversible? There is reason to think that at least for some individuals the answer is yes (Bick & Nelson, 2017; Debnath & others, 2020). The brain demonstrates both flexibility and resilience. Consider 14-year-old Michael Rehbein. At age 7, he began to experience uncontrollable seizures—as many as 400 a day. Doctors said the only solution was to remove the left hemisphere of his brain where the seizures were occurring. Recovery was slow, but his right hemisphere began to reorganize and take over functions that normally occur in the brain's left hemisphere, including speech (see Figure 9). A study that compared children and young adults who had brain damage in the left hemisphere (where language functions are generally controlled) to children and young adults without brain damage found that in more than 80 percent of the individuals with damage to the left hemisphere of the brain, the right hemisphere dominated the language functions usually controlled by the left side of the brain (Chilosi & others, 2019).

Neuroscientists believe that what wires the brain—or rewires it, in the case of Michael Rehbein—is repeated experience. Each time a baby tries to touch an attractive object or gazes intently at a face, tiny bursts of electricity shoot through the brain, knitting together neurons into circuits. The results are some of the behavioral milestones we discuss in this chapter.

The Neuroconstructivist View   Not long ago, scientists thought that our genes determined how our brains were "wired" and that the brain cells responsible for processing information just maturationally unfolded with little or no input from environmental experiences. Whatever brain your heredity dealt you, you were essentially stuck with. This view, however, turned out to be wrong. Instead, it has become clear that the brain has plasticity and its development depends on context (D'Souza & Karmiloff-Smith, 2017; Esteves & others, 2021).

The infant's brain depends on experiences to determine how connections are made (Tooley, Bassett, & Mackey, 2021; Vogels, 2017). Neurons grow and travel to distant places awaiting further instructions (Shenoda, 2017). After birth, the inflowing stream of sights, sounds, smells, touches, language, and eye contact help shape the brain's neural connections.

In the increasingly supported **neuroconstructivist view,** (a) biological processes (genes, for example) and environmental experiences (enriched or impoverished, for example) influence the brain's development; (b) the brain has plasticity and is influenced by contexts; and (c) development of the brain is closely linked with the child's cognitive development. These factors constrain or advance the construction of cognitive skills (Birle & others, 2021; Crone, 2017; D'Souza & Karmiloff-Smith, 2017; Pinho, Marcut, & Fonseca, 2020). The neuroconstructivist view emphasizes the importance of interactions between experience and gene expression in the brain's development, in much the same way that the epigenetic view proposes (Baroncelli & Lunghi, 2021; Moore, 2017).

SLEEP

When we were infants, sleep consumed more of our time than it does now (Lushington & others, 2014). Newborns sleep 16 to 17 hours a day, although some sleep more and others less—the range is from a low of about 10 hours to a high of about 21 hours per day. A research review concluded that infants 0 to 2 years of age slept an average of 12.8 hours out of the 24, within a range of 9.7 to 15.9 hours (Galland & others, 2012). By 6 months of age the majority of infants sleep through the night, awakening their parents only once or twice a week; yet, there is substantial variation between infants in how well they sleep through the night that also influences caregivers' sleep (Kalogeropoulos & others, 2022; Weinraub & others, 2012).

Although total sleep remains somewhat consistent for young infants, their sleep during the day does not always follow a rhythmic pattern. An infant might change from sleeping for long bouts of 7 or 8 hours to three or four shorter sessions only several hours in duration. By about 1 month of age, most infants have begun to sleep longer at night. By 6 months of age, they usually have moved closer to adult-like sleep patterns, spending their longest span of sleep at night and their longest span of waking during the day (Sadeh, 2008; Willumsen & Bull, 2020).

The most common infant sleep-related problem reported by parents is nighttime waking (Honaker & others, 2021; Hospital for Sick Children & others, 2010). Surveys indicate that 20 to 30 percent of infants have difficulty going to sleep and staying asleep at night (Sadeh, 2008). Less disrupted infant sleep is predicted by mothers' emotional availability at bedtime as well as a peaceful home environment, suggesting that better-regulated infant sleep is promoted by feelings of safety and security (Whitesell & others, 2018). Infant sleep problems have been related to a range of family difficulties, including marital conflict, and can be resolved by sensitive caregiving from both mothers and fathers (Covington & others, 2021; El-Sheikh & Kelly, 2017). Infant sleep problems can also be a source of marital discord, as parents and fathers who disagree about how to respond to infants' nighttime wakings perceive themselves as having lower-quality co-parenting relationships (Reader, Teti, & Cleveland, 2017). Maternal depression during pregnancy, early introduction of solid foods, infant TV viewing, and child-care attendance are related to shorter duration of infant sleep (Cook & others, 2020; Plancoulaine & others, 2018).

REM Sleep In REM sleep, the eyes flutter beneath closed lids; in non-REM sleep, this type of eye movement does not occur and sleep is quieter (Sankupellay & others, 2011). Figure 10 shows developmental changes in the average number of total hours spent in REM and non-REM sleep. By the time they reach adulthood, individuals spend about one-fifth of their night in REM sleep, and REM sleep usually appears about one hour after non-REM sleep. However, about half of an infant's sleep is REM sleep, and infants often begin their sleep cycle with REM sleep rather than non-REM sleep (Lopp & others, 2017). A much greater amount of time is taken up by REM sleep in infancy than at any other point in the life span (Funk & others, 2016). By the time infants reach 3 months of age, the percentage of time they spend in REM sleep falls to about 40 percent, and REM sleep no longer begins their sleep cycle.

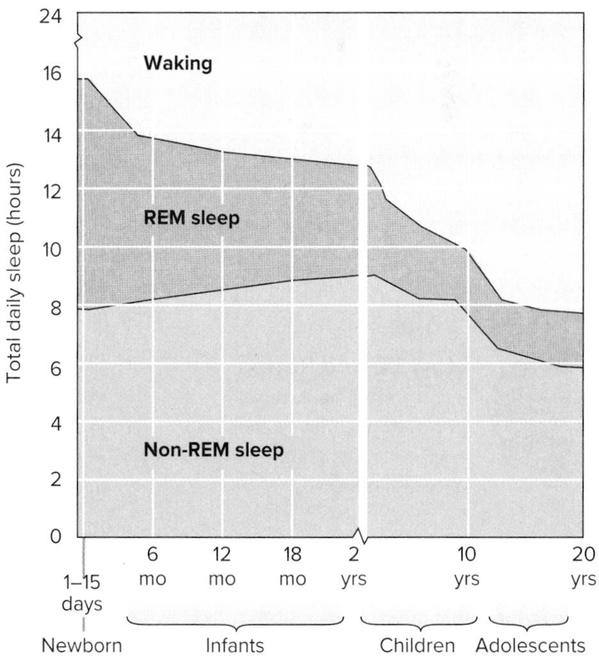

neuroconstructivist view In this view, biological processes and environmental conditions influence the brain's development; the brain has plasticity and is context dependent; and brain development is closely linked with cognitive development.

developmental **connection**

Nature and Nurture

In the epigenetic view, development is an ongoing, bidirectional interchange between heredity and environment. Connect to "Biological Beginnings."

developmental **connection**

Sleep

What are some sleep problems that can develop in childhood and adolescence? Connect to "Physical Development in Early Childhood" and "Physical Development in Adolescence."

FIGURE **10**

DEVELOPMENTAL CHANGES IN REM AND NON-REM SLEEP

Why do infants spend so much time in REM sleep? Researchers are not certain. The large amount of REM sleep may provide infants with added self-stimulation since they spend less time awake than do older children. REM sleep also might promote the brain's development in infancy (Wolfe & Ralls, 2019).

There is extensive evidence that among adults, dreaming is most common during REM sleep—although dreaming also can occur in other phases of sleep (Tsunematsu, 2023). Since infants spend more time than adults in REM sleep, can we conclude that they dream a lot? We don't know whether infants dream or not because they don't have any way of reporting dreams.

Shared Sleeping Some child experts stress that there are benefits to shared sleeping (as when an infant sleeps in the same bed with its mother). They state that it can promote breast feeding, lets the mother respond more quickly to the baby's cries, and allows her to detect breathing pauses in the baby that might be dangerous (Mileva-Seitz & others, 2017). Sharing a bed with a mother is common practice in many countries, such as Guatemala and China, whereas in others, such as the United States and Great Britain, most newborns sleep in a crib, either in the same room as the parents or in a separate room.

Shared sleeping remains a controversial issue (Barry & McKenna, 2022). Some experts recommend shared sleeping and others argue against it, although recently the recommendation trend in the United States has been to avoid infant-parent bed sharing, especially before the infant is 6 months of age (Mileva-Seitz & others, 2017). The American Academy of Pediatrics recommends against shared sleeping (Moon & others, 2022). Its members argue that in some instances bed sharing might lead to sudden infant death syndrome (SIDS), as could be the case if a sleeping mother rolls over on her baby. Bed sharing is linked with a greater incidence of SIDS, especially when parents smoke (Byard, 2018). However, bed sharing supports breast feeding, and this combination may be beneficial with respect to SIDS risk—although controversy remains, as more studies are needed (Mileva-Seitz & others, 2017).

SIDS Sudden infant death syndrome (SIDS) is a condition that occurs when infants stop breathing, usually during the night, and die suddenly without an apparent cause. SIDS is the most frequent cause of infant death in the United States, with nearly 3,000 infant deaths attributed to it annually (Heron, 2016). Risk of SIDS is highest at 2 to 4 months of age (National Institute of Child Health and Human Development, 2022).

Since 1992, the American Academy of Pediatrics (AAP) has recommended that infants be placed to sleep on their backs to reduce the risk of SIDS, and the frequency of prone sleeping (on their stomachs) among U.S. infants has dropped dramatically (Osberg, Kalstad, & Stray-Pedersen, 2021). Researchers have found that SIDS does indeed decrease when infants sleep on their backs rather than their stomachs or sides (Byard, 2021). Among the reasons given for prone sleeping being a high-risk factor for SIDS are that it reduces an infant's cardiac output and the amount of blood pumped from the left ventricle of the heart on each beat (Wu & others, 2017). However, not all studies find this effect on cardiac function (Jani & others, 2022).

In addition to sleeping in a prone position, researchers have found that the following are risk factors for SIDS:

- SIDS occurs more often in infants with abnormal brain stem functioning involving the neurotransmitter serotonin (Cummings & Leiter, 2020).
- Heart arrhythmias linked to rare genetic variants are estimated to occur in as many as 15 percent of SIDS cases, and other genetic risks have been estimated to occur in up to 35 percent of SIDS cases (Liebrechts-Akkerman & others, 2020; Neubauer & others, 2017).
- Black American and Inuit infants are four to six times as likely as all others to die of SIDS (Moon & others, 2017).
- Breast feeding for at least two months is linked to a lower incidence of SIDS, with greater protection against SIDS provided by breast feeding of longer duration (Cowgill, 2020).
- Low birth weight infants are 5 to 10 times more likely to die of SIDS than are their normal-weight counterparts (Maged & Rizzolo, 2018).

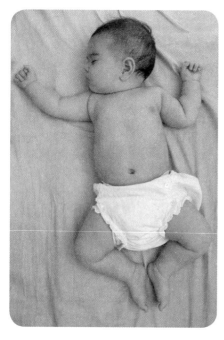

Is this a good sleep position for infants? Why or why not?

Maria Teijeiro/Cultura/Getty Images

How Would You...?

If you were a **health-care professional,** how would you advise parents about preventing SIDS?

sudden infant death syndrome (SIDS) A condition that occurs when an infant stops breathing, usually during the night, and suddenly dies without an apparent cause.

- SIDS is more likely to occur in infants who do not use a pacifier when they go to sleep than in those who do use a pacifier (Carlin & Moon, 2017). A research review of 27 studies confirmed that pacifier use is linked to a lower incidence of SIDS (Alm & others, 2016).
- Infants whose siblings have died of SIDS are five to six times as likely to die of it (Corwin, 2018).
- SIDS is more common in lower socioeconomic groups (Hogan, 2014; Moon & others, 2022).
- Infants who are exposed to cigarette smoke are more likely to die of SIDS than are infants who are not exposed (U.S. Preventive Services Task Force & others, 2021).
- SIDS is more common if infants sleep in soft bedding (Carlin & Moon, 2017).

Sleep and Cognitive Development   Might infant sleep be linked to children's cognitive development? One study revealed that infants who did most of their sleeping at night (rather than during the daytime) engaged in a higher level of executive function at age 4 (Bernier & others, 2013). Another study revealed that a lower quality of sleep at 1 year of age was linked to lower attention regulation and more behavior problems at 5 years of age (Huhdanpää & others, 2019). The link between infant sleep and children's cognitive functioning likely occurs because of sleep's role in brain maturation and memory consolidation, which may improve daytime alertness and learning. However, it is worth noting that the developmental changes in sleep and its role in cognitive development are complex and depend on many factors (Mason & others, 2021).

NUTRITION

From birth to 1 year of age, human infants nearly triple their weight and increase their length by 50 percent. What do they need to sustain this growth, and what characterizes their eating behavior?

Nutritional Needs and Eating Behavior   Individual differences among infants in terms of their nutrient reserves, body composition, growth rates, and activity patterns make defining actual nutrient needs difficult (Rolfes, Pinna, & Whitney, 2018). However, because parents need guidelines, nutritionists recommend that infants consume approximately 50 calories per day for each pound they weigh—more than twice an adult's requirement per pound.

A number of developmental changes involving eating characterize the infant's first year (Black & Hurley, 2007; Johns Hopkins Medicine, 2019). As infants' motor skills improve, they change from using suck-and-swallow movements with breast milk or formula to chew-and-swallow movements with semisolid and then more complex foods. As their fine motor control improves in the first year, they transition from being fed by others toward self-feeding. "By the end of the first year of life, children can sit independently, can chew and swallow a range of textures, are learning to feed themselves, and are making the transition to the family diet and meal patterns" (Black & Hurley, 2007, p. 1). At this point, infants need to have a diet that includes a variety of foods—especially fruits and vegetables.

Caregivers play very important roles in infants' early development of eating patterns (Hodges & others, 2020). Caregivers who are not sensitive to developmental changes in infants' nutritional needs, neglectful caregivers, and income, food, and housing security all can contribute to the development of eating problems in infants (Perez-Escamilla & Moran, 2017). One study of over 1,000 infants born in eight low- and middle-income countries followed them to 5 years of age. The healthiest cognitive and physical outcomes were found for infants who had the best diets and the most responsive caregivers, which were more common in households with more socioeconomic resources (McCormick & others, 2019).

A national study of Americans indicated that by 6 months, 37 percent of infants were already consuming snacks and that by the age of 12 months, 25 percent of daily energy intake was from snacks (Deming & others, 2017). Infants are consuming more junk food and fewer fruits and vegetables than recommended by nutrition experts. For example, 25 percent of 6- to

developmental **connection**

Nutrition

Children's eating behavior is strongly influenced by their caregivers' behavior. Connect to "Physical Development in Early Childhood."

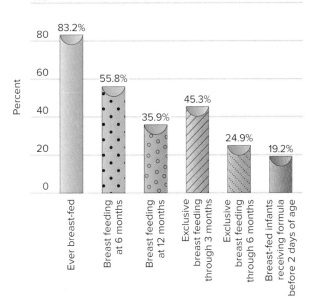

FIGURE 11

BREAST FEEDING RATES FOR INFANTS BORN IN THE UNITED STATES IN 2019. Statistics are based on data released in 2022 by the Centers for Disease Control and Prevention.
Source: https://www.cdc.gov/breastfeeding/data/reportcard.htm

Human milk or an alternative formula is a baby's source of nutrients for the first four to six months. The growing consensus is that breast feeding is better for the baby's health, although controversy still swirls about the issue of breast feeding versus bottle feeding. *Why is breast feeding strongly recommended by pediatricians?*

JGI/Blend Images

11-month-olds and 20 percent of 12- to 23-month-olds consumed no vegetables over the course of the study period in a national sample in the United States (Miles & Siega-Riz, 2017). Such poor dietary patterns early in development can result in more infants being overweight (Black & others, 2021).

Breast versus Bottle Feeding For the first four to six months of life, human milk or an alternative formula is the baby's source of nutrients and energy. The scientific consensus is that breast feeding is better for the baby's health than formula feeding (De Bruyne & Pinna, 2017; Schiff, 2017).

Since the 1970s, breast feeding by U.S. mothers has soared. In 2019, 83 percent of U.S. mothers breast-fed their newborns, and 56 percent breast-fed their 6-month-olds (Centers for Disease Control and Prevention, 2022) (see Figure 11). The World Health Organization (2021) recommends exclusive breast feeding in the first six months, followed by continued breast feeding as complementary foods are introduced, with further breast feeding for one year or longer as mutually desired by the mother and infant.

What are some of the benefits of breast feeding? The following conclusions reflect the current state of research.

Evaluation of Benefits for the Child

- *Gastrointestinal infections.* Breast-fed infants have fewer gastrointestinal infections (Stuebe & others, 2017).
- *Lower respiratory tract infections.* Breast-fed infants have fewer lower respiratory tract infections (Christensen & others, 2020).
- *Allergies.* A research review by the American Academy of Pediatrics indicated that there is no evidence that breast feeding reduces the risk of allergies in children (Greer, Sicherer, & Burks, 2019). A Danish study also found that breast feeding did not protect against allergic sensitization in early childhood and allergy-related diseases at 7 years of age (Jelding-Dannemand, Malby Schoos, & Bisgaard, 2015).
- *Asthma.* A research review by the American Academy of Pediatrics concluded that exclusive breast feeding for three months protects against wheezing in babies and may prevent asthma in older children (Greer, Sicherer, & Burks, 2019).
- *Otitis media.* Breast-fed infants are less likely to develop this middle ear infection (Meek & Noble, 2022).
- *Overweight and obesity.* Research indicates that breast-fed infants are less likely to become overweight or obese in childhood, adolescence, and adulthood (Uwaezuoke, Eneh, & Ndu, 2017).
- *Diabetes.* Breast-fed infants are less likely to develop type 1 diabetes in childhood (Esposito & others, 2019) and type 2 diabetes in adulthood (Horta & de Lima, 2019).
- *SIDS.* Breast-fed infants are less likely to experience SIDS (Landa-Rivera & others, 2022).
- *Hospitalization.* A study of more than 500,000 Scottish children found that those who were breast fed exclusively at 6 to 8 weeks of age were less likely to have ever been hospitalized in early childhood than their formula-fed counterparts (Ajetunmobi & others, 2015).
- *Cognitive development and cardiovascular health.* In a large-scale meta-analysis of 17 rigorous studies, there was a small and consistent benefit of breast feeding for children's cognitive development (Horta, Loret de Mola, & Victora, 2015). Breast feeding also may have a small beneficial effect on children's subsequent cardiovascular health (Umer & others, 2019).

Evaluation of Benefits for the Mother

- *Breast cancer.* Consistent evidence indicates a lower incidence of breast cancer in women who breast-feed their infants (Unar-Munguía & others, 2017).
- *Ovarian cancer.* Evidence also reveals a reduction in ovarian cancer in women who breast-feed their infants (Babic & others, 2020; Danial & others, 2018).
- *Type 2 diabetes and cardiovascular disease.* There is mounting evidence from many studies, research reviews, and meta-analyses indicating reduced risk for type 2 diabetes and

cardiovascular disease for breast-feeding mothers (Tschiderer & others, 2022; Victora & others, 2016).

- *Weight loss, bone health, and mental health.* In a large-scale research review, no conclusive evidence could be found for maternal benefits of breast feeding on return to pre-pregnancy weight, osteoporosis, and postpartum depression (Farías-Antúnez & others, 2020; Lambrinou, Karaglani, & Manios, 2019).

How Would You...?

If you were a **health-care professional,** how would you advise mothers about whether to breast feed or bottle feed their infants?

Which women are least likely to breast-feed? They include mothers who work full-time outside the home, mothers under age 25, mothers who did not graduate from high school, Black American mothers, and mothers in low-income circumstances (Colen & Ramey, 2014). A meta-analysis of educational and social support interventions to promote breast feeding indicates positive effects, although there is wide variation in breast feeding because there are many factors that influence the initiation and continuation of breast feeding (Kim & others, 2018). Increasingly, mothers who return to work in the infant's first year of life use a breast pump to extract breast milk that can be stored for later feeding of the infant when the mother is not present.

The World Health Organization (2021) strongly endorses breast feeding throughout the first year of life. Are there circumstances when mothers should not breast-feed? Yes. A mother should not breast-feed (1) when the mother is infected with HIV or some other infectious disease that can be transmitted through her milk, (2) if she has active tuberculosis, or (3) if she is taking any drug that may not be safe for the infant (Brown & others, 2019).

Some women cannot breast-feed their infants because of physical difficulties; others feel guilty if they terminate breast feeding early. Mothers may also worry that they are depriving their infants of important emotional and psychological benefits if they bottle-feed rather than breast-feed.

A further issue in interpreting the benefits of breast feeding was underscored in a large-scale research review (Ip & others, 2009; Velle-Forbord, Underdal, & Vanky, 2018). While highlighting a number of breast feeding benefits for children and mothers, the report issued a caution about breast feeding research: None of the findings imply causality. Breast versus formula feeding studies are correlational, not experimental, and women who breast-feed are on average wealthier, older, more educated, and likely have greater access to health-promoting supports than their formula-feeding counterparts—characteristics that could explain why breast-fed children are healthier.

developmental connection

Research Methods

How does a correlational study differ from an experimental study? Connect to "Introduction."

Malnutrition in Infancy   Many infants around the world are malnourished (FAO, IFAD, UNICEF, WFP, & WHO, 2022). Early weaning of infants from breast milk to inadequate sources of nutrients, such as unsuitable and unsanitary cow's milk formula, can cause protein deficiency and malnutrition in infants. However, as we saw in the chapter-opening story, a concern in low- and middle-income countries is the number of women who are HIV-positive and the fear that they will transmit this virus to their offspring (Remmert & others, 2020). In all countries and at all income levels, health governing bodies generally recommend against breast feeding if the mother is HIV-positive (Centers for Disease Control and Prevention, 2022).

A concern in many low- and middle-income countries is child undernutrition involving inadequate intake of micronutrients. This problem has sometimes been called the "hidden hunger" when it occurs in individuals who get adequate calories but the micronutrient content of their diet is inadequate. According to the World Health Organization (WHO) (2023), iron deficiency is the most significant micronutrient deficiency in low-income countries. More than 40 percent of the world's population of newborns to 5-year-olds are anemic, in many cases because of iron deficiency. Other micronutrient deficiencies include vitamin A (the leading cause of preventable blindness in children), zinc (can increase susceptibility to pneumonia and malaria), and iodine (can cause brain damage) (Hwalla & others, 2017; Lazarus, 2017a, b).

Two life-threatening conditions that can result from malnutrition are marasmus and kwashiorkor. **Marasmus** is caused by a severe protein-calorie deficiency and results in a wasting away of body tissues in the infant's first year. The infant becomes grossly underweight and his or her muscles atrophy. **Kwashiorkor,** caused by severe protein deficiency, usually appears between 1 and 3 years of age. Children with kwashiorkor sometimes appear to be well fed even though they are not because the disease can cause the child's abdomen and feet to swell with water

marasmus A wasting away of body tissues in the infant's first year, caused by severe protein-calorie deficiency.

kwashiorkor A condition caused by a severe deficiency in protein in which the child's abdomen and feet become swollen with water; usually appears between 1 and 3 years of age.

T. Berry Brazelton (1918–2018) was a pioneer in pediatric health care.
Courtesy of Brazelton Touchpoints Center

Age	Immunization
Birth	Hepatitis B
2 months	Diphtheria, tetanus, pertussis Polio Influenza Pneumococcal
4 months	Hepatitis B Diphtheria, tetanus, pertussis Polio Influenza Pneumococcal
6 months	Diphtheria, tetanus, pertussis Influenza Pneumococcal
1 year	Influenza Pneumococcal
15 months	Measles, mumps, rubella Influenza Varicella
18 months	Hepatitis B Diphtheria, tetanus, pertussis Polio
4 to 6 years	Diphtheria, tetanus, pertussis Polio Measles, mumps, rubella
11 to 12 years	Measles, mumps, rubella Human papillomavirus
14 to 16 years	Tetanus, diphtheria

(Benjamin & Lappin, 2020). Kwashiorkor causes a child's vital organs to collect the nutrients that are present and deprive other parts of the body of them. The child's hair becomes thin, brittle, and colorless, and the child's behavior often becomes listless.

Even if not fatal, severe and lengthy malnutrition is detrimental to physical, cognitive, and social development (Wardlaw, Smith, & Collene, 2018). One study found that Asian Indian children who had a history of malnutrition had more problems with executive functioning (cognitive processes to control behavior) than their counterparts who were not malnourished (Selvam & others, 2018). And a foundational longitudinal study revealed that Barbadians who had experienced moderate to severe protein/energy malnutrition during infancy had persisting attention deficits when they were 40 years old (Galler & others, 2012).

Researchers also have found that interventions can benefit individuals who have experienced malnutrition in infancy. Several studies in various countries have examined the effects of nutritional supplements by randomly assigning children to experimental conditions that involve nutritional supplements or control groups that do not. In Guatemala, for example, children whose mothers received nutritional supplements during pregnancy and up to 6 months postpartum and who themselves received nutritional supplements from 6 to 24 months of age were less likely to be stunted in growth (low height for age) than were children who received no supplements (Olney & others, 2018). The benefits of nutritional supplements extend beyond increased physical growth to include enhancement of cognitive and psychosocial development. In a review of 67 interventions in 20 low- and middle-income countries, nutritional supplements were found to enhance children's cognitive development; in addition to benefits of nutritional supplements to children, nutritional supplements provided to mothers during the first trimester of pregnancy were found to boost their children's cognitive development (Ip & others, 2017). To read further about providing nutritional supplements to improve infants' and young children's nutrition, see the *Caring Connections* interlude.

Adequate early nutrition is an important aspect of healthy development (Nisbett & others, 2022). In addition to sound nutrition, children need a nurturing, supportive environment (C.M. Johnson & others, 2018). One individual who was a strong advocate of caring for children was T. Berry Brazelton (1918–2018). Brazelton was often considered America's best-known pediatrician due to his numerous books, television appearances, and newspaper and magazine articles about parenting and children's health. He founded the Child Development Unit (now called the Brazelton Touchpoints Center) at Boston Children's Hospital and created the Brazelton Neonatal Behavioral Assessment Scale, a widely used measure of the newborn's health and well-being. He also conducted research studies on infants and children and was president of the Society for Research in Child Development, a leading research organization. Brazelton established a family-centered approach to child development issues that redefined pediatrics and promoted communicating with parents in easy-to-understand ways.

HEALTH

Among the most important measures used to promote infant health are immunization and accident prevention. Immunization greatly improves children's health.

Immunization   One of the most dramatic advances in infant health has been the decline of infectious disease over the last five decades because of widespread immunization for preventable diseases. Although many available immunizations can be given at any age, the recommended schedule is to begin in infancy. The recommended ages for various immunizations are presented in Figure 12.

Accident Prevention   Accidents are a major cause of death in infancy and childhood, especially from 6 to 12 months of age. Infants need to be closely monitored as they acquire increased locomotor and manipulative skills along with a strong desire to explore

FIGURE 12

RECOMMENDED IMMUNIZATION SCHEDULE FOR INFANTS AND CHILDREN

Improving the Nutrition of Infants and Young Children Living in Low-Income Families

Incomplete or insufficient nutrition is a special concern in the lives of infants in low-income families. To address this problem in the United States, the WIC (Women, Infants, and Children) program provides federal grants to states for healthy supplemental foods, health-care referrals, and nutrition education for women from low-income families beginning in pregnancy, and to infants and young children up to 5 years of age who are at nutritional risk (S.W. Ng & others, 2018). WIC serves approximately 7 million participants in the United States.

　　Positive influences on infants' and young children's nutrition and health have been found for participants in WIC (Paolicelli & others, 2021). One study revealed that a WIC program that introduced peer counseling services for pregnant women increased breast feeding substantially (McCoy & others, 2018). Another study found that entry in the first trimester of pregnancy to the WIC program in Rhode Island reduced maternal cigarette smoking (Brodsky, Viner-Brown, & Handler, 2009). And a multiple-year literacy intervention with Spanish-speaking families in the WIC program in Los Angeles increased literacy resources and activities at home, which in turn led to a higher level of school readiness in children (Whaley & others, 2011). And a longitudinal

Participants in the WIC program. *What are some of the benefits of participating in the WIC program?*
USDA Food and Nutrition Service, Supplemental Nutrition Assistance Program

analysis of nine years of infant health and mortality data in the United States indicated that WIC participation during pregnancy reduced racial and ethnic group disparities in infant mortality, low birth weight, preterm birth, and other outcomes (Testa & Jackson, 2021).

their environment (Bryant, Morrongiello, & Cox, 2022). Aspiration of foreign objects, suffocation, falls, poisoning, burns, and motor vehicle accidents are among the most common accidents in infancy (Shimony-Kanat & Benbenishty, 2018). All infants, newborns included, should be secured in special infant car seats in the backseat of a car rather than being held on an adult's lap or placed on the seat of the car.

How Would You...?
If you were a **human development and family studies professional,** how would you discuss infant safety concerns with parents?

Review *Connect* **Reflect**

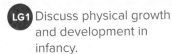 Discuss physical growth and development in infancy.

Review
- What are cephalocaudal and proximodistal patterns?
- What changes in height and weight take place in infancy?
- What are some key features of the brain and its development in infancy?
- What changes occur in sleep during infancy?
- What are infants' nutritional needs and eating patterns?
- What characterizes immunization and accident prevention in infancy?

Connect
- What types of brain research technology can be used to study infants that cannot be used to study them before they are born?

Reflect *Your Own Personal Journey of Life*
- What sleep and nutrition guidelines would you follow for enhancing the health and well-being of your own infant?

The Dynamic Systems View · Reflexes · Gross Motor Skills · Fine Motor Skills

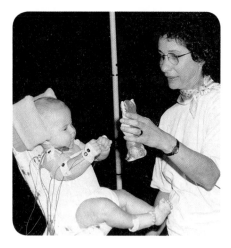

Esther Thelen (1941–2004) is shown conducting an experiment to discover how infants learn to control their arms to reach and grasp for objects. A computer device was used to monitor the infant's arm movements and to track muscle patterns. Thelen's research was conducted from a dynamic systems perspective. *What is the nature of this perspective?*

Courtesy of Dr. David Thelen

As a newborn, Ajani, whom we met in the chapter-opening story, could suck, fling his arms wide, and tightly grip a finger placed in his tiny hand. Within just two years, he would be toddling around on his own, opening doors and containers as he explored his world. Are his accomplishments inevitable? How do infants develop their motor skills, and which skills do they develop at various ages?

THE DYNAMIC SYSTEMS VIEW

Developmentalist Arnold Gesell (1934a, b) thought his painstaking observations had revealed how people develop their motor skills. He had discovered that infants and children develop rolling, sitting, standing, and other motor skills in a fixed order and within specific time frames. These observations, said Gesell, show that motor development comes about through the unfolding of a genetic plan, or maturation.

Later studies, however, demonstrated that the sequence of developmental milestones is not as fixed as Gesell indicated and not due as much to heredity as Gesell argued (Adolph, 2018). Beginning in the 1980s, the study of motor development experienced a renaissance as psychologists developed new insights about *how* motor skills develop (Adolph, 2018). One increasingly influential perspective is dynamic systems theory, proposed by Esther Thelen (1941–2004) (Thelen & Smith, 2006).

According to **dynamic systems theory,** infants assemble motor skills for perceiving and acting (Thelen & Smith, 2006). To develop motor skills, infants must perceive something in the environment that motivates them to act and use their perceptions to fine-tune their movements. Motor skills represent solutions to the infant's goals (Dineva & Schöner, 2018).

How is a motor skill developed, according to this theory? When infants are motivated to do something, they might create a new motor behavior. The new behavior is the result of many converging factors: the development of the nervous system, the body's physical properties and its possibilities for movement, the goal the child is motivated to reach, and the environmental support for the skill (Adolph, 2018; D'Souza & others, 2017). For example, babies learn to walk only when the maturation of the nervous system allows them to control certain leg muscles, when they want to move, when their legs have grown strong enough to support their weight, and when they have sufficient balance control to support their body on one leg.

Mastering a motor skill requires the infant's active efforts to coordinate several components of the skill. Infants explore and select possible solutions to the demands of a new task; they assemble adaptive patterns by modifying their current movement patterns (Adolph, 2018). The first step occurs when the infant is motivated by a new challenge—such as the desire to cross a room—and gets into the "ballpark" of the task demands by taking a couple of stumbling steps. Then, the infant "tunes" these movements to make them smoother and more effective. The tuning is achieved through repeated cycles of action and perception of the consequences of that action. According to the dynamic systems view, even culturally "universal" milestones, such as crawling, reaching, and walking, are learned through this process of adaptation: Infants modulate their movement patterns to fit a new task by exploring and selecting possible configurations (Adolph & Hoch, 2020). Motor development does appear to be similar across nations and cultures, as shown in a large study conducted in Argentina, India, South Africa, and Turkey (Ertem & others, 2018).

To see how dynamic systems theory explains motor behavior, imagine that you offer a new toy to a baby named Gabriel (Thelen & others, 1993). There is no exact program that can tell Gabriel ahead of time how to move his arm and hand and fingers to grasp the toy. Gabriel must adapt to his goal—grasping the toy—and the context. From his sitting position, he must make split-second adjustments to extend his arm, holding his body steady so that his arm and torso don't plow into the toy. Muscles in his arm and shoulder contract and stretch in a host of combinations, exerting a variety of forces. He improvises a way to reach out with one arm and wrap his fingers around the toy.

Thus, according to dynamic systems theory, motor development is not a passive process in which genes dictate the unfolding of a sequence of skills over time. Rather, the infant actively

dynamic systems theory The perspective on motor development that seeks to explain how motor skills are assembled for perceiving and acting.

puts together a skill to achieve a goal within the constraints set by the infant's body and environment. Nature and nurture, the infant and the environment, are all working together as part of an ever-developing system.

reflexes Built-in automatic reactions to stimuli.

As we examine the course of motor development, we will see how dynamic systems theory applies to some specific skills. First, though, let's examine how motor development begins with reflexes.

REFLEXES

Newborns are not completely helpless. Among other things, they have some basic reflexes. For example, newborns hold their breath and contract their throat to keep water out. **Reflexes** allow infants to respond adaptively to their environment before they have had the opportunity to learn. An overview of reflexes, some discussed below, is given in Figure 13.

Babinski reflex

Grasping reflex

Moro reflex

Reflex	Stimulation	Infant's Response	Developmental Pattern
Blinking	Flash of light, puff of air	Closes both eyes	Permanent
Babinski	Sole of foot stroked	Fans out toes, twists foot in	Disappears after 9 months to 1 year
Grasping	Palms touched	Grasps tightly	Weakens after 3 months, disappears after 1 year
Moro (startle)	Sudden stimulation, such as hearing loud noise or being dropped	Startles, arches back, throws head back, flings out arms and legs and then rapidly closes them to center of body	Disappears after 3 to 4 months
Rooting	Cheek stroked or side of mouth touched	Turns head, opens mouth, begins sucking	Disappears after 3 to 4 months
Stepping	Infant held above surface and feet lowered to touch surface	Moves feet as if to walk	Disappears after 3 to 4 months
Sucking	Object touching mouth	Sucks automatically	Disappears after 3 to 4 months
Swimming	Infant put face down in water	Makes coordinated swimming movements	Disappears after 6 to 7 months
Tonic neck	Infant placed on back	Forms fists with both hands and usually turns head to the right (sometimes called the "fencer's pose" because the infant looks like it is assuming a fencer's position)	Disappears after 2 months

FIGURE **13**

INFANT REFLEXES. This chart describes some of the infant's reflexes.

(*left to right*): PhotoAlto/Ale Ventura/Getty Images; Stockbyte/Getty Images; Erik Isakson/Getty Images

How might dynamic systems theory explain the development of this infant's walking skills?

John Lund/Drew Kelly/Blend Images LLC

rooting reflex A newborn's built-in reaction that occurs when the infant's cheek is stroked or the side of the mouth is touched. In response, the infant turns its head toward the side that was touched in an apparent effort to find something to suck.

sucking reflex A newborn's built-in reaction to automatically suck an object placed in the mouth. The sucking reflex enables nourishment before the infant has associated a nipple with food.

Moro reflex A newborn's startle response that occurs in reaction to a sudden, intense noise or movement. When startled, newborns arch their back, throw their head back, and fling out their arms and legs. Then they rapidly close their arms and legs, bringing them close to the center of the body.

grasping reflex A neonatal reflex that occurs when something touches the infant's palms. The infant responds by grasping tightly.

gross motor skills Motor skills that involve large-muscle activities, such as moving the arms and walking.

The rooting and sucking reflexes are important examples. Both have survival value for newborn humans and other mammals, who must find a nipple to obtain nourishment. The **rooting reflex** occurs when the infant's cheek is stroked or the side of the mouth is touched. In response, the infant turns its head toward the side that was touched in an apparent effort to find something to suck. The **sucking reflex** occurs when newborns suck an object placed in their mouth. This reflex enables newborns to get nourishment before they have associated a nipple with food; it also serves as a self-soothing mechanism.

Another example is the **Moro reflex,** which occurs in response to a sudden, intense noise or movement. When startled, newborns will arch their back, throw back their head, and fling out their arms and legs. Then they rapidly close their arms and legs. The Moro reflex is believed to be a way of grabbing for support while falling; it would have had survival value for our primate ancestors.

Some reflexes—coughing, sneezing, blinking, shivering, and yawning, for example—persist throughout life. They are as important for the adult as they are for the infant. Other reflexes, though, disappear several months following birth, as the infant's brain matures and it develops voluntary control over many behaviors. The rooting and Moro reflexes, for example, tend to disappear when the infant is 3 to 4 months old.

The movements involved in some reflexes eventually become incorporated into more complex, voluntary actions. One important example is the **grasping reflex,** which occurs when something touches the infant's palms. The infant responds by grasping tightly. By the end of the third month, the grasping reflex diminishes, and the infant shows a more voluntary grasp. As its motor development becomes smoother, the infant will grasp objects, carefully manipulate them, and explore their qualities.

Individual differences in reflexive behavior are apparent soon after birth. For example, the sucking capabilities of newborns vary between babies. Some newborns are efficient at forcefully sucking and obtaining milk; others are not as efficient and get tired before they are full. Most infants take several weeks to establish a sucking style that is coordinated with the way the mother is holding the infant, the way milk is coming out of the bottle or breast, and the infant's temperament—and this transition reflects actual changes in the nervous system and the brain (Muscatelli & Bouret, 2018). Cross-cultural brain science research shows that there are corresponding changes in the new mother's brain, to better coordinate and respond to the infant's needs (Bornstein & others, 2017).

The old view of reflexes was that they were exclusively genetic, built-in mechanisms that governed the infant's movements. The new perspective on infant reflexes says that they are not entirely automatic or completely beyond the infant's control. For example, infants can control such movements as alternating their legs to make a mobile jiggle or changing their sucking rate to listen to a recording (Adolph & Robinson, 2015). However, it remains unclear whether such behaviors among very young infants are truly under intentional control or are automatic behavioral routines (Bednarski, Musholt, & Wiesmann, 2022).

GROSS MOTOR SKILLS

Ask any parents about their baby, and sooner or later you are likely to hear about one or more advances in motor skills, such as "Ciara just learned to crawl," "Jing is finally sitting alone," or "Angelo took his first step last week." Parents proudly announce such milestones as their children transform themselves from babies unable to lift their heads to toddlers who grab things off the grocery store shelf, chase a cat, and participate actively in the family's social life. These milestones are examples of **gross motor skills,** skills that involve large-muscle activities, such as moving one's arms and walking.

The Development of Posture How do gross motor skills develop? As a foundation, these skills require postural control (Hadders-Algra, 2018b). For example, to track moving objects, you must be able to control your head in order to stabilize your gaze; before you can walk, you must be able to balance on one leg. Posture is more than just holding still and straight. Posture is a dynamic process that is linked with sensory information in the skin, joints, and muscles, which tell us where we are in space; in vestibular organs in the inner ear that regulate balance and equilibrium; and in vision and hearing (Thelen & Smith, 2006).

Newborn infants cannot voluntarily control their posture. Within a few weeks, though, they can hold their heads erect, and soon they can lift their heads while prone. By 2 months of age, babies can sit while supported on a lap or an infant seat, but they cannot sit independently until they are 6 or 7 months of age. Standing also develops gradually during the first year of life. By about 8 to 9 months of age, infants usually learn to pull themselves up and hold onto a chair, and they often can stand alone by about 10 to 12 months of age. Though there is general consistency across places and cultures in this developmental progression, there are important cultural differences in caregivers' understanding and beliefs about development that can influence how parents stimulate and support gross motor skills in infancy (van Schaik, Oudgenoeg-Paz, & Atun-Einy, 2018).

Newly crawling infant

Learning to Walk Locomotion and postural control are closely linked, especially in walking upright (Adolph & Hoch, 2019; Kornafel, Paremski, & Prosser, 2022). To walk upright, the baby must be able both to balance on one leg as the other is swung forward and to shift weight from one leg to the other.

Even young infants can make the alternating leg movements that are needed for walking. The neural pathways that control leg alternation are in place from a very early age, even at birth or before. Indeed, researchers have found that alternating leg movements occur during the fetal period and at birth (van Merendonk & others, 2017).

If infants can produce forward stepping movements so early, why does it take them so long to learn to walk? The key skills in learning to walk appear to be stabilizing balance on one leg long enough to swing the other forward and shifting the weight without falling. This is a difficult biomechanical problem to solve, and it takes infants about a year to do it.

Experienced walker

In learning to locomote, infants discover what kinds of places and surfaces are safe for locomotion, which involves many interactions with interesting objects (including toys) that further contribute to their development (Adolph, 2018; Herzberg & others, 2022). In a classic series of studies, Karen Adolph (1997) investigated how experienced and inexperienced crawling infants and walking infants go down steep slopes (see Figure 14). Newly crawling infants, who averaged about 8½ months in age, rather indiscriminately went down the steep slopes, often falling in the process (with an experimenter next to the slope to catch them). After weeks of practice, the crawling babies became more adept at judging which slopes were too steep to crawl down and which ones they could navigate safely. New walkers also could not judge the safety of the slopes, but experienced walkers accurately matched their skills with the steepness of the slopes. They rarely fell downhill, either refusing to go down the steep slopes or going down backward in a cautious manner. Experienced walkers perceptually assessed the situation—looking, swaying, touching, and thinking before they moved down the slope. With experience, both the crawlers and the walkers learned to avoid the risky slopes where they would fall, integrating perceptual information with the development of a new motor behavior. In this research, we again see the importance of perceptual-motor coupling in the development of motor skills. Thus, practice is very important in the development of new motor skills (Adolph & Robinson, 2015). In a follow-up study, Adolph and her colleagues (2012) observed 12- to 19-month-olds during free play. Locomotor experience was extensive, with the infants averaging 2,368 steps and 17 falls per hour.

A more recent study explored how infants plan and guide their locomotion in the challenging context of navigating a series of bridges varying in width (Kretch & Adolph, 2017). Infants' visual exploration (direction of their gaze) was assessed using a head-mounted eye-tracking device, and their locomotor actions were captured using video. The 14-month-olds engaged in visual exploration from a distance as an initial assessment before they crossed almost every bridge. The visual information led to modifications in their gait when approaching narrow bridges, and they used haptic (touch) information at the edge of the bridges. As they gained more walking experience, their exploratory behaviors became more efficient and they became more adept at deciding which bridges were safe to walk across.

Might the development of walking be linked to advances in other aspects of development? Walking experience leads to being able to gain contact with objects that were previously out of reach and to initiate interaction with parents and other adults, thereby promoting language development (Adolph & Robinson, 2015; He, Walle, & Campos, 2015; Herzberg & others, 2022). Thus, walking skills can produce a cascade of changes in the infant's development.

FIGURE 14

THE ROLE OF EXPERIENCE IN CRAWLING AND WALKING INFANTS' JUDGMENTS OF WHETHER TO GO DOWN A SLOPE. Karen Adolph (1997) found that locomotor *experience* rather than *age* was the primary predictor of adaptive responding on slopes of varying steepness. Newly crawling and walking infants could not judge the safety of the various slopes. With experience, they learned to avoid slopes where they would fall. When expert crawlers began to walk, they again made mistakes and fell, even though they had judged the same slope accurately when crawling. Adolph referred to this as the *specificity of learning* because it does not transfer across crawling and walking.

both: Dr. Karen Adolph, New York University

The First Year: Motor Development Milestones and Variations   Figure 15

summarizes important accomplishments in gross motor skills during the first year, culminating in the ability to walk easily. The timing of these milestones, especially the later ones, may vary between children by as much as several months, and experiences can accelerate or delay the onset of these milestones (Hadders-Algra, 2018b). For example, in the early 1990s, pediatricians began recommending that parents place their babies on their backs when they sleep. Following that instruction, babies who back-sleep began crawling later, typically several weeks later than babies who sleep prone (Davis & others, 1998). Also, some infants do not follow the standard sequence of motor milestones (Hadders-Algra, 2018b). For example, many infants never crawl on their belly or on their hands and knees, and this is more common in some cultures than others. Furthermore, these noncrawling infants may discover a different form of locomotion before walking, such as rolling, or they might never locomote until they can stand upright (Adolph, Hoch, & Cole, 2018).

The latest research, utilizing cell phones, accelerometers, and head-mounted eye trackers with parents and their infants, shows compelling evidence of the wide variety of gross motor accomplishments in the first year. Furthermore, the environment (e.g., the extent to which infants are held, placed in a baby carrier, or in a "baby walker") plays a major role in the progression of these motor skills (de Barbaro & Fausey, 2022; Franchak, 2019).

A comprehensive study found a number of factors that are linked to motor development in the first year of life (Flensborg-Madsen & Mortensen, 2017). Twelve developmental milestones were assessed, including grasping, rolling, sitting, and crawling; standing and walking; and overall mean of milestones. A larger size at birth (based on birth weight, birth length, and head circumference) was the aspect of pregnancy and delivery that

How Would You...?
If you were a **psychologist,** how would you advise parents who are concerned that their infant is one or two months behind the average gross motor milestones?

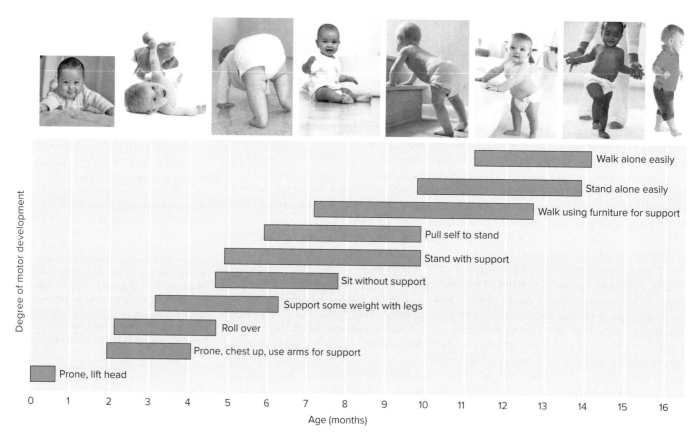

FIGURE **15**

MILESTONES IN GROSS MOTOR DEVELOPMENT. The horizontal red bars indicate the range in which most infants reach various milestones in gross motor development.

(*Photo credit left to right*) Yu Zhang/Shutterstock; StephaneHachey/E+/Getty Images; Image Source/Alamy Stock Photo; Victoria Blackie/Photodisc/Getty Images; Cohen/Ostrow/Digital Vision/Getty Images; Fotosearch/Getty Images; Tom Grill/Fuse/Getty Images; Monika Wisniewska/Amaviael/123RF

showed the strongest link to reaching motor milestones earlier. Maternal smoking in the last trimester of prenatal development was associated with reaching the motor milestones later. Also, increases in size (weight, length, and head circumference) in the first year were related to reaching the motor milestones earlier. Breast feeding also was linked to reaching the milestones earlier.

Development in the Second Year   The motor accomplishments of the first year bring increasing independence in the second year, allowing infants to explore their environment more extensively and to initiate interaction with others more readily. Motor activity during the second year is vital to the child's competent development and few restrictions, except for safety, should be placed on their adventures.

By 13 to 18 months, toddlers can pull a toy attached to a string and use their hands and legs to climb up a number of steps. By 18 to 24 months, toddlers can walk quickly or run stiffly for a short distance, balance on their feet in a squatting position while playing with objects on the floor, walk backward without losing their balance, stand and kick a ball without falling, stand and throw a ball, and jump in place.

Can parents give their babies a head start on becoming physically fit and skilled through structured exercise classes? Most infancy experts recommend against structured exercise classes for babies. But there are other ways of guiding infants' motor development. Caregivers in some cultures handle babies vigorously, and this practice might advance motor development, as we discuss in *Connecting with Diversity*.

connecting with diversity

Cultural Variations in Guiding Infants' Motor Development

The extent to which caregivers stimulate their infants' motor skills can vary by culture. For instance, in many African, Indian, and Caribbean cultures, mothers massage and stretch their infants during daily baths and at other times (Adolph & Hoch, 2020). And in sub-Saharan Africa, traditional practices in many villages involve mothers and siblings engaging babies in exercises, such as frequent exercise for trunk and pelvic muscles (Super & Harkness, 2010).

Do cultural variations make a difference in the infant's motor development? When cultural standards suggest it is a good idea for infants to engage in active exercise, some aspects of their motor development occur earlier (Adolph & Berger, 2015; Adolph, Karasik, & Tamis-LeMonda, 2010). These differences in practices also are reflected in parents' different expectations for motor development.

Many forms of restricted movement—such as Chinese sandbags, orphanage restrictions, and failure of caregivers to encourage movement in Budapest—have been found to produce substantial delays in

 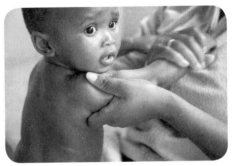

(*Left*) In the Algonquin culture in Quebec, Canada, babies are strapped to a cradle board for much of their infancy. (*Right*) In Jamaica, mothers massage and stretch their infants' arms and legs. *To what extent do cultural variations in the activity infants engage in influence the time at which they reach motor milestones?*
(*Left*) Danita Delimont/Alamy Stock Photo; (*right*) Pippa Hetherington/Earthstock/Newscom

motor development (Adolph, Hoch & Cole, 2018). In some rural Chinese provinces, babies are placed in a bag of fine sand, which acts as a diaper and is changed once a day. The baby is left alone, face up, and is visited only when being fed by the mother. Some studies of swaddling show small effects on creating delays in motor development, but other studies show no delays. Cultures that do swaddle infants usually do so early in the infant's development when the infant is not yet mobile; as the infant becomes more mobile, swaddling decreases.

fine motor skills Motor skills that involve finely tuned movements, such as finger dexterity.

FINE MOTOR SKILLS

Whereas gross motor skills involve large muscle activity, **fine motor skills** involve finely tuned movements. Grasping a toy, using a spoon, buttoning a shirt, or accomplishing anything that requires finger dexterity demonstrates fine motor skills. Infants have hardly any control over fine motor skills at birth, but newborns do have many components of what will become finely coordinated arm, hand, and finger movements.

The onset of reaching and grasping marks a significant achievement in infants' ability to interact with their surroundings. During the first two years of life, infants refine how they reach and grasp (Babik, Galloway, & Lobo, 2022). Initially, infants reach by moving their shoulders and elbows crudely, swinging their arms toward an object. Later, when infants reach for an object they move their wrists, rotate their hands, and coordinate their thumb and forefinger. Infants do not have to see their own hands in order to reach for an object or person. "Proprioceptive" cues from muscles, tendons, and joints, not sight of the limb, guide reaching by 4 months of age (Corbetta & others, 2018).

Infants refine their ability to grasp objects by developing two types of grasps. Initially, infants grip with the whole hand, which is called the *palmar grasp.* Later, toward the end of the first year, infants also grasp small objects with their thumb and forefinger, which is called the *pincer grip.* Their grasping system is very flexible. They vary their grip on an object depending on its size, shape, and texture, as well as the size of their own hands relative to the object's size. Infants grip small objects with their thumb and forefinger (and sometimes their middle finger too), whereas they grip large objects with all of the fingers of one hand or both hands.

Perceptual-motor coupling is necessary for the infant to coordinate grasping. Which perceptual system the infant is most likely to use in coordinating grasping varies with age. Four-month-old infants rely greatly on touch to determine how they will grip an object; 8-month-olds are more likely to use vision as a guide (Thomas, Karl, & Whishaw, 2015). This developmental change is efficient because vision lets infants "preshape" their hands as they reach for an object.

Especially when they can manage a pincer grip, infants delight in picking up small objects. Many develop the pincer grip and begin to crawl at about the same time, and infants at this stage of development pick up virtually everything in sight, especially small items on the floor, and put the objects in their mouth. Thus, parents need to be vigilant in regularly monitoring what objects are within the infant's reach (Morrongiello & Cox, 2016).

A young girl uses a pincer grip to pick up puzzle pieces.
Newstockimages/SuperStock

Experience plays a role in reaching and grasping. In one foundational study, 3-month-olds who were not yet engaging in reaching behavior were provided with reaching experiences. These experiences were linked to increased object exploration and attention focusing skills at 15 months of age (Libertus, Joh, & Needham, 2016). Other research studies have also found that short-term training involving practice of reaching movements can increase infants' reaching for and touching objects (Cunha & others, 2016; Righetto Greco & others, 2022).

Amy Needham and her colleagues have used "sticky mittens" to enhance young infants' active grasping and manipulation of objects. In one clever experiment, 3-month-old infants participated in play sessions wearing sticky mittens—"mittens with palms that stuck to the edges of toys and allowed the infants to pick up the toys" (Needham, Barrett, & Peterman, 2002, p. 279) (see Figure 16). Infants who used the mittens grasped and manipulated objects earlier in their development than a control group of infants who did not get to use the mittens. The infants with sticky mittens looked at the objects longer, swatted at them more during visual contact, and were more likely to mouth the objects. In subsequent research using the mittens, 3-month-old infants participated in active

FIGURE 16

INFANTS' USE OF "STICKY MITTENS" TO EXPLORE OBJECTS. Amy Needham and her colleagues (2002) found that "sticky mittens" enhanced young infants' object exploration skills.
Dr. Amy Needham

motor training using sticky mittens that allowed them to pick up toys, and these infants engaged in more sophisticated object exploration at 5.5 months of age (Wiesen, Watkins, & Needham, 2016).

Review *Connect* Reflect

 Describe infants' motor development.

Review
- What is dynamic systems theory?
- What are some reflexes that infants have?
- How do gross motor skills develop in infancy?
- How do fine motor skills develop in infancy?

Connect
- What are the differences between the grasping reflex present at birth and the fine motor grasping skills an infant develops between 4 and 12 months of age?

Reflect *Your Own Personal Journey of Life*
- Think of a motor skill that you perform. How would dynamic systems theory explain your motor skill performance?

3 How Can Infants' Sensory and Perceptual Development Be Characterized?

 Explain sensory and perceptual development in infancy.

| What Are Sensation and Perception? | The Ecological View | Visual Perception | Other Senses | Intermodal Perception | Nature, Nurture, and Perceptual Development | Perceptual-Motor Coupling |

How do sensations and perceptions develop? Can newborns see? If so, what can they perceive? What about the other senses—hearing, smell, taste, and touch? What are they like in newborns, and how do they develop? Can infants put together information from two modalities, such as sight and sound? These are among the intriguing questions that we will explore in this section.

WHAT ARE SENSATION AND PERCEPTION?

How does a newborn know that their mother's skin is soft rather than rough? How does a 5-year-old know what color their hair is? How does a 10-year-old know that a firecracker is louder than a cat's meow? Infants and children "know" these things because of information that comes through the senses. Without vision, hearing, touch, taste, smell, and other senses, we would be isolated from the world; we would live in dark silence, a tasteless, colorless, feelingless void.

Sensation occurs when information interacts with sensory *receptors*—the eyes, ears, tongue, nostrils, and skin. The sensation of hearing occurs when waves of pulsating air are collected by the outer ear and conducted through the bones of the inner ear and the *cochlea,* where mechanical vibrations are converted into electrical impulses. Then the electrical impulses move to the *auditory nerve,* which transmits them to the brain. The sensation of vision occurs as rays of light contact the eyes and become focused on the *retina,* where light is converted into electrical impulses. Then the electrical impulses are transmitted by the *optic nerve* to the visual centers of the brain.

Perception is the interpretation of what is sensed. The air waves that contact the ears might be interpreted as noise or as musical sounds, for example. The physical energy of light

sensation Reaction that occurs when information contacts sensory receptors—the eyes, ears, tongue, nostrils, and skin.

perception The interpretation of sensation.

How would you use the Gibsons' ecological theory of perception and the concept of affordance to explain the role that perception is playing in this baby's activity?

Ryan KC Wong/E+/Getty Images

being transmitted to the retina of the eye might be interpreted as a particular color, pattern, or shape, depending on how it is perceived.

THE ECOLOGICAL VIEW

Much of the research on perceptual development in infancy has been guided by the ecological view of Eleanor and James J. Gibson (E. Gibson, 1989; J. Gibson, 1979). They argue that we do not have to take bits and pieces of data from sensations and build up representations of the world in our minds. Instead, our perceptual system can select from the rich information that the environment itself provides.

According to the Gibsons' **ecological view,** we directly perceive information that exists in the world around us. Perception brings us into contact with the environment in order to interact with and adapt to it (Kretch & Adolph, 2017). Perception is designed for action. Perception gives people such information as when to duck, when to turn their bodies as they move through a narrow passageway, and when to put up their hands to catch something.

In the Gibsons' view, all objects and surfaces have **affordances,** which are opportunities for interaction offered by objects that fit within our capabilities to perform activities. A pot may afford you something to cook with, and it may afford a toddler something to bang. Adults immediately know when a chair is appropriate for sitting, when a surface is safe for walking, or when an object is within reach. We directly and accurately perceive these affordances by sensing information from the environment—the light or sound reflecting from the surfaces of the world—and from our own bodies through muscle receptors, joint receptors, and skin receptors; this information, in turn, informs the motor actions we make (Plumert, 2018).

An important developmental question is "What affordances can infants or children detect and use?" (Ishak, Franchak, & Adolph, 2014). In one classic study, when babies who could walk were faced with a squishy waterbed, they stopped and explored it, then chose to crawl rather than walk across it (Gibson & others, 1987). They combined perception and action to adapt to the demands of the task.

Studying the infant's perception has not been an easy task. What do you think some of the research challenges might be? The *Connecting with Research* interlude describes some of the ingenious ways researchers study the infant's perception.

VISUAL PERCEPTION

What do newborns see? How does visual perception develop in infancy?

Visual Acuity and Human Faces Psychologist William James (1890/1950) called the newborn's perceptual world a "blooming, buzzing confusion." More than a century later, we can safely say that he was wrong (Maurer & Lewis, 2018). Even the newborn perceives a world with some order. That world, however, is far different from the one perceived by the toddler or the adult.

Just how well can infants see? At birth, the nerves and muscles and lens of the eye are still developing. As a result, newborns cannot see small things that are far away. Estimates of the newborn's visual acuity vary from 20/240 to 20/640 on the well-known Snellen chart used for eye examinations, which means that a newborn can see at 20 feet what a normal adult can see at 240 to 640 feet. In other words, an object 20 feet away is only as clear to the newborn as it would be if it were 640 feet away from an adult with normal vision (20/20). By 6 months of age, though, *on average* vision is 20/40 (Aslin & Lathrop, 2008). Although this may seem like an initial disadvantage for newborns, this progression of visual acuity is a typical and important part of visual sensory and perceptual development (Esteban-Ibañez & others, 2022; Vogelsang & others, 2018).

Faces are possibly the most important visual stimuli in children's social environment, and it is important that they extract key information from others' faces. Infants show an interest in human faces soon after birth (Sugden & Marquis, 2017). Research shows that infants only a few hours old prefer to look at faces rather than other objects and to look at attractive faces (Lee & others, 2013).

ecological view The view that perception functions to bring organisms in contact with the environment and to increase adaptation.

affordances Opportunities for interaction offered by objects that are necessary to perform activities.

visual preference method A method developed by Fantz to determine whether infants can distinguish one stimulus from another by measuring the length of time they attend to different stimuli.

habituation Decreased responsiveness to a stimulus after repeated presentations of the stimulus.

dishabituation Recovery of a habituated response after a change in stimulation.

connecting with research

How Can We Study Newborns' Perception?

Key Points:

- Researchers study infants' perception by measuring how long they gaze at different objects (visual preference method).
- After repeated exposure to the same stimulus, an infant will stop responding to it (habituation).
- Introducing a new stimulus increases the infant's responsiveness (dishabituation).

Across many decades, scientists have developed research methods and tools sophisticated enough to examine the subtle abilities of infants and to interpret their complex actions. Following are several of these techniques.

Visual Preference Method

Robert Fantz (1963) was a pioneer in this effort. Fantz made an important discovery that advanced the ability of researchers to investigate infants' visual perception: Infants look at different things for different lengths of time. Fantz placed infants in a "looking chamber," which had two visual displays on the ceiling above the infant's head. An experimenter viewed the infant's eyes by looking through a peephole. If the infant was fixating on one of the displays, the experimenter could see the display's reflection in the infant's eyes. This arrangement allowed the experimenter to determine how long the infant looked at each display. Fantz (1963) found that infants only 2 days old look longer at patterned stimuli, such as faces and concentric circles, than at patternless red, white, or yellow discs. Infants 2 to 3 weeks old also preferred to look at patterns—a face, a piece of printed matter, or a bull's-eye—longer than at patternless red, yellow, or white discs (see Figure 17). Fantz's research method—studying whether infants can distinguish one stimulus from another by measuring the length of time they attend to different stimuli—is referred to as the **visual preference method**. Advances in 4D ultrasound technology have made it possible to examine the visual preferences of fetuses by projecting images through the mother's tissue for the fetus to see. Like newborns, fetuses prefer to look at stimuli that approximate human faces (Reid & Dunn, 2021).

Habituation and Dishabituation

Another way that researchers have studied infant perception is to present a stimulus (such as a sight or a sound) a number of times. If there is a decrease in the infant's response to the stimulus after several presentations, it indicates that the infant is no longer interested in it. If the researcher now presents a new stimulus, the infant's looking behavior will recover—indicating the infant could discriminate between the old and new stimulus (Hofrichter & others, 2021).

Habituation is the name given to decreased responsiveness to a stimulus after repeated presentations of the stimulus. **Dishabituation** is the recovery of a habituated response after a change in stimulation. Newborn infants can habituate to repeated sights, sounds, smells, or touches (Addabbo & others, 2018). Among the measures researchers use in habituation studies are sucking behavior (sucking stops when the young infant attends to a new object), heart and breathing rates, and the length of time the infant looks at an object. Figure 18 shows the results of one classic study of habituation and dishabituation with newborns (Slater, Morison, & Somers, 1988).

High-Amplitude Sucking

To assess an infant's attention to sound, researchers often use a method called high-amplitude sucking. In this method, infants are given a nonnutritive nipple to suck (like those used on bottles or pacifiers), and the nipple is connected to a sound generating system. The researcher computes a baseline high-amplitude sucking rate in a one-minute silent period (that is, the frequency or number of times the infant sucks the nipple). Following the baseline, presentation of a sound is made contingent on the rate of sucking. Initially babies suck frequently so that the same sound occurs often. Gradually, they lose interest in hearing the

FIGURE 17

FANTZ'S EXPERIMENT ON INFANTS' VISUAL PERCEPTION.
(*a*) Infants 2 to 3 weeks old preferred to look at some stimuli more than others. In Fantz's experiment, infants preferred to look at patterns rather than at color or brightness. For example, they looked longer at a face, a piece of printed matter, or a bull's-eye than at red, yellow, or white discs. (*b*) Fantz used a "looking chamber" to study infants' perception of stimuli.

David Linton, Courtesy of the Linton Family

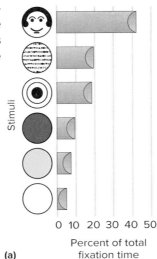

(a)

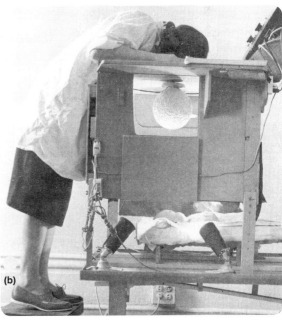

(b)

(*continued*)

(*continued*)

Habituation

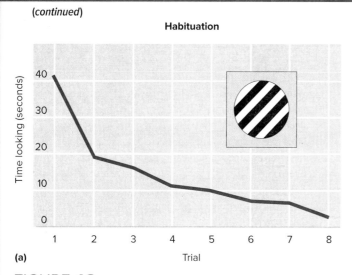

(a)

Dishabituation

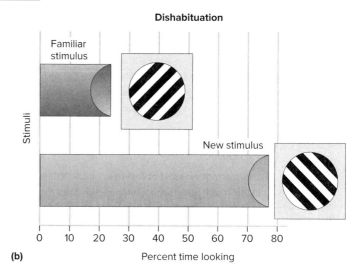

(b)

FIGURE 18

HABITUATION AND DISHABITUATION. In the first part of one study (*a*), 7-hour-old newborns were shown a stimulus. As indicated, the newborns looked at it an average of 41 seconds when it was first presented to them (Slater, Morison, & Somers, 1988). Over seven more presentations of the stimulus, they looked at it less and less. In the second part of the study (*b*), infants were presented with both the familiar stimulus to which they had just become habituated and a new stimulus (which was rotated 90 degrees). The newborns looked at the new stimulus three times as much as the familiar stimulus.

same sound so they begin to suck less often. Then the researcher changes the sound that is being presented. If the babies again increase their rate of sucking, the interpretation is that they have discriminated the sound change and are sucking more because they want to hear the interesting new sound (Pelaez & Monlux, 2017).

The Orienting Response and Tracking

A technique that can be used to determine whether an infant can see or hear is the orienting response, which involves turning one's head toward a sight or sound. However, one very important technical advance in measuring infant perception is the development of sophisticated eye-tracking equipment (Pérez-Edgar, MacNeill, & Fu, 2020; Slone & others, 2018). Figure 19 shows an infant wearing an eye-tracking headgear in a study on visually guided movement and social interaction. Typical studies of infant development use remote optics eye trackers that have a camera that is not attached to the infant's head.

One of the main reasons that infant perception researchers are so enthusiastic about sophisticated eye-tracking equipment is that "looking time" is among the most important measures of infant perceptual and cognitive development. The eye-tracking equipment allows for much greater precision than human observation in assessing various

FIGURE 19

AN INFANT WEARING EYE-TRACKING HEADGEAR. Using the ultralight, wireless, head-mounted eye-tracking equipment shown here, researchers can record where infants look while the infants freely locomote.

Courtesy of Dr. Karen Adolph, New York University

aspects of infant looking and gaze (Boardman & Fletcher-Watson, 2017). Among the areas of infant perception in which eye-tracking equipment is being used are attention, memory, and face processing (Pérez-Edgar, MacNeill, & Fu, 2020). Eye-tracking equipment also is improving our understanding of atypically developing infants, such as those who have autism or were born preterm (Wagner & others, 2018).

An illustrative eye-tracking study shed light on the effectiveness of TV programs and videos that claim to educate infants (Kirkorian, Anderson, & Keen, 2012). In this study, 1-year-olds, 4-year-olds, and adults watched *Sesame Street,* and the eye-tracking equipment recorded precisely what they looked at on the screen. The 1-year-olds were far less likely to consistently look at the same part of the screen as their older counterparts, suggesting that the 1-year-olds showed little understanding of the *Sesame Street* video but instead were attracted to what was visually salient and not by the meaningful content.

Equipment

Technology can facilitate the use of most methods for investigating the infant's perceptual abilities. Video equipment allows researchers to investigate elusive behaviors. High-speed computers make it possible to perform complex data analysis in minutes or seconds. Other equipment records respiration, heart rate, body movement, visual fixation, and sucking behavior, which provide clues to what the infant is sensing and perceiving.

What other applications of computer technology, such as motion-capture or three-dimensional modeling, do you think might someday be useful in studying children's perception?

FIGURE 20

VISUAL ACUITY DURING THE FIRST MONTHS OF LIFE. The four photographs represent a computer estimation of what a picture of a face looks like to a 1-month-old, 2-month-old, 3-month-old, and 1-year-old (which approximates the visual acuity of an adult).

Kevin Peterson/Photodisc/Getty Images

Figure 20 shows a computer estimation of what a picture of a face looks like to an infant at different ages from a distance of about 6 inches. Infants spend more time looking at their mother's face than a stranger's face as early as 12 hours after being born. By 4 months of age, infants match voices to faces, distinguish between male and female faces, and discriminate faces of their own racial and ethnic group from those of other groups (Lee, Quinn, & Pascalis, 2017; Otsuka, 2017). By 9 months of age, infants' experiences with emotional expressiveness of their families are predictive of their ability to match emotions across facial and vocal modalities (Ogren, Burling, & Johnson, 2018).

Experience has an important role in face processing in infancy and later in development. One aspect of this experience involves the concept of *perceptual narrowing,* in which infants are more likely to pay attention to faces to which they have been exposed than to faces to which they have not been exposed (Krasotkina & others, 2021; Lee, Quinn, & Pascalis, 2017). Also, as we discussed in the *Connecting with Research* interlude, young infants can perceive certain patterns. With the help of his "looking chamber," Robert Fantz (1963) revealed that even 2- to 3-week-old infants prefer to look at patterned displays rather than nonpatterned displays. For example, they prefer to look at a normal human face rather than one with scrambled features, and prefer to look at a bull's-eye target or black and white stripes rather than a plain circle. Even newborns prefer to watch biological motion of humans rather than random motion or the motion of nonbiological objects (Hirai & Senju, 2020; Sifre & others, 2018). Infants' preferences for viewing human faces and motions are important for their social and cognitive development.

Color Vision and Perceptions of Natural Scenes   The infant's color vision also improves over time (Atkinson & Braddick, 2013). By 8 weeks, and possibly as early as 4 weeks, infants can discriminate some colors. By 4 months of age, they have color preferences that mirror those of adults in some cases, preferring saturated colors such as royal blue over pale blue, for example (Bornstein, 2015). One study of 4- to 6-month-olds found that they looked longest at blue hues and shortest at green-yellow hues (Skelton & Franklin, 2020). In part, these changes in vision reflect maturation. Experience, however, is also necessary for color vision to develop normally (Röder & Kekunnaya, 2021). Over the course of the first year, infants also increasingly look at natural scenes in ways that more closely resemble how adults look at similar scenes, such as by fixating on meaningful aspects of a scene (such as an important object in one section of the scene) rather than just on aspects that are perceptually salient (such as the borders or in the center of the scene) (van Renswoude & others, 2019).

Perceptual Constancy   Some perceptual accomplishments are especially intriguing because they indicate that the infant's perception goes beyond the information provided by the senses (White & others, 2018). This is the case in perceptual constancy, in which sensory stimulation is changing but perception of the physical world remains constant. If infants did not develop perceptual constancy, each time they saw an object at a different distance or in a different orientation, they would perceive it as a different object. Thus, the development of perceptual constancy allows infants to perceive their world as stable. Two types of perceptual constancy are size constancy and shape constancy.

Size constancy is the recognition that an object remains the same even though the retinal image of the object changes as you move toward or away from the object (Chen, Sperandio, & Goodale, 2018). The farther away from us an object is, the smaller its image is on our eyes. Thus, the size of an object on the retina is not sufficient to tell us its actual size. For example, you perceive a bicycle standing right in front of you as smaller than the car parked across the

size constancy The recognition that an object remains the same even though the retinal image of the object changes as you move toward or away from the object.

shape constancy The recognition that an object's shape remains the same even though its orientation to us changes.

street, even though the bicycle casts a larger image on your eyes than the car does. When you move away from the bicycle, you do not perceive it to be shrinking even though its image on your retinas shrinks; you perceive its size to be constant.

But what about babies? Do they have size constancy? Researchers have long known that babies as young as 3 months show size constancy (Bower, 1966). However, at 3 months of age, a baby's ability is not full-blown. It continues to develop across early and middle childhood (Johnson & Hannon, 2015).

Shape constancy is the recognition that an object remains the same shape even though its orientation to us changes. Look around the room you are in right now. You likely see objects of varying shapes, such as tables and chairs. If you get up and walk around the room, you will see these objects from different sides and angles. Even though your retinal image of the objects changes as you walk and look, you will still perceive the objects as the same shape.

Do babies have shape constancy? As with size constancy, researchers have found that babies as young as 3 months have shape constancy (Bower, 1966). Three-month-old infants, however, do not have shape constancy for *irregularly* shaped objects with distinct features, edges, and shadowing (Woods & Schuler, 2014). Studies of infants' perception that rely on mental rotation of objects have found that boys, on average, are able to mentally rotate objects at a younger age than girls, an ability that has been linked to exposure in utero to different levels of testosterone and estradiol from amniotic fluid (Erdmann & others, 2019).

Perception of Occluded Objects   Once again, look around where you are now. You likely see that some objects are partly occluded by other objects that are in front of them—possibly a desk behind a chair, some books behind a backpack, or a car parked behind a tree. Do infants perceive an object as complete when it is partly occluded by an object in front of it?

In the first two months of postnatal development, infants don't perceive occluded objects as complete, instead perceiving only what is visible (Johnson, 2019). Beginning at about 2 months of age, infants develop the ability to perceive occluded objects as whole. How does perceptual completion develop? In Scott Johnson's research (Johnson & Hannon, 2015; Johnson, 2019), learning, experience, and self-directed exploration via eye movements play key roles in the development of perceptual completion in young infants.

Many of the objects in the world that are occluded appear and disappear behind closer objects, as when you are walking down the street and see cars appear and disappear behind buildings as they move or you move. Can infants predictively track briefly occluded moving objects? They develop the ability to track briefly occluded moving objects at about 3 to 5 months of age (Bremner & others, 2016). One illustrative study explored 5- to 9-month-old infants' ability to track moving objects that disappeared gradually behind an occluded partition, disappeared abruptly, or imploded (shrank quickly in size) (see Figure 21) (Bertenthal, Longo, & Kenny, 2007). In this study, the infants were more likely to accurately predict the reappearance of the moving object when it had disappeared gradually rather than when it had disappeared abruptly or imploded.

Depth Perception   Might infants even perceive depth? To investigate this question, in a classic experiment Eleanor Gibson and Richard Walk (1960) constructed a miniature cliff with a drop-off covered by glass in their laboratory. They placed infants on the edge of this visual cliff and had their mothers coax them to crawl onto the glass (see Figure 22). Most infants would not crawl out on the glass, choosing instead to remain on the opaque side, an indication that they could perceive depth. However, critics point out that the visual cliff likely is a better test of social referencing and fear of heights than depth perception.

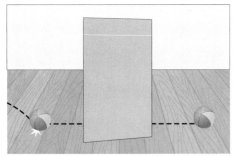

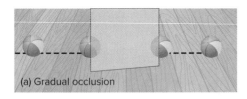

(a) Gradual occlusion

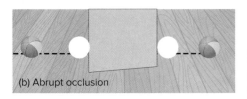

(b) Abrupt occlusion

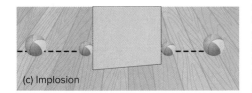

(c) Implosion

FIGURE 21

INFANTS' PREDICTIVE TRACKING OF A BRIEFLY OCCLUDED MOVING BALL. The top panel shows the visual scene that infants experienced. At the beginning of each event, a multicolored ball bounced up and down with an accompanying bounding sound, and then rolled across the floor until it disappeared behind the partition. Parts a, b, and c show the three stimulus events that the 5- to 9-month-old infants experienced: (*a*) *Gradual occlusion*—the ball gradually disappears behind the right side of the occluding partition located in the center of the display. (*b*) *Abrupt occlusion*—the ball abruptly disappears when it reaches the location of the white circle and then abruptly reappears 2 seconds later at the location of the second white circle on the other side of the occluding partition. (*c*) *Implosion*—the rolling ball quickly decreases in size as it approaches the occluding partition and rapidly increases in size as it reappears on the other side of the occluding partition.

Karen Adolph and her colleagues (Adolph, Kaplan, & Kretch, 2021; Adolph, Kretch, & LoBue, 2014) have described how for many decades it was believed that crawling infants would not cross the clear glass indicating a dangerous drop-off because they have a fear of heights. However, Adolph and her colleagues concluded that there is no research support for the view that infants have a fear of heights. Rather, research indicates that infants either crawl or walk across the glass precipice or don't do so because of their perception of the affordances it does or does not provide. Research indicates that infants' exploration of the affordances increases on more challenging cliffs (deeper ones, for example) through such behaviors as patting the glass with their hands (Ueno & others, 2011).

Although researchers do not know precisely how early in life infants perceive depth, we do know that infants develop the ability to use "binocular" cues about depth by approximately 3 to 4 months of age. Thus, Adolph and her colleagues (2014; 2021) note that the reason the visual cliff is not a great test of depth perception is that it requires infants to locomote, and infants have depth perception long before they can crawl.

OTHER SENSES

Other sensory systems besides vision also develop during infancy. We explore development in hearing, touch and pain, smell, and taste.

Hearing During the last two months of pregnancy, as the fetus nestles in its mother's womb, it can hear sounds such as music and the mother's voice (Moon, 2017). In a classic study, two psychologists wanted to find out if a fetus that heard Dr. Seuss's classic story *The Cat in the Hat* while still in the mother's womb would prefer hearing the story after birth (DeCasper & Spence, 1986). During the last months of pregnancy, 16 women read *The Cat in the Hat* to their fetuses. Then, shortly after the infants were born, the mothers read either *The Cat in the Hat* or a story with a different rhyme and pace, *The King, the Mice and the Cheese* (which had not been read aloud during prenatal development). The infants sucked on a nipple in a different way when the mothers read the two stories, suggesting that the infants recognized the pattern and tone of *The Cat in the Hat* (see Figure 23). This study illustrates not only that a fetus can hear but also that it has a remarkable ability to learn even before birth. Contemporary brain imaging research inspired by this classic study has demonstrated that the fetal brain is sensing and processing auditory signals in a sophisticated way (Draganova & others, 2018).

What kind of changes in hearing take place during infancy? They involve perception of a sound's loudness, pitch, and localization:

- *Loudness.* Immediately after birth, infants cannot hear soft sounds quite as well as adults can; a stimulus must be louder to be heard by a newborn than by an adult. For example, an adult can hear a whisper from about 4 to 5 feet away, but a newborn requires that sounds be closer to a normal conversational level to be heard at that distance. This can make it challenging for medical professionals to accurately evaluate potential hearing impairment in newborns (Kanji, Khoza-Shangase, & Moroe, 2018).

FIGURE **22**

EXAMINING INFANTS' DEPTH PERCEPTION ON THE VISUAL CLIFF.
Eleanor Gibson and Richard Walk (1960) found that most infants would not crawl out on the glass, which, according to Gibson and Walk, indicated that they had depth perception. However, critics point out that the visual cliff is a better indication of the infant's social referencing and fear of heights than of the infant's perception of depth.
Denver Post/Getty Images

(a)

(b)

FIGURE **23**

HEARING IN THE WOMB. (*a*) Pregnant mothers read *The Cat in the Hat* to their fetuses during the last few months of pregnancy. (*b*) When they were born, the babies preferred listening to a recording of their mothers reading *The Cat in the Hat*, as evidenced by their sucking on a nipple that produced this recording, rather than another story, *The King, the Mice and the Cheese*.
(*a*) Jill Braaten/McGraw Hill; (*b*) Courtesy of Dr. Melanie J. Spence

Laura Faith Kendall, Music Therapist

Laura Faith Kendall started singing and playing instruments when she was very young and has long understood the importance of music in development. After graduating from Queens University of Charlotte (North Carolina) with undergraduate degrees in psychology and music therapy, she became a board-certified music therapist.

Music therapists are specially trained health-care providers who use evidence-based music interventions to assess emotional well-being, physical health, social functioning, communication abilities, and cognitive skills through musical responses. Although music therapy can be effective with clients of various ages and needs, research indicates that creative music therapy can be particularly beneficial for preterm infants and their parents. Parents and infants are likely to be stressed after a premature birth. Participating in musical interactions can evoke feelings of joy and relaxation in parents and encourage them to interact more profoundly with their infant, resulting in greater parental well-being and stronger parent–infant bonding (Kehl & others, 2020).

Kendall currently works as the southeastern regional therapist for Music Speaks, LLC, which provides music therapy services throughout the United States. As a music therapist, Kendall has been able to use her passion for music to help people of all ages reach their developmental goals.

Music therapist Laura Faith Kendall works with an infant.
Laura Faith Kendall

By 3 months of age, infants' perception of sounds improves, although some aspects of loudness perception do not reach adult levels until 5 to 10 years of age (Trainor & He, 2013).

- *Pitch.* Infants are also less sensitive to the pitch of a sound than adults are. Pitch is the perception of the frequency of a sound. A soprano voice sounds high-pitched, a bass voice low-pitched. Infants are less sensitive to low-pitched sounds and are more likely to hear high-pitched sounds, yet from early in infancy they can demonstrate that they hear the difference (Pietraszewski & others, 2017). One study revealed that by 7 months of age, infants can process simultaneous pitches when they hear voices, but they are more likely to encode the higher-pitched voice (Marie & Trainor, 2013). By 2 years of age, infants have considerably improved their ability to distinguish sounds with different pitches.

- *Localization.* Even newborns can determine the general location from which a sound is coming—but by 7 months of age, they are more proficient at localizing sounds or detecting their origins. Their ability to localize sounds continues to improve during infancy and toddlerhood (Jutras, Lagacé, & Koravand, 2020).

Although young infants can process variations in sound loudness, pitch, and localization, these aspects of hearing continue to improve through the childhood years (Werner, 2017). Exposure to and learning from musical sounds and patterns at this stage of development can provide many benefits for both infants and their parents. See the *Connecting with Careers* profile to discover how a music therapist can provide auditory stimulation and support.

Touch and Pain   Ample evidence indicates that newborns respond to touch. For example, a touch to the cheek produces a turning of the head; a touch to the lips produces sucking movements. These are aspects of the "rooting" reflex. Even fetuses in the second and third trimesters of pregnancy respond to external stimuli by moving their heads, mouths, and arms as their mothers touch their abdomen (Nagy & others, 2021).

Newborns can also feel pain (Bellieni & others, 2016; Witt & others, 2016). This is demonstrated by their responses to customary medical procedures, such as pricking the heel for blood testing or inserting needles and tubes for newborns requiring intensive care to survive and heal after a difficult or premature birth. Research examining the behavior, physiology, and even brain activity of newborns undergoing these procedures shows that they experience pain (Bellieni & others, 2018; Verriotis & others, 2018), as do fetuses after about 20 to 22 weeks of gestation (Bellieni, 2019). Neuroimaging research is being used to measure pain responses in newborns (Yuan & others, 2022). This approach revealed that the pain threshold in newborns occurs at a lower level of stimulation than for adults, confirming newborns' heightened pain sensitivity that has been found in earlier behavioral studies (Goksan & others, 2015).

In the past, doctors performed operations on newborns without anesthesia. This practice was accepted because of the dangers of anesthesia and because of the supposition that newborns do not feel pain. Over the past few decades, major advances have been made so that anesthesia and pain relievers can be effectively used not only with newborns (Steward, 2015), but also with fetuses, which is important now that surgical procedures sometimes are conducted with fetuses in utero (Bellieni, 2019; Dick, Wimalasundera, & Nandi, 2022).

Smell Newborns can differentiate odors (Tristão & others, 2021). The expressions on their faces seem to indicate that they like the way pleasant odors such as vanilla and strawberry smell but do not like the way unpleasant odors like rotten eggs and fish smell. In one classic study, 6-day-old infants who were breast-fed showed a clear preference for smelling their mother's used breast pad rather than a clean breast pad (MacFarlane, 1975). However, when they were 2 days old, they did not show this preference, an indication that they require several days of experience to recognize this odor. Since then, many studies have shown the importance of early experience with odors in the development of olfactory perception (Schaal, 2017; Tristão & others, 2021).

Taste Sensitivity to taste is present even before birth. Human newborns learn tastes prenatally through the amniotic fluid and in breast milk after birth (Podzimek & others, 2018). In another classic study, even at only 2 hours of age, babies made different facial expressions when they tasted sweet, sour, and bitter solutions (Rosenstein & Oster, 1988). Over the first several months of age, infants begin to prefer salty tastes, which is adaptive given the important role of salt in the diet (Liem, 2017).

INTERMODAL PERCEPTION

Imagine yourself playing basketball or tennis. You are experiencing many visual inputs: the ball coming and going, other players moving around, and so on. However, you are experiencing many auditory inputs as well: the sound of the ball bouncing or being hit, the grunts and groans of the players, and so on. There is good correspondence between much of the visual and auditory information: When you see the ball bounce, you hear a bouncing sound; when a player stretches to hit a ball, you hear a groan. When you look at and listen to what is going on, you do not experience just the sounds or just the sights separately; you put all these things together. You experience a single episode. This is **intermodal perception,** which involves integrating information from two or more sensory modalities, such as vision and hearing. Most perception is intermodal (Bahrick, Todd, & Soska, 2018).

Early, exploratory forms of intermodal perception exist even in newborns. For example, newborns turn their eyes and their head toward the sound of a voice or rattle when the sound is maintained for several seconds, but this orienting behavior is reflexive and it is only with rapid brain development over the first few months of life that this orienting behavior becomes controlled (Small, Ishida, & Stapells, 2017). In another classic study, infants as young as 3½ months old looked more at their mother when they also heard her voice and longer at their father when they also heard his voice (Spelke & Owsley, 1979). Thus, even young infants can coordinate visual-auditory information involving people. These early forms of intermodal perception become sharpened with experience and development over the first year of life (Hannon, Schachner, & Nave-Blodgett, 2017), and they

intermodal perception The ability to relate and integrate information from two or more sensory modalities, such as vision and hearing.

What is intermodal perception? Which two senses is this infant using to integrate information about the blocks?
Kaori Ando/Cultura/Getty Images

continue to show developmental changes (Zhou, Cheung, & Chan, 2020). For instance, in the first six months, infants have difficulty connecting sensory input from different modes, but in the second half of the first year, they show an increased ability to make this connection mentally.

In sum, babies are born into the world with some innate abilities to perceive relations among sensory modalities, but their intermodal abilities improve considerably through experience. As with all aspects of development, in perceptual development, biological factors and experience interact and work together.

NATURE, NURTURE, AND PERCEPTUAL DEVELOPMENT

Now that we have discussed many aspects of perceptual development, let's explore one of developmental psychology's key issues as it relates to perceptual development: the nature-nurture issue. Historically, there has been a long-standing interest in how strongly infants' perception is influenced by nature, nurture, and their interaction (Panneton, Bremner, & Johnson, 2021). In the field of perceptual development, nature proponents were referred to as *nativists* and those who emphasized learning and experience were called *empiricists.*

In the strict nativist view, the ability to perceive the world in a competent, organized way is inborn or innate. A completely nativist view of perceptual development no longer is accepted in developmental psychology.

The Gibsons argued that a key question in infant perception is what information is available in the environment and how infants learn to generate, differentiate, and discriminate the information—certainly not a nativist view. The Gibsons' ecological view also is quite different from Piaget's constructivist view. According to Piaget, much of perceptual development in infancy must await the development of a sequence of cognitive stages for infants to construct more complex perceptual tasks as they learn from experience with the world. Thus, in Piaget's view, the ability to perceive size and shape constancy, a three-dimensional world, intermodal perception, and so on develops later in infancy than the Gibsons envision.

The longitudinal research of Daphne Maurer and her colleagues (Maurer, 2017; Maurer & Lewis, 2018; Rezk & others, 2021) has focused on infants born with cataracts—a thickening of the lens of the eye that causes vision to become cloudy, opaque, and distorted and thus severely restricts infants' ability to experience their visual world. Studying infants whose cataracts were removed at different points in development, they discovered that those whose cataracts were removed and new lenses placed in their eyes in the first several months after birth subsequently showed a normal pattern of visual development. However, the longer the delay in removing the cataracts, the more their visual development was impaired. In their research, Maurer and her colleagues have found that experiencing patterned visual input early in infancy is important for holistic and detailed perception of patterns and contours after infancy (Hadad, Maurer, & Lewis, 2017). Their research program illustrates how deprivation and experience influence visual development, and it identifies an early sensitive period in which visual input is necessary for normal visual development.

What roles do nature and nurture play in the infant's perceptual development?
lostinbids/E+/Getty Images

Today, it is clear that just as an extreme nativist position on perceptual development is unwarranted, an extreme empiricist position also is unwarranted. Much of very early perception develops from innate (nature) foundations, and the basic foundation of many perceptual abilities can be detected in newborns (Bornstein, Arterberry, & Mash, 2015). However, as infants develop, environmental experiences (nurture) refine or calibrate many perceptual functions, and they may be the driving force behind some functions. The accumulation of experience with and knowledge about their perceptual world contributes to infants' ability to process coherent perceptions of people and things (Bremner & others, 2017; Bremner & Spence, 2017). In sum, a full portrait of perceptual development includes the interacting influence of nature, nurture, and a developing sensitivity to information in the environment.

PERCEPTUAL-MOTOR COUPLING

As we come to the end of this chapter, we return to the important theme of perceptual-motor coupling. The distinction between perceiving and doing has been a time-honored tradition in psychology. However, a number of experts on perceptual and motor development have

questioned for some time whether this distinction makes sense. Instead, they view perception and action as being coupled (Adolph & Hoch, 2020; Slater & others, 2011; Thelen & Smith, 2006). The main thrust of research in Esther Thelen's dynamic systems approach is to explore how people assemble motor behaviors for perceiving and acting. The main theme of the ecological approach of Eleanor and James J. Gibson is to discover how perception guides action. Action can guide perception, and perception can guide action. Only by moving one's eyes, head, hands, and arms and by moving from one location to another can individuals fully experience their environment and learn how to adapt to it.

How are perception and action coupled in infants' development?
Pavlina Popovska/Getty Images

Babies, for example, continually coordinate their movements with perceptual information to learn how to maintain balance, reach for objects in space, and move across various surfaces and terrains (Kretch & Adolph, 2017). They also learn to mimic and interact socially with an engaging adult through coupling of perception and action (de Klerk, Lamy-Yang, & Southgate, 2019). They are motivated to move or to interact by what they perceive. For example, consider the sight of an attractive toy across the room. In this situation, infants must perceive the current state of their bodies and learn how to use their limbs to reach the toy. Although their movements at first are awkward and uncoordinated, babies soon learn to select patterns of movement that are appropriate for reaching their goals.

Equally important is the other part of the perception-action coupling. That is, action influences and educates perception (Adolph, 2018). For example, watching an object while exploring it with their hands helps infants to discriminate its texture, size, and hardness. Locomoting in the environment teaches babies about how objects and people look from different perspectives, or whether surfaces will support their weight. Individuals perceive in order to move and move in order to perceive. Perceptual and motor development do not occur in isolation from each other but instead are coupled.

How do infants develop new perceptual-motor couplings? Recall from our discussion earlier in this chapter that in the traditional view of Gesell, infants' perceptual-motor development is prescribed by a genetic plan to follow a fixed sequence of stages in development. The genetic determination view has been replaced by the dynamic systems view that infants learn new perceptual-motor couplings by assembling skills for perceiving and acting. New perceptual-motor coupling is not passively accomplished; rather, the infant actively develops a skill to achieve a goal within the limits set by the infant's body and the environment (de Klerk, Lamy-Yang, & Southgate, 2019; Kretch & Adolph, 2017).

Review *Connect* Reflect

 LG3 Explain sensory and perceptual development in infancy.

Review

- What are sensation and perception?
- What is the ecological view of perception?
- How does visual perception develop in infancy?
- How do hearing, touch and pain, smell, and taste develop in infancy?
- What is intermodal perception?
- What is the nativist view of perception? What is the empiricist view?
- How is perceptual-motor development coupled?

Connect

- How might the development of vision and hearing contribute to infants' gross motor development?

Reflect *Your Own Personal Journey of Life*

- How much sensory stimulation would you provide for your baby? A little? A lot? Could you overstimulate your baby? Explain.

topical connections *looking forward*

In the next chapter, you will read about the remarkable cognitive changes that characterize infant development and how infants process information about their world. Advances in infants' cognitive development—together with the development of the brain and perceptual-motor advances that were discussed in this chapter—allow infants to adapt more effectively to their world.

reach your **learning goals**

Physical Development in Infancy

1 How Do Infants Grow and Develop Physically? **LG1** Discuss physical growth and development in infancy.

Patterns of Growth

- The cephalocaudal pattern is the sequence in which growth proceeds from top to bottom. The proximodistal pattern is the sequence in which growth starts at the center of the body and moves toward the extremities.

Height and Weight

- The average North American newborn is 20 inches long and weighs 7½ pounds. Infants grow about 1 inch per month in the first year and nearly triple their weight by their first birthday. The rate of growth slows in the second year.

The Brain

- One of the most dramatic changes in the brain in the first two years of life is dendritic spreading, which increases the connections between neurons. Myelination, which speeds the conduction of nerve impulses, continues through infancy and even into adolescence.

- The cerebral cortex has two hemispheres (left and right). Lateralization refers to specialization of function in one hemisphere or the other.

- Early experiences play an important role in brain development. Neural connections are formed early in an infant's life.

- The neuroconstructivist view is an increasingly popular view of the brain's development. Before birth, genes mainly direct neurons to different locations. After birth, the inflowing stream of sights, sounds, smells, touches, language, and eye contact helps shape the brain's neural connections, as does stimulation from caregivers and others.

Sleep

- Newborns usually sleep about 18 hours a day. By 6 months of age, many infants approach adultlike sleeping patterns. REM sleep—during which most dreaming occurs—is present more in early infancy than in childhood and adulthood.

- Sleeping arrangements for infants vary across cultures. In the United States, infants are more likely to sleep alone than in many other cultures. Some experts believe shared sleeping is a risk factor for sudden infant death syndrome (SIDS), a condition that occurs when a sleeping infant suddenly stops breathing and dies without an apparent cause. Better sleep in infancy is linked to better cognitive and behavioral functioning in early childhood.

Nutrition

- A number of developmental changes characterize infants' nutritional needs and eating behavior. Caregivers play important roles in infants' development of healthy eating patterns.

- The scientific consensus is that in most instances breast feeding is superior to bottle feeding for both the infant and the mother, although the correlational nature of studies must be considered. Severe infant malnutrition is still prevalent in many parts of the world. A special concern in low- and middle-income countries is early weaning from breast milk and hygiene problems associated with bottle feeding.

| Health | • Widespread immunization of infants has led to a significant decline in infectious diseases. Accidents are a major cause of death in infancy. These accidents include the aspiration of foreign objects, suffocation, falls, and automobile accidents. |

2 How Do Infants Develop Motor Skills? Describe infants' motor development.

| The Dynamic Systems View | • Thelen's dynamic systems theory seeks to explain how motor skills are assembled for perceiving and acting. Perception and action are coupled. According to this theory, motor skills are the result of many converging factors, such as the development of the nervous system, the body's physical properties and its movement possibilities, the goal the child is motivated to reach, and environmental support for the skill. In the dynamic systems view, motor development is far more complex than the result of a genetic blueprint. |

| Reflexes | • Reflexes—built-in reactions to stimuli—govern the newborn's behavior. They include the sucking, rooting, and Moro reflexes. The rooting and Moro reflexes disappear after three to four months. Permanent reflexes include coughing and blinking. For infants, sucking is an especially important reflex because it provides a means of obtaining nutrition. |

| Gross Motor Skills | • Gross motor skills involve large-muscle activities. Key skills developed during infancy include control of posture and walking. Although infants usually learn to walk by their first birthday, the neural pathways that allow walking begin to form earlier. The time at which infants reach milestones in the development of gross motor skills may vary by as much as several months, especially for milestones in late infancy. |

| Fine Motor Skills | • Fine motor skills involve finely tuned movements. The onset of reaching and grasping marks a significant accomplishment, and this becomes more refined during the first two years of life. |

3 How Can Infants' Sensory and Perceptual Development Be Characterized? Explain sensory and perceptual development in infancy.

| What Are Sensation and Perception? | • Sensation occurs when information interacts with sensory receptors. Perception is the interpretation of sensation. |

| The Ecological View | • The Gibsons' ecological view states that we directly perceive information that exists in the world around us. Perception brings people in contact with the environment to interact with and adapt to it. Affordances provide opportunities for interaction offered by objects that fit within our capabilities to perform activities. |

| Visual Perception | • Researchers have developed a number of methods to assess the infant's perception, including the visual preference method (which Fantz used to determine young infants' interest in looking at patterned over nonpatterned displays), habituation and dishabituation, and tracking. |

| | • The infant's visual acuity increases dramatically in the first year of life. Infants' color vision improves as they develop. Young infants systematically scan human faces. By 3 months of age, infants show size and shape constancy. At approximately 2 months of age, infants develop the ability to perceive occluded objects as complete. Infants as young as 6 months have depth perception. |

| Other Senses | • The fetus can hear several weeks prior to birth. Immediately after birth, newborns can hear, but their sensory threshold is higher than that of adults. Developmental changes in the perception of loudness, pitch, and localization of sound occur during infancy. Newborns can respond to touch and feel pain. Newborns can differentiate odors, and sensitivity to taste may be present before birth. |

| Intermodal Perception | • Early, exploratory forms of intermodal perception—the ability to relate and integrate information from two or more sensory modalities—are present in newborns and become sharper over the first year of life. |

| Nature, Nurture, and Perceptual Development | • In the past among perception researchers, nature advocates were referred to as nativists and nurture proponents were called empiricists. |

- A full contemporary account of perceptual development includes the interacting roles of nature, nurture, and the developing sensitivity to information.

- Perception and action are often not isolated but rather are coupled. Individuals perceive in order to move and move in order to perceive.

key **terms**

affordances	forebrain	marasmus	sensation
cephalocaudal pattern	grasping reflex	Moro reflex	shape constancy
cerebral cortex	gross motor skills	neuroconstructivist view	size constancy
dishabituation	habituation	perception	sucking reflex
dynamic systems theory	intermodal perception	proximodistal pattern	sudden infant death syndrome
ecological view	kwashiorkor	reflexes	(SIDS)
fine motor skills	lateralization	rooting reflex	visual preference method

key **people**

Karen Adolph	Eleanor Gibson	Patricia Kuhl	John Richards
Martha Ann Bell	James J. Gibson	Daphne Maurer	Esther Thelen
T. Berry Brazelton	William James	Amy Needham	Richard Walk
Robert Fantz	Mark Johnson	Charles Nelson	

improving the **lives of children**

STRATEGIES

Supporting the Infant's Physical Development

What are some good strategies for helping the infant develop in physically competent ways?

- Be flexible about the infant's sleep patterns. Don't try to put the infant on a rigid sleep schedule. By about 4 to 5 months of age, most infants have moved closer to adultlike sleep patterns.

- Provide the infant with good nutrition. Make sure the infant has adequate energy and nutrient intake. Provide this in a loving and supportive environment. Don't put an infant on a diet. Weaning should be gradual, not abrupt.

- Breast-feed the infant, if possible. Breast feeding provides more ideal nutrition than bottle feeding. If circumstances prevent the mother from breast feeding the infant while she is away from home, she can consider "pumping."

- Give the infant extensive opportunities to explore safe environments. Infants don't need exercise classes, but they should be provided with many opportunities to actively explore safe environments. Infants should not be restricted to small, very confined environments for any length of time.

- Don't push the infant's physical development or get upset about physical norms. In the United States, there is a tendency to want our child to grow faster than other children. Remember that there is wide individual variation in healthy physical development. Just because an infant is not at the top of a physical chart doesn't mean parents should start pushing the infant's physical skills. Infants develop at different paces. Respect and nurture the infant's individuality.

RESOURCES

Typical and Atypical Functional Brain Development

Michelle de Haan and Mark Johnson
In D. Cicchetti (Ed.), *Development and Psychopathology*
(3rd ed., 2016)
New York: Oxford University Press

Leading experts discuss many aspects of the infant's developing brain, including normal and abnormal development.

Healthy Sleep Habits, Happy Child (5th ed., 2021)

Dr. Marc Weissbluth
New York: Ballantine

A leading pediatrician describes how parents can help their infants develop better sleep habits.

The Pediatrician's Guide to Feeding Babies and Toddlers (2016)

Anthony Porto and Dina DiMaggio
New York: Ten Speed Press

Good recommendations are provided for parents to guide them in making decisions about what and how to feed their infants and toddlers.

chapter 6

COGNITIVE DEVELOPMENT IN INFANCY

chapter outline

① **What Is Piaget's Theory of Infant Development?**

Learning Goal 1 Summarize and evaluate Piaget's theory of infant development.

Cognitive Processes

The Sensorimotor Stage

Evaluating Piaget's Sensorimotor Stage

② **How Do Infants Learn, Remember, and Conceptualize?**

Learning Goal 2 Describe how infants learn, remember, and conceptualize.

Conditioning

Attention

Memory

Imitation

Concept Formation

③ **How Are Individual Differences in Infancy Assessed, and Do These Assessments Predict Intelligence?**

Learning Goal 3 Discuss infant assessment measures and the prediction of intelligence.

Measures of Infant Development

Predicting Intelligence

④ **What Is the Nature of Language, and How Does It Develop in Infancy?**

Learning Goal 4 Describe the nature of language and how it develops in infancy.

Defining Language

Language's Rule Systems

How Language Develops

Biological and Environmental Influences

An Interactionist View

Jean Piaget, the famous Swiss psychologist, was a meticulous observer of his three children: Laurent, Lucienne, and Jacqueline. His books on cognitive development are filled with these observations. Here are a few of Piaget's observations of his children in infancy (Piaget, 1952):

- At 21 days of age, "Laurent found his thumb after three attempts: prolonged sucking begins each time. But, once he has been placed on his back, he does not know how to coordinate the movement of the arms with that of the mouth and his hands draw back even when his lips are seeking them" (p. 27).

- "During the third month, thumb sucking becomes less important to Laurent because of new visual and auditory interests. But, when he cries, his thumb goes to the rescue."

- Toward the end of Lucienne's fourth month, while she is lying in her crib, Piaget hangs a doll above her feet. Lucienne thrusts her feet at the doll and makes it move. "Afterward, she looks at her motionless foot for a second, then recommences. There is no visual control of her foot, for the movements are the same when Lucienne only looks at the doll or when I place the doll over her head. On the other hand, the tactile control of the foot is apparent: after the first shakes, Lucienne makes slow foot movements as though to grasp and explore" (p. 159).

- At 11 months, "Jacqueline is seated and shakes a little bell. She then pauses abruptly in order to delicately place the bell in front of her right foot; then she kicks hard. Unable to recapture it, she grasps a ball which she then places at the same spot in order to give it another kick" (p. 225).

- At 1 year, 2 months, "Jacqueline holds in her hands an object which is new to her: a round, flat box which she turns all over, shakes, [and] rubs against the bassinet. . . . She lets it go and tries to pick it up. But she only succeeds in touching it with her index finger, without grasping it. She nevertheless makes an attempt and presses on the edge. The box then tilts up and falls again" (p. 273). Jacqueline shows an interest in this result and studies the fallen box.

topical connections *looking **back***

Impressive advances occur in the development of the brain during infancy. Engaging in various physical, cognitive, and socioemotional activities strengthens the baby's neural connections. Motor and perceptual development also are key aspects of the infant's development. An important part of this development is the coupling of perceptions and actions. In this chapter, you will build on your understanding of the infant's brain, motor, and perceptual development by further examining how infants develop their competencies, focusing on how advances in their cognitive development help them adapt to their world, and how nature and nurture affect the infant's cognitive and language development.

For Piaget, these observations reflect important changes in the infant's cognitive development. Piaget believed that infants go through a series of substages as they rapidly gain new skills during their first two years.

preview

Piaget's descriptions of infants are just the starting point for our exploration of cognitive development. Excitement and enthusiasm about the study of infant cognition have been fueled by an interest in what newborns and infants know, by continued fascination about innate and learned factors in the infant's cognitive development, and by controversies about whether infants construct their knowledge (Piaget's view) or know their world more directly. In this chapter, we will highlight the historically foundational theory of Jean Piaget and will also describe the development of learning, remembering, and conceptualizing by infants; individual differences in cognitive capabilities; and language development.

1 What Is Piaget's Theory of Infant Development?

 LG1 Summarize and evaluate Piaget's theory of infant development.

| Cognitive Processes | The Sensorimotor Stage | Evaluating Piaget's Sensorimotor Stage |

Poet Nora Perry once asked, "Who knows the thoughts of a child?" As much as anyone, Piaget knew. Through careful observations of his own three children—Laurent, Lucienne, and Jacqueline—and observations of and interviews with other children, Piaget changed perceptions of the way children think about the world. We begin this chapter with an overview of this historically foundational theory of cognitive development.

Piaget's theory was a general, unifying story of how biology and experience sculpt cognitive development. Piaget thought that just as our physical bodies have structures that enable us to adapt to the world, we build mental structures that help us to adapt to the world. Adaptation involves adjusting to new environmental demands. Piaget stressed that children actively construct their own cognitive worlds; information is not just poured into their minds from the environment. He sought to discover how children at different points in their development think about the world and how systematic changes in their thinking occur.

COGNITIVE PROCESSES

What processes do children use as they construct their knowledge of the world? Piaget developed several concepts to answer this question; especially important are schemes, assimilation, accommodation, organization, equilibrium, and equilibration.

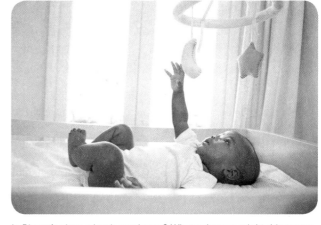

In Piaget's view, what is a scheme? What schemes might this young infant be displaying?
Wavebreak Media ltd/Alamy Stock Photo

Schemes   As the infant or child seeks to construct an understanding of the world, said Piaget (1954), the developing brain creates **schemes.** These are actions or mental representations that organize knowledge. In Piaget's theory, behavioral schemes (physical activities) characterize infancy and mental schemes (cognitive activities) develop in childhood (Thompson, 2021). A baby's schemes are structured by simple actions that can be performed on objects, such as sucking, looking, and grasping. Older children have schemes that include strategies and plans for solving problems. For example, in the descriptions at the opening of this chapter, Laurent displayed a scheme for sucking; Jacqueline displayed a scheme for investigating when she examined the box. By adulthood, we have constructed an enormous number of diverse schemes, ranging from driving a car to balancing a budget to achieving fairness.

schemes In Piaget's theory, actions or mental representations that organize knowledge.

Assimilation and Accommodation   To explain how children use and adapt their schemes, Piaget offered two concepts: assimilation and accommodation. **Assimilation** occurs when children use their existing schemes to deal with new information or experiences. **Accommodation** occurs when children adjust their schemes to take new information and experiences into account.

Think about a toddler who has learned the word *car* to identify the family's car. The toddler might call all moving vehicles on roads "cars," including motorcycles and trucks; the child has assimilated these objects to his or her existing scheme. But the child soon learns that motorcycles and trucks are not cars and fine-tunes the category to exclude motorcycles and trucks, thus accommodating the scheme.

Assimilation and accommodation operate even in very young infants. Newborns reflexively suck everything that touches their lips; they assimilate all sorts of objects into their sucking scheme. By sucking different objects, they learn about their taste, texture, shape, and so on. After several months of experience, though, they construct their understanding of the world differently by accommodating their sucking scheme. Some objects, such as fingers and the mother's breast, can be sucked, and others, such as fuzzy blankets, should not be sucked.

Organization   **Organization** in Piaget's theory is the grouping of isolated behaviors and thoughts into a higher-order system. Continual refinement of this organization is an inherent part of development. A child who has only a vague idea about how to use a hammer may also have a vague idea about how to use other tools. After learning how to use each one, the child relates these uses, grouping items into categories and organizing this knowledge.

Equilibration and Stages of Development   Assimilation and accommodation always take the child to a new understanding, according to Piaget. In trying to understand the world, the child inevitably experiences cognitive conflict, or *disequilibrium.* That is, the child is constantly faced with counterexamples to his or her existing schemes and with inconsistencies. For example, if a child believes that pouring water from a short and wide container into a tall and narrow container changes the amount of water, then the child might be puzzled by where the "extra" water came from and whether there is actually more water to drink. The puzzle creates disequilibrium; for Piaget, an internal search for equilibrium creates motivation for change. The child assimilates and accommodates, adjusting old schemes, developing new schemes, and organizing and reorganizing the old and new schemes. Eventually, the organization is fundamentally different from the old organization; it is a new way of thinking.

In short, according to Piaget, children constantly assimilate and accommodate as they seek *equilibrium*. There is considerable movement between states of cognitive equilibrium and disequilibrium as assimilation and accommodation work in concert to produce cognitive change. Piaget called this mechanism **equilibration** to describe how children shift from one stage of thought to the next.

The result of these processes, according to Piaget, is that individuals go through four stages of development. A different way of understanding the world makes each stage more advanced than the one before it. Cognition is *qualitatively* different in one stage compared with another. In other words, the way children reason at one stage is different from the way they reason at another stage. In this chapter, our focus is on Piaget's stage of infant cognitive development. In later chapters, when we study cognitive development in early, middle, and late childhood, and in adolescence, we explore the other three Piagetian stages.

THE SENSORIMOTOR STAGE

The **sensorimotor stage** lasts from birth to about 2 years of age. In this stage, infants construct an understanding of the world by coordinating sensory experiences (such as seeing and hearing) with physical, motoric actions—hence the term "sensorimotor." At the beginning of this stage, newborns have little more than reflexes with which to work. At the end of the sensorimotor stage, 2-year-olds can produce complex sensorimotor patterns and use basic symbols. We first summarize Piaget's descriptions of how infants develop. Later we consider criticisms of his view.

developmental **connection**

Cognitive Theory

Recall the main characteristics of Piaget's four stages of cognitive development. Connect to "Introduction."

assimilation Piagetian concept involving incorporation of new information into existing schemes.

accommodation Piagetian concept of adjusting schemes to fit new information and experiences.

organization Piaget's concept of grouping isolated behaviors and thoughts into a higher-order system, a more smoothly functioning cognitive system.

equilibration A mechanism that Piaget proposed to explain how children shift from one stage of thought to the next.

sensorimotor stage The first of Piaget's stages, which lasts from birth to about 2 years of age, in which infants construct an understanding of the world by coordinating sensory experiences (such as seeing and hearing) with motoric actions.

Substage	Age	Description	Example
1 Simple reflexes	Birth to 1 month	Coordination of sensation and action through reflexive behaviors.	Rooting, sucking, and grasping reflexes; newborns suck reflexively when their lips are touched.
2 First habits and primary circular reactions	1 to 4 months	Coordination of sensation and two types of schemes: habits (reflex) and primary circular reactions (reproduction of an event that initially occurred by chance). Main focus is still on the infant's body.	Repeating a body sensation first experienced by chance (sucking thumb, for example); then infants might accommodate actions by sucking their thumb differently from how they suck on a nipple.
3 Secondary circular reactions	4 to 8 months	Infants become more object-oriented, moving beyond self-preoccupation; repeat actions that bring interesting or pleasurable results.	An infant coos when a person hands an interesting toy to them; after the person takes the toy back, the infant coos again.
4 Coordination of secondary circular reactions	8 to 12 months	Coordination of vision and touch—hand-eye coordination; coordination of schemes and intentionality.	Infant manipulates a stick in order to bring an attractive toy within reach.
5 Tertiary circular reactions, novelty, and curiosity	12 to 18 months	Infants become intrigued by the many properties of objects and by the many things they can make happen to objects; they experiment with new behavior.	A block can be made to fall, spin, hit another object, and slide across the ground.
6 Internalization of schemes	18 to 24 months	Infants develop the ability to use basic symbols and form enduring mental representations.	An infant mimics the motion of a hand mixer by twirling their hand after having observed the mixer the previous day.

FIGURE 1
PIAGET'S SIX SUBSTAGES OF SENSORIMOTOR DEVELOPMENT

Substages   Piaget divided the sensorimotor stage into six substages: (1) simple reflexes; (2) first habits and primary circular reactions; (3) secondary circular reactions; (4) coordination of secondary circular reactions; (5) tertiary circular reactions, novelty, and curiosity; and (6) internalization of schemes (see Figure 1).

1. **Simple reflexes,** the first sensorimotor substage, correspond to the first month after birth. In this substage, sensation and action are coordinated primarily through reflexive behaviors such as rooting and sucking. Soon the infant produces behaviors that resemble reflexes in the absence of the usual stimulus for the reflex. For example, a newborn will suck a nipple or bottle only when it is placed directly in the baby's mouth or touched to the lips. But soon the infant might suck when a bottle or nipple is only nearby. The infant is initiating action and is actively structuring experiences in the first month of life.

2. **First habits and primary circular reactions** is the second sensorimotor substage, which develops between 1 and 4 months of age. In this substage, the infant coordinates sensation and two types of schemes: habits and primary circular reactions. A habit is a scheme based on a reflex that has become completely separated from its eliciting stimulus. For example, infants in substage 1 suck when bottles are put to their lips or when they see a bottle. Infants in substage 2 might suck even when no bottle is present. A circular reaction is a repetitive action.

   A **primary circular reaction** is a scheme based on the attempt to reproduce an event that initially occurred by chance. For example, suppose an infant accidentally sucks their fingers when they are placed near the mouth. Later, the infant searches for their fingers to suck them again, but the fingers do not cooperate because the infant cannot coordinate visual and manual actions.

   Habits and circular reactions are stereotyped—that is, the infant repeats them the same way each time. During this substage, the infant's own body continues to be the infant's center of attention. There is no outward pull by environmental events.

How might assimilation and accommodation be involved in infants' sucking?
Brand X Pictures/Stockbyte/Getty Images

simple reflexes Piaget's first sensorimotor substage, which corresponds to the first month after birth. In this substage, sensation and action are coordinated primarily through reflexive behaviors.

first habits and primary circular reactions Piaget's second sensorimotor substage, which develops between 1 and 4 months of age. In this substage, the infant coordinates sensation and two types of schemes: habits and primary circular reactions.

primary circular reaction A scheme based on the attempt to reproduce an event that initially occurred by chance.

This 17-month-old is in Piaget's stage of tertiary circular reactions. *What might infants do that suggests that they are in this stage?*

Tom Grill/Corbis/Getty Images

3. **Secondary circular reactions** is the third sensorimotor substage, which develops between 4 and 8 months of age. In this substage, the infant becomes more object-oriented, moving beyond preoccupation with the self. The infant's schemes are not intentional or goal-directed, but they are repeated because of their consequences. By chance, an infant might shake a rattle. The infant repeats this action for the sake of its fascination. This is a *secondary circular reaction:* an action repeated because of its consequences. The infant also imitates some simple actions, such as the baby talk or burbling of adults, and some physical gestures. However, the baby imitates only actions that they are already able to produce.

4. **Coordination of secondary circular reactions** is Piaget's fourth sensorimotor substage, which develops between 8 and 12 months of age. To progress into this substage, the infant must coordinate vision and touch, eye and hand. Actions become more outwardly directed. Significant changes during this substage involve the coordination of schemes and intentionality. Infants readily combine and recombine previously learned schemes in a coordinated way. They might look at an object and grasp it simultaneously, or they might visually inspect a toy, such as a rattle, and finger it simultaneously, exploring it tactilely. Actions are even more outwardly directed than before. Related to this coordination is the second achievement—the presence of intentionality. For example, infants might manipulate a stick in order to bring a desired toy within reach or they might knock over one block to reach and play with another one.

5. **Tertiary circular reactions, novelty, and curiosity** is Piaget's fifth sensorimotor substage, which develops between 12 and 18 months of age. In this substage, infants become intrigued by the many properties of objects and by the many things that they can make happen to objects. A block can be made to fall, spin, hit another object, and slide across the ground. *Tertiary circular reactions* are schemes in which the infant purposely explores new possibilities with objects, continually doing new things to them and exploring the results. This stage marks the starting point for human curiosity and interest in novelty.

6. **Internalization of schemes** is Piaget's sixth and final sensorimotor substage, which develops between 18 and 24 months of age. In this substage, the infant develops the ability to use basic or "primitive" symbols. For Piaget, a symbol is an internalized sensory image or word that represents an event. Primitive symbols permit the infant to think about concrete events without directly acting them out or perceiving them. Moreover, symbols allow the infant to manipulate and transform the represented events in simple ways. In a favorite Piagetian example, Piaget's young daughter saw a matchbox being opened and closed. Later, she mimicked the event by opening and closing her mouth. This was an obvious expression of her image of the event.

secondary circular reactions Piaget's third sensorimotor substage, which develops between 4 and 8 months of age. In this substage, the infant becomes more object-oriented, moving beyond preoccupation with the self.

coordination of secondary circular reactions Piaget's fourth sensorimotor substage, which develops between 8 and 12 months of age. Actions become more outwardly directed, and infants coordinate schemes and act with intentionality.

tertiary circular reactions, novelty, and curiosity Piaget's fifth sensorimotor substage, which develops between 12 and 18 months of age. In this substage, infants become intrigued by the many properties of objects and by the many things that they can make happen to objects.

internalization of schemes Piaget's sixth and final sensorimotor substage, which develops between 18 and 24 months of age. In this substage, the infant develops the ability to use basic symbols.

object permanence The understanding that objects continue to exist, even when they cannot directly be seen, heard, or touched.

Object Permanence   Imagine how chaotic and unpredictable your life would be if you could not distinguish between yourself and your world. Piaget thought that this was what the life of a newborn must be like, with no differentiation between the self and the world; objects have no separate, permanent existence.

By the end of the sensorimotor period, infants acquire **object permanence,** the understanding that objects continue to exist even when they cannot be seen, heard, or touched. Piaget believed that infants develop object permanence in substages that correspond to the six substages of sensorimotor development described previously.

Object permanence is studied by watching an infant's reaction when an interesting object disappears (see Figure 2). If infants search for the object, it is assumed that they believe it continues to exist.

Object permanence is just one of the basic concepts about the physical world developed by babies. To Piaget, children, even infants, are much like little scientists, examining the world to see how it works. But how can scientists determine what these "baby scientists" are finding out about the world and at what age they're finding it out? To answer this question, read the *Connecting with Research* interlude.

FIGURE 2

OBJECT PERMANENCE. Piaget argued that object permanence is one of infancy's landmark cognitive accomplishments. For this 5-month-old, "out-of-sight" is literally out of mind. The infant looks at the toy dog (*left*), but does not search for it when their view of the toy is blocked (right). Several months later, the baby searches for hidden toys, reflecting the presence of object permanence.

(both): Science History Images/Alamy Stock Photo

connecting with research

How Do Researchers Study Infants' Understanding of Object Permanence and Causality?

Key Points:

- Researchers explored infants' reasoning skills.
- Infants demonstrated object permanence and causal reasoning earlier than Piaget proposed.

Two accomplishments of infants that Piaget examined were the development of object permanence and the child's understanding of causality. Let's examine two classic research studies that address these topics.

In both studies, Renée Baillargeon and her colleagues used a research method that involves *violation of expectations*. In this method, infants see an event happen as it normally would. Then the event is changed, often in a way that violates what the infant expects to see. When infants look longer at the event that violates their expectations, it indicates they are surprised by it.

In one classic study focused on object permanence, researchers showed infants a toy car that moved down an inclined track, disappeared behind a screen, and then reemerged at the other end, still on the track (Baillargeon & DeVos, 1991). After this sequence was repeated several times, something different occurred: A toy mouse was placed behind the tracks but was hidden by the screen while the car rolled by. This was the "possible" event. Then, the researchers created an "impossible event": The toy mouse was placed on the tracks but was secretly removed after the screen was lowered so that the car seemed to go through the mouse. In this study, infants as young as 3½ months of age looked longer at the impossible event than at the

possible event, an indication that they were surprised by it. Their surprise suggested that they remembered not only the existence of the toy mouse (object permanence) but also its location.

Another classic study focused on the infant's understanding of causality (Kotovsky & Baillargeon, 1994). In this research, a cylinder rolls down a ramp and hits a toy bug at the bottom of the ramp. By 5½ and 6½ months of age, after infants have seen how far the bug will be pushed by a medium-sized cylinder, their reactions indicate that they understand that the bug will roll farther if it is hit by a large cylinder than if it is hit by a small cylinder. Thus, by the middle of the first year of life, these infants understand that the size of a moving object determines how far it will move a stationary object that it collides with.

In Baillargeon's (Lin, Stavans, & Baillargeon, 2021) view, infants have a preadapted, innate bias called the principle of persistence that explains their assumption that objects don't change their properties—including how solid they are, their location, their color, and their form—unless some external factor (a person who moves the object, for example) obviously intervenes. Shortly, we revisit the extent to which nature and nurture are at work in the changes that take place in the infant's cognitive development.

The research findings discussed in this interlude and other research indicate that infants develop object permanence and causal reasoning much earlier than Piaget proposed (Baillargeon, 2016; Lin, Stavans, & Baillargeon, 2021). Indeed, as you will see in the next section, a major theme of infant cognitive development research today is that infants are more cognitively competent than Piaget envisioned.

How does the discovery of infants' early cognitive competence affect our understanding of Piaget's research on infant development?

EVALUATING PIAGET'S SENSORIMOTOR STAGE

Piaget opened up a new way of looking at infants, but some of Piaget's explanations for the cause of cognitive changes in development are debated. In the past several decades, sophisticated experimental techniques have been devised to study infants, and there have been a large number of research studies on infant development. Much of the new research suggests that Piaget's view of sensorimotor development needs to be modified (Adolph & Hoch, 2021; Hayne & Herbert, 2021; Van de Vandervoort & Hamlin, 2018).

The A-Not-B Error   One modification concerns Piaget's claim that certain processes are crucial in transitions from one stage to the next. The data do not always support his explanations. For example, in Piaget's theory, an important feature in the progression into substage 4, *coordination of secondary circular reactions*, is an infant's inclination to search for a hidden object in a familiar location rather than to look for the object in a new location. Thus, if a toy is hidden twice, initially at location A and subsequently at location B, 8- to 12-month-old infants search correctly at location A initially. But when the toy is subsequently hidden at location B, they make the mistake of continuing to search for it at location A. **A-not-B error** (also called $A\overline{B}$ error) is the term used to describe this common mistake. Older infants are less likely to make the A-not-B error because their concept of object permanence is more complete.

However, a variety of factors affect whether infants make A-not-B errors. For example, when only the hands and arms rather than the full body of an experimenter are visible, 9-month-old infants are less likely to make A-not-B errors, suggesting that part of the error is due to infants' imitation of body movements (Boyer, Harding, & Bertenthal, 2017). Likewise, A-not-B errors are sensitive to the delay between hiding the object at B and the infant's attempt to find it (Buss, Ross-Sheehy, Reynolds, 2018). Thus, the A-not-B error might be due to a failure in memory. And A-not-B performance may be linked to attention as well. For example, 5-month-olds' more focused attention on a separate task involving a puppet was linked to better performance on an A-not-B task that involved locating an object after it was hidden from view (Marcovitch & others, 2016). Another explanation is that infants tend to repeat a previous motor behavior (MacNeill & others, 2018).

Perceptual Development and Expectation   Another necessary update is that since Piaget's time, infants' perceptual abilities and cognition have been found to be more advanced at earlier ages than Piaget theorized (Barrouillet, 2015).

Research suggests that infants begin to develop the ability to understand how the world works at a very early age (Lin, Stavans, & Baillargeon, 2021). In experiments designed to test infants' expectations of how physical objects and people will behave, infants are often placed before a puppet stage and shown a series of actions that would be either expected or unexpected, depending on one's understanding of how the world works. How long infants look at each series of actions is used as a measure of surprise because babies look longer at surprising than at expected events. Infants look longer in experiments that violate their expectations about the physical or social world than in experiments in which objects and people behave as infants expect them to. For example, by as early as 5 months of age, infants understand differences between how solid substances and liquid substances will behave and even have expectations about how potentially trickier granular substances, such as sand, will behave (Hespos & others, 2016). Likewise, from early in life, infants have expectations about how other people will behave. In a study in which infants were shown videos of a stranger either comforting or ignoring a crying infant, even 4-month-old infants were more surprised by the video in which the stranger ignored rather than comforted the infant (Jin & others, 2018).

One criticism of "looking time" studies is that this behavior might be a better measure of perceptual expectations than knowledge or understanding. Thus, researchers advocate using different types of methodologies to study infant cognition rather than relying on any single approach. For instance, newer brain-imaging techniques and measures of physiology (such as heart rate) offer options for assessing infants' cognitive development (Reynolds & Richards, 2019; Yates, Ellis, & Turk-Browne, 2021).

In sum, and contrary to Piaget's view of life within the first year following birth, infants have learned how objects behave in relation to other objects and in relation to laws of the

---

developmental **connection**

Perception

Eleanor Gibson was a pioneer in crafting the ecological view of development. Connect to "Physical Development in Infancy."

physical world, such as gravity. Infants also have learned that people generally behave in goal-directed ways toward objects (Corbetta & Fagard, 2017). As infants develop, their experiences with objects and people help them to understand physical laws and the social world, respectively (Ullman & others, 2018).

core knowledge approach View that infants are born with domain-specific innate knowledge systems, such as those involving space, number sense, object permanence, and language.

Nature and Nurture   Both nature and nurture play important roles in infant development. The **core knowledge approach** hypothesizes that infants are born with domain-specific innate knowledge systems involving space, number sense, object permanence, and language (which we discuss later in this chapter). Advocates for this viewpoint suggest that evidence of this knowledge is present earlier than Piaget surmised (Jin & Baillargeon, 2017; Spelke, 2017). Strongly influenced by evolution, the core knowledge domains are theorized to be prewired to allow infants to make sense of their world (Goupil & Kouider, 2019). In this approach, the innate core knowledge domains form a foundation around which more mature cognitive functioning and learning develop.

Researchers also have explored whether preverbal infants might have a built-in, innate sense of morality (Van de Vandervoort & Hamlin, 2018). In this research, infants as young as 4 months are more likely to make visually guided reaches toward a puppet who has acted as a helper (such as helping someone get up a hill, assisting in opening a box, or giving a ball back) rather than toward a puppet who has acted as a hinderer to others' efforts to achieve such goals (Hamlin, 2014). However, the emergence of morality in infancy may not be innate but instead may develop through reciprocal interactions between infants and others (Dahl & Killen, 2018).

The hypothesis that young infants have innate core knowledge is controversial and debated by theorists and scientists (Moore, 2009; Spencer & others, 2009). For example, one criticism is that infants in the experiments are merely responding to changes in the display that violated their expectations. Furthermore, even young infants already have experienced thousands of hours of events that inform their emerging perception and understanding of their world (Aslin, 2017; Johnston, 2008). For example, over the first six months following birth, infants gradually demonstrate the ability to discern partial or complete object occlusion (Bremner, Slater, & Johnson, 2015), which contrasts with the idea of an innate ability to know about the physical permanence of hidden objects. Similarly, there is a gradual developmental progression in how infants perceive and move their bodies through their physical environments, with cumulative experiences being crucial to the development of the needed perceptual and motor skills (Adolph, Hoch, & Cole, 2018). Current perspectives tend to emphasize both nature and nurture, working together. If core knowledge domains are present at birth, they may function as biases that provide starting points for learning, with the experiences of new and surprising events then requiring infants to update their predictions of how the physical and social worlds operate (Stahl & Feigenson, 2019).

Conclusions   In sum, many researchers conclude that certain aspects of Piaget's theory hold true—for example, that young children play an active role in constructing their knowledge. However, many also have concluded that Piaget's theory lacks precision and that infants have greater capacities than he realized. As researchers have examined the specific ways that infants learn, the field of infant cognition has become very specialized. Many researchers are at work on different questions, with no general theory emerging that can connect all of the different findings. Their theories often are local theories, focused on specific research questions, rather than grand theories like Piaget's (Kuhn, 1998).

If there is a unifying theme, it is that investigators in infant development seek to understand more precisely how developmental changes in cognition take place. As they seek to identify more precisely the contributions of nature and nurture to infant development, researchers face the difficult task of determining whether the course of acquiring information, which is very rapid in some domains, is better accounted for by an early emerging and perhaps innate set of biases (that is, core knowledge) or by the extensive input of environmental experiences to which the infant is exposed (Aslin, 2017). Among the unifying themes in the study of infant cognition are seeking to understand more precisely how developmental changes in cognition take place, to answer questions about the relative importance of nature and nurture, and to examine the brain's role in cognitive development (Amso & Tummeltshammer, 2021; Richards & Conte, 2021). Recall that exploring connections between brain, cognition, and development involves the field of developmental cognitive neuroscience.

developmental **connection**

Nature and Nurture

Nature and nurture are both important in understanding perceptual development. Connect to "Physical Development in Infancy."

What revisions in Piaget's theory of sensorimotor development do contemporary researchers recommend?
baobao ou/Flickr/Getty Images

Review *Connect* Reflect

LG1 Summarize and evaluate Piaget's theory of infant development.

Review

- What cognitive processes are important in Piaget's theory?
- What are some characteristics of Piaget's stage of sensorimotor development?
- What are some contributions and criticisms of Piaget's sensorimotor stage?

Connect

- You just read that during the first year of life infants develop an

understanding of how objects behave in relation to other objects in space. What physical developments that occur during the first year of life might contribute to the infant's understanding of these concepts?

Reflect *Your Own Personal Journey of Life*

- What are some implications of Piaget's theory of infant development for parenting?

2 How Do Infants Learn, Remember, and Conceptualize?

 Describe how infants learn, remember, and conceptualize.

Conditioning   Attention   Memory   Imitation   Concept Formation

When Piaget hung a doll above 4-month-old Lucienne's feet, as described at the beginning of the chapter, would she remember the doll? If Piaget had rewarded her for moving the doll with her foot, would the reward have affected Lucienne's behavior? If he had shown her how to shake the doll's hand, could she have imitated him? If he had shown her a different doll, could she have formed the concept of a "doll"?

Questions like these might be examined by researchers taking behavioral and social cognitive or information processing approaches. In contrast with Piaget's theory, these approaches do not describe infant development in terms of stages. Instead, they document gradual changes in the infant's ability to understand and process information about the world. In this section, we explore what researchers using these approaches can tell us about how infants learn, remember, and conceptualize.

CONDITIONING

Earlier, we described Pavlov's classical conditioning (in which, as a result of pairing, a new stimulus comes to elicit a response previously given to another stimulus) and Skinner's operant conditioning (in which the consequences of a behavior produce changes in the probability of the behavior's occurrence). Infants can learn through both types of conditioning. For example, if an infant's behavior is followed by a rewarding stimulus, the behavior is likely to recur.

Operant conditioning has been especially helpful to researchers in their efforts to determine what infants perceive (Tripathi & others, 2019). For example, infants will suck faster on a nipple when the sucking behavior is followed by a visual display, music, or a human voice (Rovee-Collier, 2008).

Carolyn Rovee-Collier (Rovee-Collier & Barr, 2010) conducted research demonstrating that infants can remember perceptual-motor information after being conditioned. In a characteristic experiment, a baby was placed in a crib underneath an elaborate mobile and one end of a ribbon would be tied to the baby's ankle and the other end to the mobile. The baby would kick and make the mobile move (see Figure 3). The movement of the mobile was the reinforcing stimulus (which increased the baby's kicking behavior) in this experiment. Weeks later, the baby was returned to the crib, but its foot was not tied to the mobile. The baby kicked, which suggests it had retained the information that if it kicked a leg, the mobile would move.

ATTENTION

Attention, the focusing of mental resources on select information, improves cognitive processing on many tasks (Bell & Broomell, 2022; Wu & Scerif, 2018). At any one time, though, people

---

- - - - - - - →

developmental connection

Theories

The behavioral and social cognitive approaches emphasize continuity rather than discontinuity in development. Connect to "Introduction."

← - - - - - - -

attention The focusing of mental resources.

can pay attention to only a limited amount of information. Even newborns can visually detect a contour and fix their attention on it. Older infants scan patterns more thoroughly. By 4 months, infants can selectively attend to an object. One study that examined 7- and 8-month-old infants' visual attention to sequences of events found that the amount of information had to be "just right"; the infants tended to look away from events that were too simple or complex, preferring instead to look at those of intermediate complexity (Kidd, Piantadosi, & Aslin, 2012).

From infancy onward, children allocate their attention in different ways (Richards & Conte, 2021). Attention in the first year of life is dominated by an *orienting/investigative process* (Colombo & Salley, 2015). This process involves directing attention to potentially important locations in the environment (that is, *where*) and recognizing objects and their features (such as color and form) (that is, *what*). From 3 to 9 months of age, infants rapidly change to deploy their attention more flexibly and quickly (Xie, Mallin, & Richards, 2018). Another important type of attention is *sustained attention,* also referred to as vigilance. New stimuli typically cause an orienting response followed by sustained attention. Sustained attention allows infants to learn about and remember characteristics of a stimulus as it becomes familiar. Infants as young as 3 months can engage in 5 to 10 seconds of sustained attention. The length of sustained attention increases over the second year (Reynolds & Romano, 2016).

Habituation and Dishabituation

Closely linked with attention are the processes of habituation and dishabituation (Wang & Feigenson, 2021). If you say the same word or show the same toy to a baby several times in a row, the baby usually pays less attention to it each time. This suggests they are bored with it and demonstrates the process of *habituation*—decreased responsiveness to a stimulus after repeated presentations of the stimulus. *Dishabituation* is the recovery of a habituated response after the stimulus changes to something new. Some of the measures that researchers use to study whether habituation is occurring include sucking behavior (sucking stops when an infant attends to a novel object), heart rates, and the length of time the infant looks at an object.

Infants' attention is strongly affected by novelty and habituation (Lloyd-Fox & others, 2019). When an object becomes familiar, attention becomes shorter, making infants more vulnerable to distraction.

Researchers study habituation to determine the extent to which infants can see, hear, smell, taste, and experience touch (Monroy & others, 2019; Sicard-Cras & others, 2022). Studies of habituation can also indicate whether infants recognize something they have previously experienced. Habituation provides a measure of an infant's maturity and well-being. Infants who have brain damage do not habituate well.

Knowing about habituation and dishabituation can help parents interact effectively with infants. Infants respond to changes in stimulation. Sensitive parents can tell when an infant shows an interest and realize that they may have to repeat something many times for the infant to process information. But if the stimulation is repeated often, the infant stops responding to the parent. In parent-infant interaction, it is important for parents to do novel things and to repeat them often until the infant stops responding. The parent stops or changes behaviors when the infant redirects their attention, and the parent notices this as part of a pattern of sensitive and responsive caregiving (Deák & others, 2018).

Joint Attention

Another aspect of attention that is an important part of infant development is **joint attention,** in which individuals focus together on the same object or event (Piazza & others, 2020). Joint attention requires (1) an ability to track another's behavior, such as following someone else's gaze; (2) one person directing another's attention; and (3) reciprocal interaction. Early in infancy, joint attention usually involves a caregiver pointing or using words to direct an infant's attention. Emerging forms of joint attention occur at about 7 to 8 months, but it is not until toward the end of the first year that joint attention skills are frequently observed (Mundy, 2018). Joint attention especially improves between 9 and 12 months of age (Boyer, Harding, & Bertenthal, 2020). In an illustrative study (Brooks & Meltzoff, 2005), at 10 to 11 months of age infants first began engaging in "gaze following," looking where another person has just looked. By their first birthday, infants have begun to direct

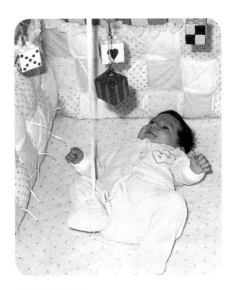

FIGURE 3

CONDITIONING AND MEMORY IN INFANTS. In Rovee-Collier's experiment, operant conditioning was used to demonstrate that infants as young as 2½ months can retain information from the experience of being conditioned. *What did infants recall in Rovee-Collier's experiment?*
Dr. Carolyn Rovee-Collier

developmental **connection**

Attention

In early childhood, children make significant advances in sustained attention. Connect to "Cognitive Development in Early Childhood."

This young infant's attention is riveted on the yellow toy duck that has just been placed there. The infant's attention to the toy duck will be strongly regulated by the processes of habituation and dishabituation. *What characterizes these processes?*
Sporrer/Rupp/Cultura/Getty Images

joint attention Individuals focusing on the same object or event; requires the ability to track another's behavior, one person directing another's attention, and reciprocal interaction.

memory A central feature of cognitive development, involving the retention of information over time.

implicit memory Memory without conscious recollection; involves skills and routine procedures that are automatically performed.

explicit memory Conscious memory of facts and experiences.

FIGURE 4

JOINT ATTENTION. A mother and her infant engaging in joint attention. *What about this photograph tells you that joint attention is occurring? Why is joint attention an important aspect of infant development?*

Tom Merton/OJO Images/Getty Images

How Would You...?

If you were a **human development and family studies professional,** what strategies would you recommend to help parents improve an infant's development of attention?

Age Group	Length of Delay
6-month-olds	24 hours
9-month-olds	1 month
10–11-month-olds	3 months
13–14-month-olds	4–6 months
20-month-olds	12 months

FIGURE 5

AGE-RELATED CHANGES IN THE LENGTH OF TIME OVER WHICH MEMORY OCCURS
Source: Bauer, P. "Learning and memory: Like a horse and carriage." In *Learning and the infant mind,* edited by Woodward, Amanda, and Amy Needham. New York: Oxford University Press, 2009.

adults' attention to objects that capture their interest using vocalizations and gestures (Cochet & Byrne, 2016).

Joint attention plays important roles in many aspects of infant development and considerably increases infants' ability to learn from other people, as illustrated in Figure 4 (Piazza & others, 2020). Nowhere is this more apparent than in observations of interchanges between caregivers and infants while the infants are learning language (Salo, Rowe, & Reeb-Sutherland, 2018). When caregivers and infants frequently engage in joint attention, infants say their first word earlier and develop a larger vocabulary (Mastin & Vogt, 2016). These differences are related to subsequent language and non-language cognitive skills in the toddler years (Masek & others, 2021; Miller & Marcovitch, 2015).

Joint attention skills in infancy and beyond also are associated with the development of self-regulation later in childhood. For example, one study in which mothers and infants were observed together and their behaviors were coded by researchers revealed that mother and school-aged children's joint attention was linked to self-regulation and other scaffolded learning skills and that these mother and child attentive behaviors were dynamic and co-coordinated during play (Leith, Yuill, & Pike, 2018). And in other research, infants who initiated joint attention at 14 months of age had higher executive function at 18 months of age (Miller & Marcovitch, 2015). Later in this chapter in our discussion of language, we further discuss joint attention as an early predictor of language development in older infants and toddlers.

MEMORY

Memory is the retention of information over time. Attention plays an important role in memory as part of a process called *encoding,* which is the process by which information gets into memory. What can infants remember, and when?

Some researchers, such as Rovee-Collier (Rovee-Collier & Barr, 2010), have concluded that infants as young as 2 to 6 months can remember some experiences through 1½ to 2 years of age. However, the infants in Rovee-Collier's experiments are displaying only implicit memory (Jabès & Nelson, 2015). **Implicit memory** refers to memory without conscious recollection—memories of skills and routine procedures that are performed automatically after being practiced and repeated. In contrast, **explicit memory** refers to the conscious memory of facts and experiences.

When people think about long-term memory, they are usually referring to explicit memory. Most researchers find that babies do not show explicit memory until the second half of the first year (Bauer & Larkina, 2016). Then explicit memory improves substantially during the second year of life (Lukowski & Bauer, 2014). In an illustrative early longitudinal study, infants were assessed several times during their second year (Bauer & others, 2000). Older infants showed more accurate memory and required fewer reminders to demonstrate their memory than younger infants. Figure 5 summarizes how long infants of different ages can remember information. Six-month-olds can remember information for 24 hours, but by 20 months of age infants can remember information they encountered 12 months earlier.

What changes in the brain are linked to infants' memory development? From about 6 to 12 months of age, the maturation of the hippocampus and the surrounding cerebral cortex, especially the frontal lobes, makes the emergence of explicit memory possible (Jabès & Nelson, 2015) (see Figure 6). Explicit memory continues to improve in the second year and beyond as these brain structures further mature and connections between them increase (Hayne & Herbert, 2021). Less is known about the areas of the brain involved in implicit memory in infancy.

Let's examine another aspect of long-term memory. Do you remember your third birthday party? Probably not. Most adults can remember little if anything from the first three years of their life (Riggins & others, 2016). This is called *infantile,* or *childhood, amnesia.* The few reported adult memories of life at age 2 or 3 are at best somewhat unclear and inaccurate (Li, Callaghan, & Richardson, 2014). Even elementary school children do not remember much from their early childhood years.

What is the cause of infantile amnesia? One reason older children and adults have difficulty recalling events from their infant and early childhood years is that during these early years the prefrontal lobes of the brain are immature; this area of the brain, and its network of connections with the hippocampus, is believed to play an important role in long-term memories (Riggins & Bauer, 2022).

Patricia Bauer and her colleagues (Bauer & Larkina, 2016; Riggins & Bauer, 2022) have studied when infantile amnesia begins to occur. In one study, children's memory for events that occurred at 3 years of age was periodically assessed through age 9 (Bauer & Larkina, 2014). By 8 to 9 years of age, children's memory of events that occurred at 3 years of age began to significantly fade away. In Bauer's (2015) view, the processes that account for these developmental changes are early, gradual development of the ability to form, retain, and later retrieve memories of personally relevant past events followed by an accelerated rate of forgetting in childhood.

In sum, most of young infants' conscious memories appear to be fragile and short-lived, although their implicit memory of perceptual-motor actions can be substantial. By the end of the second year, long-term memory is more substantial and reliable.

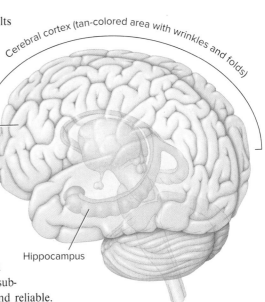

IMITATION

Can infants imitate someone else's emotional expressions? If an adult smiles, will the baby follow with a smile? If an adult protrudes their lower lip, wrinkles their forehead, and frowns, will the baby show a sad face?

Infant development researcher Andrew Meltzoff (Meltzoff & Marshall, 2018, 2020) has conducted numerous studies of infants' imitative abilities. He sees infants' imitative abilities as biologically based because infants can imitate a facial expression within the first few days after birth. He also emphasizes that the infant's imitative abilities do not resemble a hardwired response but rather involve flexibility and adaptability. In Meltzoff's observations of infants across the first 72 hours of life, the infants gradually displayed more complete imitation of an adult's facial expression, such as protruding the tongue or opening the mouth wide.

Meltzoff concludes that infants don't imitate everything they see, and they often make creative imitation errors. He also argues that beginning at birth there is an interplay between learning by observing and learning by doing (Piaget emphasized learning by doing).

Not all experts on infant development accept Meltzoff's conclusions that newborns are capable of imitation. Some say that these babies were engaging in little more than automatic responses to a stimulus (Oostenbroek & others, 2016; see Verde-Cagiao, Nieto, & Campos, 2022, for overview of different perspectives).

Deferred imitation occurs after a time delay of hours or days. Piaget held that deferred imitation doesn't occur until about 18 months of age. Meltzoff's research suggested that it occurs much earlier. In one classic early study, Meltzoff (1988) demonstrated that 9-month-old infants could imitate actions—such as pushing a recessed button in a box, which produced a beeping sound—that they had seen performed 24 hours earlier. In a subsequent study, engagement in deferred imitation at 9 months of age was a strong predictor of more extensive production of communicative gestures at 14 months of age (Heimann & others, 2006).

CONCEPT FORMATION

Along with attention, memory, and imitation, concepts are key aspects of infants' cognitive development (Oakes, 2020; Quinn, 2016). **Concepts** are cognitive groupings of similar objects, events, people, or ideas. Without concepts, you would see each object and event as unique; you would not be able to make any generalizations.

Do infants have concepts? Yes, they do, although we do not know just how early concept formation begins (Ferguson & Waxman, 2017). Using habituation experiments like those described earlier in the chapter, some researchers have found that infants as young as 3 to 4 months can group together objects with similar appearances, such as animals (Quinn, 2016). This research capitalizes on the knowledge that infants are more likely to look at a novel object than a familiar object.

How Would You...?
If you were an **educator,** how would you talk with parents about the importance of their infant developing concepts?

deferred imitation Imitation that occurs after a delay of hours or days.

concepts Cognitive groupings of similar objects, events, people, or ideas.

FIGURE 7

CATEGORIZATION IN 9- TO 11-MONTH-OLDS.
These are the stimuli used in the study that indicated
9- to 11-month-old infants categorize perceptually
similar objects as different (birds and planes) (Mandler
& McDonough, 1993).

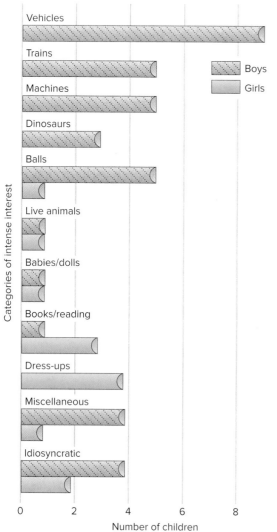

FIGURE 8

**CATEGORIZATION OF BOYS' AND GIRLS' INTENSE
INTERESTS**

Jean Mandler (2012) argues that these early categorizations are best described as *perceptual categorization*. That is, the categorizations are based on similar perceptual features of objects, such as size, color, and movement, as well as parts of objects, such as legs for animals. Mandler concludes that it is not until about 7 to 9 months of age that infants form *conceptual* categories rather than just making perceptual discriminations between different categories. In one early illustrative study of 9- to 11-month-olds, infants classified birds as animals and airplanes as vehicles even though the objects were perceptually similar—airplanes and birds with their wings spread (Mandler & McDonough, 1993) (see Figure 7).

In addition to infants categorizing items on the basis of external, perceptual features such as shape, color, and parts, they also may categorize items on the basis of prototypes, or averages, that they extract from the structural regularities of items (Althaus & others, 2020; Rakison & Lawson, 2013).

Further advances in categorization occur in the second year of life (Poulin-Dubois & Pauen, 2017). Early concepts in infancy are very broad, such as "food" or "animal." As cognitive development proceeds in the second year, these categories become more distinct and precise, such as "fruit" and then "apple," or "flying animal" and then "bird." Also, in the second year, infants often categorize objects on the basis of their shape—a strategy that they move beyond later in early childhood (Schlegelmilch & Wertz, 2021; Ware, 2017).

Learning to put things into the correct categories—what makes something one kind of thing rather than another kind of thing, such as what makes a bird a bird, or a fish a fish—is an important aspect of cognitive development. As infant development researcher Alison Gopnik (2010) once pointed out, "If you can sort the world into the right categories—put things in the right boxes—then you've got a big advance on understanding the world."

Do some very young children develop an intense, passionate interest in a particular category of objects or activities? They do—and this emerges strongly from late infancy into early childhood. One study found clear gender difference in preferences, with an intense interest in particular objects or categories stronger among boys than among girls, and preference for creative and socially interactive interests for girls more so than boys (Neitzel, Alexander, & Johnson, 2019). Categorization of boys' intense interests focused on vehicles, trains, machines, dinosaurs, and balls; girls' intense interests were more likely to involve dress-ups and books/reading (see Figure 8). When Alex (a grandson of one of the authors) was 18 to 24 months old, he already had developed an intense, passionate interest in the category of vehicles. He categorized vehicles into such subcategories as cars, trucks, earthmoving equipment, and buses. In addition to common classifications of cars into police cars, jeeps, taxis, and such, and trucks into fire trucks, dump trucks, and the like, his categorical knowledge of earthmoving equipment included bulldozers and excavators, and he categorized buses into school buses, London buses, and funky Malta buses (retro buses on the island of Malta). Later, at 2 to 3 years of age, Alex developed an intense, passionate interest in categorizing dinosaurs.

In sum, the infant's advances in processing information—through attention, memory, imitation, and concept formation—is much richer, more gradual, and less stage-like and occurs earlier than was envisioned by earlier theorists, such as Piaget (Bell & Broomell, 2022; Hayne & Herbert, 2021).

Alex, age 2, showing his intense, passionate interest in the category of vehicles while playing with a London taxi and a funky Malta bus.
Dr. John Santrock

Review *Connect* Reflect

LG2 Describe how infants learn, remember, and conceptualize.

Review

- How do infants learn through conditioning?
- What is attention? What characterizes attention in infants?
- What is memory?
- To what extent can infants remember?
- How is imitation involved in infant learning?
- When do infants develop concepts, and how does concept formation change during infancy?

Connect

- In this section, you learned that explicit memory develops in the second year as the hippocampus and frontal lobes mature and connections between them increase. What did you learn from Figure 5 in the chapter "Physical Development in Infancy" that might also contribute to improvements in a cognitive process like memory during this same time frame?

Reflect *Your Own Personal Journey of Life*

- If a friend told you that they remember a traumatic experience when they were barely 2 years old, would you believe them? Explain your answer.

3 How Are Individual Differences in Infancy Assessed, and Do These Assessments Predict Intelligence?

LG3 Discuss infant assessment measures and the prediction of intelligence.

Measures of Infant Development

Predicting Intelligence

So far in this chapter, we have discussed how the cognitive development of infants generally progresses. We have emphasized what is typical of the largest number of infants or the average infant, but the results obtained for most infants do not apply to all infants. It is advantageous to know whether an infant is developing at a typical or developmentally distinct pace during the course of infancy. If an infant advances at an especially slow rate, then some form of enrichment may be necessary. If an infant develops at a very rapid pace, parents may be advised to provide toys that stimulate cognitive growth in slightly older infants. How is an infant's cognitive development assessed?

MEASURES OF INFANT DEVELOPMENT

Individual differences in infant cognitive development have been studied primarily through the use of developmental scales or infant intelligence tests. For example, the Brazelton Neonatal Behavioral Assessment Scale (NBAS) and the Neonatal Intensive Care Unit Network Neurobehavioral Scale (NNNS) are used to evaluate newborns.

The most important early contributor to the testing of infants was Arnold Gesell (1934a, b). He developed a measure that helped to sort out typically developing from atypically developing babies. This was especially useful to adoption agencies, which had large numbers of babies awaiting placement. Gesell's examination was used widely for many years and still is frequently employed by pediatricians to distinguish between typically developing and atypically developing infants. The current version of the Gesell test has four categories of behavior:

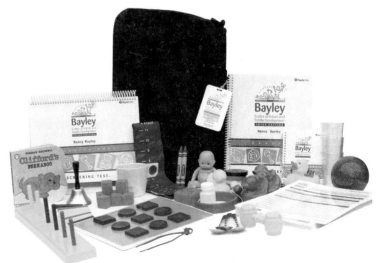

Some items used in the Bayley Scales of Infant and Toddler Development.
Amy Kiley Photography

developmental quotient (DQ) An overall score that combines subscores in motor, language, adaptive, and personal-social domains in the Gesell assessment of infants.

Bayley Scales of Infant and Toddler Development Scales developed by Nancy Bayley that are widely used in assessing infant development. The current version, the Bayley Scales of Infant and Toddler Development—Fourth Edition (Bayley-4), has five components: a cognitive scale, a language scale, a motor scale, a social-emotional scale, and an adaptive behavior scale.

motor, language, adaptive, and personal-social. The **developmental quotient (DQ)** combines subscores in these categories to provide an overall score.

The widely used **Bayley Scales of Infant and Toddler Development** were developed by Nancy Bayley (1969) to assess infant behavior and predict later development. The current version, Bayley-4, has five scales: cognitive, language, motor, social-emotional, and adaptive behavior. The first three scales are administered directly to the infant; the latter two are questionnaires given to the caregiver. The current Bayley Scales product is more appropriate for use in clinical settings than the previous editions (Gullion & others, 2019).

How should a 6-month-old perform on the Bayley cognitive scale? The 6-month-old infant should be able to vocalize pleasure and displeasure, persistently search for objects that are just out of immediate reach, and approach a mirror that is placed in front of the infant by the examiner. By 12 months of age, the infant should be able to inhibit behavior when commanded to do so, imitate words the examiner says (such as *Mama*), and respond to simple requests (such as "Take a drink").

PREDICTING INTELLIGENCE

developmental **connection**

Intelligence

The two most widely used tests of intelligence in older children, adolescents, and adults are the Stanford-Binet tests and the Wechsler scales. Connect to "Cognitive Development in Middle and Late Childhood."

The infant-testing movement grew out of the tradition of IQ testing. However, IQ tests of older children pay more attention to verbal ability. Tests for infants contain far more items related to perceptual-motor development and include measures of social interaction.

One illustrative longitudinal study examined the intelligence of 200 children from 12 months (using the Bayley scales) to 4 years (using the Stanford-Binet test) of age (Blaga & others, 2009). The results indicated considerable stability from late infancy through the preschool years. However, overall scores on tests such as the Gesell and the Bayley scales in infancy do not correlate highly with IQ scores obtained later in childhood. This is not surprising because the components tested in infancy are not the same as the components assessed by IQ tests later in childhood.

A subsequent, longer-term longitudinal study found that developmental milestones at 24 months of age were strongly linked to IQ at 5 to 6 years of age, but milestones at 4, 8, and 12 months were only slightly associated with IQ at 5 to 6 years (Peyre & others, 2017). Of the four developmental milestones (language, gross motor skills, fine motor skills, and socialization), early language skills were the best predictor of IQ. Further, early language skills were linked to which children had an IQ lower than 70 (intellectual disability) (predicted from 8 months of age) or higher than 130 (gifted) (predicted from 12 months of age) at 5 to 6 years of age.

It is important not to go too far and think that connections between cognitive development in early infancy and later cognitive development are so strong that no discontinuity takes place. Some important changes in cognitive development occur after infancy—changes that we describe in later chapters.

Review Connect Reflect

 LG3 Discuss infant assessment measures and the prediction of intelligence.

Review
- What are some measures of individual differences in infancy?
- Do tests of infants predict intelligence later in life?

Connect
- In this section, you learned that some early milestones are linked to cognitive development. Earlier in this chapter, what aspects of concept formation were also linked to cognitive development?

Reflect *Your Own Personal Journey of Life*
- Suppose your sister or brother and their spouse have their 1-year-old daughter assessed with a developmental scale, and the infant does very well on it. How confident should they be that your niece will be a "genius" when she grows up?

4 What Is the Nature of Language, and How Does It Develop in Infancy?

 LG4 Describe the nature of language and how it develops in infancy.

| Defining Language | Language's Rule Systems | How Language Develops | Biological and Environmental Influences | An Interactionist View |

In 1799, a nude boy was observed running through the woods in France. The boy was captured when he was 11 years old. He was called the Wild Boy of Aveyron and was believed to have lived in the woods alone for six years (Lane, 1976). When found, he made no effort to communicate, and he never learned to do so effectively. Turning to more recent times, a child named Genie was discovered in Los Angeles in 1970. Genie was a victim of severe abuse and spent nearly her entire life physically restrained and completely isolated from human contact. Despite intensive intervention, Genie acquired only a limited form of spoken language. Both individuals—the Wild Boy of Aveyron and Genie—raise questions about the biological and environmental determinants of language, topics that we also examine later in the chapter. First, though, we need to define language.

DEFINING LANGUAGE

Language is a form of communication—whether spoken, written, or signed—that is based on a system of symbols. Language consists of the words used by a community and the rules for varying and combining them.

Think how important language is in our everyday lives. We need language to speak with others, listen to others, read, and write. Our language enables us to describe past events in detail and to plan for the future. Language lets us pass down information from one generation to the next and create a rich cultural heritage. Language learning involves comprehending a sound system or sign system for individuals who are deaf; the world of objects, actions, and events; and how units such as words and grammar connect sound and world (Bruhn de Garavito & Schwieter, 2021; Levine, Hirsh-Pasek, & Golinkoff, 2021).

All human languages have some common characteristics (Quam & Creel, 2021). These include infinite generativity and rules for how language works. **Infinite generativity** is the ability to produce and comprehend an endless number of meaningful sentences using a finite set of words and rules. For example, using just the thousands of words available in the English language, it is possible for authors to write an infinite number of novels, poems, speeches, and other texts. Rules describe the way language works. Let's explore what these rules involve.

LANGUAGE'S RULE SYSTEMS

When nineteenth-century American writer Ralph Waldo Emerson said, "The world was built in order and the atoms march in tune," he must have had language in mind. Language is highly ordered and organized (Westbury, 2021). The organization involves five systems of rules: phonology, morphology, syntax, semantics, and pragmatics.

Phonology Every language is made up of basic sounds. **Phonology** is the sound system of the language, including the sounds that are used and how they may be combined (Bruhn de Garavito, 2021a; Vihman, 2020). For example, English has the initial consonant cluster *spr* as in *spring,* but no words begin with the cluster *rsp.*

Phonology provides a basis for constructing a large and expandable set of words out of two or three dozen phonemes (Zamuner & Thiessen, 2018). A phoneme is the basic unit of sound in a language; it is the smallest unit of sound that affects meaning (Shea & O'Neill, 2021). For example, in English the sound represented by the letter *p,* as in the words *pot* and *spot,* is a phoneme. The /p/ sound is slightly different in the two words, but this variation is not distinguished in English, and therefore the /p/ sound is a single phoneme. In some languages, such as Hindi, the variations of the /p/ sound represent separate phonemes.

Morphology **Morphology** refers to the units of meaning involved in word formation. A *morpheme* is a minimal unit of meaning; it is a word or a part of a word that cannot be broken

Language allows us to communicate with others. *What are some important characteristics of language?*
RuslanDashinsky/Getty Images

language A form of communication, whether spoken, written, or signed, that is based on a system of symbols.

infinite generativity The ability to produce an endless number of meaningful sentences using a finite set of words and rules.

phonology The sound system of the language, including the sounds that are used and how they may be combined.

morphology Units of meaning involved in word formation.

into smaller meaningful parts (Levine, Hirsh-Pasek, & Golinkoff, 2021). Every word in the English language is made up of one or more morphemes. Some words consist of a single morpheme (for example, *help*), whereas others are made up of more than one morpheme (for example, *helper* has two morphemes, *help* and *er*, with the morpheme *-er* meaning "one who," in this case "one who helps"). Thus, not all morphemes are words by themselves; for example, *pre-*, *-tion*, and *-ing* are morphemes.

Just as the rules that govern phonology describe the sound sequences that can occur in a language, the rules of morphology describe the way meaningful units (morphemes) can be combined in words (Bruhn de Garavito, 2021b). Morphemes have many jobs in grammar, such as marking tense (for example, *she walks* versus *she walked*), number (*she walks* versus *they walk*), and gender in some languages (*amigas* versus *amigos*) (Stump, 2017).

Syntax   **Syntax** involves the way words are combined to form acceptable phrases and sentences (Bruhn de Garavito, 2021c). If someone says to you, "Alex paid Tomas" or "Alex was paid by Tomas," you know who did the paying and who was paid in each case because you have a syntactic understanding of these sentence structures. You also understand that the sentence "You didn't stay, did you?" is a grammatical sentence but that "You didn't stay, didn't you?" is unacceptable and ambiguous.

If you learn another language, English syntax will not get you very far. For example, in English an adjective usually precedes a noun (as in *blue sky*), whereas in Spanish the adjective usually follows the noun (*cielo azul*). Despite the differences in their syntactic structures, however, syntactic systems in all of the world's languages have some common ground (Koeneman & Zeijstra, 2017). For example, no language we know of permits sentences like the following one:

The mouse the cat the farmer chased killed ate the cheese.

It appears that language users cannot process subjects and objects arranged in too complex a fashion in a sentence.

Semantics   **Semantics** refers to the meaning of words and sentences (Ferreira & others, 2021). Every word has a set of semantic features, which are required attributes related to meaning. *Girl* and *woman,* for example, share many semantic features but differ semantically in regard to age.

Words have semantic restrictions on how they can be used in sentences (Polišenská & others, 2021). The sentence *The bicycle talked the boy into buying a candy bar* is syntactically correct but semantically incorrect. The sentence violates our semantic knowledge that bicycles don't talk.

Pragmatics   A final set of language rules involves **pragmatics,** the appropriate use of language in different contexts. Pragmatics covers a lot of territory (Taboada, 2021). When you take turns speaking in a discussion or you adjust your loudness depending on the amount of background noise, you are demonstrating knowledge of pragmatics. You also apply the pragmatics of English when you use polite language in appropriate situations (for example, when talking to your teacher) or tell stories that are interesting, jokes that are funny, and lies that convince. Other examples include speaking formally versus informally, making requests, offering indirect directives, sharing greetings, and expressing disappointment. In each of these cases, you are demonstrating that you understand the rules of your culture for adjusting language to suit the context.

At this point, we have discussed five important rule systems involved in language. An overview of these rule systems is presented in Figure 9.

HOW LANGUAGE DEVELOPS

Whatever language they learn, infants all over the world follow a similar path in language development. What are some key milestones in this development?

Recognizing Language Sounds   Long before they begin to learn words, infants can make fine distinctions among the sounds of the language (Masapollo, Polka, & Menard, 2016). In Patricia Kuhl's (2017, 2022) research, phonemes from languages all over the world are piped through a speaker for infants to hear (see Figure 10). A box with a toy bear in it is placed where the infant can see it. A string of identical syllables is played, and then the syllables are changed (for example, *ba ba ba ba* and then *pa pa pa pa*). If the infant turns its head when

syntax The ways words are combined to form acceptable phrases and sentences.

semantics The meaning of words and sentences.

pragmatics The appropriate use of language in different contexts.

Rule System	Description	Examples
Phonology	The sound system of a language. A phoneme is the smallest sound unit in a language.	The word *chat* has three phonemes or sounds: /ch/ /ă/ /t/. Here is an example of a phonological rule in the English language: While the phoneme /r/ can follow the phonemes /t/ or /d/ in an English consonant cluster (such as *track* or *drab*), the phoneme /l/ cannot follow these letters.
Morphology	The system of meaningful units involved in word formation.	The smallest sound units that have a meaning are called morphemes, or meaning units. The word *car* is one morpheme, or meaning unit; it cannot be broken down any further and still have meaning. When the suffix *s* is added, the word becomes *cars* and has two morphemes because the *s* changed the meaning of the word, indicating that there is more than one car.
Syntax	The system that involves the way words are combined to form acceptable phrases and sentences.	In addition to having distinct types of words (e.g., nouns, verbs), word order is very important in determining meaning in many languages. For example, in English, the sentence "Sebastian pushed the bike" has a different meaning from "The bike pushed Sebastian."
Semantics	The system that involves the meaning of words and sentences.	Knowing the meaning of individual words—that is, vocabulary. For example, semantics includes knowing the meaning of such words as *orange*, *transportation*, and *intelligent*.
Pragmatics	The system of using appropriate conversation and knowledge of how to effectively use language in context.	An example is using polite language in appropriate situations, such as being mannerly when talking with one's teacher. Taking turns in a conversation also involves pragmatics.

FIGURE 9
THE RULE SYSTEMS OF LANGUAGE

the syllables change, the box lights up and the bear dances and drums, and the infant is rewarded for noticing the change.

Kuhl's (2017, 2022) research has demonstrated that from birth up to about 6 months of age, infants are "citizens of the world": they recognize when sounds change most of the time, no matter what language the syllables come from. But over the next six months, infants get even better at perceiving the changes in sounds from their "own" language, the one their parents speak, and they gradually lose the ability to recognize differences that are not important in their own language. Kuhl (2015) has found that the developmental stage when a baby's brain is most open to learning the sounds of a native language begins at 6 months for vowels and at 9 months for consonants.

Also, in the second half of the first year, infants begin to segment the continuous stream of speech they encounter into words (Karaman & Hay, 2018). Initially, they likely rely on statistical information such as the co-occurrence patterns of phonemes and syllables, which allows them to extract potential word forms (Arnon, 2019). For example, discovering that the sequence *br* occurs more often at the beginning of words while *nt* is more common at the end of words helps infants detect word boundaries. And as infants extract an increasing number of potential word forms from the speech stream they hear, they begin to associate these with concrete, perceptually available objects in their world (Saffran & Kirkham, 2018). For example, infants might detect that the spoken word "monkey" has a reliable statistical regularity of occurring in the visual presence of an observed monkey but not in the presence of other animals, such as bears (Pace & others, 2016). This statistical learning involves extracting information from the world to learn about the environment (Lany & Shoaib, 2020).

Babbling and Other Vocalizations Long before infants speak recognizable words, they produce a number of vocalizations. The functions of these early vocalizations are to practice making sounds, to communicate, and to attract attention (Lee & others, 2017; Meyer & Hunnius, 2021). Babies' sounds go through this sequence during the first year:

- *Crying.* Babies cry even at birth. Crying can signal distress, but different types of cries signal different things.
- *Cooing.* Babies first coo at about 1 to 2 months. These gurgling sounds are made in the back of the throat and usually express pleasure during interaction with the caregiver.
- *Babbling.* In the middle of the first year babies babble—that is, they produce strings of consonant-vowel combinations, such as *ba ba ba ba* (Lang & others, 2021).

FIGURE 10
FROM UNIVERSAL LINGUIST TO LANGUAGE-SPECIFIC LISTENER. In Patricia Kuhl's research laboratory, babies listen to recorded voices that repeat syllables. When the sounds of the syllables change, the babies quickly learn to look at the bear. Using this technique, Kuhl has demonstrated that babies are universal linguists until about 6 months of age, but in the next six months become language-specific listeners.

(*both*): Dr. Patricia Kuhl, Institute for Learning & Brain Sciences, University of Washington

Long before infants speak recognizable words, they communicate by producing a number of vocalizations and gestures. *At approximately what ages do infants begin to produce different types of vocalizations and gestures?*

Flying Colours/Getty Images

developmental **connection**

Cognitive Processes

What are some changes in symbolic thought in young children? Connect to "Cognitive Development in Early Childhood."

Gestures Infants start using gestures, such as showing and pointing, at about 8 to 12 months of age. They may wave bye-bye, nod to mean "yes," show an empty cup to ask for more milk, and point to a dog to draw attention to it. Some early gestures are symbolic, as when infants smack their lips to indicate food/drink. Pointing is considered by language experts to be an important index of the social aspects of language, and it follows a specific developmental sequence: from pointing without checking on adult gaze to pointing while looking back and forth between an object and the adult (Goldin-Meadow, 2018).

Lack of pointing is a significant indicator of problems in the infant's communication system (Fenlon & others, 2019). For example, failure to engage in pointing characterizes many children with autism. The ability to use the pointing gesture effectively improves in the second year of life as advances in other aspects of language communication occur (Goldin-Meadow, 2018).

A study of the functions of infants' pointing found that, just as older children ask questions, infants use gestures to obtain information (Lucca & Wilbourn, 2019). When 18-month-olds pointed at novel objects in an experiment and were provided with labels for the objects, they were less likely to persist in pointing than if the experimenter did not label the objects, suggesting that infants were pointing to obtain information.

Why might gestures such as pointing promote further language development? Infants' gestures advance their language development since caregivers often talk to them about what they are pointing to. Also, babies' first words often are for things they have previously pointed to.

First Words Babies understand their first words earlier than they speak them (Levine, Hirsh-Pasek, & Golinkoff, 2021). As early as 5 months of age, infants recognize their name when someone says it. And as early as 6 months, they recognize "Mommy" and "Daddy." On average, infants understand about 50 words at about 13 months, but they can't say this many words until about 18 months (Berko Gleason & Ratner, 2017). Thus, in infancy *receptive vocabulary* (words the child understands) considerably exceeds *spoken vocabulary* (words the child uses). Infants as young as 4 months old can understand that specific words refer to specific body parts when their parents touch their bodies while saying words referring to the body parts (Tincoff & others, 2019).

A child's first words include those that name important people (*dada*), familiar animals (*kitty*), vehicles (*car*), toys (*ball*), food (*milk*), body parts (*eye*), clothes (*hat*), household items (*clock*), and greeting terms (*bye*). These were the first words of babies 50 years ago. They are the first words of babies today, and they are the first words of babies in many different countries that speak different languages. Children often express various intentions with their single words, so that "cookie" might mean, "That's a cookie" or "I want a cookie."

The infant's spoken vocabulary rapidly increases once the first word is spoken (Levine, Hirsh-Pasek, & Golinkoff, 2021). The average 18-month-old can speak about 50 words, but the average 2-year-old can speak about 200 words. This rapid increase in vocabulary that begins at approximately 18 months is called the *vocabulary spurt* (Chow & others, 2019). Researchers can learn about which words infants and children understand and speak by observing them, but samples in observational studies are often small, and infants and children may know or speak more words than they demonstrate during a short observation period. The Wordbank project is an alternate approach that compiles many different parent report instruments from more than 75,000 children learning more than 25 languages. This "big data" approach allows researchers to explore the extent of variation across many more children and in many more languages than previously acknowledged. One major conclusion from this work is that the range of individual differences among children is quite similar across the world's languages, suggesting that the biological mechanisms and environmental influences that drive early language development are quite similar regardless of the specific language that children are learning (Frank & others, 2020).

Like the timing of a child's first word, the timing of the vocabulary spurt varies. Figure 11 shows the range for these two language milestones in 14 children. On average, these children said their first word at 13 months and had a vocabulary spurt at 19 months. However, the ages for the first word of individual children varied from 10 to 17 months and for their vocabulary spurt from 13 to 25 months.

The spurt actually involves the increase in the rate at which words are learned. That is, early on, a few words are learned every few days; then later on, a few words are learned each day; and eventually many words each day. But does early vocabulary development predict later language development? An illustrative study found that infant vocabulary development at 16 to 24 months of age was linked to vocabulary, phonological awareness, reading accuracy, and reading comprehension five years later (Duff, Tomblin, & Catts, 2015).

Cross-linguistic differences occur in word learning (Tardif, 2016). Children who are learning Mandarin Chinese, Korean, and Japanese acquire more verbs earlier in their development than do children learning English. This cross-linguistic difference reflects the richer variety of verbs in these Asian languages as well as the fact that the use of the subject, which is obligatory in English, often is optional in other languages.

Children sometimes overextend or underextend the meanings of the words they use (Berko Gleason & Ratner, 2017). *Overextension* is the tendency to apply a word to objects that are inappropriate for the word's meaning by going beyond the set of referents an adult would use. For example, children at first may say "*dada*" not only for "father" but also for other men, strangers, or boys. Another example of overextension is calling any animal with four legs a "dog." With time, overextensions decrease and eventually disappear. *Underextension* is the tendency to apply a word too narrowly; it occurs when children fail to use a word to name a relevant event or object. For example, a child might use the word *boy* to describe a 5-year-old neighbor but not apply the word to a male infant or to a 9-year-old male.

Two-Word Utterances By the time children are 18 to 24 months of age, most of their communication consists of two-word utterances (Ramsdell-Hudock, Stuart, & Parham, 2018). To convey meaning with just two words, the child relies heavily on gesture, tone, and context. The wealth of meaning children can communicate with a two-word utterance includes the following (Slobin, 1972):

- Identification: "See doggie."
- Location: "Book there."
- Repetition: "More milk."
- Negation: "Not wolf."
- Possession: "My candy."
- Attribution: "Big car."
- Agent-action: "Mama walk."
- Action–direct object: "Hit you."
- Action–indirect object: "Give Papa."
- Action-instrument: "Cut knife."
- Question: "Where ball?"

These examples are from children whose first language is English, German, Russian, Finnish, Turkish, or Samoan.

What characterizes the infant's early word learning?
Africa Studio/Shutterstock

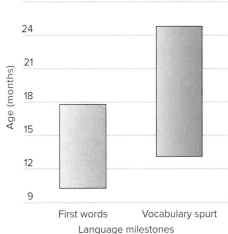

FIGURE **11**

VARIATION IN LANGUAGE MILESTONES.
What are some possible explanations for variations in the timing of these milestones?
Source: Bloom, L. "Variation in Language Milestones." In *Handbook of Child Psychology,* 5e, 309–370. New York: Wiley, 1998.

Verlee Garcia, Speech Pathologist

A speech pathologist is a health professional who works with individuals who have a communication disorder, including speech/language and hearing problems. Verlee Garcia is a speech therapist with the Las Vegas (New Mexico) City Schools. Garcia, who was born and raised on the Navajo Reservation, stuttered as a child and received speech services from second grade through high school. She recalls, "When I entered college, because I was still struggling with my own dysfluency, I began taking classes in speech-language pathology" (Neha, 2003). Garcia's experiences and natural interests led her to a career in speech-language pathology and to earning a master's degree in communications disorders from New Mexico State University.

Being a young stutterer was especially challenging for Garcia. Per her Navajo clan's beliefs, she was raised to believe that her stuttering was due to imitating or "making fun" of her grandmother, who also stuttered. "Even to this day, family members believe that I stutter because I was being disrespectful." Her experiences highlight the importance of understanding someone's culture when determining appropriate therapy. Garcia notes that "the children's individual backgrounds, attitudes, first- and second-language abilities, acculturation, and the severity of their communication disorder all have an impact on what might be suggested to clinicians." For example, with her students, she noticed that Navajo children observed an activity completely before performing it themselves, and many refrained from asking questions. She has also observed that gender and age often play a role in how much a student will respond during sessions. "Allow for a long response time," she recommends. "I have found that rushing a response only frustrates children and, more than likely, they will shut down."

What is a difference in infants' learning of nouns and verbs when comparing Mandarin Chinese and English?
Tang Ming Tung/Getty Images

telegraphic speech The use of content words without grammatical markers such as articles, auxiliary verbs, and other connectives.

Broca's area An area in the brain's left frontal lobe that is involved in speech production.

Wernicke's area An area of the brain's left hemisphere that is involved in language comprehension.

aphasia A loss or impairment of language processing caused by brain damage in Broca's area or Wernicke's area.

language acquisition device (LAD) Chomsky's term describing a biological endowment that enables the child to detect the features and rules of language, including phonology, syntax, and semantics.

Notice that the two-word utterances omit many parts of speech and are remarkably succinct. In fact, in every language, a child's first combinations of words have this economical quality; they are telegraphic. **Telegraphic speech** is the use of content words without grammatical markers such as articles, auxiliary verbs, and other connectives. Telegraphic speech is not limited to two words. "Mommy give ice cream" and "Mommy give Tommy ice cream" also are examples of telegraphic speech.

To read about the work of one individual who helps children who have speech/language and hearing problems, see *Connecting with Careers.*

BIOLOGICAL AND ENVIRONMENTAL INFLUENCES

We have discussed a number of language milestones in infancy; Figure 12 summarizes the approximate time at which infants typically reach these milestones. Despite these general patterns, there is also variability in the ages at which infants reach each milestone, depending on factors such as socioeconomic status and other environmental inputs as well as infants' development of abilities such as sustained attention (Brooks, Flynn, & Ober, 2018). But what makes this amazing development possible? Everyone who uses language in some way "knows" its rules and has the ability to create an infinite number of words and sentences. Where does this knowledge come from? Is it the product of biology? Is language learned and influenced by experiences?

Biological Influences The ability to speak and understand language requires a certain vocal apparatus as well as a nervous system with certain capabilities. The nervous system and vocal apparatus of humanity's predecessors changed over hundreds of thousands or millions of years (Cassidy, 2021). With advances in the nervous system and vocal structures, *Homo sapiens* went beyond the grunting and shrieking of other animals to develop speech (Berecz & others, 2020). Although estimates vary, many experts believe that humans acquired language about 100,000 years ago, which in evolutionary time represents a very recent acquisition. It gave humans an enormous edge over other animals and increased the chances of human survival (Arbib, 2017).

Some language scholars view the remarkable similarities in how children acquire language all over the world as strong evidence that language has a biological basis. Brain imaging studies show that language depends on networks connecting different regions of the brain (Venezia, Richards, & Hickok, 2021). Two regions involved in language were first discovered in studies of brain-damaged individuals: **Broca's area,** an area in the left frontal lobe of the brain involved in producing words (Zhang & others, 2017), and **Wernicke's area,** a region of the brain's left hemisphere involved in language comprehension (Bruckner & Kammer, 2017) (see Figure 13). Damage to either of these areas produces types of **aphasia,** which is a loss or impairment of language processing. Individuals with damage to Broca's area have difficulty producing words correctly; individuals with damage to Wernicke's area have poor comprehension and often produce incomprehensible speech.

Linguist Noam Chomsky (1957) proposed that humans are biologically prewired to learn language at a certain time and in a certain way. He said that children are born into the world with a **language acquisition device (LAD),** a biological endowment that enables the child to detect certain features and rules of language, including phonology, syntax, and semantics (McGilvray, 2017). Children are prepared by nature with the ability to detect the sounds of language, for example, and to follow rules such as how to form plurals and ask questions.

Chomsky's LAD is a theoretical construct, not a physical part of the brain. Is there evidence for the existence of an LAD? Supporters of the LAD concept cite the uniformity of language milestones across languages and cultures, evidence that children create language even in the absence of well-formed input, and biological substrates of language. But, as we will see, critics argue that even if infants have something like an LAD, it cannot explain the whole story of language acquisition.

Environmental Influences   Decades ago, behaviorists opposed Chomsky's hypothesis and argued that language represents nothing more than chains of responses acquired through reinforcement (Skinner, 1957). A baby happens to babble "Ma-ma"; Mama rewards the baby with hugs and smiles; the baby says "Mama" more and more. Bit by bit, said the behaviorists, the baby's language is built up. According to behaviorists, language is a complex learned skill, much like playing the piano or dancing.

There are several problems with the behaviorist view of language learning. First, it does not explain how people create novel sentences—sentences that people have never heard or spoken before. Second, children learn the syntax of their native language even if they are not reinforced for doing so. Social psychologist and psycholinguist Roger Brown (1973) spent long hours observing parents and their young children. He found that parents did not directly or explicitly reward or correct the syntax of most children's utterances. That is, parents did not say "good," "correct," "right," "wrong," and so on. Also, parents did not offer direct corrections such as "You should say two shoes, not two shoe." However, as we will see shortly, many parents do expand on their young children's grammatically incorrect utterances and recast many of those that have grammatical errors (Brito, 2017).

The behavioral view is no longer considered a viable explanation of how children acquire language (Berko Gleason & Ratner, 2017). But a great deal of research describes ways in which children's environmental experiences influence their language skills (Yazejian & others, 2017). Many language experts argue that a child's experiences, the particular language to be learned, and the context in which learning takes place can strongly influence language acquisition (Wilce, 2017).

Language is not learned in a social vacuum. Most children are bathed in language from a very early age (Kuhl, 2017). The Wild Boy of Aveyron, who never learned to communicate effectively, had lived in social isolation for years.

Thus, social cues play an important role in infant language learning (McGillion & others, 2017; Pace & others, 2016). Joint engagement and

FIGURE **13**

BROCA'S AREA AND WERNICKE'S AREA. Broca's area is located in the frontal lobe of the brain's left hemisphere, and it is involved in the control of speech. Wernicke's area is a portion of the left hemisphere's temporal lobe that is involved in understanding language. *How does the role of these areas of the brain relate to lateralization?*

Swissmacky/Shutterstock

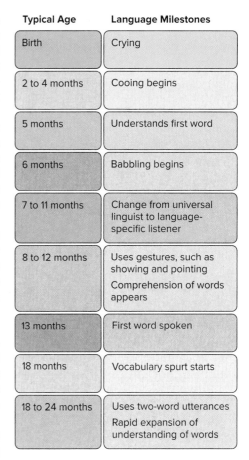

Typical Age	Language Milestones
Birth	Crying
2 to 4 months	Cooing begins
5 months	Understands first word
6 months	Babbling begins
7 to 11 months	Change from universal linguist to language-specific listener
8 to 12 months	Uses gestures, such as showing and pointing Comprehension of words appears
13 months	First word spoken
18 months	Vocabulary spurt starts
18 to 24 months	Uses two-word utterances Rapid expansion of understanding of words

FIGURE **12**

SOME LANGUAGE MILESTONES IN INFANCY. Despite great variations in the language input received by infants, around the world they follow a similar path in learning to speak.

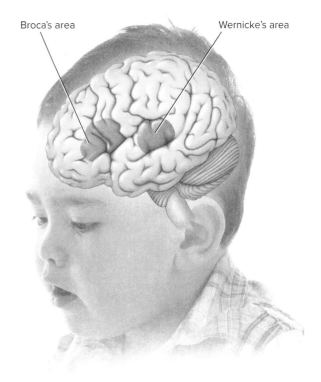

Broca's area

Wernicke's area

relevant responsiveness by a social partner predict better growth in language later in development, possibly because they improve the infant's mapping process between words and the world (Tamis-LeMonda, Kuchirko, & Song, 2014).

The support and involvement of caregivers and teachers greatly facilitate a child's language learning (Levine, Hirsh-Pasek, & Golinkoff, 2021; Morgan, 2019). In one study, the quality of early foundational communication between parent and child at age 2 accounted for more variability in language outcomes one year later than the amount of parent speech did (Hirsh-Pasek & others, 2015). In another study, both full-term and preterm infants who heard more caregiver talk based on all-day recordings at 16 months of age had better language skills (receptive and expressive language, language comprehension) at 18 months of age (Adams & others, 2018). And in yet another study, when mothers immediately smiled and touched their 8-month-old infants after they babbled, the infants subsequently made more complex speech-like sounds than when mothers responded to their infants in a random manner (Goldstein, King, & West, 2003) (see Figure 14). Furthermore, in a study of mother-infant dyads in 11 countries, mothers and infants responded contingently to one another so that infants were more likely to vocalize immediately after their mothers finished speaking to them, and mothers were more likely to speak to their infants immediately after infants finished vocalizing (Bornstein & others, 2015).

Given that social interaction is a critical component for infants to learn language effectively, might they also be able to learn language effectively through audiovisual media? Products have been marketed to parents hoping to give their infants enriching experiences. Researchers have found that infants and young children cannot effectively learn language (phonology or words) from television or videos (Zosh & others, 2017). For example, one study exposed American 9-month-olds to either English or Mandarin in interpersonal interactions with a researcher who read books and played with them over a period of time in a lab setting, in videos, or in audiorecordings. Exposure to Mandarin enabled American infants to retain the ability to distinguish sounds that occurred in Mandarin but not English, but only when they were exposed to Mandarin in interpersonal interactions rather than videos or audiorecordings (Kuhl, Tsao, & Liu, 2003). Frequent viewing of television increases the risk of delayed language development (Lin & others, 2015). Thus, just hearing language is not enough, even when infants seemingly are fully engaged in the experience.

Michael Tomasello (2018b, 2020) stresses that young children are intensely interested in their social world and that early in their development they can understand the intentions of other people. He emphasizes that children learn language in specific interactive contexts. For example, when a toddler and a father are jointly focused on a book, the father might say, "See the birdie." In this case, even a toddler understands that the father intends to name something and knows to look in the direction of the pointing. Through this kind of joint attention, early in their development children are able to use their social skills to acquire language (Piazza & others, 2020). For example, one study revealed that joint visual attention behavior at 10 to 11 months of age (before children spoke their first words) was linked to vocabulary growth at 14, 18, and 24 months of age (Brooks & Meltzoff, 2008). Another study revealed that joint attention at 12 and 18 months predicted language skills at 24 months of age (Mundy & others, 2007). Yet another study showed that infants' eye-gaze behaviors during Spanish tutoring sessions at 9.5 to 10.5 months of age predicted their second-language phonetic learning at 11 months of age, indicating a strong influence of social interaction at the earliest ages of learning a second language (Conboy & others, 2015).

Researchers also have found that the child's vocabulary development is linked to the family's socioeconomic status and the type of talk that parents direct to their children (Golinkoff & others, 2019). To read about these links, see the *Connecting with Diversity* interlude.

FIGURE 14

SOCIAL INTERACTION AND BABBLING. One study focused on two groups of mothers and their 8-month-old infants (Goldstein, King, & West, 2003). One group of mothers was instructed to smile and touch their infants immediately after the babies cooed and babbled; the other group was also told to smile and touch their infants but in a random manner, unconnected to sounds the infants made. The infants whose mothers immediately responded in positive ways to their babbling subsequently made more complex, speechlike sounds, such as "da" and "gu." The research setting for this study, which underscores how important caregivers are in the early development of language, is shown here.
Courtesy of Dr. Michael Goldstein

connecting with diversity

How Does Family Environment Affect Young Children's Language Development?

What characteristics of families influence children's language development? Parents and caregivers of children vary widely in their access to educational and economic opportunities that define family socioeconomic status (SES). SES has been linked with how much parents talk to their children and with young children's vocabulary. In their influential study, Betty Hart and Todd Risley (1995) observed and compared the language environments of children whose parents were highly educated, well-paid professionals (i.e., higher SES) and children whose parents had less education and received public assistance (i.e., lower SES). Higher-SES parents talked more to their young children, talked more about past events, and provided more elaboration than lower-SES parents did. The children of the professional parents had a much larger vocabulary at 36 months of age than the children in lower-SES homes.

More recent studies of language to which children are exposed make use of LENA recording technology, which is a small digital audio-recorder that is worn by the child in specialized clothing. The device records all speech that is "near and clear" to the child over a period of time of up to 16 hours. The system provides not only automated word counts of all adult speech, but also automated counts of the number of child vocalizations and conversational (back-and-forth) turns between caregivers and the target child. This recording technology provides a comprehensive picture of the talk that young children hear.

The LENA device can pick up on differences in the amount of talk that children hear as a function of SES as early as 18 months (Fernald, Marchman, & Weisleder, 2013; Weisleder & Fernald, 2013). In addition, these SES differences are related to children's expressions of their language skills in real time, an important early indicator of children's early language comprehension that has long-term consequences for later outcomes (Donnelly & Kidd, 2020).

Emphasis on SES, home environments, and language development risks leading to "deficit thinking" about home environments for families that lack access to socioeconomic resources. Living in a lower-SES household is not the key identifier in predicting whether children will have difficulties in language development. As long as children experience appropriate amounts of language interaction, instruction, and support, they will develop developmentally typical language skills (Florit & others, 2021; Masek & others, 2021). For example, among families with low incomes, mothers' access to higher education likely plays a key role in supporting the language environment of young children. One study of 15-month-olds in low-income families found that toddlers whose mothers had a college education had better language skills than those whose mothers did not have a college degree, and this gap continued through 3 years of age (Justice & others, 2020). And in a meta-analysis that statistically summarizes results from many studies, young children in lower-SES homes whose parents showed sensitive responsiveness experienced greater growth in language development compared with children from higher-SES homes who had less responsive parents (Madigan & others, 2019). Thus, the key for thinking about the role of family SES is to not equate it with a deficit, but to instead consider the rich variety of experiences that contribute to growth in language skills—and to be aware that many families facing barriers to socioeconomic resources do provide those experiences.

Studies using structural and functional MRI to examine the brains have shown that exposure to more conversational turns with an adult already is related to stronger functional connectivity of brain language networks (King & others, 2021). Another study of 4- to 6-year-old children showed that children who hear more conversational turns have different white-matter properties and engage in tasks differently from children who hear fewer conversational turns (Romeo & others, 2018). These effects can be long lasting. The amount of talk that children hear between 18 and 24 months is correlated with language and cognitive outcomes in adolescence (Gilkerson & others, 2018).

How can parents who face socioeconomic challenges support their infants' language development?

One intriguing component of the young child's linguistic environment is **child-directed speech,** which is language spoken in a higher pitch, slower tempo, and exaggerated intonation than normal, with simple words and sentences (Nencheva, Piazza, & Lew-Williams, 2021). It is hard to use child-directed speech when not in the presence of a baby. As soon as we start talking to a baby, though, most of us shift into child-directed speech. Much of this is automatic and something most parents are not aware they are doing. Child-directed speech serves the important functions of capturing the infant's attention, maintaining communication and social interaction between infants and caregivers, and providing infants with information about their native language by heightening differences between speech directed to children and adults (Spinelli, Fasolo, & Mesman, 2017). Even 4-year-olds speak in simpler ways to 2-year-olds than to their 4-year-old friends.

An illustrative study found that child-directed speech in a one-to-one social context at 11 to 14 months of age was linked to greater word production at 2 years of age than standard

child-directed speech Language spoken in a higher pitch than normal, with simple words and sentences.

speech and speech in a group setting (Ramirez-Esparza, Garcia-Sierra, & Kuhl, 2014). In addition, child-directed speech in a one-to-one social context at 11 to 14 months of age was also related to productive vocabulary at 2 years of age for Spanish-English bilingual infants across languages and in each individual language (Ramirez-Esparza, Garcia-Sierra, & Kuhl, 2017).

Adults often use strategies other than child-directed speech to enhance the child's acquisition of language, including recasting, expanding, and labeling:

- *Recasting* occurs when an adult rephrases something the child has said that might lack the appropriate morphology or contain some other error. The adult restates the child's immature utterance in the form of a fully grammatical sentence. For example, when a 2-year-old says, "Dog bark," the adult may respond by saying, "Oh, you heard the dog barking!" The adult sentence acknowledges that the child was heard and then adds the morphology (/ing/) and the article (the) that the child's utterance lacked.

- *Expanding* involves adding information to a child's incomplete utterance. For example, a child says, "Doggie eat," and the parent replies, "Yes, the dog is eating his food out of his special dish."

- *Labeling* is naming objects that children seem interested in. Young children are forever being asked to identify the names of objects. Roger Brown (1958) called this "the original word game." Children want more than the names of objects, though; they often want information about the object as well.

Parents use these strategies naturally and in meaningful conversations. Parents do not need to use a particular method to teach their children to talk, even for children who are slow in learning language. Children usually benefit when parents follow the child's lead, talking about things the child is interested in at the moment, and when parents provide information in ways that children can process effectively. If children are not ready to take in some information, they are likely to let you know this (perhaps by turning away). Thus, giving the child more information is not always better. Children's language acquisition also benefits from adults' undivided attention. In an experimental study in which mothers were asked to teach their 2-year-old two new words in a laboratory setting, children did not learn the new word in a condition that was interrupted by a cell phone call placed by the experimenter but did learn the new word in the uninterrupted condition, even though the mothers said the new words the same number of times in both conditions (Reed, Hirsh-Pasek, & Golinkoff, 2017). A more recent study in Israel (Lederer, Artzi, & Borodkin, 2022) found that this effect was probably due to overall lower attention and responsiveness from the parent when distracted.

Infants, toddlers, and young children also benefit when adults read books to and with them (shared reading) (Thompson, 2020). Daily reading to infants at 6 months predicts better vocabulary comprehension and production, cognition, and socioemotional competence at 12 months (O'Farrelly & others, 2018). Shared reading is especially beneficial for children's language acquisition because adults use more diverse vocabulary and more complex syntax when reading than in everyday conversation (Demir-Lira & others, 2019). For instance, one study of 9- to 18-month-old infants found that book sharing resulted in more parent talk, child talk, and interactions than other language activities (toy play, personal care, and mealtime, for example) (Clemens & Kegel, 2021). And a large meta-analysis of many studies concluded that shared picture book reading was linked to children having better expressive and receptive language (Dowdall & others, 2020).

Remember that encouragement of language development, not drill and practice, is the key. Language development is not a simple matter of imitation and reinforcement. To read further about ways that parents can facilitate children's language development, see the applications in the *Caring Connections* interlude.

AN INTERACTIONIST VIEW

If language acquisition depended only on biology, then the Wild Boy of Aveyron and Genie (discussed earlier in the chapter) should have talked without difficulty. A child's experiences influence language acquisition (Levine, Hirsh-Pasek, & Golinkoff, 2021). But we have seen that language does have strong biological foundations as well (Cassidy, 2021). No matter how much you converse with a dog, it won't learn to talk. In contrast, children are biologically prepared to learn language. Children all over the world acquire language milestones at about the same

What is shared reading and how might it benefit infants and toddlers?
Elyse Lewin/Brand X Pictures/Getty Images

How Parents Can Facilitate Infants' and Toddlers' Language Development

In three foundational books, linguist Naomi Baron (1992) in *Growing Up with Language,* developmental psychologists Roberta Golinkoff and Kathy Hirsh-Pasek (2000) in *How Babies Talk,* and scholar and policy expert Ellen Galinsky (2010) in *Mind in the Making,* provided ideas to help parents facilitate their infants' and toddlers' language development. Their suggestions are summarized below:

- **Be an active conversational partner.** Talk to your baby from the time it is born. Initiate conversation with the baby. If the baby is in a day-long child-care program, ensure that the baby receives adequate language stimulation from adults.
- **Talk in a slowed-down pace and don't worry about how you sound to other adults when you talk to your baby.** Talking in a slowed-down pace helps babies detect words in the sea of sounds they experience. Babies enjoy and attend to the high-pitched sound of child-directed speech.
- **Narrate your daily activities to the baby as you do them.** For example, talk about how you will put the baby in a high chair for lunch and ask what she would like to eat, and so on.
- **Use parent-look and parent-gesture, and name what you are looking at.** When you want your child to pay attention to something, look at it and point to it. Then name it—for example, by saying, "Look, there's an airplane."
- **When you talk with infants and toddlers, be simple, concrete, and repetitive.** Don't try to talk to them in abstract, high-level ways or think you have to say something new or different all of the time. Using familiar words often will help them remember the words.
- **Play games.** Use word games like peek-a-boo and pat-a-cake to help infants learn words.
- **Remember to listen.** Since toddlers' speech is often slow and laborious, parents are often tempted to supply words and thoughts for them. Be patient and let toddlers express themselves, no matter how painstaking the process is or how great a hurry you are in.
- **Expand and elaborate language abilities and horizons with infants and toddlers.** Ask questions that encourage answers other than "Yes" and "No." Actively repeat, expand, and recast the utterances. Your toddler might say, "Dada." You could follow with "Where's Dada?," and then you might continue, "Let's go find him."
- **Adjust to your child's idiosyncrasies instead of working against them.** Many toddlers have difficulty pronouncing words and making themselves understood. Whenever possible, make toddlers feel that they are being understood.
- **Resist making normative comparisons.** Be aware of the ages at which your child reaches specific milestones (such as the first word, first 50 words), but do not measure this development rigidly against that of other children. Such comparisons can bring about unnecessary anxiety.

It is a good idea for parents to begin talking to their babies at the start. The best language teaching occurs when the talking is begun before the infant becomes capable of intelligible speech. What are some other guidelines for parents to follow in helping their infants and toddlers develop their language skills?
Tetra Images/Getty Images

time and in about the same order. However, there are cultural variations in the type of support given to children's language development. For example, caregivers in the Kaluli culture prompt young children to use a loud voice and particular morphemes that direct the speech act performed (calling out) and to refer to names, kinship relations, and places where there has been a shared past experience that indicates a closeness to the person being addressed (Roque & Schieffelin, 2018). Tseltal Mayan infants and young children in Southern Mexico are rarely spoken to directly yet still extract information they need to learn language from the interactions that occur around them (Casillas, Brown, & Levinson, 2020).

Environmental influences are also very important in developing competence in language. Children whose parents provide them with a rich verbal environment show many positive benefits (Collins & Toppelberg, 2021). Parents who pay attention to what their children are trying to say, expand their children's utterances, read to them, and label things in the environment are providing valuable benefits for them (Odijk & Gillis, 2021).

An interactionist view emphasizes that both biology and experience contribute to language development (Sinha, 2017). How much of the language is biologically determined and how much depends on interaction with others is a subject of debate among linguists and psychologists (Adams & others, 2018; McGillion & others, 2017). However, all agree that both biological capacity and relevant experience are necessary (Green & others, 2017; Peterson & others, 2017; Warren & others, 2017).

Review *Connect* Reflect

LG4 Describe the nature of language and how it develops in infancy.

Review
- What is language?
- What are language's rule systems?
- How does language develop in infancy?
- What are some biological and environmental influences on language?
- To what extent do biological and environmental influences interact to produce language development?

Connect
- The more years children spend in homes with limited access to income, the more their physiological indices of stress are elevated. In this chapter, you learned about the role of SES in children's language acquisition and vocabulary building. How might these factors influence children's performance when they go to school?

Reflect *Your Own Personal Journey of Life*
- Would it be a good idea for you as a parent to hold large flash cards of words in front of your baby each day to help the baby learn language and improve the baby's intelligence? Why or why not?

topical connections *looking forward*

Advances in infants' cognitive development are linked to their socioemotional development. For example, you will learn about the infant's developing social orientation and understanding, which involve perceiving people as engaging in intentional and goal-directed behavior, joint attention, and cooperation. Also in "Socioemotional Development in Infancy" you will study many aspects of the infant's emotional development, temperament, attachment, and child care. And in "Cognitive Development in Early Childhood" you will read about two major theorists—Piaget and Vygotsky—and their views of how young children's thinking advances. You will see how young children become more capable of sustaining their attention; learn about the astonishing rate at which preschool children's vocabulary expands; and explore variations in early childhood education.

reach your **learning goals**

Cognitive Development in Infancy

1 What Is Piaget's Theory of Infant Development?

 LG1 Summarize and evaluate Piaget's theory of infant development.

Cognitive Processes

- In Piaget's theory, children construct their own cognitive worlds, building mental structures to adapt to their world.

- Schemes are actions or mental representations that organize knowledge. Behavioral schemes (physical activities) characterize infancy, whereas mental schemes (cognitive activities) develop in childhood. Assimilation occurs when children incorporate new information into existing schemes; accommodation refers to children's adjustment of their schemes in the face of new information.

- Through organization, children group isolated behaviors into a higher-order, more smoothly functioning cognitive system.

- Equilibration is a mechanism Piaget proposed to explain how children shift from one stage of thought to the next. As children experience cognitive conflict in trying to understand the world, they use assimilation and accommodation to attain equilibrium. The result is a new stage of thought. According to Piaget, there are four qualitatively different stages of thought.

The Sensorimotor Stage

- In sensorimotor thought, the first of Piaget's four stages, the infant organizes and coordinates sensory experiences with physical movements. The stage lasts from birth to about 2 years of age.

- The sensorimotor stage has six substages: simple reflexes; first habits and primary circular reactions; secondary circular reactions; coordination of secondary circular reactions; tertiary circular reactions, novelty, and curiosity; and internalization of schemes. One key accomplishment of this stage is object permanence, the ability to understand that objects continue to exist even though the infant is no longer observing them. Another aspect involves infants' understanding of cause and effect.

Evaluating Piaget's Sensorimotor Stage

- Piaget opened up a whole new way of looking at infant development in terms of coordinating sensory input with motoric actions. In the past decades, revisions of Piaget's view have been proposed based on research. For example, researchers have found that a stable and differentiated perceptual world is established earlier than Piaget envisioned, and infants begin to develop concepts as well. A core knowledge approach hypothesizes that infants are born with domain-specific innate knowledge systems. Critics argue that the core knowledge approach does not give adequate attention to the influence of early experiences on infants' cognitive development.

2 How Do Infants Learn, Remember, and Conceptualize?

 Describe how infants learn, remember, and conceptualize.

Conditioning

- Both classical and operant conditioning occur in infants. Operant conditioning techniques have been especially useful to researchers in demonstrating infants' perception and memory of information about perceptual-motor actions.

Attention

- Attention is the focusing of mental resources on select information, and in infancy attention is closely linked with habituation. In the first year, much of attention is of the orienting/investigative type, but sustained attention also becomes important.

- Habituation is the repeated presentation of the same stimulus, causing reduced attention to the stimulus. If a different stimulus is presented and the infant pays increased attention to it, dishabituation is occurring. Joint attention plays an important role in infant development, especially in the infant's acquisition of language.

Memory

- Memory is the retention of information over time. Infants as young as 2 to 6 months can retain information about some experiences. However, many experts argue that what we commonly think of as memory (consciously remembering the past, or explicit memory) does not occur until the second half of the first year of life. By the end of the second year, explicit memory continues to improve.

- The hippocampus and frontal lobes of the brain are involved in development of explicit memory in infancy.

- The phenomenon of not being able to remember events that occurred before the age of 2 or 3—known as infantile, or childhood, amnesia—may be due to the immaturity of the prefrontal lobes of the brain at that age.

Imitation

- Meltzoff has shown that newborns can match their behaviors (such as protruding their tongue) to a model. His research also shows that deferred imitation occurs as early as 9 months of age.

Concept Formation

- Concepts are cognitive groupings of similar objects, events, people, or ideas. Mandler argues that it is not until about 7 to 9 months of age that infants form conceptual categories, although we do not know precisely when concept formation begins. Infants' first concepts are broad. Over the first two years of life, these broad concepts gradually become more differentiated. Many infants and young children develop an intense interest in a particular category (or categories) of objects.

3 How Are Individual Differences in Infancy Assessed, and Do These Assessments Predict Intelligence?

 Discuss infant assessment measures and the prediction of intelligence.

Measures of Infant Development

- Developmental scales for infants grew out of the tradition of IQ testing of older children. These scales are less verbal than IQ tests. Gesell's test is still widely used by pediatricians to distinguish between typically and atypically developing infants; it provides a developmental quotient (DQ). The Bayley scales, developed by Nancy Bayley, continue to be widely used today to assess infant development. The current version, the Bayley-4, consists of cognitive, language, motor, socioemotional, and adaptive scales.

Predicting Intelligence

- Global scores on the Gesell and Bayley scales are not good predictors of childhood intelligence. However, measures of information processing such as speed of habituation and degree of dishabituation do correlate with intelligence later in childhood. There is both continuity and discontinuity between infant cognitive development and cognitive development later in childhood.

4 What Is the Nature of Language, and How Does It Develop in Infancy?

 Describe the nature of language and how it develops in infancy.

Defining Language

- Language is a form of communication, whether spoken, written, or signed, that is based on a system of symbols. Language consists of all the words used by a community and the rules for varying and combining them. It is marked by infinite generativity.

Language's Rule Systems

- Phonology is the sound system of the language, including the sounds that are used and how they may be combined. Morphology refers to the units of meaning involved in word formation. Syntax is the way words are combined to form acceptable phrases and sentences. Semantics involves the meaning of words and sentences. Pragmatics is the appropriate use of language in different contexts.

How Language Develops

- Among the milestones in infant language development are crying (birth), cooing (1 to 2 months), babbling (6 months), making the transition from universal linguist to language-specific listener (7 to 11 months), using gestures (8 to 12 months), comprehending words (8 to 12 months), speaking of first word (13 months), vocabulary spurt (18 months), rapid expansion of understanding words (18 to 24 months), and two-word utterances (18 to 24 months).

Biological and Environmental Influences

- In evolution, language clearly gave humans an enormous advantage over other animals and increased their chance of survival. Broca's area and Wernicke's area are important locations for language processing in the brain's left hemisphere. Chomsky argues that children are born with the ability to detect basic features and rules of language. In other words, they are biologically prepared to learn language with a prewired language acquisition device (LAD). The behaviorists' view—that children acquire language as a result of reinforcement—has not been supported.

- Adults help children acquire language through child-directed speech, recasting, expanding, and labeling. Environmental influences are demonstrated by differences in the language development of children as a consequence of being exposed to different language environments in the home. Parents should talk extensively with an infant, especially about what the baby is attending to.

An Interactionist View

- Today, most language researchers believe that children everywhere are born with special social and linguistic capacities that make language acquisition possible. How much of the language is biologically determined and how much depends on interaction with others is a subject of debate among linguists and psychologists. However, all agree that both biological capacity and relevant experience are necessary.

key **terms**

accommodation
A-not-B error
aphasia
assimilation
attention
Bayley Scales of Infant and
    Toddler Development
Broca's area
child-directed speech
concepts
coordination of secondary
    circular reactions

core knowledge approach
deferred imitation
developmental
    quotient (DQ)
equilibration
explicit memory
first habits and primary circular
    reactions
implicit memory
infinite generativity
internalization of schemes
joint attention

language
language acquisition device
    (LAD)
memory
morphology
object permanence
organization
phonology
pragmatics
primary circular
    reaction
schemes

secondary circular reactions
semantics
sensorimotor stage
simple reflexes
syntax
telegraphic speech
tertiary circular reactions,
    novelty, and curiosity
Wernicke's area

key **people**

Renée Baillargeon
Naomi Baron
Nancy Bayley
Roger Brown
Noam Chomsky

Arnold Gesell
Eleanor Gibson
Roberta Golinkoff
Betty Hart
Kathy Hirsh-Pasek

Patricia Kuhl
Jean Mandler
Andrew Meltzoff
Jean Piaget
Todd Risley

Carolyn Rovee-Collier
Michael Tomasello

improving the **lives of children**

STRATEGIES

Nourishing the Infant's Cognitive Development

What are some good strategies for helping infants develop in cognitively competent ways?

- *Provide the infant with many play opportunities in a rich and varied environment.* Give the infant extensive opportunities to experience objects of different sizes, shapes, textures, and colors. Recognize that play with objects stimulates the infant's cognitive development.

- *Actively communicate with the infant.* Don't let the infant spend long bouts of waking hours in social isolation. Infants need caregivers who actively communicate with them. This active communication with adults is necessary for the infant's competent cognitive development.

- *Don't try to accelerate the infant's cognitive development.* Most experts stress that infants cognitively benefit when they learn concepts naturally. The experts emphasize that restricting infants to a passive role and showing them flash cards to accelerate their cognitive development are not good strategies.

RESOURCES

Mind in the Making (2010)

Ellen Galinsky
New York: HarperCollins

A widely read book for parents of infants and young children. Galinsky interviewed a number of leading experts in children's development and distilled their thoughts in an easy-to-read fashion. The book provides abundant examples of how to improve infants' attention, communication, cognitive skills, and learning.

Growing Up with Language (1992)

Naomi Baron
Reading, MA: Addison-Wesley

Baron focuses on three representative children and their families. She explores how children put their first words together, struggle to understand meaning, and use language as a creative tool. She shows parents how they play a key role in their child's language development.

Becoming Brilliant: What Science Tells Us about Raising Successful Children (2016)

Roberta Michnick Golinkoff and Kathy Hirsh-Pasek
Washington, DC: American Psychological Association

Targeted to parents, this book by leading experts details the fascinating world of infants' and children's cognitive development. The authors discuss implications of scientific findings on how infants and children learn for how parents and teachers can help children reach their full developmental potential.

The Development of Language (10th ed., 2022)

Jean Berko Gleason and Nan Ratner
San Diego: Plural Publishing

A number of leading experts provide up-to-date discussion of many aspects of language development, including the acquisition of language skills, language rule systems, and communication in infancy.

chapter 7

SOCIOEMOTIONAL DEVELOPMENT IN INFANCY

chapter outline

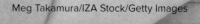

An increasing number of fathers are staying home to care for their children (Parke & Cookston, 2019). And researchers are finding positive outcomes when fathers are positively engaged with their infants (Matte-Gagné, Turgeon, Bernier, & Cyr, 2023; Volling & Cabrera, 2019). Consider 17-month-old Darius. On weekdays, Darius' father, a writer, cares for him during the day while his mother works full-time as a landscape architect. Darius' father is doing a great job of caring for him. He keeps Darius nearby while he is writing and spends lots of time talking to him and playing with him. From their interactions, it is clear that they genuinely enjoy each other.

Last month, Darius began spending one day a week at a childcare center. His parents carefully selected the center after observing a number of centers and interviewing teachers and center directors. His parents placed him in the center one day a week so Darius could get some experience with peers and his father could have time off from caregiving.

Darius' father looks to the future and imagines the soccer games Darius will play in and the many other activities he can enjoy with Darius. Remembering how little time his own father spent with him, he is dedicated to making sure that Darius has an involved, nurturing experience with his father.

When Darius' mother comes home in the evening, she spends considerable time with him. Darius shows a positive attachment to both his mother and his father.

Many fathers are spending more time with their infants today than in the past.
Tetra Images/Getty Images

topical connections *looking **back***

"Cognitive Development in Infancy" described the development of cognitive abilities in infancy, including the ability to learn, remember, and conceptualize, as well as to understand and acquire language. Up to this point, what you have read about socioemotional development has mainly focused on topics such as the social situations and emotions of parents before and after the arrival of their infants, including parents' feelings of joy, anticipation, anxiety, and stress during pregnancy; how a mother's optimism may lead to less adverse outcomes for her fetus; and parents' emotional and psychological adjustments during the postpartum period. In this chapter, you will study many intriguing aspects of infants' socioemotional development.

preview

In "Physical Development in Infancy" and "Cognitive Development in Infancy" you read about how the infant perceives, learns, and remembers. Infants also are socioemotional beings, capable of displaying emotions and initiating social interaction with people close to them. The main topics that we will explore are emotional understanding and attachment, and the social contexts of the family and child care.

1 How Do Emotions and Personality Develop in Infancy?

 LG1 Discuss emotional and personality development in infancy.

Emotional Development   Temperament   Personality Development

Anyone who has been around infants for even a brief time detects that they are emotional beings. Not only do infants express emotions, but they also differ from each other in their temperament. Some are shy and others are outgoing, for example. In this section, we explore these and other aspects of emotional and personality development in infants.

EMOTIONAL DEVELOPMENT

Imagine your life without emotion. Emotion is the color and music of life, as well as the tie that binds people together. How do psychologists define and classify emotions, and why are they important to development? How do emotions develop during the first two years of life?

What Are Emotions? For our purposes, we will define **emotion** as feeling, or affect, that occurs when a person is in a state or an interaction that is important to them, especially in relation to their well-being. Particularly in infancy, emotions play important roles in (1) communication with others and (2) behavioral organization. Through emotions, infants communicate important aspects of their lives such as joy, sadness, interest, and fear (Walle & others, 2017). In terms of behavioral organization, emotions influence infants' social responses and adaptive behavior as they interact with others in their world (Davis, Parsafar, & Brady, 2023).

One of the most common ways to classify emotions is as positive or negative (Waugh & others, 2019). Positive emotions include enthusiasm, joy, and love. Negative emotions include anxiety, anger, guilt, and sadness. Although emotion consists of more than communication, in infancy the communication aspect is at the forefront of emotion.

Biological, Cognitive, and Environmental Influences Emotions are influenced by biological foundations, cognitive processes, and a person's experiences (Aktar & Perez-Edgar, 2021; Cassidy, 2021). Biology's importance to emotion also is apparent in the early developmental changes in a baby's emotional capacities (M.J. Martin & others, 2017; Miller & others, 2017). Certain regions of the brain that develop early in life (such as the brain stem, hippocampus, and amygdala) play a role in distress, excitement, and rage, and even infants display these emotions (Ng & others, 2018; Richards & Conte, 2021). But, as we discuss later in the chapter, infants only gradually develop the ability to regulate their emotions, and this ability seems to be tied to the gradual maturation of frontal regions of the cerebral cortex that can exert control over other areas of the brain (Broomell & Bell, 2022; Xie & others, 2019).

Cognitive processes, both in immediate "in the moment" contexts and across childhood development, influence infants' and children's emotional development (Davis, Parsafar, & Brady, 2023; Jiang & others, 2017). Attention toward or away from an experience can influence infants' and children's emotional responses. For example, children who can distract themselves from a stressful encounter show a lower level of negative affect in the context and less anxiety over time (Leerkes & Bailes, 2019). Also, as children become older, they develop cognitive strategies for controlling their emotions and become more adept at modulating their emotional arousal (Kaunhoven & Dorjee, 2017).

---

developmental connection

Brain Development

The maturation of the amygdala and prefrontal cortex may be linked to adolescent risk taking. Connect to "Physical Development in Adolescence."

---

emotion Feeling, or affect, that occurs when a person is in a state or interaction that is important to them. Emotion can be characterized as positive (enthusiasm, joy, love, for example) or negative (anxiety, guilt, or sadness, for example).

Biological evolution has endowed human beings to be *emotional,* but embeddedness in relationships and culture provides diversity in emotional experiences (Dagan & Sagi-Schwartz, 2021; Muhlenbeck & others, 2020; Norona & Baker, 2017; Zachary & others, 2019). Emotional development and coping with stress are influenced by whether caregivers have maltreated or neglected their children and whether or not children's caregivers are depressed (Doyle & Cicchetti, 2018; Priel & others, 2020). When infants become stressed, they show better biological recovery from the stressors when their caregivers engage in sensitive caregiving with them (Thompson & Goodvin, 2016).

Social relationships, in turn, provide the setting for the development of a rich variety of emotions (Rattaz & others, 2022; Thompson, 2016). When toddlers hear their parents quarreling, they often react with distress and inhibit their play. Well-functioning families make each other laugh and may develop a light mood to defuse conflicts.

Cultural influences are linked to variations in emotional expression (Savina & Wan, 2017; Suarez-Alvarez & others, 2020). For example, researchers have found that East Asian infants display less frequent and less intense positive and negative emotions than non-Latino White infants (Chen, 2018). Throughout childhood, East Asian parents encourage their children to be emotionally reserved rather than emotionally expressive (Krassner & others, 2017). Further, Japanese parents try to prevent children from experiencing negative emotions, whereas non-Latina White mothers more frequently respond after their children become distressed and then help them cope (Rothbaum & Trommsdorff, 2007).

Early Emotions

A leading expert on infant emotional development, Michael Lewis (2018) distinguishes between primary emotions and self-conscious emotions. **Primary emotions** are emotions that are present in humans and other animals; these emotions appear in the first six months of the human infant's development. Primary emotions include surprise, interest, joy, anger, sadness, fear, and disgust (see Figure 1 for infants' facial expressions of some of these early emotions). In Lewis' classification, **self-conscious emotions** require self-awareness that involves consciousness and a sense of "me." Self-conscious emotions include jealousy, empathy, embarrassment, pride, shame, and guilt—most of these occurring for the first time at some point in the second half of the first year or during the second year.

Researchers such as Joseph Campos (2009) and Michael Lewis (2018) debated about how early in the infant and toddler years various emotions first appear and in what sequence. As an indication of the controversy regarding when certain emotions first are displayed by infants, consider jealousy. Lewis and others argue that jealousy does not emerge until approximately 18 months of age, whereas some other researchers assert that it is displayed much earlier (Hart, 2018).

Consider the results of two illustrative research studies. In one study, 9-month-old infants engaged in more approach-style, jealousy-related behaviors when their mothers gave attention to a social "rival" (a lifelike doll) than to a non-social rival (a book) (Mize & others, 2014). Further, in this study, the infants showed brain activity (measured using an electroencephalogram, or EEG) during the social-rival condition that is associated with jealousy. In another older study, 6-month-old infants observed their mothers in situations similar to the previous study: either giving attention to a lifelike baby doll (hugging or gently rocking it, for example) or to a book (Hart & Carrington, 2002). When mothers directed their attention to the doll, the infants were more likely to display negative emotions, such as anger and sadness, which may have indicated their jealousy (see Figure 2). However, their expressions of anger and sadness may have reflected frustration in not being able to have the novel doll to play with.

Debate about the onset of an emotion such as jealousy illustrates the complexity and difficulty of indexing early emotions. That said, some experts on infant socioemotional development, such as Jerome Kagan (2018), conclude that the structural immaturity of the infant brain makes it unlikely that emotions requiring thought—such as guilt, pride, despair, shame, empathy, and jealousy—can be experienced in the first year. Thus, both Kagan (2018) and Campos (2009) have argued that so-called self-conscious emotions

primary emotions Emotions that are present in humans and other animals, and emerge early in life; examples are joy, anger, sadness, fear, and disgust.

self-conscious emotions Emotions that require self-awareness, especially consciousness and a sense of "me"; examples include jealousy, empathy, and embarrassment.

How do Japanese mothers handle their infants' and children's emotional development differently from non-Latina White mothers?

Satoshi-K/Getty Images

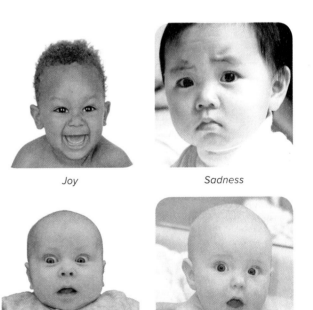

Joy   *Sadness*

Fear   *Surprise*

FIGURE 1

EXPRESSION OF DIFFERENT EMOTIONS IN INFANTS

(Joy): gelpi/123RF; *(Sadness)*: Jill Braaten/McGraw Hill; *(Fear)*: Stanislav/Shutterstock; *(Surprise)*: Photodisc Collection/EyeWire/Getty Images

FIGURE 2

IS THIS THE EARLY EXPRESSION OF JEALOUSY? In the study by Hart and Carrington (2002), the researchers concluded that the 6-month-old infants who observed their mothers giving attention to a baby doll displayed negative emotions—such as anger and sadness—which may indicate the early appearance of jealousy. However, experts on emotional development, such as Joseph Campos (2009) and Jerome Kagan (2018), argue that it is unlikely emotions such as jealousy appear in the first year. *Why do they conclude that it is unlikely jealousy occurs in the first year?*

Kenny Braun/Braun Photography

What are some different types of cries?
Don Hammond/Design Pics

basic cry A rhythmic pattern usually consisting of a cry, a briefer silence, a shorter inspiratory whistle that is higher pitched than the main cry, and then a brief rest before the next cry.

anger cry A cry similar to the basic cry, with more excess air forced through the vocal cords.

pain cry A sudden appearance of a long, initial loud cry without preliminary moaning, followed by breath holding.

don't occur until after the first year, which increasingly reflects the view of most developmental psychologists. Thus, in regard to the photograph in Figure 2, it is unlikely that the 6-month-old infant is experiencing jealousy.

Emotional Expression and Social Relationships

Emotional expressions are involved in infants' first relationships. The ability of infants to communicate emotions permits coordinated interactions with their caregivers and the beginning of an emotional bond between them (Lachman & others, 2019; Walle & Lopez, 2020). Not only do parents change their emotional expressions in response to infants' emotional expressions, but infants also modify their emotional expressions in response to their parents' emotional expressions. In other words, these interactions are mutually regulated (Ogren & Johnson, 2021). Because of this coordination, the interactions are described as reciprocal, or synchronous, when all is going well. Sensitive, responsive parents help their infants grow emotionally, whether the infants respond in distressed or happy ways (Henderson, Burrows, & Usher, 2020; Thompson, 2016). A meta-analysis of 22 studies found that when parents talked with young children more about mental states, children had a better understanding of emotions (Tompkins & others, 2018).

One illuminating study documented how babies pick up on their mothers' stress (Waters, West, & Mendes, 2014). In this study, mothers were separated from their babies to give a 5-minute speech, with half of the mothers receiving a positive evaluation, the other half a negative evaluation. Mothers who received negative feedback reported an increase in negative emotion and physiological stress, while those who were given positive feedback reported an increase in positive emotion. The babies quickly detected their mothers' stress, as reflected in an increased heart rate when reunited with them. And the greater the mother's stress response, the more her baby's heart rate increased.

Cries and smiles are two emotional expressions that infants display when interacting with parents. These are babies' first forms of emotional communication.

Crying Crying is the most important mechanism newborns have for communicating with their world. The first cry verifies that the baby's lungs have filled with air. Cries also may provide information about the health of the newborn's central nervous system. Newborns even tend to respond with cries and negative facial expressions when they hear other newborns cry (Ruffman & others, 2019). Infants as young as 4 months expect unfamiliar adults to respond to a crying baby (Jin & others, 2018).

Babies have at least three types of cries:

- **Basic cry.** A rhythmic pattern that usually consists of a cry, followed by a briefer silence, then a shorter inspiratory whistle that is somewhat higher in pitch than the main cry, then another brief rest before the next cry. Some infancy experts stress that hunger is one of the conditions that incite the basic cry.
- **Anger cry.** A variation of the basic cry in which more excess air is forced through the vocal cords. The anger cry has a loud, harsh sound to it, almost like shouting.
- **Pain cry.** A sudden long, initial loud cry followed by breath holding; no preliminary moaning is present. The pain cry is triggered by a high-intensity stimulus.

Most adults can determine whether an infant's cries signify anger or pain (Esposito & others, 2015). The accuracy of adults' perceptions of infant pain increases with caregiving experience (Corvin & others, 2022). Also, parents can interpret the cries of their own baby better than those of another baby.

Smiling   Smiling is critical as a means of developing a new social skill and is a key social signal (Dau & others, 2017; Martin & Messinger, 2018). Two types of smiling can be distinguished in infants:

- **Reflexive smile.** A smile that does not occur in response to external stimuli and appears during the first month after birth, usually during sleep.
- **Social smile.** A smile that occurs in response to an external stimulus, typically a face in the case of the young infant. Social smiling occurs as early as 4 to 6 weeks of age in response to a caregiver's voice.

The infant's social smile can have a powerful impact on caregivers (Martin & Messinger, 2018). Following weeks of endless demands, fatigue, and little reinforcement, an infant starts smiling at them and many caregivers begin to feel that their efforts are rewarded. One study found that smiling and laughter at 7 months of age were associated with self-regulation at 7 years of age (Posner & others, 2014). Another study found that parents can soothe and increase pleasurable smiling in their infant by singing a song that is familiar to them (Cirelli & Trehub, 2020).

Fear   One of a baby's earliest emotions is fear, which typically first appears at about 6 months of age and peaks at about 18 months (Gartstein, Hancock, & Iverson, 2018). However, abused and neglected infants can show fear as early as 3 months (Witherington & others, 2010). Researchers have found that infant fear is linked to guilt, empathy, and low aggression at 6 to 7 years of age (Rothbart, 2011; Shephard & others, 2019). The most frequent expression of an infant's fear involves **stranger anxiety,** in which an infant shows a fear and wariness of strangers (Brand, Escobar, & Patrick, 2020). Stranger anxiety usually emerges gradually. It first appears at about 6 months of age in the form of wary reactions. By age 9 months, the fear of strangers is often more intense, reaching a peak toward the end of the first year of life (Finelli, Zeanah, & Smyke, 2019).

Not all infants show distress when they encounter a stranger. Besides individual variations, whether an infant shows stranger anxiety also depends on the social context, infant temperament, caregiver characteristics, and characteristics of the stranger (Shapiro, 2018). Infants show less stranger anxiety when they are in familiar settings. It appears that when infants feel secure, they are less likely to show stranger anxiety.

In addition to stranger anxiety, infants experience fear of being separated from their caregivers (Granqvist & Duschinsky, 2021). The result is **separation protest**—crying when the caregiver leaves. Separation protest is initially displayed by infants at approximately 7 to 8 months and peaks at about 15 months (Keeton, Schleider, & Walkup, 2017). One classic study revealed that separation protest peaked at about 13 to 15 months in four different cultures (Kagan, Kearsley, & Zelazo, 1978). The percentage of infants who engaged in separation protest varied across cultures, but the infants reached a peak of protest at about the same age—during the first half of their second year of life.

Emotion Regulation and Coping
During the first year of life, the infant gradually develops an ability to inhibit, or minimize, the intensity and duration of emotional reactions (Dollar & Calkins, 2020). From early in infancy, babies put their thumbs in their mouths to soothe themselves. But at first, infants mainly depend on caregivers to help them soothe their emotions, as when a caregiver rocks an infant to sleep, sings lullabies to the infant, gently strokes the infant, and so on. In one illustrative study, young infants with a negative temperament used fewer emotion regulation strategies while maternal sensitivity to infants was linked to more adaptive emotion regulation (Thomas & others, 2017).

Later in infancy, when they become emotionally aroused, infants sometimes redirect their attention or distract themselves in order to reduce their arousal (Schoppmann, Schneider, & Seehagen, 2019). By 2 years of age, toddlers can use language to define their feeling states and the context that is upsetting them (Kopp, 2008). A toddler might say, "Feel bad. Dog scare." This type of communication may allow caregivers to help the child regulate emotions.

Contexts can influence emotion regulation (Geyer & Ogbonnaya, 2021; Godleski & others, 2020). Infants are often affected by fatigue, hunger, time of day, which people are around them, and where they are. Infants must learn to adapt to different contexts that require emotion regulation. Further, new demands appear as the infant becomes older and parents modify their expectations (Mitsven & others, 2021). For example, a parent may take it in stride if a 6-month-old infant screams in a grocery store but may react very differently if a 2-year-old starts screaming.

How Would You...?

If you were a **human development and family studies professional,** how would you respond to the parents of a 13-month-old baby who are concerned because their son has suddenly started crying every morning when they drop him off at child care—despite the fact that he has been going to the same child-care center for over six months?

reflexive smile A smile that does not occur in response to external stimuli. It happens during the month after birth, usually during sleep.

social smile A smile in response to an external stimulus, which, early in development, typically is a face.

stranger anxiety An infant's fear and wariness of strangers; it tends to appear in the second half of the first year of life.

separation protest Occurs when infants experience a fear of being separated from a caregiver, which results in crying when the caregiver leaves.

To soothe or not to soothe—should a crying baby be given attention and soothed, or does this attention spoil the infant? Many years ago, the behaviorist John Watson (1928) argued that parents spend too much time responding to infant crying. As a consequence, he said, parents reward crying and increase its incidence. However, infancy experts Mary Ainsworth (1979) and John Bowlby (1989) stressed that you can't respond too much to infant crying in the first year of life. They argued that a quick, comforting response to the infant's cries is an important ingredient in the development of a strong bond between the infant and the caregiver. In one of Ainsworth's classic studies, infants whose mothers responded quickly when they cried at 3 months of age cried less later in the first year of life (Bell & Ainsworth, 1972). Further, a more contemporary study revealed that mothers experiencing depression rocked and touched their crying infants less than mothers not experiencing depression (Esposito & others, 2017c).

Controversy still characterizes the question of whether or how parents should respond to an infant's cries, particularly when infants are learning to sleep through the night. Some developmentalists argue that an infant cannot be spoiled in the first year of life, a view suggesting that parents should soothe a crying infant. This reaction should help infants develop a sense of trust and secure attachment to the caregiver. One experiment showed that training mothers to soothe their newborns resulted in sounder sleep and less crying (Ozturk Donmez & Bayik Temel, 2019). Yet other research suggests that letting young infants "cry it out" (as long as their basic needs have been met) may have short-term negative effects but no long-term effects on behavior or attachment (Bilgin & Wolke, 2020; Giesbrecht & others, 2020). Thus, there are somewhat mixed results about whether infants' development is harmed when parents do not respond immediately to their cries, such as in middle-of-the-night crying. That said, when parents perceive that their infant's cry is a response to pain or fear, they should always respond immediately in a nurturing manner.

TEMPERAMENT

Do you get upset a lot? Does it take much to get you angry, or to make you laugh? Even at birth, babies seem to have different emotional styles. One infant is cheerful and happy much of the time; another baby seems to cry constantly. These tendencies reflect **temperament,** which involves individual differences in behavioral styles, emotions, and characteristic ways of responding. With regard to its link to emotion, temperament refers to individual differences in how quickly the emotion is shown, how strong it is, how long it lasts, and how quickly it fades away (Campos, 2009).

Another way to describe temperament focuses on predispositions toward emotional reactivity and self-regulation (Bates, McQuillan, & Hoyniak, 2019; Pozzi & others, 2021). *Reactivity* involves variations in the speed and intensity with which an individual responds to situations with positive or negative emotions. *Self-regulation* involves variations in the extent or effectiveness of an individual's control over emotion.

Describing and Classifying Temperament   How would you describe your temperament or the temperament of a friend? Researchers have described and classified the temperaments of individuals in different ways (Aktar & Perez-Edgar, 2021; Gartstein & Putnam, 2019). Here we examine three of those ways.

Chess and Thomas' Classification   Psychiatrists Stella Chess and Alexander Thomas (Chess & Thomas, 1977; Thomas & Chess, 1991) identified three basic types, or clusters, of temperament:

- An **easy child** is generally in a positive mood, quickly establishes regular routines in infancy, and adapts readily to new experiences.
- A **difficult child** reacts negatively and cries frequently, engages in irregular daily routines, and is slow to accept change.
- A **slow-to-warm-up child** has a low activity level, is somewhat negative, and displays a low intensity of mood.

In their longitudinal investigation, Chess and Thomas found that 40 percent of the children they studied could be classified as easy, 10 percent as difficult, and 15 percent as slow to warm up. Notice that 35 percent did not fit any of the three patterns. Researchers have found that these three basic clusters of temperament are moderately stable across the

How Would You...?

If you were a **social worker,** how would you advise a parent who is frustrated with their 18-month-old who tends to whine and cry excessively in comparison to their 3-year-old sibling?

temperament Involves individual differences in behavioral styles, emotions, and characteristic ways of responding.

easy child A temperament style in which the child is generally in a positive mood, quickly establishes regular routines, and adapts easily to new experiences.

difficult child A temperament style in which the child tends to react negatively and cry frequently, engages in irregular daily routines, and is slow to accept new experiences.

slow-to-warm-up child A temperament style in which the child has a low activity level, is somewhat negative, and displays a low intensity of mood.

childhood years. All children benefit from high-quality early child care more than low-quality child care, but child-care quality is especially important for children with a difficult temperament (Johnson, Finch, & Phillips, 2019).

Kagan's Behavioral Inhibition   Another way of classifying temperament focuses on the differences between a shy, subdued, timid child and a sociable, extraverted, bold child (Callueng, Emam, & Oakland, 2020). Jerome Kagan (2013, 2019) regards shyness with strangers (peers or adults) as one feature of a broad temperament category called *inhibition to the unfamiliar.* Beginning at about 7 to 9 months, inhibited children react to many aspects of unfamiliarity with initial avoidance, distress, or subdued affect. In Kagan's longitudinal research, inhibition shows some continuity from infancy through early childhood, although a substantial number of infants who are classified as inhibited become less so by 7 years of age. Recent research findings spanning many studies indicate that infants and young children who have an inhibited temperament are at risk for developing social anxiety disorder in adolescence and adulthood (Fox & others, 2021; Sandstrom, Uher, & Pavlova, 2020).

Rothbart and Bates' Classification   New classifications of temperament continue to be forged (Rothbart, Posner, & Sheese, 2021). Mary Rothbart and John Bates (2006) argue that three broad dimensions best represent what researchers have found to characterize the structure of temperament: extraversion/surgency, negative affectivity, and effortful control (self-regulation):

- *Extraversion/surgency* includes "positive anticipation, impulsivity, activity level, and sensation seeking" (Rothbart, 2004, p. 495). Kagan's uninhibited children fit into this category.

- *Negative affectivity* includes "fear, frustration, sadness, and discomfort" (Rothbart, 2004, p. 495). These children are easily distressed; they may fret and cry often. Kagan's inhibited children fit this category. In one study, positive affectivity and surgency at 4 months of age was linked to school readiness at 4 years of age (Gartstein, Putnam, & Kliewer, 2016).

- *Effortful control* (self-regulation) includes "attentional focusing and shifting, inhibitory control, perceptual sensitivity, and low-intensity pleasure" (Rothbart, 2004, p. 495). Infants who are high on effortful control show an ability to keep their arousal from getting too high and have strategies for soothing themselves. By contrast, children low on effortful control are often unable to control their arousal; they become easily agitated and intensely emotional (Bates, McQuillan, & Hoyniak, 2019). One study found that having better effortful control at the age of 54 months predicted lower rates of behavior problems from kindergarten to sixth grade, due in part to having fewer conflicts with teachers (Crockett & others, 2018). Another study revealed that self-regulation capacity at 4 months of age was linked to school readiness at 4 years of age (Gartstein, Putnam, & Kliewer, 2016). And in one clinical study, children with a lower level of effort control at 3 years of age were more likely to have ADHD symptoms at 13 years of age (Einziger & others, 2018).

The description of temperament so far reflects the development of normative capabilities of children, not individual differences in children. The development of these capabilities, such as effortful control, allows individual differences to emerge (Bates, McQuillan, & Hoyniak, 2019). For example, although maturation of the brain's prefrontal lobes must occur for any child's attention to improve and the child to achieve effortful control, some children develop strong effortful control but others do not. And it is these individual differences in children that are at the heart of temperament.

Biological Foundations and Experience   How does a child acquire a certain temperament? Kagan (2013, 2019) argues that children inherit a physiology that biases them to have a particular type of temperament. However, through experience they may learn to modify their temperament somewhat (Goodvin, Winer, & Thompson, 2015). For example, children may inherit a physiology that disposes them to be fearful and inhibited, but they learn to reduce their fear and inhibition to some degree.

Physiological characteristics have been linked with different temperaments (Clauss, Avery, & Blackford, 2015; Rothbart, Posner, & Sheese, 2021). In particular, an inhibited temperament

developmental **connection**

Nature and Nurture

Twin and adoption studies have been used in the effort to estimate hereditary and environmental influences on development. Connect to "Biological Beginnings."

is associated with a unique physiological pattern that includes high and stable heart rate, high level of the hormone cortisol, and high activity in the right frontal lobe of the brain (Kagan, 2018). This pattern may be tied to the excitability of the amygdala, a structure of the brain that plays an important role in fear and inhibition. And the development of effortful control is linked to advances in the brain's frontal lobes (Quiñones-Camacho & others, 2019).

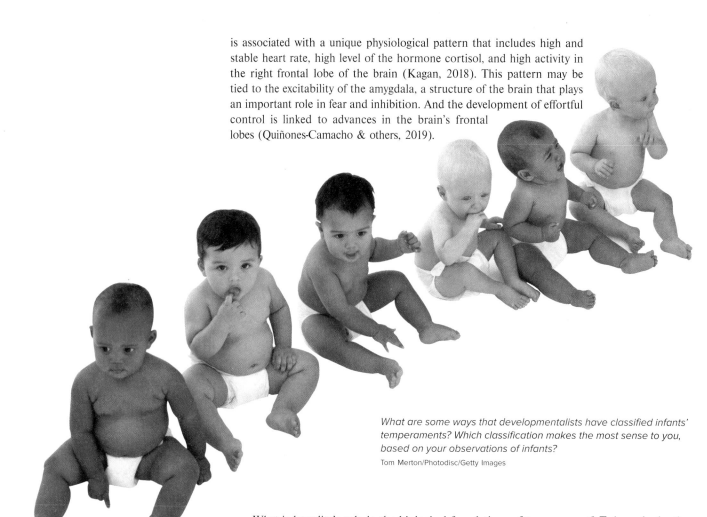

What are some ways that developmentalists have classified infants' temperaments? Which classification makes the most sense to you, based on your observations of infants?

Tom Merton/Photodisc/Getty Images

What is heredity's role in the biological foundations of temperament? Twin and adoption studies suggest that heredity has a moderate influence on differences in temperament within a group of people (Planalp & Goldsmith, 2020). Too often, though, the biological foundations of temperament are interpreted as meaning that temperament cannot develop or change. However, important self-regulatory dimensions of temperament such as adaptability, soothability, and persistence look very different in a 1-year-old and a 5-year-old (R.A. Thompson, 2015). These temperament dimensions develop and change with the growth of the neurobiological foundations of self-regulation and predict subsequent outcomes later in life (Robson, Allen, & Howard, 2020; Shiner, 2021).

Developmental Links   Is temperament in childhood linked with adjustment in adulthood? In one classic study, children who had an easy temperament at 3 to 5 years of age were likely to be well adjusted as young adults (Chess & Thomas, 1977). In contrast, many children who had a difficult temperament at 3 to 5 years of age were not well adjusted as young adults. In a more recent longitudinal study, children who had a difficult temperament at 5 and 14 years of age were more likely to have mental health problems at 21 years of age (Kingsbury & others, 2017).

Inhibition is another temperament characteristic that has been studied extensively (Bates, McQuillan & Hoyniak, 2019). A longitudinal study found that greater inhibitory control at 42 months predicted a greater decrease in shyness by the age of 84 months (Eggum-Wilkens & others, 2016). Another study found that fearful inhibition at 2 years of age predicted internalizing behavior problems at age 6, but not if children at age 3 had good inhibitory control or had a mother who was low in negative behaviors (Liu, Calkins, & Bell, 2018). And one of the longest-running longitudinal studies of fearful inhibition in infancy showed that these infants were more likely to be introverted, to have difficulties in social relationships, and to have symptoms of anxiety and depression 25 years later when they were in their mid-twenties (Tang & others, 2020).

In sum, these studies reveal some continuity between certain aspects of temperament in childhood and adjustment in early adulthood (Dagan & Sagi-Schwartz, 2021; Shiner, 2019). However, keep in mind that these connections between childhood temperament and adult adjustment are based on only a small number of studies; more research is needed to verify these linkages.

Developmental Contexts What accounts for the continuities and discontinuities between a child's temperament and an adult's personality? Physiological and heredity factors likely are involved in continuity (Clauss, Avery, & Blackford, 2015; Kagan, 2019). Links between temperament in childhood and personality in adulthood also might vary, depending on the contexts in individuals' experience (Shiner, 2019).

The reaction to an infant's or older child's temperament may depend, in part, on culture (Fan, Ren, & Li, 2020; Suh & Kang, 2020). For example, behavioral inhibition is more highly valued in China than in North America and Europe, and researchers have found that Chinese infants and toddlers are more inhibited than Western infants (Chen & others, 2019). The cultural differences in temperament are linked to parental attitudes and behaviors. Western mothers of inhibited children are less accepting of their infants' inhibited temperament, whereas Chinese mothers are more accepting. Many other cultural distinctions around the globe have been found when examining young children's temperaments and their socialization environments (Gartstein & Putnam, 2018).

In short, many aspects of a child's environment can encourage or discourage the persistence of temperament characteristics (Bates, McQuillan, & Hoyniak, 2019). For example, one illustrative study found that fathers' anxiety and depression were linked to a higher level of negative affectivity in their 6-month-olds (Potapova, Gartstein, & Bridgett, 2014). One useful way of thinking about these relationships applies the concept of goodness of fit, which we examine next.

developmental **connection**

Culture

Cross-cultural studies seek to determine culture-universal and culture-specific aspects of development. Connect to "Introduction."

Goodness of Fit Goodness of fit refers to the match between a child's temperament and the environmental demands the child must cope with. Suppose one toddler is very active but is made to sit still for long periods of time, compared to another who is a slow-to-warm-up toddler who is abruptly pushed into new situations on a regular basis. Both toddlers face a lack of fit between their temperament and environmental demands. Lack of fit can produce adjustment problems (Newland & Crnic, 2017).

Some temperament characteristics pose more parenting challenges than others, at least in modern Western societies (Bates, McQuillan, & Hoyniak, 2019; Dagan & Sagi-Schwartz, 2021). When children are prone to distress, as exhibited by frequent crying and irritability, their parents may eventually respond by ignoring the child's distress or trying to force the child to "behave." However, one classic intervention study showed that extra support and training for mothers of distress-prone infants improved the quality of mother-infant interaction (van den Boom, 1989). The training led the mothers to alter their demands on the child, improving the fit between the child and the environment. Researchers also have found that changes in infants' negative emotionality are linked to co-occurring changes in parental sensitivity, involvement, and responsivity (Vertsberger & Knafo-Noam, 2019). And a meta-analysis of 84 studies found that, compared with children with an easy temperament, children with a more difficult temperament were more vulnerable to negative parenting but also benefited more from positive parenting (Slagt & others, 2016).

An infant's temperament can vary across cultures. *What do parents need to know about a child's temperament?*
Seiji Takemura/MIXA/Getty Images

The most recent emerging ideas regarding goodness of fit involve the *differential susceptibility model* and the *biological sensitivity to context model* (Belsky, Zhang, & Sayler, 2022; Shakiba & others, 2020). These models emphasize that certain characteristics—such as a difficult temperament—that render children more vulnerable to difficulty in adverse contexts can also make them more likely to experience optimal growth in very supportive conditions. These models may help us see "negative" temperament characteristics in a new light.

To read further about some positive strategies for parenting that take into account the child's temperament, see the *Caring Connections* interlude.

How Would You...?

If you were a **social worker**, how would you apply information about an infant's temperament to maximize the goodness of fit in a clinical setting?

goodness of fit Refers to the match between a child's temperament and the environmental demands the child must cope with.

Parenting and the Child's Temperament

What are the implications of temperamental variations for parenting? Although answers to this question necessarily are speculative, the following conclusions were reached decades ago by temperament experts Ann Sanson and Mary Rothbart (1995), regarding the best parenting strategies to use in relation to children's temperament, and still hold true today:

- *Attention to and respect for individuality.* One implication is that it is difficult to generate general prescriptions for "good" parenting. A goal might be accomplished in one way with one child and in another way with another child, depending on the child's temperament. Parents need to be sensitive and flexible in responding to the infant's signals and needs. Researchers have found that decreases in infants' negative emotionality are related to higher levels of parental sensitivity, involvement, and responsiveness.
- *Structuring the child's environment.* Crowded, noisy environments can pose greater problems for some children (such as "difficult" children) than others (such as "easygoing" children). We might also expect that a fearful, withdrawing child would benefit from slower entry into new contexts.
- *The "difficult child" and packaged parenting programs.* Programs for parents often focus on dealing with children who have "difficult"

What are some good strategies for parents to adopt when responding to their infant's temperament?
Noriko Cooper/digitalskill/123RF

temperaments. In some cases, "difficult child" refers to Thomas and Chess' description of a child who reacts negatively, cries frequently, engages in irregular daily routines, and is slow to accept change. In others, the concept might be used to describe a child who is irritable, displays anger frequently, does not follow directions well, or shows some other negative characteristic. Acknowledging that some children are harder than others to parent is often helpful, and advice on how to handle specific difficult characteristics can be useful. However, whether a specific characteristic is difficult depends on its fit with the environment. To label a child "difficult" has the danger of becoming a self-fulfilling prophecy. If a child is identified as "difficult," people may treat the child in a way that actually elicits "difficult" behavior.

Too often, we pigeonhole children into categories without examining the context (Bates, McQuillan & Hoyniak, 2019). Nonetheless, caregivers need to take children's temperament into account. Research does not yet allow for many highly specific recommendations, but, in general, caregivers should (1) be sensitive to the individual characteristics of the child, (2) be flexible in responding to these characteristics, and (3) avoid applying negative labels to the child.

PERSONALITY DEVELOPMENT

Emotions and temperament represent key aspects of personality—the enduring personal characteristics of individuals. Let's now examine characteristics that often are thought of as central to personality development during infancy: trust and the development of self and independence.

Trust   According to Erik Erikson (1968), the first year of life is characterized by the trust versus mistrust stage of development. Following a life of regularity, warmth, and protection in the mother's womb, the infant faces a world that is less secure. Erikson proposed that infants learn trust when they are cared for in a consistent, warm manner. If the infant is not well fed and kept warm on a consistent basis, a sense of mistrust is likely to develop.

Trust versus mistrust is not resolved once and for all in the first year of life. It arises again at each successive stage of development, a pathway that can have positive or negative outcomes. For example, children who leave infancy with a sense of trust can still have their sense of mistrust activated at a later stage, perhaps if their parents break up under conflictual circumstances.

developmental **connection**

Personality

Erikson proposed that individuals go through eight stages in the course of human development. Connect to "Introduction."

The Developing Sense of Self   Real or imagined, the sense of self is a strong motivating force in life. When does the individual begin to sense a separate existence from others? Studying the self in infancy is difficult mainly because infants cannot tell us how they experience themselves. Infants cannot verbally express their views of the self. They also cannot understand complex instructions from researchers.

One ingenious strategy to test infants' visual self-recognition is the use of a mirror technique, in which an infant's mother first puts a dot of rouge (reddish makeup) on the infant's nose. Then an observer watches to see how often the infant touches its nose. Next, the infant is placed in front of a mirror, and observers detect whether nose touching increases. Why does this matter? The idea is that increased nose touching indicates that the infant recognizes the self in the mirror and is trying to touch or rub off the rouge because the rouge violates the infant's view of the self. Increased touching indicates that the infant realizes that it is the self in the mirror but that something is not right since the real self does not have a dot of rouge on it.

Figure 3 displays the results of two classic investigations that used the mirror technique. The researchers found that before they were 1 year old, infants did not recognize themselves in the mirror (Amsterdam, 1968; Lewis & Brooks-Gunn, 1979). Signs of self-recognition began to appear among some infants when they were 15 to 18 months old. By the time they were 2 years old, most children recognized themselves in the mirror. In sum, infants begin to develop a self-understanding called self-recognition at approximately 18 months of age (Leed, Chinn, & Lockman, 2019).

Late in the second year and early in the third year, toddlers show other emerging forms of self-awareness that reflect a sense of "me" (Goodvin, Winer, & Thompson, 2015). For example, they refer to themselves by saying "Me big"; they label internal experiences such as emotions; they monitor themselves as when a toddler says, "Do it myself"; and they say that things are theirs (Davoodi, Nelson, & Blake, 2018; Ross & others, 2017). It is during the second year that infants develop a conscious awareness of their own bodies (Waugh & Brownell, 2015). This developmental change in body awareness marks the beginning of children's representation of their own three-dimensional body shape and appearance, providing an early step in the development of their self-image and identity.

Also, researchers recently have found that the capacity to understand others may begin to develop during infancy (Rhodes & Baron, 2019; Yeung, Müller, & Carpendale, 2019). For example, infants as young as 13 months of age seem to consider another's perspective when predicting their actions (Choi & Luo, 2015).

Independence   Not only does the infant develop a sense of self in the second year of life, but independence also becomes a more central theme in the infant's life (Campione-Barr,

Erikson argued that autonomy versus shame and doubt is the key developmental theme of the toddler years. *What are some good strategies for parents to use with their toddlers?*

Marvin Fox/Moment/Getty Images

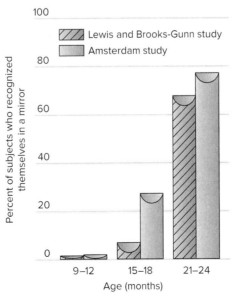

FIGURE **3**

THE DEVELOPMENT OF SELF-RECOGNITION IN INFANCY. The graph shows the findings of two studies in which infants less than 1 year of age did not recognize themselves in the mirror. A slight increase in the percentage of infant self-recognition occurred around 15 to 18 months of age. By 2 years of age, a majority of children recognized themselves. *Why do researchers study whether infants recognize themselves in a mirror?*

(photo): Digital Vision/Getty Images

How Would You...?

If you were a **human development and family studies professional,** how would you work with a parent who shows signs of being overly protective or critical to the point of impairing the toddler's independence?

developmental **connection**

Personality

Two key points in development when there is a strong push for independence are the second year of life and early adolescence. Connect to "Socioemotional Development in Adolescence."

2020). The theories of Margaret Mahler and Erik Erikson have important implications for both self-development and independence. Mahler (1979) argues that the child goes through a separation and then an individuation process. *Separation* involves the infant's movement away from the mother. *Individuation* involves the development of self.

Erikson (1968), like Mahler, stressed that independence is an important issue in the second year of life. Erikson describes the second stage of development as the stage of autonomy versus shame and doubt. Autonomy builds as the infant's mental and motor abilities develop. At this point in development, not only can infants walk, but they can also climb, open and close, drop, push and pull, and hold and let go. Infants feel pride in these new accomplishments and want to do everything themselves, whether the activity is flushing a toilet, pulling the wrapping off a package, or deciding what to eat. It is important for parents to recognize the motivation of toddlers to do what they are capable of doing at their own pace. Then they can learn to control their muscles and their impulses themselves. But when caregivers are impatient and do for toddlers what they are capable of doing themselves, shame and doubt develop. Every parent has rushed a child from time to time. It is only when parents consistently overprotect toddlers or criticize accidents (wetting, soiling, spilling, or breaking, for example) that children develop an excessive sense of shame and doubt about their ability to control themselves and their world. As we discuss in later chapters, Erikson argued that the stage of autonomy versus shame and doubt has important implications for the individual's future development.

Review *Connect* Reflect

LG1 Discuss emotional and personality development in infancy.

Review

- What is the nature of an infant's emotions, and how do they change?
- What is temperament, and how does it develop in infancy?
- What are some important aspects of personality in infancy, and how do they develop?

Connect

- Earlier in this section, you read that the early development of the hippocampus in infants plays a role in their emotions.

The hippocampus is also connected to another key cognitive process. What is that process?

Reflect *Your Own Personal Journey of Life*

- How would you describe your temperament? Does it fit one of Chess and Thomas's three styles—easy, slow to warm up, or difficult? If you have siblings, is your temperament similar to or different from theirs?

---

2 How Do Social Orientation/Understanding and Attachment Develop in Infancy?

LG2 Describe the development of social orientation/understanding and attachment in infancy.

| Social Orientation/ Understanding | Attachment and Its Development | Individual Differences in Attachment | Developmental Social Neuroscience and Attachment |

So far, we have discussed how emotions and emotional competence change as children develop. We have also examined the role of emotional style; in effect, we have seen how emotions set the tone of our experiences in life. But emotions also write the lyrics because they are at the core of our relationships with others.

SOCIAL ORIENTATION/UNDERSTANDING

In Ross Thompson's view (Thompson, 2016, 2022), infants are socioemotional beings who show a strong interest in the social world and are motivated to orient to it and understand it. In other chapters, we described many of the biological and cognitive foundations that contribute to the infant's development of social orientation and understanding. We call attention to relevant biological and cognitive factors as we explore social orientation; locomotion; intention, goal-directed behavior, and cooperation; and social referencing.

Social Orientation   From early in their development, infants are captivated by the social world. Young infants stare intently at faces and are attuned to the sounds of human voices, especially those of their caregivers (Durand & others, 2020; Singarajah & others, 2017; Sugden & Moulson, 2017). Later, they become adept at interpreting the meaning of facial expressions (Piazza & others, 2020; Weatherhead & White, 2017). *Face-to-face play* often begins to characterize caregiver-infant interactions when the infant is about 2 to 3 months of age. The focused social interaction of face-to-face play may include vocalizations, touch, and gestures. Such play is part of many mothers' efforts to create a positive emotional state in their infants and is an important part of establishing shared experience and understanding (Margolis & others, 2019; Terrace, Bigelow, & Beebe, 2022).

In part because of such positive social interchanges between caregivers and infants, it was long ago established that by 2 to 3 months of age infants respond to people differently from the way they do to objects, showing more positive emotion toward people than inanimate objects such as puppets (Legerstee, 1997). At this age, most infants expect people to react positively when the infants initiate a behavior, such as a smile or a vocalization. This finding has been discovered by use of a method called the *still-face paradigm,* in which the caregiver alternates between engaging in face-to-face interaction with the infant and remaining still and unresponsive (Gao & others, 2023). As early as 2 to 3 months of age, infants show more withdrawal, negative emotions, and self-directed behavior when their caregivers are still and unresponsive (Adamson & Frick, 2003). Infants' autonomic nervous system activity changes reliably during both the still face and recovery period using the still-face paradigm (Jones-Mason & others, 2018).

Infants also learn about the social world through contexts other than face-to-face play with a caregiver (Swingler & others, 2017; Thompson 2022). Even though infants as young as 6 months of age show an interest in each other, their interaction with peers increases considerably in the last half of the second year. As increasing numbers of U.S. infants experience child care outside the home, they are spending more time in social play with peers (Child Trends, 2016; National Center for Education Statistics, 2021). Later in the chapter, we further discuss child care.

Locomotion   Recall from earlier in the chapter how important independence is for infants, especially in the second year of life. As infants develop the ability to crawl, walk, and run, they are able to explore and expand their social world. These newly developed self-produced locomotor skills allow the infant to independently initiate social interchanges on a more frequent basis. Remember that the development of these gross motor skills reflects a number of factors, including the development of the nervous system, the goal the infant is motivated to reach, and environmental support for the skill (Adolph, 2018; Hospodar & others, 2021).

The infant's and toddler's push for independence also is likely paced by the development of locomotion skills (Adolph & Hoch, 2019). Locomotion is also important for its motivational implications. Once infants have the ability to move in goal-directed pursuits, the reward from these pursuits leads to further efforts to explore and develop skills.

Intention, Goal-Directed Behavior, and Cooperation   Perceiving people as engaging in intentional and goal-directed behavior is an important social cognitive accomplishment, and this initially occurs toward the end of the first year (Thompson, 2015). Joint attention and gaze following help the infant to understand that other people have intentions (Boyer, Harding, & Bertenthal, 2020; Stout & others, 2021). *Joint attention* occurs when the caregiver and infant focus on the same object or event. By their first birthday, infants have begun to direct the caregiver's attention to objects that capture their interest (Salo, Rowe, & Reeb-Sutherland, 2018).

Amanda Woodward and her colleagues (Colomer & Woodward, 2023; Filippi & others, 2019; Krogh-Jespersen, Henderson, & Woodward, 2020) argue that infants' ability to understand and respond to others' meaningful intentions is a critical cognitive foundation for effectively engaging in the social world. They especially emphasize that an important aspect of this ability is the capacity to grasp social knowledge quickly in order to make an appropriate social

developmental **connection**

Biological, Cognitive, and Socioemotional Processes

Discussing biological, cognitive, and socioemotional processes together reminds us of an important aspect of development: These processes are intricately intertwined. Connect to "Introduction."

A mother and her baby engage in face-to-face play. *At what age does face-to-face play usually begin, and when does it typically start decreasing in frequency?*
Tom Grill/JGI/Blend Images/Getty Images

developmental **connection**

Theories

The dynamic systems view is increasingly used to explain how infants develop. Connect to "Physical Development in Infancy."

FIGURE 4

THE COOPERATION TASK. The cooperation task consisted of two handles on a box, atop which was an animated musical toy, surreptitiously activated by remote control when both handles were pulled. The handles were placed far enough apart that one child could not pull both handles. The experimenter demonstrated the task, saying, "Watch! If you pull the handles, the doggie will sing" (Brownell, Ramani, & Zerwas, 2006).

Courtesy of Celia A. Brownell, University of Pittsburgh

response. Although processing speed is an important contributor to social engagement, other factors are involved, such as infants' motivation to interact with someone, the infant's social interactive history with the individual, the interactive partner's social membership, and culturally specific aspects of interaction.

Cooperating with others also is a key aspect of effectively engaging with others in the social world. Can infants engage in cooperation with others? One illustrative study involved presenting 1- and 2-year-olds with a simple cooperative task that consisted of pulling a lever to get an attractive toy (Brownell, Ramani, & Zerwas, 2006) (see Figure 4). Any coordinated actions of the 1-year-olds appeared to be more coincidental than cooperative, whereas the 2-year-olds' behavior was more likely to be characterized as active cooperation to reach a goal. In this study, the infants also were assessed using two social understanding tasks, observation of children's behavior in a joint attention task, and the parents' perceptions of the language the children use about the self and others. Those with more advanced social understanding were more likely to cooperate. To cooperate, the children had to connect their own intentions with the peer's intentions and put this understanding to use in interacting with the peer to reach a goal.

Social Referencing

Another important social cognitive accomplishment in infancy is developing the ability to "read" the emotions of other people (Fawcett & Kreutz, 2021; Piazza & others, 2020). **Social referencing** is the term used to describe "reading" emotional cues in others to help determine how to act in a specific situation. The development of social referencing helps infants to interpret ambiguous situations more accurately, as when they encounter a stranger and need to know whether or not to fear the person (Ehli & others, 2020). By the end of the first year, a mother's facial expression—either smiling or fearful—influences whether an infant will explore an unfamiliar environment.

Infants become better at social referencing at the end of the first year and in the second year of life (Bazhydai, Westermann, & Parise, 2020). At this age, they tend to "check" with their mother before they act; they look at her to see if she is happy, angry, or fearful.

Infants' Social Sophistication and Insight

In sum, researchers are discovering that infants are more socially sophisticated and insightful at younger ages than was previously envisioned (Thompson, 2016, 2022). Such sophistication and insight are reflected in infants' perceptions of others' actions as intentionally motivated and goal-directed and their motivation to share and participate in that intentionality by their first birthday. More advanced social cognitive skills of infants could be expected to influence their understanding and awareness of **attachment** to a caregiver.

ATTACHMENT AND ITS DEVELOPMENT

There is no shortage of theories about why infants become attached to a caregiver. Three theorists—Freud, Erikson, and Bowlby—proposed influential views.

Freud noted that infants become attached to the person or object that provides oral satisfaction. For most infants, this is the mother since she is most likely to feed the infant. Is feeding as important as Freud thought? A classic study by Harry Harlow (1958) revealed that the answer is no (see Figure 5).

Harlow removed infant monkeys from their mothers at birth; for six months they were reared by surrogate (substitute) "mothers." One surrogate mother was made of wire, the other of cloth. Half of the infant monkeys were fed by the wire mother, half by the cloth mother. Periodically, the amount of time the infant monkeys spent with either the wire or the cloth mother was computed. Regardless of which mother fed them, the infant monkeys spent far more time with the cloth mother. Even if the wire mother but not the cloth mother provided nourishment, the infant monkeys spent more time with the cloth mother. And when Harlow frightened the monkeys, those "raised" by the cloth mother ran to the mother and clung to it; those raised by the wire mother did not. Whether the mother provided comfort seemed to

social referencing "Reading" emotional cues in others to help determine how to act in a particular situation.

attachment A close emotional bond between two people.

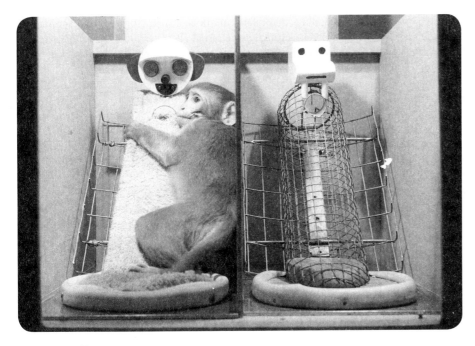
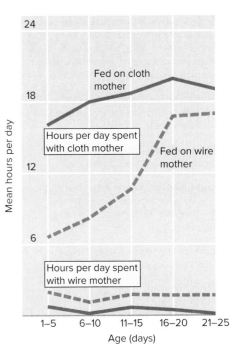

FIGURE 5

CONTACT TIME WITH WIRE AND CLOTH SURROGATE MOTHERS. Regardless of whether the infant monkeys were fed by a wire or a cloth mother, they overwhelmingly preferred to spend contact time with the cloth mother. *How do these results compare with what Freud's theory and Erikson's theory would predict about human infants?*

(photo): Al Fenn/The LIFE Picture Collection/Shutterstock

determine whether the monkeys associated the mother with security. This study clearly demonstrated that feeding is not the crucial element in the attachment process and that contact comfort is important. Follow-up studies documented other characteristics of surrogate mothers, such as warm temperature, that could confer comfort and security (Harlow & Suomi, 1970).

Physical comfort also plays a role in Erik Erikson's (1968) view of the infant's development. Recall Erikson's proposal that the first year of life represents the stage of trust versus mistrust. Physical comfort and sensitive care, according to Erikson (1968), are key to establishing a basic trust in infants. The infant's sense of trust, in turn, is the foundation for attachment and sets the stage for a lifelong expectation that the world will be a good and pleasant place to be.

The ethological perspective of British psychiatrist John Bowlby (1969, 1989) also stresses the importance of attachment in the first year of life and the responsiveness of the caregiver. Bowlby stresses that infants and their primary caregivers are biologically predisposed to form attachments to each other. He argues that the newborn is biologically equipped to elicit attachment behavior. The baby cries, clings, coos, and smiles. Later, the infant crawls, walks, and follows the mother. The immediate result is to keep the primary caregiver nearby; the long-term effect is to increase the infant's chances of survival.

Attachment does not emerge suddenly but rather develops in a series of phases, moving from a baby's general preference for human beings to a partnership with primary caregivers. Following are four such phases based on Bowlby's conceptualization of attachment (Schaffer, 1996):

- *Phase 1: From birth to 2 months.* Infants instinctively direct their attachment to human figures. Strangers, siblings, and parents are equally likely to elicit smiling or crying from the infant.

- *Phase 2: From 2 to 7 months.* Attachment becomes focused on one figure, usually the primary caregiver, as the baby gradually learns to distinguish familiar from unfamiliar people.

- *Phase 3: From 7 to 24 months.* Specific attachments develop. With increased locomotor skills, babies actively seek contact with regular caregivers, such as the mother or father.

- *Phase 4: From 24 months on.* Children become aware of others' feelings, goals, and plans and begin to take these into account in forming their own actions.

Strange Situation An observational measure of infant attachment that requires the infant to move through a series of introductions, separations, and reunions with the caregiver and an adult stranger in a prescribed order.

securely attached babies Babies that use the caregiver as a secure base from which to explore their environment.

insecure avoidant babies Babies that show insecurity by avoiding the caregiver.

insecure resistant babies Babies that often cling to the caregiver, then resist by fighting against the closeness, perhaps by kicking or pushing away.

insecure disorganized babies Babies that show insecurity by being disorganized and disoriented.

How Would You...?
If you were a **psychologist,** how would you identify an insecurely attached infant? How would you encourage a parent to strengthen the attachment bond?

Researchers' more recent findings that infants are more socially sophisticated and insightful than was previously envisioned suggest that some of the characteristics of Bowlby's phase 4, such as understanding the goals and intentions of the attachment figure, appear to be developing in phase 3 as attachment security is taking shape (Thompson, 2021).

Bowlby argued that infants develop an *internal working model* of attachment, a simple mental model of the caregiver, their relationship, and the self as deserving of nurturant care. The infant's internal working model of attachment with the caregiver influences the infant's—and later, the child's—subsequent responses to other people (Cassidy, 2016; Fearon & Roisman, 2017). The internal model of attachment also has played a pivotal role in the discovery of links between attachment and subsequent emotional understanding and self-perception (Dagan & Sagi-Schwartz, 2021; Thompson, 2016).

In sum, attachment emerges from the social cognitive advances that allow infants to develop expectations for the caregiver's behavior and to determine the affective quality of their relationship (Lopez-Maestro & others, 2017; Nelson & Fivush, 2020; Thompson, 2022). These social cognitive advances include recognizing the caregiver's face, voice, and other features, as well as developing an internal working model of expecting the caregiver to provide pleasure in social interaction and relief from distress.

INDIVIDUAL DIFFERENCES IN ATTACHMENT

Although attachment to a caregiver intensifies midway through the first year, isn't it likely that the quality of babies' attachment experiences varies? Mary Ainsworth (1979) thought so. Ainsworth created the **Strange Situation,** an observational measure of infant attachment in which the infant experiences a series of introductions, separations, and reunions with the caregiver and an adult stranger in a prescribed order (Posada & others, 2021). In using the Strange Situation, researchers hope that their observations will provide information about the infant's motivation to be near the caregiver and the degree to which the caregiver's presence provides the infant with security and confidence (Brownell & others, 2015).

Based on how babies respond in the Strange Situation, they are described as being securely attached or insecurely attached (in one of three ways) to the caregiver:

- **Securely attached babies** use the caregiver as a secure base from which to explore the environment. When in the presence of their caregiver, securely attached infants explore the room and examine toys that have been placed in it. When the caregiver departs, securely attached infants might protest mildly, and when the caregiver returns, these infants reestablish a positive interaction with them, perhaps by smiling or climbing on the caregiver's lap. Subsequently, they often resume playing with the toys in the room.

- **Insecure avoidant babies** show insecurity by avoiding the caregiver. In the Strange Situation, these babies engage in little interaction with the caregiver, are not distressed when the caregiver leaves the room, usually do not reestablish contact on their return, and may even turn their back on them. If contact is established, the infant usually leans away or looks away.

- **Insecure resistant babies** often cling to the caregiver and then resist by fighting against the closeness, perhaps by kicking or pushing away. In the Strange Situation, these babies often cling anxiously to the caregiver and don't explore the playroom. When the caregiver leaves, they often cry loudly and push away if the caregiver tries to comfort them on their return.

- **Insecure disorganized babies** are disorganized and disoriented. In the Strange Situation, these babies might appear dazed, confused, and fearful. To be classified as disorganized, babies must show strong patterns of avoidance and resistance or display certain specified behaviors, such as extreme fearfulness around the caregiver.

Evaluating the Strange Situation Does the Strange Situation capture important differences among infants? As a measure of attachment, it may be culturally biased (Gernhardt, Keller, & Rubeling, 2016; Otto & Keller, 2013). For example, a classic study from the 1980s showed that German and Japanese babies often show different patterns of attachment from those of American infants. As illustrated in Figure 6, German infants are more likely to show an avoidant attachment pattern and Japanese infants are less likely to display this pattern than U.S. infants (van IJzendoorn & Kroonenberg, 1988). The avoidant pattern in German babies likely occurs because their caregivers encourage them to be independent (Grossmann & others, 1985). Also as shown in Figure 6, Japanese babies are more likely than American babies to be categorized as resistant. This may have more to do with the Strange Situation as a measure of attachment than with attachment insecurity itself. Japanese mothers rarely allow anyone unfamiliar with their babies to care for them. Thus, the Strange Situation might create considerably more stress for Japanese infants than for American infants, who are more accustomed to separation from their mothers (Kondo-Ikemura & others, 2018). Even though there are cultural variations in attachment classification, the most frequent classification in every culture studied so far is secure attachment (Fearon & Roisman, 2017; Thompson, 2021).

Some critics stress that behavior in the Strange Situation—like other laboratory assessments—might not indicate what infants would do in a natural environment. But researchers have found that infants' behaviors in the Strange Situation are closely related to how they behave at home in response to separation and reunion with their mothers (Bailey & others, 2017). Thus, many infant researchers stress that the Strange Situation continues to show merit as a measure of infant attachment.

Caregiving Styles and Attachment

Is the style of caregiving linked with the quality of the infant's attachment? Securely attached babies have caregivers who are sensitive to their signals and are consistently available to respond to their infants' needs (Bohr & others, 2018; Luby, 2020). These caregivers often let their babies have an active part in determining the onset and pacing of interaction in the first year of life. A comprehensive review of 687 articles revealed clear evidence that maternal sensitivity is related to infant attachment and child outcomes (Deans, 2020). Yet another study found that maternal sensitivity in parenting was related to secure attachment in infants in Colombia, Mexico, Peru, and the United States (Posada & others, 2016). Although maternal sensitivity is linked to the development of secure attachment in infancy, it is important to note that the size of this effect is not overwhelmingly strong (Deans, 2020).

How do the caregivers of insecurely attached babies interact with them? Caregivers of avoidant babies tend to be unavailable or rejecting (Groh & others, 2019). They often don't respond to their babies' signals and have little physical contact with them. When they do interact with their babies, they may behave in an angry and irritable way. Caregivers of resistant babies tend to be inconsistent; sometimes they respond to their babies' needs, and sometimes they don't. In general, they tend not to be very affectionate with their babies and show little synchrony when interacting with them. Caregivers of disorganized babies often neglect or physically abuse them (Cicchetti, 2017). In some cases, these caregivers are depressed. In sum, caregivers' interactions with infants influence whether infants are securely or insecurely attached to the caregivers (Fourment & others, 2022; Leerkes & Zhou, 2018).

Interpreting Differences in Attachment

Do individual differences in attachment matter? Ainsworth notes that secure attachment in the first year of life provides an important foundation for psychological development later in life. The securely attached infant moves freely away from the mother but keeps track of where she is through periodic glances. The securely attached infant responds positively to being picked up by others and, when put back down, freely moves away to play. An insecurely attached infant, by contrast, avoids the mother or is ambivalent toward her, fears strangers, and is upset by minor, everyday separations.

If early attachment to a caregiver is important, it should influence a child's social behavior later in development. For many children, early attachments foreshadow later functioning (Dagan & Sagi-Schwartz, 2021; Thompson, Simpson, & Berlin, 2021a, b). In the extensive longitudinal study conducted by Alan Sroufe and his colleagues (2016), early secure attachment (assessed by the Strange Situation at 12 and 18 months) was linked with positive emotional health, high self-esteem, self-confidence, and socially competent interaction with peers, teachers, camp counselors, and romantic partners through adolescence. Also, a

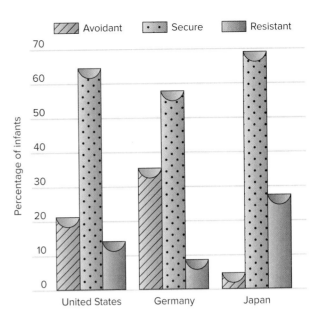

FIGURE 6

CROSS-CULTURAL COMPARISON OF ATTACHMENT. In one classic study, infant attachment in three countries—the United States, Germany, and Japan—was measured in the Ainsworth Strange Situation (van IJzendoorn & Kroonenberg, 1988). The dominant attachment pattern in all three countries was secure attachment. However, German infants were more avoidant and Japanese infants were less avoidant and more resistant than U.S. infants. *What are some explanations for differences in how German, Japanese, and American infants respond to the Strange Situation?*

How Would You...?

If you were a **health-care professional,** how would you use an infant's attachment style and/or a parent's caregiving style to determine whether an infant might be at risk for neglect or abuse?

What is the nature of secure and insecure attachment? How are caregiving styles related to attachment classification?

Corbis/age fotostock

longitudinal study found that infant attachment insecurity was linked to less effective emotion-regulation strategies (suppressing emotions, disengaging from close others, and exaggerating emotional expressions, for example) in relationship-challenging contexts 20 to 35 years later (Girme & others, 2021). Also, a meta-analysis found that secure attachment in infancy was linked to social competence with peers in childhood (Groh & others, 2014). Further, another study revealed that infant attachment insecurity (especially insecure resistant attachment) and early childhood behavioral inhibition predicted adolescent social anxiety symptoms (Lewis-Morrarty & others, 2015). And yet another meta-analysis revealed that disorganized attachment was more strongly linked to externalizing problems (aggression and hostility, for example) than were avoidant and resistant attachment (Fearon & others, 2010).

Few studies have assessed infants' attachment security to the mother and the father separately (Ahnert & Schoppe-Sullivan, 2020). However, one illustrative study revealed that infants who were insecurely attached to their mother and father ("double-insecure") at 15 months of age had more externalizing problems (out-of-control behavior, for example) in the elementary school years than their counterparts who were securely attached to at least one parent (Kochanska & Kim, 2013). A more recent study found that an infant's secure attachment to the father was not enough to reduce the infant's stress reactions when the mother-infant attachment was insecure (Kuo & others, 2019).

An important issue regarding attachment is whether infancy is a critical or sensitive period for development. Many, but not all, research studies reveal the power of infant attachment to predict subsequent development (Steele & Steele, 2019; Thompson, Simpson, & Berlin, 2021a, b; Waters & Roisman, 2018). In a meta-analytic review, early attachment predicted social competence with peers, internalizing behaviors such as anxiety, and externalizing behaviors such as aggression, but the researchers suggested that a number of other risk and protective factors could strengthen or weaken links between early attachment and subsequent development (Groh & others, 2017).

Consistently positive caregiving over a number of years is likely an important factor in connecting early attachment with the child's functioning later in development. Indeed, researchers have found that early secure attachment and subsequent experiences, especially parental care and life stresses, are linked with children's later behavior and adjustment (Sutton, 2019; Thompson, 2021). For example, a longitudinal study revealed that changes in attachment security/insecurity from infancy to adulthood were linked to stresses and supports in socioemotional contexts (Van Ryzin, Carlson, & Sroufe, 2011). These results suggest that attachment continuity may be a reflection of stable social contexts as much as early working models. The study just described (Van Ryzin, Carlson, & Sroufe, 2011) reflects an increasingly accepted view of the development of attachment and its influence on development. That is, it is important to recognize that attachment security in infancy does not always by itself produce long-term positive outcomes, but rather is linked to later outcomes through connections with the way children and adolescents subsequently experience various social contexts as they develop.

The Van Ryzin, Carlson, and Sroufe (2011) study reflects a **developmental cascade model,** which involves connections across domains over time that influence developmental pathways and outcomes (St. George & others, 2020). Developmental cascades can include connections between a wide range of biological, cognitive, and socioemotional processes (attachment, for example), and also can involve social contexts such as families, peers, schools, and culture. Further, links can produce positive or negative outcomes at different points in development, such as infancy, early childhood, middle and late childhood, adolescence, and adulthood.

A meta-analysis shows evidence for the effects just described (Pinquart, Feubner, & Ahnert, 2013). In this meta-analysis of 127 research reports, the following conclusions were reached: (1) moderate stability of attachment security occurred from early infancy to adulthood; (2) no significant stability occurred for time intervals of more than 15 years; (3) attachment stability was greater when the time span was less than 2 years than when it was more than 5 years; and (4) securely attached children at risk were less likely to maintain attachment security, while insecurely attached children at risk were likely to continue to be insecurely attached.

In addition to challenging whether secure attachment in infancy is established during a critical or sensitive period, some developmentalists argue that the secure attachment concept does not adequately consider certain biological factors in development (Esposito & others, 2017c; B.R Kim & others, 2017; Kranenburg & van IJzendoorn, 2016; Vaughn & Bost, 2016). Genetic factors, temperament, and exposure to a wide range of risk and protective factors may play a larger role than attachment per se in child development. For example, if some infants inherit a low tolerance for stress, this characteristic, rather than an insecure attachment bond, may be responsible for an inability to get along with peers. One illustrative study found that

developmental cascade model Involves connections across domains over time that influence developmental pathways and outcomes.

infants with the short version of the serotonin transporter gene (5-HTTLPR) were prone to distress and wariness but not to insecure attachment (Brumariu & others, 2016).

Another criticism of attachment theory is that it ignores the diversity of socializing agents and contexts that exists in an infant's world. A culture's value system can influence the nature of attachment (Lansford, 2022; Mesman, 2018). A series of now classic studies showed that mothers' expectations for infants to be independent were high in northern Germany, whereas Japanese mothers were more strongly motivated to keep their infants close to them (Grossmann & others, 1985; Rothbaum & others, 2000). As a result, northern German infants tended to show less distress than Japanese infants when separated from their mother. Also, in some cultures, infants show attachments to many people. Among the Hausa (who live in Nigeria), both grandmothers and siblings provide a significant amount of care for infants (Harkness & Super, 1995). Infants in agricultural societies tend to form attachments to older siblings, who are assigned a major responsibility for younger siblings' care. In a more recent study in Zambia, where siblings were substantially involved in caregiving activities, infants showed strong attachments to their mothers and their sibling caregivers (Mooya, Sichimba, & Bakermans-Kranenburg, 2016). In this study, secure attachment was the most frequent attachment classification for both mother-infant and sibling-infant relationships.

Despite these questions about the validity and applicability of attachment theory, there is ample evidence that security of attachment is important in development (Dagan & Sagi-Schwartz, 2021; Sroufe, 2016; Thompson, 2021). Secure attachment in infancy reflects a positive parent-infant relationship and provides a foundation that supports healthy socioemotional development in the years that follow.

DEVELOPMENTAL SOCIAL NEUROSCIENCE AND ATTACHMENT

In the "Introduction" chapter you read about the emerging field of *developmental social neuroscience,* which examines connections between socioemotional processes, development, and the brain (Champagne, 2021; Telzer & others, 2018; Thomas, Mareschal, & Dumontheil, 2020). Attachment is one of the main areas in which theory and research on developmental social neuroscience have focused. These connections between attachment and the brain involve the neuroanatomy of the brain, neurotransmitters, and hormones.

Theory and research on the role of the brain's regions in mother-infant attachment are emerging (Esposito & others, 2017c; Feldman, 2017; Sullivan & Wilson, 2018). Brain imaging studies have revealed connections among infants' cues such as crying, mothers' responses, and brain activity. In an intervention in which mothers were assigned to either an intervention group to reduce parenting stress or a no-intervention control group, the intervention group showed improvement in areas of the brain involved in social responses, self-awareness, and decision making (Swain & others, 2017).

Research on the role of hormones and neurotransmitters in attachment has emphasized the importance of the neuropeptide hormone *oxytocin* and the neurotransmitter *dopamine* in the formation of the maternal-infant bond (Feldman, 2017; Kim, Strathearn, & Swain, 2016; Lecompte & others, 2020). Oxytocin, a mammalian hormone that also acts as a neurotransmitter in the brain, is released during breast feeding and by contact and warmth (Hannan & others, 2023; Phillipps, Yip, & Grattan, 2020). Oxytocin is especially thought to be a likely candidate in the formation of infant-mother attachment (Feldman, 2017; Toepfer & others, 2019). Sensitive maternal caregiving is predicted by higher levels of oxytocin, suggesting a biological pathway fostering attachment relationships (Kohlhoff & others, 2017).

It is well known that oxytocin release is stimulated by birth and lactation in mothers, but might it also be released in fathers? Oxytocin is secreted in males, and one research study found that at both 6 weeks and 6 months after birth, when fathers engaged in more stimulation contact with babies, encouraged their exploration, and directed their attention to objects, the fathers' oxytocin levels increased (Gordon & others, 2010). Another study found that fathers with lower testosterone levels engaged in more optimal parenting with their infants (Weisman, Zagoory-Sharon, & Feldman, 2014). Interestingly, when fathers were administered oxytocin, their parenting behavior improved, as evidenced in increased positive affect, social gaze, touch, and vocal synchrony when interacting with their infants. More recently, a longitudinal study of first-time fathers in Japan documented changes in their brain functioning and hormone levels during the

developmental **connection**

Nature and Nurture

What is involved in gene-environment (G × E) interaction? Connect to "Biological Beginnings."

In the Hausa culture, siblings (like the older child shown here) and grandmothers provide a significant amount of care for infants. *How might these variations in care affect attachment?*

Penny Tweedie/The Image Bank/Getty Images

FIGURE **7**

REGIONS OF THE BRAIN PROPOSED AS LIKELY IMPORTANT IN INFANT-MOTHER ATTACHMENT.

Note: This illustration shows the brain's left hemisphere. The corpus callosum is the large bundle of axons that connect the brain's two hemispheres.

(girl): Takayuki/Shutterstock

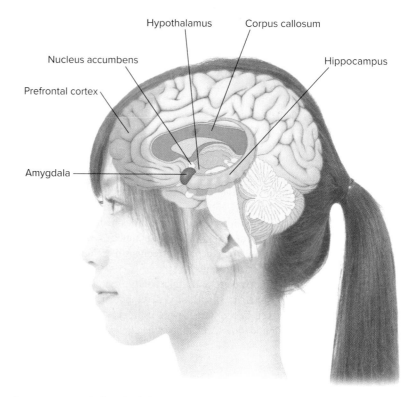

partner's pregnancy and after the infant was born—patterns that were indicative of neurobiological changes preparing fathers to be sensitive, responsive caregivers (Diaz-Rojas & others, 2023).

In mothers, the experience of pleasure and reward is reflected in the brain's dopamine circuits when mothers care for their infants and are exposed to their infants' cues, such as eye contact, smiling, and so on (Hoekzema & others, 2020). These experiences and brain changes likely promote mother-infant attachment and sensitive parenting. Also, the influence of oxytocin on dopamine in the mother's nucleus accumbens (a collection of neurons in the forebrain that are involved in pleasure) likely is important in motivating the mother's approach to the baby (Bos, 2017; Feldman, 2019). Figure 7 shows the regions of the brain we have described that are likely to play important roles in infant-mother attachment.

In sum, it is likely that a number of brain regions, neurotransmitters, and hormones are involved in the development of infant-mother attachment. Key candidates for influencing this attachment are connections between the prefrontal cortex, amygdala, and hypothalamus; the neuropeptides oxytocin and vasopressin; and the activity of the neurotransmitter dopamine in the nucleus accumbens.

developmental **connection**

Brain Development

Connections are increasingly being made between brain development and socioemotional processes. Connect to "Introduction" and "Physical Development in Adolescence."

Review Connect Reflect

LG2 Describe the development of social orientation/understanding and attachment in infancy.

Review

- How do social orientation and understanding develop in infancy?
- What is attachment, and how is it conceptualized?
- What are some individual variations in attachment? How are caregiving styles related to attachment? What are some criticisms of attachment theory?
- What characterizes the study of developmental social neuroscience and attachment?

Connect

- How might the infant's temperament be related to the way in which

attachment is classified? Look at the temperament categories we described in the first main section of this chapter and reflect on how these might be more likely to show up in infants in some attachment categories than in others.

Reflect *Your Own Personal Journey of Life*

- Imagine that you are the parent or caregiver of an infant. What could you do to improve the likelihood that your baby will form a secure attachment with you?

3 How Do Social Contexts Influence Socioemotional Development in Infancy?

The Family

Child Care

Now that we have explored the infant's emotional and personality development and attachment, let's examine the social contexts in which these occur. We begin by studying a number of aspects of the family and then turn to a social context in which infants increasingly spend time—child care.

THE FAMILY

The family can be thought of as a constellation of subsystems—a complex whole made up of interrelated, interacting parts—defined in terms of generation, gender, and role. Each family member participates in several subsystems (Chen, Hughes, & Austin, 2017; Keller & Noone, 2020). In a two-parent family, one parent and the child represent one subsystem, the other parent and child another, the two parents another, the parent-parent-child represent yet another, and so on. These subsystems have reciprocal influences on each other (Perez-Brena & others, 2022). For example, Jay Belsky (1981) emphasizes that partner relations, parenting, and infant behavior and development can have both direct and indirect effects on each other (see Figure 8). An example of a direct effect is the influence of the parents' behavior on the child. An indirect effect is how the relationship between the adult partners mediates the way a parent acts toward the child (Taraban & Shaw, 2018). For example, conflict between the parents might reduce the efficiency of parenting, in which case the partners' conflict would indirectly affect the child's behavior (Warmuth, Cummings, & Davies, 2020). The simple fact that two people are becoming parents may have profound effects on their relationship.

The Transition to Parenthood When people become parents through pregnancy, adoption, or stepparenting, they face disequilibrium and must adapt. Parents want to develop a strong attachment with their infant, but they also want to maintain strong attachments to their partner and friends, and possibly continue their careers. Parents ask themselves how the presence of this new being will change their lives. A baby places new restrictions on partners; no longer will they be able to just go out to dinner on a moment's notice, and money will not be readily available for vacations and other luxuries. Dual-career couples ask, "Will it harm the baby to place them in child care? Will we be able to find responsible baby-sitters?"

What characterizes the transition to parenting?
Drazen_/Getty Images

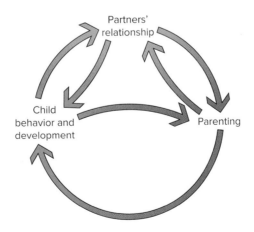

FIGURE 8

INTERACTION BETWEEN CHILDREN AND THEIR PARENTS: DIRECT AND INDIRECT EFFECTS

Illustration Source: Belsky, J. "Early Human Experiences: A Family Perspective." In *Developmental Psychology,* Vol. 59, 147–156. Washington, DC: American Psychological Association, 1981.

Katrina Wittkamp/Photodisc/Getty Images

In one important longitudinal investigation of couples from late pregnancy until 3½ years after the baby was born, couples enjoyed more positive partnership relations before the baby was born than after (Cowan & Cowan, 2000; Cowan & others, 2005). Still, almost one-third showed an increase in relationship satisfaction. Some couples said that the baby had both brought them closer together and moved them farther apart; being parents enhanced their sense of themselves and gave them a new, more stable identity as a couple. Becoming a parent also created adjustments in the adults' gendered norms. Babies opened men up to a concern with intimate relationships, and the demands of juggling work and family roles encouraged women to manage family tasks more efficiently and pay attention to their own personal growth.

Many other studies have explored the transition to parenthood (McMahon, 2023; Nomaguchi & Milkie, 2020). One illustrative study indicated that women and less avoidantly attached new parents adapted better to the introduction of child-care tasks compared with most men, especially men who were avoidantly attached (Fillo & others, 2015). In a comprehensive review of parenting and the transition to parenthood among gay, lesbian, and bisexual adults, researchers reported a key role of social support within the LGBTQ+ community for a positive transition (Leal & others, 2021). Also, in a study of dual-earner couples, a gender division of labor across the transition to parenthood occurred (Yavorsky & others, 2015). In this study, a gender gap was not present prior to the transition to parenthood, but after a child was born, women did more than 120 minutes of additional work per day compared with an additional 40 minutes for men. And in another study, when new fathers were given more responsibility for the care of their infants, they reported more closeness and co-parenting with their partner (Olsavsky & others, 2020).

The Bringing Baby Home project (Gottman Institute, 2023) is a workshop for new parents that emphasizes strengthening the couple's relationship, understanding and becoming acquainted with the baby, resolving conflict, and developing parenting skills (Gottman, 2014). Evaluations of the project over the past decade have revealed that parents who participated improved their ability to work together as parents, fathers were more involved with their baby and sensitive to the baby's behavior, mothers had a lower incidence of postpartum depression symptoms, and their babies showed better overall development compared with families in control groups (Shapiro, Gottman & Fink, 2015, 2020).

Reciprocal Socialization Socialization between parents and children is not a one-way process. Parents do socialize children, but socialization in families is reciprocal (Nishamura, Kanakogi, & Myowa-Yamakoshi, 2016; Yaremych & Volling, 2020). **Reciprocal socialization** is socialization that is bidirectional; children socialize parents just as parents socialize children. These reciprocal interchanges and mutual influence processes are sometimes referred to as *transactional* (Sameroff, 2009, 2020).

For example, the interaction of parents and their infants is sometimes symbolized as a dance in which successive actions of the partners are closely coordinated. This coordinated dance can assume the form of synchrony—that is, each person's behavior depends on the partner's previous behavior. Or the interaction can be reciprocal in a precise sense—in which the actions of the partners can be matched, as when one partner imitates the other or when there is mutual smiling.

An important example of early synchronized interaction is mutual gaze or eye contact. In one classic study, the mother and infant engaged in a variety of behaviors while they looked at each other; by contrast, when they looked away from each other, the rate of such behaviors dropped considerably (Stern & others, 1977). In a subsequent series of studies that were summarized in several meta-analyses and reviews of the literature, synchrony in parent-child relationships was positively related to children's social competence and lower levels of problem behaviors (Davis, Bilms, & Suveg, 2017; Harrist & Waugh, 2002). The types of behaviors involved in reciprocal socialization in infancy are temporally connected, mutually contingent behaviors such as one partner imitating the sound of another or the parent responding with a vocalization to the baby's arm movements.

Another example of synchronization occurs in **scaffolding**, which means adjusting the level of guidance to fit the child's performance (Abels, Osokina, & Kilale, 2023; Waldman-Levi, Finzi-Dottan, & Cope, 2020). The parent responds to the child's behavior with scaffolding, which in turn affects the child's behavior. For example, in the game peek-a-boo, parents initially cover their babies, then remove the covering, and finally register "surprise" at the babies' reappearance. As infants become more skilled at peek-a-boo, infants gradually do some of the covering and uncovering. Parents try to time their actions in such a way that the infant takes

developmental connection

Cognitive Theory

A version of scaffolding is an important aspect of Lev Vygotsky's sociocultural cognitive theory. Connect to "Physical and Cognitive Development in Early Childhood."

reciprocal socialization Socialization that is bidirectional; children socialize parents, just as parents socialize children.

scaffolding In regard to cognitive development, Vygotsky used this term to describe the changing level of support provided over the course of a teaching session, with the more-skilled person adjusting guidance to fit the child's current performance level.

turns with the parent in this and other activities like pat-a-cake and "so big." But scaffolding of infant learning also is involved in fundamental essential activities such as learning to eat and share food, as demonstrated in research among the Hadza people of northern Tanzania (Abels, Osokina, & Kilale, 2023).

Scaffolding can be used to support children's efforts at any age. One study found that when adults used explicit scaffolding (encouragement and praise) with young infants, the infants were more likely to engage in spontaneous helping behavior than were their counterparts who did not receive the scaffolding (Dahl, Goeltz, & Brownell, 2022). Also, a study of Hmong families living in the United States revealed that maternal scaffolding, especially in the form of cognitive support of young children's problem solving the summer before kindergarten, predicted the children's reasoning skills in kindergarten (Stright, Herr, & Neitzel, 2009). And another study of economically disadvantaged families revealed that an intervention designed to enhance maternal scaffolding with infants was linked to improved cognitive skills when the children were 4 years old (Obradovic & others, 2016).

Increasingly, genetic and epigenetic factors are being studied to discover not only parental influences on children but also children's influence on parents (Bakermans-Kranenburg & van IJzendoorn, 2016; Belsky & Pluess, 2016; Jiang, Wang, Yang, & Choi, 2022; Li & others, 2019). Recall that the *epigenetic view* emphasizes that development is the result of an ongoing, bidirectional interchange between heredity and the environment (Moore, 2017; Moore & Flom, 2020). For example, harsh, hostile parenting is associated with negative outcomes for children, such as being defiant and oppositional. This likely reflects bidirectional influences rather than a unidirectional parenting effect. That is, the parents' harsh, hostile parenting and the children's defiant, oppositional behavior may mutually influence each other. In this bidirectional influence, the parents' and children's behavior may have genetic linkages as well as experiential connections (Deater-Deckard, Chen, & El Mallah, 2016; Neiderhiser & Chen, 2023).

Managing and Guiding Infants' Behavior In addition to sensitive parenting that involves warmth and caring and can result in secure attachment to parents, other important aspects of parenting infants involve managing and guiding their behavior in an attempt to reduce or eliminate undesirable behaviors (Holden, 2019; Lansford, 2022). This management process includes (1) being proactive and childproofing the environment so infants won't encounter potentially dangerous objects or situations and (2) using corrective methods when infants engage in undesirable behaviors such as excessive fussing and crying, throwing objects, and so on. Encouraging and supporting proactive, planned-out behavior management of children is a major component of prevention and intervention programs for parents with young children (Resnik & others, 2023).

One of the few intensive longitudinal studies on the topic assessed discipline and corrective methods that parents had used by the time infants were 12 and 24 months old (Vittrup, Holden, & Buck, 2006) (see Figure 9). Notice in Figure 9 that the main corrective method parents used by the time infants were 12 months old was diverting the infants' attention, followed by reasoning, ignoring, and negotiating. Also note in Figure 9 that more than one-third of parents had yelled at their infant, about one-fifth had slapped the infant's hands or threatened the infant, and approximately one-sixth had spanked the infant by the first birthday.

As infants move into the second year of life and become more mobile and capable of exploring a wider range of environments, parental management of the toddler's behavior often triggers even more corrective feedback and discipline (Lawrence & others, 2019). As indicated in Figure 9, in the study described above, parental yelling increased from 36 percent at 1 year of age to 81 percent at 2 years of age, slapping the infant's hands increased from 21 percent at 1 year to 31 percent at age 2, and spanking increased from 14 percent at 1 year to 45 percent at age 2 (Vittrup, Holden, & Buck, 2006). More recent research confirms these patterns (Lawrence & others, 2019, 2021).

An important aspect of understanding why parents might increase their disciplinary corrective feedback in the second year involves their expectations for their toddlers' behavior. A national poll of parents who had children 3 years of age and younger found that parents have stricter expectations for their toddlers' ability to control their behavior than is warranted based on the maturation of the prefrontal cortex (Newton & Thompson, 2010). Thus, some of parents' corrective feedback likely arises because parents anticipate that toddlers and young

How Would You...?
If you were an **educator,** how would you explain the value of games and the role of scaffolding in the development of infants and toddlers?

Caregivers often play games such as peek-a-boo and pat-a-cake. *How is scaffolding involved in these games?*

(top): Brand X Pictures/Getty Images; (bottom): Ronnie Kaufman/Getty Images

developmental connection
Parenting
Psychologists give a number of reasons why harsh physical punishment can be harmful to children's development. Connect to "Socioemotional Development in Early Childhood."

FIGURE 9

PARENTS' METHODS FOR MANAGING AND CORRECTING INFANTS' UNDESIRABLE BEHAVIORS. Shown here are the percentages of parents who had used various corrective methods by the time infants were 12 and 24 months old.
Source: Vittrup, B., Holden, G.W., & Buck, M. "Attitudes Predict the Use of Physical Punishment: A Prospective Study of the Emergence of Disciplinary Practices." *Pediatrics, 117* (2006), 2055–2064.

Method	12 Months	24 Months
Spank with hand	14	45
Slap infant's hand	21	31
Yell in anger	36	81
Threaten	19	63
Withdraw privileges	18	52
Time-out	12	60
Reason	85	100
Divert attention	100	100
Negotiate	50	90
Ignore	64	90

An Aka pygmy father with his infant son. In the Aka culture, fathers were observed to be holding or nearby their infants 47 percent of the time.

Nick Greaves/Alamy Stock Photo

children should be exercising greater self-control over their emotions and impulses than they are capable of achieving.

A special concern is that such corrective disciplinary tactics not become abusive. Too often what starts out as mild to moderately intense discipline on the part of parents can move into highly intense anger. In "Socioemotional Development in Early Childhood," you will read more extensively about the use of punishment with children and the occurrence of child abuse.

Mothers and Fathers as Caregivers

Much of our discussion of attachment has focused on mothers as caregivers. Do mothers and fathers differ in their caregiving roles? In general, mothers on average still spend considerably more time in caregiving with infants and children than do fathers—as shown in many studies in numerous countries (Lamb & Lewis, 2015; Zammaro & Prados, 2021; Zhao, 2020). Mothers especially are more likely to engage in a managerial role with their children, coordinating their activities, making sure their health-care needs are met, and so on (Clarke-Stewart & Parke, 2014). In gay two-father family households, this "division of labor" with child care is smaller, and caregiving tends to be more equally divided than in mother-father parent dyads (Carone & Lingiardi, 2022).

However, an increasing number of U.S. fathers stay home full time with their children (Livingston, 2018). The number of stay-at-home dads in the United States was estimated to be 2 million in 2012 and through 2016 (Cowan & others, 2019a, b; Livingston, 2018). Since 2020, as greater numbers of parents began working at home to maintain social distancing during the COVID-19 pandemic, this likely has changed somewhat and has probably increased the amount of time fathers spend interacting with their children. However, the pandemic has had a bigger impact on mothers, with more of them leaving the workforce than fathers in order to care for children at home (Zamarro & Prados, 2021). Prior to the pandemic, historical data revealed that there was a 400-plus percent increase in stay-at-home fathers in the United States from 1996 to 2013. A large proportion of full-time fathers have career-focused partners who provide the main family income. Even when fathers do not stay home with their children full-time, they play many crucial roles in children's development (Volling & Palkovitz, 2021).

Observations of infants separately interacting with their mothers and fathers suggest that global measures of attachment security do not differ for fathers and mothers (Fernandes & others, 2018); a similar result appears to be emerging in the newer research on same-sex two-parent families (Carone & Lingiardi, 2022). Consider the Aka pygmy culture in Africa where fathers spend as much time interacting with their infants as do their mothers (Hewlett & MacFarlan, 2010; Meehan, Hagen, & Hewlett, 2017). When fathers are actively involved as caregivers, children are more likely to interact in similar ways with fathers and mothers (McHale & Sirotkin, 2019). Fathers' involvement is predicted by a number of factors, including residential status, education, income, beliefs about gender roles, and the quality of the father's relationship with the mother (Macon & others, 2017; Schoppe-Sullivan & others, 2021). Father involvement matters. For example, a study showed that when fathers of 3-month-old infants were withdrawn and depressed, the children had a lower level of cognitive development at 24 months of age (Sethna & others, 2017). Also in this study, when fathers of 3-month-old infants were more engaged and sensitive, as well as less controlling, the children showed a higher level of cognitive development at 24 months.

Remember, however, that although fathers can be active, nurturant, involved caregivers with their infants as Aka pygmy fathers do, in many cultures men do not follow this pattern

(Lynn, Grych, & Fosco, 2016). The most striking evidence for this is from Scandinavia, which has shown that family policies that financially support father involvement in child care have led to increased caregiving among men, but there continue to be more mothers than fathers who are full-time caregivers (Eydal, Rostgaard, & Hiilamo, 2018). As with mothers, if fathers have mental health problems, they may interact less effectively with their infants than fathers without such problems. Fathers experiencing depression interact with their infants in ways that are less playful and less engaged, and they touch their infants less compared to fathers not experiencing depression (Fisher & others, 2021; Sethna & others, 2018). And aside from potential depressive or other symptoms, other research has revealed that both fathers' and mothers' sensitivity, as assessed when infants were 10 to 12 months old, were linked to children's cognitive development at 18 months and language development at 36 months (Malmberg & others, 2016).

Do fathers behave differently toward infants than mothers do? Maternal interactions usually center on child-care activities—feeding, changing diapers, bathing. Paternal interactions are more likely to include play (Kuhns & Cabrera, 2018; Lamb & Lewis, 2015). Fathers tend to engage in more rough-and-tumble play than mothers do. They bounce infants, throw them up in the air, tickle them, and so on (Robinson, St. George, & Freeman, 2021). Mothers do play with infants, but their play is less physical and arousing than that of fathers. That aside, mothers engage in play with their children three times as often as fathers do (Cabrera & Roggman, 2017).

CHILD CARE

On every continent, children today experience multiple caregivers. Most do not have a parent staying home to care for them; instead, the children have some type of care provided by others—"child care." Some parents worry that time spent in child care will reduce their infants' emotional attachment to them, slow down the infants' cognitive development, fail to teach them how to control anger, and allow them to be unduly influenced by their peers. How extensive is the use of child care? Are the worries of these parents justified?

Parental Leave   Today far more young children are in child care than at any other time in history. About 15 million children under the age of 6 years are in child care in the United States (Child Care Aware, 2018). The availability and use of nonparental child care encountered unprecedented shifts and disruptions during the COVID-19 pandemic in the United States and many other countries (Haynie, Waterman, & Ritter, 2023). To read about child-care policies in different countries, see the *Connecting with Diversity* interlude.

Variations in Child Care   Because the United States does not have a policy of paid leave for child care, child care in the United States has become a major national concern (Berger & Carlson, 2020; Snyder, 2019). Many factors influence the effects of child care, including the age of the child, the type of child care, and the quality of the program.

Types of child care vary extensively (see Childcare.gov for more information). Child care is provided in large centers with elaborate facilities and in private homes. Some child-care centers are commercial operations; others are nonprofit centers run by religious organizations, civic groups, and employers. Some child-care providers are professionals; others are adults who want to earn extra money. Infants and toddlers are more likely to be found in family child care and informal care settings, while older children are more likely to be in child-care centers and preschool and early education programs. Figure 10 presents the primary care arrangements for children under 5 years of age in the United States in 2019 (U.S. Department of Education, National Center for Education Statistics, 2021). Updated validated data reflecting changes during the pandemic are not yet available.

In the United States, approximately 15 percent of children 5 years of age and younger attend more than one child-care arrangement. Whether and how different child-care arrangements are related to children's school readiness and behavioral adjustment depend on a number of factors, such as the quality and consistency of the care (Boller & Harding, 2020; Dearing & Zachrisson, 2017). Also, use of different types of care varies by ethnicity, socioeconomic status, geographic region, and age of the child. Parents' reports of whether good child-care options are available to them and barriers to finding good child care also vary by these factors. For example, cost is less likely to be a barrier in higher-income families, and lack of available spots is less likely to be a barrier for older children than for infants (Haynie, Waterman, & Ritter, 2023; U.S. Department of Education, National Center for Education Statistics, 2018).

How do most fathers and mothers, on average, interact differently with infants?
Hero Images Inc./Alamy Stock Photo

Child-Care Policies Around the World

Child-care policies around the world vary in eligibility criteria, leave duration, benefit level, and the extent to which parents take advantage of the policies (Bartel & others, 2018; Thébaud & Pedulla, 2022). Europe has led the way in creating new standards of parental leave: The European Union (EU) mandated a paid 14-week maternity leave nearly three decades ago in 1992. In most European countries today, working parents on leave receive from 70 to 100 percent of the worker's prior wage, and paid leave averages about 16 weeks (OECD, 2022). The United States currently allows workers up to 12 weeks of unpaid leave to care for a newborn, but only if the company has more than 50 employees within a 75-mile radius, which means that many Americans are not eligible for any leave, paid or unpaid.

Most countries restrict eligibility for benefits to women employed for a minimum time prior to childbirth. In Germany, child-rearing leave is available to almost all parents. The Nordic countries (Denmark, Finland, Iceland, Norway, and Sweden) have extensive gender-equity family leave policies for childbirth that emphasize the contributions of both women and men (Hakovirta & Eydal, 2020). For example, in Sweden, parents can take an 18-month job-protected parental leave with benefits that can be shared by parents and applied to full-time or part-time work. These policies are paid for by central government

How are child-care policies in many European countries, such as Sweden, different from those in the United States?
Juliana Wiklund/Getty Images

funding through taxation, and the policies exist because the populations generally support the need for removing financial and occupational barriers to both parents' being able to care for their young children (Greve & Hussain, 2021).

How Would You...?
If you were a **psychologist**, what factors would you encourage parents to consider in deciding whether to place their infant in child care so that both parents can return to work?

Child-care quality makes a difference (Raikes & others, 2020; Vermeer & others, 2016). What constitutes a high-quality child-care program for infants? In high-quality child care (Clarke-Stewart & Miner, 2008, p. 273):

> . . . caregivers encourage the children to be actively engaged in a variety of activities, have frequent, positive interactions that include smiling, touching, holding, and speaking at the child's eye level, respond properly to the child's questions or requests, and encourage children to talk about their experiences, feelings, and ideas.

High-quality child care also involves providing children with a safe environment, access to age-appropriate toys and participation in age-appropriate activities, and a low caregiver-to-child ratio that allows caregivers to spend considerable time with children on an individual basis. Children are more likely to experience poor-quality child care if they come from families with fewer resources (psychological, social, and economic) (Krafft, Davis, & Tout, 2017). Many researchers have examined the role of income in quality of child care (Carlin & others, 2019; Pilarz, Sandstrom, & Henly, 2022). A number of studies have demonstrated that high-quality child care can benefit children from low-income households. For example, spending more time in child care buffered the otherwise negative effects of household chaos in low-income families on children's cognitive and social outcomes at age 5 years (Berry & others, 2016). Emotionally supportive environments in caregiving settings may be particularly important for aiding children's development of stress resistance and resilience (Hatfield & others, 2021). To read about one individual who provides quality child care for low-income families, see the *Connecting with Careers* profile. Do children in low-income families get quality care at day care? For the answer to that question, as well as other information on the effects of child care on children's development, see *Connecting with Research*.

FIGURE 10

PRIMARY CARE ARRANGEMENTS IN THE UNITED STATES FOR CHILDREN THROUGH 5 YEARS OF AGE

(Bar chart)
- Parental care: 41%
- Relative care: 22%
- Nonrelative care: 12%
- Center-based care: 36%

Wanda Mitchell, Child-Care Director

Wanda Mitchell is the Center Director at the Hattie Daniels Day Care Center in Wilson, North Carolina. Her responsibilities include directing the operation of the center, which involves creating and maintaining an environment in which young children can learn effectively, and ensuring that the center meets state licensing requirements. Mitchell obtained her undergraduate degree from North Carolina A&T University, majoring in Child Development. Prior to her current position, she was an education coordinator for Head Start and an instructor at Wilson Technical Community College. Describing her career, Mitchell says, "I really enjoy working in my field. This is my passion. After graduating from college, my goal was to advance in my field."

Wanda Mitchell, child-care director, works with some of the children at her center.
Courtesy of Wanda Mitchell

What Are Some Important Findings in the Study of Early Child Care and Youth Development (SECCYD) in the United States?

Key Points:

- A seven-year study assessed child-care quality in the United States.
- Most of the nonparental child care was inadequate.
- Negative impacts were more pronounced when children received poor-quality care at home and in child-care settings.

Beginning in 1991, the National Institute of Child Health and Human Development (NICHD) began the most comprehensive longitudinal study of child-care experiences ever conducted; its findings are still highly relevant today. Data were collected on a diverse sample of almost 1,400 children and their families at 10 locations across the United States from birth through the middle school years. Researchers used multiple methods (trained observers, interviews, questionnaires, and testing) and measured many facets of children's development, including physical health, cognitive development, and socioemotional development. Following are some of the results of what is referred to as the NICHD Study of Early Child Care and Youth Development, or NICHD SECCYD (NICHD Early Child Care Research Network, 2001, 2002, 2004, 2006, 2010).

- **Patterns of use.** Many families placed their infants in child care very soon after the child's birth, and there was considerable instability in the child-care arrangements. By 4 months of age, nearly three-fourths of the infants had entered some form of nonparental child care. Almost half of the infants were cared for by a relative when they first entered care; only 12 percent were enrolled in child-care centers. Low-income families were more likely than more affluent families to use child care, but infants from low-income families who were in child care averaged as many hours as other income groups. In the preschool years, mothers who were single, those with more education, and families with higher incomes used more hours of center-based care than other families did. Minority families and mothers with less

What are some important findings from the national longitudinal study of child care conducted by the National Institute of Child Health and Human Development?
Christopher Futcher/iStock/Getty Images

education used more hours of care by relatives. Many of these patterns are still seen today in the United States, even with the disruptions of the COVID-19 pandemic (Haynie, Waterman, & Ritter, 2023).

- **Quality of care.** Evaluations of quality of care were based on characteristics such as group size, child–adult ratio, physical environment, caregiver characteristics (such as formal education, specialized training, and child-care experience), and caregiver behavior (such as sensitivity to children). An alarming conclusion was that a majority of the child care in the first three years of life was of unacceptably low quality. Positive caregiving by non-parents in child-care settings was infrequent—only 12 percent of the children studied experienced positive nonparental child care (such as positive talk and language stimulation)! Further, infants from low-income families experienced

(continued)

(continued)

lower quality of child care than infants from higher-income families. When quality of caregivers' care was high, children performed better on cognitive and language tasks, were more cooperative with their mothers during play, showed more positive and skilled interaction with peers, and had fewer behavior problems. Caregiver training and good child-staff ratios were linked with higher cognitive and social competence when children were 54 months of age. For example, high-quality infant-toddler child care was linked to better memory skills at the end of the preschool years (Li & others, 2013). These findings led to important changes in government policies and supports for improving child-care quality (Herbst, 2023).

- *Amount of child care.* The quantity of child care predicted some child outcomes. When children spent extensive amounts of time in child care beginning in infancy, they experienced less sensitive interactions with their mother, showed more behavior problems, and had higher rates of illness. Many of these comparisons involved children in child care for less than 30 hours a week versus those in child care for more than 45 hours a week. In general, though, when children spent 30 hours or more per week in child care, their development was less than optimal (Ramey, 2005).

- *Family and parenting influences.* The influence of families and parenting was not weakened by extensive child care. Parents played a significant role in helping children to regulate their emotions. Especially important parenting influences were being sensitive to children's needs, being involved with children, and cognitively stimulating them. Indeed, parental sensitivity has been the most consistent predictor of a secure attachment, with child-care experiences being relevant in many cases only when mothers engage in insensitive parenting (Friedman, Melhuish, & Hill, 2010). An important point about the extensive NICHD research is that findings show that family factors are considerably stronger and more consistent predictors of a wide variety of child outcomes than are child-care experiences (such as quality, quantity, type), and having exposure to high-quality child care can even protect young children from deleterious effects of distressed parenting (Choi, Hatton-Bowers, & Shin, 2022). The worst outcomes for children occur when both home and child-care settings are of poor quality. For example, a follow-up analysis of the NICHD SECCYD data revealed that worse socioemotional outcomes (more problem behavior, low level of prosocial behavior) for children occurred when they experienced both home and child-care environments that conferred risk (Watamura & others, 2011).

What do the research findings from this foundational longitudinal study suggest about what the U.S. child-care system is doing well? What could be improved about the system? If you were a researcher involved in this study, what other questions would you want to explore?

What are some strategies parents can follow in regard to child care? Child-care expert Kathleen McCartney (2003, p. 4) offered this advice two decades ago, and it remains true today:

- *Recognize that the quality of your parenting is a key factor in your child's development.*
- *Make decisions that will improve the likelihood you will be good parents.* "For some this will mean working full-time"—for personal fulfillment, income, or both. "For others, this will mean working part-time or not working outside the home."
- *Monitor your child's development.* "Parents should observe for themselves whether their children seem to be having behavior problems." They need to talk with their child-care providers and their pediatrician about their child's behavior.
- *Take some time to find the best child care.* Observe different child-care facilities and be certain that you like what you see. "Quality child care costs money, and not all parents can afford the child care they want. However, state subsidies, and other programs like Head Start, are available for families in need."

Review Connect Reflect

 Explain how social contexts influence the infant's development.

Review

- What are some important family processes in infant development?
- How does child care influence infant development?

Connect

- Earlier, you learned about a fine motor skills experiment involving 3-month-olds and grasping. What concept in the last section of this chapter relates to the use of "sticky mittens"?

Reflect *Your Own Personal Journey of Life*

- Imagine that a friend of yours is getting ready to put their baby in child care. What advice would you give to them? Do you think they should stay home with the baby? Why or why not? What type of child care would you recommend?

You will study socioemotional development in early childhood. Babies no more, young children make considerable progress in the development of their self, their emotions, and their social interactions. In early childhood, they show increased self-understanding and understanding of others, as well as ability to regulate their emotions. In early childhood, relationships and interactions with parents and peers expand children's knowledge of and connections with their social world. Additionally, play becomes not only something they enjoy doing on a daily basis but also a wonderful context for advancing both their socioemotional and cognitive development. Many of the advances in young children's socioemotional development become possible because of the remarkable changes in their brain and cognitive development.

reach your **learning goals**

Socioemotional Development in Infancy

1 How Do Emotions and Personality Develop in Infancy?

 Discuss emotional and personality development in infancy.

Emotional Development

- Emotion is feeling, or affect, that occurs when people are in a state or an interaction that is important to them. Emotion can be classified as either positive (for example, joy) or negative (for example, anger).

- Psychologists hold that emotions, especially facial expressions of emotions, have a biological foundation. Biological evolution endowed humans to be emotional.

- Cognitive processes also play important roles in emotional development. And embeddedness in culture and relationships provides diversity in emotional experiences.

- Emotions play key roles in parent-child relationships. Infants display a number of emotions early in their development, although researchers debate the onset and sequence of these emotions. Lewis distinguishes between primary emotions and self-conscious emotions.

- Crying is the most important mechanism newborns have for communicating with their world. Babies have at least three types of cries—basic, anger, and pain cries. Controversy swirls about whether babies should be soothed when they cry, although increasingly experts recommend immediately responding in a caring way during the first year.

- Social smiling occurs as early as 2 months of age and then increases considerably from 2 to 6 months.

- Two fears that infants develop are stranger anxiety and separation from a caregiver (which is reflected in separation protest). As infants develop, it is important for them to engage in emotion regulation.

Temperament

- Temperament is an individual's behavioral style and characteristic way of emotionally responding. Chess and Thomas classified infants as (1) easy, (2) difficult, or (3) slow to warm up. Kagan proposed that inhibition to the unfamiliar is an important temperament category. Rothbart and Bates' view of temperament emphasizes this classification: (1) extraversion/surgency, (2) negative affectivity, and (3) effortful control (self-regulation).

- Physiological characteristics are associated with different temperaments. Children inherit a physiology that biases them to have a particular type of temperament, but through experience they learn to modify their temperament style to some degree.

- Goodness of fit refers to the match between a child's temperament and the environmental demands the child must cope with. Goodness of fit can be an important aspect of a child's adjustment. Although research evidence is sketchy at this point, some general recommendations are that caregivers should (1) be sensitive to the individual characteristics of the child, (2) be flexible in responding to these characteristics, and (3) avoid negative labeling of the child.

Personality Development

- Erikson argued that an infant's first year is characterized by the stage of trust versus mistrust. Some infants develop signs of self-recognition at about 15 to 18 months of age.

- Independence becomes a central theme in the second year of life. Mahler argues that the infant separates from the mother and then develops individuation. Erikson stressed that the second year of life is characterized by the stage of autonomy versus shame and doubt.

2 How Do Social Orientation/Understanding and Attachment Develop in Infancy?

 LG2 Describe the development of social orientation/understanding and attachment in infancy.

Social Orientation/Understanding

- Infants show a strong interest in the social world and are motivated to understand it. Infants orient to the social world early in their development. Face-to-face play with a caregiver begins to occur at 2 to 3 months of age. Newly developed self-produced locomotion skills significantly expand infants' ability to initiate social interchanges and explore their social world more independently.

- Perceiving people as engaging in intentional and goal-directed behavior is an important social cognitive accomplishment, and this initially occurs toward the end of the first year. Social referencing increases during the second year of life.

Attachment and Its Development

- Attachment is a close emotional bond between two people. In infancy, contact comfort and trust are important in the development of attachment. Bowlby's ethological theory stresses that the caregiver and the infant are biologically predisposed to form an attachment. Attachment develops in four phases during infancy.

Individual Differences in Attachment

- Securely attached babies use the caregiver, usually the mother, as a secure base from which to explore the environment. Three types of insecure attachment are avoidant, resistant, and disorganized. Ainsworth created the Strange Situation, an observational measure of attachment. Ainsworth argues that secure attachment in the first year of life provides an important foundation for psychological development later in life. Caregivers of secure babies are sensitive to the babies' signals and are consistently available to meet their needs. Caregivers of avoidant babies tend to be unavailable or rejecting. Caregivers of resistant babies tend to be inconsistently available to their babies and usually are not very affectionate. Caregivers of disorganized babies often neglect or physically abuse their babies.

- The strength of the link between early attachment and later development has varied somewhat across studies. Some critics argue that attachment theorists have not given adequate attention to genetics and temperament. Other critics stress that not enough attention has been given to the diversity of social agents and contexts. Cultural variations in attachment have been found, but in all cultures studied to date, secure attachment is the most common classification.

Developmental Social Neuroscience and Attachment

- Increased interest is being directed toward the role of the brain in the development of attachment. The hormone oxytocin is a key candidate for influencing the development of maternal-infant attachment.

3 How Do Social Contexts Influence Socioemotional Development in Infancy?

 LG3 Explain how social contexts influence the infant's development.

The Family

- The transition to parenthood requires considerable adaptation and adjustment on the part of parents. Children socialize parents, just as parents socialize children. Mutual regulation and scaffolding are important aspects of reciprocal socialization. Belsky's model points out that marital relations, parenting, and infant behavior and development can have direct and indirect effects on each other. An important parental task involves managing and correcting infants' undesirable behaviors. The mother's primary role when interacting with the infant often is caregiving; fathers are more likely to engage in playful interaction.

Child Care

- More U.S. children are in child care now than at any earlier point in history. The quality of child care is uneven, and child care remains a controversial topic. Quality child care can be achieved and seems to have few adverse effects on children. In the NICHD child-care study, infants from low-income families were more likely to receive the lowest quality of care. Also, higher quality of child care was linked with fewer child problems.

key terms

anger cry	goodness of fit	primary emotions	separation protest
attachment	insecure avoidant babies	reciprocal socialization	slow-to-warm-up child
basic cry	insecure disorganized	reflexive smile	social referencing
developmental cascade model	babies	scaffolding	social smile
difficult child	insecure resistant	securely attached	Strange Situation
easy child	babies	babies	stranger anxiety
emotion	pain cry	self-conscious emotions	temperament

key people

Mary Ainsworth	Stella Chess	Margaret Mahler	John Watson
John Bates	Erik Erikson	Kathleen McCartney	Amanda Woodward
Jay Belsky	Harry Harlow	Mary Rothbart	
John Bowlby	Jerome Kagan	Alexander Thomas	
Joseph Campos	Michael Lewis	Ross Thompson	

improving the lives of children

STRATEGIES

Nurturing the Infant's Socioemotional Development

What are the best ways to help an infant develop socioemotional competencies?

- *Develop a secure attachment with the infant.* Infants need the warmth and support of one or more caregivers. The caregiver(s) should be sensitive to the infant's signals and respond in a nurturing way.

- *Be sure that both the mother and the father nurture the infant.* Infants develop best when both the mother and the father provide warm, nurturant support. Fathers need to seriously evaluate their responsibility in rearing a competent infant.

- *Select competent child care.* If the infant will be placed in child care, spend time evaluating different options. Be sure the infant–caregiver ratio is low. Also assess whether the adults enjoy and are knowledgeable about interacting with infants. Confirm that the facility is safe and provides stimulating activities.

- *Understand and respect the infant's temperament.* Be sensitive to the characteristics of each child. It may be necessary to provide extra support for distress-prone infants, for example. Avoid negative labeling of the infant.

- *Adapt to developmental changes in the infant.* An 18-month-old toddler is very different from a 6-month-old infant. Be knowledgeable about how infants develop, and adapt to the changing infant. Let toddlers explore a wider but safe environment.

- *Be physically and mentally healthy.* Infants' socioemotional development benefits when their caregivers are physically and mentally healthy. For example, a depressed parent may not respond sensitively to the infant's signals.

- *Read a good book on infant development.* Any of T. Berry Brazelton's books is a good start. One is *Touchpoints*.

RESOURCES

The Happiest Baby on the Block (Updated and revised edition, 2015)

Harvey Karp
New York: Bantam

An outstanding book on ways to calm a crying baby.

Touchpoints: Birth to Three (2006)

T. Berry Brazelton and Joshua Sparrow
Cambridge, MA: Da Capo Press

In this classic book that covers the period from birth through age 3, Brazelton and Sparrow focus on the concerns and questions parents have about the child's feelings, behavior, and development.

Raising a Secure Child (2017)

Kent Hoffman and others
New York: Guilford Press

An excellent book for parents that provides valuable information and strategies for protecting and nurturing infants.

Zero to Three

https://www.zerotothree.org/resources/for-families/

A frequently updated resource for caregivers of infants and toddlers, provided by a leading nonprofit organization dedicated to the healthy development of all young children and families.

You are troubled at seeing him spend his early years doing nothing. What! Is it nothing to be happy? Is it nothing to skip, to play, to run about all day long? Never in his life will he be so busy as now.

—JEAN-JACQUES ROUSSEAU
Swiss-born French philosopher, 18th century

FatCamera/Getty Images

Early Childhood

In early childhood, our greatest untold poem was being only 4 years old. We skipped and ran and played all the sun long, never in our lives so busy, busy being something we had not quite grasped yet. Who knew our thoughts, which we worked up into small mythologies all our own? Our thoughts and images and drawings took wings. The blossoms of our heart, no wind could touch. Our small world widened as we discovered new refuges and new people. When we said, "I," we meant something totally unique, not to be confused with any other. Section 4 consists of three chapters: "Physical Development in Early Childhood," "Cognitive Development in Early Childhood," and "Socioemotional Development in Early Childhood."

chapter 8

PHYSICAL DEVELOPMENT IN EARLY CHILDHOOD

chapter **outline**

① How Does a Young Child's Body and Brain Grow and Change?

Learning Goal 1 Discuss growth and change in the young child's body and brain.

Height and Weight

The Brain

② How Do Young Children's Motor Skills Develop?

Learning Goal 2 Describe changes in motor development in early childhood.

Gross and Fine Motor Skills

Perceptual Development

Young Children's Artistic Drawings

③ What Are Some Important Aspects of Young Children's Health?

Learning Goal 3 Characterize the health of young children.

Sleep and Sleep Problems

Nutrition

Exercise

Health, Safety, and Illness

kali9/Getty Images

Teresa Amabile remembers that when she was in kindergarten, she rushed in every day, excited and enthusiastic about getting to the easel and painting with bright colors and big brushes. Children in Teresa's class had free access to a clay table with all kinds of art materials on it. Teresa remembers going home every day and telling her mother she wanted to draw and paint. Teresa's kindergarten experience, unfortunately, was the high point of her enthusiasm for art classes in school.

A description of Teresa's further childhood experiences with art and creativity follows (Goleman, Kaufman, & Ray, 1993):

> The next year she entered a strict, traditional school, and things began to change. As she tells it, "Instead of having free access to art materials every day, art became just another subject, something you had for an hour and a half every Friday afternoon." Week after week, all through elementary school, it was the same art class. And a very restricted, even demoralizing one at that.

The children were not given any help in developing their skills. Also, the teacher graded the children on the art they produced, adding evaluation pressure to the situation. Teresa was aware at that time that her motivation for doing artwork was being completely destroyed. In her words, "I no longer wanted to go home at the end of the day and take out my art materials and draw or paint."

In spite of the negative instruction imposed upon her in art classes, Teresa Amabile continued her education and eventually obtained a Ph.D. in psychology. In part because of her positive experiences in kindergarten, she became one of the leading researchers on creativity. Her hope is that more schools will not crush children's enthusiasm for creativity, the way hers did. So many young children, like Teresa, are excited about exploring and creating, but by the time they reach the third or fourth grade, many don't like school, let alone have any sense of pleasure in their own creativity.

topical connections *looking **back***

Physical growth in infancy is dramatic. Even though physical growth in early childhood slows, it is not difficult to distinguish young children from infants when you look at them. Most young children lose their "baby fat," and their legs and trunks become longer. In addition to what you can see with the naked eye, much development also continues within the brain. In infancy, myelination of axons in the brain paved the way for development of such functions as full visual capacity. Continued myelination in early childhood provides children with much better hand-eye coordination.

preview

As young children's physical development advances, their small worlds widen. We begin this chapter by examining how young children's bodies grow and change. Then we discuss the development of young children's motor skills and conclude by exploring important aspects of their health.

1 How Does a Young Child's Body and Brain Grow and Change?

 LG1 Discuss growth and change in the young child's body and brain.

Height and Weight | The Brain

In this section, we examine the height and weight changes for boys and girls in early childhood along with individual growth patterns. In addition, we look at how the brain and nervous system continue to develop, and how young children's cognitive abilities expand.

HEIGHT AND WEIGHT

Remember from "Physical Development in Infancy" that the infant's growth in the first year is rapid. During the infant's second year, the growth rate begins to slow down, and the growth rate continues to slow across early childhood. The average child grows 2½ inches in height and gains between 5 and 7 pounds a year during early childhood. As the preschool child grows older, the percentage of increase in height and weight decreases with each additional year (World Health Organization, 2023). Figure 1 shows the average height and weight of children as they age from 2 to 6 years (adapted from charts by the Centers for Disease Control and Prevention, 2020a; see the charts at www.cdc.gov/growthcharts/clinical_charts.htm). Girls are only slightly smaller and lighter than boys during these years, a difference that continues until puberty. During the preschool years, both boys and girls slim down as the trunks of their bodies lengthen. Although their heads are still somewhat large for their bodies, by the end of the preschool years most children have lost their top-heavy look. Body fat also shows a slow, steady decline during the preschool years. The chubby baby often looks much leaner by the end of early childhood. Girls have more fatty tissue and less muscle tissue than boys.

Growth patterns vary individually (Glasper, Richardson, & Randall, 2021). Think back to your elementary school years. This was probably the first time you noticed that some children were taller than you, some shorter; some were stronger, some weaker. Much of the variation is due to heredity, but environmental experiences are involved to some extent. A classic study that reviewed the height and weight of children around the world concluded that the two most important contributors to height differences are ethnic origin and nutrition (Meredith, 1978). Urban, middle-socioeconomic-status, and firstborn children were taller than rural, lower-socioeconomic-status, and later-born children. The children whose mothers smoked during pregnancy were half an inch shorter than the children whose mothers did not smoke during pregnancy. Overall, these factors and their correlations with stature differences between children have not changed much since the 1970s (de Onis & others, 2018).

Why are some children unusually short? The primary contributing influences are congenital factors (genetic or prenatal problems), growth hormone deficiency, a physical problem that develops in childhood, maternal smoking during pregnancy, or an emotional difficulty (Polidori & others, 2020). Chronically sick children are shorter than their rarely sick counterparts. Children who have been physically abused or neglected may not secrete adequate growth hormone, the lack of which can restrict their physical growth. **Growth hormone deficiency** is the absence or deficiency of growth hormone produced by the pituitary gland to stimulate the body to grow. Growth hormone deficiency may occur during infancy or later in childhood (Danowitz & Grimberg, 2022). As many as 10,000 to 15,000 U.S. children may have growth hormone deficiency (Stanford University Medical Center, 2017). Without treatment, most children with growth hormone deficiency will not reach a height of five feet. Treatment involves regular injections of growth hormone and usually lasts several years (Derraik & others, 2019). Some children

The bodies of 5-year-olds and 2-year-olds are different. Notice that the 5-year-old not only is taller and weighs more, but also has a longer trunk and legs than the 2-year-old. *Can you think of some other physical differences between 2- and 5-year-olds?*

Michael Hitoshi/Digital Vision/Getty Images

growth hormone deficiency The absence or deficiency of growth hormone produced by the pituitary gland to stimulate the body to grow.

FIGURE **1**

HEIGHT AND WEIGHT CHANGES FROM 2 THROUGH 6 YEARS OF AGE. These graphs show the percentiles of height and weight for boys and girls from 2 through 6 years of age in the United States.

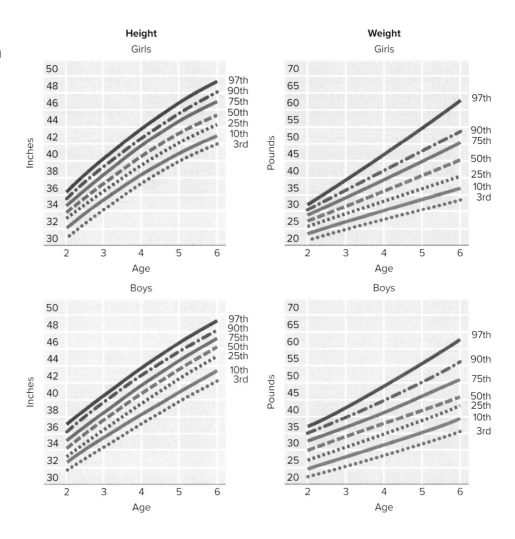

receive injections daily, others several times a week. A large study in the United States, Europe, and Japan found that girls are less likely to be treated with growth hormone than boys (Ranke & others, 2017). There also are race disparities in treatment access that disadvantage Black children compared to White children in the United States (Grimberg & others, 2018).

A large international study spanning the United States and Europe revealed that extensive growth hormone treatment in childhood was linked to an increase to close to average height (Sävendahl & others, 2019). Also, a comprehensive review concluded that accurate assessment of growth hormone deficiency is difficult and that many children diagnosed with growth hormone deficiency re-test as normal later in childhood (Murray, Dattani, & Clayton, 2016).

There has been a significant upsurge in treating very short children with growth hormone therapy (Grimberg & Allen, 2017). Some medical experts have expressed concern that many young children who are being treated with growth hormone therapy are merely short but don't have a growth hormone deficiency. In such cases, parents often perceive that there is a handicap in being short, especially for boys.

Few studies have been conducted on the psychological and social outcomes of having very short stature in childhood. One study found that children with growth hormone deficiencies were at high risk of psychiatric problems such as social anxiety disorders and were often victimized by peers (Çoban & others, 2022). A study in France found improvements on children's overall social and emotional quality of life after growth hormone treatment of children very short in stature (González Briceño & others, 2019).

THE BRAIN

One of the most important physical developments during early childhood is the continuing development of the brain and nervous system (Hyde & others, 2022). Although the brain continues to grow in early childhood, it does not grow as rapidly as in infancy. By the time children reach 3 years of age, the brain is three-quarters of its adult size. By age 6, the brain has reached about 95 percent of its adult volume (Lenroot & Giedd, 2006). Thus, the brain of a 5-year-old is nearly the size it will be when the child reaches adulthood, but as we see in later chapters, the development that occurs inside the brain continues through the remaining childhood and adolescent years (Guyer, Beard, & Venticinque, 2023).

The brain and the head grow more rapidly than any other part of the body. The top parts of the head, the eyes, and the brain grow faster than the lower portions, such as the jaw. Figure 2 reveals how the growth curve for the head and brain advances more rapidly than the growth curve for height and weight. At 5 years of age, when the brain has attained approximately 90 percent of its adult weight, the 5-year-old's total body weight is only about one-third of what it will be when the child reaches adulthood.

Neuronal Changes

In "Prenatal Development" and "Physical Development in Infancy," we discussed the brain's development during the prenatal and infancy periods. Changes in neurons in early childhood involve connections between neurons and myelination, just as in infancy (Alex & others, 2023). Communication in the brain is characterized by the transmission of information between neurons, or nerve cells. Some of the brain's increase in size during early childhood is due to the increase in the number and size of nerve endings and receptors, which allows more effective communication to occur. Neurons communicate with each other through *neurotransmitters* (chemical substances) that carry information across gaps (called *synapses*) between the neurons.

Some of the brain's increase in size also is due to the increase in **myelination,** in which nerve cells are covered and insulated with a layer of fat cells (see Figure 3). This has the effect of increasing the speed and efficiency of information traveling through the nervous system. Myelination is important in the development of a number of abilities in children and adolescents (Slater & others, 2019). For example, myelination in the areas of the brain related to hand-eye coordination is not complete until about 4 years of age. One fMRI study of children during the first five years of life (mean age: 3 years) found that children with more advanced cognitive abilities had higher levels of myelination (Deoni & others, 2016). Myelination in the areas of the brain related to focusing attention is not complete until the end of middle childhood or later.

Structural Changes

Until recently, scientists lacked adequate technology to detect sensitive changes and view detailed maps of the developing human brain. However, sophisticated brain-scanning techniques, such as magnetic resonance imaging (MRI), now allow us to better detect these changes (Kraus & Horowitz-Kraus, 2022). With high-resolution MRI, scientists have evolved spatially complex, four-dimensional growth pattern maps of the developing brain (including during late fetal development), allowing the brain to be monitored with greater sensitivity than ever before. Using these techniques, scientists have discovered that children's brains undergo dramatic anatomical changes between the ages of 3 and 15. The amount of brain material in some areas can nearly double within as little as a year, followed by a drastic loss of tissue as unneeded cells are purged and the brain continues to reorganize itself. Scientists have found that the overall size of the brain does not show dramatic growth in the 3- to 15-year age range. However, what does dramatically change are local connectivity patterns within the brain (Gozdas & others, 2019).

This rapidly growing developmental brain science literature is showing that in children from 3 to 6 years of age, the most rapid growth takes place in the frontal lobe areas involved in planning and organizing new actions and in maintaining attention to tasks. From age 6 through puberty, the most rapid growth takes place in the temporal and parietal lobes, especially areas that play major roles in language and spatial relations. At some points in

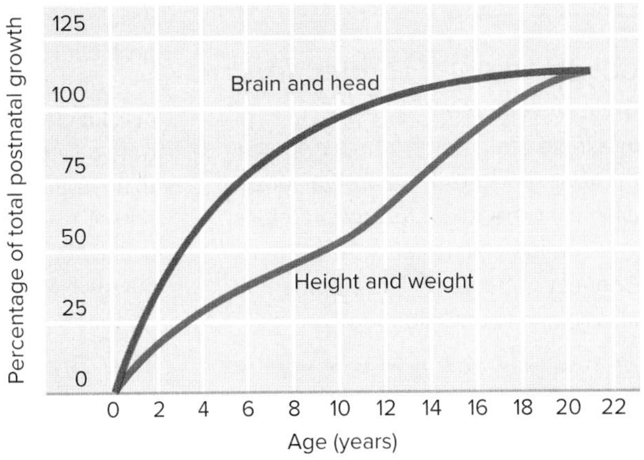

FIGURE 2

GROWTH CURVES FOR THE HEAD AND BRAIN AND FOR HEIGHT AND WEIGHT. The more rapid growth of the brain and head can easily be seen. Height and weight advance more gradually over the first two decades of life. *Source:* Damon, Albert. *Human Biology and Ecology,* Figure 10.6. New York: W. W. Norton & Company, 1977.

myelination The process in which the nerve cells are covered and insulated with a layer of fat cells, which increases the speed at which information travels through the nervous system.

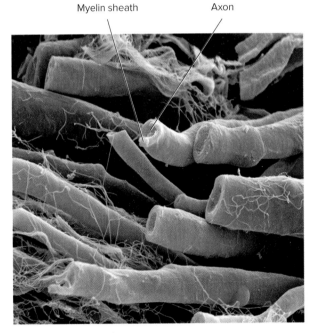

FIGURE 3

A MYELINATED NERVE FIBER. The myelin sheath, shown in gray, encases the axon (pink). This image was produced by an electron microscope that magnified the nerve fiber 12,000 times. *What role does myelination play in the brain's development and children's cognition?*

Steve Gschmeissner/Science Source

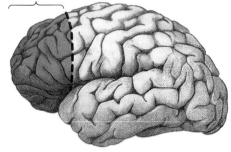

developmental **connection**

Brain Development

In middle and late childhood, cortical thickening occurs in the frontal lobes, which may be linked to improvements in language abilities such as reading. Connect to "Physical Development in Middle and Late Childhood."

development, young children's brains are better suited for particular types of learning and problem solving than are brains of older children and adults (Gualtieri & Finn, 2022).

In addition, contextual factors such as poverty and parenting quality are linked to the development of the brain (Merz & others, 2019; Moriguchi & Shinohara, 2019). In one illustrative study of children, those from the poorest homes had significant maturational lags in their frontal and temporal lobes at 4 years of age, and these lags were associated with lower school readiness skills (Hair & others, 2015). In another study, levels of maternal sensitivity in infancy were associated with structural differences in specific areas of the brain years later (Bernier & others, 2019).

The Brain and Cognitive Development   The substantial increases in memory and rapid learning that characterize infants and young children are related to cell loss, myelination, and synaptic growth. These changes in brain development are related to specific changes in cognitive and social abilities in early childhood (Schneider, Greenstreet, & Deoni, 2022). The density of synapses peaks at around 4 years of age (Gilmore, Knickmeyer, & Gao, 2018). Some scientists argue that true episodic memory (memory for the "when and where" of life's happenings, such as remembering what one had for breakfast this morning) and self-awareness do not develop until about this time (Rah, Kim, & Lee, 2022). However, recall that some infant development researchers conclude that episodic memory and self-awareness emerge during infancy (Bauer & Leventon, 2015). These aspects of the brain's maturation, combined with opportunities to experience a widening world, contribute to children's emerging cognitive abilities (Bell, Ross, & Patton, 2018; Gozdas & others, 2019). Consider a child who is learning to read and is asked by a teacher to read aloud to the class. Input from the child's eyes is transmitted to the child's brain, and then passed through many brain systems, which process the patterns of black and white into codes for letters, words, and associations. The output occurs in the form of messages to the child's lips and tongue. The child's own gift of speech is possible because brain systems are organized in ways that permit language processing.

The brain is organized according to many neural circuits, which are neural networks composed of many neurons with certain functions (Craske & others, 2023). One specific neural circuit is thought to have an important function in the development of attention and working memory (a type of short-term memory that is used like a mental workbench in performing many cognitive tasks) (Ott & Nieder, 2019). This neural circuit involves the *prefrontal cortex,* and the neurotransmitter dopamine is a key aspect of information transmission in the prefrontal cortex and this neural circuit (see Figure 4). The maturation of the prefrontal cortex is important in the development of a number of cognitive and socioemotional skills, including attention, memory, and self-regulation (Holmboe & Abigail, 2019).

In sum, scientists are beginning to chart connections between children's cognitive development in areas such as attention and memory, brain regions such as the prefrontal cortex, and the transmission of information at the level of the neuron such as the neurotransmitter dopamine. As continuing advancements in technology allow scientists to "look inside" the brain to observe its activity, we will see an increased precision in our understanding of the brain's functioning in various aspects of cognitive and social-emotional development and how these developmental processes unfold in specific environmental contexts (D'Souza & D'Souza, 2019).

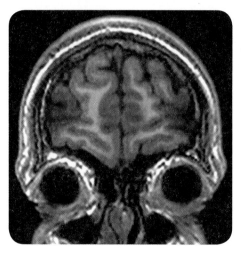

Prefrontal cortex

FIGURE **4**

THE PREFRONTAL CORTEX. The prefrontal cortex, the highest level in the brain, shows extensive development from 3 to 6 years of age and continues to grow through the remainder of childhood and adolescence. The prefrontal cortex plays important roles in attention, memory, and self-regulation. The image on the top shows a side view of the location of the prefrontal cortex. The image on the bottom (frontal view) is a composite of more than 100 fMRI images of the prefrontal cortex that were taken to assess individuals' speed of processing information under different conditions.

(MRI Scan): Dr. Sam Gilbert, Institute of Cognitive Neuroscience, UK

Review *Connect* Reflect

 LG1 Discuss growth and change in the young child's body and brain.

Review

- What changes in height and weight characterize early childhood?
- How does the brain change in young children?

Connect

- How do changes in the brain in early childhood represent advances over the child's brain at the end of infancy?

Reflect *Your Own Personal Journey of Life*

- Think back to when you were a young child. How would you characterize your body growth? Was your growth about the same as that of most children your age, or was it different?

2 How Do Young Children's Motor Skills Develop?

LG2 Describe changes in motor development in early childhood.

(Gross and Fine Motor Skills)   (Perceptual Development)   (Young Children's Artistic Drawings)

Running as fast as you can, falling down, getting right back up and running just as fast as you can . . . building towers with blocks . . . scribbling, scribbling, and scribbling some more . . . cutting paper with scissors . . . During your preschool years, you probably developed the ability to perform all of these activities.

GROSS AND FINE MOTOR SKILLS

Considerable progress is made in both gross and fine motor skills during early childhood, as preschoolers develop a sense of mastery through increased proficiency in gross motor skills such as walking and running (Goodway, Ozmun, & Gallahue, 2020). Improvement in fine motor skills—such as being able to turn the pages of a book, one at a time—also contributes to the child's sense of mastery in the second year. First, let's explore changes in gross motor skills.

Gross Motor Skills   The preschool child no longer has to make an effort simply to stay upright and to move around. As children move their legs with more confidence and carry themselves more purposefully, moving around in the environment becomes more automatic.

At 3 years of age, children enjoy simple movements, such as hopping, jumping, and running back and forth, just for the sheer delight of performing these activities. They take considerable pride in showing how they can run across a room and jump all of 6 inches. The run-and-jump will win no Olympic gold medals, but for the 3-year-old the activity is a source of considerable pride in accomplishment.

At 4 years of age, children are still enjoying the same kinds of activities, but they have become more adventurous. They scramble over low jungle gyms as they display their athletic prowess. Although they have been able to climb stairs with one foot on each step for some time, they are just beginning to be able to come down the same way. They still often revert to putting two feet on each step.

At 5 years of age, children are even more adventuresome than they were at 4. It is not unusual for self-assured 5-year-olds to perform hair-raising stunts on practically any climbing object. Five-year-olds run hard and enjoy races with each other and their parents. A summary of development in gross motor skills during early childhood is shown in Figure 5.

You probably have arrived at one important conclusion about preschool children: They are very, very active. Indeed, 3-year-old children have the highest activity level of any age in the entire human life span. They fidget when they watch television. They fidget when they sit at the dinner table. Even when they sleep, they move around quite a bit.

> **developmental connection**
> **Physical Development**
> Participation in sports can have positive or negative outcomes for children. Connect to "Physical Development in Middle and Late Childhood."

37 to 48 Months	49 to 60 Months	61 to 72 Months
Throws ball underhanded (4 feet)	Bounces and catches ball	Throws ball overhanded (25+ feet)
Pedals tricycle 10 feet	Runs 10 feet and stops	Carries a 16-pound object
Catches large ball	Pushes/pulls a wagon/doll buggy	Kicks rolling ball
Completes forward somersault (aided)	Kicks 10-inch ball toward target	Skips alternating feet
Jumps to floor from 12 inches	Carries 12-pound object	Roller skates
Hops three hops with both feet	Catches ball	Skips rope
Steps on footprint pattern	Bounces ball under control	Rolls ball to hit object
Catches bounced ball	Hops on one foot four hops	Rides bike with training wheels

FIGURE 5

THE DEVELOPMENT OF GROSS MOTOR SKILLS IN EARLY CHILDHOOD.

Note: The skills are listed in the approximate order of difficulty within each age period.

Designing and implementing a developmentally appropriate movement curriculum (one that's appropriate for the child's age and each child individually) facilitates the development of children's gross motor skills (Magistro & others, 2022). To read further about supporting young children's motor development, see the *Caring Connections* interlude.

There can be long-term negative effects for children who fail to develop basic motor skills (Snowling & others, 2019). These children will not be able to join in group games or participate

caring connections

Supporting Young Children's Motor Development

If you observe young children, you will see that they spend a great deal of time engaging in motor activities such as running, jumping, throwing, and catching. These activities can form the basis of advanced, sports-related skills that also positively influence many other aspects of development across childhood and beyond (Jiménez-Díaz, Chaves-Castro, & Salazar, 2019). For children to progress to effective, coordinated, and controlled motor performance, interaction with and instruction from supportive adults can be beneficial (Stevenson, Wainwright, & Williams, 2023).

How can early childhood educators support young children's motor development? When planning physical instruction for young children, it is important to keep in mind that their attention span is rather short, so instruction should be brief and to the point. Young children need to practice skills in order to learn them, so instruction should be followed with ample time for practice (Morrison, 2017, 2018). A large international team developed a set of benchmarks for children's overall physical activity, as well as in specific domains such as active play and organized sports and in specific settings such as at home and in school (Aubert & others, 2022).

Fitness is an important dimension of people's lives, and it is beneficial to develop a positive attitude toward exercise early in life. Preschoolers need vigorous activities for short periods of time. They can be encouraged to rest or change to a quieter activity as needed.

Movement, even within the classroom, can improve a child's stamina. Such movement activities might be as basic as practicing

Young children practicing their motor skills in an early childhood education program.
Operation 2022/Alamy Stock Photo

locomotor skills or as complex as navigating an obstacle course. A number of locomotor skills (such as walking, running, jumping, sliding, skipping, and leaping) can be practiced forward and backward. And it is important to keep practice fun, allowing children to enjoy movement for the sheer pleasure of it. Incorporating movement into academic subjects, such as math, can also increase children's enjoyment of these subjects (Liang & others, 2023).

What are some effective strategies for supporting young children's motor development?

in sports during their school years and in adulthood. However, the positive development of motor skills has benefits besides participation in games and sports. Engaging in motor skills fulfills young children's needs and desires for movement, and exercise builds muscles, strengthens the heart, and enhances aerobic capacity. In an illustrative study, Brazilian children who were randomly assigned to an intervention group that focused on improving both motor and cognitive skills improved not only in motor skills and academic skills but also in perceived competence, self-worth, and social acceptance compared to a control group (Nobre, Nobre, & Valentini, 2023). It is clear that the development of gross motor skills, and feelings of confidence about those skills, are important co-developing factors in early childhood.

Fine Motor Skills At 3 years of age, children show a more mature ability to place and handle things than they did when they were infants or toddlers. Although for some time they have had the ability to pick up the tiniest objects between their thumb and forefinger, they are still somewhat clumsy at it. Three-year-olds can build surprisingly high block towers, each block placed with intense concentration but often not in a completely straight line. When 3-year-olds play with a simple jigsaw puzzle, they are rather rough in placing the pieces. Even when they recognize the location a piece fits into, they are not very precise in positioning the piece. They often try to force the piece in the location or pat it vigorously.

By 4 years of age, children's fine motor coordination has improved substantially and is more precise. Sometimes 4-year-old children have trouble building high towers with blocks because in their efforts to place each of the blocks perfectly, they may upset those already stacked. By age 5, children's fine motor coordination has improved. Hand, arm, and body all move together under better command of the eye. Mere towers no longer interest the 5-year-old, who now wants to build a house or a castle, although adults may still need to be told what each finished project is meant to be. A summary of the development of fine motor skills in early childhood is shown in Figure 6.

How do developmentalists measure children's motor development? The **Denver Developmental Screening Test II** is a simple, inexpensive, fast method of diagnosing developmental delays in children from birth through 6 years of age. The test is individually administered and includes separate assessments of gross and fine motor skills, as well as language and personal-social ability (Ribeiro & others, 2017; Rubio-Codina & others, 2016). Among the gross motor skills this test measures are the child's ability to sit, walk, long jump, pedal a tricycle, throw a ball overhand, catch a bounced ball, hop on one foot, and balance on one foot (Yilmaz & others, 2017). Fine motor skills measured by the test include the child's ability to stack cubes, reach for objects, and draw a person. This test has had a broad international impact as well, with studies demonstrating its global validity in countries as different from each other as South Korea and the Dominican Republic (Jang & others, 2019; Sánchez-Vincitore, Schaettle, & Castro, 2019).

PERCEPTUAL DEVELOPMENT

Changes in children's perceptual development continue throughout childhood (Benassi & others, 2021). Children become increasingly efficient at detecting the boundaries between colors (such as red and orange) at 3 to 4 years of age. When children are about 4 or 5 years old, their eye

Denver Developmental Screening Test II A test used to diagnose developmental delay in children from birth to 6 years of age; includes separate assessments of gross and fine motor skills, language, and personal-social ability.

37 to 48 Months	49 to 60 Months	61 to 72 Months
Approximates a circle in drawing	Strings and laces shoelace	Folds paper into halves and quarters
Cuts paper	Cuts following a line	Traces around hand
Pastes using pointer finger	Strings 10 beads	Draws rectangle, circle, square, and triangle
Builds three-block bridge	Copies figure X	Cuts interior piece from paper
Builds eight-block tower	Opens and places clothespins (one-handed)	Uses crayons appropriately
Draws 0 and +	Builds a five-block bridge	Makes clay object with two small parts
Dresses and undresses doll	Pours from various containers	Reproduces letters
Pours from pitcher without spilling	Prints first name	Copies two short words

FIGURE 6

THE DEVELOPMENT OF FINE MOTOR SKILLS IN EARLY CHILDHOOD.
Note: The skills are listed in the approximate order of difficulty within each age period.

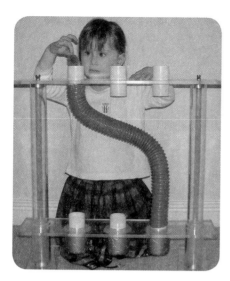

FIGURE 7

VISUAL EXPECTATIONS ABOUT THE PHYSICAL WORLD. When young children see the ball dropped into the tube, many of them will search for it immediately below the dropping point.

Dr. Bruce Hood

muscles usually are developed enough that they can move their eyes efficiently across a series of letters. Many toddler and preschool children are farsighted, unable to see close up as well as they can see far away (Mutti & others, 2018). By the time they enter kindergarten or first grade, though, most children can focus their eyes and sustain their attention effectively on close-up objects.

What are the signs of vision problems in children? They include rubbing the eyes, blinking or squinting excessively, appearing irritable when playing games that require good distance vision, shutting or covering one eye, and tilting the head or thrusting it forward when looking at something. A child who shows any of these behaviors should be examined by an ophthalmologist.

After infancy, children's visual expectations about the physical world continue to develop, due in part to continuing changes in their cognitive development. In one illustrative study, 2- to 4½-year-old children were given a task in which the goal was to find a ball that had been dropped through an opaque tube (Hood, 1995). As shown in Figure 7, if the ball is dropped into the opaque tube at the top, it will land in the box at the bottom that is farthest away. However, in this task, most of the 2-year-olds, and even some of the 4-year-olds, persisted in searching in the box immediately beneath the dropping point. For them, gravity ruled and they had failed to perceive the end location of the curved tube.

In a subsequent study, 3-year-olds were presented with a task very similar to the one shown in Figure 7 (Palmquist, Keen, & Jaswal, 2018). In the group that was told to imagine the ball rolling through the tube, the young children were more accurate in predicting where the ball would land. In another study, 3-year-olds improved their performance on the ball-dropping task shown in Figure 7 when they were instructed to follow the tube with their eyes to the bottom (Bascandziev & Harris, 2011). Thus, in these two studies, 3-year-olds were able to overcome the gravity bias and their impulsive tendencies when they were given verbal instructions from a knowledgeable adult.

How do children learn to deal with situations like that in Figure 7, and how do they come to understand other laws of the physical world? These questions are addressed by studies of cognitive development, which we discuss in more detail later.

YOUNG CHILDREN'S ARTISTIC DRAWINGS

In the story that opened the chapter, you read about Teresa Amabile's artistic skills and interest during kindergarten. The story revealed how these skills were restricted once she went to elementary school. Indeed, many young children show a special interest in drawing, just as Teresa did.

Children may use lavish colors that come close, but perhaps won't match the reality of their subjects. Form and clarity give way to bold lines flowing freely on the page. The end product matters less than the joy of creating, the fun of mixing colors, experimenting with different mediums, and getting messy in the process.

Young children often use the same formula for drawing different things. Though modified in small ways, one basic form can cover a range of objects. When children begin to draw animals, they portray them in the same way they portray humans: standing upright with a smiling face, two legs, and outstretched arms. Pointed ears may be a clue to adults about the nature of the particular beast. As children become more sophisticated, their drawing of a cat will look more catlike to an adult. It may be resting on all four paws, tail in the air, with fur standing on end.

Not all children embrace art with enthusiasm, and the same child may want to draw one day but have no interest in it the next day. For most children, however, art is an important vehicle for conveying feelings and ideas that are not easily expressed in words. For example, in one study in Saudi Arabia, children were asked to draw what they missed about preschool during the COVID-19 pandemic as a way of helping children express what was important to them and to guide educators as they prepared children to return to school (Alabdulkarim & others, 2021). Drawing and constructing also provide children with a hands-on opportunity to use their problem-solving skills to develop creative ways to represent scale, space, and motion (Feeney, Moravcik, & Nolte, 2018). Parents and child-care providers can provide a context for artistic exploration by giving children a work space where they are not overly concerned about messiness or damage. They can make supplies available, have a bulletin board display space for the child's art, and support and encourage the child's art activity. When viewing children's art, many parents take special delight in hearing about the creative process. Questions such as "Can you tell me about this?" and "What were you thinking about when you made this?" encourage children and help parents to see the world through their children's eyes. When comparing cultures and countries, there are many aspects of the encouragement and support of artistic expression in young children, though some practices vary in accordance with cultural differences (Hamilton, Jin, & Krieg, 2019).

placement stage Kellogg's term for 2- to 3-year-olds' drawings that are drawn on a page in placement patterns.

shape stage Kellogg's term for 3-year-olds' drawings consisting of diagrams in different shapes.

design stage Kellogg's term for 3- to 4-year-olds' drawings that mix two basic shapes into more complex designs.

pictorial stage Kellogg's term for 4- to 5-year-olds' drawings depicting objects that adults can recognize.

Developmental Changes and Stages   The development of fine motor skills in the preschool years allows children to become budding artists. There are dramatic changes in how children depict what they see and imagine. Art provides unique insights into children's perceptual worlds—what they are attending to, how space and distance are viewed, how they experience patterns and forms (Bullard, 2017). Rhoda Kellogg (1898–1987) was a creative teacher of preschool children who observed and guided young children's artistic efforts for many decades. She assembled an impressive array of tens of thousands of drawings produced by more than 2,000 preschool children. Adults who are unfamiliar with young children's art often view the productions of this age group as meaningless scribbles. However, Kellogg (1970) documented that young children's artistic productions are orderly, meaningful, and structured.

By their second birthday, children can scribble. Scribbles represent the earliest form of drawing. Every form of graphic art, no matter how complex, contains the lines found in children's artwork, which Kellogg called the 20 basic scribbles. These include vertical, horizontal, diagonal, circular, curving, waving or zigzag lines, and dots. As young children progress from scribbling to picture making, they go through four distinguishable stages: placement, shape, design, and pictorial (see Figure 8).

Following young children's scribbles (Figure 8a) is the **placement stage,** Kellogg's term for 2- to 3-year-olds' drawings, drawn on a page in placement patterns. One example of these patterns is the spaced border pattern shown in Figure 8b. The **shape stage** was Kellogg's term for 3-year-olds' drawings consisting of diagrams in different shapes (see Figure 8c). Young children draw six basic shapes: circles, squares or rectangles, triangles, crosses, Xs, and forms. The **design stage** was Kellogg's term for 3- to 4-year-olds' drawings in which young children mix two basic shapes into a more complex design (see Figure 8d). This stage occurs rather quickly after the shape stage. The **pictorial stage** was Kellogg's term for 4- to 5-year-olds' drawings that consist of objects that adults can recognize (see Figure 8e).

Child Art in Context   Claire Golomb (2011, 2016) has studied and conducted research on children's art for a number of decades. Golomb especially criticizes views of young children's art that describe it as primitive and a reflection of conceptual immaturity. She argues that children, like all novices, tend to use forms economically, and their comments indicate that their simplified version works. Rather than seeing children's art as reflections of their conceptual immaturity, Golomb (2011, 2016) focuses on the inventive problem solving that goes into creating these drawings.

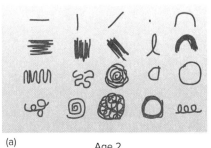

(a)
Age 2
20 basic scribbles

(b)
Age 2 to 3
Placement stage

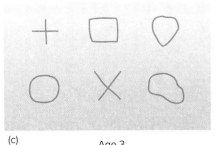

(c)
Age 3
Shape stage

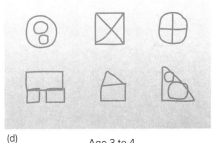

(d)
Age 3 to 4
Design stage

(e)
Age 4 to 5
Pictorial stage

At which of Kellogg's stages of children's art is this young girl's drawing?

Katy McDonnell/DigitalVision/Getty Images

FIGURE **8**

THE STAGES OF YOUNG CHILDREN'S ARTISTIC DRAWINGS

Golomb (2011, 2016) maintains that developmental changes in the way children draw are not strictly age-related but also depend on talent, motivation, familial support, and cultural values. Thus, her view contrasts with Kellogg's universal stage approach in which all children go through the same sequence in developing art skills, which we just discussed. In Golomb's view, children's art flourishes in sociocultural contexts where tools are made available and where this activity is valued. This helps explain why there are culture and country-specific preschool education standards with respect to some aspects of art education (Hamilton, Jin, & Krieg, 2019).

Review Connect Reflect

 LG2 Describe changes in motor development in early childhood.

Review
- How do gross and fine motor skills change in early childhood?
- How can young children's artistic drawings be characterized?

Connect
- Would you describe the development of gross motor skills as occurring more rapidly in infancy or in early childhood?

Reflect *Your Own Personal Journey of Life*
- Imagine that you are the director of a preschool program, and the parents ask you to develop a program to teach the children how to participate in sports. Think through how you would explain to parents why most 3-year-olds are not ready for participation in sports programs. Include in your answer information about 3-year-olds' limited motor skills, as well as the importance of helping children learn basic motor skills first rather than having unrealistic expectations for young children's development of sports skills.

3 What Are Some Important Aspects of Young Children's Health?

 LG3 Characterize the health of young children.

| Sleep and Sleep Problems | Nutrition | Exercise | Health, Safety, and Illness |

So far, we have discussed young children's body growth and change, as well as their development of motor skills. In this section, we explore another aspect of young children's physical development—health. To learn more about young children's health, we focus on how it is affected by sleep, nutrition, exercise, safety practices, and illnesses.

SLEEP AND SLEEP PROBLEMS

A good night's sleep is an important aspect of a child's development (Cremone & others, 2019). Experts recommend that young children get 10 to 13 hours of a sleep each night (National Sleep Foundation, 2023). Most young children sleep through the night and have one daytime nap.

Not only is the amount of sleep children get important, but so is uninterrupted sleep (Willumsen & Bull, 2020). However, it sometimes is difficult to get young children to go to sleep as they drag out their bedtime routine. A number of studies have found that bedtime resistance is associated with conduct problems or hyperactivity in children (Corkum & others, 2019).

Sleep expert Mona El-Sheikh (2020) recommends adjusting the following aspects of the child's environment to improve the child's sleep: making sure that the bedroom is cool, dark, and comfortable; maintaining consistent bedtimes and wake times; and building positive family relationships. Also, helping the child slow down before bedtime often contributes to less resistance in going to bed. Reading the child a story, playing quietly with the child in the bath, and letting the child sit on the caregiver's lap while listening to music are quieting activities.

It is common for children to experience one or more sleep problems at some point in their development (Shimizu & others, 2021). Reviews of the literature suggest that more than

 How Would You...?
If you were a **human development and family studies professional,** how would you advise parents of a young child who is resisting going to bed at night?

- - - - - - - - - →

developmental connection

Sleep

What sleep disorder in infancy leads to the most infant deaths, and at what age is the infant most at risk for this disorder? Connect to "Physical Development in Infancy."

← - - - - - - - -

40 percent of children experience a sleep problem at some point in their development (Williamson & others, 2019). The following research studies indicate links between children's sleep and their developmental outcomes:

- Preschool children who had better-quality observed interactions with their parents (more harmonious and reciprocal) had longer sleep duration than their counterparts who had lower-quality interactions (more indifferent and conflictual) with their parents (Dubois-Comtois & others, 2020).
- In a Chinese study, preschool children who slept seven hours per night or less had a worse school readiness profile (including language/cognitive deficits and emotional immaturity) (Tso & others, 2016). Also in this study, preschool children who used electronic devices three or more hours per day had shortened sleep durations.
- Preschool children who had a longer sleep duration were more likely to have better peer acceptance, social skills, and receptive vocabulary (Vaughn & others, 2015).
- Having nightmares at 24 months and restless sleep at 48 months were linked to ADHD at 11 years of age (Carpena & others, 2020).
- In 2- to 5-year-old children, each additional hour of daily screen time was associated with a decrease in sleep time, less likelihood of sleeping 10 hours or more per night, and later bedtime (Xu & others, 2016).

Let's now explore four specific sleep problems in children: nightmares, night terrors, sleepwalking, and sleep talking. **Nightmares** are frightening dreams that awaken the sleeper, more often toward the morning than just after the child has gone to bed at night (El Rafihi-Ferreira & others, 2019). Caregivers should not worry about young children having occasional nightmares because almost every child has them. If children have nightmares persistently, it may indicate that they are feeling too much stress during their waking hours (Akinsanya, Marwaha, & Tampi, 2017).

Night terrors are characterized by a sudden arousal from sleep and an intense fear, usually accompanied by a number of physiological reactions, such as rapid heart rate and breathing, loud screams, heavy perspiration, and physical movement (Leung & others, 2020). In most instances, the child has little or no memory of what happened during the night terror. Night terrors are less common than nightmares and occur more often in deep sleep than do nightmares. Many children who experience night terrors return to sleep rather quickly after the night terror. Children usually outgrow night terrors.

Somnambulism (sleepwalking) occurs during the deepest stage of sleep. Approximately 15 percent of children sleepwalk at least once, and from 1 to 5 percent do it regularly. It is far more common in young children if one or both of their biological parents also are sleepwalkers (Kantha, 2022). Most children outgrow the problem without professional intervention.

Sleep talkers are soundly asleep as they speak. Occasionally they make fairly coherent statements for a brief period of time. Most of the time, though, you can't understand what children are saying during sleep talking. There is nothing abnormal about sleep talking, and there is no reason to try to stop it from occurring.

What characterizes young children's sleep? What are some sleep problems in childhood?
Westend61/Getty Images

NUTRITION

Four-year-old Jamai is on a steady diet of double cheeseburgers, French fries, and chocolate milk shakes. Between meals, he gobbles up candy bars and marshmallows. He hates green vegetables. Jamai, a preschooler, already has developed poor nutritional habits. What are a preschool child's energy needs? What is a preschooler's eating behavior like?

Energy Needs Feeding and eating habits are important aspects of development during early childhood (Wedde & others, 2020). What children eat affects their skeletal growth, body shape, and susceptibility to disease. The preschool child requires up to 1,800 calories per day. Figure 9 shows the increasing energy needs of children as they move from infancy through the childhood years. Energy needs of individual children of the same age, sex, and size vary. However, an increasing number of children have an energy intake that exceeds what they need (Mireault & others, 2023). The World Health Organization offers guidelines regarding increasing fruit and vegetable consumption and decreasing intake of sugar, salt, and fats to promote healthier eating (World Health Organization, 2020).

nightmares Frightening dreams that awaken the sleeper.

night terrors Incidents characterized by sudden arousal from sleep, intense fear, and usually physiological reactions such as rapid heart rate and breathing, loud screams, heavy perspiration, and physical movement.

somnambulism Sleepwalking; occurs in the deepest stage of sleep.

sleep talker A child speaking with clear or unclear words and statements while asleep.

FIGURE 9

RECOMMENDED ENERGY INTAKES FOR CHILDREN AGES 1 THROUGH 10

Age	Weight (lb)	Height (in)	Energy needs (calories)	Calorie ranges
1 to 3	29	35	1,300	900 to 1,800
4 to 6	44	44	1,700	1,300 to 2,300
7 to 10	62	52	2,400	1,650 to 3,300

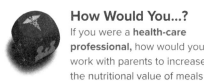

How Would You...?

If you were a **health-care professional,** how would you work with parents to increase the nutritional value of meals and snacks they provide to their young children?

What are some positive strategies parents can adopt regarding their young children's eating behavior?

Pixelfit/Getty Images

Diet, Eating Behavior, and Parental Feeding Styles A foundational national study found that from the late 1970s through the late 1990s, several dietary shifts took place in U.S. children: greater away-from-home consumption; large increases in total energy from salty snacks, soft drinks, and pizza; and large decreases in energy from low- and medium-fat milk and medium- and high-fat beef and pork (Nielsen, Siega-Riz, & Popkin, 2002). These dietary changes occurred for children as young as 2 years of age through the adult years.

Being overweight has become a serious health problem in early childhood (Centers for Disease Control and Prevention, 2022). National studies in the United States have revealed that young children's meals typically do not meet recommended guidelines for nutrients and calories (Dallacker, Hertwig, & Mata, 2018).

Young children's eating behavior is strongly influenced by their caregivers' behavior (Campbell & others, 2018). Young children's eating behavior improves when caregivers eat with children on a predictable schedule, model eating healthy food, make mealtimes pleasant occasions, and engage in certain feeding styles. Distractions from screens and media, family arguments, and competing activities should be minimized so children can focus on eating. A sensitive/responsive caregiver feeding style, in which the caregiver is nurturant, provides clear information about what is expected, and responds appropriately to children's cues, is recommended (Hart & others, 2023). Forceful and restrictive caregiver behaviors are not recommended. For example, a restrictive feeding style is linked to children being overweight (Johnson & others, 2018).

Another problem is that many parents do not recognize that their children are overweight. One large Australian study of parents with infant or preschool-aged children found that, over time, parents vastly underestimated the overweight status of heavier toddlers, preschoolers, and children (Wake, Kerr, & Jansen, 2018).

Fat and Sugar Consumption Although some health-conscious parents may be providing too little fat in their infants' and children's diets, other parents are raising their children on diets in which the percentage of fat is far too high (Hampl & others, 2023). Too many young children already have developed a pattern of not eating enough fruits and vegetables, a pattern that can have negative consequences later in development. For example, one study revealed that 2½-year-old children's liking for fruits and vegetables was related to their eating more fruits and vegetables at 7 years of age (Fletcher & others, 2017).

Our changing lifestyles, in which we often eat on the run and pick up fast-food meals, contribute to the increased fat levels in children's diets. Most fast-food meals are high in protein, especially meat and dairy products. But the average American child does not need to be concerned about getting enough protein. What must be of concern is the vast number of young children who are being raised on fast foods that are not only high in protein but also high in fat and sodium. Eating habits become ingrained very early in life; unfortunately, it is during the preschool years that many people get their first taste of fast food. The American Heart Association recommends that the daily limit for calories from fat should be approximately 35 percent.

The concern surrounding food choices involves not only excessive fat in children's diets but also excessive sugar (Hampl & others, 2023). Consider Olivia, age 3, who loves chocolate. Her mother lets her have three chocolate candy bars a day. She also drinks an average of four cans of caffeinated cola a day, and she eats sugar-coated cereal each morning at breakfast. The average American child consumes almost 2 pounds of sugar per week. One study found that children from low-income families were likely to consume more sugar than their counterparts from higher-income families (Duffy & others, 2020).

How does sugar consumption influence the health and behavior of young children? The association of sugar consumption with children's health problems—dental cavities and obesity, for example—has been widely documented (Pereira Araújo & others, 2022).

In sum, although there is individual variation in appropriate nutrition for children, their diets should be well balanced and should include fats, carbohydrates, protein, vitamins, and minerals (World Health Organization, 2020). An occasional candy bar does not hurt, but a steady diet of hamburgers, French fries, milk shakes, and candy bars should be avoided.

"Fussy Eaters," Sweets, and Snacks   Many young children get labeled as "fussy" or "difficult eaters" when they are only trying to exercise the same rights to personal taste and appetite that adults take for granted (Taylor & Emmett, 2019). Caregivers should allow for the child's developing tastes in food. However, when young children eat too many sweets—candy, cola, and sweetened cereals, for example—they can spoil their appetite and then not want to eat more nutritious foods at mealtime. Thus, caregivers need to be firm in limiting the amount of sweets young children eat.

Overweight Young Children   The Centers for Disease Control and Prevention (2022) has established categories for obesity, overweight, and at risk for being overweight. These categories are determined by body mass index (BMI), which is computed by a formula that takes into account height and weight. Children and adolescents whose BMI is at or above the 97th percentile are classified as obese; those whose BMI is at or above the 95th percentile are overweight; and those whose BMI is at or above the 85th percentile are at risk of becoming overweight.

The percentages of young children who are overweight or at risk of being overweight in the United States have increased dramatically in recent decades, but in the last several years there are indications that fewer preschool children are obese. In 2009–2010, 12.1 percent of U.S. 2- to 5-year-olds were classified as obese, compared with 5 percent in 1976–1980 and 10.4 percent in 2007–2008 (Ogden & others, 2016). However, in 2013–2014, a substantial drop in the obesity rate of 2- to 5-year-old children occurred in comparison with their counterparts in 2003–2004 (Ogden & others, 2016). In 2013–2014, 9.4 percent of 2- to 5-year-olds were obese compared with 14 percent in 2004. It is not clear why this drop occurred, but possible causes include families buying lower-calorie foods and the influence of the Special Supplemental Nutrition Program for Women, Infants, and Children that subsidizes food for women in low-income families and emphasizes consuming less fruit juice, cheese, and eggs and more whole fruits and vegetables.

What are some trends in the eating habits and weight of young children?
HearttoHeart0225/Getty Images

There are racial and ethnic differences in rates of obesity in young children. In the United States, obesity is more prevalent in Latino (26 percent) and non-Latino Black (22 percent) children than in non-Latino White (14 percent) or Asian American (11 percent) children (Centers for Disease Control and Prevention, 2018d).

The risk that overweight children will continue to be overweight when they are older has been well documented. Obesity in childhood strongly predicts obesity or being overweight in adulthood and leads to higher rates of cardiovascular and metabolic disorders, certain types of cancer, and a shorter life span into adulthood (Weihrauch-Blüher, Schwarz, & Klusmann, 2019).

At least nine countries, including the United States, have prevalence rates of childhood obesity that are over 20 percent (World Health Organization, 2021). According to the World Health Organization (2021), 38 million children under the age of 5 years were overweight or obese around the world in 2019. Further, more than 340 million children and adolescents aged 5 to 19 were overweight or obese worldwide in 2016. Childhood obesity contributes to a number of health problems in young children. For example, physicians sometimes see type 2 (adult-onset) diabetes (a condition directly linked with obesity and a low level of fitness) and hypertension in young children (Lim & others, 2022).

Being overweight also is linked to young children's psychological functioning. In one longitudinal Canadian study of over 10,000 preschoolers, children who were overweight or

developmental connection

Nutrition

A number of intervention programs have been conducted in an effort to help overweight and obese children to lose weight. Connect to "Physical Development in Middle and Late Childhood."

What are some effective strategies for preventing childhood obesity?

Larry Williams/Stone/Getty Images

obese in early childhood were more likely to need mental health services later. This effect was stronger for girls than boys (Carsley & others, 2018).

Prevention of obesity in children includes helping children and parents see food as a way to satisfy hunger and nutritional needs, not as proof of love or as a reward for good behavior. Snack foods should be low in fat, simple sugars, and salt, as well as high in fiber. Routine physical activity should be a daily occurrence (Ha & others, 2019; Powers & Dodd, 2017). A comprehensive intervention study with children attending Head Start programs found that getting parents involved in activities such as nutrition counseling, becoming more aware of their child's weight status, and developing healthy lifestyles was effective in lowering children's rates of obesity, increasing children's physical activity, reducing children's TV viewing, and improving children's eating habits (Davison & others, 2013). Other researchers also are finding that interventions with parents can reduce children's risk of being overweight or obese (Byrne & others, 2018; Moore & others, 2019). A meta-analysis and review of Internet-based parent-focused interventions concluded that they were often effective in helping obese children lose weight (Hammersley, Jones, & Okely, 2016). A recent study found that positive parenting that emphasized praise for healthy eating behavior improved young children's eating behavior (increased vegetable intake, for example) and helped overweight children lose weight better than negative comments by parents did (Rotman & others, 2020).

Malnutrition in Young Children from Low-Income Families Malnutrition continues to be a major threat to millions during the childhood years, particularly in low-income countries that have high rates of poverty (UNICEF, 2022). A meta-analysis of 80 studies conducted primarily in Asia and Africa found that interventions that communicated information about nutrition and social behavior change to parents were effective in improving children's growth (Mahumud & others, 2022).

A common nutritional problem in early childhood is iron deficiency anemia, which results in chronic fatigue (Gingoyon & others, 2022). This problem results from the failure to eat adequate amounts of quality meats and dark green vegetables. Young children from low-income families are most likely to develop iron deficiency anemia (Mitchinson & others, 2019).

Some researchers have argued that malnutrition is directly linked to cognitive deficits because of negative effects on brain development (for example, see Nyaradi & others, 2013). However, an increasing number of researchers conclude that the links between child malnutrition, physical growth, and cognitive development are more complex. For example, nutritional influences can be viewed in the context of socioemotional factors that often coincide with nutrient levels. Thus, children who vary considerably from the norm in physical growth also differ on other biological and socioemotional factors that might influence cognitive development. For example, children who are underfed often are also less supervised, less stimulated, and less educated than children who are well nourished. As we discussed earlier, poverty is an especially strong risk factor that interacts with children's nutritional status to affect physical and cognitive development (Black & others, 2017).

In addition to cognitive deficits, malnutrition may be linked to other aspects of development. One of the longest-running longitudinal studies found that U.S. children who were malnourished at 3 years of age showed more aggressive and hyperactive behavior at age 8, had more externalizing problems at age 11, and evidenced more excessive motor behavior at age 17 (Liu & others, 2004). To read about a pediatric occupational therapist who works with children to attain healthy lifestyles, please see the *Connecting with Careers* box.

---->

developmental **connection**

Health

As boys and girls reach and progress through adolescence, they exercise less. Connect to "Physical Development in Adolescence."

<----

EXERCISE

Because of their activity level and the development of large muscles, especially in the arms and legs, preschool children need daily exercise (Centers for Disease Control and Prevention, 2023). Four expert panels from Australia, Canada, the United Kingdom, and the United States issued physical activity guidelines for young children that were quite similar (Pate & others, 2015). The guidelines recommend that young children get 15 or more minutes of physical activity per hour over a 12-hour period, or about 3 hours per day total. These guidelines reflect an increase from earlier guidelines established in 2002.

Alyssa Cantal, Pediatric Occupational Therapist

Children who either are now or are at risk for becoming overweight or obese can be limited in their ability to participate in meaningful, satisfying activities (Cantal, 2019). Occupational therapy practitioners provide the vital tools, framework, and interventions needed to support the children and their families. Alyssa Cantal is an occupational therapist at Gallagher Pediatric Therapy in Fullerton, California. After receiving her undergraduate degree in human development with a minor in psychology from UC San Diego, she earned a doctorate of occupational therapy at the University of Southern California.

Cantal says her passion for working with others as well as her sister's experience as a pediatric physical therapist motivated her to pursue a career in rehabilitation. During her medical residency, she participated in "Imagining America: CREATE Your Vision," a community-based therapeutic arts program that guides children through health-related topics. In Cantal's experiences with clients, she has seen disparities in healthy weight by race, ethnicity, and physical ability. As a pediatric occupational therapist, she can play a pivotal role in promoting health, well-being, and quality of life for all children.

Alyssa Cantal, a pediatric occupational therapist, works with a group of school children to strengthen their knowledge about healthy behaviors.
Dr. Alyssa Cantal

Too often, though, preschool children are not getting enough exercise (Dowda & others, 2017). In a systematic review of studies in 11 countries that included nearly 14,000 preschoolers in child-care settings, children spent large amounts of time being sedentary. This ranged from as little as 12 minutes per hour to 55 minutes per hour of sedentary time depending on the study and sample of children and centers (O'Brien & others, 2018). Preschool children are more physically active if they spend time outdoors and live in a safe neighborhood where families feel that they can trust their neighbors (Parent & others, 2021). A comprehensive research review of 17 studies concluded that exercise was an effective strategy for reducing body fat in overweight and obese children (Kelley & Kelley, 2013). Further, in an intervention study, 60 minutes of physical activity per day in preschool academic contexts improved early literacy (Kirk & Kirk, 2016).

In sum, the child's life should be centered around physical activities, not meals. Just how important are these activities in young children's lives? See the *Connecting with Research* interlude for insight from one research study.

HEALTH, SAFETY, AND ILLNESS

In the effort to make a child's world safer, one of the main strategies is to prevent childhood injuries. And in considering young children's health, it important to examine the contexts in which they live.

Preventing Childhood Injuries   Young children's active and exploratory nature, coupled with unawareness of danger in many instances, often puts them in situations in which they are at risk for injuries. Most of young children's cuts, bumps, and bruises are minor, but some accidental injuries can produce serious injuries or even death (Heron, 2021).

In the United States, unintentional injuries (such as in motor vehicle accidents) are the leading cause of death in young children, followed by congenital anomalies and cancer

Physical Activity in Young Children Attending Preschools

Key Points:

- Researchers monitored physical activity in 3- to 5-year-olds.
- Children did not meet activity guidelines.
- Boys were more active than girls.

One classic study examined the activity levels of 281 3- to 5-year-olds in nine preschools (Pate & others, 2004). The preschool children wore accelerometers, a small activity monitor, for four to five hours a day. Height and weight assessments of the children were made to calculate their BMI.

Guidelines recommend that preschool children engage in at least two hours of physical activity per day, divided into one hour of structured activity and one hour of unstructured free play (Society of Health and Physical Educators, 2022), with some recommendations of three hours (Pate & others, 2015). In the study conducted by Pate and colleagues, the young children participated in an average of 7.7 minutes per hour of moderate to vigorous activity, usually in a block of time when they were outside. Over the course of eight hours of a preschool day, these children would get approximately one hour of moderate and vigorous physical activity—only about 50 percent of the amount recommended. The researchers concluded that young children are unlikely to engage in another hour per day of moderate and vigorous physical activity outside their eight hours spent in preschool and thus are not getting adequate opportunities for physical activity.

Gender and age differences characterized the preschool children's physical activity. Boys were more likely to engage in moderate or vigorous physical activity than girls were. Four- and 5-year-old children were more likely to be sedentary than 3-year-old children.

What are some guidelines for preschool children's exercise?
skynesher/Getty Images

The young children's physical activity levels also varied according to the particular preschool they attended. The extent to which they participated in moderate and vigorous physical activity ranged from 4.4 to 10.2 minutes per hour across the nine preschools. Thus, the policies and practices of particular preschools influence the extent to which children engage in physical activity. The researchers concluded back in 2004 that young children need more vigorous play and organized activities, and this need is equally important today.

Can you think of any other ways in which researchers could test and confirm the findings of this study?

How Would You...?

If you were a **health-care professional**, what changes would you advise parents of young children to make in order to improve the safety of their home?

(see Figure 10). In addition to motor vehicle accidents, other accidental deaths in children involve drowning, falls, burns, and poisoning (Heron, 2021).

The leading cause of death of children in the United States is firearms, which kill more children than motor vehicle accidents and other injuries (Centers for Disease Control and Prevention, 2021). In no other large or wealthy country is firearm-related death even in the top four causes of death in children (McGough & others, 2022). The United States represents only 46% of the population of large and wealthy countries but accounts for 97% of child deaths related to firearms.

Influences on children's safety include the acquisition and practice of individual skills and safety behaviors, family and home influences, school and peer influences, and the community's actions. For example, children can be restrained in car seats to reduce risk of injury and death in motor vehicle accidents, guns can be kept locked away from children, and children can be supervised in the bathtub to prevent drowning (Burr & others, 2023). Notice that these influences reflect Bronfenbrenner's ecological model of development. Ecological contexts can influence children's safety, security, and injury prevention (Sleet, 2018). We will have more to say about contextual influences on young children's health shortly.

Reducing access to firearms is essential (Behrens & others, 2023). In 12 states that passed laws requiring that firearms be made inaccessible to children, unintentional shooting deaths of children fell by almost 25 percent. In one landmark study, many parents in homes with firearms reported that their children never handled the firearms, but interviews with their children contradicted the parents' perceptions (Baxley & Miller, 2006).

Deaths of young children due to automobile accidents have declined considerably in many countries since the introduction of the seat belt, followed by the child safety or booster seat. All U.S. states and the District of Columbia have laws that require young children to be restrained in the back seats of cars, in specially designed seats or carriers; such laws also are widely prevalent throughout the world, especially in industrialized nations. In many instances, when young children are killed today in automobile accidents, they are unrestrained. Although many parents today use car seats or "booster seats" for their children, many don't install the seats properly. If the seat is not installed correctly, children are at risk for serious injury or death in automobile accidents (Egly & Ricca, 2022). Nearly all local police departments will assist parents in installing their children's car seats safely. This service is provided free of charge.

Most fatal non-vehicle-related deaths in young children occur in or around the home. Young children have drowned in bathtubs and swimming pools, been burned in fires and explosions, experienced falls from heights, and drunk or eaten poisonous substances.

Playgrounds also can be a source of children's injuries (Olsen & Kennedy, 2019). One of the major problems is that playground equipment is often not constructed over impact-absorbing surfaces such as wood chips or sand.

Contexts of Young Children's Health   Among the contexts affecting young children's health are poverty and ethnicity, home and child care, environmental tobacco smoke, and exposure to lead. In addition to discussing these issues, we will discuss the state of illness and health in the world's children.

Poverty and Ethnicity   Low income is linked with poor health in young children (Roos, Wall-Wieler, & Lee, 2019). Many health problems of young children in poverty begin before birth when their mothers receive little or no health care, which can produce a low birth weight child and other complications that may continue to affect the child years later (Davis & others, 2023). Children living in poverty may experience unsanitary conditions and live in crowded housing, which in a five-decade longitudinal study was found to be related to premature mortality in adulthood (Yu & others, 2022). Children in poverty are more likely to be exposed to lead poisoning than children growing up in higher socioeconomic conditions (Whitehead & Buchanan, 2019). The families of many children in poverty do not have adequate medical insurance, and thus the children often receive less adequate medical care than do children living in higher socioeconomic conditions (Black & others, 2017). Furthermore, early physical and cognitive development are negatively affected by inadequate nutrition and food insecurity that often accompany poverty (Alam & others, 2020).

Ethnicity is also linked to children's health in many countries (Trent, Dooley, & Dougé, 2019). For example, structural racism and barriers to health care have contributed to health disparities in the United States, with Black and Latino children having more health problems and less access to health care than non-Latino White children, including during the COVID-19 pandemic (Goyal & others, 2020). Another study, conducted in Spain, revealed that children whose parents had limited Spanish proficiency were far more likely to have fair or poor dental health status than their Spanish-proficient counterparts (Soria, Bernabé, & Perez, 2019).

Safety at Home and in Child Care   Caregivers—whether they are parents at home or teachers and supervisors in child care—play an important role in protecting the health of young children. For example, by controlling the speed of the vehicles they drive, by decreasing or eliminating their drinking—especially before driving—by not smoking around children, and by not consuming sugary sweetened beverages, caregivers enhance the likelihood that children will be healthy (Drouin, Winickoff, & Thorndike, 2019).

Young children may lack the cognitive skills—including reading ability—to discriminate between safe and unsafe household substances. And they may lack the impulse control to keep from running out into a busy street while chasing a ball. In these and many other situations, competent adult supervision and monitoring of young children are important to prevent

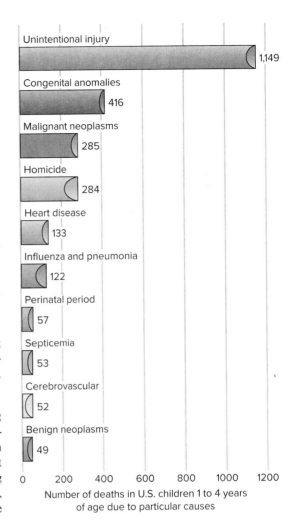

FIGURE **10**

MAIN CAUSES OF DEATH IN CHILDREN 1 THROUGH 4 YEARS OF AGE. This figure shows the number of deaths in U.S. children 1 to 4 years of age due to particular causes in 2019 (Heron, 2021).

How Would You...?

If you were a **health-care professional,** how would you talk with parents about the impact of secondhand smoke on children's health in order to encourage parents to stop smoking?

What are some negative outcomes for children when they experience environmental tobacco smoke?

Hannah Maule-Ffinch/Image Source/Getty Images

injuries (Damashek & Borduin, 2019). In communicating with young children, caregivers need to make sure that the information they give to children is cognitively simple. And an important strategy is that parents guide children in learning how to control and regulate their own health behavior.

Parents also should invest effort in finding a competent health-care provider for their children. This "includes consulting sources of information and asking questions likely to provide useful information about practice characteristics that may affect the parent-doctor relationship. Parents, for example, might seek information concerning a physician's willingness to answer questions and involve parents in decision making or at least to outline options. Parents might also inquire about the physician's style of practice and philosophies about treatment, behavior management, nutrition, and other general health maintenance practices" (Hickson & Clayton, 2002).

Environmental Tobacco Smoke   Estimates indicate that approximately 22 percent of children and adolescents in the United States are exposed to tobacco smoke in the home. A large number of studies reach the conclusion that children are at risk for health problems when they live in homes in which a parent smokes (Ramos-Lopez & others, 2021). In one review of the literature, if the mother smoked, her children were more likely to develop respiratory problems (Sly & Bush, 2019). In another study, young children whose fathers smoked were more likely to have respiratory problems such as asthma than those whose fathers did not smoke; this effect was explained, in part, by "epigenetic" alterations to the children's genes while still in the womb (Wu & others, 2019). A national study found that children with a smoker in the home were 30 percent more likely to be diagnosed with asthma than children with no smokers in the home (Xie & others, 2021). Another study showed that exposure to second-hand smoke was related to young children's sleep problems (Plancoulaine & others, 2018). And a different investigation found that young children who were exposed to environmental tobacco smoke were more likely to engage in antisocial behavior when they were 12 years old (Pagani & others, 2017).

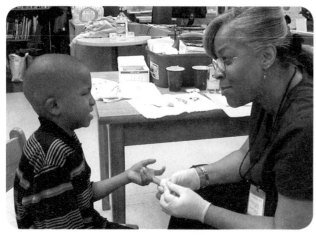

What are some negative effects of high levels of lead in children's blood?

Mike Householder/AP Images

Exposure to Lead   There are special concerns about lead poisoning in young children (Del Rio & others, 2023). Approximately 3 percent of children under 6 years of age are estimated to be at risk for lead poisoning, which might harm their development (McClure, Niles, & Kaufman, 2016). As we mentioned earlier, children in poverty are at greater risk for lead poisoning than children living in higher socioeconomic conditions (Ruckart & others, 2021). Lead can get into children's bloodstreams through ingesting food or water that is contaminated by lead, putting lead-contaminated fingers in their mouths, or inhaling dust from lead-based paint. The negative effects of high lead levels in children's blood include lower intelligence, lower achievement, attention deficit hyperactivity disorder, and elevated blood pressure (Blackowicz & others, 2017; Whitehead & Buchanan, 2019). One longitudinal study found that children who lived in high poverty neighborhoods were more likely to be exposed to lead, which in turn led to lower vocabulary skills (Wodtke, Ramaj, & Schachner, 2022). Because of such negative outcomes, the Centers for Disease Control and Prevention recommends that children be screened for the presence of lead contamination in their blood.

To read further about children's illness and health, see the *Connecting with Diversity* interlude.

The State of Illness and Health in the World's Children

Each year, UNICEF produces a report titled *The State of the World's Children*. The report each year highlights a different key issue affecting children, such as the under-5 mortality rate of a nation, children with disabilities, and mental health. UNICEF concluded in one report, for example, that the under-5 mortality rate is the result of a wide range of factors, including the nutritional health and health knowledge of mothers, the level of immunization, dehydration, availability of maternal and child health services, income and food availability in the family, availability of clean water and safe sanitation, and the overall safety of the child's environment.

UNICEF and the World Bank periodically report rankings of nations' under-5 mortality rates. In 2020, 48 nations had a lower under-5 mortality rate than the United States, with San Marino and Iceland having the lowest rates and Nigeria and Somalia having the highest rates (World Bank, 2023). The relatively high under-5 mortality rate of the United States compared with other high-income nations is due to such factors as poverty and inadequate health care. The devastating effects on the health of young children occur in countries where poverty rates are high. Individuals living in poverty are the majority in nearly one of every five nations in the world. They often experience lives of hunger, malnutrition, illness, inadequate access to health care, unsafe water, and a lack of protection from harm (UNICEF, 2023a).

A leading cause of childhood death in low-income countries is dehydration caused by diarrhea. In 1980, diarrhea was responsible for over 4.6 million childhood deaths. Oral rehydration therapy (ORT) was introduced in 1979 and quickly became the foundation for controlling diarrheal diseases. ORT now is given to the majority of children in low-income countries suffering with diarrhea, which has decreased the number of deaths due to dehydration caused by diarrhea.

Acute respiratory infections, such as pneumonia, also have killed many children under the age of 5. Many of these children's lives could have been saved with antibiotics administered by a community health worker. Undernutrition also is a contributing factor to many deaths of children under the age of 5 in low-income countries (UNICEF, 2019a).

In recent decades, there has been a dramatic increase in the number of young children who have died because of HIV/AIDS transmitted to them by their parents (UNICEF, 2023b). Deaths in young children due to HIV/AIDS especially occur in countries with high rates of poverty and low levels of education (Tomlinson & others, 2016). Education campaigns are needed for parents and health care providers to prevent parent-to-child transmission (Okusanya & others, 2022).

Many of the deaths of young children around the world can be prevented by a reduction in poverty and improvements in nutrition, sanitation, education, and health services (UNICEF, 2023a).

Many children in low-income countries die before reaching the age of 5 from dehydration and malnutrition brought about by diarrhea. *What are some of the other main causes of death in young children around the world?*
Kent Page/AP Images

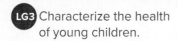
Review

- What is the nature of sleep and sleep problems in young children?
- What are young children's energy needs? What characterizes young children's eating behavior?
- What are some important aspects of exercise in the lives of young children?
- How can the nature of children's injuries be summarized? How do contexts influence children's health?

Connect

- In this section, you learned that experts recommend that young children get 10 to 13 hours of sleep a night during early childhood. How does that compare with what you learned about sleep requirements in infancy?

Reflect *Your Own Personal Journey of Life*

- If you become a parent of a young child, what precautions will you take to improve your child's health?

topical connections *looking forward*

Next, you will explore the fascinating world of young children's cognitive development, their remarkable advances in language development, and the role of education in their development. Later, you will read about the continuing changes in children's physical development in middle and late childhood. Their motor skills become smoother and more coordinated during the elementary school years. And the development of their brain—especially in the prefrontal cortex—provides the foundation for a number of cognitive and language advances, including the use of strategies and reading skills.

reach your **learning goals**

Physical Development in Early Childhood

1 How Does a Young Child's Body and Brain Grow and Change?

 Discuss growth and change in the young child's body and brain.

Height and Weight

The Brain

- The average child grows 2½ inches in height and gains between 5 and 7 pounds a year during early childhood. Growth patterns vary individually, though. Some children are unusually short because of congenital factors, growth hormone deficiency, a physical problem that develops during childhood, maternal smoking during pregnancy, or an emotional difficulty.

- By age 6, the brain has reached about 95 percent of its adult volume. Some of the brain's growth is due to increases in the number and size of nerve endings and receptors. One neurotransmitter that increases in concentration from 3 to 6 years of age is dopamine.

- Researchers have found that changes in local patterns in the brain occur from 3 to 15 years of age. From 3 to 6 years of age, the most rapid growth occurs in the frontal lobes. From age 6 through puberty, the most substantial growth takes place in the temporal and parietal lobes.

- Increasing brain maturation contributes to changes in cognitive abilities. One such link involves the prefrontal cortex, dopamine, and improved attention and working memory.

2 How Do Young Children's Motor Skills Develop?

 Describe changes in motor development in early childhood.

Gross and Fine Motor Skills

- Gross motor skills increase dramatically in early childhood. Children become increasingly adventuresome as their gross motor skills improve. It is important for early childhood educators to design and implement developmentally appropriate activities for young children's gross motor skills. Three types of these activities are fundamental movement, daily fitness, and perceptual-motor. Fine motor skills also improve substantially during early childhood.

- The Denver Developmental Screening Test II is a simple, inexpensive method of diagnosing developmental delay and includes separate assessments of gross and fine motor skills.

Perceptual Development

- Among the changes in young children's perceptual development are better detection of color boundaries and increased focusing of their eyes.

Young Children's Artistic Drawings

- The development of fine motor skills allows young children to become budding artists. Scribbling begins at 2 years of age, followed by four stages of drawing, culminating in the pictorial stage at 4 to 5 years of age.

- Golomb argues that it is important to explore the sociocultural contexts of children's art and that factors such as talent, motivation, familial support, and cultural values influence the development of children's art.

3 What Are Some Important Aspects of Young Children's Health?

 Characterize the health of young children.

Sleep and Sleep Problems

- Young children should get 10 to 13 hours of sleep each night. Most young children sleep through the night and have one daytime nap. Helping the young child slow down before bedtime often leads to less resistance in going to bed. Among the sleep problems that can develop in young children are nightmares, night terrors, somnambulism (sleepwalking), and sleep talking.

Nutrition

- Energy needs increase as children go through the early childhood years. The preschool child requires up to 1,800 calories daily. National assessments indicate that a large majority of young children in the United States do not have a healthy diet and that their eating habits have worsened over the last two decades. Too many parents are rearing young children on diets that are high in fat and sodium. Children's diets should contain well-balanced proportions of fats, carbohydrates, protein, vitamins, and minerals. A special concern is malnutrition in young children from low-income families.

Exercise

- Exercise should be a daily occurrence for young children. Guidelines recommend that they get at least two hours of exercise per day. The young child's life should be centered on physical activities rather than meals.

Health, Safety, and Illness

- In the United States, injuries (including those from firearms and motor vehicle accidents) are the leading cause of deaths among young children. Firearm deaths are especially high among young children in the United States in comparison with other countries. Among the strategies for preventing childhood injuries are restraining children in automobiles, preventing access to firearms, and making the home and playground safer.

- Among the contexts involved in children's health are poverty and ethnicity, home and child care, environmental tobacco smoke, and exposure to lead. The most devastating effects on the health of young children occur in countries with high poverty rates. Among the problems that low-income families face in these countries are malnutrition, illness, inadequate access to health care, unsafe water, and a lack of protection from harm.

- In recent decades, the trend in children's illness and health has been toward prevention as vaccines have been developed to reduce the occurrence of diseases in children. Parents play an important role in protecting young children's health. They influence their children's health by the way they behave in regard to children's illness symptoms. Parents can use a number of positive strategies in coping with the stress of having a chronically ill child. Parents need to invest effort in selecting a competent health-care provider for their children.

key **terms**

Denver Developmental	growth hormone deficiency	nightmares	shape stage
Screening Test II	myelination	pictorial stage	sleep talkers
design stage	night terrors	placement stage	somnambulism

key **people**

Teresa Amabile	Mona El-Sheikh	Claire Golomb	Rhoda Kellogg

improving the **lives of children**

STRATEGIES

Supporting Young Children's Physical Development

What are some good strategies for supporting young children's physical development?

- *Give young children plenty of opportunities to be active and explore their world.* Young children are extremely active and should not be constrained for long periods of time. Competent teachers plan daily fitness activities for young children. Preschool-aged children are too young for organized sports.

- *Make sure that young children's motor activities are fun and appropriate for their age.* Young children should enjoy the motor activities they participate in. Also, don't try to push young children into activities more appropriate for older children. For example, don't try to train a 3-year-old to ride a bicycle or enroll a 4-year-old in tennis lessons.

- *Give young children ample opportunities to engage in art.* Don't constrain young children's drawing. Let them freely create their artwork.

- *Provide young children with good nutrition.* Know how many calories preschool children need to meet their energy requirements, which are greater than in infancy. Too many young children are raised on fast foods. Monitor the amount of fat and sugar in young children's diets. Nutritious midmorning and midafternoon snacks are recommended, in addition to breakfast, lunch, and dinner. Make sure that young children get adequate iron, vitamins, and protein.

- *Make sure that young children have regular medical checkups.* These are especially important for children living in impoverished conditions, who are less likely to get such checkups.

- *Be a positive health role model for young children.* When you have young children as passengers, control the speed of the vehicle you are driving. Don't smoke in their presence. Eat healthy foods. Just by being in your presence, young children will imitate many of your behaviors.

- *Make sure children play in safe places.* Walk through the areas where children play and check for any potential hazards.

RESOURCES

Early Childhood Development Coming of Age: Science Through the Life Course (2017)
Maureen Black and her colleagues
Lancet (2017), 389 (10074), 77–90.

Leading expert Maureen Black outlines the key features needed in early childhood programs that will especially benefit at-risk children and help them reach their potential.

The Creation of Imaginary Worlds: The Role of Art, Magic, and Dreams in Child Development (2016)
Claire Golomb
London: Jessica Kinsgley Publishers

A leading expert analyzes the rich imaginary worlds of children with a special emphasis on children's art and how they express themselves through art.

American Academy of Pediatrics
www.aap.org

This Web site provides extensive information about strategies for improving children's health.

Centers for Disease Control and Prevention
www.cdc.gov/ncbddd/childdevelopment/positiveparenting/ preschoolers.html

This Web site describes major developmental milestones (including for gross and fine motor skills), safety recommendations, and health guidelines for children of different ages.

The State of the World's Children
UNICEF
Geneva, Switzerland: UNICEF

Each year, UNICEF publishes *The State of the World's Children,* which has a special focus on children's health. Enter the title of the report on a search engine and you will be able to access the entire report at no charge.

chapter 9

COGNITIVE DEVELOPMENT IN EARLY CHILDHOOD

chapter outline

Ariel Skelley/Blend Images/Getty Images

The Reggio Emilia approach is an educational program for young children that was developed in the northern Italian city of Reggio Emilia. Children of single parents and children with disabilities have priority in admission; other children are admitted according to a scale of needs. Parents pay on a sliding scale based on income.

A Reggio Emilia classroom in which young children explore topics that interest them.
Ruby Washington/The New York Times/Redux Pictures

The children are encouraged to learn by investigating and exploring topics that interest them (Bredekamp, 2017). A wide range of stimulating media and materials is available for children to use as they learn music, movement, drawing, painting, sculpting, collages, puppets and disguises, and photography, for example (Manera, 2022).

In this program, children often explore topics in a group, which fosters a sense of community, respect for diversity, and a collaborative approach to problem solving (Edwards & Gandini, 2018). Two co-teachers are present to serve as guides for children. The Reggio Emilia teachers consider a project to be an adventure, which can start from an adult's suggestion, from a child's idea, or from an event such as a snowfall or another unexpected happening. Every project is based on what the children say and do. The teachers allow children enough time to plan and craft a project.

At the core of the Reggio Emilia approach is the image of children who are competent and have rights, especially the right to outstanding care and education. Parent participation is considered essential, and cooperation is a major theme in the schools. Many early childhood education experts believe the Reggio Emilia approach provides a supportive, stimulating context in which children are motivated to explore their world in a competent and confident manner.

topical connections   looking *back*

In "Physical Development in Early Childhood" you learned how a young child's body and brain grow and change. In "Cognitive Development in Infancy" a special emphasis was the increasing consensus that infants' cognitive development is more advanced than Piaget envisioned. You learned that infants make amazing progress in their attentional, memory, concept formation, and language skills. In this chapter, you will discover that these information-processing skills continue to show remarkable advances in early childhood.

preview

Children make a number of significant cognitive advances in early childhood. In the opening section, we explore the cognitive changes described by three major theories of cognitive development. This includes consideration of the historical foundations of the contributions of Piaget and Vygotsky, followed by contemporary information processing theories and approaches that more directly consider the developing brain and its changing functions across childhood. Then we examine the dramatic changes in young children's language, and we conclude by discussing a wide range of topics involving early childhood education.

1 What Are Three Views of the Cognitive Changes That Occur in Early Childhood?

 LG1 Describe three views of the cognitive changes that occur in early childhood.

| Piaget's Preoperational Stage | Vygotsky's Theory | Information Processing |

The cognitive world of the preschool child is creative, free, and fanciful. Preschool children's imaginations work overtime, and their mental grasp of the world improves. Our coverage of cognitive development in early childhood focuses on three theories: Piaget's, Vygotsky's, and information processing.

PIAGET'S PREOPERATIONAL STAGE

Recall that during Jean Piaget's first stage of development, the sensorimotor stage, the infant progresses in the ability to organize and coordinate sensations and perceptions with physical movements and actions. The **preoperational stage,** which lasts from approximately 2 to 7 years of age, is the second Piagetian stage. In this stage, children begin to represent the world with words, images, and drawings. They form stable concepts and begin to reason. At the same time, the young child's cognitive world is dominated by egocentrism and magical beliefs.

Because Piaget called this stage "preoperational," it might sound like an unimportant waiting period. This is not the case. However, the label *preoperational* emphasizes that the child does not yet perform **operations,** which are reversible mental actions that allow children to do mentally what before they could do only physically. Mentally adding and subtracting numbers are examples of operations. *Preoperational thought* is the beginning of the ability to reconstruct in thought what has been established in behavior. The preoperational stage can be divided into two substages: the symbolic function substage and the intuitive thought substage.

The Symbolic Function Substage The **symbolic function substage** is the first substage of preoperational thought, occurring roughly between the ages of 2 and 4. In this substage, the young child gains the ability to mentally represent an object that is not present. This ability vastly expands the child's mental world; how early symbolic representation abilities develop is related to children's exposure to symbols in everyday life, such as exposure to video and print materials and drawing with parents (Salsa & Gariboldi, 2018). Young children use scribble designs to represent people, houses, cars, clouds, and so on; they begin to use language and engage in pretend play. However, although young children make distinct progress during this substage, their thought still has important limitations, two of which are egocentrism and animism.

Egocentrism is the inability to distinguish between one's own perspective and someone else's perspective. Piaget and Barbel Inhelder (1969) initially studied young children's egocentrism by devising the three mountains task (see Figure 1). The child walks around the model of the mountains and becomes familiar with what the mountains look like from different perspectives and can see that there are different objects on the mountains. The child is then seated on one side of the table on which the mountains are placed. The experimenter moves a doll to different locations around the table, at each location asking the child to select from a series of

- - - - - - - - →

developmental **connection**
Cognitive Development
Object permanence is an important accomplishment during the sensorimotor stage. Connect to "Cognitive Development in Infancy."

← - - - - - - - - - -

preoperational stage Piaget's second stage, lasting from 2 to 7 years of age, when children begin to represent the world with words, images, and drawings. In this stage, they also form stable concepts and begin to reason. At the same time, their cognitive world is dominated by egocentrism and magical beliefs.

operations Internalized actions that allow children to do mentally what before they had done only physically. Operations also are reversible mental actions.

symbolic function substage Piaget's first substage of preoperational thought, in which the child gains the ability to mentally represent an object that is not present (occurs roughly between 2 and 4 years of age).

egocentrism Piaget's concept that describes the inability to distinguish between one's own perspective and someone else's perspective.

Model of Mountains

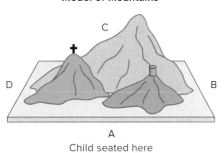

Child seated here

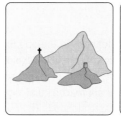

Photo 1
(View from A)

Photo 2
(View from B)

Photo 3
(View from C)

Photo 4
(View from D)

FIGURE 1

THE THREE MOUNTAINS TASK. The mountain model on the far left shows the child's perspective from view A, where the child is sitting. The four squares represent photos showing the mountains from four different viewpoints of the model—A, B, C, and D. The experimenter asks the child to identify the photo in which the mountains look as they would from position B. To identify the photo correctly, the child has to take the perspective of a person sitting at spot B. Invariably, a child who thinks in a preoperational way cannot perform this task. When asked what a view of the mountains looks like from position B, the child selects Photo 1, taken from location A (the child's own view at the time) instead of Photo 2, the correct view.

photos the one photo that most accurately reflects the view that the doll is seeing. Children in the preoperational stage often pick their own view rather than the doll's view. Preschool children frequently show the ability to take another's perspective on some tasks but not others.

Animism, another limitation of preoperational thought, is the belief that inanimate objects have lifelike qualities and are capable of action. A young child might show animism by saying, "That tree pushed the leaf off, and it fell down" or "The sidewalk made me mad; it made me fall down." A young child who uses animism fails to distinguish the appropriate occasions for using human and nonhuman perspectives (Goldman, Baumann, & Poulin-Dubois, 2022).

Possibly because young children are not very concerned about reality, their drawings are fanciful and inventive. Suns might be blue, skies green, and cars shown floating on clouds in their symbolic, imaginative world. One 3½-year-old looked at a scribble he had just drawn and described it as a pelican kissing a seal (see Figure 2a). The symbolism is simple but strong, like abstractions found in some modern art. Twentieth-century Spanish artist Pablo Picasso commented, "I used to draw like Raphael but it has taken me a lifetime to draw like young children." During the elementary school years, a child's drawings become more realistic, neat, and precise (see Figure 2b). Improvements in fine motor control and working memory contribute to increased realism in drawings as children mature (Panesi & Morra, 2022).

The Intuitive Thought Substage

The **intuitive thought substage** is the second substage of preoperational thought, occurring between approximately 4 and 7 years of age. During this substage, children begin to use primitive reasoning and want to know the answers to all sorts of questions. Consider 4-year-old Miguel, who is at the beginning of the intuitive thought substage. Although he is starting to develop his own ideas about the world he lives in, his ideas are still simple, and he is not very good at thinking things out. He has difficulty

animism The belief that inanimate objects have lifelike qualities and are capable of action.

intuitive thought substage Piaget's second substage of preoperational thought, in which children begin to use primitive reasoning and want to know the answers to all sorts of questions (occurs between about 4 and 7 years of age).

FIGURE 2

THE SYMBOLIC DRAWING OF YOUNG CHILDREN. (*a*) A 3½-year-old's symbolic drawing. Halfway into his drawing, the 3½-year-old artist said it was a "pelican kissing a seal." (*b*) This 11-year-old's drawing is neater and more realistic but also less inventive.

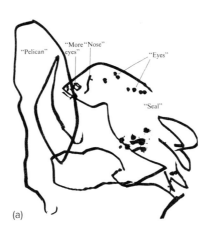

(a)

(b)

understanding events that he knows are taking place but that he cannot see. His fantasized thoughts bear little resemblance to reality. He cannot yet answer the question "What if?" in any reliable way. For example, he has only a vague idea of what would happen if a car were to hit him. He also has difficulty negotiating traffic because he cannot do the mental calculations necessary to estimate whether an approaching car will hit him when he crosses the road.

By the age of 5, children have just about exhausted the adults around them with "why" questions. The child's questions signal the emergence of interest in reasoning and in figuring out why things are the way they are. By the time children enter preschool, they ask an average of 76 questions per hour seeking information, and by the age of 5 their questions are well-formulated to elicit the information needed to learn new concepts (Kurkul & Corriveau, 2018; Kurkul, Dwyer, & Corriveau, 2022). Some of children's questions require simple, one-word answers such as naming an unfamiliar object, but "how" and "why" questions require more complex explanations.

Piaget called this substage *intuitive* because young children seem so sure about their knowledge and understanding yet are unaware of how they know what they know. That is, they know something but know it without the use of rational thinking.

Centration and the Limits of Preoperational Thought

One limitation of preoperational thought is **centration,** a centering of attention on one characteristic to the exclusion of all others. Centration is most clearly evidenced in young children's lack of **conservation,** the awareness that altering an object's or a substance's appearance does not change its basic properties. For example, to adults, it is obvious that a certain amount of liquid will have the same volume, regardless of a container's shape. But this is not at all obvious to young children. Instead, they are struck by the height of the liquid in the container; they focus on that characteristic to the exclusion of others.

The situation that Piaget devised to study conservation is his most famous task. In the conservation task, children are presented with two identical beakers, each filled to the same level with liquid (see Figure 3). They are asked if these beakers have the same amount of liquid, and they usually say yes. Next, the liquid from one beaker is poured into a third beaker, which is taller and thinner than the first two. Then, the children are asked if the amount of liquid in the tall, thin beaker is equal to that which remains in one of the original beakers. Children who are younger than 7 or 8 years old usually say no and justify their answers in terms of the differing height or width of the beakers. Older children usually answer yes and justify their answers appropriately ("If you poured the water back, the amount would still be the same").

In Piaget's theory, failing the conservation-of-liquid task is a sign that children are at the preoperational stage of cognitive development. The failure demonstrates not only centration but also an inability to mentally reverse actions. For example, in the conservation-of-matter example shown in Figure 4, preoperational children say that the longer shape has more clay because they assume that "longer is more." Preoperational children cannot mentally reverse the clay-rolling process to see that the amount of clay is the same in both the shorter ball

centration The focusing of attention on one characteristic to the exclusion of all others.

conservation The realization that altering an object's or substance's appearance does not change its basic properties.

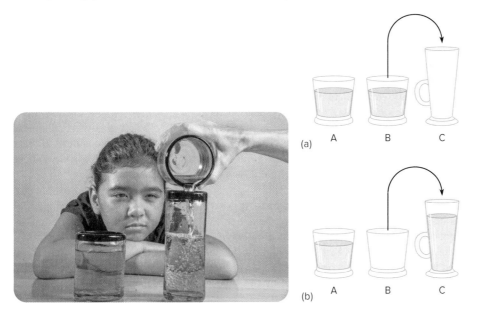

(a)

A   B   C

(b)

A   B   C

FIGURE 3

PIAGET'S CONSERVATION TASK. The beaker task is a well-known Piagetian task to determine whether a child can think operationally—that is, can mentally reverse actions and show conservation of the substance. (*a*) Two identical beakers are presented to the child. Then the experimenter pours the liquid from B into C, which is taller and thinner than A or B. (*b*) The child is asked if these beakers (A and C) have the same amount of liquid. The preoperational child says "no." When asked to point to the beaker that has more liquid, the preoperational child points to the tall, thin beaker.

(photo): Marmaduke St. John/Alamy Stock Photo

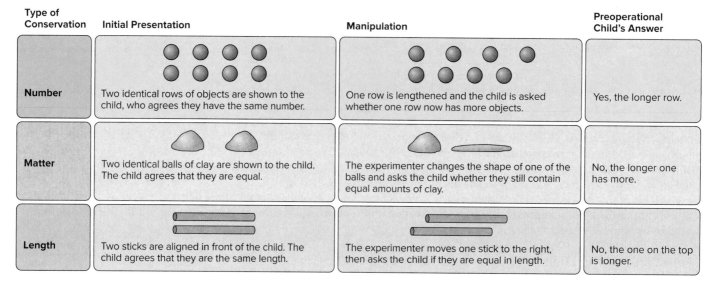

Type of Conservation	Initial Presentation	Manipulation	Preoperational Child's Answer
Number	Two identical rows of objects are shown to the child, who agrees they have the same number.	One row is lengthened and the child is asked whether one row now has more objects.	Yes, the longer row.
Matter	Two identical balls of clay are shown to the child. The child agrees that they are equal.	The experimenter changes the shape of one of the balls and asks the child whether they still contain equal amounts of clay.	No, the longer one has more.
Length	Two sticks are aligned in front of the child. The child agrees that they are the same length.	The experimenter moves one stick to the right, then asks the child if they are equal in length.	No, the one on the top is longer.

FIGURE **4**

SOME DIMENSIONS OF CONSERVATION: NUMBER, MATTER, AND LENGTH. *What characteristics of preoperational thought do children demonstrate when they fail these conservation tasks?*

shape and the longer stick shape. Researchers have discovered links between performance on Piagetian tasks and the brain's development, particularly in the prefrontal cortex (Bolton & Hattie, 2017; Fiske & Holmboe, 2019). For example, a fMRI brain imaging study of conservation of number revealed that advances in a network in the parietal and frontal lobes were linked to 9- and 10-year-olds' conservation success compared with non-conserving 5- and 6-year-olds (Houdé & others, 2011).

Some developmentalists disagree with Piaget's estimate of when children's conservation skills emerge (Bjorklund & Causey, 2018). For example, early research by Rochel Gelman (1969) showed that when the child's attention to relevant aspects of the conservation task is improved, the child is more likely to conserve. Gelman has also demonstrated that attentional training on one dimension, such as number, improves the preschool child's performance on another dimension, such as mass. Thus, Gelman argues that conservation appears earlier than Piaget thought and that attention is especially important in explaining conservation.

VYGOTSKY'S THEORY

Piaget's theory has played a key role in the history and foundations of child development research. Another historically important theory that focuses on children's cognition was proposed by Lev Vygotsky (1962). Like Piaget, Vygotsky (1896–1934) emphasized that children actively construct their knowledge and understanding. In Piaget's theory, children develop ways of thinking and understanding by their actions and interactions with the physical world. In Vygotsky's theory, children are more often described as social creatures than in Piaget's theory (Moura da Costa & Tuleski, 2017). They develop their ways of thinking and understanding primarily through social interaction (Bodrova & Leong, 2017). Their cognitive development depends on the tools provided by society, and their minds are shaped by the cultural context in which they live (Baggs & Chemero, 2020). Let's take a closer look at Vygotsky's ideas about how children learn and his view of the role of language in cognitive development.

How Would You...?
If you were an **educator,** how would you apply Vygotsky's concept of the zone of proximal development and the concept of scaffolding to help a young child complete a puzzle?

zone of proximal development (ZPD)
Vygotsky's term for the range of tasks that are too difficult for children to achieve alone but can be achieved with the guidance and assistance of adults or more-skilled children.

The Zone of Proximal Development Vygotsky's (1962) belief in the impact of social influences, especially instruction, on children's cognitive development is reflected in his concept of the zone of proximal development. **Zone of proximal development (ZPD)** is Vygotsky's term for the range of tasks that are too difficult for the child to master alone but that can be learned with guidance and assistance of adults or more-skilled children. Thus, the lower limit of the ZPD is the level of skill reached by the child working independently. The upper limit is the level of additional responsibility the child can accept with the assistance of an able instructor (see Figure 5). The ZPD captures the child's cognitive skills that are in the process of maturing and can be accomplished only with the assistance of a more-skilled person (Groot & others, 2020). Vygotsky (1962) called these the "buds" or "flowers" of development, to distinguish them from the "fruits" of development, which the child already can accomplish independently.

What are some factors that can influence the effectiveness of the ZPD in children's learning and development? Researchers have found that the following factors can enhance the ZPD's effectiveness (Gauvain, 2013): better emotion regulation, secure attachment, absence of maternal depression, and child compliance.

Scaffolding   Closely linked to the idea of the ZPD is the concept of scaffolding. **Scaffolding** means changing the level of support. Over the course of a teaching session, a more-skilled person (a teacher or an advanced peer) adjusts the amount of guidance to fit the child's current performance (Wright, 2018). When the student is learning a new task, the more-skilled person may use direct instruction. As the student's competence increases, the person gives less guidance. Around the world, caregivers and children arrange children's activities and revise children's responsibilities as they gain skill and knowledge. With guidance, children participate in cultural activities that help them acquire skills. For example, Mayan mothers in Guatemala help their daughters learn to weave through guided participation. Throughout the world, learning occurs, not just by studying or by attending classes, but also through interaction with knowledgeable people (Alcalá, Montejano, & Fernandez, 2021; Rogoff, Dahl, & Callanan, 2018).

Language and Thought   According to Vygotsky, children use speech not only for social communication but also to help in solving problems. Vygotsky (1962) further argued that young children use language to plan, guide, and monitor their behavior. This use of language for self-regulation is called *private speech.* From Piaget's perspective, private speech is egocentric and immature—but for Vygotsky, it is an important tool of thought during the early childhood years (Lantolf, 2017; Mulvihill, Matthews, & Carroll, 2023).

Vygotsky said that language and thought initially develop independently of each other and then merge. He emphasized that all mental functions have external, or social, origins. Children must use language to communicate with others before they can focus inward on their own thoughts. Children also must communicate externally and use language for a long period of time before they can make the transition from external to internal speech. This transition period occurs between 3 and 7 years of age and involves talking to oneself. After a while, the self-talk becomes second nature to children, and they can act without verbalizing. At this point, children have internalized their egocentric speech in the form of *inner speech,* which becomes their thoughts (Smolucha & Smolucha, 2021).

Vygotsky maintained that children who use a lot of private speech are more socially competent than those who don't. He argued that private speech represents an early transition in becoming more socially communicative. For Vygotsky, when young children talk to themselves, they are using language to govern their behavior and guide themselves. For example, a child working alone on a puzzle might say, "Which pieces should I put together first? I'll try those green ones first. Now I need some blue ones. No, that blue one doesn't fit there. I'll try it over here."

Researchers have found support for Vygotsky's view that private speech plays a positive role in children's development (Day & others, 2018). Preschoolers who use private speech are better able to regulate their behaviors and internalize new information (Day & Smith, 2019; Mulvihill, Matthews, & Carroll, 2023). Preschoolers who use positive private speech also are more motivated to master challenging tasks (Sawyer, 2017).

Teaching Strategies   Vygotsky's theory has been embraced by many teachers and has been successfully applied to education (Bodrova & Leong, 2017; Clara, 2017; Newman & Latifi, 2021). Here are some ways Vygotsky's theory can be incorporated in classrooms:

• *Assess the child's ZPD.* Like Piaget, Vygotsky did not hold that formal, standardized tests are the best way to assess children's learning. Rather, Vygotsky argued that assessment should focus on determining the child's zone of proximal development. The skilled helper presents the child with tasks of varying difficulty to determine the best

Upper limit
Level of additional responsibility child can accept with assistance of an able instructor

Zone of proximal development (ZPD)

Lower limit
Level of problem solving reached on these tasks by child working alone

FIGURE **5**

VYGOTSKY'S ZONE OF PROXIMAL DEVELOPMENT. Vygotsky's zone of proximal development has a lower limit and an upper limit. Tasks in the ZPD are too difficult for the child to perform alone. They require assistance from an adult or a more-skilled child. As children experience the verbal instruction or demonstration, they organize the information in their existing mental structures so that they can eventually perform the skill or task alone.
Ariel Skelley/Blend Images

developmental **connection**
Parenting
Scaffolding also is an important strategy for parents to adopt in interacting with their infants. Connect to "Socio-emotional Development in Infancy."

scaffolding In regard to cognitive development, Vygotsky used this term to describe the changing level of support provided over the course of a teaching session, with the more-skilled person adjusting guidance to fit the child's current performance level.

Lev Vygotsky (1896–1934), shown here with his daughter, reasoned that children's cognitive development is advanced through social interaction with more-skilled individuals embedded in a sociocultural backdrop. *How is Vygotsky's theory different from Piaget's?*

Courtesy of James V. Wertsch, Washington University

level at which to begin instruction. Today, standardized test results often are reported using a ZPD for reading or math instruction, such as by providing a reading level range to guide teachers and students in choosing books that are at a reading level that is neither too difficult nor too easy for the child (Poehner, Davin, & Lantolf, 2017).

- *Use the child's ZPD in teaching.* Teaching should begin toward the zone's upper limit so that the child can reach the goal with help and move to a higher level of skill and knowledge. Offer just enough assistance. You might ask, "What can I do to help you?" Or simply observe the child's intentions and attempts and provide support when needed. When the child hesitates, offer encouragement. And encourage the child to practice the skill. You may watch and appreciate the child's practice or offer support when the child forgets what to do. This practice is exemplified in "guided reading" practice between a teacher and a child who is beginning to learn to read (Nicholas, Veresov, & Clark, 2021).

- *Use more-skilled peers as teachers.* Remember that it is not just adults who are important in helping children learn. Children also benefit from the support and guidance of more-skilled children (Johnson & Cochran, 2021).

- *Monitor and encourage children's use of private speech.* Be aware of the developmental change from externally talking to oneself when solving a problem during the preschool years to privately talking to oneself in the early elementary school years. In the elementary school years, encourage children to internalize and self-regulate their talk to themselves.

- *Place instruction in a meaningful context.* Educators today are moving away from abstract presentations of material and instead are providing students with opportunities to experience learning in real-world settings. For example, instead of just memorizing math procedures, even young children can learn math strategies for use in many daily settings, including those shown in picture books (Dunphy, 2020).

- *Transform the classroom with Vygotskian ideas.* What does a Vygotskian classroom look like? Flipped classrooms in which student-centered learning activities, such as team problem-solving, are prioritized over teacher-centered delivery of information represent one approach based on Vygotsky's theory (Hew & others, 2021). Flipped classrooms can benefit students' learning by providing time for in-class practice, enabling students to receive immediate feedback from teachers and peers, and helping students take more responsibility for their own learning.

The *Caring Connections* interlude further explores the implications of Vygotsky's theory for children's education.

Evaluating Vygotsky's Theory Even though their theories were proposed at about the same time, most of the world learned about Vygotsky's theory later than they learned about Piaget's theory, so Vygotsky's theory has not yet been evaluated as thoroughly. Vygotsky's view of the importance of sociocultural influences on children's development fits with the current belief that it is important to evaluate the contextual factors in learning (Gauvain, 2018).

We already have compared certain aspects of Vygotsky's and Piaget's theories, such as Vygotsky's emphasis on the importance of inner speech in development and Piaget's view that such speech is immature. Although both theories are constructivist, Vygotsky's is a **social constructivist approach,** which emphasizes the social contexts of learning and the construction of knowledge through social interaction (van Hover & Hicks, 2017).

In moving from Piaget to Vygotsky, the conceptual shift is from the individual to collaboration, social interaction, and sociocultural activity (Bodrova & Leong, 2017). The endpoint of cognitive development for Piaget is formal operational thought. For Vygotsky, the endpoint can differ depending on which skills are considered to be the most important in a particular culture (Clara, 2017). For Piaget, children construct knowledge by transforming, organizing, and reorganizing previous knowledge. For Vygotsky, children construct knowledge through social interaction (Daniels, 2017). The implication of Piaget's theory for teaching is that children need support to explore their world and discover knowledge. The main implication of Vygotsky's theory for teaching is that students need many opportunities to learn with the teacher and more-skilled peers. In both Piaget's and Vygotsky's theories, teachers serve as facilitators and guides, rather than as directors and molders of learning. Figure 7 compares Vygotsky's and Piaget's theories.

social constructivist approach An approach that emphasizes the social contexts of learning and the fact that knowledge is mutually built and constructed; Vygotsky's theory is a social constructivist approach.

Tools of the Mind

Tools of the Mind is an early childhood education curriculum that emphasizes children's development of self-regulation and the cognitive foundations of literacy (Diamond & others, 2019). The curriculum was created by Elena Bodrova and Deborah Leong (2018) and has been implemented in hundreds of classrooms. Most of the children in the Tools of the Mind programs are at risk because of their living circumstances, which in many instances involve income, housing, and food insecurity, and caregivers with mental or physical health problems.

Tools of the Mind is grounded in Vygotsky's (1962) theory, with special attention given to cultural tools and self-regulation, the zone of proximal development, scaffolding, private speech, shared activity, and the importance of play. In a Tools of the Mind classroom, dramatic play has a central role. Teachers guide children in creating themes that are based on the children's interests, such as treasure hunt, store, hospital, and restaurant. Teachers also incorporate field trips, visitor presentations, videos, and books in the development of children's play. They help children develop a play plan, which increases the maturity of their play. Play plans describe what the children expect to do in the play period, including the imaginary context, roles, and props to be used. The play plans increase the quality of their play and self-regulation.

Scaffolding writing is another important theme in the Tools of the Mind classroom. Teachers guide children in planning their own message by drawing a line to stand for each word the child says. Children then repeat the message, pointing to each line as they say the word. Then, the child writes on the lines, trying to represent each word with some letters or symbols. Figure 6 shows how the scaffolding writing process improved a 5-year-old child's writing over the course of two months.

Research assessments of children's writing in Tools of the Mind classrooms revealed more advanced writing skills than those of children in other early childhood programs (Bodrova & Leong, 2018) (see Figure 6). For example, children in these classrooms write more complex messages, use more words, spell more accurately, show better letter recognition, and have a better understanding of the concept of a sentence.

The effectiveness of the Tools of the Mind approach was examined in 29 schools, 79 classrooms, and 759 children (Blair & Raver, 2014). Positive effects of the Tools of the Mind program were found for the cognitive processes of executive function (improved self-regulation, for example) and attention control. Further, the Tools of the Mind program improved children's reading, vocabulary, and mathematics at the end of kindergarten and into the first grade. The most significant improvements occurred in students living in high-poverty areas.

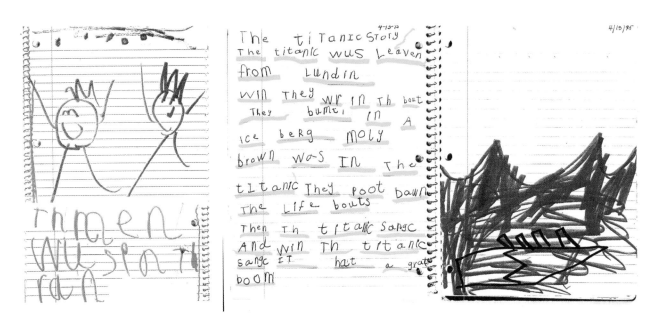

FIGURE 6

WRITING PROGRESS OF A 5-YEAR-OLD BOY OVER TWO MONTHS USING THE SCAFFOLDING WRITING PROCESS IN TOOLS OF THE MIND.

Bodrova, Elena, and Deborah J. Leong. *Tools of the Mind: A Case Study of Implementing the Vygotskian Approach in American Early Childhood and Primary Classroom*, 36–38. Geneva, Switzerland: International Bureau of Education, 2001.

	Vygotsky	Piaget
Sociocultural Context	Strong emphasis	Little emphasis
Constructivism	Social constructivist	Cognitive constructivist
Stages	No general stages of development proposed	Strong emphasis on stages (sensorimotor, preoperational, concrete operational, and formal operational)
Key Processes	Zone of proximal development, language, dialogue, tools of the culture	Schema, assimilation, accommodation, operations, conservation, classification
Role of Language	A major role; language plays a powerful role in shaping thought	Language has a minimal role; cognition primarily directs language
View on Education	Education plays a central role, helping children learn the tools of the culture	Education merely refines the child's cognitive skills that have already emerged
Teaching Implications	Teacher is a facilitator and guide, not a director; establish many opportunities for children to learn with the teacher and more-skilled peers	Also views teacher as a facilitator and guide, not a director; provide support for children to explore their world and discover knowledge

FIGURE 7

COMPARISON OF VYGOTSKY'S AND PIAGET'S THEORIES

(*Left*): A.R. Lauria/Dr. Michael Cole, Laboratory of Human Cognition, University of California, San Diego; (*right*): Bettmann/Getty Images

Criticisms of Vygotsky's theory also have surfaced (Daniels, 2017; Newman & Latifi, 2021). Some critics point out that Vygotsky was not specific enough about age-related changes. Another criticism claims that Vygotsky did not adequately describe how changes in socioemotional capabilities contribute to cognitive development. Yet another criticism is that he overemphasized the role of language in thinking. Also, his emphasis on collaboration and guidance has potential pitfalls. Might facilitators be too helpful in some cases, as when a parent becomes too overbearing and controlling? Further, some children might become unmotivated and expect help when they could have done something on their own.

INFORMATION PROCESSING

Piaget's and Vygotsky's theories provided important ideas about how young children think and how their thinking changes. More recently, the information-processing approach has generated research that illuminates how children process information during the preschool years (Dotan, Eliahou, & Cohen, 2021; Siegler & Braithwaite, 2017). What are the limitations and advances in young children's ability to pay attention to the environment, to remember, to develop strategies and solve problems, and to understand their own mental processes and those of others?

Attention Recall that attention was defined as the focusing of mental resources on select information. The child's ability to pay attention improves significantly during the preschool years, as seen in children's behavior as well as measures of brain activity and functioning (Rueda, 2018). Toddlers wander around, shift attention from one activity to another, and seem to spend little time focused on any one object or event. By comparison, the preschool child might be observed watching television for a half hour. One classic study videotaped young children in their homes (Anderson & others, 1985). In 99 families who were observed for 4,672 hours, visual attention to television dramatically increased during the preschool years. However, contemporary evidence shows that spending more time on screens in early childhood may be associated with poorer attention regulation (Anderson & Subrahmanyam, 2017; Jourdren, Bucaille, & Ropars, 2023).

Young children especially make advances in two aspects of attention—executive attention and sustained attention (Rothbart & Posner, 2015). **Executive attention** involves planning actions, allocating attention to goals, detecting and compensating for errors, monitoring progress on tasks, and dealing with novel or difficult circumstances. **Sustained attention** is focused and extended engagement with an object, task, event, or other aspect of the environment. Sustained attention also is referred to as *vigilance* (Benitez & others, 2017). One study found a considerable increase

executive attention Involves planning actions, allocating attention to goals, detecting and compensating for errors, monitoring progress on tasks, and dealing with novel or difficult circumstances.

sustained attention Keeping attention on a selected stimulus for a prolonged period of time. Sustained attention is also called *vigilance*.

from 2½ to 3½ years of age in the ability to sustain attention and then regain attention after being distracted (Danis & others, 2008). In this illustrative study, children showed more consistent control of their attention after 4½ years of age. Research indicates that although older children and adolescents show increases in vigilance, it is during the preschool years that individuals show the greatest increase in vigilance (Rothbart & Posner, 2015). One study found that preschoolers' sustained attention was linked to a greater likelihood of completing college by 25 years of age (McClelland & others, 2013). Another study showed that children's executive attention was a good predictor of their overall self-regulation (Tiego & others, 2020).

Mary Rothbart and Maria Gartstein (2008, p. 332) described why advances in executive and sustained attention are so important in early childhood, and their interpretation still holds true today:

> The development of the . . . executive attention system supports the rapid increases in effortful control in the toddler and preschool years. Increases in attention are due, in part, to advances in comprehension and language development. As children are better able to understand their environment, this increased appreciation of their surroundings helps them to sustain attention for longer periods of time.

In at least two ways, however, the preschool child's control of attention is still limited:

- *Salient versus relevant dimensions.* Preschool children are likely to pay attention to stimuli that stand out, or are salient, even when those stimuli are not relevant to solving a problem or performing a task. For example, if a flashy, attractive clown presents the directions for solving a problem, preschool children are likely to pay more attention to the clown than to the directions. After the age of 6 or 7, children attend more efficiently to the dimensions of the task that are relevant, such as the directions for solving a problem. This change reflects a shift to cognitive control of attention so that children behave less impulsively and reflect more.

- *Planfulness.* Although in general young children's planning improves as part of advances in executive attention, when experimenters ask children to judge whether two complex pictures are the same, preschool children tend to use a haphazard comparison strategy, not examining all of the details before making a judgment. By comparison, elementary-school-age children are more likely to systematically compare the details across the pictures, one detail at a time (Vurpillot, 1968) (see Figure 8).

In certain aspects of daily activity and curricula in preschool and kindergarten, children participate in exercises designed to improve their attention (Posner & Rothbart, 2007; Savina, 2021). For example, in one eye-contact exercise, the teacher sits in the center of a circle of children, and each child is required to catch the teacher's eye before being permitted to leave the group. In other exercises created to improve attention, teachers have children participate in stop-go activities during which they have to listen for a specific signal, such as a drumbeat or an exact number of rhythmic beats, before stopping the activity.

In the head-toes-knees-shoulders task, children first respond by touching the body part named by the leader but then are asked to respond in a different way, such as by touching their head when the leader says to touch their toes, which not only improves children's attention but also helps them with working memory, inhibitory control, and cognitive flexibility (Gonzalez & others, 2021; McClelland & others, 2014). Other examples include games like "red light/green light" and "Simon Says"—activities that help children practice attending to relevant information and disregarding irrelevant information.

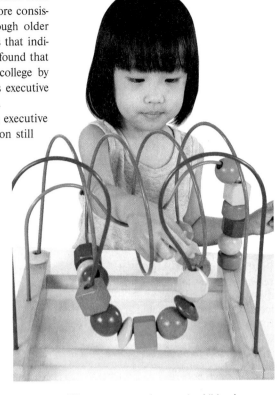

What are some advances in children's attention in early childhood?
Kiankhoon/iStock/Getty Images

FIGURE **8**

THE PLANFULNESS OF ATTENTION. In a classic study, children were given pairs of houses to examine, like the ones shown here (Vurpillot, 1968). For three pairs of houses, what was in the windows was identical (*a*). For the other three pairs, the windows had different items in them (*b*). By filming the reflection in the children's eyes, it could be determined what they were looking at, how long they looked, and the sequence of their eye movements. Children under 6 examined only a fragmentary portion of each display and made their judgment on the basis of insufficient information. By contrast, older children scanned the windows in more detailed ways and were more accurate in their judgments of which were identical.

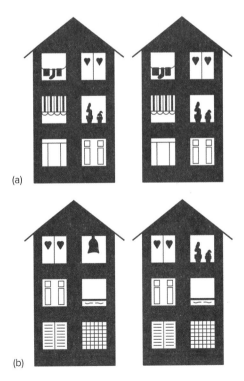

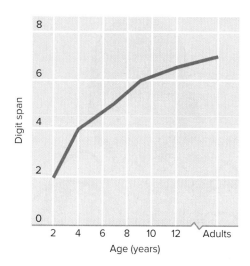

FIGURE 9

DEVELOPMENTAL CHANGES IN MEMORY SPAN. In a classic study, from 2 years of age to 7 years of age children's memory span increased about 2 digits to 5 digits (Dempster, 1981). By 12 years of age, memory span had increased on average only another 1½ digits, to 6½ digits. *What factors might contribute to the increase in memory span during childhood?*

Contemporary approaches use digital media (for example, computer tasks and games) to exercise and "train" attention (Posner, Rothbart, & Tang, 2015). There are many such games and tools available now commercially. One study of 4- to 5-year-olds found positive effects on attention skills after two weeks of training on action-like mini games (Nava, Focker, & Gori, 2020). These and other types of cognitive skills training methods—for young children as well as teens and adults—tend to be effective for training the specific skill, but for the most part the training does not appear to have general effects beyond the skill that is being practiced (Kassai & others, 2019).

Preschool children's ability to control and sustain their attention is related to school readiness and academic success (Peng & Kievit, 2020; Rothbart & Posner, 2015). For example, a now classic longitudinal study of more than 1,000 children revealed that their ability to sustain their attention at 54 months of age was linked to their school readiness, as indicated by scholastic and language skills (NICHD Early Child Care Research Network, 2005). In a follow-up study, children whose parents and teachers rated them higher on a scale of having attention problems at 54 months of age had poorer social skills in peer relations in the first and third grades than did their counterparts who were rated lower on the attention problems scale at 54 months of age (NICHD Early Child Care Research Network, 2009).

Memory *Memory*—the retention of information over time—is a central process in children's cognitive development. During infancy, memories are often fragile and, for the most part, short-lived—except for the memory of perceptual-motor actions, which can be substantial (Bauer & Larkina, 2016; Forsberg, Adams, & Cowan, 2022). In the chapter on "Cognitive Development in Infancy," we noted that in discussing an individual's capacity to remember, it is important to distinguish *implicit memory* from *explicit memory*. Implicit memory refers to memory without conscious recollection, while explicit memory refers to the conscious recollection of facts and experiences.

Explicit memory itself comes in many forms (Radvansky, 2017). One distinction occurs between relatively permanent retention, or *long-term memory*, and *short-term memory*.

Short-Term Memory In **short-term memory,** individuals retain information for up to 30 seconds if there is no rehearsal of the information. By using rehearsal (repeating information after it has been presented), we can keep information in short-term memory for a much longer period. One method of assessing short-term memory is the memory-span task. You hear a short list of stimuli—such as digits—presented at a rapid pace (one per second, for example). Then you are asked to repeat the digits.

Research with the memory-span task suggests that short-term memory increases during early childhood. For example, in a classic investigation, memory span increased from about 2 digits in 2- to 3-year-old children to about 5 digits in 7-year-old children, yet between 7 and 12 years of age memory span increased only by 1½ digits (Dempster, 1981) (see Figure 9). Keep in mind, though, that memory span varies from one individual to another.

Why does memory span increase with age? Speed and efficiency of processing information are important, especially the speed with which memorized items can be identified. The speed-of-processing explanation highlights a key point in the information-processing perspective: The speed with which a child processes information is an important aspect of the child's cognitive abilities, and there is abundant evidence that the speed with which many cognitive tasks are completed improves dramatically across the childhood years (Rose, Feldman, & Jankowski, 2015). One study found that myelination (the process by which the sheath that encases axons helps electrical signals travel faster down the axon) in a number of brain areas was linked to young children's processing speed (Chevalier & others, 2015). Many contemporary studies have replicated and extended the evidence showing the importance of processing speed to developmental improvements in memory span (e.g., Alghamdi, Murphy, & Crewther, 2021). Rehearsal of information is also important; older children rehearse the digits more than younger children do.

How Accurate Are Young Children's Long-Term Memories? In contrast with short-term memory, *long-term memory* is a relatively permanent type of memory that stores huge amounts of information for a long time. Sometimes the long-term memories of preschoolers may seem erratic, but young children can remember a great deal of information if they are given appropriate cues and prompts. One area in which children's long-term memory is being examined extensively relates to whether young children should be allowed to testify in court (Andrews & Lamb, 2017; Brown, 2022; Melinder & others, 2016). This is especially important

short-term memory The memory component in which individuals retain information for up to 30 seconds, assuming there is no rehearsal.

if a child is the sole witness to abuse, a crime, and so forth (Lamb & others, 2015). Several factors can influence the accuracy of a young child's memory:

- *There are age differences in children's susceptibility to suggestion.* Preschoolers are the most suggestible age group in comparison with older children and adults (Andrews & Lamb, 2017). For example, preschool children are more susceptible to retaining misleading or incorrect post-event information (Ceci, Hritz, & Royer, 2016). Despite these age differences, there is still concern about the accuracy of older children's recollections when they are subjected to suggestive interviews (Ahern, Kowalski, & Lamb, 2018).

- *There are individual differences in susceptibility to suggestion.* Some preschoolers as well as older children are highly resistant to interviewers' suggestions, whereas others immediately succumb to the slightest suggestion (Klemfuss & Olaguez, 2020).

- *Interviewing techniques can produce substantial distortions in children's reports about highly salient events.* Children are suggestible not just regarding peripheral details but also about the central aspects of an event. Nonetheless, young children are capable of recalling much that is relevant about an event (Lamb & others, 2015). When children do accurately recall an event, the interviewer often has a neutral tone, there is limited use of misleading questions, and there is an absence of any motivation for the child to make a false report (Magnusson & others, 2021).

Can false memories be induced in children? See the *Connecting with Research* interlude to read about a study that addresses this question.

In sum, whether a young child's eyewitness testimony is accurate or not may depend on a number of factors such as the type, number, and intensity of the suggestive techniques the child has experienced. It appears that the reliability of young children's reports has as much to do with the skills and motivation of the interviewer as with any natural limitations on young children's memory.

Autobiographical Memory   Another aspect of long-term memory that has been extensively studied in children's development is autobiographical memory (Kangaslampi, 2023).

connecting with research

Can Parents Suggest False Events to Children?

Key Points:

- Researchers examined whether parents can influence false memory formation in their children.
- Children were highly suggestive and had difficulty accurately reporting prior experience.
- The study has implications for how children's testimony should be handled in legal proceedings.

As described in Bruck and Ceci (1999, pp. 429–430), a study by Deborah Poole and D. Stephen Lindsay revealed how parents can subtly influence their young children's memories of events. Preschool children participated in four activities (such as lifting cans with pulleys) with "Mr. Science" in a university laboratory (Poole & Lindsay, 1995). Four months later, the children's parents were mailed a storybook with a description of their child's visit to see Mr. Science. The storybook described two of the activities in which the child had participated, but it also described two in which the child had not participated. Each description ended with this fabrication of what happened when it was time to leave the laboratory: "Mr. Science wiped (child's name) hands and face with a wet-wipe. The cloth got close to (child's name) mouth and tasted real yucky."

Parents read the descriptions to their children three times. Later, the children told the experimenter that they had participated in the activities that actually had only been mentioned in the descriptions read by their parents. For example, when asked whether Mr. Science had put anything yucky in their mouth, more than half of the young children said that he had. Subsequently, when asked whether Mr. Science put something in their mouth or their parent just read this to them in a story, 71 percent of the young children said that it really happened.

This study shows how subtle suggestions can influence children's inaccurate reporting of nonevents. If such inaccurate reports are pursued in follow-up questioning by an interviewer who suspected that something sexual occurred, the result could be a sexual interpretation. This study also revealed the difficulty preschool children have in identifying the source of a suggestion (called *source-monitoring errors*). Children in this study confused their parent's reading the suggestion to them with their experience of the suggestion.

How might researchers expand on this study to test the influence of other adults on children's memories? Do you think any ethical issues would arise in such research?

How did Walter Mischel and his colleagues study young children's delay of gratification? In their research, what later developmental outcomes were linked to the preschoolers' ability to delay gratification?

Amy Kiley Photography

Autobiographical memory involves memory of significant events and experiences in one's life. You are engaging in autobiographical memory when you answer questions such as: What was your first-grade teacher's personality like? What is the most traumatic event that happened to you as a child?

During the preschool years, young children's memories increasingly take on more autobiographical characteristics (Bauer & Larkina, 2016). In some areas, such as remembering a story, a movie, a song, or an interesting event or experience, young children have been shown to have reasonably good memories. From 3 to 5 years of age, they (1) increasingly remember events as occurring at a specific time and location, such as "on my birthday at the park last year," and (2) include more elements that are rich in detail in their narratives (Bauer, 2013). A culture sensitizes its members to certain objects, events, and strategies, which in turn can influence the nature of memory (Wang, 2021).

Executive Function

Recently, increasing interest has been directed toward the development of children's **executive function,** an umbrella-like concept that consists of a number of higher-level cognitive processes linked to the development of the brain's prefrontal cortex (Bell & Garcia Meza, 2020; McClelland & others, 2017; Perone, Almy & Zelazo, 2017). Executive function involves managing one's thoughts to engage in goal-directed behavior and exercise self-control (Hoskyn, Iarocci, & Young, 2017). Earlier in this chapter, we described the recent interest in *executive attention,* which comes under the umbrella of executive function.

In early childhood, executive function especially involves developmental advances in cognitive inhibition (such as inhibiting a strong tendency that is incorrect), cognitive flexibility (such as shifting attention to another item or topic), goal-setting (such as sharing a toy or mastering a skill like catching a ball), and delay of gratification (waiting longer to get a more attractive reward, for example) (McClelland, Cameron, & Alonso, 2019; McDermott & Fox, 2018). During early childhood, the relatively stimulus-driven toddler is transformed into a child capable of flexible, goal-directed problem solving that characterizes executive function (Zelazo, 2015). Walter Mischel and his colleagues (Berman & others, 2013; Mischel, Cantor, & Feldman, 1996; Mischel & Moore, 1980; Mischel & others, 2011; Schlam & others, 2013) have conducted a number of classic studies of delay of gratification with young children. One way they assess delay of gratification is to place a young child alone in a room with an alluring marshmallow that is within their reach. The children are told that they can either ring a bell at any time and eat the marshmallow or wait until the experimenter returns and then get two marshmallows. When young children waited for the experimenter to return, what did they do to help them wait? They engaged in a number of strategies to distract their attention from the marshmallow, including singing songs, picking their noses, or doing something else to keep from looking at the marshmallow. Mischel and his colleagues labeled these strategies "cool thoughts" (that is, doing non-marshmallow-related thoughts and activities), whereas they labeled what young children were doing when they looked at the marshmallow as engaging in "hot thoughts." The young children who engaged in cool thoughts were more likely to eat the marshmallow later or wait until the experimenter returned to the room. Whether children waited to eat the marshmallow was also dependent on how trustworthy children believed the person bringing the prize to be (Kidd, Palmeri, & Aslin, 2013). In one study using the delay of gratification task just described, longer delay of gratification at 4 years of age was linked to a lower body mass index (BMI) three decades later (Schlam & others, 2013).

Researcher Stephanie Carlson administers the Less Is More task to a 4-year-old boy. *What were the results of Carlson's research?*

Dawn Villella Photography

executive function An umbrella-like concept that consists of a number of higher-level cognitive processes linked to the development of the brain's prefrontal cortex. Executive function involves managing one's thoughts to engage in goal-directed behavior and exercise self-control.

Stephanie Carlson and her colleagues (Carlson, Claxton, & Moses, 2015; Prager, Sera, & Carlson, 2016; White & others, 2017; Zelazo & Carlson, 2022) also have conducted a number of research studies on young children's executive function. In one early study, Carlson and her colleagues (2005) gave young children a task called Less Is More, in which they are shown two trays of candy—one with five pieces, the other with two—and told that the tray they pick will be given to a stuffed animal seated at the table. Three-year-olds consistently selected the tray with the five pieces of candy, thus giving away more candy than they kept for themselves. However, 4-year-olds were far more likely to choose the tray with only two pieces of candy, keeping five pieces for themselves, and thus inhibiting their impulsiveness far better than the 3-year-olds did. In another study, young children were read either *Planet Opposite*—a fantasy book in which everything is turned upside down—or *Fun Town*—a reality-oriented fiction book (Carlson & White, 2013). After being read one of the books, the young children completed the Less Is More task. Sixty percent of the 3-year-olds who heard the *Planet Opposite* story chose the two pieces of candy compared with only 20 percent of their counterparts who heard the more straightforward story. The results indicated that learning about a topsy-turvy imaginary world likely helped the young children become more flexible in their thinking.

Researchers have found that advances in executive function during the preschool years are linked with math skills, language development, and school readiness (Blair, 2017; Nakamichi, Nakamichi, & Nakazawa, 2022). Some researchers have found that executive function is a better predictor of school readiness than general IQ (Duckworth & others, 2019).

The largest and longest-running longitudinal study of an important dimension of executive function—inhibitory control—found that 3- to 11-year-old children who had better inhibitory control (were more able to wait their turn, not as easily distracted, more persistent, and less impulsive) were more likely as adolescents to still be in school, less likely to engage in risk-taking behavior, and less likely to be taking drugs (Moffitt & others, 2011). In addition, 30 years after they were initially assessed, the individuals with better inhibitory control had better physical and mental health (they were less likely to be overweight, for example), had better earnings in their career, were more law-abiding, and were happier.

What are some predictors of young children's executive function? Parenting practices are linked to children's development of executive function (Bernier & others, 2017). For example, several studies have linked greater use of verbal scaffolding by parents (providing age-appropriate support during cognitive tasks) to children's more advanced executive function. A study of mothers and preschoolers in South Korea found that mothers who adjusted their level of scaffolding during a puzzle task according to the child's ongoing level of understanding had preschoolers who demonstrated better executive function than did preschoolers whose mothers were less contingent in their scaffolding (Lee, Baker, & Whitebread, 2018). Children who are born very premature are at risk of having poor executive function, but sensitive parenting and mutually responsive and harmonious parent-preschooler interactions have been found to boost the executive functioning of preschoolers who were born very preterm (Zvara & others, 2019). Experiencing peer problems (such as victimization and rejection) beginning in early childhood also is linked to lower executive function later in childhood, which in turn increases the likelihood of experiencing peer problems later in childhood (van Lier & Deater-Deckard, 2022).

Other predictors of better executive function in children that researchers have found include higher socioeconomic status (Duncan, McClelland, & Acock, 2017); some aspects of language, including vocabulary diversity and language complexity (Daneri & others, 2019); imagination (generating novel ideas, for example) (Gleason & White, 2023); and fewer sleep problems (Nieto & others, 2022).

Some developmental psychologists use their training in areas such as cognitive development to pursue careers in applied areas. To read about the work of Helen Hadani, an individual who has followed this path, see the *Connecting with Careers* profile.

connecting with careers

Helen Hadani, Toy Designer and Placemaking Innovator

Helen Hadani obtained a Ph.D. in developmental psychology from Stanford University. As a graduate student at Stanford, she worked part-time for Hasbro Toys and Apple, testing software and other computer products for young children. Her first job after graduate school was with Zowie Entertainment, which was subsequently bought by LEGO. According to Hadani, "Even in a toy's most primitive stage of development . . . you see children's creativity in responding to challenges, their satisfaction when a problem is solved or simply their delight in having fun" (Schlegel, 2000, p. 50).

Hadani is currently a fellow at the Brookings Institution, where she leads the Playful Learning Landscapes project, an initiative that brings together the fields of developmental science and *placemaking* (the process of creating desirable, quality places for people to live, work, play, and learn) with the goal of improving child and community outcomes.

Helen Hadani is a developmental psychologist who has focused on designing toys and innovative learning experiences for children and families.

Dr. Helen Shwe Hadani

theory of mind A concept that refers to awareness of one's own mental processes and the mental processes of others.

The Child's Theory of Mind   Even young children are curious about the nature of the human mind (Birch & others, 2017). They have a **theory of mind,** which refers to awareness of one's own mental processes and the mental processes of others. Studies of theory of mind investigate how children acquire the skills to notice, think about, explain, and understand the feelings and thoughts of others. Researchers are increasingly discovering that children's theory of mind is linked to cognitive processes (Birch & others, 2017; Rakoczy, 2022). For example, one study found that preschoolers' theory of mind competence is related to better social working memory (He & others, 2019).

Developmental Changes   Although the question of whether infants have a theory of mind has been heavily investigated and debated (Burge, 2018; Yates, Ellis, & Turk-Browne, 2021), the consensus is that some changes occur quite early in development, as we see next (Scott & Baillargeon, 2017). From 18 months to 3 years of age, children begin to understand three mental states:

- *Perceptions*. By 2 years of age, children recognize that another person will see what's in front of her own eyes instead of what's in front of the child's eyes, and by 3 years of age, they realize that looking leads to knowing what's inside a container.
- *Emotions*. The child can distinguish between positive (for example, happy) and negative (for example, sad) emotions. A child might say, "Daddy feels bad."
- *Desires*. All humans have some sort of desires. But when do children begin to recognize that someone else's desires may be different from their own? Toddlers recognize that if people want something, they will try to get it. For instance, a child might say, "I want my mommy."

Two- to 3-year-olds understand that desires are related to actions and to simple emotions. For example, they understand that people will search for what they want and that if they obtain it, they are likely to feel happy, but if they don't get it, they will keep searching for it and are likely to feel sad or angry (Wu, Muentener, & Schulz, 2017). Children also refer to desires earlier and more frequently than they refer to cognitive states such as thinking and knowing (Bartsch & Wellman, 1995). However, the capacity for noticing and understanding other people's cognitive states may happen earlier in development, before children can verbalize this understanding (Wu & others, 2021).

One of the landmark developments in understanding others' desires is recognizing that someone else may have desires that differ from one's own (Wellman, 2015). In one illustrative example, 18-month-olds understood that their own food preferences might not match the preferences of others—they would give an adult the food to which she says "Yummy!" even if the food was something that the infants detested (Repacholi & Gopnik, 1997). As they get older, young children can recognize and verbalize that they themselves do not like something but an adult might (Rostad & Pexman, 2015).

Between the ages of 3 and 5, children come to understand that the mind can represent objects and events accurately or inaccurately (Visu-Petra, Prodan, & Talwar, 2022). The realization that people can have *false beliefs*—beliefs that are not true—develops in a majority of children by the time they are 5 years old (see Figure 10). This point is often described as a pivotal one in understanding the mind—recognizing that beliefs are not just mapped directly into the mind from the surrounding world, but also that different people can have different, and sometimes incorrect, beliefs (Tomasello, 2018b). In a classic false-belief task, young children are shown a Band-Aids box and asked what is inside. To the children's surprise, the box actually contains pencils. When asked what a child who had never seen the box would think was inside, 3-year-olds typically respond, "Pencils." However, the 4- and 5-year-olds, grinning in anticipation of the false beliefs of other children who had not seen what is inside the box, are more likely to say "Band-Aids."

In a similar task, children are told a story about Sally and Anne: Sally places a toy in a basket and then leaves the room (see Figure 11). In her absence, Anne takes the toy from the basket and places it in a box. Children are asked where Sally will look for the toy when she returns. The major finding is that 3-year-olds tend to fail false-belief tasks, saying that Sally will look in the box (even though Sally could not know that the toy has been moved to this new location). Four-year-olds and older children tend to pass the task, correctly saying that Sally will have a "false belief"—she will think the object is in the basket, even though that belief is now false. The conclusion from these studies is that children younger than 4 years old do not understand that it is possible to have a false belief.

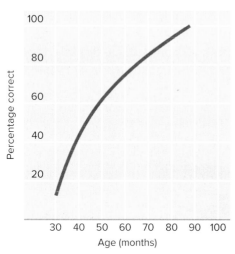

FIGURE 10

DEVELOPMENTAL CHANGES IN FALSE-BELIEF PERFORMANCE. False-belief performance—the child's understanding that a person may have a false belief that contradicts reality—dramatically increases from 2½ years of age through the middle of the elementary school years. In a foundational summary of the results of many studies, 2½-year-olds gave incorrect responses about 80 percent of the time (Wellman, Cross, & Watson, 2001). At 3 years, 8 months, they were correct about 50 percent of the time, and after that, they increasingly gave correct responses.

However, there are reasons to question the focus on this one supposedly pivotal moment in the development of a theory of mind. For example, the false-belief task is a complicated one that involves a number of factors such as the characters in the story and all of their individual actions (Wellman, 2018). Children also have to disregard their own knowledge in making predictions about what others would think, which is difficult for young children. Another important issue is that there is more to understanding the minds of others than this false-belief task would indicate.

One example of a limitation in 3- to 5-year-olds' understanding the mind is how they think about thinking. Preschoolers often underestimate when mental activity is likely occurring. For example, they sometimes think that a person who is sitting quietly or reading is not actually thinking very much (Flavell, Green, & Flavell, 1995). Their understanding of their own thinking is also limited. One study revealed that even 5-year-olds have difficulty reporting their thoughts (Flavell, Green, & Flavell, 1995). Children were asked to think quietly about the room in their home where they kept their toothbrushes. Shortly after this direction, many children denied they had been thinking at all and failed to mention either a toothbrush or a bathroom. In another study, when 5-year-olds were asked to try to have no thoughts at all for about 20 seconds, they reported that they were successful at doing this (Flavell, Green, & Flavell, 2000). By contrast, most of the 8-year-olds said they engaged in mental activity during the 20 seconds and reported specific thoughts.

It is only beyond the preschool years—at approximately 5 to 7 years of age—that children have a deepening appreciation of the mind itself rather than just an understanding of mental states. For example, they begin to recognize that people's behaviors do not necessarily reflect their thoughts and feelings. Not until middle and late childhood do children see the mind as an active constructor of knowledge or a processing center and move from understanding that beliefs can be false to realizing that the same event can be open to multiple interpretations (Brandone & Klimek, 2018). For example, in one study, children saw an ambiguous line drawing (for example, a drawing that could be seen as either a duck or a rabbit); one puppet told the child she believed the drawing was a duck while another puppet told the child he believed the drawing was a rabbit (see Figure 12). Before the age of 7, children said that there was one right answer, and it was not okay for the two puppets to have different opinions.

Although most research on children's theory of mind focuses on children around or before their preschool years, at 7 years of age and beyond there are important developments in the ability to understand the beliefs and thoughts of others (Devine & Lecce, 2021). While it is important to understand that people may have different interpretations of the same thing, it is also important to recognize that some interpretations and beliefs may still be evaluated on the basis of the merits of arguments and evidence (Osterhaus, Koerber, & Sodian, 2017). In early adolescence, children can understand that people can have mixed and ambivalent feelings and that people's thoughts, feelings, and decisions can be consistent or inconsistent in different situations (Lagattuta, Elrod, & Kramer, 2016).

Individual Differences   As in other developmental research, there are individual differences in the ages when children reach certain milestones in their theory of mind (Birch & others, 2017). For example, executive function also is connected to theory of mind development (Fujita, Devine, & Hughes, 2022). In one executive function task, children are asked to say the word *night* when they see a picture of a sun, and the word *day* when they see a picture of a moon and stars. To do this correctly, children have to engage in inhibitory control by suppressing the most realistic responses (saying the word *day* when seeing a picture of a sun, for example).

Children who perform better at such executive function tasks show a better understanding of theory of mind (Benson & Sabbagh, 2017). This connection between theory of mind and executive function has been observed across early childhood and across cultures (Fujita, Devine, & Hughes, 2022). In one study, executive function at 3 years of age predicted theory of mind at 4 years of age, and likewise executive function at 4 years of age predicted theory of mind at 5 years of age (Marcovitch & others, 2015). In this research, the reverse did not occur—that is, theory of mind at earlier ages did not predict executive function at later ages.

Young children's symbolic skills also contribute to the development of theory of mind. One study found that young children's symbolic understanding provided a foundation for their theory of mind and also for language, pretend play, and representational understanding (Diaz, 2022; Lillard & Kavanaugh, 2014).

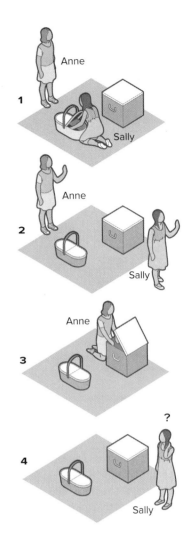

FIGURE 11

THE SALLY AND ANNE FALSE-BELIEF TASK. In the false-belief task, the skit above in which Sally has a basket and Anne has a box is shown to children. Sally places a toy in her basket and then leaves. While Sally is gone and can't watch, Anne removes the toy from Sally's basket and places it in her box. Sally then comes back and the children are asked where they think Sally will look for her toy. Children are said to "pass" the false-belief task if they understand that Sally will look in her basket first before realizing the toy isn't there.

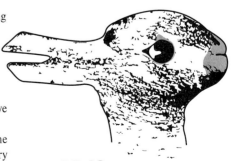

FIGURE 12
AMBIGUOUS LINE DRAWING

A young boy diagnosed with autism spectrum disorder. *What are some characteristics of children who have ASD? What are some differences in their theory of mind?*

Pollyana Ventura/Getty Images

developmental **connection**

Disorders

The current consensus is that autism is a brain neurodifference involving variations in brain structure and neurotransmitters, and that genetic factors play an important role in its occurrence. Connect to "Physical Development in Middle and Late Childhood."

developmental **connection**

Disorders

Boys are five times more likely to be diagnosed with an autism spectrum disorder than girls are. Connect to "Physical Development in Middle and Late Childhood."

Language development also likely plays a prominent role in the increasingly reflective nature of theory of mind as children go through the early childhood and middle and late childhood years (Tompkins, Farrar, & Montgomery, 2019). Researchers have found that differences in children's language skills predict performance on theory of mind tasks and also help account for the link between better theory of mind and executive function skills (Shahaeian, Haynes, & Frick, 2023).

Among other factors that influence children's development of theory of mind are advances in prefrontal cortex functioning (Maliske, Schurz, & Kanske, 2023; Powers, Chavez, & Heatherton, 2016), engaging in make-believe play (Bauer, Gilpin, & Thibodeau-Nielsen, 2021), and various aspects of social interaction (Devine & Hughes, 2018). Among the social interaction factors that advance children's theory of mind are being securely attached to parents who engage children in mental state talk ("That's a good thought you have" or "Can you tell what he's thinking?") (Devine & Hughes, 2018), having older siblings and friends who engage in mental state talk (Hughes & others, 2010), and living in a family of higher socioeconomic status (Devine & Hughes, 2018). One study found that parental engagement in mind-mindedness (viewing children as mental agents by making mind-related comments to them) advanced preschool children's theory of mind (Hughes, Devine, & Wang, 2018). Also, research indicates that children who have an advanced theory of mind are more popular with their peers and have better social skills in peer relations (Peterson & others, 2016).

Theory of Mind and Autism   Another individual difference in understanding the mind involves autism (Fletcher-Watson & Happé, 2019). Approximately 1 in 54 children is estimated to have some type of autism spectrum disorder (National Autism Association, 2022). Autism can usually be diagnosed by the age of 3 years and sometimes earlier. Children with autism show a number of behaviors different from those exhibited by other children their age, involving theory of mind, social interaction, and communication, as well as repetitive behaviors or interests (Martínez-González, Cervin, & Piqueras, 2022; von dem Hagen & Bright, 2017). One study found that theory of mind predicted the severity of autism in children (Hoogenhout & Malcolm-Smith, 2017). However, children with autism might have difficulty understanding others' beliefs and emotions not solely due to theory of mind deficits but to other aspects of cognition such as problems in focusing attention, eye gaze, face recognition, memory, executive function, language impairment, or some general intellectual impairment (Mukherjee, 2017; Boucher, 2017; Rice & others, 2022).

Children and adults with autism have difficulty in social interactions, often described as difficulties in theory of mind (Broekhof & others, 2015). These challenges are generally greater than in children the same mental age with an intellectual disability (Greenberg & others, 2018). Researchers have found that some children with autism have difficulty with aspects of theory of mind, especially in understanding others' beliefs and emotions (Fletcher-Watson & Happé, 2019). Although children with autism tend to do poorly when reasoning about false-belief tasks and task sequencing (Bulgarelli, Testa, & Molina, 2022; Peterson, Wellman, & Slaughter, 2012), they can perform much better on reasoning tasks that require an understanding of physical causality.

Review Connect Reflect

 Describe three views of the cognitive changes that occur in early childhood.

Review

- What characterizes Piaget's stage of preoperational thought?
- What does Vygotsky's theory suggest about how preschool children construct knowledge?
- What are some important ways in which information processing changes during early childhood? What characterizes children's theory of mind?

Connect

- What are some differences between the attention of young children and the attention of infants?

Reflect *Your Own Personal Journey of Life*

- If you were the parent of a 4-year-old child, would you try to train the child to develop conservation skills? Explain.

LG2 Summarize how language develops in early childhood.

| Understanding Phonology and Morphology | Changes in Syntax and Semantics | Advances in Pragmatics | Young Children's Literacy |

Toddlers move rather quickly from producing two-word utterances to creating three-, four-, and five-word combinations. Between 2 and 3 years of age, they begin the transition from saying simple sentences that express a single proposition to saying complex sentences.

As young children learn the special features of their own language, there are extensive regularities in how they acquire that particular language (Bruhn de Garavito & Schwieter, 2021). For example, children in English-speaking families learn the prepositions *on* and *in* before other prepositions. Children learning other languages also acquire the particular features of those languages in a consistent order.

UNDERSTANDING PHONOLOGY AND MORPHOLOGY

During the preschool years, most children gradually become more sensitive to the sounds of spoken words and become increasingly capable of producing all the sounds of their language (Shea & O'Neill, 2021). By the time children are 3 years of age, they can produce all the vowel sounds and most of the consonant sounds (Prelock & Hutchins, 2018). They can also recognize sounds before they can produce them.

Young children can even produce complex consonant clusters such as *str-* and *mpt* in languages such as English where consonant clusters are common. They notice rhymes, enjoy poems, make up silly names for things by substituting one sound for another (such as *bubblegum, bubblebum, bubbleyum*), and clap along with each syllable in a phrase.

By the time children move beyond two-word utterances, they demonstrate a knowledge of morphology rules (Bruhn de Garavito, 2021b). Children begin using the plural and possessive forms of nouns (such as *dogs* and *dog's*). They put appropriate endings on verbs (such as *-s* when the subject is third-person singular and *-ed* for the past tense). They use prepositions (such as *in* and *on*), articles (such as *a* and *the*), and various forms of the verb *to be* (such as "I *was* going to the store"). Some of the best evidence for changes in children's use of morphological rules occur in their overgeneralization of the rules, as when a preschool child says "foots" instead of "feet," or "goed" instead of "went."

In a classic early experiment that was designed to study children's knowledge of morphological rules, such as how to make a plural, Jean Berko (1958) presented preschool children and first-grade children with cards such as the one shown in Figure 13. Children were asked to look at the card while the experimenter read aloud the words on the card. Then the children were asked to supply the missing word. This task might sound easy, but Berko was interested in the children's ability to apply the appropriate morphological rule—in this case, to say "wugs" with the *z* sound that indicates the plural.

Although the children's answers were not perfect, they were much better than what could have been achieved by chance. What makes Berko's study impressive is that most of the words were made up for the experiment. Thus, the children could not have based their responses on remembering past instances of hearing the words. The fact that they could make the plurals or past tenses of words they had never heard before was evidence that they knew the morphological rules.

CHANGES IN SYNTAX AND SEMANTICS

Preschool children also learn and apply rules of syntax (Bruhn de Garavito, 2021c). They show a growing mastery of complex rules for how words should be ordered (Kyratzis, 2017).

Consider *wh-* questions, such as "Where is Daddy going?" or "What is that boy doing?" To ask these questions properly, the child must know two important differences between *wh-* questions and affirmative statements (for instance, "Daddy is going to work" and "That boy is waiting for the school bus"). First, a *wh-* word must be added at the beginning of the sentence. Second, the auxiliary verb must be inverted—that is, exchanged with the subject of the sentence.

This is a wug.

Now there is another one.
There are two of them.
There are two _____.

FIGURE **13**

STIMULI IN BERKO'S STUDY OF YOUNG CHILDREN'S UNDERSTANDING OF MORPHOLOGICAL RULES. In Jean Berko's (1958) study, young children were presented with cards, such as this one with a "wug" on it. Then the children were asked to supply the missing word; in supplying the missing word, they had to say it correctly, too. "Wugs" is the correct response here.

fast mapping A process that helps to explain how young children learn the connection between a word and its referent so quickly.

developmental **connection**

Language Development

The average 2-year-old can speak about 200 words. Connect to "Cognitive Development in Infancy."

Young children learn quite early where to put the *wh-* word, but they take much longer to learn the auxiliary-inversion rule. Thus, preschool children might ask, "Where Daddy is going?" and "What that boy is doing?"

Gains in semantics also characterize early childhood (van Hout, 2017). Vocabulary development is dramatic (Vukelich & others, 2020). Some experts have concluded that between 18 months and 6 years of age, young children learn approximately one new word every waking hour (Gelman & Kalish, 2006)! By the time they enter first grade, it is estimated that children know about 14,000 words (Clark, 1993).

Why can children learn so many new words so quickly? One possibility is **fast mapping,** which involves children's ability to make an initial connection between a word and its referent after only limited exposure to the word (Weatherhead & others, 2021). However, fast mapping may have more to do with knowing what a word refers to in the immediate environment than with truly learning the word because children can rarely recall the words they have apparently learned in a fast-mapping context (McMurray, Horst, & Samuelson, 2012). Researchers have found that exposure to words on multiple occasions over several days results in more successful word learning than the same number of exposures in a single day (Slone & Sandhofer, 2017).

What are some important aspects of how word learning optimally occurs? Following are six key principles in young children's vocabulary development (Harris, Golinkoff, & Hirsh-Pasek, 2011):

1. *Children learn the words they hear most often.* They learn the words that they encounter during interactions with parents, teachers, siblings, and peers, and also from books. They especially benefit from encountering words that they do not know.

2. *Children learn words for things and events that interest them.* Parents and teachers can direct young children to experience words in contexts that interest the children; playful peer interactions are especially helpful in this regard.

3. *Children learn words best in responsive and interactive contexts rather than passive contexts.* Children who participate in turn-taking opportunities, joint focusing experiences, and positive, sensitive socializing contexts with adults encounter the scaffolding necessary for optimal word learning. They learn words less effectively when they are passive learners. It is harder for children to learn words from watching television than from interacting with adults.

4. *Children learn words best in contexts that are meaningful.* Young children learn new words more effectively when new words are encountered in integrated contexts rather than as isolated facts.

5. *Children learn words best when they access clear information about word meaning.* Children whose parents and teachers are sensitive to words the children might not understand and provide support and elaboration with hints about word meaning learn words better than they do if parents and teachers quickly state a new word and don't monitor whether children understand its meaning.

6. *Children learn words best when grammar and vocabulary are considered.* Children who experience a large number of words and diversity in verbal stimulation develop a richer vocabulary and better understanding of grammar. In many cases, vocabulary and grammar development are connected.

ADVANCES IN PRAGMATICS

Changes in pragmatics also characterize young children's language development (Taboada, 2021). A 6-year-old is simply a much better conversationalist than a 2-year-old is. What are some of the improvements in pragmatics during the preschool years?

Young children begin to engage in extended discourse (Akhtar & Herold, 2017). For example, they learn culturally specific rules of conversation and politeness, and become sensitive to the need to adapt their speech in different settings. Their developing linguistic skills and increasing ability to take the perspective of others contribute to their generation of more competent narratives.

How do children's language abilities develop during early childhood?

Dean Mitchell/Vetta/Getty Images

As children get older, they become increasingly able to talk about things that are not here (Grandma's house, for example) and not now (what happened to them yesterday or might happen tomorrow, for example). A preschool child can tell you what she wants for lunch tomorrow, something that would not have been possible at the two-word stage of language development.

Around 4 to 5 years of age, children learn to change their speech style to suit the situation. For example, even 4-year-old children speak to a 2-year-old differently from the way they would talk to a same-aged peer; they use shorter sentences with the 2-year-old. They also speak to an adult differently from a same-aged peer, using more polite and formal language with the adult (Ikeda, Kobayashi, & Itakura, 2018).

Peers also can play an important role in aspects of language other than pragmatics. A study of more than 1,800 4-year-olds revealed that peers' expressive language abilities (transmitting language to others) were positively linked with young children's expressive and receptive (what a child hears and reads) language development (Mashburn & others, 2009).

YOUNG CHILDREN'S LITERACY

Growing concern about the ability of U.S. children to read and write has led to a careful examination of preschool and kindergarten children's experiences, with the hope that a positive orientation toward reading and writing can be fostered early in life (Dickinson & others, 2019; Tompkins & Rodgers, 2020). The most obvious literacy necessity is knowing a language. Children will not be able to comprehend the text they read if they don't understand the words and sentence structures. Parents and teachers need to provide young children with a supportive environment in which to develop literacy skills (Tamis-LeMonda & others, 2019). Children should be active participants and be immersed in a wide range of interesting listening, talking, writing, and reading experiences (Tompkins, 2016; Yang & others, 2021). Children's emergent literacy skills are highly correlated with their parents' literacy skills (Pakarinen & others, 2021; Taylor, Greenberg, & Terry, 2016). In one study, literacy experiences (such as how often the child was read to), the quality of the mother's engagement with her child (such as attempts to cognitively stimulate the child), and provision of learning materials (such as age-appropriate learning materials and books) were important home literacy experiences in low-income families that were linked to the children's language development in positive ways (Wood, Fitton, & Rodriguez, 2018).

Catherine Snow, a leading expert on children's language development, thinks that mealtimes are an excellent context for promoting young children's literacy. Snow and her colleague Diane Beals (Snow & Beals, 2006) described some of the ways that mealtimes can improve young children's literacy: Mealtime conversations often include information about current events and what is going on in the world; they provide an opportunity for everyday problems to be aired and solutions to be discussed; and they provide a context for learning about being polite and having good manners. Snow and colleagues have found that language use during these open and natural conversation contexts may actually have a larger impact on children's subsequent academic readiness skills than direct instruction in the home (McCormick & others, 2020).

Snow (2010) emphasizes that parents can promote literacy skills in young children at mealtime by using extended discourse, which involves talking about a topic that goes beyond a sentence or two and extends to several conversational turns. While engaging in such extended discourse, parents often use words young children haven't heard before or don't understand, which provides opportunities to expand children's vocabularies. In describing parents' use of sophisticated vocabulary in such mealtime contexts, Snow (2010, p. 128) commented:

How might mealtimes provide a context for enriching young children's literacy?
Ariel Skelley/Blend Images/Getty Images

In these dinner table conversations, of course, there's always a lot of talk about "Eat your peas" and "Keep your elbows off the table" and "Pass the noodles," but in some of the families, in addition, there's wonderfully interesting conversation about what proposals the governor just suggested for a new budget, or how the construction of the expressway is going to influence the neighborhood. And these conversations are full of wonderful words like *budget* and *governor* and *proposal* and *neighborhood*—words that children might not use and probably won't understand fully. We found that families that used words like that in their dinner table conversations had children with much larger vocabularies two years later.

So far, our discussion of early literacy has focused on U.S. children. Researchers have found that the extent to which phonological awareness is linked to learning to read effectively varies across language to some extent (McBride, 2016). Phonological awareness is less important for early reading development in languages that use characters, such as Chinese, rather than alphabets (Ruan & others, 2018). Further, rates of dyslexia (severe reading disability) differ across countries and are linked to the spelling and phonetic rules that characterize the language (McBride, Pan, & Mohseni, 2021). English is one of the more difficult languages because of its irregular spellings and pronunciations. In countries where English is spoken, the rate of dyslexia is higher than in countries where the alphabet script is more phonetically pronounced.

Books can be valuable in enhancing children's communication skills (Morrow, 2020). What are some strategies for using books effectively with preschool children? Ellen Galinsky (2010) suggested these strategies:

- *Use books to initiate conversation with young children.* Ask them to put themselves in the book characters' places and imagine what they might be thinking or feeling.
- *Use what and why questions.* Ask young children what they think is going to happen next in a story and then to see if it occurs.
- *Encourage children to ask questions about stories.*
- *Choose some books that play with language.* Creative books on the alphabet, including those with rhymes, often interest young children.

What are some strategies for supporting young children's literacy?

MBimages/Shutterstock

The advances in language that take place in early childhood lay the foundation for later development during the elementary school years, as we will see in "Cognitive Development in Middle and Late Childhood."

Review *Connect* Reflect

LG2 Summarize how language develops in early childhood.

Review

- How do phonology and morphology change during early childhood?
- What characterizes young children's understanding of syntax and semantics in early childhood?
- What advances in pragmatics occur in early childhood?
- What are some effective ways to guide young children's literacy?

Connect

- In this section, you learned that children can sometimes overgeneralize the rules for morphology. How is this different from or similar to the concept of overextension as it relates to infants' speech?

Reflect *Your Own Personal Journey of Life*

- As a parent, what would you do to improve the likelihood that your child would enter first grade with excellent literacy skills?

3 What Are Some Important Features of Young Children's Education?

LG3 Evaluate different approaches to early childhood education.

| Variations in Early Childhood Education | Educating Young Children Who Are Disadvantaged | Controversies in Early Childhood Education |

To the teachers at a Reggio Emilia program (described in the chapter opening), preschool children are active learners, exploring the world with their peers, constructing their knowledge of the world in collaboration with their community, aided but not directed by the teachers. In many ways, the Reggio Emilia approach applies ideas consistent with the views of Piaget and Vygotsky discussed in this chapter. Do educators' beliefs make a difference to the children they teach? How do other early education programs treat children, and how do the children fare? Our exploration of early childhood education focuses on variations in programs, education for children who are disadvantaged, and some controversies in early childhood education.

VARIATIONS IN EARLY CHILDHOOD EDUCATION

Attending preschool has become the norm for U.S. children. Forty-four states plus the District of Columbia and Guam have publicly funded preschool programs for 3- and 4-year-old children (Friedman-Krauss & others, 2022). Many other 3- and 4-year-old children attend private preschool programs.

There are many variations in the ways young children are educated (Morrison & others, 2022). The foundation of early childhood education has been the child-centered kindergarten.

Larry Page and Sergey Brin, founders of the highly successful Internet search engine Google, said that their early years at Montessori schools were a major factor in their success (International Montessori Council, 2006). During an interview with Barbara Walters, they said they learned how to be self-directed and self-starters at Montessori (ABC News, 2005). They commented that the Montessori experiences encouraged them to think for themselves and allowed them the freedom to develop their own interests.

James Leynse/Corbis Historical/Getty Images

The Child-Centered Kindergarten   Nurturing is a key aspect of the **child-centered kindergarten,** which emphasizes the education of the whole child and concern for his or her physical, cognitive, and socioemotional development (Bredekamp, 2020). Instruction is organized around the child's needs, interests, and learning styles. Emphasis is on the process of learning, rather than what is learned (Bredekamp, 2017; Gestwicki, 2017). The child-centered kindergarten honors three principles: Each child follows a unique developmental pattern; young children learn best through firsthand experiences with people and materials; and play is extremely important to the child's total development. *Experimenting, exploring, discovering, trying out, restructuring, speaking,* and *listening* are frequent activities in excellent kindergarten programs. Such programs are closely attuned to the developmental status of 4- and 5-year-old children.

The Montessori Approach   Montessori schools are patterned after the educational philosophy of Maria Montessori (1870–1952), an Italian physician-turned-educator who crafted a revolutionary approach to young children's education at the beginning of the twentieth century. Her work began in Rome with a group of children with an intellectual disability. She was successful in teaching them to read, write, and pass examinations designed for typically developing children. Some time later, she turned her attention to impoverished children from low-income areas of Rome and had similar success in teaching them. Her approach has since been adopted extensively in private nursery schools in the United States. The number of Montessori schools in the United States has expanded dramatically in recent years, from one school in 1959 to 355 schools in 1970 to more than 3,000 in 2021 with estimates of Montessori schools worldwide at approximately 20,000 in 2020 (National Center for Montessori in the Public Sector, 2022).

The **Montessori approach** is a philosophy of education in which children are given considerable freedom and spontaneity in choosing activities. They are allowed to move from one activity to another as they desire. The teacher acts as a facilitator rather than a director. The teacher shows the child how to perform intellectual activities, demonstrates interesting ways to explore curriculum materials, and offers help when the child requests it (Macia-Gual & Domingo-Penafiel, 2021). Montessori teachers encourage children to make decisions from an early age, which helps them to engage in self-regulated problem solving and learn to manage their time effectively. Several studies have found that children in Montessori preschool programs, compared with children in other types of preschools, have better scores on measures of early reading and math, executive functioning, social functioning, and moral reasoning, controlling for potentially confounding factors (Lillard, 2021). One illustrative study found that Latino children in low-income communities who began the school year having at-risk pre-academic and behavioral skills benefitted from a Montessori public school pre-K program, ending the year scoring above national averages for school readiness (Ansari & Winsler, 2014).

child-centered kindergarten Education that involves the whole child by considering the child's physical, cognitive, and socioemotional development and addressing the child's needs, interests, and learning styles.

Montessori approach An educational philosophy in which children are given considerable freedom and spontaneity in choosing activities and are provided with specially designed curriculum materials.

developmentally appropriate practice (DAP) Education that focuses on the typical developmental patterns of children (age appropriateness) as well as the uniqueness of each child (individual appropriateness). Such practice contrasts with developmentally inappropriate practice, which ignores the concrete, hands-on approach to learning. For example, direct teaching largely through abstract paper-and-pencil activities presented to large groups of young children is believed to be developmentally inappropriate.

Project Head Start Compensatory education designed to provide children from low-income families the opportunity to acquire skills and experiences that are important for school success.

What are some differences in developmentally appropriate and inappropriate practice?
Image100/PunchStock

Some developmentalists favor the Montessori approach, but others believe that it neglects children's social development (Gustafsson, 2018). For example, while Montessori fosters independence and the development of cognitive skills, it deemphasizes verbal interaction between the teacher and child and peer interaction. Montessori's critics also argue that its reliance on self-correction may work well for students who are highly motivated and able to focus their attention but that students with learning disabilities or learning styles that would benefit from more direct instruction may do better in preschools with more guidance from teachers.

Developmentally Appropriate and Inappropriate Education Many educators and psychologists conclude that preschool and young elementary school children learn best through active, hands-on teaching methods such as games and dramatic play. They know that children develop at varying rates and believe that schools need to allow for these individual differences (Morrison & others, 2022). They also argue that schools should focus on facilitating children's socioemotional development as well as their cognitive development. Educators refer to this type of schooling as **developmentally appropriate practice (DAP),** which is based on knowledge of the typical development of children within a particular age span (age appropriateness), as well as on the uniqueness of the individual child (individual appropriateness).

DAP emphasizes the importance of creating settings that encourage children to be active learners and reflect children's interests and capabilities (Bjorklund, 2022). Desired outcomes for DAP include thinking critically, working cooperatively, solving problems, developing self-regulatory skills, and enjoying learning. The emphasis in DAP is on the process of learning rather than on its content (Cobanoglu, Capa-Aydin, & Yildirim, 2019).

Do developmentally appropriate educational practices improve young children's development? Some researchers have found that young children in developmentally appropriate classrooms are likely to feel less stress, be more motivated, be more socially skilled, have better work habits, be more creative, have better language skills, and demonstrate better math skills than children in developmentally inappropriate classrooms. However, not all studies find DAP to have significant positive effects (Sanders & Farago, 2018). Among the reasons that it is difficult to generalize from the research findings on developmentally appropriate education is that individual programs often vary, and developmentally appropriate education is an evolving concept. Recent changes in the concept have given more attention to how strongly academic skills should be emphasized and how they should be taught.

EDUCATING YOUNG CHILDREN WHO ARE DISADVANTAGED

For many years, U.S. children from low-income families did not receive any education before they entered first grade. Often, they began first grade several steps behind their classmates in their readiness to learn. In the summer of 1965, the federal government began an effort to break the cycle of poverty and inadequate education for young children in the United States through **Project Head Start.** It is a compensatory program designed to provide children from low-income families the opportunity to acquire the skills and experiences important for success in school. After more than half a century, Head Start continues to be the largest federally funded program for U.S. children, with almost 1 million U.S. children enrolled annually (Administration for Children and Families, 2023). In 2022–2023, a tiny percentage of Head Start children were 5 years old or older, with about one-third each being children who were 4, 3, or under 3 years old.

Early Head Start was established in 1995 to serve children from birth to 3 years of age. In 2007, half of all new funds appropriated for Head Start programs were used for the expansion of Early Head Start (Burgette & others, 2017). Researchers have found positive effects for Early Head Start and that Early Head Start can serve as a buffer to protect children from risk factors in the family by offering supports to both parents and children (Paschall, Mastergeorge, & Ayoub, 2019).

Head Start programs are not all created equal. Variations in the effectiveness of Head Start are found as a function of the types of services offered as part of the program, the characteristics of the participating children, and alternative care options that may be available (Morris & others, 2018). More attention needs to be given to developing Head Start programs

connecting with careers

Rakaya Humphreys, Head Start Director

During college at Bethel University in Tennessee, Rakaya Humphreys switched her major from chemistry and premed to social science, resulting in a more rewarding way to help families who are experiencing poverty. "I experienced that too growing up in Memphis," says Humphreys. "I grew up homeless, and my mom was young when she had me, so we almost grew up together" (Shields, 2020).

Humphreys is currently the director of Head Start for the Northwest Tennessee Economic Development Council. For over 20 years, she has been involved with Head Start programs both personally and professionally. As a young mother soon after college, she enrolled her son in Head Start and, with the help of her mother, he was able to continue to participate in the program when she was deployed to Iraq for a year with the Army Reserve.

Humphreys' first job out of college was as a family advocate at Washington-Douglass Head Start in East Jackson, Tennessee. Since then, she has served in a number of coordinator and administrator positions with Head Start organizations throughout northern Tennessee.

Head Start programs foster children's readiness for school and beyond through individualized learning experiences. The program also engages parents or other key family members in positive relationships, with a focus on family well-being. Humphreys wants to ensure that her communities know that Head Start is an available resource, particularly as families have struggled during the COVID-19 pandemic. "We've kept a watchful eye on families to make sure domestic violence

Rakaya Humphreys with an Early Head Start infant.
Rakaya Humphreys

hasn't become an issue while everyone has had to stay at home. Taking care of families and making sure the children and their parents have every opportunity available to them is our goal, and that's what we strive to do every day."

---

that are of consistently high quality (Slater & others, 2021; Sommer & others, 2020). (See the *Connecting with Careers* feature that profiles one professional who has seen the benefits of Head Start, both as a recipient of its services and as an administrator.)

Mixed results have been found for Head Start (K. Lee, 2019). Some evaluations support the positive influence of quality early childhood programs on both the cognitive and social worlds of disadvantaged young children (Yazejian & others, 2017). One study found that one year of Head Start was linked to higher performance in early math, early reading, and receptive vocabulary (Miller, Farkas, & Duncan, 2016).

Also, a national evaluation of Head Start revealed that the program had a positive influence on the language and cognitive development of 3- and 4-year-olds (National Head Start Association, 2016). However, by the end of the first grade, there were few lasting benefits. One exception was a larger vocabulary for those who went to Head Start as 4-year-olds and better oral comprehension for those who went to Head Start as 3-year-olds. In many early child-care programs that do not show differences in test scores later in elementary school, program participants show delayed benefits in terms of earnings in adulthood, perhaps because Head Start improves socioemotional functioning and other factors that can have long-term benefits that may not be captured in test scores (National Head Start Association, 2016).

Positive outcomes for Early Head Start have been found. In an important experimental study of low-income families, data were collected when the children were 1, 2, and 3 years old in Early Head Start, and also at 5 years of age (2 years after leaving Early Head Start) (Love & others, 2013). In this study, positive outcomes for the Early Head Start children (compared with a control group who did not receive the Early Head Start experience) occurred at 2, 3, and 5 years of age. At 2 and 3 years of age, Early Head Start children showed higher levels of cognition, language, attention, and health, as well as fewer behavior problems, than other children from low-income families; at age 5, the Early Head Start children had better attention and

How Would You...?
If you were an **educator,** how would you design a developmentally appropriate lesson to teach kindergarten children the concept of gravity?

How Would You...?
If you were a **health-care professional,** how would you explain the importance of including health services as part of an effective Head Start program?

developmental connection

Cognitive Development

Educational issues surrounding bilingual children and children who come to school as English-language learners are important. Connect to "Cognitive Development in Middle and Late Childhood."

approaches to learning as well as fewer behavior problems, but they did not differ from control group children in early school achievement. Also, another early study revealed that Early Head Start had a protective effect on risks young children might experience in regard to parenting stress, language development, and self-control (Ayoub, Vallotton, & Mastergeorge, 2011).

One high-quality early childhood education program (although not a Head Start program) was the Perry Preschool program in Ypsilanti, Michigan, a two-year preschool program that included weekly home visits from program personnel. In analyses of the long-term effects of the program, adults who had been in the Perry Preschool program were compared with a control group of adults from the same background who had not received the enriched early childhood education (Schweinhart, 2019). Those who had been in the Perry Preschool program had fewer teen pregnancies and better high school graduation rates, and at age 40 they had fewer arrests and were more likely to be employed, own a home, and have a savings account.

CONTROVERSIES IN EARLY CHILDHOOD EDUCATION

Three controversies in early childhood education involve (1) the curriculum, (2) universal preschool education, and (3) school readiness (Greenberg, 2018; Morrison & others, 2022).

What Should the Curriculum Emphasize in Early Childhood Education?

Regarding the curriculum controversy, on one side are those who advocate a child-centered, constructivist approach along the lines of developmentally appropriate practice (Auld & Morris, 2019). Child-centered, constructivist approaches often emphasize aspects of socioemotional development, such as learning to share, take turns, and listen to directions. On the other side are those who advocate an academic, direct instruction approach. Advocates of teacher-directed, academic approaches argue that these approaches can engage children's natural curiosity and be sensitive to young children's capacities and needs while also emphasizing early skills in mathematics and literacy (Baroody, Clements, & Sarama, 2019).

In practice, many high-quality early childhood education programs include both academic and constructivist approaches. Many education experts, though, worry about academic approaches that place too much pressure on young children to achieve and don't provide any opportunities to actively construct knowledge (Faas, Wu, & Geiger, 2017). Competent early childhood programs also should focus on both cognitive development and socioemotional development, not exclusively on cognitive development (Tager, 2022).

Should All Children Be Provided with Preschool Education?

Another early childhood education controversy focuses on whether preschool education should be instituted for all U.S. 4-year-old children. Proponents of universal preschool education emphasize that quality preschools equip children for school readiness and later academic success (Cascio, 2023). For example, quality preschool programs increase the likelihood that once children go to elementary and secondary school, they will not repeat a grade or drop out of school. Proponents also point to analyses indicating that universal preschool would bring cost savings on the order of billions of dollars because of a diminished need for remedial services (van Huizen, Dumhs, & Plantenga, 2019).

Critics of universal preschool education argue that the gains attributed to preschool and kindergarten education are often overstated. They especially stress that research has not proven that nondisadvantaged children benefit academically from attending a preschool (Blau, 2021). Thus,

What are some of the controversies in early childhood education?
Ronnie Kaufman/Corbis/Getty Images

the critics say it is more important to improve preschool education for young children who are disadvantaged than to fund preschool education for all 4-year-old children. Some critics, especially homeschooling advocates, emphasize that young children should be educated by their parents, not by schools. Thus, controversy continues to surround proposals for universal preschool education.

How Would You...?
If you were a **psychologist,** how would you advise preschool teachers to balance the development of young children's skills for academic achievement with opportunities for healthy social interaction?

What Is Required for School Readiness? Educational reform has prompted considerable concern about children's readiness to enter kindergarten and first grade (Williams & others, 2019).

A foundational massive analysis using six longitudinal studies examined various factors that might be linked to school readiness and assessed the extent to which they predicted later achievement in reading and math (Duncan & others, 2007). Across all six studies, the strongest predictors of later achievement were school-entry-level math, reading, and attention skills. However, school-entry-level socioemotional behaviors, such as degrees of internalizing and externalizing problems and social skills, showed little connection to later academic achievement. Nevertheless, several subsequent studies have demonstrated the importance of children's socioemotional development, including skills such as the ability to regulate emotions and get along with peers, in children's readiness for the transition to school (Harrington & others, 2020). The relationship with the caregiver in early child-care settings also is very important, with more cooperative and playful relationships (versus more difficult and conflicted relationships) between toddlers and their preschool caregivers being most predictive of school readiness (Nguyen & others, 2020).

In some high-income countries, such as Japan, as well as in many low- and middle-income countries, the goals of early childhood education are quite different from those of programs in the United States. To read about some of the differences, see the *Connecting with Diversity* interlude.

A child's attention is an important aspect of school readiness.
Russ Rohde/age fotostock

Review Connect Reflect

LG3 Evaluate different approaches to early childhood education.

Review
- What are some variations in early childhood education?
- What are the main efforts to educate young children who are disadvantaged?
- What are three controversies about early childhood education?

Connect
- Earlier in the chapter, you read about Piaget's and Vygotsky's cognitive theories. Which side of the curriculum controversy in early childhood education—child-centered, constructivist, or direct instruction—would be supported by Piaget's and Vygotsky's theories? Why?

Reflect *Your Own Personal Journey of Life*
- What type of early childhood education program would you want your child to attend?

topical connections *looking forward*

In the next chapter, you will read about the many advances in the socioemotional development of young children. The cognitive advances we discussed in this chapter, combined with the socioemotional experiences young children have in interacting with others, pave the way for social cognitive advances in understanding the self and others. In "Physical Development in Middle and Late Childhood" and "Cognitive Development in Middle and Late Childhood," you will read about further changes in children's physical and cognitive development. In terms of physical development, the development of the brain—especially the prefrontal cortex—provides the foundation for a number of cognitive advances, including the development of strategies and reading skills.

Early Childhood Education in Japan, the United States, and Low- and Middle-Income Countries

As in the United States, there is diversity in Japanese early childhood education. Some Japanese kindergartens have specific aims, such as providing early musical training or practicing Montessori strategies. In large cities, some kindergartens are attached to universities that have elementary and secondary schools. In most Japanese preschools, however, little emphasis is put on academic instruction.

In one foundational early study, 300 Japanese and 210 American preschool teachers, child development specialists, and parents were asked about various aspects of early childhood education (Tobin, Wu, & Davidson, 1989). Only 2 percent of the Japanese respondents mentioned "to give children a good start academically" as one of their top three reasons for a society to have preschools. In contrast, over half the American respondents chose this as one of their top three choices. Japanese preschools do not teach reading, writing, and mathematics but rather skills like persistence, concentration, and the ability to function as a member of a group. The vast majority of young Japanese children are taught to read at home by their parents.

In the comparison of Japanese and American parents, more than 60 percent of the Japanese parents said that the purpose of preschool is to give children experience being a member of a group, compared with only 20 percent of the U.S. parents (Tobin, Wu, & Davidson, 1989) (see Figure 14). Lessons in living and working together grow naturally out of the Japanese culture. In many Japanese kindergartens, children wear the same uniforms, including caps, in specific colors to indicate the classrooms to which they belong. They have identical sets of equipment, kept in identical drawers and shelves. This system is not intended to turn the young children into robots, as some Americans have surmised, but to impress on them that other people, just like themselves, have needs and desires that are equally important (Hendry, 1995).

Japan is a high-income country. What about early childhood education in low- and middle-income countries? Globally, almost half of

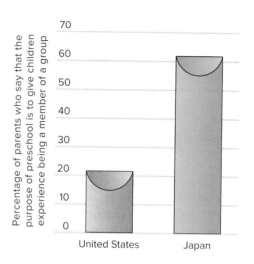

FIGURE **14**

COMPARISON OF JAPANESE AND U.S. PARENTS' VIEWS ON THE PURPOSE OF PRESCHOOL

preschool-age children are not enrolled in any preschool programs (UNICEF, 2023). In low-income countries, only about 20 percent of preschool-aged children are enrolled in preschool, and those who are enrolled often are in crowded classrooms without trained teachers or stimulating curricula. According to UNICEF, universal access to preschool education should be a priority because it sets the stage for early learning, helps students succeed in school, and eventually promotes economic growth by keeping students in school to prepare for eventual participation in the labor market. The Sustainable Development Goals guiding the international development agenda through 2030 call for universal access to at least one year of preschool for all children globally.

What characterizes early childhood education in some high-income countries like Japan (shown here)?

Andreas Meichsner/Laif/Redux Pictures

What characterizes early childhood education in some low- and middle-income countries like Jamaica (shown here)?

Nik Wheeler/Corbis NX/Getty Images

Cognitive Development in Early Childhood

1 What Are Three Views of the Cognitive Changes That Occur in Early Childhood?

 Describe three views of the cognitive changes that occur in early childhood.

Piaget's Preoperational Stage

- According to Piaget, in the preoperational stage, which lasts from about 2 to 7 years of age, children cannot yet perform operations, which are reversible mental actions, but they begin to represent the world with words, images, and drawings; to form stable concepts; and to reason.

- During the symbolic function substage, which occurs between 2 and 4 years of age, children begin to mentally represent an object that is not present; their thought is limited by egocentrism and animism.

- During the intuitive thought substage, which stretches from about 4 to 7 years of age, children begin to reason and to bombard adults with questions. Thought at this substage is called intuitive because children seem so sure about their knowledge yet are unaware of how they know what they know. Centration and a lack of conservation also characterize the preoperational stage.

Vygotsky's Theory

- Vygotsky's theory represents a social constructivist approach to development. According to Vygotsky, children construct knowledge through social interaction, and they use language not only to communicate with others but also to plan, guide, and monitor their own behavior and to help them solve problems. His theory suggests that adults should access and use the child's zone of proximal development (ZPD), which is the range of tasks that are too difficult for children to master alone but that can be learned with the guidance and assistance of adults or more-skilled children.

- Vygotsky's theory also suggests that adults and peers should teach through scaffolding, which involves changing the level of support over the course of a teaching session, with the more-skilled person adjusting guidance to fit the student's current performance level.

Information Processing

- The child's ability to attend to stimuli dramatically improves during early childhood. Advances in executive attention and sustained attention are especially important in early childhood, but the young child still attends to the salient rather than the relevant features of a task. Significant improvement in short-term memory occurs during early childhood. With good prompts, young children's long-term memories can be accurate, although young children can be led into developing false memories. During the preschool years, children's memories take on more autobiographical characteristics.

- Advances in executive function, an umbrella-like concept that consists of a number of higher-level cognitive processes linked to the development of the prefrontal cortex, occur in early childhood. Executive function involves managing one's thoughts to engage in goal-directed behavior and to exercise self-control.

- Theory of mind is the awareness of one's own mental processes and the mental processes of others. Children begin to understand mental states involving perceptions, desires, and emotions from 18 months to 3 years of age; by 5 years of age a majority realize that people can have false beliefs. It is only beyond the preschool years that children have a deepening appreciation of the mind itself rather than just an understanding of mental states. Some children with autism have difficulty with aspects of theory of mind.

2 How Do Young Children Develop Language?

 Summarize how language develops in early childhood.

Understanding Phonology and Morphology

- Young children increase their grasp of language's rule systems. In terms of phonology, most young children become more sensitive to the sounds of spoken language. Berko's classic experiment demonstrated that young children understand morphological rules.

- Preschool children learn and apply rules of syntax involving how words should be ordered. In terms of semantics, vocabulary development increases dramatically during early childhood.

- Young children's conversational skills improve, they increase their sensitivity to the needs of others in conversation, and they learn to change their speech style to suit the situation.

- There has been increased interest in young children's literacy. Young children need to develop positive images of reading and writing skills through a supportive environment. Children should be active participants in their education and be immersed in a wide range of interesting and enjoyable listening, talking, writing, and reading experiences.

3 What Are Some Important Features of Young Children's Education?

 Evaluate different approaches to early childhood education.

- The child-centered kindergarten emphasizes the education of the whole child, with particular attention to individual variation, the process of learning, and the importance of play in development. The Montessori approach allows children to choose from a range of activities while teachers serve as facilitators. Developmentally appropriate practice focuses on the typical patterns of children (age appropriateness) and the uniqueness of each child (individual appropriateness). In contrast, developmentally inappropriate practice ignores the concrete, hands-on approach to learning.

- The U.S. government has tried to reduce poverty with programs such as Head Start. Model programs have been shown to have positive effects on children who live in poverty.

- Controversy surrounds early childhood education curricula. On the one side are the child-centered, constructivist advocates; on the other are those who advocate a direct instruction, academic approach. Another controversy involves whether universal preschool education should be provided for all U.S. 4-year-olds. A third controversy focuses on school readiness and whether early academic skills or socioemotional skills are more important in predicting later academic achievement.

key **terms**

animism
centration
child-centered kindergarten
conservation
developmentally appropriate
    practice (DAP)

egocentrism
executive attention
executive function
fast mapping
intuitive thought substage
Montessori approach

operations
preoperational stage
Project Head Start
scaffolding
short-term memory
social constructivist approach

sustained attention
symbolic function substage
theory of mind
zone of proximal development
    (ZPD)

key **people**

Jean Berko
Elena Bodrova
Stephanie Carlson

Maria Gartstein
Rochel Gelman
Barbel Inhelder

Deborah Leong
Maria Montessori
Jean Piaget

Mary Rothbart
Catherine Snow
Lev Vygotsky

improving the **lives of children**

STRATEGIES

Nourish the Young Child's Cognitive Development

What are some good strategies for helping young children develop their cognitive competencies?

- *Provide opportunities for the young child's development of symbolic thought.* Give the child ample opportunities to scribble and draw. Provide the child with opportunities to engage in make-believe play. Don't criticize the young child's art and play. Let the child's imagination flourish.

- *Engage children in activities that will improve their executive function.* A good resource for such activities is: http://developingchild.harvard.edu/science/key-concepts/executive-function/

- *Monitor young children's ability to delay gratification.* Delay of gratification is a key element of many aspects of children's competence. Create exercises and activities for young children to practice their delay of gratification.

- *Encourage exploration.* Let the child select many of the activities he or she wants to explore. Don't have the child do rigid paper-and-pencil exercises that involve rote learning. The young child should not be spending lots of time passively sitting, watching, and listening.

- *Be an active language partner with the young child.* Encourage the young child to speak in entire sentences instead of using single words. Be a good listener. Ask the child lots of questions. Don't spend time correcting the child's grammar; simply model correct grammar yourself when you talk with the child. Don't correct the young child's writing. Spend time selecting age-appropriate books for the young child. Read books with the young child.

- *Become sensitive to the child's zone of proximal development.* Monitor the child's level of cognitive functioning. Know what tasks the child can competently perform alone and those that are too difficult, even with your help. Guide and assist the child in the proper performance of skills and use of tools in the child's zone of proximal development. Warmly support the young child's practice of these skills.

- *Evaluate the quality of the child's early childhood education program.* Make sure the early childhood program the child attends involves developmentally appropriate education. The program should be age appropriate and appropriate for the individual child. It should not be a high-intensity, academic-success-at-all-costs program. Don't pressure the child to achieve at this age.

RESOURCES

Becoming Brilliant: What Science Tells Us About Raising Successful Children (2016)

Roberta Michnick Golinkoff and Kathy Hirsh-Pasek
Washington, DC: American Psychological Association

Becoming Brilliant is a terrific book by two leading developmental psychologists that provides up-to-date recommendations for how children should be educated. They emphasize that too often schools give attention only to content and not enough to other key processes that will help children succeed in life: collaboration, communication, critical thinking, creative innovation, and confidence.

The Montessori Toddler: A Parents' Guide to Raising a Curious and Responsible Human Being (2019)

Simone Davies
New York: Workman Publishing

This cleverly illustrated book provides guidance for parents and other caregivers in applying many of the basic principles and practices of Montessori curriculum and pedagogy to support the development of young children.

National Association for the Education of Young Children (NAEYC)

800-424-2460
www.naeyc.org

NAEYC is an important professional organization that advocates for young children and has developed guidelines for a number of dimensions of early childhood education. It publishes the excellent journal *Young Children*.

The Gardener and the Carpenter: What the New Science of Child Development Tells Us About the Relationship Between Parents and Children (2017)

Alison Gopnik
New York: Macmillan

An excellent book for parents who want to understand how young children learn and how they can support their young children's cognitive development. Gopnik describes research on the importance of play in children's learning and the implications of these findings for parent-child relationships.

Executive Functions in Children's Everyday Lives: A Handbook for Professionals in Applied Psychology (2017)

Maureen J. Hoskyn, Grace Iarocci, and Arlene R. Young (Editors)
Oxford University Press

An exploration of many aspects of children's executive function, including chapters on the supportive role parents can play as well as how important executive function is to children's schooling and academic achievement.

chapter 10

SOCIOEMOTIONAL DEVELOPMENT IN EARLY CHILDHOOD

chapter **outline**

Rawpixel/Getty Images

Like many children, Sarah Newland loves animals. During a trip to the zoo at age 4, Sarah learned about an animal that was a member of an endangered species, and she became motivated to help. With her mother's guidance, she baked lots of cakes and cookies, and then sold them on the sidewalk outside her home. She was excited about making $35 from the cake and cookie sales, and she mailed the money to the World Wildlife Fund. Several weeks later, Sarah received a letter thanking her for the donation and requesting more money. Sarah was devastated because she thought she had taken care of the animal problem. Her mother consoled her and explained that the endangered animal problem and many others are so big that it takes continued help from many people to solve them. Her mother's guidance when Sarah was a young child must have worked because by the end of elementary school, Sarah had begun helping out at a child-care center and working with her mother to provide meals to people who were homeless.

As Sarah's mother did, sensitive parents can make a difference in encouraging young children's sense of morality. Just as parents support and guide their children to become good readers, musicians, or athletes, they also play key roles in young children's socioemotional development (*Source:* Kantrowitz, 1991).

topical connections   looking **back**

In "Socioemotional Development in Infancy" you learned that infants' socioemotional development reflects considerable progress as their caregivers (especially their parents) socialize them and as they develop more sophisticated ways of initiating social interactions with others. Development of a secure attachment is a key aspect of infancy, and the development of autonomy in the second year of life also signals an important accomplishment. As children move through infancy, it is important for caregivers to guide them in regulating their emotions. Temperament also is a central characteristic of the infant's profile, and some temperament styles are more adaptive than others. The use of child-care providers has become increasingly common in recent years, and the quality of this care varies considerably. Parents continue to play key roles in children's development in the early childhood period, but peers begin to play more important roles as well.

preview

In early childhood, children's emotional lives and personalities develop in significant ways as their small worlds widen. In addition to the continuing influence of family relationships, peers take on a more significant role in children's development and play fills the days of many young children's lives.

1 What Characterizes Young Children's Emotional and Personality Development?

 LG1 Discuss emotional and personality development in early childhood.

| The Self | Emotional Development | Moral Development | Gender |

Many changes characterize young children's socioemotional development in early childhood. Their developing minds and social experiences produce remarkable advances in the development of their self-understanding, emotional maturity, moral understanding, and gender awareness.

THE SELF

During the second year of life, children make considerable progress in self-recognition. In the early childhood years, young children develop in many ways that enable them to enhance their self-understanding.

What characterizes young children's self-understanding?

Juanmonino/Getty Images

Initiative versus Guilt In "Introduction" you read about Erik Erikson's (1968) eight developmental stages that are encountered during certain time periods in the human life span. Erikson's first stage, trust versus mistrust, describes what he considers to be the main developmental task of infancy. Erikson's psychosocial stage associated with early childhood is *initiative versus guilt.* By now, children have become convinced that they are persons of their own; during early childhood they begin to discover what kind of person they will become. They identify intensely with their parents, who most of the time appear to them to be powerful and beautiful, although often unreasonable, disagreeable, and sometimes even dangerous. During early childhood, children use their perceptual, motor, cognitive, and language skills to make things happen. They have a surplus of energy that permits them to forget failures quickly and to approach new areas that seem desirable—even if dangerous—with undiminished zest and an increased sense of direction. On their own *initiative,* then, children at this stage exuberantly move out into a wider social world.

The great governor of initiative is *guilt.* Young children's initiative and enthusiasm may bring them not only rewards but also guilt, which lowers self-esteem.

Self-Understanding and Understanding Others A number of research studies have revealed that young children are more psychologically aware—of themselves and others—than used to be thought (Thompson, 2020). This increased psychological awareness reflects young children's expanding psychological sophistication.

Self-Understanding In Erikson's portrait of early childhood, the young child clearly has begun to develop **self-understanding,** which is the representation of self, the substance and content of self-conceptions (Harter, 2015). Though not the whole of personal identity, self-understanding provides its rational underpinnings.

Early self-understanding involves self-recognition. In early childhood, young children think that the self can be described by material characteristics such as size, shape, and color. They distinguish themselves from others through many physical and material attributes. Says 4-year-old Shayla, "I'm different from Julia because I have brown hair and she has blond hair." Says 4-year-old Rafael, "I am different from Owen because I am taller, and I am different from my sister because I have a bicycle." Physical activities are also a central component of the self in

self-understanding The child's cognitive representation of self; the substance and content of the child's self-conceptions.

early childhood. For example, preschool children often describe themselves in terms of activities such as play. In sum, during early childhood, children often provide self-descriptions that involve body attributes, material possessions, and physical activities.

Although young children mainly describe themselves in terms of concrete, observable features and action tendencies, at about 4 to 5 years of age, as they hear others use psychological trait and emotion terms, they begin to include these in their own self-descriptions (Starmans, 2017). Thus, in a self-description, a 4-year-old might say, "I'm not scared. I'm always happy."

Many young children's self-descriptions are typically unrealistically positive, as reflected in the comment of the 4-year-old above who claims to be always happy, which is not true (Harter, 2015, 2016). This optimism occurs because they don't yet distinguish between their desired competence and their actual competence, tend to confuse ability and effort (thinking that differences in ability can be changed as easily as can differences in effort), don't engage in spontaneous social comparison of their abilities with those of others, and tend to compare their present abilities with what they could do at an earlier age (which usually makes them look quite good).

However, as in virtually all areas of human development, there are individual variations in young children's self-conceptions. In addition, there is increasing evidence that some children are vulnerable to negative self-attributions (Hendriks, Meesters, & Muris, 2020). For example, one study revealed that preschool children had a lower self-concept if they had insecure attachments with their fathers or mothers, and even more so if they were rejected by their peers (Pinto & others, 2015). This research indicates that young children's generally optimistic self-perceptions do not protect them from adverse, stressful family and peer group conditions.

Understanding Others   Children also make advances in their understanding of others in early childhood (Thompson, 2020). Young children's theory of mind includes understanding that other people have emotions and desires (Goffin, Kochanska, & Yoon, 2020). And, at about 4 to 5 years of age, children not only start describing themselves in terms of psychological traits but also begin to perceive others in terms of psychological traits. Thus, a 4-year-old might say, "My teacher is nice."

To understand others, it is necessary to take their perspective. **Perspective taking** is the social cognitive process involved in assuming the perspective of others and understanding their thoughts and feelings. Executive function is at work in perspective taking (Khu, Chambers, & Graham, 2020). Among the executive functions called on when young children engage in perspective taking are cognitive inhibition (controlling one's own thoughts to consider the perspectives of others) and cognitive flexibility (seeing situations in different ways).

Perspective taking in young children also is linked to the quality of their social relationships. One study found that higher perspective-taking ability in 2-year-olds predicted more stable mother-child attachment later in the preschool years (Meins, Bureau, & Ferryhough, 2018).

One type of understanding that children need to develop is an awareness that people don't always accurately describe their own beliefs (Quintanilla, Giménez-Dasí, & Gaviria, 2018). Researchers have found that even 4-year-olds understand that people may make statements that aren't true to obtain what they want or to avoid trouble (Nancarrow & others, 2018). One illustrative study revealed that 4- and 5-year-olds were increasingly skeptical of another child's claim to be sick when the children were informed that the child was motivated to avoid having to go to camp (Gee & Heyman, 2007). Another study compared preschool children's trust in an expert's comments (Landrum, Mills, & Johnston, 2013). In this study, in one condition, 5-year-olds trusted the expert's claim more than did 3-year-olds. However, in other conditions, preschoolers tended to trust a nice non-expert more than a mean expert, indicating that young children often are likely to believe someone who is nice to them even if that person is not an expert.

Another important aspect of understanding others involves understanding joint commitments. As children approach their third birthday, their collaborative interactions with others increasingly involve obligations to the partner (Warneken, 2018). One study revealed that 5-year-olds were more likely than 3-year-olds to understand when they and a partner were committed to the same goal of collaborating in joint activities (Kachel & Tomasello, 2019).

Individual differences characterize young children's social understanding (Laurent & others, 2018). Some young children are better than others at understanding what people are feeling and what they desire, for example. To some

perspective taking The social cognitive process involved in assuming the perspective of others and understanding their thoughts and feelings.

Young children are more psychologically aware of themselves and others than used to be thought. Some children are better than others at understanding people's feelings and desires—and, to some degree, these individual differences are influenced by conversations caregivers have with young children about feelings and desires.
Don Hammond/DesignPics

degree, these individual differences are linked to conversations caregivers have with young children about other people's feelings and desires, and children's opportunities to observe others talking about people's feelings and desires (Ruffman & others, 2018). For example, a parent might say to a 3-year-old, "Think about how Raphael felt when you hit him. You would feel sad if someone hit you, and Raphael felt sad, too."

Developing an understanding of how others think and feel is important to social interactions. Young children's ability to understand their own and others' emotions precedes advances in their theory of mind (Fu & others, 2023). The research has indicated that a better basic understanding of emotions in early childhood enabled them to develop a more advanced understanding of others' perspectives.

Both the extensive theory of mind research and the recent research on young children's social understanding underscore that young children are not as egocentric as Piaget and others had envisioned (Decety, Meidenbauer, & Cowell, 2018). The concept of egocentrism has become so ingrained in people's thinking about young children that too often the current research on social awareness in infancy and early childhood has been overlooked. Research increasingly shows that young children are more socially sensitive and perceptive than was previously envisioned, suggesting that parents and teachers can help them to better understand and interact in the social world by how they interact with them (Thompson, 2020). If young children are seeking to better understand various mental and emotional states (intentions, goals, feelings, desires) that they know underlie people's actions, then talking with them about these internal states can improve young children's understanding of them (Burdelski, 2019). However, the debate continues about whether young children are socially sensitive or basically egocentric.

Whichever side is taken in this debate, it is important to underscore that social interactions and relationships with others contribute significantly to young children's development of the self and understanding of others. In Thompson's (2013, p. 113) view, "When caregivers exuberantly applaud their child's accomplishments, focus their young child's attention on the consequences of misbehavior, acknowledge shared intentions, work to repair affective mismatches, or talk with their child about emotions, they act as *relational catalysts,* fostering the child's socioemotional growth and helping to refine the child's representations of who they are (and) what other people are like."

EMOTIONAL DEVELOPMENT

The young child's growing awareness of self is linked to the ability to feel an expanding range of emotions. Young children, like adults, experience many emotions during the course of a day. Their emotional development in early childhood allows them to try to make sense of other people's emotional reactions and to begin to control their own emotions (Harrington & others, 2020).

Expressing Emotions   Recall that even young infants experience emotions such as joy and fear, but to experience *self-conscious emotions,* children must be able to refer to themselves and be aware of themselves as distinct from others (Lewis, 2020). Pride, shame, embarrassment, and guilt are examples of self-conscious emotions. Self-conscious emotions do not appear to develop until self-awareness emerges at around 18 months of age. In one study, a broad capacity for self-evaluative emotion was present in the preschool years and was linked to young children's empathetic concern (Ross, 2017). In this study, young children's moral pride, pride in response to achievement, and resilience to shame were linked to a greater tendency to engage in spontaneous helping.

During the early childhood years, emotions such as pride and guilt become more common, and they are especially influenced by parents' responses to children's behavior. For example, a young child may experience shame when a parent says, "You should feel bad about biting your sister." Parents' use of different discipline strategies to invoke shame differs across cultural contexts and is especially common in China (Fung, Li, & Lam, 2017).

Understanding Emotions   Among the most important changes in emotional development in early childhood is an increased understanding of emotion (Hare & others, 2021). During early childhood, young children increasingly understand that certain situations are likely to evoke particular emotions, facial expressions indicate specific emotions, emotions affect behavior, and emotions can be used to influence others' emotions (Pollak, Camras, & Cole, 2019). In an experiment in which toddlers either did or did not participate in conversations about emotions

A young child expressing the emotion of shame, which occurs when children evaluate their actions as not living up to standards. A child experiencing shame wishes to hide or disappear. *Why is shame called a self-conscious emotion?*

Sappington Todd/BLOOMimage/Getty Images

developmental connection

Cognitive Theory

In Piaget's view, young children are egocentric in that they don't distinguish between their perspective and someone else's. Connect to "Cognitive Development in Early Childhood."

after listening to emotion-based stories, those who had participated in the conversations were more prosocial than those who had not (Ornaghi & others, 2017).

Between 2 and 4 years of age, children increase the number of terms they use to describe emotions. During this time, they are also learning about the causes and consequences of feelings (Zinsser, Gordon, & Jiang, 2021). When they are 4 to 5 years of age, children show an increased ability to reflect on emotions. They also begin to understand that the same event can elicit different feelings in different people. Moreover, they show a growing awareness that they need to manage their emotions to meet social standards.

Regulating Emotions Many researchers consider the growth of emotion regulation in children as fundamental to the development of social competence (Harrington & others, 2020). Emotion regulation can be conceptualized as an important component of self-regulation or of executive function. Recall that executive function is thought to be a key concept in describing the young child's higher-level cognitive functioning (Bell & Broomell, 2021). Cybele Raver and her colleagues (Blair, Raver, & Finegood, 2016; Raver & others, 2012, 2013) are using interventions, such as increasing caregiver emotional expressiveness, to improve young children's emotion regulation and reduce behavior problems in Head Start families. To read in greater detail about one of Cybele Raver's studies, see *Connecting with Research*.

connecting with research

Caregivers' Emotional Expressiveness, Children's Emotion Regulation, and Behavior Problems in Head Start Children

Key Points:

- Children whose caregivers expressed more negative emotions and children with poorer emotion regulation had more internalizing behavior problems.
- Children whose caregivers expressed more positive emotions had fewer externalizing behavior problems.

A foundational study by Dana McCoy and Cybele Raver (2011) explored links between caregivers' reports of their positive and negative emotional expressiveness, observations of young children's emotion regulation, and teachers' reports of the children's internalizing and externalizing behavior problems. The study focused on 97 children, most of whom were Black or Latino and whose mean age was 4 years and 3 months. The other participants in the study were the children's primary caregivers (90 mothers, 5 fathers, and 2 grandmothers).

To assess caregiver expressiveness, caregivers were asked to provide ratings on a scale from 1 (never/rarely) to 9 (very frequently) for 7 items that reflect caregiver expressiveness, such as "telling family members how happy you are" and "expressing anger at someone's carelessness." Children's emotion regulation was assessed with (a) the emotion regulation part of the PSRA (preschool self-regulation assessment) in which observers rated young children's behavior on 4 delay tasks, 3 executive function tasks, and 3 compliance tasks; (b) an assessment report on children's emotion and emotion regulation; and (c) observations of the children's real-time emotion regulation related to positive emotion (expressions of happiness, for example) and negative emotion (expressions of anger or irritability, for example). Children's internalizing and externalizing behavior problems

What did Dana McCoy and Cybele Raver discover about the importance of caregivers' emotions and children's emotion regulation in children's development?

Tatyana Dzemileva/Shutterstock

were rated by their teachers, who reported the extent to which the children had shown such behavioral problems in the last 3 months.

The researchers found that a higher level of caregiver negativity and a lower level of children's emotion regulation independently were linked to more internalizing behavior problems in the young Head Start children. Also, caregivers' reports of their positive emotional expressiveness were associated with a lower level of young children's externalizing behavior problems. The findings demonstrate the importance of family emotional climate and young children's emotion regulation in the development of young children.

The study you just read about was correlational in nature. If you were interested in conducting an experimental study of the effects of caregivers' emotional expressiveness and children's emotion regulation on children's problem behaviors, how would you conduct the study differently?

What are some differences in emotion-coaching (shown here) and emotion-dismissing parents?

kali9/E+/Getty Images

Emotion-Coaching and Emotion-Dismissing Parents Parents are important in helping young children regulate their emotions (England-Mason & Gonzalez, 2020). Depending on how they talk with their children about emotion, parents can be described as taking an *emotion-coaching* or an *emotion-dismissing* approach (Lobo & others, 2021). The distinction between these approaches is most evident in the way the parent deals with the child's negative emotions (anger, frustration, sadness, and so on). *Emotion-coaching parents* monitor their children's emotions, view their children's negative emotions as opportunities for teaching, assist them in labeling emotions, and coach them in how to deal effectively with emotions. In contrast, *emotion-dismissing parents* view their role as to deny, ignore, or change negative emotions. The pattern of emotion socialization children receive from both mothers and fathers is related to children's social competence and behavior problems (Miller-Slough & others, 2018).

Researchers have observed that emotion-coaching parents interact with their children in a less rejecting manner, use more scaffolding and praise, and are more nurturant than are emotion-dismissing parents (England-Mason & Gonzalez, 2020). Moreover, the children of emotion-coaching parents are better at soothing themselves when they get upset, more effective in regulating their negative affect, focus their attention better, and have fewer behavior problems than the children of emotion-dismissing parents (Gottman, 2017).

Knowledge of their children's emotional world can help parents guide their children's emotional development and teach them how to cope effectively with problems. Children who are better at understanding and regulating emotions are then able to form better relationships with peers and teachers, perform better academically, and show fewer behavioral problems (Denham, 2023).

What types of positive emotions are associated with young children's moral development?

Stockbyte/Getty Images

moral development Development that involves thoughts, feelings, and behaviors regarding rules and conventions about what people should do in their interactions with other people.

conscience An internal regulator of standards of right and wrong that involves an integration of moral thought, feeling, and behavior.

Regulation of Emotion and Peer Relations Emotions play a strong role in determining the success of a child's peer relationships (Herd & Kim-Spoon, 2021). Moody and emotionally negative children are more likely to experience rejection by their peers, whereas emotionally positive children are more popular. More generally, studies have shown clear links between better emotion regulation and better peer relationships and fewer behavioral and emotional problems (Denham, 2023). These social relationship and emotion regulation processes appear to operate similarly across a variety of cultural contexts (Alonso-Alberca & others, 2019).

MORAL DEVELOPMENT

Moral development involves the development of thoughts, feelings, and behaviors regarding rules and conventions about what people should do in their interactions with other people. Major developmental theories have focused on different aspects of moral development (Bock & others, 2020; Jensen, 2020; Killen & Dahl, 2018; Narváez, 2018; Turiel & Gingo, 2017).

Moral Feelings Feelings of anxiety and guilt are central to the account of moral development provided by Sigmund Freud's psychoanalytic theory. The **conscience** punishes the child for behaviors disapproved by the parents, making the child feel guilty and worthless. Freud's ideas are not backed by research, but guilt certainly can motivate moral behavior. Researchers can examine the extent to which children feel guilty when they misbehave. Grazyna Kochanska and her colleagues (Goffin, Kochanska, & Yoon, 2020; Kim & Kochanska, 2017; Kochanska & Kim, 2013; Kochanska & others, 2010) have conducted a number of studies that explore children's conscience development. Reflecting the presence of a conscience in young children, Kochanska and her colleagues, as well as other researchers, have found that young children are aware of right and wrong, have the capacity to show empathy toward others, experience guilt, indicate discomfort following a transgression, and are sensitive to violating rules (Malti, 2016).

A major focus of interest regarding young children's conscience involves children's relationships with their caregivers (Goffin, Kochanska, & Yoon, 2020). Especially important in this regard is the emergence of young children's willingness to embrace the values of their parents, an orientation that flows from a positive, close relationship (Knafo-Noam, Barni, &

Schwartz, 2020). For example, children who are securely attached are more likely to internalize their parents' values and rules (Thompson, 2019).

Other emotions, however, also contribute to the child's moral development, including positive feelings. One important example is **empathy,** which is responding to another person's feelings with an emotion that echoes the other's feelings (Gallant, Lavis, & Mahy, 2020).

To empathize is not just to sympathize; it is to put oneself in another's place emotionally. **Sympathy** is an emotional response to another person in which the observer feels sad or concerned about the other person's well-being (Eisenberg, 2020). Feeling sympathy often motivates moral behavior. For example, one study found that young children's sympathy predicted whether they would share their possessions with others (Ongley & Malti, 2014).

Infants have the capacity for some purely empathic responses, but empathy often requires the discerning of another's inner psychological states, or what is called *perspective taking*, which we discussed earlier in our coverage of self-development. Learning how to identify a wide range of emotional states in others and to anticipate what kinds of action will improve another person's emotional state help to advance children's moral development (Decety, Meidenbauer, & Cowell, 2018).

Today, many child developmentalists believe that both positive feelings—such as empathy, sympathy, admiration, and self-esteem—and negative feelings—such as anger, outrage, shame, and guilt—contribute to children's moral development (Eisenberg, 2020). When strongly experienced, these emotions influence children to act in accord with standards of right and wrong (Malti, Galarneau, & Peplak, 2021). These emotional underpinnings inform children's development of moral feelings across a wide range of cultural contexts (Narváez, 2019).

Emotions such as empathy, shame, guilt, and anxiety over other people's violations of standards are present early in development and undergo developmental change throughout childhood and beyond (Spinrad & Eisenberg, 2019). Also, connections between these emotions can occur, and the connections may influence children's development. For example, in one study, participants' tendency to feel guilty, when combined with their empathy, predicted an increase in prosocial behavior (Torstveit, Sutterlin, & Lugo, 2016).

Moral emotions provide a natural base for children's acquisition of moral values, motivating them to pay close attention to moral events. However, moral emotions do not operate in a vacuum to build a child's moral awareness, and they are not sufficient in themselves to generate moral responses. They do not give the "substance" of moral regulation—the rules, values, and standards of behavior that children need to understand and act on. Moral emotions are inextricably interwoven with the cognitive and social aspects of children's development (Narváez, 2019).

Moral Reasoning Jean Piaget (1932) extensively observed and interviewed children from the ages of 4 through 12. Piaget watched children play marbles to learn how they thought about and used the game's rules. He also asked children about ethical issues—theft, lies, punishment, and justice, for example. Piaget concluded that children go through two distinct stages of moral development:

How is this child's moral thinking likely to be different about stealing a cookie depending on whether he is in Piaget's heteronomous or autonomous stage?
Fuse/Getty Images

- From 4 to 7 years of age, children display **heteronomous morality,** the first stage of moral development in Piaget's theory. Children think of justice and rules as unchangeable properties of the world, removed from the control of people. From 7 to 10 years, children transition gradually into the next stage.

- From about 10 years of age and older, children show **autonomous morality.** They become aware that rules and laws are created by people, and, in judging an action, they consider the actor's intentions as well as the consequences.

Because young children are "heteronomous moralists," they judge the rightness or goodness of behavior by considering its consequences, not the intentions of the actor. For example, to the heteronomous moralist, breaking 12 cups accidentally is worse than breaking one cup intentionally. The heteronomous thinker also believes that rules are unchangeable and are handed down by all-powerful authorities. When Piaget suggested to young children that they use new rules in a game of marbles, they resisted. By contrast, older children—moral

empathy An affective response to another's feelings with an emotional response that is similar to the other's feelings.

sympathy An emotional response to another person in which the observer feels sad or concerned about the individual's well-being.

heteronomous morality The first stage of moral development in Piaget's theory, occurring from approximately 4 to 7 years of age. Justice and rules are conceived of as unchangeable properties of the world, removed from the control of people.

autonomous morality The second stage of moral development in Piaget's theory, displayed by older children (about 10 years of age and older). The child becomes aware that rules and laws are created by people and that, in judging an action, one should consider the actor's intentions as well as the consequences.

developmental **connection**
Cognitive Theory
Lawrence Kohlberg's theory, like Piaget's, emphasizes that peers play a much stronger role in the development of moral thinking than parents do. Connect to "Socioemotional Development in Early Childhood."

autonomists—accept change and recognize that rules are merely convenient conventions, subject to change. As children develop into "autonomous moralists," intentions become more important than consequences.

The heteronomous thinker also believes in **immanent justice,** the concept that if a rule is broken, punishment will be delivered immediately. The young child believes that a violation is connected automatically to its punishment. Thus, young children often look around worriedly after doing something wrong, expecting inevitable punishment. Older children recognize that punishment occurs only if someone witnesses the wrongdoing and that, even then, punishment is not inevitable.

How do these changes in moral reasoning occur? Piaget argued that as children develop, they become more sophisticated in thinking about social matters, especially about the possibilities and conditions of cooperation. Piaget emphasized that this social understanding comes about through the mutual give-and-take of peer relations. In the peer group, where others have power and status similar to the child's, plans are negotiated and coordinated, and disagreements are reasoned about and eventually settled. Parent-child relations, in which parents have power and children do not, are less likely to advance moral reasoning because rules are often handed down through the parent's authority.

However, young children are not as egocentric as Piaget once envisioned. Thompson (2020) further elaborated on this view, arguing that recent research indicates that young children often show a non-egocentric awareness of others' goals, feelings, and desires and how such internal states are influenced by the actions of others. These ties between advances in moral understanding and theory of mind indicate that young children possess cognitive resources that allow them to be aware of others' intentions and know when someone violates a moral prohibition. One study of 3- and 5-year-olds found that they were less likely to offer rewards to a puppet character that they had previously observed being selfish to another individual (Vogelsang & Tomasello, 2016).

However, because of limitations in their self-control skills, social understanding, and cognitive flexibility, young children's moral advancements often are inconsistent and vary across situations. They still have a long way to go before they have the capacity to develop a consistent moral character and make ethical judgments.

Moral Behavior   The behavioral and social cognitive theory of child development focuses on moral behavior rather than on moral reasoning. It holds that the processes of reinforcement, punishment, and imitation explain the development of moral behavior (Grusec & Davidov, 2021). When children are rewarded for behavior that is consistent with laws and social conventions, they are likely to repeat that behavior. When models who behave morally are provided, children are likely to adopt their actions. And, when children are punished for immoral behavior, those behaviors are likely to be reduced or eliminated. However, because punishment may have adverse side effects, as we discuss later in this chapter, it needs to be used judiciously and cautiously.

If a 4-year-old boy has been rewarded by his mother for telling the truth when he breaks a glass at home, does that mean he is likely to tell the truth to his preschool teacher when he knocks over a vase and breaks it? Not necessarily; the situation influences behavior. More than half a century ago, a comprehensive study of thousands of children in many situations—at home, at school, and at a religious facility, for example—found that the totally honest child was virtually nonexistent, and so was the child who cheated in all situations (Hartshorne & May, 1928–1930). Behavioral and social cognitive researchers emphasize that what children do in one situation is often only weakly related to what they do in other situations. A child might cheat in class but not in a game; a child might steal a piece of candy when alone but not steal it when others are present. Nevertheless, although moral behavior is influenced by situational determinants, some people are more likely than others to cheat, lie, and steal (O'Reilly & Doerr, 2020).

When provided with models who behave morally, individuals are likely to adopt their actions. In one experiment, 5- to 9-year-old children were randomly assigned to conditions in which they viewed peers or adults modeling prosocial sharing or antisocial stealing (Misch & Dunham, 2021). Children then had the chance to donate stickers to others or take them away privately. Children who had watched the prosocial model were more likely to donate than take away stickers, and younger children (5 to 6 years old) were especially susceptible to peer

developmental **connection**

Social Cognitive Theory

What are the main themes of Bandura's social cognitive theory? Connect to "Introduction."

influence in their own behavior when the peers were more similar to themselves. These findings suggest that a range of situational factors can influence moral behavior.

Social cognitive theorists also believe that the ability to resist temptation is closely tied to the development of self-control (Mischel, 2014). To achieve this self-control, children must learn to delay gratification. According to social cognitive theorists, cognitive factors are important in the child's development of self-control (Bandura, 2018).

Parenting and Young Children's Moral Development   Young children's relationship with their parents is an important aspect of moral development (Eisenberg, 2020). Especially important in this regard is the emergence of young children's willingness to embrace the values of their parents, which flows from a positive, close relationship. For example, children who are securely attached are more likely to internalize their parents' values and rules (Thompson, 2020).

In Ross Thompson's (2020) view, young children are moral apprentices, striving to understand what is moral. They can be assisted in this quest by the "sensitive guidance of adult mentors in the home who provide lessons about morality in everyday experiences" (Thompson, Meyer, & McGinley, 2006, p. 290). An important parenting strategy is to proactively avert potential misbehavior by children before it takes place (Padilla-Walker & Son, 2019). With younger children, being proactive means using diversion, such as distracting their attention or moving them to alternative activities. With older children, being proactive may involve talking with them about values that the parents deem important. Transmitting these values can help older children and adolescents to resist the temptations that inevitably emerge in contexts such as peer relations and media exposure beyond the scope of direct parental monitoring.

What are some aspects of relationships between parents and children that contribute to children's moral development?

Tanya Constantine/Blend Images/Getty Images

GENDER

Gender refers to the socially constructed characteristics of people as boys/men and girls/women. It is distinct from the biologically defined sex type of female and male. **Gender identity** involves a sense of one's own gender, including knowledge, understanding, and acceptance of being a boy/man, girl/woman, or another gender (Erickson-Schroth & Davis, 2021). One aspect of gender identity involves knowing whether you are a girl or boy or another gender (Best & Puzio, 2019). Until recently, it was thought that this aspect of gender identity emerged at about 2½ years of age. However, a study that examined the use and recognition of gender labels and gender-typed appearance revealed that gender identity likely begins to emerge before 2 years of age (Halim & others, 2017). In this study, mothers' gender role attitudes were not related to their 2-year-olds' gender-typed appearance, but 2-year-olds' own ability to recognize and use gender labels was related to their gender-typed appearance. The study suggests that children are aware of gender from a very early age and are motivated to adhere to gender stereotypes by dressing in traditionally gendered ways. Another study revealed that sex-typed toy play (boys playing with cars and girls with dolls, for example) during the preschool years predicted sex-typed behaviors five years later, regardless of whether children were being reared by lesbian, gay, or straight parents (Li, Kung, & Hines, 2017).

Gender roles are sets of expectations that prescribe how girls/women or boys/men should think, act, and feel. During the preschool years, most children increasingly act in ways that match their culture's gender roles. **Gender typing** refers to acquisition of a traditional masculine or feminine role. For example, fighting is more characteristic of a traditional masculine role and crying is more characteristic of a traditional feminine role (Helgeson, 2020).

How is gender influenced by biology? By children's social experiences? By cognitive factors?

Biological Influences   Biology plays a role in gender development. Among the possible biological influences are chromosomes, hormones, and evolution (Antfolk, 2017; Hyde & others, 2019; Johnson, 2017).

gender identity The sense of one's own gender, including knowledge, understanding, and acceptance of being a boy/man, girl/woman, or another gender.

gender role A set of expectations that prescribes how girls/women or boys/men should think, act, and feel.

gender typing Acquisition of a traditional masculine or feminine role.

Chromosomes and Hormones Biologists have learned a great deal about how sex differences develop. Recall that humans normally have 46 chromosomes arranged in pairs (see "Biological Beginnings"). The 23rd pair consists of a combination of X and Y chromosomes, usually two X chromosomes in a female and an X and a Y in a male. In the first few weeks of gestation, however, female and male embryos look alike.

Males start to differ from females when genes on the Y chromosome in the male embryo trigger the development of testes rather than ovaries; the testes secrete copious amounts of the class of hormones known as androgens, which lead to the development of male sex organs. Low levels of androgens in the female embryo allow the normal development of female sex organs.

Thus, hormones play a key role in the development of sex differences (Hyde & others, 2019). The two main classes of sex hormones are estrogens and androgens, which are secreted by the *gonads* (ovaries in females, testes in males). *Estrogens,* such as estradiol, influence the development of female genitals and secondary physical sex characteristics. *Androgens,* such as testosterone, promote the development of male secondary physical sex characteristics. Sex hormones also can influence children's socioemotional development. One study revealed that prenatal androgen exposure was related to preschool children's gender-typed behavior (Spencer & others, 2021).

The Evolutionary Psychology View How might physical differences between the sexes give rise to psychological differences between males and females? Evolutionary psychology offers one answer. According to evolutionary psychology, adaptation during human evolution produced psychological differences between men and women (Buss, 2020). Because of their differing roles in reproduction, men and women faced differing pressures when the human species was evolving (Thoni, Volk, & Cortina, 2021). In particular, because having multiple sexual liaisons improves the likelihood that men will pass on their genes, natural selection favored men who adopted short-term mating strategies. These are strategies that allow a man to win the competition with other men to be attractive to women. Therefore, say evolutionary psychologists, men evolved dispositions that favor violence, competition, and risk taking (Lewis, Al-Shawaf, & Buss, 2021).

In contrast, according to evolutionary psychologists and biologists, women's contributions to the gene pool were improved when they secured resources that ensured that their offspring would survive; this outcome was promoted by obtaining long-term mates who could provide their offspring with resources and protection (Buss, 2020). As a consequence, natural selection favored women who devoted effort to parenting and chose successful, ambitious mates who could provide their offspring with resources and protection. The evidence for this binary or "dimorphism" between males and females is found in many animal species (Morrison, Epperson, & Bale, 2020).

Critics of evolutionary psychology argue that its hypotheses are backed by speculations about prehistory, not evidence, and that in any event people are not locked into behavior that was adaptive in the evolutionary past. Critics also claim that the evolutionary view pays little attention to cultural and individual variations in gender differences (Gangestad & Chang, 2020).

Social Influences Many social scientists do not think the cause of psychological gender differences is biological dispositions. Rather, they argue that these differences are due to social experiences. Explanations for how gender differences come about through experience include both social and cognitive theories (Pang & Baumann, 2020).

Social Theories of Gender Three main social theories of gender have been proposed—social role theory, psychoanalytic theory, and social cognitive theory. Alice Eagly (2022) proposed **social role theory,** which states that psychological gender differences result from the contrasting roles of women and men. In most cultures around the world, women have less access to power and status than men, and they control fewer resources (UNICEF, 2020). Compared with men, women perform more domestic work, spend fewer hours in paid employment, receive lower pay, and are more thinly represented in the highest levels of organizations. In Eagly's view, as women adapted to roles with less power and less status in society, they showed more cooperative, less dominant profiles than men. Thus, the social hierarchy and division of labor are important causes of gender differences in power, assertiveness, and nurturing behavior (Eagly, 2022).

First imagine that this is a photograph of a baby girl. *What expectations would you have of her?* Then imagine that this is a photograph of a baby boy. *What expectations would you have of him?*

Kwame Zikomo/Purestock/SuperStock

social role theory Eagly's theory that psychological gender differences are caused by the contrasting social roles of women and men.

The **psychoanalytic theory of gender** stems from Freud's view that the preschool child develops a sexual attraction to the opposite-sex parent. This is the process known as the Oedipus complex (for boys) or Electra complex (for girls). At 5 or 6 years of age, the child renounces this attraction because of anxious feelings. Subsequently, the child identifies with the same-sex parent, unconsciously adopting the same-sex parent's characteristics. However, this theory has been discarded, and developmentalists have observed that gender development does not proceed as Freud proposed (Blakemore, Berenbaum, & Liben, 2009). Children become gender-typed much earlier than 5 or 6 years of age, and they become masculine or feminine even when the same-sex parent is not present in the family.

The social cognitive approach provides an alternative explanation of how children develop gender-typed behavior. According to the **social cognitive theory of gender,** children's gender development occurs through observing and imitating what other people say and do, and through being rewarded and punished for behaviors believed to be appropriate or inappropriate for their gender (Coyne & others, 2021). From birth onward, boys and girls are treated differently. When infants and toddlers show gender differences, adults tend to reward them. Parents often use rewards and punishments to teach their daughters to be feminine ("You are being a good girl when you play gently with your doll") and their sons to be masculine ("A boy as big as you is not supposed to cry"). Parents, however, are only one of many sources through which children learn gender roles (Coyle & Liben, 2020). Culture, schools, peers, the media, and other family members also provide gender-role models. For example, children learn about gender from observing adults in the neighborhood and engaging in screen time. As children get older, peers become increasingly important. Let's take a closer look at the influence of parents and peers.

Parental Influences   Parents, by action, by example, and by virtue of their own gender identity and expression, influence their children's gender development (Erickson-Schroth & Davis, 2021). Both mothers and fathers are psychologically important to their children's gender development (Tenenbaum & May, 2014). Cultures around the world, however, tend to give mothers and fathers different roles (Chen & Liu, 2016). For example, a study of 15- to 39-month-olds found that mothers tended to protect young children from distress, while fathers were more likely to help them in coping with frustration (Deichmann & Ahnert, 2021). A comprehensive research review provided these conclusions, which still hold true in many Western cultures today (Bronstein, 2006):

- *Mothers' socialization strategies.* In many cultures mothers socialize their daughters to be more obedient and responsible than their sons. They also place more restrictions on daughters' autonomy.
- *Fathers' socialization strategies.* Fathers show more attention to sons than to daughters, engage in more activities with sons, and put forth more effort to promote sons' intellectual development.

Thus, despite increased awareness in the United States and other Western nations of the negative outcomes of gender stereotyping, many parents continue to foster behaviors and perceptions that reflect traditional gender-role norms that influence long-term outcomes (Humlum, Nandrup, & Smith, 2019). Although there have been substantial shifts in views of gender and socialization since Bronstein's review was published, it is still the case that in many cultures and societies, gender stereotypes remain strongly held by parents, youth, and older adults alike (Koenig, 2018).

Peer Influences   Parents provide the earliest discrimination of gender roles, but before long, peers join the process of responding to and modeling masculine and feminine behavior (Schroeder & Liben, 2021). Peers extensively reward and punish gender behavior (Schroeder & Liben, 2021). For example, when children play in ways that the culture views as consistent with gender stereotypes, their peers tend to reward them (Nabbijohn & others, 2020). But peers often reject children who act in a manner that is contrary to gender stereotypes (Warren, Goldsmith, & Rimes, 2019). When binary gender stereotypes exist in a culture, there is greater pressure for boys to conform to a traditional male role than for girls to conform to a traditional female role. For example, a preschool girl who wants to wear boys' clothing receives considerably more approval than a boy who wants to wear a dress. In one study of 9- to 10-year-olds in Great Britain, gender-nonconforming boys were most at risk for peer rejection (Braun & Davidson, 2017). In this study, gender-nonconforming girls were preferred more than

psychoanalytic theory of gender A theory deriving from Freud's view that the preschool child develops a sexual attraction to the opposite-sex parent, by approximately 5 or 6 years of age renounces this attraction because of anxious feelings, and subsequently identifies with the same-sex parent, unconsciously adopting the same-sex parent's characteristics.

social cognitive theory of gender The idea that children's gender development occurs through observation and imitation of gender behavior as well as through the rewards and punishments children experience for behaviors believed to be appropriate or inappropriate for their gender.

How Would You...?
If you were a **human development and family studies professional,** how would you describe the ways in which parents influence their children's notions of gender roles?

What role does gender play in children's peer relations?
(*Left*) PeopleImages/Getty Images; (*right*) Digital Vision/Getty Images

gender-conforming girls, with children most often citing stereotypically masculine activities as the reason for this choice. Further research showed that some of these positive and negative effects in adjustment persist well through adolescence (Warren, Goldsmith, & Rimes, 2019).

Gender molds important aspects of peer relations (Riggs, Kinard, & Long, 2023). It influences the composition of children's groups, the size of groups, and interactions within a group (Rose & Smith, 2018):

- *Gender composition of children's groups.* Around the age of 3, children already show a preference to spend time with same-sex playmates. From 4 to 12 years of age, this preference for playing in same-sex groups increases, and during the elementary school years children spend a large majority of their free time with children of their own sex (see Figure 1).

- *Group size.* From about 5 years of age onward, boys are more likely to congregate in larger clusters than girls are. Boys are also more likely to participate in organized group games than girls are.

- *Interaction in same-sex groups.* Boys are more likely than girls to engage in rough-and-tumble play, competition, conflict, ego displays, risk taking, and dominance seeking. By contrast, girls are more likely to engage in "collaborative discourse," in which they talk and act in a more reciprocal manner. For example, one study of preschool children (average age: 4 years) found that children selected playmates of the same sex who engaged in similar levels of stereotypical gender-typed activities (Martin & others, 2013). In selecting a playmate, sex of the playmate was found to be more important than activity.

Cognitive Influences   One influential cognitive theory is **gender schema theory,** which states that gender typing emerges as children gradually develop gender schemas of what is gender-appropriate and gender-inappropriate in their culture (Halim & others, 2016; Martin & Cook, 2017; Weisgram, 2019). The theory has recently been revisited to encompass nonbinary and transgender perspectives (Jackson & Bussey, 2023). A schema is a cognitive structure, a network of associations that guide an individual's perceptions. A gender schema organizes the world in terms of girl/woman and boy/man. Children and adolescents are internally motivated to perceive the world and to act in accordance with their developing schemas. Bit by bit, children and adolescents pick up what is believed to be gender-appropriate and gender-inappropriate in their culture, developing gender schemas that shape how they perceive the world and what they remember (Cook & others, 2022). Children and adolescents are motivated to act in ways that conform to these learned gender schemas.

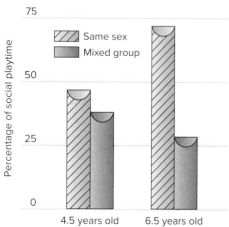

FIGURE 1

DEVELOPMENTAL CHANGES IN PERCENTAGE OF TIME SPENT IN SAME-SEX AND MIXED-GROUP SETTINGS. Observations of children show that they are more likely to play in same-sex than mixed-sex groups. This tendency increases between 4 and 6 years of age.

2 What Roles Do Families Play in Young Children's Development?

 LG2 Explain how families can influence young children's development.

| Parenting | Child Maltreatment | Sibling Relationships and Birth Order | The Changing Family in a Changing Social World |

Attachment to a caregiver is a key social relationship process during infancy. Social and emotional development is also shaped by other relationships and by temperament, contexts, and social experiences in the early childhood years and later. In this section, we discuss social relationships of early childhood beyond attachment.

PARENTING

Some media accounts portray parents as unhappy, stressed, and feeling little joy in caring for their children. However, research has found that parents were more satisfied with their lives than were nonparents, felt relatively better on a daily basis than did nonparents, and had more positive feelings related to caring for their children than to other daily activities (Nelson, Kushley, & Lyubomirsky, 2014). Also, a comprehensive research review concluded that parents are unhappy when they experience more negative emotions, financial problems, sleep problems, and troubled marriages (Nelson, Kushley, & Lyubomirsky, 2014). This review concluded that parents were happy when they experienced meaning in life, satisfaction of basic needs, more positive emotions, and positive social roles.

Good parenting takes time and effort (Grusec & Davidov, 2021). Of course, it's not just the quantity of time parents spend with children that is important for children's development—the quality of the parenting is clearly influential as well (Ewing & others, 2019). For example, studies have found that maternal scaffolding, sensitivity, and support for autonomy (as well as other aspects of positive parenting) are linked to better cognitive and social-emotional outcomes using behavioral and brain-based measures (D.B. Lee & others, 2019; Neppl & others, 2020).

Baumrind's Parenting Styles Diana Baumrind (1971, 2013) emphasized that parents should be neither punitive nor aloof. Rather, they should develop rules for their children and be affectionate with them. She described four types of parenting styles that have been examined in thousands of studies in many cultures and countries spanning the globe (Larzelere, Morris, & Harrist, 2013):

- **Authoritarian parenting** is a restrictive, punitive style in which parents exhort the child to follow their directions and respect their work and effort. The authoritarian parent places firm limits and controls on the child and allows little verbal exchange. For example, an

authoritarian parenting A restrictive, punitive parenting style in which parents exhort the child to follow their directions and to respect their work and effort. The authoritarian parent places firm limits and controls on the child and allows little verbal exchange. Authoritarian parenting is associated with children's social incompetence.

authoritative parenting A parenting style in which parents encourage their children to be independent but still place limits and controls on their actions. Extensive verbal give-and-take is allowed, and parents are warm and nurturant toward the child. Authoritative parenting is associated with children's social competence.

neglectful parenting A style of parenting in which the parent is very uninvolved in the child's life; it is associated with children's social incompetence, especially a lack of self-control.

indulgent parenting A style of parenting in which parents are highly involved with their children but place few demands or controls on them. Indulgent parenting is associated with children's social incompetence, especially a lack of self-control.

How Would You...?
If you were a **psychologist**, how would you use the research on parenting styles to design a parent education class that teaches effective skills for interacting with young children?

According to Ruth Chao, what type of parenting style do many Asian American parents use?

Blend Images/SuperStock

authoritarian parent might say, "You will do it my way or else." Authoritarian parents also might spank the child frequently, enforce rules rigidly but not explain them, and show rage toward the child. Children of authoritarian parents are often unhappy, fearful, and anxious about comparing themselves with others; fail to initiate activity; and have weak communication skills. Also, a review of a large number of studies concluded that authoritarian parenting is linked to a higher level of aggressive behavior problems (Pinquart, 2017).

- **Authoritative parenting** encourages children to be independent but still places limits and controls on their actions. Extensive verbal give-and-take is allowed, and parents are warm and nurturant toward the child. An authoritative parent might talk to the child in a comforting way and say, "You know you should not have done that. Let's talk about how you can handle the situation better next time." Authoritative parents show pleasure and support in response to children's constructive behavior. They also expect mature, independent, and age-appropriate behavior by children. Children whose parents are authoritative are often cheerful, self-controlled and self-reliant, and achievement-oriented; they tend to maintain friendly relations with peers, cooperate with adults, and cope well with stress. In one study, children of authoritative parents engaged in more prosocial behavior than their counterparts whose parents used the other parenting styles described in this section (Carlo & others, 2018). Also, in a comprehensive research review, the authoritative parenting style was most effective in predicting lower levels of obesity later in child and adolescent development (Sokol, Qin, & Poti, 2017).

- **Neglectful parenting** is a style in which the parent is uninvolved in the child's life. Children whose parents are neglectful develop the sense that other aspects of their parents' lives are more important than they are. These children tend to be socially incompetent. Many have poor self-control and don't handle independence well. They frequently have low self-esteem, are immature, and may be alienated from the family. In adolescence, they may show patterns of truancy and delinquency. In the research review of studies described under authoritarian parenting (Pinquart, 2017), neglectful parenting was associated with a higher level of externalizing problems.

- **Indulgent parenting** is a style in which parents are highly involved with their children but place few demands or controls on them. Such parents let their children do what they want. The result is that the children never learn to control their own behavior and always expect to get their way. Some parents deliberately rear their children in this way because they believe the combination of warm involvement and few restraints will produce a creative, confident child. However, children whose parents are indulgent rarely learn respect for others and tend to have difficulty controlling their behavior. They might be domineering, egocentric, and noncompliant, and have difficulties in peer relations.

These four classifications of parenting involve combinations of acceptance and responsiveness on the one hand and demand and control on the other (Larzelere, Morris, & Harrist, 2013). How these dimensions combine to produce authoritarian, authoritative, neglectful, and indulgent parenting is shown in Figure 2.

Parenting Styles in Context   Do the benefits of authoritative parenting transcend the boundaries of ethnicity, socioeconomic status (SES), and household composition? Although occasional exceptions have been found, evidence linking authoritative parenting with competence on the part of the child occurs in research across a wide range of ethnic groups, social strata, cultures, and family structures (Masud & others, 2019).

Other research with ethnic groups suggests that some aspects of the authoritarian style may be associated with positive child outcomes (Chen-Bouck, Patterson, & Chen, 2019). For example, Asian American parents exert considerable control over their children's lives. However, Ruth Chao (2007; Wu & Chao, 2017) argued that the style of parenting used by many Asian American parents, which she calls *training parents,* is distinct from the domineering control of the authoritarian style. In research on Chinese American adolescents and their parents, parental control was endorsed, as were the Confucian parental goals of perseverance, diligence in school, obedience, and responsiveness to parents' wishes (Russell, Crockett, & Chao, 2010). Similar patterns have been observed in subsequent research with mainland Chinese families (Liu & others, 2022).

An emphasis on requiring respect and obedience is also associated with the authoritarian style, but in Latino child rearing this focus may be positive rather than punitive. Rather than suppressing the child's development, it may encourage the development of an identity that is embedded in the family (Wang, Vallotton, & Bowles, 2020). Furthermore, Latino families often have several generations living together or near one another and helping each other (Bradley, 2019). In these circumstances, emphasizing respect and obedience by children is a part of maintaining a harmonious home and may be important in shaping the child's identity (Constante & others, 2019; Safa, Umaña-Taylor, & Martinez-Fuentes, 2023).

Further Thoughts on Parenting Styles   Several caveats about parenting styles are in order. First, the parenting styles do not capture the important themes of reciprocal socialization and synchrony (Aguayo & others, 2021). Keep in mind that children socialize parents, just as parents socialize children (Knafo-Noam, Barni, & Schwartz, 2020). Second, many parents use a combination of techniques rather than a single technique, although one technique may be dominant. Although consistent parenting is usually recommended, the wise parent may sense the importance of being more permissive in certain situations, more authoritarian in others, and more authoritative in yet other circumstances. In addition, parenting styles often are talked about as if both parents have the same style, although this may not be the case (Sanders, Turner, & Metzler, 2019). Finally, some critics argue that the concept of parenting style is too broad and that more research needs to be conducted to "unpack" parenting styles by studying various components and dimensions that compose the styles (Grusec & Davidov, 2021). For example, is parental monitoring more important than warmth in predicting child and adolescent outcomes?

Further, much of the parenting style research has involved mothers, not fathers. In many families, mothers will use one style, fathers another style. Especially in cultures that value traditional gender roles, fathers have an authoritarian style and mothers a more permissive, indulgent style. It has often been said that it is beneficial for parents to engage in a consistent parenting style; however, if fathers are authoritarian and aren't willing to change, children may benefit when mothers use an authoritative style.

Punishment   Use of corporal (physical) punishment is legal in every state in the United States, although corporal punishment has been outlawed in 65 countries around the world (End Violence Against Children, 2023). A national survey of U.S. parents and children found that 49 percent of parents reported that they had spanked their 0- to 9-year-old child in the last year, and 23 percent of 10- to 17-year-olds reported their parents had spanked them in the last year (Finkelhor & others, 2019). Rates of spanking differed by child gender, geographic region, ethnicity, and parental education. Different national surveys from 1988 to 2014 estimate that spanking of 5-year-old children has decreased at least 26 percent and up to 40 percent from 1988 to 2014 (Finkelhor & others, 2019). In many countries, the use of corporal punishment and beliefs in its necessity have decreased over historical time. Recent research has shown decreases in places as diverse from each other as Sierra Leone, Montenegro, Macedonia, and Ukraine (Lansford & others, 2017). In surveys of nationally representative samples in eight countries, more parents reported using corporal punishment than reported believing it is necessary to use corporal punishment to rear a child properly (see Figure 3) (Lansford & others, 2017). According to the United Nations, using corporal punishment violates children's rights to protection from abuse and exploitation (Committee on the Rights of the Child, 2020).

What are some reasons for avoiding spanking or similar punishments? They include the following:

- When adults punish a child by yelling, screaming, or spanking, they are presenting children with out-of-control models for handling stressful situations. Children may imitate this behavior.
- Punishment can instill fear, rage, or avoidance. For example, spanking the child may cause the child to avoid being near the parent and to fear the parent.

	Accepting, responsive	Rejecting, unresponsive
Demanding, controlling	Authoritative	Authoritarian
Undemanding, uncontrolling	Indulgent	Neglectful

FIGURE 2

CLASSIFICATION OF PARENTING STYLES. The four types of parenting styles (authoritative, authoritarian, indulgent, and neglectful) involve the dimensions of acceptance and responsiveness, on the one hand, and demand and control on the other. For example, authoritative parenting involves being both accepting/responsive and demanding/controlling.

Oleksiy Rezin/Shutterstock

How Would You...?
If you were a **human development and family studies professional,** how would you characterize the parenting style that prevails within your own family?

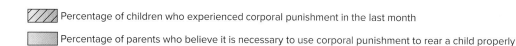

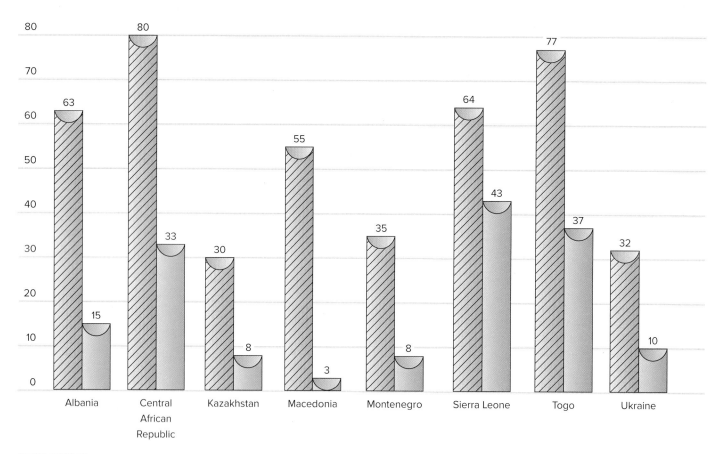

FIGURE 3

CORPORAL PUNISHMENT IN DIFFERENT COUNTRIES. Parents were asked whether they or anyone in their household had physically punished their child in the last month (yes or no) and whether they believe it is necessary to use corporal punishment to rear a child properly (yes or no). *Why are studies of corporal punishment correlational studies, and how does that affect their usefulness?*

How Would You...?

If you were a **human development and family studies professional,** how would you advise parents about why they should not spank their children? Also, what alternatives to spanking would you recommend?

- Punishment tells children what not to do rather than what to do. Children should be given constructive feedback, such as "Why don't you try this?"
- Parents might unintentionally become so angry when they are punishing the child that they become abusive.

Most child psychologists recommend handling misbehavior by reasoning with the child, especially explaining the consequences of the child's actions for others. *Time out,* in which the child is removed from a setting that offers positive reinforcement, can also be effective.

A meta-analysis of studies of 160,927 children concluded that corporal punishment by parents is related to more child aggression, antisocial behavior, depression, anxiety, mental health problems, negative relationships with parents, and impaired cognitive ability, as well as less moral internalization, lower self-esteem, and risk for physical abuse from parents (Gershoff & Grogan-Kaylor, 2016). In addition, adults who had been spanked when they were children had more mental health problems and antisocial behavior.

Debate about the effects of physical punishment on children's development continues (Larzelere & others, 2019). Individuals who question whether spanking worsens child outcomes point out that studies investigating this link are correlational. Clearly, it would be highly unethical to randomly assign parents to either spank or not spank their children in an experimental study. Recall that cause and effect cannot be determined in a correlational study. Nevertheless, a large body of research using a variety of methods, including longitudinal studies that take into account children's initial levels of problem behaviors and neuroimaging studies that examine brain structure and function, leads to the conclusion that spanking is detrimental for children's well-being (Gershoff & others, 2018). As a result of this evidence, numerous professional organizations have issued position statements urging parents not to use corporal punishment. For example, the American Academy of Pediatrics and the American Psychological Association both affirm that corporal punishment is detrimental to child development and encourage parents to use alternate forms of discipline (American Psychological Association, 2019; Sege & others, 2018).

In addition to the issue of how corporal punishment is related to child development, the issue of corporal punishment is increasingly regarded from a human rights perspective. In the Convention on the Rights of the Child, the United Nations asserted children's right to protection from all forms of violence, including corporal punishment, no matter how mild (United Nations, 1989). The Sustainable Development Goals guiding the international agenda through 2030 specifically target eliminating parents' use of corporal punishment and psychological aggression toward children (Danish Institute for Human Rights, 2018).

Coparenting   The relationship between marital conflict and the use of punishment highlights the importance of *coparenting,* which is the support that parents provide one another in jointly raising a child. Poor coordination between parents, undermining of the other parent, lack of cooperation and warmth, and disconnection by one parent are conditions that place children at risk for problems (Tomfohr-Madsen & others, 2020). One study that randomly assigned first-time parents to an intervention focused on their relationship, an intervention focused on coparenting, or a control group found that both interventions led to improvements in children's emotional and behavioral adjustment at ages 12 and 24 months compared to the control group (Tomfohr-Madsen & others, 2020). Coparenting effectively is important regardless of whether parents are living together or not (Cox & others, 2021).

Parents who do not spend enough time with their children or who have problems in child rearing can benefit from counseling and therapy. To read about the work of a marriage and family therapist, see the *Connecting with Careers* profile.

connecting with careers

Allison Tomlinson, Marriage and Family Therapist

Allison Tomlinson is a marriage and family therapist in Arlington, Texas. Her practice, Point of Change Counseling Education and Training Services, employs a team of licensed therapists who work with adults, children, and families dealing with a wide range of mental health issues. Tomlinson specializes in providing trauma therapy intervention to children and nontraditional family compositions, such as foster care and adoption.

A marriage and family therapist can assess, diagnose, and treat mental health issues such as depression, anxiety, anger, post-traumatic stress disorder, and relationship issues. A therapist may provide child and family counseling, as well as couples counseling (premarital, relationship, separation, and divorce).

Tomlinson received a bachelor's degree in social work from Texas Christian University, a master's degree in social work from Howard University, and a doctorate in marriage and family therapy from Texas Women's University. She is a licensed clinical social worker (LCSW-S) and a state of Texas board-approved supervisor. In addition to her clinical practice, Tomlinson is the Director of Undergraduate Programs in Social Work at the University of Texas–Arlington. Her practice and instruction draw on diverse career experiences in multiple areas of

Allison Tomlinson provides therapy for children and families on a wide range of mental health and relationship issues.
Allison Tomlinson

social work, including policy work through criminal justice reform with the Washington, D.C., Juvenile Detention Alternatives Initiative and the Office of Justice Programs.

CHILD MALTREATMENT

Unfortunately, punishment or neglect sometimes leads to the abuse of infants and children (Russotti & others, 2021). In 2021, 588,229 U.S. children were found to be victims of child abuse or neglect at least once during that year (U.S. Department of Health and Human Services, 2023). Three-quarters of these children were abused by a parent or parents. Laws in every state in the United States and in many other countries now require physicians and teachers to report suspected cases of child abuse, yet many cases go unreported, especially those involving battered infants.

Whereas the public and many professionals use the term *child abuse* to refer to both abuse and neglect, developmentalists increasingly use the term *child maltreatment* (Almy & Cicchetti, 2018; Doyle & Cicchetti, 2018). This term does not have quite the emotional impact of the term *abuse* and acknowledges that maltreatment includes diverse conditions.

Types of Child Maltreatment   The four main types of child maltreatment are physical abuse, child neglect, sexual abuse, and emotional abuse (U.S. Department of Health and Human Services, 2023):

- *Physical abuse* is characterized by the infliction of physical injury as a result of punching, beating, kicking, biting, burning, shaking, or otherwise physically harming a child. The parent or other person may not have intended to hurt the child; the injury may have resulted from excessive physical punishment (Knox, 2020).

- *Child neglect* is characterized by failure to provide for the child's basic needs. Neglect can be physical (abandonment, for example), educational (allowing chronic truancy, for example), or emotional (marked inattention to the child's needs, for example) (Naughton & others, 2017). Child neglect is by far the most common form of child maltreatment. In every country where relevant data have been collected, neglect occurs up to three times more often than abuse (O'Hara & others, 2015)—although there is wide variation in how neglect is defined between countries (Mathews & others, 2020).

- *Sexual abuse* includes fondling a child's genitals, intercourse, incest, rape, sodomy, exhibitionism, and commercial exploitation through prostitution or the production of pornographic materials (Russell, Higgins, & Posso, 2020).

- *Emotional abuse (psychological/verbal abuse/mental injury)* includes acts or omissions by parents or other caregivers that have caused, or could cause, serious behavioral, cognitive, or emotional problems (Kosson & others, 2021).

Although any of these forms of child maltreatment may be found separately, they often occur in combination. Emotional abuse is almost always present when other forms are identified.

How Would You...?
If you were a **health-care professional,** how would you work with parents during infant and child checkups to prevent child maltreatment?

The Context of Abuse   No single factor causes child maltreatment, and this makes it challenging to provide a unified approach to preventing it or reducing its consequences (Campbell, Wuthrich, & Norlin, 2020). A combination of factors, including the culture, family, and developmental characteristics of the child, likely contributes to child maltreatment.

The extensive violence that takes place in the United States and in many other cultures is reflected in the occurrence of violence in the family (Deater-Deckard & Lansford, 2017). A regular diet of violence appears on television shows, and parents often resort to power assertion as a disciplinary technique.

The family itself is obviously a key part of the context of abuse. Research in many countries, including the United States, Australia, and other nations as diverse from each other as Nigeria, Laos, Chile, and Vietnam, shows that family and family-associated characteristics contribute to child maltreatment. These include parenting stress, substance abuse, social isolation, single parenting, and socioeconomic difficulties (especially poverty) (Doyle & Cicchetti, 2018). The interactions of all family members need to be considered, regardless of who performs the violent acts against the child. For example, even though one parent may physically abuse the child, the behavior of the other parent, the child, and siblings also should be evaluated.

Eight-year-old Donnique Hein lovingly holds her younger sister, 6-month-old Maria Paschel, after a meal at Laura's Home, a crisis shelter run by the City Mission in a suburb of Cleveland, Ohio.
Joshua Gunter/The Plain Dealer/Landov Images

Were parents who abuse children abused by their own parents? A ground-breaking 30-year longitudinal study found that offspring of parents who had engaged in child abuse and neglect are at risk for engaging in child neglect and sexual abuse themselves (Widom, Czaja, & DuMont, 2015). About one-third of parents who were abused themselves when they were young go on to abuse their own children (Doyle & Cicchetti, 2018). Thus, some, but not a majority, of parents are involved in an intergenerational transmission of abuse. A series of classic studies long ago demonstrated that mothers who break out of the intergenerational transmission of abuse often report having had at least one warm, caring adult in their background; having a close, positive marital relationship; and having received therapy (Egeland, Jacobvitz, & Sroufe, 1988).

Developmental Consequences of Abuse   Among the consequences of child maltreatment in childhood and adolescence are poor emotion regulation, attachment problems, problems in peer relations, difficulty in adapting to school, and other psychological problems such as depression, suicide, and delinquency (Doyle & Cicchetti, 2018). As shown in Figure 4, another study showed that maltreated young children in foster care were more likely to show abnormally high levels of stress hormones than were middle-SES young children living with their birth family (Gunnar, Fisher, & The Early Experience, Stress, and Prevention Science Network, 2006). In this study, the abnormal stress hormone levels were mainly present in the foster children who experienced neglect, best described as "institutional neglect" (Carr, Duff, & Craddock, 2020). Adolescents who experienced abuse or neglect as children are more likely than adolescents who were not maltreated as children to engage in violent romantic relationships, delinquency, sexual risk taking, and substance abuse (Negriff, 2020). Other research has found that exposure to physical or sexual abuse in childhood and adolescence is linked to an increase in adolescents' and emerging adults' suicidal ideation, plans, and attempts (Paul & Ortin, 2019).

Later, during the adult years, individuals who were maltreated as children are more likely to experience pain as well as physical, emotional, and sexual problems (Beal & others, 2020). A longitudinal study that followed children from kindergarten through middle adulthood found that adults who had been physically abused in the first five years of life were more likely to have clinical levels of internalizing problems (like anxiety and depression) and externalizing problems (like antisocial behavior), were more likely to have been convicted of a crime, and had poorer physical health than adults who had not been abused (Lansford & others, 2021). Other research has revealed that young adults who had experienced child maltreatment, especially physical abuse, at any age were more likely to be depressed and to engage in suicidal ideation as adults (Angelakis, Gillespie, & Panagioti, 2019). Further, adults who had been maltreated as children often have difficulty establishing and maintaining healthy intimate relationships (Li, Zhao, & Yu, 2019). As adults, maltreated children are also at higher risk for violent behavior toward other adults—especially dating partners and marital partners (Li, Zhao, & Yu, 2019).

An important strategy for reducing the incidence of these lifelong emotional and physical problems is to prevent child maltreatment (Eddy & Sneddon, 2020). This may best be accomplished by taking a "public health" approach toward expanding supports for positive, enriching parenting and toward minimizing harsh and abusive child rearing. In "Triple P," the most widely used parenting prevention and intervention program in the world, emphasis is placed on strengthening positive parenting by building parents' self-control and sense of competency and self-worth in the parenting role (Prinz, 2020).

To read about a child welfare case manager who works with children who have been maltreated, see the *Connecting with Careers* feature.

SIBLING RELATIONSHIPS AND BIRTH ORDER

How do developmentalists characterize sibling relationships? How extensively does birth order influence behavior?

Sibling Relationships   Approximately 80 percent of American children have one or more siblings—that is, sisters and brothers (Fouts & Bader, 2017). One in six American children under the age of 18 now lives with half siblings, and increasing proportions of U.S. children also are living with stepsiblings (Knop, 2020). In a longitudinal study, a bidirectional

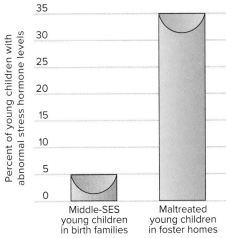

FIGURE 4

ABNORMAL STRESS HORMONE LEVELS IN YOUNG CHILDREN IN DIFFERENT TYPES OF REARING CONDITIONS

What characterizes children's sibling relationships?

(both): RubberBall Productions/Getty Images

Stacie Padilla, Child Welfare Case Manager

Child welfare case workers participate in child protection cases, from the initial investigation to case closure. An advocate for the health and safety of the child, the case worker helps families to establish and achieve goals, understanding that each family is different and requires tailored, culturally relevant services.

Stacie Padilla is a Senior Child Welfare Case Manager at Gulf Coast Jewish Family and Community Services (JFCS) in Hillsborough, Florida. She has been professionally acknowledged for her passion in supporting children throughout difficult situations (Florida Institute for Child Welfare, 2021). "My job is to help children be reunified with their parents safely, if that is a possibility," Padilla says. "And, if that is not a possibility, then my job is to find permanency to those children" (Gulf Coast JFCS, 2022).

A case manager such as Padilla may conduct home visits, attend legal hearings, and provide referrals for parents who are dealing with a myriad of issues, including mental health problems, economic stress, and substance abuse. Becoming a child welfare case worker usually involves obtaining an undergraduate degree in social work, with a master's degree often required for licensure and management positions.

With more than 400,000 children in foster care in the United States (U.S. Department of Health and Human Services, 2021), a case worker is required to balance the needs of everyone involved, including the biological parents, extended family, foster parents or other caregivers, and, most importantly, the child. A case worker navigates across multiple systems to address children's needs related to mental and physical health care, school attendance, and

Stacie Padilla, senior child welfare case manager, works to find safe and supportive environments for children.
Stacie Padilla

the legal system. Balancing all these factors can be difficult and stressful, but also extremely rewarding. "The thing that motivates me would be the children," says Padilla. "The kids are what keep me going."

association between a child's behavior and sibling relationship quality was found (Pike & Oliver, 2017). In this study, a child's behavior (prosocial behavior, presence of conduct problems, for example) at 4 years of age predicted sibling relationship quality at 7 years of age, and sibling relationship quality (degree of conflict, for example) at 4 years of age predicted child behavior at 7 years of age as well. It would be expected that improvement in sibling relationship quality or an individual child's behavior would have positive developmental outcomes.

If you grew up with siblings, you probably have some memories of aggressive, hostile interchanges. Siblings in the presence of each other when they are 2 to 4 years of age, on average, have a conflict once every 10 minutes and then the conflicts go down somewhat from 5 to 7 years of age (Kramer, 2006).

What do parents do when they encounter siblings having a verbal or physical confrontation? Several studies have shown that they do one of three things: (1) most commonly, parents will intervene and try to help them resolve the conflict by encouraging resolution through communication, followed by (2) ignoring and intentionally not intervening so that they work it out on their own, or (3) least commonly, admonishing them or telling them to physically stand up to each other (Leijten, Melendez-Torres, & Oliver, 2021). Many parents believe that siblings should learn to resolve conflict on their own.

Laurie Kramer (Kramer & others, 2019), who conducted a number of research studies on siblings, said that not intervening and letting sibling conflict escalate are not good strategies. She developed a now classic program titled "More Fun with Sisters and Brothers," which teaches 4- to 8-year-old siblings social skills for developing positive interactions (Kramer & others, 2019). Among the social skills taught in the program are how to appropriately initiate play, how to accept and refuse invitations to play, how to take another's perspective, how to deal with angry feelings, and how to manage conflict. One study of 5- to 10-year-old siblings and their parents found that training parents to mediate sibling disputes increased children's understanding of conflicts and reduced sibling conflict (Smith & Ross, 2007). Subsequent research has shown that effective parental intervention in sibling conflict is a key factor in childhood, adolescent, and even adult sibling relationships (Bouchard, Plamondon, & Lachance-Grzela, 2019).

However, conflict is only one of the many dimensions of sibling relations (Kramer & others, 2019). Sibling relations also include helping, sharing, teaching, and playing—and siblings can act as emotional supports, rivals, and communication partners.

Do parents usually favor one sibling over others—and if so, does it make a difference in a child's development? One study of 384 sibling pairs revealed that 65 percent of their mothers and 70 percent of their fathers showed favoritism toward one sibling (Shebloski, Conger, & Widaman, 2005). When favoritism of one sibling occurred, it was linked to lower self-esteem and sadness in the less-favored sibling. Indeed, equality and fairness are major concerns of siblings' relationships with each other and how they are treated by their parents (Kramer & others, 2019).

Judy Dunn (2015), a leading expert on sibling relationships, described three important characteristics of sibling relationships that have been evident for many years and across diverse family and cultural contexts:

- *Emotional quality of the relationship.* Intense positive and negative emotions are often expressed by siblings toward each other. Many children have mixed feelings toward their siblings.

- *Familiarity and intimacy of the relationship.* Siblings typically know each other very well, and this intimacy suggests that they can either provide support or tease and undermine each other, depending on the situation.

- *Variation in sibling relationships.* Some siblings describe their relationships more positively than others. Thus, there is considerable variation in sibling relationships. Above, we saw that many siblings have mixed feelings about each other, but some children mainly describe their sibling in warm, affectionate ways, whereas others primarily talk about how irritating and mean a sibling is.

Birth Order A large body of research has investigated whether having older or younger siblings is linked to the development of certain personality characteristics. An early review of the research concluded that "firstborns are the most intelligent, achieving, and conscientious, while later-borns are the most rebellious, liberal, and agreeable" (Paulhus, 2008, p. 210). Compared with later-born children, firstborn children have also been described as more adult-oriented, helpful, conforming, and self-controlled. However, when such birth order differences are reported, they often are small. Indeed, the most extensive large-scale rigorous analysis of multiple datasets showed only a small effect, and only for intelligence (Rohrer, Egloff, & Schmukle, 2015).

When birth order effects are found, what might account for even small differences? Proposed explanations usually point to variations in interactions with parents and siblings associated with being in a particular position in the family. This is especially true in the case of the firstborn child (Volling & others, 2023). The oldest child is the only one who does not have to share parental love and affection with other siblings—until another sibling comes along (on average, two years after the firstborn's arrival). An infant requires more attention than an older child; thus, the firstborn sibling receives less attention after the newborn arrives. Does this result in conflict between parents and the firstborn? In one classic research study, mothers became more negative, coercive, and restraining and played less with the firstborn following the birth of a second child (Dunn & Kendrick, 1982).

What is the only child like? The popular conception is that the only child is a "spoiled brat," with such undesirable characteristics as dependency, lack of self-control, and self-centered behavior. But researchers present a more positive portrayal of the only child. Classic studies showed that only children often are achievement-oriented and display a desirable personality, especially in comparison with later-borns and children from large families (Falbo & Poston, 1993; Jiao, Ji, & Jing, 1996). Most recently, researchers noted potential brain-based differences corresponding to cognitive and behavioral differences between only children and those with siblings (Yang & others, 2017). However, a study of more than 20,000 adults in New Zealand showed differences between those with and without siblings that did not meet the threshold for even small effect sizes, suggesting that being an only child has negligible effects on personality (Stronge & others, 2019).

A one-child policy was in place for a number of decades in China. However, in 2016, the Chinese government began allowing two children per family without a financial penalty. *In general, though, what have researchers found the only child to be like?*

Image Source/Getty Images

As popular as the ideas about birth order might be, researchers have concluded that when all of the factors that influence behavior are considered, birth order and being an only child show limited ability to predict behavior. Think about some of the other important factors in children's lives that influence their behavior beyond having siblings, or sibling birth order. They include heredity, models of competency or incompetency that parents present to children on a daily basis, peer influences, school influences, socioeconomic factors, sociohistorical factors, and cultural variations. When someone says firstborns are always like this but lastborns are always like that, the person is making overly simplistic statements that do not adequately take into account the complexity of influences on a child's development.

THE CHANGING FAMILY IN A CHANGING SOCIAL WORLD

Beyond variations in the number of siblings, the families that children experience differ in many important ways. For instance, the number of children growing up in single-parent families is large but varies markedly by country and community. As shown in Figure 5, the United States has one of the highest percentages of single-parent families in the world. Among two-parent families, there are those in which both parents work, those in which divorced parents have remarried, or those with gay or lesbian parents. Differences in culture and SES also influence families. How do these variations in families affect children?

Working Parents   In 2020, 71 percent of mothers and 92 percent of fathers with children under the age of 18 participated in the paid workforce in the United States (Bureau of Labor Statistics, 2021). The increased number of mothers in the labor force represents one historical source of change in families and society in the United States (Bastian, 2020). More than one of every two U.S. mothers with a child under the age of 5 is in the labor force; more than two of every three with a child from 6 to 17 years of age is. Maternal employment rates are highest in northern Europe because those countries (for example, Sweden and Denmark) provide substantial amounts of paid parental leave and access to nationally subsidized systems of early child care.

Most research on parental work has focused on young children and the mother's employment (Perry-Jenkins & Gerstel, 2020). However, the effects of working parents involve the father as well as the mother when factors such as work schedules and work-family stress are considered (Rose, 2021). Research indicates that the qualities of a parent's work (for example, having control over scheduling, and enjoyment in the work role) have a stronger influence on children's development than whether the parent works outside the home (Capistrant & others, 2020). For example, a large study of almost 3,000 adolescents found a negative association of the father's, but not the mother's, unemployment on the adolescents' health (Bacikova-Sleskova, Benka, & Orosova, 2015). Also, a study of dual-earner couples found that work-family enrichment experiences had positive outcomes on parenting quality, which in turn was linked to positive child outcomes. By contrast, work-family conflict experiences were associated with poorer parenting quality, which in turn was related to negative child outcomes (Vieira & others, 2016).

How does work affect parenting?
Eric Audras/PhotoAlto/Getty Images

FIGURE **5**

SINGLE-PARENT FAMILIES IN DIFFERENT COUNTRIES

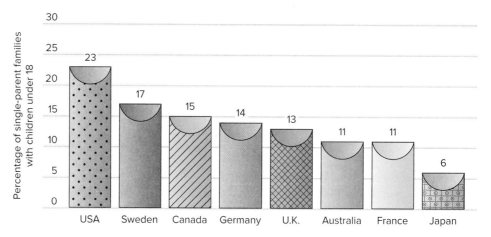

Importantly, the "conflict" parents experience, between meeting the demands of their work and taking care of their partners and children at home, is more similar than different when fathers and mothers are compared across all published studies (Shockley & others, 2017).

Work can produce positive and negative effects on parenting (Perry-Jenkins & Gerstel, 2020). Ann Crouter (2006), a researcher who has studied working couples and parenting for decades, described how parents bring their experiences at work into their homes. She concluded that parents who have poor working conditions, such as long hours, overtime work, stressful work, and lack of autonomy at work, are likely to be more irritable at home and engage in less effective parenting than their counterparts who have better working conditions. One important finding is that children (especially girls) of working mothers engage in less gender stereotyping and have more egalitarian views of gender (Goldberg & Lucas-Thompson, 2008). Interestingly, emerging evidence from research on government-mandated family and work policy changes in Scandinavia, in which fathers and mothers are required to take similar amounts of time off from work to care for family members, has shown positive effects on children's academic and social-emotional functioning (Cools, Fiva, & Kirkebøen, 2015).

developmental **connection**

Social Contexts

Research consistently shows that family factors are considerably better at predicting children's developmental outcomes than are child-care experiences. Connect to "Socioemotional Development in Infancy."

Children in Divorced Families   Divorce rates rose dramatically in the United States and many countries around the world in the late twentieth century (Braver & Lamb, 2013). The U.S. divorce rate increased rapidly in the 1960s and 1970s but has declined since the 1980s. However, the divorce rate in the United States is still much higher than that of most other countries, even when compared with nations in Europe and South America that have similar economies and family policies (OECD, 2022).

When divorce rates were at their highest level, it was estimated that around 40 percent of children born to married parents in the United States would experience their parents' divorce (Hetherington & Stanley-Hagan, 2002). The percentage of children who experience the dissolution of their parents' relationship has increased slightly in recent decades, in part because more children have parents who live together but do not marry (which means it is legally easier to separate than if they were married). Let's examine some important questions about children in divorced families:

- *Are children better adjusted in intact, never-divorced families than in divorced families?*
  Most researchers agree that children from divorced families show poorer adjustment than their counterparts in nondivorced families (Amato & Anthony, 2014; Arkes, 2015; Hetherington, 2006; Lansford, 2013; Wallerstein, 2008) (see Figure 6). The largest meta-analysis of studies to date showed consistent effects on poorer mental health in adolescence and adulthood, although the size of these effects has decreased over the past few decades as divorce and post-divorce coparenting have become more common (Auersperg & others, 2019). Those who have experienced multiple divorces are at greater risk. Children in divorced families are more likely than children in nondivorced families to have academic problems, to show externalized problems (such as acting out and delinquency) and internalized problems (such as anxiety and depression), to be less socially responsible, to have less competent intimate relationships, to drop out of school, to become sexually active at an early age, to take drugs, to associate with antisocial peers, to have low self-esteem, and to be less securely attached as young adults; however, contemporary research has moved away from simple comparisons of children whose parents have divorced and those who have not divorced to studying complex histories of instability and contextual factors in children's development (Raley & Sweeney, 2020). In one study, individuals who had experienced their parents' divorce had less satisfaction and more distress in romantic relationships in early adulthood (Roper, Fife, & Seedall, 2020). Experiencing parental divorce in childhood has even been shown to predict long-term poorer health well into middle age (Thomas & Hognas, 2015).

  Nonetheless, keep in mind that a majority of children in divorced families do not have significant adjustment problems (van der Wal, Finkenauer, & Visser, 2019). One classic study found that 20 years after their parents had divorced when they were children, approximately 80 percent of adults concluded that their parents' decision to divorce had been a wise one (Ahrons & Ahrons, 2004). There are long-term implications for children's adult relationships, though. A subsequent study concluded that experiencing parental divorce was linked to having an increased number of

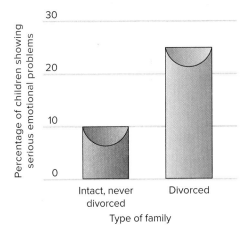

FIGURE 6

DIVORCE AND CHILDREN'S EMOTIONAL PROBLEMS. In Hetherington's research, 25 percent of children from divorced families showed serious emotional problems compared with only 10 percent of children from intact, never-divorced families. However, keep in mind that a substantial majority (75 percent) of the children from divorced families did not show serious emotional problems.

cohabiting/marital partnerships and negative partner relationships from 16 to 30 years of age (Fergusson, McLeod, & Horwood, 2014). An important point is that the outcomes just described for the life event of parental divorce were explained by a variety of other factors and social contexts—parental history of illicit drug use, experience of childhood sexual abuse, lower SES status at the child's birth, and parental history of criminality.

- *Should parents stay together for the sake of the children?* Whether parents should stay in an unhappy or conflictual marriage for the sake of their children is one of the most commonly asked questions about divorce (Morrison, Fife, & Hertlein, 2017). If the stresses and disruptions in family relationships associated with an unhappy marriage are reduced by the move to a divorced, single-parent family, divorce can be advantageous. However, if the diminished resources and increased risks associated with divorce also are accompanied by inept parenting and sustained or increased conflict, not only between the divorced couple but also among the parents, children, and siblings, the best choice for the children would be for an unhappy marriage to be retained (Hetherington & Stanley-Hagan, 2002). It is difficult to determine how these "ifs" will play out when parents either remain together in an acrimonious marriage or become divorced.

  Note that marital conflict has negative consequences for children regardless of whether the parents are married or divorced (Leys & others, 2020). One illustrative longitudinal study revealed that conflict in nondivorced families was associated with emotional problems in children (Amato, 2006). Indeed, many of the problems that children from divorced homes experience begin during the predivorce period, a time when parents are often in active conflict with each other. This conflict increases risks of adjustment problems, in part through cascading effects on other social relationships as children move through adolescence (Davies, Martin, & Cummings, 2018). Thus, when children from divorced homes show problems, the problems may be due not only to the divorce, but also to the marital conflict that led to it.

  E. Mark Cummings and his colleagues (Cummings & Davies, 2010; Cummings & Miller, 2015; Cummings & others, 2017; Cummings & Valentino, 2015) have proposed *emotional security theory,* which has its roots in attachment theory and states that children appraise marital conflict in terms of their sense of security and safety in the family. These researchers make a distinction between marital conflict that is negative for children (such as hostile emotional displays and destructive conflict tactics) and marital conflict that can be positive for children (such as marital disagreement that involves a calm discussion of each person's perspective and working together to reach a solution). In one such study, Cummings and his colleagues (Mills & others, 2021) found that destructive interparental conflict predicted more emotional insecurity, which in turn predicted worse parent-adolescent communication. In a longitudinal study by a different group of researchers, maladaptive marital conflict (for example, destructive strategies and severity of arguments) when children were 2 years old was associated with increased internalizing problems 8 years later due to an undermining of attachment security for girls, while negative emotional aftermath of conflict (due to unresolved, lingering tension in the family) increased both boys' and girls' internalizing problems (Brock & Kochanska, 2016). Cummings and his colleagues have developed an intervention that aims to reduce interparental conflict and, in turn, promote children's emotional security (Hoegler & others, 2023).

- *How much do family processes matter in divorced families?* In divorced families, family processes matter a great deal (Herrero, Martínez-Pampliega, & Alvarez, 2020). When the divorced parents have a harmonious relationship and use authoritative parenting, the adjustment of children is improved. When the divorced parents can agree on child-rearing strategies and can maintain a cordial relationship with each other, frequent visits by the noncustodial parent usually benefit the child (Karberg & Cabrera, 2020). Following a divorce, father involvement with children drops off more than mother involvement, especially for fathers of girls. Further, a recent study of noncustodial fathers in divorced families indicated that high father-child involvement and low interparental conflict were linked to positive child outcomes (Flam & others, 2016). To sum up, a comprehensive research review concluded that coparenting (coparental support, cooperation, and agreement) following divorce was associated with positive child outcomes such as reduced anxiety and depression, as well as higher levels of self-esteem and academic performance (Lamela & Figueiredo, 2016). Finally, interventions to improve post-divorce family processes also have been conducted. For example, an intervention called Fathering Through Change offered to recently separated or divorced fathers improved child adjustment by decreasing fathers' coercive parenting (DeGarmo & Jones, 2019).

- *What factors influence an individual child's vulnerability to negative consequences from living in a divorced family?* Among the factors involved in the child's risk and vulnerability are the child's adjustment prior to the divorce, as well as the child's personality, temperament, and custody situation (Hetherington, 2006). Children whose parents later divorce show poorer adjustment even *before* the breakup (Amato & Booth, 1996; Lansford, 2009), probably due to the conflict that is occurring. Children who are socially mature and responsible, who show few behavioral problems, and who have an easy temperament are better able to cope with their parents' divorce. Children with a difficult temperament often have problems coping with their parents' divorce (Karela & Petrogiannis, 2018). Joint custody works best for children when the parents can get along with each other (Herrero, Martinez-Pampliega, & Alvarez, 2020).

  Early studies by Hetherington and others reported gender differences in response to divorce, with divorce being more negative for girls than for boys in mother-custody families. However, subsequent studies have shown that gender differences are less pronounced and consistent than was previously believed (Parke, 2013). Some of the change in this pattern may be due to the increase in father custody, joint custody, and involvement of noncustodial fathers especially in their sons' lives, compared with the original studies of divorce from the 1970s and 1980s.

What concerns are involved in whether parents should stay together for the sake of the children or become divorced?
Zoey/Image Source/Getty Images

- *What role does socioeconomic status play in the lives of children in divorced families?* It was shown a few decades ago—and is still true today—that custodial mothers experience a much more substantial loss of their predivorce income in comparison with the income loss for custodial fathers (Sbarra & Whisman, 2022). This income loss for divorced mothers is accompanied by increased workloads, high rates of job instability, and residential moves to less desirable neighborhoods with inferior schools (Mortelmans, 2020).

In sum, many factors are involved in determining how divorce influences a child's development (Venta & Walker, 2021). To read about some strategies for helping children cope with their parents' divorce, see the *Caring Connections* interlude.

LGBTQ Parents   Increasingly, LGBTQ couples are creating families that include children (Walker & Taylor, 2021). Today, 15 percent of same-sex couples have at least one child under age 18 in their household (Taylor, 2020). An important aspect of gay and lesbian families with children is the sexual orientation of parents at the time of a child's birth or adoption (Patterson, 2022). The largest group of children with gay and lesbian parents are likely those who were born in the context of heterosexual relationships, with one or both parents only later identifying themselves as gay or lesbian. Gay and lesbian parents may be single or have sex partners. In addition, gays and lesbians are increasingly choosing parenthood through donor insemination or adoption. Researchers have found that the children conceived through new reproductive technologies—such as in vitro fertilization—are as well adjusted as their counterparts conceived by natural means (Golombok, 2021).

Earlier in the chapter, we described the positive outcomes of coparenting for children. One study compared the incidence of coparenting in adoptive heterosexual, lesbian, and gay couples with preschool-aged children (Farr & Patterson, 2013). Both self-reports and observations found that lesbian and gay couples shared child care more than heterosexual couples, with lesbian couples being more supportive than gay couples. Further, a subsequent study revealed more positive parenting in adoptive gay father families and fewer child externalizing problems in these families than in heterosexual families (Golombok & others, 2014).

How Would You...?
If you were a **human development and family studies professional,** how would you apply the guidelines on communicating about divorce to help parents discuss the death of a family member with their children?

Communicating with Children About Divorce

More than 30 years ago, Ellen Galinsky and Judy David (1988) developed a number of guidelines for communicating with children about divorce that are still helpful today:

- *Explain the separation.* As soon as daily activities in the home make it obvious that one parent is leaving, tell the children. If possible, both parents should be present when children are told about the separation to come. The reasons for the separation are very difficult for young children to understand. No matter what parents tell children, children can find reasons to argue against the separation. It is extremely important for parents to tell the children who will take care of them and to describe the specific arrangements for seeing the other parent.

- *Explain that the separation is not the child's fault.* Young children often believe their parents' separation or divorce is their own fault. Therefore, it is important to tell children that they are not the cause of the separation. Parents need to repeat this message a number of times.

- *Explain that it may take time to feel better.* Tell young children that it's normal not to feel good about what is happening and that many other children feel this way when their parents become separated. It is also okay for divorced parents to share some of their emotions with children by saying something like "I'm having a hard time since the separation just like you, but I know it's going to get better

after a while." Such statements are best kept brief and should not criticize the other parent.

- *Keep the door open for further discussion.* Tell your children to come to you anytime they want to talk about the separation. It is healthy for children to express their pent-up emotions in discussions with their parents and to learn that the parents are willing to listen to their feelings and fears.

- *Provide as much continuity as possible.* The less children's worlds are disrupted by the separation, the easier their transition to a single-parent family will be. This means maintaining the rules already in place as much as possible. Children need parents who care enough not only to give them warmth and nurturance but also to set reasonable limits.

- *Provide support for your children and yourself.* Parents are as important to children after a divorce or separation as they were before the divorce or separation. Divorced parents need to provide children with as much support as possible. Parents function best when other people are available to give them support as adults and as parents. Divorced parents can find people who provide practical help and with whom they can talk about their problems. For example, many individuals going through a divorce report that they benefit enormously from having a support system of friends with whom they can discuss their situation.

Another issue focuses on custody arrangements for children. Many individuals from the LGBTQ community have lost custody of their children to heterosexual spouses following divorce. For this reason, many LGBTQ parents are noncustodial parents.

Researchers have found few differences between the adjustment and mental health of children growing up with LGBTQ parents and those who are raised by heterosexual parents (Patterson, Farr, & Goldberg, 2021). Discrimination faced outside the family and processes that are important in all families, such as warmth and involvement, are more important than family structure in the adjustment of children with LGBTQ parents (Carone & others, 2021). An analysis of 72 reviews of the literature concluded that parents' sexual orientation is not related to their children's sexual orientation (Schumm & Crawford, 2019). The majority of children growing up in a household with LBGTQ parents have a heterosexual orientation as adolescents and adults.

Cultural, Ethnic, and Socioeconomic Variations Parenting can be influenced by culture, ethnicity, and socioeconomic status. Recall from Bronfenbrenner's ecological theory (discussed in the "Introduction" chapter) that a number of social contexts influence the child's development. In Bronfenbrenner's theory, culture, ethnicity, and socioeconomic status are classified as part of the macrosystem because they represent broader, societal contexts.

What are the research findings regarding the development and psychological well-being of children raised by LGBTQ parents?
Creatas/Getty Images

Cross-Cultural Studies Different cultures often give different answers to such basic questions as what the father's role in the family should be, what support systems are available to families, and how children should be disciplined (Li & Fung, 2020; Oh, Falbo, & Lee, 2020). There are important cross-cultural variations in parenting (Lansford, 2022). For example, parental monitoring varies across cultures in ways that are related to cultural expectations regarding adolescent autonomy and how much control parents should have over adolescents' decisions and activities (Soenens & Vansteenkiste, 2020).

Cultural change, brought about by such factors as increasingly frequent international travel, the Internet and electronic communications, and economic globalization, affects families in many countries around the world. There are trends toward greater family mobility, migration to urban areas, separation as some family members work in cities or countries far from home, smaller families, fewer extended-family households, and increases in maternal employment (Seltzer, 2019). These trends can change the resources that are available to children. For example, when several generations no longer live near each other, children may lose support and guidance from grandparents, aunts, and uncles. On the positive side, smaller families may produce more openness and communication between parents and children as well as increases in inheritance of financial resources and assets across generations. At the same time, there continues to be a global increase in the availability of smartphones and Internet access, which enables frequent contact among generations even across vast distances (Fingerman, Huo, & Birditt, 2020).

Ethnicity Families within different ethnic groups in the United States and many other diverse countries differ in their typical size, structure, composition, reliance on kinship networks, and levels of income and education (Gibson-Davis, Keister, & Gennetian, 2021). In the United States, large and extended families are more common among ethnic minority groups than among the non-Latino White majority. For example, in 2013 in the United States, 23 percent of Hispanic (the term used by the Census Bureau) individuals had families with five or more people (usually with three or more children), compared with 14 percent of Black American and 10 percent of non-Hispanic White families (Pew Research Center, 2015). In addition, Black American and Latino children interact more with grandparents, aunts, uncles, cousins, and more-distant relatives than do non-Latino White children in the United States (Cross, 2020).

Single-parent families are more common among Black Americans and Latino Americans than among non-Latino White Americans (Cross, 2020). Single-parent households are becoming more common throughout industrialized countries. Furthermore, in most countries, in comparison with two-parent households, single parents usually have fewer resources of time, money, and energy (Mencarini, Pasqua, & Romiti, 2019). Ethnic minority parents also have less access to higher education and are more likely to live in low-income circumstances than their non-Latino White counterparts in the United States. Still, even in challenging economic circumstances, many families, regardless of ethnicity, are resilient and their children grow up to be healthy and happy (Masten & others, 2021).

A major change in families in the last several decades in the United States, Canada, and throughout Europe has been the dramatic increase in the immigration of families from Latin America, Asia, and Africa (Chuang, 2019). Immigrant families often experience stressors uncommon to or less prominent among long-time residents, such as language barriers, dislocations and separations from support networks, the struggle to preserve identity and also acculturate, health, and changes in socioeconomic resources (Cross, Rivas-Drake, & Aramburu, 2022).

Further, an increasing number of children are growing up in transnational families, who move back and forth between the United States, Canada, and many European countries, and another country (Hiitola & others, 2020). In some cases, these children are left behind in their home country or in other cases (especially in China), they are sent back to China to be raised by grandparents during their early childhood years. Such children might benefit from money being sent home but suffer emotionally from prolonged separation from their parents.

Of course, individual families vary, and how ethnic minority and majority families deal with stress depends on many factors (Bae, 2020; Yoshikawa & others, 2016). Whether the parents are native-born or immigrants, how long the family has been in their new country, and their socioeconomic status and national origin all make a difference (Berry, 2015). The characteristics of the family's social context also influence its adaptation. What are the attitudes toward the family's ethnic group within its neighborhood or city? Can the family's children attend good schools? Are there community groups that welcome people from the family's ethnic group? Do members of the family's ethnic group form community groups of their own? To read further about ethnic minority parenting, see the *Connecting with Diversity* interlude.

connecting with diversity

Immigration and Ethnic Minority Parenting

Recent research indicates that many members of families that have recently immigrated to the United States, Canada, and many other countries adopt a bicultural orientation, selecting characteristics of the new culture that help them to survive and advance, while still retaining aspects of their culture of origin (Fang & Huang, 2020). Immigration also involves cultural brokering, which has increasingly occurred in the United States as children and adolescents serve as mediators (cultural and linguistic) for their immigrant parents (López, 2020).

Consider, for example, the experience of Latino immigrant youth in the United States. In adopting characteristics of the U.S. culture, Latino families are increasingly embracing the

How is acculturation involved in ethnic minority parenting?

Jack Hollingsworth/Ocean/Getty Images

importance of education (Arellanes, Anguaino, & Lohman, 2019). Although their school dropout rates have remained higher than for most other ethnic groups, the rates have declined every year into and through 2018 (National Center for Education Statistics, 2019). In addition to adopting aspects of American culture, immigrants often retain positive aspects of their culture of origin. Parenting in many ethnic minority families emphasizes issues associated with promoting children's ethnic pride, knowledge of their ethnic group, and awareness of discrimination (Safa, Umaña-Taylor, & Martinez-Fuentes, 2022).

How Would You...?

If you were an educator, how would you work with low-socioeconomic-status families to increase parental involvement in their children's educational activities?

Socioeconomic Status Low-income families have less access to resources than higher-income families do (Cooper & Pugh, 2020). The differential in access to resources includes nutrition, health care, protection from danger, and enriching educational and socialization opportunities, such as tutoring and lessons in various activities.

Persistent and long-standing poverty can have especially damaging effects on children (Roos, Wall-Wieler, & Lee, 2019). One illuminating study revealed that the more years children spent in poverty, the higher were their physiological indices of stress (Evans & Kim, 2007). Other research has found that persistent economic hardship as well as very early poverty are linked to lower cognitive functioning in children at 5 years of age (Schoon & others, 2012). And in another line of research, poverty-related adversity in family, school, and neighborhood contexts in early childhood has been linked to less effective executive function in middle childhood (Tomlinson & others, 2020).

In the United States and most Western cultures, differences have been found in child rearing among different SES groups. These were identified two decades ago (Hoff, Laursen, & Tardif, 2002, p. 246), and they persist today:

How might socioeconomic status and poverty be linked to parenting and young children's development?

Jens Kalaene/picture-alliance/dpa/AP Images

- "Lower-SES parents (1) are more concerned that their children conform to society's expectations, (2) create a home atmosphere in which it is clear that parents have authority over children," (3) use physical punishment more in disciplining their children, and (4) are more directive and less conversational with their children.

- "Higher-SES parents (1) are more concerned with developing children's initiative" and delay of gratification, (2) "create a home atmosphere in which children are more nearly equal participants and in which rules are discussed as opposed to being laid down" in an authoritarian manner, (3) are less likely to use physical punishment, and (4) "are less directive and more conversational" with their children.

Parents in different socioeconomic groups also tend to think differently about education (Yeung & others, 2022). Middle- and upper-income parents more often think of education as something that should be mutually encouraged by parents and teachers. By contrast, low-income parents are more likely to view education as the teacher's job, or to view access to higher education as unrealistic or unnecessary because of its immediate financial costs (Fischer, Barnes, & Kilpatrick, 2019). Thus, increased school-family linkages can especially benefit students from low-income families.

Review

- What aspects of parenting are linked with young children's development?
- What are the types and consequences of child maltreatment?
- How are sibling relationships and birth order related to young children's development?
- How is children's development affected by having two wage-earning parents, having divorced parents, or being part of a particular cultural, ethnic, and socioeconomic group?

Connect

- Given what you learned in this section, which family interactions would a researcher or marriage and family therapist likely explore in cases of child maltreatment?

Reflect *Your Own Personal Journey of Life*

- Which style or styles of parenting did your parents or caregivers use in rearing you? What effects do you think their parenting styles have had on your development?

---

3 How Are Peer Relations, Play, and Media/Screen Time Involved in Young Children's Development?

LG3 Describe the roles of peers, play, and media/screen time in young children's development.

| Peer Relations | Play | Media/Screen Time |

The family is an important social context for children's development. However, children's development also is strongly influenced by what goes on in other social contexts, such as in peer groups, at play, or while watching television and online content.

PEER RELATIONS

As children grow older, they spend an increasing amount of time with their peers—children of about the same age or maturity level.

What are the functions of a child's peer group? One of its most important functions is to provide a source of information and comparison about the world outside the family. Children receive feedback about their abilities and interests from their peer group. Children evaluate what they do in terms of whether it is better than, as good as, or worse than what other children do. They also can compare what they and their peers like, and do not like, to spend their time doing. It is hard to make these judgments at home because siblings are usually older or younger.

Good peer relations can be necessary for normal socioemotional development (Bukowski, Laursen, & Rubin, 2018; Casper, Card, & Barlow, 2020). Special concerns focus on children who are withdrawn or aggressive. Withdrawn children who are rejected by peers or are victimized and feel lonely are at risk for depression. Children who are aggressive with their peers are at risk of developing a number of problems, including delinquency and dropping out of school (Ersan, 2020).

Developmental Changes   Recall from our discussion of gender that by about the age of 3, children prefer to spend time with same-sex rather than opposite-sex playmates, and this preference increases across early childhood. During these same years, the frequency of peer interaction, both positive and negative, increases considerably (Bukowski, Laursen, & Rubin, 2018). Many preschool children spend considerable time in peer interaction conversing with playmates about such matters as "negotiating roles and rules in play, arguing, and agreeing" (Rubin, Bukowski, & Parker, 2006). And during early childhood, children's interactions with peers become more coordinated and involve longer turns and sequences.

Why are peer relations so important in children's development?
LightFieldStudios/Getty Images

> **developmental connection**
>
> **Peers**
>
> Children's peer relations have been classified in terms of five peer statuses. Connect to "Socioemotional Development in Middle and Late Childhood."

Friends In early childhood, children distinguish between friends and nonfriends. In one experimental study, 4- and 5-year-olds were more likely to expect their friends than nonfriends to share with them; however, 3-year-olds did not yet make this distinction in their expectations about sharing (Lenz & others, 2021). For most young children, a friend is someone to play with. Young preschool children are more likely than older children to have friends who are of different gender and ethnicity (Y. Wang & others, 2019).

The Connected Worlds of Parent-Child and Peer Relations Parents influence their children's peer relations in many ways, both direct and indirect (Nocentini & others, 2019). Parents affect their children's peer relations through their interactions with their children, how they manage their children's lives, and the opportunities they provide their children, and children's experiences in peer relationships can also affect relationships with parents (Kaufman & others, 2020). For example, one study found that when mothers coached their preschool daughters about the negative aspects of peer conflicts involving relational aggression (harming someone by manipulating a relationship), the daughters engaged in lower rates of relational aggression (Werner & others, 2014).

Basic decisions by parents—their choices of neighborhoods, religious communities, schools, and their own friends—largely determine the pool from which their children select possible friends. These choices in turn affect which children their children meet, their purpose in interacting, and eventually which children become their friends.

Researchers also have found that children's peer relations are linked to a number of aspects of parenting, such as sensitivity and harshness (Ringoot & others, 2022). Early attachments to caregivers provide a connection to children's peer relations not only by creating a secure base from which children can explore social relationships beyond the family but also by conveying a working model of relationships (Booth-LaForce & Groh, 2018).

Do these results indicate that children's peer relations always are wedded to parent-child relationships? Although parent-child relationships influence children's subsequent peer relations, children also learn other modes of relating through their relationships with peers. For example, rough-and-tumble play occurs mainly with other children, not in parent-child interaction. In times of stress, children often turn to parents rather than peers for support. In parent-child relationships, children learn how to relate to authority figures. With their peers, children are likely to interact on a much more equal basis and to learn a mode of relating based on mutual influence.

PLAY

An extensive amount of peer interaction during childhood involves play, but social play is only one type of play. *Play* is a pleasurable activity that is engaged in for its own sake, and its functions and forms vary.

Play's Functions Play is essential to the young child's health (Lucas, 2020). Theorists have focused on different aspects of play and highlighted a long list of functions (Lucas, 2020).

According to Freud and Erikson, play helps the child master anxieties and conflicts (Demanchick, 2015). Because tensions are relieved in play, the child can cope more effectively with life's problems. Play permits the child to work off excess physical energy and to release pent-up tensions. Therapists use *play therapy* both to allow the child to work off frustrations and to analyze the child's conflicts and ways of coping with them (Clark, 2016). Children may feel less threatened and be more likely to express their true feelings in the context of play (Perryman & others, 2020).

Play also is an important context for cognitive development (Christie, 2022). Piaget (1962) maintained that play advances children's cognitive development. At the same time, he said that children's cognitive development constrains the way they play. Play permits children to practice their competencies and acquired skills in a relaxed, pleasurable way. Piaget thought that cognitive structures need to be exercised, and play provides the perfect setting for this exercise. For example, children who have just learned to add or multiply begin to play with numbers in different ways as they perfect these operations, laughing as they do so.

Margo Harrison/123RF

Lev Vygotsky (1962) also considered play to be an excellent setting for cognitive development. He was especially interested in the symbolic and make-believe aspects of play, as when a child substitutes a stick for a horse and rides the stick as if it were a horse. For young children, the imaginary situation is real. Parents should encourage such imaginary play because it advances the child's cognitive development, especially creative thought.

Another classic theoretical foundation for play was established by Daniel Berlyne (1960), who described play as exciting and pleasurable in itself because it satisfies our exploratory drive. This drive involves curiosity and a desire for information about something new or unusual. Play is a means whereby children can safely explore and seek out new information. Play encourages exploratory behavior by offering children the possibilities of novelty, complexity, uncertainty, surprise, and incongruity.

More recently, play has been described as an important context for the development of language, communication, and self-regulation skills (Baron & others, 2020; Taggart, Eisen, & Lillard, 2018). Language and communication skills may be enhanced through discussions and negotiations regarding roles and rules in play as young children practice various words and phrases. These types of social interactions during play can benefit young children's literacy skills (Jones & Christensen, 2022). And, as we saw in "Cognitive Development in Early Childhood," play is a central focus of the child-centered kindergarten and is thought to be an essential aspect of early childhood education (Henniger, 2017; Morrison, 2018).

Types of Play   The contemporary perspective on play emphasizes both the cognitive and the social aspects of play (Evans & others, 2022). Among the most widely studied types of children's play today are sensorimotor and practice play, pretense/symbolic play, social play, constructive play, and games (Fromberg & Bergen, 2015).

Sensorimotor and Practice Play   **Sensorimotor play** is behavior by infants to derive pleasure from exercising their sensorimotor schemes. The development of sensorimotor play follows Piaget's description of sensorimotor thought. Infants initially engage in exploratory and playful visual and motor transactions in the second quarter of the first year of life. For example, at 9 months of age, infants begin to select novel objects for exploration and play, especially responsive objects such as toys that make noise or bounce. At 12 months of age, infants enjoy making things work and exploring cause and effect.

Practice play involves the repetition of behavior when new skills are being learned or when physical or mental mastery and coordination of skills are required for games or sports. Sensorimotor play, which often involves practice play, is primarily confined to infancy, whereas practice play can be engaged in throughout life. During the preschool years, children often engage in practice play. Although practice play declines in the elementary school years, practice play activities such as running, jumping, sliding, twirling, and throwing balls or other objects are frequently observed on the playgrounds at elementary schools.

Pretense/Symbolic Play   **Pretense/symbolic play** occurs when the child transforms aspects of the physical environment into symbols. Between 9 and 30 months of age, children increase their use of objects in symbolic play. They learn to transform objects—substituting them for other objects and acting toward them as if they were these other objects (Lillard & Taggart, 2019). For example, a preschool child treats a chair as if it were a horse and says, "I'm riding the horse," as she grabs the back of the chair. Many experts on play have long considered the preschool years the "golden age" of symbolic/pretense play that is dramatic or sociodramatic in nature (Rubin, Bukowski, & Parker, 2006). This type of make-believe play often appears at about 18 months of age and reaches a peak at 4 to 5 years of age, then gradually declines.

Some child psychologists conclude that pretend play is an important aspect of young children's development and often reflects advances in their cognitive development, especially as an indication of symbolic understanding (Kang & others, 2016). For example, Catherine Garvey (2000) and Angeline Lillard (2006; Lillard & Taggart, 2019) emphasize that hidden in young children's pretend play narratives are remarkable capacities for role-taking, balancing of social roles, metacognition (thinking about thinking), testing of the reality-pretense distinction, and numerous nonegocentric capacities that reveal the remarkable cognitive skills of young children.

Social Play   **Social play** involves interaction with peers. Social play increases dramatically during the preschool years. For many children, social play is the main context for social interactions with peers (Solovieva & Quintanar, 2017).

developmental **connection**

Cognitive Theory

Vygotsky emphasized the importance of culture and social interaction in children's cognitive development. Connect to "Cognitive Development in Early Childhood."

A preschool "superhero" at play.
Michelle D. Milliman/Shutterstock

sensorimotor play Behavior engaged in by infants to derive pleasure from exercising their existing sensorimotor schemas.

practice play Play that involves repetition of behavior when new skills are being learned or when physical or mental mastery and coordination of skills are required for games or sports.

pretense/symbolic play Play in which the child transforms aspects of the physical environment into symbols.

social play Play that involves social interactions with peers.

What are some different types of play?
McGraw Hill

Constructive Play   **Constructive play** combines sensorimotor/practice play with symbolic representation. Constructive play occurs when children engage in the self-regulated creation of a product or a solution. Constructive play increases in the preschool years as symbolic play increases and sensorimotor play decreases. Constructive play is also a frequent form of play in the elementary school years, both inside and outside the classroom.

Games   **Games** are activities that are engaged in for pleasure and that have rules. Often they involve competition. Preschool children may begin to participate in social games that involve simple rules of reciprocity and turn-taking. However, games take on a much more important role in the lives of elementary school children. After age 12, playground and neighborhood games decline in popularity (Fromberg & Bergen, 2015). With the advent of digital games on mobile devices, game playing has become widely available and used by older children, adolescents, and adults (Pew Research Center, 2018).

In sum, play ranges from an infant's simple exercise of a new sensorimotor skill to a preschool child's riding a tricycle to an older child's participation in organized games. Note that children's play can involve a combination of the play categories we have discussed. For example, social play can be sensorimotor (rough-and-tumble), symbolic, or constructive.

Trends in Play   Kathy Hirsh-Pasek, Roberta Golinkoff, and their colleagues emphasize the importance of play for children's healthy development, and they stress that early childhood programs should give children plenty of time to play rather than trying to promote school readiness by substituting more didactic forms of learning (Hassinger-Das, Hirsh-Pasek, & Golinkoff, 2017; Yogman & others, 2018). They underscore that learning in playful contexts captivates children's minds in ways that enhance their cognitive and socioemotional development—Singer, Golinkoff, and Hirsh-Pasek's (2006) first book on play was titled *Play = Learning.* Among the cognitive benefits of play they described are these skills: creative,

What are some of the benefits of play for children, according to Hirsh-Pasek and her colleagues?
Temple University, photo by Joseph V. Labolito

constructive play Play that combines sensorimotor/practice play with symbolic representation. Constructive play occurs when children engage in self-regulated creation or construction of a product or a solution.

games Activities engaged in for pleasure that include rules and often competition with one or more individuals.

abstract thinking; imagination; attention, concentration, and persistence; problem-solving; social cognition, empathy, and perspective taking; language; and mastering new concepts. Among the socioemotional experiences and development they believe play promotes are enjoyment, relaxation, and self-expression; cooperation, sharing, and turn-taking; anxiety reduction; and self-confidence. With so many positive cognitive and socioemotional outcomes of play, clearly it is important that we find more time for play in young children's lives.

MEDIA/SCREEN TIME

If the amount of time spent in an activity is any indication of its importance, there is no doubt that media/screen time plays important roles in children's and adolescents' lives

(Stienwandt & others, 2022). Few developments in society in the past 50 years have had a greater impact on children, adolescents, and society at large than television, digital gaming, and the Internet. Television continues to have a strong influence on children's development, but children's use of other media and information/communication devices has led to the use of the term *screen time,* which includes how much time individuals spend watching television or DVDs, playing video games, and using computers or handheld electronic devices such as smartphones. Contemporary pediatric guidelines recommend that children younger than 2 years have no screen time and that children between the ages of 2 and 5 years be limited to one hour of screen time per day. A meta-analysis of 63 studies including 89,163 participants found that only 25 percent of children younger than 2 and 36 percent of children ages 2 to 5 were meeting the guidelines (McArthur & others, 2022).

Compared with their counterparts in other developed countries, children in the United States have considerably more screen time (see Figure 7). The American Academy of Pediatrics (2021) recommends that 2- to 5-year-olds have no more than one hour of screen time a day. The Academy also recommends that media consumption by this age group should consist of high-quality programs, such as *Sesame Street,* as well as educationally and socioculturally rich apps for young children. Many children spend more time with various screen media than they do interacting with their parents and peers, and this disparity continues to grow with the proliferation of small handheld devices that are now commonly used by toddlers and preschoolers every day in many industrialized countries (Levine & others, 2019).

Among other concerns about young children having so much screen time are decreased time spent in play, less time interacting with peers, lower levels of physical activity, increased risk of overweight and obesity, poor sleep habits, and higher rates of aggression. The total amount of screen time as well as the content they view and conditions in which children interact with media are all important. For example, in a meta-analysis of studies conducted between 1960 and 2019, more screen time was related to poorer language skills for children ages 12 and younger, but the quality of screen use mattered too (Madigan & others, 2020). Children who watched educational programs and co-viewed with their parents had better language skills than those who viewed purely for entertainment and watched alone.

Learning from media is difficult for infants and toddlers, and they learn much more easily from direct experiences with people. At about 3 years of age, children can learn from media with educational material if the media use effective strategies such as repeating concepts a number of times, use images and sounds that capture young children's attention, and use children's rather than adults' voices. However, the vast majority of media that young children experience is geared toward entertainment rather than education (Callaghan & Reich, 2018).

Screen time can have a negative influence on children by making them passive learners, distracting them from doing homework, teaching them stereotypes, providing them with violent models of aggression, presenting them with unrealistic views of the world, and increasing sleep problems (Calvert, 2015). Further, researchers have found that a high level of TV viewing in early childhood predicts adolescent habits and outcomes years later. One of the largest longitudinal studies from Canada found effects years later on weight, eating habits, and academic

How does screen time influence children's development?
Luca Cappelli/Getty Images

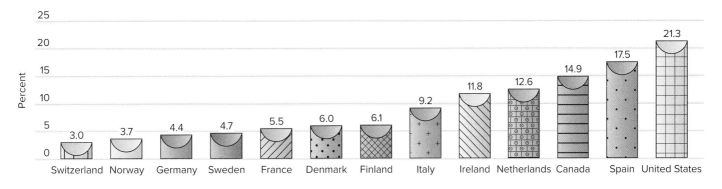

FIGURE 7

PERCENTAGE OF 9-YEAR-OLD CHILDREN WHO REPORT HAVING MORE THAN FIVE HOURS OF SCREEN TIME PER WEEKDAY

How Would You...?

If you were a **human development and family studies professional,** how would you talk with parents about strategies for improving their children's screen time?

engagement (Simonato & others, 2018). A comprehensive review of the literature noted that many of the behavioral and health risks arising from extensive screen viewing reflect impacts on sleep and wake-time habits (LeBourgeois & others, 2017).

However, television also can have a positive influence on children's development by presenting motivating educational programs, increasing their information about the world beyond their immediate environment, and providing models of prosocial behavior (de Leeuw & van der Laan, 2018). A comprehensive meta-analysis of studies conducted in 15 countries found that watching *Sesame Street* had the following positive outcomes for children: (1) developing cognitive skills (literacy and numeracy, for example); (2) learning about the world (health and safety knowledge, for example); and (3) increasing social reasoning and encouraging tolerant and accepting attitudes toward out-groups (Mares & Pan, 2013). Newer technologies, especially interactive touchscreen games, hold promise for motivating children to learn and become better problem solvers (Blumberg & others, 2019). At the same time, there is mounting evidence that digital training to enhance skills (for example, memory, attention, reaction time) will not have general or long-lasting positive effects on cognitive ability, even if there are short-term effects on some very specific skills (Sala, Tatlidil, & Gobet, 2018).

Effects of Screen Time on Children's Aggression

The extent to which children are exposed to violence and aggression during screen time raises special concern (Miles-Novelo & others, 2022). For example, some cartoon shows average more than 25 violent acts per hour. Research reviews have concluded that children and adolescents who experience a heavy diet of media violence are more likely to perceive the world as a dangerous place and to view aggression as more acceptable than their counterparts who see media violence less frequently (Groves, Prot, & Anderson, 2020). This pattern of effects may be due to the reinforcement of beliefs and attributions about others and can be a source of aggression intent and behavior—an effect that may grow over time with development and prolonged exposure into adulthood (Anderson & Bushman, 2018).

In addition to television violence, there is increased concern about children who play violent video games, especially those that are highly realistic. Meta-analyses have demonstrated consistent links between playing violent video games and children's aggressive behavior, even after taking into account the propensity for children who are already aggressive to choose more violent media content (Greitemeyer, 2022).

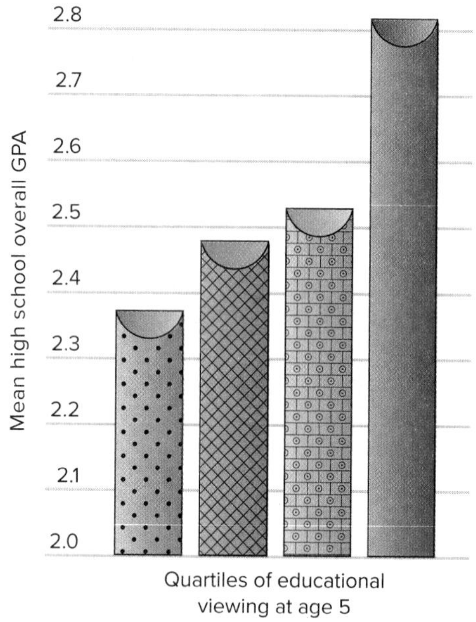

Effects of Screen Time on Children's Prosocial Behavior

Television also can teach children that it is better to behave in positive, prosocial ways than in negative, antisocial ways (Maloy & others, 2017; Prot & others, 2017; Truglio & Kotler, 2014). In an early study, Aimee Leifer (1973) selected episodes from the television show *Sesame Street* that reflected positive social interchanges in which children were taught how to use their social skills. For example, in one interchange, two men were fighting over the amount of space available to them; they gradually began to cooperate and to share the space. Children who watched these episodes copied these behaviors, and in later social situations they applied the prosocial lessons they had learned. More recent research also has found that playing prosocial video games is related to more subsequent prosocial thoughts and behaviors (Li & Zhang, 2023).

Screen Time, Achievement, and Cognitive Development

Watching television has been linked with lower school achievement (Adelantado-Renau & others, 2019). However, some types of television—such as educational programming for young children—may enhance achievement. For example, in one classic longitudinal study, viewing educational programs such as *Sesame Street* and *Mr. Rogers' Neighborhood* as preschoolers was associated with a host of desirable characteristics in adolescence: getting higher grades, reading more books, placing a higher value on achievement, being more creative, and behaving less aggressively (Anderson & others, 2001) (see Figure 8). These associations were more consistent for boys than girls. In contrast and on a less positive note, a more recent research review concluded that higher levels of screen time (mostly involving TV viewing) were associated with lower levels of cognitive development in early childhood (Carson & others, 2015).

FIGURE 8

EDUCATIONAL TV VIEWING AND HIGH SCHOOL GRADE-POINT AVERAGE FOR BOYS. When boys watched more educational television (especially *Sesame Street*) as preschoolers, they had higher grade-point averages in high school (Anderson & others, 2001). The graph displays the boys' early TV-viewing patterns in quartiles and the means of their grade-point averages. The bar on the left is for the lowest 25 percent of boys who viewed educational TV programs, the next bar the next 25 percent, and so on, with the bar on the right for the 25 percent of the boys who watched the most educational TV shows as preschoolers.

Y-axis: Mean high school overall GPA (2.0 to 2.8)
X-axis: Quartiles of educational viewing at age 5

Review *Connect* Reflect

LG3 Describe the roles of peers, play, and media/screen time in young children's development.

Review

- How do peers affect young children's development?
- What are some theories about the purposes of various types of play?
- How do media and screen time influence children's development?

Connect

- Earlier in the chapter, you read about Laurie Kramer's program for teaching

siblings social skills to reduce sibling conflict. Would her recommendations also apply to reducing conflict in peer relationships? Explain.

Reflect *Your Own Personal Journey of Life*

- What guidelines would you adopt for your own children's screen time/media use?

⌐topical connections *looking forward*

This chapter brings your exploration of early childhood to a close. In the next chapter you will begin to study middle and late childhood, especially the physical, brain, and motor skill changes that occur during this period of development. The middle and late childhood years also produce further changes in children's socioemotional development, which you will study in "Socioemotional Development in Middle and Late Childhood." Development of self-understanding and understanding others becomes more sophisticated, emotional understanding improves, and moral reasoning advances. Children in this age group spend less time with parents, but parents still play very important roles in children's lives, especially in guiding their academic achievement and managing their opportunities. Peer status and friendship become more important in children's peer relations, and school takes on a stronger academic focus.

---

reach your **learning goals**

Socioemotional Development in Early Childhood

1 What Characterizes Young Children's Emotional and Personality Development?

LG1 Discuss emotional and personality development in early childhood.

The Self

- In Erikson's theory, early childhood is a period when development involves resolving the conflict of initiative versus guilt. The toddler's rudimentary self-understanding develops into the preschooler's representation of the self in terms of body attributes, material possessions, and physical activities. At about 4 to 5 years of age, children also begin to use traitlike self-descriptions. Young children display more sophisticated self-understanding and understanding of others than was previously thought.

Emotional Development

- Young children's range of emotions expands during early childhood as they increasingly experience self-conscious emotions such as pride, shame, and guilt. Between 2 and 4 years of age, children use an increasing number of terms to describe emotion and learn more about the causes and consequences of feelings. At 4 to 5 years of age, children show an increased ability to reflect on emotions and to understand that a single event can elicit different emotions in different people. They also show a growing awareness of the need to manage emotions to meet social standards.

- Emotion-coaching parents have children who engage in more effective self-regulation of their emotions than do emotion-dismissing parents. Emotion regulation plays an important role in successful peer relations.

- Moral development involves thoughts, feelings, and behaviors regarding rules and regulations about what people should do in their interactions with others. Freud's psychoanalytic theory emphasizes the importance of feelings in the development of morality. Positive emotions, such as empathy, also contribute to the child's moral development. Piaget analyzed moral reasoning and concluded that children from 4 to 7 years of age display heteronomous morality, judging behavior by its consequences.

- According to behavioral and social cognitive theorists, moral behavior develops as a result of reinforcement, punishment, and imitation, and there is considerable situational variability in moral behavior. Conscience refers to an internal regulation of standards of right and wrong that involves an integration of moral thought, feeling, and behavior. Young children's conscience emerges out of relationships with parents. Parents influence young children's moral development by developing quality parent-child relationships, by being proactive in helping children avert misbehavior, and by engaging children in conversational dialogue about moral issues.

- Gender refers to the characteristics of people as boys/men or girls/women. Gender identity involves a sense of one's own gender, including knowledge, understanding, and acceptance of being a boy/man, girl/woman, or another gender. A gender role is a set of expectations that prescribes how girls/women or boys/men should think, act, and feel. Gender typing refers to the acquisition of a traditional masculine or feminine role.

- Biological influences on gender development include chromosomes and hormones. However, biology is not the sole determinant of gender development; children's socialization experiences matter a great deal. Social role theory and social cognitive theory emphasize various aspects of social experiences in the development of gender characteristics.

- Parents influence children's gender development, and peers are especially adept at rewarding stereotypically gender-appropriate behavior. Gender schema theory emphasizes that gender typing emerges as children develop schemas of their culture's perceptions of gender-appropriate and gender-inappropriate behaviors.

2 What Roles Do Families Play in Young Children's Development?

 LG2 Explain how families can influence young children's development.

- Authoritarian, authoritative, neglectful, and indulgent are four main parenting styles. Authoritative parenting is the most widely used style around the world and is the style most often associated with children's social competence. However, ethnic variations in parenting styles suggest that in some ethnic groups, some aspects of authoritarian control may benefit children. Some criticisms of the categorization of parenting styles have been made, such as its failure to capture the themes of reciprocal socialization and synchrony. There are a number of reasons not to use physical punishment to discipline children. Coparenting has positive effects on children's development.

- Child maltreatment may take the form of physical abuse, child neglect, sexual abuse, and emotional abuse. Child maltreatment places the child at risk for academic, emotional, and social problems. Adults who suffered child maltreatment are also vulnerable to a range of problems.

- Siblings interact with each other in positive and negative ways. Birth order is related in certain ways to child characteristics, but by itself it is not a good predictor of behavior.

- In general, having both parents employed full-time outside the home does not have negative effects on children. However, the nature of parents' work can affect their parenting quality.

- Divorce can have negative effects on children's adjustment, but so can an acrimonious relationship between parents who stay together for their children's sake. If divorced parents develop a harmonious relationship and practice authoritative parenting, children's adjustment improves.

- Researchers have found few differences between children growing up in LGBTQ families and children growing up in heterosexual families.

- Cultures vary on a number of issues regarding families. Black American and Latino children are more likely than non-Latino White American children to live in single-parent families and larger families and to have extended-family connections.

- Low-income families have less access to resources than higher-income families. Lower-SES parents create a home atmosphere that involves more authority and physical punishment with children than higher-SES parents. Higher-SES parents are more concerned about developing children's initiative and delay of gratification.

3 How Are Peer Relations, Play, and Media/ Screen Time Involved in Young Children's Development?

LG3 Describe the roles of peers, play, and media/screen time in young children's development.

Peer Relations

Play

Media/Screen Time

- Peers are powerful socialization agents. Peers provide a source of information and comparison about the world outside the family.

- Play's functions include affiliation with peers, tension release, advances in cognitive development, exploration, and provision of a safe haven. The contemporary perspective on play emphasizes both the cognitive and social aspects of play. Among the most widely studied types of children's play are sensorimotor play, practice play, pretense/symbolic play, social play, constructive play, and games.

- There is substantial concern about the increase in media/screen time in young children. Extensive media/screen time in young children is linked to a number of negative developmental outcomes. Screen time can have both negative developmental influences (such as turning children into passive learners and presenting them with models of aggressive behavior) and positive influences (such as providing models of prosocial behavior). Media violence is not the only cause of children's aggression, but it can induce aggression. Prosocial behavior during screen time can teach children positive behavior. High levels of overall screen time are linked to lower achievement in school, but exposure to educational media in early childhood is linked to higher academic achievement.

key terms

authoritarian parenting	gender identity	moral development	sensorimotor play
authoritative parenting	gender role	neglectful parenting	social cognitive theory of gender
autonomous morality	gender schema theory	perspective taking	social play
conscience	gender typing	practice play	social role theory
constructive play	heteronomous morality	pretense/symbolic play	sympathy
empathy	immanent justice	psychoanalytic theory of gender	
games	indulgent parenting	self-understanding	

key people

Diana Baumrind	Erik Erikson	Kathy Hirsh-Pasek	Cybele Raver
Daniel Berlyne	Sigmund Freud	Grazyna Kochanska	Ross Thompson
Ruth Chao	Catherine Garvey	Lawrence Kohlberg	Lev Vygotsky
Ann Crouter	Elizabeth Gershoff	Laurie Kramer	
E. Mark Cummings	Roberta Golinkoff	Angeline Lillard	
Judy Dunn	Susan Harter	Jean Piaget	

improving the **lives of children**

STRATEGIES

Guiding Young Children's Socioemotional Development

How can young children's socioemotional skills be nourished? These strategies can help:

- *Look for opportunities to help children with their emotions.* Parents, teachers, and other adults can help children understand and handle their emotions in socially acceptable ways.

- *Present positive moral models for the child and use emotional situations to promote moral development.* Children benefit when they are around people who engage in prosocial rather than antisocial behavior. Encourage children to show empathy and learn to deal with their emotions.

- *Be an authoritative parent.* Children's self-control and social competence benefit when both parents are authoritative—that is, when they are neither punitive and overcontrolling nor permissive or neglectful. Authoritative parents are nurturant, engage the child in verbal give-and-take, monitor the child, and use nonpunitive control.

- *Adapt to the child's developmental changes.* Parents should use less physical manipulation and more reasoning or withholding of special privileges in disciplining a 5-year-old in comparison with strategies used for disciplining a 2-year-old.

- *Communicate effectively with children in a divorced family.* Good strategies are to explain the separation and say it is not the child's fault, assure the child that it may take time to feel better, keep the door open for further discussion, provide as much continuity as possible, and supply a support system for the child.

- *Provide the child with opportunities for peer interaction.* Children learn a great deal from the mutual give-and-take of peer relations. Make sure the child gets considerable time to play with peers rather than watching TV or attending an academic early childhood program for the entire day.

- *Provide the child with many opportunities for play.* Positive play experiences can greatly support the young child's socioemotional development.

- *Monitor the child's media/screen time.* Keep exposure to media violence to a minimum with no more than one hour of screen time per day. Develop a set of guidelines for the child's media/screen time, especially emphasizing quality programs such as *Sesame Street.*

RESOURCES

Societal Contexts of Child Development (2014)
Elizabeth Gershoff, Rashmita Mistry, and Danielle Crosby (Eds.)
New York: Oxford University Press

Leading experts describe many aspects of social contexts that influence children's development and have implications for improving children's lives.

The Future of Families (2013)
Ross Parke
New York: Wiley

One of the world's leading experts on children's socioemotional development, Ross Parke, explores the wide diversity in family forms that increasingly characterize children's lives, including fathers as single parents, same-gender parents, new reproductive technologies, and immigrant families.

The Early Years Matter: Education, Care, and the Well-Being of Children, Birth to 8 (2014)
Marylou Hyson and Heather Biggar Tomlinson
New York: Teachers College Press

This book by leading experts on early childhood provides teachers, child-care providers, and other stakeholders in early childhood education with an overview of the importance of birth to age 8 for children's success and well-being.

The Co-Parenting Handbook: Raising Well-Adjusted and Resilient Kids from Little Ones to Young Adults Through Divorce or Separation (2017)
Karen Bonnell, with Kristin Little
Seattle, WA: Sasquatch Books

A parenting coach and child specialist help guide parents through the family transition as they collaborate to support their children's healthy adjustment.

Gender and Development (2019)
Janet Momsen
New York: Routledge

This book describes the role of gender in low- and middle-income countries, particularly in relation to the United Nations Sustainable Development Goals related to gender equity.

Parents and Digital Technologies (2016)
Suzie Hayman and John Coleman
New York: Oxford University Press

An excellent book with recommendations to help parents develop effective strategies for communicating with children about technology, as well as set boundaries and establish rules.

Each forward step we take we leave some phantom of ourselves behind.

—JOHN LANCASTER SPALDING
American Educator, 19th Century

FatCamera/E+/Getty Images

Middle and Late Childhood

In middle and late childhood, children are on a different plane, belonging to a generation and feeling all their own. It is the wisdom of the human life span that at no time are children more ready to learn than during the period of expansive imagination at the end of early childhood. Children develop a sense of wanting to make things—and not just to make them, but to make them well and even perfectly. They seek to know and to understand. They are remarkable for their intelligence and for their curiosity. Their parents continue to be important influences in their lives, but their growth also is shaped by peers and friends. They don't think much about the future or about the past, but they enjoy the present moment. Section 5 consists of three chapters: "Physical Development in Middle and Late Childhood," "Cognitive Development in Middle and Late Childhood," and "Socioemotional Development in Middle and Late Childhood."

chapter 11

PHYSICAL DEVELOPMENT IN MIDDLE AND LATE CHILDHOOD

chapter outline

FatCamera/Getty Images

The following comments were made by Angie, an elementary-school-age girl:

When I was eight years old, I weighed 125 pounds. My clothes were the size that large teenage girls wear. I hated my body and my classmates teased me all the time. I was so overweight and out of shape that when I took a P.E. class my face would get red and I had trouble breathing. I was jealous of the kids who played sports and weren't overweight like I was.

I'm nine years old now and I've lost 30 pounds. I'm much happier and proud of myself. How did I lose the weight? My mom took me to a pediatrician who specializes in helping children lose weight and keep it off. The pediatrician counseled my mom about my eating and exercise habits, then had us join a group that he had created for overweight children and their parents. My mom and I go to the group once a week and we've now been participating in the program for six months. I no longer eat fast-food meals and my mom is cooking more healthy meals. Now that I've lost weight, exercise is not as hard for me and I don't get teased by the kids at school. My mom's pretty happy too because she's lost 15 pounds herself since we've been in the counseling program.

Not all overweight children are as successful as Angie at reducing their weight. Indeed, being overweight in childhood has become a major national concern in the United States. Later in the chapter, we explore in detail the topic of being overweight in childhood, including its causes and outcomes.

topical connections   *looking **back***

In the last chapter you concluded your study of early childhood by looking at socioemotional development in young children, the accompanying moral development that takes place, and children's growing sense of self and gender. You became familiar with the role of family, siblings, peers, play, and the media in early childhood. You learned that children grow more slowly in early childhood than in infancy, but they still grow an average of 2½ inches and 5 to 7 pounds a year. In early childhood, the most rapid growth in the brain occurs in the prefrontal cortex.

preview

Considerable progress in children's physical development continues to take place in the middle and late childhood years. Children grow taller, heavier, and stronger. They become more adept at using their physical skills. We begin the chapter by exploring the changes that characterize body growth and motor skills, then examine the central issues in children's health, and conclude by discussing children with disabilities and their education.

1 What Changes Take Place in Body Growth, the Brain, and Motor Development?

 LG1 Discuss changes in body growth, the brain, and motor development in middle and late childhood.

Skeletal and Muscular Systems · The Brain · Motor Development

The period of middle and late childhood involves slow, consistent growth. This is a period of calm before the rapid growth spurt of adolescence (Hockenberry, Wilson, & Rodgers, 2017). Among the important aspects of body growth and proportion in this developmental period are those involving skeletal and muscular systems, the brain, and motor development.

SKELETAL AND MUSCULAR SYSTEMS

During the elementary school years, children grow an average of 2 to 3 inches a year until, at the age of 11, the average girl is 4 feet, 9 inches tall, and the average boy is 4 feet, 7¾ inches tall. The average 8-year-old girl and the average 8-year-old boy weigh 56 pounds (National Center for Health Statistics, 2022). During middle and late childhood, children gain about 5 to 7 pounds a year. The weight increase is due mainly to increases in the size of the skeletal and muscular systems, as well as the size of some body organs. Muscle mass and strength gradually increase as "baby fat" decreases. The loose movements of early childhood give way to improved muscle tone. The increase in muscular strength is due both to heredity and to exercise. Children also double their strength capabilities during these years. A summary of the changes in height and weight in middle and late childhood appears in Figure 1.

Proportional changes are among the most pronounced physical changes in middle and late childhood (Hockenberry, Wilson, & Rodgers, 2021). Head circumference, waist circumference, and leg length decrease in relation to body height. A less noticeable physical change is that bones continue to ossify (harden) during middle and late childhood.

THE BRAIN

The development of brain-imaging techniques, such as magnetic resonance imaging (MRI), has led to increased research on changes in the brain during middle and late childhood and on how these brain changes are linked to improvements in cognitive development (de Haan & Johnson, 2016; Kraus & Horowitz-Kraus, 2022). One such change

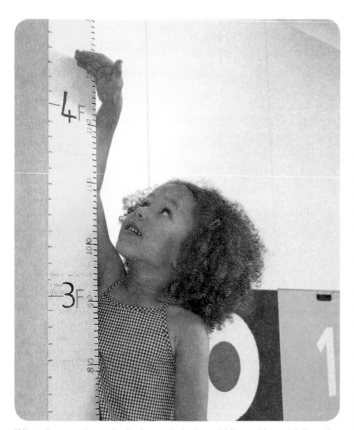

What characterizes physical growth during middle and late childhood?
Chris Windsor/Digital Vision/Getty Images

Age	Female Percentiles			Male Percentiles		
	25th	50th	75th	25th	50th	75th
6	43.75	45.00	46.50	44.25	45.75	47.00
7	46.00	47.50	49.00	46.25	48.00	49.25
8	48.00	49.75	51.50	48.50	50.00	51.50
9	50.25	53.00	53.75	50.50	52.00	53.50
10	52.50	54.50	56.25	52.50	54.25	55.75
11	55.00	57.00	58.75	54.50	55.75	57.25

WEIGHT (POUNDS)

Age						
6	39.25	43.00	47.25	42.00	45.50	49.50
7	43.50	48.50	53.25	46.25	50.25	55.00
8	49.00	54.75	61.50	51.00	55.75	61.50
9	55.75	62.75	71.50	56.00	62.00	69.25
10	63.25	71.75	82.75	62.00	69.25	78.50
11	71.75	81.25	94.25	69.00	77.75	89.00

FIGURE **1**

CHANGES IN HEIGHT AND WEIGHT IN MIDDLE AND LATE CHILDHOOD. *Note:* The percentile tells how the child compares with other children of the same age. The 50th percentile tells us that half of the children of a particular age are taller (heavier) or shorter (lighter). The 25th percentile tells us that 25 percent of the children of that age are shorter (lighter) and 75 percent are taller (heavier).

involves increased myelination, which improves the speed of processing information and communication in the higher regions of the brain, such as the cerebral cortex. The increase in myelination during middle and late childhood is linked to more effective processing of information on cognitive tasks (Kwon & others, 2020; Wendelken & others, 2016). Recall from our discussion in "Physical Development in Early Childhood" that myelination is the process of encasing axons with fat cells.

Total brain volume stabilizes by the end of late childhood, but significant changes in various structures and regions of the brain continue to occur. In particular, the brain pathways and circuitry involving the prefrontal cortex, the highest level in the brain, continue to increase (Denes, 2016). These advances in the prefrontal cortex are linked to children's improved attention, reasoning, and cognitive control (Bell, 2023; Bell & Broomell, 2022). (See Figure 6 for the location of the prefrontal cortex in the brain.)

Leading developmental cognitive neuroscientist Mark Johnson and his colleagues (2009, 2021) have found and summarized the research evidence that the prefrontal cortex likely orchestrates the functions of many other brain regions during development. As part of its neural organizational role, the prefrontal cortex may provide an advantage to neural networks and connections that include the prefrontal cortex. According to these and other researchers, the prefrontal cortex coordinates the best neural connections for solving a problem at hand.

Changes also occur in the thickness of the cerebral cortex (cortical thickness) in middle and late childhood. Studies using brain scans have found that cortical thickness is related to general intelligence as well as to improvements in specific abilities related to reading, attention, and other abilities that develop during middle and late childhood (Schmitt & others, 2019). Cortical thickening in the temporal and frontal lobe areas that function in language may account for improvements in language abilities such as reading. Cortical thickness appears to reach its peak in early or middle childhood, then gradually decreases over the rest of the life span (Frangou & others, 2022).

As children develop, activation of some brain areas increases, while that of others decreases (Denes, 2016). One shift in activation that occurs as children develop is from diffuse, larger areas to more focal, smaller areas (Bigler, 2021). This shift is characterized by synaptic pruning, in which areas of the brain not being used lose synaptic connections and those being used show increased connections. In one study, researchers found less diffusion and more focal activation in the prefrontal cortex from 7 to 30 years of age (Durston & others, 2006). The activation change was linked to advances in executive function, especially in cognitive control, which involves flexible and effective control in a number of areas. These areas include focusing attention, reducing interfering thoughts, inhibiting motor actions, and being flexible in switching between competing choices (Chevalier & others, 2019; Friedman & Robbins, 2022).

developmental **connection**

Brain Development

Synaptic pruning is an important aspect of the brain's development, and the pruning varies by region across children's development. Connect to "Physical Development in Infancy."

Age	Motor skills
6	Children can skip. Children can throw with proper weight shift and step. Girls and boys can vertically jump 7 inches. Girls can do a standing long jump of 33 inches, boys 36 inches. Children can cut and paste. Children enjoy making simple figures in clay.
7	Children can balance on one foot without looking. Children can walk 2-inch-wide balance beams. Children can hop and jump accurately into small squares. Children can participate in jumping jack exercise. Girls can throw a ball 25 feet, boys 45 feet. Girls can vertically jump 8 inches, boys 9 inches. Girls can do a standing long jump of 41 inches, boys 43 inches.
8	Children can engage in alternate rhythmic hopping in different patterns. Girls can throw a ball 34 feet, boys 59 feet. Girls can vertically jump 9 inches, boys 10 inches. Girls can perform a standing long jump of 50 inches, boys 55 inches. Children's grip strength increases. Children can use common tools, such as a hammer.
9	Girls can throw a ball 41 feet, boys 71 feet. Girls can vertically jump 10 inches, boys 11 inches. Girls can perform a standing long jump of 53 inches, boys 57 inches. Children's perceptual-motor coordination becomes smoother.
10	Children can judge and intercept pathways of small balls thrown from a distance. Girls can throw a small ball 49 feet, boys 94 feet. Girls can vertically jump 10 inches, boys 11 inches.

FIGURE **2**

CHANGES IN MOTOR SKILLS DURING MIDDLE AND LATE CHILDHOOD

MOTOR DEVELOPMENT

During middle and late childhood, children's motor development becomes much smoother and more coordinated than it was in early childhood (Hockenberry, Wilson, & Rodgers, 2021). For example, only one child in a thousand can hit a tennis ball over the net at the age of 3, yet by the age of 10 or 11 most children can learn to play the sport. Running, climbing, jumping rope, swimming, bicycle riding, and skating are just a few of the many physical skills elementary school children can master. And, when mastered, these skills are a source of great pleasure and accomplishment for children. In gross motor skills involving large muscle activity, boys usually outperform girls on average, although proficiency in a wide range of skills overlaps between sexes.

As children move through the elementary school years, they gain greater control over their bodies and can sit for longer periods of time. However, elementary school children are far from being physically mature, and they need to be active. Elementary school children become more fatigued by long periods of sitting than by running, jumping, or bicycling (Wuest & Walton-Fisette, 2024). Physical action is essential for children to refine their developing skills, such as batting a ball, skipping rope, or balancing on a beam. An important principle of practice for elementary school children, therefore, is that they should be physically active whenever possible.

Increased myelination of the nervous system is reflected in the improvement of fine motor skills during middle and late childhood. Children use their hands as sophisticated tools. Six-year-olds can hammer, paste, tie shoes, and fasten clothes. By 7 years of age, children's hands have become steadier. At this age, children prefer a pencil to a crayon for printing, reversal of letters is less common, and printing becomes smaller. At 8 to 10 years of age, children can use their hands independently with more ease and precision. Fine motor coordination develops to the point at which children use cursive writing rather than printing. Letter size becomes smaller and more even. At 10 to 12 years of age, children begin to show manipulative skills similar to the abilities of adults. They can now master the complex, intricate, and rapid movements needed to produce fine-quality crafts or to play a difficult piece on a musical instrument. Girls usually outperform boys in fine motor skills on average, although there is a wide range within both sexes. A summary of changes in motor skills in middle and late childhood appears in Figure 2. Note that some children perform these skills earlier or later than other children.

Review *Connect* Reflect

 LG1 Discuss changes in body growth, the brain, and motor development in middle and late childhood.

Review

- How do skeletal and muscular systems change in middle and late childhood?
- What characterizes changes in the brain during middle and late childhood?
- How do children's gross and fine motor skills change in middle and late childhood?

Connect

- In this section, you learned about advances in the prefrontal cortex.

Earlier, you read about the prefrontal cortex's role in executive function. What executive function skills were described as important in early childhood cognitive development?

Reflect *Your Own Personal Journey of Life*

- Look again at Figure 2. On which of the motor skills were you especially competent? On which skills were you less competent? What hereditary and environmental factors do you think influenced your motor skills?

Nutrition | Exercise and Sports | Overweight Children | Diseases | Accidents and Injuries

Although we have become a health-conscious nation, many children as well as adults do not practice good health habits. Too much junk food and too much sedentary behavior describe the habits of far too many children. We begin our exploration of children's health with nutrition and exercise, then turn to a number of health problems that can emerge during this period of development.

NUTRITION

During middle and late childhood, children's average body weight doubles. Children exert considerable energy as they engage in many different motor activities. To support their growth and active lives, children need to consume more food than they did in early childhood. From 1 to 3 years of age, infants and toddlers should consume about 1,300 calories per day. At 4 to 6 years of age, young children should take in around 1,700 calories per day. From 7 to 10 years of age, children should consume about 2,400 calories per day; however, depending on the child's size, the range of recommended calories for 7- to 10-year-olds is 1,650 to 3,300 per day.

Within these calorie ranges, it is important to impress on children the value of a balanced diet to promote their growth (Sorte & others, 2020). Children usually eat as their families eat, so the quality of their diet often depends largely on their family's pattern of eating (Campbell & others, 2018). Most children acquire a taste for an increasing variety of food in middle and late childhood. However, with the availability of fast-food restaurants and media inducements, too many children fill up on food that has "empty calories" that do not promote effective growth. Many of these empty-calorie foods have a high content of sugar, starch, and excess fat.

Parents and teachers alike can help children learn to eat better (Finnane & others, 2017). For example, they can help children learn about what a healthy diet entails, including healthy food choices and appropriate serving sizes for their age and level of activity (USDA, 2023).

Children should begin their day by eating a healthy breakfast. According to nutritionists, breakfast should make up about one-fourth of the day's calories. A nutritious breakfast helps children have more energy and be more alert in the morning hours of school.

EXERCISE AND SPORTS

How much exercise do children get? What are children's sports like? These topics and more are explored in the following section of this chapter.

Exercise American children and adolescents are not getting enough exercise (C.Y. Pan & others, 2019; Wuest & Walton-Fisette, 2024). Increasing children's exercise levels has positive outcomes (Sun & others, 2021).

A large number of studies document the importance of exercise in children's physical development. For example, one study of more than 6,000 elementary school children revealed that 55 minutes or more of moderate-to-vigorous physical activity daily was associated with a lower incidence of obesity (Nemet, 2016). Vigorous physical activity has benefits for children above and beyond the benefits of moderate physical activity (Sardinha & others, 2022). Interventions have found that even brief interruptions in sedentary behavior (with 3 minutes of moderate-intensity walking every 30 minutes across 3 hours) improve glucose metabolism and are a promising strategy for reducing metabolic risk in overweight and obese children (Broadney & others, 2018).

Exercise not only improves children's physical health but also boosts their cognitive skills (Petruzzello & others, 2018; Sun &

What are some good strategies for increasing children's exercise?
Alistair Berg/Getty Images

developmental **connection**

Exercise

Guidelines recommend that pre-school children engage in two hours of physical activity per day. Connect to "Physical Development in Early Childhood."

others, 2021). Researchers have found that aerobic exercise benefits children's attention, memory, effortful and goal-directed thinking and behavior, creativity, and academic success (C.Y. Pan & others, 2019; Tomporowski, 2016). In a fMRI study of physically unfit 8- to 11-year-old overweight children, a daily instructor-led aerobic exercise program that lasted eight months was effective in improving the efficiency or flexible modulation of neural circuits that support better cognitive functioning (Krafft & others, 2014). Further, a meta-analysis concluded that children who engage in regular physical activity have better cognitive inhibitory control (Jackson & others, 2016). Another study that examined fMRI in children with ADHD who received an aerobic activity intervention showed improvements in their attention skills corresponding to changes in frontal-lobe functioning (Jiang & others, 2022).

Parents play important roles in children's exercise and physical activity (Lindsay & others, 2018; Petersen & others, 2020). Growing up with parents who regularly exercise provides positive models of exercise for children. Peers can also play an important role in children's physical activity (Hu & others, 2021).

Some of the blame for inactivity in middle and late childhood also falls on the nation's schools, many of which fail to provide daily physical education classes (Dauenhauer & others, 2019). Many children's school weeks do not include adequate physical education classes, and even when physical education classes are mandated, children may not exercise vigorously in such classes, and such classes may not change children's BMI. For example, in a study in which schools were randomly assigned to conditions that implemented a physical education requirement or did not do so, those children in schools with and without the physical education requirement did not differ in BMI trajectories over the course of three years (Ickovics & others, 2019a).

Screen time, including watching videos or using computers, tablets, or cell phones, also is linked with low activity levels and obesity in children (Potter & others, 2018; Ramirez-Coronel & others, 2023). A two-decade longitudinal study found that a higher incidence of TV viewing in childhood was linked with being overweight, or obese in adulthood at ages 26–45 (Tahir, Willett, & Forman, 2019).

Sports   Despite the growing concern about lack of exercise, many children become involved in sports every year. Both in schools and in community agencies, children's sports programs have changed the shape of many children's lives (Foss & others, 2018).

Participation in sports can have both positive and negative consequences for children. Participation can provide exercise and self-esteem, opportunities to learn how to compete and be persistent, and a setting for developing peer relations and friendships. One study found that 8-year-old children who continued to participate in sports over the next 24 months were rated by their parents as having a higher health-related quality of life than children who did not participate in sports (Vella & others, 2014). In this study, the positive effects of sports participation were stronger for girls than for boys. Further, research indicates that participating in sports reduces the likelihood that children will become obese (Lee, Pope, & Gao, 2018). One longitudinal study of nearly 400 Spanish children and teens revealed that youth who participated in organized sports activities and other activities that improved their actual motor skills as well as their perceived competence at motor skills were far more physically active than their nonparticipating counterparts (Menescardi & others, 2023). Also, a study of 7- to 9-year-olds found that participating in organized leisure-time sports for approximately one year was linked to decreased cardiovascular risk (Hebert & others, 2017).

However, sports also can bring pressure to achieve and win, physical injuries, burnout, and stressful expectations for success as an athlete (Foss & others, 2018). Injuries are a special concern when children participate in sports (Marshall & others, 2022). Studies have found differences in the types of sports injuries that occur as a function of age and sex (Valasek & others, 2019). In addition, children who specialize in one sport (defined as playing that sport to the exclusion of others for more than 6 months of the year) are more likely to sustain overuse injuries, leading some experts to recommend that children play a variety of sports rather than specializing in one sport at a young age (Weekes & others, 2019). There also is concern about the occurrence of concussions in youth football and other contact sports, such as soccer, hockey, and lacrosse (Waltzman & Sarmiento, 2019). Medical and research professionals have identified the key importance of parents and other caregivers as crucial in detecting the presence of potential concussions among children (Haarbauer-Krupa & others, 2021). In the *Caring Connections* interlude, you can read about some positive strategies for parents to follow regarding their children's sports participation.

Ryan McVay/Photodisc/Getty Images

How Would You...?

If you were a **human development and family studies professional,** what advice would you offer to parents who want to make their children's participation in sports enjoyable?

Parents, Coaches, and Children's Sports

Most sports psychologists stress that it is important for parents to show an interest in their children's sports participation. Most children want their parents to watch them perform in sports. Many children whose parents do not come to watch them play in sporting events feel that their parents do not adequately support them. However, some children become extremely nervous when their parents watch them

What are some of the potential positive and negative aspects of children's participation in sports? What are some guidelines that can benefit parents and coaches of children in sports?
SW Productions/Photodisc/Getty Images

perform, or they get embarrassed when their parents cheer too loudly or make a fuss. If children request that their parents not watch them perform, parents should respect their children's wishes.

Parents should compliment their children for their sports performance, and if they don't become overinvolved, they can help their children build their physical skills and emotional maturity—discussing with them how to deal with a difficult coach, how to cope with a tough loss, and how to put in perspective a poorly played game (Knight, 2017).

The following are some guidelines that can benefit both parents and coaches of children who participate in sports (based on a variety of sources available through organizations and research groups such as Women's Sports Foundation [2023] and the Families in Sports Lab at Utah State University [2023]):

The Do's

- Make sports fun; the more children enjoy sports, the more they will want to play.
- Remember that it is okay for children to make mistakes; it means they are trying.
- Allow children to ask questions about the sport and discuss the sport in a calm, supportive manner.
- Show respect for the child's sports participation.
- Be positive and convince the child that he or she is making a good effort.
- Be a positive role model for the child in sports.

The Don'ts

- Yell or scream at the child.
- Condemn the child for poor play or continue to bring up failures long after they happen.
- Point out the child's errors in front of others.
- Expect the child to learn something immediately.
- Expect the child to become a pro.
- Ridicule or make fun of the child.
- Compare the child to siblings or to more talented children.
- Make sports all work and no fun.

Now let's turn our attention to additional children's health issues. For most children, middle and late childhood is a time of excellent health. Disease and death are less prevalent in this period than in other periods of childhood and adolescence. However, some children do have health problems, such as obesity, cancer, diabetes, cardiovascular disease, asthma, and injuries due to accidents.

OVERWEIGHT CHILDREN

Being overweight is an increasingly prevalent health problem in the United States and elsewhere (Centers for Disease Control and Prevention, 2022a). Recall that being overweight is defined in terms of body mass index (BMI), which is computed by a formula that takes into

developmental **connection**

Nutrition and Weight

In one international comparison of 34 countries, the United States had the second highest rate of childhood obesity. Connect to "Physical Development in Early Childhood."

Jules Frazier/Photodisc/Getty Images

account height and weight. Also, children at or above the 95th percentile of BMI are included in the obese category, whereas children at or above the 85th percentile are described as being overweight (Centers for Disease Control and Prevention, 2022a). Over the last three decades, the percentage of U.S. children who are overweight has increased dramatically and is likely to continue to grow unless children's lifestyles change dramatically (Schiff, 2021).

It is not just in the United States that children are becoming more overweight. Childhood obesity is one of the most pressing public health challenges of the twenty-first century, according to the World Health Organization (2020), which reported that 38 million children under the age of 5 years were overweight or obese globally in 2019.

Researchers have found that being overweight as a child is a risk factor for being obese as an adult (Thompson, Manore, & Vaughan, 2017; Weihrauch-Blüher, Schwarz, & Klusmann, 2019). For example, a foundational longitudinal study revealed that girls who were overweight in childhood were 11 to 30 times more likely to be obese in adulthood than girls who were not overweight in childhood (Thompson & others, 2007). This pattern has been found in many subsequent studies regardless of the children's sex (Simmonds & others, 2016).

What Factors Are Linked with Being Overweight in Childhood?
Heredity and environmental contexts are related to being overweight in childhood (Silventoinen & Konttinen, 2020). Genetic analysis indicates that heredity is an important factor in children becoming overweight (Donatelle, 2017). Overweight parents tend to have overweight children (Hollis & Robinson, 2019). For example, one early study found that the greatest risk factor for being overweight at 9 years of age was having a parent who is overweight (Agras & others, 2004). Also, in a 14-year longitudinal study, parental weight change predicted children's weight change (Andriani, Liao, & Kuo, 2015). And one study revealed that having two overweight/obese parents significantly increased the likelihood of a child being overweight/obese (Xu & others, 2011). Characteristics such as body type, height, body fat composition, and metabolism are inherited from parents (Blake, 2017). Environmental factors that influence whether children become overweight include availability of food (especially food high in fat content), use of energy-saving devices, levels of physical activity, parents' eating habits and monitoring of children's eating habits, the context in which a child eats, and screen time (Hemmingsson & others, 2023; Potter & others, 2018). A more recent study found that positive parenting that emphasized praise for healthy eating behavior improved young children's eating behavior (increased vegetable intake, for example) and was more effective in supporting children's weight loss than were negative comments by parents (Rotman & others, 2020).

Consequences of Being Overweight in Childhood
The increasing percentage of overweight children in recent decades is cause for great concern because being overweight raises the risk for many medical and psychological problems (Thavamani & others, 2020). Diabetes, hypertension (high blood pressure), and elevated blood cholesterol levels are common in children who are overweight (Liang & others, 2020; Villasis-Keever & others, 2021).

Once considered rare in childhood, hypertension has become increasingly common in overweight children (Flynn & others, 2023; Tanrikulu, Agirbasli, & Berenson, 2017). A Chinese study revealed that high blood pressure in 23 percent of boys and 15 percent of girls was linked to being overweight or obese (Dong & others, 2015). In another study, a larger waist circumference and a higher body mass index (BMI) combined to place children at higher risk for cardiovascular disease (de Koning & others, 2015). Social and psychological consequences of being overweight in childhood include low self-esteem, depression, and some exclusion of obese children from peer groups (Lin & others, 2018). In a study in Taiwan, obese children were found to have fewer friends and less rewarding peer relationships, which in turn contributes to greater social isolation and feelings of alienation from peers (Chen & Lu, 2022). And in one nationally representative sample of American children, being overweight was related to a number of later negative physical and psychological outcomes, effects that were partly accounted for by overweight children's greater likelihood of being bullied (Lee, Jeong, & Roh, 2018).

What are some concerns about overweight children?
Image Source/Getty Images

Treatment of Children Who Are Overweight Many experts recommend a program that involves a combination of diet, exercise, and behavior modification to help children lose weight. Exercise is an extremely important component of a successful weight-loss program for overweight children (Fairclough & others, 2017; Jebeile & others, 2022). Exercise increases the child's lean body mass, which increases the child's resting metabolic rate. These changes result in more calories being burned in the resting state.

Children's activity levels are influenced by their motivation to engage in energetic activities, as well as by caregivers who model an active lifestyle and are motivated to provide children with opportunities to be active (Morgan & others, 2016; Rajjo, Erickson, & Biggs, 2022). In a typical behavior modification program, children are taught to monitor their own behavior, keeping a food diary while attempting to lose weight. The diary should record not only the type and amount of food eaten but also when, with whom, and where it was eaten. That is, do children eat in front of a screen by themselves, or at times when they are angry or depressed? A food diary identifies behaviors that need to be changed.

Parents play an important role in preventing children from becoming overweight (Morgan & others, 2016; Verduci & others, 2022). In a Japanese study, the family pattern that was linked to the highest overweight/obesity in children was a combination of irregular mealtimes and the most screen time for both parents (Watanabe & others, 2016). Parents can encourage healthy eating habits in children by eating meals together as a family, having healthy snacks available, and limiting children's access to sugar-sweetened beverages and sodas. They also can help reduce the likelihood their children will become overweight by reducing children's screen time, getting children involved in sports and other physical activities, and being healthy, physically active models themselves (Ren & others, 2017). As we learned in Angie's story at the beginning of the chapter, a combination of behavior modification techniques, parental involvement, and a structured program can effectively help overweight children. Intervention programs that emphasize getting parents to engage in more healthful lifestyles themselves, as well as to feed their children nutrient-dense food and get them to exercise more, can produce weight reduction in overweight and obese children (Muthuri & others, 2016). For example, in a 3-month intervention that compared weight loss of children randomly assigned to different intervention conditions, children lost the most weight if they participated jointly with their parents in the intervention, effects that were sustained up to 2 years following the intervention (Yackobovitch-Gavan & others, 2018). To read further about helping overweight children lose weight, see *Caring Connections.*

Some intervention programs with overweight children are conducted through schools and often focus on teaching children and parents about making healthy food choices, exercising more, and reducing screen time (Sanders & others, 2021). A promising strategy is to provide students with healthier foods to eat at school. Several states now have laws that require healthier foods to be sold in vending machines at schools. An exhaustive review and meta-analysis of 100 studies reported that school-based interventions to improve nutrition and healthy eating behavior in schools can have a positive impact on weight management and nutritious snack consumption (e.g., eating fruit) (Pineda, Bascunan, & Sassi, 2021).

How Would You...?

If you were a **health-care professional,** how would you use your knowledge of risk factors for being overweight to design a workshop to help parents and children learn about healthy lifestyle choices?

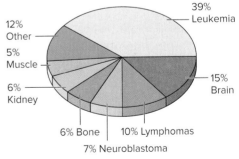

What can parents do to prevent their children from being overweight or obese?

Ariel Skelley/DigitalVision/Getty Images

DISEASES

Four childhood diseases that can be especially harmful to children's development are cancer, diabetes, cardiovascular disease, and asthma.

Cancer Cancer is the leading cause of disease-related deaths during childhood, with approximately 10,500 new cases of childhood cancer diagnosed each year in the United States (National Cancer Institute, 2023). As treatments have become more effective, death rates from childhood cancer have declined by 79 percent in the last four decades.

Cancers in children mainly attack the white blood cells (leukemia), brain, bone, lymphatic system, muscles, kidneys, and nervous system. All are characterized by an uncontrolled proliferation of abnormal cells (Marcoux & others, 2017). As indicated in Figure 3, the most common cancer in children is leukemia, a cancer in which bone marrow manufactures an abundance of abnormal white blood cells, which crowd out normal cells, making the child susceptible to bruising and infection (Buchmann & others, 2022; Shago, 2017).

FIGURE 3

TYPES OF CANCER IN CHILDREN. Cancers in children have a different profile from adult cancers, which attack mainly the lungs, colon, breast, prostate, and pancreas.

Parenting Strategies for Helping Overweight Children Lose Weight

Most parents with an overweight child want to help the child to lose weight but aren't sure of the best ways to accomplish this goal. Keep in mind the research we have discussed that indicates overweight children are likely to become overweight adolescents and adults, so it is important for parents to help their children attain a healthy weight and maintain it. Following are some recommended ways that parents can help their overweight children lose weight (Centers for Disease Control and Prevention, 2023a; Matthiessen, 2013; Moninger, 2013; Niec & others, 2022):

- **Work on a healthy project together and involve the child in the decision-making process.** Get the child involved in an activity that can promote weight loss, such as purchasing pedometers for all family members and developing goals for how many steps to take each day. By involving the child in making decisions about the family's health, the hope is that the child will begin to take responsibility for their own health.
- **Be a healthy model for your child.** In many aspects of life, what people do is more influential than what they say. For example, if parents are overweight and engaging in unhealthy behaviors such as eating unhealthy fast food and not exercising, then telling their overweight children to lose weight is unlikely to be effective.
- **Engage in physical activities with children.** Parents and children can engage in activities like bicycling, jogging, hiking, and swimming together. Parents might say something like "Let's take a walk after dinner this evening. It would be fun and could help us both get in better shape."
- **Give children choices in what they want to do to lose weight.** Take them to the grocery store with you and let them select the fruits and vegetables they are willing to eat. Let them choose which sport or type of exercise they would like to do.
- **Eat healthy family meals together on a regular basis.** Children who eat meals together with their family are less likely to be overweight.
- **Reduce screen time.** Children who spend large numbers of hours per day in screen time are more likely to be overweight than their counterparts whose screen time takes up a smaller part of their day.

What are some concerns about children's cardiovascular health and obesity?
Blend Images-JGI/Jamie Grill/Getty Images

type 1 diabetes An autoimmune disease in which the body's immune system destroys insulin-producing cells.

type 2 diabetes The most common type of diabetes, in which the body is able to produce insulin, but the amount may be insufficient or the body's cells may be unable to use it.

When cancer strikes children, it behaves differently from the way it attacks adults. Children frequently have a more advanced stage of cancer when they are first diagnosed. When cancer is first diagnosed in adults, it has spread to distant parts of the body in only about 20 percent of the cases; however, that figure rises to 80 percent in children. Most cancers in adults result from lifestyle factors, such as smoking, diet, occupation, and exposure to other cancer-causing agents. By contrast, little is known about the causes of childhood cancers. Researchers are searching for possible genetic links to childhood cancers (Karlsson & others, 2018; Körber & others, 2023).

Because of advancements in cancer treatment, children with cancer are surviving longer (National Cancer Institute, 2023). Approximately 80 percent of children with acute lymphoblastic leukemia are cured with current chemotherapy treatment.

Diabetes Diabetes is one of the most common chronic diseases in children and adolescents. Rates of diabetes in children have increased in the United States and other countries (Lawrence & others, 2021). **Type 1 diabetes** is an autoimmune disease in which the body's immune system destroys insulin-producing cells, so the body produces little or no insulin (the hormone that regulates the body's blood sugar level) (Mitchell, 2017).

In **type 2 diabetes,** the most common type of diabetes, the body is able to produce insulin, but the amount may be insufficient or the body's cells may be unable to use it. Risk factors for type 2 diabetes include being overweight and/or physically inactive, having relatives with this disease, or belonging to certain ethnic groups (Harnois-Leblanc & others, 2023). Native Americans, Black Americans, Latinos, and Asian Americans are at greater risk than non-Latino White Americans for developing diabetes (Hasson & others, 2013; Lawrence & others, 2021).

Cardiovascular Disease Cardiovascular disease is uncommon in children. Nonetheless, environmental experiences and behavior in the childhood years can sow the seeds for cardiovascular disease in adulthood (Schaefer & others, 2017). Many

connecting with research

Heart Smart

Key Points:

- One of the first and largest comprehensive cardiovascular health and fitness studies and interventions in the world.
- A wide variety of proven approaches to assessing health and hopefully increasing healthy habits has been implemented through schools.
- Findings indicate strong and lasting effects on health from childhood, ranging from effects of poor diet to lack of exercise.

The Bogalusa Heart Study, also called Heart Smart, is a large-scale investigation designed to improve children's cardiovascular health. It involves an ongoing evaluation of 8,000 boys and girls in Bogalusa, Louisiana, who now are well into adulthood (Harville & others, 2017; Moukaled & others, 2023; Tanrikulu, Agirbasli, & Berenson, 2017). Heart Smart intervention takes place in schools. Since 95 percent of children and adolescents aged 5 to 18 are in school, school is an efficient context in which to educate individuals about health. Special attention is given to teachers, who serve as role models. Teachers who value the role of health in life and who engage in health-enhancing behavior present children and adolescents with positive models for health. Teacher in-service education is conducted by an interdisciplinary team of specialists, including physicians, psychologists, nutritionists, physical educators, and exercise physiologists. The school's staff is introduced to information about heart health, the nature of cardiovascular disease, and risk factors for heart disease. Coping behavior, exercise behavior, and eating behavior are discussed with the staff, and a Heart Smart curriculum is explained.

The Heart Smart curriculum for grade 5 includes strategies for improving cardiovascular health, eating behavior, and exercise. The physical education component of Heart Smart involves two to four class periods each week devoted to a "Superkids-Superfit" exercise program. The physical education instructor teaches skills required by the school system plus aerobic activities aimed at cardiovascular conditioning, including jogging, racewalking, interval workouts, rope skipping, circuit training, aerobic dance, and games. Classes begin and end with five minutes of walking and stretching.

The school lunch program serves as an intervention site, where sodium, fat, and sugar levels are decreased. Children and adolescents are given reasons that they should eat healthy foods, such as a tuna sandwich, and why they should not eat unhealthy foods, such as a hot dog with chili. The school lunch program includes a salad bar where children and adolescents can serve themselves. The amount and type of snack foods sold on the school premises are monitored.

High-risk children—those with elevated blood pressure, cholesterol, and high weight—are identified as part of Heart Smart. A multidisciplinary team of physicians, nutritionists, nurses, and behavioral counselors works with the high-risk boys and girls and their parents through group-oriented activities and individual-based family counseling. High-risk boys and girls and their parents receive diet, exercise, and relaxation prescriptions in an intensive 12-session program, followed by long-term monthly evaluations.

Extensive assessment is a part of this ongoing program. Short-term and long-term changes in children's knowledge about cardiovascular disease and changes in their behavior are assessed.

Following are some findings from the Bogalusa Heart Study:

- Cardiovascular risk factors, including high BMI, were significantly correlated across generations (Harville & others, 2019).
- Mothers' pre-pregnancy BMI predicted their daughters' high blood pressure and other cardiovascular risk factors into adolescence and adulthood (Harville, Apolzan, & Bazzano, 2019).
- High levels of body fat and elevated blood pressure beginning in childhood were linked to premature death from coronary heart disease in adulthood (Berenson & others, 2016).
- Higher body mass index (BMI) in childhood was linked to the likelihood of developing diabetes in adulthood (Zhang & others, 2019).
- Individuals in underserved communities were far more likely to have multiple cardiovascular disease indicators in adulthood (Moukaled & others, 2023).

How do you think parents, siblings, and peers might influence children's health behavior such as exercise habits and food choices?

elementary-school-aged children already possess one or more of the risk factors for cardiovascular disease, such as hypertension and obesity (Pool & others, 2021). Hypertension and high blood pressure during childhood are under-recognized and under-diagnosed (Basalely & others, 2023). Nevertheless, treating these conditions is important not only for children's health but also to prevent health problems stemming from early hypertension and high blood pressure that otherwise will likely continue and worsen into adulthood (Baker-Smith & others, 2018).

How might research studies help us improve children's cardiovascular health? The Bogalusa Heart Study discussed in the *Connecting with Research* interlude seeks to answer this question.

Asthma **Asthma** is a chronic lung disease that involves episodes of airflow obstruction (Pavord & others, 2023). Symptoms of an asthma attack include shortness of breath, wheezing, or tightness in the chest. The incidence of asthma has risen steadily in recent decades, possibly because of increased air pollution (Ding & others, 2017). Asthma is the most common chronic disease in U.S. children, being present in 16 percent of Black children and 7 percent of White children (Centers for Disease Control and Prevention, 2022b). Asthma is the primary reason for absences from school, and it is responsible for a number of pediatric admissions to emergency rooms and hospitals (Rutman & others, 2016). Children with asthma account for more than 600,000 emergency room visits per year in the United States, with one in six children with asthma visiting the emergency room annually (Centers for Disease Control and Prevention, 2022b; Rutman & others, 2016).

The exact causes of asthma are not known, but it is believed that the disease results from hypersensitivity to environmental substances that triggers an allergic reaction (Altug & others, 2013). Research reviews have concluded that there are numerous risk factors for asthma, such as being male, having one or both parents with asthma, and/or having allergy sensitivity, stress early in life, infections, obesity, and exposure to environmental tobacco smoke, indoor allergens, and outdoor pollutants (Feleszko & others, 2006; Toskala & Kennedy, 2015). There is increasing concern about children's exposure to secondhand smoke as a contributor to asthma (Puranik & others, 2017). One illustrative study found that secondhand smoke more than doubled the odds of hospitalization for children with asthma (Jin, Seiber, & Ferketich, 2013).

Corticosteroids, which generally are inhaled, are the most effective anti-inflammatory drugs for treating asthmatic children (Di Cicco & others, 2023). Often, parents have kept asthmatic children from exercising because they feared that exercise might provoke an asthma attack. However, today it is believed that children with asthma should be encouraged to exercise, provided their asthma is under control, and participation should be evaluated on an individual basis (Minic & Sovtic, 2017). Physical activity is a possible protective factor against asthma development (Lu & others, 2022). Some asthmatic children lose their symptoms in adolescence and adulthood (Trivedi & Denton, 2019).

What are some of the risk factors for developing asthma during childhood?
Jean-Paul CHASSENET/123RF

How Would You...?
If you were a **health-care professional**, how would you work with school-age children to reduce their chances of injury due to accidents?

ACCIDENTS AND INJURIES

Injuries are the leading cause of death during middle and late childhood. The most common cause of severe injury and death during this period is motor vehicle accidents, either as pedestrians or as passengers (Centers for Disease Control and Prevention, 2018b; Heron, 2021). For this reason, safety advocates recommend the use of safety-belt restraints and child booster seats in vehicles because they can greatly reduce the severity of motor vehicle injuries (Hafner & others, 2017). For example, one study found that child booster seats reduced the risk for serious injury very substantially (Shaw & others, 2022). Other serious injuries in this age group involve bicycles, skateboards, roller skates, and other sports equipment.

Most accidents occur in or near the child's home or school. The most effective prevention strategy is to educate the child about proper use of equipment and the hazards of risk-taking behaviors (Souza & others, 2017). Safety helmets, protective eye and mouth shields, and protective padding are recommended for children who engage in active sports.

Caregivers play a key role in preventing childhood injuries (Cosottile & Damashek, 2022). A landmark study that was conducted in four countries (Ethiopia, Peru, Vietnam, and India) revealed that depression in caregivers was consistently linked to children's risk of all types of injury assessed (burns, serious falls, broken bones, and near-fatal injury) (Howe, Huttly, & Abramsky, 2006), perhaps because caregivers who are depressed are less likely to provide direct supervision to their children.

Dealing with a serious medical issue, such as a debilitating injury, can be quite traumatic for a child and the child's family. See the *Connecting with Careers* profile to read about a child life specialist who works to ease the recovery process.

connecting with careers

Ariana Lorenzo, Child Life Specialist

While playing soccer for St. Thomas University in Florida, Ariana Lorenzo began volunteering at a local children's hospital and learned about the important role a child life specialist can play in the lives of children and their families as children are recovering from illness and injury (HCA Florida Healthcare, 2022). Because children process information differently from adults, they have distinct needs for managing the effects of stress and trauma. Children may experience emotions such as fear, shame, confusion, and loneliness, which can inhibit their natural development and have lasting negative effects on their well-being (Association of Child Life Professionals, 2022).

Becoming a certified child life specialist requires an undergraduate degree, either from an approved program or with additional targeted courses, and a clinical internship. Lorenzo currently works as a child life specialist at Kendall Regional Medical Center in Miami, Florida.

According to Lorenzo, every day is different, based on the children she is working with and what situation they are facing. One of her cases involved 12-year-old Nick Howell, who spent more than two months in the hospital recovering from serious burns from attempting a TikTok challenge. His care team included Lorenzo, who was there every step of the way with Howell and his family. The complicated and lengthy care he underwent turned into a relationship that his family and the staff say they'll cherish forever. "They pushed me, enough to believe in myself to finish . . . and that's where I am now," Howell said (Jorges, 2022).

Review Connect Reflect

 Characterize children's health in middle and late childhood.

Review

- What are key aspects of children's nutrition in middle and late childhood?
- What roles do exercise and sports play in children's development?
- What are the consequences of being overweight in childhood?
- Which four diseases are especially harmful to children?
- What is the most common cause of severe injury and death in childhood?

Connect

- What are some positive and negative parental practices that are likely to play a role in children's eating patterns in middle and late childhood?

Reflect *Your Own Personal Journey of Life*

- How good were your eating habits as a child? How much did you exercise in middle and late childhood? Are your eating and exercise habits today similar to or different from your eating and exercise habits as a child? Why are they similar or different?

3 What Are the Prevalent Disabilities in Children?

 Summarize information about children with disabilities.

| Who Are Children with Disabilities? | The Range of Disabilities | Educational Issues |

In the previous section of this chapter, our discussion of children's health focused on nutrition and exercise. In addition, we discussed some of the most common health problems, including obesity, cancer, diabetes, cardiovascular disease, and asthma. In this section, we turn our attention to children with disabilities and the issues involved in their education.

WHO ARE CHILDREN WITH DISABILITIES?

Of all children from 3 to 21 years of age in the United States, 15 percent received special education or related services in 2020–2021, an increase of 2 percent from a decade earlier (Condition of Education, 2022). Figure 4 shows the four largest groups of students with a

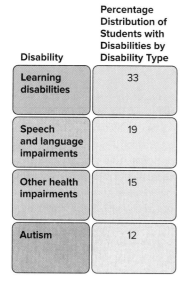

Disability	Percentage Distribution of Students with Disabilities by Disability Type
Learning disabilities	33
Speech and language impairments	19
Other health impairments	15
Autism	12

FIGURE 4

U.S. CHILDREN WITH A DISABILITY WHO RECEIVE SPECIAL EDUCATION SERVICES. Figures are for the 2020–2021 school year and represent the four categories with the highest numbers and percentages of children. Note that some children with more severe attention deficit hyperactivity disorder are included in the learning disabilities category (Condition of Education, 2022).

learning disability Disability in which a child has difficulty in learning that involves understanding or using spoken or written language, and the difficulty can appear in listening, thinking, reading, writing, or spelling, or math. To be classified as a learning disability, the learning problem is not primarily the result of visual, hearing, or motor disabilities; intellectual disabilities; emotional disorders; or environmental, cultural, or economic disadvantage.

disability who were served by federal programs during the 2021–2022 school year (Condition of Education, 2022). As indicated in Figure 4, students with a learning disability were by far the largest group of students with a disability to be given special education, followed by children with speech or language impairments, other health impairments, and autism. Note that the U.S. Department of Education includes both students with a learning disability and some students with more severe ADHD in the category of learning disability.

Educators now prefer to speak of "children with disabilities" rather than "handicapped or disabled children" in order to focus on the person rather than the disability (Heward, Alber-Morgan, & Konrad, 2017). The term "handicapping conditions" is still used to describe impediments imposed by society that restrict the learning and functioning of individuals with a disability. For example, in the case of children who use a wheelchair and do not have access to a bathroom, transportation, and so on, this exemplifies handicapping conditions.

THE RANGE OF DISABILITIES

In this section, we examine learning disabilities, attention deficit hyperactivity disorder, speech disorders, sensory disorders, physical disorders, emotional and behavioral disorders, and autism spectrum disorder. Later, we will study intellectual disabilities.

Learning Disabilities   Mateo's second-grade teacher complains that his spelling is awful. Eight-year-old Tim says reading is really hard, and often the words don't make much sense. Alisha has good oral language skills but has considerable difficulty in computing correct answers to arithmetic problems. Each of these students may have a learning disability.

Characteristics and Identification   The U.S. government created a definition of learning disabilities in 1997 and then reauthorized the definition with a few minor changes in 2004. Following is a description of the government's definition of what determines whether a child should be classified as having a learning disability. A child with a **learning disability** has difficulty in learning that involves understanding or using spoken or written language, and the difficulty can appear in listening, thinking, reading, writing, spelling, or mathematics (Turnbull & others, 2020; Werner, Berg, & Höhr, 2019). To be classified as a learning disability, the learning problem is not primarily the result of visual, hearing, or motor disabilities; intellectual disabilities; emotional disorders; or environmental, cultural, or economic disadvantage (Friend, 2018).

About three times as many boys as girls are classified as having a learning disability. Among the explanations for this difference are a greater biological vulnerability among boys and referral bias (that is, boys are more likely to be referred by teachers for treatment because of their behavior) (Lai, Lin, & Ameis, 2022; Mowlem & others, 2019).

Most learning disabilities are lifelong. Compared with children without a learning disability, children with a learning disability are more likely to show poor academic performance, high dropout rates, and poor employment and postsecondary education records (Aro & others, 2019). Because of their poor prognosis if left untreated, it is important to develop effective diagnostic, monitoring, and intervention systems in and out of school settings to help children with learning disabilities reach their full potential (Grigorenko & others, 2020). Despite the problems they encounter, many children with a learning disability grow up to lead lives engaged in productive work. For example, actress Whoopi Goldberg and investment company owner Charles Schwab have learning disabilities.

Diagnosing whether a child has a learning disability is often a difficult task. Because federal guidelines are just that—guidelines—it is up to each state, or in some cases each school system within a state, to determine how to define and implement diagnosis of learning disabilities. The same child might be diagnosed as having a learning disability in one school system and receive services but not be diagnosed and not receive services in another school system. In such cases, parents sometimes will move to a new location to obtain or to avoid the diagnosis.

Initial identification of a possible learning disability usually is made by the classroom teacher. If a learning disability is suspected, the teacher calls on specialists. An interdisciplinary team of professionals is best suited to determine whether a student has a learning disability. Individual psychological evaluations (of intelligence) and educational assessments (such as current level of achievement) are required, and there can be substantial variation across school districts in the approaches taken (Hallahan, Kauffman, & Pullen, 2018; Lockwood & others, 2022). In addition, tests of visual-motor skills, language, and memory may be used.

Reading, Writing, and Math Difficulties   The most common academic areas in which children with a learning disability have problems are reading, writing, and math (Dohla & Heim, 2016). A problem with reading affects the vast majority of children with a learning disability (Astle & others, 2022). Such children have difficulty with phonological skills, which involve being able to understand how sounds and letters match up to make words, and also can have problems in comprehension. **Dyslexia** is a category reserved for individuals with a severe impairment in their ability to read and spell (Remien & Marwaha, 2021).

Dysgraphia is a learning disability that involves difficulty in handwriting (Cabrero & De Jesus, 2021). Children with dysgraphia may write very slowly, their writing products may be virtually illegible, and they may make numerous spelling errors because of their inability to match up sounds and letters.

Dyscalculia, also known as developmental arithmetic disorder, is a learning disability that involves difficulty in math computation (Cardenas & others, 2021). A child may have both a reading and a math disability, and there are cognitive features that characterize both types of disabilities, such as difficulties in working memory (Werner, Berg, & Höhr, 2019).

Causes and Intervention Strategies   The precise causes of learning disabilities are multifaceted and very complex (Heward, Alber-Morgan, & Konrad, 2017; Muktamath, Hegde, & Chand, 2022). However, some possible causes have been proposed. Learning disabilities tend to run in families, with higher rates among children having one parent with a disability such as dyslexia or dyscalculia.

Researchers currently are exploring the role of genetics in learning disabilities (Erbeli, Rice, & Paracchini, 2022). Also, some learning disabilities are likely to be caused by problems during prenatal development or delivery. For example, a number of studies have found that learning disabilities are more prevalent in low birth weight and preterm infants (O'Reilly & others, 2020; R. Taylor & others, 2016).

Researchers also use brain-imaging techniques, such as magnetic resonance imaging and event-related potentials, to examine any regions of the brain that might be involved in learning disabilities (Jagger-Rickels, Kibby, & Constance, 2018; Li & others, 2020) (see Figure 5). This research indicates that it is unlikely learning disabilities stem from disorders in a single, specific brain location. More likely, learning disabilities are due to problems integrating information from multiple brain regions or to subtle defects in brain structure and function.

A number of effective approaches can be used to improve educational outcomes of students with learning disabilities (Alquraini & Rao, 2020). Many interventions have focused on improving the child's reading ability (Temple & others, 2018). Intensive instruction over a period of time by a competent teacher can help many children (Swanson & Berninger, 2018). For example, a brain-imaging study involved 15 children with severe reading difficulties who had not shown adequate progress in response to reading instruction in the first grade and were given eight weeks of intensive instruction in phonological decoding skills followed by eight weeks of intensive instruction in word recognition skills (Simos & others, 2007). The intervention led to significant improvement in a majority of the children's reading skills as well as changes in brain regions involved in reading.

Attention Deficit Hyperactivity Disorder   Seven-year-old Andreana has attention deficit hyperactivity disorder, and the outward signs are fairly typical. She has trouble attending to the teacher's instructions and is easily distracted. She has trouble sitting still for more than a few minutes at a time, and her handwriting is messy. Andreana's mother describes her as unfocused and fidgety.

Characteristics   **Attention deficit hyperactivity disorder (ADHD)** is a disability in which children consistently show one or more of the following characteristics over a period of time: (1) inattention, (2) hyperactivity, and (3) impulsivity. For an ADHD diagnosis, onset of these characteristics early in childhood is required, and the characteristics must be debilitating for the child.

Inattentive children have difficulty focusing on any one thing and may get bored with a task after only a few minutes. Problems in sustaining

dyslexia A category of learning disabilities involving a severe impairment in the ability to read and spell.

dysgraphia A learning disability that involves difficulty in handwriting.

dyscalculia Also known as developmental arithmetic disorder; a learning disability that involves difficulty in math computation.

attention deficit hyperactivity disorder (ADHD) A disability in which children consistently show one or more of the following characteristics: (1) inattention, (2) hyperactivity, and (3) impulsivity.

How Would You...?
If you were an **educator,** how would you explain the nature of learning disabilities to a parent whose child had recently been diagnosed with a learning disability?

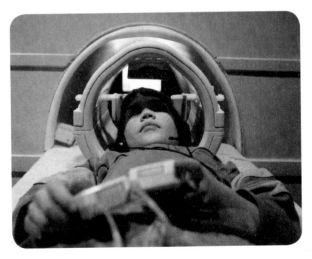

FIGURE 5

BRAIN SCANS AND LEARNING DISABILITIES. An increasing number of studies are using MRI brain scans to examine the brain pathways involved in learning disabilities. Shown here is 9-year-old Patrick Price, who has dyslexia. Patrick is going through an MRI scanner disguised by drapes to look like a child-friendly castle. Inside the scanner, children must lie virtually motionless as words and symbols flash on a screen, and they are asked to identify them by clicking different buttons.
Manuel Balce Ceneta/AP Images

Many children with ADHD show impulsive behavior. *How would you handle this situation if you were a teacher and noticed this happening in your classroom?*
Nicole Hill/Rubberball/Getty Images

How Would You...?

If you were a **health-care professional,** how would you respond to the following remarks by a parent? "I do not believe that ADHD is a real disorder. Children are supposed to be active."

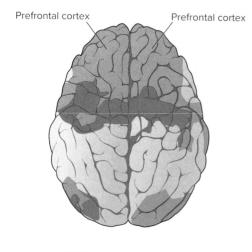

Prefrontal cortex   Prefrontal cortex

■ Greater than 2 years' delay
■ 0 to 2 years' delay

FIGURE **6**

REGIONS OF THE BRAIN IN WHICH CHILDREN WITH ADHD HAD A DELAYED PEAK IN THE THICKNESS OF THE CEREBRAL CORTEX.
Note: The greatest delays occurred in the prefrontal cortex.

attention are the most common type of attention problem in children with ADHD. Hyperactive children show high levels of physical activity, almost always seeming to be in motion. Impulsive children have difficulty curbing their reactions and don't do a good job of thinking before they act. Depending on the characteristics that children with ADHD display, they can be diagnosed as having (1) ADHD with predominantly inattention, (2) ADHD with predominantly hyperactivity/impulsivity, or (3) ADHD with both inattention and hyperactivity/impulsivity.

Diagnosis and Developmental Status   The number of children diagnosed with and treated for ADHD has increased substantially over the past few decades (Hallahan, Kauffman, & Pullen, 2023). The Centers for Disease Control and Prevention (2023b) estimates that ADHD has continued to increase in 4- to 17-year-old children, going from 8 percent in 2003 to 9.5 percent in 2007 and to nearly 10 percent by 2019. Approximately 13.2 percent of U.S. boys and 5.6 percent of U.S. girls have ever been diagnosed with ADHD. The disorder occurs as much as four to nine times more often in boys than in girls. There is controversy about the increased diagnosis of ADHD, however (Friend, 2018). Some experts attribute the increase mainly to heightened awareness of the disorder. Others are concerned that many children are being diagnosed without undergoing extensive professional evaluation based on input from multiple sources.

One illustrative study examined the possible misdiagnosis of ADHD (Bruchmiller, Margraf, & Schneider, 2012). In this study, child psychologists, psychiatrists, and social workers were given vignettes of children with ADHD (some vignettes matched the diagnostic criteria for the disorder, while others did not). Whether each child was male or female varied. The researchers assessed whether the mental health professionals gave a diagnosis of ADHD to the child described in the vignette. The professionals overdiagnosed ADHD almost 20 percent of the time, and regardless of the symptoms described, boys were twice as likely as girls to be given a diagnosis of ADHD.

Although signs of ADHD are often present during the preschool years, children with ADHD are not usually classified until the elementary school years (Allan & Lonigan, 2019). The increased academic and social demands of formal schooling, as well as stricter standards for behavioral control, often illuminate the problems of the child with ADHD. Elementary school teachers typically report that this type of child has difficulty in working independently, completing seatwork, and organizing work. Restlessness and distractibility also are often noted. These problems are more likely to be observed in repetitive or difficult tasks, or tasks the child perceives to be boring (such as completing worksheets or doing homework).

Experts previously thought that most children "grow out" of ADHD. However, recent evidence suggests that many children who are diagnosed with ADHD continue to have problems with attention and related aspects of executive functioning into adolescence and adulthood (Lin & Gau, 2019; Tallberg & others, 2022).

Causes and Treatment   Definitive causes of ADHD have not been found. However, a number of genetic and environmental causes have been proposed (Magnus & others, 2021). Some children likely inherit a tendency to develop ADHD from their parents (Huang & others, 2019). Other children likely develop ADHD because of damage to their brain during prenatal or postnatal development (Debnath & others, 2021). Among early possible contributors to ADHD are cigarette and alcohol exposure, as well as a high level of maternal stress during prenatal development and low birth weight (Biederman & others, 2020; Manzari & others, 2019).

As with learning disabilities, the development of brain-imaging techniques is leading to a better understanding of the brain's role in ADHD (Zou & Yang, 2021). One landmark study revealed that peak thickness of the cerebral cortex occurred three years later (10.5 years) in children with ADHD than in children without ADHD (peak at 7.5 years) (Shaw & others, 2007). The delay was more prominent in the prefrontal regions of the brain that are especially important in attention and planning (see Figure 6). Another more recent study also found delayed development of the brain's frontal lobes in children with ADHD, linked to delayed or decreased myelination (Bouziane & others, 2018). Researchers are exploring the roles that various neurotransmitters, such as serotonin and dopamine, might play in ADHD (Cai & others, 2021). For example, one study found that the dopamine transporter gene

DAT 1 was involved in decreased cortical thickness in the prefrontal cortex of children with ADHD (Fernandez-Jaen & others, 2015).

The delays in brain development just described are in areas linked to executive function (Karr & others, 2021). A focus of increasing interest in studies of children with ADHD is their difficulty on tasks involving executive function, such as behavioral inhibition when necessary, use of working memory, and effective planning (Kofler & others, 2019). Researchers also have found deficits in theory of mind in children with ADHD (Pineda-Alhucema & others, 2018).

Adjustment and optimal development also are difficult for children who have ADHD, so it is important that the diagnosis be accurate (Adisetiyo & Gray, 2017). Children diagnosed with ADHD have an increased risk of problematic peer relations, school dropout, adolescent pregnancy, substance use problems, and antisocial behavior (Obsuth & others, 2020; Tistarelli & others, 2020). For example, a research review concluded that in comparison with typically developing girls, girls with ADHD had more problems in friendship, peer interaction, social skills, and peer victimization (Kok & others, 2016). Another research review concluded that ADHD in childhood was linked to the following long-term outcomes: failure to complete high school, other mental and substance use disorders, criminal activity, and unemployment (Erskine & others, 2016). Childhood ADHD also is associated with long-term underachievement in math and reading (Arnold & others, 2020).

Stimulant medication such as Ritalin (methylphenidate) or Adderall (amphetamine and dextroamphetamine) is effective in improving the attention of many children with ADHD, but it usually does not improve their attention to the same level as children who do not have ADHD (Cortese & others, 2018). Stimulant medications are effective in treating ADHD during the short term, but longer-term benefits of stimulant medications are not yet as clear (Rajeh & others, 2017; Rosenau & others, 2021). Behavioral interventions can also be effective in reducing behavior problems among children with ADHD (Papadopoulos & others, 2019). Researchers have often found that a combination of medication (such as Ritalin) and behavior management may improve the behavior of children with ADHD better than medication alone or behavior management alone, although this does not happen in all cases (Caye & others, 2019).

The sheer number of ADHD diagnoses has prompted speculation that psychiatrists, parents, and teachers might be labeling normal childhood behavior as psychopathology (Gascon & others, 2022; Mash & Wolfe, 2016). One reason for concern about overdiagnosing ADHD is that the form of treatment in the majority of cases is psychoactive drugs, including stimulants such as Ritalin and Adderall (Garfield & others, 2012). Further, there is increasing concern that children who are given stimulant drugs such as Ritalin or Adderall are at risk for developing substance abuse problems in adolescence and adulthood, although research results are preliminary and have been mixed (Ivanov & others, 2022).

Researchers have been exploring the possibility that neurofeedback might improve the attention of children with ADHD (Alegria & others, 2017; Moreno-García, Cano-Crespo, & Rivera, 2022). *Neurofeedback* trains individuals to become more aware of their physiological responses so that they can attain better control over their brain's prefrontal cortex, where executive control primarily occurs. Individuals with ADHD have higher levels of electro-encephalogram (EEG) abnormalities, such as lower beta waves that involve attention and memory, and lower sensorimotor rhythms (which involve control of movements). Neurofeedback produces audiovisual profiles of brain waves so that individuals can learn how to modify EEG functioning. In one illustrative study, 7- to 14-year-olds with ADHD were randomly assigned either to take Ritalin or to undergo 40 sessions of a neurofeedback treatment (Meisel & others, 2013). Both groups showed a lower level of ADHD symptoms six months after the treatment, but only the neurofeedback group performed better academically.

A meta-analysis of 11 studies suggested that ADHD symptoms, hyperactivity, inattention, executive functioning, and on-task behavior of children with ADHD can be improved through yoga, mindfulness, and meditation (Chimiklis & others, 2018). Another meta-analysis concluded that mindfulness training significantly improved the attention of children with ADHD (Cairncross & Miller, 2020). However, these approaches are not recommended as the first treatment of choice.

Exercise also is being investigated as a possible treatment for children with ADHD (Den Heijer & others, 2017; C.Y. Pan & others, 2019). A meta-analysis concluded that physical

developmental connection

Cognitive Processes

Working memory is a "mental workbench" that includes a central executive function whereby individuals monitor and control information. Connect to "Cognitive Development in Middle and Late Childhood."

How is neurofeedback being used to reduce ADHD symptoms in children?
Jerilee Bennett/KRT/Newscom

developmental connection

Cognitive Processes

Mindfulness training is being used to improve students' executive function. Connect to "Cognitive Development in Middle and Late Childhood."

exercise is effective in reducing cognitive symptoms of ADHD in individuals 3 to 25 years of age (Tan, Pooley, & Speelman, 2016). A second meta-analysis concluded that short-term aerobic exercise is effective in reducing symptoms such as inattention, hyperactivity, and impulsivity (Cerrillo-Urbina & others, 2015). Another meta-analysis indicated that exercise is associated with better executive function in children with ADHD (Vysniauske & others, 2020). A comprehensive review showed that the average effect was modest to moderate in size (Huang & others, 2023).

Among the reasons given as to why exercise might reduce ADHD symptoms in children are (1) better allocation of attention resources, (2) positive influence on prefrontal cortex functioning, and (3) exercise-induced dopamine regulation (Chang & others, 2012; Huang & others, 2023).

Despite the encouraging recent studies of the use of neurofeedback, mindfulness training, and exercise to improve the attention of children with ADHD, it has not been determined whether these non-drug therapies are as effective as stimulant drugs and/or whether they benefit children as add-ons to stimulant drugs to provide a combination treatment (Den Heijer & others, 2017).

Speech Disorders   Speech disorders include articulation disorders, voice disorders, and fluency disorders (Duffy, 2020). **Articulation disorders** are problems in pronouncing sounds correctly (Bernthal, Bankson, & Flipsen, 2017). A child's articulation at 6 to 7 years is still not always error-free, but it should be by age 8. A child with an articulation problem may find communication with peers and the teacher difficult or embarrassing. As a result, the child may avoid asking questions, participating in discussions, or talking with peers. Articulation problems can usually be improved or resolved with speech therapy, although it may take months or years.

Voice disorders are reflected in speech that is hoarse, harsh, too loud, too high-pitched, or too low-pitched. Children with a cleft palate often have a voice disorder that makes their speech difficult to understand. If a student speaks in a way that is consistently difficult to understand, the child should be referred to a speech therapist (Bernthal, Bankson, & Flipsen, 2017).

Fluency disorders often involve what is commonly called "stuttering." Stuttering occurs when a child's speech has a spasmodic hesitation, prolongation, or repetition (Druker, Mazzucchelli, & Beilby, 2019). The anxiety many children feel because they stutter can make their stuttering worse. Speech therapy is recommended.

Sensory Disorders   Sensory disorders include visual and hearing impairments. Sometimes these impairments are described as part of a larger category called "communication disorders" that also encompasses speech and language disorders.

Visual Impairments   Some children may have mild vision problems that have not been corrected. If children frequently squint, hold books close to their face when they read, rub their eyes often, say that things look blurred, or mention that words move around on the page, they should be referred to appropriate professionals to have their vision checked. In many cases, corrective lenses will solve the child's vision problem. However, a small proportion of children (about 1 in 1,000) have more serious visual problems and are classified as visually impaired. This category includes children with low vision and blind children.

Children with **low vision** have visual acuity of between 20/70 and 20/2000 (on the Snellen scale, in which 20/20 is normal) with corrective lenses. Children with low vision can read with the aid of large-print books or a magnifying glass. Children who are **educationally blind** cannot use their vision in learning and must use their hearing and touch to learn. Approximately 1 in every 3,000 children is educationally blind. Almost half of these children were born blind, and another one-third lost their vision during the first year of life. Many children who are educationally blind have normal intelligence and function very well academically with appropriate supports and learning aids. 3-D printing provides an important technology support for students with visual impairments. Haptic devices (involving the sense of touch) and technology that makes use of audio rather than visual cues have been found to increase the learning and exploration of students with a visual impairment (Cappagli & others, 2019).

An important task when working with a visually impaired child is to determine the modality (such as touch or hearing) through which the child learns best. Preferential seating in the front of the classroom is also helpful.

articulation disorders Problems in pronouncing sounds correctly.

voice disorders Disorders reflected in speech that is hoarse, harsh, too loud, too high-pitched, or too low-pitched.

fluency disorders Various disorders that involve what is commonly called "stuttering."

low vision Visual acuity between 20/70 and 20/2000.

educationally blind Unable to use one's vision in learning and needing to use hearing and touch to learn.

Hearing Impairments A hearing impairment can make learning difficult for children. Children who are born deaf or experience a significant hearing loss in the first several years of life may not develop normal speech and language (Brown, 2020; Waldman & Cleary, 2017). Some children in middle and late childhood have hearing impairments that have not yet been detected. If children turn one ear toward the speaker, frequently ask to have something repeated, don't follow directions, or frequently complain of earaches, colds, and allergies, their hearing needs to be evaluated by a specialist, such as an audiologist (Centers for Disease Control and Prevention, 2023c).

Many children with hearing impairment receive supplementary instruction beyond general classroom instruction, but when hearing loss is undetected and untreated, children are more likely to struggle in school because they have language difficulties (Bell, Mouzourakis, & Wise, 2022; LeClair & Saunders, 2019). Educational approaches for children with hearing impairments fall into two categories: oral and manual (Murray, Hall, & Snoddon, 2019):

- **Oral approaches** include using lip reading, speech reading (relying on visual cues to teach reading), and use of whatever hearing the child has.
- **Manual approaches** involve sign language and finger spelling. Sign language is a system of hand movements that symbolize words. Finger spelling consists of "spelling out" each word by placing the hand in different positions.

A total communication approach that includes both oral and manual approaches is increasingly being used with children who are hearing impaired (Hallahan, Kauffman, & Pullen, 2023).

Today many children with hearing impairments are educated in the regular classroom, and their learning is supported by the use of tools such as preferential, specific seating and the assistance of hearing aids, cochlear implants, and other amplification devices (Ching & others, 2018; Furno, Demchak, & Bingham, 2020).

Physical Disorders

Physical disorders in middle and late childhood include orthopedic impairments such as cerebral palsy. Many children with physical disorders require special education as well as related services. The related services may include transportation, physical therapy, school health services, and psychological services.

Orthopedic impairments involve restricted movement or lack of control over movement due to muscle, bone, or joint problems. The severity of problems ranges widely. Orthopedic impairments can be caused by prenatal or perinatal problems, or they can result from diseases or accidents during the childhood years. With the help of adaptive devices and medical technology, many children with orthopedic impairments function well in the classroom (Lewis, Wheeler, & Carter, 2017).

Cerebral palsy is a disorder that involves a lack of muscular coordination, shaking, and unclear speech. Cerebral palsy can be caused by many factors, including lack of oxygen at birth and other environmental and genetic factors (Patel & others, 2020). In the most common type of cerebral palsy, which is called spastic, children's muscles are stiff and difficult to move. The rigid muscles often pull the limbs into contorted positions. In a less common type, ataxia, children's muscles are rigid one moment and floppy the next moment, making movements clumsy and jerky.

Computers can be effective tools to help children with cerebral palsy learn. If they have the coordination to use the keyboard, they can do their written work on the computer. A pen with a light can be added to a computer and used by the child as a pointer. Children with cerebral palsy sometimes have unclear speech. For these children, speech and voice synthesizers, communication boards, and page turners can improve their communication.

Emotional and Behavioral Disorders

Most children have minor emotional difficulties at some point during their school years. A small percentage have problems so serious and persistent that they are classified as having an emotional or a behavioral disorder (La Salle & others, 2018; Lambert & others, 2022). **Emotional and behavioral disorders** consist of serious, persistent problems that involve relationships, aggression, depression, fears associated with

oral approaches Educational approaches to support children with hearing impairments, including lip reading, speech reading, and use of whatever hearing the child has.

manual approaches Educational approaches to support children with hearing impairments, including sign language and finger spelling.

orthopedic impairments Restrictions in movement abilities due to muscle, bone, or joint problems.

cerebral palsy A disorder that involves a lack of muscular coordination, shaking, and unclear speech.

emotional and behavioral disorders Serious, persistent problems that involve relationships, aggression, depression, fears associated with personal or school matters, as well as other inappropriate socioemotional characteristics.

Special input devices can help students with physical disabilities use computers more effectively. Many students with physical disabilities such as cerebral palsy cannot use a conventional keyboard and mouse but can use alternative keyboards effectively.

Wendy Maeda/The Boston Globe/Getty Images

personal or school matters, as well as other inappropriate socioemotional characteristics (Lewis, Asbury, & Plomin, 2017; Weersing & others, 2017). The most recent evidence from a meta-analysis of studies in eight countries, including the United States, showed that about 14 percent of 1- to 7-year-old children are diagnosed with an emotional or behavioral disorder (Vasileva & others, 2021).

Autism Spectrum Disorders   **Autism spectrum disorders (ASDs)** are characterized by problems in social interaction, problems in verbal and nonverbal communication, and repetitive behaviors (Lord & others, 2020). Children with these disorders may also show atypical responses to sensory experiences (National Institute of Mental Health, 2017). Intellectual disability is present in some children with ASD, while others show average or above-average intelligence (Klinger & Dudley, 2019). Autism spectrum disorders can often be detected in children as early as 1 to 3 years of age and attempts are increasingly being made to identify ASDs during infancy by using eye-tracking methods to assess infants' attention and through parents' reports of concerns about infants' development (Alcañiz & others, 2022; M. Miller & others, 2018).

Estimates of the prevalence of ASD tracked over time indicate that the estimated proportion of 8-year-old children with autism spectrum disorder had increased to 1 in 54 (Centers for Disease Control and Prevention, 2020). Also, in 2018–2019, 11 percent of all children receiving special education in U.S. schools were diagnosed with autism (compared with only 6.5 percent in 2010-2011) (National Center for Education Statistics, 2020b). Further, in one major survey, autism spectrum disorder was identified four times more often in boys than in girls (Centers for Disease Control and Prevention, 2020). Researchers and clinicians are striving to identify ways to diagnose autism as early as possible, to be able to begin intervention when the child is developing most rapidly (Hudry & others, 2022).

Children with ASD show some deficits in cognitive processing of information. For example, one study found that a lower level of working memory was the executive function most strongly associated with autism spectrum disorders (Ziermans & others, 2017). Children with these disorders may also show atypical responses to sensory experiences (National Institute of Mental Health, 2017).

In 2013, the American Psychiatric Association proposed that in the new *DSM-V* psychiatric classification of disorders, autistic disorder (which was formerly considered a severe autism spectrum disorder), Asperger syndrome (which was formerly considered a relatively mild autism spectrum disorder), and several other autistic variations ought to be consolidated in the overarching category of autism spectrum disorder (Autism Research Institute, 2013). Today, distinctions are made in terms of the severity of problems based on amount of support needed due to challenges involving social communication, restricted interests, and repetitive behaviors.

What causes autism spectrum disorders? The current consensus is that ASD is a brain dysfunction characterized by abnormalities in brain structure and neurotransmitters (Takumi & others, 2020). A lack of connectivity between brain regions may be a key factor in ASD (McKinnon & others, 2019; Nair & others, 2018).

Genetic factors play a role in the development of autism spectrum disorders (Li & others, 2020). Twin studies document heritability estimates between 80 and 90 percent, but environmental factors, such as lead exposure or micronutrient deficiencies, also play a role in the manifestation of autism spectrum disorders (Willfors, Tammimies, & Bölte, 2017). There is no evidence that family socialization causes ASD.

Many children with ASD benefit from a well-structured classroom, individualized teaching, and small-group instruction (Davis & Rispoli, 2018). As with children who have an intellectual disability, behavior modification techniques are sometimes effective in helping children with ASD learn (Alberto & Troutman, 2017; Wheeler & Richey, 2019).

EDUCATIONAL ISSUES

The legal requirement that schools serve all children with a disability is fairly recent. Beginning in the mid-1960s and into the mid-1970s, legislators, the federal courts, and the U.S. Congress laid down special educational rights for children with disabilities. Prior to that time, most children with a disability were either refused enrollment or inadequately served by schools. In 1975, **Public Law 94-142,** the Education for All Handicapped Children Act, required that all students with disabilities be given a free, appropriate public education and be provided the funding to help implement this education.

- - - - - - - →
developmental connection

Disabilities

Children with ASD have difficulty in developing a theory of mind, especially in understanding others' beliefs and emotions. Connect to "Cognitive Development in Early Childhood."

← - - - - - - -

autism spectrum disorders (ASDs) Also called pervasive developmental disorders, this category ranges from severe to milder disorders. Children with these disorders are characterized by problems with social interaction, verbal and nonverbal communication, and repetitive behaviors.

Public Law 94-142 The Education for All Handicapped Children Act, created in 1975, which requires that all children with disabilities be given a free, appropriate public education and which provides the funding to help with the costs of implementing this education.

In 1990, Public Law 94-142 was recast as the **Individuals with Disabilities Education Act (IDEA).** IDEA was amended in 1997 and then reauthorized in 2004. IDEA spells out broad mandates for providing services to all children with disabilities (U.S. Department of Education, 2019). These include evaluation and eligibility determination, appropriate education and an individualized education plan (IEP), and education in the least restrictive environment (LRE).

Evaluation and Eligibility Determination

Children who are thought to have a disability are evaluated to determine their eligibility for services under IDEA. Schools are prohibited from planning special education programs in advance and offering them on a space-available basis.

Children must be evaluated before a school can begin providing special services (Etscheidt & others, 2023). Parents should be involved in the evaluation process. Reevaluation is required at least every three years (sometimes every year), when requested by parents, or when conditions suggest that a reevaluation is needed. A parent who disagrees with the school's evaluation can obtain an independent evaluation, which the school is required to consider in providing special education services. If the evaluation finds that the child has a disability and requires special services, the school must provide them to the child.

The IDEA has many specific provisions involving the parents of a child with a disability. These include requirements that schools send notices to parents of proposed actions, of attendance at meetings regarding the child's placement or individualized education plan, and of the right to appeal school decisions to an impartial evaluator.

Appropriate Education and the Individualized Education Plan (IEP)

The IDEA requires that students with disabilities have an **individualized education plan (IEP),** a written statement that spells out a program tailored specifically for the student with a disability. In general, the IEP should be (1) related to the child's learning capacity, (2) specially constructed to meet the child's individual needs and not merely a copy of what is offered to other children, and (3) designed to provide educational benefits.

Under IDEA, the child with a disability must be educated in the **least restrictive environment (LRE),** a setting as similar as possible to the one in which children who do not have a disability are educated. And schools must make an effort to educate children with a disability in the regular classroom. The term **inclusion** means educating a child with special educational needs full-time in the regular classroom (U.S. Department of Education, 2019). In the 2016–2017 school year, 63 percent of U.S. students with a disability spent more than 80 percent of their school day in a general classroom (compared with only 33 percent in 1990) (National Center for Education Statistics, 2018).

Not long ago, it was considered appropriate to educate children with disabilities outside the regular classroom. However, today, schools must make every effort to provide inclusion for children with disabilities (Kauffman & others, 2022; U.S. Department of Education, 2019). These efforts can be very costly financially and very time consuming in terms of faculty effort. The principle of least restrictive environment compels schools to examine possible modifications of the regular classroom before moving the child with a disability to a more restrictive placement. Also, regular classroom teachers often need specialized training to help some children with a disability, and state educational agencies are required to provide such training.

Many of the legal changes regarding children with disabilities have been extremely positive. Compared with several decades ago, far more children today are receiving competent, specialized services. For many children, inclusion in the regular classroom, with modifications or supplemental services, is appropriate (Turnbull & others, 2020). However, some leading experts on special education argue that the effort to use inclusion to educate children with disabilities has become too extreme in some cases. For example, inclusion sometimes involves making accommodations in the regular classroom that do not always benefit children with disabilities (Maag, Kauffman, & Simpson, 2019). A more individualized approach that does not always involve full inclusion but provides options such as special education outside the regular classroom may be needed. James Kauffman and his colleagues (2004, p. 620) acknowledge that children with disabilities "*do* need the services of specially trained professionals to achieve their full potential. They *do* sometimes need altered curricula or

Increasingly, children with disabilities are being taught in the regular classroom, as is this child with an intellectual disability.
E.D. Torial/Alamy Stock Photo

Individuals with Disabilities Education Act (IDEA) The IDEA spells out broad mandates for providing services to all children with disabilities (IDEA is a renaming of Public Law 94-142); these include evaluation and eligibility determination, appropriate education and an individualized education plan (IEP), and education in the least restrictive environment (LRE).

individualized education plan (IEP) A written statement that spells out a program tailored to a child with a disability. The plan should be (1) related to the child's learning capacity, (2) specially constructed to meet the child's individual needs and not merely a copy of what is offered to other children, and (3) designed to provide educational benefits.

least restrictive environment (LRE) The concept that a child with a disability must be educated in a setting that is as similar as possible to the one in which children who do not have a disability are educated.

inclusion Educating a child with special educational needs full-time in the regular classroom.

Ethnic Minority Students in Special Education

Researchers, educators, and policymakers have several concerns about ethnic minority students in special education programs and classes:

- Students may be unserved or receive services that do not meet their needs.
- Students may be misclassified or inappropriately labeled.
- Placement in special education classes may be a form of discrimination.

In some analyses, ethnic minority students have been found to be overrepresented in special education, particularly for some stigmatizing disability classifications such as emotional disturbances and intellectual disabilities (Connor & others, 2019). However, in other analyses that control for confounding factors such as family income and other student characteristics, ethnic minority students have been found to be less likely to be identified for special education services (Morgan & others, 2017). The findings are controversial and have been interpreted in different ways but raise concerns regarding whether ethnic minority students are receiving appropriate services guaranteed under IDEA (Gordon, 2017; Harry & Klingner, 2022).

More appropriate inclusion of ethnic minority students in special education is a complex problem and requires the creation of a successful school experience for all students. Recommendations for ensuring that the needs of ethnic minority students are met in special education include the following:

- Reviewing school practices to identify and address factors that might contribute to having school difficulties.
- Forming policy-making groups that include community members and promote partnerships with service agencies and cultural organizations.
- Helping families get social, medical, mental health, and other support services.
- Training more teachers from ethnic minority backgrounds and providing all teachers with more extensive course work and training in educating children with disabilities and in understanding diversity issues.

adaptations to make their learning possible." However, "we sell students with disabilities short when we pretend that they are not different from typical students. We make the same error when we pretend that they must not be expected to put forth extra effort if they are to learn to do some things—or learn to do something in a different way." As is true of general education, an important aspect of special education should be to challenge students with disabilities "to become all they can be."

One concern about special education involves whether the needs of students from ethnic minority backgrounds are being met in special education programs and classes (Connor & others, 2019). The *Connecting with Diversity* interlude addresses this issue.

Review Connect Reflect

 LG3 Summarize information about children with disabilities.

Review
- Who are children with disabilities?
- What are some characteristics of the range of children's disabilities?
- What are some important issues in the education of children with disabilities?

Connect
- Earlier, you learned about the development of attention in infancy and early childhood. How might ADHD be linked to attention difficulties during infancy and early childhood?

Reflect *Your Own Personal Journey of Life*
- Think about your own schooling and how children with learning disabilities or ADHD either were or were not diagnosed. Were you yourself diagnosed, or were you aware of other such individuals in your classes? Were they helped by specialists? Consider their educational experiences and whether you think schools could have done a better job of helping.

This chapter introduced you to the physical and brain changes of middle and late childhood. In "Physical Development in Adolescence," you will read about how the slow physical growth of middle and late childhood gives way to the dramatic changes of puberty in early adolescence. Significant changes also occur in the adolescent's brain, and such changes may be linked to an increase in risk taking and sensation seeking. In "Cognitive Development in Middle and Late Childhood," you will explore developmental changes in children's cognition in middle and late childhood, including Piaget's theory and a number of changes in children's information processing. You'll also read about some important processes that influence children's achievement and changes in language development in older children, including reading skills.

reach your **learning goals**

Physical Development in Middle and Late Childhood

1 What Changes Take Place in Body Growth, the Brain, and Motor Development?

LG1 Discuss changes in body growth, the brain, and motor development in middle and late childhood.

Skeletal and Muscular Systems

- The period of middle and late childhood involves slow, consistent growth. During this period, children grow an average of 2 to 3 inches a year. Muscle mass and strength gradually increase. Among the most pronounced changes are decreases in head circumference, waist circumference, and leg length in relation to body height.

The Brain

- Changes in the brain continue to occur in middle and late childhood, and these changes, such as increased myelination, are linked to improvements in cognitive functioning. In particular, there is an increase in pathways involving the prefrontal cortex—changes that are related to improved attention, reasoning, and cognitive control. During middle and late childhood, less diffusion and more focal activation occur in the prefrontal cortex, changes that are associated with an increase in cognitive control.

Motor Development

- During middle and late childhood, motor development becomes much smoother and more coordinated. Children gain greater control over their bodies and can sit and pay attention for longer periods of time. However, their lives should be filled with physical activity.

- Gross motor skills are expanded during this period, and children refine such skills as hitting a tennis ball, jumping rope, or balancing on a beam. Increased myelination of the nervous system is reflected in improved fine motor skills, such as more legible handwriting and the ability to play a difficult piece on a musical instrument.

2 What Are the Central Issues in Children's Health?

LG2 Characterize children's health in middle and late childhood.

Nutrition

- During middle and late childhood, weight doubles and considerable energy is expended in motor activities. To support their growth, children need to consume more calories than they did when they were younger. A balanced diet is important. A special concern is that too many children fill up on "empty-calorie" foods that are high in sugar, starch, and excess fat and low in nutrients. A nutritious breakfast promotes higher energy and better alertness in school.

| Exercise and Sports | • Every indication suggests that children in the United States are not getting enough exercise. Excessive screen time, parents who are poor role models for exercise, and inadequate physical education classes in schools are among the culprits. Children's participation in sports can have both positive and negative consequences. |

- Although the increase of child obesity in the United States has begun to level off, over the last four decades the percentage of U.S. children who are overweight has tripled. An increasing number of children in many countries worldwide are overweight.

Overweight Children

- Being overweight in middle and late childhood substantially increases the risk of being overweight in adolescence and adulthood. Factors linked with being overweight in childhood include heredity and environmental contexts. Being overweight in childhood is related to a number of problems. Diet, exercise, and behavior modification are recommended for helping children to lose weight.

Diseases

- Cancer is the second leading cause of death in children (after accidents). Childhood cancers have a different profile from that of adult cancers. Diabetes is also a common disease in childhood. Cardiovascular disease is uncommon in children, but the precursors to adult cardiovascular disease are often already apparent in children. Asthma is the most common chronic disease in U.S. children.

Accidents and Injuries

- The most common cause of severe injury and death in childhood is motor vehicle accidents.

3 What Are the Prevalent Disabilities in Children?

 LG3 Summarize information about children with disabilities.

Who Are Children with Disabilities?

- Students with a learning disability are by far the largest group of students with a disability who receive special education. Substantial percentages also include children with speech or language impairments, intellectual disabilities, and emotional disturbance.

- The term "children with disabilities" is now recommended rather than "handicapped children." The newer terminology is intended to focus more on the child than on the disability.

The Range of Disabilities

- Children's disabilities cover a wide range and include learning disabilities, ADHD, speech disorders, sensory disorders, physical disorders, emotional and behavioral disorders, and autism spectrum disorders.

- A child with a learning disability has difficulty in learning that involves understanding or using spoken or written language, and the difficulty can appear in listening, thinking, reading, writing, and spelling. A learning disability also may involve difficulty in doing mathematics. To be classified as a learning disability, the learning problem is not primarily the result of visual, hearing, or motor disabilities; intellectual disabilities; or emotional disorders or due to environmental, cultural, or economic disadvantage. Diagnosing whether a child has a learning disability is difficult. About three times as many boys as girls have a learning disability.

- The most common academic problem for children with a learning disability is difficulty reading. Dyslexia is a severe impairment in the ability to read and spell. Dysgraphia is a learning disability that involves difficulty in handwriting. Dyscalculia is a learning disability that involves difficulties in math computation. Controversy surrounds the "learning disability" category. Many interventions targeted for learning disabilities focus on improving the child's reading ability and include such strategies as improving letter and word decoding skills.

- Attention deficit hyperactivity disorder (ADHD) is a disability in which children consistently show problems in one or more of the following areas: inattention, hyperactivity, and impulsivity. For an ADHD diagnosis, the characteristics must appear early in childhood and be debilitating for the child. Although signs of ADHD may be present in early childhood, diagnosis of ADHD often doesn't occur until the elementary school years. Many experts recommend a combination of academic, behavioral, and medical interventions to help students with ADHD learn and adapt.

- Speech disorders include articulation disorders, voice disorders, and fluency disorders. Sensory disorders include visual and hearing impairments. Physical disorders that children may have include orthopedic impairments and cerebral palsy. Emotional and behavioral disorders consist of serious, persistent problems that involve relationships, aggression, depression, fears associated with personal or school matters, as well as other inappropriate socioemotional characteristics.

- Autism spectrum disorders (ASDs) involve abnormalities in social relationships and communication. ASDs also are characterized by repetitive behaviors. The current consensus is that autism spectrum disorders involve an organic brain dysfunction. Autism spectrum disorders range from mild to severe forms.

Educational Issues

- Beginning in the 1960s and 1970s, the educational rights of children with disabilities were articulated. In 1975, Public Law 94-142 required school systems to provide all children with a free, appropriate public education. In 1990, Public Law 94-142 was renamed and called the Individuals with Disabilities Education Act (IDEA). Children who are thought to have a disability are evaluated to determine their eligibility for services. An individualized education plan (IEP) is a written plan that spells out a program tailored to the needs of a child with a disability. The concept of a least restrictive environment (LRE) is contained in the IDEA. The term *inclusion* means educating children with disabilities full-time in the general classroom. The trend is toward greater use of inclusion.

key **terms**

articulation disorders	dyslexia	Individuals with Disabilities	orthopedic impairments
asthma	educationally blind	Education Act (IDEA)	Public Law 94-142
attention deficit hyperactivity	emotional and behavioral	learning disability	type 1 diabetes
disorder (ADHD)	disorders	least restrictive environment	type 2 diabetes
autism spectrum disorders (ASDs)	fluency disorders	(LRE)	voice disorders
cerebral palsy	inclusion	low vision	
dyscalculia	individualized education plan	manual approaches	
dysgraphia	(IEP)	oral approaches	

key **people**

Mark Johnson   James Kauffman

improving the **lives of children**

STRATEGIES

Nurturing Children's Physical Development and Health

What are some good strategies for supporting children's physical development and health in the middle and late childhood years?

- *Elementary school children should be physically active whenever possible.* Goals should especially include reducing screen time and increasing participation in activities such as swimming, skating, and bicycling.

- *Parents should monitor children's eating behavior.* Children need more calories now than they did when they were younger. However, a special concern is the increasing number of obese children. Children who are overweight need to have a medical checkup, to revise their diet, and to participate in a regular exercise program.

- *Elementary schools need to develop more and better physical education programs.* Only about one of every three elementary school children participates in a physical education program daily. Many of those who don't are exercising much during the program.

- *Parents need to engage in physical activities that they can enjoy together with their children.* Suggested activities include running, bicycling, hiking, and swimming.

- *Parents should try to make their children's experiences in sports positive ones.* They should stress the benefits of sports rather than displaying a win-at-all-costs philosophy.

- *Parents should help children avoid accidents and injuries.* They should educate their children about the hazards of risk-taking behaviors and improper use of equipment.

RESOURCES

Routledge Handbook of Talent Identification and Development in Sport (2017)

Edited by Joseph Baker and his colleagues
New York: Routledge

Extensive information and strategies that can help parents become more effective in raising children who are talented in sports in positive ways.

Children's HeartLink

www.childrensheartlink.org

This organization provides treatment for needy children with heart disease and support for rheumatic fever prevention programs. It also supports the education of medical professionals from other countries and provides technical advice and medical equipment and supplies.

Council for Exceptional Children (CEC)

www.cec.sped.org

The CEC maintains an information center on the education of children and adolescents with disabilities and publishes materials on a wide variety of topics.

Learning Disabilities Association of America (LDA)

www.ldaamerica.org

The LDA provides education and support for parents of children with learning disabilities, interested professionals, and others. More than 500 chapters are in operation nationwide, offering information services, pamphlets, and book recommendations.

Autism Spectrum Disorders (2nd ed.) (2017)

E. Amanda Boutot
Upper Saddle River, NJ: Pearson

This book on various aspects of autism spectrum disorders describes research and practical approaches for improving the lives of children with autism spectrum disorders.

Exceptional Learners (15th ed.) (2023)

Daniel Hallahan, James Kauffman, and Paige Pullen
Upper Saddle River, NJ: Pearson

This excellent book by leading experts provides a very up-to-date examination of many child disabilities, including learning disabilities, ADHD, and autism spectrum disorders, as well as effective strategies for teaching children who have these conditions.

chapter 12

COGNITIVE DEVELOPMENT IN MIDDLE AND LATE CHILDHOOD

chapter **outline**

① **What Is Piaget's Theory of Cognitive Development in Middle and Late Childhood?**

Learning Goal 1 Discuss Piaget's stage of concrete operational thought and apply Piaget's theory to education.

Concrete Operational Thought

Evaluating Piaget's Concrete Operational Stage

Applications to Education

② **What Is the Nature of Children's Information Processing?**

Learning Goal 2 Describe changes in information processing in middle and late childhood.

Memory

Thinking

Metacognition

③ **What Changes in Language Development Occur in Middle and Late Childhood?**

Learning Goal 3 Summarize language development in middle and late childhood.

Vocabulary, Grammar, and Metalinguistic Awareness

Reading and Writing

Dual-Language and Second-Language Learning

④ **How Can Children's Intelligence Be Described?**

Learning Goal 4 Characterize children's intelligence.

Intelligence and Its Assessment

Types of Intelligence

Interpreting Differences in IQ Scores

Extremes of Intelligence

⑤ **What Characterizes Children's Achievement?**

Learning Goal 5 Explain the development of achievement in children.

Extrinsic and Intrinsic Motivation

Sustained Attention, Effort, and Task Persistence

Mastery Motivation and Mindset

Self-Efficacy

Goal Setting, Planning, and Self-Monitoring/Self-Regulation

Social Relationships and Contexts

Steve Debenport/E+/Getty Images

Marva Collins, challenging a child to achieve.

Elizabeth Flores/Milwaukee Journal Sentinel

On the first day of school, Chicago teacher Marva Collins told her students, many of whom were repeating the second grade,

"I know most of you can't spell your name. You don't know the alphabet, you don't know how to read. . . . I promise you that you will. None of you has ever failed. School may have failed you. Well, goodbye to failure, children. Welcome to success. You will read hard books in here and understand what you read. You will write every day. . . . But you must help me to help you. If you don't give anything, don't expect anything. Success is not coming to you, you must come to it." (Dweck, 2006, pp. 188–189)

Her second-grade students usually had to start with the lowest level of reader available, but by the end of the school year most of the students were reading at or above their grade level.

Collins, who passed away in 2015 but left a legacy of students and educators who were inspired by her efforts, took inner-city children who were just beginning the period of middle childhood and who were living in low-income circumstances, and challenged them to be all they could be. She did not accept failure by her students and taught students to be responsible for their behavior every day of their lives. Collins told students that being excellent at something is not a one-time thing but a habit, that determination and persistence are what move the world, and that thinking others will make you successful is a sure way to fail.

-topical **connections**   *looking **back***

You have studied the physical changes that characterize development in middle and late childhood, including the substantial advances in the development of the brain. Early childhood is a period in which young children increasingly engage in symbolic thought. Young children's information-processing skills also improve considerably—executive and sustained attention advance, short-term memory gets better, and their understanding of the human mind makes considerable progress. Young children also increase their knowledge of language's rule systems, and their literacy benefits from active participation in a wide range of language experiences. Many young children attend an early childhood education program, and there are many variations in these programs. In this chapter, you will study a number of advances in children's cognitive development during the elementary school years.

preview

In the current chapter, we explore many aspects of achievement. First, we will examine three main aspects of cognitive changes—the concrete operational stage of Piaget's cognitive developmental theory, information processing, and intelligence—that characterize middle and late childhood. Then we will look at language changes and explore children's achievement.

1 What Is Piaget's Theory of Cognitive Development in Middle and Late Childhood?

LG1 Discuss Piaget's stage of concrete operational thought and apply Piaget's theory to education.

Concrete Operational Thought

Evaluating Piaget's Concrete Operational Stage

Applications to Education

According to Jean Piaget (1952), the preschool child's thought is preoperational. Preschool children can form stable concepts, and they have begun to reason, but their thinking is flawed by egocentrism and magical belief systems. However, Piaget underestimated the cognitive skills of preschool children. Many researchers argue that under the right conditions, young children may display abilities that are characteristic of Piaget's next stage of cognitive development, the stage of concrete operational thought, and many argue that stages are not the best way to characterize children's cognitive development (Bolton & Hattie, 2017). Here we cover the characteristics of concrete operational thought, an evaluation of Piaget's portrait of this stage, and applications of Piaget's ideas to education.

> **developmental connection**
>
> **Cognitive Processes**
>
> Centration, a centering of attention on one characteristic to the exclusion of others, is present in young children's lack of conservation. Connect to "Cognitive Development in Early Childhood."

CONCRETE OPERATIONAL THOUGHT

Piaget proposed that the *concrete operational stage* lasts from approximately 7 to 11 years of age. In this stage, children can perform **concrete operations,** and they can reason logically as long as they can apply their reasoning to specific or concrete examples. Remember that *operations* are mental actions that are reversible, and *concrete operations* are operations that are applied to real, concrete objects.

The conservation tasks described in "Cognitive Development in Early Childhood" indicate whether children are capable of concrete operations. For example, recall that in one task involving conservation of matter, the child is presented with two identical balls of clay. The experimenter rolls one ball into a long, thin shape; the other remains in its original ball shape. The child is then asked if there is more clay in the ball or in the long, thin piece of clay. By the time children reach the age of 7 or 8, most answer that the amount of clay is the same. To answer this problem correctly, children have to imagine rolling the elongated clay back into a ball. This type of thinking involves a reversible mental action applied to a real, concrete object. Concrete operations allow the child to consider several characteristics rather than to focus on a single property of an object. In other words, the child's thinking is decentered—that is, the child does not focus or center on a single characteristic but rather several characteristics at a time. In the clay example, the preoperational child is likely to focus on height or width. The concrete operational child coordinates information about both dimensions.

What other abilities are characteristic of children who have reached the concrete operational stage? One important skill is the ability to classify or divide things into different sets or subsets and to consider their interrelationships. Consider the family tree of four generations that is shown in Figure 1 (Furth & Wachs, 1975). This family tree suggests that the grandfather (A) has three children (B, C, and D), each of whom has two children (E through J), and that one of these children (J) has three children (K, L, and M). A child who comprehends the classification system can move up and down a level, across a level, and up and down and across within the system. The concrete operational child understands that person J can at the same time be father, brother, and grandson, for example. So, for

concrete operations Reversible mental actions applied to real, concrete objects.

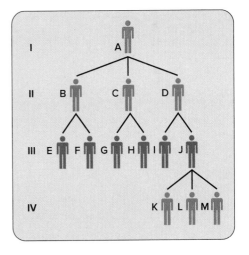

FIGURE 1

CLASSIFICATION: AN IMPORTANT ABILITY IN CONCRETE OPERATIONAL THOUGHT. A family tree of four generations (*I to IV*): The preoperational child has trouble classifying the members of the four generations; the concrete operational child can classify the members vertically, horizontally, and obliquely (up and down and across). For example, the concrete operational child understands that a family member can be a son, a brother, and a father, all at the same time.

instance, a boy who is one of two boys in a family can correctly answer the question "Does your brother have a brother?"

Children who have reached the concrete operational stage are also capable of **seriation,** which is the ability to order objects along a quantitative dimension (such as length). To see if students can serialize, a teacher might haphazardly place eight sticks of different lengths on a table. The teacher then asks the students to order the sticks by length. Many young children end up with two or three small groups of "big" sticks or "little" sticks, rather than a correct ordering of all eight sticks. The concrete operational thinker simultaneously understands that each stick must be longer than the one that precedes it and shorter than the one that follows it.

Another aspect of reasoning about the relations between classes is **transitivity,** which is the ability to logically combine relations among objects to come to certain conclusions. In this case, consider three sticks (A, B, and C) of differing lengths. A is the longest, B is intermediate in length, and C is the shortest. Does the child understand that if A is longer than B and B is longer than C, then A is longer than C? In Piaget's theory, concrete operational thinkers do; preoperational thinkers do not.

Learning science and mathematics is an important cultural experience that promotes the development of operational thought. *Might Piaget have underestimated the roles of culture and schooling in children's cognitive development?*
BSIP SA/Alamy Stock Photo

EVALUATING PIAGET'S CONCRETE OPERATIONAL STAGE

Has Piaget's portrait of the concrete operational child stood the test of research? Recall that in Piaget's theory, various aspects of a stage should emerge at the same time. In fact, however, some concrete operational abilities do not appear in synchrony. For example, children do not learn to conserve at the same time that they learn to classify complex relationships.

Furthermore, education and culture exert stronger influences on children's development than Piaget maintained (Kirmayer & others, 2020; Riccio & Castro, 2021). Some preoperational children can be trained to reason at a concrete operational stage. And the age at which children acquire conservation skills is related to how much practice their culture provides in these skills. However, great caution is needed in taking a procedure, such as a standard Piagetian task, and applying it in a new cultural context in which the materials and even the manner of an adult questioning a child about a problem to which the adult already knows the answer may be quite unusual, leading children to respond in ways that do not reflect knowledge they hold in situations that are closer to their lived experiences (Rogoff, Dahl, & Callanan, 2018).

Thus, although Piaget was a leader in the history of the study of cognitive development, his conclusions about the concrete operational stage have been challenged. Later, after we examine the final stage in his theory of cognitive development, we will evaluate Piaget's contributions and discuss the criticisms of his theory.

Neo-Piagetians, who are contemporary scholars who build on Piaget's ideas, argue that Piaget got some things right but that his theory needs considerable revision. They place greater emphasis on how children use attention, memory, and strategies to process information (Morra & Panesi, 2017). According to neo-Piagetians, a more accurate portrayal of children's thinking requires attention to children's strategies, the speed at which children process information, the particular task involved, and the division of problems into smaller, more precise steps (Demetriou & others, 2018; Fitamen, Blaye, & Camos, 2019; Siegler & Alibali, 2020). These are issues addressed by the information-processing approach, and we discuss some of them later in this chapter.

Another alternative to concrete operational thought comes from Lev Vygotsky. Vygotsky, like Piaget, held that children construct their knowledge of the world. But Vygotsky did not propose stages of cognitive development, and he emphasized the importance of social interaction, the social contexts of learning, and the young child's use of language to plan, guide, and monitor behavior (Clara, 2017).

APPLICATIONS TO EDUCATION

Although Piaget was not an educator, he provided a conceptual framework for viewing learning and education. Following are some ideas in Piaget's theory that can be applied to teaching children (Waite-Stupiansky, 2017):

seriation The concrete operation that involves ordering objects along a quantitative dimension (such as length).

transitivity The ability to logically combine relations to draw certain conclusions.

neo-Piagetians Developmentalists who have elaborated on Piaget's theory, giving more emphasis to information processing, strategies, and precise cognitive steps.

1. *Take a constructivist approach.* Piaget emphasized that children learn best when they are active and seek solutions for themselves. Piaget opposed teaching methods that treat children as passive learners. The educational implication of Piaget's view is that, in all subjects, students learn best by making discoveries, reflecting on them, and discussing them, rather than by blindly imitating the teacher or doing things by rote.

2. *Facilitate rather than direct learning.* Effective teachers design situations that allow students to learn by doing. These situations promote students' thinking and discovery. Teachers listen, watch, and question students, to help them gain a better understanding.

3. *Consider the child's knowledge and level of thinking.* Students do not come to class with empty minds. They have concepts of space, time, quantity, and causality. These ideas differ from the ideas of adults. Teachers need to interpret what a student is saying and respond in a way that is not too far from the student's level. Also, Piaget suggested that it is important to examine children's mistakes in thinking, not just what they get correct, to help guide them to a higher level of understanding.

What are some educational strategies that can be derived from Piaget's theory?

John Lund/Marc Romanelli/Blend Images/The Agency Collection/Getty Images

4. *Promote the student's intellectual health.* When Piaget came to lecture in the United States, he was asked, "What can I do to get my child to a higher cognitive stage sooner?" He was asked this question so often here compared with other countries that he called it the American question. Piaget believed that children's learning should occur naturally. Children should not be pushed and pressured into achieving too much too early in their development, before they are maturationally ready. In the Piagetian view, this is not the best way for children to learn. It places too much emphasis on speeding up intellectual development, involves passive learning, and will not lead to positive outcomes.

5. *Turn the classroom into a setting of exploration and discovery.* What do actual classrooms look like when the teachers adopt Piaget's views? Montessori methods build on Piaget's work (Povell, 2017). The teachers emphasize students' own exploration and discovery. The classrooms are less structured than what we think of as a typical classroom. Workbooks and predetermined assignments are not used. Rather, the teachers observe the students' interests and natural participation in activities to determine what the course of learning will be. For example, a math lesson might be constructed around counting the day's lunch money or dividing supplies among students. Games are often used in the classroom to stimulate mathematical thinking.

Review *Connect* Reflect

 LG1 Discuss Piaget's stage of concrete operational thought and apply Piaget's theory to education.

Review
- How can concrete operational thought be characterized?
- How can Piaget's concrete operational stage be evaluated?
- How can Piaget's theory be applied to education?

Connect
- How is the application of Piaget's theory to children's education similar to or different from the application of Vygotsky's theory to their education?

Reflect *Your Own Personal Journey of Life*
- Imagine that you are an elementary school teacher. Based on Piaget's theory, in what important ways is your thinking likely to differ from that of the children in your classroom? What adjustments in thinking might you need to make when you communicate with the children?

2 What Is the Nature of Children's Information Processing?

LG2 Describe changes in information processing in middle and late childhood.

Memory | Thinking | Metacognition

short-term memory Limited-capacity memory system in which information is usually retained for up to 30 seconds if there is no rehearsal of the information. Using rehearsal, people can keep the information in short-term memory longer.

long-term memory A relatively permanent type of memory that holds huge amounts of information for a long period of time.

working memory A mental "workbench" where individuals manipulate and assemble information when making decisions, solving problems, and comprehending written and spoken language.

During middle and late childhood, most children dramatically improve their ability to sustain and control attention. They pay more attention to task-relevant stimuli such as teacher instructions than to salient stimuli such as the colors in the teacher's attire. Other changes in information processing during middle and late childhood involve memory, thinking, and metacognition (Bjorklund, 2022). In the following pages, we examine each of these areas.

MEMORY

Short-term memory is a memory system with a limited capacity in which information is usually retained for 15 to 30 seconds unless strategies are used to retain it longer. It increases considerably during early childhood, but after age 7 the rate of improvement slows down. **Long-term memory,** a relatively permanent and unlimited, long-lasting type of memory, increases with age during middle and late childhood. In part, improvements in both types of memory reflect children's increased knowledge and their increased use of strategies to retain information (Bjorklund, 2022).

Working Memory When psychologists first analyzed short-term memory, they described it as if it were a passive storage room with shelves to store information until it is moved to long-term memory. But we do many other things with the information stored in short-term memory. For example, the words in this sentence are part of your short-term memory, and you are manipulating them to form a meaningful whole as you read them. The concept of **working memory** is used to describe how we manipulate the information in short-term memory.

Alan Baddeley (2018, 2021) defines working memory as a kind of mental "workbench" where individuals manipulate and assemble information when they make decisions, solve problems, and comprehend written and spoken language (see Figure 2). Working memory is the mental space in which people process and manipulate information. It is what we often refer to as consciousness. In working memory, we attend to new information or what we are currently thinking about. A *central executive* supervises and controls the flow of information as we work on it. This executive helps us use selective attention, inhibition, planning and decision making, and troubleshooting. Recall that *executive function* is an umbrella-like concept that comprises a number of higher-level cognitive processes. One of those cognitive processes is working memory, especially its central executive dimension.

Working memory uses information from long-term memory in its work and transfers information to long-term memory for longer storage. Working memory is a foundational cognitive activity, with the frontoparietal brain network playing a key role in its development (Rosenberg & others, 2020).

Working memory develops slowly. Even by 8 years of age, children can only hold in memory half the items that adults can remember (Kharitonova, Winter, & Sheridan, 2015). Working memory is linked to many aspects of children's development (Camos & Barrouillet, 2018; Vernucci & others, 2020). For example, children who have better working memory have better language comprehension, math skills, and problem-solving skills than their counterparts with less effective working memory (Nelwan & others, 2022; Tsubomi & Watanabe, 2017). In

Working Memory

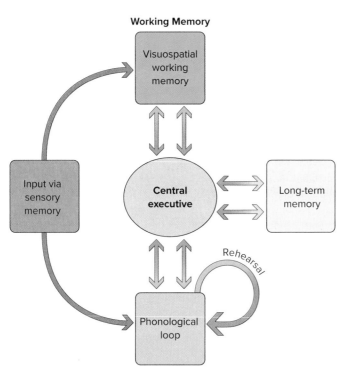

FIGURE 2

WORKING MEMORY. In Baddeley's classic working memory model, working memory is like a mental workbench where a great deal of information processing is carried out. Working memory consists of three main components: the phonological loop and visuospatial working memory serve as assistants, helping the central executive do its work. Input from sensory memory goes to the phonological loop, where information about speech is stored and rehearsal takes place, and visuospatial working memory, where visual and spatial information, including imagery, are stored. Working memory is a limited-capacity system, and information is stored there for only a brief time. Working memory interacts with long-term memory, using information from long-term memory in its work and transmitting information to long-term memory for longer storage. Most recently, Baddeley added an "episodic buffer" component to help explain how information about the timing and location of memories gets stored and used.

one study, research with first- to third-graders indicated that working memory improvement predicted math problem-solving growth in bilingual children (Swanson, Arizmendi, & Li, 2021).

Knowledge and Expertise   Much of the research on the role of knowledge in memory has compared experts and novices (Newberry, Feller, & Bailey, 2021). *Experts* have acquired extensive knowledge about a particular content area; this knowledge influences what they notice and how they organize, represent, and interpret information. These skills in turn affect their ability to remember, reason, and solve problems. When individuals have expertise about a particular subject, their memory also tends to be good regarding material related to that subject (Gobet, 2018).

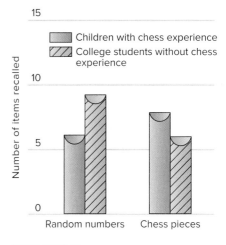

Tetra Images/Alamy Stock Photo

For example, one illustrative study found that 10- and 11-year-olds who were very experienced chess players ("experts") were able to remember more information about the location of chess pieces than college students who were not chess players ("novices") (Chi, 1978) (see Figure 3). In contrast, when the college students were presented with "non-chess" stimuli, they were able to remember them better than the children were. The children's expertise in chess gave them superior memories, but only for items involving chess.

There are developmental changes in expertise that help explain improvements in memory with age. Older children usually have more expertise about many subjects than younger children do, which can contribute to their better memory for each subject. However, it is important to consider that expertise is gained in a broader context of family, school, neighborhood, and culture.

Strategies   Long-term memory depends on the learning activities individuals engage in when learning and remembering information (Dawson & Guare, 2018). A key learning activity involves the use of **strategies,** which consist of deliberate mental activities to improve the processing of information (Graham & others, 2021). For example, organizing information is a strategy that older children, adolescents, and adults use to remember information more effectively. Strategies do not occur automatically; they require effort and work. Strategies, which are also called *control processes,* are under the learner's conscious control and can be used to improve memory. An important strategy is **elaboration,** which involves engaging in more extensive processing of information (Kretschmer-Trendowicz & others, 2019).

When individuals engage in elaboration, their memory benefits (Wu & Jobson, 2019). Thinking of examples, especially those related to yourself, is a good way to elaborate information. Thinking about personal associations with information makes the information more meaningful and helps children to remember it (Hutchison, Ross, & Cunningham, 2021). For example, if the word *win* is on a list of words a group of children is asked to remember, some of the children might think of the last time they won a race with some friends.

Fuzzy Trace Theory   Might something other than knowledge and strategies be responsible for improvement in memory during the elementary school years? Charles Brainerd and Valerie Reyna (2014) argue that what they call *fuzzy traces* account for much of this improvement. Their **fuzzy trace theory** states that memory is best understood by considering two types of memory representations: (1) verbatim memory and (2) gist. *Verbatim memory* consists of the precise details of the information, whereas *gist* refers to the central idea of the information. When gist is used, fuzzy traces are built up that contain the main idea but not all the details of the information. Although individuals of all ages extract gist, young children are more prone to try to store and retrieve verbatim traces. During middle childhood, children begin to use gist more and, according to the theory, its use contributes to the improved memory and reasoning of older children because fuzzy traces are more enduring and less likely to be forgotten than verbatim traces (Kiraly & others, 2017).

Autobiographical Memory   Recall that *autobiographical memory* involves memory of significant events and experiences in one's life. You are engaging in autobiographical memory when you answer questions such as: Who were your favorite elementary school teachers and

FIGURE 3

THE ROLE OF EXPERTISE IN MEMORY. Notice that when 10- to 11-year-old children and college students were asked to remember a string of random numbers that had been presented to them, the college students fared better. However, the 10- to 11-year-olds who had a great deal of experience playing chess ("experts") had better memory for the location of chess pieces on a chess board than the college students with no chess experience ("novices") (Chi, 1978).

strategies Deliberate mental activities designed to improve the processing of information.

elaboration An important strategy that involves engaging in more extensive processing of information.

fuzzy trace theory States that memory is best understood by considering two types of memory representations: (1) verbatim memory trace and (2) fuzzy trace, or gist. According to this theory, older children's better memory is attributed to the fuzzy traces created by extracting the gist of information.

what were they like? What is the most traumatic event that happened to you as a child? As children go through middle and late childhood, and through adolescence, their autobiographical narratives broaden and become more elaborated (Bauer & Larkina, 2018). Researchers have found that children develop more detailed, coherent, and evaluative autobiographical memories when their mothers reminisce with them in elaborated and evaluative ways (Fivush, 2019a).

Culture influences children's autobiographical memories. Family narratives and stories pass down memories from one generation to the next, and these family memories may be especially salient in cultures in which individuals are highly "interdependent" with each other (Reese & others, 2017). In all cultures, the information that is exchanged and remembered happens in culturally defined and appropriate ways that support memory development and functioning (Q. Wang, 2021).

Improving Children's Memory Some strategies adults can adopt when guiding children to remember information more effectively and longer include assisting them to organize information, elaborate the information, and develop images of the information. Another good strategy is to encourage children to understand the material that needs to be remembered rather than rotely memorizing it. Two additional strategies adults can use to guide children's retention of memory have been proposed:

- *Repeat new information in various ways and link it to what children already know.* To improve children's memory, it is helpful to consolidate the information children are learning and connect or link it to other information they already know (Bauer, 2009). For instance, variations on a lesson theme increase the number of associations in memory storage, and linking expands the network of associations in memory storage; both strategies expand the routes for retrieving information from storage.

- *Embed memory-relevant language when instructing children.* Teachers vary considerably in how much they use memory-relevant language that encourages students to remember information. In research that involved extensive observations of a number of early-elementary teachers in the classroom, Peter Ornstein and colleagues (summarized in Ornstein & Coffman, 2020) found that many teachers rarely used strategy suggestions or metacognitive (thinking about thinking) questions. In this research, when lower-achieving students were placed in classrooms in which teachers frequently embedded memory-relevant information in their teaching, students' achievement increased.

THINKING

Four important aspects of thinking are executive function, critical thinking, creative thinking, and scientific thinking

Executive Function There has been a surge of interest in studying children's *executive function,* an umbrella-like concept that encompasses a number of higher-level cognitive processes linked to the development of the brain's prefrontal cortex. Executive function involves managing one's thoughts to engage in goal-directed behavior and exercise self-control (Bell & Garcia Meza, 2020; Muller & others, 2017).

How might executive function change in middle and late childhood and affect children's success in school? The following dimensions of executive function are important for 4- to 11-year-old children's cognitive development and school success (Kassai & others, 2019):

- *Self-control/inhibition.* Children need to develop self-control that will allow them to concentrate and persist on learning tasks, to inhibit their tendencies to repeat incorrect responses, and to resist the impulse to do something now that is not useful or productive.

- *Working memory.* Children need to use working memory efficiently to process the masses of information they will encounter as they go through school and beyond.

- *Flexibility.* Children need to be flexible in their thinking to consider different strategies and perspectives.

A number of diverse activities have been found to increase children's executive function, including computerized training that uses games to improve working memory (Chocko &

Anthony Harvie/Photographer's Choice/Getty Images

others, 2017), aerobic exercise (Zhang & others, 2023), scaffolding of self-regulation (Bardack & Obradović, 2019), mindfulness (Geronimi, Arellano, & Woodruff-Borden, 2020), and some types of school curricula such as the Montessori curriculum that emphasize learning through play and other child-centered approaches (Doebel & Lillard, 2023).

Ann Masten and her colleagues (Distefano & others, 2021; Masten & Labella, 2016; Monn & others, 2017) have found that executive function and parenting skills are linked to success in school among children in families who lack housing. Masten believes that executive function and good parenting skills are related. In her words, "When we see kids with good executive function, we often see adults around them that are good self-regulators. Parents model, they support, and they scaffold these skills" (Masten, 2012, p. 11). This developing, scaffolded self-regulation perhaps is even more important as a protective factor in children's development in the face of stressors that arise from housing and income insecurity.

Critical Thinking   **Critical thinking** involves thinking reflectively and productively, as well as evaluating evidence (Baron, 2020; Sternberg & Halpern, 2020). When people think critically, they examine the information given to them and try to understand what it means and also why it may mean that. That is, critical thinking involves going beyond the information given. In this release, the "Connect" and "Reflect" questions at the end of each section challenge you to think critically about a topic or an issue related to the discussion.

Schools vary in the degree to which they teach students to think critically and to develop a deep understanding of concepts. Deep understanding occurs when students are stimulated to rethink previously held ideas. Many instructional approaches ask students to recite, define, describe, state, and list, rather than to analyze, infer, connect, synthesize, criticize, create, evaluate, think, and rethink. As a result, many students often think on a superficial level, staying on the surface of problems rather than stretching their minds and becoming deeply engaged in meaningful thinking. However, this limitation can be addressed through teaching methods that emphasize critical thinking and creativity (Grigg & Lewis, 2019).

Mindfulness—being alert, mentally present, and cognitively flexible while going through life's everyday activities and tasks—is an important aspect of thinking critically (Farrar & Tapper, 2018). Mindful children and adults maintain an active awareness of the circumstances in their life and are motivated to find the best solutions to tasks (Lux, Decker, & Nease, 2020). Mindful individuals create new ideas, are open to new information, and are able to use multiple perspectives. By contrast, individuals who are not concentrating on what they are doing in the present and are distracted by other thoughts and information are more likely to be entrapped in old ideas, engage in automatic behavior, and operate from a single perspective.

Mindfulness is an important mental process that children can engage in to improve a number of cognitive and socioemotional skills, such as executive function, focused attention, emotion regulation, and empathy. Mindfulness training can be implemented in schools through practices such as using age-appropriate activities that increase children's reflection on moment-to-moment experiences, resulting in improved self-regulation (Amundsen & others, 2020; Sheinman & others, 2018). For example, mindfulness training has been found to improve children's attention and self-regulation (Poehlmann-Tynan & others, 2016), achievement (Singh & others, 2016), and coping strategies in stressful situations (Dariotis & others, 2016). These individual study results have been affirmed in more recent meta-analyses of such training in school settings (Dunning & others, 2019). In addition to mindfulness, activities such as yoga, meditation, and tai chi have been suggested as candidates for improving children's cognitive and socioemotional development. Mindfulness-based interventions are helpful not only for students but also for teachers. For example, mindfulness-based interventions reduce public school teachers' stress, produce a better mood at school and at home, improve interactions with students, and improve sleep (Crain, Schonert-Reichl, & Roeser, 2017; Roeser & others, 2022; C. Taylor & others, 2016).

Creative Thinking   **Creative thinking** is the ability to think in novel and unusual ways and to come up with unique solutions to problems. Thus, intelligence and creativity are not the same thing (Sternberg, 2018c). This difference was recognized by J.P. Guilford (1967), who distinguished between **convergent thinking,** which produces one correct answer and characterizes the kind of thinking that is required on conventional tests of intelligence, and **divergent thinking,** which produces many different answers to the same question and characterizes creativity. For example, a typical item on a conventional intelligence test is "How many quarters will you get in return for 60 dimes?" In contrast, the following question has many possible

developmental **connection**
Education
A criticism of standardized testing in school, which is often accompanied by teachers spending a lot of class time preparing children for these tests or "teaching to the test," is that it does not give adequate attention to critical thinking skills. Connect to "Socioemotional Development in Middle and Late Childhood."

How might mindfulness training be implemented in schools?
Ariel Skelley/Blend Images/Vetta/Getty Images

critical thinking The ability to think reflectively and productively, as well as to evaluate the evidence.

mindfulness Being alert, mentally present, and cognitively flexible while going through life's everyday activities and tasks.

creative thinking The ability to think in novel and unusual ways and to come up with unique solutions to problems.

convergent thinking Thinking that produces one correct answer and is characteristic of the kind of thinking tested by standardized intelligence tests.

divergent thinking Thinking that produces many different answers to the same question and is characteristic of creativity.

How Would You...?
If you were a **psychologist,** how would you talk with teachers and parents about ways to improve children's creative thinking?

answers: "What image comes to mind when you hear the phrase 'sitting alone in a dark room' or 'some unique uses for a paper clip'?"

A special concern is that creative thinking may be declining in U.S. children. One influential study of approximately 300,000 U.S. children and adults found that creativity scores rose until 1990, but since then have been steadily declining (Kim, 2010). Among the likely causes of the creativity decline are the number of hours U.S. children spend watching TV and playing video games instead of engaging in creative activities, as well as the lack of emphasis on creative thinking skills in schools (Sternberg & Kaufman, 2018b). Some countries, though, are placing increasing emphasis on creative thinking in schools. However, it has been challenging to systematically implement creative thinking through curricula in schools, as revealed in analyses of many countries (Patston & others, 2021).

An important goal is to help children become more creative (Bereczki & Kárpáti, 2018). The *Caring Connections* interlude recommends some ways to accomplish this goal.

Scientific Thinking   Like scientists, children ask fundamental questions about reality and seek answers to problems that seem surprising or unanswerable to other people (such as "Why is the sky blue?"). Do children generate hypotheses, perform experiments, and reach conclusions about their data in ways resembling those of scientists?

Scientific reasoning often is aimed at identifying causal relations. Like scientists, children place a great deal of emphasis on causal mechanisms.

There also are important differences between the reasoning of children and the reasoning of scientists (Kuhn, 2013). Children are more influenced by coincidence than by an overall pattern (Kuhn, 2013). Often, children maintain their old theories regardless of the evidence (Lehrer & Schauble, 2015).

Children sometimes have difficulty reconciling seemingly contradictory new information with their existing beliefs. Children, and even many adults, also have difficulty designing experiments that can distinguish among alternative causes. Instead, they tend to bias the experiments in favor of whatever hypothesis they began with. Sometimes they see the results as supporting their original hypothesis even when the results directly contradict it. Thus, although there are important similarities between children and scientists in their basic curiosity and in the kinds of questions they ask, there are also important differences in the degree to which they can separate ideas and evidence and in their ability to design conclusive experiments (Lehrer & Schauble, 2015).

Effective science teaching helps children distinguish between fruitful errors and misconceptions and detect plainly wrong ideas that need to be replaced by more accurate conceptions (Contant & others, 2018). Too often, the skills scientists use, such as careful observation, graphing, self-regulatory thinking, and knowing when and how to apply one's knowledge to solve problems, are not routinely taught in schools (Manz, Lehrer, & Schauble, 2020). Children have many concepts that are incompatible with science and reality. Effective teachers perceive and understand a child's underlying scientific concepts, and then use the concepts as a scaffold for learning (Contant & others, 2018).

It is important for teachers to initially scaffold students' science learning, extensively monitor their progress, and ensure that they are learning science content because these practices are most essential to scientific reasoning and critical thinking (Novak & Treagust, 2018). Thus, in pursuing science investigations, students need to learn inquiry skills and science content simultaneously (Manz, Lehrer, & Schauble, 2020).

developmental **connection**

Cognitive Processes

Theory of mind—awareness of one's own mind and the mental processes of others—involves metacognition. Connect to "Cognitive Development in Early Childhood."

METACOGNITION

One expert in children's thinking, Deanna Kuhn (1999, 2017), argues that to help students become better thinkers, schools should pay more attention to helping students develop skills that entail knowing about their own (and others') ways of thinking and knowing. In other words, schools should do more to develop **metacognition,** which is knowing about thinking (de Boer & others, 2018; Norman, 2017). Metacognition can take many forms, including thinking about and knowing when and where to use particular strategies for learning or solving problems (Fergus & Bardeen, 2017). Conceptualization of metacognition includes several dimensions of executive function, such as planning (deciding how much time to focus on the task, for example), evaluation (monitoring progress toward task completion, for example), and self-regulation (modifying strategies as work on the task progresses, for example) (Bellon, Fias, & Smedt, 2020; Dos Santos Kawata & others, 2021; Pennequin & others, 2020).

How Would You...?
If you were an **educator,** how would you advise teachers and parents regarding ways to improve children's metacognitive skills?

metacognition Cognition about cognition, or knowing about thinking.

Guiding Children's Creativity

An important goal of teachers is to help children become more creative (Bereczki & Kárpáti, 2018; Kaufman & Sternberg, 2021). Following are some of the best strategies for accomplishing this goal.

- *Encourage creative thinking on a group and individual basis.* **Brainstorming** is a technique in which individuals are encouraged to come up with creative ideas in a group, play off each other's ideas, and say practically whatever comes to mind that seems relevant to a particular issue. Participants are usually told to hold off from criticizing others' ideas, at least until the end of the brainstorming session.

- *Provide environments that stimulate creativity.* Some environments nourish creativity, while others inhibit it. Parents and teachers who encourage creativity often rely on children's natural curiosity (Moore, Tank, & English, 2018). They provide exercises and activities that stimulate children to find insightful solutions to problems, rather than ask a lot of questions that require rote answers (Reis & Renzulli, 2020). Teachers also encourage creativity by taking students on field trips to locations where creativity is valued, such as science, discovery, and children's museums that offer rich opportunities to stimulate creativity.

- *Don't overcontrol students.* Telling children exactly how to do things might leave them feeling that originality is a mistake and exploration is a waste of time. If, instead of dictating which activities they should engage in, you let children select activities that match their interests and you support their inclinations, you will be less likely to inhibit their natural curiosity (Bereczki & Kárpáti, 2018; Hennessey, 2021). When parents and teachers are always hovering over students, they make the students feel that they are constantly being watched while they are working. When children are under constant surveillance, their creative risk taking and adventurous spirit diminish. Children's creativity also is diminished when adults have grandiose expectations for children's performance and expect perfection from them.

- *Encourage internal motivation.* Excessive use of prizes, such as gold stars, money, or toys, can stifle creativity by undermining the intrinsic pleasure students derive from creative activities (Malik & Butt, 2017). Creative children's motivation is the satisfaction generated by the work itself. Competition for prizes and formal evaluations often undermine intrinsic motivation and creativity (Hennessey, 2021). However, this should not rule out material rewards altogether.

- *Guide children to help them think in flexible ways.* Creative thinkers approach problems in many different ways, rather than getting

What are some good strategies for guiding children in thinking more creatively?
Ariel Skelley/DigitalVision/Getty Images

locked into rigid patterns of thought. Give children opportunities to exercise this flexibility in their thinking.

- *Build children's confidence.* To expand children's creativity, encourage children to believe in their own ability to create something innovative and worthwhile. Building children's confidence in their creative skills aligns with Bandura's (2018) concept of *self-efficacy,* the belief that one can master a situation and produce positive outcomes.

- *Guide children to be persistent and delay gratification.* Most highly successful creative products take years to develop. Most creative individuals work on ideas and projects for months and years without being rewarded for their efforts (Sternberg, 2020c). Children don't become experts at sports, music, or art overnight. It usually takes many years of working at something to become an expert at it; the same is true for a creative thinker who produces a unique, worthwhile product.

- *Encourage children to take intellectual risks.* Creative individuals take intellectual risks and seek to discover or invent something never before discovered or invented (Sternberg, 2020c). They risk spending a lot of time on an idea or project that may not work. Failure can be useful in the creative process (Hannigan, 2018). Creative people often see failure as an opportunity to learn.

- *Introduce children to creative people.* Teachers can invite creative people to their classrooms and ask them to describe what helps them become creative or to demonstrate their creative skills. A writer, poet, painter, musician, scientist, or another creative individual can bring their ideas and work to the class, turning it into an opportunity to stimulate students' own creativity.

A number of early developmental studies classified as "metacognitive" focused on *metamemory,* or knowledge about memory (Schneider, 2015). This includes general knowledge about memory, such as knowing that recognition tests are easier than recall tests. It also encompasses knowledge about one's own memory, such as a student's ability to monitor whether they have studied enough for a test as well as evaluating the reliability of your own working memory (Forsberg, Blume, & Cowan, 2021).

brainstorming A technique in which individuals are encouraged to come up with creative ideas in a group, play off each other's ideas, and say practically whatever comes to mind that seems relevant to a particular issue.

Young children do have some general knowledge about memory (Fivush, 2019b). By 5 or 6 years of age, children usually already know that familiar items are easier to learn than unfamiliar ones, that short lists are easier to remember than long ones, that recognition is easier than recall, and that forgetting is more likely to occur over time (Lyon & Flavell, 1993). However, in other ways young children's metamemory is limited. They don't understand that related items are easier to remember than unrelated ones and that remembering the gist of a story is easier than remembering information verbatim (Kreutzer, Leonard, & Flavell, 1975). By the fifth grade, however, students understand that gist recall is easier than verbatim recall.

Young children also have only limited knowledge about their own memory. They have an inflated opinion of their memory abilities. For example, in one classic study a majority of young children predicted that they would be able to recall all 10 items on a list of 10 items. When tested for this, none of the young children managed this feat (Flavell, Friedrichs, & Hoyt, 1970). As they move through the elementary school years, children give more realistic evaluations of their memory skills (Bjorklund, 2022).

In addition to metamemory, metacognition includes knowledge about strategies. Strategies have been the focus of a number of microgenetic investigations (Siegler, 2016a, b). A number of microgenetic studies (so called because they involve examination of changes as they occur in real time) have focused on a specific aspect of academic learning, such as how children learn whole number arithmetic, fractions, and other areas of math (Voutsina, George, & Jones, 2019). Using the microgenetic approach, researchers have shown that developing and knowing when to use effective strategies doesn't occur abruptly but gradually. This research has also found considerable variability in children's use of strategies, even revealing that they may use an incorrect strategy in solving a math problem for which they had used a correct strategy several trials earlier (Siegler & Braithwaite, 2017).

Cognitive developmentalist John Flavell is a pioneer in providing insights about children's thinking. Among his many contributions are establishing the field of metacognition and conducting numerous studies in this area, including metamemory and theory of mind studies.
Dr. John Flavell

Michael Pressley's (1951–2006) views about education have been very influential, suggesting that the key to education is helping students learn a rich repertoire of strategies that result in solutions to problems. Good thinkers routinely use strategies and effective planning to solve problems. Good thinkers also know when and where to use strategies. Understanding when and where to use strategies often results from monitoring the learning situation—that is, knowing what is needed to understand or solve the problem at hand (Pressley & McCormick, 2007).

Pressley and his colleagues (Pressley, 2007; Pressley & Hilden, 2006) spent considerable time observing strategy instruction by teachers and strategy use by students in elementary and secondary school classrooms. They concluded that strategy instruction tends to be far less complete and intense than what students need in order to learn how to use strategies effectively. They argued that education ought to be restructured so that students are provided with more opportunities to become competent strategic learners.

What are some developmental changes in metacognition?
Sigrid Olsson/PhotoAlto/The Agency Collection/Getty Images

Review Connect Reflect

 Describe changes in information processing in middle and late childhood.

Review
- What characterizes children's memory in middle and late childhood?
- What is involved in thinking critically, thinking creatively, and thinking scientifically?
- What is metacognition?

Connect
- In discussing memory, thinking, and metacognition, the topic of recommended educational strategies came up. Compare these recommendations in this main section with those you have already learned.

Reflect *Your Own Personal Journey of Life*
- When you were in elementary school, did classroom instruction prepare you adequately for critical and creative thinking? If you were a parent of an 8-year-old, what would you do to guide your child to think more critically and creatively?

3 What Changes in Language Development Occur in Middle and Late Childhood?

 LG3 Summarize language development in middle and late childhood.

| Vocabulary, Grammar, and Metalinguistic Awareness | Reading and Writing | Dual-Language and Second-Language Learning |

Knowledge of vocabulary words is a part of virtually all intelligence tests, and this and other aspects of language development are important aspects of children's intelligence. As they enter school, children gain new skills that make it possible for them to learn to read and write—these include increasingly using language to talk about things that are not physically present, learning what a word is, and learning how to recognize and talk about sounds (Gleason & Ratner, 2023). They have to learn the alphabetic principle—that the letters of the alphabet represent sounds of the language in languages that use alphabets, and that characters represent concepts in languages such as Chinese. As children develop during middle and late childhood, changes in their vocabulary and grammar also take place (Bruhn de Garavito, 2021c).

VOCABULARY, GRAMMAR, AND METALINGUISTIC AWARENESS

During middle and late childhood, changes occur in the way children organize their mental vocabulary. When asked to say the first word that comes to mind when they hear a word, young children typically provide a word that often follows the word in a sentence. For example, when asked to respond to "dog," a young child may say "barks," or to the word "eat" say "lunch." At about 7 years of age, children begin to respond with a word that is the same part of speech as the stimulus word. For example, children may now respond to the word "dog" with "cat" or "horse." To "eat," they now might say "drink." These responses are evidence that children's conceptual categorization changes and that language reflects this mental change (Gleason & Ratner, 2023).

The process of categorizing becomes easier as children increase their vocabulary (Clark, 2017). Children's vocabulary grows from an average of about 14,000 words at 6 years of age to an average of about 40,000 words by 11 years of age.

Children make similar advances in grammar (Hoff, Quinn, & Giguere, 2018). During the elementary school years, children's improvement in logical reasoning and analytical skills helps them understand such constructions as the appropriate use of comparatives (*shorter, deeper*) and subjunctives ("If you were president ..."). During the elementary school years, children become increasingly able to understand and use complex grammar, such as the following sentence: *The student who kicked the ball wore a hat.* They also learn to use language in a more connected way, producing connected discourse. They become able to relate sentences to one another to produce descriptions, definitions, and narratives that make sense. Children must be able to do these things orally before they can be expected to deal with them in written assignments.

These advances in vocabulary and grammar during the elementary school years are accompanied by the development of **metalinguistic awareness,** which is knowledge about language, such as knowing what a preposition is or being able to discuss the sounds of a language (Dong & others, 2020; Yeon, Bae, & Joshi, 2017). Metalinguistic awareness allows children "to think about their language, understand what words are, and even define them" (Berko Gleason, 2009, p. 4). It improves considerably during the elementary school years (Winne, 2017). Defining words becomes a regular part of classroom discourse, and children increase their knowledge of syntax as they study and talk about the components of sentences, such as subjects and verbs (Crain, 2012; Zipke, 2021). And reading also feeds into metalinguistic awareness as children try to comprehend written text.

Children also make progress in understanding how to use language in culturally appropriate ways—*pragmatics* (Nadasdi, 2021). By the time they enter adolescence, most children know the rules for the use of language in everyday contexts—that is, what is appropriate to say and what is inappropriate to say.

metalinguistic awareness Knowledge about language, such as knowing what a preposition is or being able to discuss the sounds of a language.

READING AND WRITING

Two key aspects of language development in middle and late childhood are reading and writing.

Reading Before learning to read, children learn to use language to talk about things that are not present; they learn what a word is; and they learn how to recognize sounds and talk about them. Children who begin elementary school with a robust vocabulary have an advantage in learning to read: vocabulary development plays an important role in reading comprehension.

How should children be taught to read? For many years, the debate focused on the phonics approach versus the whole-language approach (Dewitz & others, 2020).

The **phonics approach** emphasizes that reading instruction should teach basic rules for translating written symbols into sounds. Early phonics-centered reading instruction should involve simplified materials. Only after children have learned correspondence rules that relate spoken phonemes to the alphabet letters that are used to represent them should they be given complex reading materials, such as books and poems (Bear & others, 2020).

In contrast, the **whole-language approach** stresses that reading instruction should parallel children's natural language learning. In some whole-language classes, beginning readers are taught to recognize whole words or even entire sentences, and to use the context of what they are reading to guess at the meaning of words. With this approach, children are given reading materials in a complete form, such as stories and poems, so that they learn to understand language's communicative function. Reading is connected with listening and writing skills. Although there are variations in whole-language programs, most share the premise that reading should be integrated with other skills and subjects, such as science and social studies, and that it should focus on real-world material. Thus, a class might read newspapers, magazines, or books and then write about and discuss what they have read.

Which approach is better? Early in development, a strong foundation for oral language (for example, vocabulary) is important for building pre-reading skills. Next, phonics becomes important, and then later, comprehension and language knowledge more generally become important again as children put things together. It is not that either phonics or whole language is necessarily more important but rather that there is a developmental sequence where one approach is more important than the other at different times in development.

Beyond the phonics/whole-language issue in learning to read, becoming a good reader includes learning to read fluently, or smoothly, without having to pause to sound out words (Jamshidifarsani & others, 2019; Kim, Quinn, & Petscher, 2021). Many beginning or poor readers do not recognize words automatically. Their processing capacity is consumed by the demands of word recognition, so they have less capacity to devote to comprehension of groupings of words as phrases or sentences. As their processing of words and passages becomes more automatic, it is said that their reading becomes more *fluent* (Dewitz & others, 2020). Metacognitive strategies, such as learning to monitor one's reading progress, getting the gist of what is being read, and summarizing also are important in becoming a good reader (Zarger, Adams, & McDonald Connor, 2020).

Writing Children's writing emerges out of their early scribbles, which appear at around 2 to 3 years of age (Pinto & Incognito, 2021). In early childhood, children's motor skills usually develop to the point that they can begin printing letters. Most 4-year-olds can print their first names. Five-year-olds can reproduce letters and copy several short words. They gradually learn to distinguish the distinctive characteristics of letters, such as whether the lines are curved or straight, open or closed. Through the early elementary grades, many children continue to reverse letters such as *b* and *d* and *p* and *q* (Temple & others, 2018). At this age, if other aspects of the child's development are normal, letter reversals do not predict literacy problems. Also, as they begin to write, children often invent spellings. Usually they base these spellings on the sounds of words they hear (Ouellette & Sénéchal, 2017).

Parents and teachers should encourage children's early writing but not be overly concerned about the formation of letters or spelling. Printing errors are a natural part of the child's growth. Corrections of spelling and printing should be selective and made in positive ways that do not discourage the child's writing and creativity.

Like becoming a good reader, becoming a good writer takes many years and lots of practice (Feldgus, Cardonick, & Gentry, 2017). Children should be given many writing opportunities (Graham & Alves, 2021). As their language and cognitive skills improve with good instruction, so will their writing skills. For example, developing a more sophisticated understanding of syntax

This teacher is helping a student sound out words. Researchers have found that phonics instruction is a key aspect of teaching students to read, especially beginning readers and students with less developed reading skills.
Mordolff/Getty Images

phonics approach The idea that reading instruction should teach basic rules for translating written symbols into sounds.

whole-language approach An approach to reading instruction based on the idea that instruction should parallel children's natural language learning. Reading materials should be whole and meaningful.

and grammar serves as an underpinning for better writing. So do such cognitive skills as organization and logical reasoning. Through the course of the school years, students develop increasingly sophisticated methods of organizing their ideas. In early elementary school, they narrate and describe or write short poems. In late elementary and middle school, they can combine narration with reflection and analysis in projects such as book reports.

Monitoring one's writing progress is especially important in becoming a good writer (Harris & Graham, 2017). This includes being receptive to feedback and applying what one learns in writing one paper to making the next paper better. In one study, Self-Regulated Strategy Development (SRSD) was implemented with second-grade students who were at risk for writing failure (Harris, Graham, & Adkins, 2015). The students were taught a general planning strategy, general writing strategies (a catchy opening, effective vocabulary, clear organization, and an effective ending). The intervention produced positive results for story writing quality, motivation, and effort, as well as meaningful generalization to other types of writing.

The metacognitive strategies needed to be a competent writer are linked with those required to be a competent reader because the writing process involves competent reading and rereading during composition and revision (Feldgus, Cardonick, & Gentry, 2017). Further, researchers have found that strategy instruction involving planning, drafting, revising, and editing improves older elementary school children's metacognitive awareness and writing competence (Graham & others, 2021).

As with reading, teachers play a critical role in students' development of writing skills (Graham & Alves, 2021). Effective writing instruction provides guidance about planning, drafting, and revising, not only in elementary school but through college. A meta-analysis (use of statistical techniques to combine the results of studies) revealed that the following interventions were the most effective in improving fourth- through twelfth-grade students' writing quality: (1) strategy instruction, (2) summarization, (3) peer assistance, and (4) setting goals (Graham & Perin, 2007).

Classroom observations made by Michael Pressley and his colleagues (2007) indicate that students become good writers when teachers spend considerable time on writing instruction and are passionate about teaching students to write. Their observations also indicate that classrooms with students who receive higher scores on writing assessments have walls that overflow with examples of effective writing.

This student in middle childhood is busily writing in a notebook. Effective instruction is important to developing writing skills. For example, Beverly Gallagher, a third-grade teacher in Princeton, New Jersey, works with students to stimulate their interest in writing. She created the Imagine the Possibilities program, which brings nationally known poets and authors to her school. She phones each student's parents periodically to describe their child's progress and new interests. She invites students from higher grades to work with small groups in her class so that she can spend more one-on-one time with students. Each student keeps a writer's notebook to record thoughts, inspirations, and special words that intrigue them. Students get special opportunities to sit in an author's chair, where they read their writing to the class. (*Source:* USA Today, *2000*)

Darrin Henry/Shutterstock

DUAL-LANGUAGE AND SECOND-LANGUAGE LEARNING

Many different scenarios account for how and when children learn two or more languages. Some people learn a first language and then a second language later in life. Others learn two languages from birth. Are there sensitive periods in learning a second language? That is, if individuals want to learn a second language, how important is the age at which they begin to learn it? For many years, it was claimed that if individuals did not learn a second language before puberty, they would never reach native-language speakers' proficiency in the second language (Johnson & Newport, 1991). However, research indicates a more complex conclusion: Sensitive periods likely vary across different language systems (Frankenhuis & Fraley, 2017). Thus, for late language learners, such as adolescents and adults, new vocabulary is easier to learn than new sounds or new grammar (DeKeyser, 2018). For example, children's ability to pronounce words with a native-like accent in a second language typically decreases with age, with an especially sharp drop occurring after the age of about 10 to 12. Also, adults tend to learn a second language faster than children, but their final level of second-language attainment is not as high as children's.

Some aspects of children's ability to learn a second language are transferred more easily to the second language than others (Pace & others, 2021). Children who are fluent in two languages perform better than their single-language counterparts on tests of control of attention, concept formation, analytical reasoning, cognitive flexibility, and cognitive complexity (Bialystok, 2018; Tao & others, 2021). Recent research also documented that bilingual children are better at theory of mind tasks (Rubio-Fernandez, 2017). They also are more conscious of the structure of spoken and written language and better at noticing errors of grammar and meaning, skills that benefit their reading ability (Bialystok, 2018). A study of 6- to 10-year-olds found that early bilingual exposure was a key factor in bilingual children outperforming monolingual children on phonological awareness and word learning (Jasinska & Petitto, 2018). Vocabulary size in bilingual children is related to a number of factors, including metalinguistic awareness and whether they have a preference for one language over the other (Altman, Goldstein, & Armon-Lotem, 2018).

Students in the United States are far behind their counterparts in many other countries in learning a second language. For example, in Russia, schools have 10 grades, called *forms,* which roughly correspond to the 12 grades in American schools. Russian children begin school at age 7 and begin learning English in the third form. Because of this emphasis on teaching English, most Russian citizens under the age of 40 are able to speak at least some English. The United States is the only technologically advanced Western nation that does not have a national foreign language requirement at the high school level, even for students in rigorous academic programs. In contrast, there are nearly 60 countries that are officially and legally bilingual or trilingual, spanning many countries and languages across Africa, Asia, the Americas, Oceania, and Europe (Jezak, 2021).

American students who do not learn a second language may be missing more than the chance to acquire a skill. Some research suggests that bilingualism may have a positive effect on children's cognitive development (Yow & others, 2017). An especially important developmental question that many parents of infants and young children have is whether to teach them two languages simultaneously or just teach one language at a time to avoid confusion. The answer is that teaching infants and young children two languages simultaneously (as when a mother's native language is English and her husband's is Spanish) has numerous benefits and few drawbacks (Bialystok, 2018).

connecting with diversity

English Language Learners

What is the best way to teach English language learners (ELLs)? ELLs have been taught in one of two main ways: (1) instruction in English only or (2) a *dual-language* (formerly called *bilingual*) approach that involves instruction in their home language and English (Herrell & Jordan, 2020). In a dual-language approach, instruction is given in both the ELL child's first language and English for varying amounts of time at certain grade levels. One of the arguments in favor of the dual-language approach is the research discussed earlier demonstrating that bilingual children have more advanced information-processing skills than monolingual children (Tao & others, 2021).

If a dual-language strategy is used, too often it has been thought that children need only one or two years of this type of instruction. However, a longitudinal study of immigrant children in the Los Angeles public schools found that most children needed four to seven years to become proficient in a new language and that even after nine years, one-fourth of students were not yet considered fully proficient (Thompson, 2015). Importantly, bilingualism has been found to narrow gaps in executive functioning and self-regulation otherwise found between children from higher versus lower socioeconomic backgrounds (Hartanto & Yang,

What have researchers found about the effectiveness of ELL instruction?
RichLegg/E+/Getty Images

2019). Thus, especially for immigrant children who have less access to socioeconomic resources, more years of dual-language instruction may be needed than they currently are receiving.

What have researchers found regarding outcomes of ELL programs? Drawing conclusions about the effectiveness of ELL programs is difficult because of variations across programs in the number of years they are in effect, type of instruction, quality of schooling other than ELL instruction, teachers, children, and other factors. In research studies comparing English-only versus dual-language programs, dual-language programs have shown benefits for students' academic achievement even after controlling for students' proficiency in English (MacSwan & others, 2017).

Experts generally support the combined home language and English approach because (1) children have difficulty learning a subject when it is taught in a language they do not understand and (2) when both languages are integrated in the classroom, children learn the second language more readily and participate more actively. Most large-scale studies have found that the academic achievement of ELLs is higher in dual-language programs than in English-only programs (MacSwan & others, 2017).

Salvador Tamayo, Teacher of English Language Learners

Salvador Tamayo is a middle school broadcasting communications teacher in West Chicago, Illinois. He received a National Educator Award from the Milken Family Foundation for his work in educating English language learners (ELLs). Tamayo is especially adept at integrating technology into his ELL classes. He and his students created several award-winning Web sites about the West Chicago City Museum, the local Latino community, and the history of West Chicago. His students also developed an "I Want to Be an American Citizen" Web site to assist family and community members in preparing for the U.S. citizenship test. Tamayo mentors a student club in which participants learn to produce, write, and anchor school broadcasts, such as an informational podcast on Latinos In Action, a group that aims to empower Latino youth to lead and strengthen their communities through college and career readiness.

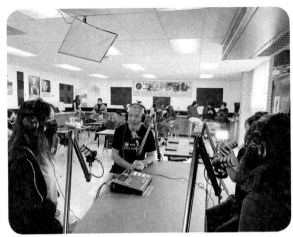

Salvador Tamayo works with broadcasting communications students in West Chicago.
Sal Tamayo

Most children who learn two languages are not exposed to the same quantity and quality of each language. Nonetheless, bilingual children do not show delays in the rate at which they acquire language overall (Hoff, 2015). In one study, by 4 years of age children who continued to learn both Spanish and English languages had a total vocabulary growth that was greater than that of monolingual children (Hoff & others, 2014). The most recent research suggests that the benefits may depend on contexts and specific skills that are being assessed (Grundy, 2020). In addition, it can be difficult to know the cognitive benefits of bilingualism because there is so much variation across families in the amount and ways of speaking in both languages (Hoff, 2018).

In the United States, many immigrant children go from being monolingual in their home language to being bilingual in that language and in English, only to end up monolingual speakers of English. This *subtractive dual-language learning* can have negative effects on children, who can become ashamed of their home language.

A current controversy related to dual-language learning involves dual-language education (Diaz-Rico, 2020). To read about this controversy, see the *Connecting with Diversity* interlude. And to read about an educator who works with English language learners, see *Connecting with Careers*.

Review *Connect* Reflect

LG3 Summarize language development in middle and late childhood.

Review

- What are some changes in vocabulary, grammar, and metalinguistic awareness in the middle and late childhood years?
- What controversy surrounds teaching children to read? What are some positive ways for children to learn how to write competently?
- What characterizes dual-language learning and second-language learning? What issues are involved in dual-language instruction?

Connect

- In an earlier main section in this chapter, you read about

metacognition. Compare that concept with the concept of metalinguistic awareness discussed in this section.

Reflect *Your Own Personal Journey of Life*

- Did you learn a second language as a child? If so, do you think it was beneficial to you? Why or why not? If you did not learn a second language as a child, do you wish you had? Why or why not?

4 How Can Children's Intelligence Be Described?

LG4 Characterize children's intelligence.

| Intelligence and Its Assessment | Types of Intelligence | Interpreting Differences in IQ Scores | Extremes of Intelligence |

Twentieth-century English novelist Aldous Huxley said that children are remarkable for their curiosity and intelligence. Intelligence is a topic of great interest to psychologists, educators, and many others, including parents. What do we mean when we use the word *intelligence,* and can intelligence be measured or assessed?

INTELLIGENCE AND ITS ASSESSMENT

Despite the general sense that intelligence is important and the commonly held belief that we know it when we see it, intelligence has been very difficult to define. Some experts describe intelligence as problem-solving skills. Others describe it as the ability to adapt to and learn from life's everyday experiences. In general, these ideas are used to define **intelligence** as the ability to solve problems and learn from one's everyday life experiences.

Other than trying to define intelligence, there is also much interest in individual differences in intelligence and how to assess these differences (Bjorklund, 2022; Coyle, 2021). **Individual differences** are the stable, consistent ways in which people are different from each other (Schermer & Saklofske, 2021). Individual differences are found in personality and many other domains, but it is in the domain of intelligence that the most attention has been directed at individual differences (Estrada & others, 2017; Giofre & others, 2017). For example, an intelligence test purports to inform us about whether a student can reason better than others of the same age who have taken the test (Jaarsveld & Lachmann, 2017). Let's go back in history and see what the first intelligence test was like.

The Binet Tests   In 1904, the French Ministry of Education asked psychologist Alfred Binet to devise a method of identifying children who were unable to learn in school. School officials wanted to reduce crowding by placing students who did not benefit from regular classroom teaching in special schools. Binet and his student Theophile Simon developed an intelligence test to meet this request. The test, called the 1905 Scale, consisted of 30 questions on topics ranging from the ability to touch one's ear to the ability to draw designs from memory and to define abstract concepts.

Binet used the results of these tests to develop the concept of **mental age (MA),** an individual's level of mental development relative to that of others. Not much later, in 1912, William Stern created the concept of **intelligence quotient (IQ),** a person's mental age (MA) divided by chronological age (CA), multiplied by 100. That is: $IQ = MA/CA \times 100$. If mental age is the same as chronological age, then the person's IQ is 100. If mental age is above chronological age, then IQ is greater than 100. If mental age is below chronological age, then IQ is less than 100. This is called a standardized score because regardless of a person's age, if the person scores at the same level of mental development considered normative or standard for his or her age, the person would have a score of 100.

The Binet test has been revised many times to incorporate advances in the understanding of intelligence and intelligence tests (Wasserman, 2018). The most well-known revisions are called the *Stanford–Binet tests* (the revisions have been done at Stanford University). By administering the test to large numbers of people of different ages (from preschool through late adulthood) from different backgrounds, researchers have found that scores on the Stanford–Binet approximate a normal distribution (see Figure 4). A **normal distribution** is symmetrical, with a majority of the scores falling in the middle of the possible range of scores and few scores appearing toward the extremes of the range.

The Wechsler Scales   Another set of tests widely used to assess students' intelligence is called the Wechsler scales (Elkana & others, 2020; Wechsler, 1939). Developed by

intelligence The ability to solve problems and to adapt to and learn from experiences.

individual differences The stable, consistent ways in which people differ from each other.

mental age (MA) Binet's measure of an individual's level of mental development, compared with that of others.

intelligence quotient (IQ) A person's mental age divided by chronological age, multiplied by 100; devised in 1912 by William Stern.

normal distribution A symmetrical distribution with most scores falling in the middle of the possible range of scores and few scores appearing toward the extremes of the range.

Percent of cases under the normal curve								
0.13%	2.14%	13.59%	34.13%	34.13%	13.59%	2.14%	0.13%	

Cumulative percentages	0.1%	2.3%	15.9%	50.0%	84.1%	97.7%	99.9%

Stanford–Binet IQs	55	70	85	100	115	130	145

FIGURE 4

THE NORMAL CURVE AND STANFORD–BINET IQ SCORES. The distribution of IQ scores approximates a normal curve. Most of the population falls in the middle range of scores. Notice that extremely high and extremely low scores are very rare. Slightly more than two-thirds of the scores fall between 84 and 116. Only about 1 in 50 individuals has an IQ of more than 132, and only about 1 in 50 individuals has an IQ of less than 68.

psychologist David Wechsler, they include the Wechsler Preschool and Primary Scale of Intelligence–Fourth Edition (WPPSI-IV) to test children from 2 years 6 months to 7 years 3 months of age; the Wechsler Intelligence Scale for Children–Fifth Edition (WISC-V) for children and adolescents 6 to 16 years of age (see Figure 5); and the Wechsler Adult Intelligence Scale–Fourth Edition (WAIS-IV).

The WISC-V not only provides an overall IQ score but also yields five sub-scores (Verbal Comprehension, Working Memory, Processing Speed, Fluid Reasoning, and Visual Spatial) (Wright, 2020). These scores allow the examiner to determine whether the individual is strong or weak in different aspects of intelligence.

TYPES OF INTELLIGENCE

Is it more appropriate to think of a child's intelligence as a general ability that characterizes the way an individual thinks all or most of the time or as a number of specific abilities? Robert Sternberg and Howard Gardner have proposed influential theories oriented to this second viewpoint.

Sternberg's Triarchic Theory   Robert J. Sternberg (2021a, b) developed the **triarchic theory of intelligence,** which states that intelligence comes in three forms:

- *Analytical intelligence,* referring to the ability to analyze, judge, evaluate, compare, and contrast.
- *Creative intelligence,* consisting of the ability to create, design, invent, originate, and imagine.
- *Practical intelligence,* involving the ability to use, apply, implement, and put ideas into practice.

Sternberg (2021a, b) says that all individuals, including children, differ in intelligence across these three components. These differences can have

Verbal Subscales

Similarities

A child must think logically and abstractly to answer a number of questions about how things might be similar.

Example: "In what way are a lion and a tiger alike?"

Comprehension

This subscale is designed to measure an individual's judgment and common sense.

Example: "What is the advantage of keeping money in a bank?"

Nonverbal Subscales

Block Design

A child must assemble a set of multicolored blocks to match designs that the examiner shows.
Visual-motor coordination, perceptual organization, and the ability to visualize spatially are assessed.

Example: "Use the four blocks on the left to make the pattern on the right."

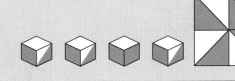

FIGURE 5

SAMPLE SUBSCALES OF THE WECHSLER INTELLIGENCE SCALE FOR CHILDREN—FIFTH EDITION (WISC-V). The WISC now includes 16 subscales. Three of the subscales are shown here. Simulated items are similar to those found in the Wechsler Intelligence Scale for Children, Fifth Edition.
Source: Wechsler Intelligence Scale for Children, Fifth Edition (WISC-V), Upper Saddle River, NJ: Pearson Education, Inc., 2014.

Robert J. Sternberg developed the triarchic theory of intelligence.

Robert Sternberg

consequences for children's experience and success in school. Students with high analytical intelligence tend to be favored in conventional schooling. They often do well with direct instruction, in which the teacher lectures and gives students tests based on what they have been taught in the lessons. They often are considered to be "smart" students who get good grades, show up in high-level tracks, do well on traditional tests of intelligence and the SAT, and later get admitted to competitive colleges.

In contrast, children who are high in creative intelligence do not often score in the top rung of their class. Many teachers have specific expectations about how assignments should be done, and creatively intelligent students may not conform to those expectations. Instead of giving more conventional answers, they give unique answers, for which they might get reprimanded or marked down. No teacher wants to discourage creativity, but Sternberg stresses that too often a teacher's desire to increase students' knowledge suppresses creative thinking.

Like children high in creative intelligence, children who are high in practical intelligence often do not relate well to the demands of school. However, many of these children do well outside the classroom's walls. They may have excellent social skills and good common sense. As adults, some become successful managers, entrepreneurs, or politicians in spite of having undistinguished school records.

Gardner's Eight Frames of Mind Howard Gardner (1983; Chen & Gardner, 2018) suggests that there are eight types of intelligence, or "frames of mind." These are described here, with examples of the types of occupations in which they function as strengths (Campbell, Campbell, & Dickinson, 2004):

- *Verbal:* the ability to think in words and use language to express meaning (occupations: authors, journalists, speakers)
- *Mathematical:* the ability to carry out mathematical operations (occupations: scientists, engineers, accountants)
- *Spatial:* the ability to think three-dimensionally (occupations: architects, artists, sailors)
- *Bodily-kinesthetic:* the ability to manipulate objects and be physically adept (occupations: surgeons, craftspeople, dancers, athletes)
- *Musical:* a sensitivity to pitch, melody, rhythm, and tone (occupations: composers, musicians, sensitive listeners)
- *Interpersonal:* the ability to understand and interact effectively with others (occupations: teachers, mental health professionals)
- *Intrapersonal:* the ability to understand oneself (occupations: theologians, psychologists)
- *Naturalist:* the ability to observe patterns in nature and understand natural and human-made systems (occupations: farmers, botanists, ecologists, landscapers)

According to Gardner, everyone has all of these intelligences to varying degrees. As a result, we prefer to learn and process information in different ways. People learn best when they can do so in a way that uses their stronger intelligences.

Evaluating the Multiple-Intelligence Approaches Sternberg's and Gardner's approaches have much to offer in thinking about what intelligence is and how it is useful to us. They have stimulated teachers to think more broadly about what makes up children's competencies (Sternberg, 2018a). And they have motivated educators to develop programs that instruct students in multiple areas of thinking or domains. These approaches have also contributed to interest in assessing intelligence and classroom learning in innovative ways, such as by evaluating a broader range of skills and interests, as described in assessment methods that use student portfolios.

Still, doubts about multiple-intelligence approaches persist. A number of psychologists think that the multiple-intelligence views have taken the idea that there are a number of different types of intelligence too far. Some argue that a research base to

Children learn not only in classrooms but also by engaging in meaningful activities of everyday life.

Alistair Berg/DigitalVision/Getty Images

support the three intelligences of Sternberg or the eight intelligences of Gardner has not yet emerged (Hagmann-von Arx, Lemola, & Grob, 2018). A number of psychologists continue to support the concept of general intelligence (Hill & others, 2018). For example, in a survey of 102 experts on intelligence around the world, most supported the concept of general intelligence (Rindermann, Becker, & Coyle, 2020). They point out that people who excel at one type of intellectual task are likely to excel at other intellectual tasks (Zaboski, Kranzler, & Gage, 2018). Thus, individuals who do well at memorizing lists of digits are also likely to be good at solving verbal problems and spatial layout problems. This general intelligence includes abstract reasoning or thinking, the capacity to acquire knowledge, and problem-solving ability (Floyd & others, 2021).

Advocates of the concept of general intelligence also point to its success in predicting school and job success (Demetriou & Spanoudis, 2018). For example, scores on tests of general intelligence are substantially correlated with school grades and achievement test performance, both at the time of the test and years later (Sackett, Shewach, & Dahlke, 2020). A meta-analysis of 240 independent samples and more than 100,000 individuals found a correlation of +0.54 between intelligence and school grades (Roth & others, 2015). However, remember that many factors in addition to intelligence, such as motivation, contribute to success in school and the workplace (Van Iddekinge & others, 2018).

The argument between those who support the concept of general intelligence and those who advocate the multiple-intelligences view is ongoing (Chen & Gardner, 2018; Kornhaber, 2020). For instance, Sternberg (2018) accepts that there is a general intelligence for the kinds of analytical tasks that traditional IQ tests assess, but he thinks that the range of tasks those tests measure is far too narrow.

INTERPRETING DIFFERENCES IN IQ SCORES

The IQ scores that result from tests such as the Stanford–Binet and Wechsler scales provide information about children's mental abilities. However, the significance of performance on an intelligence test is debated (Sternberg, 2021a, b). Historically, this has been called the nature-nurture debate.

Researchers agree that both heredity and environment influence intelligence. Twin and adoption studies demonstrate that intelligence is partly inherited genetically, but genes also contribute to the kinds of environments that individuals tend to select for themselves, and environments then further contribute to intelligence (Sauce & Matzel, 2018). For example, individuals who are genetically predisposed to higher intelligence may be more likely to choose to spend their time in academic activities and environments, such as reading or joining the school math team, and these academic environments then further enhance their intelligence.

Genetic Influences Have scientists been able to pinpoint specific genes that are linked to intelligence? Using genome-wide association studies—a method that looks at individuals' entire genome in relation to observed traits—researchers have identified polygenic patterns that contribute to intelligence (von Stumm & Plomin, 2021). These studies have found that genetic information contributes between 20 and 50 percent of the heritability of intelligence.

One strategy for examining the role of heredity in intelligence is to compare the IQs of identical and fraternal twins. Recall that identical twins have exactly the same genetic makeup but fraternal twins, siblings who happen to be born at the same time, do not. If intelligence is genetically determined, say some investigators, the IQs of identical twins should be more similar than the IQs of fraternal twins. A research review of many studies found that the correlation of intelligence between identical twins was stronger than the correlation of intelligence between fraternal twins (Grigorenko, 2000) (see Figure 6).

Today, researchers agree that genetics and environment interact to influence intelligence. Modifications in environment can change individuals' IQ scores considerably.

Environmental Influences Although genetic endowment influences a child's intellectual ability, the environmental experiences of children do make a difference (Haier, 2017; Mayer, 2020). In one classic study, researchers went into homes and observed how extensively parents from low- and middle-income families talked and communicated with their

How Would You...?
If you were a **psychologist,** how would you use Gardner's theory of multiple intelligences to respond to a child who is distressed to receive a below-average score on a traditional intelligence test?

developmental **connection**

Nature and Nurture

The epigenetic view emphasizes that development is an ongoing, bidirectional interchange between heredity and environment. Connect to "Biological Beginnings."

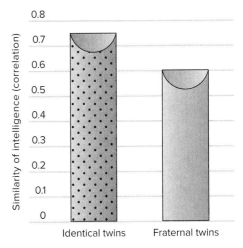

FIGURE 6

TWIN SIMILARITY (CORRELATION) IN INTELLIGENCE TEST SCORES AND TWIN TYPE. The graph represents a summary of research findings that have calculated the intelligence test score similarity of genetically identical twins compared with non-identical fraternal twins. A small difference in twin-similarity correlations has been found, with a higher correlation for identical twins (.75) and a lower correlation for fraternal twins (.60).

young children (Hart & Risley, 1995). They found that the middle-income parents were much more likely to communicate with their young children than the low-income parents were. How much the parents communicated with their children in the first three years of their lives was correlated with the children's Stanford–Binet IQ scores at age 3. And a research analysis by Richard Nisbett and his colleagues (2012) supported the importance of environmental influences on intelligence: A 12- to 18-point increase in IQ was found when children are adopted from low-income families into middle- and upper-income families. And another illustrative study revealed that children with more highly educated (especially college-educated) mothers and/or children born into higher-income families showed higher scores on math achievement tests than children who had less-educated mothers and came from lower-income families (Ang, Rodgers, & Wanstrom, 2010). The important message from this research is that parent education, an environmental factor, can contribute in substantial ways to children's performance on IQ tests.

Schooling also influences intelligence. In a meta-analysis of 42 data sets including over 600,000 participants, each additional year of formal education was found to raise IQ scores by 1 to 5 points, even taking into account that people with a higher propensity for intelligence stay in school longer (Ritchie & Tucker-Drob, 2018). The biggest effects have been found when large groups of children are deprived of formal education for an extended period, resulting in poorer performance on the factors that IQ tests measure. For example, an increase in IQ of 8 to 13 points in children ages 6 to 9 years between 2004 and 2016 in Khartoum, Sudan, could be attributed to the absence of compulsory schooling in the earlier cohorts of children (Dutton & others, 2018). Another possible effect of education can be seen in rapidly increasing IQ test scores around the world (Flynn, 2018, 2020). IQ scores have been increasing so quickly that a high percentage of people regarded as having average intelligence in 1900 would be considered below average in intelligence today (see Figure 7). If a representative sample of people today took the Stanford–Binet test version used in 1932, about 25 percent would be defined as having very superior intelligence, a label usually accorded to less than 3 percent of the population. Because the increase has taken place within a relatively short time, it can't be due to heredity but is likely due to environmental factors, such as increasing levels of education attained by a much greater percentage of the world's population, or to other environmental factors such as the increased amount of various types of information to which people are exposed, including more information being presented in two-dimensional form (e.g., media, photos, books, films, video games). In fact, not all aspects of intelligence have increased over time, and some have increased more than others. Spatial thinking has shown a considerable rise, which suggests that changes in the way information is presented spatially may be contributing to the increase in IQ scores over the last several generations (Bratsberg & Rogeberg, 2018). Additional factors, such as prenatal and postnatal nutrition, are related to intelligence (Mahmassani & others, 2022), and have been proposed as explanations for historical changes in intelligence test scores (Bratsberg & Rogeberg, 2018). This worldwide increase in intelligence test scores over a short time frame is called the *Flynn effect* after the researcher who discovered it—James Flynn (2018, 2020).

Researchers are concerned about improving the early environment of children who are at risk for lower performance on intelligence tests (Black & others, 2017). These efforts are

FIGURE 7

INCREASING IQ SCORES FROM 1932 TO 1997. As measured by the Stanford–Binet intelligence test, American children seem to be getting "smarter." Scores of a group tested in 1932 fell along a bell-shaped curve with half below 100 and half above. Studies show that if children took that same test today, half would score above 120 on the 1932 scale. Very few of them would score in the "very low IQ score" end, on the left side, and about one-fourth would rank in the "very high" range.
Source: Neisser, Ulric. From *The Increase in IQ Scores from 1932 to 1997*. Copyright by The executors to the Estate of Urlic Neisser. All rights reserved. Used with permission.

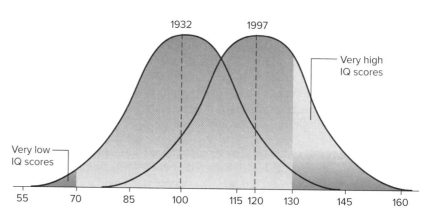

especially aimed at low-income families who, for various reasons, face more difficulty providing an intellectually stimulating environment for their children. Programs that educate and support parents and other caregivers to provide cognitive stimulation for their children, as well as support services such as quality child-care programs, can make a difference in a child's intellectual development (Morrison, 2018). In one illustrative two-year intervention study with very low-income families, maternal scaffolding and cognitive stimulation, such as reading to children regularly, improved young children's intellectual functioning (Obradovic & others, 2016).

In a study at the University of North Carolina at Chapel Hill conducted by Craig Ramey and his associates (Ramey, 2018, 2019), 111 young children from low-income, poorly educated families were assigned randomly to either an intervention group, which received full-time, year-round child care along with medical and social work services, or a control group, which received medical and social benefits but no child care. The child-care program included game-like learning activities aimed at improving language, motor, social, and cognitive skills.

The success of the program in improving IQ was evident by the time the children were 3 years of age. At that age, the experimental group showed normal IQs averaging 101, a 17-point advantage over the control group. Follow-up results suggest that the effects are long-lasting. More than a decade later, at age 15, children from the intervention group still maintained an IQ advantage of 5 points over the control-group children (97.7 to 92.6) (Ramey, 2018, 2019). They also did better on standardized tests of reading and math, and were less likely to be held back a year in school. Also, the greatest IQ gains were made by the children whose mothers had especially low IQs—below 70. At age 15, these children showed a 10-point IQ advantage over a group of children whose mothers' IQs were below 70 but who had not experienced the child-care intervention. By age 30, the children who had experienced the early intervention were almost four times more likely to have graduated from college, were more likely to be employed full-time, and were less likely to be receiving public assistance (Ramey, 2018, 2019). A benefit-cost ratio of 7.3:1 suggests a large financial return on the investment in early childhood cognitive enrichment (Ramey, 2018).

Revisiting the Nature-Nurture Issue   In sum, there is a consensus among psychologists that both heredity and environment influence intelligence (Sternberg, 2021a, b). As in other areas of development, genetic factors interact with factors in the environment to influence intelligence.

Culture and Intelligence   Is intelligence seen the same way in all cultures, or is there cultural variability in what people consider intelligent?

Culture and Culture-Fair Tests   Cultural groups, and individuals within cultures, vary in the way they describe what it means to be intelligent (Gonthier, 2022). People in Western cultures tend to view intelligence in terms of reasoning and thinking skills, but individuals can demonstrate intellectual skills in different ways. Sternberg (2017a) has reported many instances of this around the world. For example, some of the children in an Inuit community in Canada who performed poorly in traditional classrooms were able to navigate for long distances between villages in the Arctic during winter with no visible landmarks. Likewise, Kenyan children who performed poorly in school were able to administer hundreds of herbal treatments for illnesses, suggesting that intelligence encompasses a broader array of intellectual abilities than those captured in traditional tests. Among many cultural groups in Africa, a child who takes on responsibilities and respects elders is considered intelligent (Serpell, 2019). Because of differences across cultures in what intelligence is, researchers have tried to devise ways of assessing intelligence in a culture-fair way, one that recognizes and accounts for these differences.

Culture-fair tests are tests of intelligence that are intended to be free of cultural bias. Two types of culture-fair tests have been devised. The first includes items that are familiar to children from all socioeconomic and ethnic backgrounds, or items that at least are familiar to the children taking the test. For example, a child might be asked how a bird and a dog are different, on the assumption that all children have been exposed to birds and dogs. The second type of culture-fair test has no verbal questions but instead might have the child engage in tasks such as arranging a set of blocks to match a picture of a pattern.

Why is it so hard to create culture-fair tests? Most tests tend to reflect what the dominant culture thinks is important (Ang, Ng, & Rockstuhl, 2020). Time limits on tests will bias the

culture-fair tests Tests of intelligence that are designed to be free of cultural bias.

stereotype threat Anxiety that one's behavior might confirm a negative stereotype about one's group.

test against groups not concerned with time. If languages differ, the same words might have different meanings for different language groups. Even pictures can produce bias because some cultures have less experience with drawings and photographs than others (Anastasi & Urbina, 1997). Furthermore, the reliance on visual-spatial reasoning tests to reduce bias may actually introduce new biases because these assessments still rely on the use of standardized items that typically do not involve commonly experienced information in many cultures (Gonthier, 2022). Within the same culture, different subgroups could have different attitudes, values, and motivation, and these could affect their performance on intelligence tests. For instance, items that ask why buildings should be made of brick are biased against children who have little or no experience with brick houses. Questions about railroads, furnaces, snow, distances between cities, and so on can be biased against groups who have less experience than others with these contexts. Recall, too, that cultures define intelligence differently. Because of such difficulties in creating culture-fair tests, Robert Sternberg (2020c) concludes that there are no culture-fair tests, only *culture-relevant* or *culture-reduced tests.*

Ethnic and Gender Variations Sometimes intelligence tests are used to compare one demographic group to another. In any group comparison, it is important to keep in mind that average scores of groups are being compared and that the overlap in the distribution of scores is extensive. Group averages sometimes favor one group over another, such as when one gender outperforms the other or one ethnic group outperforms others on a test of general intelligence or specific cognitive abilities.

One potential influence on intelligence test performance (as well as performance in many other domains, such as motor and artistic skills) is **stereotype threat,** the anxiety that one's behavior might confirm a negative stereotype about one's group (von Hippel, Kalokerinos, & Zacher, 2017; Wasserberg, 2017). However, for racial and ethnic group variations in schools in the United States, stereotype threat explains less of the variance in test performance than do other factors, such as schools' racial climate, teacher participation in cultural competence training initiatives, faculty diversity, and a variety of demographic factors related to exposure to discrimination (Whaley, 2018, 2020).

Using Intelligence Tests Psychological tests are tools. Like all tools, their effectiveness depends on the knowledge, skill, and integrity of the user. A hammer can be used to build a beautiful kitchen cabinet, or it can be used as a weapon of assault. Like a hammer, psychological tests can be used for positive purposes, or they can be badly abused. Here are some cautions about IQ testing that can help you avoid the pitfalls of using information about a child's intelligence test score in negative ways:

- *Use caution in interpreting an overall IQ score.* In evaluating a child's intelligence, it is wiser to think of intelligence as consisting of a number of features. Keep in mind the different types of intelligence described by Sternberg and Gardner. By considering the different aspects of intelligence, you will find that every child has areas of strength.

- *Know that IQ is not a sole indicator of competence.* Another concern about IQ tests occurs when they are used as the main or sole assessment of competence. A high IQ is not the ultimate human value. As we have seen in this chapter, it is important to consider students' intellectual competence not only in areas such as verbal skills but also in their creative and practical skills.

- *Avoid stereotyping and preconceived expectations.* A special concern is that the scores on an IQ test easily can lead to stereotypes and preconceived expectations about students. Sweeping generalizations are too often made on the basis of an IQ score. An IQ test should always be considered a measure of current performance. It is not a measure of fixed potential. Maturational changes and enriched environmental experiences can advance a student's intelligence.

How Would You...?

If you were a **social worker,** how would you explain the role and purpose of intelligence test scores to a parent whose child is preparing to take a standardized intelligence test?

EXTREMES OF INTELLIGENCE

Intelligence tests have been used to discover indications of intellectual disability or intellectual giftedness, the extremes of intelligence. Keeping in mind the theme that an intelligence test should not be used as the sole indicator of intellectual disability or giftedness, we will explore the nature of these intellectual extremes.

Intellectual Disability The most distinctive feature of intellectual disability (formerly called mental retardation) is intellectual functioning that is developmentally not typical given the person's age (Elliott & Resing, 2020). Long before formal tests were developed to assess intelligence, individuals with an intellectual disability were identified by a lack of age-appropriate skills in learning and caring for themselves. Once intelligence tests were developed, they were used to identify the degree of intellectual disability. However, it was found that when two individuals with an intellectual disability had the same low IQ, one might be married, employed, and involved in the community and the other might require constant supervision in an institution. Such differences in social competence led psychologists to include deficits in adaptive behavior in their definition of intellectual disability (Smith & others, 2018).

Intellectual disability is a condition of limited mental ability in which the individual (1) has a low IQ, usually below 70 on a traditional intelligence test; (2) has difficulty adapting to the demands of everyday life; and (3) first exhibits these characteristics by age 18 (Heward, Alber-Morgan, & Konrad, 2017). The age limit is included in the definition of intellectual disability because, for example, we don't usually think of a college student who suffers massive brain damage in a car accident, resulting in an IQ of 60, as having an "intellectual disability." The low IQ and low adaptiveness should be evident in childhood, not after normal functioning is interrupted by damage of some form. About 5 million Americans fit this definition of intellectual disability.

Some cases of intellectual disability have an organic cause and are thus known as **organic intellectual disability** (Mir & Kuchay, 2019). Down syndrome is one form of organic intellectual disability, and it occurs when an extra chromosome is present. Other causes of organic intellectual disability include fragile X syndrome, an abnormality in the X chromosome that was discussed in "Biological Beginnings"; prenatal malformation; metabolic disorders; and diseases that affect the brain. Most people who suffer from organic intellectual disability have IQs between 0 and 50.

When no evidence of organic brain damage can be found, cases are labeled **cultural-familial intellectual disability.** Individuals with this type of disability have IQs between 55 and 70. Psychologists suspect that this type of disability often results from growing up in a below-average intellectual environment. Children with this type of disability can be identified in schools, where they often fail tests, need tangible rewards (candy rather than praise), and are highly sensitive to what others expect of them. However, as adults, they are usually not noticeably different from others, perhaps because adult settings don't tax their cognitive skills as much as school did. It may also be that they increase their intelligence as they move toward adulthood.

Giftedness There have always been people whose abilities and accomplishments outshine those of others—the "whiz kid" in class, the star athlete, the "natural" musician. People who are **gifted** have above-average intelligence (an IQ of 130 or higher, although this is an arbitrary threshold) and/or superior talent for something. When it comes to programs for the gifted, most school systems select children who have intellectual superiority and academic aptitude, whereas children who are talented in the visual and performing arts (arts, drama, dance) or athletics or have other special aptitudes tend to be overlooked (Elliott & Resing, 2020; Gubbels & others, 2016).

Characteristics Estimates vary but indicate that approximately 6 percent of U.S. students are classified as gifted by school districts (National Association for Gifted Children, 2023). This percentage is likely conservative because it focuses only on children who are gifted intellectually and academically.

Despite speculation that giftedness is linked with having a mental disorder, no relation between giftedness and mental disorder has been found. Similarly, the idea that gifted children are maladjusted is a myth, as Lewis Terman (1925) found when he conducted an extensive study of 1,500 children whose Stanford–Binet IQs averaged 150. The children in Terman's study were socially well adjusted, and many went on to become successful doctors, lawyers, professors, and scientists. Studies support the conclusion that gifted people tend to be more mature than others, have fewer emotional problems, and grow up in a positive family climate (Worrell & others, 2019). For example, one study revealed that parents and teachers identified gifted elementary school children as having fewer emotional and behavioral risks than other children (Eklund & others, 2015). In this study, when children who are gifted did have

What causes a child to develop Down syndrome? In which major classification of intellectual disability does the condition fall?
George Doyle/Stockbyte/Getty Images

developmental **connection**
Conditions, Diseases, and Disorders
Down syndrome is caused by the presence of an extra copy of chromosome 21. Connect to "Biological Beginnings."

intellectual disability A condition of limited mental ability in which an individual has a low IQ, usually below 70 on a traditional test of intelligence, and has difficulty adapting to the demands of everyday life.

organic intellectual disability Involves physical causes such as a genetic disorder or brain damage.

cultural-familial intellectual disability Condition in which there is no evidence of organic brain damage but the individual's IQ generally is between 55 and 70.

gifted Having above-average intelligence (an IQ of 130 or higher) and/or superior talent for something.

At 2 years of age, art prodigy Alexandra Nechita (shown here as an adolescent) colored in coloring books for hours and also took up pen and ink. She had no interest in toys or friends. By age 5 she was using watercolors. Once she started school, she would paint as soon as she got home. At the age of 8, she saw the first public exhibit of her work. Since then, working quickly and impulsively on canvases as large as 5 feet by 9 feet, she has completed hundreds of paintings, some of which sell for close to $100,000 apiece. As an adult, she continues to paint today—relentlessly and passionately. It is, she says, what she loves to do. *What are some characteristics of children who have such exceptional skills?*

Koichi Kamoshida/Newsmakers/Hulton Archive/Getty Images

How Would You...?
If you were an **educator,** how would you structure educational programs for children who are gifted that would challenge and expand their unique abilities?

problems, they were more likely to have internalized problems, such as anxiety and depression, than externalized problems, such as acting out and high levels of aggression.

Three key criteria characterize gifted children, whether in art, music, or academic domains (Winner & Drake, 2018):

1. *Precocity.* Gifted children are precocious. They begin to master an area earlier than their peers. Learning in their domain is more effortless for them than for ordinary children. In most instances, these gifted children are precocious because they have an inborn high ability in a particular domain or domains.

2. *Finding their own distinct ways of learning (i.e., "marching to their own drummer").* Gifted children learn in qualitatively different ways from ordinary children. One way that they "march to a different drummer" is that they need minimal help, or scaffolding, from adults to learn. In many instances, they resist any kind of explicit instruction. They often make discoveries on their own and solve problems in unique ways.

3. *A passion to master an ability or skill set.* Gifted children are driven to understand the domain in which they have high ability. They display an intense, obsessive interest and an ability to focus. They motivate themselves and do not need to be "pushed" by their parents.

A fourth area in which some children who are gifted may excel involves *information-processing skills.* Some research has found that children who are gifted learn at a faster pace, process information more rapidly, are better at reasoning, use more effective learning strategies, and monitor their understanding better than other students. However, some studies also show no such differences and indicate that the population of children who are gifted have a wide range of information-processing capacities (Bucaille & others, 2022).

Nature and Nurture   Giftedness, like other aspects of development, is a product of both heredity and environment. Individuals who are gifted often demonstrate special abilities from an early age and even before having formal training (Comeau & others, 2018). This suggests the importance of potentially innate ability in giftedness. However, researchers have also found that individuals with world-class status in the arts, mathematics, science, and sports all report strong family support and years of training and practice (Ericsson, 2020). Deliberate practice is an important characteristic of individuals who become experts in a particular domain.

Developmental Changes and Domain-Specific Giftedness   Can we predict from infancy who will be gifted as children, adolescents, and adults? Individuals who are highly gifted are typically not gifted in many domains, and research on giftedness is increasingly focused on domain-specific developmental trajectories (Chang & Lane, 2018; Reis & Renzulli, 2020). During the childhood years, the domain in which individuals are gifted usually emerges. Thus, at some point in the childhood years, the child who is to become a gifted artist or the child who is to become a gifted mathematician begins to show expertise in that domain. Identifying an individual's domain-specific talent and providing the person with individually appropriate and optional educational opportunities should be accomplished at the very latest by adolescence (Lo & Porath, 2017). During adolescence, individuals who are talented become less reliant on parental support and increasingly pursue their own interests.

Some children who are gifted become gifted adults, but many gifted children do not become gifted and highly creative adults. In Terman's research on children with superior IQs, the children typically became experts in a well-established domain, such as medicine, law, or business. However, they did not become major creators (Winner, 2000). That is, they did not create a new domain or revolutionize an old domain. Another reason that gifted children may not become gifted adults is that the criteria for giftedness change. Without the regular testing that occurs during school to identify gifted children, being labeled as gifted as an adult often depends on a major achievement in a particular field, such as becoming an award-winning author or a celebrated concert pianist.

Education of Children Who Are Gifted   A number of experts argue that the education of children who are gifted in the United States requires a significant overhaul (Sternberg, Ambrose, & Karami, 2022). Some educators also conclude that the inadequate education of children who are gifted has been compounded by the federal government's emphasis on standardized testing that seeks to raise the achievement level of students who are not doing well academically at the expense of enriching the education of children who are gifted (Ecker-Lyster & Niileksela, 2017).

Geoffrey Moon, Gifted Education Specialist

Geoffrey Moon is a gifted education program support specialist for the Santa Fe (New Mexico) Public School District. President of the New Mexico Association for the Gifted, Moon says the ultimate goal is that the high school students being celebrated for their academic achievements "proportionately represent the community's diversity of race, culture, gender, socioeconomic level, language, and disability" (Moon, 2022). He says that the process of identifying students' strengths and their possibilities, enriching the curriculum with creativity and critical thinking, and accelerating students more quickly to higher levels of study are all key to achieving that goal, and that the process needs to start early in their education.

Moon has a bachelor of arts in theatre arts from Southwestern College and a master of arts in teaching in special education with an emphasis in gifted education from Western New Mexico University. His

Geoffrey Moon is a gifted education program support specialist in Santa Fe, New Mexico.
Geoffrey Moon

professional interests include creativity, developing equity for historically underrepresented populations, and program design. He has received the Gifted Coordinator award from the National Association of Gifted Children. He has also participated in MathAmigos, a community organization that brings math mentorship, circles, and contests to local students and teachers.

Too often, children who are gifted are socially isolated and underchallenged in the classroom (Roberts & Inman, 2021; Winner & Drake, 2018). It is not unusual for them to be ostracized and labeled. A child who is gifted may be the only such child in the room and thus lacks the opportunity to learn with students of like ability. Raising standards can benefit all children, but when some children are still underchallenged, one option is to allow them to attend advanced classes in their domain of exceptional ability—for example, some especially precocious middle school students take college classes in their area of expertise (Worrell & others, 2019).

A final concern is that Black American, Latino, and Native American children are underrepresented in gifted programs (Worrell & others, 2019). Much of the underrepresentation involves the lower test scores for children in minoritized racial and ethnic groups, which arise from factors such as test bias and fewer opportunities to learn and practice the skills that are commonly being tested (Owens & others, 2018). There is growing awareness of the importance of addressing inequity in how gifted students are identified, to address this underrepresentation (Wright, Ford, & Moore, 2022).

A number of people work in various capacities in school systems with children who are gifted. See the *Connecting with Careers* profile to read about one professional who works in gifted education.

Review **Connect** Reflect

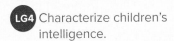 Characterize children's intelligence.

Review

- What is intelligence? How can the Binet tests and the Wechsler scales be characterized?
- What are some different views of multiple intelligences? How can the multiple-intelligences approach be evaluated?
- What are some issues in interpreting differences in IQ scores? Explain them.
- What is intellectual disability? How can children's giftedness be described?

Connect

- In this section, you learned how intellectual disability is assessed and

classified. What have you learned about the prevalence of Down syndrome in the population and the factors that might cause a child to be born with Down syndrome?

Reflect *Your Own Personal Journey of Life*

- A computer app is being sold to parents so they can test their child's IQ. Several parents tell you that they purchased the app and assessed their children's IQ. Why might you be skeptical about giving your children an IQ test and interpreting the results?

Extrinsic and Intrinsic Motivation	Sustained Attention, Effort, and Task Persistence	Mastery Motivation and Mindset	Self-Efficacy	Goal Setting, Planning, and Self-Monitoring/ Self-Regulation	Social Relationships and Contexts

Human beings are motivated to do well at what we attempt, to gain mastery over the world in which we live, to explore unknown environments with enthusiasm and curiosity, and to achieve the heights of success. In this section, we explore how children can effectively achieve their potential.

EXTRINSIC AND INTRINSIC MOTIVATION

Extrinsic motivation involves external incentives such as rewards and punishments (Evertson & Emmer, 2017). By contrast, **intrinsic motivation** is based on internal factors such as self-determination, curiosity, challenge, and effort (Flannery, 2017). Some individuals study hard because they want to make good grades or avoid parental disapproval (extrinsic motivation; Liu & others, 2020). Others study hard because they are internally motivated to achieve high standards in their work (intrinsic motivation; Chaudhuri, 2020). Current evidence strongly favors establishing a classroom climate in which students are intrinsically motivated to learn (Fong & others, 2019). For example, in an experiment in which children were provided with either positive or negative feedback delivered in either a controlling (for example, telling the child what to do) or autonomy-supportive (for example, encouraging the child to find a solution) way found that children were most intrinsically motivated to complete a similar task in the future and persisted longer in the face of challenges when adults had provided positive feedback delivered in an autonomy-supportive way on their prior activities (Mabbe & others, 2018).

One view of intrinsic motivation emphasizes self-determination (Ryan & Deci, 2019). In this view, children want to believe that they are doing something because of their own will, not because of external success or rewards. An overwhelming conclusion of motivation research is that teachers should encourage students to become intrinsically motivated (Harackiewicz & Knogler, 2017). For example, teachers should create learning environments that promote students' cognitive engagement, effort, and self-responsibility for learning (Järvelä & others, 2018; Schunk, 2020). Researchers have found that students' internal motivation and intrinsic interest in school tasks increase when students have some choice and are given opportunities to take personal responsibility for their learning (Reeve & Cheon, 2021; Shin & Bolkan, 2021). That said, the real world includes both intrinsic and extrinsic motivation, and too often intrinsic and extrinsic motivation have been pitted against each other as polar opposites. In many aspects of students' lives, both intrinsic and extrinsic motivation are at work (Schunk, 2020). Keep in mind, though, that many psychologists believe that extrinsic motivation by itself is not a good strategy.

SUSTAINED ATTENTION, EFFORT, AND TASK PERSISTENCE

Of course, it is important not only to perceive that effort is an important aspect of achieving, but in working toward a goal it also is important to actually engage in sustained attention, effort, and task persistence in school, work, and a career (Moilanen, Padilla-Walker, & Blaacker, 2018). Recall that *sustained attention* is the ability to maintain attention to a selected stimulus for a prolonged period of time. Sustained attention requires effort, and as individuals develop through childhood and adolescence, school tasks, projects, and work become more complex and require longer periods of sustained attention, effort, and task persistence than in childhood.

Might the capacity of children and adolescents to persist at tasks be linked to their career success in adulthood? A number of studies have revealed that task persistence, attentional

A student gives a presentation to her class. *How might the student's motivation while preparing the presentation influence what she learned from the project?*
FatCamera/Getty Images

extrinsic motivation Response to external incentives such as rewards and punishments.

intrinsic motivation Internal factors such as self-determination, curiosity, challenge, and effort.

control, and related aspects of sustained effort in early and middle childhood are related to occupational success in middle age (Ahmed & others, 2021; Andersson & Bergman, 2011).

MASTERY MOTIVATION AND MINDSET

Cognitive engagement and efforts toward self-improvement characterize children with a mastery motivation. These children also have a growth mindset—a belief that they can produce positive outcomes if they put forth sufficient effort.

Mastery Motivation   Developmental psychologist Carol Dweck and colleagues (2013, 2019) have found that children often show two distinct responses to difficult or challenging circumstances. Individuals who display **mastery motivation** are task-oriented; they concentrate on learning strategies and the process of achievement rather than focusing on their ability or the intended outcome. Those with a **helpless orientation** seem trapped by the experience of difficulty, and they attribute their difficulty to lack of ability. They frequently make comments such as "I'm not very good at this," even though they might earlier have demonstrated their ability through many successes. And, once they view their behavior as failure, they often feel anxious, and their performance worsens even further.

In contrast, mastery-oriented children often instruct themselves to pay attention, to think carefully, and to remember strategies that have worked for them in previous situations. They frequently report feeling challenged and excited by difficult tasks, rather than being threatened by them (Dweck & Yeager, 2018).

Another issue in motivation involves whether to adopt a mastery or a performance orientation. Children with a **performance orientation** are focused on achievement outcomes, believing that winning is what matters most and that happiness results from winning. Does this mean that mastery-oriented individuals do not like to win and that performance-oriented individuals are not motivated to experience the self-efficacy that comes from being able to take credit for one's accomplishments? No. A matter of emphasis or degree is involved, though. For mastery-oriented individuals, winning isn't everything; for performance-oriented individuals, skill development and self-efficacy take a backseat to winning.

A final point needs to be made about mastery and performance goals: They are not always mutually exclusive. Students can be both mastery- and performance-oriented, and researchers have found that mastery goals combined with performance goals often benefit students' success (Schunk, 2020).

Mindset   Carol Dweck's (2016, 2019) analysis of motivation for achievement stresses the importance of developing a **mindset,** which she defines as the cognitive view individuals develop for themselves. She concludes that individuals have one of two mindsets: (1) a *fixed mindset,* in which they believe that their qualities are carved in stone and cannot change; or (2) a *growth mindset,* in which they believe their qualities can change and improve through their effort. A fixed mindset is similar to a helpless orientation; a growth mindset is much like having a mastery motivation.

In *Mindset,* Dweck (2006) argued that individuals' mindsets influence whether they will be optimistic or pessimistic, shape their goals and how hard they will strive to reach those goals, and affect many aspects of their lives, including achievement and success in school and sports. Dweck says that mindsets begin to be shaped as children and adolescents interact with parents, teachers, and coaches, who themselves have either a fixed mindset or a growth mindset.

In research by Dweck and her colleagues, students from lower-income families were less likely to have a growth mindset than their counterparts from

Carol Dweck's Brainology program is designed to cultivate children's growth mindset.
Dr. Carol S. Dweck

wealthier families (Claro, Paunesku, & Dweck, 2016). However, the achievement of students from lower-income families who did have a growth mindset was more likely to be protected from the negative effects of less access to financial resources.

Dweck and her colleagues (Haimovitz & Dweck, 2016; Dweck, 2016) incorporated information about the brain's plasticity into their effort to improve students' motivation to achieve and succeed. In one study, they assigned two groups of seventh-grade students to eight sessions of either (1) study skills instruction or (2) study skills instruction plus information about the importance of developing a growth mindset (called *incremental theory* in the research) (Blackwell, Trzesniewski, & Dweck, 2007). One of the exercises in the growth mindset group, titled "You Can Grow Your Brain," emphasized that the brain is like a muscle that can change and grow as it is exercised and develops new connections. Students were informed that the more you challenge your brain to learn, the more your brain cells grow. Both groups had a pattern of declining math scores prior to the intervention. Following the intervention, the group who received only the study skills instruction continued to have declining scores, but the group who received a combination of study skills instruction and the growth mindset emphasis on exercising the brain reversed the downward trend and improved their math achievement.

In other work, Dweck has been creating a computer-based workshop, "Brainology," to teach students that their intelligence can change (Blackwell & Dweck, 2008; Dweck, 2012). Students experience six modules about how the brain works and how they can make their brain improve. After the workshop was tested in 20 New York City schools, students strongly endorsed the value of the computer-based brain modules. Said one student, "I will try harder because I know that the more you try the more your brain knows" (Dweck & Master, 2009, p. 137).

Dweck and her colleagues (Good, Rattan, & Dweck, 2012) also have found that a growth mindset can prevent negative stereotypes from undermining achievement. For example, they found that believing that math ability can be learned protected women from negative gender stereotyping about math. And other research indicates that people will work and resist temptations more during stressful circumstances if they regard willpower as a virtually unlimited resource (Bernecker & others, 2017). Other researchers have explored whether peer mindsets can influence a child's mindset (Sheffler & Cheung, 2020). In one study, the mindset of a student's classmates in the second month of the school year predicted the student's mindset near the end of the school year (King, 2020).

SELF-EFFICACY

Like having a growth mindset, **self-efficacy**—the belief that one can master a situation and produce favorable outcomes—is an important cognitive view for children to develop. Albert

What characterizes students with high self-efficacy?
Juice Images/Glow Images

self-efficacy The belief that one can master a situation and produce favorable outcomes.

Bandura (2018), whose social cognitive theory was discussed earlier, emphasizes that self-efficacy is a critical factor in whether or not students achieve. Self-efficacy has much in common with mastery motivation and intrinsic motivation. Self-efficacy is the belief that "I can"; helplessness is the belief that "I cannot" (Stipek, 2002). Students with high self-efficacy endorse such statements as "I know that I will be able to learn the material in this class" and "I expect to be able to do well at this activity."

Dale Schunk (2020) has applied the concept of self-efficacy to many aspects of students' achievement. In his view, self-efficacy influences a student's choice of activities. Students with low self-efficacy for learning may avoid many learning tasks, especially those that are challenging. By contrast, their high-self-efficacy counterparts eagerly work at learning tasks (Zimmerman, Schunk, & DiBenedetto, 2017). High-self-efficacy students are more likely to expend effort and persist longer at a learning task than low-self-efficacy students. Self-efficacy contributes to students' career aspirations. For example, ninth-grade students with high self-efficacy in science are more interested in exploring STEM careers (Mau & Li, 2018).

Children's achievement is influenced by their parents' self-efficacy. For example, adolescents have higher self-efficacy when their parents also have high self-efficacy (Di Giunta & others, 2018), and adolescents engage in fewer problem behaviors when their parents have higher self-efficacy related to managing behavior problems (Babskie, Powell, & Metzger, 2017).

GOAL SETTING, PLANNING, AND SELF-MONITORING/SELF-REGULATION

Goal setting, planning, and self-monitoring/self-regulation are important aspects of achievement (Eckhoff & Weiss, 2020; Schunk, 2020). Researchers have found that self-efficacy and achievement improve when individuals set goals that are specific, proximal, and challenging (DiBenedetto & Schunk, 2018). An example of a nonspecific, fuzzy goal is "I want to be successful." A more concrete, specific goal is "I want to do well on my spelling test this week."

Individuals can set both long-term (distal) and short-term (proximal) goals. It is okay for individuals to set some long-term goals, such as "I want to graduate from high school" or "I want to go to college," but they also need to create short-term goals that serve as steps along the way. "Getting an A on the next math test" is an example of a short-term, proximal goal. So is "Doing all of my homework by 4 p.m. Sunday."

Another good strategy is for individuals to set challenging goals (Greco & Kraimer, 2020). A challenging goal is a commitment to self-improvement. Strong interest and involvement in activities are sparked by challenges. Goals that are easy to reach generate little interest or effort. However, goals should be optimally matched to the individual's skill level. If goals are unrealistically high, the result will be repeated failures that lower the individual's self-efficacy.

Yet another good strategy is to develop personal goals about desired and undesired future circumstances (Höchli, Brügger, & Messner, 2018). Personal goals can be a key aspect of an individual's motivation for coping and dealing with life's challenges and opportunities (Burns, Martin, & Collie, 2019). However, it is not enough to simply set goals. It also is important to plan how to reach the goals (Höchli, Brügger, & Messner, 2018). Being a good planner means managing time effectively, setting priorities, and being organized.

Individuals should not only plan their next week's activities but also monitor how well they are sticking to their plan (Zimmerman, Schunk, & DiBenedetto, 2017). Once engaged in a task, they need to monitor their progress, judge how well they are doing on the task, and evaluate the outcomes to regulate what they do in the future (Schunk, 2020).

How Would You...?
If you were an **educator**, how would you encourage enhanced self-efficacy in a student who says, "I can't do this work"?

SOCIAL RELATIONSHIPS AND CONTEXTS

Children's relationships with parents, peers, friends, teachers, mentors, and others can profoundly affect their achievement, and social relationships, especially with peers and non-kin adults, become increasingly important from early to middle childhood. Social contexts of ethnicity and culture also are important for children's achievement.

Parents   Parents' child-rearing practices are linked to children's achievement (Grolnick & Pomerantz, 2022; Pomerantz, 2017). Here are some positive parenting practices that result in improved motivation and achievement: knowing enough about the child to provide the right amount of challenge and the right amount of support; providing a positive emotional climate that motivates children to internalize their parents' values and goals; and modeling motivated achievement behavior, such as working hard and persisting with effort at challenging tasks.

In addition to general child-rearing practices, parents provide various activities or resources at home that may influence students' interest and motivation to pursue various activities over time (Wigfield & others, 2015). For example, reading to one's preschool children and providing reading materials in the home are positively related to students' later reading achievement and motivation (Demir-Lira & others, 2019). These parenting and home environment factors are connected in crucial ways with the school and neighborhood contexts that can support academic achievement (Skinner & others, 2022).

How Would You...?

If you were an **educator,** how would you describe the importance of teachers in children's achievement?

Teachers   Teachers play an important role in students' achievement. When researchers have observed classrooms, they have found that effective, engaging teachers provide support for students to make good progress but also encourage them to become self-regulated achievers (Schunk, 2020). The encouragement takes place in a very positive environment, one in which students are constantly being motivated to try hard and to develop self-efficacy.

Teachers' expectations influence students' motivation and performance (Zhu, Urhahne, & Rubie-Davies, 2018). Students', teachers', and parents' expectations are all important to consider in relation to students' motivation and achievement. If teachers or parents have high expectations for students' success in school, these high expectations can serve as a buffer when students' own expectations fall short (Wigfield & Gladstone, 2019). When teachers' and parents' expectations are high, they can provide encouragement and different opportunities to help students achieve. However, some teachers can have inaccurately high expectations for their students that do not reflect the level at which their students are currently learning and achieving, and this can interfere with student success (Urhahne & Wijnia, 2021).

Ethnicity   The diversity that exists among children in underrepresented racial and ethnic groups is evident in their achievement (Chen & Graham, 2018). In addition to recognizing diversity of achievement within every cultural group, it also is important to distinguish between difference and deficiency (Koppelman, 2017). Too often, the achievement levels of ethnic minority students—especially Black Americans, Latinos, and Native Americans—have been interpreted as *deficits* by middle-socioeconomic-status White standards, when they simply are *culturally different and distinct* (Sharma & Lazar, 2019). An especially important factor is lack of access to adequate learning resources to support students' learning (Schunk, 2020).

The school experiences of students from different ethnic groups vary considerably (Koppelman, 2017). A special challenge for many students from underrepresented ethnic groups is the harm arising from negative stereotypes and discrimination. The racial climate of the school as well as teachers' racial and ethnic identities and cultural competence have implications for biases and expectations encountered by students, which in turn affect students' achievement (Lash, Akpovo, & Cushner, 2022; Whaley, 2020). Many underrepresented ethnic students also must learn to manage the sometimes conflicting expectations and values of their neighborhood and their school, a lack of representation among available role models, and, as discussed earlier, struggling schools (McLoyd, 2019; Schunk, 2020). Even students who are motivated to learn and achieve may find it difficult to learn and perform effectively in such contexts. To learn more about one researcher's investigation and ideas for solutions, read *Connecting with Research.*

Cross-Cultural Comparisons   International assessments indicate that the United States has not fared well compared with many other countries in the areas of math and science. Since the early 1990s, the poorer math and science performance of children and adolescents in the United States compared with other countries has been well publicized. In the most recent large-scale international comparison of 15-year-olds in over 70 countries, the top scores in reading, math, and science were held by countries in Asia and Northern Europe (OECD, 2019). In this study, U.S. 15-year-olds placed 13th in reading, 37th in math, and 18th in science.

Figure 8 shows international comparisons of reading and math scores in this study. There is extensive, ongoing analysis of country differences in educational policies and practices that might explain these wide-ranging differences (Gomendio, 2023). The large international assessments are continuing; it will be important to see whether and how scores have changed during and following the COVID-19 pandemic.

Math		Reading	
1. B-S-J-Z (China)	591	1. B-S-J-Z (China)	555
2. Singapore	569	2. Singapore	549
3. Macao (China)	558	3. Macao (China)	525
4. Hong Kong (China)	551	4. Hong Kong (China)	524
5. Chinese Taipei	531	5. Estonia	523
6. Japan	527	6. Canada	520
7. Korea	526	7. Finland	520
8. Estonia	523	8. Ireland	518
9. Netherlands	519	9. Korea	514
10. Poland	516	10. Poland	512
11. Switzerland	515	11. Sweden	506
12. Canada	512	12. New Zealand	506
13. Denmark	509	**13. United States**	**505**
14. Slovenia	509	14. United Kingdom	504
15. Belgium	508	15. Japan	504
16. Finland	507	16. Australia	503
17. Sweden	502	17. Chinese Taipei	503
18. United Kingdom	502	18. Denmark	501
19. Norway	501	19. Norway	499
20. Germany	500	20. Germany	498
21. Ireland	500	21. Slovenia	495
22. Czech Republic	499	22. Belgium	493
23. Austria	499	23. France	493
24. Latvia	496	24. Portugal	492
25. France	495	25. Czech Republic	490
26. Iceland	495	26. Netherlands	485
27. New Zealand	494	27. Austria	484
28. Portugal	492	28. Switzerland	484
29. Australia	491	29. Croatia	479
30. Russia	488	30. Latvia	479
31. Italy	487	31. Russia	479
32. Slovak Republic	486	32. Italy	476
33. Luxembourg	483	33. Hungary	476
34. Spain	481	34. Lithuania	476
35. Lithuania	481	35. Iceland	474
36. Hungary	481	36. Belarus	474
37. United States	**478**	37. Israel	470
38. Belarus	472	38. Luxembourg	470
39. Malta	472	39. Ukraine	466
40. Croatia	464	40. Turkey	466

FIGURE 8

INTERNATIONAL COMPARISON OF 15-YEAR-OLDS' READING AND MATH SCORES.
Source: OECD (2019). *PISA 2018 insights and interpretations.* Paris, France: OECD.

connecting with research

Do Parental Expectations Influence Black Boys' Math Scores?

Key Points:

- A research study explored influences on Black male adolescents' academic performance.
- Higher parental expectations for students' educational attainment were correlated with higher student expectations and better performance on a math test.

Researcher Lawrence Jackson, who strives to be an inspiration to other Black boys and men, found extra motivation to pursue a career in psychology from his observations that there were few Black researchers at national conventions (Gradworld FSU, 2019). His research explores the factors that influence young Black boys' academic achievement. In one study, he explored the associations among what Black high school students expected of themselves regarding educational achievement, what their parents expected of them, and their performance on a math test (Jackson & others, 2020).

How do parents' and adolescents' educational expectations influence their education?
Digital Vision/Getty Images

The data for the research came from the large-scale High School Longitudinal Study sponsored by the National Center for Education Statistics. Among the 23,000 students from 944 high schools who participated in the study, the focus was on Black boys in ninth grade, resulting in 1,282 participants for this analysis. A standardized test of algebraic skills was used as a measure of current academic performance. Also, students' and parents' expectations for the students' future educational attainment were assessed. Both the parents and students were asked the following question: "How far in school do you think he/you will get?" The response options were:

0 = Don't know
1 = Less than high school completion
2 = Complete high school
3 = Start associate's degree
4 = Complete associate's degree
5 = Start bachelor's degree
6 = Complete bachelor's degree
7 = Start master's degree
8 = Complete master's degree
9 = Start professional degree
10 = Complete professional degree

The findings indicated that the parents' educational expectations for their children were slightly higher than what their children expected. Most parents responded between 2.64 and 9.2, with their average score at 5.92. Placed in context of the responses to the expectation question, this reveals that most parents expected their child to complete high school, and on average they basically expected the completion of a bachelor's degree. Most of the Black boys responded between 1.54 and 8.88, with their average score of 5.21. This reveals that the students were less certain than their parents that they would complete high school or attain a bachelor's degree.

Other analyses revealed that better performance on the math test was related to higher educational expectancy expressed by parents and by students. Also, when parents expected higher educational achievement from their Black sons, the sons also had higher educational expectations for themselves. In addition, higher parental expectations were associated with higher math scores, even in cases where the Black boys themselves had low educational expectations.

What activities or forms of support might teachers and schools offer to parents or extended family members to create more hope and higher expectations for adolescent Black boys' educational achievement?

Review Connect Reflect

 LG5 Explain the development of achievement in children.

Review

- How does extrinsic motivation differ from intrinsic motivation?
- What roles do sustained attention, effort, and task persistence play in achievement?
- How does mastery motivation differ from helpless and performance orientations?
- What is mindset, and how does it influence children's achievement?
- What is self-efficacy, and how is it involved in achievement?
- What functions do goal setting, planning, and self-monitoring play in achievement?
- How are social relationships and contexts involved in children's achievement?

Connect

- In this section, you read about extrinsic and intrinsic motivation. Which theory discussed in the "Introduction" chapter places the most emphasis on the importance of extrinsic motivation in children's development?

Reflect *Your Own Personal Journey of Life*

- Think about several of your own past schoolmates who showed low motivation in school. Why do you think they behaved that way? What teaching strategies might have helped them?

┌-topical connections *looking forward*

In the next chapter you will study many aspects of children's socioemotional development during the elementary school years, including changes in the self, emotional development, moral development, and gender. You'll also explore changes in parent-child relationships, peer relationships, and schooling in middle and late childhood.

In "Cognitive Development in Adolescence" you will read about how adolescent thought is more abstract, idealistic, and logical than children's. The transition to middle school or junior high is difficult for many individuals because it coincides with so many physical, cognitive, and socioemotional changes in development.

Cognitive Development in Middle and Late Childhood

1 What Is Piaget's Theory of Cognitive Development in Middle and Late Childhood?

 LG1 Discuss Piaget's stage of concrete operational thought and apply Piaget's theory to education.

Concrete Operational Thought

Evaluating Piaget's Concrete Operational Stage

Applications to Education

- Concrete operational thought involves operations, conservation, classification, seriation, and transitivity. Thought is not as abstract as it is later in development.

- Critics argue that elements of a stage do not appear at the same time, and that education and culture have more influence on development than Piaget predicted. Neo-Piagetians place more emphasis on how children process information, strategies, speed of information processing, and the division of cognitive problems into more precise steps.

- Application of Piaget's ideas to education especially involves a constructivist approach that focuses on the teacher as a guide rather than a director and turns the classroom into a setting for exploration and discovery.

2 What Is the Nature of Children's Information Processing?

 LG2 Describe changes in information processing in middle and late childhood.

Memory

Thinking

Metacognition

- Long-term memory increases in middle and late childhood. Working memory is an important memory process that involves manipulating and assembling information. Knowledge and expertise influence memory. Strategies such as organization, imagery, and elaboration can be used by children to improve their memory. Fuzzy trace theory has been proposed to explain developmental changes in memory.

- Advances in executive function in middle and late childhood include self-control/inhibition, working memory, and cognitive flexibility. Critical thinking involves thinking reflectively and productively, as well as evaluating evidence. Mindfulness is an important aspect of critical thinking. A special concern is the lack of emphasis on critical thinking in many schools.

- Creative thinking is the ability to think in novel and unusual ways and to come up with unique solutions to problems and involves divergent, as opposed to convergent, thinking. A number of strategies can be used to encourage children's creative thinking. Children think like scientists in some ways, but in other ways they don't.

- Metacognition is knowing about thinking, or cognition about cognition. Most metacognitive studies have focused on metamemory. Pressley views the key to education as helping students learn a rich repertoire of strategies.

3 What Changes in Language Development Occur in Middle and Late Childhood?

 LG3 Summarize language development in middle and late childhood.

Vocabulary, Grammar, and Metalinguistic Awareness

- In middle and late childhood, children become more analytical and logical in their approach to words and grammar. They become increasingly able to use complex grammar in ways that make sense. Improvements in metalinguistic awareness—knowledge about language—are evident during the elementary school years as children increasingly define words, expand their knowledge of syntax, and increase their understanding of how to use language in culturally appropriate ways.

<table>
<tr><td>

Reading and Writing

</td><td>

- An ongoing debate about reading instruction focuses on the phonics approach versus the whole-language approach. The phonics approach concentrates on the sounds of language and often relies on simplified reading material. The whole-language approach stresses that reading instruction should parallel children's natural language learning and recommends giving children materials such as books and newspapers. An increasing number of experts now conclude that although both approaches can benefit children, direct instruction in phonics is a key aspect of learning to read in English and other languages that use alphabets.

- Children's writing emerges out of scribbling. Advances in children's language and cognitive development provide the underpinnings for improved writing.

</td></tr>
<tr><td>

Dual-Language and Second-Language Learning

</td><td>

- Research indicates a complex conclusion about whether there are sensitive periods in learning a second language. Some research suggests that children who are fluent in two languages have more advanced information-processing skills than children who use only one language.

- Instruction for English language learners (ELLs) has taken one of two main forms: (1) instruction in English only or (2) dual-language instruction in the child's home language and English. Some research has found a higher level of academic achievement when the dual-language approach is used.

</td></tr>
</table>

4 How Can Children's Intelligence Be Described?

 Characterize children's intelligence.

<table>
<tr><td>

Intelligence and Its Assessment

</td><td>

- Intelligence consists of problem-solving skills and the ability to adapt to and learn from life's everyday experiences. Interest in intelligence often focuses on individual differences and assessment. Widely used intelligence tests today include the Stanford–Binet tests and Wechsler scales. Results on these tests may be reported in terms of an overall IQ or in terms of performance on specific areas of the tests.

</td></tr>
<tr><td>

Types of Intelligence

</td><td>

- Sternberg proposed that intelligence comes in three main forms: analytical, creative, and practical. Gardner described eight types of intelligence: verbal, math, spatial, bodily-kinesthetic, interpersonal skills, intrapersonal skills, musical skills, and naturalist skills. The multiple-intelligence approaches have expanded our conception of intelligence, but critics argue that the research base for these approaches is not well established.

</td></tr>
<tr><td>

Interpreting Differences in IQ Scores

</td><td>

- IQ scores are influenced by both genetics and the environment. Parenting, home environments, schools, and intervention programs can influence these scores. Intelligence test scores have risen considerably around the world in recent decades—a phenomenon known as the Flynn effect—and this rise supports the role of environment in intelligence.

- Group differences in IQ scores reflect many influences, including cultural bias. Tests may be biased against groups that are not familiar with a standard form of English, with the content that is being tested, or with the testing situation.

</td></tr>
<tr><td>

Extremes of Intelligence

</td><td>

- Intellectual disability involves low IQ and problems in adapting to the demands of everyday life. One classification of intellectual disability distinguishes organic and cultural-familial intellectual disability.

- A child who is gifted has above-average intelligence and/or superior talent for something. Three characteristics of gifted children are precocity, individuality, and a passion to master a domain.

</td></tr>
</table>

5 What Characterizes Children's Achievement?

 Explain the development of achievement in children.

<table>
<tr><td>

Extrinsic and Intrinsic Motivation

</td><td>

- Extrinsic motivation involves external incentives such as rewards and punishments. Intrinsic motivation is based on internal factors such as self-determination, curiosity, challenge, and effort. Giving children some choice and providing opportunities for personal responsibility increase intrinsic motivation.

</td></tr>
</table>

- Sustained attention, effort, and task persistence are key aspects of achievement. As children develop, school tasks, projects, and work become more complex and require longer periods of sustained attention, effort, and task persistence.

- Individuals with a mastery motivation focus on the task and use solution-oriented strategies. Mastery motivation is preferred over a helpless orientation (in which individuals are overwhelmed by the experience of difficulty and attribute their difficulty to lack of ability) or a performance orientation (being concerned with achievement outcomes—winning is what matters).

- Mindset is the cognitive view, either fixed or growth, that individuals develop for themselves. Dweck argues that a key aspect of promoting children's development is guiding them in developing a growth mindset.

- Self-efficacy is the belief that one can master a situation and produce positive outcomes. Bandura stresses that self-efficacy is a critical factor in whether children will achieve.

- Setting specific, proximal (short-term), and challenging goals benefits children's self-efficacy and achievement. Being a good planner means managing time effectively, setting priorities, and being organized. Self-monitoring is a key aspect of self-regulation that benefits children's learning.

- Among the social relationships and contexts that are linked to children's achievement are those that involve parenting, teachers, ethnicity, and culture. There are substantial differences between countries in academic test performance that arise from many complex factors.

key **terms**

brainstorming	extrinsic motivation	mastery motivation	phonics approach
concrete operations	fuzzy trace theory	mental age (MA)	self-efficacy
convergent thinking	gifted	metacognition	seriation
creative thinking	helpless orientation	metalinguistic awareness	short-term memory
critical thinking	individual differences	mindfulness	stereotype threat
cultural-familial intellectual disability	intellectual disability	mindset	strategies
culture-fair tests	intelligence	neo-Piagetians	transitivity
divergent thinking	intelligence quotient (IQ)	normal distribution	triarchic theory of intelligence
elaboration	intrinsic motivation	organic intellectual disability	whole-language approach
	long-term memory	performance orientation	working memory

key **people**

Alan Baddeley	Howard Gardner	Peter Ornstein	Dale Schunk
Albert Bandura	Sandra Graham	Jean Piaget	Theophile Simon
Alfred Binet	J. P. Guilford	Eva Pomerantz	William Stern
Charles Brainerd	Lawrence Jackson	Michael Pressley	Robert J. Sternberg
Carol Dweck	Deanna Kuhn	Craig Ramey	Lewis Terman
James Flynn	Ann Masten	Valerie Reyna	David Wechsler

improving the **lives of children**

STRATEGIES

Supporting Children's Cognitive Development

What are some effective ways to help elementary and middle school children develop their cognitive skills?

- *Facilitate rather than direct children's learning.* Design situations that let children learn by doing and that actively promote their thinking and discovery. Listen, watch, and question children to help them attain a better understanding of concepts.

- *Provide opportunities for children to think critically.* Encourage children to think reflectively, rather than automatically accepting information as correct. Ask children questions about similarities and differences in things. Ask them questions of clarification, such as "What is the main point?" and "Why?" Ask children to justify their opinion. Ask them "what if" questions.

- *Be a good cognitive role model.* Model thinking and self-reflection for the child to see and hear. When children are around people who think critically and reflectively, they incorporate these cognitive styles into their own thinking repertoire.

- *Encourage collaboration with other children.* Children learn not only from adults but from other children as well. Cross-age teaching, in which older children who are competent thinkers interact with younger children, can be especially helpful. Collaborative problem solving teaches children how to work cooperatively with others.

- *Stimulate children's creative thinking.* Encourage children to take risks in their thinking. Don't overcontrol by telling children precisely what to do; let their originality come through. Don't set up grandiose expectations; it can hurt creativity. Encourage the child to think freely and come up with as many different ways of doing something as possible.

RESOURCES

ERIC Database
www.eric.ed.gov

ERIC provides wide-ranging references to many educational topics, including educational practices, parent-school relations, and community programs.

National Association for Gifted Children (NAGC)
www.nagc.org

The NAGC is an association of academics, educators, and librarians. Its goal is to improve the education of gifted children. It publishes periodic reports on the education of gifted children and the journal *Gifted Children Quarterly*.

Mindset (2006)
Carol Dweck

New York: Random House

An outstanding classic that emphasizes how important it is for parents, teachers, and other adults to guide children in developing a growth rather than a fixed mindset.

Motivating Students to Learn (5th ed.) (2020)
Kathryn Wentzel

New York: Routledge

A contemporary look at many aspects of schools and teaching that influence students' achievement.

chapter 13

SOCIOEMOTIONAL DEVELOPMENT IN MIDDLE AND LATE CHILDHOOD

chapter outline

FatCamera/Getty Images

For years, author and journalist Steve Hartman has been broadcasting stories of kindness and generosity in unexpected places, including from young children. In one story, Hartman (2022) and his two school-age children discussed the importance of honesty. They shared with viewers what happened when a fifth-grade Girl Scout, Charlotte, was very open about which of the various types of cookies her troop was selling were tasty and which ones were not. She understood this was her opinion, but she also felt that the people who were buying her cookies needed useful information that was more honest compared to the advertising. This led to record-breaking sales for Charlotte. When interviewed later by Hartman and his family, she said that her honesty had been learned not only from Girl Scouts but also from her parents and other important people in her life.

By late childhood, most children have developed friendships, learned to interact with adults other than their parents, and developed ideas about fairness and other moral concepts, such as honesty.

Honesty is just one important concept. Can children understand such complex concepts as discrimination, economic inequality, affirmative action, and comparable worth? Probably not, if you use those terms when talking with them. But in a now classic study, developmental psychologist Phyllis Katz (1987) found that children can understand situations that involve those concepts. Katz asked elementary-school-age children to pretend that they had taken a long ride on a spaceship to a make-believe planet called Pax. Once there, the children find problematic situations. For example, citizens of Pax who had dotted noses couldn't get jobs. Instead, the jobs went to the people with striped noses. "What would you do in this situation?" Katz asked the children.

She asked them for their opinions about various situations on this faraway planet. For example, what should a teacher do when two students were tied for

┌-topical connections   *looking **back***

In "Socioemotional Development in Early Childhood," you learned that young children are in Erikson's stage of initiative versus guilt, parents continue to play an important role in their development, and an authoritative style of parenting is more likely than other parenting styles to have positive outcomes for children. In early childhood, peer relationships take on a more significant role as children's social worlds widen. Play has a special place in young children's lives and is an important context for both cognitive and socioemotional development. In the preceding chapter you studied children's cognitive development in middle and late childhood, including Piaget's view of children's thinking, their intelligence, language skills, and achievement. In this chapter, you will explore continuing advances in many aspects of children's socioemotional development.

a prize or when they had been fighting? The elementary school children often came up with interesting solutions to problems. All but one thought that not giving a job to a qualified applicant who had different physical characteristics (a dotted rather than a striped nose) was unfair. Overall, the types of rules the children believed a society should abide by were quite sensible—almost all included the need for equitable sharing of resources and work and prohibitions against aggression.

preview

The years of middle and late childhood bring many changes to children's social and emotional lives. The development of their self-concepts, emotions, moral reasoning, and gendered behavior is significant. Transformations in their relationships with parents and peers also occur, and schooling takes on a more academic flavor.

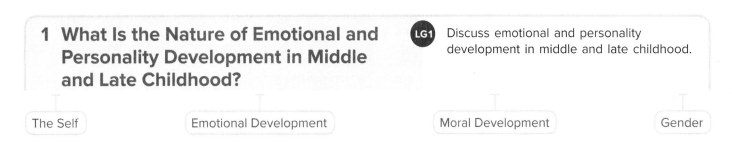

1 What Is the Nature of Emotional and Personality Development in Middle and Late Childhood?

LG1 Discuss emotional and personality development in middle and late childhood.

| The Self | Emotional Development | Moral Development | Gender |

In this section, we explore how the self continues to develop during middle and late childhood and the emotional changes that take place during these years. We also discuss children's moral development and many aspects of the role that gender plays in their development in middle and late childhood.

THE SELF

What is the nature of the child's self-understanding, understanding of others, and self-esteem during the elementary school years? What role does self-regulation play in children's achievement?

The Development of Self-Understanding In middle and late childhood, especially from 8 to 11 years of age, children increasingly describe themselves in terms of psychological characteristics and traits, in contrast to the more concrete self-descriptions of younger children. Older children are more likely to describe themselves with terms such as "popular, nice, helpful, mean, smart, and dumb" (Harter, 2016).

In addition, during the elementary school years, children become more likely to recognize social aspects of the self (Harter, 2012, 2016). In addition to including social groups in their self-descriptions, children in elementary school are increasingly aware of racism, discrimination, and power hierarchies that affect their self-understanding as well as their relationships with other people (Rizzo & Killen, 2020).

Children's self-understanding in the elementary school years also includes increasing reference to social comparison (Harter, 2012, 2016). At this point in development, children are more likely to distinguish themselves from others in comparative rather than in absolute terms. That is, elementary-school-aged children are no longer as likely to think about what they do or do not do, but are more likely to think about what they can do in comparison with others.

Consider a foundational series of studies in which Diane Ruble (1983) investigated children's use of social comparison in their self-evaluations. Children were given a difficult

How Would You...?
If you were a **psychologist,** how would you explain the role of social comparison in the development of a child's sense of self?

What are some changes in children's understanding of others in middle and late childhood?

Asiseeit/E+/Getty Images

task and then offered feedback on their performance, as well as information about the performances of other children their age. The children were then asked for self-evaluations. Children younger than 7 made virtually no reference to the information about other children's performances. However, many children older than 7 included socially comparative information in their self-descriptions.

Social comparisons become even more pronounced as children enter early adolescence. For example, in a qualitative study using in-depth interviews to understand academic identity of Black and White American 12- and 13-year-olds, Black students in honors courses had more positive academic and racial identity than did Black students tracked into non-honors courses, suggesting that social comparisons figured prominently in students' self-understanding (Legette, 2018).

In sum, in middle and late childhood, self-description increasingly involves psychological and social characteristics, including social comparison.

Understanding Others Earlier, we described the advances and limitations of young children's understanding of others. In middle and late childhood, children show an increase in *perspective taking,* the ability to take other people's perspectives and understand their thoughts and feelings (Lagattuta & Kramer, 2021). Research indicates that children and adolescents who do not have good perspective-taking skills are more likely to have difficulty in peer relationships and engage in more aggressive and oppositional behavior (Morosan & others, 2017; Nilsen & Basco, 2017; O'Kearney & others, 2017).

In Robert Selman's (2003) view, at about 6 to 8 years of age, children begin to understand that others may have a different perspective because some people have more access to information. Then, he says, in the next several years, children become aware that each individual is aware of the other's perspective and that putting oneself in the other's place is a way of judging the other person's intentions, purposes, and actions.

Perspective taking is especially thought to be important in relation to whether children develop prosocial or antisocial attitudes and behavior. In terms of prosocial behavior, taking another's perspective improves children's likelihood of understanding and sympathizing with others who are distressed or in need. One study revealed that when 10-year-old children were put in a negative emotional state and presented with stories of someone in need, children who had better emotion regulation were more likely to engage in increased empathy and prosocial behavior (Hein, Röder, & Fingerle, 2018).

In middle and late childhood, children also become more skeptical of others' claims (Amemiya & others, 2021; Heyman, Fu, & Lee, 2013). Even 4-year-old children show some skepticism of others' claims. In middle and late childhood, children become increasingly skeptical of some sources of information about psychological traits. For example, in one study, 8- to 11-year-olds and adults were less likely than younger children to accept the accuracy or usefulness of another person's boasting (Lockhart, Goddu, & Keil, 2018). Compared with 5- to 7-year-olds, the more psychologically sophisticated 8- to 11-year-olds also showed a better understanding that others' self-reports on socially desirable tendencies should be scrutinized. A different study of 6- to 9-year-olds revealed that older children were less trusting and more skeptical of others' distorted claims than were younger children (Mills & Elashi, 2014). Children also become more aware across middle childhood of the situational factors that should influence whether and how skeptical you should be (Amemiya & others, 2021).

How Would You...?

If you were an **educator,** how would you work with children to help them develop a healthy self-concept concerning their academic ability?

self-esteem The global evaluative dimension of the self. Self-esteem is also referred to as self-worth or self-image.

self-concept Domain-specific evaluations of the self.

Self-Esteem and Self-Concept High self-esteem and a positive self-concept are important characteristics of children's well-being (Arens & Niepel, 2023; Harter, 2016; Kadir & Yeung, 2018). Investigators sometimes use the terms *self-esteem* and *self-concept* interchangeably or do not precisely define them, but there is a meaningful difference between them. **Self-esteem** refers to global evaluations of the self; it is also called self-worth or self-image. For example, a child may perceive that they are not merely a person but a good person. **Self-concept** refers to domain-specific evaluations of the self. Children can make self-evaluations in many domains of their lives—academic, athletic, appearance, and so on. In sum, self-esteem refers to global self-evaluations, self-concept to domain-specific evaluations.

For most children, high self-esteem and a positive self-concept are important aspects of their well-being (Arens & Niepel, 2023; Harter, 2016). However, for some children, self-esteem reflects perceptions that do not always match reality (Becht & others, 2017; Jordan & Zeigler-Hill, 2013). Children's self-esteem might reflect a belief about whether they are intelligent and attractive, for example, but that belief is not necessarily accurate. Thus, high self-esteem may refer to accurate, justified perceptions of one's worth as a person and one's successes and accomplishments, but it can also refer to an arrogant, grandiose, unwarranted sense of superiority over others (Brummelman, Thomaes, & Sedikides, 2016). In the same manner, low self-esteem may reflect either an accurate perception of one's shortcomings or a distorted, even pathological insecurity and inferiority (Stadelmann & others, 2017).

What are the consequences of low self-esteem? Low self-esteem has been implicated in overweight and obesity, anxiety, depression, suicide, and delinquency (Hill, 2016; Masselink & others, 2018; Reed-Fitzke, 2019; Paxton & Damiano, 2017; Rieger & others, 2016). One of the longest-running longitudinal studies also revealed that youth with low self-esteem had lower life satisfaction at 30 years of age (Birkeland & others, 2012).

What are some issues involved in understanding children's self-esteem in school?
Inti St Clair/Digital Vision/Getty Images

Another study found that low and decreasing self-esteem in adolescence was linked to adult depression two decades later (Steiger & others, 2014).

The foundations of self-esteem and self-concept emerge from the quality of parent-child interaction in infancy and childhood. Children with high self-esteem are more likely to be securely attached to their parents and to have parents who engage in sensitive caregiving (Thompson, 2020). And in a longitudinal study, the quality of children's home environment (which involved assessment of parenting quality, cognitive stimulation, and the physical home environment) was linked to their self-esteem in early adulthood (Orth, 2018).

Although variations in self-esteem have been linked with many aspects of children's development, much of the research is *correlational* rather than *experimental*. Recall that correlation does not equal causation. Thus, if a correlational study finds an association between children's low self-esteem and low academic achievement, low academic achievement could cause the low self-esteem as much as low self-esteem causes low academic achievement (Scherrer & Preckel, 2019). In fact, there are only moderate correlations between school performance and self-esteem. Inflated praise, although well intended, may cause children with low self-esteem to avoid important learning experiences such as tackling challenging tasks (Brummelman, Crocker, & Bushman, 2016).

Researchers have found that adults who provide inflated praise are more likely to praise the personal qualities (such as intelligence) than the behavior (such as hard work) of children with low self-esteem. However, person-oriented praise may backfire. Children who had been praised for their personal qualities rather than behavior are less likely to persist in the face of difficulties. If individuals have been praised for their intelligence but then fail, they may think there is nothing they can do to improve their performance in the future. But, if children have been praised for their hard work and fail, they may think that they need to work harder in the future. Holding an *incremental theory of intelligence* (believing that intelligence can be improved by working hard) and having *learning goals* (wanting to learn to understand the material better rather than just to get a good grade) are both related to better school performance (Gunderson & others, 2018). Having positive feelings about being challenged and learning also contributes to achievement (Lichtenfeld & others, 2023).

Although self-esteem historically has been thought to derive from doing well at activities that individuals believe are important for themselves, cross-cultural research suggests that self-esteem is more closely tied to doing well at activities that one's cultural group believes are important. In a large study of more than 5,000 young people in 19 countries, self-esteem was not related to personal values but rather to fulfilling values of other people in that culture. For example, in Western Europe and parts of South America, self-esteem was related to individual freedom and feeling in control of one's life, whereas in the Middle East, Africa, and Asia, self-esteem was related to perceiving oneself as fulfilling obligations to others and doing one's duty (Becker & others, 2014). In addition, cultures differ in the importance placed on self-esteem. For example, European American mothers often spontaneously mention building children's self-esteem as important for promoting positive adjustment. By contrast, Taiwanese mothers

Increasing Children's Self-Esteem

Four ways children's self-esteem can be improved include identifying the causes of low self-esteem, providing emotional support and social approval, helping children achieve, and helping children cope (Harter, 2012, 2016):

- *Identify the causes of low self-esteem.* Intervention should target the causes of low self-esteem. Children have the highest self-esteem when they perform competently in domains that are important to them. Therefore, children should be encouraged to identify and value areas of competence. These areas might include academic skills, athletic skills, physical attractiveness, and social acceptance.
- *Provide emotional support and social approval.* Some children with low self-esteem come from conflicted families or conditions in which they experienced abuse or neglect—situations in which support was not available. In some cases, alternative sources of support can be arranged either informally through the encouragement of a teacher, a coach, or another significant adult, or more formally through programs such as Big Brothers and Big Sisters.
- *Help children achieve.* Achievement also can improve children's self-esteem. For example, the straightforward teaching of real skills to children often results in increased achievement and, thus, in enhanced self-esteem. Children develop higher self-esteem because

How can parents help children develop healthy self-esteem?
MoMo Productions/DigitalVision/Getty Images

they know the important tasks that will achieve their goals, and they have performed them or similar behaviors in the past.
- *Help children cope.* Self-esteem is often increased when children face a problem and try to cope with it, rather than avoid it. If coping rather than avoidance prevails, children often face problems realistically, honestly, and nondefensively. This produces favorable self-evaluative thoughts, which lead to the self-generated approval that raises self-esteem.

rarely mention self-esteem, and if they do, they describe it as a vulnerability that can lead to rudeness, poor self-control, and stubbornness (Miller & Cho, 2018).

What are some good strategies for effectively increasing self-esteem in children who have a poor self-image? See the *Caring Connections* interlude for some answers to this question.

Self-Regulation   One of the most important aspects of the self in middle and late childhood is the increased capacity for self-regulation (Blair, 2016; Clark & others, 2023; Eisenberg, Smith, & Spinrad, 2016). Self-regulation generally increases rapidly from the age of 3 to 7 years, with the majority of children showing the most rapid growth in self-control during preschool but approximately 20 percent not showing substantial gains in self-regulation until elementary school (Montroy & others, 2016). This increased capacity is characterized by deliberate efforts to manage one's behavior, emotions, and thoughts that lead to increased social competence and achievement (Duncan, McClelland, & Acock, 2017; Flanagan & Symonds, 2022; Galinsky & others, 2017; Neuenschwander & Blair, 2017; Usher & Schunk, 2018). This may be even more important for children facing adversity. For example, one study revealed that children in low-income families who had a higher level of self-regulation earned higher grades in school than their counterparts who had a lower level of self-regulation (Buckner, Mezzacappa, & Beardslee, 2009). Also, a study of almost 17,000 3- to 7-year-old children revealed that self-regulation was a protective factor for children growing up in low-socioeconomic-status (low-SES) conditions (Flouri, Midouhas, & Joshi, 2014). In this study, 7-year-old children with low self-regulation living in low-SES conditions had more emotional problems than their 3-year-old counterparts. Thus, low self-regulation was linked to a widening gap in low-SES children's emotional problems over time. And in another study, higher levels of self-control assessed at 4 years of age were linked to improvements in the math and reading achievement of early elementary school children living in predominantly rural and low-income contexts (Blair & others, 2015).

The increased capacity for self-regulation is linked to developmental advances in the brain's prefrontal cortex, a topic that was discussed in "Cognitive Development in Middle and Late Childhood." In that discussion, increased focal activation in the prefrontal cortex was linked to improved cognitive control. Such cognitive control includes self-regulation (Clark & others, 2023; Schunk & Greene, 2018). An app for iPads has been developed to help children improve their self-regulation (for more information, go to www.selfregulationstation .com/sr-ipad-app/).

Industry versus Inferiority

Earlier, we discussed Erik Erikson's (1968) eight stages of human development. His fourth stage, industry versus inferiority, appears during middle and late childhood. The term *industry* expresses a dominant theme of this period: Children become interested in how things are made and how they work. When children are encouraged in their efforts to make, build, and work—whether they are building a model airplane, constructing a tree house, fixing a bicycle, solving an addition problem, or cooking—their sense of industry increases. However, parents who see their children's efforts at making things as "mischief" or "making a mess" can cause children to develop a sense of inferiority.

Children's social worlds beyond their families also contribute to a sense of industry. School becomes especially important in this regard. Consider children who are slightly below average in intelligence. They are too bright to be in special classes but not bright enough to be in gifted classes. Failing frequently in their academic efforts, they develop a sense of inferiority. By contrast, consider children whose sense of industry is disparaged at home. A series of sensitive and committed teachers may revitalize their sense of industry. Thus, children's relationships with parents and teachers are important for children's industry, including engagement in school (Heatly & Votruba-Drzal, 2017; Hofkens & Pianta, 2022).

EMOTIONAL DEVELOPMENT

Preschoolers become more adept at talking about their own and others' emotions. They also show a growing awareness of the need to control and manage their emotions to meet social standards. In middle and late childhood, children further develop their understanding and self-regulation of emotion (Calkins & Perry, 2016; Cole & Jacobs, 2018; Hong & others, 2021).

Developmental Changes

Developmental changes in emotions during middle and late childhood include the following (Cole & Jacobs, 2018):

- *Improved emotional understanding.* For example, children in elementary school develop an increased ability to understand such complex emotions as pride and shame. These emotions become less tied to the reactions of other people; they become more self-generated and integrated with a sense of personal responsibility. Also, during middle and late childhood as part of their understanding of emotions, children can engage in "mental time travel," in which they anticipate and recall the cognitive and emotional aspects of events (Kramer & Lagattuta, 2018).

- *Increased understanding that more than one emotion can be experienced in a particular situation.* A third-grader, for example, may realize that achieving something might involve both anxiety and joy.

- *Increased tendency to be aware of the events leading to emotional reactions.* A fourth-grader may become aware that her sadness today is influenced by her friend's moving to another town last week.

- *Ability to suppress or conceal negative emotional reactions.* When one of his classmates irritates him, a fifth-grader has learned to tone down his anger more effectively than he used to.

- *The use of self-initiated strategies for redirecting feelings.* In the elementary school years, children become more reflective about their emotional lives and increasingly use strategies to control their emotions. They become more effective at cognitively managing their emotions, such as soothing themselves after an upset.

- *A capacity for genuine empathy.* For example, a fourth-grader feels compassion for a distressed person and experiences vicariously the sadness the distressed person is feeling.

developmental **connection**

Erikson's Theory

Initiative versus guilt is Erikson's early childhood stage, and identity versus identity confusion is his adolescence stage. Connect to "Socioemotional Development in Early Childhood" and "Socioemotional Development in Adolescence."

What characterizes Erikson's stage of industry versus inferiority?
Beau Lark/Fancy/Glow Images

What are some developmental changes in emotion during the middle and late childhood years?
Kevin Dodge/The Image Bank/Getty Images

How does attachment change during middle and late childhood?

Hero Images/Fancy/Corbis

Attachment in Middle and Late Childhood You have read about the importance of secure attachment in infancy and the role of sensitive parenting in attachment (Dagan & Sagi-Schwartz, 2021; Roisman & Cicchetti, 2017; Thompson, 2016). The attachment process continues to be an important aspect of children's development beyond infancy. In middle and late childhood, attachment becomes more sophisticated, and as children's social worlds expand to include peers, teachers, and others, they typically spend less time with parents.

Kathryn Kerns and her colleagues (Movahed Abtahi & Kerns, 2017; Gastelle & Kerns, 2022; Kerns & Seibert, 2016) have studied links between attachment to parents and various child outcomes in middle and late childhood. They have found that during this period of development, secure attachment is associated with less anxiety and depression in children, as well as more positive emotions (Kerns & Brumariu, 2016; Obeldobel & Kerns, 2020). Children who are more securely attached to their mothers also are less likely to be excluded by their peers at school and less likely to behave aggressively toward peers, providing evidence that parent-child relationships set the stage for children's relationships outside the family (Seibert & Kerns, 2015).

Social-Emotional Education Programs An increasing number of social-emotional educational programs have been developed to improve many aspects of children's and adolescents' lives. Two such programs are the Second Step program (2023) created by the Committee for Children (2017) and the Collaborative for Academic, Social, and Emotional Learning (CASEL, 2023). Many social-emotional education programs only target young children, but Second Step can be implemented in pre-K through eighth grade, and CASEL can be used with pre-K through twelfth-grade students.

What characterizes social-emotional programs for children?

Antonio Perez/Chicago Tribune/MCT/Newscom

- *Second Step* focuses on the following aspects of social-emotional learning from pre-K through the eighth grade: (1) pre-K: self-regulation and cognitive skills that improve their attention and help them control their behavior; (2) K–grade 5: making friends, self-regulation of emotion, and solving problems; and (3) grades 6–8: communication skills, coping with stress, and decision making to avoid engaging in problem behaviors.
- *CASEL* targets five core social and emotional learning domains: (1) self-awareness (recognizing one's emotions and how they affect behavior, for example); (2) self-management (self-control, coping with stress, and impulse control, for example); (3) social awareness (perspective taking and empathy, for example); (4) relationship skills (developing positive relationships and communicating effectively with individuals from diverse backgrounds, for example); and (5) responsible decision making (engaging in ethical behavior and understanding the consequences of one's actions, for example).

Programs such as Second Step and CASEL are delivered by teachers or other school personnel to entire classes during the school day. Delivering the program to all students rather than singling out students who are struggling has the advantage of being able to encourage classroom-wide change while avoiding the stigmatization of individual students.

Coping with Stress An important aspect of children's lives is learning how to cope with stress (Fisher & others, 2021). As children get older, they are able to more accurately appraise a stressful situation and determine how much control they have over it. Researchers who study how children cope with stress have identified five main strategies: problem solving, emotional suppression, cognitive reappraisal, distraction, and avoidance (Compas & others, 2017). Older children are better than younger children at intentionally shifting their thoughts to something that is less stressful. Older children are also better at reframing, or changing their perception of a stressful situation through a process known as cognitive reappraisal. For example, younger children may be very disappointed that their teacher did not say hello to them when they arrived at school. Older children may reframe this type of situation and think, "She may have been busy with other things and just forgot to say hello." Children who manage stress through problem solving or cognitive reappraisal have less anxiety and other adverse effects than do children who suppress their emotions or avoid dealing with the problems causing stress (Compas & others, 2017).

Disasters can especially harm children's development and produce adjustment problems (Acharya, Bhatta, & Assannangkornchai, 2018). Among the outcomes for children who experience disasters are acute stress reactions, depression, panic disorder, and post-traumatic stress disorder (Danielson & others, 2017; Masten & others, 2021). Proportions of children developing these problems following a disaster depend on factors such as the nature and severity of the disaster, as well as the support available to the children. Also, children who have developed a number of coping techniques have the best chance of adapting and functioning competently in the face of disasters and trauma (Ungar, 2015).

Following are descriptions of studies of how various aspects of traumatic events and disasters affect children:

What are some effective strategies to help surviving children cope with traumatic events, such as the attack by a gunman at Robb Elementary School in Uvalde, Texas, in May 2022, when 19 children and two teachers were killed?
Brandon Bell/Getty Images

- In a large meta-analysis of 15 studies and almost 23,000 children, anxiety, depression, irritability, boredom, inattention, and fear were the main new-onset psychological problems that emerged during the COVID-19 pandemic (Kumar Panda & others, 2021).
- A year after the 2015 earthquake in Nepal, 51 percent of children continued to have moderate to severe PTSD symptoms, which were stronger for younger than older children (Acharya, Bhatta, & Assannangkornchai, 2018).
- Children's exposure to community violence is related to a number of detrimental outcomes. For example, children who were exposed to short-term violence in their community following a contested political election in Kenya had an increase in behavior problems such as aggression (Skinner & others, 2014). Likewise, Palestinian children exposed to chronic ethnic and political violence are at risk for both aggressive behavior and emotional distress (Niwa & others, 2016).

In research on disasters and trauma, the term *dose-response effects* is often used. A widely supported finding in this research area is that the more severe the disaster or trauma (dose) is, the worse the adaptation and adjustment (response) following the event (Narayan & Masten, 2019).

From 2020 to 2022, the abrupt emergence and worldwide spread of the novel coronavirus (COVID-19) took everyone by surprise and increased the stress and anxiety levels of many adults and children. To slow the spread of the virus, a majority of schools closed and many adults began to work from home. In such stressful circumstances, it is important for parents to stay calm, educate themselves about the ongoing issues related to the disaster (in this case, the virus), and communicate accurate information to their children. It is especially important for children to understand that such disruptions are not permanent and that eventually their lives will return to normal, although with possible adaptations. These and other factors play a crucial role in how families have coped during the pandemic (Prime, Wade, & Browne, 2020).

Children who have a number of coping techniques have the best chance of adapting and functioning competently in the face of disasters, traumas, and other stressful life events. Following are some recommendations for helping children cope with the stress of especially devastating events (Centers for Disease Control and Prevention, 2018c):

- *Reassure children of their safety and security.* This step may need to be taken numerous times.
- *Allow children to retell events and be patient in listening to them.*
- *Encourage children to talk about any disturbing or confusing feelings.* Tell them that these are normal feelings after a stressful event.
- *Help children make sense of what happened.* Children may misunderstand what took place.
- *Protect children from reexposure to frightening situations and reminders of the trauma.* This strategy includes limiting conversations about the event in front of the children.

Child and adolescent psychiatrists are among the mental health professionals who help youth cope with stress, including traumatic experiences. To read about a psychiatrist who treats children and adolescents, see *Connecting with Careers*.

How Would You...?
If you were a **social worker,** how would you counsel a child who had been exposed to a traumatic event?

developmental **connection**
Peer Relationships and Friendships
The coronavirus pandemic has caused many children, adolescents, and adults to engage in "social distancing." Connect to "Socioemotional Development in Adolescence."

MORAL DEVELOPMENT

Recall our description of Piaget's view of moral development. Piaget proposed that younger children are characterized by *heteronomous morality* but that, by 10 years of age, they have moved into a higher stage called *autonomous morality.* According to Piaget, older children

connecting with careers

Melissa Jackson, Child Psychiatrist

Dr. Melissa Jackson is a child and adolescent psychiatrist in Miami, Florida. She obtained a medical degree from the University of Florida and then completed an internship and residency in psychiatry at Advocate Lutheran General Hospital in Chicago, followed by a fellowship in child and adolescent psychiatry at the University of Southern California. Among the problems and disorders that Dr. Jackson treats are post-traumatic stress disorder, ADHD, anxiety, autism, depression, and a number of behavioral issues. In addition to her psychiatric treatment of children, she founded Health for Honduras, which includes trips to Honduras to provide services to children in orphanages.

To become a child and adolescent psychiatrist like Dr. Jackson, you would need to obtain an undergraduate degree, then earn a medical degree, spend three to four years as a resident physician in general psychiatry, and complete a two-year fellowship in the subspecialty of child and adolescent psychiatry. An important aspect of being a psychiatrist is that psychiatrists can prescribe medication, which psychologists cannot do.

Dr. Melissa Jackson with her dog Prince, who is available by request for additional comfort and support during sessions. Many of her child clients can't wait until their next session to see Prince.
Melissa Jackson, MD

Lawrence Kohlberg, the architect of a provocative cognitive developmental theory of moral development. *What is the nature of his theory?*
Harvard University Archives, UAV 605.295.8, Box 7, Kohlberg

preconventional reasoning The lowest level in Kohlberg's theory of moral development. The individual's concept of good and bad is interpreted primarily in terms of external rewards and punishment.

consider the intentions of the individual, believe that rules are subject to change, and are aware that punishment does not always follow wrongdoing. Let's now explore some other views of moral development.

Kohlberg's Theory A second major perspective on moral development was proposed by Lawrence Kohlberg (1958, 1986). Basing his perspective partly on Piaget's theory, Kohlberg suggested that there are six stages of moral development. These stages, he argued, are universal. Development from one stage to another, said Kohlberg, was fostered by taking the perspective of others and experiencing a conflict between one's current moral thinking and a more advanced level of moral reasoning.

Kohlberg arrived at his view after 20 years of using a unique interview with children. In the interview, children were presented with stories in which characters face moral dilemmas. The following is the most famous example:

> In Europe a woman was near death from a special kind of cancer. There was one drug that the doctors thought might save her. It was a form of radium that a druggist [i.e., a pharmacist] in the same town had recently discovered. The drug was expensive to make, but the druggist was charging ten times what the drug cost him to make. He paid $200 for the radium and charged $2,000 for a small dose of the drug. The sick woman's husband, Heinz, went to everyone he knew to borrow the money, but he could only get together $1,000, which is half of what it cost. He told the druggist that his wife was dying and asked him to sell it cheaper or let him pay later. But the druggist said, "No, I discovered the drug, and I am going to make money from it." So Heinz got desperate and broke into the man's store to steal the drug for his wife. (Kohlberg, 1969, p. 379)

After reading the story, the interviewee answers a series of questions about the moral dilemma. Should Heinz have stolen the drug? Was stealing it right or wrong? Why? Is it a husband's duty to steal the drug for his wife if he can get it no other way? Would a good husband steal? Did the pharmacist have the right to charge that much when there was no law setting a limit on the price? Why or why not?

The Kohlberg Stages Based on answers to questions like these, three levels of moral thinking (each with two stages) could be defined (see Figure 1). The progression through the levels and stages involves the person's morality gradually becoming more internal rather than being based on the external or superficial reasons they would have given when they were younger.

LEVEL 1	LEVEL 2	LEVEL 3
Preconventional Level **No Internalization**	**Conventional Level** **Intermediate Internalization**	**Postconventional Level** **Full Internalization**
Stage 1 Heteronomous Morality	**Stage 3** Mutual Interpersonal Expectations, Relationships, and Interpersonal Conformity	**Stage 5** Social Contract or Utility and Individual Rights
Children obey because adults tell them to obey. People base their moral decisions on fear of punishment.	*Individuals value trust, caring, and loyalty to others as a basis for moral judgments.*	*Individuals reason that values, rights, and principles undergird or transcend the law.*
Stage 2 Individualism, Instrumental Purpose, and Exchange	**Stage 4** Social Systems Morality	**Stage 6** Universal Ethical Principles
Individuals pursue their own interests but let others do the same. What is right involves equal exchange.	*Moral judgments are based on understanding and the social order, law, justice, and duty.*	*The person has developed moral judgments that are based on universal human rights. When faced with a dilemma between law and conscience, a personal, individualized conscience is followed.*

FIGURE 1

KOHLBERG'S THREE LEVELS AND SIX STAGES OF MORAL DEVELOPMENT. Kohlberg argued that people everywhere develop their moral reasoning by passing through these age-based stages. *Where does Kohlberg's theory stand on the nature-nurture and continuity-discontinuity issues?*

Preconventional reasoning is the lowest level. At this level, good and bad are interpreted in terms of external rewards and punishments.

- *Stage 1.* **Heteronomous morality** is the first stage in preconventional reasoning. At this stage, moral thinking is tied to punishment. For example, children think that they must obey because they fear punishment for disobedience.
- *Stage 2.* **Individualism, instrumental purpose, and exchange** is the second stage of preconventional reasoning. At this stage, individuals reason that pursuing their own interests is the right thing to do, but they let others do the same. Thus, they think that what is right involves an equal exchange. They reason that if they are nice to others, others will be nice to them in return.

Conventional reasoning is the second, or intermediate, level. At this level, individuals have certain standards, but they are the standards set by others, such as parents or the government.

- *Stage 3.* **Mutual interpersonal expectations, relationships, and interpersonal conformity** is Kohlberg's third stage, in which individuals value trust, caring, and loyalty to others as a basis for moral judgments. Children and adolescents often adopt their parents' moral standards at this stage, seeking to be thought of by their parents as being "good."
- *Stage 4.* **Social systems morality** is the fourth stage, in which moral judgments are based on understanding the social order, law, justice, and duty. For example, adolescents may reason that in order for a community to work effectively, it needs to be protected by laws that everyone follows.

Postconventional reasoning is the highest level, when the individual recognizes alternative moral courses, explores the options, and then decides on a personal moral code.

- *Stage 5.* **Social contract or utility and individual rights** is the fifth stage, when individuals reason that values, rights, and principles undergird or transcend the law. A person evaluates the validity of actual laws and realizes that social systems can be examined in terms of the degree to which they preserve and protect fundamental human rights and values.
- *Stage 6.* **Universal ethical principles** is the sixth and highest stage, in which the person has developed a moral standard based on universal human rights. When faced with a conflict between law and conscience, the person reasons that conscience should be followed, even when it brings risk.

Kohlberg held that before age 9, most children use level 1, preconventional reasoning based on external rewards and punishments, when they consider moral choices. By early

heteronomous morality The first stage of moral development in Piaget's theory, occurring from approximately 4 to 7 years of age. Justice and rules are conceived of as unchangeable properties of the world, removed from the control of people. Kohlberg adapted Piaget's ideas in his first stage of preconventional reasoning in which moral thinking is tied to punishment.

individualism, instrumental purpose, and exchange The second Kohlberg stage in preconventional reasoning. At this stage, individuals pursue their own interests but also let others do the same.

conventional reasoning The second, or intermediate, level in Kohlberg's theory of moral development. At this level, individuals abide by certain standards, but they are standards set by others such as parents or the government.

mutual interpersonal expectations, relationships, and interpersonal conformity Kohlberg's third stage of moral development. At this stage, individuals value trust, caring, and loyalty to others as a basis of moral judgments.

social systems morality The fourth stage in Kohlberg's theory of moral development. Moral judgments are based on understanding the social order, law, justice, and duty.

postconventional reasoning The highest level in Kohlberg's theory of moral development. At this level, the individual recognizes alternative moral courses, explores the options, and then decides on a personal moral code.

social contract or utility and individual rights The fifth Kohlberg stage. At this stage, individuals reason that values, rights, and principles undergird or transcend the law.

universal ethical principles The sixth and highest stage in Kohlberg's theory of moral development. Individuals develop a moral standard based on universal principles of human rights.

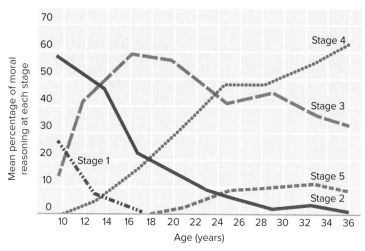

FIGURE 2

AGE AND THE PERCENTAGE OF INDIVIDUALS AT EACH KOHLBERG STAGE.
In a classic longitudinal study of males from 10 to 36 years of age, at age 10 most moral reasoning was at stage 2 (Colby & others, 1983). At 16 to 18 years of age, stage 3 became the most frequent type of moral reasoning, and it was not until the mid-twenties that stage 4 became the most frequent. Stage 5 did not appear until 20 to 22 years of age, and it never characterized more than 10 percent of the individuals. In this study, the moral stages appeared somewhat later than Kohlberg envisioned, and stage 6 was absent. *Do you think it matters that all of the participants in this study were males? Why or why not?*

How Would You...?

If you were a **human development and family studies professional,** how would you explain the progression of moral reasoning skills that develop during the elementary school years?

---

developmental connection

Peers

Kohlberg argued that the mutual give-and-take of peer relations is more important than parenting in enhancing children's moral reasoning. Connect to "Socioemotional Development in Early Childhood."

---

justice perspective A moral perspective that focuses on the rights of the individual and in which individuals independently make moral decisions.

care perspective The moral perspective of Carol Gilligan, which views people in terms of their connectedness with others and emphasizes interpersonal communication, relationships with others, and concern for others.

---

adolescence, their moral reasoning is increasingly based on the application of standards set by others. Most adolescents reason at stage 3, with some signs of stages 2 and 4. By early adulthood, a small number of individuals reason in postconventional ways. A classic 20-year longitudinal investigation found that use of stages 1 and 2 decreased with age (Colby & others, 1983) (see Figure 2). Stage 4, which did not appear at all in the moral reasoning of 10-year-olds, was reflected in the moral thinking of 62 percent of 36-year-olds. Stage 5 did not appear until age 20 to 22 and never characterized more than 10 percent of individuals. This study showed that the moral stages appeared somewhat later than Kohlberg initially envisioned, and reasoning at the higher stages, especially stage 6, was rare. Although stage 6 has been removed from the interview scoring manual, it still is considered to be theoretically important.

Influences on the Kohlberg Stages Moral reasoning at each stage is based on the individual's level of cognitive development, but Kohlberg argued that advances in children's cognitive development did not ensure development of moral reasoning. Instead, moral reasoning also reflects children's experiences in dealing with moral questions and moral conflict.

Several investigators have tried to advance individuals' levels of moral development by having a model present arguments that reflect moral thinking one stage above the individuals' established levels—or by observing whether a child's parents essentially do this when discussing moral conflicts. This approach applies the concepts of equilibrium and conflict that Piaget used to explain cognitive development. By presenting arguments slightly beyond the children's level of moral reasoning, the researchers created a disequilibrium that motivated the children to restructure their moral thought. The upshot of studies using this approach is that virtually any plus-stage discussion, for any length of time, seems to promote more advanced moral reasoning (Walker, 1982).

Kohlberg emphasized that peer interaction and perspective taking are critical aspects of the social stimulation that challenges children to change their moral reasoning. Whereas adults characteristically impose rules and regulations on children, the give-and-take among peers gives children an opportunity to take the perspective of another person and to generate rules democratically. Kohlberg stressed that in principle, encounters with any peers can produce perspective-taking opportunities that may advance a child's moral reasoning. Comprehensive reviews of cross-cultural studies involving Kohlberg's theory and similar types of measures have revealed strong support for a link between perspective-taking skills and more advanced moral judgments (Gibbs, 2019).

Kohlberg's Critics Kohlberg's theory has provoked debate, research, and criticism (Gray & Graham, 2018; Hoover & others, 2018; Killen & Dahl, 2018; Narváez, 2018). Key criticisms involve the significance of concern for others, the link between moral thought and moral behavior, whether moral reasoning is conscious/deliberative or unconscious/automatic, the role of emotion, the importance of culture and the family in moral development, and domain theory.

Gender and the Care Perspective The most publicized criticism of Kohlberg's theory has come from Carol Gilligan (1982, 1992, 1996), who has argued that Kohlberg's theory reflects a gender bias. According to Gilligan, Kohlberg's theory is based on a male norm that puts abstract principles above relationships and concern for others and sees the individual as standing alone and independently making moral decisions. It puts justice at the heart of morality. In contrast to Kohlberg's **justice perspective,** which focuses on the rights of the individual, Gilligan argues for a **care perspective,** which is a moral perspective that views people in terms of their connectedness with others and emphasizes interpersonal communication, relationships with others, and concern for others. According to Gilligan, Kohlberg greatly underplayed the care perspective, perhaps because he was a man, because most of his research was with men rather than women, and because he used men's responses as a model for his theory.

In extensive interviews with girls from 6 to 18 years of age, Gilligan and her colleagues found that girls consistently interpret moral dilemmas in terms of human relationships and base these interpretations on watching and listening to other people (Gilligan, 1992; Gilligan & others, 2003). However, a meta-analysis (a statistical analysis that combines the results of many different studies) casts doubt on Gilligan's claim of substantial gender differences in moral judgment (Jaffee & Hyde, 2000). A review concluded that girls' moral orientations are "somewhat more likely to focus on care for others than on abstract principles of justice, but they can use both moral orientations when needed (as can boys . . .)" (Blakemore, Berenbaum, & Liben, 2009, p. 132).

Moral Thought and Moral Behavior Kohlberg's theory has been criticized for placing too much emphasis on moral thought and not enough emphasis on moral behavior. Moral reasons can sometimes be a shelter for immoral behavior. Corrupt CEOs and politicians endorse the loftiest of moral virtues in public before their own behavior is exposed. Whatever the latest public scandal, you will probably find that the culprits displayed virtuous thoughts but engaged in immoral behavior. No one wants a nation of cheaters and thieves who can reason at the postconventional level. The cheaters and thieves may know what is right yet still do what is wrong. Heinous actions can be cloaked in a mantle of moral virtue. Moral disengagement is the psychological process by which individuals separate themselves from the harmful effects of their actions (Bandura, 2015, 2016). By blaming victims, diffusing responsibility, and justifying their behavior as serving worthy causes, individuals sometimes feel good about themselves even when they are behaving immorally.

Conscious/Deliberative versus Unconscious/Automatic Social psychologist Jonathan Haidt (2013, 2017) argues that a major flaw in Kohlberg's theory is his view that moral thinking is deliberative and that individuals go around all the time contemplating and reasoning about morality. Haidt believes that moral thinking is more often an intuitive gut reaction, with deliberative moral reasoning serving as an after-the-fact justification. Thus, in his view, much of morality begins with rapid evaluative judgments of others rather than with strategic reasoning about moral circumstances (Graham & Valdesolo, 2017).

The Role of Emotion Kohlberg argued that emotion has negative effects on moral reasoning. However, increasing evidence indicates that emotions play an important role in moral thinking (Gui, Gan, & Liu, 2016; Schalkwijk & others, 2016). Researchers have found that individuals who have damage to a particular region in the brain's prefrontal cortex lose the ability to integrate emotions into their moral judgments (Damasio, 1994). Losing their intuitive feelings about what is right or wrong, they can't adequately decide which actions to take and have trouble making choices involving moral issues.

Research with healthy individuals also has shown that the moral decisions individuals make are linked to the intensity and activation of emotion in the same region of the prefrontal cortex mentioned and in the amygdala (Shenhav & Greene, 2014).

Culture and Moral Reasoning Kohlberg emphasized that his stages of moral reasoning are universal, but some critics claim his theory is culturally biased (Christen, Narváez, & Gutzwiller, 2017; Graham & Valdesolo, 2017; Gray & Graham, 2018). Both Kohlberg and his critics may be partially correct. One early review of 45 studies in 27 cultures around the world, mostly non-European, provided support for the universality of Kohlberg's first four stages (Gibbs, 2019). Individuals in diverse cultures developed through these four stages in sequence as Kohlberg predicted. More recent research revealed support for the qualitative shift from stage 2 to stage 3 across cultures (Gibbs & others, 2007). Stages 5 and 6, however, have not been found in all cultures (Gibbs & others, 2007; Snarey, 1987). Furthermore, critics assert that Kohlberg's scoring system does not recognize the higher-level moral reasoning of certain cultures and thus does not acknowledge that moral reasoning is more culture-specific than Kohlberg envisioned (Gibbs, 2019). For example, it appears that notions of morality in personal domains, such as lying to avoid taking credit for a good deed or lying to benefit a group versus an individual, vary across cultures, depending on the extent to which self-benefiting behavior is socially encouraged or discouraged (Helwig, 2017).

Darcia Narváez and Tracy Gleason (2013) have described cohort effects regarding moral reasoning. In recent years, postconventional moral reasoning has been declining in college students, not down to the next level (conventional) but to the lowest level (personal interests) (Thoma & Bebeau, 2008). Narváez and Gleason (2013) also argue that declines in prosocial

Carol Gilligan. *What is Gilligan's view of moral development?*
Dr. Carol Gilligan

behavior have occurred in recent years and that humans, especially those living in Western cultures, are "on a fast train to demise." They emphasize that the solution to improving people's moral lives lies in better child-rearing strategies and social supports for families and children. In more recent commentary, Narváez and her colleagues (Christen, Narváez, & Gutzwiller, 2017) stress that we need to make better progress in dealing with an increasing array of temptations and possible wrongdoings in a human social world in which complexity is accumulating over time.

In sum, although Kohlberg's approach does capture much of the moral reasoning voiced in various cultures around the world, his approach misses or misconstrues some important moral concepts in particular cultures (Gibbs, 2019; Miller & Bland, 2014).

Families and Moral Development   Kohlberg argued that family processes are essentially unimportant in children's moral development. As noted earlier, he argued that parent-child relationships usually provide children with little opportunity for give-and-take or perspective taking. Rather, Kohlberg said that such opportunities are more likely to be provided by children's peer relations.

Did Kohlberg underestimate the contribution of family relationships to moral development? A number of developmentalists emphasize that conversations between parents and children about situations and relationships involving moral issues are important for children's moral development (Carlo & others, 2018). In addition, parents' *inductive discipline,* which uses reasoning and focuses children's attention on the consequences of their actions for others, positively influences moral development (Grusec & Davidov, 2021). These developmentalists also stress that parents' moral values influence children's development of moral thoughts (Carlo & others, 2018; Eisenberg, Spinrad, & Knafo-Noam, 2015; Laible & Thompson, 2007). Nonetheless, most developmentalists agree with Kohlberg, and Piaget, that peers play an important role in the development of moral reasoning.

Domain Theory: Moral, Social Conventional, and Personal Reasoning   The **domain theory of moral development** states that there are different domains of social knowledge and reasoning, including moral, social conventional, and personal domains. In domain theory, children's and adolescents' moral, social conventional, and personal knowledge and reasoning emerge from their attempts to understand and deal with different forms of social experience (Jambon & Smetana, 2018; Killen & Dahl, 2018; Mulvey & others, 2016; Smetana, 2017; Turiel, 2015; Turiel & Gingo, 2017).

Some of the domain theorists and researchers argue that Kohlberg did not adequately distinguish between moral reasoning and social conventional reasoning. **Social conventional reasoning** focuses on conventional rules that have been established by social consensus in order to control behavior and maintain the social system. The rules themselves are arbitrary, such as raising your hand in class before speaking, not cutting in front of someone standing in line to buy movie tickets, and stopping at a stop sign when driving. There are sanctions if we violate these conventions, although they can be changed by consensus.

In contrast, moral reasoning focuses on ethical issues and rules of morality. Unlike conventional rules, moral rules are not arbitrary. They are obligatory, widely accepted, and somewhat impersonal (Killen & Dahl, 2018; Turiel & Gingo, 2017). Rules pertaining to lying, cheating, stealing, and physically harming another person are moral rules because violation of these rules affronts ethical standards that exist apart from social consensus and convention. Moral judgments involve concepts of justice, whereas social conventional judgments are concepts of social organization. Violating moral rules is usually more serious than violating conventional rules.

The social conventional approach is a serious challenge to Kohlberg's approach because Kohlberg argued that social conventions are a stop-over on the road to higher moral sophistication For social conventional reasoning advocates, social conventional reasoning is not lower than postconventional reasoning but rather something that needs to be disentangled from the moral thread (Dahl & Killen, 2018; Jambon & Smetana, 2018; Turiel & Gingo, 2017).

Recently, a distinction also has been made between moral and conventional issues, which are viewed as legitimately subject to adult social regulation, and personal issues, which are more likely subject to the child's or adolescent's independent decision making and personal discretion (Killen & Dahl, 2018; Turiel & Gingo, 2017). Personal issues include control over one's body, privacy, and choice of friends and activities. Thus, some actions belong to a *personal* domain, not governed by moral strictures or social norms. A study of 5- to 9-year-old

domain theory of moral development Theory that traces social knowledge and reasoning to moral, social conventional, and personal domains. These domains arise from children's and adolescents' attempts to understand and deal with different forms of social experience.

social conventional reasoning Focuses on conventional rules established by social consensus, as opposed to moral reasoning that stresses ethical issues.

American and Chinese children found that older children were more likely to say that judgments about personal issues were up to the child to decide (Smetana & others, 2014).

In domain theory, boundaries are developed regarding adult authority, which can produce parent-adolescent conflict. Adolescents have a large personal domain and most parents can live with that; however, parents have a larger moral domain than adolescents think is reasonable (Jambon & Smetana, 2018; Turiel & Gingo, 2017).

Prosocial Behavior   Children engage in both immoral antisocial acts such as lying and cheating and prosocial moral behavior such as showing empathy or acting altruistically (Carlo & others, 2018; Misch & Dunham, 2021; Spinrad, Eisenberg, & Valiente, 2019). Even during the preschool years children may care for others or comfort others in distress, but prosocial behavior occurs more often in adolescence than in childhood (Eisenberg & Spinrad, 2016).

William Damon (1988) once described how sharing develops. During their first years, when children share, it is usually not for reasons of empathy but for the fun of the social play ritual or out of imitation. Then, at about 4 years of age, a combination of empathic awareness and adult encouragement produces a sense of obligation on the part of the child to share with others. Most 4-year-olds are not selfless saints, however. Children believe they have an obligation to share but do not necessarily think they should be as generous to others as they are to themselves. By the age of 5, children's own sharing is closely aligned with their expectations regarding others' sharing (Paulus & Moore, 2014). An extensive body of research in many diverse cultures indicates fairly similar patterns of development in early childhood (Callaghan & Corbit, 2018).

Children's sharing comes to reflect a more complex sense of what is just and right during middle and late childhood. By the start of the elementary school years, children begin to express objective ideas about fairness, but children's notions of fairness depend on their cultural context. In one study, 4- to 11-year-old children in three different locations—Germany, a rural area in Kenya that primarily relies on gardening and livestock for food, and a rural foraging tribe in Namibia—were asked to "go fishing" by catching metal objects in a fish tank using a magnetic rod (Schäfer, Haun, & Tomasello, 2015). Each child was paired with another child who fished in an adjacent tank. In some cases, the children "caught" the same number of fish, but in other cases the experimenter rigged the outcome so one child caught three times as many fish as the other. In a third case, the children did not fish but were simply given an unequal number of objects from the tanks. Next, each pair of children was given the same number of sweets as their total catch and asked to divide the sweets between themselves without adult input. The German children divided the sweets in a way consistent with ideas of merit and distributive justice—if children "caught" three times as many fish, they received three times as many sweets. By contrast, the children from the two African groups largely ignored merit and divided the sweets equally, perhaps because they had been socialized from an early age to share equally as a way of maintaining harmony and balancing asymmetries.

In sum, moral development is a multifaceted, complex concept. Included in this complexity are thoughts, feelings, behaviors, personality, relationships, domains, and prosocial behavior.

How does children's sharing develop?
Creatas/Getty Images

GENDER

Gilligan's claim that Kohlberg's theory of moral development reflects gender bias reminds us of the pervasive influence of gender on development. Long before elementary school, boys and girls show preferences for different toys and activities. Preschool children display a gender identity and gender-typed behavior that reflects biological, cognitive, and social influences. Here we will examine gender stereotypes, gender similarities and differences, and gender-role classification.

Gender Stereotypes   Broad categories that reflect general impressions and beliefs about girls/women and boys/men reflect **gender stereotypes.** Gender stereotyping continues to change during middle and late childhood (Brannon, 2017; Foster-Hanson & Rhodes, 2023; Halim & others,

gender stereotypes General impressions and beliefs about girls/women and boys/men.

2016). Five-year-old boys and girls are equally likely to say that boys and girls are "really, really smart," but by the age of 6, girls are likely to say that more boys than girls are "really, really smart" and to avoid activities that are described as being for children who are "really, really smart" (Bian & others, 2017). In a review of 78 studies in which children in kindergarten through twelfth grade were asked to draw a scientist, children in more recent decades were more likely to draw female scientists than were children in earlier decades (D.I. Miller & others, 2018). However, even children in recent decades were more likely to draw male than female scientists, particularly at older ages, suggesting persistent stereotypes associating science with men. Analysis of 65 million words of language and text directed at children and adults shows that gender stereotypes remain pervasive (Charlesworth & others, 2021). In another study, 5-year-olds who were more engaged with Disney princess media and products showed more female gender stereotypical behavior one year later, even after statistically accounting for their earlier gender stereotypical behavior (Coyne & others 2016). To study children's ability to resist gender stereotypes, researchers told children about gender stereotype conforming groups (girls doing ballet, boys playing football) and gender stereotype nonconforming groups (girls playing football, boys doing ballet). Children believed it would be easier for girls than for boys to challenge gender stereotypes and that exclusion from the peer group was a possible consequence of challenging gender stereotypes, but they also believed themselves to be personally able to resist gender stereotypes (Mulvey & Killen, 2015). In subsequent research, this team found that children who preferred counterstereotype toys and playing with peers who had similar counterstereotyping preferences were also more inclusive and less stereotyped in their expectations of their peers (Sims & others, 2022).

Gender and Sex Similarities and Differences What is the reality behind gender stereotypes? Let's examine some of the differences between sex and gender groups, keeping the following information in mind:

- The differences are averages and do not apply to all girls/women or all boys/men.
- Even when gender differences occur, there often is considerable overlap between boys/men and girls/women.
- The majority of the research that has been conducted on sex and gender similarities and differences has assumed that participants are cisgender (i.e., that they have a gender identity that matches their assigned sex at birth).
- The differences may be due primarily to biological factors, sociocultural factors, or both.

First, we examine physical similarities and differences, and then we turn to cognitive and socioemotional similarities and differences.

Physical Development Females have about twice the body fat of males, most of it concentrated around breasts and hips. In males, fat is more likely to go to the abdomen. On average, males grow to be 10 percent taller than females. Other physical differences are less obvious. From conception on, females have a longer life expectancy than males, and females are less likely than males to develop physical or mental disorders. The risk of coronary disease is twice as high in males as in females.

Do sex differences matter when it comes to brain structure and function? Human brains are more alike than different, whether the brain belongs to a male or a female (Ruigrok & others, 2014). The most comprehensive meta-analysis of three decades of brain studies concluded that there was virtually no average difference between genders or sexes (Eliot & others, 2021). Still, the following differences have been identified:

- On average, not correcting for overall body size, female brains are approximately 10 percent smaller than male brains. However, differences in brain size are typically found during adulthood rather than childhood.
- Some specific regions of the brain are larger in males, whereas other specific regions of the brain are larger in females.
- Portions of the corpus callosum—the band of tissues through which the brain's two hemispheres communicate—may be larger in females than in males, although some studies have found this not to be the case (Shiino & others, 2017).
- The average gender differences in specific brain regions map onto gender differences in functions controlled by those regions. However, these effects do not always replicate, and they are usually very small differences (Eliot & others, 2021).

Although some differences in brain structure and function have been found, either many of these differences are small or research is inconsistent regarding the differences. Janet Shibley Hyde and her colleagues (2019) have concluded that in most instances it is more accurate to describe these variations as a mosaic rather than as male-typical and female-typical brains. Also, when sex differences in the brain have been detected, in many cases they have not been directly linked to psychological differences (Grabowska, 2020). In addition, similarities and differences in the brains of males and females may be due to biological or experiential factors (Hyde & others, 2019).

Cognitive and Socioemotional Development In the largest synthesis of research to date regarding gender differences and similarities in cognitive and socioemotional development, data from over 20,000 individual studies and 12 million participants were used to examine whether gender differences are found in a number of psychological domains (Zell, Krizan, & Teeter, 2015). Overall, when gender differences were found, 46 percent were characterized as being small and 39 percent as very small. Across all of the cognitive and socioemotional domains examined, 84 percent of the distributions of the variables overlapped between males and females. Gender differences were consistent across ages, generations, and cultural contexts.

Despite this overall pattern suggesting more gender similarities than differences, there were 10 areas that showed moderate to large differences between males and females (Zell, Krizan, & Teeter, 2015). Men scored higher than women in aggression, masculinity, spatial rotation ability, attention to physical attractiveness in mate selection, confidence in physical abilities, and performance in same-sex groups. Women scored higher than men in reactions to painful stimuli, fear, attachment to peers, and interest in people rather than things.

One area that emerged in the research synthesis as a domain with moderate to large differences between males and females is visuospatial skills, which include being able to rotate objects mentally and determine what they would look like when rotated. These types of skills are important in courses such as plane and solid geometry and geography. However, even when gender differences are found, most of the distribution of males' and females' visuospatial skills overlaps (Hyde, 2014) (see Figure 3).

Five areas of socioemotional development in which gender similarities and differences have been studied extensively are aggression, relationships, emotion, prosocial behavior, and school achievement.

One of the most consistent gender differences is that boys are more physically aggressive than girls are (Hyde, 2014). The difference occurs in all cultures and appears very early in children's development (Dayton & Malone, 2017). The physical aggression difference is especially pronounced when children are provoked. Both biological and environmental factors have been proposed to account for gender differences in aggression. Biological factors include heredity and hormones. Environmental factors include cultural expectations, adult and peer models, and social agents that reward aggression in boys and punish aggression in girls.

Although boys are consistently more physically aggressive than girls, might girls show at least as much verbal aggression, such as yelling, as boys do? When verbal aggression is examined, gender differences typically disappear (Björkqvist, 2018).

Recently, increased interest has been directed toward *relational, social, and indirect aggression,* which involves harming someone by manipulating a relationship (Brandes & others, 2021). Relational aggression includes behaviors such as trying to make others dislike a certain individual by spreading malicious rumors about the person (Chen & Cheng, 2020). Mixed findings have characterized research on whether girls show more relational aggression than boys, but one consistency in findings is that relational aggression comprises a greater percentage of girls' overall aggression than is the case for boys (Björkqvist, 2018; Casper, Card, & Barlow, 2020).

Gender differences occur in some aspects of emotion (Connolly & others, 2019). Women express emotion more than

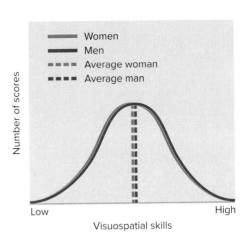

FIGURE 3

VISUOSPATIAL SKILLS OF MEN AND WOMEN. Notice that, although an average man's visuospatial skills are higher than an average woman's, scores almost entirely overlap. Not all men have better visuospatial skills than women—the overlap indicates that although the average man's score is higher, many women outperform men on such tasks.

What might be some explanations for why boys tend to be more physically aggressive than girls?
Fuse/Corbis/Getty Images

What are some contexts and activities that indicate girls are more "people oriented" than boys are?

Lucky Business/Shutterstock

How Would You...?

If you were a **psychologist,** how would you discuss gender similarities and differences with a parent or teacher who is concerned about a child's academic progress and social skills?

rapport talk The language of conversation and a way of establishing connections and negotiating relationships; more characteristic of girls/women than of boys/men.

report talk Talk that conveys information; more characteristic of boys/men than girls/women.

do men, are better at decoding emotion, smile more, cry more, and are happier (Chaplin, 2015). Men report experiencing and expressing more anger than do women (Kring, 2000). And one meta-analysis found that women are better than men at recognizing nonverbal displays of emotion (Thompson & Voyer, 2014). However, another meta-analysis found that overall gender differences in children's emotional expression were small, with girls showing more positive emotions (sympathy, for example) and more internalized emotions (sadness and anxiety, for example) (Chaplin & Aldao, 2013). In this analysis, the gender difference in positive emotions became more pronounced with age as girls more strongly expressed positive emotions than boys in middle and late childhood and in adolescence.

An important skill is to be able to regulate and control one's emotions and behavior (Gagne, Liew, & Nwadinobi, 2021). Boys usually develop self-regulation later and more slowly than girls do (van Tetering & others, 2020). This low self-control can translate into behavior problems.

Researchers have found that, on average, girls are more "people oriented" and boys are more "things oriented" (Hyde, 2014). In a research review, this conclusion was supported by findings that girls spend more time and energy building relationships, while boys spend more time alone, playing video games, and playing sports; that girls work at part-time jobs that are people-oriented such as waitressing and babysitting, while boys are more likely to take part-time jobs that involve manual labor and using tools; and girls are interested in careers that are more people-oriented, such as teaching and social work, while boys are more likely to be interested in object-oriented careers, such as mechanics and engineering (Perry & Pauletti, 2011). Evidence from research over the past decade suggests that these potential gender differences also are seen in various forms of social and other digital media (Ward & Grower, 2020).

Are there gender differences in communication in relationships? Sociolinguist Deborah Tannen (2013) distinguishes between rapport talk and report talk:

- **Rapport talk** is the language of conversation and a way of establishing connections and negotiating relationships. On average, girls enjoy rapport talk and conversation that is relationship-oriented more than boys do.
- **Report talk** is talk that gives information. Public speaking is an example of report talk. On average, boys are more likely to hold center stage through report talk with verbal performances such as storytelling, joking, and lecturing with information.

Note, however, that some researchers criticize Tannen's ideas as being overly simplified and suggest that communication between genders is far more complex than Tannen indicates (Palczewski, DeFrancisco, & McGeough, 2017). An analysis of recorded conversations between same-sex and mixed-sex pairs of undergraduates found several gender differences in self-disclosure and negotiation. For example, during negotiations, women were more likely to use affiliative strategies such as making requests and indirect suggestions, whereas men were more likely to make direct suggestions; women were more likely to self-disclose and to respond with elaborations in response to others' self-disclosures, whereas men were more likely to make negative comments in response to others' disclosure. However, all of these differences were small.

Are there gender differences in prosocial behavior? Across childhood and adolescence, females engage in more prosocial behavior (Eisenberg & Spinrad, 2016). The biggest gender difference occurs for kind and considerate behavior, with a smaller difference in sharing. Prosocially reaching out to offer help and support to friends also is observed in girls and boys alike, but the emotional effects on the helper may show a small gender difference (Armstrong-Carter & others, 2020).

Are there gender differences in school contexts? There is strong evidence that girls outperform boys in reading and writing. Girls have consistently outperformed boys in reading and writing skills in the National Assessment of Educational Progress in fourth-, eighth-, and twelfth-grade assessments. For example, in the most recent report from this national assessment (2019), girls had higher reading achievement than boys in both fourth- and eighth-grade assessments, with girls 11 points higher (269) than boys (258) in the eighth grade. These differences may emerge early in schooling. In a study of preschool children, girls outperformed boys in attention, language, and early literacy skills (Brandlistuen & others, 2021).

Keep in mind that measures of achievement in school or scores on standardized tests may reflect many factors besides cognitive ability. For example, performance in school may in part reflect attempts to conform to gender roles or differences in motivation, self-regulation, or other socioemotional characteristics (Klug & others, 2016; Pang & Baumann, 2020; Wigfield & others, 2015).

There are longstanding concerns that schools and teachers have biases against both boys and girls (Denessen & others, 2020; Glock & Kleen, 2017). What evidence exists that the classroom setting is biased against boys? Here are some factors to consider (DeZolt & Hull, 2001):

- Compliance, following rules, and being neat and orderly are valued and reinforced in many classrooms. These are behaviors that usually characterize girls more than boys.
- A large majority of teachers are women, especially at the elementary school level. This trend may make it more difficult for boys than for girls to identify with their teachers and model their teachers' behavior. Men teachers perceive boys more positively and see them as being more educationally competent than do women teachers.
- Boys are more likely than girls to have a learning disability or ADHD, or to drop out of school.
- Boys are more likely than girls to be criticized by their teachers.
- School personnel tend to stereotype boys' behavior as problematic.

What are some possible gender biases in the classroom?

Neustockimages/Vetta/Getty Images

What evidence is there that the classroom setting is biased against girls? Consider the following examples (Sadker, Zittleman, & Koch, 2019):

- In a typical classroom, girls are more compliant and boys are more rambunctious. Boys demand more attention, and girls are more likely to quietly wait their turn. Teachers are more likely to scold and reprimand boys, as well as send boys to school authorities for disciplinary action. Educators worry that girls' tendency to be compliant and quiet comes at a cost: diminished assertiveness and not receiving attention they may need.
- In many classrooms, teachers spend more time watching and interacting with boys, whereas girls work and play quietly on their own. Most teachers don't intentionally favor boys by spending more time with them, yet somehow the classroom frequently ends up with this type of gendered profile (Bassi & others, 2018).
- Boys get more instruction than girls and more help when they have trouble with a question. Teachers often give boys more time to answer a question, more hints at the correct answer, and further tries if they give the wrong answer.
- Boys are more likely than girls to get lower grades and to be grade repeaters, yet girls are less likely to believe that they will be successful in college work (Terrier, 2020).

Thus, there is evidence of gender bias against boys and girls in schools. Many school personnel are not aware of their gender-biased attitudes. These attitudes are deeply entrenched in and supported by the general culture. Increasing awareness of gender bias in schools is clearly an important strategy in reducing such bias (Wang, Rubie-Davies, & Meissel, 2018).

Might single-sex education be better for children than coeducational schooling? The argument for single-sex education is that it reduces in-school exposure to gender biases and stereotypes and sexual harassment. Single-sex public education has increased dramatically in recent years. In 2002, only 12 public schools in the U.S. provided single-sex education; by the 2014–2015 school year, there were 170 public schools for boys and 113 for girls, with 21,000 girls and 17,000 boys enrolled (Mitchell & others, 2017). This trend has accelerated, as more school districts have policies permitting school choice and charter school attendance in single-sex schools (Herr, Grant, & Price, 2020). Also, some schools offer single-sex classrooms as an option in some grades.

What are some recent changes in single-sex education in the United States? What does research say about whether single-sex education is beneficial?

J.B. Forbes/St. Louis Post-Dispatch/Newscom

developmental **connection**

Community and Culture

Bronfenbrenner's ecological theory emphasizes the importance of contexts; in his theory, the macrosystem includes cultural beliefs and values. Connect to "Introduction."

In China, women and men are usually socialized to behave, feel, and think differently. The old patriarchal traditions of male dominance have not been completely changed. Chinese women still make considerably less money than Chinese men do, and, in rural China (such as here in the Lixian Village of Sichuan), male dominance still governs many women's lives.

Diego Azubel/EPA/Newscom

Despite the increase in single-sex education, a review of 184 studies that included 1.6 million students from 21 countries concluded that the highest-quality studies showed that same-sex education did not provide benefits over mixed-sex education (Pahlke & others, 2014). In another review, Diane Halpern and her colleagues (Halpern, Beninger, & Straight, 2011) concluded that same-sex education is misguided, misconstrued, and unsupported by valid scientific evidence. They emphasize that among the many arguments against same-sex education, the strongest is its reduction of opportunities for boys and girls to work together in a supervised, purposeful environment. This view has been supported in more recent reviews of the research, yet the idea that same-sex education is effective against reducing gendered biases continues to be debated (Herr, Grant, & Price, 2020).

Gender in Context The nature and extent of gender differences may depend on the context (Leaper, 2015; Liben, 2017). The importance of considering gender in context is nowhere more apparent than when we examine what is culturally prescribed behavior for girls and boys in different countries around the world (Chuang & Tamis-Lemonda, 2009). Although there has been greater acceptance of androgyny and similarities in boys' and girls' behavior in the United States, in many countries gender roles have remained gender-specific (UNICEF, 2018a). For example, in many Middle Eastern countries, the division of labor between males and females is dramatic. Males are socialized and schooled to work in the public sphere, females in the private world of home and child rearing. For example, in a number of Middle Eastern countries, the dominant view is that the man's duty is to provide for his family and the woman's is to care for her family and household. China and India also have been male-dominant cultures. Although women have made some strides in China and India, especially in urban areas, the male role is still dominant.

In a study of eighth-grade students in 36 countries, in every country girls had more egalitarian attitudes about gender roles than boys did (Dotti Sani & Quaranta, 2017). In this study, girls had more egalitarian gender attitudes in countries with higher levels of societal gender equality. In another recent study of 15- to 19-year-olds in the country of Qatar, males had more negative views of gender equality than females did (Al-Ghanim & Badahdah, 2017).

Gender identity encompasses children's understanding of themselves in terms of cultural construals of what it means to be a boy or a girl. Gender identity becomes more salient during adolescence but has precursors in childhood. Some of the most important issues in the study of gender identity involve understanding children who identify with the gender associated with their sex assigned at birth (cisgender children) and those who identify with gender that is different from their sex assigned at birth (transgender children). Prevalence rates are difficult to obtain accurately because of barriers to disclosure, but estimates are that approximately 0.5 to 0.7 percent of youth ages 10 to 17 years identify as transgender (Herman & others, 2017; Potter & others, 2021).

In studies of socially transitioned transgender children (i.e., children who refer to themselves using pronouns of the gender with which they identify rather than the sex assigned to them at birth but with no hormonal or surgical interventions involved), children report that by the age of 3 years, they identified with their current gender (Olson & Gülgöz, 2018). In a study of 5- to 12-year-old transgender children, researchers found the participants had cognitive patterns more consistent with their expressed gender than their sex assigned at birth (Olson, Key, & Eaton, 2015). In terms of expressed preferences related to clothes, toys, and other gender-stereotypical items and activities, transgender children were indistinguishable from cisgender children who had the same gender identity. Transgender children and their siblings are less likely than unrelated children to endorse gender stereotypes and more likely to befriend peers who are transgender or binary gender nonconforming (Olson & Enright, 2018). Prejudice, discrimination, bullying, family rejection, and lack of self-acceptance are all concerns for transgender children (Sherman & others, 2020). Family support is especially important for transgender children's mental health. Socially transitioned transgender children have been found to have markedly lower levels of anxiety and depression than children with gender dysphoria who continue to live as the gender tied to the sex they were assigned at birth (Olson & others, 2016).

Review Connect Reflect

 LG1 Discuss emotional and personality development in middle and late childhood.

Review

- What changes take place in the self during middle and late childhood?
- How does emotion change during middle and late childhood?
- What is Kohlberg's theory of moral development, and how has it been criticized? How does prosocial behavior develop?

Connect

- What are gender stereotypes, and what are some important gender differences?
- How is the concept of joint attention similar to or different from the concept of perspective taking you learned about in this section?

Reflect *Your Own Personal Journey of Life*

- A young man who had been sentenced to serve 10 years for selling a small amount of marijuana walked away from a prison camp six months after he was sent there. Many years later, he is now in his fifties and has been a model citizen. Should he be sent back to prison? Why or why not? At which Kohlberg stage should your response be placed? Do you think the stage at which you placed your response accurately captures the level of your moral thinking? Explain.

---

2 What Are Some Changes in Parenting and Families in Middle and Late Childhood?

LG2 Describe changes in parenting and families in middle and late childhood.

| Developmental Changes in Parent-Child Relationships | Parents as Managers | Family Structure |

Our discussion of parenting and families in this section focuses on how parent-child interactions typically change in middle and late childhood, the importance of parents being effective managers of children's lives, and how elementary school children are affected by living in different family structures.

DEVELOPMENTAL CHANGES IN PARENT-CHILD RELATIONSHIPS

As children move into the middle and late childhood years, parents spend considerably less time with them (Grusec, 2017). In one study, parents spent less than half as much time with their children aged 5 to 12 in caregiving, instruction, reading, talking, and playing than they did when the children were younger (Del Giudice, 2014). Although parents spend less time with their children in middle and late childhood than in early childhood, parents continue to be extremely important in their children's lives. In an analysis of the contributions of parents in middle and late childhood, the following conclusion was reached: "Parents serve as gatekeepers and provide scaffolding as children assume more responsibility for themselves and . . . regulate their own lives" (Huston & Ripke, 2006, p. 422).

Parents especially play an important role in supporting and stimulating children's academic achievement in middle and late childhood (Collins & Madsen, 2019). The value parents place on education can determine whether children do well in school. Parents not only influence children's in-school achievement, but they also make decisions about children's out-of-school activities. Whether children participate in sports, music, and other activities is heavily influenced by the extent to which parents sign up children for such activities or encourage their participation (Goshin & others, 2021).

What are some changes in the focus of parent-child relationships in middle and late childhood?
Sasi Ponchaisang/123RF

Parents' use of different discipline strategies also changes as children move from early to middle childhood. As children in elementary school become better able to understand complex reasoning, parents are more likely to appeal to children's self-esteem, make comments that are designed to increase the child's sense of guilt, emphasize that children are responsible for their own actions, and manipulate privileges to regulate children's behavior. Spanking is against the law in over 60 countries, but in countries where spanking is still legal, elementary school children tend to receive less physical discipline than they did as preschoolers.

During middle and late childhood, some control is transferred from parent to child. The process is gradual, and it produces coregulation rather than control by either the child or the parent alone. Parents continue to exercise general supervision and control, while children are allowed to engage in moment-to-moment self-regulation (Koehn & Kerns, 2017). The major shift to autonomy does not occur until early adolescence. For example, in a classic study in Chile, the Philippines, and the United States, expectations for autonomy increased with age (Darling, Cumsille, & Peña-Alampay, 2005). However, expectations that children need to obey their parents even if they disagree with them were stronger in the Philippines than in Chile or the United States. Variations in expectations about autonomy and control differ within the United States, too. For example, in another classic study, Chinese American parents scored higher than European American parents on a type of control known as *guan* or "training," which involves parents socializing children to behave in culturally appropriate ways (Chao, 1994).

PARENTS AS MANAGERS

Parents can play important roles as managers of children's opportunities, as monitors of their behavior, and as social initiators and arrangers (Rosenblum, Navon, & Meyer, 2021). Mothers are more likely than fathers to take a managerial role in parenting.

Researchers have found that family management practices are positively related to students' grades and self-responsibility, and negatively to school-related problems (Vernon-Feagans, Willoughby, & Garrett-Peters, 2016). Among the most important family management practices in this regard are maintaining a structured and organized family environment, such as establishing routines for homework, chores, meals, bedtime, and so on, and effectively monitoring the child's behavior. A research review of family functioning in Black American students' academic achievement found that when parents monitored their sons' academic achievement by ensuring that homework was completed, restricted time spent on nonproductive distractions (such as video games and TV), and participated in dialogue with teachers and school personnel, their sons' academic achievement benefited (Mandara, 2006). Likewise, research with Asian American families has found that one of the most important ways that Asian American parents demonstrate care for their children is by providing support for their children's education. For example, Chinese American mothers were more likely than European American mothers to say that they show warmth to their children by providing for children's daily routine needs (e.g., making favorite foods) and guiding their children's learning (e.g., providing educational opportunities) (Cheah & others, 2015). In sum, to help children and adolescents reach their full potential, a parent needs to be an effective manager—one who finds information, makes contacts, helps structure choices, and provides guidance. Parents who fulfill this important managerial role help children and adolescents to avoid pitfalls and to work their way through a myriad of choices and decisions (Beckmeyer & Russell, 2018).

FAMILY STRUCTURE

Children grow up in many different kinds of families. Because rates of cohabitation have increased and people are waiting until older ages before marrying, the proportion of children being born to unmarried parents has also increased. In the United States, 40 percent of children are now born to unmarried parents (Michas, 2023). Divorces occur at a much higher rate in remarriages than in first marriages (Mayol-García, Gurrentz, & Kreider, 2021). Of children whose parents are married, approximately half will experience their parents' divorce. In addition, about half of children whose parents divorce will have a stepparent within four years of the separation. Thus, children may be reared by a single mother, single father, two biological or adoptive parents, one biological parent and a stepparent, or other combinations of adults who may or may not be biologically related to the child. Family structure is not static. Children may experience changes in family structure as their parents enter and leave romantic partnerships.

Divorce can pose challenges for children's development. So too can living in a stepfamily.

Remarried parents face some unique tasks. The couple must define and strengthen their marriage and at the same time renegotiate the biological parent-child relationships and establish stepparent-stepchild and stepsibling relationships (Ganong & Coleman, 2017). The complex histories and multiple relationships make adjustment difficult in a stepfamily (Bean & others, 2021). A majority of stepfamily couples do not stay remarried. And some remarried individuals are more adult-focused, responding more to the concerns of their partner, while others are more child-focused, responding more to the concerns of the children (Ganong & others, 2022).

In some cases, the stepfamily may have been preceded by the death of a spouse. However, by far the largest number of stepfamilies are preceded by divorce rather than death, and remarriage following divorce happens more quickly than after the death of a spouse, especially for men (Watkins & Waldron, 2017). Three common types of stepfamily structure are (1) stepfather, (2) stepmother, and (3) blended or complex. In stepfather and stepmother families, the parent who had custody of the children and remarried then introduced a stepfather or stepmother into their children's lives. In a blended or complex stepfamily, both parents bring children from previous relationships to live in the newly formed stepfamily. Children may also be part of more than one stepfamily if both of their biological parents enter into relationships with different partners.

How does living in a stepfamily influence a child's development?
kali9/Getty Images

In E. Mavis Hetherington's (2006) classic longitudinal study, children and adolescents who had been in a simple stepfamily (stepfather or stepmother) for a number of years were adjusting better than they did in the early years of the remarried family and were functioning well in comparison with children and adolescents in conflicted nondivorced families and children and adolescents in complex (blended) stepfamilies. More than 75 percent of the adolescents in long-established simple stepfamilies described their relationships with their stepparents as "close" or "very close." Hetherington (2006) concluded that in long-established simple stepfamilies, adolescents seem to eventually benefit from the presence of a stepparent and the resources provided by the stepparent. The overall pattern of results from this classic study have been replicated in a large research literature over the two decades since Hetherington published these results (Saint-Jacques & others, 2018).

Although many studies compare the social, emotional, behavioral, and academic adjustment of children living in different family structures, relationship quality is often found to be a better predictor of children's adjustment than family structure per se. For example, changes in families that result in more parent-child conflict, poorer parent-child relationship quality, or more financial distress lead to an increase in children's emotional and behavioral problems, regardless of family structure (Murry & Lippold, 2018). Likewise, parenting stress was found to be a better predictor of child behavior problems than family type in a comparison of gay father, lesbian mother, and heterosexual parent families with adopted children in the U.K. (Golombok & others, 2014). Parenting practices that promote children's well-being appear to operate in similar ways in all family structures.

How Would You...?
If you were a **human development and family studies professional,** what advice would you offer to divorced parents about strategies to ease their children's adjustment to remarriage?

Review *Connect* Reflect

 LG2 Describe changes in parenting and families in middle and late childhood.

Review
- What changes characterize parent-child relationships in middle and late childhood?
- How can parents be effective managers of their children's lives?

Connect
- In this section, you learned about how living in a stepfamily can influence children's development. What have

you learned about how living in a divorced family can influence children's development?

Reflect *Your Own Personal Journey of Life*
- What was your relationship with your parents like when you were in elementary school? How do you think it influenced your development?

3 What Changes Characterize Peer Relationships in Middle and Late Childhood?

LG3 Identify changes in peer relationships in middle and late childhood.

Developmental Changes — Peer Status — Social Cognition — Bullying — Friends

Having positive relationships with peers is especially important in middle and late childhood (Nesi & others, 2017; Rubin & Barstead, 2018; Wentzel & Muenks, 2016; Wentzel & Ramani, 2016). Engaging in positive interactions with peers, resolving conflicts with peers in nonaggressive ways, and having quality friendships in middle and late childhood not only create positive outcomes at this time in children's lives but also are linked to more positive relationship outcomes in adolescence and adulthood (Huston & Ripke, 2006). For example, in one of the longest longitudinal studies conducted on the subject, being popular with peers and engaging in low levels of aggression at 8 years of age were related to higher levels of occupational status at 48 years of age (Huesmann & others, 2006). Another early illustrative study found that peer competence (a composite measure that included social contact with peers, popularity with peers, friendship, and social skills) in middle and late childhood was linked to having better relationships with co-workers in early adulthood (Collins & van Dulmen, 2006).

What are some statuses that children have with their peers?
Wavebreak Media Ltd/123RF

popular children Children who are frequently nominated as a best friend and are rarely disliked by their peers.

average children Children who receive an average number of both positive and negative nominations from peers.

neglected children Children who are infrequently nominated as a best friend but are not disliked by their peers.

rejected children Children who are infrequently nominated as a best friend and are actively disliked by their peers.

controversial children Children who are frequently nominated both as someone's best friend and as being disliked.

DEVELOPMENTAL CHANGES

As children enter the elementary school years, reciprocity becomes especially important in peer interchanges. Researchers estimate that the percentage of time spent in social interaction with peers increases from approximately 10 percent at 2 years of age to more than 30 percent in middle and late childhood (Rubin, Bukowski, & Parker, 2006). In one classic study, a typical day in elementary school included approximately 300 episodes with peers (Barker & Wright, 1951). As children move through middle and late childhood, the size of their peer group increases, and peer interaction is less closely supervised by adults (Rubin, Bukowski, & Parker, 2006). Until about 12 years of age, children's preference for same-sex peer groups increases (Corsaro, 2018).

PEER STATUS

Which children are likely to be popular with their peers and which ones tend to be disliked? Developmentalists address these and similar questions by examining *sociometric status,* a term that describes the extent to which children are liked or disliked by their peer group (van der Wilt & others, 2018). Sociometric status is typically assessed by asking children to rate how much they like or dislike each of their classmates. Or it may be assessed by asking children to nominate the children they like the most and those they like the least.

Developmentalists have distinguished five peer statuses (Cillessen & Bukowski, 2018):

- **Popular children** are frequently nominated as a best friend and are rarely disliked by their peers.

- **Average children** receive an average number of both positive and negative nominations from their peers.

- **Neglected children** are infrequently nominated as a best friend but are not disliked by their peers.

- **Rejected children** are infrequently nominated as someone's best friend and are actively disliked by their peers.

- **Controversial children** are frequently nominated both as someone's best friend and as being disliked.

Popular children have a number of social skills that contribute to their being well liked. They give out reinforcements, listen carefully, maintain open lines of communication with peers, are happy, control their negative emotions, act like themselves, show enthusiasm and concern for others, and are self-confident without being conceited (Rubin, Bukowski, & Bowker, 2015). These patterns have been observed in youth in schools in the United States, Canada, China, throughout Europe, and elsewhere (Rytioja, Lappalainen, & Savolainen, 2019; Zhang & others, 2018).

Researchers have distinguished between *sociometric popularity,* which is characterized by being well-liked by peers, and *perceived popularity,* which is measured by asking children which of their peers are "popular" or "unpopular." Perceived popularity is only moderately correlated with being well-liked, meaning that some children who are perceived by their peers as being popular are well-liked, but others are not (McDonald & Asher, 2018).

Neglected children engage in low rates of interaction with their peers and are often described as shy by peers. The goal of many training programs for neglected children is to help them attract attention from their peers in positive ways and to hold that attention by asking questions, by listening in a warm and friendly way, and by saying things about themselves that relate to the peers' interests. They also are taught to enter groups more effectively.

Rejected children often have more serious adjustment problems than those who are neglected (McDonald & Asher, 2018). One classic longitudinal study evaluated 112 boys over a period of seven years from fifth grade until the end of high school (Kupersmidt & Coie, 1990). The best predictor of whether rejected children would engage in delinquent behavior or drop out of school later during adolescence was aggression toward peers in elementary school. Another longitudinal study of boys and girls that followed them from kindergarten through the end of high school found that rejection and victimization from peers was a strong, consistent predictor of decreases in school engagement and academic achievement (Ladd, Ettekal, & Kochenderfer-Ladd, 2017).

John Coie (2004, pp. 252–253) described three reasons aggressive, peer-rejected boys have problems in social relationships:

- "First, the rejected, aggressive boys are more impulsive and have problems sustaining attention. As a result, they are more likely to be disruptive of ongoing activities in the classroom and in focused group play.
- Second, rejected, aggressive boys are more emotionally reactive. They are aroused to anger more easily and probably have more difficulty calming down once aroused. Because of this they are more prone to become angry at peers and attack them verbally and physically. . . .
- Third, rejected children have fewer social skills in making friends and maintaining positive relationships with peers."

Not all rejected children are aggressive (Rubin & others, 2018). Although aggression and its related characteristics of impulsiveness and disruptiveness underlie rejection about half the time, approximately 10 to 20 percent of rejected children are shy.

How can rejected children be trained to interact more effectively with their peers? Rejected children may be taught to more accurately assess whether the intentions of their peers are negative. They may be asked to engage in role playing or to discuss hypothetical situations involving negative encounters with peers, such as when a peer cuts into a line ahead of them. In some programs, children are shown videotapes of appropriate peer interaction and asked to draw lessons from what they have seen. Today, there are a variety of social skills training tools and interventions that can be implemented with individuals, small groups, or even whole schools (DiPerna & others, 2018).

SOCIAL COGNITION

A boy accidentally trips and knocks another boy's soft drink out of his hand. The second boy misconstrues the encounter as hostile, and his interpretation leads him to retaliate aggressively against the boy who tripped. Through repeated encounters of this kind, the aggressive boy's classmates come to perceive him as habitually acting in inappropriate ways.

This example demonstrates the importance of *social cognition*—thoughts about social matters, such as the aggressive boy's interpretation of an encounter as hostile and his classmates'

How Would You...?

If you were a **social worker,** how would you help a neglected child become more involved in peer activities?

How Would You...?

If you were a **psychologist**, how would you characterize differences in the social cognition of aggressive children compared with children who behave in less hostile ways?

perception of his behavior as inappropriate (Carpendale & Lewis, 2015; Vetter & others, 2013). Children's social cognition about their peers becomes increasingly important for understanding peer relationships in middle and late childhood. Of special interest are the ways in which children process information about peer relations and their social knowledge (Dodge 2011a, b; White & Kistner, 2011).

Kenneth Dodge (2011a, b) argues that children go through five steps in processing information about their social world. They decode social cues, interpret, generate possible responses, evaluate responses, and enact. Dodge has found that aggressive children are more likely to perceive another child's actions as hostile when the child's intention is ambiguous. And, when aggressive children search for cues to determine a peer's intention, they respond more rapidly, less efficiently, and less reflectively than do nonaggressive children. In a study of children in nine countries (China, Colombia, Italy, Jordan, Kenya, the Philippines, Sweden, Thailand, and the United States), children in all nine countries were more likely to report that they would react aggressively if they believed a peer acted with hostile intent than with benign intent, and children's hostile attribution biases predicted more child- and mother-reported aggression, even statistically accounting for children's prior aggression (Dodge & others, 2015).

Social knowledge also is involved in children's ability to get along with peers (Carpendale & Lewis, 2015). They need to know what goals to pursue in poorly defined or ambiguous situations, how to initiate and maintain a social bond, and what scripts to follow to get other children to be their friends. For example, as part of the script for getting friends, it helps to know that saying nice things, regardless of what the peer does or says, will make the peer like the child more.

BULLYING

Many studies have been conducted (primarily in North America and Europe, but also in Asia, Africa, and South America) showing that significant numbers of students are victimized by bullies (Chen & others, 2018). In the latest available data for a national sample of 6- to 17-year-olds in the United States (Lebrun-Harris & others, 2018), nearly one in four youth reported being a victim of bullying; in contrast, only one in 16 reported being a bully. Victimization was somewhat more common among children than among adolescents.

What characterizes bullying? Bullies often display anger and hostility, and in many cases are morally disengaged (Chen & others, 2018). A review of 154 studies found that characteristics of families and parenting, such as child abuse and neglect and witnessing domestic violence, increased the likelihood of children's bullying, whereas characteristics such as parental support and adaptive communication reduced the likelihood of children's bullying (Nocentini & others, 2019).

Who is likely to be bullied? A number of studies have indicated some general patterns (Salmivalli & others, 2021). Victimization is more common among boys, particularly during the early middle school years. Researchers also have found that anxious, socially withdrawn, and aggressive children are often the victims of bullying. Anxious and socially withdrawn children may be victimized because they are nonthreatening and unlikely to retaliate if bullied, whereas aggressive children may be the targets of bullying because their behavior is irritating to bullies (Rubin & others, 2018).

Overweight and obese children are often bullied (Puhl & King, 2013). A review of 18 studies of more than 56,000 students found that sexual minority youth were moderately more likely to be victimized at school than were heterosexual youth (Toomey & Russell, 2016). Having supportive friends was linked to a lower level of bullying and victimization (Kendrick, Jutengren, & Stattin, 2012).

Social contexts such as poverty, family, and peer contexts also influence bullying (Prinstein & Giletta, 2016; Salmivalli & Peets, 2021). Ethnic minority children living in poverty who had behavioral problems are more likely to become bullies, as are children whose mothers have suboptimal mental health (Shetgiri & others, 2012). Also in this study, children whose parents talked with them more and had met all or most of their friends, and who always or usually completed their homework, were less likely to become bullies. A meta-analysis indicated that positive parenting behavior (including having good communication and a warm relationship, being involved, and engaging in supervision of their children) was related to a lesser likelihood that a child would become either a bully or a victim at school (Lereya, Samara, & Wolke, 2013).

The social context of the peer group also plays an important role in bullying (Prinstein & Giletta, 2016; Troop-Gordon, 2017; Zych, Farrington, & Ttofi, 2018). Research indicates that 70 to 80 percent of victims and their bullies are in the same school classroom (Salmivalli & Peets, 2018). Classmates are often aware of bullying incidents and witness bullying. Peers who witness bullying sometimes are passive bystanders, but in other cases intervene to help the victim or join in with the bully (Jenkins & Nickerson, 2017; Salmivalli & others, 2021). In many cases, bullies torment victims to gain higher status in the peer group, and bullies need others to witness their power displays. Many bullies are not rejected by the peer group (Pouwels, Lansu, & Cillessen, 2018). In one study, bullies sometimes became friends with one another and influenced each other's bullying (Rambaran, Dijkstra, & Veenstra, 2020). In another study, collaborative behavior and liking one another occurs even between two aggressive youth who first meet each other, suggesting why some bullies affiliate with each other (Andrews & others, 2019).

Who is likely to be bullied? What are some outcomes of bullying?
Lopolo/Shutterstock

What are the outcomes of bullying? Researchers have found that children who are bullied are more likely to experience depression, engage in suicidal ideation, and attempt suicide than their counterparts who have not been the victims of bullying (Arseneault, 2017; Brunstein-Klomek & others, 2019). Peer victimization during the elementary school years is a leading indicator of internalizing problems (depression, for example) in adolescence (Schwartz & others, 2014). Also, a longitudinal study found that children who were bullied at 6 years of age were more likely to have excess weight gain when they were 12 to 13 years of age (Sutin & others, 2016). And three meta-analyses concluded that engaging in bullying during middle school is linked to an increased likelihood of antisocial and criminal behavior later in adolescence and adulthood (Kim & others, 2011; Losel & Bender, 2011; Ttofi & others, 2011). Further, bullying can have long-term effects, including difficulty in forming lasting relationships and getting along with co-workers (Wolke & Lereya, 2015).

Several meta-analyses of many studies have revealed a small but significant link between peer victimization and lower academic achievement (Nakamoto & Schwartz, 2010; Schoeler & others, 2018). A large study of more than 27,000 Australian adolescents revealed that victims had more health problems (such as headaches, dizziness, sleep problems, and anxiety) than their peers (Agostini, Lushington, & Dorrian, 2019). In addition, another study revealed that being a victim of bullying in childhood was linked to increased use of mental health services by the victims five decades later (Evans-Lacko & others, 2017).

Also, there is concern about peer bullying and harassment on the Internet (called *cyberbullying*) (Bauman & Bellmore, 2015; Zych, Farrington, & Ttofi, 2018). One longitudinal study found that adolescents experiencing social and emotional difficulties were more likely to be both cyberbullied and traditionally bullied than traditionally bullied only (Cross, Lester, & Barnes, 2015). In this study, adolescents targeted in both ways stayed away from school more than their counterparts who were traditionally bullied only. And another study revealed that adolescents who were bullied both in a direct way and through cyberbullying had more behavioral problems and lower self-esteem than adolescents who were only bullied in one of these two ways (Wolke, Lee, & Guy, 2017). Information about preventing cyberbullying and other types of bullying can be found at www.stopbullying.gov.

What leads some children to become bullies and others to fall victim to bullying? To read further about bullying, see the *Connecting with Research* interlude.

Extensive interest is being directed to preventing and treating bullying and victimization (Flannery & others, 2016; Gower, Cousin, & Borowsky, 2017; Hall, 2017; Menesini & Salmivalli, 2017; Muijs, 2017; Smith, 2019). School-based interventions vary greatly, ranging from involving the whole school in an antibullying campaign to providing individualized social skills training (Divecha & Brackett, 2019; Huang & others, 2019). An example of a teacher intervention in elementary and secondary schools sought to decrease bullying by focusing on increasing bullies' empathy and condemning their behavior. The intervention was effective in increasing the bullies' intent to stop being a bully (Garandeau & others, 2016). In contrast, blaming the bully had no effect.

One of the most promising bullying intervention programs has been created by Dan Olweus (2013). This program focuses on 6- to 15-year-olds, with the goal of decreasing opportunities and rewards for bullying. School staff are instructed in ways to improve peer relations and make schools safer. When properly implemented, the program reduces bullying by 30 to 70 percent (Olweus, Limber, & Breivik, 2019). Information on how to implement the program can be obtained from

What Are the Perspective Taking and Moral Motivation of Bullies, Bully-Victims, Victims, and Prosocial Children?

Key Points:

- Teacher and peer ratings were used to classify children as bullies, bully-victims, victims, or prosocial children.
- Bully-victims, but not bullies, were deficient in perspective taking.
- Bullies and bully-victims were deficient in moral motivation.

One illustrative study explored the roles that perspective taking and moral motivation play in the lives of bullies, bully-victims, victims, and prosocial children (Gasser & Keller, 2009), who are defined as follows:

- *Bullies* are highly aggressive toward other children but are not victims of bullying.
- *Bully-victims* are not only highly aggressive toward other children but also the recipients of other children's bullying.
- *Victims* are passive, nonaggressive respondents to bullying.
- *Prosocial children* engage in positive behaviors such as sharing, helping, comforting, and empathizing.

Teacher and peer ratings in 34 classrooms were used to classify 212 7- to 8-year-old boys and girls into the aforementioned four categories. On a 5-point scale (from never to several times a week), teachers rated (1) how often the child bullied others and (2) how often the child was bullied. The ratings focused on three types of bullying and being victimized: physical aggression, verbal aggression, and excluding others. On a 4-point scale (from not applicable to very clearly applicable), teachers also rated children's prosocial behavior on three items: "willingly shares with others," "comforts others if necessary," and "empathizes with others." Peer ratings assessed children's nominations of which children in the classroom acted as bullies, were victimized by bullies, and engaged in prosocial behavior. Combining the teacher and peer ratings after eliminating those that did not agree on which children were bullies, victims, or prosocial children, the final sample consisted of 49 bullies, 80 bully-victims, 33 victims, and 50 prosocial children.

Children's perspective-taking skills were assessed using theory of mind tasks, and moral motivation was examined by interviewing children about aspects of right and wrong in stories about children's transgressions. In one theory of mind task, children were tested to see whether they understood that people may have false beliefs about another individual. In another theory of mind task, children were assessed to determine whether they understood that people sometimes hide their emotions by showing an emotion different from what they really feel. A moral interview also was conducted in which children were told four moral transgression stories (with content about being unwilling to share with a classmate, stealing candy from a classmate, hiding a victim's shoes, and verbally bullying a victim) and then asked to judge whether the acts were right or wrong and how the participants in the stories likely felt.

The results of the study indicated that only bully-victims—but not bullies—were deficient in perspective taking. Further analysis revealed that both aggressive groups of children—bullies and bully-victims—had a deficiency in moral motivation. The analyses were consistent with a portrait of bullies as socially competent and knowledgeable in terms of perspective-taking skills and being able to effectively interact with peers. However, bullies use this social knowledge for their own manipulative purposes. The analysis also confirmed the picture of the bully as being morally insensitive. Subsequent research in multiple countries has made clear that moral disengagement plays a key role in victimizing others (Chen & others, 2018).

What possible solutions to the problem of bullying do these research results suggest? What else would you want to know about the relationship between bullies and their victims before you proposed possible remedies?

How Would You...?

If you were an **educator,** how would you design and implement a bullying-reduction program at your school?

the Center for the Prevention of Violence at the University of Colorado: www.colorado.edu/cspv/blueprints. Also, a research review concluded that interventions focused on the whole school, such as Olweus', are more effective than interventions involving classroom curricula or social skills training (Cantone & others, 2015). School counselors also play a crucial role in preventing and addressing bullying. Learn more about this in the *Connecting with Careers* feature.

FRIENDS

Like adult friendships, children's friendships are typically characterized by similarity (Laninga-Wijnen & others, 2019; Rubin, Bukowski, & Bowker, 2015). Throughout childhood, friends are more similar than dissimilar in terms of age, sex, gender, race, and many other factors (Prinstein & Giletta, 2016). Friends often have similar attitudes toward school, similar educational aspirations, and closely aligned achievement orientations, and the strength of these similarities grows across the transition into early adolescence (Veenstra & Laninga-Wijnen, 2022).

Yolanda Curry, High School Counselor

Graduating with a degree in journalism from the University of Missouri–Columbia, Yolanda Curry planned a career in communications. After a number of years and numerous jobs in video production and marketing, she found herself sitting in church one day, listening to the story of a young person in her community who had committed suicide. "It just really touched my heart. I just kind of said to myself that I wanted to do something to help other young people not go down that path, even if it was just one individual" (Hurwitz, 2021).

Curry started a service club at her child's school, hoping to encourage students to help others and, in her words, "change some perspectives." The principal suggested that Curry consider a career as a school counselor. She took a job as a paraprofessional educator, then completed her master's degree. Today she is a counselor at St. Charles West High School in St. Charles, Missouri.

Curry began counseling shortly before the onset of the COVID-19 pandemic. During her tenure, students have dealt with transitioning to and from virtual learning. Some have developed anxiety and depression that was not present before the pandemic or have seen their pre-existing problems at home magnified by the increased stress created by social distancing. One of Curry's strategies is what she calls a "one-minute check-in." She pulls a student aside and asks a few questions to find out how they're doing. "That has been helpful because there have been some kids that I never would have guessed are dealing with certain issues, like anxiety or maybe bullying," Curry said.

Although Curry's daily responsibilities range from dealing with behavioral issues to reviewing class schedules to helping with

High school counselor Yolanda Curry presents an award to an outstanding senior.
Wagner Portrait Group, Yolanda Curry and Awa Diallo

college applications, she says building relationships with students is her most important role. "Just taking a few minutes, to get to know students and just let them know that you care about them, that you're there for them, really does open them up to being able to receive from you later."

Why are children's friendships important? Willard Hartup (1983, 1996, 2009) has studied peer relations and friendship for more than four decades. He recently concluded that friends can provide cognitive and emotional resources from childhood through old age. Friends can foster self-esteem and a sense of well-being.

More specifically, children's friendships can serve six functions (Gottman & Parker, 1987):

- *Companionship.* Friendship provides children with a familiar partner and playmate, someone who is willing to spend time with them and join in collaborative activities.

- *Stimulation.* Friendship provides children with interesting information, excitement, and amusement.

- *Physical support.* Friendship provides resources and assistance.

- *Ego support.* Friendship provides the expectation of support, encouragement, and feedback, which helps children maintain an impression of themselves as competent, attractive, and worthwhile individuals.

- *Social comparison.* Friendship provides information about where the child stands vis-à-vis others and whether the child is doing okay.

- *Affection and intimacy.* Friendship provides children with a warm, close, trusting relationship with another individual. **Intimacy in friendships** is characterized by self-disclosure and the sharing of private thoughts.

What are some characteristics of children's friendships?
Kwame Zikomo/PureStock/Getty Images

intimacy in friendships Self-disclosure and the sharing of private thoughts.

Although having friends can be a developmental advantage, friendships are not all alike (Choukas-Bradley & Prinstein, 2016; Sørlie, Hagen, & Nordahl, 2021). People differ in the

developmental **connection**

Peers

Beginning in early adolescence, teenagers typically prefer to have a smaller number of friendships that are more intense and intimate. Connect to "Socioemotional Development in Adolescence."

company they keep—that is, who their friends are. Developmental advantages occur when children have friends who are socially skilled and supportive (Chow, Tan, & Buhrmester, 2015; Kindermann, 2016). However, it is disadvantageous to have coercive and conflict-ridden friendships (Normand & others, 2022; Schneider, 2016).

The importance of friendship has been demonstrated for children in most cultures, but the specific functions served by friends may differ across cultures (Chen, Lee, & Chen, 2018). For example, in individualistic countries, such as Canada and the United States, friends often offer compliments and make each other feel good about themselves. In collectivistic countries, such as China and Korea, friends are less likely to offer compliments that would focus on the individual rather than the group and instead are more likely to offer instrumental support, such as helping with homework (Zhu, 2021).

Review Connect Reflect

 Identify changes in peer relationships in middle and late childhood.

Review

- What developmental changes characterize peer relationships in middle and late childhood?
- How does children's peer status influence their development?
- How is social cognition involved in children's peer relationships?
- What is the nature of bullying?
- What are children's friendships like?

Connect

- Earlier in the chapter you read that most developmentalists agree that peers play an important role in the

development of moral reasoning. Of the five peer statuses that you read about in this section, in which group do you think children would have the least opportunity to find answers to their moral reasoning questions, and why would this be the case?

Reflect *Your Own Personal Journey of Life*

- Which of the five peer statuses characterized you as a child? Did your peer status change in adolescence? How do you think your peer status as a child influenced your development?

4 What Are Some Important Aspects of Schools?

LG4 Characterize contemporary approaches to student learning and sociocultural diversity in schools.

Contemporary Approaches to Student Learning

Socioeconomic Status, Race, and Ethnicity

For most children, entering the first grade signals new obligations. They form new relationships and develop new standards by which to judge themselves. School provides children with a rich source of new ideas to shape their sense of self. They will spend many years in schools as members of small societies in which there are tasks to be accomplished, people to socialize with and be socialized by, and rules that define and limit behavior, feelings, and attitudes. By the time students graduate from high school, they will have spent 12,000 hours in the classroom.

CONTEMPORARY APPROACHES TO STUDENT LEARNING

Controversy swirls about the best way to teach children because so many approaches exist (Kauchak & Eggen, 2021; Popham, 2020). There also is considerable interest in finding the best way to hold schools and teachers accountable for whether children are learning (Popham, 2017).

constructivist approach A learner-centered approach that emphasizes the importance of individuals actively constructing their knowledge and understanding with guidance from the teacher.

Constructivist and Direct Instruction Approaches The **constructivist approach** is learner centered and emphasizes the importance of individuals actively constructing their knowledge and understanding with guidance from the teacher. In the constructivist view, teachers should not attempt to simply pour information into children's minds. Rather, children should be encouraged to explore their world, discover knowledge, reflect, and think critically with careful monitoring and meaningful guidance from the teacher (Kauchak & Eggen, 2021). The constructivist belief is that for too long in American education children have been required to sit still, be passive learners, and rotely memorize irrelevant as well as relevant information. Today, constructivism may include an emphasis on collaboration—children working together in their efforts to know and understand (J.A. Johnson & others, 2018; Sadker, Zittleman, & Koch, 2022).

By contrast, the **direct instruction approach** is structured and teacher centered. It is characterized by teacher direction and control, high teacher expectations for students' progress, maximum time spent by students on academic tasks, and efforts by the teacher to keep negative emotional expression to a minimum. An important goal in the direct instruction approach is maximizing student learning time (Kauchak & Eggen, 2021; Webb & Metha, 2017).

Is this classroom more likely constructivist or direct instruction? Explain.
Elizabeth Crews

Advocates of the constructivist approach argue that the direct instruction approach turns children into passive learners and does not adequately challenge them to think in critical and creative ways (Sadker, Zittleman, & Koch, 2022). The direct instruction enthusiasts say that the constructivist approaches do not give enough attention to the content of a discipline, such as history or science. They also believe that the constructivist approaches are too relativistic and vague.

Some experts in educational psychology believe that many effective teachers use both a constructivist *and* a direct instruction approach rather than relying on either approach exclusively (J.A. Johnson & others, 2018; Parkay, 2020). Further, some circumstances may call more for a constructivist approach, others for a direct instruction approach. For example, experts increasingly recommend an explicit, intellectually engaging direct instruction approach when teaching students with a reading or a writing disability (Temple & others, 2018; Tompkins & Rodgers, 2020).

Accountability   Since the 1990s, the U.S. public and governments at every level have demanded increased accountability from schools. One result was the spread of state-mandated tests to measure what students had or had not learned (Chappuis, 2020). Many states identified objectives for students in their state and created tests to measure whether students were meeting those objectives. This approach became national policy in 2002 when the No Child Left Behind (NCLB) legislation was signed into law and continues in the 2015 Every Student Succeeds Act (ESSA), which scales back but does not eliminate standardized testing. ESSA is giving states much more flexibility in implementing the law than was the case for NCLB (Burnette, 2021).

Advocates argue that statewide standardized testing will have a number of positive effects. These include improved student performance; more time teaching the subjects that are tested; high expectations for all students; identification of poorly performing schools, teachers, and administrators; and improved confidence in schools as test scores rise.

What are some issues involved in the Every Student Succeeds legislation?
Ocean/Comstock Images/Corbis

Standardized tests can help educators identify students who are struggling as well as content areas in need of more instruction. For example, on the most recent national tests available in the United States (in 2019), only 35 percent of fourth-grade students and 34 percent of eighth-grade students were identified as proficient or better in reading, and 41 percent of fourth-grade students and 34 percent of eighth-grade students were identified as proficient or better in math (Irwin & others, 2021). These numbers represent an increase from previous years but still indicate gaps in knowledge.

Critics argue that standardized tests do more harm than good (Ladd, 2017; Sadker & Zittleman, 2016). One long-standing criticism stresses that using a single test as the sole indicator of students' progress and competence presents a very narrow view of students' skills (Lewis, 2007).

direct instruction approach A structured, teacher-centered approach that is characterized by teacher direction and control, mastery of academic skills, high expectations for students' progress, and maximum time spent on learning tasks.

This criticism is similar to the one leveled at IQ tests, which we described in "Cognitive Development in Middle and Late Childhood." To assess student progress and achievement, many psychologists and educators emphasize that a number of measures should be used, including tests, quizzes, projects, portfolios, classroom observations, and so on. Also, the standardized tests don't measure creativity, motivation, persistence, flexible thinking, or social skills (Stiggins, 2008). Critics point out that teachers end up spending far too much class time "teaching to the test" by drilling students and having them memorize isolated facts at the expense of teaching that focuses on thinking skills, which students need for success in life (Ladd, 2017). Also, some individuals are concerned that in the era of standardized tests, scant attention is paid to students who are gifted because so much energy is devoted to raising the achievement level of students who are not doing well (Ballou & Springer, 2017).

In addition to keeping schools accountable for student achievement, standardized tests often are used to compare how students in different countries perform relative to one another in math, science, and other subjects. For example, the Program for International Student Assessment (PISA) and Trends in International Math and Science Study (TIMSS) have been used to create country rankings of students' performance on benchmark tests at certain grade levels (Irwin & others, 2021). Fourth-grade students in the United States ranked 9th in science and 15th in math among 58 countries that participated in the 2019 TIMSS. Educational methods in countries that perform well on international tests have been adopted in other countries to try to improve learning and boost student achievement. For example, because Singapore consistently is at the top of the rankings in students' math and science scores, educators in some other countries have adopted content and instructional practices that incorporate the national math curriculum used in elementary schools in Singapore (Jaciw & others, 2016; Lindorff, Hall, & Sammons, 2019).

In 2009, the Common Core State Standards Initiative was endorsed by the National Governors Association in an effort to implement more rigorous state guidelines for educating students. The Common Core State Standards specify what students should know and the skills they should develop at each grade level in various content areas (Common Core State Standards Initiative, 2023). A large majority of states have agreed to implement the Standards, but they have generated considerable controversy. Critics argue that they are simply a further effort by the federal government to control education and that they emphasize a "one-size-fits-all" approach that pays little attention to individual variations in students. Supporters say that the Standards provide much-needed detailed guidelines and important milestones for students to achieve.

SOCIOECONOMIC STATUS, RACE, AND ETHNICITY

Children with less access to socioeconomic resources and who are among underrepresented racial and ethnic groups face more challenges in school than do their middle-socioeconomic-status, White counterparts (Koppleman, 2019; Nastasi & Naser, 2021). Why? Critics argue that schools have not done a good job of educating low-income or minoritized students to adequately address the many barriers to achievement (Banks, 2020). Let's further explore the roles of socioeconomic status and ethnicity in schools.

Educating Students in Low-Income Neighborhoods Many children living in poverty face problems that present barriers to their learning (Lampert & others, 2020). They might have parents who struggle with supporting their child's learning because they are burdened with securing basic resources, or who don't have enough money to pay for educational materials and experiences, such as books and trips to zoos and museums. One study revealed that children born into poverty had lower test scores at 3, 5, and 7 years of age and that children who lived in poverty continuously had cognitive development scores at age 7 that were nearly 20 percentile ranks lower than children who had never lived in poverty, even after statistically controlling for a wide variety of other factors that can affect children's cognitive development (Dickerson & Popli, 2016).

In the United States, the vast majority of children and adolescents attend neighborhood public schools, which are funded almost entirely by local school and property taxes. Thus, schools in lower-income areas often have fewer resources than schools in higher-income neighborhoods (Curtis & Bandy, 2016). In lower-income areas, schools are more likely to be staffed by young teachers with less experience than are schools in higher-income neighborhoods

(Gollnick & Chinn, 2021). As a result, many schools in lower-income neighborhoods struggle to provide students with environments that are conducive to effective learning (Hix-Small, 2020; Osher & others, 2020). Much of the focus has emphasized improving educational and economic outcomes for youth in schools in low-income areas. However, the students' social and emotional functioning also needs to be given attention (Crosnoe & Leventhal, 2014; Hoskins & Schweig, 2022).

Schools and school programs are the focus of some income and poverty program interventions (Dragoset & others, 2017). In an intervention with first-generation immigrant children attending high-poverty schools in Boston, Massachusetts, the City Connects program has been successful in improving children's math and reading achievement at the end of elementary school (Dearing & others, 2016). The program is directed by a full-time school counselor or social worker in each school. Annual reviews of children's needs are conducted during the first several months of the school year. Then site coordinators and teachers collaborate to develop a student support plan that might include an after-school program, tutoring, mentoring, or family counseling. For children identified as having intense needs (about 8 to 10 percent), a wider team of professionals becomes involved, possibly including school psychologists, principals, nurses, and/or community agency staff, to create additional supports. Follow-up analysis has shown that programs such as City Connects are cost effective, in addition to showing impacts on youth outcomes (Bowden & others, 2020). To read further about programs to assist low-income families and children, see the *Connecting with Diversity* interlude.

Race and Ethnicity in Schools   More than one-third of all Black and almost one-third of all Latino students attend schools in the 47 largest city school districts in the United States, compared with only 5 percent of all non-Latino White and 22 percent of all Asian American students. Many of these urban schools are still informally segregated, are grossly underfunded, and lack adequate resources to provide opportunities for children to learn effectively (Cushner, McClelland, & Safford, 2022; Garcia, 2020). Thus, the effects of SES and the race and ethnicities of students in schools are often intertwined (Banks, 2020; Umaña-Taylor & Douglass, 2017).

connecting with diversity

The New Hope Intervention Program

As we have just discussed, far too many schools in low-income neighborhoods struggle to provide environments that are conducive to effective learning.

Might intervention with low-income families and children improve children's school performance? In an illustrative and influential experimental study, Aletha Huston and her colleagues (Gupta, Thornton, & Huston, 2008) evaluated the effects of New Hope—a program designed to increase parental employment and increase family income—on adolescent development. They randomly assigned families with 6- to 10-year-old children living in low-income households to the New Hope program or to a control group. New Hope offered adults who were living in low-income households and were employed 30 or more hours a week benefits that were designed to increase family income (a wage supplement that ensured that net income increased as parents earned more) and to provide work supports through subsidized child care (for any child under age 13) and health insurance. Management services were provided to New Hope participants to assist them in job searches and other needs. The New Hope program was available to the experimental group families for three years (until the children were 9 to 13 years old).

Five years after the program began and two years after it had ended, the program's effects on the children were examined when they were 11 to 15 years old. Compared with adolescents in the control group, New Hope adolescents were more competent at reading, had better school performance, were less likely to be in special education classes, had more positive social skills, and were more likely to be in formal after-school arrangements. New Hope parents reported better psychological well-being and a greater sense of self-efficacy in managing their adolescents than control group parents did. In further assessment, the influence of the New Hope program on 9- to 19-year-olds after they left the program was evaluated (McLoyd & others, 2011). Positive outcomes especially occurred for Black boys, who became more optimistic about their future employment and career prospects after experiencing the New Hope program. Subsequent research across the whole country and many such programs has shown that with concerted effort and the use of interventions that have been shown to work, the United States can enact policies to improve the learning, health, and well-being of children by reducing poverty and its negative effects (Le Menestrel & Duncan, 2019).

Even outside large urban districts, school segregation remains a factor in U.S. education (Gollnick & Chinn, 2021). Almost one-third of all Black and Latino students attend schools in which 90 percent or more of the students are in minoritized groups (Banks, 2020).

The school experiences of students from different ethnic groups vary considerably (Koppelman, 2017). Black and Latino students are less likely than non-Latino White or Asian American students to be enrolled in academic, college preparatory programs and are over-represented in remedial and special education programs. Asian American students are more likely than students in other ethnic groups to take advanced math and science courses in high school. Black students are twice as likely as Latino, Native American, or White students to experience suspension from school.

The comparisons just described do not address the reasons for the educational dispari-ties. Many more students in underrepresented racial groups have grown up in poverty conditions, attended less well-funded schools, and experienced discrimination, bias, and prejudice (U.S. Department of Education, Office of Civil Rights, 2018). For example, in regard to Black American students being suspended from school more than students from other racial and ethnic groups, research shows that Black students are more likely to be given more severe punishment than non-Latino White students for the same behaviors (Jarvis & Okonofua, 2020).

Following are some effective strategies for improving relationships among students from diverse backgrounds:

How Would You...?

If you were an **educator** in a very diverse school, how would you strive toward providing effective learning experiences for all your students?

- *Turn the class into a jigsaw classroom.* When Elliot Aronson was a professor at the University of Texas at Austin, the school system contacted him for ideas on how to reduce the increasing racial tension in classrooms. Aronson (1986) developed the concept of a "jigsaw classroom," in which students from different cultural backgrounds are placed in a cooperative group in which they have to construct different parts of a project to reach a common goal. Aronson used the term *jigsaw* because he likened the technique to a group of students cooperating to put different pieces together to complete a jigsaw puzzle. How might this work? Team sports, drama productions, music performances, and academic projects are examples of contexts in which students participate cooperatively to reach a common goal.

- *Encourage students to have positive personal contact with diverse other students.* Mere contact does not do the job of improving relationships with diverse others. For example, busing students from minoritized groups to predominantly White schools, or vice versa, has not reduced prejudice or improved intergroup relations. What matters is what happens after children get to school. Especially beneficial in improving relations between diverse groups is sharing one's worries, successes, failures, coping strategies, interests, and other personal information with peers who have diverse backgrounds and experiences. When this happens, people tend to look at others as individuals rather than as members of a homogeneous "other" group.

In *The Shame of the Nation,* Jonathan Kozol (2005) criticized the inadequate quality and lack of resources in many U.S. schools, especially those in the poverty areas of inner cities that have high concentrations of ethnic minority children. Kozol praises teachers like Angela Lively (*above*), who keeps a box of shoes in her Indianapolis classroom for students in need.
Michael Conroy/AP Images

- *Reduce bias.* Teachers can reduce bias by displaying images of children from diverse racial, ethnic, and cultural groups, selecting play materials and classroom activities that encourage cultural understanding, helping students resist racism and stereotyping, and working with parents to reduce children's exposure to bias and prejudice at home. Exercises and activities that help students see others' perspectives can reduce bias as well. These help students "step into the shoes" of peers who are culturally different and to discover what it feels like to be treated in fair or unfair ways.

- *View the school and community as a team.* James Comer (2010) advocates a community-wide team-based approach as the best way to educate children. Three important aspects of the Comer School Development Project (SDP) are (1) a governance and management team that develops a comprehensive school plan, assessment strategy, and staff development plan; (2) a mental health or school support team; and (3) a parents' program. Comer believes that the entire school community should have a cooperative rather than an adversarial attitude. The SDP model is currently operating in more than 1,000 schools in 26 states, the District of Columbia, Trinidad and Tobago, South Africa, England, and Ireland.

- *Be a competent cultural mediator.* Teachers can play a powerful role as cultural mediators by being sensitive to biased content in materials and classroom interactions, learning more about different racial and ethnic groups, being aware of their own and children's stereotyping attitudes, viewing students of color positively, and getting diverse groups of parents and caregivers involved as partners with teachers in educating children (Cushner, McClelland, & Safford, 2022).

Dr. James P. Comer is, perhaps, best known for founding the School Development Program in 1968, which promotes the collaboration of parents, educators, and the surrounding community to improve social, emotional, and academic outcomes for children. Comer grew up in a low-income neighborhood in East Chicago, Indiana, and credits his parents with valuing the importance of education. He received a bachelor's degree from Indiana University, a medical degree from Howard University, a Master of Public Health degree from the University of Michigan, and psychiatry training from the Yale University School of Medicine's Child Study Center. He currently is the Maurice Falk professor of Child Psychiatry at the Yale University Child Study Center and Associate Dean for Student Affairs in the School of Medicine. During his years at Yale, Dr. Comer has concentrated on promoting a focus on child development as a way of improving schools.

James P. Comer, MD

Review **Connect** Reflect

 LG4 Characterize contemporary approaches to student learning and sociocultural diversity in schools.

Review

- What are two major contemporary issues in educating children?
- How do socioeconomic status, race, and ethnicity influence schooling?

Connect

- Earlier, you read about Carol Dweck's concept of mindset. How could the concept of mindset be applied to improving the education of elementary school children?

Reflect *Your Own Personal Journey of Life*

- How would you rate the quality of teachers in your elementary school? Were their expectations for achievement too high or too low? Describe the best elementary school teacher you had and the worst.

¡topical connections *looking **forward***

This chapter concludes the discussion of development in middle and late childhood. In "Physical Development in Adolescence" you will read about the dramatic changes of puberty, how the brain changes in adolescence, sexuality, and various aspects of adolescents' health. In "Cognitive Development in Adolescence" you will examine impressive advances in adolescents' thinking and the challenges of educating adolescents effectively. And in "Socioemotional Development in Adolescence" you will learn that adolescents spend far more time thinking about their identity—who they are, what they are all about, and where they are going in life—than they did when they were children. Transformations in relationships with parents and peers also characterize adolescence.

Socioemotional Development in Middle and Late Childhood

1 What Is the Nature of Emotional and (LG1) Personality Development in Middle and Late Childhood?

Discuss emotional and personality development in middle and late childhood.

The Self

- In middle and late childhood, self-understanding increasingly involves social and psychological characteristics, including social comparison. Children increase their perspective taking in middle and late childhood, and their social understanding shows increasing psychological sophistication as well.

- Self-concept refers to domain-specific evaluations of the self. Self-esteem refers to global evaluations of the self and is also referred to as self-worth or self-image. Self-esteem is only moderately related to school performance but is more strongly linked to initiative. Four ways to increase self-esteem are to (1) identify the causes of low self-esteem, (2) provide emotional support and social approval, (3) help children achieve, and (4) help children cope.

- Erikson's fourth stage of development, industry versus inferiority, characterizes the middle and late childhood years.

Emotional Development

- Developmental changes in emotion include increasing one's understanding of complex emotions such as pride and shame, detecting that more than one emotion can be experienced in a particular situation, taking into account the circumstances that led to an emotional reaction, improving the ability to suppress or conceal negative emotions, and using self-initiated strategies to redirect feelings.

- In middle and late childhood, attachment becomes more sophisticated as children's social worlds expand. As children get older, they use a greater variety of coping strategies and more cognitive strategies.

Moral Development

- Kohlberg argued that moral development consists of three levels—preconventional, conventional, and postconventional—and six stages (two at each level). Kohlberg maintained that these stages were age-related. Influences on movement through the stages include cognitive development, imitation and cognitive conflict, peer relationships, and perspective taking.

- Criticisms of Kohlberg's theory have been made, especially by Gilligan, who advocates a stronger care perspective. Other criticisms focus on the inadequacy of moral reasoning to predict moral behavior or to account for the intuitiveness of moral thought, the role of emotion, and cultural and family influences.

- The domain theory of moral development states that there are different domains of social knowledge and reasoning, including moral, social conventional, and personal.

- Prosocial behavior involves positive moral behaviors such as sharing. Most sharing in the first three years is not done for empathy, but at about 4 years of age empathy contributes to sharing. By the start of the elementary school years, children express objective ideas about fairness.

Gender

- Gender stereotypes are broad categories that reflect impressions and beliefs about girls/women and boys/men. A number of physical differences exist between males and females.

- Boys and girls are more similar than different on a wide range of measures of cognitive and socioemotional development.

- In terms of socioemotional differences, on average, boys are more physically aggressive than girls, while girls are more people oriented and boys are more "things" oriented.

- Gender bias exists in schools, and recent interest has been directed to single-sex schooling. It is important to think about gender in terms of context.

2 What Are Some Changes in Parenting and Families in Middle and Late Childhood?

 Describe changes in parenting and families in middle and late childhood.

Developmental Changes in Parent-Child Relationships

Parents as Managers

Family Structure

- Parents spend less time with children during middle and late childhood than they did in early childhood. Parents especially play an important role in supporting and stimulating children's academic achievement. Discipline changes, and control is more coregulatory.

- Parents have important roles as managers of children's opportunities, as monitors of their behavior, and as social initiators and arrangers. On average, mothers are more likely than fathers to function in these parental management roles.

- As in divorced families, children living in stepparent families have more adjustment problems than their counterparts in nondivorced families. However, a majority of children in stepfamilies do not have adjustment problems. Parent-child relationship quality is more important for children's adjustment than is family structure.

3 What Changes Characterize Peer Relationships in Middle and Late Childhood?

 Identify changes in peer relationships in middle and late childhood.

Developmental Changes

Peer Status

Social Cognition

Bullying

Friends

- Among the developmental changes in peer relations in middle and late childhood are increased preference for same-sex groups, increased time spent in peer interaction, expansion in the size of the peer group, and less supervision of the peer group by adults.

- Popular children are frequently nominated as best friends and are rarely disliked by their peers. Average children receive an average number of both positive and negative nominations from their peers. Neglected children are infrequently nominated as a best friend but are not disliked by their peers. Rejected children are infrequently nominated as a best friend and are actively disliked by their peers. Controversial children are frequently nominated both as best friends and as being disliked by peers. Rejected children are especially at risk for a number of problems.

- Social information-processing skills and social knowledge are two important dimensions of social cognition in peer relationships.

- Significant numbers of children are bullied, and this can result in short-term and long-term negative effects for both the victims and the bullies.

- Like adult friends, children who are friends tend to be similar to each other. Children's friendships serve six functions: companionship, stimulation, physical support, ego support, social comparison, and intimacy/affection.

4 What Are Some Important Aspects of Schools?

 Characterize contemporary approaches to student learning and sociocultural diversity in schools.

Contemporary Approaches to Student Learning

Socioeconomic Status, Race, and Ethnicity

- Contemporary approaches to student learning include the constructivist approach (a learner-centered approach) and the direct instruction approach (a teacher-centered approach).

- In the United States, standardized testing of elementary school students has been mandated by national legislation and has been controversial. Standardized tests are meant to boost student achievement by keeping schools accountable and identifying students who need additional help and topics that need to be taught more clearly.

- Children living in low-income families and neighborhoods face many barriers to learning at school as well as at home. The effects of SES, race, and ethnicity on schools are intertwined, as many U.S. schools are segregated and there is unequal access to effective learning environments based on the financial resources of the neighborhood schools being compared.

key **terms**

average children
care perspective
constructivist
    approach
controversial children
conventional reasoning
direct instruction approach
domain theory of moral
    development

gender stereotypes
heteronomous morality
individualism, instrumental
    purpose, and exchange
intimacy in friendships
justice perspective
mutual interpersonal
    expectations, relationships,
    and interpersonal conformity

neglected children
popular children
postconventional
    reasoning
preconventional
    reasoning
rapport talk
rejected children
report talk

self-concept
self-esteem
social contract or utility and
    individual rights
social conventional
    reasoning
social systems
    morality
universal ethical principles

key **people**

Elliot Aronson
John Coie
James Comer
William Damon

Kenneth Dodge
Erik Erikson
Carol Gilligan
Willard Hartup

E. Mavis Hetherington
Aletha Huston
Kathryn Kerns
Lawrence Kohlberg

Dan Olweus
Diane Ruble
Deborah Tannen

improving the **lives of children**

STRATEGIES

Guiding Children's Socioemotional Development

What are some good strategies for nourishing children's socioemotional skills?

- *Improve children's self-esteem.* This can be accomplished by identifying the causes of the child's low self-esteem, providing emotional support and social approval, and helping the child achieve.

- *Help children understand their emotions and cope with stress.* When children are experiencing considerable stress, try to remove at least one stressor from their lives. Also help the child learn effective coping strategies.

- *Nurture children's moral development.* Parents can improve their children's morality by being warm and supportive rather than punitive, using reasoning when disciplining, providing opportunities for children to learn about others' perspectives and feelings, involving children in family decision making, and modeling prosocial moral behavior.

- *Adapt to developmental changes in children.* Because parents typically spend less time with children in middle and late childhood, it is

important to strengthen children's self-control. As in early childhood, authoritative parenting tends to be more effective than authoritarian, neglectful, or indulgent parenting.

- *Improve children's peer and friendship skills.* Peer relationships and friendships become increasingly important to elementary school children. Adults can talk with children about the benefits of being nice, engaging in prosocial behavior, and providing support to peers and friends. Parents also can communicate to children that being aggressive, self-centered, and inconsiderate of others harms peer relationships and friendships.

- *Create schools that support children's socioemotional development.* Not only do good teachers know how to challenge and stimulate children's cognitive development, but they also know how to make children feel good about themselves. Too much of elementary school education involves negative feedback. We need more classrooms in which children are excited about learning. This learning should be designed to increase children's self-esteem, not threaten their emotional well-being. Parents need to encourage and support their children's educational accomplishments but not set unrealistic achievement expectations.

RESOURCES

The Dreamkeepers: Successful Teachers of African American Children (3rd ed.) (2022)
Gloria Ladson-Billings
New York: Jossey-Bass

An outstanding book by a leading expert that provides an in-depth exploration of Black American children, their teachers, and their families in many different contexts.

National Stepfamily Resource Center
www.stepfamilies.info

This Web site provides a clearinghouse and support network for stepparents, remarried parents, and their children.

Stop Bullying
www.stopbullying.gov/
Washington, DC

An excellent resource for learning more about identifying and preventing cyberbullying and other forms of bullying, and what to do if they happen.

In no order of things is adolescence the simple time of life.

—JEAN ERSKINE STEWART
American Writer, 20th Century

Adolescence

Adolescents try on one face after another, seeking to find a face of their own. Their generation of young people is the fragile cable by which the best and the worst of their parents' generation is transmitted to the present. In the end, there are only two lasting bequests parents can leave youth— one is roots, the other wings. Section 6 contains three chapters: "Physical Development in Adolescence," "Cognitive Development in Adolescence," and "Socioemotional Development in Adolescence."

chapter 14

Physical Development in Adolescence

chapter outline

Thirteen-year-old Robbie Blackwell has been forging birthday gifts for years, opting instead for donations to be given to the Hamilton County, Indiana, "Pets Healing Vets" program. Robbie's efforts have raised more than $30,000 for the program that pairs veterans with emotional support animals (Pointer, 2021).

"There are 35 animals paired through the program and each of those animals, the cost for care for them annually is thousands of dollars," says Jennifer Hatcher, senior outreach manager for the Humane Society for Hamilton County. "And so this is literally helping save so many lives at both ends of the leash."

Another teen, Joshua Nelson, graduated from high school in 2021 and was awarded a Presidential Scholarship from Southeast Missouri State University in Cape Girardeau, Missouri. Because the scholarship covered most of his college expenses, Joshua donated $1,000 of his personal college savings to establish the Joshua Nelson Leaders in Action Scholarship to benefit other students involved in his high school's Multicultural Achievement Council, a program that encourages historically underrepresented students to maximize their academic potential and become college and career ready. Joshua's benevolence attracted additional donations, which have helped the scholarship fund grow for future students who demonstrate leadership skills and abilities (CNN, 2021).

Negative stories about adolescents are often the ones we hear the most. But there are many adolescents like Robbie and Joshua who contribute in positive ways to their communities and competently make the transition through adolescence.

Darrell Montalvo-Luna (*left*) is awarded the "Joshua Nelson Leaders In Action Scholarship" by Joshua Nelson (*right*), who established the scholarship with his own savings.
Yolanda Curry

-topical connections *looking **back***

You have explored the physical, cognitive, and socioemotional development that characterizes children in the elementary school years. In regard to physical development, you learned that growth continues but at a slower pace than in infancy and early childhood. In middle and late childhood, gross motor skills become much smoother and more coordinated, and fine motor skills also improve. Significant advances in the development of the brain's prefrontal cortex also occur in middle and late childhood. In this chapter, you will study how the slower physical growth in middle and late childhood is replaced by the dramatic changes of puberty and continued transformations in the brain.

preview

Adolescence is an important juncture in the lives of many individuals, a time when many health habits—good or bad—are formed and ingrained. In this chapter, we explore what adolescence is, examine its physical and psychological changes, discuss adolescent sexuality, and then describe several adolescent problems and health issues.

1 What Is the Nature of Adolescence?

 LG1 Discuss views and developmental transitions that involve adolescence.

Positive and Negative Views of Adolescence

Developmental Transitions

As in development during childhood, a number of genetic, biological, environmental, and social factors interact in adolescent development. As children during their first decade of life, adolescents experienced thousands of hours of interactions with parents, peers, and teachers, but now in their second decade of life they face dramatic biological changes, new experiences, and new developmental tasks. Relationships with parents take a different form, moments with peers become more intimate, and dating occurs for the first time, as do sexual exploration and possibly intercourse. The adolescent's thoughts are more abstract and idealistic. Biological changes trigger a heightened interest in body image. Adolescence has both continuity and discontinuity with childhood.

POSITIVE AND NEGATIVE VIEWS OF ADOLESCENCE

There is a long history of worrying about how adolescents will turn out. In 1904, G. Stanley Hall proposed the "storm-and-stress" view that adolescence is a turbulent time charged with conflict and mood swings. However, when Daniel Offer and his colleagues (1988) conducted a landmark study of the self-images of adolescents in the United States, Australia, Bangladesh, Hungary, Israel, Italy, Japan, Taiwan, Turkey, and West Germany, at least 73 percent of the adolescents displayed a healthy self-image. Although there were differences among them, the adolescents were happy most of the time, they enjoyed life, they perceived themselves as able to exercise self-control, they valued work and school, and they expressed confidence about their sexual selves. In addition, they expressed positive feelings toward their families, and they felt they had the capability to cope with life's stresses—not exactly a storm-and-stress portrayal of adolescence.

However, in matters of taste and manners, the young people of every generation have seemed radical, unnerving, and different from adults—different in how they look, in how they behave, in the music they enjoy, in their hairstyles, and in the clothing they choose. It would be an enormous error, though, to perceive adolescents' enthusiasm for trying on new identities and enjoying moderate amounts of outrageous behavior as hostility toward parental and societal standards. "Acting out" and "boundary testing" are time-honored ways in which adolescents move toward accepting, rather than rejecting, parental values.

Social policy is the course of action designed by the national government to influence the welfare of its citizens. Currently, many researchers in adolescent development are designing studies that ideally will facilitate wise and effective social policy decision making (Rodriguez Vega & Yoshikawa, 2023).

Peter Benson and his colleagues (Benson, 2010; Benson & Scales, 2011; Scales, Benson, & Roehlkepartain, 2011) argued that the United States has a fragmented social policy for youth that too often has focused only on the negative developmental

Growing up has never been easy. However, adolescence is not best viewed as a time of rebellion, crisis, pathology, and deviance. A far more accurate vision of adolescence describes it as a time of evaluation, of decision making, of commitment, and of carving out a place in the world. Most of the problems of today's youth are not with the youth themselves. What adolescents need is access to a range of legitimate opportunities and to long-term support from adults who deeply care about them. *What might be some examples of such support and caring?*
Alistair Berg/Getty Images

developmental **connection**

Community

Service learning is linked to many positive outcomes for adolescents. Connect to "Cognitive Development in Adolescence."

deficits of adolescents, especially health-compromising behaviors such as drug use and delinquency, and not focused enough on positive strengths of teenagers. According to Benson and his colleagues (2004), taking a strength-based approach to social policy for youth, also referred to as *positive youth development (PYD),*

> adopts more of a wellness perspective, places particular emphasis on the existence of healthy conditions, and expands the concept of health to include the skills and competencies needed to succeed in employment, education, and life. It moves beyond the eradication of risk and deliberately argues for the promotion of well-being. (Benson & others, 2004, p. 783)

Research indicates that youth benefit enormously when they have caring adults in their lives in addition to parents or guardians (Scales, Roehlkepartain, & Houltberg, 2022). Caring adults—such as coaches, neighbors, teachers, mentors, and after-school leaders—can serve as role models, confidants, advocates, and resources. Relationships with caring adults are powerful when youth know they are respected, that they matter to the adult, and that the adult wants to be a resource in their lives.

Most adolescents negotiate the lengthy path to adult maturity successfully, but too many do not. Ethnic, cultural, gender, socioeconomic, age, and lifestyle factors influence the actual life trajectory of each adolescent (Cook & others, 2018; Velez & Spencer, 2018). Different portrayals of adolescence emerge, depending on the particular group of adolescents being described. Today's adolescents are exposed to a complex menu of lifestyle options through technology, and many face the temptations of drug use and sexual activity at ever younger ages. Too many adolescents are not provided with adequate opportunities and support to become competent adults (Noret, Hunter, & Rasmussen, 2020).

DEVELOPMENTAL TRANSITIONS

Developmental transitions are often important junctures in people's lives. Such transitions include moving from the prenatal period to birth and infancy, from infancy to early childhood, and from early childhood to middle and late childhood. For adolescents in every nation and culture, two important transitions are from childhood to adolescence and from adolescence to adulthood. Let's explore these transitions.

Childhood to Adolescence   The transition from childhood to adolescence involves a number of biological, cognitive, and socioemotional changes. Among the biological changes are the growth spurt, hormonal changes, and sexual maturation that come with puberty. In early adolescence, changes take place in the brain that allow for more advanced thinking. Also at this time, adolescents begin to stay up later at night and sleep later in the morning.

Among the cognitive changes that occur during the transition from childhood to adolescence are increases in abstract, idealistic, and logical thinking. As they make this transition, adolescents begin to think in more egocentric ways, often sensing that they are onstage, unique, and invulnerable. In response to these changes, parents place more responsibility for decision making on the young adolescents' shoulders.

Among the socioemotional changes adolescents undergo are a quest for independence, conflict with parents, and a desire to spend more time with peers. Conversations with friends become more intimate and include more self-disclosure. As children enter adolescence, they attend schools that are larger and more impersonal than their neighborhood grade schools. Achievement becomes a more serious business, and academic challenges increase. At this time, increased sexual maturation produces a much greater interest in romantic relationships. Young adolescents also experience greater mood swings than they did when they were children.

In sum, the transition from childhood to adolescence is complex and multidimensional, involving change in many different aspects of an individual's life. The complexities of these changes can have different consequences for different youth, and in different cultural contexts (Crockett & others, 2019). Negotiating this transition successfully requires considerable adaptation and thoughtful, sensitive support from caring adults.

Adolescence to Adulthood: Emerging Adulthood   Another important transition occurs from adolescence to adulthood (Arnett, Robinson, & Lachman, 2020). It has been said that adolescence begins in biology and ends in culture. That is, the transition from childhood to adolescence begins with the onset of pubertal maturation, whereas the transition from adolescence to adulthood is determined by cultural standards and experiences. Around the world, it is increasingly common to delay entry into adulthood because the information society in which we now live requires that youth obtain more education than their parents' generation received. Thus, the transition between adolescence and adulthood can be long, while adolescents develop more effective skills to become full members of society.

Today, the transition from adolescence to adulthood is referred to as emerging adulthood (Lowe & Arnett, 2019). The age range for **emerging adulthood** is approximately 18 to 25 years. Experimentation and exploration characterize the emerging adult. At this point in their development, many individuals are still exploring which career path they want to follow, what they want their identity to be, and which lifestyle they want to adopt (Parmenter & others, 2022). Emerging adulthood is now found in many cultures and countries (Kuang & others, 2023).

Jeffrey Arnett (2006) concluded that five key features characterize emerging adulthood:

- *Exploring identity, especially in love and work.* Emerging adulthood is the time during which key changes in identity take place for many individuals.

- *Experiencing instability.* Residential changes peak during early adulthood, a time during which there also is often instability in love, work, and education.

- *Being self-focused.* According to Arnett (2006, p. 10), emerging adults "are self-focused in the sense that they have little in the way of social obligations, little in the way of duties and commitments to others, which leaves them with a great deal of autonomy in running their own lives."

- *Feeling in-between.* Many emerging adults don't consider themselves adolescents or full-fledged adults.

- *Experiencing the age of possibilities, a time when individuals have an opportunity to transform their lives.* Arnett (2006) describes two ways in which emerging adulthood is the age of possibilities. First, many emerging adults are optimistic about their future.

What are some physical, cognitive, and socioemotional changes involved in the transition from childhood to adolescence? What characterizes emerging adulthood?

(*Top*): Bowdenimages/iStock/Getty Images; (*bottom*) Rawpixel.com/Shutterstock

Second, for emerging adults who have experienced difficult times while growing up, emerging adulthood presents an opportunity to steer their lives in a more positive direction.

One comprehensive review and analysis of research on resilience in the transition to adulthood concluded that the increased freedom that is available to emerging adults in Western society places a premium on the capacity to plan ahead, delay gratification, and make positive choices (Burt & Paysnick, 2012). Also emphasized in resilient adaptation during emerging adulthood was the importance of forming positive close relationships—to some degree with parents, but more often with supportive romantic partners, close friends, and mentors.

Joseph and Claudia Allen (2009) wrote a book titled *Escaping the Endless Adolescence: How We Can Help Our Teenagers Grow Up Before They Grow Old*, and opened the book with a chapter titled "Is Twenty-five the New Fifteen?" They argue that in recent decades adolescents have experienced a world that places more challenges on maturing into a competent adult. In their words (p. 17),

> Generations ago, fourteen-year-olds used to drive, seventeen-year-olds led armies, and even average teens contributed labor and income that helped keep their families afloat. While facing other problems, those teens displayed adultlike maturity far more quickly than today's, who are remarkably well kept, but cut off from most of the responsibility, challenge, and growth-producing feedback of the adult world. Parents of twenty-somethings used to lament, "They grow up so fast." But that seems to be replaced with, "Well, . . . Mary's living at home a bit while she sorts things out."

The Allens conclude that what is happening to the current generation of adolescents is that after adolescence, they are experiencing "more adolescence" instead of adequately being launched into the adult years. Even many adolescents who have gotten good grades and then

emerging adulthood Occurring from approximately 18 to 25 years of age, this transitional period between adolescence and adulthood is characterized by experimentation and exploration.

developmental **connection**

Families

Secure attachment to parents increases the likelihood that adolescents will be socially competent. Connect to "Socioemotional Development in Adolescence."

as emerging adults continued to achieve academic success in college later find themselves in their mid-twenties not knowing how to find a meaningful job, manage their finances, or live independently.

The Allens offer the following suggestions for helping adolescents become more mature on their way to adulthood:

- *Provide them with opportunities to be contributors.* Help them move away from being consumers by creating more effective work experiences (quality work apprenticeships, for example) or service learning opportunities that allow adolescents to make meaningful contributions.

- *Give candid, quality feedback to adolescents.* Don't just shower praise and material things on them, but let them see how the real world works. Don't protect them from criticism, constructive or negative. Protecting them in this way only leaves them ill-equipped to deal with the ups and downs of the real world of adulthood.

- *Create positive adult connections with adolescents.* Many adolescents deny that they need parental support or attachment to parents, but to help them develop maturity on the way to adulthood, they do. Exploring a wider social world than in childhood, adolescents need to be connected to parents and other adults in positive ways to be able to handle autonomy maturely.

- *Challenge adolescents to become more competent.* Adults need to do fewer things for adolescents that they can accomplish for themselves. Providing adolescents with opportunities to engage in tasks that are just beyond their current level of ability stretches their minds and helps them to make progress along the road to maturity.

Review Connect Reflect

LG1 Discuss views and developmental transitions that involve adolescence.

Review
- What are some positive and negative views of adolescence?
- What are two key developmental transitions involving adolescence?

Connect
- How could positive youth development (PYD) be incorporated into a nation's social policy?

Reflect *Your Own Personal Journey of Life*
- You likely experienced some instances of stereotyping as an adolescent. What are some examples of circumstances in which you feel that you were stereotyped as an adolescent?

2 What Are the Physical and Psychological Aspects of Puberty?

 LG2 Describe puberty's characteristics, developmental changes, psychological dimensions, and the development of the brain.

| Sexual Maturation, Height, and Weight | Hormonal Changes | Timing and Variations in Puberty | Psychological Dimensions of Puberty | The Brain |

One father remarked that the problem with his teenage son was not that he grew, but that he did not know when to stop growing. As we will see, there is considerable variation in the timing of the adolescent growth spurt. In addition to pubertal changes, other physical changes involve sexuality and brain development.

"Puberty" is not the same as "adolescence." For most of us, puberty ends long before adolescence does, although puberty is the most important marker of the beginning of adolescence. **Puberty** is a brain-neuroendocrine process occurring primarily in early adolescence that provides stimulation for the rapid physical changes that take place in this period of

puberty A brain-neuroendocrine process occurring primarily in early adolescence that provides stimulation for the rapid physical changes that accompany this period of development.

development (Dorn & Susman, 2019). Rather than a specific event, puberty is a process that unfolds through a series of coordinated neuroendocrine changes. Among the most noticeable changes are signs of sexual maturation and increases in height and weight.

SEXUAL MATURATION, HEIGHT, AND WEIGHT

Male pubertal characteristics typically develop in the following order: increase in penis and testicle size and onset of sperm production (sometimes called **spermarche**), appearance of straight pubic hair, minor voice change, first ejaculation (sometimes called *semenarche,* which usually occurs through masturbation or a wet dream), appearance of curly pubic hair, onset of maximum growth in height and weight, growth of hair in armpits, more detectable voice changes, and, finally, growth of facial hair.

What is the order of appearance of physical changes in females? First, either the breasts enlarge or pubic hair appears. Later, hair appears in the armpits. As these changes occur, the female grows in height, her hips widen, and her ovaries, labia, clitoris, vagina, and uterus grow. **Menarche**—a girl's first menstruation—typically arrives later in the pubertal transition. Initially, her menstrual cycles may be highly irregular. For the first several years, she may not ovulate every menstrual cycle; some girls do not ovulate at all until a year or two after menstruation begins. No voice changes comparable to those in pubertal males occur in pubertal females. By the end of puberty, the female's breasts have become fully formed.

Marked weight gains coincide with the onset of puberty. During early adolescence, girls tend to outweigh boys, but by about age 14 boys begin to surpass girls. Similarly, at the beginning of adolescence, girls tend to be as tall as or taller than boys of the same age, but by the beginning of the high school years most boys have matched or surpassed girls in height.

As indicated in Figure 1, the growth spurt (shown in the figure as the annual rate of height gain in inches per year) occurs approximately two years earlier for girls than for boys. The mean age at the beginning of the growth spurt in girls is 9; for boys, it is 11. The peak rate of pubertal change occurs at 11½ years for girls and 13½ years for boys. During their growth spurt, girls increase in height about 3½ inches per year, and for boys it is about 4 inches per year. Boys and girls who are shorter or taller than their peers before adolescence are likely to remain so during adolescence; however, as many as 30 percent of the variations in individuals' heights in late adolescence cannot be explained by earlier height differences in the elementary school years.

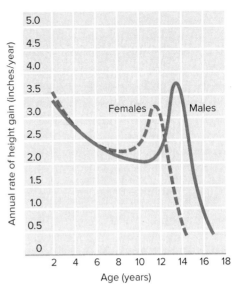

FIGURE 1

PUBERTAL GROWTH SPURT. This figure shows the average rate of height gain (in inches per year) from early childhood through the end of adolescence. On average, the peak of the growth spurt during puberty occurs two years earlier for girls (11½) than for boys (13½). *How are hormones related to the growth spurt and to the difference between the average height of adolescent boys and girls?*

HORMONAL CHANGES

Behind the first whisker in boys and the widening of hips in girls is a flood of **hormones,** powerful chemical substances secreted by the endocrine glands and carried through the body by the bloodstream (Frederiksen & others, 2020). The endocrine system's role in puberty involves the interaction of the hypothalamus, the pituitary gland, and the gonads (see Figure 2). The **hypothalamus** is a structure in the brain that is involved with eating and sex. The **pituitary gland** is an important endocrine gland that controls growth and regulates other glands; among these, the **gonads**—the testes in males, the ovaries in females—are particularly important in giving rise to pubertal changes in the body.

How do the gonads, or sex glands, work? The pituitary sends a signal via **gonadotropins**—hormones that stimulate the testes or ovaries—to the appropriate gland to manufacture hormones. These hormones give rise to such changes as the production of sperm in males and menstruation and the release of eggs from the ovaries in females. The pituitary gland, through interaction with the hypothalamus, detects when the optimal level of hormones is reached and responds and maintains it with additional gonadotropin secretion.

Not only does the pituitary gland release gonadotropins that stimulate the testes and ovaries, but through interaction with the hypothalamus the pituitary gland also secretes hormones that either directly lead to growth and skeletal maturation or produce growth effects through interaction with the thyroid gland, located at the base of the throat.

The concentrations of certain hormones increase dramatically during adolescence (Spaziani & others, 2021). **Testosterone** is a hormone associated in boys with genital maturation, an increase in height, and a change in voice. **Estradiol** is a type of estrogen; in girls it is

spermarche The beginning of sperm production in boys.

menarche A girl's first menstrual period.

hormones Powerful chemical substances secreted by the endocrine glands and carried through the body by the bloodstream.

hypothalamus A structure in the brain that monitors eating and sex.

pituitary gland An important endocrine gland that controls growth and regulates other glands.

gonads The sex glands—the testes in males, the ovaries in females.

gonadotropins Hormones that stimulate the testes or ovaries.

testosterone A hormone associated in boys with the development of the genitals, an increase in height, and a change in voice.

estradiol A hormone associated in girls with breast, uterine, and skeletal development.

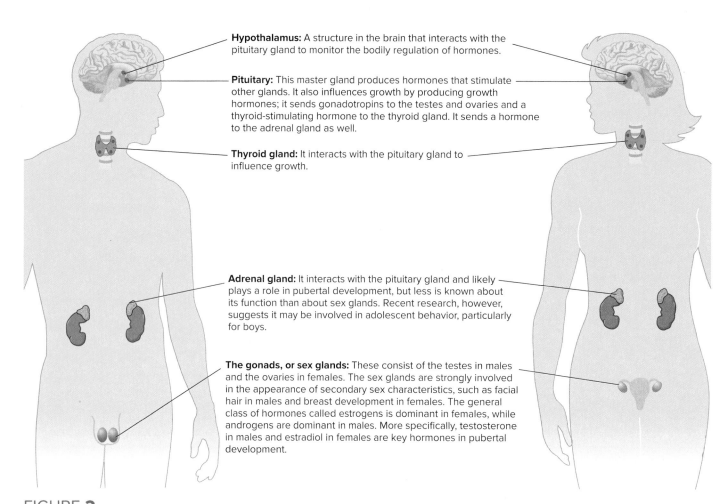

FIGURE **2**

THE MAJOR ENDOCRINE GLANDS INVOLVED IN PUBERTAL CHANGE

associated with breast, uterine, and skeletal development. In a foundational study, testosterone levels increased eighteenfold in boys but only twofold in girls during puberty; estradiol increased eightfold in girls but only twofold in boys (Nottelmann & others, 1987). Thus, both testosterone and estradiol are present in the hormonal makeup of both boys and girls, but testosterone dominates in male pubertal development and estradiol in female pubertal development (Bakhtiani & Geffner, 2022).

The same influx of hormones that grows hair on a male's chest and increases the fatty tissue in a female's breasts may also contribute to psychological development in adolescence (Andersen & others, 2022). However, a comprehensive research review concluded that there is insufficient research to confirm that the changes in testosterone levels during puberty are linked to mood and behavior in adolescent males (Duke, Balzer, & Steinbeck, 2014); to put it simply, hormonal effects by themselves do not account for adolescent development. For example, a number of studies have shown that social factors (for example, support or stress) influence many aspects of psychological and biological functioning and are much better predictors of adolescents' mental and behavioral health and problems than hormone levels (Susman, 2019). Behavior and moods also can affect hormones. Stress, eating patterns, exercise, sexual activity, tension, and depression can activate or suppress various aspects of the hormonal system (Joos & others, 2018). In sum, the hormone-behavior link is highly complex (Dorn & Susman, 2019).

TIMING AND VARIATIONS IN PUBERTY

In the United States—where children mature up to a year earlier than children in most other areas of the world—the average age of menarche has declined significantly since the mid-nineteenth century (Eckert-Lind & others, 2020). A research review of 30 studies in different countries around the world concluded that the age at which breast development began in girls (called thelarche) was earlier by almost three months per decade from 1977 to 2013 (Eckert-Lind & others, 2021). Fortunately, however, we are unlikely to see pubescent toddlers since what has happened in the past century is likely the result of improved nutrition and health.

For most boys, the pubertal sequence may begin as early as age 10 or as late as 13½ and may end as early as age 13 or as late as 17. Thus, the normal range is wide enough that, given two boys of the same chronological age, one might complete the pubertal sequence before the other one has begun it. For girls, menarche is considered within the normal range if it appears between the ages of 9 and 15.

Why do the changes of puberty occur when they do, and how can variations in their timing be explained? Puberty is not an environmental accident. Programmed into the genes of every human being is the timing for the emergence of puberty (Argente & others, 2023). Puberty does not take place at 2 or 3 years of age and it does not occur in the twenties. Scientists have been conducting molecular genetic studies in an attempt to identify specific genes that are linked to the onset and progression of puberty (Manotas & others, 2022).

However, puberty is not determined by genes alone. Nutrition, health, family stress, and other environmental factors also affect puberty's timing and makeup (Argente & others, 2023). For example, childhood obesity contributes to an earlier onset of puberty (Wang & others, 2023). Experiences that are linked to earlier pubertal onset also include an urban environment, low socioeconomic status, adoption, father absence, family conflict, maternal harshness, child maltreatment, and early substance use (Papadimitriou, 2016; Sun & others, 2017). In many cases, puberty comes months earlier in these situations, and this earlier onset of puberty is likely explained by high rates of conflict and stress in these social contexts. A foundational study of more than 15,000 girls in China revealed that girls living in an urban environment started puberty earlier than their counterparts who lived in a rural environment (Sun & others, 2012). Exposure to trauma, such as child sexual abuse, is also linked to earlier pubertal onset (Colich & McLaughlin, 2022).

PSYCHOLOGICAL DIMENSIONS OF PUBERTY

A host of psychological changes accompanies pubertal development. These changes involve body image and early and late maturation (Pfeifer & Allen, 2021).

Body Image   Preoccupation with body image is strong throughout adolescence, but it is especially acute during early adolescence, a time when adolescents are more dissatisfied with their bodies than in late adolescence (Miranda & others, 2021).

Gender differences characterize adolescents' perceptions of their bodies, and these gender differences are often exacerbated by heavy social media use (Harriger, Thompson, & Tiggemann, 2023). In general, throughout puberty girls are less happy with their bodies and have more negative body images than boys do (Cabaco & others, 2021). As pubertal change proceeds, girls often become more dissatisfied with their bodies, probably because their body fat increases. In contrast, boys become more satisfied as they move through puberty, probably because their muscle mass increases. However, when the entirety of adolescence is considered, adolescents' body images become more positive as they move through adolescence and into emerging adulthood (Gattario & Frisén, 2019).

Early and Late Maturation   Recall that some people enter puberty early, others late, and still others on time. Adolescents who mature earlier or later than their peers perceive themselves differently (Hoyt & others, 2020). In the groundbreaking Berkeley Longitudinal Study conducted decades ago, early-maturing boys perceived themselves more positively and had more successful peer relations than did their late-maturing counterparts (Jones, 1965). When the late-maturing boys were in their thirties, however, they had developed a stronger sense of identity than the early-maturing boys had (Peskin, 1967). This may have occurred because the late-maturing boys had more time to explore life's options, or because the early-maturing boys continued to focus on their advantageous physical status instead of on career development and achievement. Contemporary research on early maturation effects for boys is mixed with regard to negative and positive outcomes (Klopack & others, 2020).

How do early and late maturation influence adolescent development?
SDI Productions/Getty Images

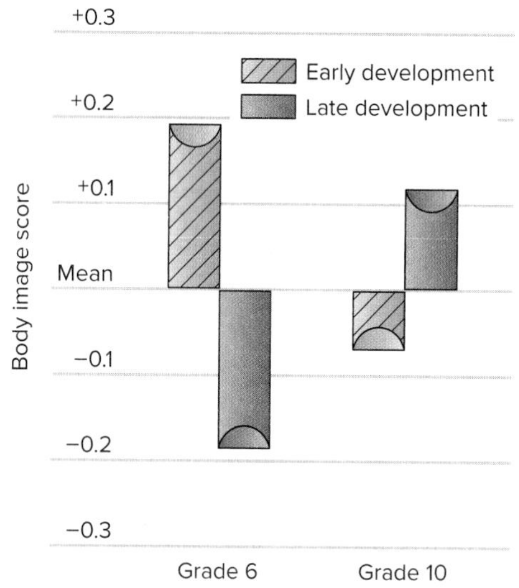

FIGURE **3**

EARLY- AND LATE-MATURING ADOLESCENT GIRLS' PERCEPTIONS OF BODY IMAGE IN EARLY AND LATE ADOLESCENCE. The sixth-grade girls in this classic study had positive body image scores if they were early maturers but negative body image scores if they were late maturers (Simmons & Blyth, 1987). Positive body image scores indicated satisfaction with their figures. By the tenth grade, however, it was the late maturers who had positive body image scores.

For girls, early and late maturation have been linked with body image. In the sixth grade, early-maturing girls show greater satisfaction with their figures than do late-maturing girls, but by the tenth grade late-maturing girls are more satisfied (Simmons & Blyth, 1987) (see Figure 3 for an illustration from a classic study). One possible reason for this developmental change is that in late adolescence early-maturing girls are shorter and stockier, whereas late-maturing girls are taller and thinner. Thus, late-maturing girls in late adolescence have bodies that more closely approximate the prevailing Western ideal of feminine beauty—tall and thin.

Many researchers have found that early maturation increases girls' vulnerability to a number of problems (Black & Rofey, 2018). Early-maturing girls are more likely to smoke, drink, be depressed, have an eating disorder, engage in delinquency, struggle for earlier independence from their parents, have older friends, start dating earlier, and have earlier sexual experiences (Chen, Rothman, & Jaffee, 2017). An eight-year longitudinal study in the United States found that early maturation predicted a stable higher level of depression for adolescent girls (Copeland & others, 2019). Longitudinal research also found that early-maturing girls are more likely to become pregnant and bear children as teenagers and are less likely to graduate from high school, which predicts depressive symptoms and antisocial behavior into adulthood (Mendle, Ryan, & McKone, 2019). Apparently as a result of their social and cognitive immaturity, combined with early physical development, early-maturing girls are more prone to problem behaviors, not recognizing the possible long-term effects on their development.

In the short term, early maturation often has more favorable outcomes for boys, especially in early adolescence. However, late-maturing boys may do better over the long term, especially in terms of identity and career development. Research increasingly has found that early-maturing girls are more vulnerable to a number of problems.

THE BRAIN

Along with the rest of the body, the brain is changing during adolescence. As advances in technology take place, significant strides will also likely be made in charting developmental changes in the adolescent brain (Modabbernia & others, 2021). What do we know now?

The dogma of the "unchanging brain" has been discarded and researchers are mainly focused on context-induced plasticity of the brain over time (Aoki, Romeo, & Smith, 2017). The development of the brain mainly changes in a bottom-up, top-down sequence, with sensory, appetitive (eating, drinking), sexual, sensation-seeking, and risk-taking brain linkages maturing first and higher-level brain linkages such as self-control, planning, and reasoning maturing later (Zelazo, 2013).

Using MRI brain scans, scientists have discovered that adolescents' brains undergo significant structural changes (Andrews, Ahmed, & Blakemore, 2021; Garcia-Tabuenca & others, 2021). The **corpus callosum,** where fibers connect the brain's left and right hemispheres, thickens in adolescence, and this change improves adolescents' ability to process information (Danielsen & others, 2020). We have discussed advances in the development of the *prefrontal cortex*—the highest level of the frontal lobes involved in reasoning, decision making, and self-control. However, the prefrontal cortex does not finish maturing until emerging adulthood—approximately 18 to 25 years of age—or later (Kolk & Rakic, 2022).

At a lower, subcortical level, the **limbic system,** which is the seat of emotions and where rewards are experienced, matures much earlier than the prefrontal cortex and is almost completely developed by early adolescence (Romeo, 2017). The limbic system structure that is especially involved in emotion is the **amygdala.** Figure 4 shows the locations of the prefrontal cortex, limbic system, amygdala, and corpus callosum.

With the onset of puberty, the levels of neurotransmitters change (Cohen & Casey, 2017; Monahan & others, 2016). For example, an increase in the neurotransmitter dopamine occurs in both the prefrontal cortex and the limbic system during adolescence (Dai & Scherf, 2019). Increases in dopamine have been linked to increased risk taking and the use of addictive drugs (Steinberg & others, 2018). Researchers have found that dopamine plays an important role in reward seeking during adolescence (Ladouceur & others, 2019).

Earlier, we described the increased focal activation that is linked to synaptic pruning in a specific region, such as the prefrontal cortex. In middle and late childhood, while there is increased focal activation within a specific brain region such as the prefrontal cortex, there also are only limited connections across distant brain regions. By the time individuals reach emerging adulthood, there are increased connections across brain areas (Lebel, Treit, &

corpus callosum The location where fibers connect the brain's left and right hemispheres.

limbic system A lower, subcortical system in the brain that is the seat of emotions and experience of rewards.

amygdala A part of the brain that is the seat of emotions.

Beaulieu, 2019). The evidence shows that increased connections (referred to as brain networks) are especially prevalent across more distant brain regions. Thus, as children develop, greater efficiency and focal activation occur in local areas of the brain, and simultaneously there is an increase in brain networks across different brain regions (Markant & Thomas, 2013).

Many of the changes in the adolescent brain that we have described involve the rapidly emerging fields of *cognitive developmental neuroscience* and *social developmental neuroscience,* which involve connections between development, the brain, and cognitive or socioemotional processes (Andrews, Ahmed, & Blakemore, 2021; Forbes & others, 2021). For example, consider leading researcher Charles Nelson's (2003) view that although adolescents are capable of very strong emotions, their prefrontal cortex has not adequately developed to the point at which they can control these passions. It is as if their brain does not have the brakes to slow down their emotions. Or consider this interpretation of the development of emotion and cognition in adolescents: "early activation of strong 'turbo-charged' feelings with a relatively unskilled set of 'driving skills' or cognitive abilities to modulate strong emotions and motivations" (Dahl, 2004, p. 18).

Of course, a major issue is which comes first, biological changes in the brain or experiences that stimulate these changes (Tooley & others, 2020). In a longitudinal study, 11- to 18-year-olds who lived in poverty conditions had diminished brain functioning at 25 years of age (Brody & others, 2017). However, the adolescents from poverty backgrounds whose families participated in a supportive parenting intervention did not show this diminished brain functioning in adulthood. Another illustrative study found that the prefrontal cortex thickened and more brain connections formed when adolescents resisted peer pressure (Paus & others, 2008). Scientists have yet to determine whether the brain changes come first or whether the brain changes are the result of experiences with peers, parents, and others (Webber & others, 2017). Once again, we encounter the question of how nature and nurture interact that is so prominent in examining development through the life span. Nonetheless, there is adequate evidence that environmental experiences make important contributions to the brain's development (Humphreys & others, 2019).

In closing this section on the development of the brain in adolescence, a further caution is in order. Much of the research on neuroscience and the development of the brain in adolescence is correlational, and thus causal statements need to be scrutinized.

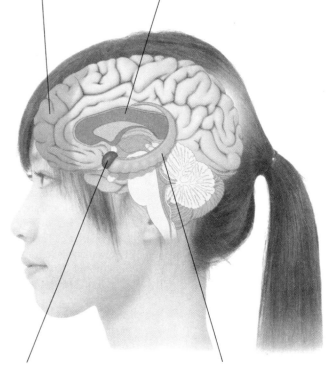

Prefrontal cortex
This "judgment" region reins in intense emotions but doesn't finish developing until at least emerging adulthood.

Corpus callosum
These nerve fibers connect the brain's two hemispheres; they thicken in adolescence to process information more effectively.

Amygdala
Limbic system structure especially involved in emotion.

Limbic system
A lower, subcortical system in the brain that is the seat of emotions and experience of rewards. This system is almost completely developed in early adolescence.

FIGURE 4

THE PREFRONTAL CORTEX, LIMBIC SYSTEM, AMYGDALA, AND CORPUS CALLOSUM
Takayuki/Shutterstock

Review Connect Reflect

 LG2 Describe puberty's characteristics, developmental changes, psychological dimensions, and the development of the brain.

Review

- What is puberty? What characterizes sexual maturation and the pubertal growth spurt?
- What are some hormonal changes in puberty?
- How has the timing of puberty changed, and what are some variations in puberty?
- What are some psychological dimensions of pubertal change?
- What developmental changes occur in the brain during adolescence?

Connect

- What developmental changes in the brain occur in middle and late childhood?

Reflect *Your Own Personal Journey of Life*

- Did you experience puberty early, late, or on time? How do you think the timing of your puberty influenced your development?

Developing a Sexual Identity	Timing and Trends in Adolescent Sexual Behavior	Sexual Risk Taking in Adolescence

Not only are adolescents characterized by substantial changes in physical growth and the development of the brain, but adolescence also is a bridge between the asexual child and the sexual adult (Diamond, 2023). Adolescence is a time of sexual exploration and experimentation, of sexual fantasies and realities, of incorporating sexuality into one's identity. Adolescents have an intense curiosity about sexuality. They are concerned about whether they are sexually attractive, how to do sex, and what the future holds for their sexual lives. Although most adolescents experience times of vulnerability and confusion, the majority will eventually develop a mature sexual identity.

Every society gives some attention to adolescent sexuality. In some societies, adults resolutely protect adolescent females from males by chaperoning them, while other societies promote very early marriage. Then there are societies that allow some sexual experimentation. These sociocultural variations transmit important information to adolescents about the sexual identity and behavioral norms that are deemed appropriate in that cultural context (Pulerwitz & others, 2019).

In the United States and most industrialized countries, the sexual culture is widely available to adolescents. In addition to any advice adolescents get from parents, they learn a great deal about sex from television, videos, magazines, the lyrics of popular music, and the Internet (Masterson & Messina, 2023). In some schools, sexting occurs frequently, as indicated in a study of 656 high school students at one school in which 15.8 percent of males and 13.6 percent of females reported sending and 40.5 percent of males and 30.6 percent of females reported receiving explicit sexual pictures on cell phones (Strassberg, Cann, & Velarde, 2017). And an illustrative study of Swedish adolescents found that in the context of unwanted sexual texts, adolescents reported having a range of emotional reactions and developing a range of responses, such as blocking particular peers or standing up for themselves in other ways (Lunde & Joleby, 2023).

DEVELOPING A SEXUAL IDENTITY

Mastering emerging sexual feelings and forming a sense of sexual identity are multifaceted and lengthy processes (Diamond, 2023). They involve learning to manage sexual feelings (such as sexual arousal and attraction), developing new forms of intimacy, and learning the skills to regulate sexual behavior to avoid undesirable consequences. Developing a sexual identity also involves more than just sexual behavior. Sexual identities emerge in the context of physical factors, social factors, and cultural factors, with most societies placing constraints on the sexual behavior of adolescents.

An adolescent's sexual identity involves activities, interests, styles of behavior, and an indication of sexual orientation (whether an individual has same-sex and/or other-sex attractions) (Kahn & Halpern, 2019). For example, some adolescents have a high anxiety level about sex, others a low level. Some adolescents are strongly aroused sexually, others less so. Some adolescents are very active sexually, others not at all. Some adolescents are sexually inactive in response to their strong religious upbringing; others go to religious services regularly, yet their religious training does not inhibit their sexual activity.

It is commonly believed that some youth quietly struggle with their sexual orientation in childhood, do not engage in heterosexual dating, and gradually recognize that they are LGBTQ in mid to late adolescence. Many youth do follow this developmental pathway, but others do not (Diamond, 2023). Many youth, not only those who eventually identify as LGBTQ, have diverse patterns of initial sexual attraction (Diamond, 2023).

The majority of sexual minority adolescents have competent and successful paths of development through adolescence and become healthy adults. However, in a large-scale study, sexual minority adolescents did engage in a higher prevalence of health-risk behaviors (greater drug use and sexual risk taking, for example) compared with heterosexual adolescents (Kann &

connecting with careers

Terrance Weeden, Pediatrician

"Queer Black youth don't get enough reminders of their beauty and potential. Let's remedy that," says Dr. Terrance Weeden, a pediatrician and an adolescent medicine fellow at the Ann & Robert H. Lurie Children's Hospital of Chicago, Illinois (Weeden, 2021). Weeden's clinical and research interests include LGBTQ+ health care and eradicating health and health-care disparities among youth in underserved communities. In an open letter to LGBTQ+ and Black youth, Weeden writes "to inspire and instill the confidence and boldness in you that I wish I had when I was younger."

A health-related career became an interest early on for Weeden after his father died of cancer when he was 3 years old. "I realized that I wanted to become a pediatrician during my ninth-grade biology class since it captured two of my passions—science and children" (Philadelphia College of Osteopathic Medicine, 2022).

Dr. Weeden received his bachelor's degree in biomedical sciences at Auburn University in Alabama. While at the Philadelphia College of Osteopathic Medicine in Suwanee, Georgia, he received his master's degree in biomedical sciences and his doctorate degree in osteopathic medicine. He completed his residency at the University of South Alabama Children's & Women's Hospital in Mobile, Alabama.

Pediatrician Terrance Weeden is addressing disparities in the health care of LGBTQ+ youth.
Terrance Weeden, DO

Weeden is a vocal advocate for the health-care rights of all youth. "I aspire to become a successful pediatrician who profoundly impacts the lives of my patients and the community that I choose to serve," he says. "I want to be a positive role model for children, particularly those of minority and underprivileged backgrounds, and to inspire and empower a future generation of physicians."

others, 2016b). This can be attributed in part to the higher levels of stigma and discrimination faced by sexual minority youth (Coulter & others, 2019).

To read about the work of one pediatrician who works with LGBTQ+ youth, see the *Connecting with Careers* profile.

TIMING AND TRENDS IN ADOLESCENT SEXUAL BEHAVIOR

The timing of sexual initiation varies by country as well as by gender and other sociodemographic characteristics. What is the current profile of sexual activity of adolescents? In the most recent large U.S. national survey conducted in 2021, 30 percent of high school students reported ever having sex, 21 percent were currently sexually active (as defined by having sex with at least one person in the last three months), and 6 percent reported having sex with four or more partners (Centers for Disease Control and Prevention, 2023). These behaviors did not differ by race or ethnicity, except that Asian American adolescents were less likely than those in other racial/ethnic groups to report ever having sex, currently being sexually active, or having four or more partners. Being sexually active carries risks for adolescents' health.

What trends in adolescent sexual activity have occurred in the last decade? From 2011 to 2021, the percentage of high school students who reported ever having had sex, who reported currently being sexually active, and who reported having sex with four or more partners declined, as did the percentage of students who reported using a condom the last time they had sexual intercourse (Centers for Disease Control and Prevention, 2023) (see Figure 5).

Until recently, at all grade levels adolescent males have been more likely than adolescent females to report having had sexual intercourse and being sexually active. However, a 2009 national survey was the first time that a higher

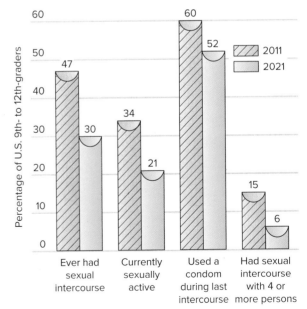

FIGURE 5

SEXUAL ACTIVITY OF U.S. ADOLESCENTS FROM 2011 TO 2021 (CENTERS FOR DISEASE CONTROL AND PREVENTION, 2023)

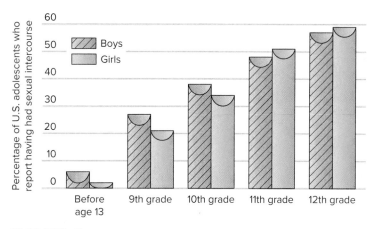

FIGURE **6**

TIMING OF INITIATION OF SEXUAL INTERCOURSE AMONG U.S. ADOLESCENTS (KANN & OTHERS, 2016A)

How Would You...?

If you were a **psychologist,** how would you describe the historical changes in adolescents' sexual experiences?

developmental **connection**

Self and Identity

One of the most important aspects of the self in middle and late childhood is the increased capacity for self-regulation. Connect to "Socioemotional Development in Middle and Late Childhood."

What are some risks for early initiation of sexual intercourse?
Stockbyte/Punchstock/Getty Images

percentage of twelfth-grade females than twelfth-grade males reported having experienced sexual intercourse (Eaton & others, 2010). This reversal continued through 2021 (Centers for Disease Control and Prevention, 2023). In 2015, the reversal also occurred at the eleventh grade, with more eleventh-grade females reporting they had experienced sexual intercourse than eleventh-grade males (Kann & others, 2016a) (see Figure 6). However, a higher percentage of ninth- and tenth-grade males reported they had experienced sexual intercourse than their female counterparts (Kann & others, 2016a). Adolescent males also are more likely than their female counterparts to describe sexual intercourse as an enjoyable experience.

Research indicates that oral sex is now a common occurrence for U.S. adolescents. In a national survey, 51 percent of U.S. 15- to 19-year-old boys and 47 percent of girls in the same age range said they had engaged in oral sex (Child Trends, 2015). U.S. youth may perceive oral sex to be more acceptable and produce fewer health risks. The onset and frequency of oral sex in adolescence also intersect with condom use and other preventative measures (Holway & Hernandez, 2018). Thus, how adolescents initiate their sex lives may have positive or negative consequences for their sexual health.

SEXUAL RISK TAKING IN ADOLESCENCE

Many adolescents are not emotionally prepared to handle sexual experiences, especially in early adolescence. Early sexual activity is linked with risky behaviors such as drug use, delinquency, and school-related problems (Letourneau & others, 2017). A large study of more than 3,000 Swedish adolescents revealed that sexual intercourse before age 14 was linked to risky behaviors such as an increased number of sexual partners, experience of oral and anal sex, negative health behaviors (smoking, drug and alcohol use), and antisocial behavior (being violent, stealing, running away from home) at 18 years of age (Kastbom & others, 2015). Further, a study found that early sexual debut (first sexual intercourse before age 13) was associated with sexual risk taking, substance use, violent victimization, and suicidal thoughts/attempts in both sexual minority (in this study, gay, lesbian, and bisexual) adolescents and heterosexual youth (Lowry & others, 2017). And a number of international studies of adolescent girls have found that early menarche is linked to earlier initiation of sexual intercourse (Whitworth & others, 2023).

A number of family factors are associated with sexual risk taking (Alexopoulos & Cho, 2019; Holmes & others, 2019). For example, one study revealed that adolescents who in the eighth grade reported greater parental knowledge and more family rules about dating were less likely to initiate sex from the eighth to tenth grade (Ethier & others, 2016). In another study, difficulties and disagreements between Latino adolescents and their mothers about sex and dating were linked to the adolescents' sexual initiation (Guilamo-Ramos & others, 2019). And another study revealed that the parenting practice associated most closely with a lower level of risky sexual behavior by adolescents was supportive parenting (Simons & others, 2016). Also, having siblings who use alcohol or cannabis or are themselves sexually active is a risk factor for adolescents' own risky sexual behavior (Thomas & others, 2022).

Socioeconomic status/poverty, peer, school, and sport contexts provide further information about sexual risk taking in adolescents (Belsky, 2019; Widman & others, 2016). Cross-cultural studies have shown that the percentage of sexually active young adolescents is higher in low-income areas of inner cities (Gausman & others, 2019). One longitudinal study found that adolescents who associated with more deviant peers in early adolescence were likely to have more sexual partners at age 16 (Lansford & others, 2010). Further, a research review found that school connectedness was linked to positive sexuality and mental health outcomes for sexual minority as well as majority youth (Colvin, Egan, & Coulter, 2019). Also, a study of high school students revealed that better academic achievement was a protective factor in keeping boys and girls from engaging in risky sexual and other behaviors (Frankel & others, 2018). And another study found that adolescent males who play sports engage in a higher level of sexual risk taking, while adolescent females who play sports engage in a lower level of sexual risk taking (Lipowski & others, 2016).

Weak self-regulation (difficulty controlling one's emotions and behavior) is strongly implicated in sexual risk taking. For example, a large study of 88,815 high school students in Minnesota found that students with poorer self-regulation were more likely to have initiated sexual activity and to engage in risky sexual behavior (Song & Qian, 2020). A comprehensive review of the literature revealed that a high level of impulsiveness was linked to adolescent and adult sexual risky behaviors (Bőthe & others, 2019).

Contraceptive Use   Are adolescents increasingly using contraceptives? Nationally representative data from the United States indicate that only 52 percent of sexually active adolescents reported using a condom the last time they had sexual intercourse, and only 33 percent reported using effective hormonal birth control—birth control pills, an intrauterine device (IUD) or implant, a shot, a patch, or a birth control ring—the last time they had sexual intercourse with an opposite-sex partner (Centers for Disease Control and Prevention, 2023). International research reveals some improvements in contraceptive use, but rates vary widely, especially in lower-income countries where access to preventative health care for adolescents is limited (Ba & others, 2019; Kalamar & others, 2018).

Too many sexually active adolescents still do not use contraceptives, use them inconsistently, or use contraceptive methods that are not highly effective (Diedrich, Klein, & Peipert, 2017; Francis & Gold, 2017; Jaramillo & others, 2017). A large international study found that among adolescent girls living in low- or middle-income countries, contraceptive use was lowest for those who were already married, yet there were large country and regional differences in rates of use (Coll & others, 2019). Younger adolescents are less likely than older adolescents to take contraceptive precautions. Males who report having intercourse with younger female partners are also less likely to report using a condom (Nguyen & Violette, 2022).

Recently, a number of leading medical organizations and experts have recommended that adolescents use long-acting reversible contraception (LARC). These include the Society for Adolescent Health and Medicine (2018), the American Academy of Pediatrics and American College of Obstetricians and Gynecologists (2018), and the World Health Organization (2017). LARC includes intrauterine devices (IUDs) and contraceptive implants, which are much more effective than birth control pills and condoms in preventing unwanted pregnancies (Goldstuck & Cheung, 2019).

Sexually Transmitted Infections   Some forms of contraception, such as birth control pills or implants, do not protect against sexually transmitted infections, or STIs. **Sexually transmitted infections (STIs)** are diseases that are contracted primarily through sexual contact. This contact is not limited to vaginal intercourse but includes oral-genital and anal-genital contact as well. STIs are an increasing health problem. Approximately 25 percent of sexually active adolescents are estimated to become infected with an STI each year. Each year, approximately half of all new STIs occur in young people ages 15 to 24, yet only 5 percent of high school students report having been tested for an STI in the last year (Centers for Disease Control and Prevention, 2023). Among the main STIs adolescents can get are bacterial infections (such as gonorrhea, syphilis, and chlamydia), and STIs caused by viruses—genital herpes, genital warts, and **AIDS** (acquired immune deficiency syndrome). Figure 7 describes these sexually transmitted infections.

No single STI has had a greater impact on sexual behavior, or created more fear, in recent decades than AIDS. AIDS is caused by the human immunodeficiency virus (HIV), which destroys the body's immune system. Following exposure to HIV, an individual is vulnerable to germs that a normal immune system could destroy.

In 2018, 21 percent of all new HIV infections in the United States occurred among individuals 13 to 24 years of age (Centers for Disease Control and Prevention, 2019b). Worldwide, the greatest concern about AIDS is in sub-Saharan Africa, where it has reached epidemic proportions (World Health Organization, 2022). Adolescent girls in many African countries are especially vulnerable to becoming infected with HIV by adult men. Approximately six times as

How Would You...?
If you were a **social worker,** how would you design an educational campaign to increase adolescents' effective use of contraception?

A 13-year-old boy pushes his friends around in his barrow during a break from his work as a barrow boy in a community in sub-Saharan Africa. He became the breadwinner in the family after both of his parents died of AIDS.
Louise Gubb/Corbis/Getty Images

sexually transmitted infections (STIs)
Diseases that are contracted primarily through sexual contact. This contact is not limited to vaginal intercourse but includes oral-genital contact and anal-genital contact as well.

AIDS Acquired immune deficiency syndrome; caused by the human immunodeficiency virus (HIV), which destroys the body's immune system.

STI	Description/cause	Incidence	Treatment
Gonorrhea	Commonly called the "drip" or "clap." Caused by the bacterium *Neisseria gonorrhoeae*. Spread by contact between infected moist membranes (genital, oral-genital, or anal-genital) of two individuals. Characterized by discharge from penis or vagina and painful urination. Can lead to infertility.	500,000 cases annually in U.S.	Penicillin, other antibiotics
Syphilis	Caused by the bacterium *Treponema pallidum*. Characterized by the appearance of a sore where syphilis entered the body. The sore can be on the external genitals, vagina, or anus. Later, a skin rash breaks out on palms of hands and bottom of feet. If not treated, can eventually lead to paralysis or even death.	100,000 cases annually in U.S.	Penicillin
Chlamydia	A common STI named for the bacterium *Chlamydia trachomatis*, an organism that spreads by sexual contact and infects the genital organs of both sexes. A special concern is that females with chlamydia may become infertile. It is recommended that adolescent and young adult females have an annual screening for this STI.	About 3 million people in U.S. annually	Antibiotics
Genital herpes	Caused by a family of viruses with different strains. Involves an eruption of sores and blisters. Spread by sexual contact.	One of five U.S. adults	No known cure but antiviral medications can shorten outbreaks
AIDS	Caused by the human immunodeficiency virus (HIV), which destroys the body's immune system. Semen and blood are the main vehicles of transmission. Common symptoms include fevers, night sweats, weight loss, chronic fatigue, and swollen lymph nodes.	More than 300,000 cumulative cases of HIV virus in U.S. 25–34-year-olds; epidemic incidence in sub-Saharan countries	New treatments have slowed the progression from HIV to AIDS; no cure
Genital warts	Caused by the human papillomavirus (HPV), which does not always produce symptoms. Usually appear as small, hard painless bumps in the vaginal area, or around the anus. Very contagious. Certain high-risk types of this virus cause cervical cancer and other genital cancers. May recur despite treatment. A vaccine to protect against HPV is now available and recommended beginning at age 9.	About 5.5 million new cases annually; considered the most common STI in the U.S.	A topical drug, freezing, or surgery

FIGURE 7

SEXUALLY TRANSMITTED INFECTIONS

many adolescent girls as boys have AIDS in these countries. In Kenya, 25 percent of the 15- to 19-year-old girls are HIV-positive, compared with only 4 percent of boys in this age group. In Botswana, more than 30 percent of the adolescent girls who are pregnant are infected with the HIV virus. In many countries, there is a large unmet need for contraceptives, including condoms, to help prevent transmission of HIV and other STIs (World Health Organization, 2019).

There continues to be great concern about AIDS in many parts of the world, not just sub-Saharan Africa. In the United States, prevention is especially targeted at groups that show the highest incidence of AIDS. These include drug users, individuals with other STIs, young gay males, individuals living in low-income circumstances, Latinos, and Black Americans (Centers for Disease Control and Prevention, 2022b).

Adolescent Pregnancy Adolescent pregnancy is another problematic outcome of sexuality in adolescence and requires major efforts to reduce its occurrence (World Health Organization, 2020). Globally, approximately 14 percent of girls give birth before the age of 18 (UNICEF, 2022). In cross-cultural comparisons, the United States continues to have one of the highest adolescent pregnancy and childbearing rates in the industrialized world, despite a considerable decline during the 1990s. For instance, the U.S. adolescent pregnancy rate is four times as high as that in the Netherlands (World Bank, 2023). Although U.S. adolescents are no more sexually active than their counterparts in the Netherlands, their adolescent pregnancy rate is dramatically higher. In the United States, 77 percent of pregnancies to teen mothers are unintended (Office of Population Affairs, 2020). A cross-cultural comparison found that among 194 countries, 61 countries had lower pregnancy rates than the United States (World Bank, 2023). However, as you will see shortly, the adolescent pregnancy rate in the United States has dropped considerably in the last decade or more.

Despite the negative comparisons of the United States with many other high-income countries, there have been some encouraging trends in U.S. adolescent pregnancy rates. In

2020, the U.S. birth rate for 15- to 19-year-olds was 15 births per 1,000 females, the lowest rate ever recorded, which represents a substantial decrease from 62 births per 1,000 females for the same age range in 1991 (Martin, Hamilton, & Osterman, 2015; Osterman & others, 2022) (see Figure 8). Reasons for the decline include school/community health classes, increased contraceptive use, and fear of sexually transmitted infections such as AIDS.

There are ethnic group differences, on average, in the rates of adolescent pregnancy (Maslowsky & others, 2019). Latina adolescents are more likely than Black American and non-Latina White adolescents to become pregnant. For 15- to 19-year-old U.S. females in 2018, per 1,000 females the birth rate for Latinas was 29, for Black Americans 28, for non-Latina Whites 14, and for Asian Americans 7 (Office of Population Affairs, 2020). These figures represent substantial decreases (approximately a 70 percent decrease just since 2011) in adolescent pregnancy rates for Latina and Black American teens. However, Latina and Black American adolescent girls who have a child are more likely to have a second child than are non-Latina White adolescent girls (Maslowsky & others, 2019). And daughters of teenage mothers are at risk for teenage childbearing, thus perpetuating an intergenerational cycle. A study using data on over 15,000 mothers and their daughters in Ontario, Canada, revealed that daughters of mothers who became pregnant as teens were 42 to 117 percent more likely to become pregnant as teens themselves, with the rate increasing based on the number of pregnancies the mother had (Liu & others, 2018). In this study, there was a very strong association between how many times the mother became pregnant as a teen, and whether and how often the daughter became pregnant as a teen.

Turning back to the United States, why are adolescent pregnancy rates so high? We discuss possible answers to this question in the following *Connecting with Diversity* interlude.

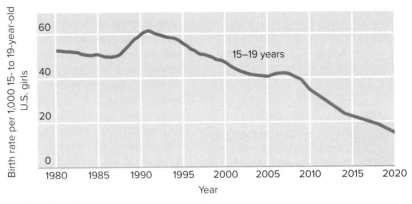

FIGURE 8

BIRTH RATES FOR U.S. 15- TO 19-YEAR-OLD GIRLS FROM 1980 TO 2020 (MARTIN, HAMILTON, & OSTERMAN, 2015; OSTERMAN & OTHERS, 2022)

connecting with diversity

Cross-Cultural Comparisons of Adolescent Pregnancy

Three reasons U.S. adolescent pregnancy rates are so high in comparison with many other countries can be found in cross-cultural studies (Boonstra, 2002, pp. 9–10):

- *"Childbearing regarded as adult activity."* European countries, as well as Canada, give a strong consensus that childbearing belongs in adulthood "when young people have completed their education, have become employed and independent from their parents and are living in stable relationships. . . . In the United States, this attitude is much less strong and much more variable across groups and areas of the country."

- *"Clear messages about sexual behavior.* While adults in other countries strongly encourage teens to wait until they have established themselves before having children, they are generally more accepting than American adults of teens having sex. In France and Sweden, in particular, teen sexual expression is seen as normal and positive, but there is also widespread expectation that sexual intercourse will take place within committed relationships. In fact, relationships among U.S. teens tend to be more sporadic and of shorter duration. Equally strong is the expectation that young people who are having sex will

take actions to protect themselves and their partners from pregnancy and sexually transmitted infections," an expectation that is much stronger in Europe than in the United States. "In keeping with this view, . . . schools in Great Britain, France, Sweden, and most of Canada" have sex education programs that provide more comprehensive information about prevention than U.S. schools do. In addition, these countries use the media more often in "government-sponsored campaigns for promoting responsible sexual behavior."

- *"Access to family-planning services.* In countries that are more accepting of teenage sexual relationships, teenagers also have easier access to reproductive health services. In Canada, France, Great Britain, and Sweden, contraceptive services are integrated into other types of primary health care and are available free or at low cost for all teenagers. Generally, teens [in these countries] know where to obtain information and services and receive confidential and nonjudgmental care. . . . In the United States, where attitudes about teenage sexual relationships are more conflicted, teens have a harder time obtaining contraceptive services. Many cannot get birth control as part of their basic health care."

How Would You...?

If you were an **educator**, how would you incorporate sex education throughout the curriculum to encourage adolescents' healthy, responsible sexual development?

The consequences of high adolescent pregnancy rates are cause for great concern (Kiani, Ghazanfarpour, & Saeidi, 2019). Adolescent pregnancy creates health risks for both the baby and the mother. Adolescent mothers are more likely to be depressed and drop out of school than their peers (Cox & others, 2019). Infants born to adolescent mothers are more likely to have low birth weights—a prominent factor in infant mortality—an outcome that is prevalent in wealthy to low-income countries around the globe (Workicho & others, 2019). Although many adolescent mothers resume their education later in life, they generally never catch up economically with women who postpone childbearing until their twenties. A meta-analysis of 35 studies found that offspring born to mothers younger than age 21 had more cognitive, externalizing, and internalizing problems across the life span than did offspring born to mothers who were 21 or older (Cresswell & others, 2022). A separate meta-analysis found that offspring of adolescent fathers also were at greater risk of being born prematurely, of having low birth weight, and of having psychological disorders later in development (Bamishigbin, Schetter, & Stanton, 2019).

A special concern is repeated adolescent pregnancy. In a large national study in the United States, the percentage of teen births that were repeat births decreased from 21 percent in 2004 to 17 percent in 2015 (Dee & others, 2017) and decreased further to 16 percent in 2017 (Maslowsky & others, 2019). In a meta-analysis, use of effective contraception, especially LARC, and education-related factors (higher level of education and school continuation) resulted in a lower incidence of repeated teen pregnancy, while depression and a history of abortion were linked to a higher percentage of repeated teen pregnancy (Maravilla & others, 2017).

Researchers have found that adolescent mothers interact less effectively with their infants than do adult mothers (Cox & others, 2019). One illustrative study revealed that adolescent mothers spent more time negatively interacting and less time in play and positively interacting with their infants than did adult mothers (Riva Crugnola & others, 2014). An intervention program, "My Baby and Me," that involved frequent, intensive home visitation coaching sessions with adolescent mothers across three years resulted in improved maternal behavior and child outcomes (Guttentag & others, 2014). And another study assessed the reading and math achievement trajectories of children born to adolescent and non-adolescent mothers with different levels of education (Tang & others, 2016). In this study, higher levels of maternal education were linked to growth in their children's achievement through the eighth grade. Nonetheless, the achievement of children born to the adolescent mothers never reached the levels of children born to adult mothers.

caring connections

Reducing Adolescent Pregnancy

In 2010, the U.S. government launched the Teen Pregnancy Prevention (TPP) program under the direction of the then-new Office of Adolescent Health. A number of studies have been funded by the program in an effort to find ways to reduce the rate of adolescent pregnancy. A meta-analysis of 52 studies found no consistent evidence that this set of programs had effects on ever having been pregnant, recent pregnancy, ever having had sexual intercourse, recent sexual activity, recent unprotected sexual activity, number of sexual partners, or proportion of recent sexual experiences that were unprotected (Juras & others, 2022). The findings suggest a pressing need to identify and implement programs that will be more successful in reducing adolescent pregnancy.

A major controversy in U.S. sex education is whether schools should have an abstinence-only program or a program that emphasizes contraceptive knowledge (Grasso & Trumbull, 2023). A number of leading experts on adolescent sexuality now conclude that sex education programs that emphasize contraceptive knowledge do not increase the incidence of sexual intercourse and are more likely to reduce the risk of adolescent pregnancy and sexually transmitted infections than abstinence-only programs (Donovan, 2017; Jaramillo & others, 2017). Despite the evidence that favors comprehensive sex education, there recently has been an increase in government funding for abstinence-only programs, which have been demonstrated to be ineffective (Guttmacher Institute, 2021). Also, in some states (Texas and Mississippi, for example), many students still get abstinence-only instruction or no sex education at all (Guttmacher Institute, 2023). A meta-analysis of 15 surveys in the United States demonstrated that 88 percent of respondents in nationally representative samples supported sexuality education in schools (Szucs & others, 2022).

Some sex education programs adopt an abstinence-plus sexuality approach that promotes abstinence while providing information on contraceptive use. Researchers today advocate for more comprehensive programs that also include information on how to communicate with a partner about consent, sexual history, pregnancy, and STIs (Grasso & Trumbull, 2023). Researchers also stress the importance of broadening sexuality education to address the needs of LGBTQ adolescents.

Though the consequences of high adolescent pregnancy rates are cause for great concern, it often is not pregnancy alone that leads to negative consequences for an adolescent mother and her offspring. Adolescent mothers are more likely to come from low-SES backgrounds (Maslowsky & others, 2019). Many adolescent mothers also were not good students before they became pregnant. However, not every adolescent female who bears a child lives a life of poverty and low achievement. Thus, although adolescent pregnancy is a high-risk circumstance, and adolescents who do not become pregnant generally fare better than those who do, some adolescent mothers do well in school and have positive outcomes (Raskin & others, 2019).

Serious, extensive efforts are needed to help pregnant adolescents and young mothers enhance their educational and occupational opportunities (Cox & others, 2019). Adolescent mothers also need help in obtaining competent child care and in planning for the future.

All adolescents can benefit from age-appropriate family-life education (Darling, Cassidy, & Ballard, 2022). Family and consumer science educators teach life skills, such as effective decision making, to adolescents. To learn more about ways to reduce adolescent pregnancy, see the *Caring Connections* interlude.

What are some consequences of adolescent pregnancy?

Katarzyna Białasiewicz/123RF

Review Connect Reflect

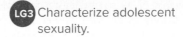 Characterize adolescent sexuality.

Review

- How do adolescents develop a sexual identity?
- What characterizes timing and trends in adolescent sexual behavior?
- What is the nature of sexual risk taking in adolescence?

Connect

- How might the development of self-regulation benefit adolescents when sexual decision making is involved?

Reflect *Your Own Personal Journey of Life*

- How would you describe your sexual identity as an adolescent? What contributed to this identity?

4 How Can Adolescents' Health and Health-Enhancing Assets Be Characterized?

 Summarize adolescents' health and eating disorders.

| Adolescent Health | Leading Causes of Death in Adolescence | Substance Use and Abuse | Eating Problems and Disorders |

To improve adolescent health, adults should aim (1) to increase adolescents' *health-enhancing behaviors,* such as eating nutritious foods, exercising, wearing seat belts, and getting adequate sleep; and (2) to reduce adolescents' *health-compromising behaviors,* such as drug abuse, violence, unprotected sexual intercourse, and dangerous driving.

How Would You...?

If you were a **health-care professional,** how would you explain the benefits of physical fitness in adolescence to adolescents, parents, and teachers?

ADOLESCENT HEALTH

Adolescence is a critical juncture in the adoption of behaviors that are relevant to health (Devenish, Hooley, & Mellor, 2017; Yap & others, 2017). Many of the behaviors that are linked to poor health habits and early death in adults begin during adolescence (Wang, Chen, & Lee, 2019). Conversely, the early formation of healthy behavior patterns, such as regular exercise and a preference for foods low in fat and cholesterol, not only has immediate health benefits but also helps in adulthood to delay or prevent disability and mortality from heart disease, stroke, diabetes, and cancer (Agostinis-Sobrinho & others, 2019).

These adolescents are attending a weight-management camp. *What types of interventions have been most successful in helping overweight adolescents lose weight?*
Homer Sykes/Alamy Stock Photo

How can adding weight-bearing exercises positively affect an adolescent's health?
Fuse/Getty Images

- - - - - - - - →

developmental **connection**

Nutrition and Weight

Being overweight at age 3 is a risk factor for subsequently being overweight at age 12. Connect to "Physical Development in Early Childhood."

← - - - - - - - -

In 2007, Texas became the first state to test students' physical fitness; today, there are many school districts that conduct these kinds of assessments. This student is performing the trunk lift. Other assessments include aerobic exercise, muscle strength, and body fat.
Vernon Bryant/Dallas Morning News

Nutrition and Weight   Concerns are growing about adolescents' nutrition and exercise habits (Powers & Dodd, 2017; Schiff, 2017). National data in the United States indicated that the percentage of obese 12- to 19-year-olds increased from 11 percent in the early 1990s to more than 22 percent in 2017–2020 (Centers for Disease Control and Prevention, 2022a). Globally, a similar upward trend in obesity rates has been observed in most countries (Ashdown-Franks & others, 2019).

Being obese in adolescence predicts obesity in emerging adulthood. For example, a study of more than 8,000 12- to 21-year-olds found that obese adolescents were more likely to develop severe obesity in emerging adulthood than were overweight or normal-weight adolescents (The & others, 2010).

And more emerging adults are overweight or obese than are adolescents. An illustrative longitudinal study tracked more than 1,500 adolescents who were classified as not overweight, overweight, or obese when they were 14 years of age (Patton & others, 2011). Across the 10-year period of the study, the percentage of overweight individuals increased from 20 percent at 14 years of age to 33 percent at 24 years of age. Obesity increased from 4 percent to 7 percent across the 10 years. Ongoing analysis of the National Health and Nutrition Examination Survey (NHANES) reveals that by early adulthood, nearly 40 percent of Americans are obese (State of Childhood Obesity, 2020).

What types of interventions and activities have been successful in reducing overweight in adolescents and emerging adults? Research indicates that dietary changes and regular exercise are key components of weight reduction in adolescence and emerging adulthood (Oden, Ward, & Raisingani, 2019; Stoner & others, 2019). For example, one study found that a combination of regular exercise and a diet plan promoted weight loss and enhanced executive function in adolescents (Xie & others, 2017). Also, a meta-analysis concluded that supervised exercise, especially aerobic exercise, was linked to a reduction of abdominal fat in adolescents (Gonzalez-Ruiz & others, 2017). Further, a clinical trial of different types of dietary changes and exercise (discussed in more detail next) among obese adolescents revealed that aerobic exercise, or aerobic plus weight-bearing exercise, were most effective at reducing fat and improving blood sugar regulation (S. Lee & others, 2019). It has become clear that all youth, regardless of demographics and living circumstances, can benefit from improved diet and more physical activity.

Exercise   There also is major concern about the low level of exercise by adolescents in many countries and cultural contexts. In a large global study of many survey datasets, researchers found that 4 out of 5 adolescents were below or far below the recommended level of physical activity from the world health agencies. There were vast world region differences, with the highest rates of insufficient physical activity found in high-income Asian countries (Guthold & others, 2020).

Researchers have found that individuals tend to become less active as they reach and progress through adolescence (Chong & others, 2020). A national survey found that in 2019, 23 percent of ninth- to twelfth-graders had engaged in physical activity for 60 minutes or more in each of the last seven days, compared with 28.7 percent in 2011 (Underwood & others, 2020). Adolescent girls were much less likely to have engaged in physical activity for 60 minutes or more per day in each of the last seven days (15.4 percent) than were boys (30.9 percent) (Underwood & others, 2020). Figure 9 shows the average amount of exercise among U.S. boys and girls from 9 to 15 years of age on weekdays and weekends. In the Gateshead Millennium Study of over 1,000 youth born in 1999 in northeast England, researchers have tracked the children as they develop through adolescence. They have found that, with the exception of a small percentage of boys whose vigorous activity increased across adolescence (due to sports participation), boys and girls alike showed large decreases across adolescence in vigorous activity (Beltran-Valls & others, 2019).

There are ethnic group differences in exercise participation rates of U.S. adolescents, and these rates vary by gender. As indicated in Figure 10, in the National Youth Risk Survey, non-Latino White boys exercised the most, Black American and Latina girls the least (Kann & others, 2016a). These differences in exercise participation rates of U.S. adolescents vary due to differences in access to and opportunities for physical exercise.

Turning to cross-country analysis, a major study conducted a comparison of adolescents in 28 countries. This study found that U.S. adolescents exercised less and ate more junk food than did adolescents in most of the other countries (World Health Organization, 2000). Just two-thirds of U.S. adolescents exercised at least twice a week compared with 80 percent or more of adolescents in Ireland, Austria, Germany, and the Slovak Republic. U.S. adolescents were more likely to eat fried food and less likely to eat fruits and vegetables than were adolescents in most other countries studied. U.S. adolescents' eating choices were similar to those of adolescents in England. More recent research has shown that although these diet and exercise habits remain highly problematic in the United States, the trends are moving toward poorer health behaviors among adolescents in many other wealthy as well as low- and middle-income countries (Guthold & others, 2020).

Just as in childhood, exercise is linked with a number of positive outcomes in adolescence (Schutte & others, 2019). Regular exercise has a positive effect on adolescents' healthy weight status (Xie & others, 2017). A number of studies converge to show that physically active children are far more likely to be active and healthy-weight adolescents (Pate & others, 2019). Another line of research shows that adolescents high in physical fitness have better connectivity between brain regions and overall brain function efficiency than adolescents low in physical fitness (Valkenborghs & others, 2019). Additional positive outcomes of exercise in adolescence are reduced triglyceride levels, lower blood pressure, and a lower incidence of type 2 diabetes (Lumpkin, 2021). An intervention that included 12 weeks of aerobic exercise for depressed teens and emerging adults showed positive effects on respiratory function and decreased depressive symptoms (Jaworska & others, 2019). A study of Chinese adolescents showed more depressive symptoms after COVID-19 appeared; however, engaging in more physical exercise during quarantine periods helped to reduce the link between the pandemic and depressive symptoms (Ren & others, 2021).

Adolescents' exercise is known to be associated with specific features of parenting and peer relationships (Hu & others, 2021). For example, a study in Ireland revealed that adolescent boys' and girls' participation in physical activities was predicted by more parental support for those activities (especially from their same-gender parent), and girls' participation in physical activities was also linked to their friends' support of those activities (Lawler & others, 2022). In a thorough research review, peer/friend support of exercise, presence of peers and friends, peer norms, friendship quality and acceptance, peer crowds, and peer victimization were linked to adolescents' physical activity (Fitzgerald, Fitzgerald, & Aherne, 2012). A meta-analysis of studies has shown that parents' support of exercise, and engaging in exercise themselves (i.e., modeling an active lifestyle for their children), are associated with higher levels of physical activity across childhood and adolescence (Yao & Rhodes, 2015).

Researchers have found that screen time is associated with a number of adolescent health problems, including a lower rate of exercise and a higher rate of sedentary behavior and cardiovascular and metabolic disorder symptoms (van Sluijs & others, 2021). Adolescents who engage in low physical activity and high screen-based activity are much more likely to be overweight or obese than are peers who are physically active (Zhu & others, 2019). The largest and most comprehensive review to

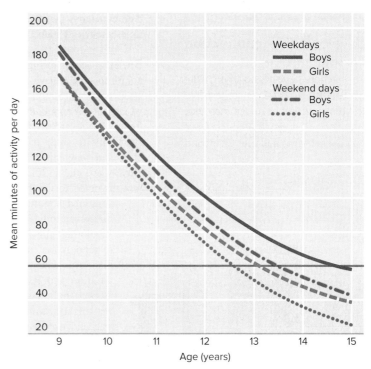

FIGURE **9**

AVERAGE AMOUNT OF MODERATE TO VIGOROUS EXERCISE ENGAGED IN BY U.S. 9- TO 15-YEAR-OLDS ON WEEKDAYS AND WEEKENDS.

Note: The federal government recommends 60 minutes of moderate to vigorous physical activity per day.

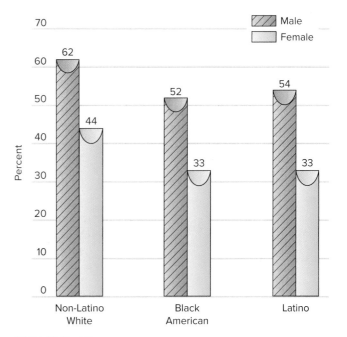

FIGURE **10**

EXERCISE RATES OF U.S. HIGH SCHOOL STUDENTS IN 2015: GENDER AND ETHNICITY (KANN & OTHERS, 2016A).

Note: Data are for high school students who were physically active doing any kind of physical activity that increased their heart rate and made them breathe hard some of the time for a total of at least 60 minutes per day on five or more of the seven days preceding the survey.

developmental **connection**

Exercise

Researchers have found that children who participate in sports are less likely to be overweight or obese than those who don't. Connect to "Physical Development in Middle and Late Childhood."

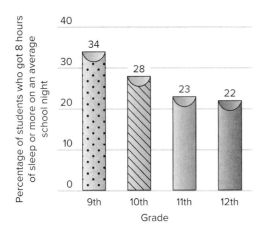

FIGURE 11

DEVELOPMENTAL CHANGES IN U.S. ADOLESCENTS' SLEEP PATTERNS ON AN AVERAGE SCHOOL NIGHT

developmental **connection**

Sleep

Experts recommend that young children get 11 to 13 hours of sleep each night. Connect to "Physical Development in Early Childhood."

melatonin A sleep-inducing hormone that is produced in the brain's pineal gland.

date concludes that these effects continue to persist in a variety of youth populations in multiple countries (Stiglic & Viner, 2019).

Sleep Might changing sleep patterns in adolescence contribute to adolescents' health-compromising behaviors? The research field has witnessed a surge of interest in adolescent sleep patterns (Simon & others, 2021; Trosman & Ivanenko, 2021). A longitudinal study in which adolescents completed daily diaries every 14 days in ninth, tenth, and twelfth grades found that regardless of how much students studied each day, when the students sacrificed sleep time to study more than usual, they had difficulty understanding what was taught in class and were more likely to struggle with class assignments the next day (Gillen-O'Neel, Huynh, & Fuligni, 2013). Also, an experimental study indicated that when adolescents' sleep was restricted to five hours for five nights, then returned to ten hours for two nights, their sustained attention was negatively affected (especially in the early morning) and did not return to baseline levels during the sleep recovery period (Agostini & others, 2017). In another study, a "natural" experiment was conducted that compared teens who were in schools that moved to a later morning start time to teens in schools that had not made this change. Results showed a positive effect of later start time on longer sleep duration and lower levels of depressive symptoms (Berger, Wahlstrom, & Widome, 2019). And a national study of more than 10,000 13- to 18-year-olds revealed that later weeknight bedtime, shorter weekend bedtime delay, and both short and long periods of weekend oversleep were linked to increased rates of anxiety, mood, substance abuse, and behavioral disorders (Zhang & others, 2017). Further, in a five-year longitudinal study beginning at 14 years of age, poor sleep patterns (for example, shorter sleep duration and greater daytime sleepiness) in mid-adolescence were associated with an increased likelihood of drinking alcohol and using marijuana at 19 years of age (Nguyen-Louie & others, 2018). Also, several studies in Sweden revealed that adolescents with a shorter sleep duration were likely to have more school absences, while shorter sleep duration and greater sleep deficits were linked to lower grade point averages (Hysing & others, 2015, 2016).

In a large national survey of youth, only 25 percent of U.S. adolescents reported getting eight or more hours of sleep on an average school night, compared with 32 percent who had reported getting this much sleep in a study conducted four years earlier (Kann & others, 2018). In this study, the percentage of adolescents getting this much sleep on an average school night decreased as they got older (see Figure 11). Also, in other research with more than 270,000 U.S. adolescents from 1991–2012, the amount of sleep they get has been decreasing in recent years (Keyes & others, 2015). This troubling trend has been accelerated by increased time on mobile devices at night (Mireku & others, 2019). Studies have confirmed that adolescents in other countries also are not getting adequate sleep. One study found large differences in amounts of sleep, especially on school-day nights, across large regions of Europe and North America (Gariepy & others, 2020).

Mary Carskadon and her colleagues (Carskadon & others, 2019; Crowley & others, 2018; Ziporyn & others, 2022) have conducted a number of research studies on adolescent sleep patterns. They found that when given the opportunity, adolescents will sleep an average of nine hours and 25 minutes a night. Most get considerably less than nine hours of sleep, especially during the week. This shortfall creates a sleep deficit, which adolescents often attempt to make up on the weekend. This chronic pattern of poor sleep may affect gene expression, through epigenetic changes in DNA. The researchers also found that older adolescents tend to be more sleepy during the day than younger adolescents. They theorized that this sleepiness was not due to academic work or social pressures. Rather, their research suggests that adolescents' biological clocks undergo a shift as they get older, delaying their period of wakefulness by about one hour. A delay in the nightly release of the sleep-inducing hormone **melatonin,** which is produced in the brain's pineal gland, seems to underlie this shift. Melatonin is secreted at about 9:30 p.m. in younger adolescents and approximately an hour later in older adolescents.

Carskadon and colleagues have argued that early school starting times may cause grogginess, inattention in class, and poor performance on tests. Based on her research, school officials in Edina, Minnesota, decided to start classes at 8:30 a.m. rather than the usual 7:25 a.m. Since then there have been fewer referrals for discipline problems, and the number of students who report being ill or depressed has decreased. The school system reports that test scores have improved for high school students, but not for middle school students. This finding supports Carskadon's suspicion that early start times are likely to be more stressful for older than for younger adolescents. Using statewide administrative data in North Carolina, later school start times were found to reduce absences and suspensions and to improve math and reading test scores (Bastian & Fuller, 2023). In another study, early school start times were linked to a higher vehicle crash rate in adolescent drivers (Vorona & others, 2014). The American Academy of Pediatrics recommended that schools institute start times from 8:30 to 9:30 a.m. to improve adolescents' academic performance and quality of life (Adolescent Sleep Working Group, AAP, 2014). This policy has been endorsed by the American Association of Sleep Technologists (2019).

Do sleep patterns change in emerging adulthood? Research indicates that they do (Nicholson, Bohnert, & Crowley, 2023). One study categorized more than 60 percent of college students as poor-quality sleepers (Lund & others, 2010). In this study, the weekday bedtimes and rise times of first-year college students were approximately 1 hour and 15 minutes later than those of seniors in high school. However, the first-year college students had later bedtimes and rise times than third- and fourth-year college students, indicating that at about 20 to 22 years of age, a reverse in the timing of bedtimes and rise times occurs. Another illustrative study used wrist actimetry sensors (devices that measure movement and stillness) with a large and ethnically diverse sample and found that overall sleep quality deteriorated for college and non-college emerging adults, and within-person inconsistency in sleep (from night to night) increased with age (Park & others, 2019).

In Mary Carskadon's sleep laboratory at Brown University, an adolescent girl's brain activity is being monitored. Later school start times lead to better academic performance and fewer behavioral problems for adolescents.
Jim LoScalzo

LEADING CAUSES OF DEATH IN ADOLESCENCE

The three leading causes of death in adolescence and emerging adulthood are accidents, homicide, and suicide (Murphy & others, 2021). Almost half of all deaths at 15 to 24 years of age are due to unintentional injuries, approximately three-fourths of them involving motor vehicle accidents. Risky driving habits, such as speeding, tailgating, texting while driving, and driving under the influence of alcohol or other drugs, may be more important contributors to these accidents than lack of driving experience. In about 50 percent of motor vehicle fatalities involving adolescents, the driver has a blood alcohol level of 0.10 percent—twice the level designated as "under the influence" in some states. A high rate of intoxication is also found in adolescents who die as pedestrians or while using recreational vehicles.

Homicide is another leading cause of death in adolescence and emerging adulthood. In the United States, this is particularly true for Black American males, who are three times more likely to be killed by guns than by natural causes. The United States is the only large or wealthy country in which guns are a leading cause of death in adolescents (McGough & others, 2022).

Suicide is the third-leading cause of death in adolescence and emerging adulthood in the United States. The suicide rate among U.S. adolescents and emerging adults tripled during the second half of the twentieth century, declined in the early 2000s, then began rising quickly again after 2010—a pattern seen in other countries such as the United Kingdom and Canada (Bould & others, 2019; Cribb, Ovid, & Bigham, 2018). Following the COVID-19 pandemic, concerns about suicide grew exponentially; in 2021, nearly 60 percent of female adolescents reported persistent feelings of sadness or hopelessness, and almost 25 percent made a suicide plan (Centers for Disease Control and Prevention, 2023).

SUBSTANCE USE AND ABUSE

Among the significant problems that can develop in adolescence are substance use and abuse, which we will discuss here. In the chapter on "Socioemotional Development in Adolescence" we will explore further the adolescent problems of juvenile delinquency, depression, and suicide.

Trends in Substance Use and Abuse
Each year since 1975, Lloyd Johnston and his colleagues at the Institute for Social Research at the

How Would You...?
If you were an **educator,** how would you use developmental research to convince your school board to change the starting time of high school?

developmental **connection**
Problems, Diseases, and Disorders
Both earlier and later experiences may be involved in adolescent suicide attempts. Connect to "Socioemotional Development in Adolescence."

Why might adolescents be especially likely to protest gun violence and advocate for reforms in gun laws?
Ken Wolter/123RF

FIGURE **12**

TRENDS IN DRUG USE BY U.S. EIGHTH-, TENTH-, AND TWELFTH-GRADE STUDENTS. This graph shows the percentage of U.S. eighth-, tenth-, and twelfth-grade students who reported having taken an illicit drug in the last 12 months from 1991 to 2022 (for eighth- and tenth-graders) and from 1975 to 2022 (for twelfth-graders) (Johnston & others, 2017; National Institute on Drug Abuse, 2022).

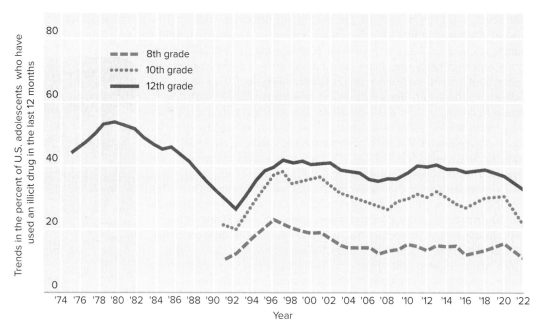

University of Michigan have monitored the drug use of America's high school seniors in a wide range of public and private high schools, in a study called Monitoring the Future. Since 1991, they also have surveyed drug use by eighth- and tenth-graders. For example, in 2021, the study surveyed 31,438 students in 308 public and private schools (National Institute on Drug Abuse, 2022). A report is released each year to provide an update on adolescents' substance use in the United States.

According to this study, the proportions of eighth-, tenth-, and twelfth-grade U.S. students who used any illicit drug declined during the late 1990s and the first two decades of the twenty-first century (Johnston & others, 2017; National Institute on Drug Abuse, 2022) (see Figure 12). The overall decline in the use of illicit drugs since the late 1990s is approximately one-third for eighth-graders, one-fourth for tenth-graders, and one-eighth for twelfth-graders. The most notable declines in drug use by U.S. adolescents in the twenty-first century have occurred for LSD, cocaine, cigarettes, sedatives, tranquilizers, and Ecstasy.

As shown in Figure 12, in which marijuana use is included, an increase in illicit drug use by U.S. adolescents occurred from 2008 to 2013. However, when marijuana use is subtracted from the illicit drug index, no increase in U.S. adolescent drug use occurred in this time frame (Johnston & others, 2017). Illicit drug use by adolescents began decreasing again in 2014 and 2015, and then an even greater decrease in U.S. adolescents' use of illicit drugs occurred in 2016, with the greatest declines occurring for eighth- and tenth-grade students (Johnston & others, 2017). These lower rates of use continued through 2022, according to the most recent data available from the survey (National Institute on Drug Abuse, 2022). The United States still has one of the highest rates of adolescent drug use among industrialized nations.

How extensive is alcohol use by U.S. adolescents? Sizable declines in adolescent alcohol use have occurred over the past decade or so (Johnston & others, 2017). Data from the Monitoring the Future study reveal that 15.2 percent of eighth-graders, 31.3 percent of tenth-graders, and 51.9 percent of twelfth-graders reported drinking alcohol in the last year. In addition, 8.3 percent of eighth-graders, 19.5 percent of tenth-graders, and 30.7 percent of twelfth-graders reported cannabis use in the past year (National Institute on Drug Abuse, 2022).

A special concern is adolescents who drive while they are under the influence of alcohol or other substances (McCarthy & McCarthy, 2019). In a large national study, one in four twelfth-graders reported that they had consumed alcohol mixed with energy drinks in the last 12 months, and this combination was linked to their unsafe driving (Martz, Patrick, & Schulenberg, 2016).

What are some trends in alcohol use by U.S. adolescents?
BananaStock/Getty Images

Cigarette smoking (in which the active drug is nicotine) is one of the most serious yet preventable health problems among adolescents and emerging adults (Macy & others, 2019). Smoking is likely to begin in grades 7 through 9, although sizable proportions of youth are still establishing regular smoking habits during high school and the transition to early adulthood. Risk factors for becoming a regular smoker in adolescence include having a friend who smokes, a weak academic orientation, and low parental support (Long & Valente, 2019).

The peer group plays an especially influential role in smoking (Long & Valente, 2019; Strong & others, 2017). In one study, the risk of current smoking was linked with having peers who smoked as well as the adolescents' perceptions of the social acceptability of smoking and other substance use (Macy & others, 2019). Age-mates may be more powerful influencers than adults. In one study, early smoking was predicted better by sibling and peer smoking than by parental smoking (Kelly & others, 2011).

Cigarette smoking among U.S. adolescents peaked in 1996 and 1997 and has declined since then (Johnston & others, 2017; National Institute on Drug Abuse, 2022). Following peak use in 1996, smoking rates for U.S. eighth-graders have fallen by 50 percent. For instance, in 2016, the percentages of adolescents who said they had smoked cigarettes in the last 30 days were 10.5 percent among twelfth-graders (down from 16 percent in 2013), 4.9 percent among tenth-graders (down from 9 percent in 2013), and 2.6 percent among eighth-graders (down from 4.5 percent in 2013). Since the mid-1990s a growing percentage of adolescents have reported that they perceive cigarette smoking as dangerous, that they disapprove of it, that they are less accepting of being around smokers, and that they prefer to date nonsmokers (Johnston & others, 2017). However, the prevalence of vaping has increased over this time period and is now a more common way for adolescents to use nicotine, as well as cannabis (National Institute on Drug Abuse, 2022). To read about a prevention scientist who has been researching prevention and intervention programs, see the *Connecting with Careers* box.

connecting with careers

Bonnie Halpern-Felsher, University Professor in Pediatrics and Director of Community Efforts to Improve Adolescents' Health

Halpern-Felsher is a professor in the Department of Pediatrics at Stanford University. Her work exemplifies how some professors not only teach and conduct research in a single discipline, like psychology, but do research in multiple disciplines and also work outside their university in the community in an effort to improve the lives of youth. Halpern-Felsher is a developmental psychologist with additional training in adolescent health. She is especially interested in understanding why adolescents engage in risk-taking and in using this research to develop intervention programs for improving adolescents' lives.

In particular, Halpern-Felsher has studied adolescent sexual decision making and reproductive health, including cognitive and socioemotional predictors of sexual behavior. Her research has included influences of parenting and peer relationships on adolescent sexual behavior. Halpern-Felsher also has served as a consultant for a number of community-based adolescent health promotion campaigns, and she has been involved in community-based efforts to reduce substance abuse in adolescence. For example, she has worked with the state of California to implement new school-based tobacco prevention educational materials. As a further indication of her strong commitment to improving adolescents' lives, Halpern-Felsher coordinates the STEP-UP program (Short-Term Research

Bonnie Halpern-Felsher (*second from left*) with some of the students she is mentoring in the STEP-UP program.
Bonnie Halpern-Felsher

Experience for Underrepresented Persons), in which she has personally mentored and supervised 22 to 25 middle and high school students every year since 2007.

E-cigarettes are battery-powered devices that contain a heating element and produce a vapor that users inhale. In most cases the vapor contains nicotine, but the specific contents of "vape" formulas are not regulated (Barrington-Trimis & others, 2018; Gorukanti & others, 2017). As a result, states are rapidly adopting standards (including some bans) on vaping products (Public Health Law Center, 2019). In 2014, for the first time in the Monitoring the Future study, e-cigarette use was assessed (Johnston & others, 2015). E-cigarette use by U.S. adolescents in 2014 surpassed tobacco cigarette use—in the 30 days preceding the survey, 9 percent of eighth-graders, 16 percent of tenth-graders, and 17 percent of twelfth-graders reported using e-cigarettes. In 2022, 12.0 percent of eighth-graders, 20.5 percent of tenth-graders, and 27.3 percent of twelfth-graders reported vaping nicotine in the past year (National Institute on Drug Abuse, 2022).

The Roles of Development, Parents, Peers, and Educational Success   A special concern involves adolescents who begin to use drugs early in adolescence or even in childhood (Donatelle & Ketcham, 2018). One of the longest-running longitudinal studies (following the same individuals from 8 to 42 years of age) found that early onset of drinking was linked to increased risk of heavy drinking in middle age (Pitkanen, Lyyra, & Pulkkinen, 2005). Another longitudinal study found that onset of alcohol use before 11 years of age was linked to increased adult alcohol dependence (Guttmannova & others, 2012). Still another longitudinal study found that earlier age at first use of alcohol was linked to risk of heavy alcohol use in early adulthood (Liang & Chikritzhs, 2015). Finally, one study examined distinct trajectories (for example, involving timing and pace) of use across adolescence; the data indicated that early- and rapid-onset trajectories of alcohol, marijuana, and substance use were associated with substance abuse in early adulthood (Nelson, Van Ryzin, & Dishion, 2015).

Parents play an important role in preventing adolescent drug abuse (Kapetanovic & others, 2019). Positive relationships with parents and others can reduce adolescents' drug use (Ladis & others, 2019; Mak & Iacovou, 2019). Researchers have found that parental monitoring is linked with a lower incidence of drug use (Merrin & others, 2019). Family routines also are important; for example, adolescents who eat dinner with their parents, who feel they can confide in their parents, and who believe that their parents understand them are less likely to use substances (Afifi & others, 2022).

Peer relations powerfully influence whether adolescents engage in substance use (Mason & others, 2019). Substance use is often initiated in the presence of peers (Henneberger, Gest, & Zadzora, 2019), and adolescents' perceptions of their peers' substance use are strongly predictive of adolescents' own substance use (Marmet & others, 2021). A longitudinal study of Appalachian youth found that risky decision making, coupled with having peers who were substance users, best predicted neurological and cognitive changes that led to more rapid increases in substance use (Kim-Spoon & others, 2019).

Educational success is a strong buffer against the emergence of drug problems in adolescence. An influential analysis by Jerald Bachman and colleagues (2008) revealed that early educational achievement considerably reduced the likelihood that adolescents would develop drug problems, including those involving alcohol abuse, smoking, and abuse of various illicit drugs. This pattern has continued to be found, with Bachman and colleagues reporting in 2016 that school absences predicted higher rates of synthetic psychoactive drug use among adolescents (Patrick & others, 2016).

Can special programs effectively reduce adolescent drinking and smoking? See the *Connecting with Research* interlude for a description of a classic program evaluation study that addressed this question.

How Would You...?

If you were a **human development and family studies professional,** how would you explain to parents the importance of parental monitoring in preventing adolescent substance abuse?

What are ways that parents have been found to influence whether their adolescent children take drugs?

LJM Photo/Design Pics/Getty Images

EATING PROBLEMS AND DISORDERS

Eating disorders have become increasingly common among adolescents (Galmiche & others, 2019). Here are some research findings involving adolescent eating disorders:

- *Body image.* Body dissatisfaction and distorted body image (i.e., body dysmorphia) play important roles in adolescent eating disorders (Murnen & Smolak, 2019). One study revealed that in general, adolescents were dissatisfied with their bodies, with males

A Classic Evaluation Study of a Family Program Designed to Reduce Drinking and Smoking in Young Adolescents

Key Points:

- The program provided adolescents and their parents with resources to facilitate discussions about substance use.
- Adolescents whose families participated in the program were less likely to use alcohol and cigarettes three months and one year later than adolescents whose families did not participate.

Few experimental studies have been conducted to determine whether family programs can reduce drinking and smoking in young adolescents. In one classic experimental study, 1,326 families throughout the United States with 12- to 14-year-old adolescents were interviewed (Bauman & others, 2002). After the baseline interviews, participants were randomly assigned either to go through the Family Matters program (experimental group) or not to experience the program (control group) (Bauman & others, 2002).

The families assigned to the Family Matters program received four mailings of booklets. Each mailing was followed by a telephone call from a health educator to "encourage participation by all family members, answer any questions, and record information" (Bauman & others, 2002, pp. 36–37). The first booklet focused on the negative consequences of adolescent substance abuse to the family. The second booklet emphasized "supervision, support, communication skills, attachment, time spent together, educational achievement, conflict reduction, and how well adolescence is understood." The third booklet asked parents to "list things that they do that might inadvertently encourage their child's use of tobacco or alcohol, identify rules that might influence the child's use, and consider ways to monitor use. Then adult family members and the child meet to agree upon rules and sanctions related to adolescent use." Booklet four deals with what "the child can do to resist peer and media pressures for use."

Two follow-up interviews with the parents and adolescents were conducted three months and one year after the experimental group completed the program. Adolescents in the Family Matters program reported lower rates of alcohol and cigarette use both at three months

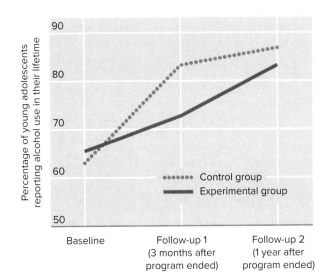

FIGURE **13**

YOUNG ADOLESCENTS' REPORTS OF ALCOHOL USE IN THE FAMILY MATTERS PROGRAM.

Note that at baseline (before the program started) the young adolescents in the Family Matters program (experimental group) and their counterparts who did not go through the program (control group) reported approximately the same lifetime use of alcohol (slightly higher use by the experimental group). However, three months after the program ended, the experimental group reported lower alcohol use, and this reduction was still present one year after the program ended, although the effect was not as strong.

and again one year after the program had been completed. Figure 13 shows the results for alcohol.

What other types of research efforts might help identify or design programs that are effective in reducing adolescent drinking and smoking?

desiring to increase their upper body through weight training and sports and females wanting to decrease the overall size of their body (Ata, Ludden, & Lally, 2007). In this study, low self-esteem and social support, weight-related teasing, and pressure to lose weight were linked to adolescents' negative body images. In a meta-analysis of longitudinal studies, reciprocal links were demonstrated, with low self-esteem predicting more eating pathology and more eating pathology predicting worse self-esteem over time (Krauss, Dapp, & Orth, 2023). Another line of research, including studies conducted outside the United States (for example, in China), has shown that poorer body image plays a key role in the link between depression and obesity in adolescence (Rao & others, 2019).

- *Parenting.* Adolescents who report observing more healthy eating patterns and exercise by their parents have more healthy eating patterns and exercise more themselves

(Yeatts, Martin, & Farren, 2019). Other research has shown that a range of parenting risk factors, such as harshness and abuse as well as parents' own eating disorders, predict the development of eating disorders in adolescence and early adulthood (Potterton & others, 2020).

- *Gender identity and sexual orientation.* Historically, research on eating disorders focused primarily on girls and women, but more recent research has expanded to include boys and men and to examine the role of sexual orientation and gender identity in relation to eating disorders (Breton, Juster, & Booji, 2023). Early evidence suggests that sexual minority youth are at higher risk for eating disorders than their heterosexual peers (Cao & others, 2023).

- *Role models and the media.* Early research showed that girls who were highly motivated to look like female celebrities were more likely than their peers to become very concerned about their weight (Field & others, 2001). Also, watching ads with "idealized" thin female images increased adolescent girls' dissatisfaction with their bodies (Hargreaves & Tiggemann, 2004). Interestingly, a meta-analysis of over 100,000 participants around the globe showed that these media exposure effects may be getting weaker, with a shift toward greater acceptance of a diversity of body types and shapes (Karazsia, Murnen, & Tylka, 2017). However, contemporary research suggests that extensive use of social media contributes to more body dissatisfaction for girls and boys (Vandenbosch, Fardouly, & Tiggemann, 2022).

Earlier in the chapter we examined the health risks and emotional consequences of being overweight or obese in adolescence. Let's now examine two other eating problems—anorexia nervosa and bulimia nervosa. Researchers consistently have discovered that the onset of anorexia nervosa and bulimia nervosa occurs in adolescence and that adult onset of these conditions is rare (Favaro & others, 2019). Scientists also have found that eating disorders, including anorexia nervosa and bulimia nervosa, are far more likely to appear in females than males.

Anorexia Nervosa   **Anorexia nervosa** is an eating disorder that involves the relentless pursuit of thinness through starvation. It is a serious disorder that can lead to death (Phillipou, Castle, & Rossell, 2019). Anorexia nervosa is about 10 times more likely to occur in females than males. Although most U.S. girls have been on a diet at some point, slightly less than 1 percent ever develop anorexia nervosa. However, extreme dieting and anorexia are found not only in the United States but also in many other countries in Asia and Europe (van Eeden, van Hoeken, & Hoek, 2021).

Three main characteristics of anorexia nervosa are (1) weighing less than 85 percent of what is considered normal for a person's age and height, (2) having an intense fear of gaining weight—a fear that does not decrease with weight loss, and (3) having a distorted image of body shape (Phillipou, Castle, & Rossell, 2019). Obsessive thinking about weight and compulsive exercise also are linked to anorexia nervosa (Back & others, 2019). Even when they are extremely thin, people with anorexia see themselves as too fat. They never think they are thin enough, especially in the abdomen, buttocks, and thighs. They usually weigh themselves frequently, often take their body measurements, and gaze critically at themselves in mirrors.

Anorexia nervosa typically begins in the early to middle teenage years, often following an episode of dieting and some type of life stress. When anorexia nervosa does occur in males, the symptoms and other characteristics (such as a distorted body image and family conflict) are usually similar to those reported by females who have the disorder (Murray, Griffiths, & Lavender, 2019).

Youth with anorexia become stressed about not being able to reach their high expectations and shift their focus to something they can control: their weight (H.B. Murray & others, 2017; Stice & others, 2017). Offspring of mothers with anorexia nervosa or related extreme dieting and exercising behaviors are at risk for becoming anorexic themselves (Watson, O'Brien, & Sadeh-Sharvit, 2018). Problems in family functioning are often found to be linked to the appearance of anorexia nervosa in adolescent girls (Machado & others, 2014), and family therapy is often the most effective treatment, especially when coupled with individual psychotherapy (Hurst & Zimmer-Gembeck, 2019).

Biology and culture are involved in anorexia nervosa. Genes play an important role in anorexia nervosa, and specific gene variants are now being identified (Watson & others,

Anorexia nervosa is a serious problem for many young people. *What are some possible causes of anorexia nervosa?*

PeopleImages/E+/Getty Images

anorexia nervosa An eating disorder that involves the relentless pursuit of thinness through starvation.

2019). Also, the physical effects of dieting may change neural networks in the brain and thus sustain the disordered pattern (Scaife & others, 2017). The "fashion image" in many contemporary media cultures likely contributes to the incidence of anorexia nervosa (Cazzato & others, 2016). The media and social media portray idealized body images that young people may try to emulate. An illustrative study found that having an increased number of friends on social media across two years was linked to enhanced motivation to be thin (Tiggemann & Slater, 2017). These pressures have historically been described as primarily affecting straight non-Latina White girls, but they affect adolescents across racial, ethnic, gender identity, and sexual orientation groups (National Association of Anorexia Nervosa and Associated Disorders, 2023).

Bulimia Nervosa   Whereas individuals with anorexia control their eating by restricting it, most people with bulimia do not (Castillo & Weiselberg, 2017). **Bulimia nervosa** is an eating disorder in which the individual consistently follows a binge-and-purge pattern. A person with bulimia goes on an eating binge and then purges by self-induced vomiting or use of a laxative. Many people binge and purge occasionally and some experiment with it, but a person is considered to have a serious bulimic disorder if the episodes occur at least twice a week for three months (Cuzzolaro, 2014).

About 90 percent of people with bulimia are females, and approximately 1 to 2 percent of U.S. females are estimated to develop bulimia nervosa. Bulimia nervosa typically begins in late adolescence or early adulthood. Many women who develop bulimia nervosa were somewhat overweight before the onset of the disorder, and the binge eating often began during an episode of dieting. Unlike people with anorexia, people who binge-and-purge typically fall within a normal weight range, which makes bulimia more difficult to detect.

As with people with anorexia, most individuals with bulimia are preoccupied with food, have a strong fear of becoming overweight, and are depressed or anxious (H.B. Murray & others, 2017; Stice & others, 2017). A meta-analysis of many studies has shown that people with bulimia, like people with anorexia, are highly perfectionistic (Kehayes & others, 2019). Gender dysphoria and eating disorders may be linked in complicated ways (Abernathey & others, 2023).

As with anorexia nervosa, about 70 percent of individuals who develop bulimia nervosa eventually recover from the disorder (Agras & others, 2004), although those who eventually recover often have relapsed multiple times (Sala & others, 2023). Drug therapy and psychotherapy have been effective in treating anorexia nervosa and bulimia nervosa (Svaldi & others, 2019). Cognitive-behavioral therapy has especially been helpful in treating bulimia nervosa (Kaidesoia, Cooper, & Fordham, 2023).

bulimia nervosa An eating disorder in which the individual consistently follows a binge-and-purge eating pattern.

How Would You...?
If you were a **health-care professional,** how would you educate parents to identify the signs and symptoms that may signal an eating disorder?

Review **Connect** Reflect

LG4 Summarize adolescents' health and eating disorders.

Review
- What are key concerns about the health of adolescents?
- What are the leading causes of death in adolescence and emerging adulthood?
- What are some characteristics of adolescents' substance use and abuse?
- What are the characteristics of the major eating disorders?

Connect
- How might eating patterns in childhood possibly contribute to eating problems in adolescence?

Reflect *Your Own Personal Journey of Life*
- What were your health habits like from the time you entered puberty to the time you completed high school? Describe your health-compromising and health-enhancing behaviors during this time. Since high school, have you reduced your health-compromising behaviors? Explain.

In this chapter, you examined some significant changes that occur in the adolescent's brain—the early development of the amygdala and the delayed development of the prefrontal cortex—that may contribute to risk taking and sensation seeking. Next, you will read about how adolescent thinking becomes more abstract, idealistic, and logical—which Piaget described as the key aspects of formal operational thought. Other topics you will explore in the next chapter include adolescents' decision making and the influence of schools in their lives.

reach your **learning goals**

Physical Development in Adolescence

1 What Is the Nature of Adolescence?

 Discuss views and developmental transitions that involve adolescence.

Positive and Negative Views of Adolescence

- Many stereotypes about adolescents are negative. Today, however, the majority of adolescents successfully negotiate the path from childhood to adulthood, although too many are not provided with adequate support and opportunities.

- It is important to view adolescents as a heterogeneous group. Adolescent behavior typically moves toward accepting, rather than rejecting, parental values. Recent interest has focused on a strength-based approach that emphasizes positive youth development.

Developmental Transitions

- Two important transitions in development are those from childhood to adolescence and from adolescence to adulthood. In the transition from childhood to adolescence, pubertal change is prominent, although cognitive and socioemotional changes occur as well.

- The concept of emerging adulthood recently has been proposed to describe the transition from adolescence to adulthood. Five key characteristics of emerging adulthood are identity exploration (especially in love and work), instability, being self-focused, feeling in-between, and experiencing opportunities to transform one's life.

2 What Are the Physical and Psychological Aspects of Puberty?

 Describe puberty's characteristics, developmental changes, psychological dimensions, and the development of the brain.

Sexual Maturation, Height, and Weight

- Puberty is a brain-neuroendocrine process occurring primarily in early adolescence that provides stimulation for the rapid physical change involved in this period of development. A number of changes occur in sexual maturation, including increased size of the penis and testicles in boys and breast growth and menarche in girls. The growth spurt involves height and weight and occurs about two years earlier for girls than for boys.

Hormonal Changes

- Extensive hormonal changes characterize puberty. The pituitary gland plays an important role in these hormonal changes. During puberty, testosterone concentrations increase considerably in boys, and estradiol increases considerably in girls.

Timing and Variations in Puberty

- In the United States, the age of menarche (a girl's first menstrual period) has declined since the mid-1800s. The basic genetic program for puberty is wired into the species, but nutrition, health, and other environmental factors affect puberty's timing and makeup. Menarche typically appears between 9 and 15 years of age. Boys can start the pubertal sequence as early as 10 years of age or as late as 17.

Psychological Dimensions of Puberty

- Adolescents show heightened interest in their bodies and body images. Younger adolescents are more preoccupied with these images than are older adolescents. Adolescent girls often have a more negative body image than do adolescent boys.

- Early maturation often favors boys, at least during early adolescence, but as adults, late-maturing boys have a more positive identity than early-maturing boys. Early-maturing girls are at risk for a number of developmental problems. They are more likely to smoke and drink and have an eating disorder and are likely to have earlier sexual experiences than later-maturing girls.

The Brain

- The thickening of the corpus callosum in adolescence is linked to improved processing of information. The limbic system and the amygdala, which are involved in emotions such as anger, mature earlier than the prefrontal cortex, which functions in reasoning and self-regulation. This gap in development may help to explain the increase in risk-taking behavior that often characterizes adolescence.

3 What Are the Dimensions of Adolescent Sexuality?

 LG3 Characterize adolescent sexuality.

Developing a Sexual Identity

- Adolescence is a time of sexual exploration and sexual experimentation. Mastering emerging sexual feelings and forming a sense of sexual identity are multifaceted. An adolescent's sexual identity includes sexual orientation, activities, interests, and styles of behavior.

Timing and Trends in Adolescent Sexual Behavior

- The timing of sexual initiation in adolescence varies by country, gender, and socioeconomic characteristics. Also, recently there has been a decline in the number of adolescents who say they have experienced various aspects of sexuality. However, a dramatic increase in oral sex has occurred recently among adolescents.

Sexual Risk Taking in Adolescence

- Having sexual intercourse in early adolescence, as well as various contextual and family factors, is associated with sexual problems and negative developmental outcomes. Large numbers of adolescents do not use contraceptives. Recently, there has been increased emphasis on having adolescents use long-acting reversible contraception.

- Sexually transmitted infections (STIs) are contracted primarily through sexual contact. Approximately one in four sexually active adolescents have an STI. Among the STIs are bacterial infections such as gonorrhea, syphilis, and chlamydia, and viral infections such as genital herpes, genital warts, and HIV.

- Although the U.S. adolescent pregnancy rate is still among the highest in high-income countries, the rate declined considerably in the last two decades. Adolescent pregnancy often increases health risks for the mother and the offspring, although it often is not pregnancy alone that places adolescents at risk. Easy access to family-planning services and comprehensive sex education programs in schools can help reduce the U.S. adolescent pregnancy rate.

4 How Can Adolescents' Health and Health-Enhancing Assets Be Characterized?

 LG4 Summarize adolescents' health and eating disorders.

Adolescent Health

- Adolescence is a critical juncture in health because many of the factors related to poor health habits and early death in the adult years begin during adolescence. Poor nutrition, lack of exercise, and inadequate sleep are concerns.

Leading Causes of Death in Adolescence

- The three leading causes of death in adolescence and emerging adulthood are accidents, homicide, and suicide.

Substance Use and Abuse

- Despite recent declines in use, the United States has one of the highest rates of adolescent drug use of any industrialized nation. Alcohol abuse is a major adolescent problem, although its rate has been dropping in recent years, as has the rate of cigarette smoking, although vaping is increasing. Drug use in childhood or early adolescence has more negative outcomes than drug use that begins in late adolescence. Parents and peers play important roles in whether adolescents take drugs.

Eating Problems and Disorders

- Eating disorders have increased in adolescence, with a substantial increase in the percentage of adolescents who are overweight. Three eating disorders that may occur in adolescence are obesity, anorexia nervosa, and bulimia nervosa.

- A combination of behavioral therapy, calorie restriction, exercise, and reduction of sedentary activities such as screen time has been more effective for overweight adolescents than school-based approaches.

- Anorexia nervosa is an eating disorder that involves the relentless pursuit of thinness through starvation. Individuals with anorexia are intensely afraid of weight gain, have a distorted body image, and weigh less than 85 percent of what would be considered normal for their height.
- Bulimia nervosa is an eating disorder in which a binge-and-purge pattern is consistently followed. Most individuals with bulimia are depressed or anxious and fearful of becoming overweight, and their weight typically falls within a normal range. About 70 percent of individuals with bulimia and anorexia eventually recover.

key terms

AIDS	emerging adulthood	hypothalamus	puberty
amygdala	estradiol	limbic system	sexually transmitted infections
anorexia nervosa	gonadotropins	melatonin	(STIs)
bulimia nervosa	gonads	menarche	spermarche
corpus callosum	hormones	pituitary gland	testosterone

key people

Claudia Allen	Peter Benson	Bonnie Halpern-Felsher	Charles Nelson
Joseph Allen	Mary Carskadon	Lloyd Johnston	Daniel Offer
Jeffrey Arnett	G. Stanley Hall		

improving the lives of children

STRATEGIES

Supporting Adolescent Physical Development and Health

What are some strategies for supporting and guiding adolescent physical development and health?

- *Develop positive expectations for adolescents.* Adolescents often are negatively stereotyped. These negative expectations have a way of becoming self-fulfilling prophecies and harming adult-adolescent communication. Don't view adolescence as a time of crisis and rebellion. View it instead as a time of evaluation, decision making, commitment, and the carving out of a place in the world.

- *Understand the many physical changes adolescents are going through.* The physical changes adolescents go through can be very perplexing to them. They are not quite sure what they are going to change into, and this can create considerable uncertainty for them.

- *Be a good health role model for adolescents.* Adolescents benefit from being around adults who are good health role models: individuals who exercise regularly, eat healthily, and don't take drugs or smoke.

- *Communicate effectively with adolescents about sexuality.* Emphasize that young adolescents should abstain from sex. If adolescents are going to be sexually active, they need to take contraceptive precautions. Adolescents also need to learn about sexuality and human reproduction before they become sexually active.

RESOURCES

Search Institute
www.search-institute.org

The Search Institute has available a large number of resources for improving the lives of adolescents. Brochures and books include resource lists and address topics such as school improvement, adolescent literacy, parent education, program planning, and adolescent health. A free quarterly newsletter is also available.

Society for Adolescent Health and Medicine (SAHM)
www.adolescenthealth.org

SAHM is a valuable source of information about competent physicians who specialize in treating adolescents. It maintains a list of recommended adolescence specialists across the United States. SAHM publishes an excellent research journal, *Journal of Adolescent Health,* that provides up-to-date coverage of many problems adolescents can develop.

Nemours KidsHealth
www.kidshealth.org

This website provides excellent advice to help parents understand, guide, and converse with their teens about many topics, including puberty, sleep problems, body image, and drugs.

You and Your Adult Child: How to Grow Together in Challenging Times (2023)
Lawrence Steinberg
New York: Simon & Schuster

A superb, well-written book on the lives of emerging adults, including extensive recommendations for parents on how to effectively guide their children through the transition from adolescence to adulthood.

Understanding the Well-Being of LGBTQI+ Populations (2021)
National Academies of Sciences, Engineering, and Medicine
Washington, DC: National Academies Press

This consensus study report reviews research on the well-being of LGBTQI+ individuals across the life span and recommends policies and practices to support their well-being.

Attack of the Teenage Brain! (2018)
John Medina
Alexandria, VA: ASCD

An engaging and accessible book by an expert in developmental neurogenetics that examines the latest brain science of puberty.

chapter 15

COGNITIVE DEVELOPMENT IN ADOLESCENCE

chapter outline

Image100 Ltd

Kim-Chi Trinh was only 9 years old in Vietnam when her father used his savings to buy passage for her on a fishing boat. It was a costly and risky sacrifice for the family, who placed Kim-Chi on the small boat, among strangers, in the hope that she eventually would reach the United States, where she would get a good education and enjoy a better life.

Kim-Chi made it to the United States and coped with a succession of three foster families. When she graduated from high school in San Diego, she had a straight-A average and a number of college scholarship offers. When asked why she excelled in school, Kim-Chi says that she had to do well because she owed it to her parents, who were still in Vietnam.

Kim-Chi is one of a wave of bright, highly motivated Asians who are immigrating to the United States. Not all Asian American youth do this well, however. Vietnamese, Cambodian, and Hmong refugees who have fallen behind in their schooling, in particular, have been at risk for school-related problems. Many refugee children's histories are replete with losses and trauma.

topical connections   looking *back*

You have explored how early adolescence is a time of dramatic physical change as puberty unfolds. Pubertal change also brings considerable interest in one's body image. And pubertal change ushers in an intense interest in sexuality. Adolescence also is a critical time in the development of behaviors related to health, such as good nutrition and regular exercise, which are health enhancing, and drug abuse, which is health compromising. Significant changes occur in the adolescent's brain—the early development of the limbic system/amygdala and the delayed development of the prefrontal cortex—that may contribute to risk taking and decision making. You have read about cognitive advances in middle childhood, including improved thinking strategies and reading skills. This chapter examines continued advances in thinking skills, moral development and values, and schools.

preview

When people think of the changes that characterize adolescents, they often focus on puberty and adolescent problems. However, some impressive cognitive changes occur during adolescence. We begin this chapter by focusing on these cognitive changes and then turn our attention to adolescents' values, moral education, and religion. In the last section of the chapter, we study the characteristics of schools for adolescents.

1 How Do Adolescents Think and Process Information? Discuss different approaches to adolescent cognition.

| Piaget's Theory | Adolescent Egocentrism | Information Processing |

Adolescents' developing power of thought opens up new cognitive and social horizons. Let's examine the characteristics of this developing power of thought, beginning with Piaget's theory (1952).

PIAGET'S THEORY

Jean Piaget proposed that at about 7 years of age children enter the *concrete operational stage* of cognitive development. They can reason logically about concrete events and objects, and they make gains in their ability to classify objects and to reason about the relationships between classes of objects. According to Piaget, the concrete operational stage lasts until the child is about 11 years old, when the fourth and final stage of cognitive development begins—the formal operational stage.

The Formal Operational Stage What are the characteristics of the formal operational stage? Formal operational thought is more abstract than concrete operational thought. Adolescents are no longer limited to actual experiences as anchors for thought. They can conjure up make-believe situations—events that are purely hypothetical possibilities or abstract propositions—and can try to reason logically and systematically about them.

The abstract quality of thinking during the formal operational stage is evident in the adolescent's verbal problem-solving ability. Whereas the concrete operational thinker needs to see the concrete elements A, B, and C to be able to make the logical inference that if A = B and B = C, then A = C, the formal operational thinker can solve this problem merely through verbal presentation.

Another indication of the abstract quality of adolescents' thought is their capacity to think about thought itself. One adolescent commented, "I began thinking about why I was thinking what I was. Then I began thinking about why I was thinking about what I was thinking about what I was." This example characterizes the adolescent's enhanced focus on thought and its abstract qualities.

Formal operational thinking also is full of idealism and possibilities, especially during the beginning of the formal operational stage, when assimilation dominates. Adolescents engage in extended speculation about ideal characteristics—qualities they desire in themselves and in others. Such thoughts often lead adolescents to compare themselves with others in regard to such ideal standards. And their thoughts are often fantasy flights into future possibilities.

developmental **connection**

Cognitive Development

Piaget's first three stages are sensorimotor, preoperational, and concrete operational. Connect to "Cognitive Development in Infancy," "Cognitive Development in Early Childhood," and "Cognitive Development in Middle and Late Childhood."

Might adolescents' ability to reason hypothetically and to evaluate what is ideal versus what is real lead them to engage in demonstrations, such as this Black Lives Matter protest? What other causes might be attractive to adolescents' newfound cognitive abilities of hypothetical-deductive reasoning and idealistic thinking?

Marcello Sgarlato/Alamy Stock Photo

hypothetical-deductive reasoning Piaget's formal operational concept that adolescents have the cognitive ability to develop hypotheses, or best guesses, about ways to solve problems.

adolescent egocentrism The heightened self-consciousness of adolescents that is reflected in their belief that others are as interested in them as they are in themselves, and in their sense of personal uniqueness and invincibility.

imaginary audience Refers to adolescents' belief that others are as interested in them as they themselves are, as well as their attention-getting behavior motivated by a desire to be noticed, visible, and "on stage."

developmental **connection**

Cognitive Development

Neo-Piagetians are developmentalists who have elaborated on Piaget's theory. They argue that cognitive development is more specific than Piaget envisioned, and they give more emphasis to information processing. Connect to "Cognitive Development in Middle and Late Childhood."

Many adolescents spend long hours in front of the mirror, checking their appearance. *How might this behavior be related to changes in adolescent cognitive and physical development?*
Syldavia/iStock/Getty Images

Adolescents also learn to think more logically about abstract concepts. Children are likely to solve problems through trial-and-error; adolescents begin to think more as a scientist thinks. This type of problem solving requires **hypothetical-deductive reasoning.** Such reasoning involves creating a hypothesis and deducing its implications, which provide ways to test the hypothesis. Thus, formal operational thinkers develop hypotheses about ways to solve problems and then systematically deduce the best path to follow to solve the problem.

Evaluating Piaget's Theory   Some of Piaget's ideas on the formal operational stage have been challenged. The stage includes much more individual variation than Piaget envisioned. Only about one in three young adolescents is a formal operational thinker. Many American adults never become formal operational thinkers, and neither do many adults in other cultures.

Furthermore, education in the logic of science and mathematics promotes the development of formal operational thinking. This point recalls a criticism of Piaget's theory: Culture and education exert stronger influences on cognitive development than Piaget maintained (Kirmayer & others, 2020; Riccio & Castro, 2021).

Piaget's theory of cognitive development has been challenged on other points as well. Piaget conceived of stages as unitary structures of thought, with various aspects of a stage emerging at the same time. However, most contemporary developmentalists agree that cognitive development is not as stage-like as Piaget envisioned (Hayne & Herbert, 2021). Furthermore, children can be trained to reason at a higher cognitive stage, and some cognitive abilities emerge earlier than Piaget predicted (Bell & Broomell, 2021). For example, even 2-year-olds are nonegocentric in some contexts. When they realize that another person does not see an object, they investigate whether the person is blindfolded or looking in a different direction. Some understanding of the conservation of number has been demonstrated as early as age 3, although Piaget did not think it emerged until 7. Other cognitive abilities can emerge later than Piaget expected. For example, college students are better at solving formal operations problems in their majors than in unfamiliar subject areas (Bjorklund & Causey, 2017).

Despite these challenges to Piaget's ideas, we owe him a tremendous debt. Piaget was the founder of the present field of cognitive development, and he established a long list of masterful concepts of enduring power and fascination: assimilation, accommodation, object permanence, egocentrism, conservation, and others. Psychologists also owe him for the current vision of children as active, constructive thinkers. And they are indebted to him for creating a theory that generated a huge volume of research on children's cognitive development (Bjorklund, 2018).

Piaget was a genius when it came to observing children. His careful observations demonstrated inventive ways to discover how children act on and adapt to their world. He also showed us how children need to make their experiences fit their schemes yet simultaneously adapt their schemes to reflect their experiences. Piaget revealed how cognitive change is likely to occur if the context is structured to allow gradual movement to the next higher level. Concepts do not emerge suddenly, full-blown, but instead develop through a series of partial accomplishments that lead to increasingly comprehensive understanding (Birch & others, 2017).

ADOLESCENT EGOCENTRISM

David Elkind (1978) described how adolescent egocentrism governs the way that adolescents think about social matters. **Adolescent egocentrism** is the heightened self-consciousness of adolescents, which is reflected in their belief that others are as interested in them as they are in themselves, as well as in their sense of personal uniqueness and invincibility. Elkind argued that adolescent egocentrism can be dissected into two types of social thinking—imaginary audience and personal fable.

The **imaginary audience** refers to the aspect of adolescent egocentrism that involves feeling that one is on stage at the center of everyone's attention. Adolescents might think that others are as keenly aware that they have a few hairs out of place as they themselves are, or that all eyes are riveted on their complexion as they walk into a classroom.

Might today's teens be drawn to social media to express their imaginary audience and sense of uniqueness? A need for peer approval can motivate teens to carefully cultivate their social media posts to make themselves appear attractive, interesting, and popular (Yau & Reich, 2019). A look at a teen's social media posts may suggest to many adults that what teens are reporting is often rather mundane and uninteresting as they update to the world at large what they are doing and having, such as: "Studying heavy. Not happy tonight." or "At Starbucks with

Jesse. Lattes are great." Possibly for adolescents, though, such posts are not trivial but rather an expression of each teen's sense of uniqueness. An illustrative study found that the frequency of posting selfies to a popular social networking site in China was related to greater self-objectification for Chinese female adolescents, especially those who believed more strongly in the imaginary audience (Zheng, Ni, & Luo, 2019). And a meta-analysis concluded that greater use of social networking sites was linked to higher levels of narcissism (Gnambs & Appel, 2018).

The **personal fable** is another part of adolescent egocentrism that involves an adolescent's sense of personal uniqueness along with a feeling of invincibility. Adolescents' sense of personal uniqueness makes them believe that no one can understand how they really feel. For example, adolescents might think that their parents cannot possibly sense the hurt they feel from a relationship breakup, or think that they cannot get harmed if they engage in a risky behavior.

However, some research challenges the idea of a personal fable. For example, some studies suggest that rather than perceiving themselves to be invulnerable, many adolescents view themselves as vulnerable (Reyna, 2018). For example, 12- to 18-year-olds greatly overestimate their chances of dying in the next year and prior to age 20 (de Bruin & Fischhoff, 2017). Some researchers have argued that the sense of invulnerability in adolescents is more complex than being due to just one factor; instead, it consists of two dimensions (Kim, Park, & Kang, 2018; Potard & others, 2018):

- *Danger invulnerability,* which involves adolescents' sense of indestructibility and tendency to take on physical risks (driving recklessly at high speeds, for example).

- *Psychological invulnerability*, which captures an adolescent's felt invulnerability related to personal or psychological distress (getting one's feelings hurt, for example).

Adolescents who score low on perceptions of risks (or high on perceptions of danger invulnerability) are more likely to engage in a given behavior than are adolescents who perceive the behavior as riskier. For example, use of electronic cigarettes for "vaping" is higher among adolescents who do not perceive their use as risky (Burrow-Sánchez & Ratcliff, 2021). In another example, adolescents who experience traumas that disrupt their sense of psychological invulnerability are more at risk of developing mental health problems (W.Y. Chen & others, 2017). In terms of psychological invulnerability, adolescents often benefit from the typical developmental challenges of exploring identity, making new friends, and learning a new skill. All of these important adolescent tasks involve a risk of failure as well as a potential for enhanced self-image following a successful outcome.

Are social media, such as Instagram and Snapchat, amplifying the expression of adolescents' imaginary audience and personal fable sense of uniqueness?
Tracy Martinez/Alamy Stock Photo

INFORMATION PROCESSING

In Deanna Kuhn's (2009) view, in the later years of childhood and continuing in adolescence, individuals approach cognitive levels that may or may not be achieved. By adolescence, considerable variation in cognitive functioning is present across individuals. This variability supports the argument that adolescents are producers of their own development, perhaps to a greater extent than are children.

Executive Function   A very important cognitive change in adolescence is improvement in *executive function.* Recall our description of *executive function* as an umbrella-like concept that consists of a number of higher-level cognitive processes linked to the development of the prefrontal cortex. Executive function involves managing one's thoughts to engage in goal-directed behavior and to exercise self-control. Executive function in early childhood especially involves developmental advances in cognitive inhibition, cognitive flexibility, and goal setting (Bell & Garcia Meza, 2020). We have described executive function advances in cognitive inhibition, as well as progress in working memory (Gerst & others, 2017).

Executive function strengthens not only during childhood but also during adolescence (Chaku, Hoyt, & Barry, 2021). This executive function "assumes a role of monitoring and managing the deployment of cognitive resources as a function of task demands. As a result, cognitive development and learning itself become more effective. . . . Emergence and strengthening of this executive (function) is arguably the single most important and consequential intellectual development to occur in the second decade of life" (Kuhn & Franklin, 2006, p. 987). We focus next on five subtypes of executive function in adolescence: working memory, cognitive control, decision making, critical thinking, and metacognition.

developmental **connection**

The Brain

The prefrontal cortex is the location in the brain where much of executive function occurs. Connect to "Physical Development in Early Childhood," "Physical Development in Middle and Late Childhood," and "Physical Development in Adolescence."

personal fable The part of adolescent egocentrism that involves an adolescent's sense of uniqueness and invincibility.

	TASK			
	VERBAL		**VISUOSPATIAL**	
Age	**Semantic Association**	**Digit/ Sentence**	**Mapping/ Directions**	**Visual Matrix**
8	1.33	1.75	3.13	1.67
10	1.70	2.34	3.60	2.06
13	1.86	2.94	4.09	2.51
16	2.24	2.98	3.92	2.68
24	2.60	3.71	4.64	3.47
Highest Working Memory Performance				
	3.02 (age 45)	3.97 (age 35)	4.90 (age 35)	3.47 (age 24)

FIGURE 1

DEVELOPMENTAL CHANGES IN WORKING MEMORY.

Note: The scores shown here are the means for each age group, and the age also represents a mean age. Higher scores reflect superior working memory performance.

Working Memory Recall that *working memory* is a kind of "mental workbench" where people manipulate and assemble information to help them make decisions, solve problems, and comprehend written and spoken language (Baddeley, Hitch, & Allen, 2021). Working memory is a foundational cognitive activity, with the frontoparietal brain network playing a key role in its development (Rosenberg & others, 2020). Working memory is an important aspect of executive function and is linked to many aspects of children's and adolescents' development (Vernucci & others, 2020). For example, an illustrative study found that adolescents with poorer working memory were more at risk for internalizing problems, such as anxiety and depression (Blok & others, 2023).

In one extensive cross-sectional study, the performances of individuals from 6 to 57 years of age were examined on both verbal and visuospatial working memory tasks (Swanson, 1999). The two verbal tasks were auditory digit sequence (the ability to remember numerical information embedded in a short sentence, such as "Now suppose somebody wanted to go to the supermarket at 8651 Elm Street") and semantic association (the ability to organize words into abstract categories) (Swanson, 1999, p. 988).

In the semantic association task, the participant was presented with a series of words (such as *shirt, saw, pants, hammer, shoes,* and *nails*) and then asked to remember how they go together. The two visuospatial tasks involved mapping/directions and a visual matrix. In the mapping/directions task, the participant was shown a street map indicating the route a bicycle (child/young adolescent) or car (adult) would take through a city. After briefly looking at the map, participants were asked to redraw the route on a blank map. In the visual matrix task, participants were asked to study a matrix showing a series of dots. After looking at the matrix for five seconds, they were asked to answer questions about the location of the dots. As shown in Figure 1, working memory increased substantially from 8 through 24 years of age—that is, through the transition to adulthood and beyond—no matter what the task. Another study using brain imaging found that these improvements in adolescence into young adulthood were due to shifts in neural functioning in particular brain regions (Simmonds, Hallquist, & Luna, 2017). Thus, the adolescent years are likely to be an important developmental period for improvement in working memory.

Cognitive Control **Cognitive control** involves effective control and flexible thinking in a number of areas, including controlling attention, reducing interfering thoughts, and being cognitively flexible (Robinson & Steyvers, 2023). Cognitive control also has been referred to as *inhibitory control* or *effortful control* to emphasize the ability to resist a strong inclination to do one thing but instead to do what is most effective.

Across childhood and adolescence, cognitive control increases with age (Bjorklund, 2022). The increase in cognitive control is thought to be due to the maturation of brain pathways and circuitry, especially those involving the prefrontal cortex (Friedman & Robbins, 2022). For example, one study found less diffusion and more focal activation in the prefrontal cortex from 7 to 30 years of age (Durston & others, 2006). The activation change was accompanied by increased efficiency in cognitive performance, especially in *cognitive control*.

Think about all the times adolescents and emerging adults need to engage in cognitive control, such as the following situations (Galinsky, 2010):

- making a real effort to stick with a task, avoiding interfering thoughts or environmental events, and instead doing what is most effective;
- stopping and thinking before acting to avoid blurting out something they might wish they hadn't said; and
- continuing to work on something that is important but boring when there is something a lot more fun to do.

The largest and longest-running longitudinal study of an important dimension of executive function—inhibitory control—found that 3- to 11-year-old children who early in development

cognitive control Involves effective control and flexible thinking in a number of areas, including controlling attention, reducing interfering thoughts, and being cognitively flexible.

had better inhibitory control (waiting their turn, not getting easily distracted, showing more persistence, and being less impulsive) were more likely to still be in school, less likely to engage in risk-taking behavior, and less likely to be taking drugs in adolescence (Moffitt & others, 2011). In addition, 30 years after they were initially assessed, the children with better inhibitory control had better physical and mental health (they were less likely to be overweight, for example), had better earnings in their career, were more law-abiding, and were happier.

Controlling Attention and Reducing Interfering Thoughts Controlling attention is a key aspect of learning and thinking in adolescence and emerging adulthood (Bjorklund, 2022). Distractions that can interfere with attention in adolescence and emerging adulthood come from the external environment. Examples include other students talking while the student is trying to listen to a lecture, or when someone uses social media on their laptop during a lecture and looks at messages and friends' photos. Other intrusive distractions can come from competing thoughts in the individual's mind. Self-oriented thoughts, such as worrying, self-doubt, and intense emotionally laden thoughts, may especially interfere with focusing attention on thinking tasks and also can affect mental health (Blake, Trinder, & Allen, 2018).

Being Cognitively Flexible *Cognitive flexibility* involves being aware that options and alternatives are available and adapting to the situation (Akdeniz & Ahçı, 2023). Before adolescents and emerging adults adapt their behavior in a situation, they must become aware that they need to change their way of thinking and be motivated to do so. Having confidence in their ability to adapt their thinking to a particular situation, an aspect of *self-efficacy,* also is important in being cognitively flexible (Bandura, 2018). To evaluate how cognitively flexible you are, take the quiz in Figure 2 (Galinsky, 2010).

Decision Making Adolescence is a time of increased decision making—which friends to choose; which person to date; whether to have sex, buy a car, go to college, and so on (Edelson & Reyna, 2023). How competent are adolescents at making decisions? Overall, the research shows that older adolescents are more competent than younger adolescents, who in turn are more competent than children. Compared with children, young adolescents are more likely to generate different options, examine a situation from a variety of perspectives, anticipate the consequences of decisions, and consider the credibility of sources.

However, older adolescents' (as well as adults') decision-making skills are far from perfect, and having the capacity to make competent decisions does not guarantee they will be made in everyday life, where breadth of experience often comes into play (Kuhn, 2009). As an example, driver-training courses improve adolescents' cognitive and motor skills to levels equal to, or sometimes superior to, those of adults. However, driver training has not been effective in reducing adolescents' high rate of traffic accidents. Still, graduated driver licensing (GDL) does reduce crash and fatality rates for adolescent drivers (U.S. Department of Transportation, 2021).

How Would You...?
If you were an **educator,** how would you incorporate decision-making exercises into the school curriculum for adolescents?

CIRCLE THE NUMBER THAT BEST REFLECTS HOW YOU THINK FOR EACH OF THE FOUR ITEMS:

	Exactly Like You	Very Much Like You	Somewhat Like You	Not Too Much Like You	Not At All Like You
1. When I try something that doesn't work, it's hard for me to give it up and try another solution.	1	2	3	4	5
2. I adapt to change pretty easily.	5	4	3	2	1
3. When I can't convince someone of my point of view, I can usually understand why not.	5	4	3	2	1
4. I am not very quick to take on new ideas.	1	2	3	4	5

Add your numbers for each of the four items: Total Score: _____
If your overall score is between 20 and 15, then you rate high on cognitive flexibility. If you scored between 9 and 14, you are in the middle category, and if you scored 8 or below, you likely could improve.

FIGURE **2**

HOW COGNITIVELY FLEXIBLE ARE YOU?

What are some of the decisions adolescents have to make? What characterizes their decision making?

Jack Affleck/Getty Images

GDL components include a learner's holding period, practice-driving certification, night-driving restriction, and passenger restriction. GDL is now commonly used throughout North America, Europe, and Australia, as well as certain countries on other continents.

Most people make better decisions when they are calm than when they are emotionally aroused, which often is the case for adolescents (Icenogle & others, 2019). Recall from our discussion of brain development in "Physical Development in Adolescence" that adolescents have a tendency to be emotionally intense, in part due to puberty-related hormonal and other neurobiological changes (Andersen & others, 2022). Thus, the same adolescent who makes a wise decision when calm may make an unwise decision when emotionally aroused. In the heat of the moment, then, adolescents' emotions may especially overwhelm their decision-making ability (Duell & Steinberg, 2020).

The social context plays a key role in adolescent decision making (Defoe & others, 2020). For example, adolescents' willingness to make risky decisions is more likely to occur in contexts where alcohol, drugs, and other temptations are readily available (Reyna, 2018). This body of research reveals that the presence of peers in risk-taking situations increases the likelihood that adolescents will make risky decisions (Shulman & others, 2016a, b). In one study of risk taking involving a simulated driving task, the presence of peers increased the likelihood of an adolescent's decision to engage in risky driving by 50 percent but had no effect on adults (Gardner & Steinberg, 2005). In another study, adolescents took greater risks and showed stronger preference for immediate rewards when they were with three same-aged peers than when they were alone (Silva, Chein, & Steinberg, 2016). The presence of peers may activate the brain's reward system, especially its dopamine pathways (Eckstrand, Lenniger, & Forbes, 2022).

Psychological science has informed several Supreme Court decisions regarding the extent to which adolescents can be held legally responsible for their behavior (Icenogle & others, 2019). For example, the Supreme Court abolished the death penalty for 16- and 17-year-olds in *Roper v. Simmons,* arguing that adolescents younger than 18 did not have the psychological maturity to be held accountable for their crimes.

Adolescents need more opportunities to practice and discuss realistic decision making. Many real-world decisions on matters such as sex, drugs, and dangerous driving occur in an atmosphere of stress that includes time constraints and emotional involvement. One strategy for improving adolescent decision making in such circumstances is to provide more opportunities for them to engage in role playing and group problem solving. Another strategy is for parents to involve adolescents in appropriate decision-making activities.

To better understand adolescent decision making, Valerie Reyna and her colleagues (Reyna, 2021; Reyna, Müller, & Edelson, 2023) have proposed the **fuzzy-trace theory dual-process model,** which states that decision making is influenced by two cognitive systems—"verbatim" analytical (literal and precise) and gist-based intuitional (simple bottom-line meaning)—which operate in parallel. Basing judgments and decisions on simple gist is viewed as more beneficial than analytical thinking to adolescents' decision making. In this view, adolescents don't benefit from engaging in reflective, detailed, higher-level cognitive analysis about a decision, especially in high-risk, real-world contexts where they would get bogged down in trivial detail. In such contexts, adolescents need to rely on their awareness that some circumstances are simply so dangerous that they must be avoided at all costs.

In risky situations, it is important for an adolescent to quickly get the *gist,* or meaning, of what is happening and perceive that the situation is a dangerous context, which can cue personal values that will protect the adolescent from making a risky decision (Rahimi-Golkhandan &

fuzzy-trace theory dual-process model
States that decision making is influenced by two systems—"verbatim" analytical (literal and precise) and gist-based intuition (simple bottom-line meaning)—which operate in parallel; in this model, gist-based intuition benefits adolescent decision making more than analytical thinking does.

others, 2017). One experiment showed that encouraging gist-based thinking about risks (along with factual information) reduced self-reported risk taking up to one year after exposure to the curriculum (Reyna & Mills, 2014). However, some experts on adolescent cognition argue that in many cases adolescents benefit from both analytical and gist-based systems, arising in part from continuing improvements in executive function (Kuhn, 2009).

Critical Thinking   In "Cognitive Development in Middle and Late Childhood" we defined *critical thinking* as thinking reflectively and productively and evaluating evidence. Here we discuss how critical thinking changes in adolescence. Among the factors that provide a basis for improvement in critical thinking during adolescence are the following:

- Increased speed, automaticity, and capacity of information processing, which free cognitive resources for other purposes.
- Greater breadth of content knowledge in a variety of domains.
- Increased ability to construct new combinations of knowledge.
- A greater range and more spontaneous use of strategies and procedures for obtaining and applying knowledge, such as planning, considering the alternatives, and cognitive monitoring.

Adolescence is an important period in the development of critical-thinking skills. However, if an individual has not developed a solid basis of fundamental literacy and math skills during childhood, critical-thinking skills are unlikely to fully mature in adolescence—although some youth can "catch up" to their peers over development (Geary & others, 2017).

Metacognition   Recall from the chapter on "Cognitive Development in Middle and Late Childhood" that *metacognition* involves thinking about thinking, or "knowing about knowing" (Dos Santos Kawata & others, 2021). Metacognition helps people to perform many cognitive tasks more effectively (Smortchkova & Shea, 2020). Metacognition is increasingly recognized as a very important cognitive skill not only in adolescence but also in emerging adulthood (Scheider, Tibken, & Richter, 2022). In comparison with children, adolescents have a greater capacity to monitor and manage cognitive resources to effectively meet the demands of a learning task (Kuhn, 2022). This increased metacognitive ability results in improved cognitive functioning and learning. Two studies illustrate this pattern. The first revealed that from 12 to 14 years of age, young adolescents increasingly used metacognitive skills and used them more effectively in math and history classes (van der Stel & Veenman, 2010). For example, 14-year-olds monitored their own text comprehension more frequently and more effectively than their younger counterparts did. The other study described how college professors can embed metacognitive strategies, such as helping students monitor their own learning to be more accurate about gaps in knowledge, into their teaching practices to improve students' learning (Voorhees & others, 2022).

developmental **connection**

Cognitive Processes

Mindfulness is an important aspect of critical thinking. Connect to "Cognitive Development in Middle and Late Childhood."

developmental **connection**

Cognitive Processes

Developing effective strategies is a key aspect of metacognition. Connect to "Cognitive Development in Middle and Late Childhood."

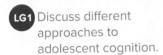

Review *Connect* Reflect

LG1 Discuss different approaches to adolescent cognition.

Review

- What is Piaget's view of adolescent cognitive development?
- What is adolescent egocentrism?
- How does information processing change during adolescence?

Connect

- Egocentrism has been mentioned in the context of early childhood cognitive development. How is egocentrism in adolescence similar to or different from egocentrism in early childhood?

Reflect *Your Own Personal Journey of Life*

- Think back to your early adolescent years. How would you describe the level of your thinking at that point in your development? Has your cognitive development changed since you were a young adolescent? Explain.

2 What Characterizes Adolescents' Values, Moral Development and Education, and Religion?

 LG2 Describe adolescents' values, moral development and education, and religion.

| Values | Moral Development and Education | Religion |

values Beliefs and attitudes about the way things should be.

service learning A form of education that promotes social responsibility and service to the community.

What are the values of adolescents today? How can moral education be characterized? How powerful is the influence of religion in adolescents' lives?

VALUES

Values are beliefs and attitudes about the way things should be. They involve what is important to us. We attach values to all sorts of things: politics, religion, money, sex, education, helping others, family, friends, career, cheating, self-respect, and so on.

How Would You...?

If you were an **educator,** how would you devise a program to increase adolescents' motivation to participate in service learning?

Changing Values One way of measuring what people value is to ask them what their goals are. Over the past five decades, traditional-aged college students have shown an increased concern for personal well-being and a decreased concern for the well-being of others, especially for the disadvantaged (Eagan & others, 2016). As shown in Figure 3, first-year college students today are more strongly motivated to be well-off financially and less motivated to develop a meaningful philosophy of life than were their counterparts of 20 or even 10 years ago. In 2015, 82 percent of students (the highest percent ever in this survey) viewed becoming well-off financially as an "essential" or a "very important" objective compared with only 42 percent in 1971.

There are, however, some signs that U.S. college students are shifting toward a stronger interest in the welfare of society. In the survey just described, interest in developing a meaningful philosophy of life increased from 39 percent to 46.5 percent of U.S. first-year college students from 2003 through 2015 (Eagan & others, 2016) (see Figure 3).

Service Learning **Service learning** is a form of education that promotes social responsibility and service to the community. In service learning, adolescents engage in activities such as tutoring, helping older adults, working in a hospital, assisting at a child-care center, or cleaning up a vacant lot to make a play area. An important goal of service learning is for adolescents to become less self-centered and more strongly motivated to help others (Filges & others, 2022). A meta-analysis of 10 service-learning programs in the United States identified eight important standards to be considered in the implementation of such programs: "(1) Meaningful service, (2) Link to curriculum, (3) Reflection, (4) Diversity, (5) Youth voice, (6) Community partnerships, (7) Progress monitoring and (8) Sufficient duration and intensity" (Filges & others, 2022, p. 1).

Service learning takes education out into the community (Hart & others, 2017). Adolescent volunteers tend to have parents who are also civically engaged, and as they enter adulthood they tend to continue to volunteer more than individuals who did not volunteer in high school (Ramey & others, 2022). Also, some research suggests there may be complex gender differences in adolescents' participation in service learning and

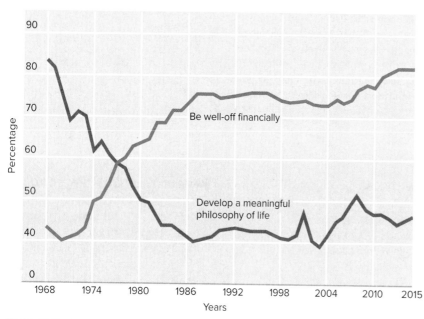

FIGURE 3

CHANGING LIFE GOALS OF FIRST-YEAR COLLEGE STUDENTS, 1968 TO 2015. In the last five decades, a significant change has occurred in first-year college students' life goals. A far greater percentage of today's first-year college students state that an "essential" or "very important" life goal is to be well-off financially, and far fewer state that developing a meaningful philosophy of life is an "essential" or "very important" life goal.

community service activities, and in what they take away from these experiences (Flanagan & others, 2015).

Researchers have found that service learning is related to positive adolescent adjustment in a number of ways (Hart & Wandeler, 2018). For example, adolescents engaged in service learning have higher grades in school, increased goal setting, higher self-esteem, a greater sense of being able to make a difference for others, and an increased likelihood that they will serve as volunteers in the future. A study of more than 4,000 high school students revealed that those who worked directly with individuals in need were better adjusted academically, whereas those who worked for organizations had better civic outcomes (Schmidt, Shumow, & Kackar, 2007). However, results from a meta-analysis of studies that had a clearly defined control group in addition to the service learning group were less conclusive about the benefits of service learning (Filges & others, 2022).

Researchers also have explored the role that civic engagement might play in adolescents' identity and moral development (Wray-Lake & Ballard, 2023). One study found that compared with adolescents who had a diffused identity status, those who were identity achieved were more involved in volunteering in their community (Crocetti, Jahromi, & Meeus, 2012). (Identity statuses of adolescents are further discussed in the chapter on "Socioemotional Development in Adolescence.") In this study, adolescents' volunteer activity also was linked to their values, such as social responsibility, and the view that they, along with others, could make an impact on their community. Another study of more than 5,000 adolescents in Chile showed distinct profiles reflecting different levels and types of civic engagement. School programs had a major effect on adolescents' community engagement (Martínez & others, 2020).

The benefits of service learning, for both the volunteer and the recipient, suggest that more students should be required to participate in such programs (Tsiorvas & Eady, 2023). However, the most rigorously conducted longitudinal studies show that engagement must be voluntary and supported in adolescence for it to have lasting effects; forcing teenagers to volunteer increases participation in the short term but has no lasting effects into adulthood (Henderson, Brown, & Pancer, 2019).

What are some of the positive outcomes associated with service learning? See the *Connecting with Research* interlude for the results of one study that asked this question.

What are some of the positive effects of service learning?
Hero Images/Getty Images

MORAL DEVELOPMENT AND EDUCATION

What are some changes that occur in moral development during adolescence? What characterizes moral education?

Moral Stages   Recall that Lawrence Kohlberg argues that adolescents' moral reasoning is more likely to be at the conventional level of moral development and that some adolescents, emerging adults, and adults reach the highest level of moral development—post-conventional reasoning. Also recall that Kohlberg's theory has been criticized for a number of reasons, including its cultural and gender bias, inadequate attention to parenting influences, and other shortcomings (Killen & Dahl, 2018; Narváez, 2018). Darcia Narváez and Tracy Gleason (2013) have described cohort effects regarding moral reasoning. In recent years, post-conventional moral reasoning has been declining in college students, not down to the next level (conventional), but to the lowest level (personal interests). Narváez and Gleason (2013) also argue that declines in prosocial behavior have occurred in recent years and that humans, especially those living in Western cultures, are "on a fast train to demise." They believe the solution to improving people's moral lives lies in better childrearing strategies and social supports for families and children. And they emphasize the importance of expanding and improving moral education.

Prosocial Behavior   Prosocial behavior increases in adolescence. Why might this happen? Cognitive changes involving advances in abstract, idealistic, and logical reasoning as well as increased empathy and emotional understanding likely are involved. With such newfound cognitive abilities, young adolescents increasingly sympathize with members of abstract groups with whom they have little experience, such as people living in poverty in other countries (Padilla-Walker, Carlo, & Memmott-Elison, 2018). The increase in volunteer opportunities in adolescence also contributes to more frequent prosocial behavior.

Evaluating a Service-Learning Program Designed to Increase Civic Engagement

Key Points:

- Students who were required to participate in service-learning activities increased their civic engagement.
- Involvement in service learning likely increases students' expectations for their future civic engagement if they were not already initially inclined to volunteer.

In one study, the possible benefits of a service-learning requirement for high school students were explored (Metz & Youniss, 2005). One group of students had a service-learning requirement, while the other group did not. Each group of students was also divided according to whether or not they were motivated to serve voluntarily. The participants in the study were 174 students (class of 2000) who were not required to engage in service learning and 312 students (classes of 2001 and 2002) who were required to accumulate 40 hours of community service. The school was located in a middle- to upper-middle-SES suburban community outside Boston, Massachusetts. The focus of the study was to compare the 2001 and 2002 classes, which were the first ones to have a 40-hour community service requirement, with the class of 2000, the last year in which the school did not have this requirement. For purposes of comparison, the 2001 and 2002 classes were combined into one group to be compared with the 2000 class.

The service-learning requirement for the 2001 and 2002 classes was designed to give students a sense of participating in the community in positive ways. Among the most common service-learning activities that students engaged in were "tutoring, coaching, assisting at shelters or nursing homes, organizing food or clothing drives, and assisting value-centered service organizations or churches" (p. 420). To obtain credit for the activities, students were required to write reflectively about the activities and describe how the activities benefited both the recipients and themselves. Students also had to obtain an adult's or supervisor's signature to document their participation.

Detailed self-reported records of students' service in grades 10 through 12 were obtained. In addition to describing the number of service hours they accumulated toward their requirement, they also were asked to indicate any voluntary services they provided in addition to the required 40 hours. Since students in the 2000 class had no required service participation, all of their service was voluntary.

The students rated themselves on four 5-point scales of civic engagement: (1) their likelihood of voting when reaching 18; (2) the likelihood they would "volunteer" or "join a civic organization" after graduating from high school; (3) their future unconventional civic involvement (such as boycotting a product, demonstrating for a cause, or participating in a political campaign); and (4) their political interest and understanding (how much they discuss politics with parents and friends, read about politics in magazines and newspapers, or watch the news on TV).

The results indicated that students who were already inclined to engage in service learning scored high on the four scales of civic engagement throughout high school and showed no increase in service after it was required. However, students who were less motivated to engage in service learning increased their civic engagement on three of the four scales (future voting, joining a civic organization after graduating from high school, and interest and understanding) after they were required to participate. In sum, this research documented that a required service-learning program can especially benefit the civic engagement of students who are inclined not to engage in service learning, at least in the short term.

How might you design a study to identify positive outcomes of service learning that did not rely on self-reports?

Two important aspects of prosocial behavior that have been studied in adolescence are forgiveness and gratitude. **Forgiveness** is an aspect of prosocial behavior that occurs when the injured person releases the injurer from possible behavioral retaliation. An overview of the research literature on the development of forgiveness showed that a number of factors are involved, including personal characteristics, peers, and family influences (van der Wal, Karremans, & Cillessen, 2017). One study of the development of forgiveness from ages 5 to 10 found that children of all ages tend to give others the benefit of the doubt by offering forgiveness when information about transgressors' intent and remorse is not available (Amir & others, 2021). Older children are more likely than younger children to pay attention to intentions and to be more forgiving of accidental than purposeful transgressions.

Gratitude is a feeling of thankfulness and appreciation, especially in response to someone doing something kind or helpful (Tudge & Frietas, 2018). Interest in studying adolescents' gratitude or lack thereof is increasing. Consider the following evidence:

- Young adolescent Chinese students who have more gratitude also have better well-being at school (Ekema-Agbaw, McCutchen, & Geller, 2016).

forgiveness An aspect of prosocial behavior that occurs when an injured person releases the injurer from possible behavioral retaliation.

gratitude A feeling of thankfulness and appreciation, especially in response to someone doing something kind or helpful.

- Gratitude is linked to a number of positive aspects of development in young adolescents, including satisfaction with one's family, optimism, and prosocial behavior (Bausert & others, 2018).

- Adolescents' expression of gratitude is linked to having fewer depressive and anxious symptoms (Rey, Sánchez-Álvarez, & Extremera, 2018).

- Researchers have found that parents socialize gratitude in their children in four main ways: modeling their own gratitude, daily scaffolding (prompting children to notice what they have received and express appreciation), niche selection (choosing experiences for their children to allow them to experience and express gratitude), and conversations with children about gratitude moments and missed opportunities for gratitude (Hussong, Coffman, & Halberstadt, 2021).

- A longitudinal study assessed the gratitude of adolescents from middle to high school in the United States (Bono & others, 2019). Across this period of adolescent development, growth in gratitude was both a predictor of, and an outcome of, decreases in antisocial behavior and increases in prosocial behavior. These links were explained, in part, by improvements in overall life satisfaction that were associated with growth in gratitude.

What are characteristics of gratitude in adolescence?
Pamela Moore/iStock/Getty Images

Compared with antisocial behavior such as juvenile delinquency, less attention has been given to research on prosocial behavior in adolescence. Although the research literature is growing, we still do not have adequate research information about such topics as how youth perceive prosocial norms and how school policies and peers influence prosocial behavior (Dijkstra & Gest, 2015).

Moral Education Two views on moral education involve (1) the hidden curriculum and (2) character education.

The Hidden Curriculum More than 80 years ago, educator John Dewey (1933) recognized that, even when schools do not offer specific programs in moral education, they provide moral education through a "hidden curriculum." The **hidden curriculum** is conveyed by the moral atmosphere that is a part of every school. The moral atmosphere is created by school and classroom rules, the moral orientation of teachers and school administrators, and text materials. Teachers serve as models of ethical or unethical behavior. Classroom rules and peer relationships at school transmit attitudes about cheating, lying, stealing, and consideration for others. And, by creating and enforcing rules and regulations, the school administration infuses the school with a value system.

Research interest has been directed toward the role of classroom and school climates as part of the hidden curriculum. Darcia Narváez (2022) argues that attention should be given to the concept of "sustaining climates." In her view, a sustaining classroom climate is more than a positive learning environment and more than a caring context. Sustaining climates involve focusing on students' sense of purpose, social engagement, community connections, and ethics. In sustaining classroom and school climates, students learn skills for flourishing and reaching their potential and help others to do so as well.

Character Education **Character education** is a direct education approach that involves teaching students a basic moral literacy to prevent them from engaging in immoral behavior and doing harm to themselves or others. The argument is that behaviors such as lying, stealing, and cheating are wrong, and students should be taught this throughout their education (Parks & Oslick, 2021).

In the character education approach, every school is expected to have an explicit moral code that is clearly communicated to students. According to traditional views of character education, any violations of the code should be met with sanctions, although more recent approaches advocate a more democratic solution. Instruction in specified moral concepts, such as cheating, can take the form of example and definition, class discussions and role playing, or rewarding students for proper behavior. More recently, an emphasis on the importance of

hidden curriculum Dewey's concept that every school has a pervasive moral atmosphere, even if it doesn't have an official program of moral education.

character education A direct education approach that involves teaching students a basic moral literacy to prevent them from engaging in immoral behavior and doing harm to themselves and others.

Why do students cheat? What are some strategies teachers can adopt to prevent cheating?

Eric Audras/PhotoAlto/Getty Images

encouraging students to develop a care perspective has been accepted as a relevant aspect of character education. Rather than just instructing adolescents to refrain from engaging in morally deviant behavior, a care perspective emphasizes educating students about the importance of engaging in prosocial behaviors such as considering others' feelings, being sensitive to others, and helping others (Shin & Lee, 2021).

Cheating   A concern involving moral education is whether students cheat and how to handle cheating if it is discovered (Ramberg & Modin, 2019). Academic cheating can take many forms, including plagiarism, using "cheat sheets" during an exam, copying from a neighbor during a test, purchasing papers, and falsifying lab results. A foundational survey of almost 30,000 high school students in the United States revealed that 64 percent of the students said they had cheated on a test in school during the past year, and 36 percent of the students reported that they had plagiarized information from the Internet for an assignment in the past year (Josephson Institute of Ethics, 2008). Over the past decade, evidence has mounted in many countries showing similarly concerning levels of academic dishonesty (M. Pan & others, 2019).

Why do students cheat? Among the reasons students give for cheating are pressure to get high grades, time constraints, poor teaching, and lack of interest. A growing body of international and cross-cultural research shows some consistent patterns: Cheating is least likely if adolescents or young adults are morally focused on honesty, believe that cheating is wrong, and think they have control over their decisions and actions (Chudzicka-Czupała & others, 2016).

A long history of research also implicates the power of the situation in determining whether students will cheat (Waltzer & Dahl, 2021). For example, students are more likely to cheat when they are not being closely monitored during a test, when they know their peers are cheating, when they know whether another student has been caught cheating, and when student scores are made public. More broadly, the culture of the school has a major impact. A large study of high schoolers in Stockholm, Sweden, revealed that cheating was least common in schools that had a culture emphasizing fairness and honesty, and in which school administrators and teachers were engaged with the students (Ramberg & Modin, 2019).

Among the strategies for decreasing academic cheating are preventive measures such as making sure students are aware of what constitutes cheating and what the consequences will be if they cheat, closely monitoring students' behavior while they are taking tests, and emphasizing the importance of being a moral, responsible individual who practices academic integrity. In promoting academic integrity, many colleges have instituted an honor code policy that emphasizes self-responsibility, fairness, trust, and scholarship (Tatum, 2022). However, few secondary schools have developed honor code policies. The Center for Academic Integrity (www.academicintegrity.org) offers an extensive selection of materials to help schools develop academic integrity policies. To be most effective, Darcia Narváez (2022) emphasizes an integrative approach to moral education. This approach would encompass both the reflective moral thinking and commitment to justice advocated in Kohlberg's approach and the process of developing a particular moral character emphasized in the character education approach.

How Would You...?

If you were an **educator,** how would you try to reduce the incidence of cheating in your school?

RELIGION

Can religion, religiousness, and spirituality be distinguished from each other? Based on their analysis of theory and results of prior research studies, Pamela King and her colleagues (King, Hardy, & Noe, 2021) make the following distinctions:

- **Religion** is an organized set of beliefs, practices, rituals, and symbols that increases an individual's connection to a sacred or transcendent other (God, higher power, or ultimate truth).

religion An organized set of beliefs, practices, rituals, and symbols that increases an individual's connection to a sacred or transcendent other (God, higher power, or ultimate truth).

- **Religiousness** (or *religiosity*) refers to the degree of affiliation with an organized religion, participation in its prescribed rituals and practices, connection with its beliefs, and involvement in a community of believers.
- **Spirituality** involves experiencing something beyond oneself in a transcendent manner and living in a way that benefits others and society.

Religious issues are important to adolescents around the globe (King, Hardy, & Noe, 2021; Sugimura & others, 2019). However, in the twenty-first century, a downtrend in religious interest has occurred among young adults. In the United States, by 2015 there was about a 15 percent difference in religious service participation for middle-aged adults compared with young adults—and this gap continues to grow. Globally, over 80 percent of people identify with a religion (Pew-Templeton Global Religious Future Project, 2022). However, large differences emerge across countries, with adolescents in higher-income countries (especially in Europe) typically more secular than adolescents in lower-income countries (Jensen, 2021).

One illustrative longitudinal study revealed that religiousness declined in U.S. adolescents between age 14 and age 20 (Koenig, McGue, & Iacono, 2008) (see Figure 4). In this study, religiousness was assessed on the basis of criteria such as frequency of prayer, frequency of discussing religious teachings, frequency of deciding moral actions for religious reasons, and the overall importance of religion in everyday life. As indicated in Figure 4, more change in religiousness occurred from 14 to 18 years of age than from 20 to 25 years of age. Also, the researchers found that frequency of attending religious services was highest at 14 years of age, declined from 14 to 18 years of age, and increased at 20 years of age.

The Positive Role of Religion in Adolescents' Lives
Researchers have found that various aspects of religion are linked with positive outcomes for adolescents and adults alike (Chen & VanderWeele, 2018). One study revealed that women in late adolescence who had been exposed to maltreatment when they were children had higher self-esteem and better interpersonal relationships if they held views of God as benevolent rather than punishing (Waldron, Scarpa, & Kim-Spoon, 2018). Churchgoing may also benefit adolescents academically because religious communities encourage socially acceptable behavior, which includes doing well in school. Churchgoing also may benefit students because churches often offer positive role models for students.

Religion also plays a role in adolescents' health and whether they experience troubled emotions or engage in problem behaviors (Eskin & others, 2019). A meta-analysis found that religiosity was positively related to well-being, self-esteem, and three of the Big Five factors of personality (conscientiousness, agreeableness, openness) (Yonker, Schnabelrauch, & DeHaan, 2012). In this meta-analysis, religiosity was negatively associated with risk behavior and depression. For example, in a national sample of more than 17,000 12- to 17-year-olds, those who believed their religious views influenced their thinking and the lives of their friends in positive ways were less likely to experience major depressive disorder (King, Topalian, & Vidourek, 2020). Also, adolescents who have a religious affiliation are less likely to start using alcohol or drugs (Rosmarin & others, 2023). Many religious adolescents also internalize their religion's message about caring and concern for people (King, Mangan, & Riveros, 2023).

Religious counselors often advise people about mental health and coping. To read about the work of one religious counselor, see *Connecting with Careers*.

Developmental Changes
Adolescence can be an important developmental period in religious identity and behavior (Scarlett & Warren, 2010). Even if children have been indoctrinated into a religion by their parents, because of advances in their cognitive development they may begin to question what their own religious beliefs truly are.

Cognitive Changes
Many of the cognitive changes thought to influence religious development involve Piaget's cognitive developmental theory, which we discussed earlier in this chapter. In comparison with children, adolescents think more abstractly, idealistically, and logically. The increase in abstract thinking lets adolescents consider various ideas about religious and spiritual concepts. For example, an adolescent might ask how a loving God can possibly exist given the extensive suffering of many people in the world. Adolescents' increased

FIGURE 4

DEVELOPMENTAL CHANGES IN RELIGIOUSNESS FROM 14 TO 25 YEARS OF AGE.

Note: The religiousness scale ranged from 0 to 32, with higher scores indicating stronger religiousness (Koenig, McGue, & Iacono, 2008).

What are some positive influences of religion on adolescents' development?

Christopher Futcher/E+/Getty Images

religiousness Degree of affiliation with an organized religion, participation in prescribed rituals and practices, connection with its beliefs, and involvement in a community of believers.

spirituality Experiencing something beyond oneself in a transcendent manner and living in a way that benefits others and society.

Gabriel Dy-Liacco, University Professor and Pastoral Counselor

Gabriel Dy-Liacco is a professor of religious and pastoral counseling at Divine Mercy University in Virginia. He obtained his Ph.D. in pastoral counseling from Loyola University in Maryland and has worked as a psychotherapist in mental health settings such as a substance-abuse program, military family center, psychiatric clinic, and community mental health center. Earlier in his career he was a pastoral counselor at the Pastoral Counseling and Consultation Centers of Greater Washington, D.C., and taught at Loyola. As a pastoral counselor, he works with adolescents and adults in the aspects of their lives that they show the most concern about—psychological, spiritual, or the interface of both. Having lived in Peru, Japan, and the Philippines, he brings considerable multicultural experience to teaching and counseling settings.

Gabriel Dy-Liacco is a university professor and pastoral counselor.
Dr. Gabriel Dy-Liacco

idealistic thinking provides a foundation for thinking about whether religion provides the best route to a better, more ideal world in the future. And adolescents' increased logical reasoning gives them the ability to develop hypotheses and systematically sort through different answers to spiritual questions (Good & Willoughby, 2008).

Erikson's Theory and Identity

During adolescence, especially in late adolescence and the college years, identity development becomes a central focus. In Erik Erikson's (1968) theory, adolescents grapple with identity versus role confusion and seek answers to questions like "Who am I?" "What am I all about as a person?" and "What kind of life do I want to lead?" As part of their search for identity, adolescents begin to grapple in more sophisticated, logical ways with such questions as "Why am I on this planet?" "Is there really a God or higher spiritual being, or have I just been believing what my parents and culture embedded in my mind?" "What really are my religious views?" It is during the transition to adulthood that these questions begin to get answered, as individuals become more autonomous and their identities are solidified.

Contemporary developmental research increasingly tries to understand how individuals perceive and navigate the intersectionality of their identities, including their religious identity (Azmitia & others, 2023). For example, one study of the role of church attendance, prayer, and faith practices found that Black adolescents' racial/ethnic identity was shaped in part by messages they received at church (Martin, Butler-Barnes, & Hope, 2023). And a longitudinal study of Muslim adolescents in Indonesia found that peers influenced adolescents' religious identities (Shen & others, 2023).

Religious Beliefs and Parenting

Religious institutions created by adults are designed to introduce certain beliefs to children and thereby ensure that they will carry on a religious tradition. Various societies utilize Sunday schools, parochial education, tribal transmission of religious traditions, and parental teaching of children at home to further this aim.

Does this socialization work? In many cases it does (Krok, 2018). In general, adults tend to adopt the religious teachings of their upbringing. One study revealed that parents' religiousness assessed during youths' adolescence was positively related to youths' own religiousness during adolescence, which in turn was linked to their religiousness following the transition to adulthood (Spilman & others, 2013).

However, when examining religious beliefs and adolescence, it is important to consider the quality of the parent-adolescent relationship. Adolescents who have a positive relationship with their parents are likely to adopt their parents' religious affiliation. But when conflict or low quality characterizes parent-adolescent relationships, adolescents are more likely to become atheists or seek a religious affiliation that is different from that of their parents (Langston, Speed, & Coleman, 2020).

Religiousness and Sexuality in Adolescence and Emerging Adulthood

One area of religion's influence on adolescent and emerging adult development involves sexual activity. Although variability and change in religious teachings make it difficult to generalize about religious doctrines, most religions discourage premarital sex. Thus, the degree of adolescent and emerging adult participation in religious organizations may be more important than affiliation with a specific religion as a determinant of premarital sexual attitudes and behavior. Adolescents and emerging adults who frequently attend religious services are likely to hear messages about abstaining from sex. Involvement of adolescents and emerging adults in religious organizations also enhances the probability that they will become friends with adolescents who have restrictive attitudes toward premarital sex. An illustrative study using a nationally representative sample of Black Americans revealed that adolescents with high religiosity were less likely to have had sexual intercourse (Taggart & others, 2018).

A longitudinal study of a nationally representative sample of Americans found that attending religious services regularly during adolescence predicted a lower likelihood of having engaged in oral, vaginal, or anal sex in early adulthood (Vasilenko, 2022). Also, a review of research conducted over the last 30 years concluded that *spirituality* (believing in a higher power, for example) was more protective in terms of reducing adolescents' risky behavior than was merely attending religious services (S.A. Hardy & others, 2019). And in another study of Black American adolescent girls, those who reported that religion was of low or moderate importance to them had a younger sexual debut than their counterparts who indicated that religion was extremely important to them (George Dalmida & others, 2017).

Review Connect Reflect

 LG2 Describe adolescents' values, moral development and education, and religion.

Review

- What characterizes adolescents' values? What is service learning?
- What are some variations in moral education?
- In what ways are adolescents' religious experiences and spirituality related to their behaviors?

Connect

- Earlier, we described five characteristics of emerging adults.

Might some of those characteristics be linked to an individual's religiousness and spirituality? Explain.

Reflect *Your Own Personal Journey of Life*

- What were your values, religious beliefs, and spiritual interests in middle school and high school? Have they changed since then? If so, how?

---

3 What Is the Nature of Schools for Adolescents?

 LG3 Characterize schools for adolescents.

| The American Middle School | The American High School | Individuals Who Drop Out of High School |

The impressive changes in adolescents' cognition lead us to examine the nature of schools for adolescents. Earlier, we discussed various ideas about the effects of schools on children's development. Here, we focus more exclusively on the nature of secondary schools.

THE AMERICAN MIDDLE SCHOOL

One worry expressed by educators and psychologists is that middle schools (most often consisting of grades 6 through 8) tend to be watered-down versions of high schools, mimicking their curricular and extracurricular schedules. The critics argue that unique curricular and extracurricular activities reflecting a wide range of individual differences in biological and psychological development in early adolescence should be incorporated into junior high and middle schools. The critics also stress that many high schools foster passivity rather than autonomy, and they urge schools to create a variety of pathways on which students can achieve an identity.

The Transition to Middle or Junior High School

The transition to middle school from elementary school interests developmentalists because, even though it is a normative experience for virtually all children, the transition can be stressful (Lovette-Wilson, Orange, & Corrales, 2022). Why? The transition takes place at a time when many changes—in the individual, in the family, and in school—are occurring simultaneously. These changes include puberty and related concerns about body image; the emergence of at least some aspects of formal operational thought, including accompanying changes in social cognition; increased responsibility and independence in association with decreased dependence on parents; moving from a small, contained classroom structure to a larger, more impersonal school structure; switching from one teacher to many teachers and from a small, homogeneous set of peers to a larger, more heterogeneous set of peers; and adjusting to an increased focus on achievement and performance.

This list includes a number of negative, stressful features, but there can be positive aspects to the transition from elementary school to middle school or junior high school. Students are more likely to feel grown up, to have more subjects from which to select, to have more opportunities to spend time with peers and to locate compatible friends, and to enjoy increased independence from direct parental monitoring—and they may be more challenged intellectually by academic work.

When students make the transition from elementary school to middle or junior high school, they experience the **top-dog phenomenon,** the circumstance of moving from the top position (in elementary school, being the oldest, biggest, and most powerful students in the school) to the lowest position (in middle or junior high school, being the youngest, smallest, and least powerful students in the school). Researchers who have charted the transition from elementary to middle school find that the first year of middle school can be difficult for many students. For example, one illustrative study revealed that compared with students in elementary school, students in the first year of middle school had lower levels of adaptive coping and higher levels of maladaptive coping (Skinner & Saxton, 2020). Students' academic motivation and engagement often drop during school transitions, especially if students perceive themselves as lacking control and efficacy to meet new academic challenges (Bagnall, Fox, & Skipper, 2021). School transitions and adjustment following the transitions are less stressful for students who have relationships with teachers characterized by high levels of warmth and low levels of conflict (Pham, Murray, & Gau, 2022). More than 90 percent of U.S. students also report that their parents are helpful during the transition to middle school (Fite & others, 2019). One reason that school transitions can be difficult is that they tend to disrupt friendships. For example, in a longitudinal study in 26 middle schools in the United States, over two-thirds of friendships were either gained or lost in the first year of middle school; greater instability in friendships was predictive of less school engagement and lower grades (Lessard & Juvonen, 2018).

Effective Middle Schools

How effective are the middle schools U.S. students attend? The Carnegie Council on Adolescent Development (1989) issued an extremely negative evaluation of U.S. middle schools. In the report—*Turning Points: Preparing American Youth for the Twenty-First Century*—the conclusion was reached that most young adolescents attend massive, impersonal schools; learn from seemingly irrelevant curricula; trust few adults in school; and lack access to health care and counseling. The Carnegie report recommended the following changes:

- Developing smaller "communities" or "houses" to lessen the impersonal nature of large middle schools.
- Lowering student-to-counselor ratios from several-hundred-to-1 to 10-to-1.
- Involving parents and community leaders in schools.

The transition from elementary to middle or junior high school occurs at the same time as a number of other developmental changes. *What are some of these other developmental changes?*

Creatas Images/PunchStock/Getty Images

top-dog phenomenon The circumstance of moving from the top position (in elementary school, being the oldest, biggest, and most powerful students) to the lowest position (in middle or junior high school, being the youngest, smallest, and least powerful students).

How Would You...?

If you were an **educator,** how would you improve middle schools?

- Developing curricula that produce students who are literate, understand the sciences, and have a sense of health, ethics, and citizenship.

- Having teachers team-teach in more flexibly designed curriculum blocks that integrate several disciplines, instead of presenting students with disconnected, rigidly separated 50-minute segments.

- Boosting students' health and fitness with more in-school programs and helping students who need public health care to get it.

Turning Points 2000 (Jackson & Davis, 2000) continued to endorse the recommendations set forth in *Turning Points 1989.* One new recommendation in the 2000 report stated that it is important to teach a curriculum grounded in rigorous academic standards for what students should know and should be able to learn. A second new recommendation was to engage in instruction that encourages students to achieve higher standards and become lifelong learners. Three decades after the original report, educators are still calling for reforms to improve middle schools (Yeager, Dahl, & Dweck, 2018).

Extracurricular Activities   Adolescents in U.S. schools usually have a wide array of extracurricular activities they can participate in beyond their academic courses. These activities include such diverse programs as sports, academic clubs, band, drama, and art clubs. Researchers have found that participation in extracurricular activities is linked to higher grades, increased school engagement, a reduced likelihood of dropping out of school, improved probability of going to college, higher self-esteem, and lower rates of depression, delinquency, and substance abuse (Feraco & others, 2022). Adolescents benefit from a breadth of extracurricular activities more than focusing on a single extracurricular activity. The quality of the extracurricular activities also matters (Feraco & others, 2022). High-quality extracurricular activities that are likely to promote positive adolescent development provide competent and supportive adult mentors, opportunities for increasing school connectedness, challenging and meaningful activities, and opportunities for improving skills. To read about one individual who improves adolescents' lives by serving as a school activities director, see *Connecting with Careers.*

What are the benefits of participating in extracurricular activities?

Hero Images/Corbis/Glow Images

connecting with careers

Willie Howard, High School Activities Director

Willie Howard has known tremendous success on the football field, including a college and professional football career and being named Minnesota's High School Coach of the Year (Robbinsdale Area Schools, 2022). His newer role as activities director for Cooper High School in New Hope, Minnesota, supports his passion for taking on more leadership responsibilities and improving opportunities for all students. "Cooper's in my blood," says Howard. "I wanted to put my name into the hat in order to lead not only the football program, but to be able to lead our activities, from the drama department to the music department to all other sports and being able to bring some more energy to all the programs" (CCX Media Community News, 2022).

Howard has also served as an assistant principal and dean of students at his school, and he has been an active supporter of various student programs over the years. "I truly believe in order to be a part of a community, you have to be invested in so many things."

Speaking from experience, which includes suffering an injury that ended his professional football career after only eight games, Howard gives talks on appreciating their higher education opportunities to athletes who are hoping to play in college. "Because an education can never be taken away," he tells them. "The millions of dollars that you envision can be taken overnight. In essence, that's what happened to me" (Thompson, 2011).

Howard received a bachelor of arts degree from Stanford University, a master of arts degree in educational leadership from Concordia University, and a master of science from Minnesota State University—Mankato, with a specialization in educational leadership and K–12 administrative and principal licensure. His postgraduate studies focused on the expertise to successfully lead today's racially and ethnically diverse schools.

What are some concerns about the American high school?

Hill Street Studios/Blend Images

THE AMERICAN HIGH SCHOOL

Many high school graduates not only are poorly prepared for college but also are poorly prepared to meet the demands of the modern, high-performance workplace (Price & Corrin, 2020). High school curricula are being revised to reflect the importance of twenty-first-century competencies, which include digital literacy, innovative thinking, critical thinking and communication, citizenship, self-regulated learning, and collaborative learning (van de Oudeweetering & Voogt, 2018).

The transition to high school can be problematic for adolescents, just as the transition to middle school can. These problems may include the following (Eccles & Roeser, 2015): High schools are often even larger, more bureaucratic, and more impersonal than middle schools are; there isn't much opportunity for students and teachers to get to know each other, which can lead to distrust; and teachers too infrequently choose content that is relevant to students' interests. Such experiences likely undermine the motivation of students.

Another major problem with U.S. high schools is that the negative social aspects of adolescents' lives undermine their academic achievement. For example, some adolescents become immersed in complex peer group cultures that demand conformity (Crosnoe, Pivnick, & Benner, 2018). High school is supposed to be about getting an education, but for many youth it involves navigating the social worlds of peer relations that may or may not value education and academic achievement. Adolescents who fail to fit in become stigmatized.

Ethnic diversity is important in middle and high schools. In a longitudinal study of approximately 6,000 ethnically diverse sixth-graders as they made the transition to middle school, ethnic diversity was found to buffer many of the challenges of the school transition (Graham, 2018). In particular, ethnic diversity within schools improved adolescents' mental health, intergroup attitudes, and school adjustment by helping them form and maintain cross-ethnic friendships, develop complex social identities, and decrease their perceptions of vulnerability.

---- ➤

developmental **connection**

Schools

The New Hope intervention program is designed to enhance the development of children and adolescents growing up in poverty. Connect to "Socioemotional Development in Middle and Late Childhood."

◄ ----

A special concern regarding secondary schools—middle and high schools—involves adolescents who are growing up in economically disadvantaged contexts (Nastasi & Naser, 2021). Many children living in poverty face problems that present barriers to their learning (Lampert & others, 2020). They might have parents who struggle with supporting their child's learning because they are burdened with securing basic resources or who don't have enough money to pay for educational materials and experiences, such as books or trips to zoos and museums. During the 2020 COVID-19 pandemic in which schools were closed in most countries around the world, educational disparities became even more pronounced between adolescents in economically advantaged versus disadvantaged contexts. For example, adolescents in more advantaged contexts had more access to the Internet to facilitate the transition to online learning, whereas adolescents from more economically disadvantaged contexts had more disruptions in their learning (Esposito & Principi, 2020).

Some innovative programs indicate that improving certain characteristics of schools raises achievement levels for adolescents from economically disadvantaged backgrounds, including adolescents in low- and middle-income countries (Wils, Sheehan, & Shi, 2018). A number of characteristics of teachers, such as motivation, and school climates, such as providing opportunities for teachers' professional development, have been found to improve adolescents' school performance (Didion, Toste, & Filderman, 2020).

Are American secondary schools different from those in other countries? To explore this question, see the *Connecting with Diversity* interlude.

What challenges did students face when schools couldn't provide in-person instruction due to the COVID-19 pandemic?

Prostock-studio/Alamy Stock Photo

INDIVIDUALS WHO DROP OUT OF HIGH SCHOOL

Dropping out of high school has been viewed as a serious educational and societal problem for many decades. When adolescents leave high school before graduating, they approach adult

Cross-Cultural Comparisons of Secondary Schools

Most countries recognize that high-quality, universal education of children and youth is critical for the success of any country. However, countries vary considerably in their ability to fulfill this mission. The Sustainable Development Goals guiding the international development agenda through 2030 prioritize ensuring inclusive and equitable education for all, including free access to primary and secondary school for both boys and girls (United Nations, 2023). In low- and middle-income countries, adolescent girls are less likely to be enrolled in school than are boys.

Secondary schools in different countries share a number of features but differ in many ways. Let's explore the similarities and differences in secondary schools in seven countries: Australia, Brazil, Germany, Japan, China, Russia, and the United States.

Most countries mandate that children begin school at 6 to 7 years of age and stay in school until they are 14 to 17 years of age. Brazil requires students to go to school only until they are 14 years old, whereas Russia mandates that students stay in school until they are 17. Germany, Japan, Australia, and the United States require school attendance until at least 15 to 16 years of age, with some states, such as California, raising the mandatory age to 18.

Most secondary schools around the world are divided into two or more levels, such as middle school (or junior high school) and high school. However, Germany's schools are divided according to three educational ability tracks: (1) the main school provides a basic level of education, (2) the middle school gives students a more advanced education, and (3) the academic school prepares students for entrance to a university. German schools, like most European schools, offer a classical education, which includes courses in Latin and Greek. Japanese secondary schools have an entrance exam, but secondary schools in the other countries do not. Only Australia and Germany have comprehensive exit exams.

The United States and Australia are among the few countries in the world in which sports are an integral part of the public school system. Only a few private schools in other countries have their own sports teams, sports facilities, and highly organized sports events.

In Brazil, students are required to take Portuguese (the native language) and four foreign languages (Latin, French, English, and Spanish). Brazil requires these languages because of the country's international character and emphasis on trade and commerce. Seventh-grade students in Australia take courses in sheep husbandry and weaving,

The juku, or "cramming school," is available to Japanese children and adolescents in the summer and after school. It provides coaching to help them improve their grades and entrance exam scores for high schools and universities.
urbancow/E+/Getty Images

two areas of economic and cultural interest in the country. In Japan, students take a number of Western courses in addition to their basic Japanese courses; these courses include Western literature and languages (in addition to Japanese literature and language), Western physical education (in addition to Japanese martial arts classes), and Western sculpture and handicrafts (in addition to Japanese calligraphy). The Japanese school year is also much longer than that of other countries (225 days versus 180 days in the United States, for example).

Countries differ in the extent to which curricula are variable versus nationally standardized (Sorbring & Lansford, 2019). For example, in China, a national curriculum, textbooks, and even pedagogy result in educational experiences that are largely similar regardless of which school a student attends. By contrast, in the United States there are over 13,000 independent school districts that vary widely in curriculum, teaching materials, and other resources, largely because public schools receive much of their funding from personal property taxes, which vary by geographic region and even by neighborhood. Insufficient numbers of adequately trained teachers, lack of resources provided to schools, and barriers to equity compromise many students' access to quality education around the world (United Nations, 2023).

life with educational deficiencies that severely curtail their economic and social well-being (McFarland & others, 2020). In this section, we study the scope of the problem, the causes of dropping out, and ways to reduce dropout rates.

Dropout Rates In the last half of the twentieth century and the first decade of the twenty-first century, U.S. high school dropout rates declined (National Center for Education

Statistics, 2023). In the 1940s, more than half of U.S. 16- to 24-year-olds had dropped out of school; by 2020, this rate had dropped to 5.3 percent. The lowest dropout rate in 2020 occurred for Asian American adolescents (2.4 percent), followed by Black adolescents (4.2 percent), non-Latino White adolescents (4.8 percent), and Latino adolescents (7.4 percent) (National Center for Education Statistics, 2023). The dropout rates have dropped considerably since 2000, when the dropout rate for non-Latino Whites was 6.9 percent, for Black Americans 13.1 percent, and for Latinos 27.8 percent. Gender differences characterize U.S. dropout rates, with males more likely to drop out than females (6.2 versus 4.4 percent) (National Center for Education Statistics, 2023).

The average U.S. high school dropout rates just described mask some very high dropout rates in low-income areas of inner cities. For example, in cities such as Detroit, Cleveland, and Chicago, dropout rates can reach 50 percent or higher. Also, the percentages cited here are for 16- to 24-year-olds. When dropout rates are calculated in terms of students who do not graduate from high school in four years, the percentage of students is also much higher. Thus, in considering high school dropout rates, it is important to examine age, the number of years it takes to complete high school, and various contexts including ethnicity, gender, and school location.

Causes of Dropping Out of School   Students drop out of school for school-related, economic, family-related, peer-related, and personal reasons. School-related problems are consistently associated with dropping out of school (Dupéré & others, 2018). Students who dropped out of high school were three times as likely to have experienced a major recent stressful life event compared with average students as well as high-risk students who stayed in school (Dupéré & others, 2018).

How Would You...?
If you were an **educator,** how would you reduce the school dropout rate of high-risk adolescents?

Reducing the Dropout Rate   A number of interventions have been developed to prevent students from dropping out of high school; programs that involve regular check-ins

caring connections

The "I Have a Dream" Program

"I Have a Dream" (IHAD) is an innovative, comprehensive, long-term dropout prevention program administered by the National "I Have a Dream" Foundation in New York. The program is currently operating in nine states and New Zealand ("I Have a Dream" Foundation, 2023). Local IHAD projects around the country "adopt" entire grades (usually the third or fourth) from public elementary schools, or corresponding age cohorts from public housing developments. These children are then provided with a program of academic, social, cultural, and recreational activities throughout their elementary, middle school, and high school years. An important part of this program is that it is personal rather than institutional: IHAD sponsors and staff develop close, long-term relationships with the children. When participants complete high school, IHAD provides the tuition assistance necessary for them to attend a state or local college or vocational school.

The IHAD program was created in 1981 when philanthropist Eugene Lang made an impromptu offer of college tuition to a class of graduating sixth-graders at P.S. 121 in East Harlem. Statistically, 75 percent of the students should have dropped out of school; instead, 90 percent graduated and 60 percent went on to college. Other evaluations of IHAD programs have found dramatic improvements in grades, test scores, and school attendance, as well as a reduction in

These adolescents are participating in the "I Have a Dream" (IHAD) Program, a comprehensive, long-term dropout prevention program that has been very successful. *What are some other strategies for reducing high school dropout rates?*
Courtesy of "I Have a Dream" Foundation of Boulder County (www.ihadboulder.org)

behavioral problems of participants. Ninety percent of program participants graduate from high school, compared with 74 percent of their low-income peers who do not participate in the program. In addition, participants are three times more likely to earn a bachelor's degree than their low-income peers ("I Have a Dream" Foundation, 2023).

with trusted adults and mentoring programs have been found to be particularly effective. High schools can also reduce dropout rates by creating caring environments and relationships and offering community-service opportunities.

Early detection of children's school-related difficulties, and getting children engaged with school in positive ways, are important strategies for reducing the dropout rate. The Bill and Melinda Gates Foundation has provided funding for efforts to reduce the dropout rate in schools where dropout rates are high. One strategy that is being emphasized in the Gates' funding is keeping students who are at risk for dropping out of school with the same teachers through their high school years. The hope is that the teachers will get to know these students much better, their relationship with the students will improve, and they will be able to monitor and guide the students toward graduating from high school. Initiatives by the Bill and Melinda Gates Foundation involve creating a new generation of courseware that adapts to students' learning needs and blending face-to-face instruction with digital tools that help students to learn independently.

One program that has been very effective in reducing school dropout rates is described in the *Caring Connections* interlude.

An important educational goal is to increase the high school graduation rate of Native American youth. An excellent strategy to accomplish this goal is high-quality early childhood educational programs such as this one at St. Bonaventure Indian School on the Navajo Nation in Thoreau, New Mexico.
Jim West/Alamy Stock Photo

Review Connect Reflect

LG3 Characterize schools for adolescents.

Review
- What is the transition from elementary to middle school like? What are some criticisms of, and recommendations for improving, U.S. middle schools?
- How can the American high school be improved so that students are better prepared for the demands of the modern workplace?
- What are some of the reasons adolescents drop out of school?

Connect
- What impact might the concept of parents as "managers" have on reducing the high school dropout rate?

Reflect *Your Own Personal Journey of Life*
- What was your own middle or junior high school like? How did it compare to schools in other countries?

topical connections *looking forward*

The next chapter concludes our exploration of the journey through childhood and adolescence. You will read about how adolescents spend more time thinking about their identity—who they are, what they are all about, and where they are going in life—than they did when they were children. Time spent with peers increases in adolescence, and friendships become more intense and intimate. Dating and romantic relationships also become more central to the lives of most adolescents. Parents continue to have an important influence on adolescent development. Having good relationships with parents provides support for adolescents as they seek greater autonomy and explore a widening social world. Problems that adolescents can develop include juvenile delinquency, depression, and suicide.

Cognitive Development in Adolescence

1 How Do Adolescents Think and Process Information?

 Discuss different approaches to adolescent cognition.

Piaget's Theory

- During the formal operational stage, Piaget's fourth stage of cognitive development, thinking is more abstract, idealistic, and logical than during the concrete operational stage. Adolescents become capable of hypothetical-deductive reasoning. However, many adolescents are not formal operational thinkers but are consolidating their concrete operational thought. Piaget made a number of important contributions to understanding children's development, but his theory has undergone considerable criticism.

Adolescent Egocentrism

- Elkind proposed that adolescents, especially young adolescents, develop an egocentrism that includes both an imaginary audience (the belief that others are as interested in the adolescent as the adolescent is) and a personal fable (a sense of uniqueness and invincibility).

Information Processing

- Key changes in information processing especially involve executive function. These changes focus on working memory, cognitive control, decision making, critical thinking, and metacognition. It is increasingly thought that executive function strengthens during adolescence.

- Adolescence is a time of increased decision making. Older adolescents make better decisions than younger adolescents, who in turn are better at this skill than children are. Being able to make competent decisions, however, does not mean adolescents actually will make such decisions in everyday life, where breadth of experience comes into play. One proposal to explain effective adolescent decision making is the fuzzy-trace theory dual-process model.

- Adolescence is an important transitional period in critical thinking because of cognitive changes such as increased speed, automaticity, and capacity of information processing; greater breadth of content knowledge; increased ability to construct new combinations of knowledge; and increased use of spontaneous strategies.

2 What Characterizes Adolescents' Values, Moral Development and Education, and Religion?

 Describe adolescents' values, moral development and education, and religion.

Values

- Values are beliefs and attitudes about the way things should be. Over the past five decades, traditional-aged college students have shown an increased concern for personal well-being and a decreased interest in the welfare of others. Recently, U.S. first-year college students have shown an increased interest in developing a meaningful philosophy of life.

- Service learning is a form of education that promotes social responsibility and service to the community. Service learning is increasingly required by schools and has positive effects on adolescent development.

Moral Development and Education

- Reseach indicates that cohort effects characterize adolescents' moral reasoning with more adolescents today reasoning at a lower moral level than in the past. Adolescents engage in more prosocial behavior than do children.

- Two important aspects of adolescents' prosocial behavior that are increasingly being studied are forgiveness and gratitude. Aspects of moral education include Dewey's hidden curriculum and character education.

- Cheating is a moral education concern and can take many forms. Various aspects of the situation influence whether students will cheat or not. An integrative moral education approach has been advocated for preventing academic cheating in schools.

| Religion | • Distinctions have been made between the concepts of religion, religiousness (or religiosity), and spirituality. Religious issues are important to adolescents. Adolescence may be a special juncture in religious development for many individuals. |

• Distinctions have been made between the concepts of religion, religiousness (or religiosity), and spirituality. Religious issues are important to adolescents. Adolescence may be a special juncture in religious development for many individuals.

• Various aspects of religion are linked with positive outcomes in adolescent development. Religiosity is linked to lower drug use and delinquency rates, less school truancy, and lower rates of depression.

• Erikson's ideas on identity can be applied to understanding the questions about religion that arise during adolescence. Piaget's theory provides a theoretical foundation for understanding developmental changes in religiousness. When adolescents have a positive relationship with their parents, they often adopt their parents' religious beliefs. Links have been found between adolescents' sexual behavior and their religiousness.

3 What Is the Nature of Schools for Adolescents?

 LG3 Characterize schools for adolescents.

The American Middle School

• The transition to middle or junior high school coincides with many physical, cognitive, and socioemotional changes. The transition involves moving from the top-dog position to the lowest position, and this transition is difficult for many adolescents.

• U.S. middle schools have been criticized as too massive and impersonal, with curricula that are often irrelevant. Recommendations for improving U.S. middle schools include developing small communities of students within the schools, maintaining lower student-to-counselor ratios, and raising academic standards.

• Participation in extracurricular activities is associated with positive academic and psychological outcomes.

The American High School

• The American high school needs to prepare students for today's workplace by providing them with an education that gives them skills in digital literacy, innovative thinking, critical thinking and communication, citizenship, self-regulated learning, and collaborative learning.

Individuals Who Drop Out of High School

• Many individuals who drop out of high school have educational deficiencies that limit their economic and social well-being for much of their adult lives. Progress has been made in lowering the dropout rate for all racial/ethnic groups, although disparities across groups remain. Males are more likely to drop out of high school than females. Dropping out of school is associated with demographic, family-related, peer-related, school-related, economic, and personal factors.

key **terms**

adolescent egocentrism
character education
cognitive control
forgiveness
fuzzy-trace theory dual-process model

gratitude
hidden curriculum
hypothetical-deductive reasoning

imaginary audience
personal fable
religion
religiousness

service learning
spirituality
top-dog phenomenon
values

key **people**

John Dewey
David Elkind

Erik Erikson
Pamela King

Lawrence Kohlberg
Deanna Kuhn

Darcia Narváez
Jean Piaget

improving the **lives of children**

STRATEGIES

Supporting Adolescents' Cognitive Development

What are some good strategies for nourishing adolescents' cognitive development?

- *Provide support for adolescents' information processing.* Provide opportunities and guide adolescents to develop their executive function skills such as cognitive control; to gain practice in making good decisions, especially in real-world settings; to think critically; and to engage in self-regulatory learning.

- *Give adolescents opportunities to discuss moral dilemmas.* Provide adolescents with group opportunities to discuss the importance of cooperation, trust, and caring.

- *Create better schools for adolescents.* Schools for adolescents need to emphasize socioemotional development as well as cognitive development.

- *Take individual variation in adolescents seriously.*

- *Develop curricula that involve high expectations for success and the support to attain that success.*

- *Develop smaller communities within each school.*

- *Involve parents and community leaders more.*

- *Break down the barriers between school and work to reduce the high school dropout rate.*

- *Provide adolescents with information about careers.* Adolescents do not get adequate information about careers. Career decision making needs to be given a higher priority in schools.

RESOURCES

Building Our Best Future: Thinking Critically About Ourselves and Our World—Student Edition (2019)
Deanna Kuhn
Mauritius: Lambert Academic Publishing

This book is geared for high school and college students interested in learning how to make big and small decisions that will benefit themselves, their communities, and even the world.

APA Handbook of Adolescent and Young Adult Development (2023)
Edited by Lisa J. Crockett, Gustavo Carlo, & John E. Schulenberg
Washington, DC: American Psychological Association

Leading experts provide up-to-date discussions of a wide range of topics, including decision making, civic engagement, and identity.

Handbook of Research on Learning and Instruction (2016)
Edited by Richard E. Mayer and Patricia A. Alexander
New York: Routledge

Leading experts in educational psychology provide an up-to-date account of a wide-ranging set of topics related to how children and adolescents learn and how to help them learn.

National Dropout Prevention Center
www.dropoutprevention.org

Acts as a clearinghouse for information about dropout prevention and at-risk youth and publishes the *National Dropout Prevention Newsletter*.

Below the Surface: Talking with Teens about Race, Ethnicity, and Identity (2019)
Deborah Rivas-Drake and Adriana J. Umaña-Taylor
Princeton, NJ: Princeton University Press

This volume provides a wealth of useful information for parents, teachers, and others to help young people develop positive racial-ethnic identities and positive interracial relationships.

chapter 16

SOCIOEMOTIONAL DEVELOPMENT IN ADOLESCENCE

chapter outline

① What Characterizes Identity, Emotional Development, and Gender Classification in Adolescence?

Learning Goal 1 Discuss identity, emotional development, and gender classification during adolescence.

Identity
Emotional Development
Gender Classification

② What Is the Nature of Parent-Adolescent Relationships?

Learning Goal 2 Describe changes that take place in adolescents' relationships with their parents.

Parental Monitoring and Adolescents' Information Management
Autonomy and Attachment
Parent-Adolescent Conflict

③ What Aspects of Peer Relationships Are Important in Adolescence?

Learning Goal 3 Characterize the changes that occur in peer relationships during adolescence.

Friendship
Peer Groups
Romantic Relationships

④ Why Is Culture an Important Context for Adolescent Development?

Learning Goal 4 Explain how culture influences adolescent development.

Cross-Cultural Comparisons
Race/Ethnicity
Media and Technology

⑤ What Are Some Socioemotional Problems in Adolescence?

Learning Goal 5 Identify adolescent problems in socioemotional development and strategies for helping adolescents with problems.

Juvenile Delinquency
Depression and Suicide
The Interrelation of Problems and Successful Prevention/Intervention Programs

John Giustina/The Image Bank/Getty Images

Greta Thunberg is a well-known Swedish environmental activist who, as a teenager, took on world leaders with her pleas to pass effective legislation to combat climate change. She is not alone.

In upstate New York, 16-year-old Scout Pronto Breslin founded Hudson Valley Wild, a wildlife rehabilitation clinic. According to Breslin, "The birds there often come in with blood poisoning because of illegal toxins from chemical runoff and fertilizer." She encourages other teens to get involved in the climate change movement through local initiatives such as composting in their schools.

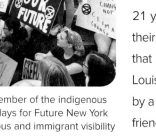

Xiye Bastida, a climate activist and a member of the indigenous Otomi-Toltec nation, leads a rally at Fridays for Future New York City. She is a leading voice for indigenous and immigrant visibility in climate activism.

Henny Garfunkel/Redux

Xiye Bastida of New York City led her high school in the city's first big student climate strike. A member of the indigenous Mexican Otomi-Toltec nation, Bastida helped form Fridays for Future, in which students discuss or "go on strike" on climate issues. She has been a leading voice for indigenous and immigrant visibility in climate activism.

Sixteen-year-old Jayden Foytlin of Rayne, Louisiana, was one of 21 young people who sued the U.S. government in 2015 for violating their rights to a livable planet. The plaintiffs were from communities that had been directly affected by global warming. Foytlin's home in Louisiana was flooded by storms. Although their case was dismissed by a federal appeals court, Foytlin says the experience gave her lasting friendships. "We all share one thing in common—we really care about where we're from, and how we are going to continue to live [here]."

Katharine Wilkinson, who works with the solutions-focused climate organization Project Drawdown, says it's no coincidence that teenage girls are especially visible right now as climate leaders. "The youth movement is such a great example of the way in which girls and young women are stepping into the heart of this space and showing us what it looks like to lead with courage and imagination and incredible moral clarity" (Kamenetz, 2020).

-topical connections   *looking **back***

In other chapters, you explored changes in the physical and cognitive development of adolescents. You read about socioemotional development in middle and late childhood, including how self-understanding and understanding others become more sophisticated, emotional understanding improves, and moral reasoning advances. In Erikson's view, in middle and late childhood, children are in the industry versus inferiority stage. Children at this developmental stage spend more time with peers, but parents continue to play important roles in their development, especially in guiding their academic achievement and managing their opportunities. Peer status and friendship become more important in children's peer relationships, and school takes on a stronger academic focus. In this chapter, we will examine a key feature of adolescent development—exploring an identity. We will also look at changing relationships with parents and peers, then consider some problems that can develop during adolescence, such as delinquency.

preview

Significant changes characterize socioemotional development in adolescence. These changes include increased efforts to understand oneself, a search for identity, and emotional fluctuations. Changes also occur in the social contexts of adolescents' lives, with transformations occurring in relationships with families and peers. Adolescents are also at risk for developing socioemotional problems such as delinquency and depression.

1 What Characterizes Identity, Emotional Development, and Gender Classification in Adolescence?

LG1 Discuss identity, emotional development, and gender classification during adolescence.

- Identity
- Emotional Development
- Gender Classification

The adolescents described in the opening to this chapter are activists striving to make the world a better place. Their confidence, positive identity, and emotional maturity sound at least as impressive as their activities. In this section, we examine how adolescents develop characteristics like these.

IDENTITY

"Who am I? What am I all about? What am I going to do with my life? What is different about me? How can I make it on my own?" These questions reflect the search for an identity. By far the most comprehensive and provocative theory of identity development is Erik Erikson's. In this section, we examine his views on identity. We also discuss contemporary research on how identity develops and how social contexts influence that development.

What Is Identity?   Identity is a self-portrait composed of many pieces, including these:

- The career and work path the person wants to follow (vocational/career identity)
- Whether the person is conservative, liberal, or middle-of-the-road (political identity)
- The person's spiritual beliefs (religious identity)
- Whether the person is single, married, divorced, and so on (relationship identity)
- The extent to which the person is motivated to achieve and is intellectual (achievement, intellectual identity)
- Whether the person is heterosexual, gay, lesbian, or bisexual, and how they identify in terms of gender (sexual and gender identities)
- Which part of the world or country a person is from and how intensely the person identifies with this cultural heritage (cultural/ethnic identity)
- The things a person likes to do, which can include sports, music, hobbies, and so on (interests)
- The individual's personality characteristics (such as being introverted or extraverted, anxious or calm, friendly or hostile, and so on) (personality)
- The individual's body image (physical identity)

Synthesizing the identity components can be a lengthy process, with many negations and affirmations of various roles and facets (Meeus, 2023). Decisions are not made once and for all, but have to be made again and again. Identity development does not happen neatly, and it does not happen cataclysmically (Lu, Benet-Martínez, & Robins, 2020).

What are some important dimensions of identity?
JGI/Jamie Grill/Tetra images/Getty Images

identity versus identity confusion Erikson's fifth developmental stage, which occurs at about the time of adolescence. At this time, adolescents are faced with deciding who they are, what they are all about, and where they are going in life.

psychosocial moratorium Erikson's term for the gap between childhood security and adult autonomy.

crisis Marcia's term for a period of identity development during which the individual is exploring alternatives.

Erik Erikson
Bettmann/Getty Images

Erikson's View

Questions about identity surface as common, virtually universal, concerns during adolescence. Some decisions made during adolescence might seem trivial: whether to study or play, whether to take a part-time job after school, whom to date, whether to break up with someone or stay in the relationship, whether or not to be politically active, and so on. Over the years of adolescence, however, such decisions begin to form the core of what the individual is all about as a human being—what is called his or her identity.

It was Erik Erikson (1968) who first understood the importance of questions about identity in understanding adolescent development. The fact that identity is now believed to be a key aspect of adolescent development is a result of Erikson's thinking and analysis.

We discussed Erikson's theory in the "Introduction" chapter. Recall that his fifth developmental stage, which individuals experience during adolescence, is **identity versus identity confusion.** During this time, said Erikson, adolescents are faced with deciding who they are, what they are all about, and where they are going in life.

The search for an identity during adolescence is aided by a **psychosocial moratorium,** which is Erikson's term for the gap between childhood security and adult autonomy. During this period, society leaves adolescents relatively free of responsibilities and able to try out different identities. Adolescents in effect search their culture's identity files, experimenting with different roles and personalities. They may want to pursue one career one month (lawyer, for example) and another career the next month (doctor, actor, teacher, social worker, or astronaut, for example). They may dress neatly one day, sloppily the next. This experimentation is a deliberate effort on the part of adolescents to find out where they fit into the world. Most adolescents eventually discard undesirable roles.

Youth who successfully cope with conflicting identities emerge with a new sense of self that is both refreshing and acceptable. Adolescents who do not successfully resolve this identity crisis suffer what Erikson calls *identity confusion.* The confusion takes one of two courses: Individuals withdraw, isolating themselves from peers and family, or they immerse themselves in the world of peers and lose their identity in the crowd.

Some critics argue that the identity status approach does not produce enough depth in understanding identity development (Klimstra & Adams, 2022). One way that researchers are now examining identity changes in depth is to use a *narrative approach.* This involves asking individuals to tell their life stories and evaluate the extent to which their stories are meaningful and integrated (Booker, Fivush, & Graci, 2022). In one study, researchers found three major factors in identity narratives: motivational and affective themes (such as goals and emotions), autobiographical reasoning (such as reported changes in understanding about oneself or an experience), and structural aspects (such as temporal sequencing and the amount of detail provided) (McLean & others, 2020).

Developmental Changes

Although questions about identity may be especially important during adolescence, identity formation neither begins nor ends during these years. It begins with the appearance of attachment, the development of the sense of self, and the emergence of independence in infancy; the process reaches its final phase with a life review and integration in old age. Even Erikson's (1968) work emphasized that identity development emerges in infancy and develops across the life span and within each stage of development. What is important about identity development in adolescence, especially late adolescence, is that for the first time, physical development, cognitive development, and socioemotional development advance to the point at which the individual can sort through and synthesize childhood identities and identifications to construct a viable path toward adult maturity.

How do individual adolescents go about the process of forming an identity? Eriksonian researcher James Marcia (1993, 1994) argues that Erikson's theory of identity development contains four identity statuses, or ways of resolving the identity crisis: identity diffusion, identity foreclosure, identity moratorium, and identity achievement. What determines an individual's identity status? Marcia classifies individuals based on the existence or extent of their crisis or commitment (see Figure 1). **Crisis** is defined as a period of identity development during which the individual is exploring alternatives. Most researchers use the term *exploration* rather than *crisis* because crisis carries a negative connotation. "Crises" are necessary and normal for development and can be thought of as

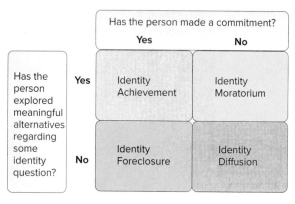

FIGURE 1
MARCIA'S FOUR STATUSES OF IDENTITY

radical turning points in development. **Commitment** is a personal investment in identity. The four statuses of identity are as follows:

- **Identity diffusion,** the status of individuals who have not yet experienced a crisis or made any commitments. Not only are they undecided about occupational and ideological choices, but they are also likely to show little interest in such matters.
- **Identity foreclosure** is the status of individuals who have made a commitment but have not experienced a crisis. This occurs most often when parents hand down commitments to their adolescents, usually in an authoritarian way, before adolescents have had a chance to explore different approaches, ideologies, and vocations on their own.
- **Identity moratorium** is the status of individuals who are in the midst of a crisis but whose commitments are either absent or only vaguely defined.
- **Identity achievement** is the status of individuals who have undergone a crisis and have made a commitment.

How Would You...?

If you were a **psychologist,** how would you apply Marcia's theory of identity formation to describe your current identity status or the identity status of adolescents you know?

How does identity change in emerging adulthood?

Tom Grill/Corbis

Emerging Adulthood and Beyond A longitudinal study of more than 5,000 young people in Japan, ranging in age from early adolescence to emerging adulthood, found that greater identity synthesis (as opposed to confusion) was related to greater life satisfaction (Hatano & others, 2022). And a large meta-analysis of 124 studies by Jane Kroger and her colleagues (2010) revealed that during adolescence and emerging adulthood, identity moratorium status rose steadily to age 19 and then declined; identity achievement rose across late adolescence and emerging adulthood; and foreclosure and diffusion statuses declined across the high school years but fluctuated during the late teens and emerging adulthood. The studies also found that a large proportion of individuals were not identity achieved by the time they reached their twenties.

Indeed, developmental experts are moving toward a consensus that the key changes in identity are more likely to take place in emerging adulthood (18 to 25 years of age) or later than in adolescence (Meeus, 2023). Why might college produce some key changes in identity? Increased complexity in the reasoning skills of college students, combined with a wide range of new experiences that highlight contrasts between home and college and between themselves and others, stimulates them to reach a higher level of integrating various dimensions of their identity (Murray & Arnett, 2019). College serves as a virtual "laboratory" for identity development through such experiences as diverse coursework and exposure to peers from diverse backgrounds. Also, one of emerging adulthood's themes is not having many social commitments, which gives individuals considerable independence in developing a life path (Nader & Robinson, 2023). To read about one academic advisor who helps students find their way, see *Connecting with Careers*.

Resolution of the identity issue during adolescence and emerging adulthood does not mean that a person's identity will be stable through the remainder of life (Mehta & others, 2020). Many individuals who develop positive identities follow what are called "MAMA" cycles—that is, their identity status changes from *moratorium* to *achievement* to *moratorium* to *achievement* (Marcia, 1994). These cycles may be repeated throughout life (Kim, Lee, & Yang, 2023). Marcia (2002) argues that the first identity is just that—it should not be viewed as the final product.

In short, questions about identity come up throughout life. An individual who develops a healthy identity is flexible and adaptive, open to changes in society, in relationships, and in careers. This openness ensures numerous reorganizations of identity throughout the individual's life.

Family Influences Parents are important figures in the adolescent's development of identity (Branje, 2022). Researchers have found that a family atmosphere that promotes both individuality and connectedness is important to the adolescent's identity development (Grotevant & Cooper, 1998):

- **Individuality** consists of two dimensions: self-assertion (the ability to have and communicate a point of view) and separateness (the use of communication patterns to express how one is different from others).
- **Connectedness** also consists of two dimensions: mutuality, which involves sensitivity to and respect for others' views, and permeability, which involves openness to others' views.

In general, then, research indicates that identity formation is enhanced by family relationships that sustain both individuation, which encourages adolescents to develop their own point of view, and connectedness, which provides a secure base from which adolescents can explore their widening social worlds (Sugimura & others, 2018).

commitment Marcia's term for the part of identity development in which individuals show a personal investment in identity.

identity diffusion Marcia's term for the status of individuals who have not yet experienced a crisis (explored alternatives) or made any commitments.

identity foreclosure Marcia's term for the status of individuals who have made a commitment but have not experienced a crisis.

identity moratorium Marcia's term for the status of individuals who are in the midst of a crisis, but their commitments are either absent or vaguely defined.

identity achievement Marcia's term for the status of individuals who have undergone a crisis and have made a commitment.

individuality Characteristic consisting of two dimensions: self-assertion (the ability to have and communicate a point of view) and separateness (the use of communication patterns to express how one is different from others).

connectedness Characteristic consisting of two dimensions: mutuality (sensitivity to and respect for others' views) and permeability (openness to others' views).

Anna Boyer-Chadwick, Academic Advisor

Anna Boyer-Chadwick is an academic advisor at the University of Texas–San Antonio. After graduating from Central Washington University with a bachelor's degree in psychology, she completed a master's degree in educational leadership at the University of Nevada–Las Vegas. Prior to becoming an academic advisor, Boyer-Chadwick worked in several different areas in higher education, including housing/residence life, orientation, and student conduct (UTSA Pride Faculty & Staff Association, 2022).

At UTSA, each student is assigned an academic advisor who helps them to develop meaningful, personalized pathways toward academic success; to stay on track; and to achieve their ultimate career goals. UTSA's Resilience and Retention (R & R) Advising Program, which is targeted toward students who are academically dismissed or denied admission into the major of their choice and are at a high risk of dropping out of college, has seen tremendous success in the form of increased retention and graduation rates. Participating students sign a success agreement, commit to using at least two academic support resources, and meet monthly with R & R advisors to discuss finances, career knowledge, and skills that can be gained from any degree. Upon achievement of a 2.0 grade point average, the student transitions to another advisor, such as Boyer-Chadwick, for college completion. The R & R program has become a nationally recognized model for Latino

Anna Boyer-Chadwick (*left*) counsels a college student.
Anna Boyer-Chadwick

student success, winning a number of awards, including the Outstanding Advising Program Merit Award from the National Academic Advising Association (NACADA). Boyer-Chadwick has also been recognized individually by NACADA for her work as an advisor (Boerger, 2020).

Boyer-Chadwick also participates in the UTSA Pride Faculty & Staff Association, whose mission is to help create a safe and supportive professional environment for the university's LGBTQIA+ employees and their families.

Peer/Romantic Relationships   Researchers have found that the capacity to explore one's identity during adolescence and emerging adulthood is linked to the quality of friendships and romantic relationships (Sugimura & others, 2022). For example, a study of Jamaicans spanning emerging adulthood found that identity achievement was associated with greater openness to and less fear of intimacy with partners and friends (Strudwick-Alexander, 2017). A study of immigrant and nonimmigrant adolescents in Greece found that national identity and friendship networks developed in tandem, with identity influencing friendship choices, and friends influencing identity development (Umaña-Taylor & others, 2020).

In terms of links between identity and romantic relationships in adolescence and emerging adulthood, two individuals in a romantic relationship are both in the process of constructing their own identities, and each person provides the other with a context for identity exploration. The extent of their secure attachment with each other can influence how the partners construct their own identity (Kerpelman & Pittman, 2018).

Cultural and Racial/Ethnic Identity   Identity developments are influenced by culture and race/ethnicity (Jones & Rogers, 2023). Most research on identity development has historically been based on data obtained from adolescents and emerging adults in the United States and Canada, especially those who are non-Latino Whites (Schwartz & others, 2015). Many of these individuals have grown up in cultural contexts that value individual autonomy. However, in many countries around the world, adolescents and emerging adults have grown up influenced by a collectivist emphasis on fitting in with the group and connecting with others. The collectivist emphasis is especially prevalent in Asian countries such as Japan (Sugimura & others, 2018). Researchers have found that self-oriented identity exploration may not be the main process through which identity achievement is attained in East Asian countries. Rather, East Asian adolescents and emerging adults may develop their identity through identification with and commitment to others in the cultural group (Sugimura, Umemura, & Nelson, 2021). This emphasis on interdependence includes an emphasis on adolescents and emerging adults accepting and embracing social and family roles. Thus, some patterns of identity development, such as the foreclosed status, may be more adaptive in non-Western cultures (Hassan, Vignoles, & Schwartz, 2018; G.L. Stein & others, 2018).

Identity development may take longer in some countries than in others (Schwartz & others, 2015). For example, research indicates that Italian youth may postpone significant identity exploration beyond adolescence and emerging adulthood, not settling on an identity until their mid- to late-twenties (Crocetti, Rabaglietti, & Sica, 2012). This delayed identity development is strongly influenced by many Italian youths living at home with their parents until 30 years of age and older.

Many aspects of sociocultural contexts may influence ethnic identity (Lilgendahl & others, 2018). Adolescents and emerging adults in the cultural majority of their country or community are unlikely to view their majority status as part of their identity. However, for many adolescents and emerging adults who have emigrated or grown up as members of an underrepresented racial/ethnic group, cultural dimensions likely are an important aspect of their identity.

An influential life-span model of ethnic-racial identity describes five dimensions of ethnic-racial identity: ethnic-racial awareness, affiliation, attitudes, behaviors, and knowledge (Williams & others, 2020). For decades and throughout the world, racial/ethnic minority groups have strived to maintain their racial/ethnic identities while functioning within the majority culture. **Racial/ethnic identity** is an enduring aspect of the self that includes a sense of membership in a racial/ethnic group as well as alignment with the attitudes and feelings related to that membership (Lu, Benet-Martínez, & Robins, 2020; Meeus, 2023; Salcido & Stein, 2023; Umaña-Taylor & Hill, 2020; Yoon & others, 2017). Thus, for adolescents from racial/ethnic minority groups, the process of identity formation has an added dimension: the choice between two or more sources of identification—their own racial/ethnic group and the mainstream, or majority culture (Gonzales & others, 2017; Tang, McLoyd, & Hallman, 2016). Adolescents also often adopt a **bicultural identity** or multicultural identities that encompass different cultural environments in which they are embedded and that can reflect their experiences with immigration and globalization (Ferguson, Iturbide, & Raffaelli, 2020). That is, they identify in some ways with their ethnic group and in other ways with the majority culture (Ferguson, Causadias, & Simenec, 2023).

Pride in one's racial/ethnic identity group has positive outcomes (Wittrup & others, 2019). For example, in one study, having pride in one's ethnic group and having a strong ethnic identity were linked to more engagement in the classroom for Cherokee adolescents (Bakth, Hoffman, & Schacter, 2022). And in another study, strong ethnic group affiliation and connection served a protective function in reducing risk for psychiatric problems (Anglin & others, 2016). Several longitudinal studies document that the ethnic identity of adolescents is influenced by positive and diverse friendships (Rivas-Drake & others, 2017; Santos, Komienko, & Rivas-Drake, 2017).

For racial/ethnic minority individuals, adolescence and emerging adulthood are often special junctures in their development (Azmitia & others, 2023). Although children are aware of some ethnic and cultural differences, individuals consciously confront their ethnicity for the first time in adolescence or emerging adulthood. Unlike children, adolescents and emerging adults are able to interpret ethnic and cultural information, to reflect on the past, and to speculate about the future. To read about one researcher who studies racial/ethnic identity and uses her findings to support youth, see *Connecting with Careers*.

The indicators of changing identity often differ for each succeeding generation (Huynh, Benet-Martínez, & Nguyen, 2018; Phinney & Vedder, 2013). For example, consider the generational differences among those who emigrated to the United States. First-generation immigrants are likely to be secure in their identities and unlikely to change much; they may or may not develop a new identity. The degree to which they begin to feel "American" appears to be related to whether or not they learn English, develop social networks beyond their ethnic group, and become culturally competent in their new country. Second-generation immigrants are more likely to think of themselves as "American," possibly because citizenship is granted at birth. Their ethnic identity is likely to be linked to retention of their ethnic language and social networks. In the third and later generations, the issues become more complex. Historical, contextual, and political factors that are unrelated to acculturation may affect the extent to which members of this generation retain their ethnic identities.

One adolescent girl, 16-year-old Michelle Chin, made these comments about ethnic identity development: "My parents do not understand that teenagers need to find out who they are, which means a lot of experimenting, a lot of mood swings, a lot of emotions and awkwardness. Like any teenager, I am facing an identity crisis. I am still trying to figure out whether I am a Chinese American or an American with Asian eyes."

Red Chopsticks/Getty Images

How Would You...?

If you were a **human development and family studies professional,** how would you design a community program that assists ethnic minority adolescents to develop a healthy bicultural identity?

racial/ethnic identity An enduring, basic aspect of the self that includes a sense of membership in a racial/ethnic group and the attitudes and feelings related to that membership.

bicultural identity Identity formation that occurs when adolescents identify in some ways with their racial/ethnic group and in other ways with the majority culture.

connecting with careers

Adriana Umaña-Taylor, Professor and Researcher of Ethnic-Racial Identity

Adriana Umaña-Taylor is a professor of education in the Harvard Graduate School of Education, where she leads the Adolescent Ethnic-Racial Identity Development (AERID) Laboratory. She obtained her undergraduate degree in psychology at the University of Texas at Austin and her doctoral degree in human development and family studies at the University of Missouri–Columbia. She has led several multidisciplinary efforts, including anthropology, sociology, developmental psychology, counseling psychology, and education, to advance the understanding of ethnic-racial identity.

Umaña-Taylor works to apply her research to reduce ethnic-racial disparities and promote social justice. She is currently leading a longitudinal study of how adolescents develop their ethnic and racial identities in the context of their peer relationships within school settings. She has collaborated with school districts to examine how ethnic-racial identity develops in social contexts including peer groups, families, schools, and neighborhoods. She developed The Identity Project, an intervention curriculum designed to provide adolescents of any ethnic-racial background with the tools and strategies to help them explore and understand their evolving identity in relation to their race and ethnicity.

Adriana Janette Umaña-Taylor is a professor who studies ethnic and racial identity. She uses her research to reduce ethnic-racial disparities and promote social justice.
Dr. Adriana Janette Umaña-Taylor

With Deborah Rivas-Drake, she coauthored *Below the Surface: Talking with Teens about Race, Ethnicity, and Identity,* which is designed to prepare parents and educators to discuss issues of race, ethnicity, and identity with adolescents as they navigate the question "Who Am I?"

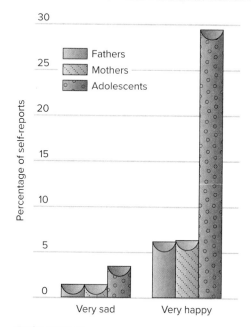

FIGURE 2

SELF-REPORTED EXTREMES OF EMOTION BY ADOLESCENTS, MOTHERS, AND FATHERS USING THE EXPERIENCE SAMPLING METHOD. In the study by Reed Larson and Maryse Richards (1994), adolescents and their mothers and fathers were beeped at random times by researchers using the experience sampling method. The researchers found that adolescents were more likely to report emotional extremes than their parents were.

EMOTIONAL DEVELOPMENT

Adolescence has long been described as a time of emotional turmoil (Hall, 1904). In its extreme form, this view is inaccurate because adolescents are not constantly in a state of "storm and stress." Nonetheless, early adolescence is a time when emotional highs and lows increase (Heshmati & others, 2023). In many instances, the intensity of the emotions of young adolescents seems out of proportion to the events that elicit them (Guyer, Silk, & Nelson, 2016). Young adolescents might sulk a lot, not knowing how to adequately express their feelings. With little or no provocation, they might blow up at their parents or siblings or use defense mechanisms to displace their feelings onto another person.

In a foundational research study, Reed Larson and Maryse Richards (1994) found that adolescents reported more extreme emotions and more fleeting emotions than their parents did. For example, adolescents were five times more likely to report being "very happy" and three times more likely to report being "very sad" than their parents were (see Figure 2). These findings lend support to the perception of adolescents as moody and changeable. Larson and colleagues also found that from the fifth through ninth grades, both boys and girls experience a 50 percent decrease in being "very happy" (Larson & Lampman-Petraitis, 1989). In this same study, adolescents were more likely than preadolescents to report mildly negative mood states. Many subsequent studies, including those examining biological and brain-based pubertal changes, have found similar results (Vijayakumar & others, 2019).

It is important for adults to recognize that moodiness is a *normal* aspect of early adolescence and that most adolescents make it through these moody times to become competent adults. Nonetheless, for some adolescents, such emotions can reflect serious problems. The ability to effectively manage and regulate one's emotions is a key dimension of positive outcomes in adolescent development, just as it is in children's development. Emotion regulation consists of effectively managing arousal to adapt to changing conditions and reach a goal (Liew, Morris, & Kerr, 2023). Arousal involves a state of alertness or activation, which can reach levels that are too high for effective functioning in adolescence. Anger, for example, often requires regulation (Karababa, 2020). One study found that young adolescents in

Taiwan who used a cognitive reappraisal strategy (i.e., changing the interpretation of an experience to better regulate emotions) rather than a suppression strategy (i.e., trying not to feel an emotion) were more likely to have a positive self-concept, which in turn was associated with having fewer internalizing problems such as depression (Hsieh & Stright, 2012).

With increasing age, adolescents are more likely to improve their use of cognitive strategies for regulating emotion, to modulate their emotional arousal, to become more adept at managing situations to minimize negative emotion, and to choose effective ways to cope with stress. Of course, there are wide variations in individuals' ability to regulate their emotions (Karababa, 2020). Indeed, a prominent feature of adolescents with problems is that they often have difficulty managing their emotions.

GENDER CLASSIFICATION

Not long ago, it was accepted that boys should grow up to be masculine (powerful, assertive, for example) and girls to be feminine (sensitive to others, caring, for example). In the 1970s, however, as females and males became dissatisfied with the burdens imposed by their stereotypic roles, alternatives to femininity and masculinity were proposed. Instead of describing masculinity and femininity as one continuum in which more of one means less of the other, two dimensions were proposed, along with an acknowledgment that individuals could have masculine as well as feminine traits.

In the 1970s, this thinking led to the development of the concept of **androgyny,** the presence of positive masculine and feminine characteristics in the same person (Bem, 1977; Spence & Helmreich, 1978). The androgynous boy might be assertive (masculine) and nurturing (feminine). The androgynous girl might be powerful (masculine) and sensitive to others' feelings (feminine). Measures were developed to assess androgyny, such as the Bem Sex Role Inventory (Bem, 1977).

Gender experts such as Sandra Bem (1977) have argued that androgynous individuals are more flexible, competent, and mentally healthy than their masculine or feminine counterparts. Current evidence suggests that androgenous individuals are healthier, evidenced both in behavior and in brain functioning (Luo & Sahakian, 2022). To some degree, though, which gender-role classification is best depends on the context involved (Mustafa & Nazir, 2018). This emphasis on considering contexts in understanding gender identity was described in terms of *functional flexibility*. In this view, gender identity is positively linked to adjustment, and competence involves flexibility in adapting to specific situations (Martin, Cook, & Andrews, 2017). For example, in close relationships, feminine and androgynous orientations might be more desirable. However, masculine and androgynous orientations might be more desirable in traditional academic and work settings because of the achievement demands in these contexts.

Contemporary views of gender classification also consider the possibility of being **transgender,** which refers to individuals who adopt a gender identity that differs from the one assigned to them at birth (Lee & Rosenthal, 2023). For example, an individual may have a female body but identify more strongly with being masculine than being feminine, or have a male body but identify more strongly with being feminine than masculine. Some individuals also may not want to be labeled "he" or "she" but prefer a more neutral label such as "they" or "ze" (Johnson & others, 2020).

Because of the nuances and complexities involved in such gender categorizations, some experts have recently argued that a better overarching umbrella term might be *trans* to identify a variety of gender identities and expressions different from the sex they were assigned at birth (Thelwall & others, 2023). The variety of gender identities might include transgender, gender queer, nonbinary, gender expansive, and gender nonconforming (individuals whose behavior/appearance does not conform to social expectations for what is appropriate for their gender). Another term, *cisgender,* can be used to describe individuals whose gender identity and expression correspond with the sex assigned at birth (Chew & others, 2020).

Prevalence rates are difficult to obtain accurately because of barriers to disclosure, but estimates are that approximately 1.4 percent of youths ages 13 to 17 years in the United States identify as transgender (Herman, Flores, & O'Neill, 2022), an estimate that has doubled since the last national estimates approximately seven years ago. In studies of socially transitioned transgender children (i.e., children who refer to themselves using pronouns of the gender with which they identify rather than their sex at birth but with no hormonal or surgical interventions involved), children report that by the age of 3 years, they identified with their current gender (Olson & Gülgöz, 2018). In a study of 5- to 12-year-old transgender children, transgender

androgyny The presence of positive masculine and feminine characteristics in the same individual.

transgender A broad term that refers to individuals who adopt a gender identity that differs from the sex assigned to them at birth.

Amber Riggle (*second from right*) is an active advocate for the rights of her transgender son, Max (*left*), and is a founding member of the Human Rights Campaign's Parents for Transgender Equality National Council.

Steven Simione/FilmMagic/Getty Images

children had cognitive patterns more consistent with their expressed gender than their natal sex (Olson, Key, & Eaton, 2015). In terms of expressed preferences related to clothes, toys, and other gender-stereotypical items and activities, transgender children were indistinguishable from cisgender children who had the same gender identity. Transgender children and their siblings are less likely than unrelated children to endorse gender stereotypes and more likely to befriend peers who are gender nonconforming (Olson & Enright, 2018).

Prejudice, discrimination, bullying, family rejection, and lack of self-acceptance are all concerns for transgender children (Zapata, 2023). Family support is especially important for transgender children's mental health. Socially transitioned transgender children have been found to have markedly lower levels of anxiety and depression than children with gender dysphoria who continue to live as their natal sex (Olson & others, 2016).

Transgender individuals can be straight, gay, lesbian, or bisexual. A comprehensive research review concluded that transgender youth have higher rates of depression, suicide attempts, and eating disorders than their cisgender peers (Connolly & others, 2016). Among the explanations for this higher rate of disorders are the distress of living in the wrong body and the discrimination and misunderstanding they experience as gender minority individuals (Chew & others, 2020).

Among adolescents who identify themselves as transgender persons, some eventually adopt a gender identity that is consistent with the sex assigned at birth (King, 2017). In a five-year longitudinal study of children who socially transitioned, 7.3 percent retransitioned at least once, but at the end of the five-year period, 94 percent identified as binary transgender (Olson & others, 2022). Other transgender individuals seek surgery to go from a male body to a female body or vice versa, but most do not. Some just receive hormonal treatments, such as biological females who use testosterone to enhance their masculine characteristics, or biological males who use estrogen to increase their feminine characteristics. Still other transgender individuals have a gender identity that does not fit within one of two traditional binary categories (Bower-Brown, Zadeh, & Jadva, 2023). To read about one person who conducts research and psychotherapy with transgender individuals, see the *Connecting with Careers* interlude.

connecting with careers

Stephanie Budge, Psychotherapist Specializing in Transgender Research

Stephanie Budge is a leading expert on transgender research, issues, and psychotherapy. She is a professor in the Department of Counseling at the University of Wisconsin–Madison, where she obtained her Ph.D. in counseling psychology. Her research examines emotional development and coping in transgender youth and adults, as well as psychotherapy with transgender clients. Budge also works nationally and internationally in training individuals to provide help related to LGBTQ issues, with a focus on increasing practitioners' self-efficacy, knowledge, and skills.

At the University of Wisconsin–Madison, Budge has given pro-bono therapy to transgender youth and adults. Budge has received the LGBTQ Outstanding Community Contributions award from the American Psychological Association and the LGBT Early Career Award from the Society for Counseling Psychology. She is currently associate editor of two journals: *Psychotherapy* and *Psychology of Sexual Orientation and Gender Diversity*. Budge also serves on the editorial board of the *International Journal of Transgender Health*.

Dr. Stephanie Budge is a leading expert on transgender youth and adults.

Dr. Stephanie Budge

2 What Is the Nature of Parent-Adolescent Relationships?

 LG2 Describe changes that take place in adolescents' relationships with their parents.

| Parental Monitoring and Adolescents' Information Management | Autonomy and Attachment | Parent-Adolescent Conflict |

As you read about parent-adolescent relationships in this section, keep in mind that a positive family climate for adolescents involves not only effective parenting but also a positive relationship between adolescents' parents, whether they are married or divorced. Families are best conceptualized as systems in which relationships between coparents, siblings, and extended family members are important in understanding parent-adolescent relationships (Updegraff & Perez-Brena, 2023).

Adolescence typically alters the relationship between parents and their children. Among the most important aspects of family relationships that change during adolescence are those that involve parental monitoring, autonomy, attachment, and parent-adolescent conflict.

PARENTAL MONITORING AND ADOLESCENTS' INFORMATION MANAGEMENT

We have discussed the important role that parents play as managers of their children's development. A key aspect of the managerial role of parenting is effective monitoring, which is especially important as children move into the adolescent years (Booth & Shaw, 2020). A current interest also focuses on adolescents' management of their parents' access to information, especially the extent to which adolescents disclose or conceal information about their activities (Son & Padilla-Walker, 2022).

Parental monitoring includes supervising adolescents' choice of social settings, activities, and friends, as well as their academic efforts. Numerous studies have found that more parental monitoring is related to better child and adolescent outcomes, including less victimization by peers (Khetarpal & others, 2022), lower rates of alcohol and marijuana use (Spirito & others, 2021), and less delinquent behavior (Jaggers & others, 2021). A qualitative study to gain in-depth understanding of factors that affect parents' knowledge of adolescents' whereabouts,

What roles do parental monitoring and adolescents' information management play in adolescent development?

RichLegg/Getty Images

friends, and activities found that adolescents were more willing to disclose information to their parents when they spent time together, when parents were affectionate, and when adolescents perceived their parents as giving good advice (Pizarro, Surkan, & Bustamante, 2021). In a longitudinal study of the transition to adolescence of youth in nine countries, researchers found that lower levels of parental monitoring played a key role in the link between neighborhood and household chaos and danger, and youth behavioral and emotional problems (Deater-Deckard & others, 2019). And in a comprehensive meta-analysis, a higher level of parental monitoring and rule enforcement were linked to adolescents' later initiation of sexual intercourse and increased use of condoms (Dittus & others, 2015).

A current interest involving parental monitoring focuses on adolescents' management of their parents' access to information, especially strategies for disclosing or concealing information about their activities (Son & Padilla-Walker, 2022). When parents engage in positive parenting practices, adolescents are more likely to disclose information. For example, disclosure increases when parents ask adolescents questions and when adolescents' relationship with parents is characterized by a high level of trust, acceptance, and quality (McElvaney, Greene, & Hogan, 2014). Researchers have found that adolescents' disclosure to parents about their whereabouts, activities, and friends is linked to positive adolescent adjustment and less depression (Dykstra, Willoughby, & Evans, 2020).

Three ways that parents can engage in parental monitoring are solicitation (asking questions), control (setting rules), and when youth don't comply, snooping. In an illustrative study, snooping was perceived by both adolescents and parents as the most likely of these three strategies to violate youths' privacy rights (Hawk, Becht, & Branje, 2016). Also, in this study, snooping was a relatively infrequent parental monitoring tactic but was a better indicator of problems in adolescent and family functioning than were solicitation and control.

AUTONOMY AND ATTACHMENT

With most adolescents, parents are likely to find themselves engaged in a delicate balancing act, weighing competing needs for autonomy and control, for independence and connection.

The Push for Autonomy   The typical adolescent's push for autonomy and responsibility puzzles and angers many parents. As parents see their teenager slipping from their grasp, they may have an urge to take stronger control. Heated emotional exchanges may ensue, with either side calling names, making threats, and doing whatever seems necessary to gain control. Parents may seem frustrated because they *expect* their teenager to heed their advice, to want to spend time with the family, and to grow up to do what is right. Most parents anticipate that their teenager will have some difficulty adjusting to the changes that adolescence brings, but few parents imagine and predict just how strong an adolescent's desires will be to spend time with peers or how intensely adolescents will want to show that it is they—not their parents—who are responsible for their successes and failures.

Stacey Christensen, age 16: "I am lucky enough to have open communication with my parents. Whenever I am in need or just need to talk, my parents are there for me. My advice to parents is to let your teens grow at their own pace, be open with them so that you can be there for them. We need guidance; our parents need to help but not be too overwhelming."

Stockbyte/Getty Images

Adolescents' ability to attain autonomy and gain control over their behavior is acquired through appropriate adult reactions to their desire for control (Distefano, Masten, & Motti-Stefanidi, 2021). At the onset of adolescence, the average individual does not have the knowledge to make appropriate or mature decisions in all areas of life. As the adolescent pushes for autonomy, the wise adult relinquishes control in those areas where the adolescent can make reasonable decisions, but continues to guide the adolescent to make reasonable decisions in areas in which the adolescent's knowledge is more limited. Gradually, adolescents acquire the ability to make mature decisions on their own. This pattern is seen in a study that found that from 16 to 20 years of age, adolescents perceived that they had increasing independence and improved relationships with their parents (Hadiwijaya & others, 2017). Note that in some cultures, boys are given more independence than girls. In one classic study, this tendency was especially true in U.S. families with a traditional gender-role orientation (Bumpus, Crouter, & McHale, 2001). However, a meta-analysis of many studies suggested these gender differences are small (Endendijk & others, 2016).

In contexts where adolescents experience a high level of risk, such as high-crime communities, and in cultural groups that place a high value on family solidarity and deference to parents, parental control either has not been linked to problem behaviors or has been shown to benefit adolescent outcomes. Relatedly, expectations about the appropriate timing of adolescent autonomy often vary across cultures, parents, and adolescents (Soenens & Vansteenkiste, 2020). A review of research on parental autonomy support among Black, White, Latino, and Asian American families concluded that understanding this aspect of parenting needs to be grounded in cultural concepts related to independence and expectations of parents (Benito-Gomez & others, 2020).

The Role of Attachment   Recall that one of the most widely discussed aspects of socioemotional development in infancy is secure attachment to caregivers (Brown & Cox, 2020). In the past few decades, researchers also have explored whether secure attachment might be an important concept in adolescents' relationships with their parents (De Meulenaere & others, 2022). For example, Joseph Allen and his colleagues (Allen & others, 2018; Allen & Tan, 2016) found that securely attached adolescents were less likely than those who were insecurely attached to engage in problem behaviors such as juvenile delinquency and drug abuse. In one longitudinal study, Allen and colleagues (Allen & Allen, 2009) found that secure attachment at 14 years of age was linked to a number of positive outcomes at 21 years of age, including relationship competence, financial/career competence, and fewer problematic behaviors. A subsequent study involving adolescents and emerging adults ages 12 to 20 years found that insecure attachment to mothers was related to more depressive symptoms (Rivers & others, 2022). Further, in a study of Latino families, a higher level of secure attachment with mothers was associated with less heavy drug use by adolescents (Gattamorta & others, 2017). A systematic review of 19 studies concluded that secure attachment to parents during adolescence is related to better peer relationships in terms of communication, support, intimacy, trust, and quality (Delgado & others, 2022).

Secure attachment in adolescence appears to be linked to parenting styles. A study of Chinese adolescents revealed that authoritative parenting positively predicted parent-adolescent attachment, which in turn was associated with a higher level of adolescent self-esteem and positive attachment to peers (Cai & others, 2013). And a longitudinal study of children in the United States revealed that secure attachment in adolescence and emerging adulthood was predicted by observations of maternal sensitivity across childhood and adolescence (Waters, Ruiz, & Roisman, 2017).

> developmental **connection**
> **Attachment**
> In secure attachment, babies use the caregiver as a secure base from which to explore the environment. Connect to "Socioemotional Development in Infancy."

PARENT-ADOLESCENT CONFLICT

Although parent-adolescent conflict increases in early adolescence, it does not reach the tumultuous proportions G. Stanley Hall envisioned at the beginning of the twentieth century (Smetana & Rote, 2019). Rather, much of the conflict involves the everyday expectations of family life, such as keeping a bedroom clean, dressing neatly, getting home by a certain time, and not talking for hours on the phone. The conflicts rarely involve major dilemmas such as drugs or delinquency.

Conflict with parents often escalates during early adolescence, remains somewhat stable during the high school years, and then lessens in emerging adulthood. One study revealed that young adult college students were more satisfied with their communication with their parents if they did not live with their parents while attending college (Sumner & Ramirez, 2019). Furthermore, the everyday conflicts that characterize parent-adolescent relationships may actually serve a positive developmental function. These minor disputes and negotiations facilitate the adolescent's transition from being dependent on parents to becoming an autonomous individual.

As shown in Figure 3, the old model of parent-adolescent relationships suggested that as adolescents mature they detach themselves from parents and move into a world of autonomy apart from parents. The old model also suggested that parent-adolescent conflict is intense and stressful throughout adolescence. The new model emphasizes that parents serve as important attachment figures and support systems while adolescents explore a wider, more complex social world. The new model also emphasizes that, in most families, parent-adolescent conflict is moderate rather than severe and that the everyday negotiations and minor disputes not only are normal but also can serve the positive developmental function of helping the adolescent make the transition from childhood dependency to adult independence.

Conflict with parents increases in early adolescence. *What is the nature of this conflict in a majority of American families?*
Juanmonino/Getty Images

How Would You...?
If you were a **social worker,** how would you counsel parents who are experiencing stress about anticipated family conflicts as their child enters adolescence?

Old Model

Autonomy, detachment from parents; parent and peer worlds are isolated

Intense, stressful conflict throughout adolescence; parent-adolescent relationships are filled with storm and stress on virtually a daily basis

New Model

Attachment and autonomy; parents are important support systems and attachment figures; adolescent-parent and adolescent-peer worlds have some important connections

Moderate parent-adolescent conflict is common and can serve a positive developmental function; conflict greater in early adolescence

FIGURE **3**

OLD AND NEW MODELS OF PARENT-ADOLESCENT RELATIONSHIPS

Klaus Vedfelt/DigitalVision/Getty Images

Still, a high degree of conflict characterizes some parent-adolescent relationships (Mokhtarnia & others, 2023). One long-ago established estimate of the proportion of parents and adolescents who engage in prolonged, intense, repeated, unhealthy conflict was about one in five families (Montemayor, 1982). This prolonged, intense conflict was associated with various adolescent problems: moving out of the home, juvenile delinquency, school dropout, pregnancy and early marriage, membership in religious cults, and drug abuse. More recent longitudinal research continues to find that more parent-adolescent conflict is related to worse adjustment, including depression, anxiety, and aggression (Martin & others, 2019).

Cross-cultural studies reveal that parent-adolescent conflict is lower in some countries than in the United States, but higher in others. In the largest international longitudinal study to date of changes in youth-parent positive and negative relationship features as children enter early adolescence, researchers identified substantial differences in hostility across nine countries spanning five continents. The highest to lowest levels of hostility were reported in Jordan, Kenya, China, Philippines, Thailand, Colombia, Sweden, Italy, and the United States (Deater-Deckard & others, 2018). In a five-country study, adolescents who had less destructive conflict with their parents were less likely to experience an increase in emotional and behavioral problems in early adulthood during the COVID-19 pandemic, suggesting the protective role of low-conflict parent-adolescent relationships (Skinner & others, 2021).

When families emigrate to another country, adolescents typically acculturate more quickly to the norms and values of their new country than do their parents (Sun & Geeraert, 2021). This likely occurs because of immigrant adolescents' exposure in school to the language and culture of the host country (Motti-Stefanidi, 2023). The norms and values immigrant adolescents experience are especially likely to diverge from those of their parents in areas such as autonomy and romantic relationships. Such divergences are likely to increase parent-adolescent conflict in immigrant families. These conflicts aren't always expressed openly but are often present in underlying, internal feelings. For example, immigrant adolescents may feel that their parents want them to give up their personal interests for the sake of the family, and the adolescents don't think this is fair. Such acculturation-based conflict focuses on issues related to core cultural values and is likely to occur in immigrant families who come to the United States to live (Safa & Umaña-Taylor, 2021). In one study of Chinese American families, parent-adolescent conflict was linked to a sense of alienation between parents and adolescents, which in turn was related to more depressive symptoms, delinquent behavior, and lower academic achievement (Hou, Kim, & Wang, 2016).

To read about some effective strategies for parenting adolescents, see the *Caring Connections* interlude.

caring connections

Strategies for Parenting Adolescents

Competent adolescent development is most likely when adolescents have parents who:

- *Show them warmth and respect, and avoid the tendency to be too controlling or too permissive.*
- *Serve as positive role models for adolescents.*
- *Demonstrate sustained interest in their lives.* Parents need to spend time with their adolescents and monitor their lives.
- *Understand and adapt to the adolescents' cognitive and socio-emotional development.*

- *Communicate expectations for high standards of conduct and achievement.*
- *Display constructive ways of dealing with problems and conflict.* Moderate conflict is a normal expression of the adolescent's desire for independence and search for an identity.
- *Understand that adolescents don't become adults overnight. Adolescence is a long journey.*

Review Connect Reflect

LG2 Describe changes that take place in adolescents' relationships with their parents.

Review

- What role does parental monitoring and adolescents' disclosure of information about their activities play in adolescent development?
- How do needs for autonomy and attachment develop in adolescence?
- What characterizes parent-adolescent conflict?

Connect

- Adolescence is identified as the second time in an individual's life when the drive for autonomy is especially strong. When is the other time, and what characterizes it?

Reflect *Your Own Personal Journey of Life*

- How much autonomy did your parents give you in adolescence? Too much? Too little? How intense was your conflict with your parents during adolescence? What kinds of conflicts did you have? Would you behave differently toward your own adolescents from the way your parents did with you? If so, how?

3 What Aspects of Peer Relationships Are Important in Adolescence?

 LG3 Characterize the changes that occur in peer relationships during adolescence.

Friendship   Peer Groups   Romantic Relationships

Peers play powerful roles in the lives of adolescents (Veenstra & Laninga-Wijnen, 2023). Peer relationships undergo important changes in adolescence, including changes in friendships and in peer groups and the beginning of romantic relationships. In middle and late childhood, the focus of peer relationships is on being liked by classmates and on being included in games or lunchroom conversations. Being overlooked or, worse yet, being rejected can have damaging effects on children's development that sometimes are carried forward to adolescence.

FRIENDSHIP

For most children, being popular with their peers is a strong motivator. In early adolescence, being popular with peers continues to be important, but teenagers also typically begin to prefer to have a smaller number of friendships that are more intense and intimate than those of young children.

Harry Stack Sullivan (1953) was the most influential early theorist to discuss the importance of adolescent friendships. In contrast with other theorists who focused almost exclusively on parent-child relationships, Sullivan argued that friends are also important in shaping the development of children and adolescents. Everyone, said Sullivan, has basic social needs, such as the need for tenderness (secure attachment), playful companionship, social acceptance, intimacy, and sexual relations. Whether or not these needs are fulfilled largely determines our emotional well-being (Whisman, Salinger, & Sbarra, 2022). For example, if the need for playful companionship goes unmet, then we become bored and depressed; if the need for social acceptance is not met, we suffer a diminished sense of self-worth.

During adolescence, said Sullivan, friends become increasingly important in meeting social needs. In particular, Sullivan argued, the need for intimacy intensifies during early adolescence and motivates teenagers to seek out close friends. If adolescents fail to forge such close friendships, they experience loneliness and a reduced sense of self-worth.

Many of Sullivan's ideas have withstood the test of time. For example, in a classic series of studies, adolescents reported disclosing intimate and personal information to their friends more often than did younger children (Buhrmester, 1998) (see Figure 4). This same

What changes take place in friendship during the adolescent years?
SW Productions/Brand X Pictures/Getty Images

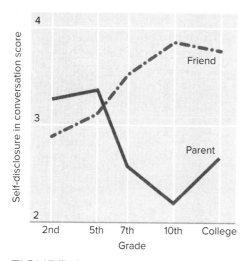

FIGURE **4**

DEVELOPMENTAL CHANGES IN SELF-DISCLOSING CONVERSATIONS. Self-disclosing conversations with friends increased dramatically in adolescence while declining in an equally dramatic fashion with parents. However, self-disclosing conversations with parents began to pick up somewhat during the college years. The measure of self-disclosure involved a 5-point rating scale completed by the children and youth, with a higher score representing greater self-disclosure. The data shown represent the means for each age group.

developmental pattern persists into adulthood, and is still found today in both "face-to-face" and social media communication methods (David-Barrett & others, 2016). Adolescents also say they depend more on friends than on parents to satisfy their needs for companionship, reassurance of worth, and intimacy. The ups and downs of experiences with friends shape adolescents' well-being (Cook, 2020).

People differ in the company they keep—that is, who their friends are. Although having friends can be a developmental advantage, not all friendships are alike, and the quality of friendship is also important to consider (de Moor & others, 2021). Developmental advantages occur when adolescents have friends who are socially skilled, supportive, and oriented toward academic achievement (Fletcher, Ross, & Zhang, 2020). It is a developmental disadvantage to have coercive, conflict-ridden, and poor-quality friendships. For example, one study revealed that having friends who engage in delinquent behavior is associated with early onset and more persistent delinquency (Evans, Simons, & Simons, 2016). Another study found that adolescents adapted their smoking and drinking behavior to that of their best friends (C. Wang & others, 2016). The importance of friendship has been demonstrated for children in most cultures, but the specific functions served by friends may differ across cultures (Chen, Lee, & Chen, 2018). For example, in individualist countries, such as Canada and the United States, friends often offer compliments and make each other feel good about themselves. In collectivist countries, such as China and Korea, friends are less likely to offer compliments that would focus on the individual rather than the group and instead are more likely to offer instrumental support, such as helping with homework.

Although most adolescents develop friendships with individuals who are close to their own age, some adolescents become best friends with younger or older individuals. Do older friends encourage adolescents to engage in delinquent behavior or early sexual behavior? Pubertal timing is important, as boys and girls who mature earlier than their same-age peers are more likely to gravitate to older peers who engage in substance use and other problem behaviors (Bucci & Staff, 2020).

PEER GROUPS

How extensive is peer pressure in adolescence? What roles do cliques and crowds play in adolescents' lives? As we see next, researchers have found that the standards of peer groups and the influence of crowds and cliques become increasingly important during adolescence.

Peer Pressure   Young adolescents conform more to peer standards than children do (Laursen & Faur, 2022). Around the eighth and ninth grades, conformity to peers—especially to their antisocial standards—peaks (Closson, Hart, & Hogg, 2017). At this point, adolescents are most likely to go along with a peer to steal hubcaps off a car, draw graffiti on a wall, or steal cosmetics from a store counter.

Which adolescents are most likely to conform to peers? Mitchell Prinstein and his colleagues (Duell & others, 2021; Prinstein, 2007; Prinstein & Giletta, 2021; Prinstein & others, 2009) have conducted research and analysis addressing this question. They conclude that adolescents who are uncertain about their social identity, which can appear in the form of low self-esteem and high social anxiety, are most likely to conform to peers. This uncertainty often increases during times of change, such as school and family transitions. Also, adolescents are more likely to conform when they are in the presence of someone they perceive to have higher status than themselves. Other research has found that boys are more likely to be influenced by peer pressure involving sexual behavior than are girls (Widman & others, 2016).

What characterizes peer pressure in adolescence?

Christin Rose/Image Source/Getty Images

clique A small group that ranges from 2 to about 12 individuals, averaging about 5 or 6 individuals, and may form because adolescents engage in similar activities.

Cliques and Crowds   Cliques and crowds assume more important roles in the lives of adolescents than in the lives of children (Ferguson & Ryan, 2019). **Cliques** are small groups that range from 2 to about 12 individuals and average about 5 or 6 individuals. The clique members are usually of the same sex and about the same age.

Cliques can form because adolescents engage in similar activities, such as being in a club or on a sports team (Martin & others, 2020). Several adolescents may form a clique because they have spent time with each other, share mutual interests, and enjoy each other's company. Not necessarily friends, they often develop a friendship if they stay in the clique. What do adolescents do in cliques? They share ideas and hang out together. Often they develop an in-group identity in which they believe that their clique is better than other cliques.

Crowds are larger than cliques and less personal. Adolescents are usually members of a crowd based on reputation, and they may or may not spend much time together. Many crowds are defined by the activities adolescents engage in (such as "jocks" who are good at sports or "nerds" who are highly academic) (Moran & others, 2019). Reputation-based crowds often appear for the first time in early adolescence and usually become less prominent in late adolescence (Collins & Steinberg, 2006).

What characterizes adolescents' cliques and crowds?
MB Images/iStock/Getty Images

Crowd membership can have serious consequences for adolescent development. In one classic study, crowd membership was associated with adolescent self-esteem (Brown & Lohr, 1987). The crowds included jocks (athletically oriented students), populars (well-known students who led social activities), normals (middle-of-the-road students who made up the masses), druggies or toughs (students who are known for illicit drug use or other delinquent activities), and nobodies (students who are low in social skills or intellectual abilities). The self-esteem of the jocks and the populars was highest, whereas that of the nobodies was lowest. One group of adolescents not in a crowd had self-esteem equivalent to that of the jocks and the populars; this group was the independents, who indicated that crowd membership was not important to them. Keep in mind that these data are correlational; self-esteem could increase an adolescent's probability of becoming a crowd member, just as crowd membership could increase the adolescent's self-esteem.

So far, we have discussed many aspects of friendship and peer relationships in adolescence. A final point about these very important socioemotional interactions is how the abrupt appearance of the coronavirus (COVID-19) in 2020 quickly affected the ways interactions with friends and peers took place. One of the most widely recommended changes in response to the virus outbreak emphasized *social distancing,* which involves maintaining a distance of at least 6 feet (2 meters) from others to prevent transmission of the virus. For many individuals, social distancing and lockdowns during which they were required to stay home increased feelings of social isolation and decreased the sense of connection with peers and friends that is so important to children and adolescents (Loades & others, 2020). This separation from peers is one factor that may have contributed to adolescents' increase in anxiety, depression, and suicidal ideation during the pandemic (Magson & others, 2021). Positive online experiences with peers helped mitigate loneliness during the pandemic when in-person interactions were not possible (Magis-Weinberg & others, 2021).

developmental **connection**

Emotional Development

The COVID-19 pandemic and other events like it can cause a great deal of anxiety and stress for children and youth. Parents can guide them in using a number of effective strategies to cope with such stressful circumstances. Connect with "Socioemotional Development in Middle and Late Childhood."

ROMANTIC RELATIONSHIPS

Adolescents spend considerable time engaging in romantic relationships or thinking about doing so (Connolly, Shulman, & Benvenuto, 2023). "Dating" can be a form of recreation, a source of status, and a setting for learning about close relationships, as well as a way of finding a mate.

Types of Dating and Developmental Changes   A number of dating variations and developmental changes characterize dating and romantic relationships. First, we examine heterosexual romantic relationships, and then we turn to romantic relationships among gay, lesbian, and bisexual youth.

Heterosexual Romantic Relationships   Three stages characterize the development of romantic relationships in adolescence in many but certainly not all national and cultural groups (Connolly & McIsaac, 2009):

crowd A larger group than a clique, one that is usually formed based on reputation; members may or may not spend much time together.

What are some developmental changes in romantic relationships in adolescence?

Hero Images/Getty Images

- *Entering into romantic attractions and affiliations at about 11 to 13 years of age.* This initial stage is triggered by puberty. From 11 to 13, adolescents become intensely interested in romance, and it dominates many conversations with same-sex friends. Developing a crush on someone is common, and the crush often is shared with a same-sex friend. Young adolescents may or may not interact with the individual who is the object of their infatuation. When dating occurs, it usually occurs in a group setting.

- *Exploring romantic relationships at approximately 14 to 16 years of age.* At this point in adolescence, two types of romantic involvement occur: casual dating and group dating. *Casual dating* emerges between individuals who are mutually attracted. These dating experiences are often short-lived, last a few months at best, and usually endure for only a few weeks. Dating in groups is common and reflects embeddedness in the peer context. Friends often act as a third-party facilitator of a potential dating relationship by communicating their friend's romantic interest and determining whether this attraction is reciprocated.

- *Consolidating dyadic romantic bonds at about 17 to 19 years of age.* At the end of the high school years, more serious romantic relationships develop. This is characterized by strong emotional bonds more closely resembling those in adult romantic relationships. These bonds often are more stable and enduring than earlier bonds, typically lasting one year or more.

Two variations on these stages in the development of romantic relationships in adolescence involve early and late bloomers (Connolly & McIsaac, 2009). *Early bloomers* include 15 to 20 percent of 11- to 13-year-olds who say that they currently are in a romantic relationship and 35 percent who indicate that they have had some prior experience in romantic relationships. One study found that early bloomers externalized problem behaviors through adolescence to a greater extent than their on-time and late-bloomer counterparts (Connolly & others, 2013). *Late bloomers* comprise approximately 10 percent of 17- to 19-year-olds who say that they have had no experience with romantic relationships and another 15 percent who report that they have not engaged in any romantic relationships that lasted more than four months.

Romantic Relationships in Gay, Lesbian, and Bisexual Youth

More recently, researchers have been studying romantic relationships in gay, lesbian, and bisexual youth (Connolly, Shulman, & Benvenuto, 2023; Kaestle, 2019; Rosario, 2019; Russell & Dorri, 2023; Savin-Williams, 2016, 2017). Many date other-sex peers, a practice that can help them to clarify their sexual orientation or disguise it from others. Still other gay and lesbian youth have some same-sex sexual experience, often with peers who are "experimenting," and then go on to a primarily heterosexual orientation (Savin-Williams, 2016). In the United States and many other industrialized nations, it is becoming more common for adolescent gay, lesbian, and bisexual youth to come out and be in romantic relationships that reflect their identity (Költő & others, 2018). Recent research also increasingly recognizes fluidity in sexual orientation and gender identity and expression (Diamond, 2021).

What characterizes romantic relationships in LGBTQ youth?

Johner Images/Getty Images

How Would You...?
If you were a **human development and family studies professional,** how would you explain to parents the developmental challenges faced by a gay or lesbian adolescent?

Sociocultural Contexts and Dating

The sociocultural context exerts a powerful influence on adolescents' dating patterns (Stein & others, 2018; Yoon & others, 2017). This influence is illustrated by differences in dating patterns among ethnic groups within the United States.

Values, religious beliefs, and traditions often dictate at what age dating begins, how much freedom in dating is allowed, whether dates must be chaperoned by adults or parents, and the roles of males and females in dating (Taggart & others, 2018). For example, Latino and Asian American cultures have more conservative standards regarding adolescent dating than do White and Black American cultures. Dating may become a source of conflict within a family if the parents have immigrated from cultures in which dating begins at a late age, little freedom in dating is allowed, dates are chaperoned, and dating by adolescent girls is especially restricted. When immigrant adolescents choose to adopt the ways of the new culture (such as uncharperoned dating), they often clash with parents and extended-family members who have more traditional values (Shenhav, Campos, & Goldberg, 2017).

In one qualitative study in which Latino adolescents participated in focus group discussions, adolescents perceived their parents as being more protective in relation to their daughters' than their sons' romantic relationships and sexual behaviors (Killoren & others, 2023). These differences were perceived as reflecting cultural values related to family honor and respect as well as gender role expectations. Another study found that mother-daughter conflict in Mexican American families was linked to an increase in daughters' romantic involvement (Tyrell & others, 2016). These research findings illustrate how adolescents' behavior in romantic relationships reflects the influence of cultural context and family and community expectations and roles.

Dating and Adjustment   Researchers have linked dating and romantic relationships with how well adjusted adolescents are (Loeb & others, 2020). In large part, whether romantic partners enhance or diminish adolescents' adjustment depends on the quality of the romantic relationship and the adjustment of the romantic partner. For example, a review of studies using data from the National Longitudinal Study of Adolescent to Adult Health concluded that experiencing violence in a dating relationship increases the likelihood of adolescents' later heavy drinking, marijuana use, and prescription opioid misuse (Austin & others, 2022). However, a different study found that having a supportive romantic relationship in adolescence was linked to positive outcomes for adolescents who had a negative relationship with their mother (Szwedo, Hessel, & Allen, 2017). In another study, adolescents who engaged in a higher level of intimate disclosure at age 10 reported a higher level of companionship in romantic relationships at 12 and 15 years of age (Kochendorfer & Kerns, 2017). In this study, those who reported more conflict in friendships had a lower level of companionship in romantic relationships at 15 years of age.

Dating and romantic relationships at an unusually early age also have been linked with several problems (Emerson & others, 2023). For example, early dating and "going with" someone are associated with adolescent pregnancy and problems at home and school (Garthe, Sullivan, & Behrhorst, 2018). In one early study on this topic, girls' early romantic involvement was linked with lower grades, less active participation in class discussions, and other school-related problems (Buhrmester, 2001).

Recently, romantic attraction has taken place not only in person but also over the Internet and through texting. Some critics argue that online romantic relationships lose the interpersonal connection, whereas others emphasize that the Internet may benefit shy or anxious individuals who find it difficult to meet potential partners in person (Cameron & Mascarenas, 2020). One problem with online relationships is that many individuals misrepresent their characteristics, such as how old they are, how attractive they are, and their educational attainment or occupation.

Connecting Online   Is looking for love online likely to work out? It didn't work out well in 2012 for Notre Dame linebacker Manti Te'o, whose online girlfriend turned out to be a "catfish," someone who fakes an identity online. However, approximately 48 percent of 18- to 29-year-olds reported in 2019 that they had used a dating app (Pew Research Center, 2020). Lesbian, gay, and bisexual young people are roughly twice as likely as straight young people to use dating apps. About 12 percent of U.S. adults say that they have been in a committed relationship with or married someone they met through a dating app.

Connecting online for love turned out positively for two Columbia University graduate students, Michelle Przybyksi and Andy Lalinde (Steinberg, 2011). They lived several blocks away from each other, so soon after they communicated online through Datemyschool.com, an online dating site exclusively for college students, they met in person, really hit it off, applied for a marriage license 10 days later, and eventually got married.

However, an editorial by Samantha Nickalls (2012) in *The Tower*, the student newspaper at Arcadia University in Philadelphia, argued that online dating sites might be okay for people in their thirties and older but not for college students. She commented:

> The dating pool of our age is huge. Huge. After all, marriage is not on most people's minds when they're in college, but dating (or perhaps just hooking up) most certainly is. A college campus, in fact, is like living a dating service because the majority of people are looking for the same thing you are. As long as you put yourself out there, flirt a bit, and be friendly, chances are that people will notice.

(*Left*) Manti Te'o; (*right*) Michelle Przybyksi and Andy Lalinde.

(*Left*): Cal Sport Media/Alamy Stock Photo; (*right*): Michelle and Andres Lalinde

If this doesn't work for you right away, why should it really matter? As a college student, you have so many other huge things going on in your life—your career choice, your transition from kid to adult, your crazy social life. Unless you are looking to get married at age 20 (which is a whole other issue that I could debate for hours), dating shouldn't be the primary thing on your mind anyway. Besides, as the old saying goes, the best things come when you least expect them.

Oftentimes, you find the best dates by accident—not by hunting them down.

What do you think? Is it a good idea to search online for romantic relationships? What are some cautions that need to be taken if you pursue an online romantic relationship?

Review *Connect* Reflect

LG3 Characterize the changes that occur in peer relationships during adolescence.

Review

- What changes take place in friendship during adolescence?
- What are adolescents' peer groups like?
- What is the nature of adolescent dating and romantic relationships?

Connect

- Piece together the information discussed earlier about sexual development in adolescence with the coverage of dating and romantic relationships in this chapter to construct a profile of positive adolescent development.

Reflect *Your Own Personal Journey of Life*

- What were your peer relationships like during adolescence? What peer groups were you involved in? How did they influence your development? What were your dating and romantic relationships like in adolescence? If you could change anything about the way you experienced peer relationships in adolescence, what would it be?

4 Why Is Culture an Important Context for Adolescent Development?

LG4 Explain how culture influences adolescent development.

| Cross-Cultural Comparisons | Race/Ethnicity | Media and Technology |

We live in an increasingly diverse world, one in which there is increasing contact between adolescents from different cultures and racial/ethnic groups. In this section, we explore these differences as they relate to adolescents, and then examine media influences on adolescents.

CROSS-CULTURAL COMPARISONS

What traditions remain for adolescents around the globe? What circumstances are changing adolescents' lives?

(a)

Traditions and Changes in Adolescence Around the Globe   Consider some of the variations of adolescence around the world (Lerner & others, 2019):

- In a 2018 survey of more than 160,000 households in India, over 90 percent of couples in their twenties said their marriage had been arranged by their families (S., 2021).
- In the Philippines and a number of other rapidly developing nations, many female adolescents sacrifice their own futures by migrating to the city to earn money that they send home to their families (Montgomery & others, 2016).
- "Street youth" in Kenya, Brazil, and other nations learn to survive under highly stressful circumstances. In some cases abandoned by their parents, they may engage in delinquency or prostitution to provide for their economic needs (Neiva-Silva & others, 2023).

(b)

Thus, depending on the culture being observed, adolescence may involve many different experiences (Pereira & others, 2023). Some cultures have retained their traditions regarding adolescence, but rapid global change is altering the experience of adolescence in many places, presenting new opportunities and challenges to young people's health and well-being. Around the world, adolescents' experiences may differ significantly.

Gender   The experiences of male and female adolescents in many cultures continue to be quite different (Peitzmeier & others, 2016). In 51 percent of countries, boys have more access to primary school education than do girls, and in 76 percent of countries boys have more access to upper secondary school education than do girls (UNICEF, 2022). In many countries, adolescent females have less freedom than males to pursue a variety of careers and engage in various leisure activities. Gender differences in sexual expression are widespread, especially in India, Southeast Asia, Latin America, and Arab countries, where there are more adult restrictions on the cross-sex contact and sexual activity of adolescent females than on that of males. These gender differences do appear to be narrowing over time, however. In some countries, educational and career opportunities for women are expanding, and control over adolescent girls' romantic and sexual relationships is weakening (Noble & others, 2019).

(c)

(*a*) Asian Indian adolescent in a marriage ceremony. (*b*) Muslim school in Middle East with boys only. (*c*) Street youth in Rio de Janeiro.

(a): Allison Joyce/Getty Images; (b): Yvan Cohen/LightRocket/Getty Images; (c): Celia Mannings/Alamy Stock Photo.

Family   In some countries, adolescents grow up in closely knit families with extensive extended-kin networks that retain a traditional way of life. For example, in Arab countries, adolescents often are taught strict codes of conduct and family loyalty (Sortheix & others, 2023). However, in many Western countries such as the United States, parenting emphasizes individuality, and much larger numbers of adolescents are growing up in divorced families and stepfamilies.

In many countries around the world, parents or adolescents migrate to urban areas to find work and to be able to send funds home to support the family (Chow & others, 2023). Unfortunately, although migration may be necessary for financial reasons, it may reduce the ability of families to spend time with their children and adolescents (Liu & others, 2020).

Peers   Some cultures give peers a stronger role in adolescence than others do. In most Western nations, peers figure prominently in adolescents' lives, in some cases taking on roles that would otherwise be assumed by parents. For example, among street youth in South America, the peer network serves as a surrogate family that supports survival in dangerous and stressful settings (Kennedy & others, 2017).

To read about how adolescents around the world spend their time, see the *Connecting with Diversity* interlude.

Rites of Passage   Another variation in the experiences of adolescents in different cultures is whether the adolescents go through a rite of passage. Some societies have elaborate ceremonies that signal the adolescent's move to maturity and achievement of adult status (Schroeder, Tallarico, & Bakaroudis, 2022). A **rite of passage** is a ceremony or ritual that marks an individual's transition from one status to another. Most rites of passage focus on the

rite of passage A ceremony or ritual that marks an individual's transition from one status to another. Most rites of passage focus on the transition to adult status.

How Adolescents Around the World Spend Their Time

In a classic series of studies, Reed Larson and Suman Verma (Larson, 2001; Larson & Verma, 1999) have examined how adolescents spend their time in work, play, and developmental activities such as school. U.S. adolescents spend about 60 percent as much time on schoolwork as East Asian adolescents do, mainly because U.S. adolescents do less homework than East Asians do. Contemporary evidence in the United States suggests that adolescents are spending more time sleeping and doing homework today compared with adolescents in the late 1990s when this study was conducted (Livingston, 2019).

What U.S. adolescents have in greater quantities than do adolescents in other industrialized countries is discretionary time (Larson, McGovern, & Orson, 2018; Larson, Walker, & McGovern, 2018). About 40 to 50 percent of U.S. adolescents' waking hours (not counting summer vacations) is spent in discretionary activities, compared with 25 to 35 percent in East Asia and 35 to 45 percent in Europe. Whether this additional discretionary time is a liability or an asset for U.S. adolescents, of course, depends on how they use it.

According to Larson, U.S. adolescents may have more unstructured time than is beneficial for their development. Indeed, when adolescents are allowed to choose what to do with their time, they typically engage in unchallenging activities such as hanging out and watching

How do East Asian and U.S. adolescents spend their time differently?
DragonImages/iStock/Getty Images

content on their phones. Although relaxation and social interaction are important aspects of adolescence, it seems unlikely that spending large numbers of hours per week in unchallenging activities fosters development. Structured voluntary activities may provide more promise for adolescent development than unstructured time, especially if adults give responsibility to adolescents, challenge them, and provide competent guidance in these activities (Larson, McGovern, & Orson, 2018; Larson, Walker, & McGovern, 2018).

These Congolese Kota boys painted their faces as part of the rite of passage to adulthood. *What rites of passage do adolescents have in other countries and cultural groups?*

Daniel Laine/Gamma Rapho

transition to adult status. In some traditional cultures, rites of passage are the avenue through which adolescents gain access to sacred adult practices, to knowledge, and to sexuality. These rites often involve dramatic practices intended to facilitate the adolescent's separation from the immediate family, especially the mother. The transformation is usually characterized by some form of ritual death and rebirth, or by contact with the spiritual world. Bonds are forged between the adolescent and the adult instructors through shared rituals, hazards, and secrets to allow the adolescent to enter the adult world. This kind of ritual provides a forceful and discontinuous entry into the adult world at a time when the adolescent is perceived to be ready for the change.

An especially rich tradition of rites of passage for adolescents has prevailed in African cultures, especially sub-Saharan Africa (Scupin & DeCorse, 2017). Under the influence of Western industrialized culture, many of these rites are disappearing today, although they are still prevalent in locations where formal education is not as readily available.

Even in diverse Western or industrialized nations, certain religious and social groups still have initiation ceremonies that indicate that an advance in maturity has been reached: the Jewish bar and bat mitzvah, the Catholic confirmation, and social debuts in traditional southern U.S. culture, for example. School graduation ceremonies come the closest to being culture-wide rites of passage in the United States and most industrial nations.

RACE/ETHNICITY

Earlier in this chapter, we explored the identity development of racial/ethnic minority adolescents. Here we further examine immigration and the relationship between race/ethnicity and socioeconomic status.

Immigration   In the United States, high rates of immigration have contributed to the growing proportion of ethnic minority adolescents and emerging adults in the population (Frey, 2019). Immigrant families are those in which at least one of the parents is born outside of the country of residence. Variations in immigrant families involve whether one or both parents are foreign born, whether the child was born in the host country, and the ages at which immigration took place for both the parents and the children (Van Hook & Glick, 2020).

Different models have been proposed as to whether children and adolescents in immigrant families are more vulnerable or more successful in relation to the general population of children and adolescents (Zhou & Gonzalez, 2019). Historically, an *immigrant risk model* was emphasized, concluding that youth of immigrants had a lower level of well-being and were at risk for more problems. For example, one study found that the longer immigrant youth from the Dominican Republic lived in the United States, the higher their risk for mental health problems in comparison with youth residing in the Dominican Republic (Peña & others, 2016).

An *immigrant paradox model* also has been proposed, emphasizing that despite the many cultural, socioeconomic, language, and other obstacles that immigrant families face, youth from some immigrant groups show a higher level of well-being and fewer problems than native-born youth (Marks & Garcia-Coll, 2018). Based on current research, some support exists for each model (Brady & Stevens, 2019). How immigrant youth fare depends on opportunities available in the country of destination, discrimination they might experience, their families' socioeconomic status, and a range of other factors (Motti-Stefanidi, 2023).

What are some cultural adaptations that many immigrant adolescents who come to the United States and other countries likely need to make?

Caroline Woodham/Photographer's Choice/Getty Images

What are some of the circumstances immigrants face that challenge their adjustment? Immigrants often experience stressors uncommon to or less prominent among longtime residents. These include language barriers, dislocations and separations from support networks, the dual struggle to preserve identity and to acculturate, and changes in SES status (Suárez-Orozco, López Hernández, & Cabral, 2021). In a study comparing Asian, Latino, and non-Latino White immigrant adolescents, immigrant Asian adolescents had the highest level of depression and the lowest self-esteem, and were the most likely to report experiencing discrimination (Lo & others, 2017).

Some individuals in immigrant families are dealing with the problem of being undocumented. Living in an undocumented family can affect children's and adolescents' developmental outcomes if parents' fear of deportation keeps them from signing up for services for which they may be eligible, through conditions linked to low-wage work and lack of benefits, and through stress, which may carry over into the home (Cross & others, 2020; Yoshikawa, Whipps, & Rojas, 2017). Consequently, when working with adolescents and their immigrant families, counselors need to adapt intervention programs to optimize cultural sensitivity (Sue & others, 2019).

The ways in which racial/ethnic minority families deal with stress depend on many factors (Burnette & others, 2019; Non & others, 2019). Whether the parents are native-born or immigrants, how long the family has been in the United States, its socioeconomic status, and its national origin all make a difference. Several studies have revealed that parents' education before migrating was strongly linked to their children's academic achievement (Zhang, Cheng, & Barrella, 2022). Another study of over 470,000 youth in Canada found that both first- and second-generation immigrant youth had lower rates of conduct disorders, ADHD, and mood disorders (like anxiety and depression) than nonimmigrant youth and that first-generation immigrant youth generally had lower rates of these problems than second-generation youth (Gadermann & others, 2022).

Jason Leonard, age 15: "I want America to know that most of us Black teens are not troubled people from broken homes and headed to jail. . . . In my relationships with my parents, we show respect for each other and we have values in our house. We have traditions we celebrate together, including Christmas and Kwanzaa."

Comstock Images/Getty Images

Race/Ethnicity and Socioeconomic Status   Too often the research on racial/ethnic minority adolescents has failed to tease apart the influences of race/ethnicity, immigration, and socioeconomic status. These factors can interact in ways that exaggerate the influence of race/ethnicity because racial/ethnic minority individuals are overrepresented in the lower socioeconomic levels in our societies (McLoyd, 2019). Consequently, researchers too often have given racial/ethnic explanations for aspects of adolescent development that were largely due instead to socioeconomic status.

Many racial/ethnic minority families are headed by affluent and educated adults. However, poverty contributes to the stressful life experiences of many racial/ethnic minority adolescents (Gonzales & others, 2016). Thus, many racial/ethnic minority adolescents experience a double

The 2020 deaths of Black Americans, such as George Floyd and Breonna Taylor, in encounters with police and the accompanying widespread endorsement of the Black Lives Matter movement across all racial/ethnic groups have stimulated increased concern about ongoing bias, prejudice, and discrimination against racial/ethnic minority individuals. *What might be some topics and strategies parents could use with their adolescents to help them cope with these stressful circumstances and guide their conduct in such matters? What might parents do to socialize their adolescents to be anti-racist?*
Tom Barlow Brown/SOPA Images/LightRocket/Getty Images

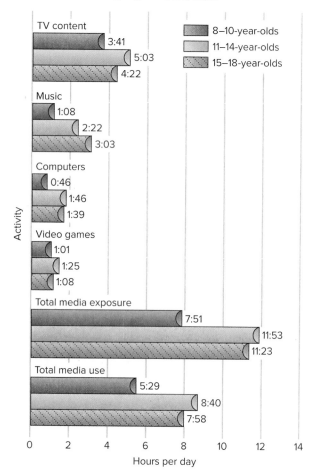

FIGURE 5

DEVELOPMENTAL CHANGES IN THE AMOUNT OF TIME U.S. 8- TO 18-YEAR-OLDS SPEND WITH DIFFERENT TYPES OF MEDIA

disadvantage: (1) prejudice, discrimination, and bias either personally in social interactions or societally through institutional practices that reflect systemic racism and (2) the stressful effects of poverty (McLoyd, 2019).

MEDIA AND TECHNOLOGY

Earlier, we discussed the role of screen time in children's development. Here we examine changes in screen time and media content exposure from childhood to adolescence.

Media Use   If the amount of time spent in an activity is any indication of its importance, there is no doubt that media play important roles in adolescents' lives (Lever-Duffy & McDonald, 2018). To better understand various aspects of U.S. adolescents' media use, the Kaiser Family Foundation (KFF) funded national surveys in 1999, 2004, and 2009. The 2009 survey included more than 2,000 young people 8 to 18 years old and documented that adolescent media use has increased dramatically in the last decade (Rideout, Foehr, & Roberts, 2010). Today's youth live in a world in which they are surrounded by media. In this survey, in 2009, 8- to 10-year-olds used media 5 hours and 29 minutes a day, but 11- to 14-year-olds used media an average of 8 hours and 40 minutes a day, and 15- to 18-year-olds an average of 7 hours and 58 minutes a day (see Figure 5). The more recent trends over the past decade indicate that these shifts toward even more media use in adolescence have only continued to increase (Blumberg & others, 2019).

A major trend in the use of technology is the dramatic increase in media multitasking (Aagard, 2019; Wang, Sigerson, & Cheng, 2019). In the 2009 KFF survey, when the amount of time spent multitasking was included in computing total media use, 11- to 14-year-olds spent nearly 12 hours a day (compared with almost 9 hours a day when multitasking was not included) exposed to media (Rideout, Foehr, & Roberts, 2010). In this survey, 39 percent of seventh- to twelfth-graders said "most of the time" they use two or more media concurrently, such as surfing the Web while listening to music. In some cases, media multitasking—such as text messaging, listening to music, and updating a YouTube account—is engaged in at the same time as doing homework. It is hard to imagine that this allows a student to do homework efficiently.

Consider the following studies that involve media multitasking:

- Heavy multimedia multitaskers were less likely than light media multitaskers to delay gratification and more likely to endorse intuitive, but wrong, answers on a cognitive reflection task (Schutten, Stokes, & Arnell, 2017).

- In a research review, a higher level of media multitasking was linked to lower levels of school achievement, executive function, and growth mindset in adolescents (Cain & others, 2016).

- For 8- to 12-year-old girls, a higher level of media multitasking was linked to negative social well-being, while a higher level of face-to-face communication was associated with positive social-well-being indicators, such as greater social success, feeling more normal, and having fewer friends whom parents thought were a bad influence (Pea & others, 2012).

- In a study of college students, media multitasking led to attention biases in taking in negative information, which in turn predicted more depression and anxiety (Li & Fan, 2022).

Technology and Digitally Mediated Communication   Culture involves change, and nowhere is that change more apparent than in the technological revolution individuals are experiencing with increased use of computers, smartphones, and the Internet (Blumberg & others, 2019). Society relies on some basic nontechnological competencies—for example, good communication skills, positive attitudes, and the ability to solve problems and to think deeply and creatively. But how people pursue these competencies is changing in ways and at a speed that few people had to cope with in previous eras. For youth to be adequately prepared for tomorrow's jobs, technology needs to become an integral part of their lives.

Mobile media, such as cell phones and tablets, are mainly driving the increased media use by adolescents. For example, in 2004, 39 percent of U.S. adolescents owned a cell phone, a figure that had jumped to 66 percent in 2009 and to 87 percent in 2016, and it continues to increase today (Common Sense Media, 2019).

Given the ubiquity of online experiences in adolescents' lives, a number of concerns have been raised about the negative effects these experiences may be having on adolescents' physical and mental health (Twenge, 2020). One study found that less screen time was linked to adolescents' better health-related quality of life (Wong & others, 2017). Another study indicated that

How much time do adolescents spend using different types of media?
Antonio Guillem/Shutterstock

a higher level of social media use was associated with a higher level of heavy drinking by adolescents (Brunborg, Andreas, & Kvaavik, 2017). However, screen time and social media use can also have benefits for adolescents. For example, when in-person interactions were restricted during the COVID-19 pandemic, an important way that adolescents were able to stay connected with their friends was through social media and other online interactions, such as playing video games together (Calandri, Cattelino, & Graziano, 2023). Balancing both positive and negative effects, researchers have called for more nuanced perspectives of understanding the who, what, and when of social media use to understand possible benefits and detriments of its use (Hamilton, Nesi, & Choukas-Bradley, 2022).

Clearly, parents need to monitor and regulate adolescents' use of the Internet. The three main ways that parents engage with adolescents around their online lives are by restricting, regulating, and discussing content (Beyens, Keijsers, & Coyne, 2022). For example, parents can set time limits on the amount of screen time adolescents are allowed; can enforce rules about when and where adolescents can be on their phones, such as not

What characterizes the online social environment of adolescents and emerging adults?
Anne Ackermann/Digital Vision/Alamy Stock Photo

allowing adolescents to sleep with their phones in their bedrooms; and can discuss with adolescents what they are doing online and whether any of it is troubling. A synthesis of 32 articles published between 2017 and 2021 found that parents who engage with adolescents' media use in more autonomy-supportive rather than restrictive ways have adolescents who spend less time on social media and report less problematic social media use (Beyens, Keijsers, & Coyne, 2022).

Review Connect Reflect

 Explain how culture influences adolescent development.

Review

- What are some differences in the lives of adolescents in various cultures? How do adolescents around the world spend their time? What are some examples of rites of passage?
- How does race/ethnicity influence adolescent development?
- What characterizes adolescents' use of media and technology?

Connect

- How do race/ethnicity and poverty influence children's development?

Reflect *Your Own Personal Journey of Life*

- What is your race/ethnicity? Have you ever been stereotyped because of your race/ethnicity? In what ways is your racial/ethnic identity similar to or different from the mainstream culture?

5 What Are Some Socioemotional Problems in Adolescence?

LG5 Identify adolescent problems in socioemotional development and strategies for helping adolescents with problems.

| Juvenile Delinquency | Depression and Suicide | The Interrelation of Problems and Successful Prevention/Intervention Programs |

Earlier, we described several adolescent problems: substance abuse, sexually transmitted infections, and eating disorders. In this chapter, we examine the problems of juvenile delinquency, depression, and suicide. We also explore interrelationships among adolescent problems and describe how such problems can be prevented or remedied.

JUVENILE DELINQUENCY

The label **juvenile delinquent** is applied to an adolescent who breaks the law or engages in behavior that is considered illegal. Like other categories of disorders, juvenile delinquency is a broad concept, encompassing legal infractions that range from littering to murder. For both male and female delinquents, rates for property offenses are higher than rates for other offenses (such as offenses against persons, drug offenses, and public order offenses). Arrest rates of adolescent males for delinquency consistently are much higher than arrest rates among adolescent females (U.S. Department of Justice, 2021).

One issue in juvenile justice is whether an adolescent who commits a crime should be tried as an adult. In a study of more than 5,000 individuals ranging in age from 10 to 30 in 11 countries, improvements in aspects of psychosocial maturity involved in decision making in emotionally charged situations continued beyond age 18 (Icenogle & others, 2019). Findings from this study suggested a maturity gap between adolescent decision making in controlled settings and adolescent decision making in arousing situations. The findings argue strongly against court placement based solely on the nature of an offense and take into account the offender's developmental maturity. Note that it was not until 2005 (in *Roper v. Simmons*) that the U.S. Supreme Court ruled that juveniles cannot be executed. Internationally, the vast majority of countries have signed onto the United Nation's International Covenant on Civil and Political Rights (ICCPR), which bans the execution of minors. Enforcement of this standard varies widely across countries, however (Death Penalty Information Center, 2019).

A distinction is made between early-onset—before age 11—and late-onset—after 11—antisocial behavior of minors. Early-onset antisocial behavior is associated with more negative developmental outcomes than late-onset antisocial behavior. Early-onset antisocial behavior is more likely to persist into emerging adulthood and is more frequently associated with mental health and relationship problems than is late-onset antisocial behavior (McGee & Moffitt, 2019).

Causes of Delinquency What causes delinquency? Although delinquency is less exclusively a phenomenon of lower socioeconomic status (SES) than it was in the past, some characteristics of lower-SES circumstances might promote delinquency (Macionis, 2017). One of the largest studies to date of more than 10,000 children and adolescents found that having a family environment characterized by poverty and child maltreatment was linked to higher odds of entering the juvenile justice system in adolescence (Vidal & others, 2017). The norms of some lower-SES peer groups and gangs are antisocial, or counterproductive, to the goals and norms of society at large. Getting into and staying out of trouble are prominent features of life for some adolescents in low-income neighborhoods. Also, adolescents in communities with high crime rates observe many models who engage in criminal activities (Tillyer & Walter, 2019). These communities may be characterized by poverty, unemployment, and feelings of alienation toward being middle class (Henslin, 2017). Quality schooling, educational funding, and organized neighborhood activities may be lacking in these communities.

Certain characteristics of family support systems are also associated with delinquency (Ray & others, 2017). Parental monitoring of adolescents is especially important in determining whether an adolescent becomes a delinquent (Bendezu & others, 2018). For example, a large international longitudinal study of young adolescents in low- and middle-income countries (for example, Colombia, the Philippines, and Kenya) found that low levels of monitoring, along

What are some factors that are linked to whether adolescents engage in delinquent acts?
Fertnig/iStock/Getty Images

juvenile delinquent An adolescent who breaks the law or engages in behavior that is considered illegal.

with harsh, rejecting parenting, played a key role in linking exposure to dangerous and chaotic homes and neighborhoods to growth in delinquent behavior problems (Deater-Deckard & others, 2019). Another illustrative study found that a developmental pathway from behavior problems in childhood to delinquency in adolescence could be disrupted by parental monitoring, which reduced adolescents' opportunities to spend time with antisocial peers (Jaggers & others, 2021). A comprehensive review of the international literature showed that authoritative parenting (warm but firm, with limit setting) was most effective at deterring delinquent behavior, in part because of its impact on adolescents' interpretation of this type of parenting as an indicator of adults' legitimate authority (Ruiz-Hernández & others, 2019).

A growing research base indicates that family therapy is often effective in reducing delinquency (Henderson, Hogue, & Dauber, 2019). A meta-analysis found that of five program types (case management, individual treatment, youth court, restorative justice, and family treatment), family treatment was the only one that was linked to reduced recidivism among juvenile offenders (Schwalbe & others, 2012). Also, in a subsequent study, family therapy improved juvenile court outcomes beyond what was achieved in non-family-based treatment, especially in reducing criminal behavior and rearrests (Dakof & others, 2015).

Siblings also can influence delinquency (Walters, 2019). A meta-analysis of 18 longitudinal studies found that both older and younger siblings who engaged in deviant behaviors increase their siblings' risk for future delinquency, regardless of the gender or age of the siblings (Maneiro & others, 2022). Peer relationships also can influence delinquency. Research on deviant peer contagion has demonstrated how peers can reinforce one another's antisocial behaviors by laughing or going along with plans to engage in delinquency (Kornienko, Ha, & Dishion, 2020).

Lack of academic success is associated with delinquency (Kim & Lee, 2019). And a number of cognitive factors such as low self-control, low intelligence, and lack of sustained attention are linked to delinquency (Rydell & Brocki, 2019). Further, research indicates that having callous-unemotional personality traits predicts an increased risk of engaging in delinquency, especially for adolescent males (Simmons & others, 2020).

How Would You...?
If you were a **psychologist,** how would you seek to lower the risk of juvenile delinquency?

DEPRESSION AND SUICIDE

What is the nature of depression in adolescence? What causes an adolescent to commit suicide?

Depression   Depression is more likely to occur in adolescence than in childhood and more likely to occur in adulthood than in adolescence. Researchers have found a linear increase in major depressive disorder from 15 to 22 years of age (Chee, Wang, & Cheung, 2020). However, an early onset of a mood disorder, such as major depressive disorder in adolescence, is linked with more negative outcomes than late onset of a mood disorder (Cui & others, 2023). For example, early onset is associated with further recurrences of depression and with an increased risk of being diagnosed with an anxiety disorder, substance abuse, eating disorder, suicide attempt, and unemployment at a future point in development (Clayborne, Varin, & Colman, 2019).

How serious a problem is depression in adolescence? In 2021, 57 percent of adolescent girls and 29 percent of adolescent boys in the United States reported persistent feelings of sadness and hopelessness (Centers for Disease Control and Prevention, 2023). Across all racial and ethnic groups, the percentage of adolescents who report feeling persistently sad or hopeless has increased over time, from 36 percent of girls and 21 percent of boys in 2011. The most recent numbers could in part be a reflection of increases in depression that accompanied stay-at-home orders and other disruptions during the COVID-19 pandemic, but the increase also reflects an upward trajectory that began well before the pandemic (Centers for Disease Control and Prevention, 2023). In 2021, 42 percent of high school students felt so sad or hopeless almost every day for at least two consecutive weeks that they stopped engaging in their usual activities.

Among the reasons for the different rates of depression for girls and boys are that females tend to ruminate (that is, to spend long periods of time thinking about things) in their depressed mood and amplify it; female self-images, especially their body images, are more negative than male self-images; females face more discrimination than males do; and puberty occurs earlier for girls than for boys (Kouros, Morris, & Garber, 2016). As a result, girls experience a confluence of changes and life experiences in adolescence that can increase depression (Hyde & Mezulis, 2020).

What are some characteristics of adolescents who become depressed? What are some factors that are linked with suicide attempts by adolescents?

Science Photo Library/age fotostock

Globally, approximately 14 percent of 10- to 19-year-olds have a mental disorder, with depression, anxiety, and behavior disorders the most prevalent (World Health Organization, 2021). Do sex differences in adolescent depression hold for other cultures? Across countries, girls and women have higher rates of depression than boys and men (de la Torre & others, 2021). Although rates of depression vary across countries, many of the predictors of depression, such as stressful life events and poverty, are similar (Porter & others, 2021).

Is adolescent depression linked to problems in emerging and early adulthood? One decade-long longitudinal study initially assessed U.S. adolescents when they were 16 to 17 years of age and then again every two years until they were 26 to 27 years of age (Naicker & others, 2013). In this study, significant effects that persisted after 10 years were depression recurrence, stronger depressive symptoms, migraine headaches, poor self-rated health, and low levels of social support. Adolescent depression was not associated with employment status, personal income, marital status, and educational attainment a decade later. In another longitudinal study involving individuals from 14 to 24 years of age, mild to moderate levels of early adolescent depressive behaviors were linked to lower maternal relationship quality, less positive romantic relationships, and greater loneliness in emerging adulthood (Allen & others, 2014).

Certain family factors place adolescents at increased risk for depression (Buehler, 2020). These include having a depressed parent, emotionally unavailable parents, parents with high marital conflict, and parents with financial problems. Other research has revealed that mother-daughter co-rumination (extensively discussing, rehashing, and speculating about problems) is linked to increased anxiety and depression in adolescent daughters (Douglas, Williams, & Reynolds, 2017). In addition to genetic factors, one of the reasons that parental depression is a risk factor for the development of adolescents' own depression is that parents who are depressed parent less consistently and adaptively than parents who are not depressed (Pine & Garber, 2023).

Poor peer relationships also are associated with adolescent depression (Cui & others, 2020). One study found that adolescents who were isolated from their peers and whose caregivers emotionally neglected them were at significant risk for developing depression (Christ, Kwak, & Lu, 2017). Best friendships can protect adolescents from increases in depression over time but appear to be protective only if the initial level of depression in both friends is relatively low (van der Mey-Baijens & others, 2023). Adolescents who are bullies and victims of bullying also have higher rates of depression than adolescents who are not bullies or victims (Sutter & others, 2023). Problems in adolescent romantic relationships also can trigger depression (Goodman & others, 2019).

A comprehensive meta-analysis found that adolescents who are obese were more likely to have depression (Arrondo & others, 2022). Other chronic physical health problems also are associated with an increased risk of depression (Thapar & others, 2022). And depression also often co-occurs with substance use and other mental health problems such as anxiety (Workman & others, 2023).

What type of treatment is most effective in reducing depression in adolescence? A research review concluded that treatment of adolescent depression needs to take into account the severity of the depression, suicidal tendencies, and social factors (American Psychological Association, 2023). In this review, cognitive-behavioral therapy and interpersonal therapy were recommended for adolescents with mild depression and in combination with drug therapy for adolescents experiencing moderate or severe depression. However, caution needs to be exercised when prescribing antidepressants, such as Prozac (fluoxetine) for adolescents, and back in 2004 the U.S. Food and Drug Administration assigned warnings to such drugs stating that they slightly increase the risk of suicidal behavior in adolescents. However, a subsequent research review concluded that Prozac and other SSRIs (selective serotonin reuptake inhibitors) show clinical benefits for adolescents at risk for moderate and severe depression (Cousins & Goodyer, 2015).

Suicide Suicidal behavior is rare in childhood but escalates in adolescence and then increases further in emerging adulthood, although there are wide individual differences in the developmental trajectory of suicide behavior (Goldston & others, 2016). Public health data show that suicide is the second or third leading cause of death in 10- to 19-year-olds depending on the country, among industrialized nations (National Center for Health Statistics, 2023). These data also show that emerging adults have triple the rate of suicide of adolescents.

In 2021, 22 percent of high school students in the United States seriously considered committing suicide, and 18 percent made a suicide plan (Centers for Disease Control and Prevention,

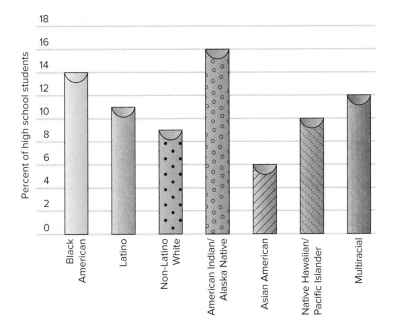

FIGURE 6

SUICIDE ATTEMPTS BY U.S. ADOLESCENTS FROM DIFFERENT RACIAL/ETHNIC GROUPS.

Note: Data shown are for one-year rates of self-reported suicide attempts (Centers for Disease Control and Prevention, 2022).

2023). Ten percent of high school students had attempted suicide in the last year, and 3 percent injured themselves seriously enough in the attempt as to require medical attention.

Females are more likely to attempt suicide than males, but males are more likely to succeed in committing suicide (Werbart Törnblom & others, 2020). Males use more lethal means, such as guns, in their suicide attempts, whereas adolescent females are more likely to cut their wrists or take an overdose of sleeping pills—methods less likely to result in death. In 2021, 30 percent of high school females and 14 percent of high school males seriously considered committing suicide, and 13 percent of high school females and 7 percent of high school males in the United States attempted suicide (Centers for Disease Control and Prevention, 2023).

Both early and later experiences are involved in suicide attempts (Bjorkenstam, Kosidou, & Bjorkenstam, 2017). The adolescent might have a long-standing history of family instability and unhappiness. Lack of affection and emotional support, high control, and pressure for achievement by parents during childhood are likely to show up as factors in suicide attempts. Adolescents who have experienced abuse also are at risk for suicidal ideation and attempts. For example, in one study, child maltreatment was linked to adolescent suicide attempts (Hadland & others, 2015). Further, in several subsequent studies, maltreatment and family dysfunction during the childhood years were linked with suicide attempts in adulthood (Park, 2017; Turner & others, 2017; Wadman, Hiller, & St Clair, 2019). Family relationships also can be involved in adolescent suicide (J.D. King & others, 2018). A suicide clinic study indicated that adolescents who were being treated experienced lower family cohesion than nonclinical adolescents and adolescents being treated at a "general" psychiatric clinic (Jakobsen, Larsen, & Horwood, 2017).

Recent and current stressful circumstances, such as getting poor grades in school or experiencing the breakup of a romantic relationship, may trigger suicide attempts (Im, Oh, & Suk, 2017). Peer victimization is linked to adolescent suicide (Peng & others, 2020). For example, one study that compared methods of bullying found that peer victimization was linked to suicidal ideation and suicide attempts, with cyberbullying more strongly associated with suicidal ideation than traditional bullying (van Geel, Vedder, & Tanilon, 2014). By contrast, another study found that higher levels of school connectedness were associated with decreased suicidal ideation in female and male adolescents and with lower rates of suicide attempts in female adolescents (Langille & others, 2015). Still another study revealed that playing sports predicted lower suicidal ideation in boys and venting by talking to others was associated with lower suicidal ideation in girls (Kim & others, 2014).

Cultural contexts also are linked to suicide attempts, and adolescent suicide attempts vary across racial/ethnic groups in the United States. As indicated in Figure 6, the latest data from the national U.S. Youth Risk Behavior Survey indicate that 16 percent of American Indian/Alaska Native high school students reported that they had attempted suicide in the previous year. Asian American high school students reported the lowest incidence of suicide attempts.

How Would You...?
If you were a **psychologist,** how would you talk with someone who has just threatened suicide?

Just as genetic factors are associated with depression, they also are associated with suicide (Levey & others, 2019). The closer a person's genetic relationship is to someone who has committed suicide, the more likely that person is to commit suicide.

What is the psychological profile of the suicidal adolescent? Suicidal adolescents often have depressive symptoms (Thompson & Swartout, 2018). Although not all depressed adolescents are suicidal, depression is the most frequently cited factor associated with adolescent suicide (Werbart Törnblom & others, 2020). Other research has shown that both depression and hopelessness were predictors of whether adolescents repeated a suicide attempt over a six-month period (Consoli & others, 2015). In another study, the most significant factor in a first suicide attempt during adolescence was a major depressive episode, while for children it was child maltreatment (Peyre & others, 2017). A sense of hopelessness, low self-esteem, and high self-blame also are associated with adolescent suicide (Flores & others, 2020).

THE INTERRELATION OF PROBLEMS AND SUCCESSFUL PREVENTION/INTERVENTION PROGRAMS

Earlier, we discussed many adolescent problems: substance abuse; juvenile delinquency; school-related problems, such as dropping out of high school; adolescent pregnancy and sexually transmitted infections; eating disorders; depression; and suicide. Four problems that affect many adolescents are (1) drug abuse, (2) juvenile delinquency, (3) sexual problems, and (4) school-related problems. The adolescents most at risk have more than one of these problems. Researchers are increasingly finding that problem behaviors in adolescence are interrelated (Feldstein Ewing & others, 2016). For example, heavy substance abuse is related to early sexual activity, lower grades, dropping out of school, and delinquency (Swartzendruber & others, 2016). Early initiation of sexual activity is associated with the use of cigarettes and alcohol, use of marijuana and other illicit drugs, lower grades, dropping out of school, and delinquency (Chan & others, 2015). In contrast, older adolescents who generally abstain from substance use have more optimism, are more involved in their schools, and hold attitudes (along with their friends) that substance use is risky and unhealthy (King & others, 2019). Delinquency is related to early sexual activity, early pregnancy, substance abuse, and dropping out of school (Liddon & others, 2016).

What are some strategies for preventing and intervening in adolescent problems?

AleksandrYu/iStock/Getty Images

One of the reasons that adolescents sometimes exhibit a range of problem behaviors is that these different problem behaviors are predicted by the same set of risk factors, such as externalizing behaviors and problematic family and peer relationships during childhood. In addition, during adolescence, engaging in one type of risky behavior, such as binge drinking, might also lead to other types of risky behavior, such as having unprotected sexual intercourse. And consequences of one type of problem behavior, such as early sexual relationships leading to an unplanned pregnancy, may lead to additional problem behavior, such as dropping out of school.

A review of the programs that have been successful in preventing or reducing adolescent problems found the following common components (Farrington & others, 2017):

1. *Intensive individualized attention.* In successful programs, high-risk adolescents are attached to a responsible adult who gives the adolescent attention and deals with the adolescent's specific needs. This theme occurs in a number of programs. In a successful substance-abuse program, a student assistance counselor is available full-time for individual counseling and referral for treatment.

2. *Community-wide multiagency collaborative approaches.* The basic philosophy of community-wide programs is that a number of different programs and services have to be in place. In one successful substance-abuse program, a community-wide health promotion campaign has been implemented that uses local media and community education, in concert with a substance-abuse curriculum in the schools.

3. *Early identification and intervention.* Reaching younger children and their families before children develop problems, or at the beginning of their problems, is a successful strategy (Almy & Cicchetti, 2018). One preschool program served as an excellent model for the prevention of delinquency, pregnancy, substance abuse, and dropping out of school. Operated by the High/Scope Foundation in Ypsilanti, Michigan, the Perry Preschool had a long-term positive impact on its students. This enrichment program, directed by David Weikart, served disadvantaged Black American children from 1962 to 1967. They attended a high-quality two-year preschool program and received weekly home visits from program personnel. Based on official police records, by age 19, individuals who had attended the Perry Preschool program were less likely to have been arrested and reported fewer adult offenses than a control group did. The Perry Preschool students also were less likely to drop out of school, and teachers rated their social behavior as more competent than that of a control group who had not received the enriched preschool experience (Schweinhart & others, 2005). Subsequent analysis of the effects on extended family and next-generation children showed similarly positive and lasting effects (Heckman & Karapakula, 2019).

What other effects can intervention programs achieve? For a description of one successful program, see the *Connecting with Research* interlude.

connecting with research

Fast Track

Key Points:

- A 10-year intervention for children who were at high risk of conduct problems was successful at reducing antisocial behavior into adulthood, especially for children highest in early risk.
- The intervention reduced later antisocial behavior by decreasing hostile-attribution biases, improving responses to social problems, and devaluing aggression.

A program that attempts to lower the risk of juvenile delinquency and other problems is Fast Track (Conduct Problems Prevention Research Group, 2007, 2010, 2011, 2013, 2016; Godwin & Conduct Problems Prevention Research Group, 2020). Schools in four areas (Durham, North Carolina; Nashville, Tennessee; Seattle, Washington; and rural central Pennsylvania) were identified as high-risk based on neighborhood crime and poverty data. Researchers screened more than 9,000 kindergarten children in the four geographic areas and randomly assigned 891 of the highest-risk and moderate-risk children to intervention or control conditions. The average age of the children when the intervention began was 6.5 years. The 10-year intervention consisted of behavior management training of parents, social cognitive skills training of children, reading tutoring, home visitations, mentoring, and a revised classroom curriculum that was designed to increase socioemotional competence and decrease aggression.

The extensive intervention was most successful for children and adolescents who were identified as the highest risk in kindergarten, lowering their incidence of conduct disorder, attention deficit hyperactivity disorder, any externalized disorder, and antisocial behavior. Positive outcomes for the intervention occurred as early as the third grade and continued through adulthood. For example, the comprehensive Fast Track intervention was successful in reducing youth arrest rates (Conduct Problems Prevention Research Group, 2010). Also, one study found that the intervention's impact on adolescents' antisocial behavior was linked to three social cognitive processes: reducing hostile-attribution biases, improving responses to social problems, and devaluing aggression (Dodge, Godwin, & Conduct Problems Prevention Research Group, 2013). Approximately one-third of Fast Track's reduction in later crime outcomes in emerging adulthood was attributed to improvements in social and self-regulation skills, such as prosocial behavior, emotion regulation, and problem solving, at 6 to 11 years of age (Sorensen, Dodge, & Conduct Problems Prevention Research Group, 2016). Assignment to the Fast Track intervention also decreased suicidal ideation and hazardous drinking in adolescence and young adulthood and decreased opioid use in young adulthood (Godwin & Conduct Problems Prevention Research Group, 2020). The Fast Track intervention also improved the home environments that participants provided to their own children as they became parents (Rothenberg & others, 2023). For a comprehensive overview of the entire project and its research findings, see Bierman and others (2019).

How might educators apply the results of this research to their daily work with adolescents in school settings?

LG5 Identify adolescent problems in socioemotional development and strategies for helping adolescents with problems.

Review
- What is juvenile delinquency? What causes it?
- What is the nature of depression and suicide in adolescence?
- How are adolescent problems interrelated? What are some components of successful prevention/intervention programs for adolescents?

Connect
- What have you learned about the connection between bullying and the development of problems in bullies and victims?

Reflect *Your Own Personal Journey of Life*
- As an adolescent, did you have any of the problems discussed in this chapter? If you had one or more of the problems, why do you think you developed the problem(s)? If you did not have any of the problems, what prevented you from developing them?

reach your **learning goals**

Socioemotional Development in Adolescence

1 What Characterizes Identity, Emotional Development, and Gender Classification in Adolescence?

LG1 Discuss identity, emotional development, and gender classification during adolescence.

Identity

- Identity development is a complex process that happens in bits and pieces. Erikson argues that identity versus identity confusion is the fifth stage of the human life span, which individuals experience during adolescence. A psychosocial moratorium during adolescence allows the personality and role experimentation that are important aspects of identity development.

- James Marcia proposed four identity statuses—identity diffusion, foreclosure, moratorium, and achievement—that are based on crisis (exploration) and commitment. Increasingly, experts argue that major changes in identity occur in emerging adulthood rather than adolescence. Individuals often follow moratorium-achievement-moratorium-achievement ("MAMA") cycles in their lives.

- Parents are important figures in adolescents' identity development. Identity development is facilitated by family relationships that promote both individuality and connectedness. Adolescents develop many types of identity, including racial/ethnic identity, sexual orientation and gender identity, political identity, and more.

Emotional Development

- Adolescents report more extreme and fleeting emotions than their parents, and as individuals go through early adolescence they are less likely to report being very happy. However, it is important to view moodiness as a normal aspect of early adolescence.

- Although pubertal change is associated with an increase in negative emotions, hormonal influences are often small, and environmental experiences may contribute more to the emotions of adolescence than hormonal changes do. Emotion regulation helps to prevent the development of problems in adolescence.

Gender Classification

- Gender-role classification focuses on the degree to which individuals are masculine, feminine, or androgynous. Androgyny means having positive feminine and masculine characteristics.

- Recently, considerable research interest has been directed to the gender category of transgender, which refers to individuals who adopt a gender identity that differs from the sex assigned to them at birth.

2 What Is the Nature of Parent-Adolescent Relationships?

 LG2 Describe changes that take place in adolescents' relationships with their parents.

Parental Monitoring and Adolescents' Information Management

Autonomy and Attachment

Parent-Adolescent Conflict

- A key aspect of the managerial role in parent-adolescent relationships involves parental monitoring. A current focus of interest is adolescents' willingness to disclose information about their activities to parents.

- Many parents have a difficult time handling the adolescent's push for autonomy, even though the push is one of the hallmarks of adolescence. Adolescents do not simply move into a world isolated from parents; instead, attachment to parents increases the probability that an adolescent will be socially competent.

- Parent-adolescent conflict increases in early adolescence. The conflict is usually moderate rather than severe, and the increased conflict may serve the positive developmental function of promoting autonomy and identity. A subset of adolescents experience high parent-adolescent conflict, which is linked with negative outcomes.

3 What Aspects of Peer Relationships Are Important in Adolescence?

 LG3 Characterize the changes that occur in peer relationships during adolescence.

Friendship

Peer Groups

Romantic Relationships

- Harry Stack Sullivan was the most influential theorist to discuss the importance of adolescent friendships. He argued that there is a dramatic increase in the psychological importance and intimacy of close friendships in early adolescence.

- Groups of children are less formal and less heterogeneous than groups of adolescents. The pressure to conform to peers is strong during adolescence, especially during the eighth and ninth grades. Cliques and crowds assume more importance in the lives of adolescents than in the lives of children. Membership in certain crowds—especially jocks and populars—is associated with increased self-esteem. Independents also show high self-esteem.

- Three stages characterize the development of romantic relationships in adolescence: (1) entry into romantic attractions and affiliations at about 11 to 13 years of age, (2) exploring romantic relationships at approximately 14 to 16 years of age, and (3) consolidating dyadic romantic bonds at about 17 to 19 years of age. A special concern is early dating, which is associated with a number of problems.

- Most LGBTQ youths have had some same-sex sexual experience, but fewer have had same-sex romantic relationships. Many LGBTQ youth date other-sex peers, which can help them to clarify their sexual orientation or disguise it from others.

- Adolescents who date have more problems, such as substance abuse, than those who do not date, but they also have greater acceptance from peers. Culture can exert a powerful influence on dating. Many adolescents from immigrant families face conflicts with their parents about dating.

4 Why Is Culture an Important Context for Adolescent Development?

 LG4 Explain how culture influences adolescent development.

Cross-Cultural Comparisons

- There are similarities and differences in adolescents across different countries. In some countries, traditions are being continued in the socialization of adolescents, whereas in others, the experiences of adolescents are changing substantially. The ways in which adolescents fill their time vary, depending on the culture in which they live.

- Rites of passage are ceremonies that mark an individual's transition from one status to another, especially into adulthood. In non-industrialized cultures, rites of passage are often well defined. In contemporary America, universal, formal rites of passage to adulthood are ill-defined, but certain religious groups have ceremonies, such as the Jewish bat and bar mitzvah and the Catholic confirmation. The high school graduation ceremony has become a nearly universal rite of passage for U.S. adolescents.

- Many of the families that have immigrated to the United States in recent decades come from collectivist cultures in which there is a strong sense of family obligation. Much of the research on racial/ethnic minority adolescents has not teased apart the influences of race/ethnicity and socioeconomic status. Because of this failure, too often researchers have given racial/ethnic explanations for characteristics that were largely due to socioeconomic factors. Poverty contributes to the stress of many racial/ethnic minority adolescents.

Media and Technology

- In terms of exposure, a significant increase in media use occurs in 11- to 14-year-olds. Adolescents are spending more time in media multitasking. The social environment of adolescents has increasingly become digitally mediated. The Internet continues to serve as the main focus of digitally mediated social interaction for adolescents but now encompasses a variety of digital devices, including cell phones (especially smartphones) and tablet computers.

- Adolescents' online time can have positive or negative outcomes. Large numbers of adolescents and college students engage in social networking on sites such as TikTok and Instagram. A special concern is the difficulty parents face in monitoring the information their children are accessing.

5 What Are Some Socioemotional Problems in Adolescence?

 LG5 Identify adolescent problems in socioemotional development and strategies for helping adolescents with problems.

Juvenile Delinquency

- A juvenile delinquent is an adolescent who breaks the law or engages in conduct that is considered illegal. Heredity, identity problems, community influences, and family experiences have been proposed as causes of juvenile delinquency.

Depression and Suicide

- Adolescents and emerging adults have higher rates of depression than children do. Female adolescents and emerging adult women are more likely to have mood and depressive disorders than their male counterparts. Adolescent suicide is a leading cause of death in U.S. 10- to 19-year-olds. Both early and later factors are likely involved in suicide's causes.

The Interrelation of Problems and Successful Prevention/Intervention Programs

- Researchers are increasingly finding that problem behaviors in adolescence are interrelated. A number of common components are found in programs that successfully prevent or reduce adolescent problems: providing individual attention to high-risk adolescents, developing community-wide intervention, and providing early identification and intervention.

key terms

androgyny
bicultural identity
clique
commitment
connectedness

crisis
crowd
identity achievement
identity diffusion
identity foreclosure

identity moratorium
identity versus
   identity confusion
individuality
juvenile delinquent

psychosocial
   moratorium
racial/ethnic identity
rite of passage
transgender

key people

Erik Erikson
Jane Kroger

Reed Larson
James Marcia

Maryse Richards
Harry Stack Sullivan

Adriana Umaña-Taylor

improving the **lives of children**

STRATEGIES

Supporting Adolescents' Socioemotional Development

What are some good strategies for helping adolescents improve their socioemotional competencies?

- *Let adolescents explore their identity.* Adolescence is a time of identity exploration. Adults should encourage adolescents to try out different options as they seek to identify what type of life they want to pursue.

- *Engage in effective monitoring of adolescents' activities.* Especially important is using strategies for getting adolescents to disclose information about their activities.

- *Understand the importance of autonomy and attachment.* A common stereotype is that parents are less important in adolescent development than in child development. However, parents continue to play a crucial role in adolescents' development by serving as a resource and support system, especially in stressful times. Value the adolescent's motivation for independence. However, continue to monitor the adolescent's whereabouts, although less intrusively and directly than in childhood.

- *Keep parent-adolescent conflict from being turbulent, and use good communication skills with the adolescent.* Adolescents' socioemotional development benefits when conflict with parents is either low or moderate. Keep communication channels open with the adolescent. Be an active listener and show respect for the adolescent's advancing developmental status. As it was during childhood, authoritative parenting is the best choice in most situations. Communicate expectations for high standards of achievement and conduct.

- *Recognize the importance of peers, youth organizations, and mentors.* Respected peers need to be used more frequently in programs that promote health and education. Adolescents need greater access to youth organizations staffed by caring peers and adults. Mentors can play a strong role in supporting adolescents' socioemotional development.

- *Help adolescents better understand the nature of differences, diversity, and value conflicts.* Adolescents need to be encouraged to take the perspective of adolescents from diverse ethnic backgrounds.

- *Give adolescents individualized attention.* One of the reasons adolescents develop problems is that they have not received adequate attention.

- *Provide better community-wide collaboration for helping youth.* In successful programs, a number of different services and programs cooperate to help adolescents.

- *Prevent adolescent problems through early identification and intervention.* The seeds of many adolescent problems are already in place in childhood.

RESOURCES

The Fast Track Program for Children at Risk: Preventing Antisocial Behavior (2019)
Conduct Problems Prevention Research Group
New York: Guilford Press

This book describes the largest long-term preventive intervention study ever conducted to prevent later problems associated with early conduct problems.

The Grown-Up's Guide to Teenage Humans (2018)
Josh Shipp
New York: Harper Wave

A best-selling guide to adults (parents, teachers, professionals, and all adults in our communities), with helpful insights about how to be the supportive adult caregiver or mentor that every adolescent needs.

Age of Opportunity (2014)
Laurence Steinberg
Boston: Houghton Mifflin Harcourt

An outstanding book by a leading expert on adolescent development with valuable information for adults who parent, teach, or counsel adolescents.

Handbook of Adolescent Digital Media Use and Mental Health (2022)
Edited by Jacqueline Nesi, Eva H. Telzer, & Mitchell J. Prinstein
New York: Cambridge University Press

Leading international researchers describe contemporary research on how digital media use is related to adolescents' brain development, relationships, identity, daily behaviors, and psychological adjustment.

National Adolescent Suicide Hotline
800-273-TALK [8255]

This hotline can be used 24 hours a day by teenagers contemplating suicide, as well as by their parents.

Substance Abuse and Mental Health Services Administration
www.samhsa.gov

This website provides information about a wide variety of issues related to drinking and drug use problems, including adolescent use and addiction.

glossary

A

accommodation Piagetian concept of adjusting schemes to fit new information and experiences.

active (niche-picking) genotype-environment correlations Correlations that exist when children seek out environments they find compatible and stimulating. *Niche-picking* refers to finding a setting that is suited to one's genetically influenced interests or abilities.

adolescence The developmental period of transition from childhood to early adulthood, entered at approximately 10 to 12 years of age and ending at 18 to 22 years of age.

adolescent egocentrism The heightened self-consciousness of adolescents that is reflected in their belief that others are as interested in them as they are in themselves, and in their sense of personal uniqueness and invincibility.

adoption study A study in which investigators seek to discover whether, in behavior and psychological characteristics, adopted children are more like their adoptive parents, who provided a home environment, or more like their biological parents, who contributed their heredity. Another form of the adoption study compares adopted and biological siblings.

affordances Opportunities for interaction offered by objects that are necessary to perform activities.

afterbirth The third stage of birth, when the placenta, umbilical cord, and other membranes are detached and expelled from the uterus.

AIDS Acquired immune deficiency syndrome; caused by the human immunodeficiency virus (HIV), which destroys the body's immune system.

amnion The fetal life-support system, which consists of a thin bag or envelope that contains a clear fluid in which the developing embryo floats.

amygdala A part of the brain that is the seat of emotions.

analgesics Drugs used to alleviate pain, such as tranquilizers, barbiturates, and narcotics.

androgyny The presence of positive masculine and feminine characteristics in the same individual.

anesthesia Drugs used in late first-stage labor and during expulsion of the baby to block sensation in an area of the body or to block consciousness.

anger cry A cry similar to the basic cry, with more excess air forced through the vocal cords.

animism The belief that inanimate objects have lifelike qualities and are capable of action.

anorexia nervosa An eating disorder that involves the relentless pursuit of thinness through starvation.

A-not-B error This occurs when infants make the mistake of selecting the familiar hiding place (A) rather than the new hiding place (B) of an object as they progress into substage 4 in Piaget's sensorimotor stage.

Apgar Scale A widely used method to assess the newborn's chances of survival and determine whether medical attention is needed.

aphasia A loss or impairment of language processing caused by brain damage in Broca's area or Wernicke's area.

articulation disorders Problems in pronouncing sounds correctly.

assimilation Piagetian concept involving incorporation of new information into existing schemes.

asthma A chronic lung disease that involves episodes of airflow obstruction.

attachment A close emotional bond between two people.

attention The focusing of mental resources.

attention deficit hyperactivity disorder (ADHD) A disability in which children consistently show one or more of the following characteristics: (1) inattention, (2) hyperactivity, and (3) impulsivity.

authoritarian parenting A restrictive, punitive parenting style in which parents exhort the child to follow their directions and to respect their work and effort. The authoritarian parent places firm limits and controls on the child and allows little verbal exchange. Authoritarian parenting is associated with children's social incompetence.

authoritative parenting A parenting style in which parents encourage their children to be independent but still place limits and controls on their actions. Extensive verbal give-and-take is allowed, and parents are warm and nurturant toward the child. Authoritative parenting is associated with children's social competence.

autism spectrum disorders (ASDs) Also called pervasive developmental disorders, this category ranges from severe to milder disorders. Children with these disorders are characterized by problems with social interaction, verbal and nonverbal communication, and repetitive behaviors.

autonomous morality The second stage of moral development in Piaget's theory, displayed by older children (about 10 years of age and older). The child becomes aware that rules and laws are created by people and that, in judging an action, one should consider the actor's intentions as well as the consequences.

average children Children who receive an average number of both positive and negative nominations from peers.

B

basic cry A rhythmic pattern usually consisting of a cry, a briefer silence, a shorter inspiratory whistle that is higher pitched than the main cry, and then a brief rest before the next cry.

Bayley Scales of Infant and Toddler Development Scales developed by Nancy Bayley that are widely used in assessing infant development. The current version, the Bayley Scales of Infant and Toddler Development—Fourth Edition (Bayley-4), has five components: a cognitive scale, a language scale, a motor scale, a social-emotional scale, and an adaptive behavior scale.

behavior genetics The field that seeks to discover the influence of heredity and environment on individual differences in human traits and development.

bicultural identity Identity formation that occurs when adolescents identify in some ways with their racial/ethnic group and in other ways with the majority culture.

biological processes Changes in an individual's body.

blastocyst The inner mass of cells that develops during the germinal period. These cells later develop into the embryo.

bonding A close connection, especially a physical bond, between parents and their newborn in the period shortly after birth.

brainstorming A technique in which individuals are encouraged to come up with creative ideas in a group, play off each other's ideas, and say practically whatever comes to mind that seems relevant to a particular issue.

Brazelton Neonatal Behavioral Assessment Scale (NBAS) A test performed within 24 to 36 hours after birth to assess newborns' neurological development, reflexes, and reactions to people.

breech position Position of the baby within the uterus that causes the buttocks to be the first part to emerge from the vagina.

Broca's area An area in the brain's left frontal lobe that is involved in speech production.

Bronfenbrenner's ecological theory An environmental systems theory that focuses on five environmental systems: microsystem, mesosystem, exosystem, macrosystem, and chronosystem.

bulimia nervosa An eating disorder in which the individual consistently follows a binge-and-purge eating pattern.

C

care perspective The moral perspective of Carol Gilligan, which views people in terms of their connectedness with others and emphasizes interpersonal communication, relationships with others, and concern for others.

case study An in-depth look at a single individual.

centration The focusing of attention on one characteristic to the exclusion of all others.

cephalocaudal pattern The sequence in which the earliest growth always occurs at the top—the head—with physical growth and feature differentiation gradually working from top to bottom.

cerebral cortex Tissue that covers the forebrain like a wrinkled cap and includes two halves, or hemispheres.

cerebral palsy A disorder that involves a lack of muscular coordination, shaking, and unclear speech.

cesarean delivery Delivery in which the baby is removed from the mother's uterus through an incision made in her abdomen. This also is sometimes referred to as a cesarean section.

character education A direct education approach that involves teaching students a basic moral literacy to prevent them from engaging in immoral behavior and doing harm to themselves and others.

child-centered kindergarten Education that involves the whole child by considering the child's physical, cognitive, and socioemotional development and addressing the child's needs, interests, and learning styles.

child-directed speech Language spoken in a higher pitch than normal, with simple words and sentences.

chromosomes Threadlike structures that come in 23 pairs, with one member of each pair coming from each parent. Chromosomes contain the genetic substance DNA.

clique A small group that ranges from 2 to about 12 individuals, averaging about 5 or 6 individuals, and may form because adolescents engage in similar activities.

cognitive control Involves effective control and flexible thinking in a number of areas, including controlling attention, reducing interfering thoughts, and being cognitively flexible.

cognitive processes Changes in an individual's thought, intelligence, and language.

cohort effects Effects due to a person's time of birth, era, or generation but not to actual age.

commitment Marcia's term for the part of identity development in which individuals show a personal investment in identity.

concepts Cognitive groupings of similar objects, events, people, or ideas.

concrete operations Reversible mental actions applied to real, concrete objects.

connectedness Characteristic consisting of two dimensions: mutuality (sensitivity to and respect for others' views) and permeability (openness to others' views).

conscience An internal regulator of standards of right and wrong that involves an integration of moral thought, feeling, and behavior.

conservation The realization that altering an object's or substance's appearance does not change its basic properties.

constructive play Play that combines sensorimotor/practice play with symbolic representation. Constructive play occurs when children engage in self-regulated creation or construction of a product or a solution.

constructivist approach A learner-centered approach that emphasizes the importance of individuals actively constructing their knowledge and understanding with guidance from the teacher.

context The settings, influenced by historical, economic, social, and cultural factors, in which development occurs.

continuity-discontinuity issue The issue regarding whether development involves gradual, cumulative change (continuity) or distinct stages (discontinuity).

controversial children Children who are frequently nominated both as someone's best friend and as being disliked.

conventional reasoning The second, or intermediate, level in Kohlberg's theory of moral development. At this level, individuals abide by certain standards, but they are standards set by others such as parents or the government.

convergent thinking Thinking that produces one correct answer and is characteristic of the kind of thinking tested by standardized intelligence tests.

coordination of secondary circular reactions Piaget's fourth sensorimotor substage, which develops between 8 and 12 months of age. Actions become more outwardly directed, and infants coordinate schemes and act with intentionality.

core knowledge approach View that infants are born with domain-specific innate knowledge systems, such as those involving space, number sense, object permanence, and language.

corpus callosum The location where fibers connect the brain's left and right hemispheres.

correlation coefficient A number based on statistical analysis that is used to describe the degree of association between two variables.

correlational research A research design whose goal is to describe the strength of the relationship between two or more events or characteristics.

creative thinking The ability to think in novel and unusual ways and to come up with unique solutions to problems.

crisis Marcia's term for a period of identity development during which the individual is exploring alternatives.

critical thinking The ability to think reflectively and productively, as well as to evaluate the evidence.

cross-cultural studies Comparisons of one culture with one or more other cultures. These comparisons provide information about the degree to which children's development is similar, or universal, across cultures, and the degree to which it is culture-specific.

cross-sectional approach A research strategy in which individuals of different ages are compared at one time.

crowd A larger group than a clique, one that is usually formed based on reputation; members may or may not spend much time together.

cultural-familial intellectual disability Condition in which there is no evidence of organic brain damage but the individual's IQ generally is between 50 and 70.

culture The behavior patterns, beliefs, and all other products of a group that are passed on from generation to generation.

culture-fair tests Tests of intelligence that are designed to be free of cultural bias.

D

deferred imitation Imitation that occurs after a delay of hours or days.

Denver Developmental Screening Test II A test used to diagnose developmental delay in children from birth to 6 years of age; includes separate assessments of gross and fine motor skills, language, and personal-social ability.

descriptive research A research design that has the purpose of observing and recording behavior.

design stage Kellogg's term for 3- to 4-year-olds' drawings that mix two basic shapes into more complex designs.

development The pattern of movement or change that begins at conception and continues through the human life span.

developmental cascade model Involves connections across domains over time that influence developmental pathways and outcomes.

developmental quotient (DQ) An overall score that combines subscores in motor, language, adaptive, and personal-social domains in the Gesell assessment of infants.

developmentally appropriate practice (DAP) Education that focuses on the typical developmental patterns of children (age appropriateness) as well as the uniqueness of each child (individual appropriateness). Such practice contrasts with *developmentally inappropriate practice*, which ignores the concrete, hands-on approach to learning. For example, direct teaching largely through abstract paper-and-pencil activities presented to large groups of young children is believed to be developmentally inappropriate.

difficult child A temperament style in which the child tends to react negatively and cry frequently, engages in irregular daily routines, and is slow to accept new experiences.

direct instruction approach A structured, teacher-centered approach that is characterized by teacher direction and control, mastery of academic skills, high expectations for students' progress, and maximum time spent on learning tasks.

dishabituation Recovery of a habituated response after a change in stimulation.

divergent thinking Thinking that produces many different answers to the same question and is characteristic of creativity.

DNA A complex molecule with a double helix shape; contains genetic information.

domain theory of moral development Theory that traces social knowledge and reasoning to moral, social conventional, and personal domains. These domains arise from children's and adolescents' attempts to understand and deal with different forms of social experience.

doula A caregiver who provides continuous physical, emotional, and educational support to the mother before, during, and after childbirth.

Down syndrome A chromosomally transmitted form of intellectual disability that is caused by the presence of an extra copy of chromosome 21.

dynamic systems theory The perspective on motor development that seeks to explain how motor skills are assembled for perceiving and acting.

dyscalculia Also known as developmental arithmetic disorder; a learning disability that involves difficulty in math computation.

dysgraphia A learning disability that involves difficulty in handwriting.

dyslexia A category of learning disabilities involving a severe impairment in the ability to read and spell.

E

early childhood The developmental period that extends from the end of infancy to about 5 to 6 years of age; sometimes called the preschool years.

early-later experience issue The issue of the degree to which early experiences (especially infancy) or later experiences are the key determinants of the child's development.

easy child A temperament style in which the child is generally in a positive mood, quickly establishes regular routines, and adapts easily to new experiences.

eclectic theoretical orientation An orientation that does not follow any one theoretical approach but rather selects from each theory whatever is considered the best in it.

ecological view The view that perception functions to bring organisms in contact with the environment and to increase adaptation.

ectoderm The outermost layer of cells, which becomes the nervous system and brain, sensory receptors (ears, nose, and eyes, for example), and skin parts (hair and nails, for example).

educationally blind Unable to use one's vision in learning and needing to use hearing and touch to learn.

egocentrism Piaget's concept that describes the inability to distinguish between one's own perspective and someone else's perspective.

elaboration An important strategy that involves engaging in more extensive processing of information.

embryonic period The period of prenatal development that occurs two to eight weeks after conception. During the embryonic period, the rate of cell differentiation intensifies, support systems for the cells form, and organs appear.

emerging adulthood Occurring from approximately 18 to 25 years of age, this transitional period between adolescence and adulthood is characterized by experimentation and exploration.

emotion Feeling, or affect, that occurs when a person is in a state or interaction that is important to them. Emotion can be characterized as positive (enthusiasm, joy, or love, for example) or negative (anxiety, guilt, or sadness, for example).

emotional and behavioral disorders Serious, persistent problems that involve relationships, aggression, depression, fears associated with personal or school matters, as well as other inappropriate socioemotional characteristics.

empathy An affective response to another's feelings with an emotional response that is similar to the other's feelings.

endoderm The inner layer of cells, which develops into digestive and respiratory systems.

epigenetic view Emphasizes that development reflects an ongoing, bidirectional interchange between heredity and environment.

equilibration A mechanism that Piaget proposed to explain how children shift from one stage of thought to the next.

Erikson's theory Includes eight stages of human development. Each stage consists of a unique developmental task that confronts individuals with a crisis that must be resolved.

estradiol A hormone associated in girls with breast, uterine, and skeletal development.

ethnic gloss The use of an ethnic label such as Black American or Latino in a superficial way that portrays an ethnic group as being more homogeneous than it really is.

ethnicity A characteristic based on cultural heritage, nationality, race, religion, and language.

ethology Stresses that behavior is strongly influenced by biology, is tied to evolution, and is characterized by critical or sensitive periods.

evocative genotype-environment correlations Correlations that exist when the child's genetically influenced characteristics elicit certain types of physical and social environments.

evolutionary psychology Branch of psychology that emphasizes the importance of adaptation, reproduction, and "survival of the fittest" in shaping behavior.

executive attention Involves planning actions, allocating attention to goals, detecting and compensating for errors, monitoring progress on tasks, and dealing with novel or difficult circumstances.

executive function An umbrella-like concept that consists of a number of higher-level cognitive processes linked to the development of the brain's prefrontal cortex. Executive function involves managing one's thoughts to engage in goal-directed behavior and exercise self-control.

experiment A carefully regulated procedure in which one or more of the factors believed to influence the behavior being studied are manipulated, while all other factors are held constant.

explicit memory Conscious memory of facts and experiences.

extrinsic motivation Response to external incentives such as rewards and punishments.

F

fast mapping A process that helps to explain how young children learn the connection between a word and its referent so quickly.

fertilization A stage in reproduction when an egg and a sperm fuse to create a single cell, called a zygote.

fetal alcohol spectrum disorders (FASD) A cluster of abnormalities and problems that appears in the offspring of mothers who drink alcohol heavily during pregnancy.

fetal period The prenatal period of development that begins two months after conception and lasts for seven months on average.

fine motor skills Motor skills that involve finely tuned movements, such as finger dexterity.

first habits and primary circular reactions Piaget's second sensorimotor substage, which develops between 1 and 4 months of age. In this substage, the infant coordinates sensation and two types of schemes: habits and primary circular reactions.

fluency disorders Various disorders that involve what is commonly called "stuttering."

forebrain The region of the brain that is farthest from the spinal cord and includes the cerebral cortex and several structures beneath it.

forgiveness An aspect of prosocial behavior that occurs when an injured person releases the injurer from possible behavioral retaliation.

fragile X syndrome A genetic disorder involving an abnormality in the X chromosome, which becomes constricted and often breaks.

fuzzy-trace theory A theory stating that memory is best understood by considering two types of memory representations: (1) verbatim memory trace and (2) gist. In this theory, older children's better memory is attributed to the fuzzy traces created by extracting the gist of information.

fuzzy-trace theory dual-process model States that decision making is influenced by two systems—"verbatim" analytical (literal and precise) and gist-based intuition (simple bottom-line meaning)—which operate in parallel; in this model, gist-based intuition benefits adolescent decision making more than analytical thinking does.

G

games Activities engaged in for pleasure that include rules and often competition with one or more individuals.

gender The characteristics of people as girls/women and boys/men.

gender identity The sense of one's own gender, including knowledge, understanding, and acceptance of being a boy/man, girl/woman, or another gender.

gender role A set of expectations that prescribes how girls/women or boys/men should think, act, and feel.

gender schema theory The theory that gender typing emerges as children gradually develop gender schemas of what is considered gender-appropriate and gender-inappropriate in their culture.

gender stereotypes General impressions and beliefs about girls/women and boys/men.

gender typing Acquisition of a traditional masculine or feminine role.

gene × environment (G × E) interaction The interaction of a specific measured variation in the DNA and a specific measured aspect of the environment.

genes Units of hereditary information composed of DNA. Genes help cells to reproduce themselves and manufacture the proteins that maintain life.

genotype A person's genetic heritage; the actual genetic material.

germinal period The period of prenatal development that takes place in the first two weeks after conception. It includes the creation of the zygote, continued cell division, and the attachment of the zygote to the uterine wall.

gifted Having above-average intelligence (an IQ of 130 or higher) and/or superior talent for something.

gonadotropins Hormones that stimulate the testes or ovaries.

gonads The sex glands—the testes in males, the ovaries in females.

goodness of fit Refers to the match between a child's temperament and the environmental demands the child must cope with.

grasping reflex A neonatal reflex that occurs when something touches the infant's palms. The infant responds by grasping tightly.

gratitude A feeling of thankfulness and appreciation, especially in response to someone doing something kind or helpful.

gross motor skills Motor skills that involve large-muscle activities, such as moving the arms and walking.

growth hormone deficiency The absence or deficiency of growth hormone produced by the pituitary gland to stimulate the body to grow.

H

habituation Decreased responsiveness to a stimulus after repeated presentations of the stimulus.

helpless orientation An orientation in which one seems trapped by the experience of difficulty and attributes one's difficulty to a lack of ability.

heteronomous morality The first stage of moral development in Piaget's theory, occurring from approximately 4 to 7 years of age. Justice and rules are conceived of as unchangeable properties of the world, removed from the control of people. Kohlberg adapted Piaget's ideas in his first stage of preconventional reasoning in which moral thinking is tied to punishment.

hidden curriculum Dewey's concept that every school has a pervasive moral atmosphere, even if it doesn't have an official program of moral education.

hormones Powerful chemical substances secreted by the endocrine glands and carried through the body by the bloodstream.

hypothalamus A structure in the brain that monitors eating and sex.

hypothesis A specific assumption or prediction that can be tested to determine its accuracy.

hypothetical-deductive reasoning Piaget's formal operational concept that adolescents have the cognitive ability to develop hypotheses, or best guesses, about ways to solve problems.

I

identity achievement Marcia's term for the status of individuals who have undergone a crisis and have made a commitment.

identity diffusion Marcia's term for the status of individuals who have not yet experienced a crisis (explored alternatives) or made any commitments.

identity foreclosure Marcia's term for the status of individuals who have made a commitment but have not experienced a crisis.

identity moratorium Marcia's term for the status of individuals who are in the midst of a crisis, but their commitments are either absent or vaguely defined.

identity versus identity confusion Erikson's fifth developmental stage, which occurs at about the time of adolescence. At this time, adolescents are faced with deciding who they are, what they are all about, and where they are going in life.

imaginary audience Refers to adolescents' belief that others are as interested in them as they themselves are, as well as their attention-getting behavior motivated by a desire to be noticed, visible, and "on stage."

immanent justice The expectation that, if a rule is broken, punishment will be delivered immediately.

implicit memory Memory without conscious recollection; involves skills and routine procedures that are automatically performed.

inclusion Educating a child with special educational needs full-time in the regular classroom.

individual differences The stable, consistent ways in which people differ from each other.

individualism, instrumental purpose, and exchange The second Kohlberg stage in preconventional reasoning. At this stage, individuals pursue their own interests but also let others do the same.

individuality Characteristic consisting of two dimensions: self-assertion (the ability to have and communicate a point of view) and separateness (the use of communication patterns to express how one is different from others).

individualized education plan (IEP) A written statement that spells out a program tailored to a child with a disability. The plan should be (1) related to the child's learning capacity, (2) specially constructed to meet the child's individual needs and not merely a copy of what is offered to other children, and (3) designed to provide educational benefits.

Individuals with Disabilities Education Act (IDEA) The IDEA spells out broad mandates for providing services to all children with disabilities (IDEA is a renaming of Public Law 94-142); these include evaluation and eligibility determination, appropriate education and an individualized education plan (IEP), and education in the least restrictive environment (LRE).

indulgent parenting A style of parenting in which parents are highly involved with their children but place few demands or controls on them. Indulgent parenting is associated with children's social incompetence, especially a lack of self-control.

infancy The developmental period that extends from birth to 18 to 24 months of age.

infinite generativity The ability to produce an endless number of meaningful sentences using a finite set of words and rules.

information-processing theory Emphasizes that individuals manipulate information, monitor it, and strategize about it. Central to this theory are the processes of memory and thinking.

insecure avoidant babies Babies that show insecurity by avoiding the caregiver.

insecure disorganized babies Babies that show insecurity by being disorganized and disoriented.

insecure resistant babies Babies that often cling to the caregiver, then resist by fighting against the closeness, perhaps by kicking or pushing away.

intellectual disability A condition of limited mental ability in which an individual has a low IQ, usually below 70 on a traditional test of intelligence, and has difficulty adapting to the demands of everyday life.

intelligence The ability to solve problems and to adapt to and learn from experiences.

intelligence quotient (IQ) A person's mental age divided by chronological age, multiplied by 100; devised in 1912 by William Stern.

intermodal perception The ability to relate and integrate information from two or more sensory modalities, such as vision and hearing.

internalization of schemes Piaget's sixth and final sensorimotor substage, which develops between 18 and 24 months of age. In this substage, the infant develops the ability to use basic symbols.

intimacy in friendships Self-disclosure and the sharing of private thoughts.

intrinsic motivation Internal factors such as self-determination, curiosity, challenge, and effort.

intuitive thought substage Piaget's second substage of preoperational thought, in which children begin to use primitive reasoning and want to know the answers to all sorts of questions (occurs between about 4 and 7 years of age).

involution The process by which the uterus returns to its prepregnant size.

J

joint attention Individuals focusing on the same object or event; requires the ability to track another's behavior, one person directing another's attention, and reciprocal interaction.

justice perspective A moral perspective that focuses on the rights of the individual and in which individuals independently make moral decisions.

juvenile delinquent An adolescent who breaks the law or engages in behavior that is considered illegal.

K

kangaroo care A way of holding a preterm infant so that there is skin-to-skin contact.

Klinefelter syndrome A chromosomal disorder in which males have an extra X chromosome, making them XXY instead of XY.

kwashiorkor A condition caused by a severe deficiency in protein in which the child's abdomen and feet become swollen with water; usually appears between 1 and 3 years of age.

L

laboratory A controlled setting in which many of the complex factors of the "real world" are absent.

language A form of communication, whether spoken, written, or signed, that is based on a system of symbols.

language acquisition device (LAD) Chomsky's term describing a biological endowment that enables the child to detect the features and rules of language, including phonology, syntax, and semantics.

lateralization Specialization of function in one hemisphere of the cerebral cortex or the other.

learning disability Disability in which a child has difficulty in learning that involves understanding or using spoken or written language, and the difficulty can appear in listening, thinking, reading, writing, or spelling, or math. To be classified as a learning disability, the learning problem is not primarily the result of visual, hearing, or motor disabilities; intellectual disabilities; emotional disorders; or environmental, cultural, or economic disadvantage.

least restrictive environment (LRE) The concept that a child with a disability must be educated in a setting that is as similar as possible to the one in which children who do not have a disability are educated.

limbic system A lower, subcortical system in the brain that is the seat of emotions and experience of rewards.

longitudinal approach A research strategy in which the same individuals are studied over a period of time, usually several years or more.

long-term memory A relatively permanent type of memory that holds huge amounts of information for a long period of time.

low birth weight infants Babies that weigh less than 5½ pounds at birth.

low vision Visual acuity between 20/70 and 20/2000.

M

manual approaches Educational approaches to support children with hearing impairments, including sign language and finger spelling.

marasmus A wasting away of body tissues in the infant's first year, caused by severe protein-calorie deficiency.

mastery motivation An approach to achievement in which one is task oriented, focusing on learning strategies and the achievement process rather than ability or the outcome.

meiosis A specialized form of cell division that occurs to form eggs and sperm (also known as *gametes*).

melatonin A sleep-inducing hormone that is produced in the brain's pineal gland.

memory A central feature of cognitive development, involving the retention of information over time.

menarche A girl's first menstrual period.

mental age (MA) Binet's measure of an individual's level of mental development, compared with that of others.

mesoderm The middle layer of cells, which becomes the circulatory system, bones, muscles, excretory system, and reproductive system.

metacognition Cognition about cognition, or knowing about thinking.

metalinguistic awareness Knowledge about language, such as knowing what a preposition is or being able to discuss the sounds of a language.

middle and late childhood The developmental period that extends from about 6 to 11 years of age; sometimes called the elementary school years.

Millennials The generation born after 1980, which is the first generation to come of age and enter emerging adulthood in the new millennium; members of this generation are characterized by their ethnic diversity and their connection to technology.

mindfulness Being alert, mentally present, and cognitively flexible while going through life's everyday activities and tasks.

mindset Dweck's concept referring to the cognitive view individuals develop for themselves; individuals have either a fixed or a growth mindset.

mitosis Cellular reproduction in which the cell's nucleus duplicates itself with two new cells being formed, each containing the same DNA as the parent cell, arranged in the same 23 pairs of chromosomes.

Montessori approach An educational philosophy in which children are given considerable freedom and spontaneity in choosing activities and are provided with specially designed curriculum materials.

moral development Development that involves thoughts, feelings, and behaviors regarding rules and conventions about what people should do in their interactions with other people.

Moro reflex A newborn's startle response that occurs in reaction to a sudden, intense noise or movement. When startled, newborns arch their back, throw their head back, and fling out their arms and legs. Then they rapidly close their arms and legs, bringing them close to the center of the body.

morphology Units of meaning involved in word formation.

mutual interpersonal expectations, relationships, and interpersonal conformity Kohlberg's third stage of moral development. At this stage, individuals value trust, caring, and loyalty to others as a basis of moral judgments.

myelination The process in which the nerve cells are covered and insulated with a layer of fat cells, which increases the speed at which information travels through the nervous system.

N

natural childbirth Method developed in 1914 by English obstetrician Grantly Dick-Read that attempts to reduce the mother's pain by decreasing her fear through education about childbirth and breathing methods and relaxation techniques during delivery.

naturalistic observation Observing behavior in real-world settings.

nature-nurture issue The issue regarding whether development is primarily influenced by nature or nurture. Both "nature" (biological inheritance) and "nurture" (environmental experiences) are important to development.

neglected children Children who are infrequently nominated as a best friend but are not disliked by their peers.

neglectful parenting A style of parenting in which the parent is very uninvolved in the child's life; it is associated with children's social incompetence, especially a lack of self-control.

Neonatal Intensive Care Unit Network Neurobehavioral Scale (NNNS) An "offspring" of the NBAS, the NNNS provides a more comprehensive analysis of the newborn's behavior, neurological and stress responses, and regulatory capacities.

neo-Piagetians Developmentalists who have elaborated on Piaget's theory, giving more emphasis to information processing, strategies, and precise cognitive steps.

neuroconstructivist view In this view, biological processes and environmental conditions influence the brain's development; the brain has plasticity and is context dependent; and brain development is closely linked with cognitive development.

neurogenesis The formation of new neurons.

neurons The term for nerve cells, which handle information processing at the cellular level.

night terrors Incidents characterized by sudden arousal from sleep, intense fear, and usually physiological reactions such as rapid heart rate and breathing, loud screams, heavy perspiration, and physical movement.

nightmares Frightening dreams that awaken the sleeper.

normal distribution A symmetrical distribution with most scores falling in the middle of the possible range of scores and few scores appearing toward the extremes of the range.

O

object permanence The understanding that objects continue to exist, even when they cannot directly be seen, heard, or touched.

operations Internalized actions that allow children to do mentally what before they had done only physically. Operations also are reversible mental actions.

oral approaches Educational approaches to support children with hearing impairments, including lip reading, speech reading, and use of whatever hearing the child has.

organic intellectual disability Involves physical causes such as a genetic disorder or brain damage.

organization Piaget's concept of grouping isolated behaviors and thoughts into a higher-order system, a more smoothly functioning cognitive system.

organogenesis Process of organ formation that takes place during the first two months of prenatal development.

orthopedic impairments Restrictions in movement abilities due to muscle, bone, or joint problems.

oxytocin A hormone that is sometimes administered during labor to stimulate contractions.

P

pain cry A sudden appearance of a long, initial loud cry without preliminary moaning, followed by breath holding.

passive genotype-environment correlations Correlations that exist when the biological parents, who are genetically related to the child, provide a rearing environment for the child.

perception The interpretation of sensation.

performance orientation An orientation in which one focuses on achievement outcomes; winning is what matters most, and happiness is thought to result from winning.

personal fable The part of adolescent egocentrism that involves an adolescent's sense of uniqueness and invincibility.

perspective taking The social cognitive process involved in assuming the perspective of others and understanding their thoughts and feelings.

phenotype The way an individual's genotype is expressed in observed and measurable characteristics.

phenylketonuria (PKU) A genetic disorder in which the individual cannot properly metabolize phenylalanine, an amino acid. PKU is now easily detected—but if left untreated, results in intellectual disability and hyperactivity.

phonics approach The idea that reading instruction should teach basic rules for translating written symbols into sounds.

phonology The sound system of the language, including the sounds that are used and how they may be combined.

Piaget's theory States that children actively construct their understanding of the world and go through four stages of cognitive development.

pictorial stage Kellogg's term for 4- to 5-year-olds' drawings depicting objects that adults can recognize.

pituitary gland An important endocrine gland that controls growth and regulates other glands.

placement stage Kellogg's term for 2- to 3-year-olds' drawings that are drawn on a page in placement patterns.

placenta A disk-shaped group of tissues in which small blood vessels from the mother and the offspring intertwine but don't join.

popular children Children who are frequently nominated as a best friend and are rarely disliked by their peers.

postconventional reasoning The highest level in Kohlberg's theory of moral development. At this level, the individual recognizes alternative moral courses, explores the options, and then decides on a personal moral code.

postpartum depression Involves a major depressive episode characterized by strong feelings of sadness, anxiety, or despair in new mothers, making it difficult for them to carry out daily tasks.

postpartum period The period after childbirth when the mother adjusts, both physically and psychologically, to the process of childbearing. This period lasts for about six weeks, or until her body has completed its adjustment and has returned to a near-prepregnant state.

practice play Play that involves repetition of behavior when new skills are being learned or when physical or mental mastery and coordination of skills are required for games or sports.

pragmatics The appropriate use of language in different contexts.

preconventional reasoning The lowest level in Kohlberg's theory of moral development. The individual's concept of good and bad is interpreted primarily in terms of external rewards and punishment.

prenatal period The time from conception to birth.

preoperational stage Piaget's second stage, lasting from 2 to 7 years of age, when children begin to represent the world with words, images, and drawings. In this stage, they also form stable concepts and begin to reason. At the same time, their cognitive world is dominated by egocentrism and magical beliefs.

prepared childbirth Developed by French obstetrician Ferdinand Lamaze, this childbirth method is similar to natural childbirth but teaches a special breathing technique to control pushing in the final stages of labor and also provides a more detailed anatomy and physiology course.

pretense/symbolic play Play in which the child transforms aspects of the physical environment into symbols.

preterm infants Babies born three weeks or more before the pregnancy has reached its full term.

primary circular reaction A scheme based on the attempt to reproduce an event that initially occurred by chance.

primary emotions Emotions that are present in humans and other animals, and emerge early in life; examples are joy, anger, sadness, fear, and disgust.

Project Head Start Compensatory education designed to provide children from low-income families the opportunity to acquire skills and experiences that are important for school success.

proximodistal pattern The sequence in which growth starts at the center of the body and moves toward the extremities.

psychoanalytic theories Describe development as primarily unconscious and heavily colored by emotion. Behavior is merely a surface characteristic, and the symbolic workings of the mind have to be analyzed to understand behavior. Early experiences with parents are emphasized.

psychoanalytic theory of gender A theory deriving from Freud's view that the preschool child develops a sexual attraction to the opposite-sex parent, by approximately 5 or 6 years of age renounces this attraction because of anxious feelings, and subsequently identifies with the same-sex parent, unconsciously adopting the same-sex parent's characteristics.

psychosocial moratorium Erikson's term for the gap between childhood security and adult autonomy.

puberty A brain-neuroendocrine process occurring primarily in early adolescence that provides stimulation for the rapid physical changes that accompany this period of development.

Public Law 94-142 The Education for All Handicapped Children Act, created in 1975, which requires that all children with disabilities be given a free, appropriate public education and which provides the funding to help with the costs of implementing this education.

R

racial/ethnic identity An enduring, basic aspect of the self that includes a sense of membership in a racial/ethnic group and the attitudes and feelings related to that membership.

rapport talk The language of conversation and a way of establishing connections and negotiating relationships; more characteristic of girls/women than of boys/men.

reciprocal socialization Socialization that is bidirectional; children socialize parents, just as parents socialize children.

reflexes Built-in automatic reactions to stimuli.

reflexive smile A smile that does not occur in response to external stimuli. It happens during the month after birth, usually during sleep.

rejected children Children who are infrequently nominated as a best friend and are actively disliked by their peers.

religion An organized set of beliefs, practices, rituals, and symbols that increases an individual's connection to a sacred or transcendent other (God, higher power, or higher truth).

religiousness Degree of affiliation with an organized religion, participation in prescribed rituals and practices, connection with its beliefs, and involvement in a community of believers.

report talk Talk that conveys information; more characteristic of boys/men than girls/women.

rite of passage A ceremony or ritual that marks an individual's transition from one status to another. Most rites of passage focus on the transition to adult status.

rooting reflex A newborn's built-in reaction that occurs when the infant's cheek is stroked or the side of the mouth is touched. In response, the infant turns its head toward the side that was touched in an apparent effort to find something to suck.

S

scaffolding In regard to cognitive development, Vygotsky used this term to describe the changing level of support provided over the course of a teaching session, with the more-skilled person adjusting guidance to fit the child's current performance level.

schemes In Piaget's theory, actions or mental representations that organize knowledge.

scientific method   An approach that can be used to obtain accurate information. It includes these steps: (1) conceptualize the problem, (2) collect data, (3) draw conclusions, and (4) revise research conclusions and theory.

secondary circular reactions   Piaget's third sensorimotor substage, which develops between 4 and 8 months of age. In this substage, the infant becomes more object-oriented, moving beyond preoccupation with the self.

securely attached babies   Babies that use the caregiver as a secure base from which to explore their environment.

self-concept   Domain-specific evaluations of the self.

self-conscious emotions   Emotions that require self-awareness, especially consciousness and a sense of "me"; examples include jealousy, empathy, and embarrassment.

self-efficacy   The belief that one can master a situation and produce favorable outcomes.

self-esteem   The global evaluative dimension of the self. Self-esteem is also referred to as self-worth or self-image.

self-understanding   The child's cognitive representation of self; the substance and content of the child's self-conceptions.

semantics   The meaning of words and sentences.

sensation   Reaction that occurs when information contacts sensory receptors—the eyes, ears, tongue, nostrils, and skin.

sensorimotor play   Behavior engaged in by infants to derive pleasure from exercising their existing sensorimotor schemas.

sensorimotor stage   The first of Piaget's stages, which lasts from birth to about 2 years of age, in which infants construct an understanding of the world by coordinating sensory experiences (such as seeing and hearing) with motoric actions.

separation protest   Occurs when infants experience a fear of being separated from a caregiver, which results in crying when the caregiver leaves.

seriation   The concrete operation that involves ordering objects along a quantitative dimension (such as length).

service learning   A form of education that promotes social responsibility and service to the community.

sexually transmitted infections (STIs)   Diseases that are contracted primarily through sexual contact. This contact is not limited to vaginal intercourse but includes oral-genital contact and anal-genital contact as well.

shape constancy   The recognition that an object's shape remains the same even though its orientation to us changes.

shape stage   Kellogg's term for 3-year-olds' drawings consisting of diagrams in different shapes.

short-term memory   A limited-capacity memory system in which information is usually retained for up to 30 seconds if there is no rehearsal of the information. Using rehearsal, people can keep the information in short-term memory longer.

sickle-cell anemia   A genetic disorder that affects the red blood cells and occurs most often in people of sub-Saharan African descent.

simple reflexes   Piaget's first sensorimotor substage, which corresponds to the first month after birth. In this substage, sensation and action are coordinated primarily through reflexive behaviors.

size constancy   The recognition that an object remains the same even though the retinal image of the object changes as you move toward or away from the object.

sleep talker   A child speaking with clear or unclear words and statements while asleep.

slow-to-warm-up child   A temperament style in which the child has a low activity level, is somewhat negative, and displays a low intensity of mood.

small for gestational age infants   Babies whose birth weight is below normal when the length of pregnancy is considered.

social cognitive theory   The view of psychologists who emphasize behavior, environment, and cognition as the key factors in development.

social cognitive theory of gender   The idea that children's gender development occurs through observation and imitation of gender behavior as well as through the rewards and punishments children experience for behaviors believed to be appropriate or inappropriate for their gender.

social constructivist approach   An approach that emphasizes the social contexts of learning and the fact that knowledge is mutually built and constructed; Vygotsky's theory is a social constructivist approach.

social contract or utility and individual rights   The fifth Kohlberg stage. At this stage, individuals reason that values, rights, and principles undergird or transcend the law.

social conventional reasoning   Focuses on conventional rules established by social consensus, as opposed to moral reasoning that stresses ethical issues.

social play   Play that involves social interactions with peers.

social policy   A government's course of action designed to promote the welfare of its citizens.

social referencing   "Reading" emotional cues in others to help determine how to act in a particular situation.

social role theory   Eagly's theory that psychological gender differences are caused by the contrasting social roles of women and men.

social smile   A smile in response to an external stimulus, which, early in development, typically is a face.

social systems morality   The fourth stage in Kohlberg's theory of moral development. Moral judgments are based on understanding the social order, law, justice, and duty.

socioeconomic status (SES)   An individual's position within society based on occupational, educational, and economic characteristics.

socioemotional processes   Changes in an individual's relationships with other people, changes in emotions, and changes in personality.

somnambulism   Sleepwalking; occurs in the deepest stage of sleep.

spermarche   The beginning of sperm production in boys.

spirituality   Experiencing something beyond oneself in a transcendent manner and living in a way that benefits others and society.

standardized test   A test with uniform procedures for administration and scoring. Many standardized tests allow a person's performance to be compared with the performance of other individuals.

stereotype threat   Anxiety that one's behavior might confirm a negative stereotype about one's group.

Strange Situation   An observational measure of infant attachment that requires the infant to move through a series of introductions, separations, and reunions with the caregiver and an adult stranger in a prescribed order.

stranger anxiety   An infant's fear and wariness of strangers; it tends to appear in the second half of the first year of life.

strategies   Deliberate mental activities designed to improve the processing of information.

sucking reflex   A newborn's built-in reaction to automatically suck an object placed in the mouth. The sucking reflex enables nourishment before the infant has associated a nipple with food.

sudden infant death syndrome (SIDS)   A condition that occurs when an infant stops breathing, usually during the night, and suddenly dies without an apparent cause.

sustained attention   Keeping attention on a selected stimulus for a prolonged period of time. Sustained attention is also called *vigilance*.

symbolic function substage   Piaget's first substage of preoperational thought, in which the child gains the ability to mentally represent an object that is not present (occurs roughly between 2 and 4 years of age).

sympathy   An emotional response to another person in which the observer feels sad or concerned about the individual's well-being.

syntax   The ways words are combined to form acceptable phrases and sentences.

T

telegraphic speech   The use of content words without grammatical markers such as articles, auxiliary verbs, and other connectives.

temperament   Involves individual differences in behavioral styles, emotions, and characteristic ways of responding.

teratogen   Any agent that can potentially cause a physical birth defect. The field of study that investigates the causes of birth defects is called *teratology*.

tertiary circular reactions, novelty, and curiosity   Piaget's fifth sensorimotor substage, which develops between 12 and 18 months of age. In this substage, infants become intrigued by the many properties of objects and by the many things that they can make happen to objects.

testosterone   A hormone associated in boys with the development of the genitals, an increase in height, and a change in voice.

theory   An interrelated, coherent set of ideas that helps to explain and make predictions.

theory of mind   A concept that refers to awareness of one's own mental processes and the mental processes of others.

top-dog phenomenon   The circumstance of moving from the top position (in elementary school, being the oldest, biggest, and most powerful students) to the lowest position (in middle or junior high school, being the youngest, smallest, and least powerful students).

transgender   A broad term that refers to individuals who adopt a gender identity that differs from the one assigned to them at birth.

transitivity   The ability to logically combine relations to draw certain conclusions.

triarchic theory of intelligence   Sternberg's theory that intelligence has three components: analytical intelligence, creative intelligence, and practical intelligence.

trophoblast   The outer layer of cells that develops in the germinal period. These cells later provide nutrition and support for the embryo.

Turner syndrome   A chromosomal disorder in females in which either an X chromosome is missing, making the person XO instead of XX, or the second X chromosome is partially deleted.

twin study   A study in which the behavioral similarity of identical twins is compared with the behavioral similarity of fraternal twins.

type 1 diabetes   An autoimmune disease in which the body's immune system destroys insulin-producing cells.

type 2 diabetes   The most common type of diabetes, in which the body is able to produce insulin, but the amount may be insufficient or the body's cells may be unable to use it.

U

umbilical cord   Contains two arteries and one vein, and connects the baby to the placenta.

universal ethical principles   The sixth and highest stage in Kohlberg's theory of moral development. Individuals develop a moral standard based on universal principles of human rights.

V

values   Beliefs and attitudes about the way things should be.

visual preference method   A method developed by Fantz to determine whether infants can distinguish one stimulus from another by measuring the length of time they attend to different stimuli.

voice disorders   Disorders reflected in speech that is hoarse, harsh, too loud, too high-pitched, or too low-pitched.

Vygotsky's theory   A sociocultural cognitive theory that emphasizes how culture and social interaction guide cognitive development.

W

Wernicke's area   An area of the brain's left hemisphere that is involved in language comprehension.

whole-language approach   An approach to reading instruction based on the idea that instruction should parallel children's natural language learning. Reading materials should be whole and meaningful.

working memory   A mental "workbench" where individuals manipulate and assemble information when making decisions, solving problems, and comprehending written and spoken language.

X

XYY syndrome   A chromosomal disorder in which males have an extra Y chromosome.

Z

zone of proximal development (ZPD)   Vygotsky's term for the range of tasks that are too difficult for children to achieve alone but can be achieved with the guidance and assistance of adults or more-skilled children.

zygote   A single cell formed through fertilization.

references

A

Aagaard, J. (2019). Multitasking as distraction: A conceptual analysis of media multitasking. *Theory and Psychology, 29*(1), 87–99.

ABC News (2005, December 12). Larry Page and Sergey Brin. Retrieved June 24, 2006, from www.Montessori.org/enews/barbara_Walters.html

Abels, M., Osokina, M., & Kilale, A.M. (2023). Sharing food with infants in Hadza communities in Tanzania. *Infant Behavior and Development, 70,* 101805.

Abernathey, L., Kahn, N., Sequeira, G., & Richardson, L. (2023). Understanding associations between gender diversity, eating disorders and other psychiatric comorbidities among adolescents. *Journal of Adolescent Health, 72*(3), S28.

Abreu-Villaça, Y., & others (2018). Hyperactivity and memory/learning deficits evoked by developmental exposure to nicotine and/or ethanol are mitigated by cAMP and cGMP signaling cascades activation. *Neurotoxicology, 66,* 150–159.

Acharya, S., Bhatta, D.N., & Assannangkornchai, S. (2018). Post-traumatic stress disorder symptoms among children of Kathmandu 1 year after the 2015 earthquake in Nepal. *Disaster Medicine and Public Health Preparedness, 12,* 486–492.

Ackerman, J.P., Riggins, T., & Black, M.M. (2010). A review of the effects of prenatal cocaine exposure among school-aged children. *Pediatrics, 125,* 554–565.

Adams, K.A., & others (2018). Caregiver talk and medical risk as predictors of language outcomes in full term and preterm toddlers. *Child Development, 89*(5), 1674–1690.

Adamson, L., & Frick, J. (2003). The still face: A history of a shared experimental paradigm. *Infancy, 4,* 451–473.

Addabbo, M., Longhi, E., Marchis, I.C., Tagliabue, P., & Turati, C. (2018). Dynamic facial expressions of emotions are discriminated at birth. *PloS One, 13*(3), e0193868.

Adelantado-Renau, M., & others (2019). Association between screen media use and academic performance among children and adolescents: A systematic review and meta-analysis. *JAMA Pediatrics, 173*(11), 1058–1067.

Adisetiyo, V., & Gray, K.M. (2017). Neuroimaging the neural correlates of increased risk for substance use disorders in attention-deficit/hyperactivity disorder: A systematic review. *The American Journal on Addictions, 26,* 99–111.

Administration for Children and Families (2023). *Head Start.* Retrieved March 14, 2023, from www.acf.hhs.gov/ecd/early-learning/head-start

Adolescent Sleep Working Group, AAP (2014). School start times for adolescents. *Pediatrics, 134,* 642–649.

Adolph, K.E. (1997). Learning in the development of infant locomotion. *Monographs of the Society for Research in Child Development, 62*(3, Serial No. 251).

Adolph, K.E. (2018). Motor development. In M.H. Bornstein & others (Eds.), *SAGE encyclopedia of lifespan human development.* Sage.

Adolph, K.E., & Berger, S.E. (2015). Physical and motor development. In M.H. Bornstein & M.E. Lamb (Eds.), *Developmental science* (7th ed.). Psychology Press.

Adolph, K.E., & Franchak, J.M. (2017). The development of motor behavior. *Wiley Interdisciplinary Reviews: Cognitive Scince, 8*(1-2), e1430.

Adolph, K.E., & Hoch, J.E. (2019). Motor development: Embodied, embedded, enculturated, and enabling. *Annual Review of Psychology, 70,* 141–164.

Adolph, K.E., & Hoch, J.E. (2020). The importance of motor skills for development. In M.M. Black, A. Singhal, & C.H. Hillman (Eds.), *Building future health and well-being of thriving toddlers and young children* (pp. 136–144). Karger.

Adolph, K.E., & Hoch, J.E. (2021). The importance of motor skills for development. *Nestle Nutrition Institute Workshop 95 Book Series.* Karger.

Adolph, K.E., Hoch, J.E., & Cole, W.G. (2018). Development (of walking): 15 suggestions. *Trends in Cognitive Sciences, 22*(8), 699–711.

Adolph, K.E., Kaplan, B.E., & Kretch, K.S. (2021). Infants on the edge: Beyond the visual cliff. In A.M. Slater & P.C. Quinn (Eds.), *Developmental psychology: Revisiting the classic studies* (2nd ed., pp. 51–72). Sage.

Adolph, K.E., Karasik, L.B., & Tamis-LeMonda, C.S. (2010). Motor skills. In M. Bornstein (Ed.), *Handbook of cultural developmental science.* Psychology Press.

Adolph, K.E., Kretch, K.S., & LoBue, V. (2014). Fear of height in infants? *Current Directions in Psychological Science, 23,* 60–66.

Adolph, K.E., & others (2012). How do you learn to walk? Thousands of steps and dozens of falls per day. *Psychological Science, 23,* 1387–1394.

Adolph, K.E., & Robinson, S.R. (2015). Motor development. In R.M. Lerner (Eds.), *Handbook of child psychology and developmental science* (7th ed.). Wiley.

Afifi, T.O., & others (2022). Protective factors for decreasing nicotine, alcohol, and cannabis use among adolescents with a history of adverse childhood experiences (ACEs). *International Journal of Mental Health and Addiction, 21,* 2255–2273.

Agarwal, A., & others (2021). Male infertility. *The Lancet, 397,* 319–333.

Agostini, A., Lushington, K., & Dorrian, J. (2019). The relationships between bullying, sleep, and health in a large adolescent sample. *Sleep and Biological Rhythms, 17*(2), 173–182.

Agostini, A., & others (2017). An experimental study of adolescent sleep restriction during a simulated school week: Changes in phase, sleep staging, performance, and sleepiness. *Journal of Sleep Research, 26*(2), 227–235.

Agostinis-Sobrinho, C., & others (2019). Lifestyle patterns and endocrine, metabolic, and immunological biomarkers in European adolescents: The HELENA study. *Pediatric Diabetes, 20*(1), 23–31.

Agras, W.S., & others (2004). Report of the National Institutes of Health workshop on overcoming barriers to treatment research in anorexia nervosa. *International Journal of Eating Disorders, 35,* 509–521.

Agricola, E., & others (2016). Investigating paternal preconception risk factors for adverse pregnancy outcomes in a population of Internet users. *Reproductive Health, 13,* 37.

Aguayo, L., & others (2021). Cultural socialization in childhood: Analysis of parent–child conversations with a direct observation measure. *Journal of Family Psychology, 35,* 138–148.

Ahern, E., Kowalski, M., & Lamb, M.E. (2018). A case study perspective: The experiences of young persons testifying to child sexual exploitation in British Criminal Court. *Journal of Child Sexual Abuse, 28,* 321–334.

Ahmed, S.F., Kuhfeld, M., Watts, T.W., Davis-Kean, P.E., & Vandell, D.L. (2021). Preschool executive function and adult outcomes: A developmental cascade model. *Developmental Psychology, 57*(12), 2234.

Ahnert, L., & Schoppe-Sullivan, S.J. (2020). Fathers from an attachment perspective. *Attachment and Human Development, 22,* 1–3.

Ahring, K.K., & others (2018). Comparison of glycomacropeptide with phenylalanine free-synthetic amino acids in test meals to PKU patients: No significant differences in biomarkers, including plasma Phe levels. *Journal of Nutrition and Metabolism, 2018,* 6352919.

Ahrons, C., & Ahrons, C.R. (2004). *We're still family: What grown children have to say about their parents' divorce.* Harper Collins.

Ainsworth, M.D.S. (1979). Infant-mother attachment. *American Psychologist, 34,* 932–937.

Ajetunmobi, O.M., & others (2015). Breastfeeding is associated with reduced childhood hospitalization: Evidence from a Scottish birth cohort (1997–2009). *Journal of Pediatrics, 166,* 620–625.

Akdeniz, S., & Ahçı, Z.G. (2023). The role of cognitive flexibility and hope in the relationship between loneliness and psychological adjustment: A moderated mediation model. *Educational and Developmental Psychologist, 40,* 74–85.

Akhtar, N., & Herold, K. (2017). Pragmatic development. Reference module in *Neuroscience and Biobehavioral Psychology*. doi:10.1016/B978-0-12-809324-5.05868-5

Akingbuwa, W.A., Hammerschlag, A.R., Bartels, M., & Middeldorp, C.M. (2021). Systematic review: Molecular studies of common genetic variation in child and adolescent psychiatric disorders. *Journal of the American Academy of Child & Adolescent Psychiatry, 61*, 227–242.

Akinsanya, A., Marwaha, R., & Tampi, R.R. (2017). Prazosin in children and adolescents with posttraumatic stress disorder who have nightmares: A systematic review. *Journal of Clinical Psychopharmacology, 37*, 84–88.

Akiyama, M. (2021). Multi-omics study for interpretation of genome-wide association study. *Journal of Human Genetics, 66*(1), 3–10.

Aktar, E., & Perez-Edgar, K. (2021). Infant emotion development and temperament. In J.J. Lockman & C. Tamis-LeMonda (Eds.), *Cambridge handbook of infant development*. Cambridge University Press.

Alabdulkarim, S.O., Khomais, S., Hussain, I.Y., & Gahwaji, N. (2021). Preschool children's drawings: A reflection on children's needs within the learning environment post COVID-19 pandemic school closure. *Journal of Research in Childhood Education, 36*, 203–218.

Alam, M.A., & others (2020). Impact of early-onset persistent stunting on cognitive development at 5 years of age: Results from a multi-country cohort study. *PLOS ONE, 15*(2), e0229663.

Alberico, S., & others (2014). The role of gestational diabetes, pre-pregnancy body mass index, and gestational weight gain on the risk of newborn macrosoma: Results from a prospective multicenter study. *BMC Pregnancy and Childbirth, 14*(1), 23.

Alberto, P.A., & Troutman, A.C. (2017). *Applied behavior analysis for teachers* (9th ed.). Pearson.

Alcalá, L., Montejano, M.D.C., & Fernandez, Y.S. (2021). How Yucatec Maya children learn to help at home. *Human Development, 65*(4), 191–203.

Alcañiz, M., & others (2022). Eye gaze as a biomarker in the recognition of autism spectrum disorder using virtual reality and machine learning: A proof of concept for diagnosis. *Autism Research, 15*(1), 131–145.

Alegria, A.A., & others (2017). Real-time fMRI neurofeedback in adolescents with attention deficit hyperactivity disorder. *Human Brain Mapping, 38*(6), 3190–3209.

Alex, A.M., & others (2023). Genetic influences on the developing young brain and risk for neuropsychiatric disorders. *Biological Psychiatry, 93*, 905–920.

Alexopoulos, C., & Cho, J. (2019). A moderated mediation model of parent–child communication, risk taking, alcohol consumption, and sexual experience in early adulthood. *Archives of Sexual Behavior, 48*(2), 589–597.

Alghamdi, R.J., Murphy, M.J., & Crewther, S.G. (2021). The contribution of visual processing speed to visual and auditory working memory in early school years. *Psychology & Neuroscience, 14*(4), 454–467.

Al-Ghanim, & Badahdah, A.M. (2017). Gender roles in the Arab world: Development and psychometric properties of the Arab Adolescents Gender Roles Attitude Scale. *Sex Roles, 77*, 169–177.

Ali, J.B., Thomas, R.L., Raymond, S.M., & Bremner, A.J. (2021). Sensitivity to visual-tactile colocation on the body prior to skilled reaching in early infancy. *Child Development, 92*(1), 21–34.

Allameh, Z., Tehrani, H.G., & Ghasemi, M. (2015). Comparing the impact of acupuncture and pethidine on reducing labor pain. *Advanced Biomedical Research, 4*, 46.

Allan, D.M., & Lonigan, C.J. (2019). Examination of the structure and measurement of inattentive, hyperactive, and impulsive behaviors from preschool to grade 4. *Journal of Abnormal Child Psychology, 47*, 975–987.

Allen, J., & Allen, C. (2009). *Escaping the endless adolescence*. Ballantine.

Allen, J.P., Chango, J., Szwedo, D., & Schad, M. (2014). Long-term sequelae of subclinical depressive symptoms in early adolescence. *Development and Psychopathology, 26*, 171–180.

Allen, J.P., Grande, L., Tan, J., & Loeb, E. (2018). Parent and peer predictors of change in attachment security from adolescence to adulthood. *Child Development, 89*(4), 1120–1132.

Allen, J.P., & Tan, J. (2016). The multiple facts of attachment in adolescence. In J. Cassidy & P.R. Shaver (Eds.), *Handbook of attachment* (3rd ed.). Guilford Press.

Alm, B., Wennergren, G., Mollborg, P., & Lagercrantz, H. (2016). Breastfeeding and dummy use have a protective effect on sudden infant death syndrome. *Acta Pediatrica, 105*, 31–38.

Almy, B., & Cicchetti, D. (2018). Developmental cascades. In M.H. Bornstein & others (Eds.), *SAGE encyclopedia of lifespan human development*. Sage.

Alonso-Alberca, N., & others (2019). Cross-cultural validity of the Emotion Matching Task. *Journal of Child and Family Studies, 29*(4), 1159–1172.

Alquraini, T.A., & Rao, S.M. (2020). Developing and sustaining readers with intellectual and multiple disabilities: A systematic review of literature. *International Journal of Developmental Disabilities, 66*, 91–103.

Al-Shawaf, L., Zreik, K., & Buss, D.M. (2021). Thirteen misunderstandings about natural selection. In T.K. Shackelford & V.A. Weekes-Shackelford (Eds.), *Encyclopedia of evolutionary psychological science*. Springer.

Althaus, N., Gliozzi, V., Mayor, J., & Plunkett, K. (2020). Infant categorization as a dynamic process linked to memory. *Royal Society Open Science, 7*(10), 200328.

Altman, C., Goldstein, T., & Armon-Lotem, S. (2018). Vocabulary, metalinguistic awareness and language dominance among bilingual preschool children. *Frontiers in Psychology, 9*, 1953.

Altug, H., & others (2013). Effects of air pollution on lung function and symptoms of asthma, rhinitis, and eczema in primary school children. *Environmental Science and Pollution Research International, 20*(9), 6455.

Amato, P.R. (2006). Marital discord, divorce, and children's well-being: Results from a 20-year longitudinal study of two generations. In A. Clarke-Stewart & J. Dunn (Eds.), *Families count*. Cambridge University Press.

Amato, P.R., & Anthony, C.J. (2014). Estimating the effects of parental divorce and death with fixed effects. *Journal of Marriage and the Family, 76*, 370–386.

Amato, P.R., & Booth, A. (1996). A prospective study of divorce and parent-child relationships. *Journal of Marriage and the Family, 58*, 356–365.

Amemiya, J., Liu, Z., Compton, B.J., & Heyman, G.D. (2021). Children's judgements of positive claims people make about themselves. *Infant and Child Development, 30*(2), e2212.

American Academy of Pediatrics (2021). Beyond screen time: A parent's guide to media use. *Pediatric Patient Education*. https://doi.org/10.1542/peo_document099

American Association of Sleep Technologists (2019). Position statement. Retrieved November 29, 2019, from www.aastweb.org/position-statement

American College of Obstetricians and Gynecologists (2019a). Cesarean delivery on maternal request. ACOG Committee Opinion No. 761. *Obstetrics & Gynecology, 133*, e73-e77.

American College of Obstetricians and Gynecologists (2019b). Committee opinion, Number 650 (December 2015, reaffirmed 2019). ACOG.

American Pregnancy Association (2023). Mercury levels in fish. Retrieved January 14, 2023, from https://americanpregnancy.org/pregnancy-health/mercury-levels-in-fish/

American Psychological Association (2003). *Psychology: Scientific problem solvers*. APA Books.

American Psychological Association (2019). *Resolution on physical discipline of children by parents*. Available https://www.apa.org/about/policy/physical-discipline.pdf

American Psychological Association (2023). *Depression treatments for children and adolescents*. Available https://www.apa.org/depression-guideline/children-and-adolescents

American Public Health Association (2006). *Understanding the health culture of recent immigrants to the United States*. Retrieved July 28, 2006, from http://www.apha.org/ppp/red/Intro.htm

Amir, D., Ahl, R.E., Parsons, W.S., & McAuliffe, K. (2021). Children are more forgiving of accidental harms across development. *Journal of Experimental Child Psychology, 205*, 105081.

Amole, M.C., Cyranowski, J.M., Wright, A.G.C., & Swartz, H.A. (2017). Depression impacts the physiological responsiveness of mother-daughter dyads during social interaction. *Depression Anxiety, 34*, 118–126.

Amrithraj, A.I., & others (2017). Gestational diabetes alters functions in offspring's umbilical cord cells with implications for cardiovascular health. *Endocrinology, 158*(7), 2102–2112.

Amso, D., & Tummeltshammer, K. (2021). Infant visual attention. In J.J. Lockman & C.S. Tamis-LeMonda (Eds.), *Cambridge handbook of infant development*. Cambridge University Press.

Amsterdam, R.K. (1968). *Mirror behavior in children under two years of age.* Unpublished doctoral dissertation. University of North Carolina, Chapel Hill.

Amundsen, R., & others (2020). Mindfulness in primary school children as a route to enhanced life satisfaction, positive outlook, and effective emotional regulation. *BMC Psychology, 8*(1), 71.

Anastasi, A., & Urbina, S. (1997). *Psychological testing* (11th ed.). Prentice Hall.

Andersen, E., & others (2022). Methods for characterizing ovarian and adrenal hormone variability and mood relationships in peripubertal females. *Psychoneuroendocrinology, 141,* 105747.

Anderson, A.J., Perone, S., & Gartstein, M.A. (2022). Context matters: Cortical rhythms in infants across baseline and play. *Infant Behavior and Development, 66,* 101665.

Anderson, C.A., & Bushman, B.J. (2018). Media violence and the general aggression model. *Journal of Social Issues, 74,* 386–413.

Anderson, D.R., Huston, A.C., Schmitt, K., Linebarger, D.L., & Wright, J.C. (2001). Early childhood viewing and adolescent behavior: The recontact study. *Monographs of the Society for Research in Child Development, 66*(1, Serial No. 264).

Anderson, D.R., & Subrahmanyam, K. (2017). Digital screen media and cognitive development. *Pediatrics, 140*(Suppl. 2), S57–S61.

Anderson, D.R., Torch, E.P., Held, D.E., Collins, P.A., & Nathan, J.G. (1985, April). *Television viewing at home: Age trends in visual attention and time with TV.* Paper presented at the biennial meeting of the Society for Research in Child Development, Toronto.

Andersson, H., & Bergman, L.R. (2011). The role of task persistence in young adolescence for successful educational and occupational attainment in middle adulthood. *Developmental Psychology, 47,* 950–960.

Andescavage, N.N., & others (2017). Complex trajectories of brain development in the healthy human fetus. *Cerebral Cortex, 27*(11), 5274–5283.

Anding, J.E., & others (2016). Couple comorbidity and correlates of postnatal depressive symptoms in mothers and fathers in the first two weeks following delivery. *Journal of Affective Disorders, 190,* 300–309.

Andreassi, M.G., & others (2021). Reproductive outcomes and Y chromosome instability in radiation-exposed male workers in cardiac catheterization laboratory. *Environmental and Molecular Mutagenesis, 61,* 361–368.

Andrews, J.L., Ahmed, S.P., & Blakemore, S.-J. (2021). Navigating the social environment in adolescence: The role of social brain development. *Biological Psychiatry, 89,* 109–118.

Andrews, N.C., Hanish, L.D., Updegraff, K.A., DeLay, D., & Martin, C.L. (2019). Dyadic peer interactions: The impact of aggression on impression formation with new peers. *Journal of Abnormal Child Psychology, 47*(5), 839–850.

Andrews, S.J., & Lamb, M.E. (2017). The structural linguistic complexity of lawyers' questions and children's responses in Scottish criminal courts. *Child Abuse and Neglect, 65,* 182–193.

Andriani, H., Liao, C.Y., & Kuo, H.W. (2015). Parental weight changes as key predictors of child weight changes. *BMC Public Health, 15,* 645.

Ang, S., Ng, K.Y., & Rockstuhl, T. (2020). Cultural intelligence. In R.J. Sternberg (Ed.), *Cambridge handbook of intelligence* (2nd ed.). Cambridge University Press.

Ang, S., Rodgers, J.L., & Wanstrom, L. (2010). The Flynn effect within subgroups in the U.S.: Gender, race, income, education, and urbanization differences in the NYLS-children data. *Intelligence, 38,* 367–384.

Angelakis, I., Gillespie, E.L., & Panagioti, M. (2019). Childhood maltreatment and adult suicidality: A comprehensive systematic review with meta-analysis. *Psychological Medicine, 49*(7), 1057–1078.

Anglin, D.M., Lui, F., Espinosa, A., Tikhonov, A., & Ellman, L. (2018). Ethnic identity, racial discrimination, and attenuated psychotic symptoms in an urban population of emerging adults. *Early Intervention in Psychiatry, 12*(3), 380–390.

Ansari, A., & Winsler, A. (2014). Montessori public school pre-K programs and the school readiness of low-income Black and Latino children. *Journal of Educational Psychology, 106,* 1066–1079.

Antfolk, J. (2017). Age limits. *Evolutionary Psychology, 15*(1), 1474704917690401.

Antonopoulos, C., & others (2011). Maternal smoking during pregnancy and childhood lymphoma: A meta-analysis. *International Journal of Cancer, 129,* 2694–2703.

Aoki, C., Romeo, R.D., & Smith, S.S. (2017). Adolescence as a critical period for developmental plasticity. *Brain Research, 1654*(Pt. B), 85–86.

Apperley, L., & others (2018). Mode of clinical presentation and delayed diagnosis of Turner syndrome: A single Centre UK study. *International Journal of Pediatric Endocrinology, 2018,* 4.

Arbib, M.A. (2017). Toward the language-ready brain: Biological evolution and primate comparisons. *Psychonomic Bulletin & Review, 24,* 142–150.

Arck, P.C & others (2018). Prenatal immune and endocrine modulators of offspring's brain development and cognitive functions later in life. *Frontiers in Immunology, 9,* 2186.

Arellanes, J.A., Anguiano, R.P.V., & Lohman, B.J. (2019). Bettering the educational attainment for Latino families: How families view the education of their children. *Journal of Latinos and Education, 18*(4), 349–362.

Arens, A.K., & Niepel, C. (2023). Formation of academic self-concept and intrinsic value within and across three domains: Extending the reciprocal internal/external frame of reference model. *British Journal of Educational Psychology, 93*(2), 545–570.

Argente, J., & others (2023). Molecular basis of normal and pathological puberty: From basic mechanisms to clinical implications. *The Lancet Diabetes & Endocrinology, 11,* 203–216.

Arkes, J. (2015). The temporal effects of divorces and separations on children's academic achievement and problem behavior. *Journal of Divorce and Remarriage, 56,* 25–42.

Armstrong-Carter, E., & others (2020). Daily links between helping behaviors and emotional well-being during late adolescence. *Journal of Research on Adolescence, 30*(4), 943–955.

Arnett, J.J. (2006). Emerging adulthood: Understanding the new way of coming of age. In J.J. Arnett & J.L. Tanner (Eds.), *Emerging adults in America.* American Psychological Association.

Arnett, J.J., Robinson, O., & Lachman, M.E. (2020). Rethinking adult development: Introduction to the special issue. *American Psychologist, 75,* 425–430.

Arnold, L.E., Hodgkins, P., Kahle, J., Madhoo, M., & Kewley, G. (2020). Long-term outcomes of ADHD: Academic achievement and performance. *Journal of Attention Disorders, 24*(1), 73–85.

Arnon, I. (2019). Statistical learning, implicit learning, and first language acquisition: A critical evaluation of two developmental predictions. *Topics in Cognitive Science, 11,* 504–519.

Aro, T., & others (2019). Associations between childhood learning disabilities and adult-age mental health problems, lack of education, and unemployment. *Journal of Learning Disabilities, 52,* 71–83.

Aronson, E. (1986, August). *Teaching students things they think they already know about: The case of prejudice and desegregation.* Paper presented at the meeting of the American Psychological Association, Washington, DC.

Arrondo, G., & others (2022). Associations between mental and physical conditions in children and adolescents: An umbrella review. *Neuroscience & Biobehavioral Reviews, 137,* 104662.

Arseneault, L. (2017). The long-term impact of bullying victimization on mental health. *World Psychiatry, 16,* 27–28.

Arya, S., Mulla, Z.D., & Plavsic, S.K. (2018). Outcomes of women delivering at very advanced maternal age. *Journal of Women's Health, 27*(11), 1378–1384.

Ashdown-Franks, G., & others (2019). Leisure-time sedentary behavior and obesity among 116,762 adolescents aged 12–15 years from 41 low- and middle-income countries. *Obesity, 27*(5), 830–836.

Askeland, K.G., & others (2017). Mental health in internationally adopted adolescents: A meta-analysis. *Journal of the American Academy of Child and Adolescent Psychiatry, 56,* 202–213.

Aslin, R.N. (2017). Statistical learning: A powerful mechanism that operates by mere exposure. *Wiley Interdisciplinary Reviews: Cognitive Science, 8*(1-2), e1373.

Aslin, R.N., & Lathrop, A.L. (2008). Visual perception. In M.M. Haith & J.B. Benson (Eds.), *Encyclopedia of infant and early childhood development.* Elsevier.

Assanand, S., Dias, M., Richardson, E., & Waxler-Morrison, N. (1990). The South Asians. In N. Waxler-Morrison, J.M. Anderson, & E. Richardson (Eds.), *Cross-cultural caring.* UBC Press.

Association of Child Life Professionals (2022). *The case for child life.* https://www.childlife.org/the-child-life-profession/the-case-for-child-life

Astle, D.E., Holmes, J., Kievit, R., & Gathercole, S.E. (2022). Annual Research Review: The transdiagnostic revolution in neurodevelopmental disorders. *Journal of Child Psychology and Psychiatry, 63*(4), 397–417.

Ata, R.N., Ludden, A.B., & Lally, M.M. (2007). The effect of gender and family, friend, and media influences on eating behaviors and body image during adolescence. *Journal of Youth and Adolescence, 36*, 1024–1037.

Atkins, K.L., Fogarty, S., & Feigel, M.L. (2021). Acupressure and acupuncture use in the peripartum period. *Clinical Obstetrics and Gynecology, 64*, 558–571.

Atkinson, J., & Braddick, O. (2013). Visual development. In P.D. Zelazo (Ed.), *Handbook of developmental psychology.* Oxford University Press.

Aubert, S., & others (2022). Global matrix 4.0 physical activity report card grades for children and adolescents: Results and analyses from 57 countries. *Journal of Physical Activity and Health, 19*, 700–728.

Auersperg, F., & others (2019). Long-term effects of parental divorce on mental health—A meta-analysis. *Journal of Psychiatric Research, 119*, 107–115.

Auld, E., & Morris, P. (2019). The OECD and IELS: Redefining early childhood education for the 21st century. *Policy Futures in Education, 17*, 11–26.

Austin, A.E., & others (2022). An illustrative review of substance use—Specific insights from the National Longitudinal Study of Adolescent to Adult Health. *Journal of Adolescent Health, 71*, S6–S13.

Autism Research Institute (2013). *DSM-V: What changes may mean.* Retrieved May 7, 2013, from www.autism.com/index.php/news_dsmV

Ayoub, C., Vallotton, C.D., & Mastergeorge, A.M. (2011). Developmental pathways to integrated social skills: The role of parenting and early intervention. *Child Development, 82*, 583–600.

Azar, S., & Wong, T.E. (2017). Sickle cell disease: A brief update. *Medical Clinics of North America, 101*, 375–393.

Azmitia, M., Peraza, P.D.G., Thomas, V., Ajayi, A.A., & Syed, M. (2023). The promises and challenges of using an intersectional framework to study identity development during adolescence and early adulthood. In L.J. Crockett, G. Carlo, & J.E. Schulenberg (Eds.), *APA handbook of adolescent and young adult development* (pp. 391–405). American Psychological Association.

B

Babic, A., & others (2020). Association between breastfeeding and ovarian cancer risk. *JAMA Oncology, 6*(6), e200421–e200421.

Babik, I., Galloway, J.C., & Lobo, M.A. (2022). Early exploration of one's own body, exploration of objects, and motor, language, and cognitive development relate dynamically across the first two years of life. *Developmental Psychology, 58*(2), 222–235.

Babskie, E., Powell, D.N., & Metzger, A. (2017). Variability in parenting self-efficacy across prudential adolescent behaviors. *Parenting, 17*, 242–261.

Bachman, J.G., & others (2008). *The education-drug use connection.* Psychology Press.

Bachmann, N., & others (2017). Novel deletion of 11p15.5 imprinting center region 1 in a patient with Beckwith-Wiedemann syndrome provides insight into distal enhancer regulation and tumorigenesis. *Pediatric and Blood Cancer, 64*(3), 10.1002/pbc.26241.

Bacikova-Sleskova, M., Benka, J., & Orosova, O. (2015). Parental employment status and adolescents' health: The role of financial situation, parent-adolescent relationship, and adolescents' resilience. *Psychology and Health, 30*, 400–422.

Back, J., & others (2019). Psychological risk factors for exercise dependence. *International Journal of Sport and Exercise Psychology, 19*(4), 461–472.

Ba, D.M., & others (2019). Prevalence and predictors of contraceptive use among women of reproductive age in 17 sub-Saharan African countries: A large population-based study. *Sexual & Reproductive Healthcare, 21*, 26–32.

Baddeley, A., Hitch, G., & Allen, R. (2021). A multicomponent model of working memory. In R.H. Logie, V. Camos, & N. Cowan (Eds.), *Working memory: State of the science* (pp. 10–43). Oxford University Press.

Baddeley, A.D. (2018). *Working memories: Postmen, divers and the cognitive revolution.* Routledge.

Baddeley, A.D. (2021). Developing the concept of working memory: The role of neuropsychology. *Archives of Clinical Neuropsychology, 36*(6), 861–873.

Bae, S.M. (2020). The relationship between bicultural identity, acculturative stress, and psychological well-being in multicultural adolescents: Verification using multivariate latent growth modelling. *Stress and Health, 36*(1), 51–58.

Baer, R.J. & others (2019). Maternal factors influencing late entry into prenatal care: A stratified analysis by race or ethnicity and insurance status. *The Journal of Maternal-Fetal & Neonatal Medicine, 32*(20), 3336–3342.

Baggs, E., & Chemero, A. (2020). Thinking with other minds. *Behavioral Brain Sciences, 43*, e92.

Bagnall, C.L., Fox, C.L., & Skipper, Y. (2021). When is the "optimal" time for school transition? An insight into provision in the US. *Pastoral Care in Education, 39*(4), 348–376.

Bahrick, L.E., Todd, J.T., & Soska, K.C. (2018). The Multisensory Attention Assessment Protocol (MAAP): Characterizing individual differences in multisensory attention skills in infants and children and relations with language and cognition. *Developmental Psychology, 54*, 2207–2225.

Bailey, H.N., & others (2017). Deconstructing maternal sensitivity: Predictive relations to mother-child attachment in home and laboratory settings. *Social Development, 26*(4), 679–693.

Baillargeon, R., & DeVos, J. (1991). Object permanence in young children: Further evidence. *Child Development, 62*, 1227–1246.

Bakeman, R., & Brown, J.V. (1980). Early interaction: Consequences for social and mental development at three years. *Child Development, 51*, 437–447.

Bakermans-Kranenburg, M.J., & van IJzendoorn, M.H. (2016). Attachment, parenting, and genetics. In J. Cassidy & P.R.Shaver (Eds.), *Handbook of parenting* (3rd ed.). Guilford Press.

Baker-Smith, C.M., & others (2018). Diagnosis, evaluation, and management of high blood pressure in children and adolescents. *Pediatrics, 142*, e20182096.

Bakhtiani, P., & Geffner, M. (2022). Early puberty. *Pediatrics in Review, 43*, 483–492.

Bakth, F.N., Hoffman, A.J., & Schacter, H.L. (2022). Investigating the relation between ethnic-racial identity and classroom engagement among Cherokee adolescents: Cultural socialization as a moderator. *Cultural Diversity and Ethnic Minority Psychology, 28*, 182–192.

Ballou, D., & Springer, M.G. (2017). Has NCLB encouraged educational triage? Accountability and the distribution of achievement gains. *Education Finance and Policy, 12*, 77–106.

Bamishigbin, N., Schetter, C.D., & Stanton, A.L. (2019). The antecedents and consequences of adolescent fatherhood: A systematic review. *Social Science & Medicine, 232*, 106–119.

Ban, L., Gibson, J.E., West, J., & Tata, L.J. (2010). Association between perinatal depression in mothers and the risk of infections in offspring: A population-based cohort study. *BMC Public Health, 10*, 799–806.

Bandura, A. (1998, August). *Swimming against the mainstream: Accentuating the positive aspects of humanity.* Paper presented at the meeting of the American Psychological Association, San Francisco, CA.

Bandura, A. (2016). *Moral disengagement: How people do harm and live with themselves.* Worth.

Bandura, A. (2018). Toward a psychology of human agency: Pathways and reflections. *Perspectives on Psychological Science, 13*(2), 130–136.

Banks, J.A. (2020). *Diversity, transformative knowledge, and civic education.* Routledge.

Barbieri, R.L. (2019). Female infertility. In J. Strauss & R. Barbieri, *Yen and Jaffe's reproductive endocrinology* (8th ed., pp. 556–581). Elsevier.

Bardack, S., & Obradović, J. (2019). Observing teachers' displays and scaffolding of executive functioning in the classroom context. *Journal of Applied Developmental Psychology, 62*, 205–219.

Barker, R., & Wright, H.F. (1951). *One boy's day.* Harper & Row.

Baron, A., & others (2020). The play's the thing: Associations between make-believe play and self-regulation in the Tools of the Mind Early Childhood Curriculum. *Early Education and Development, 31*(1), 66–83.

Baron, J. (2020). Why science succeeds, and sometimes doesn't. In R.J. Sternberg & D.F. Halpern (Eds.), *Critical thinking in psychology* (2nd ed.). Cambridge University Press.

Baron, N.S. (1992). *Growing up with language.* Addison-Wesley.

Baroncelli, L., & Lunghi, C. (2021). Neuroplasticity of the visual cortex: In sickness and in health. *Experimental Neurology, 335,* 113515.

Baroody, A.J., Clements, D.H., & Sarama, J. (2019). Teaching and learning mathematics in early childhood programs. In C.P. Brown, M.B. McMullen, & Umaña (Eds.), *The Wiley handbook of early childhood care and education.* Wiley.

Barrington-Trimis, J.L., & others (2018). Type of e-cigarette device used by adolescents and young adults: Findings from a pooled analysis of 8 studies of 2,166 vapers. *Nicotine and Tobacco Research, 20*(2), 271-274.

Barrouillet, P. (2015). Theories of cognitive development: From Piaget to today. *Developmental Review, 38,* 1-12.

Barry, E.S., & McKenna, J.J. (2022). Reasons mothers bedshare: A review of its effects on infant behavior and development. *Infant Behavior and Development, 66,* 101684.

Bartel, A.P., & others (2018). Paid family leave, fathers' leave-taking, and leave-sharing in dual-earner households. *Journal of Policy Analysis and Management, 37*(1), 10-37.

Bartsch, K., & Wellman, H.M. (1995). *Children talk about the mind.* Oxford University Press.

Basalely, A., Hill-Horowitz, T., & Sethna, C.B. (2023). Ambulatory blood pressure monitoring in pediatrics, an update on interpretation and classification of hypertension phenotypes. *Current Hypertension Reports, 25*(1), 1-11.

Bascandziev, I., & Harris, P.L. (2011). The role of testimony in young children's solution of a gravity-driven invisible displacement task. *Cognitive Development, 25,* 233-246.

Bassi, M., & others (2018). Failing to notice? Uneven teachers' attention to boys and girls in the classroom. *IZA Journal of Labor Economics, 7*(1), 1-22.

Bastian, J. (2020). The rise of working mothers and the 1975 earned income tax credit. *American Economic Journal: Economic Policy, 12,* 44-75.

Bastian, K.C., & Fuller, S.C. (2023). Late but right on time? School start times and middle grade students' engagement and achievement outcomes in North Carolina. *American Journal of Education, 129,* 177-203.

Bates, J.E., McQuillan, M.E., & Hoyniak, C.P. (2019). Parenting and temperament. In M.H. Bornstein (Ed.), *Handbook of parenting* (3rd ed.). Routledge.

Bauer, P.J. (2009). Learning and memory: Like a horse and carriage. In A. Needham & A. Woodward (Eds.), *Learning and the infant mind.* Oxford University Press.

Bauer, P.J. (2013). Memory. In P.D. Zelazo (Ed.), *Oxford handbook of developmental psychology.* Oxford University Press.

Bauer, P.J. (2015). A complementary processes account of the development of childhood amnesia and a personal past. *Psychological Review, 122,* 204-231.

Bauer, P.J., & Larkina, M. (2014). The onset of childhood amnesia in childhood: A prospective investigation of the course and determinants of forgetting of early-life events. *Memory, 22,* 907-924.

Bauer, P.J., & Larkina, M. (2016). Predicting and remembering and forgetting of autobiographical memories in children and adults: A 4-year prospective study. *Memory, 24,* 1345-1368.

Bauer, P.J., & Larkina, M. (2018). Predictors of age-related and individual variability in autobiographical memory in childhood. *Memory, 27,* 63-78.

Bauer, P.J., & Leventon, S.J. (2015). The development of declarative memory in infancy and implications for social learning. In S.D. Calkins (Ed.), *Handbook of biopsychosocial development.* Guilford Press.

Bauer, P.J., Wenner, J.A., Dropik, P.I., & Wewerka, S.S. (2000). Parameters of remembering and forgetting in the transition from infancy to early childhood. *Monographs of the Society for Research in Child Development, 65*(4, Serial No. 263).

Bauer, R.H., Gilpin, A.T., & Thibodeau-Nielsen, R.B. (2021). Executive functions and imaginative play: Exploring relations with prosocial behaviors using structural equation modeling. *Trends in Neuroscience and Education, 25,* 100165.

Baugh, N., & others (2017). The impact of maternal obesity and excessive gestational weight gain on maternal and infant outcomes in Maine: Analysis of pregnancy risk assessment monitoring results from 2000 to 2010. *Journal of Pregnancy, 2016,* 5871313.

Bauman, K.E., & others (2002). Influence of a family program on adolescent smoking and drinking prevalence. *Prevention Science, 3,* 35-42.

Bauman, S., & Bellmore, A. (2015). New directions in cyberbullying research. *Journal of School Violence, 14*(1), 1-10.

Baumrind, D. (1971). Current patterns of parental authority. *Developmental Psychology Monographs, 4*(1, Pt. 2).

Baumrind, D. (2013). Authoritative parenting revisited: History and current status. In R. Larzelere, A.S. Morris, & A.W. Harrist (Eds.), *Authoritative parenting.* American Psychological Association.

Bausert, S., Froh, J.J., Bono, G., Rose-Zornick, R., & Rose, Z. (2018). Gratitude in adolescence. In J. Tudge & L. Freitas (Eds.), *Developing gratitude in children and adolescents.* Cambridge University Press.

Baxley, F., & Miller, M. (2006). Parental misperceptions about children and firearms. *Archives of Pediatric and Adolescent Medicine, 160,* 542-547.

Bayley, N. (1969). *Manual for the Bayley Scales of Infant Development.* Psychological Corporation.

Bazhydai, M., Westermann, G., & Parise, E. (2020). "I don't know but I know who to ask": 12-month-olds actively seek information from knowledgeable adults. *Developmental Science, 23*(5), e12938.

Beal, S.J., & others (2020). Heightened risk of pain in young adult women with a history of childhood maltreatment: A prospective longitudinal study. *Pain, 161*(1), 156-165.

Bean, R.C., Ledermann, T., Higginbotham, B.J., & Galliher, R.V. (2021). Adjustment difficulties and marital stability in remarriages: The role of stepfamily constellation. *Marriage and Family Review, 57,* 721-740.

Bear, D.R., & others (2020). *Words their way* (7th ed.). Pearson.

Beatson, R., Molloy, C., Perini, N., Harrop, C., & Goldfeld, S. (2021). Systematic review: An exploration of core componentry characterizing effective sustained nurse home visiting programs. *Journal of Advanced Nursing, 77,* 2581-2594.

Becht, A.I., & others (2017). Clear self, better relationships: Adolescents' self-concept clarity and relationship quality with parents and peers across 5 years. *Child Development, 88*(6), 1823-1833.

Becker, M., & others (2014). Cultural bases for self-evaluation: Seeing oneself positively in different cultural contexts. *Personality and Social Psychology Bulletin, 40,* 657-675.

Beckmeyer, J.J., & Russell, L.T. (2018). Family structure and family management practices: Associations with positive aspects of youth well-being. *Journal of Family Issues, 39*(7), 2131-2154.

Bednarski, F.M., Musholt, K., & Wiesmann, C.G. (2022). Do infants have agency? The importance of control for the study of early agency. *Developmental Review, 64,* 101022.

Behrens, D., & others (2023). Firearm injury prevention advocacy: Lessons learned and future directions. *Pediatric Clinics of North America, 70*(1), 67-82.

Bell, E.F., & others (2022). Mortality, in-hospital morbidity, care practices, and 2-year outcomes for extremely preterm infants in the US, 2013-2018. *JAMA, 327*(3), 248-263.

Bell, M.A. (2023, in press). *Child development at the intersection of emotion and cognition* (2nd ed.). American Psychological Association.

Bell, M.A., & Broomell, A.P.R. (2021). Development of inhibitory control from infancy to early childhood. In O. Houde & G. Borst (Eds.), *Cambridge handbook of cognitive development.* Cambridge University Press.

Bell, M.A., & Garcia Meza, T. (2020). Executive function. In J.B. Benson (Ed.), *Encyclopedia of infant and early childhood development.* Elsevier.

Bell, M.A., Ross, A.P., & Patton, L.K. (2018). Emotion regulation. In M.H. Bornstein & others (Eds.), *SAGE encyclopedia of lifespan human development.* Sage.

Bell, R., Mouzourakis, M., & Wise, S.R. (2022). Impact of unilateral hearing loss in early development. *Current Opinion in Otolaryngology & Head and Neck Surgery, 30*(5), 344-350.

Bell, S.M., & Ainsworth, M.D.S. (1972). Infant crying and maternal responsiveness. *Child Development, 43,* 1171-1190.

Bellieni, C.V. (2019). New insights into fetal pain. *Seminars in Fetal and Neonatal Medicine, 24*(4), 101001.

Bellieni, C.V., & others (2016). How painful is a heelprick or a venipuncture in a newborn? *Journal of Maternal-Fetal and Neonatal Medicine, 29,* 202-206.

Bellieni, C.V., & others (2018). Pain perception in NICU: A pilot questionnaire. *The Journal of Maternal-Fetal & Neonatal Medicine, 31,* 1921-1923.

Bellon, E., Fias, W., & de Smedt, B. (2020). Metacognition across domains: Is the association between arithmetic and metacognitive monitoring domain-specific? *PLoS One, 15*(3), e0229932.

Belsky, J. (1981). Early human experience: A family perspective. *Developmental Psychology, 17,* 3-23.

Belsky, J. (2019). Early-life adversity accelerates child and adolescent development. *Current Directions in Psychological Science, 28,* 241-246.

Belsky, J., & Pluess, M. (2016). Differential susceptibility to environmental influences. In D. Cicchetti (Ed.), *Developmental psychopathology* (3rd ed.). Wiley.

Belsky, J., Zhang, X., & Sayler, K. (2022). Differential susceptibility 2.0: Are the same children affected by different experiences and exposures? *Development and Psychopathology, 34*(3), 1025-1033.

Beltran-Valls, M.R., & others (2019). Longitudinal changes in vigorous-intensity physical activity from childhood to adolescence: Gateshead Millennium Study. *Journal of Science and Medicine in Sport, 22*(4), 450-455.

Bem, S.I. (1977). On the utility of alternative procedures for assessing psychological androgyny. *Journal of Consulting and Clinical Psychology, 45,* 196-205.

Bembenutty, H. (2021). School environments that facilitate delay of gratification. In F.C. Worrell & others (Eds.), *Cambridge handbook of applied school psychology.* Cambridge University Press.

Benassi, M., & others (2021). Developmental trajectories of global motion and global form perception from 4 years to adulthood. *Journal of Experimental Child Psychology, 207,* 105092.

Bendezu, J.J., & others (2018). Longitudinal relations among parental monitoring strategies, knowledge, and adolescent delinquency in a racially diverse at-risk sample. *Journal of Clinical Child and Adolescent Psychology, 47*(Suppl. 1), S21-S34.

Benitez, V.L., & others (2017). Sustained selective attention predicts flexible switching in preschoolers. *Journal of Experimental Child Psychology, 156,* 29-42.

Benito-Gomez, M., Williams, K.N., McCurdy, A., & Fletcher, A.C. (2020). Autonomy-supportive parenting in adolescence: Cultural variability in the contemporary United States. *Journal of Family Theory and Review, 12,* 7-26.

Benjamin, O., & Lappin, S.L. (2020). Kwashiorkor. *StatPearls.*

Benson, J.E., & Sabbagh, M.A. (2017). Executive function helps children think about and learn about others' mental states. In M.J. Hoskyns & others (Eds.), *Executive functions in children's everyday lives.* Oxford University Press.

Benson, P.L. (2010). *Parent, teacher, mentor, friend: How every adult can change kids' lives.* Search Institute Press.

Benson, P.L., Mannes, M., Pittman, K., & Ferber, T. (2004). Youth development, developmental assets, and public policy. In R. Lerner & L. Steinberg (Eds.), *Handbook of adolescent psychology* (2nd ed.). Wiley.

Benson, P.L., & Scales, P.C. (2011). Thriving and sparks: Development and emergence of new core concepts in positive youth development. In R.J.R. Levesque (Ed.), *Encyclopedia of adolescence.* Springer.

Bera, A., & others (2014). Effects of kangaroo care on growth and development of low birthweight babies up to 12 months of age: A controlled clinical trial. *Acta Pediatrica, 103,* 643-650.

Berdasco-Muñoz, E., Nazzi, T., & Yeung, H.H. (2019). Visual scanning of a talking face in preterm and full-term infants. *Developmental Psychology, 55*(7), 1353.

Berecz, B., & others (2020). Carrying human infants—An evolutionary heritage. *Infant Behavior and Development, 60,* 101460.

Bereczki, E.O., & Kárpáti, A. (2018). Teachers' beliefs about creativity and its nurture: A systematic review of the recent research literature. *Educational Research Review, 23,* 25-56.

Berenson, G.S., Srinivasan, S.R., Xu, J.H., & Chen, W. (2016). Adiposity and cardiovascular risk factor variables in childhood are associated with premature death from coronary heart disease in adults: The Bogalusa Heart Study. *American Journal of Medical Science, 352,* 448-454.

Berger, A.T., Wahlstrom, K.L., & Widome, R. (2019). Relationships between sleep duration and adolescent depression: A conceptual replication. *Sleep Health, 5*(2), 175-179.

Berger, L.M., & Carlson, M.J. (2020). Family policy and complex contemporary families: A decade in review and implications for the next decade of research and policy practice. *Journal of Marriage and Family, 82*(1), 478-507.

Berko, J. (1958). The child's learning of English morphology. *Word, 14,* 150-177.

Berko Gleason, J. (2009). The development of language: An overview. In J. Berko Gleason & N.B. Ratner (Eds.), *The development of language* (7th ed.). Allyn & Bacon.

Berko Gleason, J., & Ratner, N.B. (Eds.) (2017). *The development of language* (9th ed.). Pearson.

Berlyne, D.E. (1960). *Conflict, arousal, and curiosity.* McGraw-Hill.

Berman, M.G., & others (2013). Dimensionality of brain networks linked to life-long individual differences in self-control. *Nature Communications, 4,* 1373.

Bernecker, K., Herrmann, M., Brandstatter, V., & Job, V. (2017). Implicit theories about willpower predict subjective well-being. *Journal of Personality, 85,* 136-150.

Bernier, A., Calkins, S.D., & Bell, M.A. (2016). Longitudinal associations between the quality of mother-infant interactions and brain development across infancy. *Child Development, 87,* 1159-1174.

Bernier, A., & others (2013). Sleep and cognition in preschool years: Specific links to executive functioning. *Child Development, 84*(5), 1542-1553.

Bernier, A., & others (2017). Parenting and young children's executive function development. In M.J. Hoskyn & others (Eds.), *Executive functions in children's everyday lives.* Oxford University Press.

Bernier, A., & others (2019). Mother-infant interaction and child brain morphology: A multidimensional approach to maternal sensitivity. *Infancy, 24*(2), 120-138.

Bernthal, J.E., Bankson, N.W., & Flipsen, P. (2017). *Articulation and phonological disorders* (8th ed.). Pearson.

Berry, D., & others (2016). Household chaos and children's cognitive and socio-emotional development in early childhood: Does childcare play a buffering role? *Early Childhood Research Quarterly, 34,* 115-127.

Berry, J.W. (2015). Acculturation. In J.E. Grusec & P.D. Hastings (Eds.), *Handbook of socialization* (2nd ed.). Guilford Press.

Bertenthal, B.I., Longo, M.R., & Kenny, S. (2007). Phenomenal permanence and the development of predictive tracking in infancy. *Child Development, 78,* 350-363.

Bertini, G., & others (2019). Abnormal neurological soft signs in babies born to smoking mothers were associated with lower breastfeeding for first three months. *Acta Paediatrica, 108*(7), 1256-1261.

Best, D.L., & Puzio, A.R. (2019). Gender and culture. In D. Matsumoto & H.C. Hwang (Eds.), *Handbook of culture and psychology* (2nd ed.). Oxford University Press.

Best, K.P., & others (2021). Maternal late-pregnancy serum unmetabolized folic acid concentrations are not associated with infant allergic disease: A prospective cohort study. *The Journal of Nutrition, 151,* 1553-1560.

Betts, K.S., Williams, G.M., Najman, J.M., & Alati, R. (2014). Maternal depressive, anxious, and stress symptoms during pregnancy predict internalizing problems in adolescence. *Depression and Anxiety, 31,* 9-18.

Beyens, I., Keijsers, L., & Coyne, S.M. (2022). Social media, parenting, and well-being. *Current Opinion in Psychology, 47,* 101350.

Bialystok, E. (2018). Bilingualism and executive function: What's the connection? In D. Miller, F. Bayram, J. Rothman, & L. Serratrice (Eds.), *Bilingual cognition and language: The state of the science across its subfields.* John Benjamins.

Bian, L., & others (2017). Gender stereotypes about intellectual ability emerge early and influence children's interests. *Science, 355,* 389-391.

Bick, J., & Nelson, C.A. (2017). Early experience and brain development. *Wiley Interdisciplinary Review of Cognitive Science, 8*(1-2), 10.1002/wcs.1387.

Biederman, J., & others (2020). Is paternal smoking at conception a risk for ADHD? A controlled study in youth with and without ADHD. *Journal of Attention Disorders, 11,* 1493-1496.

Bierman, K.L., & others (2019). *The Fast Track program for children at risk: Preventing antisocial behavior.* Guilford Press.

Biffi, A., & others (2020). Use of antidepressants during pregnancy and neonatal outcomes: An umbrella review of meta-analyses of observational studies. *Journal of Psychiatric Research, 124,* 99–108.

Bigler, E.D. (2021). Charting brain development in graphs, diagrams, and figures from childhood, adolescence, to early adulthood: Neuroimaging implications for neuropsychology. *Journal of Pediatric Neuropsychology, 7,* 1–28.

Bilgin, A., & Wolke, D. (2020). Parental use of "cry it out" in infants: No adverse effects on attachment and behavioral development at 18 months. *Journal of Child Psychology and Psychiatry, 61,* 1184–1193.

Bina, R. (2020). Predictors of postpartum depression service use: A theory-informed, integrative systematic review. *Women and Birth, 33*(1), e24–e32.

Bindler, R.C., & others (2017). *Clinical manual for maternity and pediatric nursing* (5th ed.). Pearson.

Birch, S.A., & others (2017). Perspectives on perspective taking: How children think about the minds of others. *Advances in Child Development and Behavior, 52,* 185–226.

Birkeland, M.S., Melkevick, O., Holsen, I., & Wold, B. (2012). Trajectories of global self-esteem development during adolescence. *Journal of Adolescence, 35,* 43–54.

Birle, C., & others (2021). Cognitive function: Holarchy or holacracy? *Neurological Science, 42,* 89–99.

Bjorkenstam, C., Kosidou, K., & Bjorkenstam, E. (2017). Childhood adversity and risk of suicide: Cohort study of 548,721 adolescents and young adults in Sweden. *BMJ, 357,* 1334.

Bjorklund, D. (2022). *Children's thinking: Cognitive development and individual differences* (7th ed.). Sage.

Bjorklund, D.F. (2018). A metatheory for cognitive development (or "Piaget is dead" revisited). *Child Development, 89,* 2288–2302.

Bjorklund, D.F. (2020). *Child development in evolutionary perspective.* Cambridge University Press.

Bjorklund, D.F. (2022). Children's evolved learning abilities and their implications for education. *Educational Psychology Review, 34,* 2243–2273.

Bjorklund, D.F., & Causey, K.B. (2017). *Children's thinking: Cognitive development and individual differences* (6th ed.). Sage.

Björkqvist, K. (2018). Gender differences in aggression. *Current Opinion in Psychology, 19,* 39–42.

Black, J.J., & Rofey, D.L. (2018). An overview of common psychiatric problems among adolescent and young adult females: Focus on mood and anxiety. *Best Practices in Research and Clinical Obstetrics and Gynecology, 48,* 165–173.

Black, M.M., & Hurley, K.M. (2007). Helping children develop healthy eating habits. In R.E. Tremblay, R.G. Barr, R. Peters, & M. Boivin (Eds.), *Encyclopedia of early childhood development* (Rev. Ed.). Retrieved March 11, 2008, from http://www.child-encyclopedia.com/pdf/expert/child-nutrition/according-experts/helping-children-develop-healthy-eating-habits

Black, M.M., & others (2017). Early childhood development coming of age: Science through the life course. *Lancet, 389,* 77–90.

Black, M.M., & others (2021). Toddler obesity prevention: A two-generation randomized attention-controlled trial. *Maternal & Child Nutrition, 17*(1), e13075.

Blackowicz, M.J., & others (2017). The impact of low-level lead toxicity on school performance among Hispanic subgroups in the Chicago public schools. *International Journal of Environmental Research and Public Health, 13*(8), 774.

Blackwell, L.S., & Dweck, C.S. (2008). *The motivational impact of a computer-based program that teaches how the brain changes with learning.* Unpublished manuscript, Department of Psychology, Stanford University, Palo Alto, CA.

Blackwell, L.S., Trzesniewski, K.H., & Dweck, C.S. (2007). Implicit theories of intelligence predict achievement across an adolescent transition: A longitudinal study and an intervention. *Child Development, 78,* 246–263.

Blaga, O.M., & others (2009). Structure and continuity of intellectual development in early childhood. *Intelligence, 37,* 106–113.

Blair, C. (2016). The development of executive functions and self-regulation: A bidirectional psychobiological model. In K.D. Vohs & R. Baumeister (Eds.), *Handbook of self-regulation* (3rd ed.). Guilford Press.

Blair, C. (2017). Educating executive function. *Wiley Interdisciplinary Reviews. Cognitive Science. 8*(1–2), 10.1002/wcs.1403

Blair, C., & others (2015). Multiple aspects of self-regulation uniquely predict mathematics but not letter-word knowledge in the early elementary grades. *Developmental Psychology, 5,* 459–472.

Blair, C., & Raver, C.C. (2014). Closing the achievement gap through modification and neuroendocrine function: Results from a cluster randomized controlled trial of an innovative approach for the education of children in kindergarten. *PLoS One, 9*(11), e112393.

Blair, C., Raver, C.C., & Finegood, E.D. (2016). Self-regulation and developmental psychopathology: Experiential canalization of brain and behavior. In D. Cicchetti (Ed.), *Developmental psychopathology* (3rd ed.). Wiley.

Blake, J.S. (2017). *Nutrition and you* (4th ed.). Pearson.

Blake, M.J., Trinder, J.A., & Allen, N.B. (2018). Mechanisms underlying the association between insomnia, anxiety, and depression in adolescence: Implications for behavioral sleep interventions. *Clinical Psychology Review, 63,* 25–40.

Blakemore, J.E.O., Berenbaum, S.A., & Liben, L.S. (2009). *Gender development.* Psychology Press.

Blanche, S. (2020). Mini review: Prevention of mother–child transmission of HIV: 25 years of continuous progress toward the eradication of pediatric AIDS? *Virulence, 11*(1), 14–22.

Blanck-Lubarsch M., & others (2020). Children with fetal alcohol syndrome (FAS): 3D-analysis of palatal depth and 3D-metric facial length. *International Journal of Environmental Research and Public Health, 17*(1), 95.

Blanc-Petitjean, P., & others (2020). Evaluation of the implementation of a protocol for the restrictive use of oxytocin during spontaneous labor. *Journal of Gynecology, Obstetrics and Human Reproduction, 49*(2), 101664.

Blanton, S.H. (2021). Linkage analysis. In W.K. Scott & M.D. Ritchie (Eds.), *Genetic analysis of complex diseases* (3rd ed.). Wiley.

Blau, D.M. (2021). The effects of universal preschool on child and adult outcomes: A review of recent evidence from Europe with implications for the United States. *Early Childhood Research Quarterly, 55,* 52–63.

Blencowe, H., & others (2019). National, regional, and worldwide estimates of low birthweight in 2015, with trends from 2000: A systematic analysis. *The Lancet Global Health, 7*(7), e849–e860.

Blok, E., & others (2023). Cognitive performance in children and adolescents with psychopathology traits: A cross-sectional multicohort study in the general population. *Development and Psychopathology, 35,* 926–940.

Blood, J.D., & others (2015). The variable heart: High frequency and very low frequency correlates of depressive symptoms in children and adolescents. *Journal of Affective Disorders, 186,* 119–126.

Blotière, P.-O., Damase-Michel, C., Weill, A., & Maura, L. (2021). Dispensing of potentially harmful prescription drugs in 1.8 million pregnant women in France: A nationwide study based on two risk classification systems. *Drug Safety, 44,* 1323–1339.

Blum, J.W., Beaudoin, C.M., & Caton-Lemos, L. (2005). Physical activity patterns and maternal well-being in postpartum women. *Maternal and Child Health Journal, 8,* 163–169.

Blumberg, F.C., & others (2019). Digital games as a context for children's cognitive development: Research recommendations and policy considerations. *SRCD Social Policy Report, 32*(1), 1–33.

Boardman, J.P., & Fletcher-Watson, S. (2017). What can eye-tracking tell us? *Archives of Disease in Childhood, 102*(4), 301–302.

Bock, T., Narváez, D., Singh, R., & Tarsha, M.S. (2020). Guiding children for virtue. In T. Tsyrlina-Spady & P. Renn (Eds.), *Nurture, care, respect, and trust: Transformative pedagogy inspired by Janusz Korczak.* Myers Education Press.

Bodrova, E., & Leong, D.J. (2017). The Vygotskian and post-Vygotskian approach: Focusing on "the future child." In L.E. Cohen & S. Waite-Stupiansky (Eds.), *Theories of early childhood education.* Routledge.

Bodrova, E., & Leong, D.J. (2018). Tools of the Mind: A Vygotskian early childhood curriculum. In M. Fleer & B. van Oers (Eds.), *International handbook of early childhood education* (pp. 1095-1111). Springer.

Boerger, M. (2020, December 18). Academic Advising's award-winning services advance student success. *UTSA Today*. Retrieved April 27, 2022, from https://www.utsa.edu/today/2020/12/story /academic-advising-awards.html

Boerma, T., & others (2018). Global epidemiology of use of and disparities in Caesarean sections. *The Lancet, 392*(10155), 1341-1348.

Boghossian, N.S., & others (2018). Morbidity and mortality in small for gestational age infants at 22 to 29 weeks' gestation. *Pediatrics, 141*(2), e20172533.

Bohr, Y., & others (2018). Evaluating caregiver sensitivity to infants: Measures matter. *Infancy, 23*(5), 730-747.

Boller, K., & Harding, J.F. (2020). Child care: Policy, characteristics, and associations with children's development. In J.B. Benson (Ed.), *Encyclopedia of infant and early childhood development* (2nd ed.). Elsevier.

Bollig, K.J., Mainigi, M., Senapati, S., Lin, A.E., Levitsky, L.L., & Bamba, V. (2023). Turner syndrome: Fertility counselling in childhood and through the reproductive lifespan. *Current Opinion in Endocrinology, Diabetes and Obesity, 30*(1), 16-26.

Bolton, S., & Hattie, J. (2017). Cognitive and brain development: Executive function, Piaget, and the prefrontal cortex. *Archives of Psychology, 1*(3).

Bono, G., & others. (2019). Gratitude's role in adolescent antisocial and prosocial behavior: A 4-year longitudinal investigation. *Journal of Positive Psychology, 14*, 230-243.

Booker, J.A., Fivush, R., & Graci, M.E. (2022). Narrative identity informs psychological adjustment: Considering three themes captured across five time points and two event valences. *Journal of Personality, 90*, 324-342.

Booth, J.M., & Shaw, D.S. (2020). Relations among perceptions of neighborhood cohesion and control and parental monitoring across adolescence. *Journal of Youth and Adolescence, 49*(1), 74-86.

Booth-LaForce, C., & Groh, A.M. (2018). Parent-child attachment and peer relations. In W.M. Bukowski, B. Laursen, & K.H. Rubin (Eds.), *Handbook of peer interactions, relationships, and groups* (pp. 349-370). Guilford Press.

Border, R., & others (2019). No support for historical candidate gene or candidate gene-by-interaction hypotheses for major depression across multiple large samples. *American Journal of Psychiatry, 176*(5), 376-387.

Bordoni, L., & others (2017). Obesity-related genetic polymorphisms and adiposity indices in a young Italian population. *IUBMB Life, 69*, 98-105.

Borle, K., Morris, E., Inglis, A., & Austin, J. (2018). Risk communication in genetic counseling: Exploring uptake and perception of recurrence numbers, and their impact on patient outcomes. *Clinical Genetics, 94*, 239-245.

Bornstein, M.H. (2015). Emergence and early development of color vision and color perception. In A.J. Elliott & others (Eds.), *Handbook of color psychology* (pp. 149-179). Cambridge University Press.

Bornstein, M.H. (Ed.) (2018). *SAGE encyclopedia of lifespan human development*. Sage.

Bornstein, M.H., Arterberry, M., & Mash, C. (2015). Perceptual development. In M.H. Bornstein & M.E. Lamb (Eds.), *Developmental science* (7th ed.). Psychology Press.

Bornstein, M.H., & others (2017). Neurobiology of culturally common maternal responses to infant cry. *Proceedings of the National Academy of Sciences, 114*(45), E9465-E9473.

Bos, P.A. (2017). The endocrinology of human caregiving and its intergenerational transmission. *Development and Psychopathology, 29*(3), 971-999.

Bőthe, B., & others (2019). Revisiting the role of impulsivity and compulsivity in problematic sexual behaviors. *The Journal of Sex Research, 56*(2), 166-179.

Bouchard, G., Plamondon, A., & Lachance-Grzela, M. (2019). Parental intervention style and adult sibling conflicts: The mediating role of involvement in sibling bullying. *Journal of Social and Personal Relationships, 36*(8), 2585-2602.

Bouchard, T.J. (1995, August). *Heritability of intelligence*. Paper presented at the meeting of the American Psychological Association, New York.

Bouchard, T.J. (2008). Genes and human psychological traits. In P. Carruthers, S. Laurence, & S. Stich (Eds.), *The innate mind: Foundations for the future* (Vol. 3). Oxford University Press.

Boucher, J. (2017). *Autism Spectrum Disorder: Characteristics, causes and practical issues*. Sage.

Boucoiran, I., & Castillo, E. (2018). Rubella in pregnancy. *Journal of Obstetrics and Gynaecology Canada, 40*(12), 1646-1656.

Bould, H., & others (2019). Rising suicide rates among adolescents in England and Wales. *The Lancet, 394*, 116-117.

Bourn, D. (2022). *Diagnostic genetic testing: Core concepts and the wider context for human DNA analysis*. Springer.

Bouziane, C., & others (2018). ADHD and maturation of brain white matter: A DTI study in medication naive children and adults. *NeuroImage: Clinical, 17*, 53-59.

Bovbjerg, M.L., Cheyney, M., & Everson, C. (2016). Maternal and newborn outcomes following waterbirth: The Midwives Alliance of North America Statistics Project, 2004 to 2009 cohort. *Journal of Midwifery and Women's Health, 61*, 11-20.

Bowden, A.B., Shand, R., Levin, H.M., Muroga, A., & Wang, A. (2020). An economic evaluation of the costs and benefits of providing comprehensive supports to students in elementary school. *Prevention Science, 21*, 1126-1135.

Bower, T.G.R. (1966). Slant perception and shape constancy in infants. *Science, 151*, 832-834.

Bower-Brown, S., Zadeh, S., & Jadva, V. (2023). Binary-trans, non-binary and gender-questioning adolescents' experiences in UK schools. *Journal of LGBT Youth, 20*, 74-92.

Bowers, M.E., & Yehuda, R. (2020). Intergenerational transmission of stress vulnerability and resilience. In A. Chen (Ed.), *Stress resilience* (pp. 257-267). Academic Press.

Bowersock, A., & Lin, C.Y. (2020). Caring for and counseling the peripartum runner. In M. Harrast (Ed.), *Clinical care of the runner* (pp. 259-269). Elsevier.

Bowlby, J. (1969). *Attachment and loss* (Vol. 1). Hogarth Press.

Bowlby, J. (1989). *Secure and insecure attachment*. Basic Books.

Boyce, W.T., Levitt, P., Martinez, F.D., McEwen, B.S., & Shonkoff, J.P. (2021). Genes, environments, and time: The biology of adversity and resilience. *Pediatrics, 147*(2), e20201651.

Boyer, T.W., Harding, S.M., & Bertenthal, B.I. (2017). Infants' motor simulation of observed actions is modulated by the visibility of the actor's body. *Cognition, 164*, 107-115.

Boyer, T.W., Harding, S.M., & Bertenthal, B.I. (2020). The temporal dynamics of joint attention: Effects of others' gaze cues and manual actions. *Cognition, 197*, 104151.

Braccio, S., Sharland, M., & Ladhani, S.N. (2016). Prevention and treatment of mother-to-child syphilis. *Current Opinion on Infectious Diseases, 29*, 268-274.

Bradley, R.H. (2019). Home life and health among Native American, African American, and Latino adolescents. *Health Psychology, 38*(8), 738-747.

Brady, S.E., & Stevens, M.C. (2019). Is immigration a culture? A qualitative approach to exploring immigrant student experiences within the United States. *Translational Issues in Psychological Science, 5*(1), 17-28.

Brainerd, C.J., & Reyna, V.E. (2014). Dual processes in memory development: Fuzzy-trace theory. In P. Bauer & R. Fivush (Eds.), *Wiley-Blackwell handbook of children's memory*. Wiley.

Bramante, C.T., Spiller, P., & Landa, M. (2018). Fish consumption during pregnancy: An opportunity, not a risk. *JAMA Pediatrics, 172*(9), 801-802.

Brand, R.J., Escobar, K., & Patrick, A.M. (2020). Coincidence or cascade? The temporal relation between locomotor behaviors and the emergence of stranger anxiety. *Infant Behavior and Development, 58*, 101423.

Brandes, C.M., & others (2021). Towards construct validity of relational aggression. *Multivariate Behavioral Research, 56*, 161-162.

Brandlistuen, R.E., & others (2021). Gender gaps in preschool age: A study of behavior, neurodevelopment, and pre-academic skills. *Scandinavian Journal of Public Health, 49*, 503-510.

Brandone, A.C., & Klimek, B. (2018). The developing theory of mental state control: Changes in beliefs about the controllability of emotional experience from elementary school through adulthood. *Journal of Cognition and Development, 19*, 509-531.

Brandt, J.S., & others (2019). Advanced paternal age, infertility, and reproductive risks: A review of the literature. *Prenatal Diagnosis, 39*(2), 81–87.

Branje, S. (2022). Adolescent identity development in context. *Current Opinion in Psychology, 45,* 101286.

Brannon, L. (2017). *Gender.* Routledge.

Bratsberg, B., & Rogeberg, O. (2018). Flynn effect and its reversal are both environmentally caused. *Proceedings of the National Academy of Sciences, 115,* 6674–6678.

Braun, S.S., & Davidson, A.J. (2017). Gender (non)conformity in middle childhood: A mixed methods approach to understanding gender-typed behavior, friendship, and peer preference. *Sex Roles, 77,* 16–29.

Braver, S.L., & Lamb, M.E. (2013). Marital dissolution. In G.W. Peterson & K.R. Bush (Eds.), *Handbook of marriage and the family* (3rd ed.). Springer.

Bredekamp, S. (2017). *Effective practices in early childhood education* (3rd ed.). Pearson.

Bredekamp, S. (2020). *Effective practices in early childhood education* (4th ed.). Pearson.

Breland, A., McCubbin, A., & Ashford, K. (2019). Electronic nicotine delivery systems and pregnancy: Recent research on perceptions, cessation, and toxicant delivery. *Birth Defects Research, 111*(17), 1284–1293.

Bremner, A.J., & Spence, C. (2017). The development of tactile stimulation. *Advances in Child Development and Behavior, 52,* 227–268.

Bremner, J.G., & others (2017). Limits of object persistence: Young infants perceive continuity of vertical and horizontal trajectories but not 45-degree oblique trajectories. *Infancy, 22,* 303–322.

Bremner, J.G., Slater, A.M., & Johnson, S.P. (2015). Perception of object persistence: The origins of object permanence in infancy. *Child Development Perspectives, 9,* 7–13.

Bremner, J.G., Slater, A.M., Mason, U.C., Spring, J., & Johnson, S.P. (2016). Perception of occlusion by young infants: Must the occlusion event be congruent with the occluder? *Infant Behavior and Development, 44,* 240–248.

Breton, C.V., & others (2021). Exploring the evidence for epigenetic regulation of environmental influences on child health across generations. *Communications Biology, 4,* 769.

Breton, É., Juster, R.-P., & Booji, L. (2023). Gender and sex in eating disorders: A narrative review of the current state of knowledge, research gaps, and recommendations. *Brain and Behavior, 13*(4), e2871.

Brito, N.H. (2017). Influence of the home linguistic environment on early language development. *Policy Insights from the Behavioral and Brain Sciences, 4,* 155–162.

Broadney, M.M., & others (2018). Effects of interrupting sedentary behavior with short bouts of moderate physical activity on glucose tolerance in children with overweight and obesity: A randomized crossover trial. *Diabetes Care, 41,* 2220–2228.

Broccia, M., & others (2023). Heavy prenatal alcohol exposure and overall morbidities: A Danish nationwide cohort study from 1996 to 2018. *Lancet Public Health, 8,* e36–e46.

Brock, R.L., & Kochanska, G. (2016). Interparental conflict, children's security with parents, and long-term risk of internalizing problems: A longitudinal study from ages 2 to 10. *Development and Psychopathology, 28,* 45–54.

Brodsky, J.L., Viner-Brown, S., & Handler, A.S. (2009). Changes in maternal cigarette smoking among pregnant WIC participants in Rhode Island. *Maternal and Child Health Journal, 13,* 822–831.

Brody, G.H., & others (2017). Protective prevention effects on the association of poverty with brain development. *JAMA Pediatrics, 17,* 46–52.

Brodzinsky, D.M., & Goldberg, A.E. (2016). Contact with birth family in adoptive families headed by lesbian, gay male, and heterosexual parents. *Children and Youth Services Review, 62,* 9–17.

Brodzinsky, D.M., & Pinderhughes, E. (2002). Parenting and child development in adoptive families. In M.H. Bornstein (Ed.), *Handbook of parenting* (Vol. I). Erlbaum.

Broekhof, E., & others (2015). The understanding of intentions, desires, and beliefs in young children with autism spectrum disorder. *Journal of Autism and Developmental Disorders, 45,* 2035–2045.

Bronfenbrenner, U., & Morris, P.A. (2006). The ecology of developmental processes. In W. Damon & R. Lerner (Eds.), *Handbook of child psychology* (6th ed.). Wiley.

Bronstein, P. (2006). The family environment: Where gender role socialization begins. In J. Worell & C.D. Goodheart (Eds.), *Handbook of girls' and women's psychological health.* Oxford University Press.

Brooks, P.J., Flynn, R.M., & Ober, T.M. (2018). Sustained attention in infancy impacts vocabulary acquisition in low-income toddlers. *Proceedings of the 42nd Annual Boston University Conference on Language Development.* Cascadilla Press.

Brooks, R., & Meltzoff, A.N. (2005). The development of gaze in relation to language. *Developmental Science, 8,* 535–543.

Brooks, R., & Meltzoff, A.N. (2008). Infant gaze following and pointing predict accelerated vocabulary growth through two years of age: A longitudinal, growth curve modeling study. *Journal of Child Language, 35,* 207–220.

Broomell, A.P., & Bell, M.A. (2022). Longitudinal development of executive function from infancy to late childhood. *Cognitive Development, 63*(3), 101229.

Brown, B.B., & Lohr, M.J. (1987). Peer-group affiliation and adolescent self-esteem: An integration of ego-identity and symbolic-interaction theories. *Journal of Personality and Social Psychology, 52,* 47–55.

Brown, D.A. (2022). Memory Development and the Forensic Context. In M. Courage & N. Cowan (Eds.), *The Development of Memory in Infancy and Childhood* (pp. 337–371). Psychology Press.

Brown, E.C., & others (2016). A systematized review of primary school whole class child obesity interventions: Effectiveness, characteristics, and strategies. *BioMed Research International, 2016,* 4902714.

Brown, G.L., & Cox, M.J. (2020). Pleasure in parenting and father-child attachment security. *Attachment & Human Development, 22*(1), 51–65.

Brown, R. (1958). *Words and things.* Free Press.

Brown, R. (1973). *A first language: The early stages.* Harvard University Press.

Brown, S.M., Aljefri, K., Waas, R., & Hampton, P. (2019). Systematic medications used in treatment of common dermatological conditions: Safety profile with respect to pregnancy, breast feeding, and content in seminal fluid. *Journal of Dermatological Treatment, 30*(1), 2–18.

Brown, T.H. (2020). Childhood hearing impairment. *Paediatrics and Child Health, 30*(1), 6–13.

Browne, K., & others (2019). The joint effects of obesity and pregestational diabetes on the risk of stillbirth. *The Journal of Maternal-Fetal & Neonatal Medicine, 31*(3), 332–338.

Brownell, C.A., Lemerise, E.A., Pelphrey, K.A., & Roisman, G.I. (2015). Measuring socioemotional behavior and development. In R.M. Lerner (Ed.), *Handbook of child psychology and developmental science* (7th ed.). Wiley.

Brownell, C.A., Ramani, G.B., & Zerwas, S. (2006). Becoming a social partner with peers: Cooperation and social understanding in one- and two-year-olds. *Child Development, 77,* 803–821.

Bruchmiller, K., Margraf, J., & Schneider, S. (2012). Is ADHD diagnosed in accord with diagnostic criteria? Overdiagnosis and influence of client gender on diagnosis. *Journal of Consulting and Clinical Psychology, 80,* 128–138.

Bruck, M., & Ceci, S.J. (1999). The suggestibility of children's memory. *Annual Review of Psychology, 50,* 419–439.

Bruckner, S., & Kammer, T. (2017). Both anodal and cathodal transcranial direct current stimulation improves semantic processing. *Neuroscience, 343,* 269–275.

Bruhn de Garavito, J. (2021a). Phonology: Sound patterns and contrasts. In J. Bruhn de Garavito & J.W. Schieter (Eds.), *Introducing linguistics.* Cambridge University Press.

Bruhn de Garavito, J. (2021b). Morphology: Word structure. In J. Bruhn de Garavito & J.W. Schieter (Eds.), *Introducing linguistics.* Cambridge University Press.

Bruhn de Garavito, J. (2021c). Syntax: Phrase and sentence structure. In J. Bruhn de Garavito & J.W. Schieter (Eds.), *Introducing linguistics.* Cambridge University Press.

Bruhn de Garavito, J., & Schwieter, J.W. (2021). *Introducing linguistics.* Cambridge University Press.

Brumariu, L.E., & others (2016). Attachment and temperament revisited: Infant distress, attachment disorganisation and the serotonin transporter polymorphism. *Journal of Reproductive and Infant Psychology, 34*(1), 77–89.

Brummelman, E., Crocker, J., & Bushman, B.J. (2016). The praise paradox: When and why praise backfires in children with low self-esteem. *Child Development, 10,* 111–115.

Brummelman, E., Thomaes, S., & Sedikides, C. (2016). Separating narcissism from self-esteem. *Current Directions in Psychological Science, 25*(1), 8-13.

Brummelte, S., & Galea, L.A. (2016). Postpartum depression: Etiology, treatment, and consequences for maternal care. *Hormones and Behavior, 77,* 153-166.

Brunborg, G.S., Andreas, J.B., & Kvaavik, E. (2017). Social media use and episodic heavy drinking among adolescents. *Psychological Reports, 120,* 475-490.

Brunstein-Klomek, A., & others (2019). Bi-directional longitudinal associations between different types of bullying victimization, suicide ideation/attempts, and depression among a large sample of European adolescents. *Journal of Child Psychology and Psychiatry, 60*(2), 209-215.

Bryant, L., Morrongiello, B.A. & Cox, A. (2023). Parents' home-safety practices to prevent injuries during infancy: From sitting to walking independently. *Journal of Child & Family Studies, 32,* 1102-1112.

Bucaille, A., & others (2022). Neuropsychological profile of intellectually gifted children: A systematic review. *Journal of the International Neuropsychological Society, 28*(4), 424-440.

Bucci, R., & Staff, J. (2020). Pubertal timing and adolescent delinquency. *Criminology, 58,* 537-567.

Buchmann, S., & others (2022). Remission, treatment failure, and relapse in pediatric ALL: An international consensus of the Ponte-di-Legno Consortium. *Blood, The Journal of the American Society of Hematology, 139*(12), 1785-1793.

Buckingham-Howes, S., Berger, S.S., Scaletti, L.A., & Black, M.M. (2013). Systematic review of prenatal cocaine exposure and adolescent development. *Pediatrics, 131,* e1917-e1936.

Buckley, J.P., Hamra, G.B., & Braun, J.M. (2019). Statistical approaches for investigating periods of susceptibility in children's environmental health research. *Current Environmental Health Reports, 6*(1), 1-7.

Buckner, J.C., Mezzacappa, E., & Beardslee, W.R. (2009). Self-regulation and its relations to adaptive functioning in low-income youths. *American Journal of Orthopsychiatry, 79,* 19-30.

Budani, M.C., & Tiboni, G.M. (2017). Ovotoxicity of cigarette smoke: A systematic review of the literature. *Reproductive Toxicology, 72,* 164-181.

Buehler, C. (2020). Family processes and children's and adolescents' well-being. *Journal of Marriage and Family, 82*(1), 145-174.

Buhrmester, D. (1998). Need fulfillment, interpersonal competence, and the developmental contexts of early adolescent friendship. In W.M. Bukowski & A.F. Newcomb (Eds.), *The company they keep: Friendship in childhood and adolescence.* Cambridge University Press.

Buhrmester, D. (2001, April). *Does age at which romantic involvement starts matter?* Paper presented at the meeting of the Society for Research in Child Development, Minneapolis.

Bukasa, A., & others (2018). Rubella infection in pregnancy and congenital rubella in United Kingdom, 2003 to 2016. *Euro Surveillance, 23*(19), 17-00381.

Bukowski, R., & others (2008, January). *Folic acid and preterm birth.* Paper presented at the meeting of the Society for Maternal-Fetal Medicine, Dallas.

Bukowski, W., Laursen, B., & Rubin, K. (2018). *Handbook of peer relationships, interactions, and groups* (2nd ed.). Guilford Press.

Bulbena-Cabre, A., Nia, A.B., & Perez-Rodriguez, M.M. (2018). Current knowledge on gene-environment interactions in personality disorders: An update. *Current Psychiatry Reports, 20,* 74.

Bulgarelli, D., Testa, S., & Molina, P. (2022). Theory of mind development in Italian children with specific language impairment and autism spectrum disorder: delay, deficit, or neither? *Journal of Autism and Developmental Disorders, 52*(12), 5356-5366.

Bullard, J. (2017). *Creating environments for learning: Birth to age eight* (3rd ed.). Pearson.

Bumpus, M.F., Crouter, A.C., & McHale, M. (2001). Parental autonomy granting during adolescence: Exploring gender differences in context. *Developmental Psychology, 37,* 163-173.

Burdelski, M. (2019). Emotion and affect in language socialization. In S. Pritzker & others (Eds.), *The Routledge handbook of language and emotion* (pp. 28-46). Routledge.

Bureau of Labor Statistics, U.S. Department of Labor (2021). *Labor force participation declines for mothers and fathers in 2020.* Available https://www.bls.gov/opub/ted/2021/labor-force-participation-declines-for-mothers-and-fathers-in-2020.htm

Burge, T. (2018). Do infants and nonhuman animals attribute mental states? *Psychological Review, 125,* 409-434.

Burgette, J.M., & others (2017). Impact of Early Head Start in North Carolina on dental care use among children younger than 3 years. *American Journal of Public Health, 107,* 614-620.

Burnette, C.E., & others (2019). The Family Resilience Inventory: A culturally grounded measure of current and family-of-origin protective processes in Native American families. *Family Process, 59*(2), 695-708.

Burnette, D. (2021, April 14). How COVID-19 will make fixing America's worst-performing schools harder. *Education Week.*

Burns, E.C., Martin, A.J., & Collie, R.J. (2019). Understanding the role of personal best (PB) goal setting in students' declining engagement: A latent growth model. *Journal of Educational Psychology, 111*(4), 557-572.

Burr, W.H., & others (2023). Injury prevention anticipatory guidance by patient age group. *Academic Pediatrics, 23,* 610-615.

Burrow-Sánchez, J.J., & Ratcliff, B.R. (2021). Adolescent risk and protective factors for the use of electronic cigarettes. *Journal of Prevention and Health Promotion, 2,* 100-134.

Burt, K.B., & Paysnick, A.A. (2012). Resilience in the transition to adulthood. *Development and Psychopathology, 24,* 493-505.

Buss, A.T., Ross-Sheehy, S., & Reynolds, G.D. (2018). Visual working memory in early development: A developmental cognitive neuroscience perspective. *Journal of Neurophysiology, 120,* 1472-1483.

Buss, D.M. (2020). Evolutionary psychology is a scientific revolution. *Evolutionary Behavioral Sciences, 14,* 316-323.

Byard, R.W. (2018). The autopsy and pathology of Sudden Infant Death Syndrome. In *SIDS Sudden infant and early childhood death: The past, the present and the future.* University of Adelaide Press.

Byard, R.W. (2021). SIDS or suffocation—The problem continues. *Acta Pediatrica, 110*(1), 364-364.

Byrne, J.L., & others (2018). A brief eHealth tool delivered in primary care to help parents prevent childhood obesity: A randomized controlled trial. *Pediatric Obesity, 13*(11), 659-667.

Byrou, S., & others (2018). Fast temperature-gradient COLD PCR for the enrichment of the paternally inherited SNPs in cell free fetal DNA: An application to non-invasive prenatal diagnosis of β-thalassaemia. *PLos ONE, 13*(7), e0200348.

Byrska-Bishop, M., & others (2022). High-coverage whole-genome sequencing of the expanded 1000 Genomes Project cohort including 602 trios. *Cell, 185*(18), 3426-3440.

C

Cabaco, A.S., & others (2021). Psychopathological risk factors associated with body image, body dissatisfaction, and weight-loss dieting in school-age adolescents. *Children, 8*(2), 105.

Cabrera, N.J., & Roggman, L. (2017). Father play: Is it special? *Infant Mental Health Journal, 38,* 706-708.

Cabrero, F.R., & De Jesus, O. (2021). Dysgraphia. *StatPearls.*

Cai, M., & others (2013). Adolescent-parent attachment as a mediator of relationships between parenting and adolescent social behavior and wellbeing in China. *International Journal of Psychology, 48,* 1185-1190.

Cai, Y., & others (2021). The neurodevelopmental role of dopaminergic signaling in neurological disorders. *Neuroscience Letters, 741,* 135540.

Cain, M.S., Leonard, J.A., Gabriel, J.D., & Finn, A.S. (2016). Media multitasking in adolescence. *Psychonomic Bulletin and Review, 23,* 1932-1941.

Caino, S., & others (2010). Short-term growth in head circumference and its relationship with supine length in healthy infants. *Annals of Human Biology, 37,* 108-116.

Cairncross, M., & Miller, C.J. (2020). The effectiveness of mindfulness-based therapies for ADHD: A meta-analytic review. *Journal of Attention Disorders, 24,* 627-643.

Calandri, E., Cattelino, E., & Graziano, F. (2023). Is playing video games during COVID-19 lockdown related to adolescent well-being? The role of emotional self-efficacy and positive coping. *European Journal of Developmental Psychology, 20*, 533–549.

Calkins, S.D., & Perry, N.B. (2016). The development of emotion regulation. In D. Cicchetti (Ed.), *Developmental psychopathology* (3rd ed.). Wiley.

Callaghan, M.N., & Reich, S.M. (2018). Are educational preschool apps designed to teach? An analysis of the app market. *Learning, Media and Technology, 43*(3), 280–293.

Callaghan, T., & Corbit, J. (2018). Early prosocial development across cultures. *Current Opinion in Psychology, 20*, 102–106.

Callueng, C.M., Emam, M., & Oakland, T. (2020). Temperament styles from Egypt and the United States: A cross-cultural examination. *Community Mental Health, 56*, 581–585.

Calvert, S.L. (2015). Children and digital media. In R.M. Lerner (Ed.), *Handbook of child psychology and developmental science* (7th ed.). Wiley.

Cameron, C.A., & Mascarenas, A. (2020). Digital social media in adolescents' negotiating real virtual romantic relationships. In *The psychology and dynamics behind social media interactions* (pp. 83–106). IGI Global.

Camos, V., & Barrouillet, P. (2018). *Working memory in development*. Routledge.

Campbell, K.A., Wuthrich, A., & Norlin, C. (2020). We have all been working in our own little silos forever: Exploring a cross-sector response to child maltreatment. *Academic Pediatrics, 20*(1), 46–54.

Campbell, K.L., & others (2018). Factors in the home environment associated with toddler diet: An ecological momentary assessment study. *Public Health Nutrition, 21*, 1855–1864.

Campbell, L., Campbell, B., & Dickinson, D. (2004). *Teaching and learning through multiple intelligence* (3rd ed.). Allyn & Bacon.

Campione-Barr, N. (2020). Development of autonomy. In S. Hupp & others (Eds.), *The encyclopedia of child and adolescent development*. Wiley.

Campos, J.J. (2009). Unpublished review of J.W. Santrock's *Life-span development* (13th ed.). McGraw Hill.

Candilis-Huisman, D. (2019). The NBAS: Supporting the newborn and its family at birth. In G. Apter & others (Eds.), *Early interaction and developmental psychopathology* (pp. 181–193). Springer.

Cantal, A. (2019). Managing obesity in pediatrics: A role for occupational therapy. American Occupational Therapy Association. https://www.aota.org/-/media/Corporate/Files/Publications/CE-Articles/CE-Article-January-2019-Obesity-Pediatrics.pdf

Cantone, E., & others (2015). Interventions on bullying and cyberbullying in schools: A systematic review. *Clinical Practice and Epidemiology in Mental Health, 11*(Suppl. 1), S58–S76.

Cao, Z., Cini, E., Pellegrini, D., & Fragkos, K.C. (2023). The association between sexual orientation and eating disorders-related eating behaviours in adolescents: A systematic review and meta-analysis. *European Eating Disorders Review, 31*, 46–64.

Capistrant, B.D., & others (2020). Earner status, marital satisfaction, and division of childcare among Mexican American and Caucasian couples. *Smith College Studies in Social Work, 90*(3), 156–180.

Cappagli, G., & others (2019). Audio motor training improves mobility and spatial cognition in visually impaired children. *Scientific Reports, 9*, 3303.

Cardenas, S., & others (2021). Arithmetic processing in children with dyscalculia: An event-related potential study. *PeerJ, 9*, e10489.

Carlin, C., Davis, E.E., Krafft, C., & Tout, K. (2019). Parental preferences and patterns of child care use among low-income families: A Bayesian analysis. *Children and Youth Services Review, 99*, 172–185.

Carlin, R.E., & Moon, R.Y. (2017). Risk factors, protective factors, and current recommendations to reduce sudden infant death syndrome: A review. *JAMA Pediatrics, 17*, 175–180.

Carlo, G., & others (2018). Longitudinal relations among parenting styles, prosocial behaviors, and academic outcomes in U.S. Mexican adolescents. *Child Development, 89*(2), 577–592.

Carlson, S.M., Claxton, L.J., & Moses, L.J. (2015). The relation between executive function and theory of mind is more than skin deep. *Journal of Cognition and Development, 16*, 186–197.

Carlson, S.M., Davis, A.C., & Leach, J.G. (2005). Executive function and symbolic representation in preschool children. *Psychological Science, 16*, 609–616.

Carlson, S.M., & White, R.E. (2013). Executive function, pretend play, and imagination. In M. Taylor (Ed.), *The Oxford handbook of the development of imagination* (pp. 161–174). Oxford University Press.

Carmina, E., Stanczyk, F.Z., & Lobo, R.A. (2019). Evaluation of hormonal status. In J. Strauss & R. Barbieri (Eds.), *Yen and Jaffe's reproductive endocrinology* (8th ed., pp. 887–914). Elsevier.

Carnegie Council on Adolescent Development (1989). *Turning points: Preparing American youth for the twenty-first century.* Carnegie Foundation.

Carone, N., Bos, H.M.W., Shenkman, G., & Tasker, F. (2021) Editorial: LGBTQ parents and their children during the family life cycle. *Frontiers in Psychology, 12*, 643647.

Carone, N., & Lingiardi, V. (2022). Untangling caregiving role from parent gender in coparenting research: Insights from gay two-father families. *Frontiers in Psychology, 13*, 863050.

Carpena, R.X., & others (2020). The role of sleep duration and sleep problems during childhood in the development of ADHD in adolescence: Findings from a population-based cohort. *Journal of Attention Disorders, 24*, 590–600.

Carpendale, J.I.M., & Lewis, C. (2015). The development of social understanding. In R.M. Lerner (Ed.), *Handbook of child psychology and developmental science* (7th ed.). Wiley.

Carr, A., Duff, H., & Craddock, F. (2020). A systematic review of reviews of the outcome of severe neglect in underresourced childcare institutions. *Trauma, Violence, & Abuse, 21*, 484–497.

Carskadon, M.A., & others (2019). A pilot prospective study of sleep patterns and DNA methylation-characterized epigenetic aging in young adults. *BMC Research Notes, 12*(1), 583.

Carsley, S., & others (2018). Overweight and obesity in preschool aged children and risk of mental health service utilization. *International Journal of Obesity, 43*, 1325–1333.

Carson, V., & others (2015). Systematic review of sedentary behavior and cognitive development in early childhood. *Preventive Medicine, 78*, 15–22.

Cascio, E.U. (2023). Does universal preschool hit the target? Program access and preschool impacts. *Journal of Human Resources, 58*(1), 1–42.

CASEL (2017). *Collaborative for Academic, Social, and Emotional Learning.* Retrieved June 3, 2017, from www.casel.org

CASEL (2023). *Advancing social-emotional learning.* https://casel.org/

Casillas, M., Brown, P., & Levinson, S.C. (2020). Early language experience in a Tseltal Mayan village. *Child Development, 91*, 1819–1835.

Casper, D.M., Card, N.A., & Barlow, C. (2020). Relational aggression and victimization during adolescence: A meta-analytic review of unique associations with popularity, peer acceptance, rejection, and friendship characteristics. *Journal of Adolescence, 80*, 41–52.

Caspi, A., & others (2003). Influence of life stress on depression: Moderation by a polymorphism in the 5-HTT gene. *Science, 301*, 386–389.

Cassidy, A.R. (2016). Executive function and psychosocial adjustment in healthy children and adolescents: A latent variable modeling investigation. *Child Neuropsychology, 22*, 292–317.

Cassidy, M. (2021). *Biological evolution.* Cambridge University Press.

Castillo, M., & Weiselberg, E. (2017). Bulimia nervosa/purging disorder. *Current Problems in Pediatric and Adolescent Health Care, 47*, 85–94.

Causadias, J.M., & Umaña-Taylor, A.J. (2018). Reframing marginalization and youth development: Introduction to the special issue. *American Psychologist, 73*(6), 707.

Caye, A., Swanson, J.M., Coghill, D., & Rohde, L.A. (2019). Treatment strategies for ADHD: An evidence-based guide to select optimal treatment. *Molecular Psychiatry, 24*, 390–408.

Cazzato, V., & others (2016). The effects of body exposure on self-body image and esthetic appreciation in anorexia nervosa. *Experimental Brain Research, 234*, 695–709.

CCX Media Community News (2022, August 12). Cooper's Willie Howard becomes school's activities director. Retrieved January 27, 2023, from https://www.youtube.com/watch?v=B0_R4JywVAA

Ceci, S.J., Hritz, A., & Royer, C.E. (2016). Understanding suggestibility. In W. O'Donohue & M. Fanetti (Eds.), *A guide to evidence-based practice.* Springer.

Centers for Disease Control and Prevention (2020). *Autism spectrum disorders.*

Centers for Disease Control and Prevention (2021). *About underlying cause of death, 1999–2020.* Available https://wonder.cdc.gov/ucd-icd10.html

Centers for Disease Control and Prevention (2022a). *About child and teen BMI.*

Centers for Disease Control and Prevention (2022a). *Childhood obesity facts.* Available https://www.cdc.gov/obesity/data/childhood.html

Centers for Disease Control and Prevention (2022b). *HIV by group.* Available https://www.cdc.gov/hiv/group/index.html

Centers for Disease Control and Prevention (2022). *Breastfeeding, breastfeeding and special circumstances: Maternal or infant illnesses or conditions.* https://www.cdc.gov/breastfeeding/breastfeeding-special-circumstances/maternal-or-infant-illnesses/hiv.html

Centers for Disease Control and Prevention (2022b). *Vital signs: Asthma in children.* https://www.cdc.gov/vitalsigns/childhood-asthma/index.html. Accessed 8 April 2023.

Centers for Disease Control and Prevention (2023a). *Tips to help children maintain a healthy weight.* https://www.cdc.gov/healthyweight/children/index.html. Accessed 2 April 2023.

Centers for Disease Control and Prevention (2023b). *Data and statistics on ADHD.* https://www.cdc.gov/ncbddd/adhd/data.html. Accessed 11 April 2023.

Centers for Disease Control and Prevention (2023c). *Hearing loss in children.* https://www.cdc.gov/ncbddd/hearingloss/index.html. Accessed 12 April 2023.

Centers for Disease Control and Prevention (2023). *How much physical activity do children need?* Available https://www.cdc.gov/physicalactivity/basics/children/index.htm

Centers for Disease Control and Prevention (2023). *Premature birth.* Available https://www.cdc.gov/reproductivehealth/features/premature-birth/index.html

Centers for Disease Control and Prevention (2023). *Youth risk behavior survey 2011–2021.* Available https://www.cdc.gov/healthyyouth/data/yrbs/pdf/YRBS_Data-Summary-Trends_Report 2023_508.pdf

Centers for Disease Control and Prevention (2018b). *Child health.* https://www.cdc.gov/nchs/fastats/child-health.htm

Centers for Disease Control and Prevention (2018c). *Coping with disaster and traumatic events.* Atlanta, GA: U.S. Department of Health and Human Services.

Centers for Disease Control and Prevention (2018d). *Defining childhood obesity: BMI for children and teens.* Retrieved May 20, 2020, from https://www.cdc.gov/obesity/childhood/defining.html

Centers for Disease Control and Prevention (2019b). *HIV among youth/age/HIV by group.* Atlanta, GA: Author.

Centers for Disease Control and Prevention (2020). *Clinical growth charts.* Retrieved May 20, 2020, from http://www.cdc.gov/growthcharts/clinical_charts.htm

Cerrillo-Urbina, A.J., & others (2015). The effects of physical exercise in children with attention deficit hyperactivity disorder: A systematic review and meta-analysis of randomized controlled trials. *Child Care, Health, and Development, 41,* 779–788.

Chaku, N., Hoyt, L.T., & Barry, K. (2021). Executive functioning profiles in adolescence: Using person-centered approaches to understand heterogeneity. *Cognitive Development, 60,* 101119.

Chambers, G.M., & others (2020). Funding and public reporting strategies for reducing multiple pregnancy from fertility treatments. *Fertility and Sterility, 114,* 715–721.

Champagne, F.A. (2021). Dynamic epigenetic impact of the environment on the developing brain. In J.J. Lockman & C. Tamis-LeMonda (Eds.), *Cambridge handbook of infant development.* Cambridge University Press.

Chan, C.H., & others (2015). Sexual initiation and emotional/behavior problems in Taiwanese adolescents: A multivariate response profile analysis. *Archives of Sexual Behavior, 44,* 717–727.

Chang, Y.H.A., & Lane, D.M. (2018). It takes more than practice and experience to become a chess master: Evidence from a child prodigy and adult chess players. *Journal of Expertise, 1*(1), 6–34.

Chang, Y.K., Liu, S., Yu, H.H., & Lee, Y.H. (2012). Effect of acute exercise on executive function in children with attention deficit hyperactivity disorder. *Archives of Clinical Neuropsychology, 27,* 225–237.

Chansakul, T., & Young, G.S. (2017). Neuroimaging in pregnant women. *Seminars in Neurology, 37*(6), 712–723.

Chao, R.K. (1994). Beyond parental control and authoritarian parenting style: Understanding Chinese parenting through the cultural notion of training. *Child Development, 65,* 1111–1119.

Chao, R.K. (2007, March). *Research with Asian Americans. Looking back and moving forward.* Paper presented at the meeting of the Society for Research in Child Development, Boston.

Chaplin, T.M. (2015). Gender and emotion expression: A developmental contextual perspective. *Emotion Review, 7,* 14–21.

Chaplin, T.M., & Aldao, A. (2013). Gender differences in emotion in children: A meta-analytic review. *Psychological Bulletin, 139*(4), 735–765.

Chappuis, J. (2020). *Classroom assessment for student learning–Doing it right–Using it well* (3rd ed.). Pearson.

Charles, C. (2018). Water for labour and birth. In V. Chapman & C. Charles (Eds.), *The midwife's labour and birth handbook.* Wiley.

Charlesworth, T.E., & others (2021). Gender stereotypes in natural language: Word embeddings show robust consistency across child and adult language corpora of more than 65 million words. *Psychological Science, 32*(2), 218–240.

Charpak, N., Montealegre-Pomar, A., & Bohorquez, A. (2021). Systematic review and meta-analysis suggest that the duration of kangaroo mother care has a direct impact on neonatal growth. *Acta Paediatrica, 110,* 45–59.

Charpak, N., & others (2017). Twenty-year follow-up of kangaroo mother care versus traditional care. *Pediatrics, 139*(1), e20162063.

Chaudhuri, J.D. (2020). Stimulating intrinsic motivation in millennial students: A new generation approach. *Anatomical Sciences Education, 13,* 250–271.

Cheah, C.S.L., Li, J., Zhou, N., Yamamoto, Y., & Leung, C.Y.Y. (2015). Understanding Chinese immigrant and European American mothers' expressions of warmth. *Developmental Psychology, 51,* 1802–1811.

Chee, J.N., Wang, K., & Cheung, A. (2020). Depression in children and adolescents. In Roger S. McIntyre (Ed.), *Major depressive disorder* (pp. 175–184). Elsevier.

Chen, D.R., & Lu, H.H. (2022). Social alienation of adolescents with obesity in classrooms: A multilevel approach. *Journal of Adolescence, 94*(1), 81–91.

Chen, F.R., Rothman, E.F., & Jaffee, S.R. (2017). Early puberty, friendship group characteristics, and dating abuse in U.S. girls. *Pediatrics, 139*(6), e20162847.

Chen, G., Zhao, Q., Dishion, T., & Deater-Deckard, K. (2018). The association between peer network centrality and aggression is moderated by moral disengagement. *Aggressive Behavior, 44,* 571–580.

Chen, H., & Cheng, C.L. (2020). Parental psychological control and children's relational aggression: Examining the roles of gender and normative beliefs about relational aggression. *Journal of Psychology, 154,* 159–175.

Chen, H., & others (2023). Indoor air pollution from coal combustion and tobacco smoke during the periconceptional period and risk for neural tube defects in offspring in five rural counties of Shanxi Province, China, 2010–2016. *Environment International, 171,* 107728.

Chen, J., & others (2023). A trans-omics assessment of gene-gene interaction in early stage NSCLC. *Molecular Oncology, 17,* 173–187.

Chen, J., Sperandio, I., & Goodale, M.A. (2018). Proprioceptive distance cues restore perfect size constancy in grasping, but not perception, when vision is limited. *Current Biology, 28*(6), 927–932.

Chen, J.-Q., & Gardner, H. (2018). Assessment from the perspective of multiple-intelligences theory: Principles, practices, and values. In D.P. Flanagan & E.M. McDonough (Eds.), *Contemporary intellectual assessment: Theories, tests, and issues* (4th ed.). Guilford Press.

Chen, K.M., White, K., Shabbeer, J., & Schmid, M. (2018). Maternal age trends support uptake of non-invasive prenatal testing (NIPT) in the low-risk population. *The Journal of Maternal-Fetal & Neonatal Medicine, 20,* 1–4.

Chen, P.J., & others (2017). Effects of prenatal yoga on women's stress and immune function across pregnancy: A randomized controlled trial. *Complementary Therapies in Medicine, 31,* 109–117.

Chen, R., Hughes, A.C., & Austin, J.P. (2017). The use of theory in family therapy research: Content analysis and update. *Journal of Marital and Family Therapy, 43*(3), 514–525.

Chen, X. (2018). Culture, temperament, and social and psychological adjustment. *Developmental Review, 50,* 42–53.

Chen, X., & Graham, S. (2018). Doing better but feeling worse: An attributional account of achievement–self-esteem disparities in Asian American students. *Social Psychology of Education, 21,* 937–949.

Chen, X., Lee, J., & Chen, L. (2018). Culture and peer relationships. In W.W. Bukowski, B. Laursen, & K.H. Rubin (Eds.), *Handbook of peer interactions, relationships, and groups* (pp. 552–570). Guilford Press.

Chen, X., & Liu, C. (2016). Culture, peer relationships, and developmental psychopathology. In D. Cicchetti (Ed.), *Developmental psychopathology* (3rd ed.). Wiley.

Chen, X., & others (2019). Developmental trajectories of shyness-sensitivity from middle childhood to early adolescence in China: Contributions of peer preference and mutual friendship. *Journal of Abnormal Child Psychology, 47*(7), 1197–1209.

Chen, Y., & VanderWeele, T.J. (2018). Associations of religious upbringing with subsequent health and well-being from adolescence to young adulthood: An outcome-wide analysis. *American Journal of Epidemiology, 187,* 2355–2364.

Chen-Bouck, L., Patterson, M.M., & Chen, J. (2019). Relations of collectivism socialization goals and training beliefs to Chinese parenting. *Journal of Cross-Cultural Psychology, 50*(3), 396–418.

Cheng, C.A., & others (2017). Pregnancy increases stroke risk up to 1 year postpartum and reduces long-term risk. *Quarterly Journal of Medicine, 110*(6), 355–360.

Cheong, J.L., & others (2020). Early environment and long-term outcomes of preterm infants. *Journal of Neural Transmission, 127*(1), 1–8.

Chess, S., & Thomas, A. (1977). Temperamental individuality from childhood to adolescence. *Journal of Child Psychiatry, 16,* 218–226.

Chevalier, N., & others (2015). Myelination is associated with processing speed in early childhood: Preliminary insights. *PLoS One, 10,* e0139897.

Chevalier, N., & others (2019). Differentiation in prefrontal cortex recruitment during childhood: Evidence from cognitive control demands and social contexts. *Developmental Cognitive Neuroscience, 36,* 100629.

Chew, D., & others (2020). Youths with a non-binary gender identity: A review of their sociodemographic and clinical profile. *The Lancet Child & Adolescent Health, 4*(4), 320–330

Chi, M.T. (1978). Knowledge structures and memory development. In R.S. Siegler (Ed.), *Children's thinking: What develops?* Erlbaum.

Child Care Aware (2018). *2018 fact sheet.* http://usa .childcareaware.org/wp-content/uploads/2018/08/2018-state-fact-sheets.pdf

Child Trends (2015, November). *Oral sex behaviors among teens.* Child Trends.

Child Trends (2016). *Child care.* Retrieved January 12, 2020, from https://www.childtrends.org /?indicators5child-care

Chilosi, A.M., & others (2019). Hemispheric language organization after congenital left brain lesions: A comparison between functional transcranial Doppler and functional MRI. *Journal of Neuropsychology, 13,* 46–66.

Chimiklis, A.L., & others (2018). Yoga, mindfulness, and meditation interventions for youth with ADHD: Systematic review and meta-analysis. *Journal of Child and Family Studies, 27,* 3155–3168.

Ching, T.Y.C., Dillon, H., Leigh, G., & Cupples, L. (2018). Learning from the Longitudinal Outcomes of Children with Hearing Impairment (LOCHI) study: Summary of 5-year findings and implications. *International Journal of Audiology, 57,* S105–S111.

Chippenham & Johnston-Willis Hospitals (2022). Perinatal Nurse Navigation for Expecting Moms. Accessed online at www.youtube.com/watch?v =LMIDPd3DEtY

Chocko, A., & others (2017). Sequenced neurocognitive and behavioral parent training for the treatment of ADHD in school-age children. *Child Neuropsychology, 24,* 427–450.

Choi, J.K., Hatton-Bowers, H., & Shin, J. (2022). Predicting toddlers' problematic behaviors: The role of poverty, parenting, and childcare. *Early Child Development and Care, 192*(2), 313–330.

Choi, L., & An, J.Y. (2021). Genetic architecture of autism spectrum disorder: Lessons from large-scale genomic studies. *Neuroscience & Biobehavioral Reviews, 128,* 244–257.

Choi, Y.J., & Luo, Y. (2015). 13-month-olds' understanding of social interaction. *Psychological Science, 26,* 274–283.

Chomsky, N. (1957). *Syntactic structures.* Mouton.

Chong, K.H., & others (2020). Changes in physical activity, sedentary behavior, and sleep across the transition from primary to secondary school: A systematic review. *Journal of Science and Medicine in Sport, 23,* 498–505.

Choudhary, M., & others (2016). To study the effect of kangaroo mother care on pain response in preterm neonates and to determine the behavioral and physiological responses to painful stimuli in preterm neonates: A study from western Rajasthan. *Journal of Maternal-Fetal and Neonatal Medicine, 29,* 826–831.

Choukas-Bradley, S., & Prinstein, M.J. (2016). Peer relationships and the development of psychopathology. In M. Lewis & D. Rudolph (Eds.), *Handbook of developmental psychopathology* (3rd ed.). Springer.

Chow, C., Zhou, X., Fu, Y., Jampaklay, A., & Jordan, L.P. (2023). From left-behind children to youth labor migrants: The impact of household networks, gendered migration, and relay migration in Southeast Asia. *Social Sciences, 12*(3), 135.

Chow, C.M., Tan, C.C., & Buhrmester, D. (2015). Interdependence of depressive symptoms, school involvement, and academic performance between adolescent friends: A dyadic analysis. *British Journal of Educational Psychology, 85,* 316–331.

Chow, J., Aimola Davies, A.M., Fuentes, L.J., & Plunkett, K. (2019). The vocabulary spurt predicts the emergence of backward semantic inhibition in 18-month-old toddlers. *Developmental Science, 22*(2), e12754.

Christ, S.L., Kwak, Y.Y., & Lu, T. (2017). The joint impact of parental psychological neglect and peer isolation on adolescents' depression. *Child Abuse and Neglect, 69,* 151–162.

Christen, M., Narváez, D., & Gutzwiller, E. (2017). Comparing and integrating biological and cultural moral progress. *Ethical Theory and Moral Practice, 20,* 55–73.

Christensen, L.B., Johnson, R.B., & Turner, L.A. (2020). *Research methods, design, and analysis* (13th ed., loose leaf). Pearson.

Christensen, N., & others (2020). Breastfeeding and infections in early childhood: A cohort study. *Pediatrics, 146*(5).

Christensen, Z.P., Freedman, E.G., & Foxe, J.J. (2021). Caffeine exposure in utero is associated with structural brain alterations and deleterious neurocognitive outcomes in 9–10 year old children. *Neuropharmacology, 186,* 108479.

Christiansen, C., & others (2021). Novel DNA methylation signatures of tobacco smoking with trans-ethnic effects. *Clinical Epigenetics, 13*(1), 1–13.

Christie, S. (2022). Why play equals learning: Comparison as a learning mechanism in play. *Infant and Child Development, 31,* e2285.

Chuang, S.S. (2019). The complexities of immigration and families: Theoretical perspectives and current issues. In B.H. Fiese & others (Eds.), *APA handbook of contemporary family psychology: Applications and broad impact of family psychology* (pp. 437–455). American Psychological Association.

Chuang, S.S., & Tamis-Lemonda, C. (2009). Gender roles in immigrant families: Parenting views, practices, and child development. *Sex Roles, 60,* 451–455.

Chudley, A.E. (2017). Teratogenic influences on cerebellar development. In H. Marzban (Ed.), *Development of the cerebellum from molecular aspects to diseases* (pp. 275–300). Springer.

Chudzicka-Czupała, A., & others (2016). Application of the theory of planned behavior in academic cheating research—Cross-cultural comparison. *Ethics & Behavior, 26,* 638–659.

Cicchetti, D. (2017). A multilevel developmental approach to the prevention of psychopathology in children and adolescents. In J.N. Butcher & others (Eds.), *APA handbook of psychopathology.* APA Books.

Cillessen, A.H.N., & Bukowski, W.W. (2018). Sociometric perspectives. In W.W. Bukowski, B. Laursen, & K.H. Rubin (Eds.), *Handbook of peer interactions, relationships, and groups*. Guilford Press.

Cirelli, L.K., & Trehub, S.E. (2020). Familiar songs reduce infant distress. *Developmental Psychology, 56*(5), 861.

Clara, M. (2017). How instruction influences conceptual development: Vygotsky's theory revisited. *Educational Psychologist, 52,* 50–62.

Clark, C.A., & others (2023). Psychometric properties of a combined go/no-go and continuous performance task across childhood. *Psychological Assessment, 35*(4), 353–365.

Clark, C.D. (2016). *Play and well-being.* Routledge.

Clark, E.V. (1993). *The lexicon in acquisition.* Cambridge University Press.

Clark, E.V. (2017). *Language in children.* Psychology Press.

Clarke-Stewart, A.K., & Miner, J.L. (2008). Effects of child and day care. In M.M. Haith & J.B. Benson (Eds.), *Encyclopedia of infant and early childhood development.* Elsevier.

Clarke-Stewart, A.K., & Parke, R.D. (2014). *Social development* (2nd ed.). Wiley.

Claro, S., Paunesku, D., & Dweck, C.S. (2016). Growth mindset tempers the effect of poverty on academic achievement. *Proceedings of the National Academy of Sciences USA, 113,* 8664–8868.

Clauss, J.A., Avery, S.N., & Blackford, J.U. (2015). The nature of individual differences in inhibited temperament and risk for psychiatric disease: A review and meta-analysis. *Progress in Neurobiology, 127–128,* 23–45.

Clauss-Ehlers, C.S., Roysircar, G., & Hunter, S.J. (2021). *Applying multiculturalism.* APA Books.

Clayborne, Z.M., Varin, M., & Colman, I. (2019). Systematic review and meta-analysis: Adolescent depression and long-term psychosocial outcomes. *Journal of the American Academy of Child & Adolescent Psychiatry, 58*(1), 72–79.

Clemens, L.F., & Kegel, C.A. (2021). Unique contribution of shared book reading on adult-child language interaction. *Journal of Child Language, 48*(2), 373–386.

Closson, L.M., Hart, N.C., & Hogg, L.D. (2017). Does the desire to conform to peers moderate links between popularity and indirect victimization in early adolescence? *Social Development, 26*(3), 489–502.

CNN (2021, June 10). *Missouri teen gives away college savings after earning scholarship.* Retrieved February 1, 2022, from https://www.youtube.com/watch?v=rhWrb72zr04

Çoban, Ö.G., & others (2022). Psychiatric disorders and peer-victimization in children and adolescents with growth hormone deficiency. *Clinical Pediatrics, 61*(10), 684–691.

Cobanoglu, R., Capa-Aydin, Y., & Yildirim, A. (2019). Sources of teacher beliefs about developmentally appropriate practice: A structural equation model of the role of teacher efficacy beliefs. *European Early Childhood Education Research Journal, 27,* 195–207.

Cochet, H., & Byrne, R.W. (2016). Communication in the second and third year of life: Relationships between nonverbal social skills and language. *Infant Behavior and Development, 44,* 189–198.

Cohen, A.O., & Casey, B.J. (2017). The neurobiology of adolescent self-control. In T. Egner (Ed.), *Wiley handbook of cognitive control.* Wiley.

Cohen, R.J. (2022). *Psychological testing and assessment* (10th ed.). McGraw Hill.

Cohen, W.R., & Friedman, E.A. (2020). Guidelines for labor assessment: Failure to progress? *American Journal of Obstetrics and Gynecology, 222,* 342.e1–342.e4.

Coie, J. (2004). The impact of negative social experiences on the development of antisocial behavior. In J.B. Kupersmidt & K.A. Dodge (Eds.), *Children's peer relations: From development to intervention.* American Psychological Association.

Colby, A., Kohlberg, L., Gibbs, J., & Lieberman, M. (1983). A longitudinal study of moral judgment. *Monographs of the Society for Research in Child Development* (Serial No. 201).

Cole, P.M., & Jacobs, A.E. (2018). From children's expressive control to emotion regulation: Looking back, looking ahead. *European Journal of Developmental Psychology, 15,* 658–677.

Colemenares, F., & Hernandez-Lloreda, M.V. (2017). Cognition and culture in evolutionary context. *Spanish Journal of Psychology, 19,* E101.

Colen, C.G., & Ramey, D.M. (2014). Is breast truly best? Estimating the effects of breastfeeding on long-term health and well-being in the United States using sibling comparisons. *Social Science and Medicine, 109C,* 55–65.

Colich, N.L., & McLaughlin, K.A. (2022). Accelerated pubertal development as a mechanism linking trauma exposure with depression and anxiety in adolescence. *Current Opinion in Psychology, 46,* 101338.

Coll, C.D.V.N., & others (2019). Contraception in adolescence: The influence of parity and marital status on contraceptive use in 73 low- and middle-income countries. *Reproductive Health, 16*(1), 21.

Collins, B.A., & Toppelberg, C.O. (2021). The role of socioeconomic and sociocultural predictors of Spanish and English proficiencies of young Latino children of immigrants. *Journal of Child Language, 48,* 129–156.

Collins, W.A., & Madsen, S.D. (2019). Parenting during middle and late childhood. In M.H. Bornstein (Ed.), *Handbook of parenting* (3rd ed., pp. 81–110). Routledge.

Collins, W.A., & Steinberg, L. (2006). Adolescent development in interpersonal context. In W. Damon & R. Lerner (Eds.), *Handbook of child psychology* (6th ed.). Wiley.

Collins, W.A., & van Dulmen, M. (2006). The significance of middle childhood peer competence for work and relationships in early childhood. In A.C. Huston & M.N. Ripke (Eds.), *Developmental contexts in middle childhood.* Cambridge University Press.

Colombo, J., & Salley, B. (2015). Biopsychosocial perspectives on attention in infancy. In S.D. Calkins (Ed.), *Handbook of infant biopsychosocial development.* Guilford Press.

Colomer, M., & Woodward, A. (2023). Should I learn from you? Seeing expectancy violations about action efficiency hinders social learning in infancy. *Cognition, 230,* 105293.

Colvin, S., Egan, J.E., & Coulter, R.W. (2019). School climate and sexual and gender minority adolescent mental health. *Journal of Youth and Adolescence, 48*(10), 1938–1951.

Comeau, G., Lu, Y., Swirp, M., & Mielke, S. (2018). Measuring the musical skills of a prodigy: A case study. *Intelligence, 66,* 84–97.

Comer, J. (2010). Comer School Development Program. In J. Meece & J. Eccles (Eds.), *Handbook of research on schools, schooling, and human development.* Routledge.

Committee on the Rights of the Child (2020). Retrieved February 29, 2020, from https://www.ohchr.org/en/hrbodies/crc/pages/crcindex.aspx

Common Core State Standards Initiative (2023). *Common Core state standards.* https://learning.ccsso.org/common-core-state-standards-initiative

Common Sense Media (2019). *The Common Sense census: Media use by tweens and teens, 2019.* Available https://www.commonsensemedia.org/research/the-common-sense-census-media-use-by-tweens-and-teens-2019

Compas, B.E., & others (2017). Coping, emotion regulation, and psychopathology in childhood and adolescence: A meta-analysis and narrative review. *Psychological Bulletin, 143,* 939–991.

Compton, R.J. (2016). *Adoption beyond borders.* Oxford University Press.

Conboy, B.T., Brooks, R., Meltzoff, A.N., & Kuhl, P.K. (2015). Social interaction in infants' learning of second-language phonetics: An exploration of brain-behavior relations. *Developmental Neuropsychology, 40,* 216–229.

Condition of Education (2022). *National Center for Education Statistics, Condition of Education, 2021-2022.*

Conduct Problems Prevention Research Group (2010). The difficulty of maintaining positive intervention effects: A look at disruptive behavior, deviant peer relations, and social skills during the middle school years. *Journal of Early Adolescence, 30*(4), 593–624.

Congdon, J.L., & others (2016). A prospective investigation of prenatal mood and childbirth perceptions in an ethnically diverse, low-income sample. *Birth, 43*(2), 159–166.

Connolly, H.L., & others (2019). Sex differences in emotion recognition: Evidence for a small overall female superiority on facial disgust. *Emotion, 19,* 455–464.

Connolly, J., Shulman, S., & Benvenuto, K. (2023). Romantic relationships in adolescence and early adulthood. In L.J. Crockett, G. Carlo, & J.E. Schulenberg (Eds.), *APA handbook of adolescent and young adult development* (pp. 243-258). American Psychological Association.

Connolly, J.A., & McIsaac, C. (2009). Romantic relationships in adolescence. In R.M. Lerner & L. Steinberg (Eds.), *Handbook of adolescent psychology* (3rd ed.). Wiley.

Connolly, J.A., Nguyen, H.N., Pepler, D., Craig, W., & Jiang, D. (2013). Developmental trajectories of romantic stages and associations with problem behaviors during adolescence. *Journal of Adolescence, 36,* 1013-1024.

Connolly, M.D., & others (2016). The mental health of transgender youth: Advances in understanding. *Journal of Adolescent Health, 59,* 489-495.

Connor, D., Cavendish, W., Gonzalez, T., & Jean-Pierre, P. (2019). Is a bridge even possible over troubled waters? The field of special education negates the overrepresentation of minority students: A DisCrit analysis. *Race, Ethnicity and Education, 22,* 723-745.

Conrad, A., Butcher, B., Oral, R., Ronnenberg, M., & Peek-Asa, C. (2021). Trends in shaken baby syndrome diagnosis codes among young children hospitalized for abuse. *Injury Epidemiology, 8*(1), 1-11.

Consoli, A., & others (2015). Risk and protective factors for suicidality at 6-month follow-up in adolescent inpatients who attempted suicide: An exploratory model. *Canadian Journal of Psychiatry, 60*(2, Suppl. 1), S27-S36.

Constante, K., & others (2019). Ethnic socialization, family cohesion, and ethnic identity development over time among Latinx adolescents. *Journal of Youth and Adolescence, 49*(4), pp. 895-906.

Contant, T.L., & others (2018). *Teaching science through inquiry-based instruction* (13th ed.). Pearson.

Conte, S., & Richards, J.E. (2022). Cortical source analysis of event-related potentials: A developmental approach. *Developmental Cognitive Neuroscience, 54,* 101092.

Cook, E.C. (2020). Affective and physiological synchrony in friendships during late adolescence. *Journal of Social and Personal Relationships, 37*(4), 1296-1316.

Cook, F., & others (2020). Profiles and predictors of infant sleep problems across the first year. *Journal of Developmental & Behavioral Pediatrics, 41*(2), 104-116.

Cook, R.E., Martin, C.L., Nielson, M.G., & Xiao, S.X. (2022). Contemporary cognitive approaches to gender development: New schemas, new directions, and new conceptualizations of gender. In D.P. VanderLaan & W.I. Wong (Eds.), *Gender and sexuality development.* Springer.

Cools, S., Fiva, J.H., & Kirkebøen, L.J. (2015). Causal effects of paternity leave on children and parents. *The Scandinavian Journal of Economics, 117*(3), 801-828.

Cook, S.H., & others (2018). Sexual orientation moderates the association between parental overprotection and stress biomarker profiles. *Psychology & Sexuality, 9*(3), 204-220.

Cooper, K. & Stewart, K. (2017). *Does money affect children's outcomes? An update.* CASEpapers (203). Centre for Analysis of Social Exclusion, The London School of Economics and Political Science.

Cooper, M., & Pugh, A.J. (2020). Families across the income spectrum: A decade in review. *Journal of Marriage and Family, 82*(1), 272-299.

Copeland, W.E., & others (2019). Early pubertal timing and testosterone associated with higher levels of adolescent depression in girls. *Journal of the American Academy of Child & Adolescent Psychiatry, 58,* 1197-1206.

Corbetta, D., & Fagard, J. (2017). Infants' understanding and production of goal-directed actions in the context of social and object-related interactions. *Frontiers in Psychology, 8,* 787.

Corbetta, D., Wiener, R.F., Thurman, S.L., & McMahon, E. (2018). The embodied origins of infant reaching: Implications for the emergence of eye-hand coordination. *Kinesiology Review, 7,* 10-17.

Corkum, P., & others (2019). Healthy sleep practices (sleep hygiene) in children with ADHD. In H. Hiscock & E. Sciberras (Eds.), *Sleep and ADHD* (pp. 119-149). Academic Press.

Corominas, J., & others (2020). Identification of ADHD risk genes in extended pedigrees by combining linkage analysis and whole-exome sequencing. *Molecular Psychiatry, 25*(9), 2047-2057.

Corsaro, W.A. (2018). *The sociology of childhood* (5th ed.). Sage.

Corsi, D.J., & others (2019). Association between self-reported prenatal cannabis use and maternal, perinatal, and neonatal outcomes. *JAMA, 322*(2), 145-152.

Cortese, S., & others (2018). Comparative efficacy and tolerability of medications for attention-deficit hyperactivity disorder in children, adolescents, and adults: A systematic review and network meta-analysis. *The Lancet, 5,* 727-738.

Corvin, S., Fauchon, C., Peyron, R., Reby, D., & Mathevon, N. (2022). Adults learn to identify pain in babies' cries. *Current Biology, 32*(15), R824-R825.

Corwin, M.J. (2018). *Patient education: Sudden infant death syndrome.* https://www.uptodate.com/contents/sudden-infant-death-syndrome-sids-beyond-the-basics

Cosottile, M., & Damashek, A. (2022). Effects of cell phone use on caregiver supervision and child injury risk. *Journal of Pediatric Psychology, 47*(1), 86-93.

Coulter, R.W., & others (2019). Mental health, drug, and violence interventions for sexual/gender minorities: A systematic review. *Pediatrics, 144*(3), e20183367.

Cousins, L., & Goodyer, I.M. (2015). Antidepressants and the adolescent brain. *Journal of Psychopharmacology, 29,* 545-555.

Covington, L., & others (2021). Longitudinal associations among diet quality, physical activity, and sleep onset consistency with body mass index z-score among toddlers in low-income families. *Annals of Behavioral Medicine, 55*(7), 653-664.

Cowan, C.P., & Cowan, P.A. (2000). *When partners become parents.* Erlbaum.

Cowan, M.K., & Bunn, J. (2016). *Microbiology fundamentals* (2nd ed.). McGraw Hill.

Cowan, P., Cowan, C., Ablow, J., Johnson, V.K., & Measelle, J. (2005). *The family context of parenting in children's adaptation to elementary school.* Erlbaum.

Cowan, P.A., & others (2019a). Supporting father involvement: A father-inclusive couples group approach to parenting interventions. In H. Steele & M. Steele (Eds.), *Handbook of attachment interventions.* Guilford Press.

Cowan, P.A., & others (2019b). Fathers' and mothers' attachment styles, couple conflict, parenting quality, and children's behavior problems: An intervention test of mediation. *Attachment and Human Development, 21,* 532-550.

Cowgill, B. (2020). Back to the breast: An historical overview of the perceived connections between sudden infant death syndrome and breastfeeding. *Journal of Human Lactation, 36,* 310-317.

Cox, J.E., & others (2019). A Parenting and Life Skills Intervention for Teen Mothers: A Randomized Controlled Trial. *Pediatrics, 143*(3), e20182303.

Cox, R.B., Brosi, M., Spencer, T., & Masri, K. (2021). Hope, stress, and post-divorce child adjustment: Development and evaluation of the Co-Parenting for Resilience Program. *Journal of Divorce and Remarriage, 62,* 144-163.

Coyle, E.F., & Liben, L.S. (2020). Gendered packaging of a STEM toy influences children's play, mechanical learning, and mothers' play guidance. *Child Development, 91*(1), 43-62.

Coyle, G.T.R. (2021). Defining and measuring intelligence. In A.K. Barbey & others (Eds.), *Cambridge handbook of intelligence and cognitive neuroscience.* Cambridge University Press.

Coyne, S.M., & others (2016). Pretty as a princess: Longitudinal effects of engagement with Disney princesses on gender stereotypes, body esteem, and prosocial behavior in children. *Child Development, 87,* 1909-1925.

Coyne, S.M., & others (2021). Dressing up with Disney and make-believe with Marvel: The impact of gendered costumes on gender typing, prosocial behavior, and perseverance during early childhood. *Sex Roles, 85,* 301-312.

Craemer, K.A., & others (2019). Nutrition and exercise strategies to prevent excessive pregnancy weight gain: A meta-analysis. *American Journal of Perinatology Reports, 9*(01), e92-e120.

Crain, S. (2012). Sentence scope. In E.L. Bavin (Ed.), *Cambridge handbook of child language.* Cambridge University Press.

Crain, T.L., Schonert-Reichl, K.A., & Roeser, R.W. (2017). Cultivating teacher mindfulness: Effects of a randomized controlled trial on work, home, and sleep outcomes. *Journal of Occupational Health Psychology, 22*(2), 138-152.

Craske, M.G., Herzallah, M.M., Nusslock, R., & Patel, V. (2023). From neural circuits to communities: An integrative multidisciplinary roadmap for global mental health. *Nature Mental Health, 1,* 12-24.

Creanga, A.A., Catalano, P.M., & Bateman, B.T. (2022). Obesity in pregnancy. *New England Journal of Medicine, 387,* 248-259.

Cremone, A., & others (2019). Sleep tight, act right: Negative affect, sleep and behavior problems during early childhood. *Child Development, 89*(2), e42-e59.

Cresswell, L., & others (2022). Cognitive and mental health of young mothers' offspring: A meta-analysis. *Pediatrics, 150*(5), e2022057561.

Cribb, R., Ovid, N., & Bigham, B. (2018, September 14). More than 5,800 youth suicides across Canada signals mental health "crisis." *The (Toronto) Star.* Retrieved June 13, 2020, from https://www.thestar .com/news/investigations/2018/09/14/youth-suicide-is-like-a-cancer-experts-warn.html

Crocetti, E., Jahromi, P., & Meeus, W. (2012). Identity and civic engagement in adolescence. *Journal of Adolescence, 35,* 521-532.

Crocetti, E., Rabaglietta, E., & Sica, L.S. (2012). Personal identity in Italy. *New Directions in Child and Adolescent Development, 138,* 87-102.

Crockett, L.J., & others (2018). Temperamental anger and effortful control, teacher-child conflict, and externalizing behavior across the elementary school years. *Child Development, 89*(6), 2176-2195.

Crockett, L.J., & others (2019). Puberty education in a global context: Knowledge gaps, opportunities, and implications for policy. *Journal of Research on Adolescence, 29*(1), 177-195.

Crone, E. (2017). *The adolescent brain.* Routledge.

Crosby, J.R. (2021). Preventing and minimizing stereotype threat in school settings. In F.C. Worrell, T.L. Hughes, & D.D. Dixson (Eds.), *Cambridge handbook of applied school psychology.* Cambridge University Press.

Crosnoe, R., & Leventhal, T. (2014). School- and neighborhood-based interventions to improve the lives of disadvantaged children. In E.T. Gershoff, R.S. Mistry, & D.A. Crosby (Eds.), *The societal context of child development.* Oxford University Press.

Crosnoe, R., Pivnick, L., & Benner, A.D. (2018). The social contexts of high schools. In B. Schneider (Ed.), *Handbook of the sociology of education in the 21st century.* Springer.

Cross, C.J. (2020). Racial/ethnic differences in the association between family structure and children's education. *Journal of Marriage and Family, 82*(2), 691-712.

Cross, D., Lester, L., & Barnes, A. (2015). A longitudinal study of the social and emotional predictors and consequences of cyber and traditional bullying victimization. *International Journal of Public Health, 60,* 207-217.

Cross, F.L., & others (2020). Illuminating ethnic-racial socialization among undocumented Latinx parents and its implications for adolescent psychosocial functioning. *Developmental Psychology, 56,* 1458-1474.

Cross, F.L., Rivas-Drake, D., & Aramburu, J. (2022). Latinx immigrants raising children in the land of the free: Parenting in the context of persecution and fear. *Qualitative Social Work, 21,* 559-579.

Croteau-Chonka, E.C., & others (2016). Examining the relationships between cortical maturation and white matter myelination throughout early childhood. *Neuroimage, 125,* 413-421.

Crouter, A.C. (2006). Mothers and fathers at work. In A. Clarke-Stewart & J. Dunn (Eds.), *Families count.* Cambridge University Press.

Crowley, K., Callahan, M.A., Tenenbaum, H.R., & Allen, E. (2001). Parents explain more to boys than to girls during shared scientific thinking. *Psychological Science, 12,* 258-261.

Crowley, S.J., & others (2018). An update on adolescent sleep: New evidence informing the perfect storm model. *Journal of Adolescence, 67,* 55-65.

Cui, L., & others (2020). Longitudinal links between maternal and peer emotion socialization and adolescent girls' socioemotional adjustment. *Developmental Psychology, 56*(3), 595-607.

Cui, L., & others (2023). Age of onset for major depressive disorder and its association with symptomatology. *Journal of Affective Disorders, 320,* 682-690.

Cummings, E.M., & Davies, P.T. (2010). *Marital conflict and children: An emotional security perspective.* Guilford Press.

Cummings, E.M., Merrilees, C.E., Taylor, L.C., Goeke-Morey, M., & Shirlow, P. (2017). Emotional insecurity about the community: A dynamic, within-person mediator of child adjustment in contexts of political violence. *Development and Psychopathology, 29*(1), 27-36.

Cummings, E.M., & Miller, L.M. (2015). Emotional security theory: An emerging theoretical model for youths' psychological and physiological responses across multiple developmental contexts. *Current Directions in Psychological Science, 24,* 208-213.

Cummings, E.M., & Valentino, K.V. (2015). Developmental psychopathology. In R.M. Lerner (Ed.), *Handbook of child psychology and developmental science* (7th ed.). Wiley.

Cummings, K.J., & Leiter, J.C. (2020). Take a deep breath and wake up: The protean role of serotonin preventing sudden death in infancy. *Experimental Neurology, 326,* 113165.

Cunha, A.B., & others (2016). Effect of short-term training on reaching behavior in infants: A randomized controlled trial. *Journal of Motor Behavior, 48,* 132-142.

Curtis, L.A., & Bandy, T. (2016). *The Quantum Opportunities Program: A randomized controlled evaluation.* Milton S. Eisenhower Foundation.

Cushner, K., McClelland, A., & Safford, P. (2022).*Human diversity in education* (10th ed.). McGraw Hill.

Cuzzolaro, M. (2014). Eating and weight disorders: Studies on anorexia, bulimia, and obesity turn 19. *Eating and Weight Disorders, 19,* 1-2.

D

Dagan, O., & Sagi-Schwartz, A. (2021). Infant attachment (to mother and father) and its place in human development: Five decades of promising research (and an unsettled issue). In J.J. Lockman & C.S. Tamis-LeMonda (Eds.), *Cambridge handbook of infant development.* Cambridge University Press.

Dahl, A., Goeltz, M. T., & Brownell, C. A. (2022). Scaffolding the emergence of infant helping: A longitudinal experiment. *Child Development, 93*(3), 751-759.

Dahl, A., & Killen, M. (2017). The development of moral reasoning from infancy to adulthood. In J. Wixted (Ed.), *Stevens' handbook of experimental psychology and cognitive neuroscience.* Wiley.

Dahl, A., & Killen, M. (2018). A developmental perspective on the origins of morality in infancy and early childhood. *Frontiers in Psychology, 9,* 1736.

Dahl, R.E. (2004). Adolescent brain development: A period of vulnerabilities and opportunities. *Annals of the New York Academy of Sciences, 1021,* 1-22.

Dai, J., & Scherf, K.S. (2019). Puberty and functional brain development in humans: Convergence in findings? *Developmental Cognitive Neuroscience,* 100690.

Dakof, G.A., & others (2015). A randomized clinical trial of family therapy in juvenile drug court. *Journal of Family Psychology, 29,* 232-241.

Dallacker, M., Hertwig, R., & Mata, J. (2018). The frequency of family meals and nutritional health in children: A meta-analysis. *Obesity Reviews, 19*(5), 638-653.

Damashek, A., & Borduin, C. (2019). The moderating role of maternal supervision in the relation of social-ecological risk factors to children's minor injuries. *Journal of Clinical Psychology in Medical Settings, 27*(3), 507-517.

Damasio, A.R. (1994). Descartes' error and the future of human life. *Scientific American, 271*(4), 144.

Damon, W. (1988). *The moral child.* Free Press.

Daneri, M.P., & others (2019). Maternal language and child vocabulary mediate relations between socioeconomic status and executive function during early childhood. *Child Development, 90,* 2001-2018.

Danial, F.N.M., Cade, J.E., Greenwood, D.C., & Burley, V.J. (2018). Breastfeeding is associated with the risk of ovarian cancer in the UK Women's Cohort Study. *Proceedings of the Nutrition Society, 77,* e224.

Daniels, H. (Ed.). (2017). *Introduction to Vygotsky* (3rd ed.). Routledge.

Danielsen, V.M., & others (2020). Lifespan trajectories of relative corpus callosum thickness: Regional differences and cognitive relevance. *Cortex, 130,* 327-341.

Danielson, C.K., & others (2017). Clinical decision-making following disasters: Efficient identification of PTSD risk in adolescents. *Journal of Abnormal Child Psychology, 48,* 117-128.

Danis, A., & others (2008). A continuous performance task in preschool children: Relations between attention and performance. *European Journal of Developmental Psychology, 43,* 576–589.

Danish Institute for Human Rights (2018). *The human rights guide to the Sustainable Development Goals.* Available http://sdg.humanrights.dk/

Danowitz, M., & Grimberg, A. (2022). Clinical indications for growth hormone therapy. *Advances in Pediatrics, 69*(1), 203–217.

Dariotis, J.K., & others (2016). A qualitative evaluation of student learning and skills use in a school-based mindfulness and yoga program. *Mindfulness, 7,* 76–89.

Darling, C.A., Cassidy, D., & Ballard, S.M. (2022). *Family life education: Working with families across the lifespan* (4th ed.). Waveland Press.

Darling, N., Cumsille, P., & Peña-Alampay, L. (2005). Rules, legitimacy of parental authority, and obligation to obey in Chile, the Philippines, and the United States. In J. Smetana (Ed.), *New directions for child and adolescent development. Changing boundaries of parental authority during adolescence* (pp. 47–60). Jossey-Bass.

Darsareh, F., Nourbakhsh, S., & Dabiri, F. (2018). Effect of water immersion on labor outcomes: A randomized clinical trial. *Nursing and Midwifery Studies, 7*(3), 111–115.

Darwom, Z., & others (2017). Fathers' views and experiences of their own mental health during pregnancy and the first postnatal year: A qualitative interview study of men participating in the UK Born and Bred in Yorkshire (BaBY) cohort. *BMC Pregnancy and Childbirth, 17*(1), 45.

Dau, A.L., & others (2017). Postpartum depressive symptoms and maternal sensitivity: An exploration of possible social media-based measures. *Archives of Women's Mental Health, 20,* 221–224.

Dauenhauer, B., Keating, X., Stoepker, P., & Knipe, R. (2019). State physical education policy changes from 2001 to 2016. *Journal of School Health, 89*(6), 485–493.

Daunhauer, L.A. (2018). Down syndrome. In M.H. Bornstein & others (Eds.), *SAGE encyclopedia of lifespan human development.* Sage.

Davenport, M.H., & others (2019). Prenatal exercise is not associated with fetal mortality: A systematic review and meta-analysis. *British Journal of Sports Medicine, 53*(2), 108–115.

David-Barrett, T., & others (2016). Communication with family and friends across the life course. *PloS One, 11*(11), e0165687.

Davidson, J.R., & others (2022). Fetal magnetic resonance imaging (MRI) enhances the diagnosis of congenital body anomalies. *Journal of Pediatric Surgery, 57*(2), 239–244.

Davidson, T., & others (2021). Genome-wide stress sensitivity moderates the stress-depression relationship in a nationally representative sample of adults. *Scientific Reports, 11,* 20332.

Davies, P.T., Martin, M.J., & Cummings, E.M. (2018). Interparental conflict and children's social problems: Insecurity and friendship affiliation as cascading mediators. *Developmental Psychology, 54*(1), 83–97.

Davies, R., Davis, D., Pearce, M., & Wong, N. (2015). The effect of waterbirth on neonatal

mortality and morbidity: A systematic review and meta-analysis. *JBI Database of Systematic Reviews and Implementation Reports, 13,* 180–231.

Davis, A.C. (2021). Resolving the tension between feminism and evolutionary psychology: An epistemological critique. *Evolutionary Behavioral Sciences, 15,* 368–388.

Davis, B.E., Moon, R.Y., Sachs, M.C., & Ottolini, M.C. (1998). Effects of sleep position on infant motor development. *Pediatrics, 102,* 1135–1140.

Davis, E.L., Parsafar, P., & Brady, S.M. (2023). Early antecedents of emotion differentiation and regulation: Experience tunes the appraisal thresholds of emotional development in infancy. *Infant Behavior and Development, 70,* 101786.

Davis, K.M., Jones, K.A., Yee, L.M., & Feinglass, J. (2023). Modeling the likelihood of low birth weight: Findings from a Chicago-area health system. *Journal of Racial and Ethnic Health Disparities, 10,* 1768–1775.

Davis, M., Bilms, J., & Suveg, C. (2017). In sync and in control: A meta-analysis of parent–child positive behavioral synchrony and youth self-regulation. *Family Process, 56*(4), 962–980.

Davis, T.N., & Rispoli, M. (2018). Introduction to the special issue: Interventions to reduce challenging behavior among individuals with autism spectrum disorder. *Behavior Modification, 42,* 307–313.

Davison, S.M., & others (2013). CHILE: An evidence-based preschool intervention for obesity prevention in Head Start. *Journal of School Health, 83,* 223–229.

Davoodi, T., Nelson, L.J., & Blake, P.R. (2018). Children's conceptions of ownership for self and other: Categorical ownership versus strength of claim. *Child Development, 91*(1), 163–178.

Dawson, P., & Guare, R. (2018). *Executive skills in children and adolescents: A practical guide to assessment and intervention* (3rd ed.). Guilford Press.

Day, K.L., & Smith, C.L. (2019). Maternal behaviors in toddlerhood as predictors of children's private speech in preschool. *Journal of Experimental Child Psychology, 177,* 132–140.

Day, K.L., Smith, C.L., Neal, A., & Dunsmore, J.C. (2018). Private speech moderates the effects of effortful control on emotionality. *Early Education and Development, 29,* 161–177.

Dayton, C.J., & Malone, J.C. (2017). Development and socialization of physical aggression in very young boys. *Infant Mental Health, 38,* 150–165.

Deans, C.L. (2020). Maternal sensitivity, its relationship with child outcomes, and interventions that address it: A systematic literature review. *Early Child Development and Care, 190*(2), 252–275.

Dearing, E., & others (2016). Can community and school-based supports improve the achievement of first-generation immigrant children attending high-poverty schools? *Child Development, 87,* 883–897.

Dearing, E., & Zachrisson, H.D. (2017). Concern over internal, external, and incidence validity in studies of child-care quantity and externalizing behavior problems. *Child Development Perspectives, 11*(2), 133–138.

Deater-Deckard, K. (2016). Is self-regulation "all in the family"? Testing environmental effects using

within-family quasi-experiments. *International Journal of Behavioral Development, 40,* 224–233.

Deater-Deckard, K., Chen, N., & El Mallah, S. (2016). Gene-environment interplay in coercion. In T. Dishion and J. Snyder (Eds.), *Oxford handbook of coercive dynamics in close relationships* (pp. 23–38). Oxford University Press.

Deater-Deckard, K., & Lansford, J.E. (2017). Cultural norms and definitions of violence. In P. Sturmey (Ed.), *The Wiley handbook of violence and aggression.* Wiley.

Deater-Deckard, K., & others (2018). Within- and between-person and group variance in behavior and beliefs in cross-cultural longitudinal data. *Journal of Adolescence, 62,* 207–217.

Deater-Deckard, K., & others (2019). Chaos, danger, and maternal parenting in families: Links with adolescent adjustment in low- and middle-income countries. *Developmental Science, 22*(5), e12855.

Death Penalty Information Center (DPIC) (2019). *Execution of juveniles in the U.S. and other countries.* Retrieved June 15, 2020, from https://deathpenaltyinfo.org/execution-juveniles-us-and-other-countries

De Baca, T.C., & Ellis, B.J. (2021). Evolutionary perspectives on parenting. In V.A. Weekes-Shackelford & T.K. Shackelford (Eds.), *The Oxford handbook of evolutionary psychology and parenting.* Oxford University Press.

de Barbaro, K., & Fausey, C.M. (2022). Ten lessons about infants' everyday experiences. *Current Directions in Psychological Science, 31*(1), 28–33.

Dębińska, A., Danielewicz, H., Drabik-Chamerska, A., Kalita, D., & Boznański, A. (2019). Genetic polymorphisms in pattern recognition receptors are associated with allergic diseases through gene–gene interactions. *Advances in Clinical and Experimental Medicine, 28*(8), 1087–1094.

Debnath, R., & others (2020). The long-term effects of institutional rearing, foster care intervention, and disruptions in care on brain electrical activity in adolescence. *Developmental Science, 23*(1), e12872.

Debnath, R., & others (2021). Investigating brain electrical activity and functional connectivity in adolescents with clinically elevated levels of ADHD symptoms in alpha frequency band. *Brain Research, 1750,* 147142.

de Boer, H., Donker, A.S., Kostons, D.D., & van der Werf, G.P. (2018). Long-term effects of metacognitive strategy instruction on student academic performance: A meta-analysis. *Educational Research Review, 24,* 98–115.

de Bruin, W.B., & Fischhoff, B. (2017). Eliciting probabilistic expectations: Collaborations between psychologists and economists. *Proceedings of the National Academy of Sciences, 114,* 3297–3304.

De Bruyne, L.K., & Pinna, K. (2017). *Nutrition for health and healthcare* (6th ed.). Cengage.

DeCasper, A.J., & Spence, M.J. (1986). Prenatal maternal speech influences newborns' perception of speech sounds. *Infant Behavior and Development, 9,* 133–150.

Decety, J., Meidenbauer, K.L., & Cowell, J.M. (2018). The development of cognitive empathy and concern in preschool children: A behavioral neuroscience investigation. *Developmental Science, 21*(3), e12570.

De Deurwaerdere, P., & Di Giovanni, G. (2021). 5-HT interaction with other neurotransmitters: An overview. *Progress in Brain Research, 259,* 1-5.

Dee, D.L., & others (2017). Trends in repeat births and use of postpartum contraception among teens—United States 2004-2015. *Monthly Mortality Weekly Reports (MMWR), 66,* 422-426.

DeFoe, I.N., & others (2020). Is the peer presence effect on heightened adolescent risky decision-making present only in males? *Journal of Youth and Adolescence, 49,* 693-705.

DeGarmo, D.S., & Jones, J.A. (2019). Fathering Through Change (FTC) intervention for single fathers: Preventing coercive parenting and child problem behaviors. *Development and Psychopathology, 31,* 1801-1811.

De Genna, N.M., Goldschmidt, L., Day N.L., & Cornelius, M.D. (2016). Prenatal and postnatal maternal trajectories of cigarette use predict adolescent cigarette use. *Nicotine and Tobacco Research, 18,* 988-992.

De Genna, N.M., & others (2018). Prenatal exposures to tobacco and cannabis: Associations with adult electronic cigarette use. *Drug and Alcohol Dependence, 188,* 209-215.

de Haan, M. (2015). Neuroscientific methods with children. In R.M. Lerner (Ed.), *Handbook of child psychology and developmental science* (7th ed.). Wiley.

de Haan, M., & Johnson, M.H. (2016). Typical and atypical human functional brain development. In D. Cicchetti (Ed.), *Developmental psychopathology* (3rd ed.). Wiley.

Dehcheshmeh, F.S., & Rafiel, H. (2015). Complementary and alternative therapies to relieve labor pain: A comparative study between music therapy and Hoku point ice massage. *Complementary Therapies in Clinical Practice, 21,* 229-232.

Deichmann, F., & Ahnert, L. (2021). The terrible twos: How children cope with frustration and tantrums and the effect of maternal and paternal behaviors. *Infancy, 26,* 469-493.

DeKeyser, R.M. (2018). Age in learning and teaching grammar. In J.I. Liontas (Ed.), *The TESOL encyclopedia of English language teaching.* Wiley.

de Klerk, C.C., Lamy-Yang, I., & Southgate, V. (2019). The role of sensorimotor experience in the development of mimicry in infancy. *Developmental Science, 22*(3), e12771.

de Koning, L., Denhoff, E., Kellogg, M.D., & de Ferranti, S.D. (2015). Associations of total and abdominal adiposity with risk marker patterns in children at high risk for cardiovascular disease. *BMC Obesity, 2,* 15.

de la Torre, J.A., & others (2021). Prevalence and variability of current depressive disorder in 27 European countries: A population-based study. *Lancet Public Health, 6,* e729-e738.

de Leeuw, R.N., & van der Laan, C.A. (2018). Helping behavior in Disney animated movies and children's helping behavior in the Netherlands. *Journal of Children and Media, 12*(2), 159-174.

Delgado, E., Serna, C., Martinez, I., & Cruise, E. (2022). Parental attachment and peer relationships in adolescence: A systematic review. *International Journal of Environmental Research and Public Health, 19*(3), 1064.

Del Giudice, M. (2014), Middle childhood: An evolutionary-developmental synthesis. *Child Development Perspectives, 8,* 193-200.

Del Rio, M., & others (2023). An interdisciplinary team-based approach for significantly reducing lower-level lead poisoning in U.S. children. *Toxicology Reports, 10,* 76-86.

Demanchick, S.P. (2015). The interpretation of play: Psychoanalysis and beyond. In J.E. Johnson & others (Eds.), *Handbook of the study of play.* Rowman & Littlefield.

Demetriou, A., Makris, N., Kazi, S., Spanoudis, G., & Shayer, M. (2018). The developmental trinity of mind: Cognizance, executive control, and reasoning. *Wiley Interdisciplinary Reviews: Cognitive Science,* e1461.

Demetriou, A., & Spanoudis, G. (2018). *Growing minds: A developmental theory of intelligence, brain, and education.* Routledge.

De Meulenaere, J., Stas, L., Antrop, I., Buysse, A., & Lemmens, G.M. (2022). Adolescent attachment: A social relations perspective on family relations. *Family Process, 61,* 764-778.

Deming, D.M., & others (2017). Cross-sectional analysis of eating patterns and snacking in the US Feeding Infants and Toddlers Study 2008. *Public Health Nutrition, 20,* 1584-1592.

Demir-Lira, O.E., Applebaum, L.R., Goldin-Meadow, S., & Levine, S.C. (2019). Parents' early book reading to children: Relation to children's later language and literacy outcomes controlling for other parent language input. *Developmental Science, 22*(3), 12764.

de Moor, E.L., Van der Graaff, J., van Doeselaar, L., Klimstra, T.A., & Branje, S. (2021). With a little help from my friends? Perceived friendship quality and narrative identity in adolescence. *Journal of Research on Adolescence, 31,* 384-401.

Dempster, F.N. (1981). Memory span: Sources of individual and developmental differences. *Psychological Bulletin, 80,* 63-100.

Denes, G. (2016). *Neural plasticity across the lifespan.* Psychology Press.

Denessen, E., & others (2020). Implicit measures of teachers' attitudes and stereotypes, and their effects on teacher practice and student outcomes: A review. *Learning and Instruction, 78,* 101437.

Denham, S.A. (2023). *The development of emotional competence in young children.* Guilford Press.

Den Heijer, A.E., & others (2017). Sweat it out? The effects of physical exercise on cognition and behavior in children and adults with ADHD: A systematic literature review. *Journal of Neural Transmission, 124*(Suppl. 1), S3-S26.

Dennis, C.L., & Vigod, S. (2020). Preventing postpartum depression: Fatigue management is a place to start. *Evidence-Based Nursing, 23*(1), 25-25.

Deoni, S., Dean, D.III, Joelson, S., O'Regan, J., & Schneider, N. (2018). Early nutrition influences developmental myelination and cognition in infants and young children. *Neuroimage, 178,* 649-659.

Deoni, S.C., & others (2016). White matter maturation profiles through early childhood predict general cognitive ability. *Brain Structure and Function, 221*(2), 1189-1203.

de Onis, M., & others (2018). Prevalence thresholds for wasting, overweight and stunting in children under 5 years. *Public Health Nutrition, 22*(1), 1-5.

Derraik, J.G., & others (2019). Idiopathic short stature and growth hormone sensitivity in prepubertal children. *Clinical Endocrinology, 91,* 110-117.

DeSantis, L. (1998). Building healthy communities with immigrants and refugees. *Journal of Transcultural Nursing, 9,* 20-31.

DeSisto, C.L., & others (2018). Deconstructing a disparity: Explaining excess preterm birth among US-born Black women. *Annals of Epidemiology, 28*(4), 225-230.

Dessì, A., and others (2018). Exposure to tobacco smoke and low birth weight: From epidemiology to metabolomics. *Expert Review of Proteomics, 15*(8), 647-656.

Devaney, S.A., Palomaki, G.E., Scott, J.A., & Bianchi, D.W. (2011). Noninvasive fetal sex determination using cell-free fetal DNA: A systematic review and meta-analysis. *Journal of the American Medical Association, 306,* 627-636.

Devenish, B., Hooley, M., & Mellor, D. (2017). The pathways between socioeconomic status and adolescent outcomes: A systematic review. *American Journal of Community Psychology, 59*(1-2), 218-238.

Devine, R.T., & Hughes, C. (2018). Family correlates of false belief understanding in early childhood: A meta-analysis. *Child Development. 89*(3), 971-987.

Devine, R.T., & Lecce, S. (Eds.). (2021). *Theory of mind in middle childhood and adolescence: Integrating multiple perspectives.* Routledge.

Dewey, J. (1933). *How we think.* D.C. Heath.

Dewitz, P.F., & others (2020). *Teaching reading in the 21st century* (6th ed.). Pearson.

DeZolt, D.M., & Hull, S.H. (2001). Classroom and school climate. In J. Worell (Ed.), *Encyclopedia of women and gender.* Academic Press.

Deák, G.O., Krasno, A.M., Jasso, H., & Triesch, J. (2018). What leads to shared attention? Maternal cues and infant responses during object play. *Infancy, 23,* 4-28.

Di, H.K., & others (2022). Maternal smoking status during pregnancy and low birth weight in offspring: Systematic review and meta-analysis of 55 cohort studies published from 1986 to 2020. *World Journal of Pediatrics, 18,* 176-185.

Diamond, A., Lee, C., Senften, P., Lam, A., & Abbott, D. (2019). Randomized control trial of Tools of the Mind: Marked benefits to kindergarten children and their teachers. *PloS One, 14*(9), e0222447.

Diamond, L.M. (2021) The new genetic evidence on same-gender sexuality: Implications for sexual fluidity and multiple forms of sexual diversity. *The Journal of Sex Research, 58,* 818-837.

Diamond, L.M. (2023, in press). What develops in the biodevelopment of sexual orientation? *Archives of Sexual Behavior.*

Díaz, V. (2022). Minds in action: Evidence that linguistic diversity helps children build a theory of mind. *Bilingualism: Language and Cognition, 25*(1), 70-80.

Diaz-Rico, L.T. (2020). *A course for teaching English learners* (3rd ed.). Pearson.

Diaz-Rojas, F., & others (2023). Development of the paternal brain in humans throughout pregnancy. *Journal of Cognitive Neuroscience, 35*(3), 396-420.

DiBenedetto, M.K., & Schunk, D.H. (2018). Self-efficacy in education revisited through a sociocultural lens. In G.A.D. Liem & D.M. McInerney (Eds.), *Big theories revisited 2.* Information Age Publishing.

Di Cicco, M., Ghezzi, M., Kantar, A., Song, W.J., Bush, A., Peroni, D., & D'Auria, E. (2023). Pediatric obesity and severe asthma: Targeting pathways driving inflammation. *Pharmacological Research, 188,* 106658.

Dick, J.R., Wimalasundera, R., & Nandi, R. (2022). Maternal and fetal anaesthesia for fetal surgery. *Obstetric Anesthesia Digest, 42*(1), 49.

Dickerson, A., & Popli, G.K. (2016). Persistent poverty and children's cognitive development: Evidence from the UK Millennium Cohort Study. *Journal of the Royal Statistical Society, 179,* 535-558.

Dickinson, D.K., & others (2019). Effects of teacher-delivered book reading and play on vocabulary learning and self-regulation among low-income preschool children. *Journal of Cognition and Development, 20,* 136-164.

Didion, L., Toste, J.R., & Filderman, M.J. (2020). Teacher professional development and student reading achievement: A meta-analytic review of the effects. *Journal of Research on Educational Effectiveness, 13,* 29-66.

Diedrich, J.T., Klein, D.A., & Peipert, J.F. (2017). Long-acting reversible contraception in adolescents: A systematic review and meta-analysis. *American Journal of Obstetrics and Gynecology, 364,* e1-e12.

Diego, M.A., Field, T., & Hernandez-Reif, M. (2014). Preterm infant weight gain is increased by massage therapy and exercise via different underlying mechanisms. *Early Human Development, 90,* 137-140.

Di Giunta, L., & others (2018). Parents' and early adolescents' self-efficacy about anger regulation and early adolescents' internalizing and externalizing problems: A longitudinal study in three countries. *Journal of Adolescence, 64,* 124-135.

Dijkstra, J.K., & Gest, S.D. (2015). Peer norm salience for academic achievement, prosocial behavior, and bullying: Implications for adolescent school experiences. *Journal of Early Adolescence, 35,* 79-96.

Dilworth-Bart, J.E., & others (2018). Longitudinal associations between self-regulation and the academic and behavioral adjustment of young children born preterm. *Early Childhood Research Quarterly, 42,* 193-204.

Di Mascio, D., & others (2016). Exercise during pregnancy in normal-weight women and risk of preterm birth: A systematic review and meta-analysis of randomized controlled trials. *American Journal of Obstetrics and Gynecology, 215,* 561-571.

Dimock, M. (2019, January 17). *Defining generations: Where millennials end and generation Z begins.* Pew Research Center.

Dineva, E., & Schöner, G. (2018). How infants' reaches reveal principles of sensorimotor decision making. *Connection Science, 30,* 53-80.

Ding, L., Zhu, D., Peng, D., & Zhao, Y. (2017). Air pollution and asthma attacks in children: A case-crossover analysis in the city of Chongqing. *Environmental Pollution, 22*(Pt. A), 348-353.

DiPerna, J.C., Lei, P., Cheng, W., Hart, S.C., & Bellinger, J. (2018). A cluster randomized trial of the Social Skills Improvement System–Classwide Intervention Program (SSIS-CIP) in first grade. *Journal of Educational Psychology, 110*(1), 1-16.

Distefano, R., Masten, A.S., & Motti-Stefanidi, F. (2021). Autonomy-supportive parenting in immigrant and non-immigrant youth during early adolescence. *Journal of Child and Family Studies, 30,* 1171-1183.

Distefano, R., & others (2021). Self-regulation as promotive for academic achievement in young children across risk contexts. *Cognitive Development, 58,* 101050.

Dittus, P.J., & others (2015). Parental monitoring and its associations with adolescent sexual risk behavior: A meta-analysis. *Pediatrics, 136,* e1587-e1599.

Divecha, D., & Brackett, M. (2020). Rethinking school-based bullying prevention through the lens of social and emotional learning: A bioecological perspective. *International Journal of Bullying Prevention, 2,* 93-113.

Dodge, K.A. (2011a). Context matters in child and family policy. *Child Development, 82,* 433-442.

Dodge, K.A. (2011b). Social information processing models of aggressive behavior. In M. Mikulincer & P.R. Shaver (Eds.), *Understanding and reducing aggression, violence, and their consequences.* American Psychological Association.

Dodge, K.A., Godwin, J., & Conduct Problems Prevention Research Group (2013). Social-information-processing patterns mediate the impact of preventive intervention on adolescent antisocial behavior. *Psychological Science, 24,* 456-465.

Dodge, K.A., & others (2015). Hostile attributional bias and aggressive behavior in global context. *Proceedings of the National Academy of Sciences, 112,* 9310-9315.

Doebel, S., & Lillard, A.S. (2023). How does play foster development? A new executive function perspective. *Developmental Review, 67,* 101064.

Dohla, D., & Heim, S. (2016). Developmental dyslexia and dysgraphia: What can we learn from one about the other? *Frontiers in Psychology, 6,* 2045.

Dollar, J., & Calkins, S.D. (2020). Emotion regulation and its development. In J.B. Benson (Ed.), *Encyclopedia of infant and early childhood development* (2nd ed.). Elsevier.

Donatelle, R.J. (2017). *Health* (12th ed.). Pearson.

Donatelle, R.J., & Ketcham, P. (2018). *Access to health* (15th ed.). Pearson.

Dong, B., Wang, Z., Wang, H.J., & Ma, J. (2015). Population attributable risk of overweight and obesity for high blood pressure in Chinese children. *Blood Pressure, 24,* 230-236.

Dong, Y., & others (2020). Reading comprehension and metalinguistic knowledge in Chinese readers: A meta-analysis. *Frontiers in Psychology, 10,* 3037.

Donnelly, S., & Kidd, E. (2020). Individual differences in lexical processing efficiency and vocabulary in toddlers: A longitudinal investigation. *Journal of Experimental Child Psychology, 192,* 104781.

Donovan, M.K. (2017). The looming threat to sex education: A resurgence of federal funding for abstinence-only programs? *Guttmacher Policy Review, 20,* 44-47.

Doob, C.B. (2021). *Poverty, racism, and sexism: The reality of oppression in America.* Routledge.

Dorn, L.D., & Susman, E.J. (2019). Fostering the developmental science of puberty: Tackling deficits and enhancing dissemination. *Journal of Adolescent Health, 64*(5), 561-562.

dos Santos, J.F., & others (2018). Maternal, fetal and neonatal consequences associated with the use of crack cocaine during the gestational period: A systematic review and meta-analysis. *Archives of Gynecology and Obstetrics, 298*(3), 487-503.

Dos Santos Kawata, K., & others (2021). Development of metacognition in adolescence: The Congruency-Based Metacognition Scale. *Frontiers in Psychology, 11,* 565231.

Dotan, D., Eliahou, O., & Cohen, S. (2021). Serial and syntactic processing in the visual analysis of multi-digit numbers. *Cortex, 134,* 162-180.

Dotti Sani, G.M., & Quaranta, M. (2017). The best is yet to come? Attitudes toward gender roles among adolescents in 36 countries. *Sex Roles, 77,* 30-45.

Douglas, J.L., Williams, D., & Reynolds, S. (2017). The relationship between adolescent rumination and maternal rumination, criticism and positivity. *Behavioural and Cognitive Psychotherapy, 45*(3), 300-311.

Dowda, M., & others (2017). Physical activity and changes in adiposity in the transition from elementary to middle school. *Child Obesity, 13,* 53-62.

Dowdall, N., & others (2020). Shared picture book reading interventions for child language development: A systematic review and meta-analysis. *Child Development, 91,* e383-e399.

Doyle, C., & Cicchetti, D. (2018). Child maltreatment. In M.H. Bornstein & others (Eds.), *SAGE encyclopedia of lifespan human development.* Sage.

Draganova, R., & others (2018). Fetal auditory evoked responses to onset of amplitude modulated sounds. A fetal magnetoencephalography (fMEG) study. *Hearing Research, 363,* 70-77.

Dragoset, L., & others (2017). School improvement grants: Implementation and effectiveness. NCEE 2017-4013. *ERIC,* ED572215.

Drexler, K.A., Quist-Nelson, J., & Weil, A.B. (2022). Intimate partner violence and trauma-informed care in pregnancy. *American Journal of Obstetrics & Gynecology, 4,* 100542.

Drouin, O., Winickoff, J.P., & Thorndike, A.N. (2019). Parents' social norms and children's exposure to three behavioral risk factors for chronic disease. *Journal of Behavioral Public Administration, 2*(1).

Druker, K.C., Mazzucchelli, T.G., & Beilby, J.M. (2019). An evaluation of an integrated fluency and resilience program for early developmental stuttering disorders. *Journal of Communication Disorders, 78*, 69-83.

D'Souza, D., & D'Souza, H. (2019). Emergent and constrained: Understanding brain and cognitive development. *Journal of Neurolinguistics, 49*, 228-231.

D'Souza, H., & Karmiloff-Smith, A. (2017). Neurodevelopmental disorders. *Wiley Interdisciplinary Reviews. Cognitive Science, 8*(1-2), e1398.

D'Souza, H., & others (2017). Specialization of the motor system in infancy: From broad tuning to selectively specialized purposeful actions. *Developmental Science, 20*(4), doi:10.1111/desc.12409

Du, M.C., & others (2019). Effects of physical exercise during pregnancy on maternal and infant outcomes in overweight and obese pregnant women: A meta-analysis. *Birth, 46*(2), 211-221.

Dubois-Comtois, K., & others (2020). Family environment and preschoolers' sleep: The complementary role of both parents. *Sleep Medicine, 58*, 114-122.

Duckworth, A.L., Taxer, J.L., Eskreis-Winkler, L., Galla, B.M., & Gross, J.J. (2019). Self-control and academic achievement. *Annual Review of Psychology, 70*, 373-399.

Duell, N., Hoorn, J., McCormick, E.M., Prinstein, M.J., & Telzer, E.H. (2021). Hormonal and neural correlates of prosocial conformity in adolescents. *Developmental Cognitive Neuroscience, 48*, 100936.

Duell, N., & Steinberg, L. (2020). Differential correlates of positive and negative risk taking in adolescence. *Journal of Youth and Adolescence, 49*, 1162-1178.

Duff, D., Tomblin, J.B., & Catts, H. (2015). The influence of reading on vocabulary growth: A case for a Matthew effect. *Journal of Speech, Language, and Hearing Research, 58*, 853-864.

Duffy, E.W., & others (2020). Developing a national research agenda to reduce consumption of sugar-sweetened beverages and increase safe water access and consumption among 0- to 5-year-olds: A mixed methods approach. *Public Health Nutrition, 23*(1), 22-33.

Duffy, J.R. (2020). *Motor speech disorders: Substrates, differential diagnosis, and management* (4th ed.). Elsevier Health Sciences.

du Fossé, N.A., & others (2022). Toward more accurate prediction of future pregnancy outcome in couples with unexplained recurrent pregnancy loss: Taking both partners into account. *Fertility and Sterility, 117*, 144-152.

Duke, S.A., Balzer, B.W., & Steinbeck, K.S. (2014). Testosterone and its effects on human male adolescent mood and behavior: A systematic review. *Journal of Adolescent Health, 55*, 315-322.

Duncan, G.J. (2021). A roadmap to reducing child poverty. *Academic Pediatrics, 21*(8), S97-S101.

Duncan, G.J., Magnuson, K., & Votruba-Drzal, E. (2017). Moving beyond correlations in assessing the consequences of poverty. *Annual Review of Psychology, 68*, 413-434.

Duncan, G.J., & others (2007). School readiness and later achievement. *Developmental Psychology, 43*, 1428-1446.

Duncan, R., McClelland, M.M., & Acock, A.C. (2017). Relations between executive function, behavioral regulation, and achievement: Moderation by family income. *Journal of Applied Developmental Psychology, 49*, 21-30.

Dunn, J. (2015). Siblings. In J.E. Grusec & P.D. Hastings (Eds.), *Handbook of socialization* (2nd ed.). Guilford Press.

Dunn, J., & Kendrick, C. (1982). *Siblings.* Harvard University Press.

Dunning, D.L., & others (2019). Research review: The effects of mindfulness-based interventions on cognition and mental health in children and adolescents—A meta-analysis of randomized controlled trials. *Journal of Child Psychology and Psychiatry, 60*(3), 244-258.

Dunphy, L. (2020). A picture book pedagogy for early childhood mathematics education. In A. MacDonald, L. Danaia, & S. Murphy (Eds.), *STEM education across the learning continuum* (pp. 67-85). Springer.

Dupéré, V., & others (2018). High school dropout in proximal context: The triggering role of stressful life events. *Child Development, 89*, e107-e122.

Durand, K., & others (2020). Does any mother's body odor stimulate interest in mother's face in 4-month-old infants? *Infancy, 25*, 151-164

Durston, S., & others (2006). A shift from diffuse to focal cortical activity with development. *Developmental Science, 9*, 1-8.

Dutton, E., & others (2018). A Flynn effect in Khartoum, the Sudanese capital, 2004-2016. *Intelligence, 68*, 82-86.

Dweck, C.S. (2006). *Mindset.* Random House.

Dweck, C.S. (2012). Mindsets and human nature: Promoting change in the Middle East, the school yard, the racial divide, and willpower. *American Psychologist, 67*, 614-622.

Dweck, C.S. (2013). Social development. In P. Zelazo (Ed.), *Oxford handbook of developmental psychology.* Oxford University Press.

Dweck, C.S. (2016, March 11). *Growth mindset revisited.* Invited presentation at Leaders to Learn From, Education Week, Washington, DC.

Dweck, C.S. (2019). The choice to make a difference. *Perspectives on Psychological Science, 14*(1), 21-25.

Dweck, C.S., & Master, A. (2009). Self-theories and motivation: Students' beliefs about intelligence. In K.R. Wentzel & A. Wigfield (Eds.), *Handbook of motivation at school.* Routledge.

Dweck, C.S., & Yeager, D.S. (2018). Mindsets change the imagined and actual future. In G. Oettingen, A.T. Sevincer, & P.M. Gollwitzer (Eds.), *The psychology of thinking about the future.* Guilford Press.

Dykstra, V.W., Willoughby, T., & Evans, A.D. (2020). A longitudinal examination of the relation between lie-telling, secrecy, parent–child relationship quality, and depressive symptoms in late-childhood and adolescence. *Journal of Youth and Adolescence, 49*, 438-448.

E

Eagan, K., & others (2016). *The American freshman: National norms fall 2015.* Higher Education Research Institute, UCLA.

Eagly, A.H. (2022). A quest for social psychology that spans the psychological and the social. In S. Kassin (Ed.), *Pillars of social psychology: Stories and retrospectives* (pp. 105-113). Cambridge University Press.

Eason, A.D., & Parris, B.A. (2018). Clinical applications of self-hypnosis: A systematic review and meta-analysis of randomized controlled trials. *Psychology of Consciousness: Theory, Research, and Practice, 6*(3), 262-278.

Eaton, D.K., & others (2010). Youth risk behavior surveillance—United States, 2009. *MMWR Surveillance Summary, 59*, 1-142.

Eccles, J.S., & Roeser, R.W. (2015). School and community influences on human development. In M.H. Bornstein & M.E. Lamb (Eds.), *Developmental science* (7th ed.). Psychology Press.

Ecker-Lyster, M., & Niileksela, C. (2017). Enhancing gifted education for underrepresented students: Promising recruitment and programming strategies. *Journal for the Education of the Gifted, 40*, 79-95.

Eckert-Lind, C., & others (2021). Worldwide secular trends in age at pubertal onset assessed by breast development among girls: A systematic review and meta-analysis. *JAMA Pediatrics, 174*(4), e195881.

Eckhoff, D.O., & Weiss, J. (2020). Goal setting: A concept analysis. *Nursing Forum, 55*, 275-281.

Eckstrand, K.L., Lenniger, C.J., & Forbes, E.E. (2022). Development of reward circuitry during adolescence: Depression, social context, and considerations for future research on disparities in sexual and gender minority youth. *Annual Review of Developmental Psychology, 4*, 231-252.

Eddy, J.M., & Sneddon, D. (2020). Rigorous research on existing child maltreatment prevention programs: Introduction to the special section. *Prevention Science, 21*(1), 1-3.

Edelson, S.M., & Reyna, V.F. (2023). Decision making in adolescence and early adulthood. In L.J. Crockett, G. Carlo, & J.E. Schulenberg (Eds.), *APA handbook of adolescent and young adult development* (pp. 107-122). American Psychological Association.

Edwards, C.P., & Gandini, L. (2018). The Reggio Emilia approach to early childhood education. In J.L. Roopnarine & others (Eds.), *Handbook of international perspectives on early childhood education*. Routledge.

Edwards, L.M., Le, H.N., & Garnier-Villarreal, M.A. (2021). Systematic review and meta-analysis of risk factors for postpartum depression among Latinas. *Maternal and Child Health Journal, 25,* 554-564.

Egeland, B., Jacobvitz, D., & Sroufe, L.A. (1988). Breaking the cycle of abuse. *New Directions for Child Development, 11,* 77-92.

Eggermann, T., & others (2021). Growth restriction and genomic imprinting—Overlapping phenotypes support the concept of an imprinting network. *Genes, 12,* 585.

Eggum-Wilkens, N.D., Reichenberg, R.E., Eisenberg, N., & Spinrad, T.L. (2016). Components of effortful control and their relations to children's shyness. *International Journal of Behavioral Development, 40,* 544-554.

Egly, J., & Ricca, R. (2022). Injury prevention. In A.P. Kennedy Jr., R.C. Ignacio, & R. Ricca (Eds.), *Pediatric trauma care*. Springer.

Ehli, S., and others (2020). Determining the function of social referencing: The role of familiarity and situational threat. *Frontiers in Psychology, 11,* 538228.

Einziger, T., & others (2018). Predicting ADHD symptoms in adolescence from early childhood temperament traits. *Journal of Abnormal Child Psychology, 46*(2), 265-276.

Eisenberg, N. (2020). Emotion, regulation, and moral development. *Annual Review of Psychology, 51,* 665-697.

Eisenberg, N., Smith, C.L., & Spinrad, T.L. (2016). Effortful control: Relations with emotion regulation, adjustment, and socialization in childhood. In K.D. Vohs & R.F. Baumeister (Eds.), *Handbook of self-regulation* (3rd ed.). Guilford Press.

Eisenberg, N., Spinrad, T.L., & Knafo-Noam, A. (2015). Prosocial development. In R.M. Lerner (Ed.), *Handbook of child psychology and developmental science* (7th ed.). Wiley.

Ekema-Agbaw, M.L., McCutchen, J.A., & Geller, E.S. (2016). Intervening to promote statements of gratitude: Informative incongruity between intention and behavior. *Journal of Prevention and Intervention in the Community, 44,* 144-154.

Eklund, K., Tanner, N., Stoll, K., & Anway, L. (2015). Identifying emotional and behavioral risk among gifted and nongifted children: A multi-gate, multi-informant approach. *School Psychology Quarterly, 30,* 197-211.

Elansary, M., & others (2022). Maternal stress and early neurodevelopment: Exploring the protective role of maternal growth mindset. *Journal of Developmental & Behavioral Pediatrics, 43*(2), e103-e109.

Eliot, L., & others (2021). Dump the "dimorphism": Comprehensive synthesis of human brain studies reveals few male-female differences beyond size. *Neuroscience & Biobehavioral Reviews, 125,* 667-697.

Elkana, O., & others (2020). WAIS Information Subtest as an indicator of crystallized cognitive abilities and brain reserve among highly educated older adults: A three-year longitudinal study. *Applied Neuropsychology: Adult, 27,* 525-531.

Elkind, D. (1978). Understanding the young adolescent. *Adolescence, 13,* 127-134.

Elliott, J.G., & Resing, W.C. (2020). Extremes of intelligence. In R.J. Sternberg (Ed.), *Human intelligence*. Cambridge University Press.

El Rafihi-Ferreira, R., & others (2019). Predictors of nighttime fears and sleep problems in young children. *Journal of Child and Family Studies, 28*(4), 941-949.

El-Sheikh, M. (2020). *Auburn sleep expert offers advice on better sleep*. https://ocm.auburn.edu/experts/2020/01/061423-sleep-expert.php

El-Sheikh, M., & Kelly, R.J. (2017). Family functioning and children's sleep. *Child Development Perspectives, 11,* 264-269.

Eltonsy, S., Martin, B., Ferreira, E., & Blais, L. (2016). Systematic procedure for the classification of proven and potential teratogens for use in research. *Birth Defects Research A: Clinical and Molecular Teratology, 106,* 285-297.

Emerson, A., Pickett, M., Moore, S., & Kelly, P.J. (2023). A scoping review of digital health interventions to promote healthy romantic relationships in adolescents. *Prevention Science, 24,* 625-639.

End Violence Against Children (2023). *Countdown to universal prohibition*. Available https://endcorporalpunishment.org/countdown/

Endendijk, J.J., Groeneveld, M.G., Bakermans-Kranenburg, M.J., & Mesman, J. (2016). Gender-differentiated parenting revisited: Meta-analysis reveals very few differences in parental control of boys and girls. *PLoS One, 11*(7), e0159193.

Engels, A.C., & others (2016). Sonographic detection of central nervous system in the first trimester of pregnancy. *Prenatal Diagnosis, 36,* 266-273.

England-Mason, G., & Gonzalez, A. (2020). Intervening to shape children's emotion regulation: A review of emotion socialization parenting programs for young children. *Emotion, 20*(1), 98-104.

Erbeli, F., Rice, M., & Paracchini, S. (2022). Insights into dyslexia genetics research from the last two decades. *Brain Sciences, 12*(1), 27.

Erdmann, K. (2019). Sex-specific relationships between infants' mental rotation ability and amiotic sex hormones. *Neuroscience Letters, 707,* 134298.

Erdogan, S.U., Yanikkerem, E., & Goker, A. (2017). Effects of low back massage on perceived birth pain and satisfaction. *Complementary Therapies in Clinical Practice, 28,* 169-175.

Erickson-Schroth, L., & Davis, B. (2021). *Gender*. Oxford University Press.

Ericsson, K.A. (2020). Towards a science of the acquisition of expert performance in sports: Clarifying the differences between deliberate practice and other types of practice. *Journal of Sports Sciences, 38*(2), 159-176.

Erikson, E.H. (1950). *Childhood and society*. W.W. Norton.

Erikson, E.H. (1968). *Identity: Youth and crisis*. W.W. Norton.

Ersan, C. (2020). Physical aggression, relational aggression and anger in preschool children: The mediating role of emotion regulation. *The Journal of General Psychology, 147*(1), 18-42.

Erskine, H.E., & others (2016). Long-term outcomes of attention-deficit/hyperactivity disorder and conduct disorder: A systematic review and meta-analysis. *Journal of the American Academy of Child and Adolescent Psychiatry, 55,* 841-850.

Ertem, I.O., & others (2018). Similarities and differences in child development from birth to age 3 years by sex and across four countries: A cross-sectional, observational study. *The Lancet Global Health, 6*(3), e279-e291.

Eskin, M., & others (2019). The role of religion in suicidal behavior, attitudes and psychological distress among university students: A multinational study. *Transcultural Psychiatry, 56,* 853-877.

Esposito, G., & others (2015). Judgment of infant cry: The roles of acoustic characteristics and sociodemographic characteristics. *Japanese Psychological Research, 57*(2), 126-134.

Esposito, G., & others (2017c). The development of attachment: Integrating genes, brain, behavior, and environment. *Behavioural Brain Research, 325*(B), 87-89.

Esposito, S., & others (2019). Environmental factors associated with type 1 diabetes. *Frontiers in Endocrinology, 10,* 592.

Esposito, S., & Principi, N. (2020). School closure during the coronavirus disease 2019 (COVID-19) pandemic: An effective intervention at the global level? *JAMA Pediatrics, 174*(10), 921-922.

Esteban-Ibañez, E., & others (2022). Age norms for grating acuity and contrast sensitivity in children using eye tracking technology. *International Ophthalmology, 42*(3), 747-756.

Esteves, M., & others (2021). Asymmetrical brain plasticity: Physiology and pathology. *Neuroscience, 454,* 3-14.

Estrada, E., & others (2017). Separating power and speed components of standardized intelligence measures. *Intelligence, 61,* 159-168.

Ethier, K.A., Harper, C.R., Hoo, E., & Ditts, P.J. (2016). The longitudinal impact of perceptions of parental monitoring on adolescent initiation of sexual activity. *Journal of Adolescent Health, 59,* 570-576.

Etscheidt, S.L., Skaar, N.R., Clopton, K.L., & Schmitz, S.L. (2023). Securing school-based mental health services through a six-step IEP approach. *TEACHING Exceptional Children,* 00400599221146318.

Evans, G.W., & English, G.W. (2002). The environment of poverty. *Child Development, 73,* 1238-1248.

Evans, G.W., & Kim, P. (2007). Childhood poverty and health: Cumulative risk exposure and stress dysregulation. *Psychological Science, 18,* 953-957.

Evans, N.S., Todaro, R.D., Golinkoff, R.M., & Hirsh-Pasek, K. (2022). Getting comfortable with uncertainty: The road to creativity in preschool children. In R.A. Beghetto & G.J. Jaeger (Eds.), *Uncertainty: A catalyst for creativity, learning and development.* Springer.

Evans, S.Z., Simons, L.G., & Simons, R.L. (2016). Factors that influence trajectories of delinquency throughout adolescence. *Journal of Youth and Adolescence, 45,* 156-171.

Evans-Lacko, S., & others (2017). Childhood bullying victimization is associated with the use of mental health services over five decades: A longitudinal nationally representative study. *Psychological Medicine, 47,* 127-135.

Evertson, C.M., & Emmer, E.T. (2017). *Classroom management for elementary teachers* (10th ed.). Pearson.

Ewing, E.S.K., & others (2019). Understanding of emotions and empathy: Predictors of positive parenting with preschoolers in economically stressed families. *Journal of Child and Family Studies, 28*(5), 1346-1358.

Eydal, G.B., Rostgaard, T., & Hiilamo, H. (2018). Family policies in the Nordic countries: aiming at equality. In *Handbook of family policy.* Edward Elgar Publishing.

F

Faas, S., Wu, S.C., & Geiger, S. (2017). The importance of play in early childhood education: A critical perspective on current policies and practices in Germany and Hong Kong. *Global Education Review, 4,* 75-91.

Fairclough, S.J., & others (2017). Fitness, fatness, and the reallocation of time between children's daily movement behaviors: An analysis of compositional data. *International Journal of Behavioral Nutrition and Physical Activity, 14*(1), 64.

Falbo, T., & Poston, D.L. (1993). The academic, personality, and physical outcomes of only children in China. *Child Development, 64,* 18-35.

Families in Sports Lab (2023). *Families in sports lab.* Retrieved March 18, 2023, from https://cehs.usu.edu/families-in-sport-lab/

Fan, J., Ren, L., & Li, X. (2020). Contributions of child temperament and marital quality to coparenting among Chinese families. *Children and Youth Services Review, 108,* 104610.

Fan, P., Zhang, Z., Liu, Y., & Xiong, Y. (2023). Parent-performed infant massage for improving parental mental state within 18 months postpartum: A systematic review. *Journal of Psychosocial Nursing and Mental Health Services, 61,* 52-59.

Fang, L., & Huang, Y.T. (2020). "I'm in between": Cultural identities of Chinese youth in Canada. *Families in Society, 101*(1), 1044389419891333.

Fantz, R.L. (1963). Pattern vision in newborn infants. *Science, 140,* 286-297.

FAO, IFAD, UNICEF, WFP & WHO (2022). *In brief to the state of food security and nutrition in the world 2022: Repurposing food and agricultural policies to make healthy diets more affordable.* FAO.

Farías-Antúnez, S., Santos, I.S., Matijasevich, A., & de Barros, A.J.D. (2020). Maternal mood symptoms in pregnancy and postpartum depression: Association with exclusive breastfeeding in a population-based birth cohort. *Social Psychiatry and Psychiatric Epidemiology, 55*(5), 635-643.

Farr, R.H. (2017). Does parental sexual orientation matter? A longitudinal follow-up of adoptive families with a school-age child. *Developmental Psychology, 53,* 252-264.

Farr, R.H., & Patterson, C.J. (2013). Coparenting among lesbian, gay, and heterosexual couples: Associations with adopted children's outcomes. *Child Development, 84,* 1226-1240.

Farrar, S., & Tapper, K. (2018). The effect of mindfulness on rational thinking. *Appetite, 123,* 468.

Farrington, D.P., Gaffney, H., Lösel, F., & Ttofi, M.M. (2017). Systematic reviews of the effectiveness of developmental prevention programs in reducing delinquency, aggression, and bullying. *Aggression and Violent Behavior, 33,* 91-106.

Favaro, A., & others (2019). The age of onset of eating disorders. In *Age of onset of mental disorders* (pp. 203-216). Springer.

Fawcett, C., & Kreutz, G. (2021). Twelve-month-old infants' physiological responses to music are affected by others' positive and negative reactions. *Infancy, 26*(6), 784-797.

Fazio, L.K., DeWolf, M., & Siegler, R.S. (2016). Strategy use and strategy choice in fraction magnitude comparison. *Journal of Experimental Psychology: Learning, Memory, and Cognition, 42,* 1-16.

Fearon, R., & Roisman, G. (2017). Attachment theory: Progress and future directions. *Current Opinion in Psychology, 15,* 131-136.

Fearon, R.P., & others (2010). The significance of insecure attachment and disorganization in the development of children's externalizing behavior: A meta-analytic study. *Child Development, 81,* 435-456.

Feeney, S., Moravcik, E., & Nolte, S. (2018). *Who am I in the lives of children?* (11th ed.). Pearson.

Feldgus, E., Cardonick, I., & Gentry, R. (2017). *Kid writing in the 21st century.* Hameray Publishing Group.

Feldman, R. (2017). The neurobiology of human attachments. *Trends in Cognitive Science, 21,* 80-89.

Feldman, R. (2019). The social neuroendocrinology of human parenting. In Bornstein, M.H. (Ed.), *Handbook of parenting* (pp. 220-249). Routledge.

Feldstein Ewing, S.W., & others (2016). Developmental cognitive neuroscience of adolescent sexual risk and alcohol use. *AIDS Behavior, 20*(Suppl. 1), S97-S108.

Feleszko, W., & others (2006). Parental tobacco smoking is associated with IL-13 secretion in children with allergic asthma. *Journal of Allergy and Clinical Immunology, 117,* 97-102.

Fenlon, J., & others (2019). Comparing sign language and gesture: Insights and pointing. *Glossa: A Journal of General Linguistics, 4*(1), 2.

Feraco, T., Resnati, D., Fregonese, D., Spoto, A., & Meneghetti, C. (2022). Soft skills and extracurricular activities sustain motivation and self-regulated learning at school. *Journal of Experimental Education, 90,* 550-569.

Fergus, T.A., & Bardeen, J.R. (2017). The metacognitions questionnaire—30. *Assessment, 26*(2), 223-234

Ferguson, B., & Waxman, S. (2017). Linking language and categorization in infancy. *Journal of Child Language, 44,* 527-552.

Ferguson, G.M., Causadias, J.M., & Simenec, T.S. (2023). Acculturation and psychopathology. *Annual Review of Clinical Psychology, 19,* 381-411.

Ferguson, G.M., Iturbide, M.I., Raffaelli, M. (2020). Proximal and remote acculturation: Adolescents' perspectives of biculturalism in two contexts. *Journal of Adolescent Research, 35,* 431-460.

Ferguson, S.M., & Ryan, A.M. (2019). It's lonely at the top: Adolescent students' peer-perceived popularity and self-perceived social contentment. *Journal of Youth and Adolescence, 48*(2), 341-358.

Fergusson, D.M., McLeod, G.F., & Horwood, L.J. (2014). Parental separation/divorce in childhood and partnership outcomes at age 30. *Journal of Child Psychology and Psychiatry, 55,* 352-360.

Fernald, A., Marchman, V.A., & Weisleder, A. (2013). SES differences in language processing skill and vocabulary are evident at 18 months. *Developmental Science, 16,* 234-248.

Fernandes, C., & others (2018). Mothers, fathers, sons, and daughters: Are there sex differences in the organization of secure base behavior during early childhood? *Infant Behavior and Development, 50,* 213-223.

Fernandez-Jaen, A., & others (2015). Cortical thickness differences in the prefrontal cortex in children and adolescents with ADHD in relation to dopamine transporter (DAT1) genotype. *Psychiatry Research, 233,* 409-117.

Ferreira, R.A., & others (2021). Word learning in two languages: Neural overlap and representational differences. *Neuropsychologia, 150,* 107703.

Field, A.E., & others (2001). Peer, parent, and media influences on the development of weight concerns and frequent dieting among preadolescent and adolescent girls and boys. *Pediatrics, 107,* 54-60.

Field, T. (2021). Massage therapy research review. *International Journal of Psychological Research and Reviews, 4,* 45.

Field, T.M. (2010). Postpartum depression effects on early interactions, parenting, and safety practices: A review. *Infant Behavior and Development, 33,* 1-6.

Field, T.M., Diego, M., & Hernandez-Reif, M. (2008). Prematurity and potential predictors. *International Journal of Neuroscience, 118,* 277-289.

Field, T.M., Diego, M., & Hernandez-Reif, M. (2010). Preterm infant massage therapy research: A review. *Infant Behavior and Development, 33,* 115-124.

Filges, T., Dietrichson, J., Viinholt, B.C.A., & Dalgaard, N.T. (2022). Service learning for improving academic success in students in grade K to 12: A systematic review. *Campbell Systematic Reviews, 18,* e1210.

Filippi, C., & others (2019). Neural correlates of infant action processing relate to theory of mind in early childhood. *Developmental Science,* e12876.

Fillo, J., Simpson, J.A., Rholes, W.S., & Kohn, J.L. (2015). Dads doing diapers: Individual and relational outcomes associated with the division of childcare across the transition to parenthood. *Journal of Personality and Social Psychology, 108,* 298–316.

Findley, T.O., & Northrup, H. (2021). The current state of prenatal detection of genetic conditions in congenital heart defects. *Translational Pediatrics, 10,* 2157–2170.

Finelli, J., Zeanah, C., & Smyke, A. (2019). Attachment disorders in early childhood. In C. Zeanah (Ed.), *Handbook of infant mental health* (4th ed.). Guilford Press.

Finet, C., Vermeer, H.J., Juffer, F., Bijttebier, P., & Bosmans, G. (2020). Adopted children's behavioral adjustment over time: Pre-adoption experiences and adoptive parenting. *Journal of Early Adolescence, 40,* 453–479.

Fingerman, K.L., Huo, M., & Birditt, K.S. (2020). A decade of research on intergenerational ties: Technological, economic, political, and demographic changes. *Journal of Marriage and Family, 82*(1), 383–403.

Finkelhor, D., Turner, H., Wormuth, B.K., Vanderminden, J., & Hamby, S. (2019). Corporal punishment: Current rates from a national survey. *Journal of Child and Family Studies, 28,* 1991–1997.

Finnane, J.M., Jansen, E., Mallan, K.M., & Daniels, L.A. (2017). Mealtime structure and responsive feeding practices are associated with less food fussiness and more food enjoyment in children. *Journal of Nutrition Education and Behavior, 49,* 11–18.

Fischer, S., Barnes, R.K., & Kilpatrick, S. (2019). Equipping parents to support their children's higher education aspirations: A design and evaluation tool. *Educational Review, 71*(2), 198–217.

Fisher, R.S., & others (2021). Coping trajectories and the health-related quality of life of childhood cancer survivors. *Journal of Pediatric Psychology, 46*(8), 960–969.

Fisher, S.D., & others (2021). Expanding the international conversation with fathers' mental health: Toward an era of inclusion in perinatal research and practice. *Archives of Women's Mental Health, 24*(5), 841–848.

Fiske, A., & Holmboe, K. (2019). Neural substrates of early executive function development. *Developmental Review, 52,* 42–62.

Fiske, A., & others (2022). The neural correlates of inhibitory control in 10-month-old infants: A functional near-infrared spectroscopy study. *NeuroImage, 257,* 119241.

Fitamen, C., Blaye, A., & Camos, V. (2019). The role of goal cueing in kindergarteners' working memory. *Journal of Experimental Child Psychology, 187,* 104666.

Fite, P., Frazer, A., DiPierro, M., & Abel, M. (2019). Youth perceptions of what is helpful during the middle school transition and correlates of transition difficulty. *Children and Schools, 41,* 55–64.

Fitzgerald, A., Fitzgerald, N., & Aherne, C. (2012). Do peers matter? A review of peer and/or friends' influence on physical activity among American adolescents. *Journal of Adolescence, 35,* 941–958.

FitzGerald, T.L., & others (2018). Body structure, function, activity, and participation in 3- to 6-year-old children born very preterm: An ICF-based systematic review and meta-analysis. *Physical Therapy, 98*(8), 691–704.

Fivush, R. (2019a). *Family narratives and the development of an autobiographical self: Social and cultural perspectives on autobiographical memory.* Routledge.

Fivush, R. (2019b). Sociocultural developmental approaches to autobiographical memory. *Applied Cognitive Psychology, 33,* 489–497.

Flam, K.K., Sandler, I., Wolchik, S., & Tein, J.Y. (2016). Non-residential father-child involvement, interparental conflict, and mental health of children following divorce: A person-focused approach. *Journal of Youth and Adolescence, 45,* 581–593.

Flanagan, C.A., Kim, T., Collura, J., & Kopish, M.A. (2015). Community service and adolescents' social capital. *Journal of Research on Adolescence, 25,* 295–309.

Flanagan, R.M., & Symonds, J.E. (2022). Children's self-talk in naturalistic classroom settings in middle childhood: A systematic literature review. *Educational Research Review, 35*(3), 100432.

Flannery, D.J., & others (2016). Bullying prevention: A summary of the report of the National Academies of Sciences, Engineering, and Medicine: Committee on the Biological and Psychological Effects of Peer Victimization: Lessons for bullying prevention. *Prevention Science, 17,* 1044–1053.

Flannery, M. (2017). Self-determination theory: Intrinsic motivation and behavior change. *Oncology Nursing Forum, 44,* 155–156.

Flavell, J.H., Friedrichs, A., & Hoyt, J. (1970). Developmental changes in memorization processes. *Cognitive Psychology, 1,* 324–340.

Flavell, J.H., Green, F.L., & Flavell, E.R. (1995). The development of children's knowledge about attentional focus. *Developmental Psychology, 31,* 706–712.

Flavell, J.H., Green, F.L., & Flavell, E.R. (2000). Development of children's awareness of their own thoughts. *Journal of Cognition and Development, 1,* 97–112.

Flensborg-Madsen, T., & Mortensen, E.L. (2017). Predictors of motor developmental milestones during the first year of life. *European Journal of Pediatrics, 176,* 109–119.

Fletcher, J.M., Ross, S.L., & Zhang, Y. (2020). The consequences of friendships: Evidence on the effect of social relationships in school on academic achievement. *Journal of Urban Economics, 116,* 103241.

Fletcher, S., & others (2017). Tracking of toddler fruit and vegetable preferences to intake and adiposity later in childhood. *Maternal and Child Nutrition, 13*(2), e12290.

Fletcher-Watson, S., & Happé, F. (2019). *Autism: A new introduction to psychological theory and current debate.* Routledge.

Flores, J.P., Swartz, K.L., Stewart, E.A., & Wilcox, H.C. (2020). Co-occurring risk factors among US high school students at risk for suicidal thoughts and behaviors. *Journal of Affective Disorders, 266,* 743–752.

Florida Institute for Child Welfare (2021, May 19). Accessed from https://www.facebook.com/FSUChildWelfare/posts/2957852384535481

Florit, E., & others (2021). Home language activities and expressive vocabulary of toddlers from low-SES monolingual families and bilingual immigrant families. *International Journal of Environmental Research and Public Health, 18*(1), 296.

Flouri, E., Midouhas, E., & Joshi, H. (2014). Family poverty and trajectories of children's emotional and behavioral problems: The moderating role of self-regulation and verbal cognitive ability. *Journal of Abnormal Child Psychology, 42,* 1043–1056.

Floyd, R.G., Farmer, R.L., Schneider, W.J., & McGrew, K.S. (2021). Theories and measurement of intelligence. In L.M. Glidden, L. Abbeduto, L.L. McIntyre, & M.J. Tassé (Eds.), *APA handbook of intellectual and developmental disabilities: Foundations* (pp. 385–424). American Psychological Association.

Flynn, J.R. (2018). Reflections about intelligence over 40 years. *Intelligence, 70,* 73–83.

Flynn, J.R. (2020). Secular changes in intelligence. In R.J. Sternberg (Ed.), *Cambridge handbook of intelligence* (2nd ed.). Cambridge University Press.

Flynn, J.T., & others (Eds.) (2023). *Pediatric hypertension* (5th ed.). Springer.

Fong, C.J., Patall, E.A., Vasquez, A.C., & Stautberg, S. (2019). A meta-analysis of negative feedback on intrinsic motivation. *Educational Psychology Review, 31,* 121–162.

Foox, J., & others (2021). Performance assessment of DNA sequencing platforms in the ABRF Next-Generation Sequencing Study. *Nature Biotechnology, 39,* 1129–1140.

Forbes, E.E., & others (2021). A social affective neuroscience model of risk and resilience in adolescent depression: Preliminary evidence and application to sexual and gender minority adolescents. *Biological Psychiatry, Cognitive Neuroscience, and Neuroimaging, 6,* 186–199.

Forsberg, A., Adams, E.J., & Cowan, N. (2022). The development of visual memory. In T. Brady & W. Bainbridge (Eds.), *Visual memory* (pp. 298–314). Routledge.

Forsberg, A., Blume, C.L., & Cowan, N. (2021). The development of metacognitive accuracy in working memory across childhood. *Developmental Psychology, 57*(8), 1297.

Foss, K.D.B., Thomas, S., Khoury, J.C., Myer, G.D., & Hewett, T.E. (2018). A school-based neuromuscular training program and sport-related injury incidence: A prospective randomized controlled clinical trial. *Journal of Athletic Training, 53,* 20-28.

Foster-Hanson, E., & Rhodes, M. (2023). Stereotypes as prototypes in children's gender concepts. *Developmental Science, 26,* e13345.

Fourment, K., Espinoza, C., Ribeiro, A.C.L., & Mesman, J. (2022). Latin American Attachment studies: A narrative review. *Infant Mental Health Journal, 43*(4), 653-676.

Fouts, H.N., & Bader, L.R. (2017). Transitions in siblinghood: Integrating developments, cultural, and evolutionary perspectives. In D. Narváez & others (Eds.), *Contexts for young child flourishing.* Oxford University Press.

Fox, E.L., & others (2018). Who knows what: An exploration of the infant feeding message environment and intracultural differences in Port-au-Prince, Haiti. *Maternal & Child Nutrition, 14*(2), e12537.

Fox, N.A., & others (2021). Understanding the emergence of social anxiety in children with behavioral inhibition. *Biological Psychiatry, 89,* 681-689.

Franchak, J.M. (2019). Changing opportunities for learning in everyday life: Infant body position over the first year. *Infancy, 24,* 187-209.

Francis, J.K.R., & Gold, M.A. (2017). Long-acting reversible contraception for adolescents: A review. *JAMA Pediatrics, 171*(7), 694-701.

Frangou, S., & others (2022). Cortical thickness across the lifespan: Data from 17,075 healthy individuals aged 3-90 years. *Human Brain Mapping, 43*(1), 431-451.

Frank, M.C., Braginsky, M., Marchman, V.A., & Yurovsky, D. (2020). *Variability and consistency in early language learning: The Wordbank Project.* MIT Press.

Franke, B., & Buitelaar, J.K. (2018). Gene-environment interactions. In T. Banaschewski, D. Coghill, & A. Zuddas (Eds.), *Oxford textbook of attention deficit hyperactivity disorder.* Oxford University Press.

Frankel, A.S., & others (2018). Sexting, risk behavior, and mental health in adolescents: An examination of 2015 Pennsylvania Youth Risk Behavior Survey data. *Journal of School Health, 88*(3), 190-199.

Frankenhuis, W.E., & Fraley, R.C. (2017). What do evolutionary models teach us about sensitive periods in psychological development? *European Psychologist, 22,* 141-150.

Franzago, M., & others (2020). Genes and diet in the prevention of chronic diseases in future generations. *International Journal of Molecular Science 21,* 7.

Frederiksen, H., & others (2020). Sex-specific estrogen levels and reference intervals from infancy to late adulthood determined by LC-MS/MS. *Journal of Endocrinology and Metabolism, 105*(3), 764-768.

Freeman, S., & others (2017). *Biological science* (6th ed.). Pearson.

Freud, S. (1917). *A general introduction to psychoanalysis.* Washington Square Press.

Frey, W.H. (2018). *Diversity explosion: How new racial demographics are remaking America.* Brookings Institution Press.

Frey, W.H. (2019). *America's not full. Its future rests with young immigrants.* Washington, DC: Brookings Institution. Retrieved March 11, 2020, from https://www.brookings.edu/blog/the-avenue/2019/04/10/america-is-not-full-its-future-rests-with-young-immigrants/

Frick, A.P. (2021). Advanced maternal age and adverse pregnancy outcomes. *Best Practice & Research Clinical Obstetrics & Gynaecology, 70,* 92-100.

Friedman, N.P., & Robbins, T.W. (2022). The role of prefrontal cortex in cognitive control and executive function. *Neuropsychopharmacology, 47,* 72-89.

Friedman, S.L., Melhuish, E., & Hill, C. (2010). Childcare research at the dawn of a new millennium: An update. In G. Bremner & T. Wachs (Eds.), *Wiley-Blackwell handbook of infant development* (2nd ed.). Wiley-Blackwell.

Friedman-Krauss, & others (2022). *The State of Preschool 2021: State Preschool Yearbook.* National Institute for Early Education Research.

Friend, M. (2018). *Special education* (5th ed.). Pearson.

Fromberg, D., & Bergen, D. (2015). *Play from birth to twelve* (3rd ed.). Routledge.

Fry, R., & Parker, K. (2018, November 15). *Early benchmarks show "post-millennials" on track to be most diverse, best-educated generation yet.* Pew Research Center.

Fu, N., & others (2023). A systematic review of measures of theory of mind for children. *Developmental Review, 67,* 101061.

Fujita, N., Devine, R.T., & Hughes, C. (2022). Theory of mind and executive function in early childhood: A cross-cultural investigation. *Cognitive Development, 61,* 101150.

Fung, H., Li, J., & Lam, C.K. (2017). Multi-faceted discipline strategies of Chinese parenting. *International Journal of Behavioral Development, 41,* 472-481.

Funk, C.M., & others (2016). Local slow waves in superficial layers of primary cortical areas during REM sleep. *Current Biology, 26,* 396-403.

Furno, L., Demchak, M., & Bingham, A. (2020). Young children with hearing impairment and other diagnoses: Effects of sound-field amplification. *Rural Special Education Quarterly, 39*(3), 152-166.

Furth, H.G., & Wachs, H. (1975). *Thinking goes to school.* Oxford University Press.

G

Gadermann, A.M. (2022). Prevalence of mental health disorders among immigrant, refugee, and nonimmigrant children and youth in British Columbia, Canada. *JAMA Network Open, 5*(2), e2144934.

Gagne, J.R., Liew, J., & Nwadinobi, O.K. (2021). How does the broader construct of self-regulation relate to emotion regulation in young children? *Developmental Review, 60,* 100965.

Gaillard, A., & others (2014). Predictors of postpartum depression: Prospective study of 264 women followed during pregnancy and postpartum. *Psychiatry Research, 215,* 341-346.

Galbally, M., & others (2020). The mother, the infant and the mother-infant relationship: What is the impact of antidepressant medication in pregnancy. *Journal of Affective Disorders, 272,* 363-370.

Galinsky, E. (2010). *Mind in the making.* HarperCollins.

Galinsky, E., & David, J. (1988). *The preschool years: Family strategies that work—From experts and parents.* Times Books.

Galinsky, E., & others (2017). Civic science for public use: Mind in the Making and Vroom. *Child Development, 88*(5), 1409-1418.

Galland, B.C., Taylor, B.J., Edler, D.E., & Herbison, P. (2012). Normal sleep patterns in infants and children: A systematic review of observational studies. *Sleep Medicine Review, 16,* 213-222.

Gallant, C.M., Lavis, L., & Mahy, C.E. (2020). Developing an understanding of others' emotional states: Relations among affective theory of mind and empathy measures in early childhood. *British Journal of Developmental Psychology, 38*(2), 151-166.

Galler, J.R., & others (2012). Infant malnutrition is associated with persisting attention deficits in middle childhood. *Journal of Nutrition, 142,* 788-794.

Galmiche, M., & others (2019). Prevalence of eating disorders over the 2000-2018 period: A systematic literature review. *The American Journal of Clinical Nutrition, 109*(5), 1402-1413.

Gangestad, S.W., & Chang, L. (2020). The contents and discontents of the nature-nurture debate. In F.M. Cheung & D.F. Halpern (Eds.), *Cambridge handbook of the international psychology of women.* Cambridge University Press.

Ganong, L., & Coleman, M. (Eds.) (2017). *Stepfamily relationships: Development, dynamics, and interventions.* Springer.

Ganong, L., Coleman, M., Sanner, C., & Berkley, S. (2022). Effective stepparenting: Empirical evidence of what works. *Family Relations, 71,* 900-917.

Gao, M., & others (2023). Dynamics of mother-infant parasympathetic regulation during face-to-face interaction: The role of maternal emotion dysregulation. *Psychophysiology, 60*(6), e14248.

Garandeau, C.F., Vartio, A., Poskiparta, E., & Salmivalli, C. (2016). School bullies' intention to change behavior following teacher interventions: Effects of empathy arousal, condemning of bullying, and blaming the perpetrator. *Prevention Science, 17,* 1034-1043.

Garcia, E. (2020). Schools are still segregated, and Black children are paying a price. ERIC #ED603475.

Garcia-Tabuenca, Z., & others (2021). Development of the brain connectome follows puberty-dependent nonlinear trajectories. *Neuroimage, 229,* 117769.

Gardner, H. (1983). *Frames of mind.* Basic Books.

Gardner, M., & Steinberg, L. (2005). Peer influence on risk taking, risk preference, and risky decision making in adolescence and adulthood: An experimental study. *Developmental Psychology, 41,* 625-635.

Garfield, C.F., & others (2012). Trends in attention deficit hyperactivity disorder ambulatory diagnosis and medical treatment in the United States 2000-2010. *Academic Pediatrics, 12,* 110-116.

Garg, N., Schiebinger, L., Jurafsky, D., & Zou, J. (2018). Word embeddings quantify 100 years of gender and ethnic stereotypes. *Proceedings of the National Academy of Sciences, 115*(16), E3635-E3644.

Gariepy, G., & others (2020). How are adolescents sleeping? Adolescent sleep patterns and sociodemographic differences in 24 European and North American countries. *Journal of Adolescent Health, 66*(6), S81-S88.

Garthe, R.C., Sullivan, T.N., & Behrhorst, K.L. (2018). A latent class analysis of early adolescent peer and dating violence: Associations with symptoms of depression and anxiety. *Journal of Interpersonal Violence, 36*(5-6), 2031-2049.

Gartstein, M.A., Hancock, G.R., & Iverson, S.L. (2018). Positive affectivity and fear trajectories in infancy: Contributions of mother-child interaction factors. *Child Development, 89,* 1519-1534.

Gartstein, M., & Putnam, S. (Eds.) (2018). *Toddlers, parents, and culture.* Routledge.

Gartstein, M.A., & Putnam, S.P. (Eds.) (2019). *Toddlers, parents and culture: findings from the joint effort toddler temperament consortium.* Routledge.

Gartstein, M.A., Putnam, S., & Kliewer, R. (2016). Do infant temperament characteristics predict core academic abilities in preschool-aged children? *Learning and Individual Differences, 45,* 299-306.

Gartstein, M.A., & Skinner, M.K. (2018). Prenatal influences on temperament development: The role of environmental epigenetics. *Development and Psychopathology, 30,* 1269-1303.

Garvey, C. (2000). *Play* (Enlarged Ed.). Harvard University Press.

Gascon, A., Gamache, D., St-Laurent, D., & Stipanicic, A. (2022). Do we over-diagnose ADHD in North America? A critical review and clinical recommendations. *Journal of Clinical Psychology, 78*(12), 2363-2380.

Gasser, L., & Keller, M. (2009). Are the competent morally good? Perspective taking and moral motivation of children involved in bullying. *Social Development, 18*(4), 798-816.

Gastelle, M., & Kerns, K.A. (2022). A systematic review of representational and behavioral measures of parent-child attachment available for middle childhood. *Human Development, 66*(1), 1-29.

Gattamorta, K.A., & others (2017). Psychiatric symptoms, parental attachment, and reasons for use as correlates of heavy substance use among treatment-seeking Hispanic adolescents. *Substance Use and Misuse, 52,* 392-400.

Gattario, K.H., & Frisén, A. (2019). From negative to positive body image: Men's and women's journeys from early adolescence to emerging adulthood. *Body Image, 28,* 53-65.

Gausman, J., & others (2019). Clustered risk: An ecological understanding of sexual activity among adolescent boys and girls in two urban slums in Monrovia, Liberia. *Social Science & Medicine, 224,* 106-115.

Gauvain, M. (2013). Sociocultural contexts of development. In P.D. Zelazo (Ed.), *Oxford handbook of developmental psychology.* Oxford University Press.

Gauvain, M. (2018). Collaborative problem solving: Social and developmental considerations. *Psychological Science in the Public Interest, 19,* 53-58.

Geary, D.C., Nicholas, A., Li, Y., & Sun, J. (2017). Developmental change in the influence of domain-general abilities and domain-specific knowledge on mathematics achievement: An eight-year longitudinal study. *Journal of Educational Psychology, 109,* 680-693.

Gee, C.L., & Heyman, G.D. (2007). Children's evaluations of other people's self-descriptions. *Social Development, 16,* 800-818.

Gelman, R. (1969). Conservation acquisition: A problem of learning to attend to relevant attributes. *Journal of Experimental Child Psychology, 7,* 67-87.

Gelman, S.A., & Kalish, C.W. (2006). Conceptual development. In W. Damon & R. Lerner (Eds.), *Handbook of child psychology* (6th ed.). Wiley.

Gennetian, L.A., & Miller, C. (2002). Children and welfare reform: A view from an experimental welfare reform program in Minnesota. *Child Development, 73,* 601-620.

George Dalmida, S., & others (2017). Sexual risk behaviors of African American adolescent females: The role of cognitive and risk factors. *Journal of Transcultural Nursing, 29*(1): 74-83.

Gernhardt, A., Keller, H., & Rubeling, H. (2016). Children's family drawings as expressions of attachment representations across cultures: Possibilities and limitations. *Child Development, 87,* 1069-1078.

Geronimi, E.M.C., Arellano, B., & Woodruff-Borden, J. (2020). Relating mindfulness and executive function in children. *Clinical Child Psychology and Psychiatry, 25,* 435-445.

Gershoff, E.T., & Grogan-Kaylor, A. (2016). Spanking and child outcomes: Old controversies and new meta-analyses. *Journal of Family Psychology, 30,* 453-469.

Gershoff, E.T., & others (2018). The strength of the causal evidence against physical punishment of children and its implications for parents, psychologists, and policymakers. *American Psychologist, 73,* 626-638.

Gerst, E.H., Dirino, P.T., Fletcher, J.M., & Yoshida, H. (2017). Cognitive and behavioral rating measures of executive function predictors of academic outcomes in children. *Child Neuropsychology, 23*(4), 381-407.

Gesell, A.L. (1934a). *An atlas of infant behavior.* Yale University Press.

Gesell, A.L. (1934b). *Infancy and human growth.* Macmillan.

Gestwicki, C. (2017). *Developmentally appropriate practice* (6th ed.). Cengage.

Geyer, C., & Ogbonnaya, I.N. (2021). The relationship between maternal domestic violence and infant and toddlers' emotional regulation: Highlighting the need for preventive services. *Journal of Interpersonal Violence, 36,* 1029-1048.

Gibbs, J.C. (2014). *Moral development and reality: Beyond the theories of Kohlberg and Hoffman* (3rd ed.). Pearson.

Gibbs, J.C. (2019). *Moral development and reality: Beyond the theories of Kohlberg, Hoffman, and Haidt* (4th ed.). Oxford University Press.

Gibbs, J.C., Basinger, K.S., Grime, R.L., & Snarey, J.R. (2007). Moral judgment development across cultures: Revisiting Kohlberg's universality claims. *Developmental Review, 27,* 443-500.

Gibson, E.J. (1989). Exploratory behavior in the development of perceiving, acting, and the acquiring of knowledge. *Annual Review of Psychology, 39,* 1-42.

Gibson, E.J., & others (1987). Detection of the traversability of surfaces by crawling and walking infants. *Journal of Experimental Psychology: Human Perception and Performance, 13,* 533-544.

Gibson, E.J., & Walk, R.D. (1960). The "visual cliff." *Scientific American, 202*(4), 64-71.

Gibson, J.J. (1979). *The ecological approach to visual perception.* Houghton Mifflin.

Gibson-Davis, C., Keister, L.A., & Gennetian, L.A. (2021). Net worth poverty in child households by race and ethnicity, 1989-2019. *Journal of Marriage and Family, 83,* 667-682.

Giesbrecht, G.F., & others (2020). Parental use of "cry out" in a community sample during the first year of life. *Journal of Developmental and Behavioral Pediatrics, 41,* 379-387.

Gilkerson, J., & others (2018). Language experience in the second year of life and language outcomes in late childhood. *Pediatrics, 142,* e20174276.

Gillen-O'Neel, C., Huynh, V.W., & Fuligni, A.J. (2013). To study or to sleep? The academic costs of extra studying at the expense of sleep. *Child Development, 84*(1), 133-142.

Gilligan, C. (1982). *In a different voice.* Harvard University Press.

Gilligan, C. (1992, May). *Joining the resistance: Girls' development in adolescence.* Paper presented at the symposium on development and vulnerability in close relationships, Montreal, Quebec.

Gilligan, C. (1996). The centrality of relationships in psychological development: A puzzle, some evidence, and a theory. In G.G. Noam & K.W. Fischer (Eds.), *Development and vulnerability in close relationships.* Erlbaum.

Gilligan, C., Spencer, R., Weinberg, M.K., & Bertsch, T. (2003). On the listening guide: A voice-centered relational model. In P.M. Carnic & J.E. Rhodes (Eds.), *Qualitative research in psychology.* American Psychological Association.

Gilmore, J.H., Knickmeyer, R.C., & Gao, W. (2018). Imaging structural and functional brain development in early childhood. *Nature Reviews Neuroscience, 19*(3), 123.

Gingoyon, A., & others (2022). Chronic iron deficiency and cognitive function in early childhood. *Pediatrics, 150*(6), e2021055926.

Giofre, D., & others (2017). Intelligence measures as diagnostic tools for children with specific learning disabilities. *Intelligence, 61,* 140-145.

Girme, Y.U., & others (2021). Infants' attachment insecurity predicts attachment-relevant emotion regulation in adulthood. *Emotion, 21,* 260-272.

Giuntella, O. (2017). Why does the health of Mexican immigrants deteriorate? New evidence from linked birth records. *Journal of Health Economics, 54,* 1-16.

Glasper, E., Richardson, J., & Randall, D. (2021). *A textbook of children's and young people's nursing* (3rd ed.). Elsevier.

Gleason, J., & Ratner, N. (2023). *The development of language* (10th ed.). Plural Publishing.

Gleason, J.L., & others (2021). Association between maternal caffeine consumption and metabolism and neonatal anthropometry: A secondary analysis of the NICHD fetal growth studies–singletons. *JAMA Network Open, 4*(3), e213238.

Gleason, T.R., & White, R.E. (2023). Pretend play as abstraction: Implications for early development and beyond. *Neuroscience & Biobehavioral Reviews, 147,* 105090.

Glock, S., & Kleen, H. (2017). Gender and student misbehavior: Evidence from implicit and explicit measures. *Teaching and Teacher Education, 67,* 93-103.

Gnambs, T., & Appel, M. (2018). Narcissism and social networking behavior: A meta-analysis. *Journal of Personality, 86*(2), 200-212.

Gobet, F. (2018). The future of expertise: The need for a multidisciplinary approach. *Journal of Expertise, 1,* 107-113.

Godfrey, K.M., & others (2017). Influence of maternal obesity on the long-term health of offspring. *Lancet. Diabetes and Endocrinology, 5,* 53-64.

Godleski, S.A., & others (2020). Parent socialization of emotion in a high-risk sample. *Developmental Psychology, 56,* 489-502.

Godwin, J., & Conduct Problems Prevention Research Group (2020). The Fast Track intervention's impact on behaviors of despair in adolescence and young adulthood. *Proceedings of the National Academy of Sciences, 117,* 31748-31753.

Goffin, K.C., Kochanska, G., & Yoon, J.E. (2020). Children's theory of mind as a mechanism linking parents' mind-mindedness in infancy with children's conscience. *Journal of Experimental Child Psychology, 193,* 104784.

Goksan, S., & others (2015). fMRI reveals neural activity overlap between adult and infant pain. *eLife, 4,* e06356.

Goldberg, A.E., Tornello, S., Farr, R., Smith, J.Z., & Miranda, L. (2020). Barriers to adoption and foster care and openness to child characteristics among transgender adults. *Children and Youth Services Review, 109,* 104699.

Goldberg, W.A., & Lucas-Thompson, R. (2008). Maternal and paternal employment, effects of. In M.M. Haith & J.B. Benson (Eds.), *Encyclopedia of infant and early childhood development.* Elsevier.

Goldin-Meadow, S. (2018). Taking a hands-on approach to learning. *Policy Insights from the Behavioral and Brain Sciences, 5,* 163-170.

Goldman E.J., Baumann, A.E., & Poulin-Dubois, D. (2022). Preschoolers' anthropomorphizing of robots: Do human-like properties matter? *Frontiers in Psychology, 13,* 1102370.

Goldstein, M.H., King, A.P., & West, M.J. (2003). Social interaction shapes babbling: Testing parallels between birdsong and speech. *Proceedings of the National Academy of Sciences, 100*(13), 8030-8035.

Goldston, D.B., & others (2016). Developmental trajectories of suicidal thoughts and behaviors from adolescence through adulthood. *Journal of the American Academy of Child & Adolescent Psychiatry, 55*(5), 400-407.

Goldstuck, N.D., & Cheung, T.S. (2019). The efficacy of intrauterine devices for emergency contraception and beyond: A systematic review update. *International Journal of Women's Health, 11,* 471-479.

Goleman, D., Kaufman, P., & Ray, M. (1993). *The creative spirit.* Plume.

Golinkoff, R.M., & Hirsh-Pasek, K. (2000). *How babies talk: The magic and mystery of language in the first three years of life.* Penguin.

Golinkoff, R.M., Hoff, E., Rowe, M.L., Tamis-LeMonda, C.S., & Hirsh-Pasek, K. (2019). Language matters: Denying the existence of the 30-million-word gap has serious consequences. *Child Development, 90*(3), 985-992.

Gollnick, D.M., & Chinn, P.C. (2021). *Multicultural education in a pluralistic society* (11th ed.). Pearson.

Golomb, C. (2011). *The creation of imaginary worlds.* Jessica Kingsley.

Golomb, C. (2016). *The development of artistically gifted children.* Psychology Press.

Golombok, S. (2021). Love and truth: What really matters for children born through third-party assisted reproduction. *Child Development Perspectives, 15,* 103-109.

Golombok, S., & others (2014). Adoptive gay father families: Parent-child relationships and children's psychological adjustment. *Child Development, 85,* 456-468.

Gomendio, M. (2023). PISA: Mission failure. *Education Next, 23*(2), 16-22.

Gómez-Roig, M.D., & others (2021). Environmental exposure during pregnancy: Influence on prenatal development and early life: A comprehensive review. *Fetal Diagnosis and Therapy, 48,* 245-257.

Gonthier, C. (2022). Cross-cultural differences in visuo-spatial processing and the culture-fairness of visuo-spatial intelligence tests: An integrative review and a model for matrices tasks. *Cognitive Research: Principles and Implications, 7*(1), 11.

Gonzales, C.R., & others (2021). The Head-Toes-Knees-Shoulders Revised (HTKS-R): Development and psychometric properties of a revision to reduce floor effects. *Early Childhood Research Quarterly, 56,* 320-332.

Gonzales, N.A., & others (2016). Culturally adaptive preventive interventions for children and adolescents. In D. Cicchetti (Ed.), *Developmental psychopathology* (3rd ed.). Wiley.

Gonzales, R., & others (2017). Ethnic identity development and acculturation preferences among minority and majority youth: Group norms and contact. *Child Development, 88,* 743-760.

González Briceño, L.G., & others (2019). Improved general and height-specific quality of life in children with short stature after 1 year on growth hormone. *The Journal of Clinical Endocrinology & Metabolism, 104*(6), 2103-2111.

González-Ruiz, K., & others (2017). The effects of exercise on abdominal fat and liver enzymes in pediatric obesity: A systematic review and meta-analysis. *Child Obesity, 13*(4), 272-282.

Good, C., Rattan, A., & Dweck, C.S. (2012). Why do women opt out? Sense of belonging and women's representation in mathematics. *Journal of Personality and Social Psychology, 102,* 700-717.

Good, M., & Willoughby, T. (2008). Adolescence as a sensitive period for spiritual development. *Child Development Perspectives, 2,* 32-37.

Goodman, R.J., & others (2019). Close relationships and depression: A developmental cascade approach. *Development and Psychopathology, 31*(4), 1451-1465.

Goodman, W.B., & others (2022). Evaluation of a Family Connects dissemination to four high-poverty rural counties. *Maternal and Child Health Journal, 26,* 1067-1076.

Goodvin, R., Winer, A.C., & Thompson, R.A. (2015). The individual child: Temperament, emotion, self, and personality. In M. Bornstein & M.E. Lamb (Eds.), *Developmental science* (7th ed.). Psychology Press.

Goodway, J., Ozmun, J., & Gallahue, D. (2020). *Understanding motor development* (8th ed.). Jones & Bartlett Learning.

Gopnik, A. (2010). Commentary. In R.E. Gitlivsky, *Mind in the making.* HarperCollins.

Gordon, I., Zagoory-Sharon, O., Leckman, J.F., & Feldman, R. (2010). Oxytocin and the development of parenting in humans. *Biological Psychiatry, 68,* 377-382.

Gordon, N. (2017). *Race, poverty, and interpreting overrepresentation in special education.* Brookings.

Gordon, R., & others (2020). Working memory and high-level cognition in children: An analysis of timing and accuracy in complex span tasks. *Journal of Experimental Child Psychology, 191,* 104736.

Gorukanti, A., & others (2017). Adolescents' attitudes towards e-cigarette ingredients, safety, addictive properties, social norms, and regulation. *Preventive Medicine, 94,* 65-71.

Goshin, M., Dubrov, D., Kosaretsky, S., & Grigoryev, D. (2021). The strategies of parental involvement in adolescents' education and extracurricular activities. *Journal of Youth and Adolescence, 50,* 906-920.

Goswami, R.G., & Thakur, M.B. (2019). Folk beliefs of food avoidance and prescription among menstruating and pregnant Karbi women of Kamrup district, Assam. *Journal of Ethnic Foods, 6,* 19.

Gottlieb, A., & DeLoache, J. (2017). *A world of babies* (2nd ed.). Cambridge University Press.

Gottlieb, G. (2007). Probabilistic epigenesis. *Developmental Science, 10,* 1–11.

Gottman, J.M. (2014). *Research on parenting.* Retrieved February 25, 2014, from www.gottman.com/parenting/research

Gottman, J.M. (2017). *Research on parenting.* Retrieved January 5, 2017, from www.gottman.com/parenting/research

Gottman, J.M., & Parker, J.G. (Eds.). (1987). *Conversations of friends.* Cambridge University Press.

Gottman Institute (2023). *Bringing baby home.* Retrieved xxx from www.gottman.com/professionals/training/bringing-baby-home/

Gould, S.J. (1981). *The mismeasure of man.* W.W. Norton.

Goupil, L., & Kouider, S. (2019). Developing a reflective mind: From core metacognition to explicit self-reflection. *Current Directions in Psychological Science, 28,* 403–408.

Gower, A.L., Cousin, M., & Borowsky, I.W. (2017). A multilevel, statewide investigation of school district anti-bullying policy quality and student bullying involvement. *Journal of School Health, 87,* 174–181.

Goyal, M.K., & others (2020). Racial and/or ethnic and socioeconomic disparities of SARS-CoV-2 infection among children. *Pediatrics, 146*(4), e2020009951.

Gozdas, E., & others (2019). Developmental changes in functional brain networks from birth through adolescence. *Human Brain Mapping, 40*(5), 1434–1444.

Grabowska, A. (2020). Sex differences in the brain. In F.M. Cheung & D.F. Halpern (Eds.), *Cambridge handbook of the international psychology of women.* Cambridge University Press.

Gradworld FSU (2019). *Lawrence Jackson.* Retrieved August 29, 2019, from https://gradworld.fsu.edu/graduates/lawrence-jackson/

Graham, J., & Valdesolo, P. (2017). Morality. In K. Deaux & M. Snyder (Eds.), *Oxford handbook of personality and social psychology.* Oxford University Press.

Graham, M.E., & others (2023). Assisted reproductive technology: Short- and long-term outcomes. *Developmental Medicine & Child Neurology, 65*(1), 38–49.

Graham, S. (2018). Race/ethnicity and social adjustment of adolescents: How (not if) school diversity matters. *Educational Psychologist, 53,* 64–77.

Graham, S., & Alves, R. (2021). Research and teaching writing. *Reading and Writing: An Interdisciplinary Journal, 34,* 1613–1621.

Graham, S., & others (2021). Writing strategy interventions. In D. Dinsmore & others (Eds.), *Handbook of strategies and strategic processing.* Routledge.

Graham, S., & Perin, D. (2007). A meta-analysis of writing instruction for adolescent students. *Journal of Educational Psychology, 99,* 445–476.

Granqvist, P., & Duschinsky, R. (2021). Attachment theory and research. In *Oxford research encyclopedia of psychology.* https://doi.org/10.1093/acrefore/9780190236557.013.51

Grant, J.H., & others (2018). Implementing group prenatal care in southwest Georgia through public–private partnerships. *Maternal and Child Health Journal, 22*(11), 1535–1542.

Grant-Marsney, H., Grotevant, H.D., & Sayer, A. (2015). Links between adolescents' closeness to adoptive parents and attachment style in young adulthood. *Family Relations, 64,* 221–232.

Grasso, K.L., & Trumbull, L.A. (2023). Sexuality and safer sex communication: What is left out of sexuality education in the United States? In W.J. Taverner (Ed.), *Sex education research.* Routledge.

Gravetter, F.J., & others (2021). *Essentials of statistics for the behavioral sciences* (10th ed.). Cengage.

Gravetter, R.J., & Forzano, L.B. (2019). *Research methods for the behavioral sciences* (6th ed.). Cengage.

Gray, K., & Graham, J. (2018). *The atlas of moral psychology.* Guilford Press.

Graziano, A., & Raulin, M. (2020). *Research methods* (9th ed., loose leaf). Pearson.

Greco, L.M., & Kraimer, M.I. (2020). Goal-setting in the career-management process: An identity theory perspective. *Journal of Applied Psychology, 105,* 40–57.

Green, J., & others (2017). Randomized trial of parent-mediated intervention for infants at high risk for autism: Longitudinal outcomes to age 3 years. *Journal of Child Psychology and Psychiatry, 58*(12), 1330–1340.

Green, T., Flash, S., & Reiss, A.L. (2019). Sex differences in psychiatric disorders: What we can learn from sex chromosome aneuploidies. *Neuropsychopharmacology, 44,* 9–21.

Greenberg, D.M., Warrier, V., Allison, C., & Baron-Cohen, S. (2018). Testing the empathizing-systemizing theory of sex differences and the extreme male brain theory of autism in half a million people. *Proceedings of the National Academy of Sciences, 115,* 12152–12157.

Greenberg, E.H. (2018). Public preferences for targeted and universal preschool. *AERA Open, 4*(1), 1–20.

Greer, F.R., Sicherer, S.H., & Burks, A.W. (2019). The effects of early nutritional interventions on the development of atopic disease in infants and children: The role of maternal dietary restriction, breastfeeding, hydrolyzed formulas, and timing of introduction of allergenic complementary foods. *Pediatrics, 143*(4), e20190281.

Greitemeyer, T. (2022). The dark and bright side of video game consumption: Effects of violent and prosocial video games. *Current Opinion in Psychology, 46,* 101326.

Greve, B., & Hussain, M.A. (2022). Support for governmental income redistribution in Nordic countries. *European Review, 30*(3), 426–444.

Grigg, R., & Lewis, H. (2019). *Teaching creative and critical thinking in schools.* Sage.

Grigorenko, E. (2000). Heritability and intelligence. In R.J. Sternberg (Ed.), *Handbook of intelligence.* Cambridge University Press.

Grigorenko, E.L., & others (2020). Understanding, educating, and supporting children with specific learning disabilities: 50 years of science and practice. *American Psychologist, 75,* 37–51.

Grimberg, A., & Allen, D.B. (2017). Growth hormone treatment for growth hormone deficiency and idiopathic short stature: New guidelines shaped by the presence and absence of evidence. *Current Opinion in Pediatrics, 29*(4), 466–471.

Grimberg, A., & others (2018). Racial/ethnic disparities in US pediatric growth hormone treatment. *Hormone Research in Paediatrics, 90*(2), 102–108.

Groh, A.M., & others (2014). The significance of attachment security for children's social competence with peers: A meta-analytic study. *Attachment and Human Development, 16,* 103–136.

Groh, A.M., & others (2017). Attachment and temperament in the early life course: A meta-analytic review. *Child Development, 88*(3), 770–795.

Groh, A.M., & others (2019). Mothers' physiological and affective responding to infant distress: Unique antecedents of avoidant and resistant attachments. *Child Development, 90*(2), 489–505.

Grolnick, W.S., & Pomerantz, E.M. (2022). Should parents be involved in their children's schooling? *Theory into Practice, 61*(3), 325–335.

Groot, F., & others (2020). Simulation at the frontier of the zone of proximal development: A test in acute care of inexperienced learners. *Academic Medicine, 95,* 1098–1105.

Grossmann, K., Grossmann, K.E., Spangler, G., Suess, G., & Unzner, L. (1985). Maternal sensitivity and newborns' orientation responses as related to quality of attachment in northern Germany. In I. Bretherton & E. Waters (Eds.), *Growing points of attachment theory and research. Monographs of the Society for Research in Child Development, 50*(1–2, Serial No. 209).

Grotevant, H.D., & Cooper, C.R. (1998). Individuality and connectedness in adolescent development: Review and prospects for research on identity, relationship, and context. In E. Skoe & A. von der Lippe (Eds.), *Personality development in adolescence: A cross-national and life-span perspective.* Routledge.

Grotevant, H.D., McRoy, R.G., Wrobel, G.M., & Ayers-Lopez, S. (2013). Contact between adoptive and birth families: Perspectives from the Minnesota/Texas Adoption Research Project. *Child Development Perspectives, 7,* 193–198.

Grotevant, H.D., Wrobel, G.M., Fiorenzo, L., Lo, A.Y., & McRoy, R.G. (2019). Trajectories of birth family contact in domestic adoptions. *Journal of Family Psychology, 33*(1), 54–63.

Groves, C.L., Prot, S., & Anderson, C.A. (2020). Violent media use and violent outcomes. In M.N. Potenza, K.A. Faust, & D. Faust (Eds.), *The Oxford handbook of digital technologies and mental health* (pp. 202–211). Oxford University Press.

Grundy, J.G. (2020). The effects of bilingualism on executive functions: An updated quantitative analysis. *Journal of Cultural Cognitive Science, 4,* 177–199.

Grusec, J.E. (2017). A domains-of-socialization perspective on children's social development. In N. Budwig, E. Turiel, & P.D. Zelazo (Eds.), *New perspectives on human development*. Cambridge University Press.

Grusec, J.E., & Davidov, M. (2021). *Socializing children*. Cambridge University Press.

Gualtieri, S., & Finn, A.S. (2022). The sweet spot: When children's developing abilities, brains, and knowledge make them better learners than adults. *Perspectives on Psychological Science, 17*(5), 1322–1338.

Gubbels, J., Segers, E., Keuning, J., & Verhoeven, L. (2016). The Aurora-*a* Battery as an assessment of triarchic intellectual abilities in upper primary grades. *Gifted Child Quarterly, 60*, 226–238.

Gui, D.Y., Gan, T., & Liu, C. (2016). Neural evidence for moral intuition and the temporal dynamics of interactions between emotional processes and moral cognition. *Social Neuroscience, 11*, 380–394.

Guilamo-Ramos, V., & others (2019). Misalignment of sexual and reproductive health priorities among older Latino adolescents and their mothers. *Contraception, 99*(3), 179–183.

Guilford, J.P. (1967). *The structure of intellect*. McGraw Hill.

Gulf Coast JFCS (2022). A day in the lives of child welfare case management with Gulf Coast JFCS. Accessed from https://www.youtube.com /watch?v=WVRGbt6uqwM

Gullion, L., & others (2019). The impact of early neuroimaging and developmental assessment in a preterm infant diagnosed with cerebral palsy. *Case Reports in Pediatrics, 2019*, 9612507.

Gump, B.B., & others (2009). Trajectories of maternal depression symptoms over her child's life span: Relation to adrenocortical, cardiovascular, and emotional functioning in children. *Development and Psychopathology, 21*, 207–225.

Gundersen, O.E. (2021). The fundamental principles of reproducibility. *Philosophical Transactions of the Royal Society A, 379*(2197), 20200210.

Gunderson, E.A., & others (2018). The specificity of parenting effects: Differential relations of parent praise and criticism to children's theories of intelligence and learning goals. *Journal of Experimental Child Psychology, 173*, 116–135.

Gunnar, M.R., Fisher, P.A., & The Early Experience, Stress, and Prevention Science Network (2006). Bringing basic research on early experience and stress neurobiology to bear on preventive interventions for neglected and maltreated children. *Development and Psychopathology, 18*, 651–677.

Güntürkün, O., Ströckens, F., & Ocklenburg, S. (2020). Brain lateralization: A comparative perspective. *Physiological Reviews, 100*(3), 1019–1063.

Gupta, A., Thornton, J.W., & Huston, A.C. (2008). Working families should not be poor—The New Hope project. In D.R. Crane & T.B. Heaton (Eds.), *Handbook of families and poverty*. Sage.

Gustafsson, C. (2018). Montessori education. In M. Fleer & B. van Oers (Eds.), *International handbook of early childhood education*. Springer.

Guthold, R., & others (2020). Global trends in insufficient physical activity among adolescents: A pooled analysis of 298 population-based surveys with 1.6 million participants. *The Lancet: Child and Adolescent Health, 4*, 23–35.

Gutierrez, B.C., & others (2020). The heroes and the helpless: The development of benevolent sexism in children. *Sex Roles, 82*(9), 558–569.

Guttentag, C.L., & others (2014). "My Baby and Me": Effects of an early, comprehensive parenting intervention on at-risk mothers and their children. *Developmental Psychology, 50*, 1482–1496.

Guttmacher Institute (2021). *Federally funded abstinence-only programs: Harmful and ineffective*. Available https://www.guttmacher.org/sites/default /files/factsheet/abstinence-only-programs-fact-sheet .pdf

Guttmacher Institute (2023). *Sex and HIV education*. Available https://www.guttmacher.org/state-policy /explore/sex-and-hiv-education

Guttmannova, K., & others (2012). Examining explanatory mechanisms of the effects of early alcohol use on young adult alcohol competence. *Journal of Studies of Alcohol and Drugs, 73*, 379–390.

Guyer, A.E., Beard, S.J., & Venticinque, J.S. (2023). Brain development during adolescence and early adulthood. In L.J. Crockett, G. Carlo, & J.E. Schulenberg (Eds.), *APA handbook of adolescent and young adult development* (pp. 21–37). American Psychological Association.

Guyer, A.E., Silk, J.S., & Nelson, E.E. (2016). The neurobiology of the emotional adolescent: From the inside out. *Neuroscience and Neurobehavioral Reviews, 70*, 74–85.

H

Ha, A.S., & others (2019). Promoting physical activity in children through family-based intervention: Protocol of the "Active 1+ FUN" randomized controlled trial. *BMC Public Health, 19*(1), 218.

Haack, K. (2022). Gender equality and the development of UN policy. In *Women's Access, Representation and Leadership in the United Nations* (pp. 23–71). Palgrave Macmillan.

Haarbauer-Krupa, J.K., & others (2021). Factors associated with concussion symptom knowledge and attitudes towards concussion care-seeking among parents of children aged 5–10 years. *Journal of Safety Research, 78*, 203–209.

Hadad, B.S., Maurer, D., & Lewis, T.L. (2017). The role of early visual input in the development of contour interpolation: The case of subjective contours. *Developmental Science, 20*(3), e12379.

Hadders-Algra, M. (2018a). Early human brain development: Starring the subplate. *Neuroscience & Biobehavioral Reviews, 92*, 276–290.

Hadders-Algra, M. (2018b). Early human motor development: From variation to the ability to vary and adapt. *Neuroscience & Biobehavioral Reviews, 90*, 411–427.

Hadiwijaya, H., Klimstra, T.A., Vermunt, J.K., Branje, S.J.T., & Meeus, W.H.J. (2017). On the development of harmony, turbulence, and independence in parent-adolescent relationships: A five-wave longitudinal study. *Journal of Youth and Adolescence, 46*, 1772–1788.

Hadland, S.E., & others (2015). Suicide attempts and childhood maltreatment among street youth: A prospective cohort study. *Pediatrics, 136*, 440–449.

Hafner, J.W., & others (2017). Child passenger restraint system misuse in rural versus urban children: A multisite case-control study. *Pediatric Emergency Care, 33*(10), 663–669.

Hagmann-von Arx, P., Lemola, S., & Grob, A. (2018). Does IQ = IQ? Comparability of intelligence test scores in typically developing children. *Assessment, 25*, 691–701.

Haidt, J. (2013). *The righteous mind*. Random House.

Haidt, J. (2017). *Three stories about capitalism*. Pantheon.

Haier, R.J. (2017). *The neuroscience of intelligence*. Cambridge University Press.

Haimovitz, K., & Dweck, C.S. (2016). What predicts children's fixed and growth intelligence mind-sets? Not their parents' views of intelligence but their parents' views of failure. *Psychological Science, 27*(6), 859–869.

Hair, N.L., Hanson, J.L., Wolfe, B.L., & Pollack, S.D. (2015). Association of poverty, brain development, and academic achievement. *JAMA Pediatrics, 169*, 822–829.

Hakovirta, M., & Eydal, G.B. (2020). Shared care and child maintenance policies in Nordic countries. *International Journal of Law, Policy and the Family, 34*(1), 43–59.

Halfon, N., & Forrest, C.B. (2018). The emerging theoretical framework of life course health development. In N. Halfon & others (Eds.), *Handbook of life course health development* (pp. 19–43). Springer.

Halim, M.L., & others (2016). Children's dynamic gender identities: Cognition, context, and culture. In B. Balter & C.S. Tamis-LeMonda (Eds.), *Child psychology* (3rd ed.). Routledge.

Halim, M.L.D., & others (2017). Gender attitudes in early childhood: Behavioral consequences and cognitive antecedents. *Child Development, 88*, 882–899.

Hall, G.S. (1904). *Adolescence* (Vols. 1 & 2). Prentice Hall.

Hall, J., & others (2023). Addressing reproductive health needs across the life course: An integrated, community-based model combining contraception and preconception care. *The Lancet Public Health, 8*, e76–e84.

Hall, W. (2017). The effectiveness of policy recommendations for school bullying: A systematic review. *Journal of the Society for Social Work and Research, 8*, 45–69.

Hallahan, D.P., Kauffman, J.M., & Pullen, P.C. (2018). *Exceptional learners* (14th ed.). Pearson.

Hallahan, D.P, Kauffman, J.K., & Pullen, P.C. (2023). *Exceptional learners: An introduction to special education* (15th ed.). Pearson.

Halpern, D.F., Beninger, A.S., & Straight, C.A. (2011). Sex differences in intelligence. In R.J. Sternberg & S.B. Kaufman (Eds.), *Handbook of intelligence*. Cambridge University Press.

Hamilton, A., Jin, Y., & Krieg, S. (2019). Early childhood arts curriculum: A cross-cultural study. *Journal of Curriculum Studies, 51*(5), 698–714.

Hamilton, J.L., Nesi, J., & Choukas-Bradley, S. (2022). Reexamining social media and socioemotional well-being among adolescents through the lens of the COVID-19 pandemic: A theoretical review and directions for future research. *Perspectives on Psychological Science, 17*, 662–679.

Hamlin, J.K. (2014). The origins of human morality: Complex socio-moral evaluations by preverbal infants. In J. Decety & Y. Christen (Eds.), *New frontiers in social neuroscience*. Springer.

Hammack, P.L., Hughes, S.D., Atwood, J.M., Cohen, E.M., & Clark, R.C. (2022). Gender and sexual identity in adolescence: A mixed-methods study of labeling in diverse community settings. *Journal of Adolescent Research, 37*, 167–220.

Hammersley, M.L., Jones, R.A., & Okely, A.D. (2016). Parent-focused childhood and adolescent overweight and obesity eHealth interventions: A systematic review and meta-analysis. *Journal of Medical Internet Research, 18*(7), e203.

Hampl, S.E., & others (2023). Clinical practice guideline for the evaluation and treatment of children and adolescents with obesity. *Pediatrics, 151*(2), e2022060640.

Han, J.Y., & others (2015). The effects of prenatal exposure to alcohol and environmental tobacco smoke on risk for ADHD: A large population-based study. *Psychiatry Research, 225*, 164–168.

Hanc, T., & others (2018). Perinatal risk factors and ADHD in children and adolescents: A hierarchical structure of disorder predictors. *Journal of Attention Disorders, 22*(9), 855–863.

Hannan, F.M., Elajnaf, T., Vandenberg, L.N., Kennedy, S.H., & Thakker, R.V. (2023). Hormonal regulation of mammary gland development and lactation. *Nature Reviews Endocrinology, 19*(1), 46–61.

Hannigan, S. (2018). A theoretical and practice-informed reflection on the value of failure in art. *Thinking Skills and Creativity, 30*, 171–179.

Hannon, E.E., Schachner, A., & Nave-Blodgett, J.E. (2017). Babies know bad dancing when they see it: Older but not younger infants discriminate between synchronous and asynchronous audiovisual musical displays. *Journal of Experimental Child Psychology, 159*, 159–174.

Hanson, M., & others (2017). Interventions to prevent obesity before conception, during pregnancy, and postpartum. *Lancet: Diabetes and Endocrinology, 5*, 65–76.

Harackiewicz, J.M., & Knogler, M. (2017). Interest: Theory and application. In A.J. Elliott, C.S. Dweck, & D.S. Yeager (Eds.), *Handbook of competence and motivation* (2nd ed.). Guilford Press.

Harden, K.P. (2021). "Reports of my death were greatly exaggerated": Behavior genetics in the postgenomic era. *Annual Review of Psychology, 72*, 37–60.

Hardy, S.A., Nelson, J.M., Moore, J.P., & King, P.E. (2019). Processes of religious and spiritual influence in adolescence: A systematic review of 30 years of research. *Journal of Research on Adolescence, 29*, 254–275.

Hare, B.D., & others. (2018). Two weeks of variable stress increases Gamma-H2AX levels in the mouse bed nucleus of the stria terminalis. *Neuroscience, 373*, 137–144.

Hare, M.M., & others (2021). Intervention response among preschoolers with ADHD: The role of emotion understanding. *Journal of School Psychology, 84*, 19–31.

Hargreaves, D.A., & Tiggemann, M. (2004). Idealized body images and adolescent body image: "Comparing" boys and girls. *Body Image, 1*, 351–361.

Harkness, S., & Super, E.M. (1995). Culture and parenting. In M.H. Bornstein (Ed.), *Handbook of parenting* (Vol. 3). Erlbaum.

Harlow, H.F., & Suomi, S.J. (1970). Nature of love: Simplified. *American Psychologist, 25*(2), 161–168.

Harlow, H.R. (1958). The nature of love. *American Psychologist, 13*, 673–685.

Harnois-Leblanc, S., & others (2023). Estimating causal effects of physical activity and sedentary behaviours on the development of type 2 diabetes in at-risk children from childhood to late adolescence: An analysis of the QUALITY cohort. *The Lancet Child & Adolescent Health, 7*(1), 37–46.

Harriger, J.A., Thompson, J.K., & Tiggemann, M. (2023). TikTok, TikTok, the time is now: Future directions in social media and body image. *Body Image, 44*, 222–226.

Harrington, E.M., Trevino, S.D., Lopez, S., & Giuliani, N.R. (2020). Emotion regulation in early childhood: Implications for socioemotional and academic components of school readiness. *Emotion, 20*(1), 48–53.

Harris, J., Golinkoff, R.M., & Hirsh-Pasek, K. (2011). Lessons from the crib for the classroom: How children really learn vocabulary. In S.B. Neuman & D.K. Dickinson (Eds.), *Handbook of early literacy research* (Vol. 3). Guilford Press.

Harris, K.R., & Graham, S. (2017). Self-regulated strategy development: Theoretical bases, critical instructional elements, and future research. In R. Fidalgo, K.R. Harris, & M. Braaksma (Eds.), *Design principles for teaching effective writing*. Brill.

Harris, K.R., Graham, S., & Adkins, M. (2015). Practice-based professional development and self-regulated strategy development for tier 2, at-risk writers in second grade. *Contemporary Educational Psychology, 40*, 5–16.

Harrison, C.L., & others (2021). Weight management across preconception, pregnancy, and postpartum: A systematic review and quality appraisal of international clinical practice guidelines. *Obesity Reviews, 22*, e13310.

Harrist, A.W., & Waugh, R.M. (2002). Dyadic synchrony: Its structure and function in children's development. *Developmental Review, 22*(4), 555–592.

Harry, B., & Klingner, J. (2022).*Why are so many students of color in special education? Understanding race and disability in schools* (3rd ed.). Teachers College Press.

Hart, B., & Risley, T.R. (1995). *Meaningful differences in the everyday experience of young Americans*. Paul H. Brookes.

Hart, C.N., & others (2023). Maternal responsiveness and toddler body mass index z-score: Prospective analysis of maternal and child mealtime interactions. *Appetite, 180*, 106348.

Hart, D., & others (2017). Morality and mental health. In C. Markey (Ed.), *Encyclopedia of mental health*. Elsevier.

Hart, S., & Carrington, H. (2002). Jealousy in 6-month-old infants. *Infancy, 3*, 395–402.

Hart, S., & Wandeler, C. (2018). The impact of action civics service-learning on eighth-grade students' civic outcomes. *International Journal of Research on Service-Learning and Community Engagement, 6*(1), Article 11.

Hart, S.L. (2018). Jealousy and attachment: Adaptations to threat posed by the birth of a sibling. *Evolutionary Behavioral Sciences, 12*(4), 263–275.

Hart, T.L., Petersen, K.S., & Kris-Etherton, P.M. (2022). Nutrition recommendations for a healthy pregnancy and lactation in women with overweight and obesity—Strategies for weight loss before and after pregnancy. *Fertility and Sterility, 118*, 434–446.

Hartanto, A., & Yang, H. (2019). Does early active bilingualism enhance inhibitory control and monitoring? A propensity-matching analysis. *Journal of Experimental Psychology: Learning, Memory, and Cognition, 45*(2), 360.

Harter, S. (2012). *The construction of the self* (2nd ed.). Wiley.

Harter, S. (2015). Self-processes and developmental psychopathology. In D. Cicchetti & D. Cohen (Eds.), *Developmental psychopathology* (2nd ed., pp. 370–418). Wiley.

Harter, S. (2016). I-self and me-self processes affecting developmental psychopathology and mental health. In D. Cicchetti (Ed.), *Developmental psychopathology* (3rd ed.). Wiley.

Hartman, S. (2022). Kindness 101: Girl scout teaches us all a lesson in honesty. https://www.cbsnews.com/video/kindness-101-girl-scout-teaches-us-all-a-lesson-in-honesty/

Hartshorne, H., & May, M.S. (1928–1930). *Moral studies in the nature of character: Studies in deceit* (Vol. 1); *Studies in self-control* (Vol. 2); *Studies in the organization of character* (Vol. 3). Macmillan.

Hartup, W.W. (1983). The peer system. In P.H. Mussen (Ed.), *Handbook of child psychology* (4th ed., Vol. 4). Wiley.

Hartup, W.W. (1996). The company they keep: Friendships and their development significance. *Child Development, 67*, 1–13.

Hartup, W.W. (2009). Critical issues and theoretical viewpoints. In K.H. Rubin, W.M. Bukowski, & B. Laursen (Eds.), *Handbook of peer interactions, relationships, and groups*. Guilford Press.

Harville, E.W., Apolzan, J.W., & Bazzano, L.A. (2019). Maternal pre-pregnancy cardiovascular risk factors and offspring and grandoffspring health: Bogalusa daughters. *International Journal of Environmental Research and Public Health, 16*(1), 15.

Harville, E.W., & others (2017). Multigenerational cardiometabolic risk as a predictor of birth outcomes: The Bogalusa Heart Study. *Journal of Pediatrics, 181,* 154–162.

Hassan, B., Vignoles, V.L., & Schwartz, S.J. (2018). Reconciling social norms with personal interests: Indigenous styles of identity formation among Pakistani youth. *Emerging Adulthood, 7*(3), 194–207.

Hassinger-Das, B., Hirsh-Pasek, K., & Golinkoff, R.M. (2017). The case of brain science and guided play. *Young Children, 72,* 45–50.

Hasson, R.E., & others (2013). Sociocultural and socioeconomic influences on type 2 diabetes risk in overweight/obese African-American and Latino-American children and adolescents. *Journal of Obesity, 2013,* 512914.

Hatano, K., & others (2022). Trajectories in sense of identity and relationship with life satisfaction during adolescence and young adulthood. *Developmental Psychology, 58,* 977–989.

Hatfield, B.E., Finders, J.K., Zandbergen, D.L., & Lewis, H. (2021). Associations between consistent and high-quality teacher-child interactions and preschool children's self-regulation and activity in the stress response system. *Early Education and Development, 33*(7), 1222–1236.

Hawk, S.T., Becht, A., & Branje, S. (2016). "Snooping" as a distinct monitoring strategy: Comparison with overt solicitation and control. *Journal of Research on Adolescence, 26,* 443–458.

Hawkes, K. (2020). Cognitive consequences of our grandmothering life history: Cultural learning begins in infancy. *Philosophical Transactions of the Royal Society B, 375,* 20190501.

Hayne, H., & Herbert, J.S. (2021). Infant memory. In J.J. Lockman & C.S. Tamis-LeMonda (Eds.), *Cambridge handbook of infant development.* Cambridge University Press.

Haynie, K., Waterman, C., & Ritter, J. (2023). *The Year in Child Care: 2021 Data, Analysis and Recommendations.* Child Care Aware® of America.

HCA Florida Healthcare (2022). *Meet Ariana Lorenzo, the Child Life Specialist at Kendall Hospital.* Retrieved April 18, 2022, from https://www.youtube.com/watch?v=oDe1-SpLfY

He, J., Guo, D., Zhai, S., Shen, M., & Gao, Z. (2019). Development of social working memory in preschoolers and its relation to theory of mind. *Child Development, 90,* 1319–1332.

He, M., Walle, E.A., & Campos, J.J. (2015). A cross-national investigation between infant walking and language development. *Infancy, 20,* 283–305.

Heaman, M.I., & others (2019). The association of inadequate and intensive prenatal care with maternal, fetal, and infant outcomes: A population-based study in Manitoba, Canada. *Journal of Obstetrics and Gynaecology Canada, 41*(7), 947–959.

Heatly, M.C., & Votruba-Drzal, E. (2017). Parent- and teacher-child relationships and engagement at school entry: Mediating, interactive, and transactional associations across contexts. *Developmental Psychology, 53,* 1042–1062.

Hébert, F., Causeur, D., & Emily, M. (2022). Omnibus testing approach for gene-based gene-gene interaction. *Statistics in Medicine, 41,* 2854–2878.

Hebert, J.J., & others (2017). The prospective association of organized sports participation with cardiovascular disease risk in children (the CHAMPS study-DK). *Mayo Clinic Proceedings, 92,* 57–65.

Heckman, J.J., & Karapakula, G. (2019). *Intergenerational and intragenerational externalities of the Perry Preschool Project* (No. w25889). National Bureau of Economic Research.

Heimann, M., & others (2006). Exploring the relation between memory, gestural communication, and the emergence of language in infancy: A longitudinal study. *Infant and Child Development, 15,* 233–249.

Hein, S., Röder, M., & Fingerle, M. (2018). The role of emotion regulation in situational empathy-related responding and prosocial behaviour in the presence of negative affect. *International Journal of Psychology, 53*(6), 477–485.

Helgeson, V.S. (2020). *The psychology of gender* (6th ed.). Routledge.

Helwig, C.C. (2017). Identifying universal developmental processes amid contextual variations in moral judgment and reasoning. *Human Development, 60,* 342–349.

Hemmingsson, E., Nowicka, P., Ulijaszek, S., & Sørensen, T.I. (2023). The social origins of obesity within and across generations. *Obesity Reviews, 24*(1), e13514.

Henderson, A., Brown, S.D., & Pancer, S.M. (2019). Curriculum requirements and subsequent civic engagement: Is there a difference between "forced" and "free" community service? *British Journal of Sociology, 70,* 1297–1322.

Henderson, C.E., Hogue, A., & Dauber, S. (2019). Family therapy techniques and one-year clinical outcomes among adolescents in usual care for behavior problems. *Journal of Consulting and Clinical Psychology, 87*(3), 308–312.

Henderson, H.A., Burrows, C.A., & Usher, L.V. (2020). Emotional development. In B. Hopkins & others (Eds.), *Cambridge encyclopedia of child development.* Cambridge University Press.

Hendricks-Munoz, K.D., & others (2013). Maternal and neonatal nurse perceived value of kangaroo mother care and maternal care partnership in the neonatal intensive care unit. *American Journal of Perinatology, 30*(10), 875–880.

Hendriks, E., Meesters, C., & Muris, P. (2020). Self-conscious emotions. In S. Hupp & J. Jewell (Eds.), *The encyclopedia of child and adolescent development* (pp. 1–9). Wiley.

Hendry, J. (1995). *Understanding Japanese society.* Routledge.

Henneberger, A.K., Gest, S.D., & Zadzora, K.M. (2019). Preventing adolescent substance use: A content analysis of peer processes targeted within universal school-based programs. *Journal of Primary Prevention, 40,* 213–230.

Hennequin, G., Agnes, E.J., & Vogels, T.P. (2017). Inhibitory plasticity: Balance, control, and codependence. *Annual Review of Neuroscience, 40,* 557–579.

Hennessey, B. (2021). Motivation and creativity. In J.C. Kaufman & R.J. Sternberg (Eds.), *Creativity.* Cambridge University Press.

Henniger, M.L. (2017). *Teaching young children* (6th ed.). Pearson.

Henslin, J.M. (2017). *Essentials of sociology* (12th ed.). Pearson.

Herbst, C.M. (2023). Child care in the United States: Markets, policy, and evidence. *Journal of Policy Analysis and Management, 42*(1), 255–304.

Herd, T., & Kim-Spoon, J. (2021). A systematic review of associations between adverse peer experiences and emotion regulation in adolescence. *Clinical Child and Family Psychology Review, 24,* 141–163.

Herman, J.L., Flores, A.R., Brown, T.N.T., Wilson, B.D.M., & Conron, K.J. (2017). *Age of individuals who identify as transgender in the United States.* The Williams Institute.

Herman, J.L., Flores, A.R., & O'Neill, K.K. (2022). *How many adults and youth identify as transgender in the United States?* UCLA Williams Institute.

Hernandez-Reif, M., Diego, M., & Field, T. (2007). Preterm infants show reduced stress behaviors and activity after 5 days of massage therapy. *Infant Behavior and Development, 30,* 557–561.

Heron, M. (2016). Deaths: Leading causes for 2013. *National Vital Statistics Reports, 65*(2), 1–95.

Heron, M. (2021). Deaths: Leading causes for 2019. *National Vital Statistics Reports, 70*(9), 1–113.

Herr, K., Grant, K., & Price, J. (2020). Sex segregated schools to challenge gender and racial bias. In *Oxford research encyclopedia of education.* https://doi.org/10.1093/acrefore/9780190264093.013.1337

Herrell, A.L., & Jordan, M. (2020). *50 strategies for teaching English language learners* (6th ed.). Pearson.

Herrero, M., Martínez-Pampliega, A., & Alvarez, I. (2020). Family communication, adaptation to divorce and children's maladjustment: The moderating role of coparenting. *Journal of Family Communication, 2*(2), 114–128.

Herzberg, O., Fletcher, K.K., Schatz, J.L., Adolph, K.E., & Tamis-LeMonda, C.S. (2022). Infant exuberant object play at home: Immense amounts of time-distributed, variable practice. *Child Development, 93*(1), 150–164.

Heshmati, S., & others (2023). Negative emodiversity is associated with emotional eating in adolescents: An examination of emotion dynamics in daily life. *Journal of Adolescence, 95,* 115–130.

Hespos, S.J., Ferry, A.L., Anderson, E.M., Hollenbeck, E.N., & Rips, L.J. (2016). Five-month-old infants have general knowledge of how nonsolid substances behave and interact. *Psychological Science, 27,* 244–256.

Hetherington, E., & others (2018). Vulnerable women's perceptions of individual versus group prenatal care: Results of a cross-sectional survey. *Maternal and Child Health Journal, 22*(11), 1632–1638.

Hetherington, E.M. (2006). The influence of conflict, marital problem solving, and parenting on children's adjustment in nondivorced, divorced, and remarried families. In A. Clarke-Stewart & J. Dunn (Eds.), *Families count.* Cambridge University Press.

Hetherington, E.M., & Stanley-Hagan, M. (2002). Parenting in divorced and remarried families. In M.H. Bornstein (Ed.), *Handbook of parenting* (2nd ed., Vol. 3). Erlbaum.

Hew, K.F., Bai, S., Dawson, P., & Lo, C.K. (2021). Meta-analyses of flipped classroom studies: A review of methodology. *Educational Research Review, 33,* 100393.

Heward, W.L., Alber-Morgan, S., & Konrad, M. (2017). *Exceptional children* (11th ed.). Pearson.

Hewlett, B.S., & MacFarlan, S.J. (2010). Fathers' roles in hunter-gatherer and other small-scale cultures. In M.E. Lamb (Ed.), *The role of the father in child development* (5th ed.). Wiley.

Heyman, G.D., Fu, G., & Lee, K. (2013). Selective skepticism: American and Chinese children's reasoning about evaluative feedback. *Developmental Psychology, 49,* 543–553.

Hickson, G.B., & Clayton, E.W. (2002). Parents and children's doctors. In M.H. Bornstein (Ed.), *Handbook of parenting* (Vol. 5). Erlbaum.

Hiitola, J., & others (Eds.) (2020). *Family life in transition: Borders, transnational mobility, and welfare society in Nordic countries.* Routledge.

Hikino, K., & others (2022). Genome-wide association study of colorectal polyps identified highly overlapping polygenic architecture with colorectal cancer. *Journal of Human Genetics, 67*(3), 149–156.

Hill, E.M. (2016). The role of narcissism in health-risk and health-protective behaviors. *Journal of Health Psychology, 21,* 2021–2032.

Hill, W.D., & others (2018). A combined analysis of genetically correlated traits identifies 187 loci and a role for neurogenesis and myelination in intelligence. *Molecular Psychiatry, 24*(2), 169–181.

Hirai, M., & Senju, A. (2020). The two-process theory of biological motion processing. *Neuroscience & Biobehavioral Reviews, 111,* 114–124.

Hirsh-Pasek, K., & others (2015). The contribution of early communication quality to low-income children's language success. *Psychological Science, 26,* 1071–1083.

Hix-Small, H. (2020). Poverty and child development. In B. Hopkins & others (Eds.), *Cambridge encyclopedia of child development.* Cambridge University Press.

Ho, P., & others (2021). Neonatal and infant mortality associated with spina bifida: A systematic review and meta-analysis. *PLoS ONE, 16*(5), e0250098.

Höchli, B., Brugger, A., & Messner, C. (2018). How focusing on superordinate goals motivates broad, long-term goal pursuit: A theoretical perspective. *Frontiers in Psychology, 9,* 1879.

Hockenberry, M.J., Wilson, D., & Rodgers, C.C. (2017). *Wong's essentials of pediatric nursing* (10th ed.). Mosby.

Hockenberry, M.J., Wilson, D. & Rogers, C.C. (2021) *Wong's essentials of pediatric nursing* (11th ed.). Elsevier.

Hodges, E.A., Propper, C.B., Estrem, H., & Schultz, M.B. (2020). Feeding during infancy: Interpersonal behavior, physiology, and obesity risk. *Child Development Perspectives, 14*(3), 185–191.

Hoefnagels, M. (2021). *Biology* (5th ed.). McGraw Hill.

Hoegler, S., Mills, A.L., Feda, A., & Cummings, E.M. (2023). Randomized preventive intervention for families: Adolescents' emotional insecurity and attachment to fathers. *Journal of Family Psychology, 37,* 79–91.

Hoekzema, E., & others (2020). Becoming a mother entails anatomical changes in the ventral striatum of the human brain that facilitate its responsiveness to offspring cues. *Psychoneuroendocrinology, 112,* 104507.

Hoff, E. (2015). Language development. In M.H. Bornstein & M.E. Lamb (Eds.), *Developmental science* (7th ed.). Psychology Press.

Hoff, E. (2018). Bilingual development in children of immigrant families. *Child Development Perspectives, 12*(2), 80–86.

Hoff, E., Laursen, B., & Tardif, T. (2002). Socioeconomic status and parenting. In M.H. Bornstein (Ed.), *Handbook of parenting* (2nd ed.). Erlbaum.

Hoff, E., & others (2014). Expressive vocabulary development in children from bilingual homes: A longitudinal study from two to four years. *Early Childhood Research Quarterly, 29,* 433–444.

Hoff, E., Quinn, J.M., & Giguere, D. (2018). What explains the correlation between growth in vocabulary and grammar? New evidence from latent change score analyses of simultaneous bilingual development. *Developmental Science, 21*(2), e12536.

Hofheimer, J.A., & others (2022). Psychosocial and medical adversity associated with neonatal neurobehavior in infants born before 30 weeks gestation. *Pediatric Research, 87,* 721–729.

Hofkens, T.L., & Pianta, R.C. (2022). Teacher–student relationships, engagement in school, and student outcomes. In A. Reschly & S. Christensen (Eds.), *Handbook of research on student engagement* (pp. 431–449). Springer International Publishing.

Hofrichter, R., Siddiqui, H., Morrisey, M.N., & Rutherford, M.D. (2021). Early attention to animacy: Change-detection in 11-month-olds. *Evolutionary Psychology, 19*(2), 14747049211028220.

Hogan, C. (2014). Socioeconomic factors affecting infant sleep-related deaths in St. Louis. *Public Health Nursing, 31,* 10–18.

Holden, G. (2019). *Parenting and the dynamics of childrearing* (Reprinted). Routledge.

Hollams, E.M., de Klerk, N.H., Holt, P.G., & Sly, P.D. (2014). Persistent effects of maternal smoking during pregnancy on lung function and asthma in adolescents. *American Journal of Respiratory and Critical Care Medicine, 189,* 401–407.

Holler-Wallscheid, M.S., & others (2017). Bilateral recruitment of prefrontal cortex in working memory is associated with task demand but not with age. *Proceedings of the National Academy of Sciences U.S.A., 114,* E830–E839.

Hollis, J., & Robinson, S. (2019). A link between maternal and childhood obesity. In D. Bagchi (Ed.), *Global perspectives on childhood obesity* (2nd ed., pp. 125–136). Elsevier.

Holmboe, K., & Abigail, F. (2019). Neural substrates of early executive function development. *Developmental Review, 52,* 42–62.

Holmes, C., & others (2019). Structural home environment effects on developmental trajectories of self-control and adolescent risk taking. *Journal of Youth and Adolescence, 48*(1), 43–55.

Holmes, L.B. (2020). Memories of the Teratology Society: 1972–2020. *Birth Defects Research, 112,* 935–941.

Holway, G.V., & Hernandez, S.M. (2018). Oral sex and condom use in a US national sample of adolescents and young adults. *Journal of Adolescent Health, 62*(4), 402–410.

Holzman, L. (2016). *Vygotsky at work and play* (2nd ed.). Routledge.

Honaker, S.M., & others (2021). Screening for problematic sleep in a diverse sample of infants. *Journal of Pediatric Psychology, 46*(7), 824–834.

Hong, Y., McCormick, S.A., Deater-Deckard, K., Calkins, S.D., & Bell, M.A. (2021). Household chaos, parental responses to emotion, and child emotion regulation in middle childhood. *Social Development, 30*(3), 786–805.

Hood, B.M. (1995). Gravity rules for 2- to 4-year-olds? *Cognitive Development, 10,* 577–598.

Hoogenhout, M., & Malcolm-Smith, S. (2017). Theory of mind predicts severity level in autism. *Autism, 21,* 242–252.

Hooper, S.R., & others (2018). Developmental trajectories of executive functions in young males with fragile X syndrome. *Research in Developmental Disabilities, 81,* 73–88.

Hoover, J., & others (2018). Into the wild: Building value through moral pluralism. In K. Gray & J. Graham (Eds.), *Atlas of moral psychology.* Guilford Press.

Horta, B.L., & de Lima, N.P. (2019). Breastfeeding and type 2 diabetes: Systematic review and meta-analysis. *Current Diabetes Reports, 19*(1), 1–6.

Horta, B.L., Loret de Mola, C., & Victora, C.G. (2015). Breastfeeding and intelligence: A systematic review and meta-analysis. *Acta Paediatrica, 104,* 14–19.

Hoskins, J.E.S., & Schweig, J.D. (2022). SEL in context: School mobility and social-emotional learning trajectories in a low-income, urban school district. *Education and Urban Society.* doi:10.1177/00131245221106735.

Hoskyn, M.J., Iarocci, G., & Young, A.R. (Eds.) (2017). *Executive functions in children's everyday lives.* Oxford University Press.

Hospital for Sick Children & others (2010). *Infant sleep.* Hospital for Sick Children.

Hospodar, C.M., Hoch, J.E., Lee, D.K., Shrout, P.E., & Adolph, K.E. (2021). Practice and proficiency: Factors that facilitate infant walking skill. *Developmental Psychobiology, 63*(7), e22187.

Hou, Y., Kim, S.Y., & Wang, Y. (2016). Parental acculturative stressors and adolescent adjustment through interparental and parent-child relationships in Chinese American families. *Journal of Youth and Adolescence, 45,* 1466–1481.

Houdé, O., & others (2011). Functional magnetic resonance imaging study of Piaget's conservation-of-number task in preschool and school-age children: A neo-Piagetian approach. *Journal of Experimental Child Psychology, 110*(3), 332–346.

Hove, L., & others (2022). Placental transfer and vascular effects of pharmaceutical drugs in the human placenta *ex vivo:* A review. *Placenta, 122,* 29–45.

Howard, E.D., & Low, L.K. (2020). It's time to dial up doula care. *The Journal of Perinatal & Neonatal Nursing, 34*(1), 4–7.

Howe, L.D., Huttly, S.R., & Abramsky, T. (2006). Risk factors for injuries in young children in four developing countries: The Young Lives Study. *Tropic Medicine and International Health, 11,* 1557–1566.

Hoyt, L.T., & others (2020). Timing of puberty for boys and girls: Implications for population health. *SSM-Population Health, 10,* 100549.

Hrdy, S.B., & Burkart, J.M. (2020). The emergence of emotionally modern humans: Implications for language and learning. *Philosophical Transactions of the Royal Society B, 375,* 20190499.

Hsieh, M., & Stright, A.D. (2012). Adolescents' emotion regulation strategies, self-concept, and internalizing problems. *Journal of Early Adolescence, 32,* 876–901.

Hu, D., Zhou, S., Crowley-McHattan, Z.J., & Liu, Z. (2021). Factors that influence participation in physical activity in school-aged children and adolescents: A systematic review from the social ecological model perspective. *International Journal of Environmental Research and Public Health, 18*(6), 3147.

Hu, H., & others (2007). Fetal lead exposure at each stage of pregnancy as a predictor of infant mental development. *Environmental Health Perspectives, 114,* 1730–1735.

Huang, H., & others (2023). Chronic exercise for core symptoms and executive functions in ADHD: A meta-analysis. *Pediatrics, 151*(1), e2022057745.

Huang, X., & others (2019). LPHN3 gene variations and susceptibility to ADHD in Chinese Han population: A two-stage case-control association study and gene-environment interactions. *European Child & Adolescent Psychiatry, 28,* 861–873.

Huang, Y., Espelage, D.L., Polanin, J.R., & Hong, J.S. (2019). A meta-analytic review of school-based anti-bullying programs with a parent component. *International Journal of Bullying Prevention, 1*(1), 32–44.

Hudry, K., & others (2022). Performance of the Autism Observation Scale for Infants with community-ascertained infants showing early signs of autism. *Autism, 25,* 490–501.

Huesmann, L.R., Dubow, E.F., Eron, L.D., & Boxer, P. (2006). Middle childhood family-contextual and personal factors as predictors of adult outcomes. In A.C. Huston & M.N. Ripke (Eds.), *Developmental contexts in middle childhood: Bridges to adolescence and adulthood.* Cambridge University Press.

Hughes, C., Devine, R.T., & Wang, Z. (2018). Does parental mind-mindedness account for cross-cultural differences in preschoolers' theory of mind? *Child Development, 89*(4), 1296–1310.

Hughes, C., Marks, A., Ensor, R., & Lecce, S. (2010). A longitudinal study of conflict and inner state talk in children's conversations with mothers and younger siblings. *Social Development, 19,* 822–837.

Hughson J.A.P., & others (2018). The rise of pregnancy apps and the implications for culturally and linguistically diverse women: Narrative review. *JMIR Mhealth Uhealth, 6*(11), e189.

Huhdanpää, H., & others (2019). Sleep difficulties in infancy are associated with symptoms of inattention and hyperactivity at the age of 5 years: A longitudinal study. *Journal of Developmental and Behavioral Pediatrics, 40*(6), 432.

Humlum, M.K., Nandrup, A.B., & Smith, N. (2019). Closing or reproducing the gender gap? Parental transmission, social norms and education choice. *Journal of Population Economics, 32*(2), 455–500.

Humphreys, K.L., & others (2019). Stressful life events, ADHD symptoms, and brain structure in early adolescence. *Journal of Abnormal Child Psychology, 47*(3), 421–432.

Hurst, K., & Zimmer-Gembeck, M. (2019). Family-based treatment with cognitive behavioural therapy for anorexia. *Clinical Psychologist, 23*(1), 61–70.

Hurwitz, S. (2021, November 19). A lost young life changed counselor Yolanda Curry's forever. *St. Louis American.*

Hussong, A.M., Coffman, J.L., & Halberstadt, A.G. (2021). Parenting and the development of children's gratitude. *Child Development Perspectives, 15,* 235–241.

Huston, A.C., & Ripke, M.N. (2006). Experiences in middle childhood and children's development: A summary and integration of research. In A.C. Huston & M.N. Ripke (Eds.), *Developmental contexts in middle childhood.* Cambridge University Press.

Hutchison, J., Ross, J., & Cunningham, S.J. (2021). Development of evaluative and incidental self-reference effects in childhood. *Journal of Experimental Child Psychology, 210,* 105197.

Huttenlocher, P.R., & Dabholkar, A.S. (1997). Regional differences in synaptogenesis in human cerebral cortex. *Journal of Comparative Neurology, 37*(2), 167–178.

Huynh, Q.L., Benet-Martínez, V., & Nguyen, A.M.D. (2018). Measuring variations in bicultural identity across US ethnic and generational groups: Development and validation of the Bicultural Identity Integration Scale–Version 2 (BIIS-2). *Psychological Assessment, 30*(12), 1581.

Hwalla, N., & others (2017). The prevalence of micronutrient deficiencies and inadequacies in the Middle East and approaches to interventions. *Nutrients, 9*(3), 229.

Hyde, J.S. (2014). Gender similarities and differences. *Annual Review of Psychology, 65,* 373–398.

Hyde, J.S., Bigler, R.S., Joel, D., Tate, C.C., & van Anders, S.M. (2019). The future of sex and gender in psychology: Five challenges to the gender binary. *American Psychologist, 74,* 171–193.

Hyde, J.S., & Mezulis, A.H. (2020). Gender differences in depression: Biological, affective, cognitive, and sociocultural factors. *Harvard Review of Psychiatry, 28*(1), 4–13.

Hyde, J.S., & others (2019). The future of sex and gender in psychology: Five challenges to the gender binary. *American Psychologist, 74*(2), 171–193.

Hyde, L.W., & others (2022). Parents, neighborhoods, and the developing brain. *Child Development Perspectives, 16,* 148–156.

Hysing, M., & others (2015). Sleep and school attendance in adolescence: Results from a large population-based study. *Scandinavian Journal of Public Health, 43,* 2–9.

Hysing, M., & others (2016). Sleep and academic performance in later adolescence: Results from a large population-based study. *Journal of Sleep Research, 25,* 318–324.

I

"I Have a Dream" Foundation (2023). Our impact. Available https://www.ihaveadreamfoundation.org/

Icenogle, G., & others (2019). Adolescents' cognitive capacity reaches adult levels prior to their psychosocial maturity: Evidence for a "maturity gap" in a multinational, cross-sectional sample. *Law and Human Behavior, 43,* 69–85.

Ickovics, J.R., & others (2019a). Implementing school-based policies to prevent obesity: Cluster randomized trial. *American Journal of Preventive Medicine, 56,* e1–e11.

Ikeda, A., Kobayashi, T., & Itakura, S. (2018). Sensitivity to linguistic register in 20-month-olds: Understanding the register-listener relationship and its abstract rules. *PLOS One, 13*(4), e0195214.

Im, Y., Oh, W.O., & Suk, M. (2017). Risk factors for suicide ideation among adolescents: Five-year national data analysis. *Archives of Psychiatric Nursing, 31,* 282–286.

International Montessori Council (2006). Larry Page and Sergey Brin, founders of Google.com, credit their Montessori education for much of their success on prime-time television. Retrieved June 24, 2006, from http://www.Montessori.org/enews/Barbara_walters.html

Ip, P., & others (2017). Impact of nutritional supplements on cognitive development of children in developing countries: A meta-analysis. *Scientific Reports, 7,* 10611.

Ip, S., Chung, M., Raman, G., Trikaliinos, T.A., & Lau, J. (2009). A summary of the Agency for Healthcare Research and Quality's evidence report on breastfeeding in developed countries. *Breastfeeding Medicine, 4* (Suppl. 1), S17–S30.

Irwin, V., & others (2021). *Report on the condition of education 2021(NCES 2021-144).* U.S. Department of Education, National Center for Education Statistics. Retrieved May 1, 2022, from https://nces.ed.gov/pubsearch/pubsinfo.asp?pubid=2021144

Ishak, S., Franchak, J.M., & Adolph, K.E. (2014). Fear of height in infants. *Current Directions in Psychological Science, 23,* 60–66.

Ishikawa, M., & Itakura, S. (2019). Physiological arousal predicts gaze following in infants. *Proceedings of the Royal Society B, 286*(1896), 20182746.

Issel, L.M., & others (2011). A review of prenatal home-visiting effectiveness for improving birth outcomes. *Journal of Obstetric, Gynecologic, and Neonatal Nursing, 40*(2), 157–165.

Ivanov, I., Bjork, J.M., Blair, J., & Newcorn, J.H. (2022). Sensitization-based risk for substance abuse in vulnerable individuals with ADHD: Review and re-examination of evidence. *Neuroscience & Biobehavioral Reviews, 135,* 104575.

J

Jaarsveld, S., & Lachmann, T. (2017). Intelligence and creativity in problem solving: The importance of test features in cognition research. *Frontiers in Psychology, 8,* 134.

Jabès, A., & Nelson, C.A. (2015). 20 years after "The ontogeny of human memory: A cognitive neuroscience perspective," where are we? *International Journal of Behavioral Development, 39,* 293–303.

Jaciw, A.P., & others (2016). Assessing impacts of *Math in Focus,* a "Singapore Math" program. *Journal of Research on Educational Effectiveness, 9,* 473–502.

Jackson, A., & Davis, G. (2000). *Turning points 2000.* Teachers College Press.

Jackson, E.F., & Bussey, K. (2023). Broadening gender self-categorization development to include transgender identities. *Social Development, 32,* 17–31.

Jackson, L.J., & others (2020). Expect the best, not the worst: The impact of parental expectation on Black males' math scores. *Journal of Black Studies, 51*(8), 767–778.

Jackson, S.L. (2016). *Research methods* (5th ed.). Cengage.

Jackson, W.M., & others (2016). Physical activity and cognitive development: A meta analysis. *Journal of Neurosurgery and Anesthesiology, 28,* 373–380.

Jacoby, N., Overfeld, J., Brinder, E.B., & Heim, C.M. (2016). Stress neurobiology and developmental psychopathology. In D. Cicchetti (Ed.), *Developmental psychopathology* (3rd ed.). Wiley.

Jaffee, S., & Hyde, J.S. (2000). Gender differences in moral orientation: A meta-analysis. *Psychological Bulletin, 126,* 703–726.

Jagger-Rickels, A.C., Kibby, M.Y., & Constance, J.M. (2018). Global gray matter morphometry differences between children with reading disability, ADHD, and comorbid reading disability/ADHD. *Brain and Language, 185,* 54–66.

Jaggers, J.W., Sonsteng-Person, M., Griffiths, A., Gabbard, W.J., & Turner, M.M. (2021). Behavioral problems and psychological distress among seriously delinquent youth: Assessing a mediational pathway of parental monitoring, peer delinquency, and violence exposure. *Youth & Society, 53,* 230–251.

Jakobsen, I.S., Larsen, K.J., & Horwood, J.L. (2017). Suicide risk assessment in adolescents—C-SSRS, K20, and READ. *Crisis, 38*(4), 247–254.

Jambon, M., & Smetana, J.G. (2018). Individual differences in prototypical moral and conventional judgments and children's proactive and reactive aggression. *Child Development, 89*(4), 1343–1359.

James, W. (1890/1950). *The principles of psychology.* Dover.

Jamshidifarsani, H., Garbaya, S., Lim, T., Blazevic, P., & Ritchie, J.M. (2019). Technology-based reading intervention programs for elementary grades: An analytical review. *Computers & Education, 128,* 427–451.

Jang, C.H., & others (2019). Clinical usefulness of the Korean Developmental Screening Test (K-DST) for developmental delays. *Annals of Rehabilitation Medicine, 43*(4), 490–496.

Jani, P., & others (2022). Regional oxygenation, perfusion and body and/or head position: Are preterm infants adversely impacted? A systematic review. *Paediatric Respiratory Reviews, 43,* 26–37.

Jaramillo, N., & others (2017). Associations between sex education and contraceptive use among heterosexually active adolescent males in the United States. *Journal of Adolescent Health, 60,* 534–540.

Jarris, P.E., & others (2017). Group prenatal care compared with traditional prenatal care: A systematic review and meta-analysis. *Obstetrics and Gynecology, 129,* 384–385.

Jaruratanasirikul, S., & others (2017). A population-based study of Down syndrome in Southern Thailand. *World Journal of Pediatrics, 13,* 63–69.

Järvelä, S., Hadwin, A., Malmberg, J., & Miller, M. (2018). Contemporary perspectives of regulated learning in collaboration. In F. Fischer & others (Eds.), *International handbook of the learning sciences.* Routledge.

Jarvis, S.N., & Okonofua, J.A. (2020). School deferred: When bias affects school leaders. *Social Psychological and Personality Science, 11*(4), 492–498.

Jasinska, K.K., & Petitto, L-A. (2018). Age of bilingual exposure is related to the contribution of phonological and semantic knowledge to successful reading development. *Child Development, 89*(1), 310–331.

Jaworska, N., & others (2019). Aerobic exercise in depressed youth: A feasibility and clinical outcomes pilot. *Early Intervention in Psychiatry, 13*(1), 128–132.

Jebeile, H., Kelly, A.S., O'Malley, G., & Baur, L.A. (2022). Obesity in children and adolescents: Epidemiology, causes, assessment, and management. *The Lancet Diabetes & Endocrinology, 10*(5), 351–365.

Jelding-Dannemand, E., Malby Schoos, A.M., & Bisgaard, H. (2015). Breast-feeding does not protect against allergic sensitization in early childhood and allergy-associated disease at age 7 years. *Journal of Allergy and Clinical Immunology, 136,* 1302–1308.

Jenkins, L.N., & Nickerson, A.B. (2017). Bullying participant roles and gender as predictors of bystander intervention. *Aggressive Behavior, 43,* 281–290.

Jensen, L.A. (Ed.) (2020). *The Oxford handbook of moral development.* Oxford University Press.

Jensen, L.A. (2021). The cultural psychology of religiosity, spirituality, and secularism in adolescence. *Adolescent Research Review, 6,* 277–288.

Jeong, J., Franchett, E.E., Ramos de Oliveira, C.V., Rehmani, K., & Yousafzai, A.K. (2021). Parenting interventions to promote early child development in the first three years of life: A global systematic review and meta-analysis. *PLoS Medicine, 18*(5), e1003602.

Jezak, M. (Ed.). (2021). *Compendium of language management in Canada (CLMC): The 55 bilingual countries in the world.* University of Ottawa. https://www.uottawa.ca/clmc/55-bilingual-countries-world

Ji, B.T., & others (1997). Paternal cigarette smoking and the risk of childhood cancer among offspring of nonsmoking mothers. *Journal of the National Cancer Institute, 89,* 235–244.

Jia, S., & others (2019). Maternal, paternal, and neonatal risk factors for neural tube defects: A systematic review and meta-analysis. *International Journal of Developmental Neuroscience, 78,* 227–235.

Jiang, K., & others (2022). How aerobic exercise improves executive function in ADHD children: A resting-state fMRI study. *International Journal of Developmental Neuroscience, 82*(4), 295–302.

Jiang, Q., Wang, D., Yang, Z., & Choi, J. K. (2022). Bidirectional relationships between parenting stress and child behavior problems in multi-stressed, single-mother families: A cross-lagged panel model. *Family Process, 62*(2), 671–686.

Jiang, Z., & others (2017). Event-related theta oscillatory substrates for facilitation and interference effects of negative emotion on children's cognition. *International Journal of Psychophysiology, 116,* 26–31.

Jiao, S., Ji, G., & Jing, Q. (1996). Cognitive development of Chinese urban only children and children with siblings. *Child Development, 67,* 387–395.

Jiménez-Díaz, J., Chaves-Castro, K., & Salazar, W. (2019). Effects of different movement programs on motor competence: A systematic review with meta-analysis. *Journal of Physical Activity and Health, 16*(8), 657–666.

Jin, K., & Baillargeon, R. (2017). Infants possess an abstract expectation of ingroup support. *Proceedings of the National Academy of Sciences, 114,* 8199–8204.

Jin, K.S., & others (2018). Young infants expect an unfamiliar adult to comfort a crying baby: Evidence from a standard violation-of-expectation task and a novel infant-triggered-video task. *Cognitive Psychology, 102,* 1–20.

Jin, Y., Seiber, E.E., & Ferketich, A.K. (2013). Secondhand smoke and asthma: What are the effects on healthcare utilization among children? *Prevention Medicine, 57,* 125–128.

Jo, J., & Lee, Y.J. (2017). Effectiveness of acupuncture in women with polycystic ovarian syndrome undergoing in vitro fertilization or intracytoplasmic sperm injection: A systematic review and meta-analysis. *Acupuncture in Medicine, 35*(3), 162–170.

Johansson, F., Watts, P.C., Sniegula, S., & Berger, D. (2021). Natural selection mediated by seasonal time constraints increases the alignment between evolvability and developmental plasticity. *Evolution, 75,* 464–475.

Johansson, J.V., Segerdahl, P., Ugander, U.H., Hansson, M.G., & Langenskiöld, S. (2018). Making sense of genetic risk: A qualitative focus-group study of healthy participants in genomic research. *Patient Education & Counseling, 101,* 422–427.

Johansson, M., Benderix, Y., & Svensson, I. (2020). Mothers' and fathers' lived experiences of postpartum depression and parental stress after childbirth: A qualitative study. *International Journal of Qualitative Studies on Health and Well-being, 15*(1), 1722564.

John, R.M. (2017). Imprinted genes and the regulation of placental endocrine function: Pregnancy and beyond. *Placenta, 56,* 86–90.

Johns Hopkins Medicine (2019). *Feeding guide for the first year.* https://www.hopkinsmedicine.org/health /wellness-and-prevention/feeding-guide-for-the-first-year

Johnson, A.D., Finch, J.E., & Phillips, D.A. (2019). Associations between publicly funded preschool and low-income children's kindergarten readiness: The moderating role of child temperament. *Developmental Psychology, 55*(3), 623–636.

Johnson, C.M., & others (2018). Observed parent–child feeding dynamics in relation to child body mass index and adiposity. *Pediatric Obesity, 13,* 222–231.

Johnson, J.A., & others (2018). *Foundations of American education* (17th ed.). Pearson.

Johnson, J.S., & Newport, E.L. (1991). Critical period effects on universal properties of language: The status of subjacency in the acquisition of a second language. *Cognition, 39,* 215–258.

Johnson, K.C., & others (2020). Trans adolescents' perceptions and experiences of their parents' supportive and rejecting behaviors. *Journal of Counseling Psychology, 67*(2), 156.

Johnson, M. (2008, April 30). Commentary in R. Highfield, *Harvard's baby brain research lab.* Retrieved January 24, 2008, from http://www .telegraph.co.uk/science/science-news/3341166 /Harvards-baby-brain-research-lab.html

Johnson, M.D. (2017). *Human biology* (8th ed.). Pearson.

Johnson, M.H., Charman, T., Pickles, A., & Jones, E.J. (2021). Annual research review: Anterior modifiers in the emergence of neurodevelopmental disorders (AMEND)—A systems neuroscience approach to common developmental disorders. *Journal of Child Psychology and Psychiatry, 62*(5), 610–630.

Johnson, M.H., Grossmann, T., & Cohen-Kadosh, K. (2009). Mapping functional brain development: Building a social brain through interactive specialization. *Developmental Psychology, 45,* 151–159.

Johnson, M.H., Jones, E., & Gliga, T. (2015). Brain adaptation and alternative developmental trajectories. *Development and Psychopathology, 27,* 425–442.

Johnson, S.J., & Cochran, H.A. (2021). Collaborative research into the "hidden worlds" of children's peer reading. *Journal of Early Childhood Research, 19*(3), 381–395.

Johnson, S.P. (2019). Development of visual-spatial attention. In T. Hodgson (Ed.), *Processes of visuospatial attention and working memory* (pp. 37–58). Springer.

Johnson, S.P., & Hannon, E.E. (2015). Perceptual development. In R. Lerner & others (Eds.), *Handbook of child psychology and developmental science* (7th ed., pp. 63–112). Wiley.

Johnson, W., & others (2007). Genetic and environmental influences on the Verbal-Perceptual-Image Rotation (VPR) Model of the Structure of Mental Abilities in the Minnesota Study of Twins Reared Apart. *Intelligence, 35,* 542–562.

Johnston, C. (2022). Diagnosis and management of genital herpes: Key questions and review of the evidence for the 2021 Centers for Disease Control and Prevention sexually transmitted infections treatment guidelines. *Clinical Infectious Diseases, 74,* S134–S143.

Johnston, C., & others (2017). Skin-to-skin care for procedural pain in infants. *Cochrane Database of Systematic Reviews, 2,* CD008435.

Johnston, L.D., O'Malley, P.M., Bachman, J.G., & Schulenberg, J.E. (2015). *Monitoring the Future national results on drug use: 2014 overview, key findings on adolescent drug use.* Institute of Social Research, University of Michigan.

Jones, B.P., & others (2021). Options for acquiring motherhood in absolute uterine factor infertility; adoption, surrogacy and uterine transplantation. *The Obstetrician & Gynaecologist, 23*(2), 138.

Jones, C.M., & Rogers, L.O. (2023). Family racial/ethnic socialization through the lens of multiracial Black identity: A m(ai)cro analysis of meaning-making. *Race and Social Problems, 15,* 59–78.

Jones, J., & Placek, P. (2017). *Adoption: By the numbers.* National Council for Adoption.

Jones, L., & others (2012). Pain management for women in labor: An overview of systematic reviews. *Cochrane Database of Systematic Reviews, 3,* CD009234.

Jones, M.C. (1965). Psychological correlates of somatic development. *Child Development, 36,* 899–911.

Jones, M.E., & Christensen, A.E. (2022). *Constructing strong foundations of early literacy.* Routledge.

Jones-Mason, K., & others (2018). Autonomic nervous system functioning assessed during the still-face paradigm: A meta-analysis and systematic review of methods, approach and findings. *Developmental Review, 50,* 113–139.

Joos, C.M., & others (2018). Neither antecedent nor consequence: Developmental integration of chronic stress, pubertal timing, and conditionally adapted stress response. *Developmental Review, 48,* 1–23.

Jordan, C.H., & Zeigler-Hill, V. (2013). Secure and fragile forms of self-esteem. In V. Zeigler-Hill (Ed.), *Self-esteem.* Psychology Press.

Jorges, V. (2022). *Boy who was severely burned reunites with hospital staff who helped him recover.* NBC Miami. https://www.nbcmiami.com/news /local/boy-who-was-severely-burned-reunites-with-hospital-staff-who-helped-him-recover /2684892/

Josephson Institute of Ethics (2008). *The ethics of American youth 2008.* Josephson Institute.

Jourdren, M., Bucaille, A., & Ropars, J. (2023). The impact of screen exposure on attention abilities in young children: a systematic review. *Pediatric Neurology, 142,* 76–88.

Juras, R., & others (2022). Meta-analysis of federally funded adolescent pregnancy prevention program evaluations. *Prevention Science, 23,* 1169–1195.

Juraska, J.M., & Willing. J. (2017). Pubertal onset as a critical transition for neural development and cognition. *Brain Research, 1654*(Pt. B), 87–94.

Justice, L.M., & others (2020). Language disparities related to maternal education emerge by two years in a low-income sample. *Maternal and Child Health Journal, 24,* 1419–1427.

Jutras, B., Lagacé, J., & Koravand, A. (2020). The development of auditory functions. *Handbook of Clinical Neurology, 173,* 143–155.

K

Kachel, U., & Tomasello, M. (2019). 3- and 5-year-old children's adherence to explicit and implicit joint commitments. *Developmental Psychology, 55*(1), 80–88.

Kadir, M.S., & Yeung, A.S. (2018). Academic self-concept. In V. Zeigler-Hill & T.K. Shackelford (Eds.), *Encyclopedia of personality and individual differences.* Springer.

Kaestle, C.E. (2019). Sexual orientation trajectories based on sexual attractions, partners, and identity: A longitudinal investigation from adolescence through young adulthood using a US representative sample. *The Journal of Sex Research, 56*(7), 811–826.

Kagan, J. (2013). Temperamental contributions to inhibited and uninhibited profiles. In P. D. Zelazo (Ed.), *Oxford handbook of developmental psychology.* Oxford University Press.

Kagan, J. (2018). Brain and emotion. *Emotion Review, 10*(1), 79–86.

Kagan, J. (2019). Distinction between moods and temperament. In A.S. Fox & others (Eds.), *The nature of emotion* (2nd ed.). Oxford University Press.

Kagan, J., Kearsley, R.B., & Zelazo, P.R. (1978). *Infancy: Its place in human development.* Harvard University Press.

Kagan, J., & Snidman, N. (1991). Infant predictors of inhibited and uninhibited behavioral profiles. *Psychological Science, 2,* 40–44.

Kahn, N.F., & Halpern, C.T. (2019). Is developmental change in gender-typed behavior associated with adult sexual orientation? *Developmental Psychology, 55*(4), 855–865.

Kaidesoia, M., Cooper, Z., & Fordham, B. (2023). Cognitive behavioral therapy for eating disorders: A map of the systematic review evidence base. *International Journal of Eating Disorders, 56,* 295–313.

Kalaitzopoulos, D.R., & others (2018). Effect of methamphetamine hydrochloride on pregnancy outcome: A systematic review and meta-analysis. *Journal of Addiction Medicine, 12*(3), 220–226.

Kalamar, A.M., & others (2018). Developing strategies to address contraceptive needs of adolescents: Exploring patterns of use among sexually active adolescents in 46 low- and middle-income countries. *Contraception, 98*(1), 36–40.

Kalisch-Smith, J.I., & Moritz, K.M. (2017). Detrimental effects of alcohol exposure around conception: Putative mechanisms. *Biochemistry and Cell Biology, 96*(2), 107–116.

Kalogeropoulos, C., & others (2022). Sleep patterns and intraindividual sleep variability in mothers and fathers at 6 months postpartum: A population-based, cross-sectional study. *BMJ Open, 12*(8), e060558.

Kamenetz, A. (2020, January 19). *"You need to act now": Meet 4 girls working to save the warming world.* NPR. Retrieved April 22, 2022, from https://www.npr.org/2020/01/19/797298179/you-need-to-act-now-meet-4-girls-working-to-save-the-warming-world

Kanakis, G.A., & Nieschlag, E. (2018). Klinefelter syndrome: More than hypogonadism. *Pediatric Reproductive Endocrinology, 86,* 135–144.

Kang, E., Klein, E., Lillard, A., & Lerner, M. (2016). Predictors and moderators of spontaneous pretend play in children with and without autism spectrum disorder. *Frontiers in Psychology, 7,* 1577.

Kangaslampi, S. (2023). Earliest versus other autobiographical memories of school-age children. *Current Psychology,* 1–11.

Kanji, A., Khoza-Shangase, K., & Moroe, N. (2018). Newborn hearing screening protocols and their outcomes: A systematic review. *International Journal of Pediatric Otorhinolaryngology, 115,* 104–109.

Kann, L., & others (2016a, June 10). Youth Risk Behavior Surveillance–United States 2015. *Mobidity & Mortality Weekly Report (MMWR), 65,* 1–174.

Kann, L., & others (2016b, August 12). Sexual identity, sex of sexual contacts, and health-related behaviors among students in grades 9–12–United States and selected sites, 2015. *MMWR Surveillance Summary, 65*(9), 1–202.

Kann, L., & others (2018, June 15). Youth risk behavior surveillance–United States, 2017. *MMWR: Morbidity and Mortality Weekly Report (MMWR), 67,* 1–479.

Kannan, P. (2020). Nutrition in labor. In A. Sharma (Ed.), *Labour room emergencies* (pp. 257–264). Springer.

Kanter, J., & others (2022). Biologic and clinical efficacy of LentiGlobin for sickle cell disease. *New England Journal of Medicine, 386*(7), 617–628.

Kantha, S.S. (2022). Somnambulism: Recent findings. In V. Chaban (Ed.), *Nursing–New insights for clinical care* (pp. 1–12). InTechOpen.

Kantrowitz, B. (1991, Summer). The good, the bad, and the difference. *Newsweek,* pp. 48–50.

Kapetanovic, S., & others (2019). Does one size fit all?–Linking parenting with adolescent substance use and adolescent temperament. *Journal of Research on Adolescence, 30,* 443–457.

Karababa, A. (2020). The relationship between trait anger and loneliness among early adolescents: The moderating role of emotion regulation. *Personality and Individual Differences, 159,* 109856.

Karaman, F., & Hay, J.F. (2018). The longevity of statistical learning: When infant memory decays, isolated words come to the rescue. *Journal of Experimental Psychology: Learning, Memory, and Cognition, 44,* 221–232.

Karazsia, B.T., Murnen, S.K., & Tylka, T.L. (2017). Is body dissatisfaction changing across time? A cross-temporal meta-analysis. *Psychological Bulletin, 143*(3), 293–320.

Karberg, E., & Cabrera, N.J. (2020). Children's adjustment to parents' break up: The mediational effects of parenting and co-parenting. *Journal of Family Issues, 41*(10), 1810–1833.

Karela, C., & Petrogiannis, K. (2018). Risk and resilience factors of divorce and young children's emotional well-being in Greece: A correlational study. *Journal of Educational and Developmental Psychology, 8*(2), 68–81.

Karlsson, J., & others (2018). Four evolutionary trajectories underlie genetic intratumoral variation in childhood cancer. *Nature Genetics, 50,* 944–950.

Karr, J.E., & others (2021). Sensitivity and specificity of an executive function screener at identifying children with ADHD and reading disability. *Journal of Attention Disorders, 25,* 134–140.

Kassai, R., Futo, J., Demetrovics, Z., & Takacs, Z.K. (2019). A meta-analysis of the experimental evidence on the near- and far-transfer effects among children's executive function skills. *Psychological Bulletin, 145*(2), 165–188.

Kastbom, A.A., & others (2015). Sexual debut before the age of 14 leads to poorer psychosocial health and risky behavior in later life. *Acta Pediatrica, 104,* 91–100.

Katz, P.A. (1987, August). *Children and social issues.* Paper presented at the meeting of the American Psychological Association, New York.

Kauchak, D., & Eggen, P. (2021). *Introduction to teaching* (7th ed.). Pearson.

Kauer, R., Callaghan, T., & Regan, A.K. (2023). Disparities in prenatal immunization rates in rural and urban US areas by indicators of access to care. *Journal of Rural Health, 39,* 142–152.

Kauffman, J.M., Burke, M.D., & Anastasiou, D. (2022). Hard LRE choices in the era of inclusion: Rights and their implications. *Journal of Disability Policy Studies, 34*(1), 61–72.

Kauffman, J.M., McGee, K., & Brigham, M. (2004). Enabling or disabling? Observations on changes in special education. *Phi Delta Kappan, 85,* 613–620.

Kaufman, J.C., & Sternberg, R.J. (Eds.). (2021). *Creativity: An Introduction.* Cambridge University Press.

Kaufman, T.M.L., Kretschmer, T., Huitsing, G., & Veenstra, R. (2020). Caught in a vicious cycle? Explaining bidirectional spillover between parent-child relationships and peer victimization. *Development and Psychopathology, 32,* 11–20.

Kaufman, Y., Carlini, S.V., & Deligiannidis, K.M. (2022). Advances in pharmacotherapy for postpartum depression: A structured review of standard-of-care antidepressants and novel neuroactive steroid antidepressants. *Therapeutic Advances in Psychopharmacology, 12,* 20451253211065859.

Kaunhoven, R.J., & Dorjee, D. (2017). How does mindfulness modulate self-regulation in pre-adolescent children? An integrative neurocognitive review. *Neuroscience and Biobehavioral Reviews, 74*(Pt. A), 163–184.

Kavanaugh, B.C., & others (2022). Parental age and autism severity in the Rhode Island Consortium for Autism Research and Treatment (RI-CART) study. *Autism Research, 15,* 86–92.

Kavle, J.A., & Landry, M. (2018). Addressing barriers to maternal nutrition in low- and middle-income countries: A review of the evidence and programme implications. *Maternal & Child Nutrition, 14*(1), e12508.

Kawwass, J.F., & Badell, M.L. (2018). Maternal and fetal risk associated with assisted reproductive technology. *Obstetrics and Gynecology, 132,* 763–772.

Kees, J. & others (2020). Evidence-based cannabis policy: A framework to guide marketing and public policy research. *Journal of Public Policy & Marketing, 39*(1), 76–92.

Keeton, C., Schleider, J., & Walkup, J. (2017). Separation anxiety, generalized anxiety, and social anxiety. In B.J. Sadock & others (Eds.), *Kaplan & Sadock's comprehensive textbook of psychiatry* (10th ed.). Lippincott Williams & Wilkins.

Kehayes, I.L.L., & others (2019). Are perfectionism dimensions risk factors for bulimic symptoms? A meta-analysis of longitudinal studies. *Personality and Individual Differences, 138,* 117–125.

Kehl, S.M., & others (2020). Creative music therapy with premature infants and their parents: A mixed-method pilot study on parents' anxiety, stress, and depressive symptoms and parent-infant attachment. *International Journal of Environmental Research and Public Health, 18*(1), 265.

Keith, K.D. (Ed.). (2019). *Cross-cultural psychology: Contemporary perspectives* (2nd ed). Wiley.

Keller, M.N., & Noone, R.J. (2020). *Handbook of Bowen family systems theory and research methods.* Routledge.

Kelley, G.A., & Kelley, K.S. (2013). Effects of exercise in the treatment of overweight and obese children and adolescents: A systematic review and analysis. *Journal of Obesity, 2013*, 783103.

Kellogg, R. (1970). *Understanding children's art: Readings in developmental psychology today.* CRM.

Kelly, A.B., & others (2011). The influence of parents, siblings, and peers on pre- and early-teen smoking: A multilevel model. *Drug and Alcohol Review, 30*, 381–387.

Kendler, K.S., Ohlsson, H., Sundquist, K., & Sundquist, J. (2018). Sources of parent-offspring resemblance for major depression in a national Swedish extended adoption study. *JAMA Psychiatry, 75*, 194–200.

Kendrick, K., Jutengren, G., & Stattin, H. (2012). The protective role of supportive friends against bullying perpetration and victimization. *Journal of Adolescence, 35*(4), 1069–1080.

Kennedy, M.C., & others (2017). Social relationships and social support among street-involved youth. *Journal of Youth Studies, 20*(10), 1328–1345.

Kennell, J.H. (2006). Randomized controlled trial of skin-to-skin contact from birth versus conventional incubator for physiological stabilization in 1200 g to 2199 g newborns. *Acta Paediatrica, 95*, 15–16.

Kerns, K.A., & Brumariu, L.E. (2016). Attachment in middle childhood. In J. Cassidy & P. Shaver (Eds.), *Handbook of attachment* (3rd ed.). Guilford Press.

Kerns, K.A., & Seibert, A.C. (2016). Finding your way through the thicket: Promising approaches to assessing attachment in middle childhood. In E. Waters, B. Vaughn, & H. Waters (Eds.), *Measuring attachment.* Guilford Press.

Kerpelman, J.L., & Pittman, J.F. (2018). Erikson and the relational context of identity: Strengthening connections with attachment theory. *Identity, 18*(4), 306–314.

Kerstis, B., & others (2016). Association between parental depressive symptoms and impaired bonding with the infant. *Archives of Women's Mental Health, 19*, 87–94.

Keunen, K., Counsell, S.J., & Benders, M.J. (2017). The emergence of functional architecture during early brain development. *NeuroImage, 160*, 2–14.

Keyes, K.M., Maslowsky, J., Hamilton, A., & Schulenberg, J. (2015). The great sleep recession: Changes in sleep duration among U.S. adolescents, 1991–2012. *Pediatrics, 135*, 460–468.

Khaleque, A. (2021). *Parenting and child development: Across ethnicity and culture.* Praeger.

Kharitonova, M., Winter, W., & Sheridan, M.A. (2015). As working memory grows: A developmental account of neural bases of working memory capacity in 5- to 8-year-old children and adults. *Journal of Cognitive Neuroscience, 27*, 1775–1788.

Khatun, M., & others (2017). Do children born to teenage parents have lower adult intelligence? A prospective birth cohort study. *PloS One, 12*(3), e0167395.

Khetarpal, S.K., Szoko, N., Culyba, A.J., Shaw, D., & Ragavan, M.I. (2022). Associations between parental monitoring and multiple types of youth violence victimization: A brief report. *Journal of Interpersonal Violence, 37*, NP19216–NP19222.

Khoury, J.E., & Milligan, K. (2019). Comparing executive functioning in children and adolescents with fetal alcohol spectrum disorders and ADHD: A meta-analysis. *Journal of Attention Disorders, 23*(14), 1801–1815.

Khu, M., Chambers, C.G., & Graham, S.A. (2020). Preschoolers flexibly shift between speakers' perspectives during real-time language comprehension. *Child Development, 91*(3), e619–e634.

Kiani, M.A., Ghazanfarpour, M., & Saeidi, M. (2019). Adolescent pregnancy: A health challenge. *International Journal of Pediatrics, 7*(7), 9749–9752.

Kidd, C., Palmeri, H., & Aslin R.N. (2013). Rational snacking: Young children's decision-making on the marshmallow task is moderated by beliefs about environmental reliability. *Cognition, 126*, 109–114.

Kidd, C., Piantadosi, S.T., & Aslin, R.N. (2012). The Goldilocks effect: Human infants allocate attention to visual sequences that are neither too simple nor too complex. *PLoS One, 7*(5), e36399.

Kieler, M., Hofmann, M., & Schabbauer, G. (2021). More than just protein building blocks: How amino acids and related metabolic pathways fuel macrophage polarization. *The FEBS Journal, 288*, 3694–3714.

Killen, M., & Dahl, A. (2018). Moral judgment: Reflective, interactive, spontaneous, challenging, and always evolving. In K. Gray & J. Graham (Eds.), *Atlas of moral psychology* (pp. 20–30). Guilford Press.

Killoren, S.E., & others (2023, in press). Latinx adolescents' perspectives on romantic relationships and sexuality: Exploring the roles of parents and siblings. *Journal of Social and Personal Relationships.*

Kim, B.R., & others (2017). Trajectories of mothers' emotional availability: Relations with infant temperament in predicting attachment security. *Attachment and Human Development, 19*, 38–57.

Kim, H.J., Yang, J., & Lee, M.S. (2015). Changes of heart rate variability during methylphenidate treatment in attention-deficit hyperactivity disorder children: A 12-week prospective study. *Yonsei Medical Journal, 56*, 1365–1371.

Kim, J., & Lee, Y. (2019). Does it take a school? Revisiting the influence of first arrest on subsequent delinquency and educational attainment in a tolerant educational background. *Journal of Research in Crime and Delinquency, 56*(2), 254–302.

Kim, K.H. (2010, May). Unpublished data. School of Education, College of William & Mary, Williamsburg, VA.

Kim, M.J., Catalano, R.F., Haggerty, K.P., & Abbott, R.D. (2011). Bullying at elementary school and problem behavior in young adulthood: A study of bullying, violence, and substance use from age 11 to age 21. *Criminal Behavior and Mental Health, 21*, 36–44.

Kim, P., Strathearn, L., & Swain, J.E. (2016). The maternal brain and its plasticity in humans. *Hormones and Behavior, 77*, 113–123.

Kim, S., & Kochanska, G. (2017). Relational antecedents and social implications of the emotion of empathy: Evidence from three studies. *Emotion, 17*(6), 981–992.

Kim, S.K., Park, S., Oh, J., Kim, J., & Ahn, S. (2018). Interventions promoting exclusive breastfeeding up to six months after birth: A systematic review and meta-analysis of randomized controlled trials. *International Journal of Nursing Studies, 80*, 94–105.

Kim, S.M., Han, D.H., Trksak, G.H., & Lee, Y.S. (2014). Gender differences in adolescent coping behaviors and suicidal ideation: Findings from a sample of 73,238 adolescents. *Anxiety, Stress, and Coping, 27*, 439–454.

Kim, Y., Lee, Y., & Yang, E. (2023, in press). Vocational identity of emerging adults: The inter-relationships of vocational identity dimensions. *Journal of Adult Development.*

Kim, Y., Park, I., & Kang, S. (2018). Age and gender differences in health risk perception. *Central European Journal of Public Health, 26*(1), 54–59.

Kim, Y.S.G., Quinn, J.M., & Petscher, Y. (2021). What is text reading fluency and is it a predictor or an outcome of reading comprehension? A longitudinal investigation. *Developmental Psychology, 57*(5), 718–732.

Kim-Spoon, J., & others (2019). Brains of a feather flocking together? Peer and individual neurobehavioral risks for substance use across adolescence. *Development and Psychopathology, 31*, 1661–1674.

Kindermann, T.A. (2016). Peer group influences on students' academic achievement and social behavior. In K. Wentzel & G. Ramani (Eds.), *Handbook of social influences in school contexts.* Psychology Press.

King, K.A., Topalian, A., & Vidourek, R.A. (2020). Religiosity and adolescent major depressive episodes among 12–17-year-olds. *Journal of Religion and Health, 59*, 2611–2622.

King, K.M., & others (2017). Externalizing behavior across childhood as reported by parents and teachers: A partial measurement invariance model. *Assessment, 25*(6), 744–758.

King, L.S., Camacho, M.C., Montez, D.F., Humphreys, K.L., & Gotlib, I.H. (2021). Naturalistic language input is associated with resting-state functional connectivity in infancy. *Journal of Neuroscience, 41*(3), 424–434.

King, P.E., Hardy, S.A., & Noe, S. (2021). Developmental perspectives on adolescent religious and spiritual development. *Adolescent Research Review, 6*, 253–264.

King, P.E., Mangan, S., & Riveros, R. (2023). Religion, spirituality, and youth thriving: Investigating the roles of the developing mind and meaning-making. In E.B. Davis, E.L. Worthington Jr., & S.A. Schnitker (Eds.), *Handbook of positive psychology, religion, and spirituality* (pp. 263–278). Springer.

King, R.B. (2020). Mindsets are contagious: The social contagion of implicit theories of intelligence among classmates. *British Journal of Educational Psychology, 90*, 349–363.

King, S.M., McGee, J., Winters, K.C., & DuPont, R.L. (2019). Correlates of substance use abstinence and non-abstinence among high school seniors: Results from the 2014 Monitoring the Future Survey. *Journal of Child & Adolescent Substance Abuse, 28*(2), 105–112.

Kingsbury, A.M., & others (2017). Does having a difficult child lead to poor mental health outcomes? *Public Health, 146*, 46–55.

Király, I., Takacs, S., Kaldy, Z., & Blaser, E. (2017). Preschoolers have better long-term memory for rhyming text than adults. *Developmental Science, 20*(3), e12398.

Kirk, S.M., & Kirk, E.P. (2016). Sixty minutes of physical activity per day included within preschool academic lessons improves early literacy. *Journal of School Health, 86*, 155–163.

Kirkorian, H.L., Anderson, D.R., & Keen, R. (2012). Age differences in online processing of video: An eye movement study. *Child Development, 83*, 497–507.

Kirmayer, L.J., Worthman, C.M., Kitayama, S., Lemelson, R., & Cummings, C. (Eds.) (2020). *Culture, mind, and brain: Emerging concepts, models, and applications.* Cambridge University Press.

Klahr, A.M., & Burt, S.A. (2014). Elucidating the etiology of individual differences in parenting: A meta-analysis of behavioral genetic research. *Psychological Bulletin, 140*, 544–586.

Klausen, T., Hansen, K.J., Munk-Jørgensen, P., & Mohr-Jensen, C. (2017). Are assisted reproductive technologies associated with categorical or dimensional aspects of psychopathology in childhood, adolescence or early adulthood? Results from a Danish prospective nationwide cohort study. *European Child and Adolescent Psychiatry, 26*, 771–778.

Klemfuss, J.Z., & Olaguez, A.P. (2020). Individual differences in children's suggestibility: An updated review. *Journal of Child Sexual Abuse, 29*, 158–182.

Klimstra, T.A., & Adams, B.G. (2022). Perspectives on personal identity development in Western and non-Western contexts. In B.G. Adams & F.J.R. van de Vijver (Eds.), *Non-Western identity*. Springer.

Klinger, L.G., & Dudley, K.M. (2019). Autism spectrum disorder. In M.J. Prinstein & others (Eds.), *Treatment of disorders in childhood and adolescence*. Guilford Press.

Klopack, E.T., Sutton, T.E., Simons, R.L., & Simons, L.G. (2020). Disentangling the effects of boys' pubertal timing: The importance of social context. *Journal of Youth and Adolescence, 49*, 1393–1405.

Klug, J., & others (2016). Secondary school students' LLL competencies, and their relation with classroom structure and achievement. *Frontiers in Psychology, 7*, 680.

Klug, W.S., & others (2017). *Essentials of genetics* (9th ed.). Pearson.

Knafo-Noam, A., Barni, D., & Schwartz, S.H. (2020). Parent–child value similarity. In L. Jensen (Ed.), *The Oxford handbook of moral development*. Oxford University Press.

Knight, C.J. (2017). Family influences on talent development in sport. In J. Baker & others (Eds.), *Routledge handbook of talent identification and development in sport*. Routledge.

Knocke, K., Chappel, A., Sugar, S., Lew, N.D., & Sommers, B.D. (2022). Doula care and maternal health: An evidence review. (Issue Brief No. HP-2022-24). Office of the Assistant Secretary for Planning and Evaluation, U.S. Department of Health and Human Services.

Knop, B. (2020). One in six children live with a half sibling under 18. U.S. Census Bureau. Available https://www.census.gov/library/stories/2020/01/more-children-live-with-half-siblings-than-previously-thought.html

Knox, M. (2020). Physical punishment and child maltreatment. In M. Knox (Ed.), *Clinician's toolkit for children's behavioral health* (pp. 199–217). Academic Press.

Kochanska, G., & Kim, S. (2013). Early attachment organization with both parents and future behavior problems: From infancy to middle childhood. *Child Development, 84*(1), 283–296.

Kochanska, G., Koenig, J.L., Barry, R.A., Kim, S., & Yoon, J.E. (2010). Children's conscience during toddler and preschool years, moral self, and a competent, adaptive development trajectory. *Development Psychology, 46*, 1320–1332.

Kochendorfer, L.B., & Kerns, K.A. (2017). Perceptions of parent-child attachment relationships and friendship qualities: Predictors of romantic relationship involvement and quality in adolescence. *Journal of Youth and Adolescence, 46*(5), 1009–1021.

Koehn, A.J., & Kerns, K.A. (2017). Parent-child attachment: Meta-analysis of associations with parenting behaviors in middle childhood and adolescence. *Attachment & Human Development,* 1–28.

Koeneman, O., & Zeijstra, H. (2017). *Introducing syntax*. Cambridge University Press.

Koenig, A.M. (2018). Comparing prescriptive and descriptive gender stereotypes about children, adults, and the elderly. *Frontiers in Psychology, 9*, 1086.

Koenig, L.B., McGue, M., & Iacono, W.G. (2008). Stability and change in religiousness during emerging adulthood. *Developmental Psychology, 44*, 523–543.

Kofler, M.J., & others (2019). Do working memory deficits underlie reading problems in attention-deficit/hyperactivity disorder (ADHD)? *Journal of Abnormal Child Psychology, 47*, 433–446.

Koh, E., & others (2022). *Adoption by the numbers.* National Council for Adoption. URL: https://adoptioncouncil.org/research/adoption-by-the-numbers/.

Kohlberg, L. (1958). *The development of modes of moral thinking and choice in the years 10 to 16.* Unpublished doctoral dissertation, University of Chicago.

Kohlberg, L. (1986). A current statement of some theoretical issues. In S. Modgil & C. Modgil (Eds.), *Lawrence Kohlberg*. Falmer.

Kohlhoff, J., & others (2017). Oxytocin in the postnatal period: Associations with attachment and maternal caregiving. *Comprehensive Psychiatry, 76*, 56–68.

Kok, F.M., Groen, Y., Fuermaler, A.B., & Tucha, O. (2016). Problematic peer functioning in girls with ADHD: A systematic literature review. *PLoS One, 11*, e0165118.

Kolk, S.M., & Rakic, P. (2022). Development of prefrontal cortex. *Neuropyschopharmacology, 47*, 41–57.

Kołomańska-Bogucka, D., & Mazur-Bialy, A.I. (2019). Physical activity and the occurrence of postnatal depression—A systematic review. *Medicina, 55*(9), 560.

Költő, A., & others (2018). Love and dating patterns for same- and both-gender attracted adolescents across Europe. *Journal of Research on Adolescence, 28*(4), 772–778.

Kominiarek, M.A., & Chauhan, S.P. (2016). Obesity before, during, and after pregnancy: A review and comparison of five national guidelines. *American Journal of Perinatology, 33*, 433–441.

Kondo-Ikemura, K., & others (2018). Japanese mothers' prebirth Adult Attachment Interview predicts their infants' response to the Strange Situation Procedure: The strange situation in Japan revisited three decades later. *Developmental Psychology, 54*(11), 2007–2015.

Kopp, C.B. (2008). Self-regulatory processes. In M.M. Haith & J.B. Benson (Eds.), *Encyclopedia of infant and early childhood development*. Elsevier.

Koppelman, K.L. (2017). *Understanding human differences* (5th ed.). Pearson.

Koppelman, K.L. (2020). *Understanding human differences: Multicultural education for a diverse America* (6th ed.). Pearson.

Körber, V., & others (2023). Neuroblastoma arises in early fetal development and its evolutionary duration predicts outcome. *Nature Genetics, 55*(4), 619–630.

Korja, R., & others (2017). The relations between maternal prenatal anxiety or stress and the child's early negative reactivity or self-regulation: A systematic review. *Child Psychiatry and Human Development, 48*(6), 851–869.

Kornafel, T., Paremski, A.C., & Prosser, L.A. (2023). Unweighting infants reveals hidden motor skills. *Developmental Science, 26*(2), e13279.

Kornhaber, M.L. (2020). The theory of multiple intelligences. In R.J. Sternberg (Ed.), *Cambridge handbook of intelligence* (2nd ed.). Cambridge University Press.

Kornienko, O., Ha, T., & Dishion, T.J. (2020). Dynamic pathways between rejection and antisocial behavior in peer networks: Update and test of confluence model. *Development and Psychopathology, 32,* 175-188.

Kosik-Bogacka, D., & others (2018). Concentrations of mercury (Hg) and selenium (Se) in afterbirth and their relations with various factors. *Environmental Geochemistry and Health, 40*(4), 1683-1695.

Kosson, D.S., & others (2021). Parental rejecting behaviors: Validating a behaviorally based youth-report measure of parental emotional abuse. *Assessment, 28,* 899-917.

Kostović, I., & others (2021). Fundamentals of the development of connectivity in the human fetal brain in late gestation: From 24 weeks gestational age to term. *Journal of Neuropathology & Experimental Neurology, 80,* 393-414.

Kotovsky, L., & Baillargeon, R. (1994). Calibration-based reasoning about collision events in 11-month-old infants. *Cognition, 51,* 107-129.

Kouros, C.D., Morris, M.C., & Garber, J. (2016). Within-person changes in individual symptoms of depression predict subsequent depressive episodes in adolescents: A prospective study. *Journal of Abnormal Child Psychology, 44,* 483-494.

Kozol, J. (2005). *The shame of the nation.* Crown.

Krafft, C., Davis, E.E., & Tout, K. (2017). Child care subsidies and the stability and quality of child care arrangements. *Early Childhood Research Quarterly, 39,* 14-34.

Krafft, C.E., & others (2014). An 8-month randomized controlled exercise trial alters brain activation during cognitive tasks in overweight children. *Obesity, 22,* 232-242.

Kramer, H.J., & Lagattuta, K.H. (2018). Social categorization. In M.H. Bornstein & others (Eds.), *SAGE encyclopedia of lifespan human development.* Sage.

Kramer, L. (2006, July 10). Commentary in J. Kluger, "How your siblings make you who you are" *Time,* pp. 46-55.

Kramer, L., & others (2019). Siblings. In B.H. Fiese & others (Eds.), *APA handbook of contemporary family psychology: Foundations, methods, and contemporary issues across the lifespan* (pp. 521-538). American Psychological Association.

Kramer, M.D., & Rodgers, J.L. (2020). The impact of having children on domain-specific life-satisfaction: A quasi-experimental longitudinal investigation using the Socio-Economic Panel (SOEP) data. *Journal of Personality and Social Psychology, 119,* 1497-1514.

Kranenburg, M.J., & van IJzendoorn, M.H. (2016). Attachment, parenting, and genetics. In J. Cassidy & P.R. Shaver (Eds.), *Handbook of parenting* (3rd ed.). Guilford Press.

Krasotkina, A., Götz, A., Höhle, B., & Schwarzer, G. (2021). Perceptual narrowing in face- and speech-perception domains in infancy: A longitudinal approach. *Infant Behavior and Development, 64,* 101607.

Krassner, A.M., & others (2017). East-west, collectivist-individualist: A cross-cultural examination of temperament in toddlers from Chile, Poland, South Korea, and the US. *European Journal of Developmental Psychology, 14*(4), 449-464.

Kraus, D., & Horowitz-Kraus, T. (2022). Functional MRI research involving healthy children: Ethics, safety and recommended procedures. *Acta Paediatrica, 111*(4), 741-749.

Krauss, S., Dapp, L.C., & Orth, U. (2023, in press). The link between low self-esteem and eating disorders: A meta-analysis of longitudinal studies. *Clinical Psychological Science.*

Kretch, K.S., & Adolph, K.E. (2017). The organization of exploratory behaviors in infant locomotor planning. *Developmental Science, 20*(4). doi:10.1111/desc.12421

Kretschmer-Trendowicz, A., Schnitzspahn, K.M., Reuter, L., & Altgassen, M. (2019). Episodic future thinking improves children's prospective memory performance in a complex task setting with real life task demands. *Psychological Research, 83,* 514-525.

Kreutzer, M., Leonard, C., & Flavell, J.H. (1975). An interview study of children's knowledge about memory. *Monographs of the Society for Research in Child Development, 40*(1, Serial No. 159).

Kring, A.M. (2000). Gender and anger. In A.H. Fischer (Ed.), *Gender and emotion.* Cambridge University Press.

Krishnamoorthy, D., & Kaminer, Y. (2020). The effects of prenatal exposure to marijuana on early childhood development: A systematic literature review. *Cannabis, 3,* 11-18.

Kroger, J., Martinussen, M., & Marcia, J.E. (2010). Identity change during adolescence and young adulthood: A meta-analysis. *Journal of Adolescence, 33,* 683-698.

Krogh-Jespersen, S., Henderson, A.M., & Woodward, A.L. (2020). Let's get it together: Infants generate visual predictions based on collaborative goals. *Infant Behavior and Development, 59,* 101446.

Krok, D. (2018). Examining the role of religion in a family setting: Religious attitudes and quality of life among parents and their adolescent children. *Journal of Family Studies, 24,* 203-218.

Krueger, R.F., & Johnson, W. (2021). Behavioral genetics and personality: Ongoing efforts to integrate nature and nurture. In O.P. John & R.W. Robins (Eds.), *Handbook of personality: Theory and research* (pp. 217-241). Guilford Press.

Kuang, J., & others (2023). Psychometric evaluation of the inventory of dimensions of emerging adulthood (IDEA) in China. *International Journal of Clinical and Health Psychology 23*(1), 100331.

Kuhl, P.K. (2015). Baby talk. *Scientific American, 313*(5), 64-69.

Kuhl, P.K. (2017). Big surprises from little brains. *Early Childhood Matters, 126,* 20-25.

Kuhl, P.K. (2022). Language. In E.R. Kandel & others (Eds.), *Principles of neural science* (6th ed.). McGraw Hill.

Kuhl, P.K., Tsao, F.-M., & Liu, H.-M. (2003). Foreign-language experience in infancy: Effects of short-term exposure and social interaction on phonetic learning. *Proceedings of the National Academy of Sciences, 100,* 9096-9101.

Kuhn, D. (1998). Afterword to volume 2: Cognition, perception, and language. In W. Damon (Ed.), *Handbook of child psychology* (5th ed., vol. 2). Wiley.

Kuhn, D. (1999). Metacognitive development. In L. Balter & S. Tamis-Lemonda (Eds.), *Child psychology: A handbook of contemporary issues.* Psychology Press.

Kuhn, D. (2009). Adolescent thinking. In R.M. Lerner & L. Steinberg (Eds.), *Handbook of adolescent psychology* (3rd ed.). Wiley.

Kuhn, D. (2013). Reasoning. In P.D. Zelazo (Ed.), *Oxford handbook of developmental psychology.* Oxford University Press.

Kuhn, D. (2017). *Building our best future: Thinking critically about ourselves and our world, teacher edition.* Wessex Learning.

Kuhn, D. (2022). Metacognition matters in many ways. *Educational Psychologist, 57,* 73-86.

Kuhn, D., & Franklin, S. (2006). The second decade: What develops (and how)? In W. Damon & R. Lerner (Eds.), *Handbook of child psychology* (6th ed.). Wiley.

Kuhns, C., & Cabrera, N. (2018). Fathering. In M.H. Bornstein & others (Eds.), *SAGE encyclopedia of lifespan human development.* Sage.

Kulich, S.J., & others (2021). Interdisciplinary history of intercultural communication studies: From roots to research and praxis. In D. Landis & D.P.S. Bhawuk (Eds.), *Cambridge handbook of intercultural training.* Cambridge University Press.

Kumar Panda, P., & others (2021). Psychological and behavioral impact of lockdown and quarantine measures for COVID-19 pandemic on children, adolescents, and caregivers: A systematic review and meta-analysis. *Journal of Tropical Pediatrics, 67*(1), fmaa122.

Kunkler, C., Lewis, A.J., & Almeida, R. (2022). Methamphetamine exposure during pregnancy: A meta-analysis of child developmental outcomes. *Neuroscience and Biobehavioral Reviews, 138,* 104714.

Kuo, B.C.H. (2021). Multicultural counseling training and intercultural training: A synthesis. In D. Landis & D.P.S. Bhawuk (Eds.), *Cambridge handbook of intercultural training.* Cambridge University Press.

Kuo, P.X., & others (2019). Is one secure attachment enough? Infant cortisol reactivity and the security of infant-mother and infant-father attachments at the end of the first year. *Attachment and Human Development, 21,* 426-444.

Kupersmidt, J.B., & Coie, J.D. (1990). Preadolescent peer status, aggression, and school adjustment as predictors of externalizing problems in adolescence. *Child Development, 61,* 1350-1363.

Kurkul, K.E., & Corriveau, K.H. (2018). Question, explanation, follow-up: A mechanism for learning from others? *Child Development, 89,* 280-294.

Kurkul, K.E., Dwyer, J., & Corriveau, K.H. (2022). 'What do YOU think?': Children's questions, teacher's responses and children's follow-up across diverse preschool settings. *Early Childhood Research Quarterly, 58,* 231-241.

Kwiatkowski, M.A., & others (2018). Cognitive outcomes in prenatal methamphetamine exposed children aged six to seven years. *Comprehensive Psychiatry, 80,* 24-33.

Kwon, D., & others (2020). Regional growth trajectories of cortical myelination in adolescents and young adults: Longitudinal validation and functional correlates. *Brain Imaging and Behavior, 14,* 242-266.

Kwon, R., Kasper, K., London, S., & Haas, D.M. (2020). A systematic review: The effects of yoga on pregnancy. *European Journal of Obstetrics & Gynecology and Reproductive Biology, 250,* 171-177.

Kyratzis, A. (2017). Children's co-construction of sentence and discourse in early childhood: Implictions for development. In N. Budwig & others (Eds.), *New perspectives on human development.* Cambridge University Press.

L

Laborte-Lemoyne, E., Currier, D., & Ellenberg, D. (2017). Exercise during pregnancy enhances cerebral maturation in the newborn: A randomized controlled trial. *Journal of Clinical and Experimental Neuropsychology, 39,* 347-354.

Lachman, A., & others (2019). Shared pleasure in early mother–infant interactions: A study in a high-risk South African sample. *Early Child Development and Care, 191*(2), 230-241.

Ladd, G.W., Ettekal, I., & Kochenderfer-Ladd, B. (2017). Peer victimization trajectories from kindergarten through high school: Differential pathways for children's school engagement and achievement? *Journal of Educational Psychology, 109*(6), 826-841.

Ladd, H.C. (2017). No child left behind: A deeply flawed federal policy. *Journal of Policy Analysis and Management, 36,* 461-469.

Ladewig, P.W., London, M.L., & Davidson, M. (2017). *Contemporary maternal-newborn nursing* (9th ed.). Pearson.

Ladis, B.A., & others (2019). Parent-focused preventive interventions for youth substance use and problem behaviors: A systematic review. *Research on Social Work Practice, 29*(4), 420-442.

Ladouceur, C.D., & others (2019). Neural systems underlying reward cue processing in early adolescence: The role of puberty and pubertal hormones. *Psychoneuroendocrinology, 102,* 281-291.

Lagattuta, K.H., Elrod, N.M., & Kramer, H.J. (2016). How do thoughts, emotions, and decisions align? A new way to examine theory of mind during middle childhood and beyond. *Journal of Experimental Child Psychology, 149,* 116-133.

Lagattuta, K.H., & Kramer, H.J. (2021). Advanced theory of mind in middle childhood and adulthood: Inferring mental states and emotions from life history. In R.T. Devine & S. Lecce (Eds.), *Theory of mind in middle childhood and adolescence.* Routledge.

Lahti-Pulkkinen, M., & others (2019). Consequences of maternal overweight and obesity in pregnancy on offspring diabetes: A record linkage study in Aberdeen, Scotland. *Diabetologia, 62*(8), 1412-1419.

Lai, M.C., Lin, H.Y., & Ameis, S.H. (2022). Towards equitable diagnoses for autism and attention-deficit /hyperactivity disorder across sexes and genders. *Current Opinion in Psychiatry, 35*(2), 90-100.

Laible, D.J., & Thompson, R.A. (2007). Early socialization: A relationship perspective. In J.E. Grusec & P.D. Hastings (Eds.), *Handbook of socialization.* Guilford Press.

Lamb, M.E., & Lewis, C. (2015). The role of parent-child relationships in child development. In M.H. Bornstein & M.E. Lamb (Eds.), *Developmental science* (7th ed.). Psychology Press.

Lamb, M.E., Malloy, L.C., Hershkowitz, I., & La Rooy, D. (2015). Children and the law. In R.E. Lerner (Ed.), *Handbook of child psychology and developmental science* (7th ed.). Wiley.

Lambert, M.C., Cullinan, D., Epstein, M.H., & Martin, J. (2022). Factor structure of the Scales for Assessing Emotional Disturbance-3 Rating Scale for students identified with emotional disturbance. *Behavioral Disorders, 47*(3), 187-195.

Lambrinou, C.P., Karaglani, E., & Manios, Y. (2019). Breastfeeding and postpartum weight loss. *Current Opinion in Clinical Nutrition & Metabolic Care, 22*(6), 413-417.

Lamela, D., & Figueiredo, B. (2016). Co-parenting after marital dissolution and children's mental health: A systematic review. *Jornal de Pediatria (Rio), 92,* 331-342.

Lampert, J., & others (2020). Poverty and schooling: Three cases from Australia, the United States, and Spain. *Asia-Pacific Journal of Teacher Education, 48,* 60-78.

Lampl, M. (1993). Evidence of saltatory growth in infancy. *American Journal of Human Biology, 5,* 641-652.

Lampl, M., & Schoen, M. (2017). How long bones grow children: Mechanistic paths to variation in human height growth. *American Journal of Human Biology, 29*(2). doi:10.1002/ajhb.22983

Landa-Rivera, J.L., & others (2022). Population-based survey showing that breastfed babies have a lower frequency of risk factors for sudden infant death syndrome than nonbreastfed babies. *Breastfeeding Medicine, 17*(2), 182-188.

Landrum, A.R., Mills, C.M., & Johnston, A.M. (2013). When do children trust the expert? Benevolence information influences children's trust more than expertise. *Developmental Science, 16,* 622-638.

Lane, H. (1976). *The wild boy of Aveyron.* Harvard University Press.

Lang, S., and others (2021). Prelexical phonetic and early lexical development in German-acquiring infants: Canonical babbling and first spoken words. *Clinical Linguistics & Phonetics, 35*(2), 185-200.

Langille, D.B., Asbridge, M., Cragg, A., & Rasic, D. (2015). Associations of school connectedness with adolescent suicidality: Gender differences and the role of risk of depression. *Canadian Journal of Psychiatry, 60,* 258-267.

Langston, J., Speed, D., & Coleman, T.J. (2020). Predicting age of atheism: Credibility enhancing displays and religious importance, choice, and conflict in family of upbringing. *Religion, Brain, and Behavior, 10,* 49-67.

Laninga-Wijnen, L., & others (2019). The role of academic status norms in friendship selection and influence processes related to academic achievement. *Developmental Psychology, 55*(2), 337-350

Lansford, J.E. (2009). Parental divorce and children's adjustment. *Perspectives on Psychological Science, 4,* 140-152.

Lansford, J.E. (2013). Single- and two-parent families. In J. Hattie & E. Anderman (Eds.), *International handbook of student achievement.* Routledge.

Lansford, J.E. (2022). Annual Research Review: Cross-cultural similarities and differences in parenting. *Journal of Child Psychology and Psychiatry, 63*(4), 466-479.

Lansford, J.E., & others (2010). Developmental precursors of number of sexual partners from ages 16 to 22. *Journal of Research on Adolescence, 20,* 651-677.

Lansford, J.E., & others (2017). Change over time in parents' beliefs about and reported use of corporal punishment in eight countries with and without legal bans. *Child Abuse & Neglect, 71,* 44-55.

Lansford, J.E., & others (2021). Early physical abuse and adult outcomes. *Pediatrics, 147*(1), e20200873.

Lantolf, J. (2017). Materialist dialectics in Vygotsky's methodological approach: Implications for second language education research. In C. Ratner & D. Silva (Eds.), *Vygotsky and Marx.* Routledge.

Lany, J., & Shoaib, A. (2020). Individual differences in non-adjacent statistical dependency learning in infants. *Journal of Child Language, 47,* 483-507.

Larrivee, D. (2019). In pursuit of non-invasive psychopharmacology: Developing fNIRS repertoire. *Journal of Neuroscience & Cognitive Studies, 3*(1), 1012.

Larson, J.J., & others (2019). Cognitive and behavioral impact on children exposed to opioids during pregnancy. *Pediatrics, 144*(2), e20190514.

Larson, R.W., & Lampman-Petraitis, C. (1989). Daily emotional states as reported by children and adolescents. *Child Development, 60,* 1250-1260.

Larson, R.W., McGovern, G., & Orson, C. (2018). How adolescents develop self-motivation in complex learning environments: Processes and practices in afterschool programs. In A. Renninger & S. Hidi (Eds.), *Cambridge handbook of motivation and learning.* Cambridge University Press.

Larson, R.W., & Richards, M.H. (1994). *Divergent realities.* Basic Books.

Larson, R.W., & Verma, S. (1999). How children and adolescents spend time across the world: Work, play, and developmental opportunities. *Psychological Bulletin, 125,* 701-736.

Larson, R.W., Walker, K.C., & McGovern, G. (2018). Youth programs as contexts for development of moral agency. In L.A. Jensen (Ed.), *Handbook of moral development: An interdisciplinary perspective.* Oxford University Press.

Larzelere, R.E., Morris, A.S., & Harrist, A.W. (Eds.) (2013). *Authoritative parenting.* American Psychological Association.

Larzelere, R.E., & others (2019). The insufficiency of the evidence used to categorically oppose spanking and its implications for families and psychological science: Comment on Gershoff et al. (2018). *American Psychologist, 74*(4), 497-499.

La Salle, T., George, H.P., McCoach, D.B., Polk, T., & Ivanovich, L.L. (2018). An examination of school climate, victimization, and mental health problems among middle school students self-identifying with emotional and behavioral disorders. *Behavioral Disorders, 43,* 383-392.

Lash, M., Akpovo, S.M., & Cushner, K. (2022). Developing the intercultural competence of early childhood preservice teachers: Preparing teachers for culturally diverse classrooms. *Journal of Early Childhood Teacher Education, 43*(1), 105-126.

Laurent, G., Hecht, H.K., Ensink, K., & Borelli, J.L. (2018). Emotional understanding, aggression, and social functioning among preschoolers. *American Journal of Orthopsychiatry, 90*(1), 9-21.

Laursen, B., & Faur, S. (2022). What does it mean to be susceptible to influence? A brief primer on peer conformity and developmental changes that affect it. *International Journal of Behavioral Development, 46,* 222-237.

Lawler, M., Heary, C., Shorter, G., & Nixon, E. (2022). Peer and parental processes predict distinct patterns of physical activity participation among adolescent girls and boys. *International Journal of Sport and Exercise Psychology, 20,* 497-514.

Lawrence, J., & others (2019). A longitudinal study of parental discipline up to 5 years. *Journal of Family Studies, 27*(4), 589-606.

Lawrence J.M., & others (2021). Trends in prevalence of type 1 and type 2 diabetes in children and adolescents in the US, 2001-2017. *JAMA, 326*(8), 717-727.

Lazarus, J.H. (2017a). Role of the Iodine Global Network in elimination of iodine deficiency. *Recent Patents on Endocrine, Metabolic, and Immune Drug Discovery, 10*(2), 119-122.

Lazarus, J.H. (2017b). Relevance of iodine nutrition to health in the 21st century. *Minerva Medicine, 108,* 114-115.

Leal, D., Gato, J., Coimbra, S., Freitas, D. & Tasker, F. (2021) The role of social support in the transition to parenthood among Lesbian, Gay, and Bisexual persons: A systematic review. *Sexuality Research and Social Policy, 18,* 1165-1179.

Leaper, C. (2015). Gender development from a social-cognitive perspective. In R.M. Lerner (Ed.), *Handbook of child psychology and developmental science* (7th ed.). Wiley.

Leary, M.R. (2017). *REVEL for introduction to behavioral research methods* (7th ed.). Pearson.

Lebel, C., Treit, S., & Beaulieu, C. (2019). A review of diffusion MRI of typical white matter development from early childhood to young adulthood. *NMR in Biomedicine, 32*(4), e3778.

LeBourgeois, M.K., & others (2017). Digital media and sleep in childhood and adolescence. *Pediatrics, 140*(Suppl. 2), S92-S96.

Lebrun-Harris, L.A., Sherman, L.J., Limber, S.P., Miller, B.D., & Edgerton, E.A. (2018). Bullying victimization and perpetration among US children and adolescents: 2016 National Survey of Children's Health. *Journal of Child and Family Studies, 28,* 2543-2557.

LeClair, K.L., & Saunders, J.E. (2019). Meeting the educational needs of children with hearing loss. *Bulletin of the World Health Organization, 97,* 722-724.

Lecompte, V., & others (2020). Examining the role of mother-child interactions and DNA methylation of the oxytocin receptor gene in understanding child controlling attachment behaviors. *Attachment & Human Development, 23*(1), 37-55.

Lederer, Y., Artzi, H., & Borodkin, K. (2022). The effects of maternal smartphone use on mother–child interaction. *Child Development, 93,* 556-570.

Lee, B., Jeong, S., & Roh, M. (2018). Association between body mass index and health outcomes among adolescents: The mediating role of traditional and cyber bullying victimization. *BMC Public Health, 18*(1), 674.

Lee, B.R., Kobulsky, J.M., Brodzinsky, D., & Barth, R.P. (2018). Parent perspectives on adoption preparation: Findings from the Modern Adoptive Families project. *Children and Youth Services Review, 85,* 63-71.

Lee, C.T., Tsai, M.C., Lin, C.Y., & Strong, C. (2017). Longitudinal effects of self-report pubertal timing and menarcheal age on adolescent psychological and behavioral outcomes in female youths from Northern Taiwan. *Pediatrics and Neonatology, 58*(4), 313-320.

Lee, D.B., & others (2019). Positive parenting moderates the effect of socioeconomic status on executive functioning: A three-generation approach. *Journal of Child and Family Studies, 28*(7), 1878-1885.

Lee, J.E., Pope, Z., & Gao, Z. (2018). The role of youth sports in promoting children's physical activity and preventing pediatric obesity: A systematic review. *Behavioral Medicine, 44,* 62-76.

Lee, J.Y., & Rosenthal, S.M. (2023). Gender-affirming care of transgender and gender-diverse youth: Current concepts. *Annual Review of Medicine, 74,* 107-116.

Lee, K. (2019). Impact of Head Start quality on children's developmental outcomes. *Social Work in Public Health, 27,* 1-12.

Lee, K., Quinn, P.C., & Pascalis, O. (2017). Face race processing and racial bias in early development: A perceptual-social linkage. *Current Directions in Psychological Science, 26,* 256-262.

Lee, K., Quinn, P.C., Pascalis, O., & Slater, A. (2013). Development of face processing ability in childhood. In P.D. Zelazo (Ed.), *Oxford handbook of developmental psychology.* Oxford University Press.

Lee, M.K., Baker, S., & Whitebread, D. (2018). Culture-specific links between maternal executive function, parenting, and preschool children's executive function in South Korea. *British Journal of Educational Psychology, 88,* 216-235.

Leed, J.E., Chinn, L.K., & Lockman, J.J. (2019). Reaching to the self: The development of infants' ability to localize targets on the body. *Psychological Science, 30*(7), 1063-1073.

Leedy, P.D., & Ormrod, J.E. (2019). *Practical research* (12th ed.). Pearson.

Leerkes, E.M., & Bailes, L.G. (2019). Emotional development within the family context. In V. LoBue & others (Eds.), *Handbook of emotional development* (pp. 627-661). Springer.

Leerkes, E.M., & Zhou, N. (2018). Maternal sensitivity to distress and attachment outcomes: Interactions with sensitivity to nondistress and infant temperament. *Journal of Family Psychology, 32*(6), 753-761.

Legerstee, M. (1997). Contingency effects of people and objects on subsequent cognitive functioning in 3-month-old infants. *Social Development, 6,* 307-321.

Legette, K. (2018). School tracking and youth self-perceptions: Implications for academic and racial identity. *Child Development, 89,* 1311-1327.

Lehrer, R., & Schauble, L. (2015). The development of scientific thinking. In R.M. Lerner & others (Eds.), *Handbook of child psychology and developmental science* (7th ed.). Wiley.

Leifer, A.D. (1973). *Television and the development of social behavior.* Paper presented at the meeting of the International Society for the Study of Behavioral Development, Ann Arbor, Michigan.

Leijten, P., Melendez-Torres, G.J., & Oliver, B.R. (2021). Parenting programs to improve sibling interactions: A meta-analysis. *Journal of Family Psychology, 35,* 703-708.

Leith, G., Yuill, N., & Pike, A. (2018). Scaffolding under the microscope: Applying self-regulation and other-regulation perspectives to a scaffolded task. *British Journal of Educational Psychology, 88,* 174-191.

Le Menestrel, S., & Duncan, G. (Eds.) (2019). *A roadmap to reducing child poverty.* National Academies Press.

Lenroot, R.K., & Giedd, J.N. (2006). Brain development in children and adolescents: Insights from anatomical magnetic resonance imaging. *Neuroscience and Biobehavioral Reviews, 30,* 718-729.

Lenz, S., Essler, S., Wörle, M., & Paulus, M. (2021). "Who will share with me?": Preschoolers rely on their friends more than on their nonfriends to share with them. *Journal of Experimental Child Psychology, 203,* 105037.

Lereya, S.T., Samara, M., & Wolke, D. (2013). Parenting behavior and the risk of becoming a victim and a bully/victim: A meta-analysis study. *Child Abuse and Neglect, 37*(12), 1091-1098.

Lerner, R.M., & others (2019). The end of the beginning: Evidence and absences studying positive youth development in a global context. *Adolescent Research Review, 4*(1), 1-14.

Lessard, L.M., & Juvonen, J. (2018). Losing and gaining friends: Does friendship instability compromise academic functioning in middle school? *Journal of School Psychology, 69,* 143-153.

Letourneau, E.J., McCart, M.R., Sheidow, A.J., & Mauro, P.M. (2017). First evaluation of contingency management intervention addressing adolescent substance use and sexual risk behaviors: Risk reduction therapy for adolescents. *Journal of Substance Abuse and Treatment, 72,* 56-65.

Leung, A.K.C., Leung, A.A.M., Wong, A.H.C., & Hon, K.L. (2020). Sleep terrors: An updated review. *Current Pediatric Reviews, 16*(3), 176-182.

Lever-Duffy, J., & McDonald, J. (2018). *Teaching and learning with technology* (6th ed.). Pearson.

Levey, D.F., & others (2019). Genetic associations with suicide attempt severity and genetic overlap with major depression. *Translational Psychiatry, 9,* 22.

Levine, D., Hirsh-Pasek, K., & Golinkoff, R.M. (2021). Infant word learning and emerging syntax. In J.J. Lockman & C.S. Tamis-LeMonda (Eds.), *Cambridge handbook of infant development.* Cambridge University Press

Levine, L.E., & others (2019). Mobile media use by infants and toddlers. *Computers in Human Behavior, 94,* 92-99.

Lewis, A.C. (2007). Looking beyond NCLB. *Phi Delta Kappan, 88,* 483-484.

Lewis, D.M.G., Al-Shawaf, L., & Buss, D.M. (2021). Evolutionary personality psychology. In P.T. Corr & G. Matthews (Eds.), *Cambridge handbook of personality psychology.* Cambridge University Press.

Lewis, G.J., Asbury, K., & Plomin, R. (2017). Externalizing problems in childhood and adolescence predict subsequent educational achievement but for different genetic and environmental reasons. *Journal of Child Psychology and Psychiatry, 58,* 292-304.

Lewis, M. (2015). Emotional development and consciousness. In R.M. Lerner (Ed.), *Handbook of child psychology and developmental science* (7th ed.). Wiley.

Lewis, M. (2018). The emergence of human emotions. In L. F. Barrett & others (Eds.), *Handbook of emotions* (4th ed.). Guilford Press.

Lewis, M. (2020). Selfhood. In B. Hopkins & others (Eds.), *Cambridge encyclopedia of child development.* Cambridge University Press.

Lewis, M., & Brooks-Gunn, J. (1979). *Social cognition and the acquisition of the self.* Plenum.

Lewis, R.B., Wheeler, J.J., & Carter, S.L. (2017). *Teaching students with special needs* (9th ed.). Pearson.

Lewis-Morrarty, E., & others (2015). Infant attachment security and early childhood behavioral inhibition interact to predict adolescent social anxiety symptoms. *Child Development, 86,* 598-613.

Leys, C., & others (2020). Pre-eminence of parental conflicts over parental divorce regarding the evolution of depressive and anxiety symptoms among children during adulthood. *European Journal of Trauma & Dissociation, 4*(1), 100102.

Li, G., Kung, K.T.F., & Hines, M. (2017). Childhood gender-typed behavior and adolescent sexual orientation: A longitudinal population-based study. *Developmental Psychology, 53,* 764-777.

Li, H., & others (2020). Mood instability across the perinatal period: A cross-sectional and longitudinal study. *Journal of Affective Disorders, 264,* 15-23.

Li, H., & Zhang, Q. (2023). Effects of prosocial video games on prosocial thoughts and prosocial behaviors. *Social Science Computer Review, 41,* 1063-1080.

Li, J., Deng, M., Wang, X., & Tang, Y. (2018). Teachers' and parents' autonomy support and psychological control perceived in junior-high school: Extending the dual-process model of self-determination theory. *Learning and Individual Differences, 68,* 20-29.

Li, J., & Fung, H. (2020). Culture at work: European American and Taiwanese parental socialization of children's learning. *Applied Developmental Science, 25,* 26-37.

Li, S., Callaghan, B.L., & Richardson, R. (2014). Infantile amnesia: Forgotten but not gone. *Learning and Memory, 21,* 135-139.

Li, S., & Fan, L. (2022). Media multitasking, depression, and anxiety of college students: Serial mediating effects of attention control and negative information attentional bias. *Frontiers in Psychiatry, 13,* 989201.

Li, S., Zhao, F., & Yu, G. (2019). Childhood maltreatment and intimate partner violence victimization: A meta-analysis. *Child Abuse & Neglect, 88,* 212-224.

Li, S-J., & others (2020). Uncovering the modulatory interactions of brain networks in cognition with central thalamic deep brain stimulation using functional magnetic resonance imaging. *Neuroscience, 440,* 65-84.

Li, W., Farkas, G., Duncan, G.J., Burchinal, M.R., & Vandell, D.L. (2013). Timing of high-quality child care and cognitive, language, and preacademic development. *Developmental Psychology, 49*(8), 1440-1451.

Li, Z., & others (2019). Interactive effects of family instability and adolescent stress reactivity on socioemotional functioning. *Developmental Psychology, 55*(10), 2193-2202.

Liang, K., & others (2023). A pilot movement integrity with intelligent play program (MIIP): Effects on math performance and enjoyment for preschoolers in China. *Child and Youth Care Forum, 52,* 703-719.

Liang, W., & Chikritzhs, T. (2015). Age at first use of alcohol predicts the risk of heavy alcohol use in early adulthood: A longitudinal study in the United States. *International Journal on Drug Policy, 26,* 131-134.

Liang, X., & others (2020). Prevalence and risk factors of childhood hypertension in urban-rural areas of China: A cross-sectional study. *International Journal of Hypertension, 2020,* 2374231.

Liben, L.S. (2017). Gender development: A constructivist-ecological perspective. In N. Budwig, E. Turiel, & P.D. Zelazo (Eds.), *New perspectives on human development.* Cambridge University Press.

Libertus, K., Joh, A.S., & Needham, A.W. (2016). Motor training at 3 months affects object exploration 12 months later. *Developmental Science, 19,* 1058-1066.

Licari, M.K., & others (2019). The brain basis of comorbidity in neurodevelopmental disorders. *Current Developmental Disorders Reports, 6*(1), 9-18.

Lichtenfeld, S., Pekrun, R., Marsh, H.W., Nett, U.E., & Reiss, K. (2023). Achievement emotions and elementary school children's academic performance: Longitudinal models of developmental ordering. *Journal of Educational Psychology, 115*(4), 552-570.

Lickliter, R. (2017). Developmental evolution. *Wiley Interdisciplinary Reviews. Cognitive Science, 8*(1-2). doi:10.1002/wcs.1422

Lickliter, R., & Witherington, D.C. (2017). Towards a truly developmental epigenetics. *Human Development, 60,* 124-138.

Liddon, N., & others (2016). Withdrawal as pregnancy prevention and associated risk factors among U.S. high school students: Findings from the 2011 National Youth Behavior Risk Survey. *Contraception, 93,* 126-132.

Lieberman, O.J., McGuirt, A.F., Tang, G., & Sulzer, D. (2019). Roles for neuronal and glial autophagy in synaptic pruning during development. *Neurobiology of Disease, 122,* 149-163.

Liebrechts-Akkerman, G., & others (2020). Explaining sudden infant death with cardiac arrhythmias: Complete exon sequencing of nine cardiac arrhythmia genes in Dutch SIDS cases highlights new and known DNA variants. *Forensic Science International. Genetics, 46,* 102266.

Liem, D.G. (2017). Infants' and children's salt taste perception and liking: A review. *Nutrients, 9*(9), 1011.

Liew, J., Morris, A.S., & Kerr, K.L. (2023). Emotion regulation processes as transdiagnostic in adolescence and early adulthood: A neurobioecological systems framework. In L.J. Crockett, G. Carlo, & J.E. Schulenberg (Eds.), *APA handbook of adolescent and young adult development* (pp. 91–106). American Psychological Association.

Lilgendahl, J.P., & others (2018). "So now, I wonder, what am I?": A narrative approach to bicultural identity integration. *Journal of Cross-Cultural Psychology, 49,* 1596–1624.

Lillard, A. (2006). Pretend play in toddlers. In C.A. Brownell & C.B. Kopp (Eds.), *Socioemotional development in the toddler years.* Oxford University Press.

Lillard, A.S. (2021). Montessori as an alternative early childhood education. *Early Child Development and Care, 191*(7–8), 1196–1206.

Lillard, A.S., & Kavanaugh, R.D. (2014). The contribution of symbolic skills to the development of explicit theory of mind. *Child Development, 85,* 1535–1551.

Lillard, A.S., & Taggart, J. (2019). Pretend play and fantasy: What if Montessori was right? *Child Development Perspectives, 13*(2), 85–90.

Lim, C.Y.S., & others (2022). Screening for metabolic complications of childhood and adolescent obesity: A scoping review of national and international guidelines. *Obesity Reviews, 23*(12), e13513.

Lin, C.C., & others (2020). Mercury, lead, manganese, and hazardous metals. In R. Kishi & P. Grandjean (Eds.), *Health impacts of developmental exposure to environmental chemicals* (pp. 247–277). Springer.

Lin, I.-H., Huang, C.-Y., Chou, S.-H., & Shih, C.-L. (2022). Efficacy of prenatal yoga in the treatment of depression and anxiety during pregnancy: A systematic review and meta-analysis. *International Journal of Environmental Research and Public Health, 19*(9), 5368.

Lin, L.Y., & others (2015). Effects of television exposure on developmental skills of young children. *Infant Behavior and Development, 38,* 20–26.

Lin, Y., Stavans, M., & Baillargeon, R. (2021). Infants' physical reasoning and the cognitive architecture that supports it. In O. Houde & G. Borst (Eds.), *Cambridge handbook of cognitive development.* Cambridge University Press.

Lin, Y.C., Latner, J.D., Fung, X.C., & Lin, C.Y. (2018). Poor health and experiences of being bullied in adolescents: Self-perceived overweight and frustration with appearance matter. *Obesity, 26,* 397–404.

Lin, Y.-J., & Gau, S.S.-F. (2019). Developmental changes of neuropsychological functioning in individuals with and without childhood ADHD from early adolescence to young adulthood: A 7-year follow-up study. *Psychological Medicine, 49,* 940–951.

Lindorff, A.M., Hall, J., & Sammons, P. (2019). Investigating a Singapore-based mathematics textbook and teaching approach in classrooms in England. *Frontiers in Education, 4,* 37.

Lindsay, A.C., Wasserman, M., Muñoz, M.A., Wallington, S.F., & Greaney, M.L. (2018). Examining influences of parenting styles and practices on physical activity and sedentary behaviors in Latino children in the United States: Integrative review. *JMIR Public Health and Surveillance, 4*(1), e14.

Lipowski, M., Lipowska, M., Jochimek, M., & Krokosz, D. (2016). Resilience as a factor protecting youths from risky behavior: Moderating effects of gender and sport. *European Journal of Sport Science, 16,* 246–255.

Liu, J., Raine, A., Venables, P.H., & Mednick, S.A. (2004). Malnutrition at 3 years and externalizing behavior problems at age 8, 11, and 17 years. *American Journal of Psychiatry, 161,* 2005–2013.

Liu, J., Zheng, X., Parker, M., & Fang, X. (2020). Childhood left-behind experience and employment quality of new-generation migrants in China. *Population Research and Policy Review,* 1–28.

Liu, N., & others (2018). Intergenerational teen pregnancy: A population-based cohort study. *BJOG: An International Journal of Obstetrics and Gynaecology, 125*(13), 1766–1774.

Liu, N., & others (2019). Effects of home visits for pregnant and postpartum women on premature birth, low birth weight and rapid repeat birth: A meta-analysis and systematic review of randomized controlled trials. *Family Practice, 36*(5), 533–543.

Liu, R., Calkins, S.D., & Bell, M.A. (2018). Fearful inhibition, inhibitory control, and maternal negative behaviors during toddlerhood predict internalizing problems at age 6. *Journal of Abnormal Child Psychology, 46,* 1665–1675.

Liu, R.D., & others (2022). The transmission of educational expectations from parents to early adolescents in Chinese families: The moderating role of the training parenting style. *Current Psychology,* 1–12.

Liu, X., & others (2017). Prenatal care and child growth and schooling in four low- and medium-income countries. *PLoS One, 12,* e0171299.

Liu, Y., & others (2020). Multiplicative effect of intrinsic and extrinsic motivation on academic performance: A longitudinal study of Chinese students. *Journal of Personality, 88,* 584–595.

Liu, Y., Wang, Y., Wu, Y., Chen, X., & Bai, J. (2021). Effectiveness of the CenteringPregnancy program on maternal and birth outcomes: A systematic review and meta-analysis. *International Journal of Nursing Studies, 120,* 103981.

Livingston, G. (2018, September 24). *Stay-at-home moms and dads account for about one-in-five U.S. parents.* Pew Research Center. Retrieved May 18, 2020, from https://www.pewresearch.org/fact-tank/2018/09/24/stay-at-home-moms-and-dads-account-for-about-one-in-five-u-s-parents/

Livingston, G. (2019, February 20). *The way U.S. teens spend their time is changing, but differences between boys and girls persist.* Pew Research Center.

Retrieved March 7, 2020, from https://www.pewresearch.org/fact-tank/2019/02/20/the-way-u-s-teens-spend-their-time-is-changing-but-differences-between-boys-and-girls-persist

Lloyd-Fox, S., & others (2019). Habituation and novelty detection fNIRS brain responses in 5- and 8-month-old infants: The Gambia and UK. *Developmental Science, 22*(5), e12817.

Lo, C.C., & others (2017). Racial/ethnic differences in emotional health: A longitudinal study of immigrants' adolescent children. *Community Mental Health Journal, 53,* 92–101.

Lo, C.O., & Porath, M. (2017). Paradigm shifts in gifted education: An examination vis-à -vis its historical situatedness and pedagogical sensibilities. *Gifted Child Quarterly, 61,* 343–360.

Loades, M.E., & others (2020). Rapid systematic review: The impact of social isolation and loneliness on the mental health of children and adolescents in the context of COVID-19. *Journal of the American Academy of Child and Adolescent Psychiatry, 59,* 1218–1239.e3.

Lobo, F.M., Lunkenheimer, E., Lucas-Thompson, R.G., & Seiter, N.S. (2021). Parental emotion coaching moderates the effects of family stress on internalizing symptoms in middle childhood and adolescence. *Social Development, 30,* 1023–1039.

Lockhart, K.L., Goddu, M.K., & Keil, F.C. (2018). When saying "I'm best" is benign: Developmental shifts in perceptions of boasting. *Developmental Psychology, 54*(3), 521–535.

Lockwood, A.B., Farmer, R.L., Winans, S., & Sealander, K. (2022). Specific learning disability identification practices in the USA: A survey of special education administrators. *Contemporary School Psychology, 26*(4), 535–544.

Loeb, E.L., & others (2020). Romantic relationship churn in early adolescence predicts hostility, abuse, and avoidance in relationships into early adulthood. *The Journal of Early Adolescence, 40*(8), 1195–1225.

Lohn, Z., & others (2022). Large-scale group genetic counseling: Evaluation of a novel service delivery model in a Canadian hereditary cancer clinic. *Journal of Genetic Counseling, 31*(2), 459–469.

London, M.L., & others (2017). *Maternal and child nursing care* (5th ed.). Pearson.

Long, E., & Valente, T.W. (2019). Perceived social acceptability and longitudinal trends in adolescent cigarette smoking. *Prevention Science, 20*(6), 824–832.

Loos, R.J., & Yeo, G.S. (2022). The genetics of obesity: From discovery to biology. *Nature Reviews Genetics, 23*(2), 120–133.

López, B.G. (2020). Incorporating language brokering experiences into bilingualism research: An examination of informal translation practices. *Language and Linguistics Compass, 14*(1), e12361.

Lopez-Maestro, M., & others (2017). Quality of attachment in infants less than 1500g or less than 32 weeks. Related factors. *Early Human Development, 104,* 1–6.

Lopp, S., Navidi, W., Achermann, P., LeBourgeois, M., & Diniz Behn, C. (2017). Developmental changes in ultradian sleep cycles across early childhood: Preliminary insights. *Journal of Biological Rhythms, 32*(1), 64–74.

Lord, C., & others (2020). Autism spectrum disorder. *Nature Reviews. Disease Primers, 6*(1), 5.

Lorenz, K.Z. (1965). *Evolution and the modification of behavior.* University of Chicago Press.

Losel, F., & Bender, D. (2011). Emotional and antisocial outcomes of bullying and victimization at school: A follow-up from childhood to adolescence. *Journal of Aggression, Conflict, and Peace Research, 3,* 89–96.

Lovallo, W.R., & others (2017). Joint impact of early life adversity and COMT Val158Met (rs4680) genotypes on the adult cortisol response to psychological stress. *Psychosomatic Medicine, 79,* 631–637.

Love, J.M., Chazan-Cohen, R., Raikes, H., & Brooks-Gunn, J. (2013). What makes a difference: Early Head Start evaluation findings in a developmental context. *Monographs of the Society for Research in Child Development, 78,* 1–173.

Lovette-Wilson, C., Orange, A., & Corrales, A. (2022). Factors influencing student transition from elementary to middle school. *Educational Studies, 48,* 424–441.

Lowe, K., & Arnett, J.J. (2019). Failure to grow up, failure to pay? Parents' views of conflict over money with their emerging adults. *Journal of Family Issues, 41,* 359–382.

Lowell, A., & Mayes, L. (2019). Assessment and treatment of prenatally exposed infants and children. In A. Hauptman & J. Salpekar (Eds.), *Pediatric neuropsychiatry* (pp. 131–144). Springer.

Lowry, R., & others (2017). Early sexual debut and associated risk behaviors among sexual minority youth. *American Journal of Preventive Medicine, 52,* 379–384.

Lowson, K., Offer, C., Watson, J., McGuire, B., & Renfrew, M.J. (2015). The economic benefits of increasing kangaroo skin-to-skin care and breastfeeding in neonatal units: Analysis of a pragmatic intervention in clinical practice. *International Journal of Breastfeeding, 10,* 11.

Lu, C., Benet-Martínez, V., & Robins, R.W. (2020). The development of ethnic identity from late childhood to young adulthood: Findings from a 10-year longitudinal study of Mexican-origin youth. *Social Psychological and Personality Science, 11*(5), 709–717.

Lu, J., & others (2018). A novel and compact review on the role of oxidative stress in female reproduction. *Reproductive Biology and Endocrinology, 16*(1), 80.

Lu, K., & others (2022). Self-reported physical activity and asthma risk in children. *Journal of Allergy and Clinical Immunology: In Practice, 10*(1), 231–239.

Luby, J.L. (2020). Editorial: The primacy of parenting. *Journal of Child Psychology and Psychiatry, 61,* 399–400.

Lucas, C. (2020). Taking play seriously. *The Lancet Child & Adolescent Health, 4*(1), 19.

Lucca, K., & Wilbourn, M.P. (2019). The what and the how: Information-seeking pointing gestures facilitate learning labels and functions. *Journal of Experimental Child Psychology, 178,* 417–436.

Luizon, M.R., Pereira, D.A., & Sandrim, V.C. (2018). Pharmacogenomics of hypertension and preeclampsia: Focus on gene-gene interactions. *Frontiers in Pharmacology, 9,* 168.

Lukowski, A.F., & Bauer, P. (2014). Long-term memory in infancy and early childhood. In P. Bauer & R. Fivush (Eds.), *Wiley-Blackwell handbook of children's memory.* Wiley.

Lumpkin, A. (2021). *Introduction to physical education, exercise science, and sports* (11th ed.). McGraw Hill.

Lund, H.G., Reider, B.D., Whiting, A.B., & Prichard, J.R. (2010). Sleep patterns and predictors of disturbed sleep in a large population of college students. *Journal of Adolescent Health, 46,* 124–132.

Lunde, C., & Joleby, M. (2023). Being under pressure to sext: Adolescents' experiences, reactions, and counter-strategies. *Journal of Research on Adolescence, 33,* 188–201.

Luo, Q., & Sahakian, B.J. (2022). Brain sex differences: The androgynous brain is advantageous for mental health and well-being. *Neuropsychopharmacology, 47,* 407–408.

Lushington, K., Pamula, Y., Martin, J., & Kennedy, J.D. (2014). Developmental changes in sleep: Infancy and preschool years. In A.R. Wolfson & E. Montgomery-Downs (Eds.), *Oxford handbook of infant, child, and adolescent sleep and behavior.* Oxford University Press.

Lux, C.J., Decker, K.B., & Nease, C. (2020). Supporting young children's executive function skills through mindfulness: Implications for school counselors. *Journal of School Counseling, 18,* 1.

Lykken, E.A., Shyng, C., Edwards, R.J., Rozenberg, A., & Gray, S.J. (2018). Recent progress and considerations for AAV gene therapies targeting the central nervous system. *Journal of Neurodevelopmental Disorders, 10,* 16.

Lynn, M.G., Grych, J.H., & Fosco, G.M. (2016). Influences on father involvement: Testing for unique contributions of religion. *Journal of Child and Family Studies, 25*(11), 3247–3259.

Lyon, T.D., & Flavell, J.H. (1993). Young children's understanding of forgetting over time. *Child Development, 64,* 789–800.

M

Maag, J.W., Kauffman, J.M., & Simpson, R.L. (2019). The amalgamation of special education? On practices and policies that may render it unrecognizable. *Exceptionality, 27,* 185–200.

Maas, J. (2008, March 4). Commentary in L. Szabo, "Parents with babies need time to reset inner clock." *USA Today,* p. 4D.

Mabbe, E., Soenens, B., De Muynck, G.J., & Vansteenkiste, M. (2018). The impact of feedback valence and communication style on intrinsic motivation in middle childhood: Experimental evidence and generalization across individual differences. *Journal of Experimental Child Psychology, 170,* 134–160.

Macedo, T.C.C., & others (2020). Prevalence of preeclampsia and eclampsia in adolescent pregnancy: A systematic review and meta-analysis of 291,247 adolescents worldwide since 1969. *European Journal of Obstetrics & Gynecology and Reproductive Biology, 248,* 177–186.

MacFarlane, J.A. (1975). Olfaction in the development of social preferences in the human neonate. In *Parent-infant interaction.* Ciba Foundation Symposium No. 33. Elsevier.

Machado, B., & others (2014). Risk factors and antecedent life events in the development of anorexia nervosa: A Portuguese case-control study. *European Eating Disorders Review, 22,* 243–251.

Macia-Gual, A., & Domingo-Penafiel, L. (2021). Demands in early childhood education: Montessori pedagogy, prepared environment, and teacher training. *International Journal of Research in Education and Science, 7,* 144–162.

Macionis, J.J. (2017). *Society* (14th ed.). Pearson.

MacNeill, L.A., Ram, N., Bell, M.A., Fox, N.A., & Pérez-Edgar, K. (2018). Trajectories of infants' biobehavioral development: Timing and rate of A-not-B performance gains and EEG maturation. *Child Development, 89,* 711–724.

Macon, T.A., & others (2017). Predictors of father investment of time and finances: The specificity of resources, relationships, and parenting beliefs. *Journal of Family Issues, 38*(18), 2642–2662.

MacSwan, J., Thompson, M.S., Rolstad, K., McAlister, K., & Lobo, G. (2017). Three theories of the effects of language education programs: An empirical evaluation of bilingual and English-only policies. *Annual Review of Applied Linguistics, 37,* 218–240.

Macy, J.T., & others (2019). Adolescent tolerance for deviance, cigarette smoking trajectories, and premature mortality: A longitudinal study. *Preventive Medicine, 119,* 118–123.

Madden, K., & others (2016). Hypnosis for pain management during labor and childbirth. *Cochrane Database of Systematic Reviews, 5,* CD009356.

Mader, S.S., & Windelspecht, M. (2017). *Inquiry into life.* McGraw Hill.

Madigan, S., McArthur, B.A., Anhorn, C., Eirich, R., & Christakis, D.A. (2020). Associations between screen use and child language skills: A systematic review and meta-analysis. *JAMA Pediatrics, 174,* 665–675.

Madigan, S., & others (2019). Parenting behavior and child language: A meta-analysis. *Pediatrics, 144*(4), e20183556.

Maged, M., & Rizzolo, D. (2018). Preventing sudden infant death syndrome and other sleep-related infant deaths. *Journal of the American Academy of PAs, 31*(11), 25–30.

Magistro, D., & others (2022). Two years of physically active mathematics lessons enhance cognitive function and gross motor skills in primary school children. *Psychology of Sport and Exercise, 63*, 102254.

Magis-Weinberg, L., Gys, C.L., Berger, E.L., Domoff, S.E., & Dahl, R.E. (2021). Positive and negative online experiences and loneliness in Peruvian adolescents during the COVID-19 lockdown. *Journal of Research on Adolescence, 31*, 717-733.

Magnus, W., & others (2021). Attention deficit hyperactivity disorder. *StatPearls.*

Magnusson, M., & others (2021). Preschoolers' true and false reports: Comparing effects of the Sequential Interview and NICHD protocol. *Legal and Criminological Psychology, 26*(1), 83-102.

Magson, N.R., & others (2021). Risk and protective factors for prospective changes in adolescent mental health during the COVID-19 pandemic. *Journal of Youth and Adolescence, 50*, 44-57.

Mahadik, K. (2019). Rising cesarean rates: Are primary sections overused? *The Journal of Obstetrics and Gynecology of India, 69*, 483-489.

Mahalik, J.R., Di Bianca, M., & Sepulveda, J.A. (2020). Examining father status and purpose to understand new dads' healthier lives. *Psychology of Men & Masculinities, 21*, 570-577.

Maharian, A., & others (2021). Can labour migration help households adapt to climate change? Evidence from four river basins in South Asia. *Climate and Development, 13*, 879-894.

Mahler, M. (1979). *Separation-individuation* (Vol. 2). Jason Aronson.

Mahmassani, H.A., & others (2022). Maternal diet quality during pregnancy and child cognition and behavior in a US cohort. *The American Journal of Clinical Nutrition, 115*(1), 128-141.

Mahrer, N.E., O'Hara, K.L., Sandler, I.N., & Wolchik, S.A. (2018). Does shared parenting help or hurt children in high-conflict divorced families? *Journal of Divorce & Remarriage, 59*(4), 324-347.

Mahumud, R.A., & others (2022). The effectiveness of interventions on nutrition social behaviour change communication in improving child nutritional status within the first 1000 days: Evidence from a systematic review and meta-analysis. *Maternal and Child Nutrition, 18*(1), e13286.

Mahumud, R.A., Sultana, M., & Sarker, A.R. (2017). Distribution and determinants of low birth weight in developing countries. *Journal of Preventive Medicine and Public Health, 50*(1), 18-28.

Mak, H.W., & Iacovou, M. (2019). Dimensions of the parent-child relationship: Effects on substance use in adolescence and adulthood. *Substance Use & Misuse, 54*(5), 724-736.

Malak, R., & others (2021). Application of the Neonatal Behavioral Assessment Scale to evaluate the neurobehavior of preterm neonates. *Brain Sciences, 11*(10), 1285.

Malik, M.A.R., & Butt, A.N. (2017). Rewards and creativity: Past, present, and future. *Applied Psychology, 66*, 290-325.

Maliske, L.Z., Schurz, M., & Kanske, P. (2023). Interactions within the social brain: Co-activation and connectivity among networks enabling empathy and Theory of Mind. *Neuroscience & Biobehavioral Reviews, 147*, 105080.

Malmberg, L.E., & others (2016). The influence of mothers' and fathers' sensitivity in the first year of life on children's cognitive outcomes at 18 and 36 months. *Child Care, Health, and Development, 42*(1), 1-7.

Maloy, R.W., Verock-O'Loughlin, R-E., Edwards, S.A., & Woolf, B.P. (2017). *Transforming learning with new technologies* (3rd ed.). Pearson.

Malti, T. (2016). Toward an integrated clinical-developmental model of guilt. *Developmental Review, 39*, 16-36.

Malti, T., Galarneau, E., & Peplak, J. (2021). Moral development in adolescence. *Journal of Research on Adolescence, 31*, 1097-1113.

Mandara, J. (2006). The impact of family functioning on African American males' academic achievement: A review and clarification of the empirical literature. *Teachers College Record, 108*, 206-233.

Mandler, J.M. (2012). On the spatial foundations of the conceptual system and its enrichment. *Cognitive Science, 36*(3), 421-451.

Mandler, J.M., & McDonough, L. (1993). Concept formation in infancy. *Cognitive Development, 8*, 291-318.

Maneiro, L., Ziti, Y., van Geel, M., Gómez-Fraguela, X.A., & Vedder, P. (2022). The role of deviant siblings in delinquency: A meta-analysis of longitudinal studies. *Aggression and Violent Behavior, 67*, 101780.

Manera, L. (2022). Art and aesthetic education in the Reggio Emilia Approach. *Education 3-13, 50*(4), 483-493.

Manganaro, L., & others (2018). Highlights on MRI of the fetal body. *La Radiologia Medica, 123*, 271-285.

Manotas, M.C., González, D.M., Céspedes, C., Forero, C., & Moreno, A.P.R. (2022). Genetic and epigenetic control of puberty. *Sexual Development, 16*, 1-10.

Manuck, S.B., & McCaffery, J.M. (2014). Gene-environment interaction. *Annual Review of Psychology, 65*, 41-70.

Manz, E., Lehrer, R., & Schauble, L. (2020). Rethinking the classroom science investigation. *Journal of Research in Science Teaching, 57*(7), 1148-1174.

Manzanares, S., & others (2016). Accuracy of fetal sex determination on ultrasound examination in the first trimester of pregnancy. *Journal of Clinical Ultrasound, 44*, 272-277.

Manzari, N., & others (2019). Prenatal maternal stress and risk of neurodevelopmental disorders in the offspring: A systematic review and meta-analysis. *Social Psychiatry and Psychiatric Epidemiology, 54*, 1299-1309.

Maravilla, J.C., & others (2017). Factors influencing repeated adolescent pregnancy: A review and meta-analysis. *American Journal of Obstetrics and Gynecology, 217*(5), 527-545.

March of Dimes (2017). *Multiple pregnancy and birth: Considering fertility treatments.* March of Dimes.

Marcia, J.E. (1993). The ego identity status approach to ego identity. In J. Marcia & others (Eds.), *Ego identity* (pp. 3-21). Springer.

Marcia, J.E. (1994). The empirical study of ego identity. In H.A. Bosma, T.L.G. Graafsma, H.D. Grotevant, & D.J. De Levita (Eds.), *Identity and development.* Sage.

Marcia, J.E. (2002). Identity and psychosocial development in adulthood. *Identity: An International Journal of Theory and Research, 2*, 7-28.

Marcoux, S., & others (2017). The PETALE study: Late adverse effects and biomarkers in childhood acute lymphoblastic leukemia survivors. *Pediatric Blood & Cancer, 64*(6), doi:10.1002/pbc.26361

Marcovitch, S., Clearfield, M.W., Swingler, M., Calkins, S.D., & Bell, M.A. (2016). Attentional predictors of 5-month-olds' performance on a looking A-not-B task. *Infant and Child Development, 25*, 233-246.

Marcovitch, S., & others (2015). A longitudinal assessment of the relation between executive function and theory of mind at 3, 4, and 5 years. *Cognitive Development, 33*, 40-55.

Mares, M-L., & Pan, Z. (2013). Effects of *Sesame Street*: A meta-analysis of children's learning in 15 countries. *Journal of Applied Developmental Psychology, 34*, 140-151.

Margolis, A.E., & others (2019). Profiles of infant communicative behavior. *Developmental Psychology, 55*(8), 1594-1604.

Marie, C., & Trainor, L.J. (2013). Development of simultaneous pitch encoding: Infants show a high voice superiority effect. *Cerebral Cortex, 23*(3), 660-669.

Mark, K.S. (2022). The effects of illicit drug and alcohol use in pregnancy. In E.A. Reece, G.F. Leguizamón, G.A. Macones, & A. Wiznitzer (Eds.), *Clinical obstetrics: The fetus and mother* (4th ed.). Wolters Kluwer.

Mark, K.S., & others (2015). Knowledge, attitudes, and practice of electronic cigarette use among pregnant women. *Journal of Addiction Medicine, 9*, 266-272.

Markant, J.C., & Thomas, K.M. (2013). Postnatal brain development. In P.D. Zelazo (Ed.), *Oxford handbook of developmental psychology.* Oxford University Press.

Marks, A.K., & Garcia-Coll, C. (2018). Education and developmental competencies of ethnic minority children: Recent theoretical and methodological advances. *Developmental Review, 50*, 90-98.

Marmet, S., Studer, J., Wicki, M., & Gmel, G. (2021). Cannabis use disorder trajectories and their prospective predictors in a large population-based sample of young Swiss men. *Addiction, 116*, 560-570.

Marshall, A.N., Root, H.J., Valovich McLeod, T.C., & Lam, K.C. (2022). Patient-reported outcome measures for pediatric patients with sport-related injuries: A systematic review. *Journal of Athletic Training, 57*(4), 371–384.

Marsland, S., Treyvaud, K., & Pepping, C.A. (2022). Prevalence and risk factors associated with perinatal depression in sexual minority women. *Clinical Psychology & Psychotherapy, 29,* 611–621.

Martin, C., Cook, R.E., & Andrews, N.C.Z. (2017). Reviving androgyny: A modern day perspective on flexibility of gender identity and behavior. *Sex Roles, 76,* 592–603.

Martin, C.L., & Cook, R. (2017). Cognitive perspectives on children's toy choices and play styles. In E. Wigram & L. Dinella (Eds.), *Gender-typing of children's toys.* American Psychological Association.

Martin, C.L., & others (2013). The role of sex of peers and gender-typed activities in young children's peer affiliative networks: A longitudinal analysis of selection and influence. *Child Development, 84,* 921–937.

Martin, C.L., & others (2017). A dual identity approach for conceptualizing and measuring children's gender identity. *Child Development, 88,* 167–182.

Martin, J.A., Hamilton, B.E., & Osterman, M.J. (2015, September). Births in the United States, 2014. *NCHS Data Brief, 216,* 1–8.

Martin, J.A., & others (2005, September). Births: Final data for 2003. *National Vital Statistics Reports, 54,* 1–116.

Martin, J.A., & others (2017). Births: Final data for 2015. *National Vital Statistics Reports, 66,* 1–69.

Martin, K.B., & Messinger, D.S. (2018). Smile. In M. Bornstein & others (Eds.), *SAGE encyclopedia of lifespan human development.* Sage.

Martin, L.J., McGuire, C., Robertson, M., & Saizew, K. (2020). Subgroups in the context of youth sport. In M.W. Bruner, M.A. Eys, & L.J. Martin (Eds.), *The power of groups in youth sport* (pp. 127–143). Academic Press.

Martin, M.J., & others (2017). The mediating role of cortisol reactivity and executive functioning difficulties in the pathways between childhood histories of emotional insecurity and adolescent school problems. *Development and Psychopathology, 29*(4), 1483–1498.

Martin, M.J., Sturge-Apple, M.L., Davies, P.T., & Gutierrez, G. (2019). Attachment behavior and hostility as explanatory factors linking parent–adolescent conflict and adolescent adjustment. *Journal of Family Psychology, 33,* 586–596.

Martin, P.P., Butler-Barnes, S.T., & Hope, M.O. (2023). Sitting in the pews: Theological beliefs and racial/ethnic identity among African American adolescents. *Youth and Society, 55,* 300–320.

Martínez, M.L., Cumsille, P., Loyola, I., & Castillo, J.C. (2020). Patterns of civic and political commitment in early adolescence. *Journal of Early Adolescence, 40,* 5–27.

Martínez-González, A.E., Cervin, M., & Piqueras, J.A. (2022). Relationships between emotion regulation, social communication and repetitive behaviors in Autism Spectrum Disorder. *Journal of Autism and Developmental Disorders, 52*(10), 4519–4527.

Martz, M.E., Patrick, M.E., & Schulenberg, J.E. (2016). Alcohol mixed with energy drink use among U.S. 12th grade students: Prevalence, correlates, and associations with safe driving. *Journal of Adolescent Health, 56,* 557–563.

Masapollo, M., Polka, L., & Menard, L. (2016). When infants talk, infants listen: Pre-babbling infants prefer listening to speech with infant vocal properties. *Developmental Science, 19,* 318–328.

Masek, L.R., & others (2021). Where language meets attention: How contingent interactions promote learning. *Developmental Review, 60,* 100961.

Mash, E.J., & Wolfe, D.A. (2016). *Abnormal child psychology* (6th ed.). Cengage.

Mashburn, A.J., Justice, L.M., Downer, J.T., & Pianta, R.C. (2009). Peer effects on children's language achievement during pre-kindergarten. *Child Development, 80,* 686–702.

Maslowsky, J., & others (2019). Repeat teen births in the United States cluster in poorer areas with more limited reproductive health care access. *PRC Research & Policy Brief Series.* University of Texas at Austin Population Research Center.

Mason, G.M., Lokhandwala, S., Riggins, T., & Spencer, R.M. (2021). Sleep and human cognitive development. *Sleep Medicine Reviews, 57,* 101472.

Mason, K., Duncan, T., & Losos, J. (2021). *Understanding biology* (3rd ed.). McGraw Hill.

Mason, M., & others (2019). Adolescent depression and substance use: The protective role of prosocial peer behavior. *Journal of Abnormal Child Psychology, 47*(6), 1065–1074.

Masselink, M., & others (2018). The longitudinal association between self-esteem and depressive symptoms in adolescents: Separating between-person effects from within-person effects. *European Journal of Personality, 32*(6), 653–671.

Masten, A.S. (2012). Faculty profile: Ann Masten. *The Institute of Child Development further developments.* University of Minnesota, School of Education.

Masten, A.S. (2017). Building a transactional science on children and youth affected by political violence and armed conflict. *Development and Psychopathology, 29,* 79–84.

Masten, A.S., & Labella, M.H. (2016). Risk and resilience in child development. In L. Balter & C.S. Tamis-LeMonda (Eds.), *Child psychology* (2nd ed.). Routledge.

Masten, A.S., Lucke, C. M., Nelson, K.M., & Stallworthy, I.C. (2021). Resilience in development and psychopathology: Multisystem perspectives. *Annual Review of Clinical Psychology, 17,* 521–549.

Masterson, A.M., & Messina, N.M. (2023). Love and sexual scripts: A content analysis of 19 Netflix teen series. *Journal of Children and Media, 17,* 161–179.

Mastin, J.D., & Vogt, P. (2016). Infant engagement and early vocabulary development: A naturalistic observation study of Mozambican infants from 1:1 to 2:1. *Journal of Child Language, 43*(2), 235–264.

Masud, H., Ahmad, M.S., Cho, K.W., & Fakhr, Z. (2019). Parenting styles and aggression among young adolescents: A systematic review of literature. *Community Mental Health Journal, 55,* 1015–1030.

Mathews, B., & others (2020). Improving measurement of child abuse and neglect: A systematic review and analysis of national prevalence studies. *PLoS One, 15*(1), e0227884.

Matte-Gagné, C., Turgeon, N.R., Bernier, A., & Cyr, C. (2023). Toward a better understanding of the associations among different measures of father involvement and parenting alliance. *Journal of Family Issues, 44*(1), 244–263.

Matthiessen, C. (2013). *Overweight children: Tips for parents.* Retrieved February 21, 2013, from www.webmd.com/parenting/raising-fit-kids/mood/talking-kids

Mattson, S.N., Bernes, G.A., & Doyle, L.R. (2019). Fetal alcohol spectrum disorders: A review of the neurobehavioral deficits associated with prenatal alcohol exposure. *Alcoholism: Clinical and Experimental Research, 43*(6), 1046–1062.

Mau, W.-C.J., & Li, J. (2018). Factors influencing STEM career aspirations of underrepresented high school students. *Career Development Quarterly, 66,* 246–258.

Maurer, D. (2017). Critical periods re-examined: Evidence from children treated for dense cataracts. *Cognitive Development, 42,* 27–36.

Maurer, D., & Lewis, T.L. (2018). Visual systems. In R. Gibb & B. Kolb (Eds.), *The neurobiology of brain and behavioral development* (pp. 213–233). Routledge.

May, L., Gervain, J., Carreiras, M., & Werker, J.F. (2018). The specificity of the neural response to speech at birth. *Developmental Science, 21*(3), e12564.

Mayer, R.E. (2020). Intelligence, education, and society. In R.J. Sternberg (Ed.), *Human intelligence.* Cambridge University Press.

Mayo, C.O., & Wadsworth, M.E. (2020). Poverty and economic strain. In J.D. Jewell & S. Hupp (Eds.), *Encyclopedia of child and adolescent development.* Wiley.

Mayo, J.A., & others (2019). Parental age and stillbirth: A population-based cohort of nearly 10 million California deliveries from 1991 to 2011. *Annals of Epidemiology, 31,* 32–37.

Mayol-García, Y.H., Gurrentz, B., & Kreider, R.M., (2021). Number, timing, and duration of marriages and divorces: 2016. *Current Population Reports,* P70-167. U.S. Census Bureau.

Mazul, M.C., Salm Ward, T.C., & Ngui, E.M. (2017). Anatomy of good prenatal care: Perspectives of low income African-American women on barriers and facilitators to prenatal care. *Journal of Racial Ethnic Health Disparities, 4,* 79–86.

McAllister, S., & others (2017). Healthcare professionals' attitudes, knowledge, and self-efficacy levels regarding the use of self-hypnosis in childbirth: A prospective questionnaire survey. *Midwifery, 47,* 8–14.

McArthur, B.A., Volkova, V., Tomopoulos, S., & Madigan, S. (2022). Global prevalence of meeting screen time guidelines among children 5 years and younger: A systematic review and meta-analysis. *JAMA Pediatrics, 176,* 373–383.

McBean, A.L., Kinsey, S.G., & Montgomery-Downs, H.E. (2016). Effects of a single night of postpartum sleep on childless women's daytime functioning. *Physiology and Behavior, 156,* 137-147.

McBride, C. (2016). *Children's literacy development: A cross-cultural perspective on learning to read and write* (2nd ed.). Routledge.

McBride, C., Pan, D.J., & Mohseni, F. (2021). Reading and writing words: A cross-linguistic perspective. *Scientific Studies of Reading, 26*(2), 125-138.

McCaffrey, T., Cheung, P.S., Barry, M., Punch, P., & Dore, L. (2020). The role and outcomes of music listening for women in childbirth: An integrative review. *Midwifery, 83,* 102627.

McCall, R.B., & others (2019). Early caregiver–child interaction and children's development: Lessons from the St. Petersburg-USA Orphanage Intervention Research Project. *Clinical Child and Family Psychology Review, 22,* 208-224.

McCarthy, K.N., & McCarthy, D.M. (2019). Substance-impaired driving in adolescence. In R. Zucker & S. Brown (Eds.), *The Oxford handbook of adolescent substance abuse* (pp. 447-462). Oxford University Press.

McCartney, K. (2003, July 16). Interview with Kathleen McCartney in A. Bucuvalas, "Child care and behavior." *HGSE News,* pp. 1-4. Harvard Graduate School of Education.

McCauley, H., & others (2019). "We are just obsessed with risk" Healthcare providers' views on choice of place of birth for women. *British Journal of Midwifery, 27*(10), 633-641.

McClelland, M.M., Acock, A.C., Piccinin, A., Rhea, S.A., & Stallings, M.C. (2013). Relations between preschool attention span-persistence and age 25 educational outcomes. *Early Childhood Research Quarterly, 28,* 314-324.

McClelland, M.M., Cameron, C.E., & Alonso, J. (2019). The development of self-regulation in young children. In D. Whitebread (Ed.), *Handbook of developmental psychology and early childhood education.* Sage.

McClelland, M.M., & others (2014). Predictors of early growth in academic achievement: The head-toes-knees-shoulders task. *Frontiers in Psychology, 5,* 599.

McClelland, M.M., & others (2017). Self-regulation. In N. Halfon (Ed.), *Handbook of life course health development.* Springer.

McCloskey, K., & others (2017). The association between higher maternal pre-pregnancy body mass index and increased birth weight, adiposity, and inflammation in the newborn. *Pediatric Obesity, 13*(1), 46-53.

McClure, L.F., Niles, J.K., & Kaufman, H.W. (2016). Blood lead levels in young children: US, 2009-2015. *Journal of Pediatrics, 175,* 173-181.

McCormick, B.J., & others (2019). Early life child micronutrient status, maternal reasoning, and a nurturing household environment have persistent influences on child cognitive development at age 5 years: Results from MAL-ED. *Journal of Nutrition, 149*(8), 1460-1469.

McCormick, M.P., & others (2020). Time well spent: Home learning activities and gains in children's academic skills in the prekindergarten year. *Developmental Psychology, 56*(4), 710-726.

McCoy, D.C., & Raver, C.C. (2011). Caregiver emotional expressiveness, child emotion regulation, and child behavior problems among Head Start families. *Social Development, 20,* 741-761.

McCoy, M.B., Geppert, J., Dech, L., & Richardson, M. (2018). Associations between peer counseling and breastfeeding initiation and duration: An analysis of Minnesota participants in the Special Supplemental Nutrition Program for Women, Infants, and Children (WIC). *Maternal and Child Health Journal, 22*(1), 71-81.

McCrae, R.R., De Bolle, M., Löckenhoff, C.E., & Terracciano, A. (2021). Lifespan trait development: Toward an adequate theory of personality. In J.F. Rauthmann (Ed.), *The Handbook of Personality Dynamics and Processes* (pp. 621-641). Academic Press.

McDermott, J.M., & Fox, N.A. (2018). Emerging executive functions in early childhood. In C. Zeanah (Ed.), *Handbook of infant mental health* (4th ed., pp. 120-133). Guilford Press.

McDonald, E.M., & others (2018). Primary care opportunities to prevent unintentional home injuries: A focus on children and older adults. *American Journal of Lifestyle Medicine, 12,* 96-106.

McDonald, K.L., & Asher, S.R. (2018). Peer acceptance, peer rejection, and popularity: Social-cognitive and behavioral perspectives. In W.W. Bukowski, B. Laursen, & K.H. Rubin (Eds.), Handbook of peer interactions, relationships, and groups (pp. 429-446). Guilford Press.

McElvaney, R., Greene, S., & Hogan, D. (2014). To tell or not to tell? Factors influencing young people's informal disclosures of child sexual abuse. *Journal of Interpersonal Violence, 29,* 928-947.

McEwen, C.A. (2021). Children in changing worlds: Sociocultural and temporal perspectives. *Contemporary Sociology, 50*(1), 80-82.

McFarland, J., Cui, J., Holmes, J., & Wang, X. (2020). *Trends in high school dropout and completion rates in the United States: 2019.* National Center on Education Statistics.

McGee, T.R., & Moffitt, T. (2019). The developmental taxonomy. In D. Farrington & others (Eds.), *Oxford handbook of developmental and life-course criminology* (pp. 149-158). Oxford University Press.

McGillion, M., & others (2017). A randomized controlled trial to test the effect of promoting caregiver contingent talk on language development in infants from diverse socioeconomic status backgrounds. *Journal of Child Psychology and Psychiatry, 58*(10), 1122-1131.

McGilvray, J. (Ed.) (2017). *The Cambridge companion to Chomsky.* Cambridge University Press.

McGough, M., Amin, K., Panchal, N., & Cox, C. (2022). Child and teen firearm mortality in the U.S. and peer countries. Available https://www.kff.org /global-health-policy/issue-brief/child-and-teen-firearm-mortality-in-the-u-s-and-peer-countries/

McHale, J., & Sirotkin, Y. (2019). Coparenting in diverse family systems. In M. Bornstein (Ed.), *Handbook of parenting* (3rd ed., pp. 137-166). Routledge.

McIntyre, H.D., & others (2020). Obesity in pregnancy: Epidemiology, mechanisms, nutritional and metabolic management. *Gestational Diabetes, 28,* 21-34.

McKinnon, C.J., & others (2019). Restricted and repetitive behavior and brain functional connectivity in infants at risk for developing autism spectrum disorder. *Biological Psychiatry, 4,* 50-61.

McLaughlin, K.A., Sheridan, M.A., & Nelson, C.A. (2017). Neglect as a violation of species-expectant experience: Neurodevelopmental consequences. *Biological Psychiatry, 82*(7), 462-471.

McLean, K.C., & others (2020). The empirical structure of narrative identity: The initial Big Three. *Journal of Personality and Social Psychology, 119,* 920-944.

McLoyd, V.C. (2019). How children and adolescents think about, make sense of, and respond to economic inequality: Why does it matter? *Developmental Psychology, 55*(3), 592-600.

McLoyd, V.C., Kaplan, R., Purtell, K.M., & Huston, A.C. (2011). Assessing the effects of a work-based antipoverty program for parents on youths' future orientation and employment experiences. *Child Development, 82,* 113-132.

McMahon, C.A. (2023). *Becoming a parent: Contemporary contexts and challenges in the transition to parenthood.* Cambridge University Press.

McMurray, B., Horst, J.S., & Samuelson, L.K. (2012). Word learning emerges from the interaction of online referent selection and slow associative learning. *Psychological Review, 119,* 831-877.

McMurray, B., & others (2022). Decoding the temporal dynamics of spoken word and nonword processing from EEG. *NeuroImage, 260,* 119457.

McWhorter, R.R., & Ellinger, A.D. (2018). Qualitative case study research: An initial primer. In V.C.X. Wang & T.G. Reio Jr. (Eds.), *Handbook of research on innovative techniques, trends, and analysis for optimized research methods* (pp. 185-201). IGI Global.

Meehan, C.L., Hagen, E.H., & Hewlett, B.S. (2017). Persistence of infant care patterns among Aka foragers. In V. Reyes-García & A. Pyhälä (Eds.), *Hunter-gatherers in a changing world.* Springer.

Meek, J.Y., & Noble, L. (2022). Policy statement: Breastfeeding and the use of human milk. *Pediatrics, 150*(1), e2022057988.

Meeus, W. (2023). Fifty years of longitudinal research into identity development in adolescence and early adulthood: An overview. In L.J. Crockett, G. Carlo, & J.E. Schulenberg (Eds.), *APA handbook of adolescent and young adult development* (pp. 139-157). American Psychological Association.

Megli, C.J., & Coyne, C.B. (2022). Infections at the maternal–fetal interface: An overview of pathogenesis and defence. *Nature Reviews Microbiology, 20,* 67-82.

Mehta C.M., Arnett J.J., Palmer C.G., & Nelson L.J. (2020). Established adulthood: A new conception of ages 30 to 45. *American Psychologist, 75,* 431-444.

Meins, E., Bureau, J.F., & Fernyhough, C. (2018). Mother-child attachment from infancy to the preschool years: Predicting security and stability. *Child Development, 89*(3), 1022-1038.

Meisel, V., Servera, M., Garcia-Banda, G., Cardo, E., & Moreno, I. (2013). Neurofeedback and standard pharmacological intervention in ADHD: A randomized controlled trial with six-month follow-up. *Biological Psychology, 94,* 12–21.

Melchor, I., & others (2019). Effect of maternal obesity on pregnancy outcomes in women delivering singleton babies: A historical cohort study. *Journal of Perinatal Medicine, 47*(6), 625–630.

Melinder, A., & others (2016). The emotional child witness effect survives presentation mode. *Behavioral Sciences and the Law, 34,* 113–125.

Meltzoff, A.N. (1988). Infant imitation and memory: Nine-month-old infants in immediate and deferred tests. *Child Development, 59,* 217–225.

Meltzoff, A.N., & Marshall, P.J. (2018). Human infant imitation as a social survival circuit. *Current Opinion in Behavioral Sciences, 24,* 130–136.

Meltzoff, A.N., & Marshall, P.J. (2020). Importance of body representations in social-cognitive development: New insights from infant brain science. *Progress in Brain Research, 254,* 25–48.

Mencarini, L., Pasqua, S., & Romiti, A. (2019). Single-mother families and the gender gap in children's time investment and non-cognitive skills. *Review of Economics of the Household, 17*(1), 149–176.

Mendle, J., Ryan, R.M., & McKone, K.M.P. (2019). Early menarche and internalizing and externalizing in adulthood: Explaining the persistence of effects. *Journal of Adolescent Health, 65,* 599–606.

Menescardi, C., & others (2023). The mediational role of motivation in the model of motor development in childhood: A longitudinal study. *Psychology of Sport and Exercise, 66,* 102398.

Menesini, E., & Salmivalli, C. (2017). Bullying in schools: The state of the knowledge and effective interventions. *Psychology, Health, and Medicine, 22*(Suppl. 1), S240–S253.

Menon, R., & others. (2011). Cigarette smoking induces oxidative stress and apoptosis in normal fetal membranes. *Placenta, 32*(4), 317–322.

Meredith, N.V. (1978). Research between 1960 and 1970 on the standing height of young children in different parts of the world. In H.W. Reece & L.P. Lipsitt (Eds.), *Advances in child development and behavior* (Vol. 12). Academic Press.

Merrin, G.J., & others (2019). Developmental changes in deviant and violent behaviors from early to late adolescence: Associations with parental monitoring and peer deviance. *Psychology of Violence, 9*(2), 196–208.

Merz, E.C., & others (2019). Socioeconomic disparities in chronic physiologic stress are associated with brain structure in children. *Biological Psychiatry, 86*(12), 921–929.

Mesman, J. (2018). Video observations of sensitivity in context: Integrating insights from seven cultural communities. *Attachment & Human Development,* 1–9.

Metz, E.C., & Youniss, J. (2005). Longitudinal gains in civic development through school-based required service. *Political Psychology, 26,* 413–437.

Meyer, M., & Hunnius, S. (2021). Neural processing of self-produced and externally generated events in 3-month-old infants. *Journal of Experimental Child Psychology, 204,* 105039.

Meza-Cervera, T., Tucker, A., Liu, R., & Bell, M.A. (2022). Child emotion inhibition mediates the effect of parent's adaptive cognitive emotion regulation on child frontal EEG asymmetry during reappraisal. *Developmental Psychobiology, 64*(8), e22339.

Michalczyk, M., Torbé, D., & Torbé, A. (2018). Comparison of the effect of patient-controlled epidural anesthesia (PCEA) and parenteral use of opioid analgesics on the postpartum condition of the newborn. *Journal of Education, Health and Sport, 8*(9), 277–284.

Michas, F. (2023). Percentage of births to unmarried women in the United States, 1980–2021. https://www.statista.com/statistics/276025/us-percentage-of-births-to-unmarried-women/

Middleton, R.J., & others (2017). Epigenetic silencing of the human 18 kDA translocator protein in a T cell leukemia cell line. *DNA and Cell Biology, 38,* 103–108.

Mikulincer, M., & Shaver, P.R. (2021). Attachment theory. In P.J. Corr & G. Matthews (Eds.), *Cambridge handbook of personality psychology.* Cambridge University Press.

Miles, G., & Siega-Riz, A.M. (2017). Trends in food and beverage consumption among infants and toddlers: 2005–2012. *Pediatrics, 139,* e20163290.

Miles-Novelo, A., & others (2022). Further tests of the media violence–aggression link: Replication and extension of the 7 Nations Project with multiple Latinx samples. *Psychology of Popular Media, 11,* 435–442.

Mileva-Seitz, V.R., Bakermans-Kranenburg, M.J., Battaini, C., & Luijk, M.P. (2017). Parent-child bed-sharing: The good, the bad, and the burden of evidence. *Sleep Medicine Reviews, 32,* 4–27.

Miller, A.L., & others (2017). Child cortisol moderates the association between family routines and emotion regulation in low-income children. *Development and Psychopathology, 59,* 99–110.

Miller, D.I., Nolla, K.M., Eagly, A.H., & Uttal, D.H. (2018). The development of children's gender-science stereotypes: A meta-analysis of 5 decades of U.S. draw-a-scientist studies. *Child Development, 89,* 1943–1955.

Miller, E.B., Farkas, G., & Duncan, G.J. (2016). Does Head Start differentially benefit children with risks targeted by the program's service model? *Early Childhood Research Quarterly, 34,* 1–12.

Miller, J.G., & Bland, C.G. (2014). A cultural perspective on moral development. In M. Killen & J.G. Smetana (Eds.), *Handbook of moral development* (2nd ed.). Psychology Press.

Miller, P.H. (2016). *Theories of developmental psychology* (6th ed.). Worth Publishers.

Miller, P.J., & Cho, G.E. (2018). *Self-esteem in time and place: How American families imagine, enact, and personalize a cultural ideal.* Oxford University Press.

Miller, S.E., & Marcovitch, S. (2015). Examining executive function in the second year of life: Coherence, stability, and relations to joint attention and language. *Developmental Psychology, 51,* 101–114.

Mills, A.L., Aquino, G.A., Hoegler, S., & Cummings, E.M. (2021). Interparental conflict, emotional insecurity, and parent–adolescent communication. *Journal of Family Issues, 42,* 2377–2396.

Mills, C.M., & Elashi, F.B. (2014). Children's skepticism: Developmental and individual differences in children's ability to detect and explain distorted claims. *Journal of Experimental Child Psychology, 124C,* 1–17.

Miller-Slough, R.L., & others (2018). Maternal and paternal reactions to child sadness predict children's psychosocial outcomes: A family-centered approach. *Social Development, 27,* 495–509.

Milne, E., & others (2012). Parental prenatal smoking and risk of childhood acute lymphoblastic leukemia. *American Journal of Epidemiology, 175,* 43–53.

Minatoya, M., Hanaoka, T., & Kishi, R. (2020). Environmental exposures and adverse pregnancy-related outcomes. In R. Kishi & P. Grandjean (Eds.), *Health impacts of developmental exposure to environmental chemicals: Current topics in environmental health and preventive medicine.* Springer.

Minic, P.B., & Sovtic, A.D. (2017). Exercise intolerance and exercise-induced broncho-constriction in children. *Frontiers of Bioscience, 9,* 21–32.

Mir, Y.R., & Kuchay, R.A.H. (2019). Advances in identification of genes involved in autosomal recessive intellectual disability: A brief review. *Journal of Medical Genetics, 56,* 567–573.

Miranda, V.I.A., & others (2019). The use of folic acid, iron salts and other vitamins by pregnant women in the 2015 Pelotas birth cohort: Is there socioeconomic inequality? *BMC Public Health, 19*(1), 889.

Miranda, V.P., & others (2021). Body image disorders associated with lifestyle and body composition of female adolescents. *Public Health Nutrition, 24,* 95–105.

Mireault, A., Mann, L., Blotnicky, K., & Rossiter, M.D. (2023). Evaluation of snacks consumed by young children in child care and home settings. *International Journal of Child Care and Education Policy, 17,* 1.

Mireku, M.O., & others (2019). Processed data on the night-time use of screen-based media devices and adolescents' sleep quality and health-related quality of life. *Data in Brief, 23,* 103761.

Misch, A., & Dunham, Y. (2021). (Peer) group influence on children's prosocial and antisocial behavior. *Journal of Experimental Child Psychology, 201,* 104994.

Mischel, W. (2014). *The marshmallow test: Understanding self-control and how to master it.* Random House.

Mischel, W., Cantor, N., & Feldman, S. (1996). Principles of self-regulation: The nature of will power and self-control. In E.T. Higgins & A.W. Kruglanski (Eds.), *Social psychology.* Guilford Press.

Mischel, W., & Moore, B.S. (1980). The role of ideation in voluntary delay for symbolically presented rewards. *Cognitive Therapy and Research, 4,* 211–221.

Mischel, W., & others (2011). "Willpower" over the life span: Decomposing self-regulation. *Social Cognitive and Affective Neuroscience, 6,* 252–256.

Mitanchez, D., & Chavatte-Palmer, P. (2018). Review shows that maternal obesity induces serious adverse neonatal effects and is associated with childhood obesity in their offspring. *Acta Paediatrica, 107*(7), 1156–1165.

Mitchell, C., Harwin, A., Vara-Orta, F., & Sheehan, F. (2017). Single-gender public schools in 5 charts. *Education Week, 37,* 10.

Mitchell, D.M. (2017). Growth in patients with type 1 diabetes. *Current Opinion in Endocrinology, Diabetes, and Obesity, 24,* 67–72.

Mitchinson, C., & others (2019). Anemia in disadvantaged children aged under five years: Quality of care in primary practice. *BMC Pediatrics, 19*(1), 178.

Mitsven, S., & others (2021). Infant emotional development. In J.J. Lockman & C. Tamis-LeMonda (Eds.), *Cambridge handbook of infant development.* Cambridge University Press.

Mize, K.D., Pineda, M., Blau, A.K., Marsh, K., & Jones, N.A. (2014). Infant physiological and behavioral responses to a jealousy provoking condition. *Infancy, 19,* 1–11.

Modabbernia, A., & others (2021). Multivariate patterns of brain-behavior-environment associations in the Adolescent Brain and Cognitive Development Study. *Biological Psychiatry, 89,* 510–520.

Moffitt, T.E., & others (2011). A gradient of childhood self-control predicts health, wealth, and public safety. *Proceedings of the National Academy of Sciences U.S.A, 108,* 2693–2698.

Moilanen, K.L., Padilla-Walker, L.M., & Blaacker, D.R. (2018). Dimensions of short-term and long-term self-regulation in adolescence: Associations with maternal and paternal parenting and parent-child relationship quality. *Journal of Youth and Adolescence, 47,* 1409–1426.

Mokhtarnia, I., & others (2023, in press). The Revised Parent-Adolescent Conflict Issues Checklist: Development, reliability, and validity. *Journal of Family Issues.*

Moline, H.R., & Smith, J.F. (2016). The continuing threat of syphilis in pregnancy. *Current Opinion in Obstetrics and Gynecology, 28,* 101–104.

Moller, A.B., & others (2017). Early antenatal care visit: A systematic analysis of regional and global levels and trends of coverage from 1990 to 2013. *The Lancet Global Health, 5*(10), e977–e983.

Monahan, K., Guyer, A., Sil, J., Fitzwater, T., & Steinberg, L. (2016). Integration of developmental neuroscience and contextual approaches to the study of adolescent psychopathology. In D. Cicchetti (Ed.), *Handbook of developmental psychology* (3rd ed.). Wiley.

Moninger, J. (2013). *How to talk with your child about losing weight.* Retrieved February 21, 2013, from www.parents.com/kids/teens/weight-loss/how-to-talk-to-your-child-about-losing-weight/

Monn, A.R., & others (2017). Executive function and parenting in the context of homelessness. *Journal of Family Psychology, 31,* 61–70.

Monroy, C., Shafto, C., Castellanos, I., Bergeson, T., & Houston, D. (2019). Visual habituation in deaf and hearing infants. *PlosOne, 14,* e0209265.

Montemayor, R. (1982). The relationship between parent-adolescent conflict and the amount of time adolescents spend with parents, peers, and alone. *Child Development, 53,* 1512–1519.

Montgomery, M.R., & others (2016). Urban migration of adolescent girls: Quantitative results from developing countries. In M.J. White (Ed.), *International handbook of migration and population distribution* (pp. 573–604). Springer.

Montroy, J.J., & others (2016). The development of self-regulation across early childhood. *Developmental Psychology, 52,* 1744–1762.

Moon, C. (2017). Prenatal experience with the maternal voice. In M. Filippa & others (Eds.), *Early vocal contact and preterm infant brain development* (pp. 25–37). Springer.

Moon, G. (2022, April 25). It's possible to improve state's gifted education. *Santa Fe New Mexican.* Retrieved May 3, 2022, from https://www.santafenewmexican.com/news/education/how-to-improve-gifted-education-in-new-mexico/article_7213f9f0-c3ec-11ec-83dc-c3f74c2bcae2.html

Moon, R.Y., Carlin, R.F., Hand, I., & Task Force on Sudden Infant Death Syndrome (2022). Sleep-related infant deaths: Updated 2022 recommendations for reducing infant deaths in the sleep environment. *Pediatrics, 150*(1), e2022057990.

Moon, R.Y., & others (2017). Health messaging and African-American infant sleep location: A randomized controlled trial. *Journal of Community Health, 42,* 1–9.

Moore, D.S. (2017). Behavioral epigenetics. *Wiley Interdisciplinary Reviews: Systems Biology and Medicine, 9*(1). doi:10.1002/wsbm.1333

Moore, D.S. (2018). Gene × environment interaction: What exactly are we talking about? *Research in Developmental Disabilities, 82,* 3–9.

Moore, D.S., & Flom, R. (2020). Epigenetics and behavioral development. *Infant Behavior & Development, 61,* 101477.

Moore, S.M., & others (2019). Two family interventions to reduce BMI in low-income urban youth: A randomized trial. *Pediatrics, 143*(6), e20182185.

Moore, T.J., Tank, K.M., & English, L. (2018). Engineering in the early grades: Harnessing children's natural ways of thinking. In L. English & T. Moore (Eds.), *Early mathematics learning and development.* Springer.

Mooya, H., Sichimba, F., & Bakermans-Kranenburg, M. (2016). Infant-mother and infant-sibling attachment in Zambia. *Attachment and Human Development, 18,* 618–635.

Moran, M.B., Villanti, A.C., Johnson, A., & Rath, J. (2019). Patterns of alcohol, tobacco, and substance use among young adult peer crowds. *American Journal of Preventive Medicine, 56,* e185–e193.

Moreno-García, I., Cano-Crespo, A., & Rivera, F. (2022). Results of neurofeedback in treatment of children with ADHD: A systematic review of randomized controlled trials. *Applied Psychophysiology and Biofeedback, 47*(3), 145–181.

Morgan, A.S., Mendonça, M., Thiele, N., & David, A.L. (2022). Management and outcomes of extreme preterm birth. *BMJ, 376,* e055924.

Morgan, H. (2019). Does high-quality preschool benefit children? What the research shows. *Education Science, 9,* 19.

Morgan, P.J., & others (2016). Practicalities and research considerations for conducting childhood obesity prevention interventions with families. *Children, 3*(4), 24.

Morgan, P.L., Farkas, G., Hillemeier, M.M., & Maczuga, S. (2017). Replicated evidence of racial and ethnic disparities in disability identification in U.S. schools. *Educational Researcher, 46,* 305–322

Moriguchi, Y., & Shinohara, I. (2019). Socioeconomic disparity in prefrontal development during early childhood. *Scientific Reports, 9*(1), 2585.

Morosan, L., & others (2017). Emotion recognition and perspective taking: A comparison between typical and incarcerated male adolescents. *PLoS One, 12*(1), e0170646.

Morra, S., & Panesi, S. (2017). From scribbling to drawing: The role of working memory. *Cognitive Development, 43,* 142–158.

Morris, P.A., & others (2018). New findings on impact variation from the Head Start Impact Study: Informing the scale-up of early childhood programs. *AERA Open, 4*(2), 2332858418769287.

Morrison, D.C. (Ed.) (2017). *Organizing early experience.* Routledge.

Morrison, G.S. (2018). *Early childhood education today* (14th ed.). Pearson.

Morrison, G.S., & others (2022). *Early childhood education today* (15th ed.). Pearson.

Morrison, K.E., Epperson, C.N., & Bale, T.L. (2020). Sex differences in the programming of stress resilience. In A. Chen (Ed.), *Stress resilience* (pp. 81–94). Academic Press.

Morrison, S.C., Fife, T., & Hertlein, K.M. (2017). Mechanisms behind prolonged effects of parental divorce: A phenomenological study. *Journal of Divorce and Remarriage, 58,* 44–63.

Morrongiello, B.A., & Cox, A. (2016). Motor development as a context for understanding parent safety practices. *Developmental Psychobiology, 58,* 909–917.

Morrow, L.M. (2020). *Literacy development in the early years* (9th ed.). Pearson.

Mortelmans, D. (2020). Economic consequences of divorce: A review. In M. Kreyenfeld & H. Trappe (Eds.), *Parental life courses after separation and divorce in Europe* (pp. 23–41). Springer.

Moss, K.R., & others (2021). New evidence for secondary axonal degeneration in demyelinating neuropathies. *Neuroscience Letters, 144,* 135595.

Motti-Stefanidi, F. (2023). Immigrant youth resilience in the context of challenging receiving societies. In L.J. Crockett, G. Carlo, & J.E. Schulenberg (Eds.), *APA handbook of adolescent and young adult development* (pp. 407–423). American Psychological Association.

Moukaled, S., De Anda-Duran, I., Potts, K., Fernandez Alonso, C., & Bazzano, L.A. (2023). Prevalence and patterns of cardiovascular multimorbidity in black and white adults at midlife: The Bogalusa Heart Study. *Circulation, 147*(Suppl. 1), A08–A08.

Moura da Costa, E., & Tuleski, S.C. (2017). Social constructivist interpretation of Vygotsky. In C. Ratner & D. Silva (Eds.), *Vygotsky and Marx.* Routledge.

Movahed Abtahi, M., & Kerns, K.A. (2017). Attachment and emotion regulation in middle childhood: Changes in affect and vagal tone during a social stress task. *Attachment and Human Development, 19,* 221–242.

Mowlem, F., Agnew-Blais, J., Taylor, E., & Asherson, P. (2019). Do different factors influence whether girls versus boys meet ADHD diagnostic criteria? Sex differences among children with high ADHD symptoms. *Psychiatry Research, 272,* 765–773.

Mueller, C.G., Webb, P.J., & Morgan, S. (2020). The effects of childbirth education on maternity outcomes and maternal satisfaction. *The Journal of Perinatal Education, 29*(1), 16–22.

Muhlenbeck, C., & others (2020). Attentional bias to facial expressions of different emotions—a cross-cultural comparison of Akoe Hallom and German children and adolescents. *Frontiers in Psychology, 11,* 795.

Muijs, D. (2017). Can schools reduce bullying? The relationship between school characteristics and the prevalence of bullying behaviors. *British Journal of Educational Psychology, 87*(2), 255–272.

Mukherjee, S.B. (2017). Autism spectrum disorders—Diagnosis and management. *Indian Journal of Pediatrics, 84*(4), 307–314.

Muktamath, V.R., Hegde, P., & Chand, S. (2022). Types of specific learning disability. In S. Misciagna (Ed.), *Learning Disabilities—Neurobiology, Assessment, Clinical Features and Treatments.* IntechOpen. doi:10.5772/intechopen.100809

Muller, U., Miller, M., Hutchison, S., & Ten Eycke, K. (2017). Transition to school: Executive function, emergent academic skills, and early school achievement. In M.J. Hoskyns & others (Eds.), *Executive functions in children's everyday lives.* Oxford University Press.

Mulvey, K.L., Hitti, A., Smetana, J.G., & Killen, M. (2016). Morality, context, and development. In L. Balter & C.S. Tamis-LeMonda (Eds.), *Child psychology: A contemporary handbook* (3rd ed.). Psychology Press.

Mulvey, K.L., & Killen, M. (2015). Challenging gender stereotypes: Resistance and exclusion. *Child Development, 86,* 681–694.

Mulvihill, A., Matthews, N., & Carroll, A. (2023). Task difficulty and private speech in typically developing and at-risk preschool children. *Journal of Child Language, 50*(2), 464–491.

Mundy, P. (2018). A review of joint attention and social-cognitive brain systems in typical development and autism spectrum disorder. *European Journal of Neuroscience, 47,* 497–514.

Mundy, P., & others (2007). Individual differences and the development of joint attention in infancy. *Child Development, 78,* 938–954.

Murakami, M., Suzuki, M., & Yamaguchi, T. (2017). Presenting information on regulation values improves the public's sense of safety: Perceived mercury risk in fish and shellfish and its effects on consumption intention. *PloS One, 12*(12), e0188758.

Murnen, S.K., & Smolak, L. (2019). The Cash effect: Shaping the research conversation on body image and eating disorders. *Body Image, 31,* 288–293.

Murphy, S.L., Kochanek, K.D., Xu, J., & Arias, E. (2021). *Mortality in the United States, 2020* (NCHS Data Brief, No. 427). National Center for Health Statistics. https://www.cdc.gov/nchs/products/databriefs/db427.htm.

Murray, A.L., & others (2017). Investigating diagnostic bias in autism spectrum conditions: An item response theory analysis of sex bias in the AQ-10. *Autism Research, 10,* 790–800.

Murray, H.B., & others (2017). Will I get fat? 22-year weight trajectories of individuals with eating disorders. *International Journal of Eating Disorders, 50*(7), 739–747.

Murray, J., & Arnett, J. (Eds.) (2019). *Emerging adulthood and higher education: A new student development paradigm.* Routledge.

Murray, J.J., Hall, W.C., & Snoddon, K. (2019). Education and health of children with hearing loss: The necessity of signed languages. *Bulletin of the World Health Organization, 97,* 711–716.

Murray, P.G., Dattani, M.T., & Clayton, P.E. (2016). Controversies in the diagnosis and management of growth hormone deficiency in childhood and adolescence. *Archives of Disease in Childhood, 101,* 96–100.

Murray, S.B., Griffiths, S., & Lavender, J.M. (2019). Introduction to a special issue on eating disorders and related symptomatology in male populations. *International Journal of Eating Disorders, 52,* 1339–1342.

Murry, V.M., & Lippold, M.A. (2018). Parenting practices in diverse family structures: Examination of adolescents' development and adjustment. *Journal of Research on Adolescence, 28,* 650–664.

Muscatelli, F., & Bouret, S.G. (2018). Wired for eating: How is an active feeding circuitry established in the postnatal brain? *Current Opinion in Neurobiology, 52,* 165–171.

Mustafa, G., & Nazir, B. (2018). Trust in transformational leadership: Do followers' perceptions of leader femininity, masculinity, and androgyny matter? *Journal of Values-Based Leadership, 11*(2), 13.

Muthuri, S.K., & others (2016). Relationships between parental education and overweight with childhood overweight and physical activity in 9–11-year-old children: Results from a 12-country study. *PLoS One, 11*(8), e0147746.

Mutti, D.O., & others (2018). Ocular component development during infancy and early childhood. *Optometry and Vision Science, 95*(11), 976–985.

Mydam, J., & others (2019). Low birth weight among infants born to black Latina women in the United States. *Maternal and Child Health Journal, 23*(4), 538–546.

Myers, D.G. (2010). *Psychology* (9th ed.). Worth.

Myle, A.K., & Al-Khattabi, G.H. (2021). Hemolytic disease of the newborn: A review of current trends and prospects. *Pediatric Health, Medicine and Therapeutics, 12,* 491–498.

N

Nabbijohn, A.N., & others (2020). Children's bias in appraisals of gender-variant peers. *Journal of Experimental Child Psychology, 196,* 104865.

Nadasdi, T. (2021). Sociolinguistics: Language in society. In J. Bruhn de Garavito & J.W. Schwieter (Eds.), *Introducing linguistics.* Cambridge University Press.

Nader, E.S., & Robinson, A.D. (2023). Reconceptualizing social bonds for emerging adults. *Criminal Justice and Behavior, 50,* 708–728.

Nagle, C., & others (2019). Informing the development midwifery standards for practice: A literature review for policy development. *Midwifery, 76,* 8–20.

Nagy, E., Thompson, P., Mayor, L., & Doughty, H. (2021). Do foetuses communicate? Foetal responses to interactive versus non-interactive maternal voice and touch: An exploratory analysis. *Infant Behavior and Development, 63,* 101562.

Naicker, K., Galambos, N.L., Zeng, Y., Senthilselvan, A., & Colman, I. (2013). Social, demographic, and health outcomes in the 10 years following adolescent depression. *Journal of Adolescent Health, 52,* 533–538.

Nair, S., & others (2018). Local resting state functional connectivity in autism: Site and cohort variability and the effect of eye status. *Brain Imaging and Behavior, 12*(1), 168–179.

Najjar, R., & Brooker, R.J. (2017). Delta-beta coupling is associated with paternal caregiving behaviors during preschool. *International Journal of Psychophysiology, 112,* 31–39.

Nakamichi, N., Nakamichi, K., & Nakazawa, J. (2022). Examining the indirect effects of kindergarteners' executive functions on their academic achievement in the middle grades of elementary school. *Early Child Development and Care, 192*(10), 1547–1560.

Nakamoto, J., & Schwartz, D. (2010). Is peer victimization associated with academic achievement? A meta-analytic review. *Social Development, 19,* 221–242.

Nakamura, A., & others (2019). Physical activity during pregnancy and postpartum depression: Systematic review and meta-analysis. *Journal of Affective Disorders, 246,* 29–41.

Nancarrow, A.F., Gilpin, A.T., Thibodeau, R.B., & Farrell, C.B. (2018). Knowing what others know: Linking deception detection, emotion knowledge, and Theory of Mind in preschool. *Infant and Child Development, 27*(5), e2097.

Narayan, A.J., & Masten, A.S. (2019). Resilience in the context of violence and trauma: Promotive and protective processes of positive caregiving. In J. Osofsky & B.M. Groves (Eds.), *Violence and trauma in the lives of children*. Praeger.

Narváez, D. (2018). Ethogenesis: Evolution, early experience, and moral becoming. In J. Graham & K. Gray (Eds.), *The atlas of moral psychology*. Guilford Press.

Narváez, D. (2019). Moral development and moral values: Evolutionary and neurobiological influences. In D.P. McAdams, R.L. Shiner, & J.L. Tackett (Eds.), *Handbook of personality development* (pp. 345–363). Guilford Press.

Narvaez, D. (2022). The moral education needed today: Decolonizing childhood and reconnecting children. In R.S. Webster, T. Airaksinen, P. Batra, & M. Kozhevnikova (Eds.), *Humanizing education in the 3rd millennium*. Springer.

Narváez, D., & Gleason, T.R. (2013). Developmental optimism. In D. Narváez & others (2013). *Evolution, early experience, and human development*. Oxford University Press.

Nastasi, B.K., & Naser, S.C. (2021). UN Convention on the Rights of the Child and the sustainable development goals: Implications for schools and regulators. In N.S. Rubin & R.L. Flores (Eds.), *Cambridge handbook of psychology and human rights*. Cambridge University Press.

National Academies of Sciences, Engineering, and Medicine (2020). *Birth settings in America: Outcomes, quality, access, and choice*. Available https://nap.nationalacademies.org/resource/25636/Birth%20Settings.pdf

National Association for Gifted Children (2023). *Knowledge center*. Retrieved April 18, 2023, from https://nagc.org/page/knowledge-center

National Association of Anorexia Nervosa and Associated Disorders (2023). *Eating disorder statistics*. https://anad.org/eating-disorders-statistics/

National Autism Association (2022). *Autism fact sheet*. https://nationalautismassociation.org/resources/autism-fact-sheet/

National Cancer Institute (2018). *Childhood cancers*. https://www.cancer.gov/types/childhood-cancers

National Cancer Institute (2023). *Childhood cancers*. Retrieved April 8, 2023, from https://www.cancer.gov/types/childhood-cancers

National Center for Education Statistics (2019). *The condition of education 2019: Status drop-out rates* (NCES 2019-144). U.S. Department of Education.

National Center for Education Statistics (2020b). *The condition of education 2019*. U.S. Department of Education.

National Center for Education Statistics (2021). *Early Childhood Program Participation: 2019* (NCES 2020-075REV), Table 1. URL: https://nces.ed.gov/pubsearch/pubsinfo.asp?pubid=2020075REV

National Center for Health Statistics (2022). *Growth charts*. https://www.cdc.gov/growthcharts/index.htm

National Center for Health Statistics (2023a). *Adolescent health*. Available https://www.cdc.gov/nchs/fastats/adolescent-health.htm

National Center for Education Statistics (2023b). *Dropout rates*. Available https://nces.ed.gov/fastfacts/display.asp?id=16

National Center for Montessori in the Public Sector (2022). *Research and resources: About Montessori*. https://www.public-montessori.org/montessori/

National Center on Shaken Baby Syndrome (2023). *Facts and info*. https://www.dontshake.org/learn-more/itemlist/category/13-facts-info

National Head Start Association (2016). *The Head Start Impact Study in 2016*. https://www.nhsa.org/files/resources/head_start_impact_study_2016_0.pdf

National Institute of Child Health and Human Development (2022). *Sudden infant death syndrome*. https://www.nichd.nih.gov/health/topics/sids

National Institute of Mental Health (2017). *Autism spectrum disorder*. Retrieved March 30, 2017, from www.nimh.nih.gov/health/topics/autism-spectrum-disorders-asd/index.shtml

National Institute on Drug Abuse (2022). *Most reported substance use among adolescents held steady in 2022*. Available https://nida.nih.gov/news-events/news-releases/2022/12/most-reported-substance-use-among-adolescents-held-steady-in-2022

National Sleep Foundation (2023). *How much sleep do babies and kids need?* Available https://www.sleepfoundation.org/children-and-sleep/how-much-sleep-do-kids-need#

Naughton, A.M., & others (2017). Ask me! Self-reported features of adolescents experiencing neglect or emotional maltreatment: A rapid systematic review. *Child: Care, Health, and Development, 43*(3), 348–360.

Nava, E., Focker, J., & Gori, M. (2020). Children can optimally integrate multisensory information after a short action-like mini game training. *Developmental Science, 23*(1), e12840.

Navaratnam, K., Alfirevic, Z., & Royal College of Obstetricians and Gynaecologists (2022). Amniocentesis and chorionic villus sampling: Green-top Guideline No. 8. *BJOG: An International Journal of Obstetrics & Gynaecology, 129*(1), e1–e15.

Navon, D., & Thomas, G. (2021). Screening before we know: Radical uncertainties in expanded prenatal genetics. *OBM Genetics, 5*(4), 12.

Ncube, C.N., & Mueller, B.A. (2017). Daughters of mothers who smoke: A population-based cohort study of maternal prenatal tobacco use and subsequent prenatal smoking in offspring. *Pediatric and Perinatal Epidemiology, 31*, 14–20.

Needham, A., Barrett, T., & Peterman, K. (2002). A pick-me-up for infants' exploratory skills: Early simulated experiences reaching for objects using "sticky mittens" enhances young infants' object exploration skills. *Infant Behavior and Development, 25*, 279–295.

Negriff, S. (2020). ACEs are not equal: Examining the relative impact of household dysfunction versus childhood maltreatment on mental health in adolescence. *Social Science & Medicine, 245*, 112696.

Neha, V. (2003). Home again: A native American SLP's experiences teaching in a Navaho reservation school. *ASHA Leader, 8*(3), 4. https://doi.org/10.1044/leader.FTR2.08032003.4

Neiderhiser, J.M., & Chen, T. (2023). Gene-environment interplay in adolescence and early adulthood. In L.J. Crockett, G. Carlo, & J.E. Schulenberg (Eds.), *APA handbook of adolescent and young adult development* (pp. 39–54). American Psychological Association.

Neitzel, C.L., Alexander, J.M., & Johnson, K.E. (2019). The emergence of children's interest orientations during early childhood: When predisposition meets opportunity. *Learning, Culture and Social Interaction, 23*, 100271.

Neiva-Silva, L., & others (2023). Street scars: Suicide ideation and suicide attempt among street-involved adolescents and youth in southern Brazil. *Child Abuse & Neglect, 139*, 105490.

Nelson, C.A. (2003). Neural development and lifelong plasticity. In R.M. Lerner, F. Jacobs, & D. Wertlieb (Eds.), *Handbook of applied developmental science* (Vol. 1). Sage.

Nelson, C.A., Thomas, K.M., & Haan, M. (2006). Neural bases of cognitive development. In W. Damon & R. Lerner (Eds.), *Handbook of child psychology* (6th ed.). Wiley.

Nelson, K., & Fivush, R. (2020). The development of autobiographical memory, autobiographical narratives, and autobiographical consciousness. *Psychological Reports, 123*(1), 71–96.

Nelson, S.E., Van Ryzin, M.J., & Dishion, T.J. (2015). Alcohol, marijuana, and tobacco use trajectories from ages 12 to 24 years: Demographic correlates and young adult substance use problems. *Development and Psychopathology, 27*, 253–277.

Nelson, S.K., Kushley, K., & Lyubomirsky, S. (2014). The pains and pleasures of parenting: When, why, and how is parenthood associated with more or less well-being? *Psychological Bulletin, 140*, 846–895.

Nelwan, M., Friso-van den Bos, I., Vissers, C., & Kroesbergen, E. (2022). The relation between working memory, number sense, and mathematics throughout primary education in children with and without mathematical difficulties. *Child Neuropsychology, 28*(2), 143–170.

Nemet, D. (2016). Childhood obesity, physical activity, and exercise. *Pediatric Exercise Science, 28*, 48–51.

Nencheva, M.L., Piazza, E.A., & Lew-Williams, C. (2021). The moment-to-moment pitch dynamics of child-directed speech shape toddlers' attention and learning. *Developmental Science, 24*(1), e12997.

Neppl, T.K., & others (2020). Positive parenting, effortful control, and developmental outcomes across early childhood. *Developmental Psychology, 56*(3), 444–457.

Nesi, J., & others (2017). Friends' alcohol-related social networking site activity predicts escalations in adolescent drinking: Mediation by peer norms. *Journal of Adolescent Health, 60*(6), 641–647.

Netsi, E. & others (2018). Association of persistent and severe postnatal depression with child outcomes. *JAMA Psychiatry, 75*(3), 247–253.

Neubauer, J., & others (2017). Post-mortem whole-exome analysis in a large sudden infant death syndrome cohort with a focus on cardiovascular and metabolic genetic diseases. *European Journal of Human Genetics, 25,* 404-409.

Neuenschwander, R., & Blair, C. (2017). Zooming in on children's behavior during delay of gratification: Disentangling impulsigenic and volitional processes underlying self-regulation. *Journal of Experimental Child Psychology, 154,* 146-163.

Neuman, W.L. (2020). *Social science research methods* (8th ed.). Pearson.

Newberry, K.M., Feller, D.P., & Bailey, H.R. (2021). Influences of domain knowledge on segmentation and memory. *Memory & Cognition, 49*(4), 660-674.

Newland, R.P., & Crnic, K.A. (2017). Developmental risk and goodness of fit in the mother-child relationship: Links to parenting stress and children's behaviour problems. *Infant and Child Development, 26*(2), e1980.

Newman, S., & Latifi, A. (2021). Vygotsky, education, and teacher education. *Journal of Education for Teaching, 47*(1), 4-17.

Newton, E.K., & Thompson, R.A. (2010). Parents' views of early social and emotional development: More and less meets the eye. *Zero to Three, 30*(4), 10-16.

Ng, S.K., & others (2018). The relationship between structural and functional brain changes and altered emotion and cognition in chronic low back pain. *The Clinical Journal of Pain, 34*(3), 237-261.

Ng, S.W., & others (2018). Federal nutrition program revisions impact low-income households' food purchases. *American Journal of Preventive Medicine, 54,* 403-412.

Nguyen, B.T., & Violette, C. (2022). Condom use at coitarche among men in non-steady relationships in the United States, 2006-2013. *Journal of Adolescent Health, 70,* 127-132.

Nguyen, T., & others (2020). The classroom relational environment and children's early development in preschool. *Social Development, 29*(4), 1071-1091.

Nguyen, V.T., & others (2017). Radiological studies of fetal alcohol spectrum disorders in humans and animal models: An updated comprehensive review. *Magnetic Resonance Imaging, 43,* 10-26.

Nguyen-Louie, T.T., & others (2018). Effects of sleep on substance use in adolescents: A longitudinal perspective. *Addiction Biology, 23*(2), 750-760.

NICHD Early Child Care Research Network (2001). Nonmaternal care and family factors in early development: An overview of the NICHD study of early child care. *Journal of Applied Developmental Psychology, 22,* 457-492.

NICHD Early Child Care Research Network (2002). Structure→process→outcome: Direct and indirect effects of child care quality on young children's development. *Psychological Science, 13,* 199-206.

NICHD Early Child Care Research Network (2004). Type of child care and children's development at 54 months. *Early Childhood Research Quarterly, 19,* 203-230.

NICHD Early Child Care Research Network (2005). Child care and development. Guilford Press.

NICHD Early Child Care Research Network (2006). Infant-mother attachment classification: Risk and protection in relation to changing maternal caregiving quality. *Developmental Psychology, 42,* 38-58.

NICHD Early Child Care Research Network (2009). Family-peer linkages: The mediational role of attentional processes. *Social Development, 18,* 875-895.

NICHD Early Child Care Research Network (2010). Testing a series of causal propositions relating time spent in child care to children's externalizing behavior. *Developmental Psychology, 46*(1), 1-17.

Nicholas, M., Veresov, N., & Clark, J.C. (2021). Guided reading—Working within a child's zone of proximal development. *Learning, Culture and Social Interaction, 30,* 100530.

Nicholson, L., Bohnert, A.M., & Crowley, S.J. (2023). A developmental perspective on sleep consistency: Preschool age through emerging adulthood. *Behavioral Sleep Medicine, 21,* 97-116.

Nickalls, S. (2012, March 9). Why college students shouldn't online date. *The Tower.* Arcadia University. Retrieved February 27, 2013, from http://tower.arcadia.edu/?p5754

Niec, L.N., Todd, M., Brodd, I., & Domoff, S.E. (2022). PCIT-Health: Preventing childhood obesity by strengthening the parent-child relationship. *Cognitive and Behavioral Practice, 29*(2), 335-347.

Nielsen, S.J., Siega-Riz, A.M., & Popkin, B.M. (2002). Trends in energy intake in U.S. between 1977 and 1996: Similar shifts seen across age groups. *Obesity Research, 10,* 370-378.

Nieto, M., & others (2022). Relation between nighttime sleep duration and executive functioning in a nonclinical sample of preschool children. *Scandinavian Journal of Psychology, 63*(3), 191-198.

Nilsen, E.S., & Basco, S.A. (2017). Cognitive and behavioral predictors of adolescents' communicative perspective-taking and social relationships. *Journal of Adolescence, 56,* 52-63.

Nisbett, N., & others (2022). Holding no-one back: The nutrition equity framework in theory and practice. *Global Food Security, 32,* 100605.

Nisbett, R.E., & others (2012). Intelligence: New findings and theoretical developments. *American Psychologist, 67*(2), 130-159.

Nishamura, Y., Kanakogi, Y., & Myowa-Yamakoshi, M. (2016). Infants' emotional states influence maternal behaviors during holding. *Infant Behavior and Development, 43,* 66-74.

Nivedita, K., & Shanthini, F.N. (2016). Knowledge, attitude and practices of pregnant women regarding anemia, iron rich diet and iron supplements and its impact on their hemoglobin levels. *International Journal of Reproduction, Contraception, Obstetrics and Gynecology, 5*(2), 425-431.

Niwa, E.Y., & others (2016). Growing up amid ethno-political conflict: Aggression and emotional desensitization promote hostility to ethnic out-groups. *Child Development, 87,* 1479-1492.

Noble, E., Ward, L., French, S., & Falb, K. (2019). State of the evidence: A systematic review of approaches to reduce gender-based violence and support the empowerment of adolescent girls in humanitarian settings. *Trauma, Violence, & Abuse, 20*(3), 428-434.

Nobre, G.C., Nobre, F.S.S., & Valentini, N.C. (2023, in press). Effectiveness of a mastery climate cognitive-motor skills school-based intervention in children living in poverty: Motor and academic performance, self-perceptions, and BMI. *Physical Education and Sport Pedagogy.*

Nocentini, A., & others (2019). Parents, family characteristics and bullying behavior: A systematic review. *Aggression and Violent Behavior, 45,* 41-50.

Noe-Bustamante, L., Mora, L., & Lopez, M.H. (2020). *About one-in-four U.S. Hispanics have heard of Latinx, but just 3% use it.* Pew Research Center Available https://www.pewresearch.org/hispanic/2020/08/11/about-one-in-four-u-s-hispanics-have-heard-of-latinx-but-just-3-use-it/

Nomaguchi, K., & Milkie, M.A. (2020). Parenthood and well-being: A decade in review. *Journal of Marriage and Family, 82*(1), 198-223.

Non, A.L., & others (2019). Stress across generations: A qualitative study of stress, coping, and caregiving among Mexican immigrant mothers. *Ethnicity & Health, 24*(4), 378-394.

Noor, S., & Milligan, E.D. (2018). Lifelong impacts of moderate prenatal alcohol exposure on neuroimmune function. *Frontiers in Immunology, 9,* 1107.

Nora, A., & others (2017). Children show right-lateralized effects of spoken word-form learning. *PLoS One, 12*(2), e0171034.

Norbom, L.B., & others (2021). New insights into the dynamic development of the cerebral cortex in childhood and adolescence: Integrating macro- and microstructural MRI findings. *Progress in Neurobiology, 204,* 102109.

Noret, N., Hunter, S.C., & Rasmussen, S. (2020). The role of perceived social support in the relationship between being bullied and mental health difficulties in adolescents. *School Mental Health, 12,* 156-168.

Norman, E. (2017). Metacognition and mindfulness: The role of fringe consciousness. *Mindfulness, 8,* 95-100.

Normand, S., & others (2022). Peer contagion dynamics in the friendships of children with ADHD. *Journal of Child Psychology and Psychiatry, 63*(12), 1477-1485.

Norona, A.N., & Baker, B.L. (2017). The effects of early positive parenting and developmental delay status on child emotion dysregulation. *Journal of Intellectual Disability Research, 61,* 130-143.

Nottelmann, E.D., & others (1987). Gonadal and adrenal hormone correlates of adjustment in early adolescence. In R.M. Lerner & T.T. Foch (Eds.),

Biological-psychological interactions in early adolescence. Erlbaum.

Novak, A.M., & Treagust, D.F. (2018). Adjusting claims as new evidence emerges: Do students incorporate new evidence into their scientific explanations? *Journal of Research in Science Teaching, 55,* 526–549.

Nurk, S., & others (2022). The complete sequence of a human genome. *Science, 376*(6588), 44–53.

Nutter, E., Meyer, S., Shaw-Battista, J., & Marowitz, A. (2014). Waterbirth: An integrative analysis of peer-reviewed literature. *Journal of Midwifery and Women's Health, 59,* 286–319.

Nyaradi, A., Li, J., Hickling, S., Foster, J., & Oddy, W.H. (2013). The role of nutrition in children's neurocognitive development, from pregnancy through childhood. *Frontiers of Human Neuroscience, 7,* 97.

O

Oakes, L. (2020). Infant categorization. In J. Lockman & C. Tamis-LeMonda (Eds.), *The Cambridge handbook of infant development: Brain, behavior, and cultural context* (pp. 381–409). Cambridge University Press.

Obeldobel, C.A., & Kerns, K.A. (2020). Attachment security is associated with the experience of specific positive emotions in middle childhood. *Attachment & Human Development, 22*(5), 555–567.

Obradovic, J., Yousafzai, A.K., Finch, J.E., & Rasheed, M.A. (2016). Maternal scaffolding and home stimulation: Key mediators of early intervention effects on children's cognitive development. *Developmental Psychology, 52,* 1409–1421.

O'Brien, K.T., & others (2018). Physical activity and sedentary time among preschoolers in centre-based childcare: A systematic review. *International Journal of Behavioral Nutrition and Physical Activity, 15*(1), 117.

Obsuth, I., & others (2020). Patterns of homotypic and heterotypic continuity between ADHD symptoms, externalizing and internalizing problems from age 7 to 15. *Journal of Abnormal Child Psychology, 48,* 223–236.

Oden, J., Ward, W.L., & Raisingani, M. (2019). Treatment of pediatric obesity: Past and present approaches to diet and exercise. In *Global perspectives on childhood obesity* (pp. 387–397). Academic Press.

O'Donnell, K.J., & Meaney, M.J. (2020). Epigenetics, development, and psychopathology. *Annual Review of Clinical Psychology, 16,* 327–350.

Odijk, L., & Gillis, S. (2021). Fine lexical tuning in infant-directed speech to typically developing children. *Journal of Child Language, 48*(3), 591–604.

OECD (2019). *PISA 2018: Insights and interpretations.* https://www.oecd.org/pisa/PISA%202018%20Insights%20and%20Interpretations%20FINAL%20PDF.pdf

OECD (2021). *OECD Family Database, CO2.2, Child Poverty.* https://www.oecd.org/els/CO_2_2_Child_Poverty.pdf. Accessed 13 January 2023.

OECD (2022a). *Marriage and divorce rates.* Available https://www.oecd.org/social/family/SF_3_1_Marriage_and_divorce_rates.pdf

OECD (2022b). *OECD family database, PF2.1. Parental leave systems.* URL: https://www.oecd.org/els/soc/PF2_1_Parental_leave_systems.pdf

O'Farrelly, C., Doyle, O., Victory, G., & Palamaro-Munsell, E. (2018). Shared reading in infancy and later development: Evidence from an early intervention. *Journal of Applied Developmental Psychology, 54,* 69–83.

Offer, D., Ostrov, E., Howard, K.I., & Atkinson, R. (1988). *The teenage world: Adolescents' self-image in ten countries.* Plenum.

Office of Population Affairs (2020). *Trends in teen pregnancy and childbearing.* Department of Health and Human Services. Retrieved November 27, 2019, from https://www.hhs.gov/ash/oah/adolescent-development/reproductive-health-and-teen-pregnancy/teen-pregnancy-and-childbearing/trends/index.html

Ogden, C.L., & others (2016). Trends in obesity prevalence among children and adolescents in the United States, 1988–1994 through 2013–2014. *JAMA, 315,* 2292–2299.

Ogren, M., Burling, J.M., & Johnson, S.P. (2018). Family expressiveness relates to happy emotion matching among 9-month-old infants. *Journal of Experimental Child Psychology, 174,* 29–40.

Ogren, M., & Johnson, S.P. (2021). Primary caregiver emotional expressiveness relates to toddler emotion understanding. *Infant Behavior and Development, 62,* 101508.

Oh, H., Falbo, T., & Lee, K. (2020). Culture moderates the relationship between family obligation values and the outcomes of Korean and European American college students. *Journal of Cross-Cultural Psychology, 51,* 511–525.

Oh, S., & others (2017). Prevalence and correlates of alcohol and tobacco use among pregnant women in the United States: Evidence from the NSDUH 205-2014. *Preventive Medicine, 97,* 93–99.

O'Hara, M., & others (2015). Children neglected: Where cumulative risk theory fails. *Child Abuse and Neglect, 45,* 1–8.

O'Hara, M.W., & McCabe, J.E. (2013). Postpartum depression: Current status and future directions. *Annual Review of Clinical Psychology, 9,* 379–407.

O'Kearney, R., & others (2017). Emotional abilities in children with oppositional defiance disorder (ODD): Impairments in perspective-taking and understanding mixed emotions are associated with high callous-unemotional traits. *Child Psychiatry and Human Development, 48,* 346–357.

Okusanya, B., & others (2022). Are prevention of mother-to-child HIV transmission service providers acquainted with national guideline recommendations? A cross-sectional study of primary health care centers in Lagos, Nigeria. *BMC Health Services Research, 22,* 769.

Olds, D.L., & others (2019). Prenatal and infancy nurse home visiting effects on mothers: 18-year follow-up of a randomized trial. *Pediatrics, 144*(6), e20183889.

Olney, D.K., Leroy, J., Bliznashka, L., & Ruel, M.T. (2018). PROCOMIDA, a food-assisted maternal and child health and nutrition program, reduces child stunting in Guatemala: A cluster-randomized controlled intervention trial. *The Journal of Nutrition, 148,* 1493–1505.

Olsavsky, A.L., & others (2020). New fathers' perceptions of dyadic adjustment: The roles of maternal gatekeeping and coparenting closeness. *Family Process, 59,* 571–585.

Olsen, H., & Kennedy, E. (2019). Safety of school playgrounds: Field analysis from a randomized sample. *The Journal of School Nursing, 36*(5), 369–375.

Olson, K.R., Durwood, L., DeMeules, M., & McLaughlin, K.A. (2016). Mental health of transgender children who are supported in their identities. *Pediatrics, 137,* e20153223.

Olson, K.R., & Enright, E.A. (2018). Do transgender children (gender) stereotype less than their peers and siblings? *Developmental Science, 21*(4), e12606.

Olson, K.R., & Gülgöz, S. (2018). Early findings from the TransYouth Project: Gender development in transgender children. *Child Development Perspectives, 12,* 93–97.

Olson, K.R., Key, A.C., & Eaton, N.R. (2015). Gender cognition in transgender children. *Psychological Science, 26,* 467–474.

Olson, K.R., & others (2022). Gender identity 5 years after social transition. *Pediatrics, 150*(2), e2021056082.

Olweus, D. (2013). School bullying: Development and some important challenges. *Annual Review of Clinical Psychology, 9,* 751–780.

Olweus, D., Limber, S.P., & Breivik, K. (2019). Addressing specific forms of bullying: A large-scale evaluation of the Olweus Bullying Prevention Program. *International Journal of Bullying Prevention, 1,* 70–84.

Ongley, S.F., & Malti, T. (2014). The role of moral emotions in the development of children's sharing behavior. *Developmental Psychology, 50,* 1148–1159.

Onishi, J. (2020) Epidemiology and incidence of preterm delivery. In H. Sameshima & others (Eds.), *Preterm labor and delivery: Comprehensive gynecology and obstetrics.* Springer.

Oostenbroek, J., & others (2016). Comprehensive longitudinal study challenges the existence of neonatal imitation in humans. *Current Biology, 26,* 1334–1338

O'Reilly, C.A., & Doerr, B. (2020). Conceit and deceit: Lying, cheating, and stealing among grandiose narcissists. *Personality and Individual Differences, 154,* 109627.

O'Reilly, H., Johnson, S., Ni, Y., Wolke, D., & Marlow, N. (2020). Neuropsychological outcomes at 19 years of age following extremely preterm birth. *Pediatrics, 145*(2), e20192087.

Oreland, L., & others (2017). Personality as an intermediate phenotype for genetic dissection of alcohol use disorder. *Journal of Neural Transmission, 125*(1), 107-130.

Organization for Economic Cooperation and Development (OECD) & World Health Organization (2018). Preterm birth and low birth weight. In *Health at a glance: Asia/Pacific 2018, Measuring progress towards universal health coverage.* OECD Publishing.

Ornaghi, V., & others (2017). Does training toddlers in emotion knowledge lead to changes in their prosocial and aggressive behavior toward peers at nursery? *Early Education and Development, 28,* 396-414.

Ornstein, P.A., & Coffman, J.L. (2020). Toward an understanding of the development of skilled remembering: The role of teachers' instructional language. *Current Directions in Psychological Science, 29*(5), 445-452.

Orth, U. (2018). The family environment in early childhood has a long-term effect on self-esteem: A longitudinal study from birth to age 27 years. *Journal of Personality and Social Psychology, 114*(4), 637-655.

Osberg, S., Kalstad, T.G., & Stray-Pedersen, A. (2021). Norwegian parents avoid placing infants in prone sleeping positions but frequently share beds in hazardous ways. *Acta Pediatrica, 110*(7), 2119-2125.

Osher, D., & others (2020). Drivers of human development: How relationships and context shape learning and development. *Applied Developmental Science, 24,* 6-36.

Osterhaus, C., Koerber, S., & Sodian, B. (2017). Scientific thinking in elementary school: Children's social cognition and their epistemological understanding promote experimentation skills. *Developmental Psychology, 53,* 450-462.

Osterman, M.J.K., Hamilton, B.E., Martin, J.A., Driscoll, A.K., & Valenzuela, C.P. (2022). *Births: Final data for 2020* (National Vital Statistics Reports Volume 70, Number 17). Centers for Disease Control and Prevention.

Otsuka, Y. (2017). Development of recognition memory for faces during infancy. In T. Tsukiura & S. Umeda (Eds.), *Memory in a social context* (pp. 207-225). Springer.

Ott, T., & Nieder, A. (2019). Dopamine and cognitive control in prefrontal cortex. *Trends in Cognitive Sciences, 23*(3), 213-234.

Otto, H., & Keller, H. (Eds.) (2013). *Different faces of attachment.* Cambridge University Press.

Ouellette, G., & Sénéchal, M. (2017). Invented spelling in kindergarten as a predictor of reading and spelling in Grade 1: A new pathway to literacy, or just the same road, less known? *Developmental Psychology, 53,* 77-88.

Owens, D., Middleton, T.J., Rosemond, M.M., & Meniru, M.O. (2018). Underrepresentation of Black children in gifted education programs: Examining ethnocentric monoculturalism. In J. Cannaday (Ed.), *Curriculum development for gifted education programs.* IGI Global.

Özdel, D., & Sari, H.Y. (2020). Effects of the prone position and kangaroo care on gastric residual volume, vital signs and comfort in preterm infants. *Japan Journal of Nursing Science, 17*(1), e12287.

Ozdenerol, E. (2021). The global problem in gender inequality: Putting gender on the map with GIS. In E. Ozdenerol (Ed.), *Gender Inequalities* (pp. 1-38). CRC Press.

Özel, Ş., & others (2019). Maternal second trimester blood levels of selected heavy metals in pregnancies complicated with neural tube defects. *The Journal of Maternal-Fetal & Neonatal Medicine, 32*(15), 2547-2553.

Ozturk Donmez, R., & Bayik Temel, A. (2019). Effect of soothing techniques on infants' self-regulation behaviors (sleeping, crying, feeding): A randomized controlled study. *Japanese Journal of Nursing Science, 16,* 407-419.

P

Pace, A., Levine, D.F., Morini, G., Hirsh-Pasek, K., & Golinkoff, R.M. (2016). Language acquisition: From words to world and back again. In L. Balter & C.S. Tamis-LeMonda (Eds.), *Child psychology: A contemporary handbook* (3rd ed.). Psychology Press.

Pace, A., & others (2021). Within and across language predictors of word learning processes in dual language learners. *Child Development, 92,* 35-53.

Padilla-Walker, L.M., Carlo, G., & Memmott-Elison, M.K. (2018). Longitudinal change in adolescents' prosocial behavior toward strangers, friends, and family. *Journal of Research on Adolescence, 28,* 698-710.

Padilla-Walker, L.M., & Son, D. (2019). Proactive parenting and moral development. In D.J. Laible & others (Eds.), *The Oxford handbook of parenting and moral development.* Oxford University Press.

Pagani, L.S., Levesque-Seck, F., Archambault, I., & Janosz, M. (2017). Prospective longitudinal associations between household smoke exposure in early childhood and antisocial behavior at age 12. *Indoor Air, 27,* 622-630.

Pahlke, E., Hyde, J., Shibley, A., & Carlie, M. (2014). The effects of single-sex compared with coeducational schooling on students' performance and attitudes: A meta-analysis. *Psychological Bulletin, 140,* 1042-1072.

Pais, M., & others (2021). A randomized controlled trial on the efficacy of integrated yoga on pregnancy outcome. *Holistic Nursing Practice, 35,* 273-280.

Pakarinen, E., & others (2021). Investigating bidirectional links between the quality of teacher-child relationships and children's interest and pre-academic skills in literacy and math. *Child Development, 92,* 388-407.

Palczewski, C.H., DeFrancisco, V.P., & McGeough, D.D. (2017). *Gender in communication: A critical introduction.* Sage.

Palmquist, C.M., Keen, R., & Jaswal, V.K. (2018). Visualization instructions enhance preschoolers' spatial problem-solving. *British Journal of Developmental Psychology, 36*(1), 37-46.

Pan, C.Y., & others (2019). Effects of physical exercise intervention on motor skills and executive functions in children with ADHD: A pilot study. *Journal of Attention Disorders, 23*(4), 384-397.

Pan, M., Stiles, B.L., Tempelmeyer, T.C., & Wong, N. (2019). A cross-cultural exploration of academic dishonesty: Current challenges, preventive measures, and future directions. In D. Velliaris (Ed.), *Prevention and detection of academic misconduct in higher education* (pp. 63-82). IGI Global.

Panesi, S., & Morra, S. (2022). The relation between drawing and language in preschoolers: The role of working memory and executive functions. *Cognitive Development, 61,* 101142.

Pang, J.S., & Baumann, N. (2020). At the crossroads of women's experience: Insights from and intersections between motivation, emotion, gender, and culture. In F.M. Cheung & D.F. Halpern (Eds.), *Cambridge handbook of the international psychology of women* (pp. 153-166). Cambridge University Press.

Pangas, J., & others (2019). Refugee women's experiences negotiating motherhood and maternity care in a new country: A meta-ethnographic review. *International Journal of Nursing Studies, 90,* 31-45.

Panneton, R., Bremner, J.G., & Johnson, S.P. (2021). Infancy studies come of age: Jacques Mehler's influence on the importance of perinatal experience for early language learning. *Cognition, 213,* 104543.

Paolicelli, C., & others (2021). The WIC Infant and Toddler Feeding Practices Study-2 (WIC ITFPS-2) through age 5: What we've learned, what questions remain, and how you can use this longitudinal dataset. *Current Developments in Nutrition, 5*(Suppl. 2), 173.

Papadimitriou, A. (2016). Timing of puberty and secular trend in human maturation. In P. Kumanov & A. Agarwal (Eds.), *Puberty* (pp. 121-136). Springer.

Papadopoulos, N., & others (2019). The efficacy of a brief behavioral sleep intervention in school-aged children with ADHD and comorbid autism spectrum disorder. *Journal of Attention Disorders, 23,* 341-350.

Papageorghiou, A.T., & others (2018). The INTERGROWTH-21st fetal growth standards: Toward the global integration of pregnancy and pediatric care. *American Journal of Obstetrics and Gynecology, 218,* S630-S640.

Parent, N., Guhn, M., Brussoni, M., Almas, A., & Oberle, E. (2021). Social determinants of playing outdoors in the neighbourhood: Family characteristics, trust in neighbours and daily outdoor play in early childhood. *Canadian Journal of Public Health, 112*(1), 120-127.

Park, E.M., Meltzer-Brody, S., & Stickgold, R. (2013). Poor sleep maintenance and subjective sleep quality are associated with postpartum depression symptom severity. *Archives of Women's Mental Health, 16,* 539-547.

Park, H., & others (2019). Developmental trends in sleep during adolescents' transition to young adulthood. *Sleep Medicine, 60,* 202-210.

Park, Y.M. (2017). Relationship between child maltreatment, suicidality, and bipolarity: A retrospective study. *Psychiatry Investigation, 14,* 136-140.

Parkay, F.W. (2020). *Becoming a teacher* (11th ed.). Pearson.

Parke, R.D. (2013). *Future families: Diverse forms, rich possibilities.* Wiley-Blackwell.

Parke, R.D., & Cookston, J.T. (2019). Commentary: Many types of fathers, many types of contexts: An agenda for future progress in fathering research. In B. Volling & N. Cabrera (Eds.), *Advancing research and measurement on fathering and children's development. Monographs of the Society for Research in Child Development, No. 332, 84*(1), 131-145.

Parke, R.D., Roisman, G.I., & Rose, A.J. (2020). *Social development* (3rd ed.). Wiley.

Parks, M., & Oslick, M.E. (2021). Using children's literature to embed character education in primary classrooms. *Dimensions of Early Childhood, 49,* 29-33.

Parmenter, J.G., & others (2022). Intersectionality and identity configurations: A qualitative study exploring sexual identity development among emerging adults in the United States. *Emerging Adulthood, 10,* 372-385.

Parsons, L., Howes, A., Jones, C.A., & Surtees, A.D.R. (2023). Changes in parental sleep from pregnancy to postpartum: A meta-analytic review of actigraphy studies. *Sleep Medicine Reviews, 68,* 101719.

Paschall, K.W., Mastergeorge, A.M., & Ayoub, C.C. (2019). Associations between child physical abuse potential, observed maternal parenting, and young children's emotion regulation: Is participation in Early Head Start protective? *Infant Mental Health Journal, 40,* 169-185.

Pate, R.R., & others (2015). Prevalence of compliance with a new physical activity guideline for preschool-aged children. *Childhood Obesity, 11,* 45-70.

Pate, R.R., & others (2019). Change in children's physical activity: Predictors in the transition from elementary to middle school. *American Journal of Preventive Medicine, 56*(3), e65-e73.

Pate, R.R., Pfeiffer, K.A., Trost, S.G., Ziegler, P., & Dowda, M. (2004). Physical activity among children attending preschools. *Pediatrics, 114,* 1258-1263.

Patel, D.R., Neelakantan, M., Pandher, K., & Merrick, J. (2020). Cerebral palsy in children: A clinical overview. *Translational Pediatrics, 9*(Suppl. 1), S125.

Patrick, M.E., & others (2016). Novel psychoactive substance use by US adolescents: Characteristics associated with use of synthetic cannabinoids and synthetic cathinones. *Drug and Alcohol Review, 35*(5), 586-590.

Patston, T.J., Kaufman, J.C., Cropley, A.J., & Marrone, R. (2021). What is creativity in education? A qualitative study of international curricula. *Journal of Advanced Academics, 32*(2), 207-230.

Patterson, C.J. (2022). Parental sexual orientation, parental gender identity, and the development of children. In J.J. Lockman (Ed.), *Advances in child development and behavior* (pp. 71-102). Academic Press.

Patterson, C.J., Farr, R.H., & Goldberg, A.E. (2021). LGBTQ+ parents and their children. *National Council on Family Relations Policy Brief, 6*(3).

Patton, G.C., & others (2011). Overweight and obesity between adolescence and early adulthood: A 10-year prospective study. *Journal of Adolescent Health, 48*(3), 275-280.

Paulhus, D.L. (2008). Birth order. In M.M. Haith & J.B. Benson (Eds.), Encyclopedia of infant and early childhood development. Elsevier.

Paul, E., & Ortin, A. (2019). Psychopathological mechanisms of early neglect and abuse on suicidal ideation and self-harm in middle childhood. *European Child & Adolescent Psychiatry, 28*(10), 1311-1319.

Pauliks, L.B. (2015). The effect of pregestational diabetes on fetal heart function. *Expert Review of Cardiovascular Therapy, 13,* 67-74.

Paulus, M., & Moore, C. (2014). The development of recipient-dependent sharing behavior and sharing expectations in preschool children. *Developmental Psychology, 50,* 914-921.

Paus, T., & others (2008). Morphological properties of the action-observation cortical network in adolescents with low and high resistance to peer influence. *Social Neuroscience, 3*(3), 303-316.

Pavlov, I.P. (1927). In G.V. Anrep (Trans.), *Conditioned reflexes.* Oxford University Press.

Pavord, I.D., Barnes, P.J., Lemière, C., & Gibson, P.G. (2023). Diagnosis and assessment of the asthmas. *Journal of Allergy and Clinical Immunology: In Practice, 11*(1), 1-8.

Paxton, S.J., & Damiano, S.R. (2017). The development of body image and weight bias in childhood. *Advances in Child Development and Behavior, 52,* 269-298.

Pea, R., & others (2012). Media use, face-to-face communication, media multitasking, and social well-being among 8- to 12-year-old girls. *Developmental Psychology, 48,* 327-336.

Pearson, R.M., & others (2013). Maternal depression during pregnancy and the postnatal period: Risk and possible mechanisms for offspring depression at age 18 years. *JAMA Psychiatry, 70,* 1312-1319.

Pecker, L.H., & Little, J. (2018). Clinical manifestations of sickle cell disease across the lifespan. In E. Meier, A. Abraham, & R. Fasano (Eds.), *Sickle cell disease and hematopoietic stem cell transplantation.* Springer.

Pedersen, C.B., McGrath, J., Mortensen, P.B., & Pedersen, L. (2014). The importance of the father's age to schizophrenia risk. *Molecular Psychiatry, 19,* 530-531.

Peitzmeier, S.M., & others (2016). Intimate partner violence perpetration among adolescent males in disadvantaged neighborhoods globally. *Journal of Adolescent Health, 59,* 696-702.

Pelaez, M., & Monlux, K. (2017). Operant conditioning methodologies to investigate infant learning. *European Journal of Behavior Analysis, 18,* 212-241.

Peña, J.B., & others (2016). A cross-national comparison of suicide attempts, drug use, and depressed mood among Dominican youth. *Suicide and Life-Threatening Behavior, 46*(3), 301-312.

Peng, P., & Kievit, R.A. (2020). The development of academic achievement and cognitive abilities: A bidirectional perspective. *Child Development Perspectives, 14*(1), 15-20.

Peng, W., & others (2020). Peer victimization and adolescents' suicidal ideation and suicide attempts: A moderated mediation model. *Children and Youth Services Review, 112,* 104888.

Pennequin, V., & others (2020). Metacognition and emotional regulation in children from 8 to 12 years old. *British Journal of Educational Psychology* (Suppl. 1), S1-S16.

Perchtold-Stefan, C.M., & others (2020). Humor comprehension and creative cognition: Shared and distinct neurocognitive mechanisms as indicated by EEG alpha activity. *NeuroImage, 213,* 116695.

Pereira, A.S., Vilanova, F., Dutra-Thomé, L., & Koller, S.H. (2023). Challenges of adolescence and emerging adulthood in Latin America. In L.J. Crockett, G. Carlo, & J.E. Schulenberg (Eds.), *APA handbook of adolescent and young adult development* (pp. 443-456). American Psychological Association.

Pereira Araújo, S.M., & others (2022). Pathways in the association between added sugar consumption, obesity in mother-child dyads, and chronic oral disease burden in early childhood. *European Journal of Oral Sciences, 130*(2), e12847.

Perez, E.M., & others (2015). Massage therapy improves the development of HIV-exposed infants living in a low socioeconomic, peri-urban community of South Africa. *Infant Behavior and Development, 38,* 135-146.

Perez-Brena, N.J., Duncan, J.C., Bámaca, M.Y., & Perez, R. (2022). Progress and gaps: A systematic review of the family demographics and family subsystems represented in top family science journals 2008-2018. *Journal of Family Theory & Review, 14*(1), 59-78.

Pérez-Edgar, K., MacNeill, L.A., & Fu, X. (2020). Navigating through the experienced environment: Insights from mobile eye tracking. *Current Directions in Psychological Science, 29*(3), 286-292.

Perez-Escamilla, R., & Moran, V.H. (2017). The role of nutrition in integrated early child development in the 21st century: Contribution from the *Maternal and Child Nutrition* journal. *Maternal and Child Nutrition, 13,* 3-6.

Permana, I., & others (2019). Difference of mortality and morbidity between neonates in adolescent pregnancy and young adult pregnancy. *International Journal of Clinical Pediatrics and Child Health, 1*(2), 1-8.

Perone, S., Almy, B., & Zelazo, P.D. (2017). Toward an understanding of the neural basis of executive function development. In R.L. Gibb & B. Kolb (Eds.), *The neurobiology of brain and behavioral development* (2nd ed.). Elsevier.

Perry, B.L., Aronson, B., & Pescosolido, B.A. (2021). Pandemic precarity: COVID-19 is exposing and exacerbating inequalities in the American heartland. *PNAS, 118*(8), e2020685118.

Perry, D.G., & Pauletti, R.E. (2011). Gender and adolescent development. *Journal of Research on Adolescence, 21,* 61-74.

Perry-Jenkins, M., & Gerstel, N. (2020). Work and family in the second decade of the 21st century. *Journal of Marriage and Family, 82*(1), 420-453.

Perryman, K.L., & others (2020). Child-centered play therapy and academic achievement: A prevention-based model. *International Journal of Play Therapy, 29*(2), 104-117.

Peskin, H. (1967). Pubertal onset and ego functioning. *Journal of Abnormal Psychology, 72,* 1-15.

Petersen, T.L., Møller, L.B., Brønd, J.C., Jepsen, R., & Grøntved, A. (2020). Association between parent and child physical activity: A systematic review. *International Journal of Behavioral Nutrition and Physical Activity, 17*(1), 1-16.

Peterson, C.B., & others (2017). The effects of psychotherapy treatment on outcome in bulimia nervosa: Examining indirect effects through emotion regulation, self-directed behavior, and self-discrepancy within the mediation model. *International Journal of Eating Disorders, 50*(6), 636-647.

Peterson, C.C., & others (2016). Peer social skills and theory of mind in children with autism, deafness, or typical development. *Developmental Psychology, 52,* 46-57.

Peterson, C.C., Wellman, H.M., & Slaughter, V. (2012). The mind behind the message: Advancing theory-of-mind scales for typically developing children and those with deafness, autism, or Asperger syndrome. *Child Development, 83,* 469-485.

Petruzzello, S.J., Greene, D.R., Chizewski, A., Rougeau, K.M., & Greenlee, T.A. (2018). Acute vs. chronic effects of exercise on mental health. In H. Budde & M. Wegner (Eds.), *The exercise effect on mental health: Neurobiological mechanisms.* Taylor & Francis.

Petty, J., & others (2020). Parents' views on preparation to care for extremely premature infants at home. *Nursing Children and Young People, 32*(1).

Peverill, M., & others (2021). Socioeconomic status and child psychopathology in the United States: A meta-analysis of population-based studies. *Clinical Psychology Review, 83,* 101933.

Pew Research Center (2015). *Table 40, Statistical portrait of Hispanics in the United States, 2013.* Pew Research Center.

Pew Research Center (2018). *5 facts about Americans and video games.* Available https://www.pewresearch.org/fact-tank/2018/09/17/5-facts-about-americans-and-video-games/

Pew Research Center (2020). *The virtues and downsides of online dating.* Available https://www.pewresearch.org/internet/2020/02/06/the-virtues-and-downsides-of-online-dating/

Pew-Templeton Global Religious Future Project (2022). *Key findings from the Global Religious Futures Project.* Available https://www.pewresearch.org/religion/2022/12/21/key-findings-from-the-global-religious-futures-project/

Peyre, H., & others (2017). Do developmental milestones at 4, 8, 12, and 24 months predict IQ at 5-6 years old? Results of the EDEN mother-child cohort. *Child Development, 21*(2) 272-279.

Pfeifer, J.H., & Allen, N.B. (2021). Puberty initiates cascading relationship between neurodevelopmental, social, and internalizing processes across adolescence. *Biological Psychiatry, 89,* 99-108.

Pham, Y.K., Murray, C., & Gau, J. (2022). The Inventory of Teacher-Student Relationships: Factor structure and associations with school engagement among high-risk youth. *Psychology in the Schools, 59,* 413-429.

Philadelphia College of Osteopathic Medicine (2022). *2017 graduate profiles: Terrance Weeden.* Retrieved April 19, 2022, from https://www.pcom.edu/commencement/graduate-profiles/2017-graduate-profiles/terrance-weeden.html

Phillipou, A., Castle, D.J., & Rossell, S.L. (2019). Direct comparisons of anorexia nervosa and body dysmorphic disorder: A systematic review. *Psychiatry Research, 274,* 129-137.

Phillipps, H.R., Yip, S.H., & Grattan, D.R. (2020). Patterns of prolactin secretion. *Molecular and Cellular Endocrinology, 502,* 110679.

Phillips, K., Healy, L., Smith, L., & Keenan, R. (2018). Hydroxyurea therapy in UK children with sickle cell anaemia: A single-centre experience. *Pediatric Blood & Cancer, 65.* doi:10.1002/pbc.26833

Phinney, J.S., & Vedder, P. (2013). Family relationship values of adolescents and parents: Intergenerational discrepancies and adaptation. In J.W. Berry & others (Eds.), *Immigrant youth in cultural transition.* Psychology Press.

Phua, D.Y., Kee, M.Z., & Meaney, M.J. (2019). Positive maternal mental health, parenting and child development. *Biological Psychiatry, 87*(4), 328-337.

Piaget, J. (1932). *The moral judgment of the child.* Harcourt Brace Jovanovich.

Piaget, J. (1952). *The origins of intelligence in children* (M. Cook, Trans.). International Universities Press.

Piaget, J. (1954). *The construction of reality in the child.* Basic Books.

Piaget, J. (1962). *Play, dreams, and imitation.* W.W. Norton.

Piaget, J., & Inhelder, B. (1969). *The child's conception of space* (F.J. Langdon & J.L. Lunger, Trans.). W.W. Norton.

Piazza, E.A., & others (2020). Infant and adult brains are coupled to the dynamics of natural communication. *Psychological Science, 31*(1), 6-17.

Piekarski, D.J., & others (2017). Does puberty mark a transition in sensitive periods for plasticity in the associative neocortex? *Brain Research, 1654*(Pt. B), 123-144.

Pietraszewski, D., Wertz, A.E., Bryant, G.A., & Wynn, K. (2017). Three-month-old human infants use vocal cues of body size. *Proceedings of the Royal Society B, 284*(1856), 20170656.

Pike, A., & Oliver, B.R. (2017). Child behavior and sibling relationship quality: A cross-lagged analysis. *Journal of Family Psychology, 31,* 250-255.

Pilarz, A.R., Sandstrom, H., & Henly, J.R. (2022). Making sense of childcare instability among families with low incomes: (Un)desired and (un)planned reasons for changing childcare arrangements. *RSF: The Russell Sage Foundation Journal of the Social Sciences, 8*(5), 120-142.

Pinderhughes, E.E., & Brodzinsky, D.M. (2019). Parenting in adoptive families. In M.H. Bornstein (Ed.), *Handbook of parenting* (3rd ed., Vol. 1). Routledge.

Pine, A.E., & Garber, J. (2023). Parental psychopathology and parenting. In D.J.A. Dozois & K.S. Dobson (Eds.), *Treatment of psychosocial risk factors in depression* (pp. 27-54). American Psychological Association.

Pineda, E., Bascunan, J., & Sassi, F. (2021). Improving the school food environment for the prevention of childhood obesity: What works and what doesn't. *Obesity Reviews, 22*(2), e13176.

Pineda-Alhucema, W., Aristizabal, E., Escudero-Cabarcas, J., Acosta-Lopez, J.E., & Vélez, J.I. (2018). Executive function and theory of mind in children with ADHD: A systematic review. *Neuropsychology Review, 28,* 341-358.

Pinho, J., Marcut, C., & Fonseca, R. (2020). Action remodeling, the synaptic tag and the maintenance of synaptic plasticity. *IUBMB Life, 72,* 577-589.

Pinquart, M. (2017). Associations of parenting dimensions and styles with externalizing problems of children and adolescents: An updated meta-analysis. *Developmental Psychology, 53,* 873-932.

Pinquart, M., Feubner, C., & Ahnert, L. (2013). Meta-analytic evidence for stability of attachments from infancy to early adulthood. *Attachment and Human Development, 15,* 189-218.

Pinto, A., & others (2015). Direct and indirect relations between parent-child attachments, peer acceptance, and self-esteem for preschool children. *Attachment & Human Development, 17*(6), 586-598.

Pinto, G., & Incognito, O. (2021). The relationship between emergent drawing, emergent writing, and visual-motor integration in preschool children. *Infant and Child Development, 31*(2), e2284.

Pinto Pereira, S.M., van Veldhoven, K., Li, L., & Power, C. (2016). Combined early and adult life risk factor associations for mid-life obesity in a prospective birth cohort: Assessing potential public health impact. *BMJ Open, 6*(4), e011044.

Pitkanen, T., Lyyra, A.L., & Pulkkinen, L. (2005). Age of onset of drinking and the use of alcohol in adulthood: A follow-up study from age 8-42 for females and males. *Addiction, 100,* 652-661.

Pizarro K.W., Surkan, P.J., & Bustamante, I.V. (2021). The social ecology of parental monitoring: Parent-child dynamics in a high-risk Peruvian neighborhood. *Family Process, 60,* 199-215.

Placek, C.D., Madhivanan, P., & Hagen, E.H. (2017). Innate food aversions and culturally transmitted food taboos in pregnant women in rural southwest India: Separate systems to protect the fetus? *Evolution and Human Behavior, 38,* 714-728.

Planalp, E.M., & Goldsmith, H.H. (2020). Observed profiles of infant temperament: Stability, heritability, and associations with parenting. *Child Development, 91,* e563-e580.

Plancoulaine, S., & others (2018). Night sleep duration trajectories and associated factors among preschool children from the EDEN cohort. *Sleep Medicine, 48,* 194-201.

Pluess, M., & others (2011). Serotonin transporter polymorphism moderates effects of prenatal maternal anxiety on infant negative emotionality. *Biological Psychiatry, 69,* 520–525.

Plumert, J.M. (Ed). (2018). Studying the perception-action system as a model system for understanding development. *Advances in Child Development and Behavior, 55,* 1–272.

Podzimek, Š., & others (2018). The evolution of taste and perinatal programming of taste preferences. *Physiological Research, 67,* S421–S429.

Poehlmann-Tynan, J., & others (2016). A pilot study of contemplative practices with economically disadvantaged preschoolers: Children's empathic and self-regulatory behaviors. *Mindfulness, 7,* 46.

Poehner, M.E., Davin, K.J., & Lantolf, J.P. (2017). Dynamic assessment. In E. Shohamy, I. Or, & S. May (Eds.), *Language testing and assessment. Encyclopedia of language and education* (3rd ed.). Springer.

Pointer, E. (2021, October 25*). Pay it forward: 13-year-old raises more than $30K for humane society program.* Nextstar Media Inc. Retrieved April 21, 2022, from https://fox59.com/morning-news/pay-it-forward/pay-it-forward-13-year-old-raises-30k-for-humane-society-program/

Polidori, N., & others (2020). Deciphering short stature in children. *Annals of Pediatric Endocrinology and Metabolism, 25,* 69–79.

Polišenská, K., & others (2021). Effects of semantic plausibility, syntactic complexity, and n-gram frequency on children's sentence recognition. *Journal of Child Language, 48,* 261–284.

Pollak, S.D., Camras, L.A., & Cole, P.M. (2019). Progress in understanding the emergence of human emotion. *Developmental Psychology, 55,* 1801–1811.

Pomerantz, E.M. (2017). *Center for Parent-Child Studies.* Retrieved May 31, 2017, from http://labs.psychology.illinois.edu/cpcs/

Ponting, C., & others (2020). Psychological interventions for depression and anxiety in pregnant Latina and Black women in the United States: A systematic review. *Clinical Psychology & Psychotherapy, 27,* 249–265.

Pool, L.R., & others (2021). Childhood risk factors and adulthood cardiovascular disease: A systematic review. *Journal of Pediatrics, 232,* 118–126.

Poole, D.A., & Lindsay, D.S. (1995). Interviewing preschoolers: Effects of nonsuggestive techniques, parental coaching, and leading questions on reports of nonexperienced events. *Journal of Experimental Child Psychology, 60,* 129–154.

Popalzai, E., & Kottasová, I. (2022, December 20). *Taliban suspend university education for women in Afghanistan.* CNN. Accessed at https://www.cnn.com/2022/12/20/asia/taliban-bans-women-university-education-intl/index.html

Popham, W.J. (2017). *Classroom assessment* (8th ed.). Pearson.

Popham, W.J. (2020). *Classroom assessment* (9th ed.). Pearson.

Porath, A.J., & Fried, P.A. (2005). Effects of prenatal cigarette and marijuana exposure on drug use among offspring. *Neurotoxicology and Teratology, 27,* 267–277.

Porter, C., & others (2021). Impact of the COVID-19 pandemic on anxiety and depression symptoms of young people in the global south: Evidence from a four-country cohort study. *BMJ Open, 11,* e049653.

Posada, G., & others (2016). Maternal sensitivity and child secure base use in early childhood: Studies in different cultural contexts. *Child Development, 87,* 297–311.

Posada, G., Waters, E., Vaughn, B.E., Pederson, D.R., & Moran, G. (2021). Mary Ainsworth, ethology, and maternal sensitivity. In E. Waters & others (Eds.), *Measuring attachment: Developmental assessment across the lifespan* (pp. 1–36). Guilford Press.

Posner, M.I., & Rothbart, M.K. (2007). *Educating the human brain.* American Psychological Association.

Posner, M.I., Rothbart, M.K., Sheese, B.E., & Voelker, P. (2014). Developing attention: Behavioral and brain mechanisms. *Advances in Neuroscience, 2014,* 405094.

Posner, M.I., Rothbart, M.K., & Tang, Y.Y. (2015). Enhancing attention through training. *Current Opinion in Behavioral Sciences, 4,* 1–5.

Potapova, N.V., Gartstein, M.A., & Bridgett, D.J. (2014). Paternal influences on infant temperament: Effects of father internalizing problems, parent-related stress, and temperament. *Infant Behavior and Development, 37,* 105–110.

Potard, C., Kubiszewski, V., Camus, G., Courtois, R., & Gaymard, S. (2018). Driving under the influence of alcohol and perceived invulnerability among young adults: An extension of the theory of planned behavior. *Transportation Research Part F: Traffic Psychology and Behaviour, 55,* 38–46.

Potter, A., & others (2021). Early adolescent gender diversity and mental health in the Adolescent Brain Cognitive Development study. *Journal of Child Psychology and Psychiatry, 62*(2), 171–179.

Potter, M., Spence, J.C., Boulé, N., Stearns, J.A., & Carson, V. (2018). Behavior tracking and 3-year longitudinal associations between physical activity, screen time, and fitness among young children. *Pediatric Exercise Science, 30,* 132–141.

Potterton, R., Richards, K., Allen, K., & Schmidt, U. (2020). Eating disorders during emerging adulthood: A systematic scoping review. *Frontiers in Psychology, 10,* 3062.

Poulin-Dubois, D., & Pauen, S. (2017). The development of object categories: What, when, and how? In H. Cohen & C. Lefebvre (Eds.), *Handbook of categorization in cognitive science* (2nd ed., pp. 653–671). Elsevier.

Pouwels, J.L., Lansu, T.A., & Cillessen, A.H. (2018). A developmental perspective on popularity and the group process of bullying. *Aggression and Violent Behavior, 43,* 64–70.

Povell, P. (2017). Maria Montessori: Yesterday, today, and tomorrow. In L.E. Cohen & S. Waite-Stupiansky (Eds.), *Theories of early childhood education.* Routledge.

Powers, K.E., Chavez, R.S., & Heatherton, T.F. (2016). Individual differences in response of dorsomedial prefrontal cortex predict daily social behavior. *Social Cognitive and Affective Neuroscience, 11,* 121–126.

Powers, S.K., & Dodd, S.L. (2017). *Total fitness and wellness* (7th ed.). Pearson.

Pozzi, E., & others (2021). Neural correlates of emotion regulation in adolescents and emerging adults: A meta-analytic study. *Biological Psychiatry, 89,* 194–204.

Prager, E.O., Sera, M.D., & Carlson, S.M. (2016). Executive function and magnitude skills in preschool children. *Journal of Experimental Child Psychology, 147,* 126–139.

Prelock, P.A., & Hutchins, T.L. (2018). An introduction to communication development. In P.A. Prelock & T.L. Hutchins (Eds.), *Clinical guide to assessment and treatment of communication disorders.* Springer.

Prenoveau, J.M., & others (2017). Maternal postnatal depression and anxiety and their association with child emotional negativity and behavior problems at two years. *Developmental Psychology, 53,* 50–62.

Pressley, M. (2007). Achieving best practices. In L.B. Gambrell, L.M. Morrow, & M. Pressley (Eds.), *Best practices in literacy instruction.* Guilford Press.

Pressley, M., & Hilden, K. (2006). Cognitive strategies. In W. Damon & R. Lerner (Eds.), *Handbook of child psychology* (6th ed.). Wiley.

Pressley, M., & McCormick, C.B. (2007). *Child and adolescent development for educators.* Guilford Press.

Pressley, M., Mohan, L., Fingeret, L., Reffitt, K., & Raphael Bogaert, L.R. (2007). Writing instruction in engaging and effective elementary settings. In S. Graham, C.A. MacArthur, & J. Fitzgerald (Eds.), *Best practices in writing instruction.* Guilford Press.

Price, M., & Corrin, W. (2020). *High school reform in perspective: Past successes, enduring challenges, and future considerations.* MDRC.

Priel, A., & others (2020). Maternal depression impairs child emotion understanding and executive functions: The role of dysregulated maternal care across the first decade of life. *Emotion, 20,* 1042–1058.

Prime, H., Wade, M., & Browne, D.T. (2020). Risk and resilience in family well-being during the COVID-19 pandemic. *American Psychologist, 75*(5), 631.

Prinstein, M.J. (2007). Moderators of peer contagion: A longitudinal examination of depression socialization between adolescents and their best friends. *Journal of Clinical Child and Adolescent Psychology, 36,* 159–170.

Prinstein, M.J., & Giletta, M. (2016). Peer relations and developmental psychopathology. In D. Cicchetti (Ed.), *Developmental psychopathology* (3rd ed.). Wiley.

Prinstein, M.J., & Giletta, M. (2021). Five priorities for future research on child and adolescent peer influence. *Merrill-Palmer Quarterly, 67,* 367–389.

Prinstein, M.J., Rancourt, D., Guerry, J.D., & Browne, C.B. (2009). Peer reputations and psychological adjustment. In K.H. Rubin, W.M. Bukowski, & B. Laursen (Eds.), *Handbook of peer interactions, relationships, and groups.* Guilford Press.

Prinz, R.J. (2020). Triple P–Positive Parenting Program. In E.T. Gershoff & S.J. Lee (Eds.), *Ending the physical punishment of children: A guide for clinicians and practitioners* (pp. 133–143). American Psychological Association.

Prot, S., & others (2017). Content effects: Violence in the media. *The International Encyclopedia of Media Effects, 1–19.*

Public Health Law Center (2019). *U.S. e-cigarette regulations: A 50-state review.* Retrieved November 29, 2019, from https://www.publichealthlawcenter .org/resources/us-e-cigarette-regulations-50-state-review

Puhl, R.M., & King, K.M. (2013). Weight discrimination and bullying. *Best Practice and Research: Clinical Endocrinology and Metabolism, 27,* 117–127.

Pulerwitz, J., & others (2019). Proposing a conceptual framework to address social norms that influence adolescent sexual and reproductive health. *Journal of Adolescent Health, 64*(4), S7–S9.

Puranik, S., Forno, E., Bush, A., & Celedon, J.C. (2017). Predicting severe asthma exacerbations in children. *American Journal of Respiratory and Critical Care Medicine, 195,* 854–859.

Q

Qin, J.B., & others (2014). Risk factors for congenital syphilis and adverse pregnancy outcomes in offspring of women with syphilis in Shenzhen, China: A prospective nested case-control study. *Sexually Transmitted Diseases, 41,* 13–23.

Quam, C., & Creel, S.C. (2021). Impacts of acoustic-phonetic variability on perceptual development for spoken language: A review. *Wiley Interdisciplinary Reviews. Review of Cognitive Science, 12*(5), e1558.

Quinn, P.C. (2016). What do infants know about cats, dogs, and people? Development of a "like-people" representation for nonhuman animals. In L. Esposito & others (Eds.), *The social neuroscience of human-animal interaction.* Elsevier.

Quiñones-Camacho, L.E., & others (2019). Cognitive flexibility-related prefrontal activation in preschoolers: A biological approach to temperamental effortful control. *Developmental Cognitive Neuroscience, 38,* 100651.

Quintanilla, L., Giménez-Dasí, M., & Gaviria, E. (2018). Children's perception of envy and modesty: Does depreciation serve as a mask for failure or success? *Current Psychology, 40,* 983–995.

Qumer, S., & Ghosh, D. (2019). Effectiveness of patterned breathing technique on pain during first stage of labour—A narrative review. *International Journal of Nursing Education, 11*(3), 60–62.

R

Radvansky, G.A. (2017). *Human memory* (3rd ed.). Elsevier.

Rah, Y.J., Kim, J., & Lee, S.A. (2022). Effects of spatial boundaries on episodic memory development. *Child Development, 93,* 1574–1583.

Rahimi-Golkhandan, S., & others (2017). A fuzzy trace theory of risk and time preferences in decision making: Integrating cognition and motivation. In J.R. Stevens (Ed.), *Impulsivity: How risk and time influence decision making.* Springer.

Raikes, H., & others (2020). Care, education, and support programs for children age birth to three and their parents. In J.B. Benson (Ed.), *Encyclopedia of infant and early childhood development.* Elsevier.

Raipuria, H.D., & others (2018). A literature review of midwifery-led care in reducing labor and birth interventions. *Nursing for Women's Health, 22*(5), 387–400.

Rajeh, A., & others (2017). Interventions in ADHD: A comparative review of stimulant medications and behavioral therapies. *Asian Journal of Psychiatry, 25,* 131–135.

Rajjo, T., Erickson, R., & Biggs, B. (2022). Pediatric obesity management practices: A survey of primary care providers. *Annals of Family Medicine, 20,* no. 2876.

Rakison, D.H., & Lawson, C.A. (2013). Categorization. In P.D. Zelazo (Ed.), *Oxford handbook of developmental psychology.* Oxford University Press.

Rakoczy, H. (2022). Foundations of theory of mind and its development in early childhood. *Nature Reviews Psychology, 1,* 223–235.

Raley, R.K., & Sweeney, M.M. (2020). Divorce, repartnering, and stepfamilies: A decade in review. *Journal of Marriage and Family, 82,* 81–99.

Rambaran, J.A., Dijkstra, J.K., & Veenstra, R. (2020). Bullying as a group process in childhood: A longitudinal social network analysis. *Child Development, 91,* 1336–1352.

Ramberg, J., & Modin, B. (2019). School effectiveness and student cheating: Do students' grades and moral standards matter for this relationship? *Social Psychology of Education, 22,* 517–538.

Ramchandani, P.G., & others (2008). Depression in men in the postnatal period and later psychopathology: A population cohort study. *Journal of the American Academy of Child and Adolescent Psychiatry, 47,* 390–398.

Ramey, C.T. (2018). The Abecedarian approach to social, educational, and health disparities. *Clinical Child and Family Psychology Review, 21,* 527–544.

Ramey, C.T. (2019). The Abecedarian Approach to full development in early childhood. In B.H. Wasik & S.L. Odom (Eds.), *Celebrating 50 years of child development research: Past, present, and future perspectives* (pp. 141–162). Brookes Publishing.

Ramey, H.L., Lawford, H.L., Pancer, S.M., Matsuba, M.K., & Pratt, M.W. (2022). Trajectories of youth's helping from adolescence into adulthood: The importance of social relations and values. *American Journal of Community Psychology, 69,* 134–144.

Ramey, S.L. (2005). Human developmental science serving children and families: Contributions of the NICHD study of early child care. In NICHD Early Child Care Network (Ed.), *Child care and development.* Guilford Press.

Ramírez-Coronel, A.A., & others (2023). Childhood obesity risk increases with increased screen time: A systematic review and dose–response meta-analysis. *Journal of Health, Population and Nutrition, 42*(1), 5.

Ramirez-Esparza, N., Garcia-Sierra, A., & Kuhl, P.K. (2014). Look who's talking: Speech style and social context in language input to infants are linked to concurrent and future speech development. *Developmental Science, 17,* 880–891.

Ramirez-Esparza, N., Garcia-Sierra, A., & Kuhl, P.K. (2017). The impact of early social interactions on later language development in Spanish-English bilingual infants. *Child Development, 88*(4), 1216–1234.

Ramos-Lopez, O., & others (2021). Epigenetic signatures underlying inflammation: An interplay of nutrition, physical activity, metabolic diseases, and environmental factors for personalized nutrition. *Inflammation Research, 70,* 29–49.

Ramsdell-Hudock, H.L., Stuart, A., & Parham, D.F. (2018). Utterance duration as it relates to communicative variables in infant vocal development. *Journal of Speech, Language, and Hearing Research, 61*(2), 246–256.

Rana, D., Garde, K., Elabiad, M.T., & Pourcyrous, M. (2022). Whole body massage for newborns: A report on non-invasive methodology for neonatal opioid withdrawal syndrome. *Journal of Neonatal-Perinatal Medicine, 15,* 559–565.

Rangey, P.S., & Sheth, M. (2014). Comparative effect of massage therapy versus kangaroo mother care on body weight and length of hospital stay in low birth weight preterm infants. *International Journal of Pediatrics, 2014,* 434060.

Ranke, M.B., & others (2017). Baseline characteristics and gender differences in prepubertal children treated with growth hormone in Europe, USA, and Japan: 25 Years' KIGS® experience (1987–2012) and review. *Hormone Research in Paediatrics, 87,* 30–41.

Rao, C., & Vaid, J. (2017). Morphology, orthography, and the two hemispheres: A divided visual field study with Hindi/Urdu biliterates. *Neuropsychologia, 98,* 46–55.

Rao, W.W., & others (2019). Prevalence of depressive symptoms in overweight and obese children and adolescents in mainland China: A meta-analysis of comparative studies and epidemiological surveys. *Journal of Affective Disorders, 250,* 26–34.

Raskin, M., & others (2019). Patterns of goal attainment among young mothers in a home visiting program. *Applied Developmental Science, 23*(2), 170–182.

Rasmussen, S.A., & Jamieson, D.J. (2020). Coronavirus disease 2019 (COVID-19) and pregnancy: Responding to a rapidly evolving situation. *Obstetrics and Gynecology, 135,* 999–1002.

Rattaz, V., Puglisi, N., Tissot, H., & Favez, N. (2022). Associations between parent–infant interactions, cortisol and vagal regulation in infants, and socioemotional outcomes: A systematic review. *Infant Behavior and Development, 67,* 101687.

Raver, C.C., & others (2012). Testing models of children's self-regulation within educational contexts: Implications for measurement. *Advances in Child Development and Behavior, 42,* 245–270.

Raver, C.C., & others (2013). Predicting individual differences in low-income children's executive control from early to middle childhood. *Developmental Science, 16,* 394–408.

Ray, J., & others (2017). Callous-unemotional traits predict self-reported offending in adolescent boys: The mediating role of delinquent peers and the moderating role of parenting practices. *Developmental Psychology, 53,* 319–328.

Razaz, N., & others (2016). Five-minute Apgar score as a marker for developmental vulnerability at 5 years of age. *Archives of Disease in Childhood: Fetal and Neonatal Edition, 101,* F114–F120.

Reader, J.M., Teti, D.M., & Cleveland, M.J. (2017). Cognitions about infant sleep: Interparental differences, trajectories across the first year, and coparenting quality. *Journal of Family Psychology, 31*(4), 453–463.

Recksiedler, C., Bernhardt, J., & Heintz-Martin, V. (2023). Mothers' well-being in families and family structure: Examining constellations of stressors across life domains. *Journal of Family Issues, 44*(2), 363–385.

Reece, S., Morgan, C., Parascandola, M., & Siddiqi, K. (2019). Secondhand smoke exposure during pregnancy: A cross-sectional analysis of data from Demographic and Health Survey from 30 low-income and middle-income countries. *Tobacco Control, 28,* 420–426.

Reed, J., Hirsh-Pasek, K., & Golinkoff, R.M. (2017) Learning on hold: Cell phones sidetrack parent-child interactions. *Developmental Psychology, 53,* 1428–1436.

Reed-Fitzke, K. (2019). The role of self-concepts in emerging adult depression: A systematic research synthesis. *Journal of Adult Development, 27*(1), 36–48.

Reese, E., Fivush, R., Merrill, N., Wang, Q., & McAnally, H. (2017). Adolescents' intergenerational narratives across cultures. *Developmental Psychology, 53,* 1142–1153.

Reeve, J., & Cheon, S.H. (2021). Autonomy-supportive teaching: Its malleability, benefits, and potential to improve educational practice. *Educational Psychologist, 56,* 54–77.

Regan, A.K., & Pereira, G. (2021). Patterns of combustible and electronic cigarette use during pregnancy and associated pregnancy outcomes. *Scientific Reports, 11,* 13508.

Reid, P.T., & Zalk, S.R. (2001). Academic environments: Gender and ethnicity in U.S. higher education. In J. Worell (Ed.), *Encyclopedia of women and gender.* Academic Press.

Reid, V.M., & Dunn, K. (2021). The fetal origins of human psychological development. *Current Directions in Psychological Science, 30*(2), 144–150.

Reis, S.M., & Renzulli, J.S. (2020). Intellectual giftedness. In R.J. Sternberg (Ed.), *Cambridge handbook of intelligence.* Cambridge University Press.

Reitan, A.F., & Sanderud, A. (2021). What information did pregnant women want related to risks and benefits attending X-ray examinations? *Journal of Medical Imaging and Radiation Sciences, 52,* 79–85.

Remec, Z.I., & others (2021). Next-generation sequencing in newborn screening: A review of current state. *Frontiers in Genetics, 12,* 662254.

Remien, K., & Marwaha, R. (2021). Dyslexia. *StatPearls.*

Remmert, J.E., & others (2020). Breastfeeding practices among women living with HIV in KwaZulu-Natal, South Africa: An observational study. *Maternal and Child Health Journal, 24*(2), 127–134.

Ren, H., & others (2017). Excessive homework, inadequate sleep, physical inactivity, and screen viewing time are major contributors to high pediatric obesity. *Acta Pediatrica, 106,* 120–127.

Ren, H., & others (2021). The protective roles of exercise and maintenance of daily living routines in Chinese adolescents during the COVID-19 quarantine period. *Journal of Adolescent Health, 68,* 35–42.

Repacholi, B.M., & Gopnik, A. (1997). Early reasoning about desires: Evidence from 14- and 18-month-olds. *Developmental Psychology, 33,* 12–21.

Resnik, F., Garbacz, S.A., Stormshak, E.A., & McIntyre, L.L. (2023). Family-centered prevention to enhance proactive parenting and parental self-efficacy during early elementary school. *Journal of Family Psychology, 37*(3), 380–387.

Rey, L., Sánchez-Álvarez, N., & Extremera, N. (2018). Spanish Gratitude Questionnaire: Psychometric properties in adolescents and relationships with negative and positive psychological outcomes. *Personality and Individual Differences, 135,* 173–175.

Reyna, V.F. (2018). Neurobiological models of risky decision-making and adolescent substance use. *Current Addiction Reports, 5,* 128–133.

Reyna, V.F. (2021). A scientific theory of gist communication and misinformation resistance, with implications for health, education, and policy. *Proceedings of the National Academy of Sciences, 118*(15), e1912441117.

Reyna, V.F., & Mills, B.A. (2014). Theoretically motivated interventions for reducing sexual risk taking in adolescence: A randomized controlled experiment applying fuzzy-trace theory. *Journal of Experimental Psychology: General, 143,* 1627–1648.

Reyna, V.F., Müller, S.M. & Edelson, S.M. (2023). Critical tests of fuzzy trace theory in brain and behavior: Uncertainty across time, probability, and development. *Cognitive, Affective, and Behavioral Neuroscience, 23,* 746–772.

Reynolds, G.D., & Richards, J.E. (2019). Infant visual attention and stimulus repetition effects on object recognition. *Child Development, 90,* 1027–1042.

Reynolds, G.D., & Romano, A.C. (2016). The development of attention systems and working memory in infancy. *Frontiers in Systems Neuroscience, 10,* 15.

Rezk, M., & others (2021, November). A brief period of postnatal visual deprivation permanently alters visual motion processing in early visual regions. Paper presented at *NeuroCog* conference, Louvain-la-Neuve, Belgium.

Rhodes, M., & Baron, A. (2019). The development of social categorization. *Annual Review of Developmental Psychology, 1,* 359–386.

Ribeiro, C.D., & others (2017). Development skills of children born premature with low and very low birth weight. *CoDAS, 29,* e20160058.

Riccio, C.A., & Castro, M.J. (2021). Executive function and school performance. In F.C. Worrell & others (Eds.), *Cambridge handbook of applied school psychology.* Cambridge University Press.

Rice, C.E., & others (2022). Defining in detail and evaluating reliability of DSM-5 criteria for autism spectrum disorder (ASD) among children. *Journal of Autism and Developmental Disorders, 52,* 5308–5320.

Richards, J.E., & Conte, S. (2021). Brain development in infants: Structure and experience. In J.J. Lockman & C.S. Tamis-LeMonda (Eds.), *Cambridge handbook of infant development.* Cambridge University Press.

Rideout, V.J., Foehr, U.G., & Roberts, D.F. (2010). *Generation M^2: Media in the lives of 8- to 18-year-olds.* Kaiser Family Foundation.

Rieger, S., Gollner, R., Trautwein, U., & Roberts, B.W. (2016). Low self-esteem prospectively predicts depression in the transition to young adulthood: A replication of Orth, Robins, & Roberts (2008). *Journal of Personality and Social Psychology, 110,* e16–e22.

Riggins, T., & Bauer, P.J. (2022). A developmental cognitive neuroscience approach to the study of memory. In M. Courage & N. Cowan (Eds.), *The development of memory in infancy and childhood* (pp. 1–30). Psychology Press.

Riggins, T., Geng, F., Blankenship, S.L., & Redcay, E. (2016). Hippocampal functional connectivity and episodic memory in early childhood. *Developmental Cognitive Neuroscience, 19,* 58–69.

Riggs, A.E., Kinard, D. & Long, M. (2023). Children's evaluations of gender non-conforming peers. *Sex Roles, 88,* 17–34.

Righetto Greco, A.L., Sato, N.T.D.S., Moreira, R.D.F.C., Cavalcante Neto, J.L., & Tudella, E. (2022). Sticky mittens training to improve reaching skills and manual exploration of full-term and at-risk infants: A systematic review. *Physical & Occupational Therapy in Pediatrics, 43*(2), 182–195.

Rindermann, H., Becker, D., & Coyle, T.R. (2020). Survey of expert opinion on intelligence: Intelligence research, experts' background, controversial issues, and the media. *Intelligence, 78,* 101406.

Ringoot, A.P., & others (2022). Parenting, young children's behavioral self-regulation and the quality of their peer relationships. *Social Development, 31,* 715-732.

Ritchie, S.J., & Tucker-Drob, E.M. (2018). How much does education improve intelligence? A meta-analysis. *Psychological Science, 29,* 1358-1369.

Riva Crugnola, C., Ierardi, E., Gazzotti, S., & Albizzati, A. (2014). Motherhood in adolescent mothers: Maternal attachment, mother-infant styles of interaction, and emotion regulation at three months. *Infant Behavior and Development, 37,* 44-56.

Rivas-Drake, D., & others (2017). Ethnic-racial identity and friendships in early adolescence. *Child Development, 88,* 710-724.

Rivera, S.M. (2018). Fragile X syndrome. In M.H. Bornstein & others (Eds.), *SAGE encyclopedia of lifespan human development.* Sage.

Rivers, A.S., Bosmans, G., Piovanetti Rivera, I., Ruan-Iu, L., & Diamond, G. (2022). Maternal and paternal attachment in high-risk adolescents: Unique and interactive associations with anxiety and depressive symptoms. *Journal of Family Psychology, 36,* 954-963.

Rizzo, M.T., & Killen, M. (2020). Children's evaluations of individually and structurally based inequalities: The role of status. *Developmental Psychology, 56,* 2223-2235.

Robbins, T., & others (2021). Pills and prayers: A comparative qualitative study of community conceptualisations of pre-eclampsia and pluralistic care in Ethiopia, Haiti and Zimbabwe. *BMC Pregnancy and Childbirth, 21,* 716.

Robbinsdale Area Schools (2022, June 2). *New activities director chosen for Cooper High School.* Retrieved January 27, 2023, from https://www.rdale.org/discover/news/article/~board/district-news/post/new-activities-director-chosen-for-cooper-high-school#:~:text=Jun%202%202022%20Willie%20Howard%20has%20been%20selected,with%20Robbinsdale%20Area%20Schools%20for%20over%2012%20years.

Roberts, C.P., & others (2019). Alternative treatments for syphilis during pregnancy. *Sexually Transmitted Diseases, 46*(10), 637-640.

Roberts, J.L., & Inman, T.F. (2021). *Strategies for differentiating instruction: Best practices for the classroom.* Routledge.

Robinson, E.L., St. George, J., & Freeman, E.E. (2021). A systematic review of father-child play interactions and the impacts on child development. *Children, 8*(5), 389.

Robinson, M.M., & Steyvers, M. (2023). Linking computational models of two core tasks of cognitive control. *Psychological Review, 130,* 71-101.

Robson, D.A., Allen, M.S., & Howard, S.J. (2020). Self-regulation in childhood as a predictor of future outcomes: A meta-analytic review. *Psychological Bulletin, 146*(4), 324-354.

Rode, S.S., Chang, P., Fisch, R.O., & Sroufe, L.A. (1981). Attachment patterns of infants separated at birth. *Developmental Psychology, 17,* 188-191.

Röder, B., & Kekunnaya, R. (2021). Visual experience dependent plasticity in humans. *Current Opinion in Neurobiology, 67,* 155-162.

Rodriguez Vega, S., & Yoshikawa, H. (2023). Border and asylum immigration policies and adolescent development in the United States. In L.J. Crockett, G. Carlo, & J.E. Schulenberg (Eds.), *APA handbook of adolescent and young adult development* (pp. 677-690). American Psychological Association.

Roeser, R.W., & others (2022). Mindfulness training improves middle school teachers' occupational health, well-being, and interactions with students in their most stressful classrooms. *Journal of Educational Psychology, 114*(2), 408.

Rogoff, B., Dahl, A., & Callanan, M. (2018). The importance of understanding children's lived experience. *Developmental Review, 50,* 5-15.

Rohrer, J.M., Egloff, B., & Schmukle, S.C. (2015). Examining the effects of birth order on personality. *Proceedings of the National Academy of Sciences, 112,* 14224-14229.

Roisman, G.I., & Cicchetti, D. (2017). Attachment in the context of atypical caregiving: Harnessing insights from a developmental psychopathology perspective. *Development and Psychopathology, 29*(2), 331-335.

Rolfes, S.R., Pinna, K., & Whitney, E. (2018). *Understanding normal and clinical nutrition* (11th ed.). Cengage.

Roman, L.A., & others (2022). The impact of a population-based system of care intervention on enhanced prenatal care and service utilization among Medicaid-insured pregnant women. *American Journal of Preventive Medicine, 62,* e117-e127.

Roman, M., Constantin, T., & Bostan, C.M. (2020). The efficiency of online cognitive-behavioral therapy for postpartum depressive symptomatology: A systematic review and meta-analysis. *Women and Health, 60,* 99-112.

Romeo, R.D. (2017). The impact of stress on the structure of the adolescent brain: Implications for adolescent mental health. *Brain Research, 1654,* 185-191.

Romeo, R.R., & others (2018). Language exposure relates to structural neural connectivity in childhood. *Journal of Neuroscience, 38,* 7870-7877.

Rood, J.E., & Regev, A. (2021). The legacy of the Human Genome Project. *Science, 373,* 1442-1443.

Roos, L.L., Wall-Wieler, E., & Lee, J.B. (2019). Poverty and early childhood outcomes. *Pediatrics, 143*(6), e20183426.

Ropars, S., & others (2018). The long-term effects of the Kangaroo Mother Care intervention on cognitive functioning: Results from a longitudinal study. *Developmental Neuropsychology, 43*(1), 82-91.

Roper, S.W., Fife, S.T., & Seedall, R.B. (2020). The intergenerational effects of parental divorce on young adult relationships. *Journal of Divorce and Remarriage, 61,* 249-266.

Roque, L.S., & Schieffelin, B.B. (2018). Learning how to know: Egophoricity and the grammar of Kaluli (Bosavi, Trans New Guinea), with special reference to child language. In S. Floyd, E. Norcliffe, & L.S. Roque (Eds.), *Egophoricity.* John Benjamins.

Rosario, M. (2019). Sexual orientation development of heterosexual, bisexual, lesbian, and gay individuals: Questions and hypotheses based on Kaestle's (2019) research. *Journal of Sex Research, 56*(7), 827-831.

Rose, A.J., & Smith, R.L. (2018). Gender and peer relationships. In W.M. Bukowski, B. Laursen, & K.H. Rubin (Eds.), *Handbook of peer interactions, relationships, and groups* (pp. 571-589). Guilford Press.

Rose, K.K. (2021). Parental decision making about non-parental child care. In O. Saracho (Ed.), *Contemporary perspectives on research on child care in early childhood education* (pp. 111-134). Information Age Publishing.

Rose, S.A., Feldman, J.F., & Jankowski, J.J. (2015). Pathways from toddler information processing to adolescent lexical proficiency. *Child Development, 86,* 1935-1947.

Rosenau, P.T., & others (2021). Effects of methylphenidate on executive functioning in children and adolescents with ADHD after long-term use: A randomized, placebo-controlled discontinuation study. *Journal of Child Psychology and Psychiatry, 62*(12), 1444-1452.

Rosenberg, M.D., & others (2020). Behavioral and neural signatures of working memory in childhood. *Journal of Neuroscience, 50,* 5090-5104.

Rosenblum, S., Navon, H., & Meyer, S. (2021). Being late for school as related to mothers and children's executive functions and daily routine management. *Cognitive Development, 57,* 101005.

Rosenstein, D., & Oster, H. (1988). Differential facial responses to four basic tastes in newborns. *Child Development, 59,* 1555-1568.

Rosmarin, D.H., & others (2023). Religious affiliation protects against alcohol/substance use initiation: A prospective study among healthy adolescents. *Journal of Adolescence, 95,* 372-381.

Ross, J. (2017). You and me: Investigating the role of self-evaluative emotion in preschool prosociality. *Journal of Experimental Child Psychology, 155,* 67-83.

Ross, J., & others (2017). Cultural differences in self-recognition: The early development of autonomous and related selves? *Developmental Science, 20*(3), e12387.

Rostad, K., & Pexman, P.M. (2015). Preschool-aged children recognize ambivalence: Emerging identification of concurrent conflicting desires. *Frontiers in Psychology, 6,* 425.

Rostron, B.L., & others (2020). Prevalence and reasons for use of flavored cigars and ENDS among US youth and adults: Estimates from Wave 4 of the PATH Study, 2016-2017. *American Journal of Health Behavior, 44*(1), 76-81.

Roth, B., & others (2015). Intelligence and school grades: A meta-analysis. *Intelligence, 53,* 118-137.

Rothbart, M.K. (2004). Temperament and the pursuit of an integrated developmental psychology. *Merrill-Palmer Quarterly, 50,* 492-505.

Rothbart, M.K. (2011). *Becoming who we are.* Guilford Press.

Rothbart, M.K., & Bates, J.E. (2006). Temperament. In W. Damon & R. Lerner (Eds.), *Handbook of child psychology* (6th ed.). Wiley.

Rothbart, M.K., & Gartstein, M.A. (2008). Temperament. In M.M. Haith & J.B. Benson (Eds.), *Encyclopedia of infant and early childhood development.* Elsevier.

Rothbart, M.K., & Posner, M. (2015). The developing brain in a multitasking world. *Developmental Review, 35,* 42–63.

Rothbart, M.K., Posner, M.I., & Sheese, B.E. (2021). Temperament and brain networks of personality. In P.J. Corr & G. Matthews (Eds.), *Cambridge handbook of personality psychology.* Cambridge University Press.

Rothbaum, F., & Trommsdorff, G. (2007). Do roots and wings complement or oppose one another?: The socialization of relatedness and autonomy in cultural context. In J.E. Grusec & P.D. Hastings (Eds.), *Handbook of socialization.* Guilford Press.

Rothbaum, F., Weisz, J., Pott, M., Miyake, K., & Morelli, G. (2000). Attachment and culture: Security in the United States and Japan. *American Psychologist, 55,* 1093–1104.

Rothenberg, W.A., & others (2023). Intergenerational effects of the Fast Track intervention on the home environment: A randomized control trial. *Journal of Child Psychology and Psychiatry, 64,* 820–830.

Rotman, S.A., & others (2020). Family encouragement of healthy eating habits predicts child dietary intake and weight loss in family-based behavioral weight-loss treatment. *Childhood Obesity, 16,* 218–225.

Rovee-Collier, C. (2008). The development of infant memory. In N. Cowan & M. Courage (Eds.), *The development of memory in infancy and childhood.* Psychology Press.

Rovee-Collier, C., & Barr, R. (2010). Infant learning and memory. In J.G. Bremner & T.D. Wachs (Ed.), *Wiley-Blackwell handbook of infant development* (2nd ed.). Wiley.

Ruan, Y., Georgiou, G.K., Song, S., Li, Y., & Shu, H. (2018). Does writing system influence the associations between phonological awareness, morphological awareness, and reading? A meta-analysis. *Journal of Educational Psychology, 110,* 180–202.

Rubin, D.H., Krasilnikoff, P.A., Leventhal, J.M., Weile, B., & Berget, A. (1986, August 23). Effect of passive smoking on birth weight. *The Lancet, 2*(804), 415–417.

Rubin, K.H., & Barstead, M. (2018). Social withdrawal and solitude. In M.H. Bornstein & others (Eds.), *SAGE encyclopedia of lifespan human development.* Sage.

Rubin, K.H., Bowker, J.C., Barstead, M.G., & Coplan, R.J. (2018). Avoiding and withdrawing from the peer group. In W. Bukowski & others (Eds.), *Handbook of peer relationships, interactions, and groups* (2nd ed.). Guilford Press.

Rubin, K.H., Bukowski, W.M., & Bowker, J. (2015). Children in peer groups. In R.E. Lerner (Ed.), *Handbook of child psychology and developmental science* (7th ed.). Wiley.

Rubin, K.H., Bukowski, W.M., & Parker, J.G. (2006). Peer interactions, relationships, and groups. In N. Eisenberg, W. Damon, & R.M. Lerner (Eds.), *Handbook of child psychology: Social, emotional, and personality development* (6th ed., pp. 571–645). Wiley.

Rubio-Codina, M., & others (2016). Concurrent validity and feasibility of short tests currently used to measure early childhood development in large-scale studies. *PLoS One, 11*(8), e0160962.

Rubio-Fernandez, P. (2017). Why are bilinguals better than monolinguals at false-belief tasks? *Psychonomic Bulletin and Review, 24,* 987–998.

Ruble, D. (1983). The development of social comparison processes and their role in achievement-related self-socialization. In E. Higgins, D. Ruble, & W. Hartup (Eds.), *Social cognitive development: A social-cultural perspective.* Cambridge University Press.

Ruckart, P.Z., & others (2021). Update of the blood lead reference value—United States, 2021. *Morbidity and Mortality Weekly Report (MMWR), 70*(43), 1509.

Rueda, M.R. (2018). Attention in the heart of intelligence. *Trends in Neuroscience and Education, 13,* 26–33.

Ruffman, T., & others (2018). Variety in parental use of "want" relates to subsequent growth in children's theory of mind. *Developmental Psychology, 54*(4), 677–688.

Ruffman, T. & others (2019). Lifespan differences in emotional contagion while watching emotion-eliciting videos. *PloS One, 14*(1), e0209253.

Ruigrok, A.N.V., & others (2014). A meta-analysis of sex differences in human brain structure. *Neuroscience & Biobehavioral Reviews, 39,* 34–50.

Ruiz-Hernández, J.A., & others (2019). Influence of parental styles and other psychosocial variables on the development of externalizing behaviors in adolescents: A systematic review. *European Journal of Psychology Applied to Legal Context, 11*(1), 9–21.

Russell, D., Higgins, D., & Posso, A. (2020). Preventing child sexual abuse: A systematic review of interventions and their efficacy in developing countries. *Child Abuse & Neglect, 102,* 104395.

Russell, P.J., Hertz, P.E., & McMillan, B. (2017). *Biology* (4th ed.). Cengage.

Russell, S.T., Crockett, L.J., & Chao, R.K. (2010). *Asian American parenting and parent-adolescent relationships.* Springer.

Russell, S.T., & Dorri, A.A. (2023). Sexual and gender minority youth. In L.J. Crockett, G. Carlo, & J.E. Schulenberg (Eds.), *APA handbook of adolescent and young adult development* (pp. 375–390). American Psychological Association.

Russotti, J., & others (2021). Child maltreatment and the development of psychopathology: The role of developmental timing and chronicity. *Child Abuse & Neglect, 120,* 105215.

Rutman, L., & others (2016). Standardized asthma admission criteria reduce length of stay in a pediatric emergency department. *Academic Emergency Medicine, 23,* 289–296.

Ryan, R.M., & Deci, E.L. (2019, May 22). *Self-determination theory.* Plenary talk at the International Self-Determination Theory conference, Amsterdam.

Rydell, A.M., & Brocki, K.C. (2019). Cognitive and emotional profiles of CU traits and disruptive behavior in adolescence: A prospective study. *Journal of Abnormal Child Psychology, 47*(6), 1039–1051.

Rytioja, M., Lappalainen, K., & Savolainen, H. (2019). Behavioural and emotional strengths of sociometrically popular, rejected, controversial, neglected, and average children. *European Journal of Special Needs Education, 34,* 557–571.

S

S, R. (2021). What the data tells us about love and marriage in India. Available https://www.bbc.com/news/world-asia-india-59530706

Sackett, P.R., Shewach, O.R., & Dahlke, J.A. (2020). The predictive value of intelligence. In R.J. Sternberg (Ed.), *Human intelligence.* Cambridge University Press.

Sadeh, A. (2008). Sleep. In M.M. Haith & J.B. Benson (Eds.), *Encyclopedia of infant and early childhood development.* Elsevier.

Sadker, D., Zittleman, K., & Koch, M. (2019). Gender bias: Past, present, and future. In J. Banks & C. McGee Banks (Eds.), *Multicultural education: Issues and perspectives* (pp. 83–100). Wiley.

Sadker, D.M., & Zittleman, K. (2016). *Teachers, schools, and society* (4th ed.). McGraw Hill.

Saez de Urabain, I.R., Nuthmann, A., Johnson, M.H., & Smith, T.J. (2017). Disentangling the mechanisms underlying infant fixation durations in scene perception: A computational account. *Vision Research, 134,* 43–59.

Safa, M.D., & Umaña-Taylor, A.J. (2021). Biculturalism and adjustment among U.S. Latinos: A review of four decades of empirical findings. *Advances in Child Development and Behavior, 61,* 73–127.

Safa, M.D., Umaña-Taylor, A.J., & Martinez-Fuentes, S. (2022). The role of ethnic–racial and national identities on U.S. Latino adolescents' global identity coherence and adjustment. *Cultural Diversity and Ethnic Minority Psychology.* doi:10.1037/cdp0000535

Saffran, J.R., & Kirkham, N.Z. (2018). Infant statistical learning. *Annual Review of Psychology, 69,* 181–203.

Saint-Jacques, M.C., & others (2018). Researching children's adjustment in stepfamilies: How is it studied? What do we learn? *Child Indicators Research, 11*(6), 1831–1865.

Sakai, J. (2020). How synaptic pruning shapes neural wiring during development and, possibly, in disease. *Proceedings of the National Academy of Sciences, 117*(28), 16096-16099.

Sala, G., Tatlidil, K.S., & Gobet, F. (2018). Video game training does not enhance cognitive ability: A comprehensive meta-analytic investigation. *Psychological Bulletin, 144,* 111-139.

Sala, M., & others (2023). Predictors of relapse in eating disorders: A meta-analysis. *Journal of Psychiatric Research, 158,* 281-299.

Salcido, V.V., & Stein, G.L. (2023). Examining the influence of ethnic-racial socialization and parental warmth on Latinx youth psychosocial outcomes. *Journal of Latinx Psychology, 11,* 89-103.

Salmivalli, C., Laninga-Wijnen, L., Malamut, S.T., & Garandeau, C.F. (2021). Bullying prevention in adolescence: Solutions and new challenges from the past decade. *Journal of Research on Adolescence, 31,* 1023-1046.

Salmivalli, C., & Peets, K. (2018). Bullying and victimization. In W.M. Bukowski, B. Laursen, & K.H. Rubin (Eds.), *Handbook of peer interactions, relationships, and groups.* Guilford Press.

Salo, V.C., Rowe, M.L., & Reeb-Sutherland, B.C. (2018). Exploring infant gesture and joint attention as related constructs and as predictors of later language. *Infancy, 23,* 432-452.

Salsa, A.M., & Gariboldi, M.B. (2018). Symbolic experience and young children's comprehension of drawings in different socioeconomic contexts. *Avances en Psicología Latinoamericana, 36,* 29-44.

Sameroff, A.J. (2009). The transactional model. In A.J. Sameroff (Ed.), *The transactional model of development: How children and contexts shape each other.* American Psychological Association.

Sameroff, A.J. (2020). It's More Complicated. *Annual Review of Developmental Psychology, 2,* 1-26.

Sanapo, L., & others (2021). How prenatal head ultrasound reference ranges affect evaluation of possible fetal microcephaly. *Journal of Maternal-Fetal & Neonatal Medicine, 34*(15), 2529-2534.

Sánchez-Vincitore, L.V., Schaettle, P., & Castro, A. (2019). Validation of the Malawi Developmental Assessment Tool for children in the Dominican Republic: Preliminary results. *PloS One, 14*(8), e0221162.

Sanders, G.J., Marwa, W.L., Wade, B., & Gately, P. (2021). Efficacy of a county-wide schools weight management intervention. *Perspectives in Public Health, 142*(6), 319-327.

Sanders, K., & Farago, F. (2018). Developmentally appropriate practice in the twenty-first century. In M. Fleer & B. van Oers (Eds.), *International handbook of early childhood education.* Springer.

Sanders, M.R., Turner, K.M., & Metzler, C.W. (2019). Applying self-regulation principles in the delivery of parenting interventions. *Clinical Child and Family Psychology Review, 22*(1), 24-42.

Sandstrom, A., Uher, R., & Pavlova, B. (2020). Prospective association between childhood behavioral inhibition and anxiety: a meta-analysis. *Journal of Abnormal Child Psychology, 48*(1), 57-66.

Sankupellay, M., & others (2011). Characteristics of sleep EEG power spectra in healthy infants in the first two years of life. *Clinical Neurophysiology, 122,* 236-243.

Sanson, A., & Rothbart, M.K. (1995). Child temperament and parenting. In M.H. Bornstein (Ed.), *Handbook of parenting* (Vol. 4). Erlbaum.

Santangeli, L., Sattar, N., & Huda, S.S. (2015). Impact of maternal obesity on perinatal and child outcomes. *Best Practices and Research. Clinical Obstetrics and Gynecology, 29,* 438-448.

Santirocco, M., & others (2021). Accuracy of prenatal ultrasound in the diagnosis of corpus callosum anomalies. *The Journal of Maternal-Fetal & Neonatal Medicine, 34,* 439-444.

Santos, C.E., Komienko, O., & Rivas-Drake, D. (2017). Peer influences on ethnic-racial identity development: A multi-site investigation. *Child Development, 88,* 725-742.

Santos, L.M., & others (2016). Prevention of neural tube defects by fortification of flour with folic acid: A population-based retrospective study in Brazil. *Bulletin of the World Health Organization, 94,* 22-29.

Sardi, L., & others (2020). Mobile health applications for postnatal care: Review and analysis of functionalities and technical features. *Computer Methods and Programs in Biomedicine, 184,* 105114.

Sardinha, L.B., Magalhães, J.P., Santos, D.A., & Hetherington-Rauth, M. (2022). Intensity matters: Impact of physical activity energy expenditure at moderate and vigorous intensity on total and abdominal obesity in children. *European Journal of Clinical Nutrition,* 1-5.

Sauce, B., & Matzel, L.D. (2018). The paradox of intelligence: Heritability and malleability coexist in hidden gene-environment interplay. *Psychological Bulletin, 144,* 26-47.

Saul, A., & others (2019). Polymorphism in the serotonin transporter gene polymorphisms (5-HTTLPR) modifies the association between significant life events and depression in people with multiple sclerosis. *Multiple Sclerosis Journal, 25,* 848-855.

Saunders, M.C., & others (2019). The associations between callous-unemotional traits and symptoms of conduct problems, hyperactivity and emotional problems: A study of adolescent twins screened for neurodevelopmental problems. *Journal of Abnormal Child Psychology, 47,* 447-457.

Saunders, N.R., & others (2018). Physiology and molecular biology of barrier mechanisms in the fetal and neonatal brain. *The Journal of Physiology, 596*(23), 5723-5756.

Sävendahl, L., & others (2019). Treatment of children with GH in the United States and Europe: Long-term follow-up from NordiNet® IOS and ANSWER program. *The Journal of Clinical Endocrinology & Metabolism, 104*(10), 4730-4742.

Savina, E. (2021). Self-regulation in preschool and early elementary classrooms: Why it is important and how to promote it. *Early Childhood Education Journal, 49*(3), 493-501.

Savina, E., & Wan, K.P. (2017). Cultural pathways to socio-emotional development and learning. *Journal of Relationships Research, 8,* e19.

Savin-Williams, R.C. (2016). *Becoming who I am: Young men on being gay.* Harvard University Press.

Savin-Williams, R.C. (2017). *Mostly straight: Sexual fluidity among men.* Harvard University Press.

Sawyer, J. (2017). I think I can: Preschoolers' private speech and motivation in playful versus non-playful contexts. *Early Childhood Research Quarterly, 38,* 84-96.

Saxena, M., Srivastava, N., & Banerjee, M. (2017). Cytokine gene variants as predictors of type 2 diabetes mellitus. *Current Diabetes Review, 14*(3), 307-319.

Sbarra, D.A., & Whisman, M.A. (2022). Divorce, health, and socioeconomic status: An agenda for psychological science. *Current Opinion in Psychology, 43,* 75-78.

Scaife, J.C., & others (2017). Reduced resting-state functional connectivity in current and recovered restrictive anorexia nervosa. *Frontiers in Psychology, 8,* 30.

Scales, P.C., Benson, P.L., & Roehlkepartain, E.C. (2011). Adolescent thriving: The role of sparks, relationships, and empowerment. *Journal of Youth and Adolescence, 40*(3), 263-277.

Scales, P.C., Roehlkepartain, E.C., & Houltberg, B.J (2022). *The elements of developmental relationships: A review of selected research underlying the framework.* Search Institute.

Scarlett, W.G., & Warren, A.E.A. (2010). Religious and spiritual development across the life span: A behavioral and social science perspective. In M.E. Lamb, A.M. Freund, & R.M. Lerner (Eds.), *Handbook of life-span development.* Wiley.

Scarr, S. (1993). Biological and cultural diversity: The legacy of Darwin for development. *Child Development, 64,* 1333-1353.

Schaal, B. (2017). Infants and children making sense of scents. In A. Buettner (Ed.), *Springer handbook of odor* (pp. 107-108). Springer.

Schaefer, F., & others (2017). Cardiovascular phenotypes in children with CKD: The 4C study. *Clinical Journal of the American Society of Nephrology, 12,* 19-28.

Schäfer, M., Haun, D.B.M., & Tomasello, M. (2015). Fair is not fair everywhere. *Psychological Science, 26,* 1252-1260.

Schaffer, H.R. (1996). *Social development.* Blackwell.

Schalkwijk, F., & others (2016). The conscience as a regulatory function: Empathy, shame, pride, guilt, and moral orientation in delinquent adolescents. *International Journal of Offender Therapy and Comparative Criminology, 60,* 675-693.

Scheider, W., Tibken, C., & Richter, T. (2022). The development of metacognitive knowledge from childhood to young adulthood: Major trends and educational implications. In J.J. Lockman (Ed.), *Advances in child development and behavior* (pp. 274-307). Academic Press.

Schell, L.M., & Rousham, E.K. (2022). Environmental effects on growth. In N. Cameron & L. Schell (Eds.), *Human growth and development* (3rd ed.). New York: Academic Press.

Schermer, J.A., & Saklofske, D.P.H. (2021). Personality and intelligence. In P.J. Corr & G.

Matthews (Eds.), *Cambridge handbook of personality psychology.* Cambridge University Press.

Scherrer, V., & Preckel, F. (2019). Development of motivational variables and self-esteem during the school career: A meta-analysis of longitudinal studies. *Review of Educational Research, 89,* 211–258.

Schiariti, V., Simeonsson, R.J., & Hall, K. (2021). Promoting developmental potential in early childhood: A global framework for health and education. *International Journal of Environmental Research and Public Health, 18*(4), 2007.

Schiff, W.J. (2017). *Nutrition essentials* (5th ed.). McGraw Hill.

Schiff, W.J. (2021). *Nutrition essentials* (3rd ed.). McGraw Hill.

Schlam, T.R., Wilson, N.L., Shoda, Y., Mischel, W., & Ayduk, O. (2013). Preschoolers' delay of gratification predicts their body mass 30 years later. *Journal of Pediatrics, 162,* 90–93.

Schlegel, M. (2000). All work and play. *Monitor on Psychology, 31*(11), 50–51.

Schlegelmilch, K., & Wertz, A.E. (2021). Influences on the visual categorization of naturalistic structures in infancy and early childhood. *Journal of Vision, 21*(9), 2618.

Schmidt, J.A., Shumow, L., & Kackar, H. (2007). Adolescents' participation in service activities and its impact on academic, behavioral, and civic outcomes. *Journal of Youth and Adolescence, 36,* 127–140.

Schmidt, K.L., & others (2021). Society to cell: How child poverty gets "under the skin" to influence child development and lifelong health. *Developmental Review, 61,* 100983.

Schmitt, J.E., & others (2019). The dynamic associations between cortical thickness and general intelligence are genetically mediated. *Cerebral Cortex, 29,* 4743–4752.

Schneider, B. (2016). *Childhood friendship and peer relations.* Routledge.

Schneider, N., Greenstreet, E., & Deoni, S.C. (2022). Connecting inside out: Development of the social brain in infants and toddlers with a focus on myelination as a marker of brain maturation. *Child Development, 93*(2), 359–371.

Schneider, N., & others (2022). A nutrient formulation affects developmental myelination in term infants: A randomized clinical trial. *Frontiers in Nutrition, 9,* 823893.

Schneider, W. (2015). *Memory development from early childhood through emerging adulthood.* Springer.

Schoeler, T., Duncan, L., Cecil, C.M., Ploubidis, G.B., & Pingault, J.B. (2018). Quasi-experimental evidence on short- and long-term consequences of bullying victimization: A meta-analysis. *Psychological Bulletin, 144*(12), 1229–1246.

Schoon, I., Jones, E., Cheng, H., & Maughan, B. (2012). Family hardship, family instability, and cognitive development. *Journal of Epidemiology and Community Health, 66*(8), 716–722.

Schoppe-Sullivan, S.J., Shafer, K., Olofson, E.L., & Kamp Dush, C.M. (2021). Fathers' parenting and coparenting behavior in dual-earner families: Contributions of traditional masculinity, father nurturing role beliefs, and maternal gate closing. *Psychology of Men & Masculinities, 22*(3), 538–550.

Schoppmann, J., Schneider, S., & Seehagen, S. (2019). Wait and see: Observational learning of distraction as an emotion regulation strategy in 22-month-old toddlers. *Journal of Abnormal Child Psychology, 47*(5), 851–863.

Schreiber, S., & Pick, C.G. (2019). Cannabis use during pregnancy: Are we at the verge of defining a "fetal cannabis spectrum disorder"? *Medical Hypotheses, 124,* 53–55.

Schroeder, E., Tallarico, R., & Bakaroudis, M. (2022). The impact of adolescent initiation rites in East and Southern Africa: Implications for policies and practices. *International Journal of Adolescence and Youth, 27,* 181–192.

Schroeder, K.M., & Liben, L.S. (2021). Felt pressure to conform to cultural gender roles: Correlates and consequences. *Sex Roles, 84,* 125–138.

Schumm, W., & Crawford, D. (2019). Scientific consensus on whether LGBTQ parents are more likely (or not) to have LGBTQ children: An analysis of 72 social science reviews of the literature published between 2001 and 2017. *Journal of International Women's Studies, 20,* 1–12.

Schunk, D.H. (2020). *Learning theories: An educational perspective* (8th ed.). Prentice Hall.

Schunk, D.H., & Greene, J.A. (Eds.) (2018). *Handbook of self-regulation of learning and performance* (2nd ed.). Routledge.

Schutte, N.M., & others (2019). A twin study on the correlates of voluntary exercise behavior in adolescence. *Psychology of Sport and Exercise, 40,* 99–109.

Schutten, D., Stokes, K.A., & Arnell, K.M. (2017). I want to media multitask and I want to do it now: Individual differences in media multitasking predict delay of gratification and system-1 thinking. *Cognitive Research Principles and Implications, 2*(1), 8.

Schwalbe, C.S., Gearing, R.E., MacKenzie, M.J., Brewer, K.B., & Ibrahim, R. (2012). A meta-analysis of experimental studies of diversion programs for juvenile offenders. *Clinical Psychology Review, 32,* 26–33.

Schwartz, D., & others (2014). Peer victimization during middle childhood as a lead indicator of internalizing problems and diagnostic outcomes in late adolescence. *Journal of Clinical Child and Adolescent Psychology, 44*(3), 393–404.

Schwartz, S.J., & others (2015). The identity of acculturation and multiculturalism: Situation acculturation in context. In V. Benet-Martinez & Y.Y. Hong (Eds.), *Oxford handbook of multicultural identity.* Oxford University Press.

Schweinhart, L.J. (2019). Lessons on sustaining early gains from the life-course study of Perry Preschool. In A.J. Reynolds & J.A. Temple (Eds.), *Sustaining early childhood learning gains: Program, school, and family influences.* Cambridge University Press.

Schweinhart, L.J., & others (2005). *Lifetime effects: The High/Scope Petty Preschool study through age 40.* High/Scope Press.

Scott, R.M., & Baillargeon, R. (2017). Early false-belief understanding. *Trends in Cognitive Science, 21,* 237–249.

Scupin, R., & DeCorse, C.R. (2017). *Anthropology* (8th ed.). Pearson.

Sebastiani, G., & others (2018). The effects of alcohol and drugs of abuse on maternal nutritional profile during pregnancy. *Nutrients, 10*(8), 1008.

Segal, N.L., Montoya, Y.S., & Becker, E.N. (2018). Twins reared apart and twins in families: The findings behind the fascination. *Twin Research and Human Genetics, 21,* 295–301.

Segars, J., & others (2020). Prior and novel coronaviruses, COVID-19, and human reproduction: What is known? *Fertility and Sterility, 113*(6), 1140–1149.

Sege, R.D., & others (2018). Effective discipline to raise healthy children. *Pediatrics, 142*(6), e20183112.

Seibert, A., & Kerns, K. (2015). Early mother-child attachment: Longitudinal prediction to the quality of peer relationships in middle childhood. *International Journal of Behavioral Development, 39,* 130–138.

Selman, R. (2003). *Promotion of social awareness.* Russell Sage Foundation.

Seltzer, J.A. (2019). Family change and changing family demography. *Demography, 56*(2), 405–426.

Selvam, S., & others (2018). Development of norms for executive functions in typically developing Indian urban preschool children and its association with nutritional status. *Child Neuropsychology, 24,* 226–246.

Semega, J., & others (2020, September 15). *Income and poverty in the United States: 2019.* Report No. P60-27. U.S. Census Bureau.

Sénat, M.V., & others (2018). Prevention and management of genital herpes simplex infection during pregnancy and delivery: Guidelines from the French College of Gynaecologists and Obstetricians (CNGOF). *European Journal of Obstetrics & Gynecology and Reproductive Biology, 224,* 93–101.

Serpell, R. (2019). Perspectivist challenges for ECD intervention in Africa. In A.T. Kjørholt & H. Penn (Eds.), *Early childhood and development work.* Palgrave Macmillan,

Sethna, V., & others (2017). Father-child interactions at 3 months and 24 months: Contributions to children's cognitive development at 24 months. *Infant Mental Health Journal, 38*(3), 378–390.

Sethna, V., & others (2018). Depression and playfulness in fathers and young infants: Physical play with peaks of emotional excitement in 3-month father-infant interactions. *Journal of Affective Disorders, 229,* 364–370.

Shago, M. (2017). Chromosome preparation for acute lymphoblastic leukemia. *Methods in Molecular Biology, 1541,* 19–31.

Shah, M.K., & Austin, K.R. (2014). Do home visiting services received during pregnancy improve birth outcomes? Findings from Virginia PRAMS 2007-2008. *Public Health Nursing, 31,* 405-413.

Shahaeian, A., Haynes, M., & Frick, P.J. (2023). The role of language in the association between theory of mind and executive functioning in early childhood: New longitudinal evidence. *Early Childhood Research Quarterly, 62,* 251-258.

Shakiba, N., & others (2020). Biological sensitivity to context: A test of the hypothesized U-shaped relation between early adversity and stress responsivity. *Development and Psychopathology, 32*(2), 641-660.

Shapiro, A., Gottman, J., & Fink, B. (2015). Short-term change in couples' conflict following a transition to parenthood intervention. *Couple & Family Psychology: Research & Practice, 4*(4), 239-251.

Shapiro, A.F., Gottman, J.M., & Fink, B.C. (2020). Father's involvement when bringing baby home: Efficacy testing of a couple-focused transition to parenthood intervention for promoting father involvement. *Psychological Reports, 123*(3), 806-824.

Shapiro, J.R. (2018). Stranger wariness. In M. Bornstein & others (Eds.), *SAGE encyclopedia of lifespan human development.* Sage.

Sharma, S., & Lazar, A.M. (2019). 21st century diversity, educational equity, and transformative change. In A. Sharma & A. Lazar (Eds.), *Rethinking 21st century diversity in teacher preparation, K-12 education, and school policy.* Springer.

Shaw, K.M., West, B., Kendi, S., Zonfrillo, M.R., & Sauber-Schatz, E. (2022). Urban and rural child deaths from motor vehicle crashes: United States, 2015-2019. *Journal of Pediatrics, 250,* 93-99.

Shaw, P., & others (2007). Attention-deficit/ hyperactivity disorder is characterized by a delay in cortical maturation. *Proceedings of the National Academy of Sciences USA, 104,* 19649-19654.

Shea, C., & O'Neill, S.O. (2021). Phonetics: Sound articulation and acoustics. In J. Bruhn de Garavito & J.W. Schwieter (Eds.), *Introducing linguistics.* Cambridge University Press.

Shebloski, B., Conger, K.J., & Widaman, K.F. (2005). Reciprocal links among differential parenting, perceived partiality, and self-worth: A three-wave longitudinal study. *Journal of Family Psychology, 19,* 633-642.

Sheffler, P.C., & Cheung, C.S. (2020). The role of peer mindsets in students' learning: An experimental study. *British Journal of Educational Psychology, 90*(Suppl. 1), S17-S34.

Sheinman, N., Hadar, L.L., Gafni, D., & Milman, M. (2018). Preliminary investigation of whole-school mindfulness in education programs and children's mindfulness-based coping strategies. *Journal of Child and Family Studies, 27*(1), 1316-1328.

Shen, M., DeLay, D., Purwono, U., & French, D.C. (2023). Peer relationships and Indonesian Muslim adolescents' religiosity and religious coping: Selection and influence. *Journal of Research on Adolescence, 33,* 127-140.

Shenhav, A., & Greene, J.D. (2014). Integrative moral judgment: Dissociating the roles of the amygdala and the ventromedial prefrontal cortex. *Journal of Neuroscience, 34,* 4741-4749.

Shenhav, S., Campos, B., & Goldberg, W.A. (2017). Dating out is intercultural: Experience and perceived parent disapproval by ethnicity and immigrant generation. *Journal of Social and Personal Relationships, 34*(3), 397-422.

Shenoda, B.B. (2017). An overview of the mechanisms of abnormal GABAergic interneuronal cortical migration associated with prenatal ethanol exposure. *Neurochemical Research, 42,* 1279-1287.

Shephard, E., & others (2019). Early developmental pathways to childhood symptoms of attention-deficit hyperactivity disorder, anxiety and autism spectrum disorder. *Journal of Child Psychology and Psychiatry, 60*(9), 963-974.

Sherman, D.F., & others (2020). Trans* community connection, health, and wellbeing: A systematic review. *LGBT Health, 7,* 1-14.

Shetgiri, R., Lin, H., Avila, R.M., & Flores, G. (2012). Parental characteristics associated with bullying perpetration in U.S. children aged 10 to 17 years. *American Journal of Public Health, 102,* 2280-2286.

Shields, B. (2020, July 18). Homeless to regional director: Rakaya Humphreys can help Head Start families from experience. *Jackson Sun.* URL: https: //www.jacksonsun.com/story/news/2020/07/18 /rakaya-humphreys-can-help-head-start-families-experience/5422007002/

Shiino, A., & others (2017). Sex-related difference in human white matter volumes studied: Inspection of the corpus callosum and other white matter by VBM. *Scientific Reports, 7,* 39818.

Shimizu, M., & others (2021). Trajectories of sleep problems in childhood: Associations with mental health in adolescence. *Sleep, 44*(3), zsaa190.

Shimony-Kanat, S., & Benbenishty, J. (2018). Age, ethnicity, and socioeconomic factors impacting infant and toddler fall-related trauma. *Pediatric Emerging Care, 34*(10), 696-701.

Shin, D.D., Lee, M., & Bong, M. (2022). Beyond left and right: Learning is a whole-brain process. *Theory into Practice, 61*(3), 347-357.

Shin, J., & Lee, B. (2021). The effects of adolescent prosocial behavior interventions: A meta-analytic review. *Asia Pacific Education Review, 22,* 565-577.

Shin, M., & Bolkan, S. (2021). Intellectually stimulating students' intrinsic motivation: The mediating influence of student engagement, self-efficacy, and student support. *Communication Education, 70,* 146-164.

Shiner, R. (2019). Negative emotion and neuroticism from childhood through adulthood. In D.P. McAdams & others (Eds.), *Handbook of personality development* (pp. 137-152). Guilford Press.

Shiner, R.L. (2021). Personality development in middle childhood. In O.P. John & R.W. Robins

(Eds.), *Handbook of personality: Theory and research* (pp. 284-302). Guilford Press.

Shockley, K.M., & others (2017). Disentangling the relationship between gender and work-family conflict: An integration of theoretical perspectives using meta-analytic methods. *Journal of Applied Psychology, 102*(12), 1601.

Shulman, E., Harden, K., Chein, J., & Steinberg, L. (2016). The development of impulse control and sensation-seeking in adolescence: Independent and interdependent processes? *Journal of Research on Adolescence, 26,* 37-44.

Shulman, E., & others (2016). The dual systems model: Review, reappraisal, and reaffirmation. *Developmental Cognitive Neuroscience, 17,* 103-117.

Sicard-Cras, I., & others (2022). A review of the characteristics, mechanisms and clinical significance of habituation in foetuses and newborn infants. *Acta Paediatrica, 111*(2), 245-258.

Siegel, D.H. (2013). Open adoption: Adoptive parents' reactions two decades later. *Social Work, 58,* 43-52.

Siegel, J. (2020). Neurological emergencies in pregnant patients. In A. Rabinstein (Ed.), *Neurological Emergencies* (pp. 357-375). Springer.

Siegler, R.S. (2016a). Continuity and change in the field of cognitive development and in the perspective of one cognitive developmentalist. *Child Development Perspectives, 10,* 128-133.

Siegler, R.S. (2016b). How does change occur? In R. Sternberg, S. Fiske, & D. Foss (Eds.), *Scientists make a difference: One hundred eminent behavioral and brain scientists talk about their most important contributions.* Cambridge University Press.

Siegler, R.S. (2017). Foreword: Build it and they will come. In D.G. Geary & others (Eds.), *Acquisition of complex arithmetic skills and higher order mathematics concepts.* Academic Press.

Siegler, R.S. (2022). Development of numerical knowledge. In O. Houdé & G. Borst (Eds.), *The Cambridge handbook of cognitive development.* Cambridge University Press.

Siegler, R.S., & Alibali, M.W. (2020). *Children's thinking* (5th ed.). Pearson.

Siegler, R.S., & Braithwaite, D.W. (2017). Numerical development. *Annual Review of Psychology, 68,* 187-213.

Sifre, R., & others (2018). A longitudinal investigation of preferential attention to biological motion in 2- to 24-month-old infants. *Scientific Reports, 8,* 2527.

Silva, K., Chein, J., & Steinberg, L. (2016). Adolescents in peer groups make more prudent decisions when a slightly older adult is present. *Psychological Science, 27*(3), 322-330.

Silventoinen, K., & Konttinen, H. (2020). Obesity and eating behavior from the perspective of twin and genetic research. *Neuroscience & Biobehavioral Reviews, 109,* 150-165.

Silverman, M.E., & others (2017). The risk factors for postpartum depression: A population-based study. *Depression and Anxiety, 34,* 178-187.

Simmonds, D.J., Hallquist, M.N., & Luna, B. (2017). Protracted development of executive and mnemonic brain systems underlying working memory in adolescence: A longitudinal fMRI study. *Neuroimage, 157*, 695–704.

Simmonds, M., Llewellyn, A., Owen, C.G., & Woolacott, N. (2016). Predicting adult obesity from childhood obesity: A systematic review and meta-analysis. *Obesity Reviews, 17*(2), 95–107.

Simmons, C., & others (2020). The relation between callous-unemotional traits, psychosocial maturity, and delinquent behavior among justice-involved youth. *Child Development, 91*(1), e120–e133.

Simmons, R.G., & Blyth, D.A. (1987). *Moving into adolescence.* Aldine.

Simon, E.J. (2017). *Biology* (2nd ed.). Pearson.

Simon, S.L., & others (2021). A model of adolescent sleep health and risk for type 2 diabetes. *Current Diabetes Reports, 21*(2), 4.

Simonato, I., Janosz, M., Archambault, M., & Pagani, L.S. (2018). Prospective associations between toddler televiewing and subsequent lifestyle habits in adolescence. *Preventive Medicine, 110,* 24–30.

Simons, L.G., & others (2016). Mechanisms that link parenting practices to adolescents' risky sexual behavior: A test of six competing theories. *Journal of Youth and Adolescence, 45*, 255–270.

Simos, P.G., & others (2007). Altering the brain circuits for reading through intervention: A magnetic source imaging study. *Neuropsychology, 21,* 485–496.

Sims, R.N., & others (2022). Desire to play with counterstereotypical peers is related to gender stereotypes and playmate experiences. *Developmental Psychology, 58*(3), 510–521.

Singarajah, A., & others (2017). Infant attention to same- and other-race faces. *Cognition, 159,* 76–84.

Singer, D., Golinkoff, R.M., & Hirsh-Pasek, K. (Eds.) (2006). *Play = learning: How play motivates and enhances children's cognitive and social-emotional growth.* Oxford University Press.

Singh, N.N., & others (2016). Effects of Samatha meditation on active academic engagement and math performance of students with attention-deficit/hyperactivity disorder. *Mindfulness, 7,* 68–75.

Sinha, C. (2017). Language as a biocultural niche and social institution. In *Ten lectures on language, culture and mind* (pp. 138–154). Brill.

Sireci, S.G., & Randall, J. (2021). Evolving notions of fairness in testing in the United States. In B.E. Clauser & M.B. Bunch (Eds.), *The History of Educational Measurement* (pp. 111–135). Routledge.

Skelton, A.E., & Franklin, A. (2020). Infants look longer at colours that adults like when colours are highly saturated. *Psychonomic Bulletin & Review, 27,* 78–85.

Skinner, A.T., Oburu, P., Lansford, J.E., & Bacchini, D. (2014). Childrearing violence and child adjustment after exposure to Kenyan post-election violence. *Psychology of Violence, 4,* 37–50.

Skinner, A.T., & others (2021). Parent-adolescent relationship quality as a moderator of links between COVID-19 disruption and reported changes in mothers' and young adults' adjustment in five countries. *Developmental Psychology, 57,* 1648–1666.

Skinner, B.F. (1938). *The behavior of organisms: An experimental analysis.* Appleton-Century-Crofts.

Skinner, B.F. (1957). *Verbal behavior.* Appleton-Century-Crofts.

Skinner, E.A., Kindermann, T.A., Vollet, J.W., & Rickert, N.P. (2022). Complex social ecologies and the development of academic motivation. *Educational Psychology Review, 34,* 2129–2165.

Skinner, E.A., & Saxton, E.A. (2020). The development of academic coping across late elementary and early middle school: Do patterns differ for students with differing motivational resources? *International Journal of Behavioral Development, 44,* 339–353.

Sladek, M.R., & others (2020). Testing invariance of ethnic-racial discrimination and identity measures for adolescents across ethnic-racial groups and contexts. *Psychological Assessment, 33,* 509–526.

Slagt, M., Dubas, J.S., Deković, M., & van Aken, M.A. (2016). Differences in sensitivity to parenting depending on child temperament: A meta-analysis. *Psychological Bulletin, 142,* 1068–1110.

Slater, A., Morison, V., & Somers, M. (1988). Orientation discrimination and cortical function in the human newborn. *Perception, 17,* 597–602.

Slater, A.M., Bremner, J.G., Johnson, S.P., & Hayes, R. (2011). The role of perceptual processes in infant addition/subtraction events. In L.M. Oakes, C.H. Cashon, M. Casasola, & D.H. Rakison (Eds.), *Early perceptual and cognitive development.* Oxford University Press.

Slater, D.A., & others (2019). Evolution of white matter tract microstructure across the life span. *Human Brain Mapping, 40*(7), 2252–2268.

Slater, S.J., & others (2021). Encouraging "active learning": Assessing the implementation of Head Start's physical activity requirements within the teaching and learning environment. *Journal of Physical Activity and Health, 17*(11), 1109–1117.

Sleet, D. (2018). The global challenge of child injury prevention. *International Journal of Environmental Research and Public Health, 15*(9), 1921.

Slobin, D. (1972, July). Children and language: They learn the same way around the world. *Psychology Today,* 71–76.

Slone, L.K., & others (2018). Gaze in action: Head-mounted eye tracking of children's dynamic visual attention during naturalistic behavior. *JoVE (Journal of Visualized Experiments), 141,* e58496.

Slone, L.K., & Sandhofer, C.M. (2017). Consider the category: The effect of spacing depends on individual learning histories. *Journal of Experimental Child Psychology, 159,* 34–49.

Sly, P., & Bush, A. (2019). Environmental contributions to respiratory disease in children. In R.W. Wilmott & others (Eds.), *Kendig's disorders of the respiratory tract in children* (9th ed., pp. 49–56). Elsevier.

Small, S.A., Ishida, I.M., & Stapells, D.R. (2017). Infant cortical auditory evoked potentials to lateralized noise shifts produced by changes in interaural time difference. *Ear and Hearing, 38,* 94–102.

Smetana, J.G. (2017). The development of autonomy during adolescence: A social-cognitive domain theory view. In B. Soenens, M. Vansteenkiste, & S. van Petegem (Eds.), *Autonomy in adolescent development: Towards conceptual clarity.* Psychology Press.

Smetana, J.G., & Rote, W.M. (2019). Adolescent-parent relationships: Progress, processes, and prospects. *Annual Review of Developmental Psychology, 1,* 41–68.

Smetana, J.G., Wong, M., Ball, C., & Yau, J. (2014). American and Chinese children's evaluations of personal domain events and resistance to parental authority. *Child Development, 85,* 626–642.

Smith, D.D., & others (2018). *Introduction to contemporary special education* (2nd ed.). Pearson

Smith, E.R., & others (2017). Barriers and enablers of health system adoption of kangaroo care: A systematic review of caregiver perspectives. *BMC Pediatrics, 17*(1), 35.

Smith, J., & Ross, H. (2007). Training parents to mediate sibling disputes affects children's negotiation and conflict understanding. *Child Development, 78,* 790–805.

Smith, P.K. (Ed.) (2019). *Making an impact on school bullying: Interventions and recommendations.* Routledge.

Smith, R.P. (2017). *Netter's obstetrics and gynecology* (3rd ed.). Elsevier.

Smolucha, L., & Smolucha, F. (2021). Vygotsky's theory in-play: Early childhood education. *Early Child Development and Care, 191,* 1–15.

Smortchkova, J., & Shea, N. (2020). Metacognitive development and conceptual change in children. *Review of Philosophy and Psychology, 11,* 745–763.

Snarey, J. (1987, June). A question of morality. *Psychology Today,* 6–8.

Snow, C.E. (2010). Commentary in E. Galinsky, *Meaning in the making.* Harperstudio.

Snow, C.E., & Beals, D.E. (2006, Spring). Mealtime talk that supports literacy development. *New Directions for Child and Adolescent Development, 111,* 51–66.

Snowling, M.J., & others (2019). Developmental outcomes for children at high risk of dyslexia and children with developmental language disorder. *Child Development, 90*(5), e548–e564.

Snyder, B. (2019). United States paid parental leave and infant mortality. *International Journal of Sociology and Social Policy, 40*(1–2), 145–153.

Society of Health and Physical Educators (2022). National physical education standards. https://www.shapeamerica.org/standards/pe/

Soenens, B., & Vansteenkiste, M. (2020). Taking adolescents' agency in socialization seriously: The role of appraisals and cognitive-behavioral responses in autonomy-relevant parenting. *New Directions for Child and Adolescent Development, 2*, 7–26.

Soesanti, F., & others (2019). Antenatal exposure to secondhand smoke of non-smoking mothers and growth rate of their infants. *PloS One, 14*(6), e0218577.

Sokol, R.L., Qin, B., & Poti, J.M. (2017). Parenting styles and body mass index: A systematic review of prospective studies among children. *Obesity Reviews, 18*, 281–292.

Solovieva, Y., & Quintanar, L. (2017). Play with social roles as a method for psychological development in young children. In T. Bruce & others (Eds.), *Routledge international handbook of early childhood play*. Routledge.

Somerville, L.H., & others (2018). The Lifespan Human Connectome Project in Development: A large-scale study of brain connectivity development in 5–21-year-olds. *NeuroImage, 183*, 456–468.

Sommer, T.E., & others (2020). A two-generation education intervention and children's attendance in Head Start. *Child Development, 91*, 1916–1933.

Son, D., & Padilla-Walker, L.M. (2022). Longitudinal associations among perceived intrusive parental monitoring, adolescent internalization of values, and adolescent information management. *Journal of Child and Family Studies, 31*, 48–60.

Song, W., & Qian, X. (2020). Adverse childhood experiences and teen sexual behaviors: The role of self-regulation and school-related factors. *Journal of School Health, 90*, 830–841.

Sood, A., & Sood, N. (2020) Pain relief in labor. In A. Sharma (Ed.), *Labour room emergencies*. Springer.

Sorbring, E., & Lansford, J.E. (Eds.) (2019). *School systems, parent behavior, and academic achievement: An international perspective*. Springer.

Sorensen, L.C., Dodge, K.A., & Conduct Problems Prevention Research Group (2016). How does the Fast Track intervention prevent adverse outcomes in young adulthood? *Child Development, 87*, 429–445.

Soria, R.V., Bernabé, E., & Perez, M.L.S. (2019). Acculturation and dental caries among children in Spain. *Journal of Immigrant and Minority Health, 21*(4), 699–705.

Sørlie, M.A., Hagen, K.A., & Nordahl, K.B. (2021). Development of social skills during middle childhood: Growth trajectories and school-related predictors. *International Journal of School & Educational Psychology, 9*(Suppl.1), S69–S87.

Sorte, J., Amador, C., Daeschel, I., & Brinkenmeyer, L. (2020). *Nutrition, health, and safety for young children: Promoting wellness* (4th ed.). Pearson.

Sortheix, F.M., Weber, W., Lilleoja, L., Renvik, T.A., & Sánchez-Montijano, E. (2023). Arab Mediterranean youth's values: The role of values and value congruence on intentions to emigrate. *International Journal of Intercultural Relations, 93*, 101758.

Souza, B.G., & others (2017). Parental awareness and perception for correct use of child restraint systems and airbags in Brazil. *Traffic Injury Prevention, 18*, 171–174.

Spaziani, M., & others (2021). Hypohalamo-pituitary axis and puberty. *Molecular and Cellular Endocrinology, 520*, 111094.

Spelke, E.S. (2017). Core knowledge, language, and number. *Language Learning and Development, 13*(2), 147–170.

Spelke, E.S., & Owsley, C.J. (1979). Intermodal exploration and knowledge in infancy. *Infant Behavior and Development, 2*, 13–28.

Spence, J.T., & Helmreich, R. (1978). *Masculinity and femininity: Their psychological dimensions*. University of Texas Press.

Spencer, D., & others (2021). Prenatal androgen exposure and children's gender-typed behavior and toy and playmate preferences. *Hormones and Behavior, 127*, 104889.

Spencer, J.P., & others (2009). Short arms and talking eggs: Why we should no longer abide the nativist–empiricist debate. *Child Development Perspectives, 3*, 79–87.

Spilman, S.K., Neppl, T.K., Donnellan, M.B., Schofield, T.J., & Conger, R.D. (2013). Incorporating religiosity into a developmental model of positive family functioning across generations. *Developmental Psychology, 49*(4), 762–774.

Spinelli, M., Fasolo, M., & Mesman, J. (2017). Does prosody make the difference? A meta-analysis on relations between prosodic aspects of infant-directed speech and infant outcomes. *Developmental Review, 44*, 1–18.

Spinrad, T.L., & Eisenberg, N. (2019). Prosocial emotions. In V. LoBue & others (Eds.), *Handbook of emotional development* (pp. 351–372). Springer.

Spinrad, T.L., Eisenberg, N., & Valiente, C. (2019). Parenting and children's prosocial development. In M.H. Bornstein (Ed.), *Handbook of parenting: The practice of parenting* (3rd ed., Vol. 5, pp. 91–121). Routledge.

Spirito, A., & others (2021). Predictors and moderators of marijuana and heavy alcohol use outcomes in adolescents treated for co-occurring substance use and psychiatric disorders in a randomized controlled trial. *Journal of Substance Abuse Treatment, 131*, 108536.

Sroufe, L.A. (2016). The place of attachment in development. In J. Cassidy & P.R. Shaver (Eds.), *Handbook of attachment* (3rd ed.). Guilford Press.

Stadd, K., & others (2020). A kangaroo care pathway for NICU staff and families: The proof is in the pouch. *Advances in Neonatal Care, 20*(1), 14–24.

Stadelmann, S., & others (2017). Self-esteem of 8–14-year-old children with psychiatric disorders: Disorder- and gender-specific effects. *Child Psychiatry & Human Development, 48*(1), 40–52.

Stahl, A.E., & Feigenson, L. (2019). Violations of core knowledge shape early learning. *Topics in Cognitive Science, 11*(1), 136–153.

Stanford University Medical Center (2017). *Growth hormone deficiency*. Author.

Stangor, C. (2015). *Research methods for the behavioral sciences* (5th ed.). Cengage.

Starmans, C. (2017). Children's theories of the self. *Child Development, 88*(6), 1774–1785.

Starr, C., Evers, C., & Starr, L. (2018). *Biology* (10th ed.). Cengage.

State of Childhood Obesity (2020). *National obesity monitor*. Retrieved November 27, 2019, from https://stateofchildhoodobesity.org/monitor/

Steele, H., & Steele, J. (Eds.) (2019). *Handbook of attachment-based interventions*. Guilford Press.

Steiger, A.E., Allemand, M., Robins, R.W., & Fend, H.A. (2014). Low and decreasing self-esteem during adolescence predict adult depression two decades later. *Journal of Personality and Social Psychology, 106*, 325–338.

Stein, G.L., & others (2018). The intersection of racial–ethnic socialization and adolescence: A closer examination at stage-salient issues. *Journal of Research on Adolescence, 28*(3), 609–621.

Steinberg, L. (2011). Adolescent risk-taking: A social neuroscience perspective. In E. Amsel & J. Smetana (Eds.), *Adolescent vulnerabilities and opportunities: Constructivist developmental perspectives*. Cambridge University Press.

Steinberg, L., & others (2018). Around the world, adolescence is a time of heightened sensation seeking and immature self-regulation. *Developmental Science, 21*(2), e12532.

Stern, D.N., Beebe, B., Jaffe, J., & Bennett, S.L. (1977). The infant's stimulus world during social interaction: A study of caregiver behaviors with particular reference to repetition and timing. In H.R. Schaffer (Ed.), *Studies in mother-infant interaction*. Academic Press.

Stern, M.J., & Axinn, J. (2017). *Social welfare: A history of the American response to need* (9th ed.). Pearson.

Sternberg, R., Ambrose, D., & Karami, S. (Eds.) (2022). *The Palgrave handbook of transformational giftedness for education*. Palgrave Macmillan.

Sternberg, R.J. (2017a). Intelligence and competence in theory and practice. In A.J. Elliot, C.S. Dweck, & D.S. Yeager (Eds.), *Handbook of competence and motivation: Theory and application* (pp. 9–24). Guilford Press.

Sternberg, R.J. (2018a). The triarchic theory of successful intelligence. In D.P. Flanagan & E.M. McDonough (Eds.), Contemporary intellectual assessment: Theories, tests, and issues (4th ed.). Guilford Press.

Sternberg, R.J. (2020c). Intelligence and creativity. In R.J. Sternberg (Ed.), *Cambridge handbook of intelligence*. Cambridge University Press.

Sternberg, R.J. (2021a). *Adaptive intelligence*. Cambridge University Press.

Sternberg, R.J. (2021b). *The nature of intelligence and its development in childhood*. Cambridge University Press.

Sternberg, R.J., & Halpern, D.F. (Eds.) (2020). *Critical thinking in psychology* (3rd ed.). Cambridge University Press.

Sternberg, R.J., & Kaufman, J.C. (2018b). Societal forces that erode creativity. *Teachers College Record, 120*(5).

Stevenson, A., Wainwright, N., & Williams, A. (2023). Interventions targeting motor skills in pre-school-aged children with direct or indirect parent engagement: A systematic review and narrative synthesis. *International Journal of Primary, Elementary and Early Years Education, 51,* 1003–1016.

Steward, D.J. (2015). The history of neonatal anesthesia. In J. Lerman (Ed.), *Neonatal anesthesia* (pp. 1–15). Springer.

St. George, S.M., & others (2020). A developmental cascade perspective of pediatric obesity: A systematic review of preventive interventions from infancy through late adolescence. *Obesity Reviews, 21*(2), e12939.

Stice, E., & others (2017). Risk factors that predict future onset of each *DSM-5* eating disorder: Predictive specificity in high-risk adolescent females. *Journal of Abnormal Psychology, 126,* 38–51.

Stienwandt, S., & others (2022). Family factors associated with hands-on play and screen time during the COVID-19 pandemic. *Child and Youth Care Forum, 51,* 1091–1115.

Stiggins, R. (2008). *Introduction to student-involved assessment for learning* (5th ed.). Prentice Hall.

Stiglic, N., & Viner, R.M. (2019). Effects of screen time on the health and well-being of children and adolescents: A systematic review of reviews. *BMJ Open, 9*(1), e023191.

Stipek, D.J. (2002). *Motivation to learn* (4th ed.). Allyn & Bacon.

Stone, A., & Bosworth, R.G. (2019). Exploring infant sensitivity to visual language using eye tracking and the preferential looking paradigm. *JoVE (Journal of Visualized Experiments), 147,* e59581.

Stoner, L., & others (2019). Exercise dose and weight loss in adolescents with overweight-obesity: A meta-regression. *Sports Medicine, 49*(1), 83–94.

Stout, W., & others (2021). A longitudinal study of the differential social-cognitive foundations of early prosocial behaviors. *Infancy, 26,* 271–290.

Strassberg, D.S., Cann, D., & Velarde, V. (2017). Sexting by high school students. *Archives of Sexual Behavior, 46*(6), 1667–1672.

Stright, A.D., Herr, M.Y., & Neitzel, C. (2009). Maternal scaffolding of children's problem solving and children's adjustment in kindergarten: Hmong families in the United States. *Journal of Educational Psychology, 101,* 207–218.

Strong, D.R., & others (2017). Pre-adolescent receptivity to tobacco marketing and its relationship to acquiring friends who smoke and cigarette smoking initiation. *Annals of Behavioral Medicine, 51*(5), 730–740.

Stronge, S., Shaver, J.H., Bulbulia, J., & Sibley, C.G. (2019). Only children in the 21st century: Personality differences between adults with and without siblings are very, very small. *Journal of Research in Personality, 83,* 103868.

Strudwick-Alexander, M.A. (2017). Identity achievement as a predictor of intimacy in young urban Jamaican adults. In K. Carpenter (Ed.), *Interweaving tapestries of culture and sexuality in the Caribbean* (pp. 191–221). Palgrave Macmillan.

Stuebe, A.M., & others (2017). An online calculator to estimate the impact of changes in breastfeeding rates on population health and costs. *Breastfeeding Medicine, 12*(10).

Stump, G. (2017). The nature and dimensions of complexity in morphology. *Annual Review of Linguistics, 3,* 65–83.

Suarez-Alvarez, J., & others (2020). Editorial: Bridging the gap between research and policy in fostering social and emotional skills. *Frontiers in Psychology, 11,* 426.

Suárez-Orozco, C., López Hernández, G., & Cabral, P. (2021). The rippling effects of unauthorized status: Stress, family separations, and deportation and their implications for belonging and development. In P. Tummala-Narra (Ed.), *Trauma and racial minority immigrants: Turmoil, uncertainty, and resistance* (pp. 185–203). American Psychological Association.

Sucksdorff, M., & others (2018). Lower Apgar scores and Caesarean sections are related to attention-deficit/hyperactivity disorder. *Acta Paediatrica, 107*(10), 1750–1758.

Sue, D.W., Sue, D., Neville, H.A., & Smith, L. (2019). *Counseling the culturally diverse: Theory and practice* (8th ed.). Wiley.

Sugden, N.A., & Moulson, M.C. (2017). Hey baby, what's "up"? One- and 3-month-olds experience faces primarily upright but non-upright faces offer the best views. *Quarterly Journal of Experimental Psychology, 70,* 959–969.

Sugimura, K., Gmelin, J.-O.H., van der Gaag, M.A.E., & Kunnen, E.S. (2022). Exploring exploration: Identity exploration in real-time interactions among peers. *Identity, 22,* 17–34.

Sugimura, K., Matsushima, K., Hihara, S., Takahashi, M., & Crocetti, E. (2019). A culturally sensitive approach to the relationships between identity formation and religious beliefs in youth. *Journal of Youth and Adolescence, 48,* 668–679.

Sugimura, K., & others (2018). A cross-cultural perspective on the relationships between emotional separation, parental trust, and identity in adolescents. *Journal of Youth and Adolescence, 47*(4), 749–759.

Sugimura, K., Umemura, T., & Nelson, L.J. (2021). Identity development in East Asia. In B.G. Adams & F.J.R. van de Vijver (Eds.), *Non-Western identity.* Springer.

Suh, B.L., & Kang, M.J. (2020). Maternal reactions to preschoolers' negative emotions and aggression: Gender difference in mediation of emotion regulation. *Journal of Child and Family Studies, 29*(1), 144–154.

Sullivan, H.S. (1953). *The interpersonal theory of psychiatry.* W.W. Norton.

Sullivan, R., & Wilson, D. (2018). Neurobiology of infant attachment. *Annual Review of Psychology,* (Vol. 69).

Sumner, E.M., & Ramirez, A. (2019). The effects of multimodal communication frequency, geographic distance, and coresidence on parent-child relationship quality during emerging adulthood. *Communication Research Reports, 36,* 114–125.

Sun, Q., & Geeraert, N. (2021). We are (migrant) families: The interdependence between family members' actual and perceived acculturation. *International Journal of Intercultural Relations, 82,* 74–80.

Sun, X., Li, Y., Cai, L., & Wang, Y. (2021). Effects of physical activity interventions on cognitive performance of overweight or obese children and adolescents: A systematic review and meta-analysis. *Pediatric Research, 89*(1), 46–53.

Sun, Y., & others (2012). National estimates of the pubertal milestones among urban and rural Chinese girls. *Journal of Adolescent Health, 51,* 279–284.

Sun, Y., & others (2017). Childhood social disadvantage and pubertal timing: A national birth cohort from Australia. *Pediatrics, 139*(6), e20164099.

Sunderam, S., & others (2017). Assisted reproduction technology surveillance—United States 2014. *MMWR Surveillance Summaries, 66*(6), 1–24.

Super, C.M., & Harkness, S. (2010). Culture in infancy. In J.G. Bremner & T.D. Wachs (Eds.), *Wiley-Blackwell handbook of infant development* (2nd ed.). Wiley.

Surkan, P.J., & others (2019). Paternal involvement and support and risk of preterm birth: Findings from the Boston birth cohort. *Journal of Psychosomatic Obstetrics & Gynecology, 40*(1), 48–56.

Susman, E.J. (2019). Stress, biomarkers, and resilience in childhood and adolescence: Advances in the last few decades. In A. Harrist & B. Gardner (Eds.), *Biobehavioral markers in risk and resilience research* (pp. 91–109). Springer.

Sutin, A.R., Robinson, E., Daly, M., & Terracciarno, A. (2016). Parent-reported bullying and child weight gain between 6 and 15. *Child Obesity, 12,* 482–487.

Sutter, C.C., Haugen, J.S., Campbell, L.O., & Jones, J.L.T. (2023). School and electronic bullying among adolescents: Direct and indirect relationships with sadness, sleep, and suicide ideation. *Journal of Adolescence, 95,* 82–96.

Sutton, T.E. (2019). Review of attachment theory: Familial predictors, continuity and change, and intrapersonal and relational outcomes. *Marriage & Family Review, 55*(1), 1–22.

Svaldi, J., & others (2019). Efficacy of psychotherapies and pharmacotherapies for bulimia nervosa. *Psychological Medicine, 49*(6), 898–910.

Swain, J.E., & others (2017). Parent–child intervention decreases stress and increases maternal brain activity and connectivity during own baby-cry: An exploratory study. *Development and Psychopathology, 29*(2), 535–553.

Swamy, G.K., Ostbye, T., & Skjaerven, R. (2008). Association of preterm birth with long-term survival, reproduction, and next-generation preterm birth. *Journal of the American Medical Association, 299,* 1429–1436.

Swanson, H.L. (1999). What develops in working memory? A life-span perspective. *Developmental Psychology, 35,* 986–1000.

Swanson, H.L., & Berninger, V.W. (2018). Role of working memory in the language learning mechanism by ear, mouth, eye and hand in individuals with and without specific learning disabilities in written language. In T.P. Alloway (Ed.), *Working memory and clinical developmental disorders.* Routledge.

Swanson, L.L., Arizmendi, G.D., & Li, J-T. (2021). Working memory growth predicts mathematical problem-solving growth among emergent bilingual children. *Journal of Experimental Child Psychology, 201,* 104988.

Swartzendruber, A., Sales, J.M., Rose, E.S., & DiClemente, R.J. (2016). Alcohol use problems and sexual risk among young adult African American mothers. *AIDS Behavior, 20*(Suppl. 1), S74–S83.

Swingler, M.M., & others (2017). Maternal behavior predicts infant neurophysiological and behavioral attention processes in the first year. *Developmental Psychology, 53,* 13–37.

Szucs, L.E., & others (2022). Overwhelming support for sexual health education in U.S. schools: A meta-analysis of 23 surveys conducted between 2000 and 2016. *Journal of Adolescent Health, 70,* 598–606.

Szwedo, D.E., Hessel, E.T., & Allen, J.P. (2017). Supportive romantic relationships as predictors of resilience against early adolescent maternal negativity. *Journal of Youth and Adolescence, 46,* 454–465.

T

Taboada, M. (2021). Pragmatics and discourse analysis. In J. Bruhn de Garavito & J.W. Schwieter (Eds.), *Introducing linguistics.* Cambridge University Press.

Tager, M. (2022). *Anti-racist pedagogy in the early childhood classroom.* Rowman & Littlefield.

Taggart, J., Eisen, S., & Lillard, A.S. (2018). Pretense. In M.H. Bornstein & others (Eds.), *SAGE encyclopedia of lifespan human development.* Sage.

Taggart, T., & others (2018). The role of religious socialization and religiosity in African American and Caribbean Black adolescents' sexual initiation. *Journal of Religion and Health, 57*(5), 1889–1904.

Tahir, M.J., Willett, W., & Forman, M.R. (2019). The association of television viewing in childhood with overweight and obesity throughout the life course. *American Journal of Epidemiology, 188,* 282–293.

Takumi, T., Tamada, K., Hatanaka, F., Nakai, N., & Bolton, P.F. (2020). Behavioral neuroscience of autism. *Neuroscience & Biobehavioral Reviews, 110,* 60–76.

Talge, N.M., Neal, C., Glover, V., and the Early Stress, Translational Research and Prevention Science Network: Fetal and Neonatal Experience on Child and Adolescent Mental Health (2007). Antenatal maternal stress and long-term effects on neurodevelopment: How and why? *Journal of Child Psychology and Psychiatry, 48,* 245–261.

Tallberg, P., Rastam, M., Hallin, A.L., Perrin, S., & Gustafsson, P. (2022). A longitudinal investigation of parental ratings and performance metrics for executive functioning and symptom severity in clinically referred youth with ADHD. *Applied Neuropsychology: Child, 2022,* 1–13.

Tam, V., & others (2019). Benefits and limitations of genome-wide association studies. *Nature Reviews Genetics, 1.*

Tamis-LeMonda, C.S., Custode, S., Kuchirko, Y., Escobar, K., & Lo, T. (2019). Routine language: Speech directed to infants during home activities. *Child Development, 90,* 2135–2152.

Tamis-LeMonda, C.S., Kuchirko, Y., & Song, L. (2014). Why is infant language learning facilitated by parental responsiveness? *Current Directions in Psychological Science, 23,* 121–126.

Tamminga, S., & others (2018). Older mothers and increased impact of prenatal screening: Stable livebirth prevalence of trisomy 21 in the Netherlands for the period 2000–2013. *European Journal of Human Genetics, 26*(2), 157–165.

Tan, B.W., Pooley, J.A., & Speelman, C.P. (2016). A meta-analytic review of the efficacy of physical exercise interventions on cognition in individuals with autism spectrum disorder and ADHD. *Journal of Autism and Developmental Disorders, 46,* 3126–3143.

Tang, A., & others (2020). Infant behavioral inhibition predicts personality and social outcomes three decades later. *Proceedings of the National Academy of Sciences, 117*(18), 9800–9807.

Tang, S., Davis-Kean, P.E., Chen, M., & Sexton, H.R. (2016). Adolescent pregnancy's intergenerational effects: Does an adolescent mother's education have consequences for children's achievement? *Journal of Research on Adolescence, 26,* 180–193.

Tang, S., McLoyd, V.C., & Hallman, S.K. (2016). Racial socialization, racial identity, and academic attitudes among African American adolescents: Examining the moderating influence of parent-adolescent communication. *Journal of Youth and Adolescence, 45,* 1141–1155.

Tannen, D. (2013). *You just don't understand: Women and men in conversation.* Simon and Schuster.

Tanner, M., Miettinen, P.J., Hero, M., Toppari, J., & Raivio, T. (2022). Onset and progression of puberty in Klinefelter syndrome. *Clinical Endocrinology, 96*(3), 363–370.

Tanrikulu, M.A., Agirbasli, M., & Berenson, G. (2017). Primordial prevention of cardiometabolic risk in childhood. *Advances in Experimental Medicine and Biology, 956,* 489–496.

Tao, L., & others (2021). Bilingualism and domain-general cognitive functions from a neural perspective: A systematic review. *Neuroscience and Biobehavioral Reviews, 125,* 264–295.

Taraban, L., & Shaw, D.S. (2018). Parenting in context: Revisiting Belsky's classic process of parenting model in early childhood. *Developmental Review, 48,* 55–81.

Tardif, T. (2016). Culture, language, and emotion: Explorations in development. In M.D. Sera, M. Maratsos, & S.M. Carlson (Eds.), *Minnesota Symposium on Child Psychology, Volume 38: Culture and developmental systems.* Wiley.

Tatum, H.E. (2022). Honor codes and academic integrity: Three decades of research. *Journal of College and Character, 23,* 32–47.

Taylor, C., & others (2016). Examining ways that a mindfulness-based intervention reduces stress in public school teachers: A mixed-methods study. *Mindfulness, 7,* 115–129.

Taylor, C.M., & Emmett, P.M. (2019). Picky eating in children: Causes and consequences. *Proceedings of the Nutrition Society, 78*(2), 161–169.

Taylor, D. (2020). *Same-sex couples are more likely to adopt or foster children.* U.S. Census Bureau. Available https://www.census.gov/library/stories/2020/09/fifteen-percent-of-same-sex-couples-have-children-in-their-household.html

Taylor, F.M.A., Ko, R., & Pan, M. (1999). Prenatal and reproductive health care. In E.J. Kramer, S.L. Ivey, & Y.W. Ying (Eds.), *Immigrant women's health.* Jossey-Bass.

Taylor, G., & Galichet, C. (2021). *Current capabilities for human genome editing: Report for the WHO Expert Advisory Committee on Developing Global Standards for Governance and Oversight of Human Genome Editing.* World Health Organization.

Taylor, N.A., Greenberg, D., & Terry, N.P. (2016). The relationship between parents' literacy skills and their preschool children's emergent literacy skills. *Journal of Research and Practice for Adult Literacy, Secondary, and Basic Education, 5,* 5–16.

Tcheandjieu, C., & others (2022). Large-scale genome-wide association study of coronary artery disease in genetically diverse populations. *Nature Medicine, 28*(8), 1679–1692.

Telzer, E.H., van Hoorn, J., Rogers, C.R., & Do, K.T. (2018). Social influence on positive youth development: A developmental neuroscience perspective. *Advances in Child Development and Behavior, 54,* 215–258.

Temple, C.A., & others (2018). *All children read: Teaching for literacy* (5th ed.). Pearson.

Tenenbaum, H., & May, D. (2014). Gender in parent-child relationships. In P. Leman & H.

Tenenbaum (Eds.), *Gender and development*. Psychology Press.

Tenenbaum, H.R., Callahan, M., Alba-Speyer, C., & Sandoval, L. (2002). Parent-child science conversations in Mexican-descent families: Educational background, activity, and past experience as moderators. *Hispanic Journal of Behavioral Sciences, 24*, 225-248.

Terman, L. (1925). *Genetic studies of genius. Vol. 1: Mental and physical traits of a thousand gifted children*. Stanford University Press.

Terrace, H.S., Bigelow, A.E., & Beebe, B. (2022). Intersubjectivity and the Emergence of Words. *Frontiers in Psychology, 13*, 693139.

Terrier, C. (2020). Boys lag behind: How teachers' gender biases affect student achievement. *Economics of Education Review, 77*, 101981.

Testa, A., & Jackson, D.B. (2021). Race, ethnicity, WIC participation, and infant health disparities in the United States. *Annals of Epidemiology, 58*, 22-28.

Thacher, J.D., & others (2018). Maternal smoking during pregnancy and early childhood and development of asthma and rhinoconjunctivitis—A MeDALL Project. *Environmental Health Perspectives, 126*(4), 047005.

Thanh, N.X., & Jonsson, E. (2016). Life expectancy of people with fetal alcohol syndrome. *Journal of Population Therapeutics and Clinical Pharmacology, 23*, e53-e59.

Thapar, A., Eyre, O., Patel, V., & Brent, D. (2022). Depression in young people. *Lancet, 400*, 617-631.

Thavamani, A., & others (2020). The increasing prevalence and adverse impact of morbid obesity in pediatric acute pancreatitis. *Pediatric Obesity, 15*(8), 12643.

The, N.S., & others (2010). Association of adolescent obesity with risk of severe obesity in adulthood. *Journal of the American Psychological Association, 304*, 2042-2047.

The Guardian (2019, September 10), #MeToo Bangladesh: The textile workers uniting against harassment. Retrieved January 13, 2023, from https://www.theguardian.com/global-development/2019/sep/10/metoo-bangladesh-the-textile-workers-uniting-against-harassment

Thelen, E., & others (1993). The transition to reaching: Mapping intention and intrinsic dynamics. *Child Development, 64*, 1058-1098.

Thelen, E., & Smith, L.B. (2006). Dynamic development of action and thought. In W. Damon & R. Lerner (Eds.), *Handbook of child psychology* (6th ed.). Wiley.

Thelwall, M., & others (2023). Academic LGBTQ+ terminology 1900-2021: Increasing variety, increasing inclusivity? *Journal of Homosexuality, 70*, 2514-2538.

Theo, L.O., & Drake, E. (2017). Rooming-in: Creating a better experience. *The Journal of Perinatal Education, 26*(2), 79-84.

Thoma, S.J., & Bebeau, M. (2008). *Moral judgment competency is declining over time: Evidence from 20 years of defining issues test data*. Paper presented at the meeting of the American Educational Research meeting, New York, NY.

Thomas, A., & Chess, S. (1991). Temperament in adolescence and its functional significance. In R.M. Lerner, A.C. Petersen, & J. Brooks-Gunn (Eds.), *Encyclopedia of adolescence* (Vol. 2). Garland.

Thomas, B.L., Karl, J.M., & Whishaw, I.Q. (2015). Independent development of the reach and the grasp in spontaneous self-touching by human infants in the first 6 months. *Frontiers in Psychology, 5*, 1526.

Thomas, J.C., & others (2017). Developmental origins of infant emotion regulation: Mediation by temperamental negativity and moderation by maternal sensitivity. *Developmental Psychology, 53*, 611-628.

Thomas, J.R., & Hognas, R.S. (2015). The effect of parental divorce on the health of adult children. *Longitudinal and Life Course Studies, 6*, 279-302.

Thomas, K.A., & Spieker, S. (2016). Sleep, depression, and fatigue in late postpartum. *MCN: American Journal of Maternal and Child Nursing, 41*, 104-109.

Thomas, M.S., Mareschal, D., & Dumontheil, I. (Eds.) (2020). *Educational neuroscience: Development across the life span*. Routledge.

Thomas, S.A., Micalizzi, L., Meisel, S.N., Price, D., & Spirito, A. (2022). Adolescent sibling associations among alcohol, cannabis, and sexual risk behavior: A test of interdependence. *Substance Use and Misuse, 57*, 1572-1580.

Thompson, A.E., & Voyer, D. (2014). Sex differences in the ability to recognize non-verbal displays of emotion: A meta-analysis. *Cognition and Emotion, 28*, 1164-1195.

Thompson, D.R., & others (2007). Childhood overweight and cardiovascular disease risk factors: The National Heart, Lung, and Blood Institute Growth and Health Study. *Journal of Pediatrics, 150*, 18-25.

Thompson, E.J. (2011, April 13). Willie Howard's life after the NFL. *Daily Norseman*. Retrieved January 27, 2023, from https://www.dailynorseman.com/2011/4/13/2107710/minnesota-vikings-willie-howard-life-after-the-nfl

Thompson, J., Manore, M., & Vaughan, L. (2017). *Science of nutrition* (4th ed.). Pearson.

Thompson, M.J.J. (2021). Piaget's stages of cognitive development and Erikson's stages of psychosocial development. In C. Laver-Bradbury & others (Eds.), *Child and adolescent mental health: Theory and practice*. CRC Press.

Thompson, M.P., & Swartout, K. (2018). Epidemiology of suicide attempts among youth transitioning to adulthood. *Journal of Youth and Adolescence, 47*(4), 807-817.

Thompson, R.A. (2013). Attachment and its development: Precis and prospect. In P. Zelazo (Ed.), *Oxford handbook of developmental psychology*. Oxford University Press.

Thompson, R.A. (2015). Relationships, regulation, and development. In R.M. Lerner (Ed.), *Handbook of child psychology* (7th ed.). Wiley.

Thompson, R.A. (2016). Early attachment and later development: New questions. In J. Cassidy & P.R. Shaver (Eds.), *Handbook of attachment* (3rd ed.). Guilford Press.

Thompson, R.A. (2019). Early moral development and attachment theory. In D.J. Laible & others (Eds.), *The Oxford handbook of parenting and moral development*. Oxford University Press.

Thompson, R.A. (2020a). On what is read, shared, and felt: Parent-child conversation about stories. *Attachment & Human Development, 22*(1), 85-89.

Thompson, R.A. (2020b). The development of moral self-awareness. In L.A. Jensen (Ed.), *The Oxford handbook of moral development: An interdisciplinary perspective*. Oxford University Press.

Thompson, R.A. (2021). Internal working models as developing representations. In R.A. Thompson & others (Eds.), *Attachment: The fundamental questions*. Guilford Press.

Thompson, R.A. (2022). Emotional development and the growth of moral self-awareness. In D. Dukes & others (Eds.), *The Oxford Handbook of Emotional Development*. Oxford University Press.

Thompson, R.A., & Goodvin, R. (2016). Social support and developmental psychopathology. In D. Cicchetti (Ed.), *Developmental psychopathology* (3rd ed.). Wiley.

Thompson, R.A., Meyer, S., & McGinley, M. (2006). Understanding values in relationships: The development of conscience. In M. Killen & J. Smetana (Eds.), *Handbook of moral development*. Erlbaum.

Thompson, R.A., Simpson, J.A., & Berlin, L. (2021a). Attachment theory in the twenty-first century. In R.A. Thompson & others (Eds.), *Attachment: The fundamental questions*. Guilford Press.

Thompson, R.A., Simpson, J.A., & Berlin, L. (2021b). Assembling the puzzle—Interlocking pieces, missing pieces, and the emerging picture. In R.A. Thompson & others (Eds.), *Attachment: The fundamental questions*. Guilford Press.

Thoni, C., Volk, S., & Cortina, J.M. (2021). Greater male variability in cooperation: Meta-analytic evidence for an evolutionary perspective. *Psychological Science, 32*, 50-63.

Thurman, A.J., & others (2017). Language skills of males and Fragile X syndrome or nonsyndromic autism spectrum disorder. *Journal of Autism and Developmental Disorders, 47*(3), 728-743.

Thébaud, S., & Pedulla, D.S. (2022). When do work-family policies work? Unpacking the effects of stigma and financial costs for men and women. *Work and Occupations, 49*(2), 229-263.

Tiego, J., & others (2020). Common mechanisms of executive attention underlie executive function and effortful control in children. *Developmental Science, 23*(3), 12918.

Tiggemann, M., & Slater, A. (2017). Facebook and body image concern in adolescent girls: A prospective study. *International Journal of Eating Disorders, 50*(1), 80-83.

Tillyer, M.S., & Walter, R.J. (2019). Low-income housing and crime: The influence of housing development and neighborhood characteristics. *Crime & Delinquency, 65*(7), 969-993.

Tincoff, R., Seidl, A., Buckley, L., Wojcik, C., & Cristia, A. (2019). Feeling the way to words: Parents' speech and touch cues highlight word-to-world mappings of body parts. *Language Learning and Development, 15,* 103-125.

Tinker, S.C., & others (2019). Specific birth defects in pregnancies of women with diabetes: National Birth Defects Prevention Study, 1997-2011. *American Journal of Obstetrics and Gynecology, 222*(2), 176.e1-176.e11.

Tistarelli, N., & others (2020). The nature and nurture of ADHD and its comorbidities: A narrative review of twin studies. *Neuroscience and Biobehavioral Reviews, 109,* 63-77.

Tobin, J.J., Wu, D.Y.H., & Davidson, D.H. (1989). *Preschool in three cultures.* Yale University Press.

Toepfer, P., & others (2019). A role of oxytocin receptor gene brain tissue expression quantitative trait locus rs237895 in the intergenerational transmission of the effects of maternal childhood maltreatment. *Journal of the American Academy of Child and Adolescent Psychiatry, 58,* 1207-1216.

Tomasello, M. (2018b). Great apes and human development: A personal history. *Child Development Perspectives, 12,* 189-193.

Tomasello, M. (2020). The adaptive origins of uniquely human sociality. *Philosophical Transactions of the Royal Society B. Biological Sciences, 375,* 1803.

Tomfohr-Madsen, L.M., & others (2020). Improved child mental health following brief relationship enhancement and co-parenting interventions during the transition to parenthood. *International Journal of Environmental Research and Public Health, 17*(3), 766.

Tomlinson, M., & others (2016). Improving early childhood care and development, HIV-testing, treatment and support, and nutrition in Mokhotlong, Lesotho: Study protocol for a cluster randomized controlled trial. *Trials, 17*(1), 538.

Tomlinson, R.C., & others (2020). Neighborhood poverty predicts altered neural and behavioral response inhibition. *NeuroImage, 209,* 116536.

Tompkins, G.E. (2016). *Language arts* (9th ed.). Pearson.

Tompkins, G.E., & Rodgers, E. (2020). *Literacy in the early grades* (5th ed.). Pearson.

Tompkins, V., Farrar, M.J., & Montgomery, D.E. (2019). Speaking your mind: Language and narrative in young children's theory of mind development. *Advances in Child Development and Behavior, 56,* 109-140.

Tompkins, V., & others (2018). The relation between parents' mental state talk and children's social understanding: A meta-analysis. *Social Development, 27*(2), 223-246.

Tomporowski, P.D. (2016). Exercise and cognition. *Pediatric Exercise Science, 28,* 23-27.

Tooley, U.A., Bassett, D.S., & Mackey, A.P. (2021). Environmental influences on the pace of brain development. *Nature Reviews Neuroscience, 22*(6), 372-384.

Tooley, U.A., & others (2020). Associations between neighborhood SES and functional brain network development. *Cerebral Cortex, 30*(1), 1-19.

Toomey, R.B., & Russell, S.T. (2016). The role of sexual orientation in school-based victimization: A meta-analysis. *Youth and Society, 48,* 176-201.

Törmänen, S., & others (2017). Polymorphism in the gene encoding toll-like receptor 10 may be associated with asthma after bronchiolitis. *Scientific Reports, 7.*

Torstveit, L., Sutterlin, S., & Lugo, R.G. (2016). Empathy, guilt proneness, and gender: Relative contributions to prosocial behavior. *European Journal of Psychology, 12,* 260-275.

Toskala, E., & Kennedy, D.W. (2015). Asthma risk factors. *International Forum of Allergy & Rhinology, 5*(Suppl. 1), S11-S16.

Traccis, F., Frau, R., & Melis, M. (2020). Gender differences in the outcome of offspring prenatally exposed to drugs of abuse. *Frontiers in Behavioral Neuroscience, 14,* 72.

Trainor, L.J., & He, C. (2013). Auditory and musical development. In P.D. Zelazo (Ed.), *Handbook of developmental psychology.* Oxford University Press.

Traisrisilp, K., & Tongsong, T. (2015). Pregnancy outcomes of mothers with very advanced age (40 years and more). *Journal of the Medical Association of Thailand, 98,* 117-122.

Trent, M., Dooley, D.G., & Dougé, J. (2019). The impact of racism on child and adolescent health. *Pediatrics, 144*(2), e20191765.

Trimble, J.E. (2021). Foreword: The last page and dreams of the future and the weight of the past. In C.S. Clauss-Ehlers & others, *Applying multiculturism.* APA Books.

Tripathi, T., & others (2019). A motor learning paradigm combining technology and associative learning to assess prone motor learning in infants. *Physical Therapy, 99,* 807-816.

Tristão, R.M., & others (2021). Olfactory sensory and perceptual evaluation in newborn infants: A systematic review. *Developmental Psychobiology, 63*(7), e22201.

Trivedi, M., & Denton, E. (2019). Asthma in children and adults—what are the differences and what can they tell us about asthma? *Frontiers in Pediatrics, 7,* 256.

Troop-Gordon, W. (2017). Peer victimization in adolescence: The nature, progression, and consequences of being bullied within a developmental context. *Journal of Adolescence, 55,* 116-128.

Trosman, I., & Ivanenko, A. (2021). Classification and epidemiology of sleep disorders in children and adolescents. *Child and Adolescent Psychiatric Clinics of North America, 30,* 47-64.

Truglio, R.T., & Kotler, J.A. (2014). Language, literacy, and media: What's the word on *Sesame Street?* In E.T. Gershoff, R.S. Mistry, & D.A. Crosby (Eds.), *Societal contexts of child development.* Oxford University Press.

Truzzi, A., & others (2017). Serotonin transporter gene polymorphisms and early parent-infant interactions are related to adult male heart rate responses to female crying. *Frontiers in Physiology, 8,* 111.

Tsang, T.W., & others (2016). Prenatal alcohol exposure, FASD, and child behavior: A meta-analysis. *Pediatrics, 137,* e20152542.

Tschiderer, L., & others (2022). Breastfeeding is associated with a reduced maternal cardiovascular risk: Systematic review and meta-analysis involving data from 8 studies and 1 192 700 parous women. *Journal of the American Heart Association, 11*(2), e022746.

Tsiorvas, A., & Eady, M.J. (2023). Creating a compulsory subject requiring authentic community service learning: A framework for change. In M. Winslade, T. Loughland, & M.J. Eady (Eds.), *Work-integrated learning case studies in teacher education.* Springer

Tso, W., & others (2016). Sleep duration and school readiness of Chinese preschool children. *Journal of Pediatrics, 169,* 266-271.

Tsubomi, H., & Watanabe, K. (2017). Development of visual working memory and distractor resistance in relation to academic performance. *Journal of Experimental Psychology, 154,* 98-112.

Tsunematsu, T. (2023). What are the neural mechanisms and physiological functions of dreams? *Neuroscience Research, 189,* 54-59.

Ttofi, M.M., Farrington, D.P., Losel, F., & Loeber, R. (2011). The predictive efficiency of school bullying versus later offending: A systematic/meta-analytic review of longitudinal studies. *Criminal Behavior and Mental Health, 21,* 80-89.

Tudge, J., & Freitas, L. (2018). Developing gratitude: An introduction. In J. Tudge & L. Freitas (Eds.), *Developing gratitude in children and adolescents* (pp. 1-24). Cambridge University Press.

Tudge, J.R., Navarro, J.L., Merçon-Vargas, E.A., & Payir, A. (2021). The promise and the practice of early childhood educare in the writings of Urie Bronfenbrenner. *Early Child Development and Care, 191*(7-8), 1079-1088.

Tung, W.C., & Li, Z. (2015). Pain beliefs and behaviors among Chinese. *Home Health Care Management & Practice, 27*(2), 95-97.

Turiel, E. (2015). Moral development. In R.M. Lerner (Ed.), *Handbook of child psychology and developmental science* (7th ed.). Wiley.

Turiel, E., & Gingo, M. (2017). Development in the moral domain: Coordination and the need to consider other domains of social reasoning. In N. Budwig, E. Turiel, & P.D. Zelazo (Eds.), *New perspectives on human development.* Cambridge University Press.

Turk, E., Vroomen, J., Fonken, Y., Levy, J., & van den Heuvel, M.I. (2022). In sync with your child: The potential of parent-child electroencephalography in developmental research. *Developmental Psychobiology, 64,* e22221.

Turnbull, A., & others (2020). *Exceptional lives* (9th ed.). Pearson.

Turner, S., Taillieu, T., Cheung, K., & Afifi, T.O. (2017). The relationship between childhood sexual abuse and mental health outcomes among males: Results from a nationally representative United States sample. *Child Abuse and Neglect, 66,* 64–72.

Tweed, E.J., & others (2016). Five-minute Apgar scores and educational outcomes: Retrospective cohort study of 751,369 children. *Archives of Disease in Child, Fetal, and Neonatal Medicine, 101,* F121–F126.

Twenge, J.M. (2020). Why increases in adolescent depression may be linked to the technological environment. *Current Opinion in Psychology, 32,* 89–94.

Tyndall, C., Cuzzilla, R., & Kane, S.C. (2020). The rhesus incompatible pregnancy and its consequences for affected fetuses and neonates. *Transfusion and Apheresis Science, 59*(5), 102948.

Tyrell, F.A., & others (2016). Family influences on Mexican American adolescents' romantic relationships: Moderation by gender and culture. *Journal of Research on Adolescence, 26,* 142–158.

U

Uba, L. (1992). Cultural barriers to health care for Southeast Asian refugees. *Public Health Reports, 107,* 544–549.

Ueno, M., & others (2011). The organization of wariness of heights in experienced crawlers. *Infancy, 17,* 376–392.

Ullah, M.B., & others (2019). Factors associated with diarrhea and acute respiratory infection in children under two years of age in rural Bangladesh. *BMC Pediatrics, 19*(1), 386.

Ullman, T.D., Stuhlmüller, A., Goodman, N.D., & Tenenbaum, J.B. (2018). Learning physical parameters from dynamic scenes. *Cognitive Psychology, 104,* 57–82.

Umaña-Taylor, A.J., & Douglass, S. (2017). Developing an ethnic-racial identity intervention from a developmental perspective: Process, content, and implementation of the Identity Project. In N.J. Cabrera & B. Leyendecker (Eds.), *Handbook on positive development of minority children and youth* (pp. 437–454). Springer.

Umaña-Taylor, A.J., & Hill, N.E. (2020). Ethnic-racial socialization in the family: A decade's advance on precursors and outcomes. *Journal of Marriage and Family, 82,* 244–271.

Umaña-Taylor, A.J., Kornienko, O., McDermott, E.R., & Motti-Stefanidi, F. (2020). National identity development and friendship network dynamics among immigrant and non-immigrant youth. *Journal of Youth and Adolescence, 49,* 706–723.

Umer, A., & others (2019). Association between breastfeeding and childhood cardiovascular disease risk factors. *Maternal and Child Health Journal, 23*(2), 228–239.

Unar-Munguía, M., Torres-Mejía, G., Colchero, M.A., & González de Cosío, T. (2017). Breastfeeding mode and risk of breast cancer: A dose–response meta-analysis. *Journal of Human Lactation, 33,* 422–434.

Underwood, J.M., & others (2020, August 21). Youth risk behavior surveillance—United States, 2019. *Morbidity and Mortality Weekly Report (MMWR), 69*(1).

Ungar, M. (2015). Practitioner review: Diagnosing childhood resilience: A systematic diagnosis of adaption in diverse social ecologies. *Journal of Child Psychology and Psychiatry, 56,* 4–17.

UNICEF (2018a). *Gender equality: Global annual results report.* https://www.unicef.org/media/54911/file/Global_Annual_Results_Report_2018_Gender_Equality.pdf

UNICEF (2019a). *Early childhood education.* https://www.unicef.org/education/early-childhood-education

UNICEF (2020a). *Ending child marriage: A profile of progress in Bangladesh.* Retrieved January 13, 2023, from https://reliefweb.int/sites/reliefweb.int/files/resources/Bangladesh-Child-Marriage-Final-LR-spreads-10_1.pdf. Accessed 13 January 2023.

UNICEF (2020b). *The state of the world's children, 2019.*

UNICEF (2021). Elimination of mother-to-child transmission. Retrieved January 15, 2023, from https://data.unicef.org/topic/hivaids/emtct/

UNICEF (2022). *Early childbearing.* Available https://data.unicef.org/topic/child-health/adolescent-health/

UNICEF (2022). *Girls' education.* Available https://gdc.unicef.org/resource/girls-education

UNICEF (2022). *Malnutrition.* https://data.unicef.org/topic/nutrition/malnutrition/

UNICEF (2023a). *Child poverty.* Available https://www.unicef.org/social-policy/child-poverty#

UNICEF (2023b). *HIV and AIDS.* Available https://www.unicef.org/hiv

UNICEF (2023). *Early childhood education.* Retrieved March 14, 2023, from https://www.unicef.org/education/early-childhood-education. Accessed March 14, 2023.

United Nations (1989). *Convention on the Rights of the Child.* Available https://www.ohchr.org/en/professionalinterest/pages/crc.aspx

United Nations (2023). *The 17 goals.* Available https://sdgs.un.org/goals

Updegraff, K.A., & Perez-Brena, N.J. (2023). Studying families as systems in adolescence and early adulthood. In L.J. Crockett, G. Carlo, & J.E. Schulenberg (Eds.), *APA handbook of adolescent and young adult development* (pp. 177–192). American Psychological Association.

Urhahne, D., & Wijnia, L. (2021). A review on the accuracy of teacher judgments. *Educational Research Review, 32,* 100374.

U.S. Census Bureau (2021). *Racial and ethnic diversity in the United States: 2010 census and 2020 census.* https://www.census.gov/library/visualizations/interactive/racial-and-ethnic-diversity-in-the-united-states-2010-and-2020-census.html

USDA, U.S. Food and Drug Administration (2023). *MyPlate.* Retrieved March 18, 2023, from https://www.myplate.gov/

U.S. Department of Education (2019). *About IDEA.* https://sites.ed.gov/idea/about-idea/

U.S. Department of Education, National Center for Education Statistics (2018). *Early childhood care arrangements: Choices and costs.* https://nces.ed.gov/programs/coe/indicator_tca.asp

U.S. Department of Education, National Center for Education Statistics. (2021). *Early childhood program participation: 2019* (NCES 2020-075REV), Table 1. https://nces.ed.gov/fastfacts/display.asp?id=4

U.S. Department of Health & Human Services, Administration for Children and Families, Children's Bureau. (2023). *Child Maltreatment 2021.* Available https://www.acf.hhs.gov/cb/data-research/child-maltreatment

U.S. Department of Health and Human Services, Administration for Children and Families (2021). *The AFCARS report.* Accessed from https://www.acf.hhs.gov/sites/default/files/documents/cb/afcarsreport28.pdf

U.S. Department of Health and Human Services, Administration for Children and Families (2022). *FY 2021 Adoption and Foster Care Analysis and Reporting System.* URL: https://www.acf.hhs.gov/cb/report/afcars-report-29.

U.S. Department of Health and Human Services, Office on Women's Health (2023). *Folic acid.* Retrieved January 14, 2023, from https://www.womenshealth.gov/a-z-topics/folic-acid

U.S. Department of Justice (2021). *Juvenile arrests, 2019.* Available https://ojjdp.ojp.gov/publications/juvenile-arrests-2019.pdf

U.S. Department of Transportation (2021). *Countermeasures that work—Young drivers [Traffic Tech].* Report number DOT HS 813 165. https://rosap.ntl.bts.gov/view/dot/58602

Usher, E.L., & Schunk, D.H. (2018). Social cognitive perspective of self-regulation. In D.H. Schunk & J.A. Greene (Eds.), *Handbook of self-regulation of learning and performance* (2nd ed.). Routledge.

U.S. Preventive Services Task Force & others (2021). Interventions for tobacco smoking cessation in adults, including pregnant persons: U.S. Preventive Services Task Force recommendation statement. *JAMA, 325*(3), 265–279.

UTSA Pride Faculty & Staff Association (2022). *Anna Boyer-Chadwick.* Retrieved April 27, 2022, from https://www.pridefsa.org/annaboyerchadwick

Uwaezuoke, S.N., Eneh, C.I., & Ndu, I.K. (2017). Relationship between exclusive breastfeeding and lower risk of childhood obesity: A narrative review of published evidence. *Clinical Medicine Insights: Pediatrics, 11,* 1179556517690196.

V

Valasek, A.E., Young, J.A., Huang, L., Singichetti, B., & Yang, J. (2019). Age and sex differences in overuse injuries presenting to pediatric sports medicine clinics. *Clinical Pediatrics, 58,* 770–777.

Valkenborghs, S.R., & others (2019). The impact of physical activity on brain structure and function in youth: A systematic review. *Pediatrics, 144*(4), e20184032.

van den Boom, D.C. (1989). Neonatal irritability and the development of attachment. In G.A. Kohnstamm, J.E. Bates, & M.K. Rothbart (Eds.), *Temperament in childhood.* Wiley.

Vandenbosch, L., Fardouly, J., & Tiggemann, M. (2022). Social media and body image: Recent trends and future directions. *Current Opinion in Psychology, 45,* 101289.

van de Oudeweetering, K., & Voogt, J. (2018). Teachers' conceptualization and enactment of twenty-first century competences: Exploring dimensions for new curricula. *The Curriculum Journal, 29,* 116-133.

van der Mey-Baijens, S., & others (2023). Perceived support from best friends and depressive symptoms during adolescence: Disentangling personal from dyadic level effects. *Research on Child and Adolescent Psychopathology, 51,* 469-483.

van der Stel, M., & Veenman, M.V.J. (2010). Development of metacognitive skillfulness: A longitudinal study. *Learning and Individual Differences, 20,* 220-224.

van der Wal, R.C., Finkenauer, C., & Visser, M.M. (2019). Reconciling mixed findings on children's adjustment following high-conflict divorce. *Journal of Child and Family Studies, 28*(2), 468-478.

van der Wal, R.C., Karremans, J.C., & Cillessen, A.H. (2017). Causes and consequences of children's forgiveness. *Child Development Perspectives, 11,* 97-101.

van der Wilt, F., van der Veen, C., van Kruistum, C., & van Oers, B. (2018). Popular, rejected, neglected, controversial, or average: Do young children of different sociometric groups differ in their level of oral communicative competence? *Social Development, 27*(4), 793-807.

Van de Vandervoort, J., & Hamlin, J.K. (2018). The infantile roots of sociomoral evaluations. In K. Gray & J. Graham (Eds.), *The atlas of moral psychology.* Guilford Press.

van Eeden, A.E., van Hoeken, D., & Hoek, H.W. (2021). Incidence, prevalence and mortality of anorexia nervosa and bulimia nervosa. *Current Opinion in Psychiatry, 34,* 515-524.

van Geel, M., Vedder, P., & Tanilon, J. (2014). Relationship between peer victimization, cyberbullying, and suicide in children and adolescents: A meta-analysis. *JAMA Pediatrics, 168,* 435-442.

Van Hook, J., & Glick, J.E. (2020). Spanning borders, cultures, and generations: A decade of research on immigrant families. *Journal of Marriage and Family, 82,* 224-243.

van Hout, A. (2017). Lexical and grammatical aspect. In J. Lidz, W. Snyder, & J. Peter (Eds.), *Oxford handbook of developmental linguistics.* Oxford University Press.

van Hover, S., & Hicks, D. (2017). Social constructivism and student learning in social studies.

The Wiley Handbook of Social Studies Research, 5, 270.

van Huizen, T., Dumhs, L., & Plantenga, J. (2019). The costs and benefits of investing in universal preschool: Evidence from a Spanish reform. *Child Development, 90,* e386-e406.

Van Iddekinge, C.H., Aguinis, H., Mackey, J.D., & DeOrtentiis, P.S. (2018). A meta-analysis of the interactive, additive, and relative effects of cognitive ability and motivation on performance. *Journal of Management, 44,* 249-279.

van IJzendoorn, M.H., & Kroonenberg, P.M. (1988). Cross-cultural patterns of attachment: A meta-analysis of the Strange Situation. *Child Development, 59,* 147-156.

van Lier, P., & Deater-Deckard, K. (Eds.) (2022). *Biosocial interplay during elementary school: Pathways toward maladaptation in young children.* Springer.

van Merendonk, E.J., & others (2017). Identification of prenatal behavioral patterns of the gross motor movements within the early stages of fetal development. *Infant and Child Development, 26*(5), e2012.

van Renswoude, D.R., Visser, I., Raijmakers, M.E.J., Tsang, T., & Johnson, S.P. (2019). Real-world scene perception in infants: What factors guide attention allocation? *Infancy, 24,* 693-717.

Van Rijn, S., de Sonneville, L., & Swaab, H. (2018). The nature of social cognitive deficits in children and adults with Klinefelter syndrome (47,XXY). *Genes, Brain, and Behavior, 17*(6), e12465.

Van Ryzin, M.J., Carlson, E.A., & Sroufe, L.A. (2011). Attachment discontinuity in a high-risk sample. *Attachment and Human Development, 13,* 381-401.

van Schaik, S.D., Oudgenoeg-Paz, O., & Atun-Einy, O. (2018). Cross-cultural differences in parental beliefs about infant motor development: A quantitative and qualitative report of middle-class Israeli and Dutch parents. *Developmental Psychology, 54,* 999-1010.

van Sluijs, E.M., & others (2021). Physical activity behaviours in adolescence: Current evidence and opportunities for intervention. *The Lancet, 398,* 429-442.

van Tetering, M.A.J., & others (2020). Sex differences in self-regulation in early, middle, and late adolescence: A large-scale cross-sectional study. *PLoS One, 15*(1), e0227607.

Vasilenko, S.A. (2022). Sexual behavior and health from adolescence to adulthood: Illustrative examples of 25 years of research from Add Health. *Journal of Adolescent Health, 71,* S24-S31.

Vasileva, M., Graf, R.K., Reinelt, T., Petermann, U., & Petermann, F. (2021). Research review: A meta-analysis of the international prevalence and comorbidity of mental disorders in children between 1 and 7 years. *Journal of Child Psychology and Psychiatry, 62*(4), 372-381.

Vaughn, B.E., & Bost, K.K. (2016). Attachment and temperament as intersecting developmental products and interacting developmental contexts throughout infancy and childhood. In J. Cassidy & P.R. Shaver

(Eds.), *Handbook of attachment* (3rd ed.). Guilford Press.

Vaughn, B.E., Elmore-Staton, L., Shin, N., & el-Sheikh, M. (2015). Sleep as a support for social competence, peer relations, and cognitive functioning in preschool children. *Behavioral Sleep Medicine, 13,* 92-106.

Vaz, J.D.S., & others (2021). Intergenerational breastfeeding practices among parents and children: 1993 Pelotas birth cohort. *Maternal and Child Nutrition, 17*(1), e13058.

Veenstra, R., & Laninga-Wijnen, L. (2022). Peer network studies and interventions in adolescence. *Current Opinion in Psychology, 44,* 157-163.

Veenstra, R., & Laninga-Wijnen, L. (2023). The prominence of peer interactions, relationships, and networks in adolescence and early adulthood. In L.J. Crockett, G. Carlo, & J.E. Schulenberg (Eds.), *APA handbook of adolescent and young adult development* (pp. 225-241). American Psychological Association.

Veisani, Y., & others (2019). Effect of prenatal smoking cessation interventions on birth weight: Meta-analysis. *The Journal of Maternal-Fetal & Neonatal Medicine, 32*(2), 332-338.

Velez, G., & Spencer, M.B. (2018). Phenomenology and intersectionality: Using PVEST as a frame for adolescent identity formation amid intersecting ecological systems of inequality. *New Directions for Child and Adolescent Development, 2018*(161), 75-90.

Vella, S.A., Cliff, D.P., Magee, C.A., & Okely, A.D. (2014). Sports participation and parent-reported health-related quality of life in children: Longitudinal associations. *Journal of Pediatrics, 164,* 1469-1474.

Velle-Forbord, V., Underdal, M.O., & Vanky, E. (2018). Breastfeeding and future maternal health— No causal evidence. *JAMA Internal Medicine, 178*(6), 870-871.

Vena, F., & others (2022). Risk of neural tube defects according to maternal body mass index: A systematic review and meta-analysis. *The Journal of Maternal-Fetal & Neonatal Medicine, 35,* 7296-7305.

Venezia, J.H., Richards, V.M., & Hickok, G. (2021). Speech-driven spectrotemporal receptive fields beyond the auditory cortex. *Hearing Research, 408,* 108307.

Venkatesh, K.K., & others (2019). Association of antenatal depression with clinical subtypes of preterm birth. *American Journal of Perinatology, 36*(6), 567-573.

Venta, A., & Walker, J. (2021). Divorce, separation, and loss. In A. Venta & others (Eds.), *Developmental psychopathology.* Wiley.

Veraksa, N., & Sheridan, S. (Eds.) (2018). *Vygotsky's theory in early childhood education and research.* Routledge.

Verde-Cagiao, M., Nieto, C., & Campos, R. (2022). Mother-infant co-regulation from 0 to 2 years: The role of copy behaviors. A systematic review. *Infant Behavior and Development, 68,* 101749.

Verduci, E., Di Profio, E., Fiore, G., & Zuccotti, G. (2022). Integrated approaches to combatting childhood obesity. *Annals of Nutrition and Metabolism, 78*(2), 8-19.

Vermeer, H.J., & others (2016). Quality of child care using the environment rating scales: A meta-analysis of international studies. *International Journal of Early Childhood, 48*(1), 33–60.

Vernon-Feagans, L., Willoughby, M., & Garrett-Peters, P. (2016). Predictors of behavioral regulation in kindergarten: Household chaos, parenting, and early executive functions. *Developmental Psychology, 52*, 430–441.

Vernucci, S., & others (2020). Working memory training in children: A review of basic methodological criteria. *Psychological Reports, 123*, 605–632.

Verriotis, M., & others (2018). The distribution of pain activity across the human neonatal brain is sex dependent. *NeuroImage, 178*, 69–77.

Vertsberger, D., & Knafo-Noam, A. (2019). Mothers' and fathers' parenting and longitudinal associations with children's observed distress to limitations: From pregnancy to toddlerhood. *Developmental Psychology, 55*(1), 123–134.

Vescio, T., & Kosakowska-Berezecka, N. (2021). The not so subtle and status quo maintaining nature of everyday sexism. In F.M. Cheung & D.F. Halpern (Eds.), *Cambridge handbook of the international psychology of women.* Cambridge University Press.

Vetter, N.C., & others (2013). Ongoing development of social cognition in adolescence. *Child Neuropsychology, 19*, 615–629.

Victora, C.G., & others (2016). Breastfeeding in the 21st century: Epidemiology, mechanisms, and lifelong effect. *Lancet, 387*, 475–490.

Vidal, S., & others (2017). Maltreatment, family environment, and social risk factors: Determinants of the child welfare to juvenile justice transition among maltreated children and adolescents. *Child Abuse and Neglect, 63*, 7–18.

Vieira, J.M., Matias, M., Ferreira, T., Lopez, F.G., & Matos, P.M. (2016). Parents' work-family experiences and children's problem behaviors: The mediating role of parent-child relationship. *Journal of Family Psychology, 39*, 419–430.

Vihman, M.M. (2020). *Phonological templates in development.* Oxford University Press.

Vijayakumar, N., & others (2019). Affective reactivity during adolescence: Associations with age, puberty and testosterone. *Cortex, 117*, 336–350.

Villasis-Keever, M.A., & others (2021). Cardiometabolic factors in pediatric patients with chronic diseases. *Archives of Medical Research, 52*(5), 535–543.

Visu-Petra, L., Prodan, N., & Talwar, V. (2022). Children's lies: Intersecting cognitive development, theory of mind, and socialization. In P.K. Smith & C.H. Hart (Eds.), *The Wiley-Blackwell Handbook of Childhood Social Development* (3rd ed., pp. 668–685). Wiley.

Viteri, O.A., & others (2015). Fetal anomalies and long-term effects associated with substance abuse in pregnancy: A literature review. *American Journal of Perinatology, 32*(5), 405–416.

Vittrup, B., Holden, G.W., & Buck, M. (2006). Attitudes predict the use of physical punishment: A prospective study of the emergence of disciplinary practices. *Pediatrics, 117*, 2055–2064.

Vogelsang, L., & others (2018). Potential downside of high initial visual acuity. *Proceedings of the National Academy of Sciences, 115*, 11333–11338.

Vogelsang, M., & Tomasello, M. (2016). Giving is nicer than taking: Preschoolers reciprocate based on the social intentions of the distributor. *PloS One, 11*(1), e0147539.

Vohryzek, J., Cabral, J., Vuust, P., Deco, G., & Kringelbach, M.L. (2022). Understanding brain states across spacetime informed by whole-brain modelling. *Philosophical Transactions of the Royal Society A, 380*(2227), 20210247.

Volkow, N.D., & others (2019). Self-reported medical and nonmedical cannabis use among pregnant women in the United States. *JAMA, 322*(2), 167–169.

Volling, B., & Cabrera, N. (2019). Advancing research and measurement on fathering and child development. In B. Volling & N. Cabrera (Eds.), *Advancing research and measurement on fathering and children's development. Monographs of the Society for Research in Child Development, No. 332, 84*(1), 7–17.

Volling, B.L., & others (2023). Changes in children's attachment security to mother and father after the birth of a sibling: Risk and resilience in the family. *Development and Psychopathology, 35*(3), 1404–1420.

Volling, B.L., and Palkovitz, R. (2021). Fathering: New perspectives, paradigms, and possibilities. *Psychology of Men and Masculinities, 22*, 427–432.

von dem Hagen, E.A., & Bright, N. (2017). High autistic trait individuals do not modulate gaze behavior in response to social presence but look away more when actively engaged in an interaction. *Autism Research, 10*, 359–368.

von Hippel, C., Kalokerinos, E.K., & Zacher, H. (2017). Stereotype threat and perceptions of family-friendly policies among female employees. *Frontiers in Psychology, 7*, 2043.

von Stumm, S., & Plomin, R. (2021). Using DNA to predict intelligence. *Intelligence, 86*, 101530.

Voorhees, D.H., LeMay, L.E., Nagy, E.A., & Perez, A.E. (2022). Successes with metacognition: Empowering faculty and transforming student learning. *New Directions for Community Colleges, 2022*(199), 17–33.

Vorona, R.D., & others (2014). Adolescent crash rates and school start times in two Central Virginia counties, 2009–2011: A follow-up study to a Southeastern Virginia study, 2007–2008. *Journal of Clinical Sleep Medicine, 10*, 1169–1177.

Votavova, H., & others (2012). Deregulation of gene expression induced by environmental tobacco smoke exposure in pregnancy. *Nicotine and Tobacco Research, 14*(9), 1073–1082.

Voutsina, C., George, L., & Jones, K. (2019). Microgenetic analysis of young children's shifts of attention in arithmetic tasks: underlying dynamics of change in phases of seemingly stable task performance. *Educational Studies in Mathematics, 102*, 47–74.

Vukelich, C., & others (2020). *Helping children learn language and literacy* (5th ed.). Pearson.

Vurpillot, E. (1968). The development of scanning strategies and their relation to visual differentiation. *Journal of Experimental Child Psychology, 6*(4), 632–650.

Vygotsky, L.S. (1962). *Thought and language.* MIT Press.

Vysniauske, R., Verburgh, L., Oosteriaan, J., & Molendijk, M.L. (2020). The effects of physical exercise on functional outcomes in the treatment of ADHD: A meta-analysis. *Journal of Attention Disorders, 24*(5), 644–654.

W

Wade, M., & others (2020). Telomere length and psychopathology: Specificity and direction of effects within the Bucharest Early Intervention Project. *Journal of the American Academy of Child and Adolescent Psychiatry, 59*, 140–148.

Wadman, R., Hiller, R.M., & St Clair, M.C. (2019). The influence of early familial adversity on adolescent risk behaviors and mental health: Stability and transition in family adversity profiles in a cohort sample. *Development and Psychopathology, 32*(2), 437–454.

Wagner, J.B., Luyster, R.J., Moustapha, H., Tager-Flusberg, H., & Nelson, C.A. (2018). Differential attention to faces in infant siblings of children with autism spectrum disorder and associations with later social and language ability. *International Journal of Behavioral Development, 42*, 83–92.

Wahabi, H.A., & others (2020). Systematic review and meta-analysis of the effectiveness of pre-pregnancy care for women with diabetes for improving maternal and perinatal outcomes. *PlosOne, 15*(8), e0237571.

Wainberg, M., Merico, D., Keller, M.C., Fauman, E.B., & Tripathy, S.J. (2022). Predicting causal genes from psychiatric genome-wide association studies using high-level etiological knowledge. *Molecular Psychiatry*, 1–12.

Waite-Stupiansky, S. (2017). Jean Piaget's constructivist theory of learning. In L.E. Cohen & S. Waite-Stupiansky (Eds.), *Theories of early childhood education.* Routledge.

Wake, M., Kerr, J.A., & Jansen, P.W. (2018). Child BMI over time and parent-perceived overweight. *Pediatrics, 142*(6), e20173985.

Waldenstrom, U., Cnattingius, S., Norman, M., & Schytt, E. (2015). Advanced maternal age and stillbirth risk in nulliparous and parous women. *Obstetrics and Gynecology, 126*, 355–362.

Waldenstrom, U., & others (2014). Adverse pregnancy outcomes related to advanced maternal age compared with smoking and being overweight. *Obstetrics and Gynecology, 123*, 104–112.

Waldman, Z., & Cleary, M. (2017). Hearing loss. In R. Schwartz (Ed.), *Handbook of child language disorders* (2nd ed.). Routledge.

Waldman-Levi, A., Finzi-Dottan, R., & Cope, A. (2020). Mother-child joint play: The role of maternal caregiving and reflective function. *Journal of Child and Family Studies, 29*(1), 94–104.

Waldron, J.C., Scarpa, A., & Kim-Spoon, J. (2018). Religiosity and interpersonal problems explain individual differences in self-esteem among young adults with child maltreatment experiences. *Child Abuse & Neglect, 80,* 277–284.

Walker, L. (1982). The sequentiality of Kohlberg's stages of moral development. *Child Development, 53,* 1130–1136.

Walker, L., & Taylor, D. (2021). *Same-sex couple households: 2019.* Available https://www.census.gov /content/dam/Census/library/publications/2021 /acs/acsbr-005.pdf

Walle, E.A., & Lopez, L.D. (2020). Emotion recognition and understanding in infancy and early childhood. In J.B. Benson (Ed.), *Encyclopedia of infant and early childhood development* (2nd ed.). Elsevier.

Walle, E.A., & others (2017). Infant differential behavioral responding to discrete emotions. *Emotion, 17*(7), 1078–1091.

Wallerstein, J.S. (2008). Divorce. In M.M. Haith & J.B. Benson (Eds.), *Encyclopedia of infant and early childhood development.* Elsevier.

Walsh, T.B., Davis, R.N., & Garfield, C. (2020). A call to action: Screening fathers for perinatal depression. *Pediatrics, 145*(1), e20191193.

Walters, G.D. (2019). Tracing the delinquency acquisition sequence from older siblings, to friends, to self: A mediation analysis. *Journal of Adolescence, 75,* 113–122.

Waltzer, T., & Dahl, A. (2021). Students' perceptions and evaluations of plagiarism: Effects of text and context. *Journal of Moral Education, 50,* 436–451.

Waltzman, D., & Sarmiento, K. (2019). What the research says about concussion risk factors and prevention strategies for youth sports: A scoping review of six commonly played sports. *Journal of Safety Research, 68,* 157–172.

Wan, Q., & Wen, F.Y. (2018). Effects of acupressure and music therapy on reducing labor pain. *International Journal of Clinical and Experimental Medicine, 11*(2), 898–903.

Wang, A.Y., & others (2018). Neonatal outcomes among twins following assisted reproductive technology: An Australian population-based retrospective cohort study. *BMC Pregnancy and Childbirth, 18,* 320.

Wang, C., & others (2016). Coevolution of adolescent friendship networks and smoking and drinking behaviors with consideration of parental influence. *Psychology of Addictive Behaviors, 30,* 312–324.

Wang, F., Zhang, Q., Ni, Z.H., & Lv, H.T. (2022). Effects of kangaroo care on pain relief in premature infants during painful procedures: A meta-analysis. *Journal for Specialists in Pediatric Nursing, 27,* e12390.

Wang, H.O., & others (2021). A physical perspective to the inductive function of myelin—A missing piece of neuroscience. *Frontiers in Neural Circuits, 14,* 562005.

Wang, H.Y., Sigerson, L., & Cheng, C. (2019). Digital nativity and information technology addiction: Age cohort versus individual difference approaches. *Computers in Human Behavior, 90,* 1–9.

Wang, J., & others (2019). Impact of exercise on maternal gestational weight gain: An updated meta-analysis of randomized controlled trials. *Medicine, 98*(27).

Wang, J.J., & Feigenson, L. (2021). Dynamic changes in numerical acuity in 4-month-old infants. *Infancy, 26,* 47–62.

Wang, L., & others (2023). Causal relationships between birth weight, childhood obesity and age at menarche: A two-sample Mendelian randomization analysis. *Clinical Endocrinology, 98,* 212–220.

Wang, Q. (2021). Cultural pathways and outcomes of autobiographical memory development. *Child Development Perspectives, 15*(3), 196–202.

Wang, S., Rubie-Davies, C.M., & Meissel, K. (2018). A systematic review of the teacher expectation literature over the past 30 years. *Educational Research and Evaluation, 24*(3–5), 124–179.

Wang, W., Vallotton, C.D., & Bowles, R.P. (2020). Ethnic variances in socializing young children's mastery motivation among White, African American, and Hispanic low-income families. *Early Childhood Research Quarterly, 51,* 329–337.

Wang, Y., Chen, M., & Lee, J.H. (2019). Adolescents' social norms across family, peer, and school settings: Linking social norm profiles to adolescent risky health behaviors. *Journal of Youth and Adolescence, 48*(5), 935–948

Wang, Y., & others (2019). Do you want to play with me today? Friendship stability among preschool children. *European Early Childhood Education Research Journal, 27*(2), 170–184.

Wang, Y., & Xu, M. (2020). Comparison of ropivacaine combined with sufentanil for epidural anesthesia and spinal-epidural anesthesia in labor analgesia. *BMC Anesthesiology, 20*(1), 1.

Ward, L.M., & Grower, P. (2020). Media and the development of gender role stereotypes. *Annual Review of Developmental Psychology, 2,* 177–199.

Wardlaw, G., Smith, A., & Collene, A. (2018). *Wardlaw's contemporary nutrition* (5th ed.). McGraw Hill.

Ware, E.A. (2017). Individual and developmental differences in preschoolers' categorization biases and vocabulary across tasks. *Journal of Experimental Child Psychology, 153,* 35–56.

Warmuth, K.A., Cummings, E.M., & Davies, P.T. (2020). Constructive and destructive interparental conflict, problematic parenting practices, and children's symptoms of psychopathology. *Journal of Family Psychology, 34,* 301–311.

Warneken, F. (2018). How children solve the two challenges of cooperation. *Annual Review of Psychology, 69,* 205–229.

Warren, A.S., Goldsmith, K.A., & Rimes, K.A. (2019). Childhood gender-typed behavior and emotional or peer problems: A prospective birth-cohort study. *Journal of Child Psychology and Psychiatry, 60*(8), 888–896.

Warren, S.F., & others (2017). The longitudinal effects of parenting on adaptive behavior in children with fragile X syndrome. *Journal of Autism and Developmental Disorders, 47,* 768–784.

Warrick, P. (1992, March 1). The fantastic voyage of Tanner Roberts. *Los Angeles Times,* pp. E1, E11, E12.

Warton, F.L., & others (2018). Prenatal methamphetamine exposure is associated with reduced subcortical volumes in neonates. *Neurotoxicology and Teratology, 65,* 51–59.

Wass, S.V. (2021). The origins of effortful control: How early development within arousal/regulatory systems influences attentional and affective control. *Developmental Review, 61,* 100978.

Wasserberg, M.J. (2017). Stereotype threat effects on African American and Latina/o elementary students tested together. *Journal for Multicultural Education, 11*(1), 51–60.

Wasserman, J.D. (2018). A history of intelligence assessment: The unfinished tapestry. In D.P. Flanagan & E.M. McDonough (Eds.), *Contemporary intellectual assessment: Theories, tests, and issues* (4th ed.). Guilford Press.

Wataganara, T., & others (2016). Fetal magnetic resonance imaging and ultrasound. *Journal of Perinatal Medicine, 44,* 533–542.

Watamura, S.E., Phillips, D.A., Morrissey, T.W., McCartney, K., & Bub, K. (2011). Double jeopardy: Poorer socio-emotional outcomes for children in the NICHD SECCYD who experience home and child-care environments that confer risk. *Child Development, 82,* 48–65.

Watanabe, E., Lee, J.S., Mori, K., & Kawakubo, K. (2016). Clustering patterns of obesity-related multiple lifestyle behaviors and their associations with overweight and family environments: A cross-sectional study in Japanese preschool children. *BMJ Open, 6*(11), e012773.

Waters, H.S., Waters, T.E.A., & Waters, E. (2021). From internal working models to script-like attachment representations. In R.A. Thompson & others (Eds.), *Attachment: The fundamental questions.* Guilford Press.

Waters, S.F., West, T.V., & Mendes, W.B. (2014). Stress contagion: Physiological covariation between mothers and infants. *Psychological Science, 25,* 934–942.

Waters, T.E., & Roisman, G.I. (2018). The secure base script concept: An overview. *Current Opinion in Psychology, 25,* 162–166.

Waters, T.E., Ruiz, S.K., & Roisman, G.I. (2017). Origins of secure base script knowledge and the developmental construction of attachment representations. *Child Development, 88,* 198–209.

Watkins, M.K., & Waldron, M. (2017). Timing of remarriage among divorced and widowed parents. *Journal of Divorce & Remarriage, 58*(4), 244–262.

Watson, H.J., O'Brien, A., & Sadeh-Sharvit, S. (2018). Children of parents with eating disorders. *Current Psychiatry Reports, 20*(11), 101.

Watson, H.J., & others (2019). Genome-wide association study identifies eight risk loci and implicates metabo-psychiatric origins for anorexia nervosa. *Nature Genetics, 51*(8), 1207–1214.

Watson, J.B. (1928). *Psychological care of infant and child.* W.W. Norton.

Watson, J.B., & Rayner, R. (1920). Conditioned emotional reactions. *Journal of Experimental Psychology, 3,* 1–14.

Waugh, C.E., & others (2019). People are better at maintaining positive than negative emotional states. *Emotion, 19*(1), 132-145.

Waugh, W.E., & Brownell, C.A. (2015). Development of body-part vocabulary in toddlers in relation to self-understanding. *Early Child Development and Care, 185*(7), 1166-1179.

Weatherhead, D., and others (2021). The role of audiovisual speech in fast-mapping and novel word retention in monolingual and bilingual 24-month-olds. *Brain Sciences, 11*(1), 114.

Weatherhead, D., & White, K.S. (2017). Read my lips: Visual speech influences word processing by infants. *Cognition, 160,* 103-109.

Webb, C., Bywaters, P., Scourfield, J., Davidson, G., & Bunting, L. (2020). Cuts both ways: Ethnicity, poverty, and the social gradient in child welfare interventions. *Children and Youth Services Review, 117,* 105299.

Webb, L.D., & Metha, A. (2017). *Foundations of American education* (8th ed.). Pearson.

Webber, T.A., & others (2017). Neural outcome processing of peer-influenced risk-taking behavior in late adolescence: Preliminary evidence for gene × environment interactions. *Experimental and Clinical Psychopharmacology, 25,* 31-40.

Wechsler, D. (1939). *The measurement of adult intelligence.* Williams & Wilkins.

Wedde, S., & others (2020). Associations between family meal context and diet quality among preschool-aged children in the Guelph Family Health Study. *Canadian Journal of Dietetic Practice and Research, 81,* 21-27.

Weeden, T. (2021, September 3). *Queer Black youth don't get enough reminders of their beauty and potential. Let's remedy that.* The Advocate.

Weekes, D.G., & others (2019). The effect of single sport specialization in youth sports: Does it increase the risk of injury? A prospective study. *Orthopaedic Journal of Sports Medicine, 7*(7) (Suppl. 5).

Weersing, V.R., & others (2017). Evidence base update of psychosocial treatments for child and adolescent depression. *Journal of Clinical Child and Adolescent Psychology, 46,* 11-43.

Wei, W.S., McCoy, D.C., Busby, A.K., Hanno, E.C., & Sabol, T.J. (2021). Beyond neighborhood socioeconomic status: Exploring the role of neighborhood resources for preschool classroom quality and early childhood development. *American Journal of Community Psychology, 67*(3-4), 470-485.

Weihrauch-Blüher, S., Schwarz, P., & Klusmann, J.H. (2019). Childhood obesity: Increased risk for cardiometabolic disease and cancer in adulthood. *Metabolism, 92,* 147-152.

Weinraub, M., & others (2012). Patterns of developmental change in infants' nighttime sleep awakenings from 6 through 36 months of age. *Developmental Psychology, 48,* 1511-1528.

Weisband, Y.L., & others (2018). Who uses a midwife for prenatal care and for birth in the United States? A secondary analysis of Listening to Mothers III. *Women's Health Issues, 28*(1), 89-96.

Weisgram, E.S. (2019). Reducing gender stereotypes in toys and play for smarter, stronger, and kinder kids. *American Journal of Play, 12*(1), 74-88.

Weisleder, A., & Fernald, A. (2013). Talking to children matters: Early language experience strengthens processing and builds vocabulary. *Psychological Science, 24,* 2143-2152.

Weisman, O., Zagoory-Sharon, O., & Feldman, R. (2014). Oxytocin administration, salivary testosterone, and father–infant social behavior. *Progress in Neuro-Psychopharmacology and Biological Psychiatry, 49,* 47-52.

Weiss, Y., & others (2022). Language input in late infancy scaffolds emergent literacy skills and predicts reading related white matter development. *Frontiers in Human Neuroscience, 16,* 922552.

Weissenberger, S., & others (2017). ADHD, lifestyles, and comorbidities: A call for an holistic perspective—From medical to societal intervening factors. *Frontiers in Psychology, 8,* 454.

Wellman, H.M. (2015). *Making minds.* Oxford University Press.

Wellman, H.M. (2018). Theory of mind: The state of the art. *European Journal of Developmental Psychology, 15,* 728-755.

Wellman, H.M., Cross, D., & Watson, J. (2001). Meta-analysis of theory-of-mind development: The truth about false belief. *Child Development, 72,* 655-684.

Wendelken, C., Gerrer, E., Whitaker, K.J., & Bunge, S.A. (2016). Fronto-parietal network reconfiguration supports the development of reasoning ability. *Cerebral Cortex, 26,* 2178-2190.

Wentzel, K.R., & Miele, D.B. (Eds.) (2016). *Handbook of motivation at school* (2nd ed.). Routledge.

Wentzel, K.R., & Muenks, K. (2016). Peer influence on students' motivation, academic achievement, and social behavior. In K.R. Wentzel & G. Ramani (Eds.), *Handbook of social influences in school contexts.* Routledge.

Wentzel, K.R., & Ramani, G. (2016). *Social influences on social-emotional, motivational, and cognitive outcomes in school contexts.* Taylor & Francis.

Werbart Törnblom, A., Sorjonen, K., Runeson, B., & Rydelius, P.A. (2020). Who is at risk of dying young from suicide and sudden violent death? Common and specific risk factors among children, adolescents, and young adults. *Suicide and Life-Threatening Behavior, 50*(4), 757-777.

Werner, B., Berg, M., & Höhr, R. (2019). "Math, I don't get it": An exploratory study on verbalizing mathematical content by students with speech and language impairment, students with learning disability, and students without special educational needs. In D. Kollosche & others (Eds.), *Inclusive mathematics education.* Springer.

Werner, L.A. (2017). Ontogeny of human auditory system function. In K. Cramer & others (Eds.), *Auditory development and plasticity* (pp. 161-192). Springer.

Werner, N.E., & others (2014). Maternal social coaching quality interrupts the development of relational aggression during early childhood. *Social Development, 23,* 470-486.

Wertheimer, A., & others (2021). Amniocentesis in twin gestation: The association between gestational age at procedure and complications. *Archives of Gynecology and Obstetrics, 305,* 1169-1175.

Wertz, J., & others (2018). Genetics and crime: Integrating new genomic discoveries into psychological research about antisocial behavior. *Psychological Science, 29,* 791-803.

Westbury, C. (2021). Prenominal adjective order is such a fat big deal because adjectives are ordered by likely need. *Psychonomic Bulletin & Review, 28,* 122-138.

Whaley, A.L. (2018). Advances in stereotype threat research on African Americans: Continuing challenges to the validity of its role in the achievement gap. *Social Psychology of Education, 21,* 111-137.

Whaley, A.L. (2020). Stereotype threat and psychosocial outcomes among African Americans: A population-based approach. *Journal of African American Studies, 24*(1), 56-77.

Whaley, S.E., Jiang, L., Gomez, J., & Jenks, E. (2011). Literacy promotion for families participating in the Women, Infants, and Children program. *Pediatrics, 127,* 454-461.

Whedon, M., Perry, N.B., & Bell, M.A. (2020). Relations between frontal EEG maturation and inhibitory control in preschool in the prediction of children's early academic skills. *Brain and Cognition, 146,* 105636.

Wheeler, J.J., & Richey, D.D. (2019). *Behavior management* (4th ed.). Pearson.

Whisman, M.A., Salinger, J.M., & Sbarra, D.A. (2022). Relationship dissolution and psychopathology. *Current Opinion in Psychology, 43,* 199-204.

White, B.A., & Kistner, J.A. (2011). Biased self-perceptions, peer rejection, and aggression in children. *Journal of Abnormal Child Psychology, 39,* 645-656.

White, C.N., & Poldrack, R.A. (2018). Methods for fMRI Analysis. *Stevens' handbook of experimental psychology and cognitive neuroscience, 5,* epcn515.

White, H., Jubran, R., Heck, A., Chroust, A., & Bhatt, R.S. (2018). The role of shape recognition in figure/ground perception in infancy. *Psychonomic Bulletin & Review, 25,* 1381-1387.

White, R.E., & others (2017). The "Batman effect": Improving perseverance in young children. *Child Development, 88*(5), 1563-1571.

Whitehead, L.S., & Buchanan, S.D. (2019). Childhood lead poisoning: A perpetual environmental justice issue? *Journal of Public Health Management and Practice, 25,* S115-S120.

Whiten, A. (2017). Social learning and culture in child and chimpanzee. *Annual Review of Psychology, 68,* 129-154.

Whitesell, C.J., Crosby, B., Anders, T.F., & Teti, D.M. (2018). Household chaos and family sleep during infants' first year. *Journal of Family Psychology, 32,* 622-631.

Whittington, C.M., Buddle, A.L., Griffith, O.W., & Carter, A.M. (2022). Embryonic specializations for vertebrate placentation. *Philosophical Transactions of the Royal Society B, 377,* 20210261.

Whitworth, H.S., & others (2023). Associations between age of menarche, early sexual debut and high-risk sexual behaviour among urban Tanzanian schoolgirls: A cross-sectional study. *Tropical Medicine and International Health, 28,* 237–246.

WHO Immediate KMC Study Group (2021). Immediate "kangaroo mother care" and survival of infants with low birth weight. *New England Journal of Medicine, 384,* 2028–2038.

Widman, L., Choukas-Bradley, S., Helms, S.W., & Prinstein, M.J. (2016). Adolescent susceptibility to peer influence in sexual situations. *Journal of Adolescent Health, 58,* 323–329.

Widom, C.S., Czaja, S.J., & DuMont, K.A. (2015). Intergenerational transmission of child abuse and neglect: Real or detection bias? *Science, 347,* 1480–1485.

Wie, J.H., & others (2019). Gestational age-specific risk of stillbirth during term pregnancy according to maternal age. *Archives of Gynecology and Obstetrics, 299*(3), 681–688.

Wiesen, S.E., Watkins, R.M., & Needham, A.W. (2016). Active motor training has long-term effects on infants' object exploration. *Frontiers in Psychology, 7,* 599.

Wigfield, A., & Gladstone, J.R. (2019). What does expectancy-value theory have to say about motivation and achievement in times of change and uncertainty? In E.N. Gonida & M.S. Lemos (Eds.), *Motivation in education at a time of global change.* Emerald Publishing Limited.

Wigfield, A., & others (2015). Development of achievement motivation and engagement. In R.M. Lerner (Ed.), *Handbook of child psychology and developmental science* (7th ed.). Wiley.

Wilce, J.M. (2017). *Culture and communication.* Cambridge University Press.

Wilcox, M., & others (2021). Perinatal depressive symptoms often start in the prenatal rather than postpartum period: Results from a longitudinal study. *Archives of Women's Mental Health, 24,* 119–131.

Willfors, C., Tammimies, K., & Bölte, S. (2017). Twin research in autism spectrum disorder. In M.F. Casanova, A.S. El-Baz, & J.S. Suri (Eds.), *Autism imaging and devices.* Taylor & Francis.

Williams, C.D., & others (2020). A lifespan model of ethnic-racial identity. *Research in Human Development, 17,* 99–129.

Williams, P.G., & others (2019). School readiness. *Pediatrics, 144*(2), e20191766.

Williamson, A.A., Mindell, J.A., Hiscock, H., & Quach, J. (2019). Child sleep behaviors and sleep problems from infancy to school-age. *Sleep Medicine, 63,* 5–8.

Willumsen, J., & Bull, F. (2020). Development of WHO guidelines on physical activity, sedentary behavior, and sleep for children less than 5 years of age. *Journal of Physical Activity and Health, 17,* 96–100.

Wils, A., Sheehan, P., & Shi, H. (2018). Better secondary schooling outcomes for adolescents in low- and middle-income countries: Projections of cost-effective approaches. *Journal of Adolescent Health, 65,* S25–S33.

Winne, P.H. (2017). Cognition and metacognition within self-regulated learning. In B.J. Zimmerman & D.H. Schunk (Eds.), *Handbook of self-regulation of learning and performance.* Routledge.

Winner, E. (2000). The origins and ends of giftedness. *American Psychologist, 55,* 159–169.

Winner, E., & Drake, J.E. (2018). Giftedness and expertise: The case for genetic potential. *Journal of Expertise, 1*(2), 114–120.

Witherington, D.C., Campos, J.J., Harriger, J.A., Bryan, C., & Margett, T.E. (2010). Emotion and its development in infancy. In J.G. Bremner & T.D. Wachs (Eds.), *Wiley-Blackwell handbook of infant development* (2nd ed.). Wiley.

Withers, M., Kharazmi, N., & Lim, E. (2018). Traditional beliefs and practices in pregnancy, childbirth and postpartum: A review of the evidence from Asian countries. *Midwifery, 56,* 158–170.

Witt, N., Coynor, S., Edwards, C., & Bradshaw, H. (2016). A guide to pain assessment and management in the neonate. *Current Emergency and Hospital Medicine Reports, 4,* 1–10.

Wittrup, A.R. & others (2019). Natural mentors, racial pride, and academic engagement among black adolescents: Resilience in the context of perceived discrimination. *Youth & Society, 51*(4), 463–483.

Wodtke, G.T., Ramaj, S., & Schachner, J. (2022). Toxic neighborhoods: The effects of concentrated poverty and environmental lead contamination on early childhood development. *Demography, 59*(4), 1275–1298.

Wolfe, K., & Ralls, F.M. (2019). Rapid eye movement sleep and neuronal development. *Current Opinion in Pulmonary Medicine, 25*(6), 555–560.

Wolke, D., Lee, K., & Guy, A. (2017). Cyberbullying: A storm in a teacup? *European Child and Adolescent Psychiatry, 26,* 899–908.

Wolke, D., & Lereya, S.T. (2015). Long-term effects of bullying. *Archives of Disease in Childhood, 100,* 879–885.

Women's Sports Foundation (2023). *Curriculum guide.* Retrieved March 18, 2023, from https://www.womenssportsfoundation.org/educational_resources_categories/curriculum-resources/

Wong, M., Lycett, K., Olds, T., Gold, L., & Wake, M. (2017). Use of time and adolescent health-related quality of life/wellbeing: A scoping review. *Acta Pediatrica, 106*(8), 1239–1245.

Wong, M.-L., & others (2017). The *PHF21B* gene is associated with major depression and modulates the stress response. *Molecular Psychiatry, 22,* 1015–1025.

Wood, C., Fitton, L., & Rodriguez, E. (2018). Home literacy of kindergarten Spanish-English speaking children from rural low-SES backgrounds. *AERA Open, 4*(2), 1–15.

Woods, R.J., & Schuler, J. (2014). Experience with malleable objects influences shape-based object individuation by infants. *Infant Behavior and Development, 37,* 178–186.

Workicho, A., & others (2019). Adolescent pregnancy and linear growth of infants: A birth cohort study in rural Ethiopia. *Nutrition Journal, 18*(1), 22.

Workman, J., & others (2023). Association between co-occurring anxiety and depression with drug overdose encounters in the emergency department among adolescents and young adults in the era of COVID-19. *Journal of Adolescent Health, 72,* 989–999.

Workman, L., & Reader, W. (2021). *Evolutionary psychology: An introduction* (4th ed.). Cambridge University Press.

World Bank (2023a). *Adolescent fertility rate (births per 1,000 women ages 15–19).* Available https://data.worldbank.org/indicator/SP.ADO.TFRT

World Bank (2023b). *Mortality rate, under-5 (per 1,000 live births).* https://data.worldbank.org/indicator/SH.DYN.MORT

World Health Organization (WHO) (2000, February 2). *Adolescent health behavior in 28 countries.*

World Health Organization (WHO) (2017). *Quality of care in contraceptive information and services, based on human rights standards: A checklist for health care providers.*

World Health Organization (WHO) (2019). *Contraception.* Available https://apps.who.int/iris/bitstream/handle/10665/329884/WHO-RHR-19.18-eng.pdf?ua=1

World Health Organization (WHO) (2020). *Adolescent pregnancy fact sheet.* Retrieved November 27, 2019, from https://www.who.int/en/news-room/fact-sheets/detail/adolescent-pregnancy

World Health Organization (WHO) (2020). *Healthy eating.* Available https://www.who.int/news-room/fact-sheets/detail/healthy-diet

World Health Organization (WHO) (2020). *Obesity and overweight.*

World Health Organization (WHO) (2021). *Infant and young child feeding.* https://www.who.int/news-room/fact-sheets/detail/infant-and-young-child-feeding

World Health Organization (WHO) (2021). *Mental health of adolescents.* Available https://www.who.int/news-room/fact-sheets/detail/adolescent-mental-health

World Health Organization (WHO) (2021). *Obesity and overweight.*

World Health Organization (WHO) (2022). *HIV.* Available https://www.who.int/news-room/fact-sheets/detail/hiv-aids

World Health Organization (WHO) (2023). *Child growth standards.* Available https://www.who.int/tools/child-growth-standards/standards

World Health Organization (WHO) (2023). *Health topics: Anaemia.* https://www.who.int/health-topics/anaemia

World Health Organization (WHO) (2023). *Midwifery education and care.* Available https://www.who.int/teams/maternal-newborn-child-adolescent-health-and-ageing/maternal-health/midwifery

Worrell, F.C., Subotnik, R.F., Olszewski-Kubilius, P., & Dixson, D.D. (2019). Gifted students. *Annual Review of Psychology, 70,* 551–576.

Wouldes, T.A., & Woodward, L.J. (2020). Neurobehavior of newborn infants exposed prenatally to methadone and identification of a neurobehavioral profile linked to poorer neurodevelopmental outcomes at age 24 months. *PlosOne, 15*(10), e0240905.

Wray-Lake, L., & Ballard, P.J. (2023). Civic engagement across adolescence and early adulthood. In L.J. Crockett, G. Carlo, & J.E. Schulenberg (Eds.), *APA handbook of adolescent and young adult development* (pp. 573–593). American Psychological Association.

Wright, A.J. (2020). Equivalence of remote, digital administration and traditional, in-person administration of the Wechsler Intelligence Scale for Children, Fifth Edition (WISC-V). *Psychological Assessment, 32,* 809–817.

Wright, B.L., Ford, D.Y., & Moore, J.L. (2022). Hidden in plain sight: Increasing equitable representation of underrepresented students in gifted and talented education. In J. Nyberg & J. Manzone (Eds.), *Creating equitable services for the gifted: Protocols for identification, implementation, and evaluation* (pp. 11–19). IGI Global.

Wright, V. (2018) Vygotsky and a global perspective on scaffolding in learning mathematics. In J. Zajda (Ed.), *Globalisation and education reforms.* Springer.

Wu, C., & Chao, R.K. (2017). Parent–adolescent relationships among Chinese immigrant families: An indigenous concept of qin. *Asian American Journal of Psychology, 8,* 323–338.

Wu, C.C., & others (2019). Paternal tobacco smoke correlated to offspring asthma and prenatal epigenetic programming. *Frontiers in Genetics, 10,* 471.

Wu, J., & Jobson, L. (2019). Maternal reminiscing and child autobiographical memory elaboration: A meta-analytic review. *Developmental Psychology, 55,* 2505–2521.

Wu, R., & Scerif, G. (2018). Attention. In M.H. Bornstein & others (Eds.), *SAGE encyclopedia of lifespan human development.* Sage.

Wu, T.W., Lien, R.I., Seri, I., & Noori, S. (2017). Changes in cardiac output and cerebral oxygenation during prone and supine sleep positioning in healthy term infants. *Archives of Disease in Childhood: Fetal and Neonatal Edition, 102*(6), F483–F489.

Wu, Y., Muentener, P., & Schulz, L.E. (2017). One- to four-year-olds connect diverse positive emotional vocalizations to their probable causes. *Proceedings of the National Academy of Sciences, 114,* 11896–11901.

Wu, Y., Schulz, L.E., Frank, M.C., & Gweon, H. (2021). Emotion as information in early social learning. *Current Directions in Psychological Science, 30*(6), 468–475.

Wuest, D., & Walton-Fisette, J. (2024). *Foundations of physical education, exercise science, and sport* (21st ed.). McGraw Hill.

X

Xie, C., & others (2017). Exercise and dietary program-induced weight reduction is associated with cognitive function in obese adolescents: A longitudinal study, *PeerJ, 5,* e3286.

Xie, L., & others (2021). United States prevalence of pediatric asthma by environmental smoke exposure, 2016–2017. *Journal of Asthma, 58*(4), 430–437.

Xie, W., Mallin, B.M., & Richards, J.E. (2018). Development of infant sustained attention and its relation to EEG oscillations: An EEG and cortical source analysis study. *Developmental Science, 21*(3), e12562.

Xie, W., Mallin, B.M., & Richards, J.E. (2019). Development of brain functional connectivity and its relation to infant sustained attention in the first year of life. *Developmental Science, 22*(1), e12703.

Xie, W., & others (2019). Neural correlates of facial emotion processing in infancy. *Developmental Science, 22*(3), e12758.

Xu, J., & others (2016). DNA methylation levels of imprinted and nonimprinted genes DMRs associated with defective human spermatozoa. *Andrologia, 48,* 939–947.

Xu, L., & others (2011). Parental overweight/obesity, social factors, and child overweight/obesity at 7 years of age. *Pediatric International, 53*(6), 826–831.

Y

Yackobovitch-Gavan, M., & others (2018). Intervention for childhood obesity based on parents only or parents and child compared with follow-up alone. *Pediatric Obesity, 13,* 647–655.

Yamaoka, Y., Fujiwara, T., & Tamiya, N. (2016). Association between maternal postpartum depression and unintentional injury among 4-month-old infants in Japan. *Maternal and Child Health Journal, 20,* 326–336.

Yan, T. (2021). Consequences of asking sensitive questions in surveys. *Annual Review of Statistics and Its Application, 8,* 109–127.

Yang, J., & others (2017). Only-child and non-only-child exhibit differences in creativity and agreeableness: Evidence from behavioral and anatomical structural studies. *Brain Imaging and Behavior, 11*(2), 493–502.

Yang, X., Dulay, K.M., McBride, C., & Cheung, S.K. (2021). How do phonological awareness, rapid automatized naming, and vocabulary contribute to early numeracy and print knowledge of Filipino children? *Journal of Experimental Child Psychology, 209,* 105179.

Yang, X., & others (2020). Metabolomics study and meta-analysis on the association between maternal pesticide exposome and birth outcomes. *Environmental Research, 182,* 109087.

Yang, Y.H., Marslen-Wilson, W.D., & Bozic, M. (2017). Syntactic complexity and frequency in the neurocognitive language system. *Journal of Cognitive Neuroscience, 29,* 1605–1620.

Yang, Z., Wang, M., Zhu, Z., & Liu, Y. (2022). Coronavirus disease 2019 (COVID-19) and pregnancy: A systematic review. *The Journal of Maternal-Fetal & Neonatal Medicine, 35,* 1619–1622.

Yao, C.A., & Rhodes, R.E. (2015). Parental correlates in child and adolescent physical activity: A meta-analysis. *International Journal of Behavioral Nutrition and Physical Activity, 12*(1), 10.

Yap, M.B., & others (2017). Modifiable parenting factors associated with adolescent alcohol misuse: A systematic review and meta-analysis of longitudinal studies. *Addiction, 112*(7), 1142–1162.

Yaremych, H.E., & Volling, B.L. (2020). Sibling relationships and mothers' and fathers' emotion socialization practices: A within-family perspective. *Early Child Development and Care, 190*(2), 195–209.

Yates, T.S., Ellis, C.T., & Turk-Browne, N.B. (2021). The promise of awake behaving infant fMRI as a deep measure of cognition. *Current Opinion in Behavioral Sciences, 40,* 5–11.

Yau, J.C., & Reich, S.M. (2019). "It's just a lot of work": Adolescents' self-presentation norms and practices on Facebook and Instagram. *Journal of Research on Adolescence, 29,* 196–209.

Yavorsky, J.E., & others (2015). The production of inequality: The gender division of labor across the transition to parenthood. *Journal of Marriage and Family, 77*(3), 662–679.

Yazejian, N., & others (2017). Child and parenting outcomes after 1 year of Educare. *Child Development, 88*(5), 1671–1688.

Yazigi, A., & others (2017). Fetal and neonatal abnormalities due to congenital rubella syndrome: A review of the literature. *Journal of Maternal-Fetal and Neonatal Medicine, 30,* 274–278.

Yeager, D.S., Dahl, R.E., & Dweck, C.S. (2018). Why interventions to influence adolescent behavior often fail but could succeed. *Perspectives on Psychological Science, 13,* 101–122.

Yeatts, P.E., Martin, S.B., & Farren, G.L. (2019). Adolescents' psychological well-being and their perceptions of parental encouragement to control weight. *Journal of Family Studies, 27*(4), 607–620.

Yeon, S., Bae, H.S., & Joshi, M. (2017). Cross-language transfer of metalinguistic skills: Evidence from spelling English words by Korean students in grades 4, 5, and 6. *Dyslexia, 23*(4), 428–448.

Yeung, E., Müller, U., & Carpendale, J.I. (2019). Developmental continuity between social-cognitive skills at age 2 and false belief understanding at age 4. *Cognitive Development, 50,* 157–166.

Yeung, S.S.S., King, R.B., Nalipay, J.N., & Cai, Y. (2022). Exploring the interplay between socioeconomic status and reading achievement: An expectancy-value perspective. *British Journal of Educational Psychology, 92,* 1196–1214.

Yilmaz, D., & others (2017). Screening 5- and 6-year-old children starting primary school for development and language. *Turkish Journal of Pediatrics, 58,* 136–144.

Ying, Z., & Chen, T. (2023). Mechanisms of DNA methylation and demethylation during mammalian development. In T.O. Tollefsbol (Ed.), *Handbook of epigenetics* (pp. 11–26). Academic Press.

Yogman, M., & others (2018). The power of play: A pediatric role in enhancing development in young children. *Pediatrics, 142*(3), e20182058.

Yonker, J.E., Schnabelrauch, C.A., & DeHaan, L.G. (2012). The relationship between spirituality and religiosity on psychological outcomes in adolescents and emerging adults: A meta-analytic review. *Journal of Adolescence, 35,* 299–314.

Yoon, E., & others (2017). East Asian adolescents' ethnic identity and cultural integration: A qualitative investigation. *Journal of Counseling Psychology, 64,* 65–79.

Yoshikawa, H., & others (2016). Money, time, and peers in antipoverty programs for low-income families. In C.S. Tamis-LeMonda & L. Balter (Eds.), *Child psychology: A handbook of contemporary issues.* Taylor & Francis.

Yoshikawa, H., Whipps, M.D., & Rojas, N.M. (2017). Commentary: New directions in developmentally informed intervention research for vulnerable populations. *Child Development, 88*(2), 459–465.

Yow, W.Q., & others (2017). A bilingual advantage in 54-month-olds' use of referential cues in fast mapping. *Developmental Science, 20*(1). doi:10.1111/desc.12482

Yu, J., & others (2022). Adverse childhood experiences and premature mortality through mid-adulthood: A five-decade prospective study. *The Lancet Regional Health–Americas, 15,* 100349.

Yuan, I., & others (2022). Functional near-infrared spectroscopy to assess pain in neonatal circumcisions. *Pediatric Anesthesia, 32*(3), 404-412.

Z

Zaami, S., & others (2021). Ethical, legal and social issues (ELSI) associated with non-invasive prenatal testing: Reflections on the evolution of prenatal diagnosis and procreative choices. *Genes, 12*(2), 204.

Zabaneh, D., & others (2017). Fine mapping genetic associations between the HLA region and extremely high intelligence. *Scientific Reports, 7,* 41182.

Zablah, J.E., & others (2017). Subclinical decrease in myocardial function in asymptomatic infants of diabetic mothers: A tissue doppler study. *Pediatric Cardiology, 38*(4), 801-806.

Zaboski, B.A., Kranzler, J.H., & Gage, N.A. (2018). Meta-analysis of the relationship between academic achievement and broad abilities of the Cattell-Horn-Carroll theory. *Journal of School Psychology, 71,* 42-56.

Zachary, C., & others (2019). The role of emotion regulation and socialization in behavioral parent training: A proof-of-concept study. *Behavior Modification, 43,* 3-25.

Zamarro, G., & Prados, M.J. (2021). Gender differences in couples' division of childcare, work and mental health during COVID-19. *Review of Economics of the Household, 19*(1), 11-40.

Zamuner, T.S., & Thiessen, A. (2018). A phonological, lexical, and phonetic analysis of the new words that young children imitate. *Canadian Journal of Linguistics, 63,* 609-632.

Zandoná, M.R., & others (2017). Validation of obesity susceptibility loci identified by genome-wide association studies in early childhood in South Brazilian children. *Pediatric Obesity, 12*(1), 85-92.

Zapata, J.P. (2023). Practices for promoting affirming health care for transgender and gender diverse youth. *Health Promotion Practice, 24,* 387-390.

Zarger, E., Adams, A., & McDonald Connor, C. (2020). The relations between children's comprehension monitoring and their reading comprehension and vocabulary knowledge: An eye-movement study. *Reading and Writing, 33,* 511-545.

Zaslavsky, L., & others (2021). Discovering and summarizing relationships between chemicals, genes, proteins, and diseases in PubChem. *Frontiers in Metrics and Analytics, 6,* 689059.

Zelazo, P.D. (2013). Developmental psychology: A new synthesis. In P.D. Zelazo (Ed.), *Oxford handbook of developmental psychology.* Oxford University Press.

Zelazo, P.D. (2015). Executive function: Reflection, iterative reprocessing, complexity, and the developing brain. *Developmental Review, 38,* 55-68.

Zelazo, P.D., & Carlson, S.M. (2022). Reconciling the context-dependency and domain-generality of executive function skills from a developmental systems perspective. *Journal of Cognition and Development, 24*(2), 205-222.

Zell, E., Krizan, Z., & Teeter, S.R. (2015). Evaluating gender similarities and differences using metasynthesis. *American Psychologist, 70,* 10-20.

Zhang, D., & others (2017). Is maternal smoking during pregnancy associated with an increased risk of congenital heart defects among offspring? A systematic review and meta-analysis of observational studies. *Journal of Maternal-Fetal and Neonatal Medicine, 30,* 645-657.

Zhang, J., Cheng, H.L., & Barrella, K. (2022). Longitudinal pathways to educational attainment and health of immigrant youth in young adulthood: A comparative analysis. *Journal of Child and Family Studies, 31,* 197-210.

Zhang, J., & others (2017). Sleep patterns and mental health correlates in U.S. adolescents. *Journal of Pediatrics, 182,* 137-143.

Zhang, M., Garnier, H., Qian, G., & Li, S. (2023). Effect of 11 weeks of physical exercise on physical fitness and executive functions in children. *Children, 10*(3), 485.

Zhang, T., & others (2019). Trajectories of childhood BMI and adult diabetes: The Bogalusa Heart Study. *Diabetologia, 62,* 70-77.

Zhang, X., Hashimoto, J.G., & Guizzetti, M. (2018). Developmental neurotoxicity of alcohol: Effects and mechanisms of ethanol on the developing brain. In M. Aschner & L. Costa, *Advances in neurotoxicology* (Vol. 2, pp. 115-144). Academic Press.

Zhang, X., & others (2018). Characteristics of likability, perceived popularity, and admiration in the early adolescent peer system in the United States and China. *Developmental Psychology, 54*(8), 1568-1581.

Zhao, S. (2020). Gender in families: A comparison of the gendered division of child care in rural and urban China. *Child & Youth Care Forum, 49,* 511-531.

Zheng, D., Ni, X., & Luo, Y. (2019). Selfie posting on social networking sites and female adolescents' self-objectification: The moderating role of imaginary audience ideation. *Sex Roles, 80,* 325-331.

Zhou, H., & others (2019). Quality antenatal care protects against low birth weight in 42 poor counties of Western China. *PloS One, 14*(1), e0210393.

Zhou, H., Wang, B., Sun, H., Xu, X., & Wang, Y. (2018). Epigenetic regulations in neural stem cells and neurological diseases. *Stem Cells International, 2018,* 6087143.

Zhou, H.Y., Cheung, E.F., & Chan, R.C. (2020). Audiovisual temporal integration: Cognitive processing, neural mechanisms, developmental trajectory and potential interventions. *Neuropsychologia, 140,* 107396.

Zhou, M., & Gonzales, R.G. (2019). Divergent destinies: Children of immigrants growing up in the United States. *Annual Review of Sociology, 45,* 383-399.

Zhu, M., Urhahne, D., & Rubie-Davies, C.M. (2018). The longitudinal effects of teacher judgement and different teacher treatment on students' academic outcomes. *Educational Psychology, 38,* 648-668.

Zhu, Y. (2021). 'Self' (*ziji*),'others' (*taren*) and 'collective' (*jiti*): Friendships at school embedded with China's Confucian-collectivist sociocultural values. *Children & Society, 35*(6), 916-929.

Zhu, Y.D., & others (2018). Prenatal phthalate exposure and placental size and shape at birth: A birth cohort study. *Environmental Research, 160,* 239-246.

Zhu, Z., & others (2019). Physical activity, screen viewing time, and overweight/obesity among Chinese children and adolescents: An update from the 2017 physical activity and fitness in China—The Youth Study. *BMC Public Health, 19*(1), 197.

Ziermans, T., & others (2017). Formal thought disorder and executive functioning in children and adolescents with autism spectrum disorder: Old leads and new avenues. *Journal of Autism and Developmental Disorders, 47*(6), 1756-1768.

Zill, N. (2017). *The changing face of adoption in the United States.* Institute for Family Studies.

Zimmerman, B.J., Schunk, D.H., & DiBenedetto, M.K. (2017). Role of self-efficacy and related beliefs in self-regulation of learning and performance. In A.J. Elliott, C.S. Dweck, & D.S. Yeager (Eds.). *Handbook of competence and motivation* (2nd ed.). Guilford Press.

Zinsser, K.M., Gordon, R.A., & Jiang, X. (2021). Parents' socialization of preschool-aged children's emotion skills: A meta-analysis using an emotion-focused parenting practices framework. *Early Childhood Research Quarterly, 55,* 377-390.

Zipke, M. (2021). *Playing with language: Improving elementary reading through metalinguistic awareness.* Teachers College Press.

Ziporyn, T.D., & others (2022). Adolescent sleep health and school start times: Setting the research agenda for California and beyond. *Sleep Health, 8,* 11-22.

Zosh, J., & others (2017). Putting the education back in education apps: How content and context interact to promote learning. In R. Barr & D. Linebarger (Eds.), *Media exposure during infancy and early childhood.* Springer.

Zou, H., & Yang, J. (2021). Exploring the brain lateralization in ADHD based on variability of resting state fMRI signal. *Journal of Attention Disorders, 25,* 258-264.

Zvara, B.J., Keim, S.A., Boone, K.M., & Anderson, S.E. (2019). Associations between parenting behavior and executive function among preschool-aged children born very preterm. *Early Childhood Research Quarterly, 48,* 317-324.

Zych, I., Farrington, D.P., & Ttofi, M.M. (2018). Protective factors against bullying and cyberbullying: A systematic review of meta-analyses. *Aggression and Violent Behavior, 45,* 4-19.

name index

A

Aagaard, J., 500
ABC News, 265
Abels, M., 208, 209
Abernathey, L., 447
Abigail, F., 224
Abramsky, T., 326
Abreu-Villaça, Y., 87
Acharya, S., 386, 387
Ackerman, J., 88
Acock, A., 257, 384
Adams, A., 354
Adams, B., 480
Adams, E., 254
Adams, K.A., 178, 182
Adamson, L., 199
Addabbo, M., 143
Adelantado-Renau, M., 308
Adisetiyo, V., 331
Adkins, M., 355
Administration for Children and Families, 266
Adolescent Sleep Working Group, AAP, 441
Adolph, K., 122, 134, 136–137, 139, 142, 147, 151, 162, 163, 199
Adolph, K.E., 134, 137, 151, 199
Afifi, T.O., 444
Agarwal, A., 59
Agirbasli, M., 322, 325
Agostini, A., 405, 440
Agostinis-Sobrinho, C., 437
Agras, W.S., 322, 447
Agricola, E., 93
Aguayo, L., 289
Ahçı, Z., 457
Ahern, E., 255
Aherne, C., 439
Ahmed, S., 428, 429
Ahmed, S.F., 368–369
Ahnert, L., 204, 285
Ahring, K.K., 55
Ahrons, C., 297
Ainsworth, M., 192
Ainsworth, M.D.S., 192, 202, 203
Ajetunmobi, O.M., 130
Akdeniz, S., 457
Akhtar, N., 262
Akingbuwa, W.A., 52
Akinsanya, A., 231
Akiyama, M., 50
Akpovo, S., 372
Aktar, E., 188, 192
Akter, D., 8
Alabdulkarim, S.O., 228
Alam, M.A., 237
Alber-Morgan, S., 328, 329, 365
Albert, 22
Alberto, P., 334
Alcalá, L., 249

Alcañiz, M., 334
Aldao, A., 396
Alegria, A.A., 331
Alex, A.M., 223
Alexander, J., 168
Alexander, P.A., 476
Alexopoulos, C., 432
Alfirevic, Z., 58
Alghamdi, R., 254
Al-Ghanim, K., 398
Ali, J.B., 121
Alibali, M., 344
Al-Khattabi, G., 89
Allameh, Z., 104
Allan, D., 330
Allen, C., 423–424, 489
Allen, D., 222
Allen, J., 423–424, 489, 495
Allen, J.P., 489, 504
Allen, M., 194
Allen, N., 427, 457
Allen, R., 456
Alm, B., 129
Almeida, R., 88
Almy, B., 256, 292, 507
Alonso, J., 256
Alonso-Alberca, N., 280
Alquraini, T., 329
Al-Shawaf, L., 47, 284
Althaus, N., 168
Altman, C., 356
Altug, H., 326
Alvarez, I., 298, 299
Alves, R., 354, 355
Amabile, T., 220, 228
Amato, P., 297, 299
Amato, P.R., 298
Ambrose, D., 366
Ameis, S., 328
Amemiya, J., 382
American Academy of Pediatrics, 128, 130, 242, 291, 307, 433, 441
American Association of Sleep Technologists, 441
American College of Nurse-Midwives, 102
American College of Obstetricians and Gynecologists, 80, 105, 433
American Pregnancy Association, 92
American Psychiatric Association, 334
American Psychological Association, 35, 291, 504
American Public Health Association, 83
American Society for Reproductive Medicine, 69
Amini, M., 8
Amir, D., 462
Amole, M.C., 30
Amrithraj, A.I., 91
Amso, D., 163

Amsterdam, R.K., 197
Amundsen, R., 349
An, J., 50
Anastasi, A., 364
Anastasiou, D., 335
Andersen, E., 426, 458
Anderson, A., 122
Anderson, C., 308
Anderson, D., 144, 252
Anderson, D.R., 252, 308
Andersson, H., 368–369
Andescavage, N.N., 76
Anding, J.E., 113
Andreas, J., 501
Andreassi, M.G., 89, 93
Andrews, J., 428, 429
Andrews, N., 485
Andrews, N.C., 405
Andrews, S., 254, 255
Andriani, H., 322
Ang, S., 362, 363
Angelakis, I., 293
Anglin, D.M., 483
Anguaino, R., 302
Ansari, A., 265
Antfolk, J., 283
Anthony, C., 297
Antonopoulos, C., 87
Aoki, C., 428
Apolzan, J., 325
Appel, M., 455
Apperley, L., 55
Aramburu, J., 301
Arbib, M.A., 176
Arck, P.C., 76
Arellanes, J., 302
Arellano, B., 348–349
Arens, A., 382
Argente, J., 427
Arizmendi, G.D., 346–347
Arkes, J., 297
Armon-Lotem, S., 356
Armstrong-Carter, E., 396
Arnell, K., 500
Arnett, J., 422, 423, 481
Arnett, J.J., 423
Arnold, L.E., 331
Arnon, I., 173
Aro, T., 328
Aronson, B., 9
Aronson, E., 412
Arrondo, G., 504
Arseneault, L., 405
Arterberry, M., 150
Artzi, H., 180
Arya, S., 92
Asbury, K., 333–334
Ashdown-Franks, G., 438
Ashford, K., 87
Askeland, K.G., 60
Aslin, R., 142, 165

Aslin, R.N., 163
Aspen Institute, 10
Assanand, S., 83
Assannangkornchai, S., 386, 387
Association of Child Life Professionals, 327
Astle, D.E., 329
Ata, R., 444–445
Atkins, K., 104
Atkinson, J., 145
Atun-Einy, O., 137
Aubert, S., 226
Auersperg, F., 297
Auld, E., 268
Austin, A.E., 495
Austin, J., 207
Austin, K., 82
Autism Research Institute, 334
Avery, S., 193, 195
Axinn, J., 9
Ayoub, C., 266, 268
Azar, S., 55
Azmitia, M., 466, 483

B

Ba, D.M., 433
Babic, A., 130
Babik, I., 140
Babskie, E., 371
Bachman, J.G., 444
Bachmann, N., 53
Bacikova-Sleskova, M., 296
Back, J., 446
Badahdah, A., 398
Baddeley, A., 456
Baddeley, A.D., 346
Badell, M., 59
Bader, L., 293
Bae, H., 353
Bae, S.M., 301
Baer, R.J., 81
Baggs, E., 248
Bagnall, C., 468
Bahrick, L., 149
Bailes, L., 188
Bailey, H., 347
Bailey, H.N., 203
Baillargeon, R., 161–163, 258
Bakaroudis, M., 497
Bakeman, R., 114
Baker, B., 189
Baker, J., 340
Baker, S., 257
Bakermans-Kranenburg, M., 205, 209
Baker-Smith, C.M., 325
Bakhtiani, P., 426
Bakth, F., 483
Bale, T., 284
Ballard, P., 461
Ballard, S., 437

Brand, R., 191
Brandes, C.M., 395
Brandlistuen, R.E., 397
Brandone, A., 259
Brandt, J.S., 93
Branje, S., 481, 488
Brannon, L., 393
Bratsberg, B., 362
Braun, J., 84
Braun, S., 285
Braver, S., 297
Brazelton, T.B., 107, 132, 217
Brazelton Touchpoint Center, 132
Bredekamp, S., 244, 265
Breivik, K., 405
Breland, A., 87
Bremner, A., 150
Bremner, J., 150, 163
Bremner, J.G., 146, 150
Breslin, P., 478
Breton, C.V., 64
Breton, É., 446
Bridgett, D., 195
Brigham, M., 335
Bright, N., 260
Brin, S., 265
Brito, N.H., 177
Broadney, M.M., 319
Broccia, M., 86
Brock, R., 298
Brocki, K., 503
Brodsky, J., 133
Brody, G.H., 429
Brodzinsky, D., 62
Broekhof, E., 260
Bronfenbrenner, U., 25–27, 236, 300
Bronstein, P., 285
Brooker, R., 30
Brooks, P., 176
Brooks, R., 165, 178
Brooks-Gunn, J., 197
Broomell, A., 11, 164, 168, 188,
    279, 317, 454
Brown, B., 493
Brown, D.A., 254
Brown, E.C., 89
Brown, G., 489
Brown, J., 114
Brown, P., 181
Brown, R., 177, 180
Brown, S., 461
Brown, S.M., 131
Brown, T.H., 333
Browne, D., 387
Browne, K., 91
Brownell, C., 197, 200, 209
Brownell, C.A., 202
Bruchmiller, K., 330
Bruck, M., 255
Bruckner, S., 177
Brugger, A., 371
Bruhn de Garavito, J., 171–172,
    261, 353
Brumariu, L., 386
Brumariu, L.E., 204–205
Brummelman, E., 383
Brummelte, S., 113
Brunborg, G., 501

Brunstein-Klomek, A., 405
Bryant, L., 132–133
Bucaille, A., 252, 366
Bucci, R., 492
Buchanan, S., 237, 238
Buchmann, S., 323
Buck, M., 209, 210
Buckingham-Howes, S., 88
Buckley, J., 84
Buckner, J., 384
Budani, M., 87
Budge, S., 486
Buehler, C., 504
Buhrmester, D., 408, 491, 495
Buitelaar, J., 66
Bukasa, A., 90
Bukowski, R., 91
Bukowski, W., 303, 305, 402, 403, 406
Bulbena-Cabre, A., 65
Bulgarelli, D., 260
Bull, F., 127, 230
Bullard, J., 229
Bumpus, M., 488
Bunn, J., 52
Burdelski, M., 278
Bureau, J., 277
Bureau of Labor Statistics, 296
Burge, T., 258
Burgette, J.M., 266
Burkart, J., 47
Burke, M., 335
Burks, A., 130
Burling, J., 145
Burnette, C.E., 499
Burnette, D., 409
Burns, E., 371
Burr, W.H., 236
Burrows, C., 190
Burrow-Sánchez, J., 455
Burt, K., 423
Burt, S., 63
Bush, A., 238
Bushman, B., 308, 383
Buss, A., 162
Buss, D., 47, 284
Buss, D.M., 47, 284
Bussey, K., 286
Bustamante, I., 488
Butler-Barnes, S., 466
Butt, A., 351
Byard, R.W., 128
Byrne, J.L., 234
Byrne, R., 165–166
Byrou, S., 58
Byrska-Bishop, M., 50

C

Cabaco, A.S., 427
Cabral, P., 499
Cabrera, N., 187, 211, 298
Cabrero, F., 329
Cai, M., 489
Cai, Y., 330
Cain, M.S., 500
Caino, S., 122
Cairncross, M., 331
Calandri, E., 501

Calkins, S., 122, 191, 194, 385
Callaghan, B., 166
Callaghan, M., 307
Callaghan, T., 81, 393
Callanan, M., 249, 344
Callueng, C., 193
Calvert, S.L., 307
Cameron, C., 256, 495
Camos, V., 344, 346
Campbell, B., 360
Campbell, K., 292
Campbell, K.L., 232, 319
Campbell, L., 360
Campione-Barr, N., 197–198
Campos, B., 494–495
Campos, J., 137
Campos, J.J., 189–190, 192
Campos, R., 167
Camras, L., 278
Canadian Association of
    Midwives, 102
Candilis-Huisman, D., 107
Cann, D., 430
Cano-Crespo, A., 331
Cantal, A., 235
Cantone, E., 406
Cantor, N., 256
Cao, Z., 446
Capa-Aydin, Y., 266
Capistrant, B.D., 296
Cappagli, G., 332
Card, N., 303, 395
Cardenas, S., 329
Cardonick, I., 354, 355
Carlin, C., 212
Carlin, R., 129
Carlini, S., 113
Carlo, G., 288, 392, 393, 461, 476
Carlson, E., 204
Carlson, M., 211
Carlson, S., 256
Carmina, E., 29
Carnegie Council on Adolescent
    Development, 468–469
Carone, N., 210, 300
Carpena, R.X., 231
Carpendale, J., 197, 403–404
Carr, A., 293
Carrington, H., 189
Carroll, A., 249
Carskadon, M.A., 440–441
Carsley, S., 234
Carson, V., 308
Carter, S., 333
Cascio, E.U., 268
CASEL, 386
Casey, B., 428
Casillas, M., 181
Casper, D., 303, 395
Caspi, A., 65
Cassidy, A.R., 202
Cassidy, D., 437
Cassidy, M., 176, 180, 188
Castillo, E., 90
Castillo, M., 447
Castle, D., 446
Castro, A., 227
Castro, M., 344, 454

Catalano, P., 77
Caton-Lemos, L., 112
Cattelino, E., 501
Catts, H., 175
Causadias, J., 34, 483
Causeur, D., 53
Causey, K., 248, 454
Caye, A., 331
Cazzato, V., 447
CCX Media Community News, 469
Ceci, S., 255
Center for the Prevention of Violence,
    405–406
Centers for Disease Control and
    Prevention, 87, 102, 108, 130, 131,
    221, 232–234, 236, 238, 242,
    321–322, 324, 326, 330, 333, 334,
    387, 431–434, 438, 441, 503,
    504–505
Cerrillo-Urbina, A.J., 332
Cervin, M., 260
Chaku, N., 455
Chambers, C., 277
Chambers, G.M., 59
Champagne, F.A., 13, 205
Chan, C.H., 506
Chan, R., 149–150
Chand, S., 329
Chang, L., 284
Chang, Y., 366
Chang, Y.K., 332
Chansakul, T., 90
Chao, R., 288
Chao, R.K., 288, 400
Chaplin, T., 396
Chaplin, T.M., 395–396
Chappuis, J., 409
Charles, C., 104
Charlesworth, T.E., 394
Charpak, N., 109, 111
Chaudhuri, J.D., 368
Chauhan, S., 77
Chavatte-Palmer, P., 91
Chaves-Castro, K., 226
Chavez, R., 260
Cheah, C.S.L., 400
Chee, J., 503
Chein, J., 458
Chemero, A., 248
Chen, D., 322
Chen, F., 428
Chen, G., 404, 406
Chen, H., 76, 395
Chen, J., 53, 145, 288
Chen, J.-Q., 360, 361
Chen, K.M., 55
Chen, L., 408, 492
Chen, N., 209
Chen, P.J., 79
Chen, R., 207
Chen, T., 51, 209
Chen, W.Y., 455
Chen, X., 189, 195, 285, 408, 492
Chen, Y., 465
Chen-Bouck, L., 288
Cheng, C., 395, 500
Cheng, C.A., 91
Cheng, H., 499

Geller, E., 462
Gelman, R., 248
Gelman, S., 262
Genie, 171, 180
Gennetian, L., 10, 301
Gentry, R., 354, 355
George, J., 211
George, L., 352
George Dalmida, S., 467
Gernhardt, A., 202
Geronimi, E., 348–349
Gershoff, E., 290, 312
Gershoff, E.T., 291
Gerst, E.H., 455
Gerstel, N., 296, 297
Gesell, A.L., 134, 151, 169
Gest, S., 444, 463
Gestwicki, C., 265
Geyer, C., 191
Ghasemi, M., 104
Ghazanfarpour, M., 436
Ghosh, D., 103
Gibbs, J.C., 390–392
Gibson, E., 146
Gibson, E.J., 142, 150, 151, 162
Gibson, J.J., 142, 150, 151
Gibson-Davis, C., 301
Giedd, J., 223
Giesbrecht, G.F., 192
Giguere, D., 353
Giletta, M., 404–406, 492
Gilkerson, J., 179
Gillespie, E., 293
Gilligan, C., 390–391, 393
Gillis, S., 181
Gilmore, J., 224
Gilpin, A., 260
Giménez-Dasi, M., 277
Gingo, M., 280, 392, 393
Gingoyon, A., 234
Giofre, D., 358
Girme, Y.U., 204
Giuntella, O., 34
Gladstone, J., 372
Glasper, E., 221
Gleason, J., 353
Gleason, J.L., 86
Gleason, T., 257, 391–392, 461
Glick, J., 499
Gliga, T., 123
Glock, S., 397
Glover, V., 92
Gnambs, T., 455
Gobet, F., 308, 347
Goddu, M., 382
Godfrey, K.M., 51
Godleski, S.A., 191
Godwin, J., 507
Goeltz, M., 209
Goffin, K., 277, 280
Goker, A., 104
Goksan, S., 149
Gold, M., 433
Goldberg, A., 62, 300
Goldberg, A.E., 61
Goldberg, W., 297, 328, 494–495
Goldin-Meadow, S., 174
Goldsmith, H., 194

Goldsmith, K., 285, 286
Goldstein, M., 178
Goldstein, T., 356
Goldston, D.B., 504
Goldstuck, N., 433
Goleman, D., 220
Golinkoff, R., 171–172, 174, 178, 180,
    181, 185, 262, 273, 306
Golinkoff, R.M., 178
Gollnick, D., 35, 410–412
Golomb, C., 229–230, 242
Golombok, S., 299, 401
Gomendio, M., 372
Gómez-Roig, M.D., 89
Gonthier, C., 363, 364
Gonzales, C.R., 253
Gonzales, N.A., 499
Gonzales, R., 483, 499
González, A., 280
González Briceño, L.G., 222
Good, C., 370
Good, M., 466
Goodale, M., 145
Goodman, R.J., 504
Goodman, W.B., 83
Goodvin, R., 189, 193, 197
Goodway, J., 225
Goodyer, I., 504
Gopnik, A., 168, 258, 273
Gordon, I., 205
Gordon, N., 336
Gordon, R., 22, 279
Gori, M., 254
Gorukanti, A., 444
Goshin, M., 399
Goswami, R., 83
Gottlieb, A., 9
Gottlieb, G., 64–65
Gottman, J., 208, 407
Gottman, J.M., 208, 280
Gottman Institute, 208
Gould, S.J., 48
Goupil, L., 163
Gower, A., 405
Goyal, M.K., 237
Gozdas, E., 223, 224
Grabowska, A., 395
Graci, M., 480
Gradworld FSU, 373
Graham, J., 390–391
Graham, M.E., 59, 60
Graham, S., 277, 347, 354–355, 470
Granqvist, P., 191
Grant, J.H., 82
Grant, K., 397, 398
Grant-Marsney, H., 60
Grasso, K., 436
Grattan, D., 205
Gravetter, F.J., 30
Gravetter, R., 27, 32
Gray, K., 331, 390, 391
Graziano, A., 28, 31, 33
Graziano, F., 501
Greco, I., 371
Greedan, B., 81
Green, F., 259
Green, J., 182
Green, T., 55

Greenberg, D., 263
Greenberg, D.M., 260
Greenberg, E.H., 268
Greene, J., 385, 391
Greene, S., 488
Greenstreet, E., 124, 224
Greer, F., 130
Greitemeyer, T., 308
Greve, B., 212
Griffiths, S., 446
Grigg, R., 349
Grigorenko, E., 361
Grigorenko, E.L., 328
Grimberg, A., 221–222
Grob, A., 360–361
Grogan-Kaylor, A., 290
Groh, A., 304
Groh, A.M., 203–204
Grolnick, W., 371
Groot, F., 249
Grossmann, K., 203, 205
Grossmann, T., 317
Grotevant, H., 60, 481
Grotevant, H.D., 60, 61
Groves, C., 308
Grower, P., 396
Grundy, J.G., 357
Grusec, J., 282, 287, 289, 392
Grusec, J.E., 399
Grych, J., 210–211
Gualtieri, S., 223–224
Guardian, 8
Guare, R., 347
Gubbels, J., 365
Gui, D., 391
Guilamo-Ramos, V., 432
Guilford, J.P., 349
Guizzetti, M., 86
Gulf Coast JFCS, 294
Gülgöz, S., 398, 485
Gullion, L., 170
Gump, B.B., 113
Gundersen, O.E., 15
Gunderson, E.A., 383
Gunnar, M., 293
Güntürkün, O., 124
Gupta, A., 411
Gustafsson, C., 266
Guthold, R., 438, 439
Gutierrez, B.C., 7
Guttentag, C.L., 436
Guttmacher Institute, 436
Guttmannova, K., 444
Gutzwiller, E., 391, 392
Guy, A., 405
Guyer, A., 223, 484

H

Ha, A.S., 234
Ha, T., 503
Haack, K., 8
Haan, M., 122
Haarbauer-Krupa, J.K., 320
Hadad, B., 150
Hadani, H., 257
Hadders-Algra, M., 76, 136, 138
Hadland, S.E., 505

Hafner, J.W., 326
Hagen, E., 47, 210
Hagen, K., 407
Haidt, J., 391
Haier, R.J., 361
Haimovitz, K., 370
Hair, N.L., 224
Halberstadt, A., 463
Halfon, N., 32
Halim, M.L., 286, 393–394
Halim, M.L.D., 283
Hall, G.S., 421, 484, 489
Hall, J., 101, 410
Hall, K., 6
Hall, W., 333, 405
Hallahan, D., 328, 330, 333, 340
Hallman, S., 483
Hallquist, M., 456
Halpern, A., 430
Halpern, D., 349, 398
Halpern-Felsher, B., 443
Hamilton, A., 228, 230
Hamilton, B., 435
Hamilton, J., 501
Hamlin, J., 162, 163
Hamlin, J.K., 163
Hammack, P.L., 7
Hammersley, M., 234
Hampl, S.E., 232
Hamra, G., 84
Han, J.Y., 87
Hanaoka, T., 85
Hanc, T., 106
Hancock, G., 191
Handler, A., 133
Hannan, F.M., 205
Hannigan, S., 351
Hannon, E., 146, 149
Hanson, M., 91
Happé, F., 260
Harackiewicz, J., 368
Harden, K.P., 63
Harding, J., 211
Harding, S., 162, 165, 199
Hardy, S., 464–465
Hardy, S.A., 467
Hare, B.D., 51
Hare, M.M., 278
Hargreaves, D., 446
Harkness, S., 139, 205
Harlow, H., 201
Harlow, H.F., 200–201
Harnois-Leblanc, S., 324
Harriger, J., 427
Harrington, E.M., 269, 278, 279
Harris, J., 262
Harris, K., 355
Harris, P., 228
Harrison, C.L., 91
Harrist, A., 208, 287, 288
Harry, B., 336
Hart, B., 179, 361–362
Hart, C.N., 232
Hart, D., 460
Hart, N., 492
Hart, S., 189, 461
Hart, S.L., 189

Jaworska, N., 439
Jebeile, H., 323
Jelding-Dannemand, E., 130
Jenkins, L., 405
Jensen, L.A., 280, 465
Jeong, J., 5
Jeong, S., 322
Jezak, M., 356
Ji, B.T., 93
Ji, G., 295
Jia, S., 76
Jiang, K., 320
Jiang, Q., 209
Jiang, X., 279
Jiang, Z., 188
Jiao, S., 295
Jiménez-Díaz, J., 226
Jin, K., 163
Jin, K.S., 162, 190
Jin, Y., 228, 230, 326
Jing, Q., 295
Jo, J., 104
Joh, A., 140
Johansson, F., 47
Johansson, J.V., 56
Johansson, M., 113
John, R.M., 53
Johns Hopkins Medicine, 129
Johnson, A., 193
Johnson, C.M., 132, 232
Johnson, J., 355
Johnson, J.A., 409
Johnson, K., 168
Johnson, K.C., 485
Johnson, M., 123, 316, 317
Johnson, M.D., 47, 49, 283
Johnson, M.H., 317
Johnson, R., 31
Johnson, S., 145, 146, 150,
    163, 190, 250
Johnson, S.P., 146
Johnson, W., 45, 63
Johnston, A., 277
Johnston, C., 90
Johnston, L.D., 441–444
Joleby, M., 430
Jones, B.P., 59
Jones, C., 482
Jones, E., 123
Jones, J., 61, 299
Jones, K., 352
Jones, L., 104
Jones, M., 305
Jones, M.C., 427
Jones, R., 234
Jones-Mason, K., 199
Jonsson, E., 86
Joos, C.M., 426
Jordan, C., 382–383
Jordan, M., 356
Jorges, V., 327
Josephson Institute of Ethics, 464
Joshi, H., 384
Joshi, M., 353
Jourdren, M., 252
Juras, R., 436
Juster, R.-P., 446
Justice, L.M., 179

Jutengren, G., 404
Jutras, B., 148
Juvonen, J., 468

K

Kachel, U., 277
Kackar, H., 461
Kaczynski, T., 3, 8
Kadir, M., 382
Kaestle, C.E., 494
Kagan, J., 14, 189–191, 193–195
Kahn, N., 430
Kaidesoia, M., 447
Kalaitzopoulos, D.R., 88
Kalamar, A.M., 433
Kalisch-Smith, J., 87
Kalish, C., 262
Kalogeropoulos, C., 127
Kalokerinos, E., 364
Kalstad, T., 128
Kamenetz, A., 478
Kaminer, Y., 89
Kammer, T., 177
Kanakis, G., 54
Kanakogi, Y., 208
Kane, S., 89
Kang, E., 305
Kang, M., 195
Kang, S., 455
Kangaslampi, S., 255
Kanji, A., 147
Kann, L., 430–432, 439, 440
Kannan, P., 103
Kanske, P., 260
Kanter, J., 55
Kantha, S.S., 231
Kantrowitz, B., 275
Kapetanovic, S., 444
Kaplan, B., 147
Karababa, A., 484, 485
Karaglani, E., 131
Karaman, F., 173
Karami, S., 366
Karapakula, G., 507
Karasik, L., 139
Karazsia, B., 446
Karberg, E., 298
Karela, C., 299
Karl, J., 140
Karlsson, J., 324
Karmiloff-Smith, A., 126, 127
Karp, H., 217
Kárpáti, A., 350, 351
Karr, J.E., 331
Karremans, J., 462
Kassai, R., 254, 348
Kastbom, A.A., 432
Katz, P.A., 380–381
Kauchak, D., 408, 409
Kauer, R., 81
Kauffman, J., 328, 330, 333, 335, 340
Kaufman, H., 238
Kaufman, J., 350, 351
Kaufman, P., 220
Kaufman, T.M.L., 304
Kaufman, Y., 113
Kaunhoven, R., 188

Kavanaugh, B.C., 93
Kavanaugh, R., 259
Kavle, J., 83
Kawwass, J., 59
Kearsley, R., 191
Kee, M., 93
Keen, R., 144, 228
Kees, J., 89
Keeton, C., 191
Kegel, C., 180
Kehayes, I.L.L., 447
Kehl, S.M., 148
Keijsers, L., 501
Keil, F., 382
Keister, L., 301
Keith, K.D., 6
Kekunnaya, R., 145
Keller, H., 202
Keller, M., 207, 406
Kelley, G., 235
Kelley, K., 235
Kellogg, R., 229
Kelly, A.B., 443
Kelly, R., 127
Kendall, L.F., 148
Kendler, K.S., 63
Kendrick, C., 295
Kendrick, K., 404
Kennedy, D., 326
Kennedy, E., 237
Kennedy, M.C., 497
Kennell, J.H., 114
Kenny, S., 146
Kerns, K., 386, 400, 495
Kerpelman, J., 482
Kerr, J., 232
Kerr, K., 484
Kerstis, B., 113
Ketcham, P., 444
Key, A., 398, 486
Keyes, K.M., 440
Khaleque, A., 6
Kharazmi, N., 83
Kharitonova, M., 346
Khatun, M., 108
Khetarpal, S.K., 487
Khoury, J., 86
Khoza-Shangase, K., 147
Khu, M., 277
Kiani, M., 436
Kibby, M., 329
Kidd, C., 165, 256
Kidd, E., 179
Kieler, M., 49
Kievit, R., 254
Kilale, A., 208, 209
Killen, M., 163, 280, 381, 390, 392,
    394, 461
Killoren, S.E., 495
Kilpatrick, S., 302
Kim, B.R., 51, 204
Kim, H., 30
Kim, J., 224, 503
Kim, K.H., 350
Kim, M.J., 405
Kim, P., 205, 302
Kim, S., 204, 280, 490

Kim, S.K., 131
Kim, S.M., 505
Kim, Y., 354, 455, 481
Kim-Spoon, J., 280, 444, 465
Kinard, D., 286
Kindermann, T.A., 408
King, A., 178
King, J.D., 505
King, K., 404, 465
King, L.S., 179
King, P., 464–465
King, R.B., 370
King, S.M., 506
Kingsbury, A.M., 194
Kinsey, S., 112
Király, I., 347
Kirk, E., 235
Kirk, S., 235
Kirkebøen, L., 297
Kirkham, N., 173
Kirkorian, H., 144
Kirmayer, L.J., 11, 344, 454
Kishi, R., 85
Kistner, J., 404
Klahr, A., 63
Klausen, T., 60
Kleen, H., 397
Klein, D., 433
Klemfuss, J., 255
Kliewer, R., 193
Klimek, B., 259
Klimstra, T., 480
Klinger, L., 334
Klingner, J., 336
Klopack, E.T., 427
Klug, J., 397
Klug, W.S., 52
Klusmann, J., 233, 322
Knafo-Noam, A., 195, 280–281,
    289, 392
Knickmeyer, R., 224
Knight, C.J., 321
Knocke, K., 102
Knogler, M., 368
Knop, B., 293
Knox, M., 292
Ko, R., 83
Kobayashi, T., 263
Koch, M., 397, 409
Kochanska, G., 204, 277, 280, 298
Kochenderfer-Ladd, B., 403
Kochendorfer, L., 495
Koehn, A., 400
Koeneman, O., 172
Koenig, A.M., 285
Koenig, L., 465
Koerber, S., 259
Kofler, M.J., 331
Koh, E., 61
Kohlberg, L., 281, 388–393, 461, 464
Kohlhoff, J., 205
Kok, F.M., 331
Kolk, S., 428
Kołomańska-Bogucka, D., 112, 113
Költő, A., 494
Komienko, O., 483
Kominarek, M., 77
Kondo-Ikemura, K., 203

Richter, T., 350, 459
Rideout, V., 500
Rieger, S., 383
Riggins, T., 88, 166, 167
Riggle, A., 486
Riggle, M., 486
Riggs, A., 286
Righetto Greco, A.L., 140
Rimes, K., 285, 286
Rindermann, H., 361
Ringoot, A.P., 304
Ripke, M., 402
Risley, T., 179, 361–362
Rispoli, M., 334
Ritchie, S., 362
Ritter, J., 211, 213
Riva Crugnola, C., 436
Rivas-Drake, D., 301, 476, 483, 484
Rivera, F., 331
Rivera, S.M., 54
Riveros, R., 465
Rivers, A.S., 489
Rizzo, M., 381
Rizzolo, D., 128
Robbins, T., 83, 317, 456
Robbinsdale Area Schools, 469
Roberts, C.P., 90
Roberts, D., 500
Roberts, J., 367
Roberts, T., 99–100
Robins, R., 479, 483
Robinson, A., 481
Robinson, E., 211
Robinson, M., 456
Robinson, O., 422
Robinson, S., 136, 137, 322
Robson, D., 194
Rockstuhl, T., 363
Rode, S.S., 114
Röder, B., 145
Röder, M., 382
Rodgers, C., 316
Rodgers, E., 263, 409
Rodgers, J., 32, 362
Rodriguez, E., 263
Rodriguez Vega, S., 421
Roehlkepartain, E., 421–422
Roeser, R., 349, 470
Roeser, R.W., 349
Rofey, D., 428
Rogeberg, O., 362
Rogers, C., 122, 316, 318
Rogers, L., 482
Roggman, L., 211
Rogoff, B., 249, 344
Roh, M., 322
Roisman, G., 36, 202–204, 386, 489
Rojas, N., 499
Rolfes, S., 129
Roman, L.A., 80
Roman, M., 113
Romano, A., 165
Romeo, R., 428
Romeo, R.D., 428
Romeo, R.R., 179
Romiti, A., 301
Rood, J., 49
Roos, L., 237, 302

Ropars, J., 252
Ropars, S., 109
Roper, S., 297
Roque, L., 181
Rosario, M., 494
Rose, A., 36, 286
Rose, K.K., 296
Rose, S., 254
Rosenau, P.T., 331
Rosenberg, M.D., 346
Rosenblum, S., 400
Rosenstein, D., 149
Rosenthal, S., 485
Rosmarin, D.H., 465
Ross, A., 30, 224
Ross, H., 295
Ross, J., 197, 278, 347
Ross, S., 492
Rossell, S., 446
Ross-Sheehy, S., 162
Rostad, K., 258
Rostgaard, T., 211
Rostron, B.L., 87
Rote, W., 489
Roth, B., 361
Rothbart, M., 193, 196, 252–254
Rothbart, M.K., 191, 193
Rothbaum, F., 189, 205
Rothenberg, W.A., 507
Rothman, E., 428
Rotman, S.A., 234, 322
Rousham, E., 5
Rovee-Collier, C., 164, 166
Rowe, M., 166, 199
Royal College of Obstetricians and
    Gynaecologists, 58
Royer, C., 255
Roysircar, G., 6, 36
Ruan, Y., 264
Rubeling, H., 202
Rubie-Davies, C., 372, 397
Rubin, D.H., 93
Rubin, K., 303, 305, 402, 403, 406
Rubin, K.H., 403, 404
Rubio-Codina, M., 227
Rubio-Fernandez, P., 355
Ruble, D., 381–382
Ruckart, P.Z., 238
Rueda, M.R., 252
Ruffman, T., 190, 278
Ruigrok, A.N.V., 394
Ruiz, S., 489
Ruiz-Hernández, J.A., 503
Russell, D., 292
Russell, L., 400
Russell, P., 55
Russell, S., 288, 404, 494
Russotti, J., 292
Rutman, L., 326
Ryan, A., 492
Ryan, R., 368, 428
Rydell, A., 503
Rytioja, M., 403

S

Sabbagh, M., 259
Sackett, P., 361

Sadeh, A., 127
Sadeh-Sharvit, S., 446
Sadker, D., 397, 409
Saeidi, M., 436
Saez de Urabain, I.R., 123
Safa, M., 289, 302, 490
Safford, P., 411, 413
Saffran, J., 173
Sagi-Schwartz, A., 14, 189, 195, 202, 203, 205, 386
Sahakian, B., 485
Saint-Jacques, M.C., 401
Sakai, J., 125
Saklofske, D., 358
Sala, G., 308
Sala, M., 447
Salazar, W., 226
Salcido, V., 483
Salinger, J., 491
Salley, B., 165
Salmivalli, C., 404–405
Salm Ward, T., 80
Salo, V., 166, 199
Salsa, A., 245
Samara, M., 404
Sameroff, A.J., 208
Sammons, P., 410
Samuelson, L., 262
Sanapo, L., 58
Sánchez-Álvarez, N., 463
Sánchez-Vincitore, L., 227
Sanders, G.J., 323
Sanders, K., 266
Sanders, M., 289
Sanderud, A., 90
Sandhofer, C., 262
Sandrim, V., 53
Sandstrom, A., 193
Sandstrom, H., 212
Sanford, D., 114
Sanford, R., 114
Sankupellay, M., 127
Sanson, A., 196
Santangeli, L., 91
Santirocco, M., 57
Santos, C., 483
Santos, L.M., 76
Sarama, J., 268
Sardi, L., 112
Sardinha, L.B., 319
Sari, H., 109
Sarker, A., 108
Sarmiento, K., 320
Sassi, F., 323
Sattar, N., 91
Sauce, B., 361
Saul, A., 65
Saunders, J., 333
Saunders, M.C., 63
Saunders, N.R., 73
Sävendahl, L., 222
Savina, E., 189, 253
Savin-Williams, R.C., 494
Savolainen, H., 403
Sawyer, J., 249
Saxena, M., 53
Saxton, E., 468
Sayer, A., 60

Sayler, K., 195
Sbarra, D., 299, 491
Scaife, J.C., 447
Scales, P., 421–422
Scarlett, W., 465
Scarpa, A., 465
Scarr, S., 63–64
Scerif, G., 164
Schaal, B., 149
Schabbauer, G., 49
Schachner, A., 149
Schachner, J., 238
Schacter, H., 483
Schaefer, F., 324
Schaettle, P., 227
Schäfer, M., 393
Schaffer, H.R., 201
Schalkwijk, F., 391
Schauble, L., 350
Scheider, W., 350, 459
Schell, L., 5
Scherf, K., 428
Schermer, J., 358
Scherrer, V., 383
Schetter, C., 436
Schiariti, V., 6
Schieffelin, B., 181
Schiff, W.J., 130, 322, 438
Schlam, T.R., 256
Schlegel, M., 257
Schlegelmilch, K., 168
Schleider, J., 191
Schmidt, J., 461
Schmidt, K.L., 9
Schmitt, J.E., 317
Schmukle, S., 295
Schnabelrauch, C., 465
Schneider, B., 408
Schneider, N., 124, 125, 224
Schneider, S., 191, 330
Schneider, W., 351
Schoeler, T., 405
Schoen, M., 122
Schöner, G., 134
Schonert-Reichl, K., 349
Schoon, I., 302
Schoppe-Sullivan, S., 204
Schoppe-Sullivan, S.J., 210
Schoppmann, J., 191
Schreiber, S., 89
Schroeder, E., 497
Schroeder, K., 285
Schulenberg, J., 442, 476
Schuler, J., 146
Schulz, L., 258
Schumm, W., 300
Schunk, D., 370–371, 384, 385
Schunk, D.H., 22, 368–372
Schurz, M., 260
Schutte, N.M., 439
Schutten, D., 500
Schwab, C., 328
Schwalbe, C.S., 503
Schwartz, D., 405
Schwartz, S., 280–281, 289, 483
Schwartz, S.J., 482, 483
Schwarz, P., 233, 322
Schweig, J., 411

Stump, G., 172
Suarez-Alvarez, J., 189
Suárez-Orozco, C., 499
Subrahmanyam, K., 252
Substance Abuse and Mental Health Services Administration, 511
Sucksdorff, M., 106
Sue, D.W., 499
Sugden, N., 142, 199
Sugimura, K., 465, 481–482
Suh, B., 195
Suk, M., 505
Sullivan, H.S., 491
Sullivan, R., 122, 205
Sullivan, T., 495
Sultana, M., 108
Sumner, E., 489
Sun, Q., 490
Sun, X., 319–320
Sun, Y., 427
Sunderam, S., 59
Suomi, S., 201
Super, C., 139
Super, E., 205
Surkan, P., 488
Surkan, P.J., 94
Susman, E., 424–426
Susman, E.J., 426
Sutin, A.R., 405
Sutter, C.C., 504
Sutterlin, S., 281
Sutton, T.E., 204
Suveg, C., 208
Suzuki, M., 92
Svaldi, J., 447
Svensson, I., 113
Swaab, H., 54
Swain, J., 205
Swain, J.E., 205
Swamy, G., 109
Swanson, H., 329
Swanson, H.L., 456
Swanson, L.L., 346–347
Swartout, K., 506
Swartzendruber, A., 506
Sweeney, M., 297
Swingler, M.M., 199
Symonds, J., 384
Szucs, L.E., 436
Szwedo, D., 495

T

Taboada, M., 172, 262
Tager, M., 268
Taggart, J., 305, 467
Taggart, T., 494
Tahir, M., 320
Talge, N., 92
Tallarico, R., 497
Tallberg, P., 330
Talwar, V., 258
Tam, V., 30
Tamayo, S., 357
Tamis-LeMonda, C., 139, 178, 398
Tamis-LeMonda, C.S., 263
Tamiya, N., 113

Tammimies, K., 334
Tamminga, S., 92
Tampi, R., 231
Tan, B., 331–332
Tan, C., 408
Tan, J., 489
Tang, A., 194
Tang, S., 436, 483
Tang, Y., 254
Tanilon, J., 505
Tank, K., 351
Tannen, D., 396
Tanner, M., 54
Tanrikulu, M., 322, 325
Tao, L., 355, 356
Tapper, K., 349
Taraban, L., 207
Tardif, T., 175, 302
Tatlidil, K., 308
Tatum, H.E., 464
Taylor, B., 500
Taylor, C., 104, 233, 349
Taylor, D., 299
Taylor, F., 83
Taylor, G., 55
Taylor, N., 263
Taylor, R., 329
Tcheandjieu, C., 50
Teeter, S., 395
Tehrani, H., 104
Telzer, E., 511
Telzer, E.H., 205
Temple, C.A., 329, 354, 409
Tenenbaum, H., 285
Tenenbaum, H.R., 28
Te'o, M., 495, 496
Terman, L., 365, 366
Terrace, H., 199
Terrier, C., 397
Terry, N., 263
Testa, A., 133
Testa, S., 260
Teti, D., 127
Thacher, J.D., 87
Thakur, M., 83
Thanh, N., 86
Thapar, A., 504
Thavamani, A., 322
The, N.S., 438
Thébaud, S., 212
Thelen, E., 134, 136, 151
Thelwall, M., 485
Theo, L., 115
Thibodeau-Nielsen, R., 260
Thiessen, A., 171
Thoma, S., 391
Thomaes, S., 383
Thomas, A., 192–194, 196
Thomas, B., 140
Thomas, G., 55
Thomas, J., 297
Thomas, J.C., 191
Thomas, K., 112, 122, 429
Thomas, M., 205
Thomas, S.A., 432
Thompson, A., 396
Thompson, D.R., 322
Thompson, E.J., 469

Thompson, J., 322, 427
Thompson, M., 506
Thompson, M.J.J., 157
Thompson, R., 189, 193, 197, 203–204, 209, 283, 392
Thompson, R.A., 180, 189, 190, 194, 198–200, 202–205, 277–278, 281–283, 356, 383, 386
Thoni, C., 284
Thorndike, A., 237
Thornton, J., 411
Thunberg, G., 478
Thurman, A.J., 54
Tibken, C., 350, 459
Tiboni, G., 87
Tiego, J., 253
Tiggemann, M., 427, 446, 447
Tillyer, M., 502
Tincoff, R., 174
Tinker, S.C., 91
Tistarelli, N., 331
Tobin, J., 270
Todd, J., 149
Toepfer, P., 205
Tomasello, M., 178, 258, 277, 282, 393
Tomblin, J., 175
Tomfohr-Madsen, L.M., 291
Tomlinson, A., 291
Tomlinson, M., 239
Tomlinson, R.C., 302
Tompkins, G., 263, 409
Tompkins, G.E., 263
Tompkins, V., 190, 260
Temporowski, P.D., 320
Tongsong, T., 92
Tooley, U., 127
Tooley, U.A., 429
Toomey, R., 404
Topalian, A., 465
Toppelberg, C., 181
Torbé, A., 106
Torbé, D., 106
Törmänen, S., 53
Torstveit, L., 281
Toskala, E., 326
Toste, J., 470
Tout, K., 212
Traccis, F., 85
Trainor, L., 148
Traisrisilp, K., 92
Treagust, D., 350
Trehub, S., 191
Treit, S., 428–429
Trent, M., 237
Treyvaud, K., 113
Trimble, J.E., 35
Trinder, J., 457
Trinh, K.C., 452
Trinh, R.M., 149
Trivedi, M., 326
Trommsdorff, G., 189
Tronick, E., 107
Troop-Gordon, W., 405
Trosman, I., 440
Troutman, A., 334
Truglio, R., 308

Trumbull, L., 436
Truzzi, A., 65
Trzesniewski, K., 370
Tsang, T.W., 86
Tschiderer, L., 130–131
Tsiorvas, A., 461
Tso, W., 231
Tsubomi, H., 346
Tsunematsu, T., 128
Ttofi, M., 405
Ttofi, M.M., 405
Tucker-Drob, E., 362
Tudge, J., 462
Tudge, J.R., 25, 26
Tuleski, S., 248
Tummeltshammer, K., 163
Tung, W., 83
Turiel, E., 280, 392, 393
Turk, E., 29
Turk-Browne, N., 162, 258
Turnbull, A., 328, 335
Turner, K., 289
Turner, L., 31
Turner, S., 505
Tweed, E.J., 106
Twenge, J.M., 501
Tylka, T., 446
Tyndall, C., 89
Tyrell, F.A., 495

U

Uba, L., 83
Ueno, M., 147
Uher, R., 193
Ullah, M.B., 113
Ullman, T.D., 163
Umaña-Taylor, A., 6–7, 34, 289, 302, 411, 476, 483, 484, 490
Umaña-Taylor, A.J., 6–7, 482, 484
Umemura, T., 482
Umer, A., 130
Unar-Munguía, M., 130
Underdal, M., 131
Underwood, J.M., 438
Ungar, M., 387
UNICEF, 90, 120, 131, 234, 239, 242, 270, 284, 398, 434, 497
United Nations, 291, 471
Updegraff, K., 487
Urbina, S., 364
Urhahne, D., 372
USA Today, 355
U.S. Census Bureau, 36
U.S. Department of Agriculture, 319
U.S. Department of Education, 335, 412
U.S. Department of Health and Human Services, 61, 91, 266, 292, 294
U.S. Department of Justice, 502
U.S. Department of Labor, 296
U.S. Department of Transportation, 457
U.S. Food and Drug Administration, 92
Usher, E., 384
Usher, L., 190
U.S. Preventive Services Task Force, 129

subject index

A

abstract thinking, 453–454, 465–466
abuse. *See* child maltreatment
academic achievement. *See* achievement
academic advisor, 482
accidents
  in adolescence, 441
  in early childhood, 235–239
  in infancy, 132–133
  in middle and late childhood, 326
accommodation, 158, 454
acculturation, 36, 490
achievement, 368–374
  and adolescent behavior/health, 432, 444, 505
  attention, effort, and persistence in, 368–369
  bullying and, 405
  of children born to adolescent parents, 436
  culture and, 372, 400
  gender differences in, 370, 395, 396–397
  immigrants and, 499
  international comparisons of, 372, 410
  and juvenile delinquency, 503
  media/screen time and, 307–308
  mindset and, 369–370
  motivation and, 368–370
  parents and, 371, 373, 399
  race/ethnicity and, 372, 373
  school accountability for, 409–410
  school transitions and, 468
  self-efficacy and, 370–371
  self-esteem and, 383, 384
  self-regulation and, 384
  social relationships and, 371–372, 403
  teachers and, 372
achievement identity, 479
acquired immune deficiency syndrome (AIDS).
    See HIV/AIDS
active genotype-environment correlations, 64
activism, 478
acupuncture, 104
adaptation, 46–47, 157
adaptive behavior, 47
Adderall, 331
ADHD. *See* attention deficit hyperactivity disorder
Adolescent Ethnic-Racial Identity Development
    (AERID) Laboratory, 484
adolescents
  activism of, 478
  adoption and, 62
  attachment of, 489
  autonomy and, 488–489
  body image of, 427, 428, 444–447, 503
  brain development in, 124, 125, 188, 428–429,
    439, 458
  cognitive development in, 428–429, 451–476
  conflict with parents, 489–490
  culture and, 422–423, 434–435, 494–501
  dating and romantic relationships among, 482,
    493–496
  death of, 441, 504

decision making in, 457–459
definition of, 11–12
delinquency of (*See* juvenile delinquency)
depression in, 503–507
eating problems and disorders in, 444–447
education of, 467–473
egocentrism in, 454–455
emotional development in, 484–485
Erikson's psychosocial theory on, 18, 19, 466,
  479, 480
executive function in, 455–459
exercise in, 438–440
extracurricular activities of, 469
friendships of, 482, 491–492, 504
gender identity in, 485–486
health of, 437–441
identity development in, 18, 19, 421, 466, 479–484
immigrant, 452, 482, 490, 494–495, 499
information control/disclosure by, 487–488,
  491–492
information processing in, 455–459
interrelationship of problems in, 506
intervention/prevention for, 506–507
legal responsibility of, 458, 502
maltreatment effects in, 293
media and technology use by, 306–308, 439–440,
  500–501
memory in, 455–456
metacognition in, 453, 459
moral development in, 390, 393, 461–464
nutrition and weight of, 438
parental monitoring of, 487–488, 501, 502–503
parents and, 487–491
personal domain of, 393
physical development of, 419–450
Piaget's theory on, 20–21, 453–454, 465
positive and negative views of, 421–422
pregnancy in, 92, 434–437, 495
prosocial behavior in, 420, 461–463
puberty in, 424–429
race/ethnicity and development of, 498–500
religion and, 464–467
rites of passages for, 497–498
self-image of, 421
service learning for, 459–460, 462
sexual identity of, 430–431, 479
sexuality of, 430–437, 467
sleep in, 440–441
smoking by, 88, 443–444, 455
social comparison in, 382
social policy and, 421–422
socioemotional development in, 477–511
storm-and-stress view of, 421, 484
substance use/abuse by, 440, 441–444, 445, 469,
  504, 506–507
suicide by, 441, 504–506
thinking in, 453–459
time allocation by, 498
transition from childhood, 422
transition to adulthood, 422–424
values of, 460–461

adoption, 59–62, 299
adoption studies, 63, 194, 361, 362
adrenal gland, 426
adulthood
  adolescent transition to, 422–424
  emerging (*See* emerging adulthood)
affection, in friendship, 407
affordances, 142, 147
Africa
  breast and bottle feeding in, 120
  cultural beliefs about pregnancy in, 83
  HIV/AIDS in, 433–434
  infant massage in, 139
  notions of fairness in, 393
African Americans. *See* Black Americans
afterbirth, 101
age
  chronological, 358
  mental, 358
  at parenthood, 92, 93
  at puberty, 426–427
aggression
  gender differences in, 395–396
  media and, 307, 308
  parenting style and, 289
  peer rejection and, 303, 403
  physical punishment and, 290
  relational, 304, 395
  social cognition and, 403–404
  verbal, 395
AIDS. *See* HIV/AIDS
Air-Crib, 23
alcohol
  and adolescents, 440, 442–444
  prenatal exposure to, 86–87
allergies, 130
alphabetic principle, 353
altruism, 393
ambiguous line drawing, 259
amnesia, infantile or childhood, 166–167
amniocentesis, 57, 58
amnion, 73
amphetamines, 331
amygdala, 194, 206, 391, 428, 429
analgesia, 102
anal stage, 17
analytical intelligence, 359–360
analytical thinking, 458–459
androgens, 284
androgyny, 398, 485
anemia, 131, 234
anemia, sickle-cell, 55
anencephaly, 76
anesthesia, 103, 149
anger cry, 190
animism, 246
anorexia nervosa, 446–447
A-not-B error, 162
antidepressants, 93, 113, 504
Apgar Scale, 106
aphasia, 176, 177

art and drawing, 220, 228–230, 246
articulation disorders, 332
art therapy, 235
Ascend program (Aspen Institute), 10
ASD. *See* autism spectrum disorders
Asian Americans
    adolescent pregnancy among, 435
    adolescents, 431, 452, 489, 490, 505
    diabetes in, 324
    overweight children, 233
    parenting styles of, 289
    school dropout rate for, 472
    schools and, 411–413
Asperger syndrome, reclassification of, 334
assimilation, 158, 453, 454
assisted reproductive technologies (ART), 59, 60
asthma, 130, 326
attachment
    in adolescence, 489
    biological influences on, 204–206
    caregiving styles and, 203
    child maltreatment and, 293
    culture and, 202–203, 205
    definition of, 200
    developmental social neuroscience and, 205–206
    emotional and behavioral outcomes of, 203–204
    individual differences in, 202–205
    in infancy, 192, 200–206
    in middle and late childhood, 386
    and moral development, 280–281
    to mother *vs.* father, 204, 210
    and peer relations, 304
    phases of, 201–202
    and self-esteem, 383
    theories of, 25
    and theory of mind, 260
attention
    activities to improve, 253–254
    in adolescents, 457
    definition of, 164
    in early childhood, 252–254
    executive, 252–254
    in infants, 164–166, 199
    joint, 165–166, 199
    media multitasking and, 500
    in middle and late childhood, 368–369
    sustained, 165, 252–254, 368–369, 440
attention deficit hyperactivity disorder (ADHD), 329–332
    Apgar score and, 106
    effortful control and, 193
    exercise and, 320, 331–332
    maternal stress and, 92
    sleep problems and, 231
audience, imaginary, 454–455
audiologist, 42
auditory perception, 147–148
authoritarian parenting, 287–289
authoritative parenting, 288, 489, 503
autism spectrum disorders (ASD), 260, 334
autobiographical memory, 255–256, 347–348
automatic responses, 391
autonomous morality, 281–282, 387–388
autonomy
    in adolescence, 488–489
    Erikson's psychosocial theory on, 18, 19, 197, 198
    in middle and late childhood, 400
autonomy *vs.* shame and doubt stage, 18, 197, 198

average children, 402–403
avoidance, and coping, 386
avoidant babies, 202–205
axons, 124

B

babbling, 173
Babinski reflex, 135
basic cry, 190
Bayley Scales of Infant and Toddler Development, 170
bed sharing, 128
bedtime routines, 230
behavior
    adaptive, 47
    goal-directed, 199–200
    infant and toddler, managing and guiding, 209–210
    moral, 282–283
    prosocial (*See* prosocial behavior)
behavioral inhibition, 193, 204
behavioral schemes, 157
behavioral teratology, 84
behavioral theories, 22–24
    child development issues and, 27
    evaluating, 24
    on moral development, 282–283
behavior genetics, 63
behaviorism, 22
behaviorism view, of language development, 177
beliefs, false, 258–259
Bem Sex-Role Inventory, 485
Berkeley Longitudinal Study, 427
bias
    cultural (*See* cultural bias)
    gender (*See* gender bias)
    in intelligence tests, 363–364
    in Kohlberg's theory, 390–391, 393, 461
    referral, 328
    in research, 34–36
    teacher, reducing, 412
bicultural identity, 36, 483
bilingualism, 355–357
Bill and Melinda Gates Foundation, 473
Binet intelligence tests, 358
bioecological theory, 26
biological influences. *See also* genetic influences; nature–nurture issue
    on attachment, 204–206
    on emotions, 188–189
    on gender, 283–284
    on language development, 176–177
    on reciprocal socialization, 209
    on temperament, 193–194
biological processes, 11, 12
biological sensitivity to context model, 195
birth. *See* childbirth
birth order, 295–296
birth weight, low. *See* low birth weight infants
bisexual youth, 479, 494. *See also* LGBTQ+ persons
Black Americans
    adolescent pregnancy among, 435
    adolescents, 431, 439, 441, 467, 489, 494
    diabetes in, 324
    discrimination against, 7
    educational achievement of, 372, 373
    as ethnic group, 6–7
    family variations in, 301

fathers, 93–94
    health disparities for, 237
    LGBTQ+ youth, 431
    overweight children, 233
    prenatal care for, 81
    preterm infants, 108
    school dropout rate for, 472
    schools and, 411–413
    sexually transmitted infections among, 434
    sickle-cell anemia in, 55
    single-parent families, 301
    social comparison in, 382
    sudden infant death syndrome in, 128
    terminology for describing, 7
Black Lives Matter, 453, 500
blastocyst, 72, 73
blindness, 332
blinking reflex, 135, 136
blood types, incompatible, 89
bodily-kinesthetic intelligence, 360
body image, 427, 428, 444–447, 503
body mass index (BMI), 233, 321–322
Bogalusa Heart Study, 325
bonding. *See also* attachment
    definition of, 114
    in postpartum period, 114–115
bottle feeding, 120, 130–131
Bradley Method, 103
brain
    and attachment, 205–206
    gender differences in, 394–395
    and language development, 176–177
    lateralization in, 124
    plasticity of, 126–127, 428
    sizes in primates and humans, 48
    structure and function of, 123–125
    and temperament, 194
brain development
    in adolescents, 124, 125, 188, 428–429, 439, 458
    and cognitive control, 317, 456
    and conservation, 248
    in early childhood, 222–224, 248
    early experience and, 126
    and emotions, 188
    evolutionary perspective on, 78
    in infants, 122–127
    and memory, 166–167, 224, 254
    in middle and late childhood, 248, 316–317
    nature–nurture issue and, 429
    neuroconstructivist view of, 126–127
    prenatal, 72, 76
    and theory of mind, 260
brain imaging, 29–30
    in adolescents, 428
    in attachment studies, 205
    in conservation tasks, 248
    in deprivation studies, 126
    in early childhood, 223–224
    in infants, 122–123
    in language development studies, 176
    in learning disabilities, 329
Brainology (workshop), 369, 370
brainstorming, 351
Brazelton Neonatal Behavioral Assessment Scale (NBAS), 106–107, 132, 169
breast cancer, 130
breast development, 425, 427

breast feeding
in Africa, 120
benefits of, 130–131
vs. bottle feeding, 120, 130–131
contraindications and difficulties, 131
HIV/AIDS transmission via, 131
infant reflexes and, 135, 136
as protection against SIDS, 120, 130
shared sleeping and, 128
breech position, 105
Bringing Home Baby, 208
Broca's area, 176, 177
Bronfenbrenner's ecological theory, 25–26, 236
bulimia nervosa, 446, 447
bullying, 404–406
and adolescent depression, 504
and adolescent suicide, 505
cyberbullying, 405, 505
victims of, 398, 404–406

C

caffeine, prenatal exposure to, 86
cancer
in children, 323–324
in women, breastfeeding and, 130
cardiovascular disease, 324–326, 439–440
career counselor, 41
career identity, 479
careers, in child development, 40–42
caregivers. *See also* parents/parenting
attachment to (*See* attachment)
and eating behavior, 129
emotional expressiveness of, 279
fathers as, 187, 210–211
and joint attention, 165–166, 199
and language development, 177–180
care perspective, 390–391
case studies, 29
casual dating, 494
cataracts, 150
catfishing, 495
causality
correlation *vs.*, 31, 383
infants' understanding of, 161
scientific thinking and, 350
CenteringPregnancy, 82
central executive, 346
centration, 247
cephalocaudal pattern, 121
cerebral cortex
and ADHD, 330–332
of adolescents, 428–429
and emotional development, 188
of infants, 123–125, 166–167, 188
and memory, 166–167
in middle and late childhood, 316–317
cerebral palsy, 333
cesarean delivery, 104–105
character education, 463–464
cheating, 464
Chernobyl nuclear disaster, 89
child abuse. *See* child maltreatment
childbirth, 98–117
culture and, 101
involvement of fathers in, 101, 103
medication for, 102–103
methods of, 102–105

preterm, 107–111
settings and attendants of, 101–102
stages of, 100–101
transition from fetus to newborn in, 105
child care, 211–214
for adolescent parents, 437
and intelligence, 363
international policies of, 212
safety in, 237–238
socioeconomic status and, 211–212
child-care director, 213
child-centered kindergarten, 265, 305
child development. *See also* specific types and topics
biological, cognitive, and socioemotional
processes and, 11, 12
careers in, 40–42
continuity and discontinuity in, 13–14, 22, 27
critical period of, 85, 204
early and later experience in, 14, 27
gender and, 7, 8
importance of studying, 4
issues in, 13–14, 27
nature and nurture in, 13, 27, 55, 150
parenting and, 5
periods of, 11–12
research on, challenges in, 32–36
science of, 15–36
sensitive period of, 204
child development theories, 16–27. *See also*
specific theories
child development issues and, 27
comparison of, 27
eclectic orientation and, 26–27
time line for, 26
child-directed speech, 179–181
childhood amnesia, 166–167
child life specialist, 42, 327
child maltreatment, 292–293
and adolescent suicide, 505, 506
and juvenile delinquency, 293, 502, 503
child neglect, 292
child psychiatrist, 388
children. *See also* adolescents; early childhood;
infants; middle and late childhood; *specific topics*
improving lives of, 4–10
resilience in, 8–9
social policy and, 9–10
children with disabilities, 327–336. *See also*
specific disability
educational issues related to, 334–336
range of disabilities in, 328–334
statistics related to, 327–328
child welfare worker, 42, 294
chlamydia, 433, 434
chorionic villus sampling, 57, 58
chromosomal abnormalities, 53–55
chromosomes, 49, 51–56
cell division and, 51–52
definition of, 49
sex, 51–52, 53, 284
chronological age, 358
chronosystem, 26
cigarette smoking. *See* smoking
circular reactions, 159–160, 162
cisgender, 398, 485–486
City Connects program, 411
civic engagement, 461, 462
classical conditioning, 23, 164

classification, 343–344
classrooms
flipped, 250
gender bias in, 397
jigsaw, 412
sustaining climate in, 463
clinical psychologist, 5, 41, 114
cliques, 492–493
coach, 321
cocaine, prenatal exposure to, 87–88
cochlea, 141
code of ethics, APA, 34
cognition. *See* cognitive development; thinking
cognitive control
and ADHD, 193
in adolescence, 456–457
of attention, 253–254, 457
brain development and, 193, 317, 385, 456
definition of, 456
in early childhood, 253–254, 257, 259
in infancy, 193
in middle and late childhood, 317
cognitive development
in adolescents, 428–429, 451–476
brain development and, 224
breast feeding and, 130
core knowledge approach to, 163
in early childhood, 243–273
education and, 454
exercise and, 319–320
fathers and, 210
gender and, 395–397
individual differences in, 169–170
in infants, 129, 130, 155–185
information-processing approach to, 22
measures of, 169–170
in middle and late childhood, 316–317, 341–378
and moral development, 390
nature-nurture issue and, 163
play and, 304–305
sleep and, 129
strategies for supporting, 185, 273, 378, 476
cognitive developmental neuroscience, 11, 429
cognitive developmental theories, 20–22. *See also*
Piaget's theory; Vygotsky's theory
child development issues and, 27
evaluating, 22
information-processing approach to, 22
cognitive flexibility
in adolescence, 456–457
and creativity, 351
definition of, 457
in early childhood, 253, 256, 277, 282
in middle and late childhood, 348, 349, 351, 355
and mindfulness, 349
and second-language learning, 355
self-assessment of, 457
cognitive processes
definition of, 11
explanation of, 11, 12
in infancy, 157–158
cognitive reappraisal, 386, 484–485
cohort, definition of, 12
cohort effects
on moral development, 391–392, 461
in research, 12–13, 32
Collaborative for Academic, Social, and Emotional
Learning (CASEL), 386

collectivistic cultures, 408, 482, 492
college/university professor, 40, 443, 466, 484
color vision, 145, 227
Comer School Development Project (SDP), 412-413
commitment
    definition of, 481
    and identity status, 480-481
commitments, joint, 277
Common Core State Standards Initiative, 410
communication
    about divorce, 300
    digitally mediated, 500-501
    emotions and, 188, 190
    gender differences in, 396
companionship, in friendship, 407
conception, 72, 73
concepts, 167-168
concrete operational stage, 20-21, 343-345
confidentiality, in research, 34
conformity, 389, 429, 492
connectedness, 481
conscience, 17, 280
conscious/deliberative reasoning, 391
consent, informed, 34
conservation, 247-248, 343
constancy, perceptual, 145-146
constructive play, 306
constructivist approach, 150, 250, 268, 345, 408-409
context
    definition of, 6
    sociocultural, 6-7
continuity-discontinuity issue, 13-14, 22, 27
contraceptive use, 433, 435, 436
control
    cognitive (See cognitive control)
    in parental monitoring, 488
    in parenting styles, 287-289
    self-control (See self-regulation)
control groups, 31-32
controversial children, 402-403
conventional reasoning, 389-390, 461
conventional reasoning, social, 392-393
convergent thinking, 349
cooing, 173
coordination, of secondary circular reactions, 159, 160, 162
coparenting, 291, 297, 298-299
coping. See also emotional regulation
    in infants, 191-192
    in middle and late childhood, 384, 386-387
    and self-esteem, 384
core knowledge approach, 163
coronavirus. See COVID-19
corporal punishment. See physical punishment
corpus callosum, 394, 428, 429
correlation, vs. cause, 31, 383
correlational research, 30-31, 383
co-rumination, 504
counseling, careers in, 41-42
counseling psychologist, 41
COVID-19, prenatal exposure to, 91
COVID-19 pandemic
    academic achievement during, 372
    adoption rates during, 61
    caregivers and child care during, 210, 211, 213
    depression during, 439, 503
    drawings about, 228
    economic disparities during, 9, 470

exercise benefits during, 439
    health disparities during, 237
    parent-adolescent conflict and coping with, 490
    peer relations during, 493, 501
    psychological disorders during, 387
    schools and, 407, 470
    suicide ideation during, 441
crawling, 137, 199
creative intelligence, 359-360
creative thinking, 349-350, 351
creativity, 349-351
    in art and drawings, 220, 228-230
    guiding, 351
crisis, and identity, 480-481
critical period of development, 85, 204
critical thinking, 349, 459
cross-cultural studies, 6
cross-sectional approach to research, 32
crowds (peer groups), 492-493
crying, in infants, 173, 190-192
cultural bias
    in Kohlberg's theory, 391-392, 461
    in research, 34-36
    in standardized tests, 29
cultural-familial intellectual disability, 365
cultural identity, 36, 479, 482-484
cultural mediator, teacher as, 413
culture/cultural diversity, 6-7. See also race/ethnicity
    and acculturation, 36, 490
    and achievement, 400
    and adolescent autonomy, 489
    and adolescent conflict with parents, 490
    and adolescent dating, 494-495
    and adolescent development, 422-423, 496-501
    and adolescent pregnancy, 434-435
    and adolescent suicide, 505-506
    and adoption, 61
    and attachment, 202-203, 205
    and childbirth, 101
    deficits vs. differences in, 372
    definition of, 6
    and depression, 504
    in early childhood education, 270
    and eating disorders, 444-447
    in ecological theory, 26
    and emotions, 189
    and equality (fairness), 393
    and family variations, 300-302, 497
    and friendship, 408, 492
    and gender, 284-286, 398
    generations and, 12-13
    and identity, 36, 482-484
    individualistic vs. collectivistic, 408, 482, 492
    and intelligence tests, 363-364
    and language development, 175
    and low birth weight, 108
    and memory, 348
    and moral development, 391-392
    and motor development, 139
    and parental monitoring, 400
    and parenting styles, 289, 400, 490
    and paternal involvement, 210-211
    and peer relations, 497
    and pregnancy, 83
    and self-esteem, 383-384
    and shared sleeping, 128
    and temperament, 195
culture-fair intelligence tests, 363-364

curriculum, in early childhood education, 268
cyberbullying, 405, 505
cystic fibrosis, 55, 56

D

danger invulnerability, 455
data collection methods, 27-30
dating, 493-496
death. See also suicide
    in adolescence, 441, 504
    in early childhood, 235-236, 237
    in infancy, 81, 128-129, 130
death penalty, abolished for minors, 458, 502
debriefing, in research, 34
deception, in research, 34
decision making, in adolescents, 457-459
deferred imitation, 167
deficits vs. differences, 372
dehydration, 239
deliberative reasoning, 391
delinquency. See juvenile delinquency
dendrites, 124
Denver Developmental Screening Test II, 227
dependent variables, 31
depression
    in adolescent mothers, 436
    in adolescents, 503-507
    bullying and, 405, 504
    caretaker, and accidents, 326
    child maltreatment and, 293
    in children of divorced parents, 297
    extracurricular activities and, 469
    gender differences in, 503-504
    genetic and environmental risk factors of, 65
    gratitude and, 463
    interrelationship with other adolescent problems, 506
    intervention/prevention, 506-507
    low self-esteem and, 383
    maternal (during pregnancy), 92-93
    paternal, 195
    peer relations and, 303
    physical punishment and, 290
    postpartum, 112-113
    religion and, 465
depth perception, 146-147
descriptive research, 30
design stage, of drawings, 228, 229
development. See also child development; prenatal development
    definition of, 4
    evolutionary perspective on, 46-49
    genetic foundations of, 49-56
    as lifelong process, 12
developmental cascade model, 204
developmental cognitive neuroscience, 11, 429
developmentally appropriate practice (DAP), 266
developmental quotient (DQ), 169-170
developmental social neuroscience, 11, 205-206, 429
developmental transitions, 422-424
dextroamphetamine, 331
diabetes, 55-56, 66, 91, 130-131, 322, 324
diarrhea, 239
diet. See nutrition
differential susceptibility model, 195
difficult child, 192-193, 194, 196
direct instruction approach, 409
disabilities, children with. See children with disabilities

gratitude, 462–463
gross motor skills
    definition of, 136
    in early childhood, 225–227
    in infants, 136–139, 199
    in middle and late childhood, 318
group dating, 494
growth, physical. *See* physical development
growth hormone deficiency, 221–222
growth mindset, 369–370
growth spurt, 425
guided reading, 250
gun deaths, 236, 441

H

habits, 159
habituation, 142, 143, 165
Head Start, 9, 234, 266–268
Head Start director, 267
health
    of adolescents, 437–441
    of children, 4–5, 230–240, 319–327
    global, 239
    of infants, 132–133
    poverty and, 237
    racial/ethnic disparities in, 237
health-compromising behaviors, 437
health-enhancing behaviors, 437
hearing, 141, 147–148
hearing impairment, 333
Heart Smart, 325
height
    in adolescence, 425
    in early childhood, 221–222, 223
    in infancy, 122
    in middle and late childhood, 316, 317
helpless orientation, 369
hemispheres of brain, 123–124
hemophilia, 55, 56
heredity-environment correlations, 63–64. *See also*
    nature-nurture issue
heredity-environment interaction, 52, 62–66
heroin, prenatal exposure to, 89
herpes, genital, 90, 433, 434
heteronomous morality, 281–282, 387–388, 389
hidden curriculum, 463
high-amplitude sucking, 143–144
high school, 470–473
    cross-cultural comparisons of, 471
    dropping out of, 436, 470–473
    extracurricular activities in, 469
    service learning in, 460–461
high school activities director, 469
High School Longitudinal Study, 373
hippocampus, 166–167
HIV/AIDS, 90, 120, 131, 433–434
Hoku point ice massage, 104
home births, 101
home visitation, for prenatal care, 82–83
homicide, 441
honor code policy, 464
hormones
    in attachment, 205–206
    in childbirth, 103
    definition of, 425
    in developmental research, 29
    in fetus-to-newborn transition, 105

    and gender, 284
    and gene expression, 51
    in postpartum period, 112–113
    in puberty, 29, 425–426
    and sleep, 440
    and temperament, 193–194
"hot-cold" theory of illness, 83
Human Genome Project, 49–50
human immunodeficiency virus (HIV). *See* HIV/AIDS
hunter-gatherer societies, 47
Huntington disease, 56
hypertension, in children, 322, 325
hypnosis, during childbirth, 104
hypothalamus, 206, 425–426
hypothesis, 16
hypothetical-deductive reasoning, 454

I

id, 17
IDEA. *See* Individuals with Disabilities
    Education Act
idealistic thinking, 453–454, 465–466
identical twins, 45–46, 52, 63, 109
identity/identity development, 479–484
    in adolescents, 18, 19, 421, 466, 479–484
    bicultural, 36, 483
    culture and, 36, 479, 482–484
    definition of, 479–480
    developmental changes in, 480–481
    in emerging adulthood and beyond, 423, 481–483
    Erikson's view of, 18, 19, 466, 479
    gender, 7, 283, 398, 479, 485–486
    MAMA cycles in, 481
    in middle and late childhood, 19
    racial/ethnic, 6–7, 479, 482–484
    religion and, 465, 466, 479
    sexual, 430–431, 479
identity achievement, 480–481
identity confusion, 18, 466, 480
identity diffusion, 480–481
identity foreclosure, 480–481
identity moratorium, 480–481
identity statuses, 480–481
identity *vs.* identity confusion, 18, 466, 480
IEP. *See* individualized education plan
"I Have a Dream" program, 472
imaginary audience, 454–455
imaginary play, 305
"Imagining America: CREATE Your Vision," 235
imitation, 23–24, 167
immanent justice, 282
immigrant paradox model, 499
immigrant risk model, 499
immigrants
    acculturation of, 36, 490
    adolescents as, 452, 482, 490, 494–495, 499
    as English Language Learners, 356–357
    family variations in, 301–302
    generational differences in, 483
    identity in, 482, 483
    intervention program for, 411
    research issues on, 36
    sociocultural contexts for, 6–7
    undocumented, 499
immunization, 132
implicit memory, 166, 254
imprinting, ethological, 24

imprinting, genetic, 53
inclusion, 335–336
incompatible blood types, 89
incremental theory of intelligence, 383
incremental theory of mindset, 370
independence, 197–198. *See also* autonomy
independent variables, 31
individual differences
    in attachment, 202–205
    in cognitive development, 169–170
    definition of, 358
    in intelligence, 358
    in puberty, 426–427
    in social understanding, 277–278
    in theory of mind, 259–260
individualism, 389
individualistic cultures, 408, 482, 492
individuality, 481
individualized education plan (IEP), 335–336
individual rights, 389
Individuals with Disabilities Education Act (IDEA),
    335–336
individuation, 198, 481
inductive discipline, 392
industry *vs.* inferiority stage, 18, 385
infantile amnesia, 166–167
infants
    accident prevention for, 132–133
    adoption of, 62
    attachment in, 192, 200–206
    attention in, 164–166, 199
    brain development in, 122–127
    in child care, 211–214
    cognitive development in, 129, 130, 155–185
    crying in, 173, 190–192
    definition of, 11
    emotional development in, 188–192
    Erikson's psychosocial theory on, 18, 196–198,
        201, 480
    family influences on, 207–211
    health of, 132–133
    identity development in, 480
    immunization of, 132
    intelligence in, 170
    language development in, 171–182
    low birth weight, 107–111
    managing and guiding behavior of, 209–210
    memory in, 166–167
    motor development in, 134–141, 199
    nutrition in, 129–132
    perceptual development in, 141–151
    personality development in, 196–198
    physical growth in, 121–122
    Piaget's theory on, 20–21, 156–164
    posture in, 136–137
    reflexes in, 135–136, 158–159
    self-understanding in, 197
    sleep in, 127–129
    social orientation in, 198–199
    socioemotional development in, 186–217
    supporting physical development of, 154
    temperament in, 192–196
    thinking in, 157–163
infinite generativity, 171
information processing, 252–260
    in adolescence, 455–459
    and attention, 252–254
    in autism spectrum disorders, 334

information processing—*Cont.*
  in early childhood, 252–260
  and executive function, 256–257
  in gifted children, 366
  and memory, 254–255
  in middle and late childhood, 316–317, 346–352, 404
  neurons and, 76
  and theory of mind, 258–260
information-processing theory, 22
informed consent, 34
inhibition
  behavioral, 193, 204
  cognitive, 256, 277
  and executive function, 348–349
  temperament and, 193–196
  to the unfamiliar, 193
inhibitory control. *See* cognitive control
initiative *vs.* guilt stage, 18, 276
injuries, in children, 235–237, 320, 326
inner speech, 249
insecure avoidant babies, 202–205
insecure disorganized babies, 202–205
insecure resistant babies, 202–205
institutional neglect, 293
instrumental purpose, 389
integrity *vs.* despair stage, 18
intellectual disability, 365
intellectual identity, 479
intelligence, 358–367
  in autism spectrum disorders, 334
  culture and, 363–364
  definition of, 358
  environmental influences on, 361–363
  extremes of, 364–367
  general, 361
  genetic influences on, 361
  incremental theory of, 383
  individual differences in, 358
  nature-nurture issue and, 361–363
  predicting, 170
  theories of multiple, 359–361
  types of, 359–361
intelligence quotient (IQ)
  definition of, 358
  development of, 358
  in giftedness, 365–367
  infant intelligence testing and, 170
  in intellectual disability, 365
  interpreting differences in, 361–364
  normal distribution of, 358, 359
  worldwide increase in, 362
intelligence tests, 358–359
  culture-fair, 363–364
  for infants, 170
  use and misuse of, 364
interactionist view of language, 180–182
intermodal perception, 149–150
internalization of schemes, 159, 160–161
internal working model of attachment, 202
interpersonal conformity, 389
interpersonal expectations, mutual, 389
interpersonal intelligence, 360
intersectionality, 466
interview, as data collection method, 28
intimacy in friendships, 407, 482, 491–492
intimacy *vs.* isolation stage, 18
intrapersonal intelligence, 360
intrauterine device (IUD), 433

intrinsic motivation, 368
intuitive thought substage, 246–247
in vitro fertilization, 59, 60
involution of uterus, 112
invulnerability, adolescent sense of, 455
iron deficiency, 131, 234

J

jealousy, 189–190
jigsaw classroom, 412
joint attention, 165–166, 199
joint commitments, 277
journals, 33
junior high school. *See* middle school
justice
  distributive, 393
  immanent, 282
justice perspective, 390
juvenile delinquency, 502–503
  child maltreatment and, 293, 502, 503
  extracurricular activities and, 469
  interrelationship with other adolescent problems, 506
  intervention/prevention, 506–507
  low self-esteem and, 383
  parental monitoring and, 487, 502–503

K

kangaroo care, 109–111
kindergarten. *See also* early childhood education
  child-centered, 265, 305
kindergarten teacher, 41
knowledge
  about language, 353, 356
  about memory, 351–352
  about thinking (*See* metacognition)
  core, 163
  expertise and memory, 347
Kohlberg's theory of moral development, 388–393
  critics of, 390–393, 461
  cultural bias in, 391–392, 461
  gender bias in, 390–391, 393, 461
  social convention approach *vs.,* 392–393
  stages in, 388–390, 461
kwashiorkor, 131–132

L

labeling, 180
labor. *See* childbirth
laboratory, 28
Lamaze method, 103, 117
language
  definition of, 171
  infinite generativity of, 171
  knowledge about, 353, 356
  memory-relevant, 348
  rule systems of, 171–172, 173, 261–263
  and thought, 249
language acquisition device (LAD), 176, 177
language development
  behaviorist view of, 177
  biological influences on, 176–177
  cross-linguistic differences in, 175
  culture and, 175
  dual languages and, 355–357

  in early childhood, 224, 261–264
  environmental influences on, 177–180
  and executive function, 257
  Head Start and, 267
  in infants, 171–182
  and intelligence quotient, 170
  interactionist view of, 180–182
  joint attention and, 166
  media/screen time and, 307
  in middle and late childhood, 353–357
  play and, 305
  and theory of mind, 260
late bloomers, 494
late childhood. *See* middle and late childhood
late maturation, 427–428
latency stage, 17
lateralization, 124
Latinos/Latinas, 6–7
  academic advisors for, 482
  adolescent pregnancy among, 435
  adolescents, 432, 439, 489, 494–495
  diabetes in, 324
  early childhood education for, 265
  educational achievement of, 372
  emotions of, 189
  family variations in, 301
  fathers, 93–94
  health disparities for, 237
  immigrant, 301, 302
  overweight children, 233
  parenting styles of, 289
  prenatal care for, 81
  preterm infants, 108
  school dropout rate for, 472
  schools and, 411–413
  sexually transmitted infections among, 434
  single-parent families, 301
  terminology for describing, 7
Latinx, 7
lead poisoning, 238
learning
  contemporary approaches to, 408–409
  dual- or second-language, 355–357
  gifted children and, 366
  from media, 307–308
  observational, 23–24
  play and, 306
  scaffolding and, 208–209, 249, 251, 257
  service, 460–461, 462
  sleep and, 440–441
  social-emotional, 386
learning disabilities, 328–329
least restrictive environment (LRE), 335–336
lesbians. *See also* LGBTQ+ persons
  as parents, 299–300
  romantic relationships of, 494
Less Is More task, 256
leukemia, 323–324
LGBTQ+ persons
  academic advisors for, 482
  adolescents, 430–431, 479, 494
  adoption by, 299
  parents, 299–300
  postpartum partner support from, 113–114
  romantic relationships among youth, 494
  sex education for, 436
  transgender, 7, 398, 430–431, 485–486
  transition to parenthood, 208

Moro reflex, 135, 136
morphology, 171–172, 173, 261
mothers. *See also* parents/parenting; pregnancy
  adolescent, 92, 434–437
  attachment to, 202–206, 210, 386 (*See also* attachment)
  benefits of breast feeding for, 130–131
  bonding with newborn, 114–115
  brain studies of, 206
  divorce and, 298–299
  education of, and IQ, 362
  and gender development, 285
  LGBTQ, 299–300
  as managers of children's lives, 210, 400
  parenting style of, 289
  postpartum, 111–115
  reciprocal interactions with, 190
  shared sleeping with, 128
  stepmothers, 401
  stress in, 92–93
  transition to parenthood, 207–208
  voice recognition by infant, 149
  working, 296–297
motivation
  and achievement, 368–370
  internal, encouraging, 351
  mastery, 369
  moral, 406
motor development
  culture and, 139
  dynamic systems view of, 134–135, 151
  in early childhood, 225–227
  genetics determination view of, 134, 151
  in infants, 134–141, 199
  interventions to support, 226–227
  measuring, 227
  in middle and late childhood, 318, 354
  milestones and variations in, 138–139
  perceptual development and, 150–151
motor vehicle accidents, 133, 235–237, 326
MRI. *See* magnetic resonance imaging
multiple intelligences, 359–361
multitasking, media, 500
musical intelligence, 360
music therapy, 104, 148
mutated gene, 52
mutual gaze, 208
mutual interpersonal expectations, 389
mutuality, 481
My Baby and Me program, 436
myelination, 124–125, 223, 254, 316–318, 330
myelin sheath, 124

N

narrative approach, 480
Native Americans
  adolescent suicide among, 505
  diabetes in, 324
  educational achievement of, 372
  school dropout rate for, 473
  schools and, 412
  speech disorders among, 176
nativist view, 150
natural childbirth, 103
naturalistic observation, 28
naturalist intelligence, 360
natural scenes, perceptions of, 145

natural selection, 46–47, 48
nature-nurture issue, 13
  behavior genetics and, 63
  and brain development, 429
  child development theories and, 27
  definition of, 13
  and gene-linked abnormalities, 55
  and giftedness, 366
  and infant cognition, 163
  and intelligence, 361–363
  and moral development, 163
  and motor development, 135
  and perceptual development, 150, 163
  and temperament, 193–194
near-infrared spectroscopy, functional, 30, 123
negative affectivity, 193
negative emotions, 188
neglect, 292. *See also* child maltreatment
neglected children, 402–403
neonatal intensive care unit (NICU), 71
Neonatal Intensive Care Unit Network
  Neurobehavioral Scale (NNNS), 106–107, 169
neonatal nurse, 42
neo-Piagetians, 344
neural connectivity, 76, 124–127
neural tube, 73, 76
neural tube defects, 76, 91
neuroconstructivist view, 126–127
neurofeedback, for ADHD, 331–332
neurogenesis, 76, 77
neuroimaging. *See* brain imaging
neurons, 124–127
  changing, in early childhood, 223, 224
  changing, in infants, 124–125
  connections of, 76, 124–127
  definition of, 77
  functions of, 124–127
  prenatal development of, 76
  structure of, 124
neurotransmitters, 124, 223
  in adolescents, 428–429
  and attachment, 205
newborns. *See also* infants
  assessment of, 106–107
  bonding with, 114–115
  brain of, 123
  perception in, 142–145
  physical growth in, 121–122
  posture of, 137
  preterm and low birth weight, 107–111
  reflexes in, 135–136
  skin-to-skin contact for, 109–111, 114
  sleep in, 127
  touch and pain in, 148–149
  transition from fetus to, 105
New Hope program, 411
next-generation sequencing, 50
niche-picking, 64
nicotine, 443–444. *See also* smoking
nightmares, 231
night terrors, 231
No Child Left Behind (NCLB), 409
nonbinary, 7, 485–486
nonprescription drugs, during pregnancy, 86
non-REM sleep, 127
normal distribution, 358, 359
nucleus accumbens, 206
Nurse-Family Partnership, 82–83

nurse-midwife, 42
nursing careers, 42
nurture. *See* nature-nurture issue
nutrition
  in adolescence, 438
  in early childhood, 221, 231–234
  in infants, 129–132
  in middle and late childhood, 319
  during pregnancy, 77–78, 91–92
  and puberty, 427
  and school readiness, 133

O

obedience, 290
obesity. *See* overweight and obesity
object permanence, 160–161, 454
observation, as data collection method, 27–28
observational learning, 23–24
obstetrician/gynecologist, 42
occipital lobes, 123
occluded objects, perception of, 146
occupational therapist, 235
Oedipus complex, 285
Office of Adolescent Health, 436
1000 Genomes Project, 50
only child, 295–296
open adoption, 60–61, 62
operant conditioning, 23, 164, 165
operations, 21, 245
oral approaches, in hearing impairment, 333
oral rehydration therapy (ORT), 239
oral sex, adolescents engaging in, 432
oral stage, 17
organic intellectual disability, 365
organization
  behavioral, emotions and, 188
  in Piaget's theory, 158
organogenesis, 73–74
orienting/investigative process, 165
orienting response, 144
orthopedic impairments, 333
otitis media, 130
ovarian cancer, 130
ovaries, 425–426
overextension, of words, 175
overweight and obesity
  in adolescence, 438, 439–440, 504
  breast feeding and, 130
  consequences of, 322–323
  in early childhood, 232, 233–234
  maternal, 77–78, 91–92
  media use/screen time and, 320
  in middle and late childhood, 315, 319–323
  parenting strategies in, 324
  in pregnancy, 77–78, 91–92
  and psychological functioning, 233–234
  and puberty, 427
  screen time and, 320, 323, 439–440
  and self-esteem, 383
oxytocin, 103, 205–206

P

pain, in newborns, 148–149
pain cry, 190
palmar grasp, 140
parental leave, 211, 212

parenting styles, 287–289
  authoritarian, 287–289
  authoritative, 288, 489, 503
  in context, 288–289
  culture and, 289, 400, 490
  indulgent, 288
  mothers *vs.* fathers, 289
  neglectful, 288
parents/parenting
  and achievement, 371, 373, 399
  and adolescent depression, 504
  of adolescents, 487–491
  adolescents as, 434–437
  and adolescent sexual behavior, 432
  and adolescent substance use, 444
  adoptive, 59–62
  attachment to (*See* attachment)
  and brain development, 224
  and child development, 5
  child maltreatment by (*See* child maltreatment)
  conflict with adolescents, 489–490
  coparenting, 291, 297, 298–299
  culture and, 300–302
  direct and indirect effects of, 207
  in early childhood, 232, 287–291
  and eating disorders, 445–446
  and emotional development, 280
  and executive function, 257, 349
  and exercise habits, 439
  and feeding styles, 232
  as gatekeepers, 399
  and gender development, 285
  and gratitude, 463
  and identity development, 481
  and juvenile delinquency, 502–503
  and language development, 177–180
  LGBTQ+, 299–300
  as managers of children's lives, 400, 487
  in middle and late childhood, 399–400
  monitoring by, 400, 487–488, 501, 502–503
  and moral development, 275, 280–281, 283, 392
  and peer relations, 304
  proactive strategies of, 283
  race/ethnicity and, 300–302
  reciprocal socialization and, 208–209, 289
  and religious beliefs, 466
  and self-esteem, 383
  and sibling relationships, 294–295
  socioeconomic status of, 300, 302
  and socioemotional development, 207–211
  and sports participation, 321
  and temperament, 195–196
  transition to, 207–208
  working, 296–297
parietal lobes, 123–124, 223–224
passive genotype-environment correlations, 63–64
pastoral counselor, 466
pediatrician, 42, 431
pediatric nurse, 42
pediatric occupational therapist, 235
peer groups, 492–493
peer pressure, 429, 492
peer relations
  in ADHD, 331
  in adolescence, 427–428, 482, 491–496, 497
  and adolescent delinquency, 503
  and adolescent depression, 504
  and adolescent substance use, 443, 444

attachment and, 204, 304
bullying and, 404–406
child maltreatment and, 293
culture and, 497
and decision making, 458
developmental changes in, 303, 402
in early childhood, 280, 286–287, 303–304
early *vs.* late maturation and, 427–428
and emotional regulation, 280
gender and, 285–286, 303
and gender development, 285–286
and identity development, 482
in infancy, 199
and language development, 263
in middle and late childhood, 402–408
and moral development, 282, 390, 392
of overweight children, 315, 322
parent-child relations and, 304
and self-understanding, 277
theory of mind and, 260
peer status, 402–403
perceived popularity, 403
perception, 141–142
  auditory, 147–148
  depth, 146–147
  intermodal, 149–150
  newborn, methods for studying, 143–145, 165
  of occluded objects, 146
  olfactory, 149
  taste, 149
  and theory of mind, 258
  touch and pain, 148–149
  visual, 142–147, 149–150, 227–228
perceptual categorization, 168
perceptual constancy, 145–146
perceptual development
  constructivist view of, 150
  in early childhood, 227–228
  ecological view of, 142, 150, 151
  and expectations, 162–163
  in infants, 141–151
  motor development and, 140, 150–151
  nature-nurture issue and, 150
  Piaget's theory on, 150
perceptual-motor coupling, 140, 150–151
perceptual narrowing, 145
perfectionism, and eating disorders, 446, 447
performance orientation, 369
perinatal nurse navigator, 81
permeability, 481
Perry Preschool program, 268, 507
persistence, 351, 368–369
personal fable, 455
personality
  identity and, 479
  temperament and, 195
personality development
  in early childhood, 276–287
  in infants, 196–198
  in middle and late childhood, 381–399
personal reasoning, 392–393
perspective taking
  and bullying, 406
  definition of, 277
  in early childhood, 277, 281
  in middle and late childhood, 382
  and moral development, 390
  in sibling relationships, 294–295

phallic stage, 17
phenotypes, 52
phenylketonuria (PKU), 55, 56
phonics approach, 354
phonology, 171, 173, 261
physical abuse, 292. *See also* child maltreatment
physical development
  of adolescents, 419–450
  child development careers involving, 42
  in early childhood, 219–242
  gender differences in, 394–395
  of infants, 119–154
  in middle and late childhood, 314–340
  strategies for supporting, 154, 242, 339, 450
physical disorders, 333
physical education, 320, 325
physical identity, 479
physical punishment, 209–210, 289–291, 400
  as child maltreatment, 292
  in different countries, 289, 290
  human rights perspective on, 291
  parenting styles and, 288
  poverty and, 302
  reasons to avoid, 289–290
  socioeconomic status and, 302
physical support, in friendship, 407
physiological measures, 29–30
Piaget's theory, 20–21. *See also specific stages*
  on adolescence, 20–21, 453–454, 465
  comparison with Vygotsky's theory, 21, 248, 250–252, 344
  constructivist view in, 150, 250, 345
  contributions of, 454
  criticisms of, 22, 163
  definition of, 20
  on early childhood, 20–21, 245–248, 343
  and education, 250, 264–265, 344–345
  egocentrism in, 245–246, 278, 282, 454
  evaluation of, 22, 162–163, 344, 454
  on infancy, 20–21, 156–164
  on middle and late childhood, 20–21, 343–345
  on moral development, 281–282, 387–388, 392
  perceptual development in, 150
  on play, 304, 305
pictorial stage, of drawings, 228, 229
pincer grip, 140
Pitocin, 103
pituitary gland, 425–426
placemaking, 257
placement stage, of drawings, 228, 229
placenta, 73, 74, 101
plagiarism, 464
plasticity, 126–127, 428
play, 304–306
  face-to-face, 199
  fathers *vs.* mothers and, 211
  gender and, 285–286, 303, 396
  screen time *vs.*, 307
play therapy, 304
pointing, in infants, 174
political identity, 479
polygenic inheritance, 53
popular children, 402–403
positive emotions, 188, 395–396
positive youth development (PYD), 422
positron emission tomography (PET), 126
postconventional reasoning, 389–390, 461
Post-millennial generation, 13

referral bias, 328
reflexes, 135–136, 158–159
reflexive smile, 191
reframing, 386
Reggio Emilia approach, 244, 264–265
rejected children, 402–403
relational aggression, 304, 395
relational catalysts, 278
religion, 464–467
religious counselors, 465, 466
religious identity, 465, 479
religiousness, 464–465
remarriage, 401
REM sleep, 127–128
repetition, and memory, 348
report talk, 396
reproductive technology, 59, 60
research
    bias in, 34–36
    careers in, 40–41
    child development, challenges in, 32–36
    correlational, 30–31
    data collection methods for, 27–30
    descriptive, 30
    ethical issues in, 33–34
    experimental, 31–32
    importance of, 15–16
    journal publication of, 33
    scientific method in, 15–16
    time span of, 32
research designs, 30–32
researcher, 40
research journals, 33
resilience, 8–9, 423
resistant babies, 202–205
retina, 141
rewards
    extrinsic motivation and, 368
    operant conditioning and, 23
    preconventional reasoning and, 389–390
Rh factor, 89
risk/risk taking
    adolescent decision making and, 457–459
    adolescent perception of, 455
    adolescent sexual behavior and, 432–436
    brain development and, 188
    intellectual, and creativity, 351
    religion and, 465
Ritalin, 331
rites of passage, 497–498
RNA, 52
Roe v. Wade, 61
romantic attraction, 494
romantic relationships, 493–496
    adjustment and, 495
    and identity development, 482
    sociocultural contexts of, 494–495
rooming-in arrangement, in hospitals, 115
rooting reflex, 135, 136
Roper v. Simmons, 458, 502
rubella, 90
rumination, 503–504

S

safety
    in early childhood, 235–239
    in infancy, 132–133

scaffolding, 208–209, 249, 251, 257, 349
schemes, 157–158
    definition of, 157
    internalization of, 159, 160–161
school counselor, 41, 407
school dropouts. *See* dropping out, of school
school psychologist, 41
school readiness, 268–269
    brain development and, 224
    child care and, 211
    developing skills for, 11
    effortful control and, 193
    executive function and, 257
    Montessori approach and, 265
    nutrition and, 133
    positive affectivity/surgency and, 193
    sleep and, 231
    sustained attention and, 254
schools
    accountability from, 409–410
    achievement in (*See* achievement)
    bullying in, 404–406
    cheating in, 464
    children with disabilities in, 334–336
    community-wide team-based approach in, 412–413
    contemporary approaches in, 408–409
    discipline in, 412
    diversity improvements in, 412–413
    dropping out of, 436, 470–473
    elementary, 408–413
    extracurricular activities at, 469
    gender bias at, 397
    hidden curriculum of, 463
    middle and junior high, 467–469
    physical education in, 320, 325
    race/ethnicity in, 336, 367, 372–373, 410–413, 470, 472
    start times of, 440–441
    transitions between, 468, 470
school shooting, 387
scientific method, 15–16
scientific thinking, 350
screen time. *See* media use/screen time
scribbles, 229, 245, 246
secondary circular reactions, 159, 160, 162
secondary schools, 467–473
secondhand smoke, 87, 93, 238, 326
second-language learning, 355–357
Second Step program, 386
securely attached babies, 202–205
segregation, school, 411–412
self. *See also* identity/identity development
    in adolescence, 421, 479–484
    in early childhood, 276–278
    in infancy, 197
    in middle and late childhood, 381–385
    unrealistic positive overestimation of, 277
self-assertion, 481
self-concept
    definition of, 382
    in middle and late childhood, 382–384
    of toddlers, 197
self-conscious emotions, 189–190, 278
self-control. *See* self-regulation
self-determination, 368

self-disclosure
    in friendship, 407, 491–492
    gender differences in, 396
    to parents, 487–488
self-efficacy, 351, 370–371, 457
self-esteem
    accurate *vs.* inaccurate beliefs and, 382–383
    in children of divorced parents, 297
    correlations *vs.* causes in, 383
    culture and, 383–384
    definition of, 382
    extracurricular activities and, 469
    friendship and, 407
    increasing, 384
    inflated, 383
    low, and adolescent suicide, 506
    low, consequences of, 383
    low, identifying cause of, 384
    in middle and late childhood, 382–384
    physical punishment and, 290
    religion and, 465
Self-Regulated Strategy Development (SRSD), 355
self-regulation
    and achievement, 371
    and adolescent sexual behavior, 433
    and executive function, 348–349
    gender differences in, 396
    joint attention and, 166
    in middle and late childhood, 384–385
self-talk, 249
self-understanding
    in adolescents, 479–484
    definition of, 276
    in early childhood, 276–277
    in infants, 197
    in middle and late childhood, 381–382
semantics, 172, 173, 261–262, 456
semenarche, 425
sensation, 141. *See also* perception
sensitive period of child development, 204
sensorimotor play, 305
sensorimotor stage, 20–21, 158–163
    A-not-B error and, 162
    definition of, 158
    evaluation of, 162–163
    object permanence in, 160–161
    substages of, 159–160
sensory disorders, 332–333
separateness, 481
separation, and infant independence, 198
separation protest, 191
seriation, 344
serotonin, 330
service learning, 460–461, 462
SES. *See* socioeconomic status
Sesame Street (television program), 307, 308
sex chromosomes, 51–52, 53, 284
sex determination, fetal, 58–59
sex education, 436
sex-linked chromosomal abnormalities, 54–55
sex-linked genes, 53
sex-typed play, 283
sexual abuse, 292
sexual expression, gender and, 8, 497
sexual identity, 430–431, 479
sexuality, adolescent, 430–437, 467
sexually transmitted infections (STIs), 433–434
sexual maturation, 425

sexual orientation, 430–431. *See also* LGBTQ+ persons

shaken baby syndrome, 122

The Shame of the Nation (Kozol), 412

shape constancy, 145–146

shape stage, of drawings, 228, 229

shared reading, 180

shared sleeping, 128

sharing, 393, 396

short stature, 221–222

short-term memory, 224, 254, 346

siblings, 293–296
  birth order of, 295–296
  and juvenile delinquency, 503

sickle-cell anemia, 55

sign language, 333

similarity, in friendship, 406

simple reflexes, 159

single-parent families, 301, 400

single-sex education, 397–398

size constancy, 145–146

skin-to-skin contact, for newborns, 109–111, 114

sleep
  in adolescents, 440–441
  and cognitive development, 129
  in early childhood, 230–231, 238
  in infants, 127–129
  non-REM, 127
  parental smoking and, 238
  in postpartum period, 112
  REM, 127–128
  screen time affecting, 231, 440

sleep talkers, 231

sleepwalking, 231

slow-to-warm-up child, 192–193

small for gestational age (SGA), 107–108

smell, 149

smiling, 190, 191

smoking
  in adolescence, 88, 443–444, 455
  and asthma, 326
  e-cigarettes, 87, 444, 455
  and motor development, 139
  paternal, 93, 238
  during pregnancy, 87, 88
  secondhand smoke from, 87, 93, 238
  and sudden infant death syndrome, 129

Snellen chart, 142, 332

snooping, by parents, 488

social activism, 478

social (relational) aggression, 304, 395

social cognition
  and aggression, 403–404
  in early childhood, 276–278
  in infants (social understanding), 198–200
  in middle and late childhood, 382, 403–404
  and peer relations, 403–404

social cognitive theory, 23–24
  child development issues and, 27
  definition of, 23
  evaluating, 24
  of gender, 285
  on moral development, 282–283

social comparison
  in friendship, 407
  in self-evaluation, 381–382

social constructivist approach, 250

social contract, 389

social conventional reasoning, 392–393

social developmental neuroscience, 11, 205–206, 429

social distancing, 493

social-emotional education programs, 386

socialization, reciprocal, 208–209, 289

social media
  and adolescent attention, 457
  and adolescent development, 501
  and adolescent egocentrism, 454–455
  and adolescent friendships, 491–492
  sexual content on, 430

social orientation, infancy, 198–199

social play, 305

social policy, 9–10, 421–422

social referencing, 200

social role theory, 284

social skills training, 405–406

social smile, 191

social systems morality, 389

social worker, 41–42

sociocultural cognitive theory, 21. *See also* Vygotsky's theory

sociocultural contexts, and diversity, 6–7

socioeconomic status (SES), 7. *See also* poverty
  and adolescent pregnancy, 437
  and adolescent sexual behavior, 432
  and bullying, 404
  and child care, 211–212
  and child maltreatment, 292
  definition of, 7
  divorce and, 299
  and education, 266–268, 302, 410–413, 470
  and executive function, 257
  and families, 300, 302
  of immigrants, 499
  inequalities in, 7
  and intelligence quotient, 361–363
  and juvenile delinquency, 502
  and nutrition, 234
  race/ethnicity and, 9, 499–500
  and school dropout rate, 472
  and self-regulation, 384
  and theory of mind, 260
  variations in, 7, 302

socioemotional development. *See also* emotional development; *specific topics*
  in adolescence, 477–511
  in early childhood, 274–313
  explanation of, 11
  family and, 207–211
  gender and, 395–397
  in infants, 186–217
  in middle and late childhood, 379–417
  social contexts and, 207–214
  strategies for nurturing, 217, 416

socioemotional processes, 11, 12

sociometric popularity, 403

sociometric status, 402–403

solicitation of information, by parents, 488

somnambulism, 231

sounds, recognition of, 147–148, 172–173

source-monitoring errors, 255

spanking, 209–210, 288, 289–291, 400

spatial intelligence, 360

spatial skills, 395

special education, 327–328, 334–336

special education teacher, 40–41, 334–336

speech
  child-directed, 179–181
  inner, 249
  private, 249, 250
  telegraphic, 176

speech development. *See* language development

speech disorders, 176, 332

speech therapist/pathologist, 42, 176

sperm, 51–52

spina bifida, 55, 56, 58, 76, 91

spirituality, 464–465, 467

spoken vocabulary, 174–175

sports. *See also* exercise
  in adolescence, 432–433, 438–439, 469, 493, 505
  in middle and late childhood, 320–321
  peer groups based on, 493
  and reduced risk of suicide, 505
  in U.S. schools, 471

standardized tests, 28–29, 409–410

Stanford-Binet intelligence test, 28, 170, 358

startle (Moro) reflex, 135, 136

start times, for schools, 440–441

The State of the World's Children (UNICEF), 239

stepfamilies, 400–401

stepping reflex, 135

STEP-UP program, 443

stereotyped reactions, 159

stereotypes, gender, 285–286, 370, 393–394

stereotype threat, 364

sticky mittens, 140–141

still-face paradigm, 199

stimulant medication, 331

stimulants, for ADHD, 331

stimulation, in friendship, 407

STIs. *See* sexually transmitted infections

stoicism, 83

storm-and-stress view, of adolescence, 421, 484

stranger anxiety, 191

Strange Situation, 202–203

strategies
  definition of, 347
  knowledge about, 352
  learning and remembering using, 347

strategy instruction, 352

street youth, 497

stress
  coping with, 386–387
  in COVID-19 pandemic, 387
  poverty and, 9, 302
  during pregnancy, 92–93

Study of Early Child Care and Youth Development (SECCYD), 213–214

stuttering, 176, 332

substance use/abuse
  in adolescence, 440, 441–445, 469, 504, 506–507
  and depression, 504
  extracurricular activities and, 469
  family program for reducing, 445
  intervention/prevention, 506–507
  parental monitoring and, 487
  peers and, 443
  trends in, 441–442

subtractive dual-language learning, 357

sucking behavior
  habituation in, 143
  high-amplitude, 143–144

sucking reflex, 135, 136

sudden infant death syndrome (SIDS), 128–129, 130
sugar consumption, 232–233
suggestion, susceptibility to, 255
suicide/suicidal ideation
    adolescent, 441, 504–506
    antidepressants and risk of, 504
    bullying and, 405, 505
    child maltreatment and, 293, 505, 506
    COVID-19 pandemic and, 441
    culture and, 505–506
    low self-esteem and, 383
    psychological profile of youth at risk for, 506
    race/ethnicity and, 505
superego, 17
Superkids-Superfit program, 325
survey, as data collection method, 28
"survival of the fittest," 47
Sustainable Development Goals, 270, 291, 471
sustained attention, 165, 252–254, 368–369, 440
sustaining climate, in classroom, 463
swaddling, 139
swimming reflex, 135
symbol, 158
symbolic drawings, 246
symbolic function substage, 245–246
symbolic play, 305
sympathy, 281
synapses, 124–125
synaptic density, 125, 224
synaptic pruning, 125, 317, 428
synchronous interactions, 190
syntax, 172, 173, 261–262
syphilis, 90, 433, 434
system(s)
    environmental, in ecological theory, 25–26
    family, interactions in, 487

T

task persistence, 368–369
taste, 149
Tay-Sachs disease, 55, 56
teachers. See also schools
    and achievement, 372
    and adolescent school performance, 470
    bullying intervention by, 405–406
    career opportunities for, 40–41
    as cultural mediators, 413
    diversity efforts of, 412–413
    of exceptional children, 40–41, 334–336
    gender biases of, 397
    guiding creativity, 351
    team-teaching by, 469
teaching. See education; schools
"teaching to the test," 410
team-teaching, 469
technology. See also media use/screen time
    COVID-19 pandemic and, 501
    Generation Z and, 13
    Millennials and, 12
Teen Pregnancy Prevention (TPP) program, 436
telegraphic speech, 176
television, 292, 306–308, 320
temperament, 192–196
    biological influences on, 193–194
    classification of, 192–193
    culture and, 195
    definition of, 192

developmental contexts of, 195
developmental links to, 194–195
experience and, 193–194
goodness of fit and, 195
parenting and, 195–196
temporal lobes, 123–124, 223–224, 317
teratogens, 84–91
    definition of, 84
    dose of, 84–85
    environmental, 89–90
    genetic susceptibility to, 84–85
    medications as, 86
    psychoactive drugs as, 86–89
    time of exposure, 84–85
teratology, 84–85
tertiary circular reactions, 159, 160
testes, 425–426
testimony, from children, 254–255
testosterone, 205, 425–426
tests
    intelligence (See intelligence tests)
    standardized, 28–29
thelarche, 427
theory
    child development (See child development
        theories)
    definition of, 16
theory of mind, 258–260
    in autism spectrum disorders, 260
    definition of, 258
    developmental changes in, 258–259
    in early childhood, 277, 278, 282
    individual differences in, 259–260
    and perspective taking, 406
thinking
    abstract, idealistic, and logical, 453–454,
        465–466
    in adolescence, 453–459
    analytical, vs. gist, 458–459
    convergent, 349
    creative, 349–350, 351
    critical, 349, 459
    divergent, 349–350
    in early childhood, 245–260
    in infants, 157–163
    as information processing, 22
    knowledge about (See metacognition)
    in middle and late childhood, 348–350
    scientific, 350
thought
    intuitive, 246–247
    language and, 249
    moral, 391
    preoperational, 245–248
    unconscious, 16–17, 22
Thousand Genomes Project, 50
three-mountains task, 245–246
thyroid gland, 426
time allocation, by adolescents, 498
time out, 290
tobacco. See smoking
toddlers
    assessment measures for, 169–170
    in child care, 211–214
    emotional development in, 188–192, 197
    Erikson's psychosocial theory on, 18, 19,
        197, 198
    independence in, 198

language development in, 166, 174–182
locomotion of, 137, 199
managing and guiding behavior of,
    209–210
motor development in, 136, 139
perceptual development in, 142, 148
Piaget's theory on, 20–21, 157–164
self-understanding in, 197
temperament in, 192–196
tonic neck reflex, 135
Tools of the Mind, 251
top-dog phenomenon, 468
total communication approach, 333
Touch Research Institute, 110
touch sensation, in infants, 148–149
toy designer, 257
training parents, 289, 400
transactional interactions, 208
transgender, 7, 398, 430–431, 485–486
transitivity, 344
transnational families, 301
trauma, coping with, 386–387
triarchic theory of intelligence, 359–361
trimesters, 75
Triple P program, 293
triple screen, 58
trophoblast, 72
trust vs. mistrust stage, 18, 196, 201
Turner syndrome, 54–55
twins, 52
twin studies, 45–46, 63, 109, 194, 361
two-word utterances, 175–176
type 1 diabetes, 324
type 2 diabetes, 324

U

ultrasound sonography, 57–58
umbilical cord, 73, 74, 105
unconscious/automatic responses, 391
unconscious thought, 16–17, 22
underextension, of words, 175
undocumented immigrants, 499
unfamiliar, inhibition to, 193
universal ethical principles, 389
universal preschool education, 268–269
unmarried parents, 400
utility, 389
Uvalde (Texas) school shooting, 387

V

values, 460–461
vaping, 444, 455
verbal abuse, 292
verbal aggression, 395
verbal intelligence, 360
vernix caseosa, 105
very preterm infants, 108–109
viability of fetus, 75
vigilance, 252–254
violation of expectations, 161
violence. See also child maltreatment
    in dating relationships, 495
    exposure to, 387
    media, 292, 308
vision, sensation of, 141
visual acuity, 142–145